Cities of Dragons and Elephants

Cities of Dragons and Elephants

Urbanization and Urban Development in China and India

Edited by

GUANGHUA WAN

and

MING LU

OXFORD
UNIVERSITY PRESS

OXFORD
UNIVERSITY PRESS

Great Clarendon Street, Oxford, OX2 6DP,
United Kingdom

Oxford University Press is a department of the University of Oxford.
It furthers the University's objective of excellence in research, scholarship,
and education by publishing worldwide. Oxford is a registered trade mark of
Oxford University Press in the UK and in certain other countries

First Edition published in 2019

Published in the United States of America by Oxford University Press
198 Madison Avenue, New York, NY 10016, United States of America

British Library Cataloguing in Publication Data
Data available

Library of Congress Control Number: 2019951983

ISBN 978–0–19–882922–5

DOI: 10.1093/oso/9780198829225.003.0001

Acknowledgements

The editors of this book are grateful to the Natural Science Foundation of China for financial support through its projects 71833003 and 71703088.

Contents

List of Figures

List of Tables

List of Contributors

Jie Chen is Executive Director of Real Estate Research Institute of Shanghai University of Finance and Economics. He is also a member of Academic Committee at this university. He holds a PhD in Economics from Uppsala University. He is author of four books and has published more than twenty papers in international academic journals and more than sixty papers in Chinese academic journals. He also works as a policy advisor for several Chinese government agencies as well as a consulting expert for international organizations including the World Bank.

Zhao Chen is Deputy Director and Professor at the China Center for Economic Studies (CCES), Fudan University, Shanghai, China. His research interest covers development economics as well as urban and regional economics. Currently, he works on topics including place-based policies, the Hukou system and urbanization, entrepreneurs' political participation, and FDI spillover effects. He has published in publications such as *Journal of Comparative Economics*, *Review of Income and Wealth*, *Economic Modelling*, *Manchester School*, *China Economic Review*, *Journal of the Asian Pacific Economy*, and *China Agricultural Economic Review*. He used to be Senior Associate Member at St Antony's College, Oxford University, visiting scholar at IDEI, University of Toulouse I, France, and visiting scholar of UNU-WIDER at Helsinki, Finland. He also serves as the editor of *World Economic Papers* (a core Chinese economics journal).

Surender Kumar is a Professor at the Department of Economics, Delhi School of Economics, University of Delhi, Delhi. He had been a Visiting Fellow at the University of Illinois at Urbana-Champaign (USA) and Senior JSPS Fellow at the Yokohama National University Yokohama (Japan). Prof. Kumar was one of the lead authors for IPCC AR5, Working Group II. He specializes in environmental and resource economics and climate change and energy economics. He also extends his ambit of research to productivity and efficiency measurement, urbanization, and applied econometrics. He has published five books and more than 70 research papers in various cherished journals and edited volumes.

Zhigang Li graduated from University of California, San Diego, in 2005 with a PhD in Economics. He is now the Senior Economist of Shuion land and Adjunct Professor of the Hong Kong Baptist University. Prior to the current position Dr Li taught at the School of Economics and Finance in the University of Hong Kong for a number of years. With prime research interests in the fields of regional and public economics, Dr Li has been involved in research projects covering infrastructure investment, real estate markets, environmental issues, and the fiscal system within the context of China. Applying rigorous econometric analysis on Chinese data, Dr Li has been exploring research questions that are motivated by the growth experience of China and have general implications for economic development policies in the developing world. Recent research has been published in *Journal of Urban*

Economics, *Journal of Comparative Economics*, *Ecological Economics*, *Contemporary Economic Policy*, and *China Economic Review*.

Dan Liu is a Zijiang Young Research Professor at East China Normal University (ECNU). She received her PH.D degree in economics from University of California at Davis (UCD) in August, 2012 and joined Shanghai University of Finance and Economics (SUFE) thereafter. She worked as an associate professor at SUFE from June, 2015 to November, 2018. Her research focuses on international trade, labor market outcomes and development. Her papers are published in *Journal of International Economics*, *Journal of Development Economics*, *China Economic Review*, *the World Economy*, and *Economic Letter*.

Ming Lu is Distinguished Professor of Economics, and Director of the China Centre for Development Studies at Shanghai Jiao Tong University. He is also Research Fellow of China Institute for Urban Governance (SJTU), Fudan University, and Singapore Management University. He worked as a Fulbright Scholar at Harvard University and National Bureau of Economic Research (NBER). He has consulted for the World Bank and Asian Development Bank. His recent research tries to link political economy with economic geography to analyse regional and urban issues. He is also interested in urban labour economics that studies how social interaction and knowledge spillover affect employment and economic growth in the local labour market.

Darshini Mahadevia is a Visiting Professor at the School of Arts and Sciences, Ahmedabad University, Ahmedabad. She has over twenty-five years' experience in teaching and researching in urban studies, human and gender development, poverty and inequality, and climate change. She has a PhD from the Centre for Studies in Regional Development, Jawaharlal Nehru University, New Delhi. She is a member of the editorial board of several journals and has been a visiting fellow at University of California, Los Angeles, McGill University, Montreal, and Tsinghua University, Beijing. She held the position of Dean, Faculty of Planning, from December 2012 to April 2016 and till recently as Director, Centre for Urban Equity, at CEPT University, Ahmedabad. She has more than a hundred publications as books, chapter in books, and journal articles. She has managed more than forty research projects.

Balwant Singh Mehta is a Fellow at the Institute for Human Development, Delhi. He obtained his PhD (Development Economics) from Jamia Milia Islamia, New Delhi and Post-Doctoral from the Indian Council of Social Science Research, New Delhi. His research interests include issues in employment, unemployment, urbanization, gender, child well-being, poverty, inequality, and information and communications technologies for development (ICT4D). He has published several books and numerous articles in professional journals. In recognition of his contributions, he has been selected as an 'Amy Mahan International Fellow' by the UPF, Spain; awarded a Research Fellowship in ICT4D by SIRCA, Singapore; and selected as an 'Emerging Researcher' by the IDRC, Canada. He also writes regular columns in magazines, blogs, and newspapers on nation-relevant issues.

Arup Mitra is Professor of Economics, South Asian University and Institute of Economic Growth, Delhi. His research area encompasses issues related to labour and welfare, urban development, industrial growth and productivity, corruption and gender inequalities. He has published several books on inclusive growth, urbanization, informal sector employment and slums. Besides, he has more than one hundred and fifty research papers in various journals and edited volumes. He has worked with various international organisations and government of India.

Pengtu Ni holds a Master's Degree of Economics from Shanghai Jiaotong University. Her research is mainly about urban development. She now works on investment banking business in Shenwan Hongyuan Securities Co. Ltd.

Om Prakash Mathur is Senior Fellow, Institute of Social Sciences, New Delhi. He earlier served as a Distinguished Professor of Urban Economics at the National Institute of Urban Affairs, New Delhi (2011–13), IDFC Chair in Urban Finance at the National Institute of Public Finance and Policy, New Delhi (1992–2011), Director, National Institute of Urban Affairs, New Delhi (1984–92), and Senior Economist at the United Nations Centre for Regional Development, Nagoya, Japan (1978–84). He is a member of the *Journal of the Review of Urban and Regional Development Studies*, Tokyo, Japan. Om Prakash Mathur holds a Master's degree in Economics from the Delhi School of Economics and has done graduate work at the Massachusetts Institute of Technology and Harvard University, Cambridge, MA, USA.

Sandip Sarkar is currently working as a Professor with the Institute for Human Development, New Delhi. His main areas of research interest over two decades are urbanization, industry, poverty, labour and employment, and information and communication. He is the author of numerous publications on development economics including articles in national and international journals and several books.

Kala S. Sridhar is Professor and Head, Centre for Research in Urban Affairs, Institute for Social and Economic Change, Bangalore, India. She has written several books on urban issues (published by Springer, Oxford University Press, Sage and Palgrave Macmillan), articles in journals such as Urban Studies, Regional Science and Urban Economics, China Economic Review, and chapters in leading edited books. She is the recipient of several highly competitive national awards such as the VKRV Rao award for her contributions to social sciences, and international awards by the Global Development Network (GDN) for her research, and has visited the United Nations University twice as visiting scholar. She was a senior advisor to GDN's global project on urbanization, and member of the government of Karnataka's expert committees on urban development. Globally, she is among the top 10% of authors on the Social Science Research Network, as per the latest rankings.

Cong Sun is an Associate Professor at Shanghai University of Finance and Economics. He obtained a PhD degree from Tsinghua University, Beijing, People's Republic of China. His main research area is urban and environmental economics, and he is working on people's demand for housing, living environment, and urban amenities. He has published several international refereed papers appearing in *Nature Human Behaviour*, *Journal of Regional Science*, *Ecological Economics*, *Journal of Economic Surveys*, *Transportation Research Part D: Transport and Environment*, *Transport Policy*, and *Journal of Real Estate Finance and Economics*.

Yiran Xia is an Associate Professor in the Business School of Wenzhou University in China. She completed her economics PhD at Fudan University. Her interests include labour economics, urban economics, human capital, and spatial economics. She has authored twenty papers on labour flow, migration, population distribution, accumulation and agglomeration of city-level human capital, and the training of rural workers.

Chunbing Xing is a Professor of Economics at the Business School, Beijing Normal University. He was a visiting scholar and a Post Doc in the Department of Economics, University of Western Ontario between January 2010 and December 2011. He also was a visiting scholar at the OECD Development Centre during the summer of 2008. Chunbing received his PhD in Economics from Guanghua School of Management, Peking University in 2006. His main research interests include rural–urban migration, income distribution, human capital, and wage determination in China.

Guanghua Wan is Director, Institute of World Economy, Fudan University. Previously, he was Research Director, and Head of the Poverty/Inequality Group, Asian Development Bank (ADB). Prior to ADB, he was a Senior Economist in the United Nations and taught in a number of Universities in Australia and China. Trained in development economics and econometrics, Dr Wan is a multi-award-winning scholar on the Chinese economy and an expert on Asia, with an outstanding publication record of more than a hundred professional articles and a dozen of books including two by Oxford University Press. An honorary professor at over ten top institutions in China, including Xiamen and Zhejiang Universities, Dr Wan is among the top 7 per cent of economists globally and the top 3 per cent in Asia according to the latest ranking of REPEC. Some of his publications can be downloaded here: <http://ideas.repec.org/f/pwa395.html>.

Jianghao Wang is now a research scientist in China Future City Lab, Department of Urban Studies and Planning, Massachusetts Institute of Technology (MIT). He is also an associate professor in the State Key Laboratory of Resources and Environmental Information System, Institute of Geographic Sciences and Natural Resources Research, Chinese Academy of Sciences (CAS). He is the co-founder of Beijing City Lab, an open research network for quantitative urban studies. Dr Wang has a BSc from Hohai University, China and received a PhD in GIScience from CAS. His research interests are in spatiotemporal big data mining, urban studies, and geographic information science. He has published over forty peer reviewed English articles, in journals including *Nature Human Behaviour*, *Annals of the Association of American Geographers*, *Urban Studies*, and *Regional Studies*. He has completed or been undertaking research projects granted or entrusted by the MIT International Science and Technology Initiatives, National Natural Science Foundation of China, National High Technology Research and Development Program of China, and the Key Program of Frontier Science in CAS, among others. His most recent research focuses on modeling human behaviors and understanding urban development and air pollution through the analytical lens of emerging geospatial big data.

Xianxiang Xu is Professor of Economics at Lingnan College of Sun Yat-sen University and currently head of the Department of Economics. His research mainly includes work on China's economic growth, behaviour of Chinese local officials, and deregulation of entry. In addition to his duty at Lingnan College, Professor Xu is a regular participant in policy debates on deregulation of entry.

Li Zhang is an Associate Professor of Economics at the International Business School, Sun Yat-sen University, Guangzhou. She specializes in public economics and regional economics. Her research and teaching activities have focused on issues of local government, land market, and urbanization. She is a member in the China Society of Territorial Economists. Her research projects received support from the National Social Science Foundation of China in 2013.

Yuan Zhang is a Professor at the China Center for Economic Studies, Fudan University. His research interests include household financial activities, labour migration, and rural poverty in China. He has papers published in World Development, *China Economic Review, Economics Letters, Oxford Development Studies, China Agricultural Economic Review,* and many top economic journals in China.

Siqi Zheng is the Samuel Tak Lee Associate Professor of Real Estate Development and Entrepreneurship at Center for Real Estate, and Department of Urban Studies and Planning, Massachusetts Institute of Technology (MIT). Prof. Zheng established MIT China Future City Lab and is the Faculty Director of her Lab. Her field of specialization is urban and environmental economics, urban development and real estate market, with a special focus on China. She published in many peer reviewed English journals including the *Proceedings of the National Academy of Sciences*, and *the Journal of Economic Literature, Journal of Economic Perspectives, Journal of Economic Geography, European Economic Review, Journal of Urban Economics, Regional Science and Urban Economics, Transportation Research Part A, Environment and Planning A, Ecological Economics, Journal of Regional Science, Real Estate Economics, Journal of Real Estate Finance and Economics*. A book she has co-authored, Blue Skies over Beijing: Economic Growth and the Environment in China (Princeton University Press) was published in May 2016. She has also published more than 100 papers and two books in Chinese. She is the Associated Editor of *Journal of Regional Science, China Economic Review, Journal of Economic Surveys*, and is on the editorial board of *Journal of Housing Economics* and *International Real Estate Review*. She is the President of Asian Real Estate Society (2018–2019) and Vice General Secretary of the Global Chinese Real Estate Congress.

1
Introduction

Urbanization is one of the most important phenomena in economic development. In the past three decades, Asian urban population expanded by almost one billion, and more than one billion is expected to be added in the next three decades. Clearly, both the scale and pace of urbanization in Asia are unprecedented in human history, and will dominate the global urbanization landscape. Meanwhile, Asia's urbanization will be dominated by what is happening in China and India, the two most populous and fastest growing economies in the world.

In developing countries like China and India, ongoing urbanization will continue to meet the requirements of industrial and services development. In these two large countries, the urbanization process will also lead to a spatial redistribution of population to form a more efficient urban system, especially in China, where the urbanization process is driven by interregional migration from the inland to the coast.

This volume arises from a comparative study on urbanization and urban development in China and India. Given the similarities and differences of these two giants, it is anticipated that findings, conclusions, and implications from such a comparative analysis will be useful to most governments and institutions in Asia and beyond. The main message from this study is: Asian countries like China and India will experience an urbanization path led by megacities. What the government can do is to improve liveability within cities and equalize life quality across cities.

The study intends to address the two most fundamental issues in urbanization: why and where to urbanize. The first issue relates to the scale of urbanization, and the second to urban systems or spatial distribution of urbanites in different-sized cities. The essence of the two issues lies in comparing the benefits and costs of urbanization where both markets and governments play important roles. In a market economy, the cost–benefit trade-off determines the level, speed, and place of urbanization. In general, urbanization enhances productivity and economic growth. For enterprises and consumers, urbanization means sharing production and infrastructure costs, more efficient matching of specialized workers/employers in the labour market, and better mutual learning and synergy among managers and staff from different entities. Urbanization also improves quality of life by increasing the variety of consumer goods and services. On the negative side, urban living is costlier, with higher land/housing prices and employers usually having to pay higher wages. Other costs include congestion, pollution, and

Guanghua Wan and Ming Lu., *Introduction* In: *Cities of Dragons and Elephants: Urbanization and Urban Development in China and India. Edited by:* Guanghua Wan and Ming Lu, Oxford University Press (2019).
 DOI: 10.1093/oso/9780198829225.003.0001

crime—the three major urban diseases. One should not overlook the potential gains of rural areas in terms of per capita resources and enlarged scale of operation as rural-to-urban migration proceeds.

The benefit–cost trade-off of each individual and firm leads to a spatial equilibrium of urban system where large cities have greater scale economies than smaller ones, but also higher costs. Different cities of different sizes have their own comparative advantage in certain industries, and form a rank–size relationship possibly following Zipf's law. Under this law, the size of primary cities usually correlates with national population. China and India are the world's most populous countries. If migration and flow of capital are free, people and enterprises will trade off between the benefits and costs to stay in a certain place. If we believe both China and India will follow the regularities guiding urbanization and the urban system, their urban system will gradually transform in accordance with Zipf's law. In these two countries, the primary cities, Shanghai and Mumbai, will be the world's largest cities when their urbanization process finishes in the next few decades. This means that the urban systems will follow Zipf's law and both countries will be characterized by some megacities, which will be much larger than the cities in other countries. This megacity-led urbanization will continuously inject energies into the economic and social development of China and India.

In populous countries like China and India, megacities will lead urbanization through greater productivity gains and cost-efficiency. In addition, as international trade plays an important role in economic development, coastal regions and large seaports in both China and India have grown faster and become centres of city clusters. The urban system has evolved into a core–periphery pattern centring on large seaports like Shanghai, Hong Kong, and Mumbai.

Market forces drive production factors such as capital (foreign direct investment, FDI) and labour to agglomerate in places with greater productivity. This is why big cities and the coastal areas will grow faster. However, governments often intervene as they fear urban diseases, which are often perceived as a result of urban expansion. Consequently, the urban development policy in both China and India is biased towards small- and medium-sized cities. Such kinds of policies may distort resource allocation and lead to losses of both efficiency and equity. For example, strict restriction on labour mobility in China results in underurbanization and underdevelopment of large cities.

Government intervention is needed only when the market fails to allocate resources efficiently. One particular role of government intervention is to improve positive externality or reduce negative externality. In China, both central and local governments have played a very important role in constructing infrastructure, including railways, highways, roads, undergrounds (metros), reservoirs, etc. Industrial parks are tools to attract investment and boost local economic development. In comparison, India lags behind. Human capital externality is another area where government can play a role. The government can invest in training, education, health, and R&D to accumulate human capital and amplify its returns during urbanization, especially in poor regions. Even within cities, where income inequality could be widened with inflow of both high-skilled and low-skilled labourers, public policies should target the urban poor by providing equalized public services.

During urbanization and the formation of a core–periphery urban system, nominal interregional inequality may rise, at least in the short run, if the large cities and megacities experience greater productivity gains. But urbanization also narrows the urban–rural income gap if labour mobility is free. As for interregional inequality, in the short run, the large cities and megacities also have higher living costs and more serious urban diseases, so the real income or quality of life inequality between different cities is much lower than the nominal inequality. In the long run, only if labour mobility is free can the real income be equalized interregionally, depicting an inverse U-shape relationship between economic agglomeration and interregional inequality. In both countries, a rising within-city inequality is a new challenge. In particular, urban slums are a serious problem that India has to face, while in China residential segregation is also emerging.

In the process of urbanization led by megacities, the costs of urban development, like expensive living costs, traffic congestion, and pollution, are significant. While both the government and the public may want to control the city size to reduce urban diseases, population control may result in both efficiency loss and equity loss. In China, growth led by megacities is hindered and the interregional allocative efficiency is worsened. The narrowing of interregional and urban–rural income inequality faces many obstacles, while within-city social segmentation due to different Hukou identity leads to inequality; discrimination against migrants in the labour market, social security, and public services; and social unrest in the form of unhappiness and distrust. In India, there are no institutional barriers to movement of the factors of production, i.e. capital and labour. However, subsidies of various kinds to support rural employment (rationalized on grounds of high rates of rural poverty) indirectly affect the labour market and rural–urban migration. This is one reason that explains the low share of rural–urban migration in the urbanization process. Although there is no institutional discrimination against migrants, language and cultural obstacles, and the government's reluctance to develop cities have distorted India's urbanization process in the sense that cities have not created sufficient jobs to accommodate migrants while the poorly educated rural people are not qualified for the high-end service industries in the cities. Thus, the urbanization process has not played a sufficient role in reducing the urban–rural income gap.

Based on the empirical analyses in this volume, we recommend the following policies to achieve efficiency, equity, and sustainability in China's and India's urbanization and urban development:

(1) Ensuring efficiency of factor markets is the key policy recommendation. Both countries should make considerable efforts in removing barriers to rural–urban and interregional migration. While India needs to better integrate its labour market by reducing language and cultural differences across regions, China should remove its institutional barriers to rural–urban and interregional migration by reforming its Hukou and land systems, particularly in the in large and megacities. The length of stay in cities should be the main criterion to obtain the local Hukou, while the requirement of skill should be removed. Before these migrants change their Hukou registration to a local one, access to local public services, especially compulsory education, should be equalized between local residents and migrants. Furthermore, for those households leaving the countryside, their land, including residential land, should be allowed to be traded at market prices. As more and more residential land in rural China are converted to agricultural use when migrants leave their home town permanently, the cities accommodating migrants should be allowed to use more industrial and residential land and should provide equalized services to migrants who are contributing to local development. In India, in case of distortions such as those observed in the real estate market (what is produced is not demanded and what is demanded is not produced), incentives for correcting the distortions could be considered, so that the housing market can function more efficiently.

(2) Central–local fiscal transfers should be used to equalize public services and the quality of life across regions, so that interregional labour mobility is mainly based on productivity gain rather than better public services in richer regions. During the process of urbanization, the population-losing regions should be subsidized by central government in infrastructure, schools, hospitals, and environment protection. In particular, China should place an emphasis on its 61 million-plus left-behind children by either providing them with better education and childcare, or helping them access quality education in cities. India should make concerted efforts at raising the levels of education and training for rural residents in order to meet the needs of urban industries and services. Fiscal transfers to local governments in India are determined once every five years by the state finance commissions. These are neither adequate to enable local governments to meet their functional responsibilities nor do transfers incentivize local governments to improve their fiscal performance. The recommendation for India is to strengthen the state finance commissions,

giving them some autonomy so that they canformulate a fiscal architecture that would empower local governments fiscally. In both countries, the government should be aware of the inefficiency of moving industries to small-sized cities, especially those in remote regions. Inefficient investments should be reduced for financial sustainability.

(3) Management and technology hold the key for building liveable and equitable cities. Large-scale and efficient urban transit systems are needed to meet the fast-growing demand for transportation of people and goods. Regarding technology, e-governance can be promoted for improving urban service delivery. Also, green technologies to control car usage, reduce carbon emissions, and encourage a 'greener' life can help improve traffic and the environment. To contain widening income inequality within a city, especially in large cities, government must help the poor to access education, medical and other social services. In China, public housing, social safetynet and medical servicesshould be extended to migrants. In India, landowners should be incentivized to provide better living conditions to slum dwellers by reforming the current land polices that restrict the provision of better housing.

(4) Make the government more accountable and efficient in urban development. Both China and India must work hard in combating corruptions. China should strengthen its rule of law, while India should improve the efficiency of government policy-making. In particular, China needs to improve protection of property rights, especially rural land use rights, by allowing rural collectives to decide how to use their land. Also, it is important for China to reform its fiscal system and land evaluation system to avoid overexpansion of urban areas without sufficient job creation and population urbanization. India needs to make its local governments accountable, efficient, transparent, and participatory. Currently, their functioning is suboptimal. Urban planning should be improved to introduce the best practices from other developing countries, including China, to promote industrialization and urbanization, attract FDI, construct infrastructure, develop education, and improve urban life.

PART I

URBANIZATION AND RURAL DEVELOPMENT

2
Urbanization and Rural Development in the People's Republic of China

Zhao Chen, Ming Lu, and Pengtu Ni

2.1 Introduction

With the reforms and opening up of the economy, the PRC has experienced unprecedented economic growth and progress during the last thirty years. In this process, cities have acted as the centres of economic activities and pushed high levels of economic growth. It is an inevitable trend for economic agglomeration in urbanization. This chapter presents research findings on how urbanization enhances productivity and economic growth in both rural and urban sectors. Specifically, we explore the relationship between urbanization and economic advancement. As urbanization plays the key role in agglomeration effects and cities make a major contribution to the growth of manufacturing and services, the PRC's urbanization level and pace needs close attention to assess its economic sustainability and potential. According to the 'dual economy theory' proposed by Lewis (1954), in the urbanization process the level of industrialization and urbanization should rise simultaneously to make capital accumulation and the transition of rural labour to industrial sectors possible. However, in the PRC urbanization lags far behind industrialization. We look into this gap to examine ways for better and healthier urbanization. This chapter also studies how urbanization, migration, and remittance affect productivity, capital investment, and agricultural organizations in rural areas.

2.2 Empirical Evidence on Urban Agglomeration Economies and Economic Growth

2.2.1 Growth and Productivity

2.2.1.1 Relationship Between Urbanization and Economic Growth

Urbanization enhances economic growth. At the global level, urbanization rate and GDP per capita are positively related, but the position of the PRC is below the average level at the 95 per cent confidence interval, which means its urbanization

Zhao Chen, Ming Lu, and Pengtu Ni., *Urbanization and Rural Development in the People's Republic of China* In: *Cities of Dragons and Elephants: Urbanization and Urban Development in China and India. Edited by:* Guanghua Wan and Ming Lu, Oxford University Press (2019). © Oxford University Press. DOI: 10.1093/oso/9780198829225.003.0002

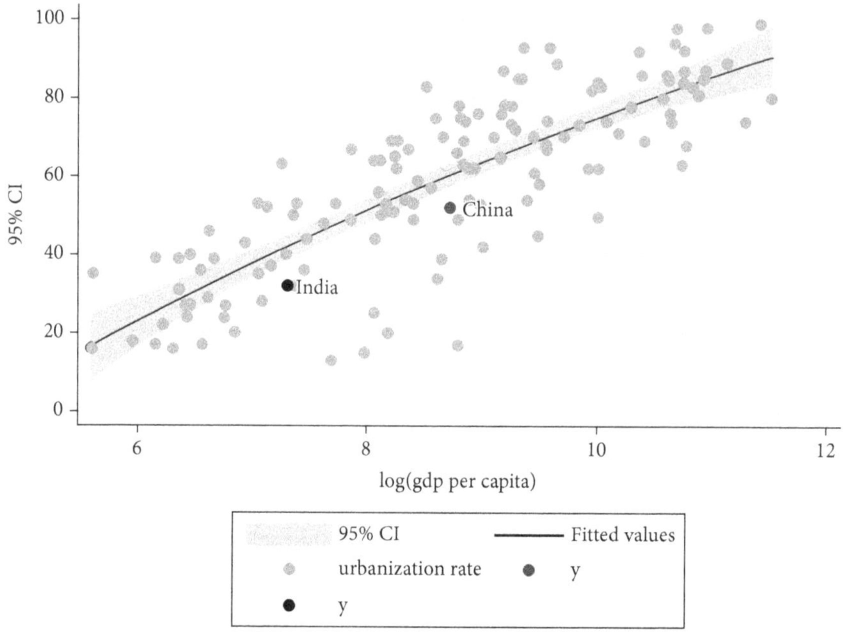

Figure 2.1. Global comparison of urbanization and GDP per capita, 2012

Source: Data are from the 2012 urbanization rate and GDP per capita in the World Bank Database. Liechtenstein and Monaco as outliers, typical city states including Singapore, Vatican City, Malta, Di San Marino, and the Maldives, and two Special Administrative Regions of the People's Republic of China (Hong Kong and Macao) have been eliminated.

lags behind its development stage by about ten percentage points (see Figure 2.1).[1] Though the PRC suffers from lagged urbanization, its urbanization is positively related to economic development, measured by average wage at the city level (see Figure 2.2).

2.2.1.2 Relationship Between Urbanization and Employment/Income

Though the relationships in Figures 2.1 and 2.2 are only correlations, endogenous growth theory and new economic geography theory argue that cities have the advantages of specialization and diversity, as well as human capital accumulation based on knowledge spillover and information exchange. Specifically, urbanization drives the increasing number and area expansion of cities, and can, thus, produce agglomeration effects. First, transaction costs are reduced and transaction efficiency is markedly improved, which are the stimulus of production and economic growth. In addition, by attracting the concentration of industries and population, cities have been the centres for knowledge spillover and technological innovation. The concentration of population and economic activities makes it easier for

[1] India is also below the average level and the 95 per cent confidence interval in Figure 2.1.

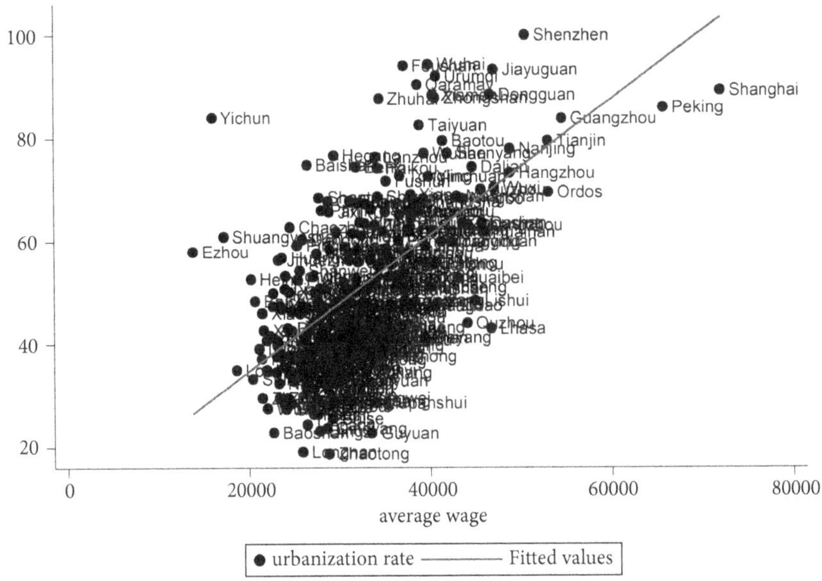

Figure 2.2. The PRC's urbanization level and average wage in 2010

Source: Urbanization rate is computed from the 2010 national population census (NBSC 2011a); average wage comes from the *China City Statistical Yearbook* (NBSC 2011b).

producers and labour to utilize the externalities of technology and knowledge, to improve productivity, and to impel capital formation.

As in other countries, the PRC's urbanization also serves as the impetus for urban agglomeration economies, improving employment opportunities and income levels.

City Size and Employment Opportunities

An urban agglomeration economy can favourably increase the possibility of employment through two main channels. On the one hand, agglomeration improves labour productivity, thus driving labour demand. On the other hand, the rise of urban income pushes the need for non-tradable commodities and expands job opportunities in non-tradable industries, especially in the cities with more high-skilled labour. High-skilled labour requires low-skilled services, bringing the 'consumption spillover' to low-skilled labour. So high-skilled and low-skilled labour can both benefit from an enlarging urban size. Urban size has a positive influence on individual employment (Lu et al. 2012). A 1 per cent rise in the city population scale increases one's employment probability by between 0.044 and 0.050 percentage points. This positive effect is mainly due to the concentration of high-skilled workers in large cities. In general, high-skilled and low-skilled workers can both benefit from the expansion of urban size.

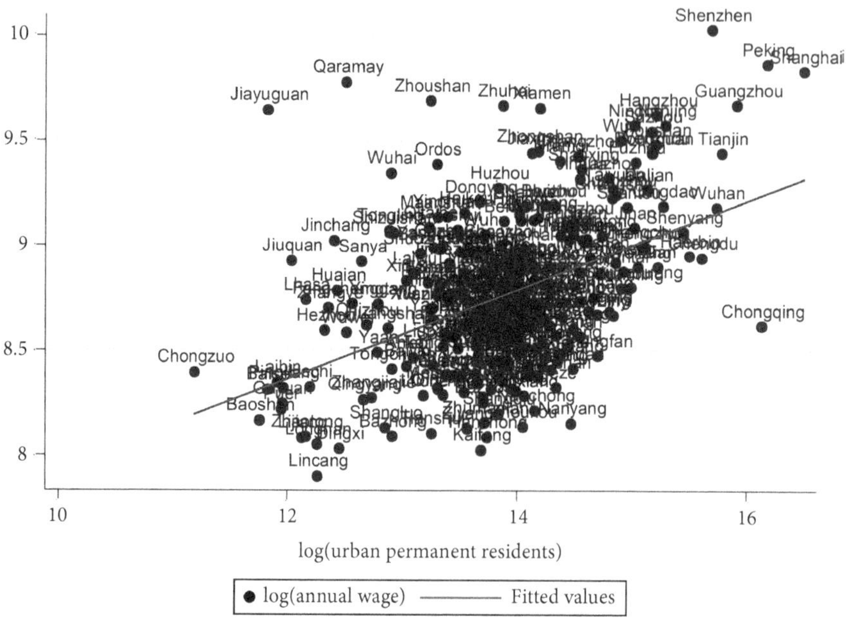

Figure 2.3. City population scale and average wage

Source: The data for 'urban permanent residents' are from the 2000 national population census; 'annual wage' is computed from the 2005 national population census.

Urban Size and Wage Level

The higher wage in larger cities is a reflection of their productivity gains. The average output and wage level are higher in big-sized cities compared with small-sized cities (Sveikauskas 1975). The doubling of city size will increase the productivity of labour by 4.77 to 6.39 per cent. The relationship between urban size and labour productivity also holds in the PRC. Au and Herderson (2006) point to an 'inverse U-shape' relationship between urban size and income per capita, indicating a positive relationship in the early stages of city development. Figure 2.3 shows the positive relationship between city size, measured by the number of urban permanent residents, and annual wage. Unlike the findings of Au and Herderson (2006), Figure 2.3 does not show an inverse U-shape relationship between city size and wage, but a linear one.

2.2.2 Sharing, Matching, and Learning

Urban agglomeration can largely improve labour productivity through the mechanism of sharing, matching, and learning. Through this mechanism, enterprises can reduce production costs by achieving economies of scale. Big cities supply more diversified products to meet the demands of consumers. Workers find it easier to get jobs, accumulate experiences, and acquire knowledge in big cities. In the three mechanisms of sharing, matching, and learning, sharing in cities has brought economies of scale, especially for transportation infrastructure facilities and diversified consumer goods. As sharing is more obvious, recent empirical research has focused on the mechanisms of matching and learning.

Due to social interactions, the expansion of urban size, especially the agglomeration of high-skilled labourers, provides more learning and innovative opportunities for workers, thus improving the productivity of labour. 'Human capital externalities' is an effect of the learning mechanism, which is significant for educational returns. This not only improves individual education levels but also the average education levels or prospects of the highly educated population in an area, usually a city, thus promoting individual wages. Empirical studies have proved the existence of human capital externalities (Rauch 1993). In the US, a 1 per cent increase in the university graduate ratio can boost labour productivity by 0.6 to 0.7 per cent (Moretti 2004a) and wage level by 0.6 to 1.2 per cent (Moretti 2004b). In the PRC, cities with a more educated labour force also have higher incomes. An additional one year of city-level education increases the individual hourly wage by 22.7 per cent (Glaeser and Lu 2013). Figure 2.4 presents a positive correlation between city-level average education and workers' annual wage in the PRC. As big cities have greater effects of human capital externalities, they can

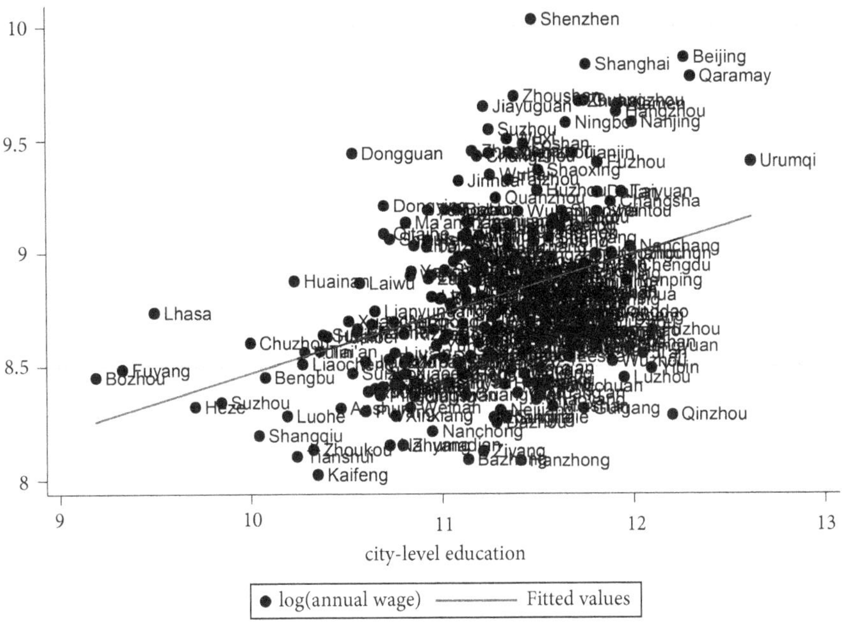

Figure 2.4. City-level education and annual wage in 2005

Source: Annual wage and average education levels are computed from the 2005 national population census.

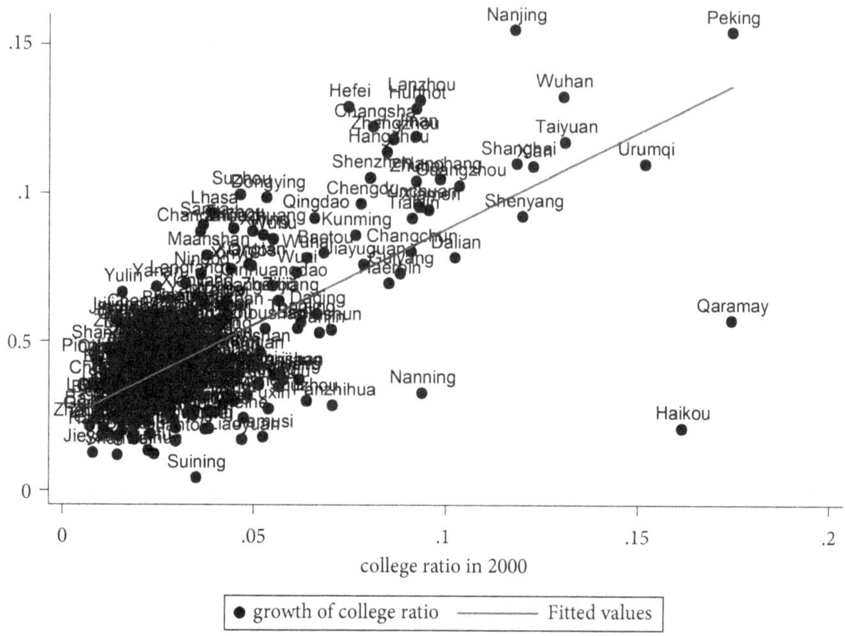

Figure 2.5. Growth of college graduate ratio (2000–10)

Source: X-axis: 2000 college graduate ratio; Y-axis: 2010 college graduate ratio–2000 college graduate ratio; 2000 and 2010 college graduate ratios are computed from the 2000 and 2010 national population census respectively.

attract more high-skilled labour. Moretti (2004c) and Glaeser and Ponzetto (2010) found that cities with higher proportions of high-skilled professions experience larger increases in the proportion of high-skilled professions. In the PRC, college graduates are moving to live and work in places that already have a higher proportion of college graduates, usually big cities. In Figure 2.5, data from the population censuses of 2000 and 2010 are analysed. In cities with high college graduate ratios in 2000, the increase in the college graduate ratio in the following ten years was higher as well. The PRC might display an unusually strong agglomeration of high-skilled labour because it still enforces the *Hukou* (household registration) system, and residents with local *Hukou* enjoy better public services and welfare of all sorts. The better social welfare in the rich cities motivates people to 'overpursue' higher education qualifications in order to obtain *Hukou* in big cities.

What are the implications of the high college graduate ratio? The agglomeration of high-skilled workers has increased the demand for low-skill workers in production and daily life, as well as greater learning effects among themselves. Moretti (2004b) used US data to check the substitution and spillover effects that high-skilled workers have on low-skilled workers. He found that a rise in the percentage of college graduates resulted in a larger wage increase for less educated labour compared with highly educated labour. In the PRC, the wages of

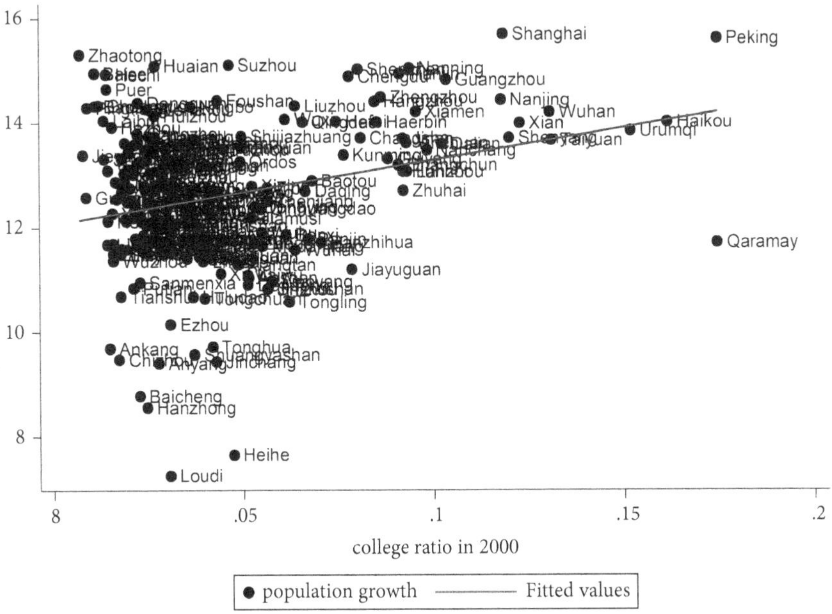

Figure 2.6. Population growth (2000–10)

Source: X-axis: 2000 college graduate ratio (%); Y-axis: log (2000 to 2010 population growth (in million) +1). The 2000 college graduate ratio is computed from the 2000 national population census. The 2000 to 2010 college population growth is computed from the 2000 and 2010 national population census respectively.

low-skilled workers are also higher in cities with higher education levels. Thus, both skilled and unskilled labour agglomerate in big cities. Figure 2.6 shows that there is a positive correlation between the 2000 college graduate ratio and the population growth over the 2000–10 period. The scatter plot shows that the variance in the data is rather large, and this big variance could be due to the severe restrictions on the flow of low-skilled workers into the cities, especially the big cities, hence inhibiting the population agglomeration effect of cities with high educational levels and large populations.

2.3 Urbanization: Level, Speed, and Regional Variation

2.3.1 Urbanization Level and Speed

The laggardness of the rate of urbanization is the first important characteristic in The PRC's urban development. Henderson (2009) illustrates that when the PRC's urbanization rate reached 46 per cent, countries with similar per capita incomes had urbanization rates of 55 per cent, while developed countries had urbanization rates of 70–85 per cent. In Figure 2.7, three categories of countries are studied:

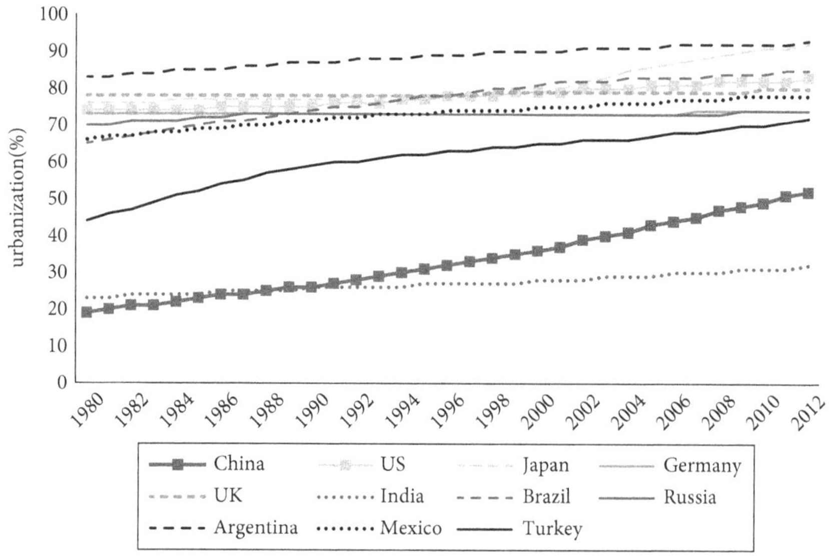

Figure 2.7. Cross-country urbanization comparison
Source: Yearly urbanization rate in the World Bank Database.

developed countries, BRIC countries, and other developing countries. Compared with the urbanization of these three categories of countries, the PRC lagged behind all in 1980. Though the PRC has been catching up in the past three plus decades, its urbanization ratio still lags behind other countries, except India.

Not only does the PRC's urbanization level lag but also the current urbanization process is not 'complete', with a huge gap between the urbanization rate of permanent residents and the rate of the urban registered residents. As many scholars have observed, the PRC has a strict *Hukou* system, which leads to the difference in numbers between the rural-to-urban migrants and the actual urban registered residents. With the advancement of urbanization, a large number of migrants have moved to cities without local registration status due to the strict Hukou system. Migrants who have resided over half a year in the cities have already been included in the category of 'permanent residents'. However, many rural-to-urban migrants who work in non-agricultural sectors in the city are still considered 'peasants' due to the current Hukou system. Considering the PRC's large scale of rural-to-urban migration, there is a large gap between the urbanization rate of permanent residents and that of urban registered residents. In 2012, the gap was as large as 17.3 percentage points and it's still widening (see Figure 2.8). As the urbanization rate of permanent residents reflects the level of urbanization more accurately, the official *China Statistical Yearbook* publication includes the migrants living in cities for more than half a year as permanent residents. The urbanization rate in this report also follows this definition, using the urbanization rate of permanent residents.

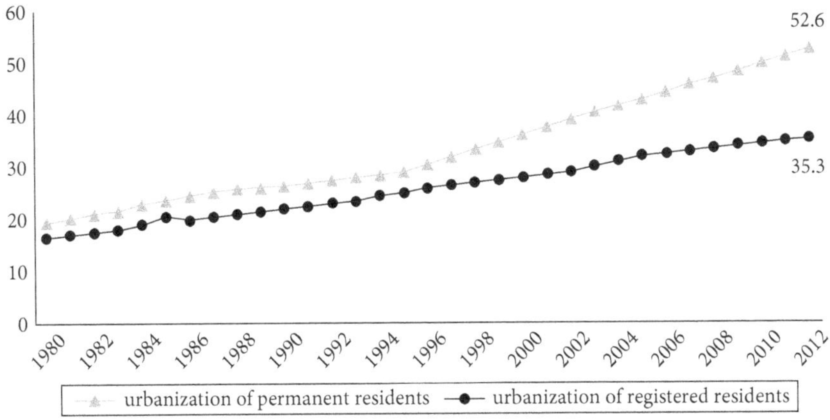

Figure 2.8. Urbanization rate of permanent residents and registered residents (%)
Source: PRC's National Plan, 'Planning for New-Type Urbanization (2014–2020)', p. 7, <http://www.gov.cn/zhengce/2014-03/16/content_2640075.htm>.

In general, urbanization in the PRC is still in its rapid growth period. Since the 'reforms and opening up', different stages of urbanization have witnessed a dramatically mounting speed, with an average annual speed of 0.26 per cent from 1980 to 1992, 0.7 per cent from 1993 to 2001, and a higher annual speed of 1.42 per cent from 2002 to 2010. Different urbanization speeds in the three periods are related to a certain model of economic development in the PRC. From 1980 to 1992, the transition to a market economy started. Reforms in agriculture were emphasized by the government as a larger proportion of people resided in rural areas. Given the restriction on interregional migration, many township-and-village enterprises were developed to absorb rural labour into manufacturing without moving them to cities. The speed of urbanization in this stage was quite slow. With the advancement of the market economy and 'opening up' during 1993 and 2001, urbanization also took a leap as a sizeable population poured into cities, pursuing more opportunities. Before 1994, the government issued food coupons (*Liangpiao*) for the urban residents to buy food in the market, while the rural residents did not have food coupons, thus facing a major obstacle to migration. Around 1994, the PRC stopped using food coupons, making rural-to-urban migration much freer. During the phase 2002 to 2010, after joining the World Trade Organization (WTO), the PRC stepped into a new era and urbanization experienced a remarkable jump to meet the needs of economic growth. In general, with time, the PRC is loosening its regulation on migration by reforming the Hukou system, though the megacities still tightly control population inflow. We believe that with Hukou system reforms and high economic growth, even if slower than before, rapid urbanization will continue in the PRC.

Although the urbanization level of the PRC lags behind many comparable countries, its speed is considerably rapid (see Figure 2.7). Is the speed of Chinese urbanization too fast? To be able to judge this, a comparison with the urbanization speed of developed countries in different time periods is required. According to Jian and Huang (2010), developed countries have all experienced rapid urbanization, especially Germany and Japan. They presented the data on urbanization in the main developed countries. From 1851 to 1861, urbanization in the UK increased from 54 per cent to 62.3 per cent, with an average growth of 0.83 percentage points per annum. From 1900 to 1910, urbanization in the US increased from 39.6 per cent to 45.7 per cent, with an average rise of 0.61 percentage points every year. In the period 1871 to 1910, urbanization in Germany ascended from 36.1 per cent to 60 per cent, while from 1890 to 1900 it increased by 11.9 percentage points and the average urbanization speed almost approached 1.2 percentage points per annum. Japan is another outstanding example with regard to urbanization speed, even faster than Germany. The urbanization rate in Japan increased from 37.5 per cent in 1950 to 56.33 per cent in 1955, with a yearly average of 3.766 percentage points. Japan also underwent a relatively faster pace of urbanization growth, with 1.3 percentage points per annum over the longer term—from 37.5 per cent in 1950 to 76.2 per cent in 1980.

Coming back to the PRC, its urbanization rose from 19.4 per cent in 1980 to 52.6 per cent in 2012 after the 'reforms and opening up'. Its yearly average urbanization speed is 1.03 per cent—a speed that is neither the highest nor unique in the world. The high economic growth in the PRC is similar to that experienced by developed countries. The PRC's urbanization speed is, therefore, reasonable in this context and has the potential to accelerate, given the PRC's below average urbanization level compared to the rest of the world and the reforms in the Hukou system.

2.3.2 Regional Variations in Urbanization Level and Speed

As a geographically large country, the PRC has huge interregional differences in urbanization levels. The urbanization rate is higher in the eastern region, which is richer than the inland region (see Figure 2.9). The eastern region has also experienced faster urbanization during the period 2000–10 (see Figure 2.10). Another indicator of regional urbanization variation is the distribution of the increase in urban permanent residents (see Figure 2.11). It is consistent with the regional distribution of the urbanization rate. These figures indicate that the eastern region has both a higher urbanization level and speed than the inland. On the one hand, this regional variation is a manifestation of unbalanced urbanization. On the

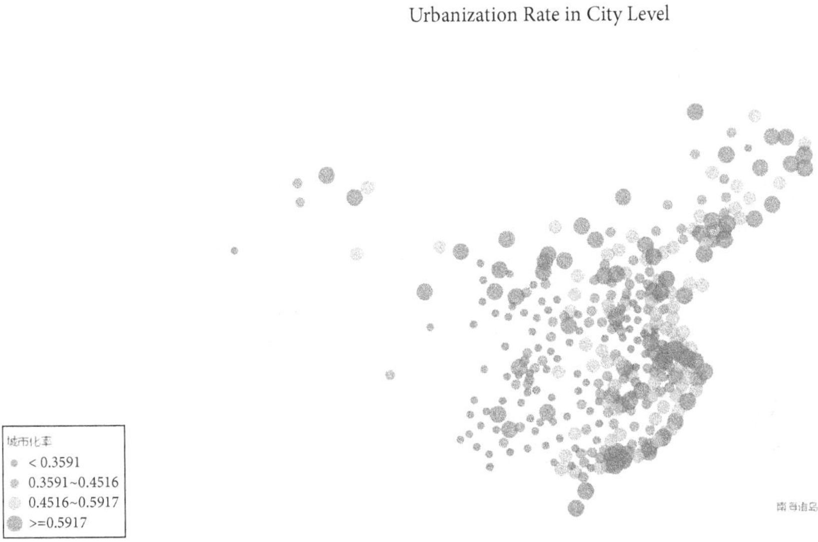

Figure 2.9. Urbanization rate at the city level in 2010

Source: The urbanization rate of 2010 is estimated from the 2010 national population census. The urbanization rate at the city level indicates the share of urban residents in the region that the city governs.

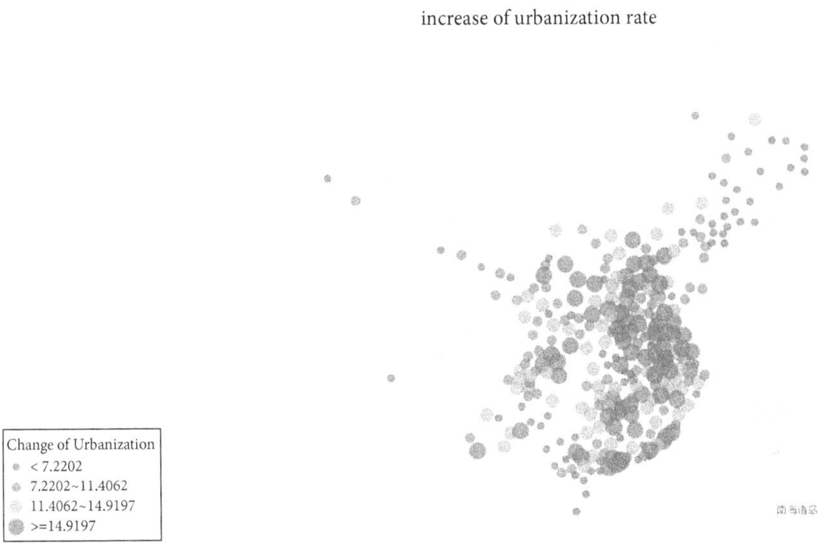

Figure 2.10. Increase in the urbanization rate during 2000 and 2010

Source: The increase in the urbanization rate is calculated on the basis of the urbanization estimates from the 2000 and 2010 national population census.

Figure 2.11. Increase in urban permanent residents during 2000 and 2010
Source: The increase in urban permanent residents is calculated on the basis of the estimates of urban permanent residents from the 2000 and 2010 national population census.

other hand, different levels of urbanization among regions exactly illustrate the agglomeration effects in more industrialized and developed areas.

2.4 The Urbanization–Industrialization Gap

2.4.1 Urbanization and Industrialization from 1980 in the PRC

Since the 'reforms and opening up', the PRC has experienced a steady rise in its urbanization level. However, the level of industrialization exceeded that of urbanization throughout the period, reflecting the characteristic of Chinese urbanization lagging behind industrialization. The most important reason for this gap is the institutional barriers that hinder rural-to-urban migration and restrict the access of migrants to public services (Chen et al. 2013). In Figure 2.12, the level of industrialization is measured by the ratio of secondary and tertiary industries' output value to GDP and the level of urbanization measured by the proportion of urban permanent residents. The gap between urbanization and industrialization was about fifty percentage points in 1980, while the gap declined to about forty percentage points in 2012. The gap between urbanization and industrialization has displayed a narrowing trend with time. It benefits from the development of the urban services sector that can absorb more rural surplus labour, largely increasing the number of urban permanent residents. However, the disparity between industrialization and urbanization is still huge.

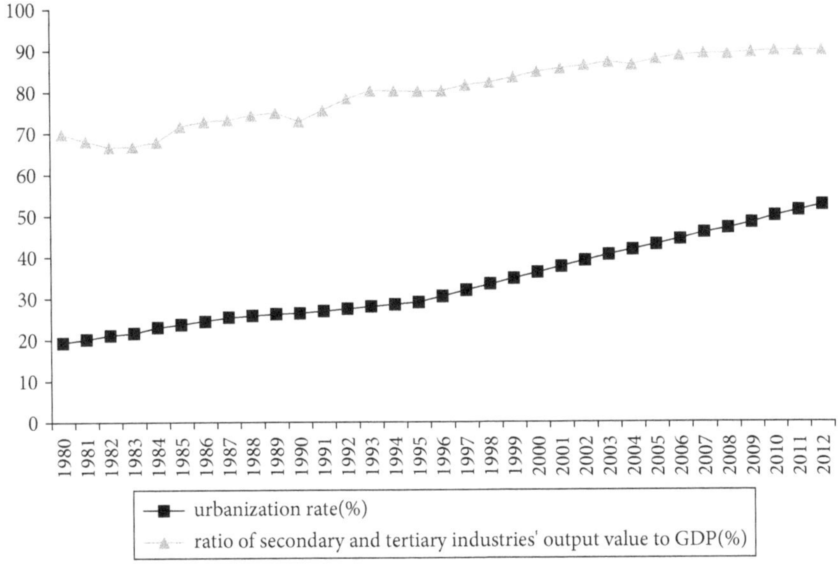

Figure 2.12. The urbanization–industrialization gap
Source: China Statistical Yearbook (NBSC 2013).

2.4.2 The Urbanization–Industrialization Gap and Average Wage at the City Level

With ongoing economic development, the services sector will create more jobs for migrants. When cities need more labour, the social costs of discriminating against migrants in public services become increasingly greater, so the policy-makers will have to remove the instruments of discrimination and allow in more migrants (Chen et al. 2013). Figure 2.13 shows that, at the city level in 2010, the gap between urbanization and industrialization was negatively related to average wage, which means economic growth can narrow the urbanization–industrialization gap.

2.4.3 Urbanization of People Lagging Behind Urbanization of Land

Usually, in a market economy, urbanization of people refers to the process of transforming rural labour into workers in the urban economy, while urban land expansion is also determined by land price. What are the implications of urbanization lagging behind industrialization? It directly reflects the fact that the reallocation of populations to cities is not in sync with the development of urban industry. Obviously, this is not because the development of industry in the PRC's

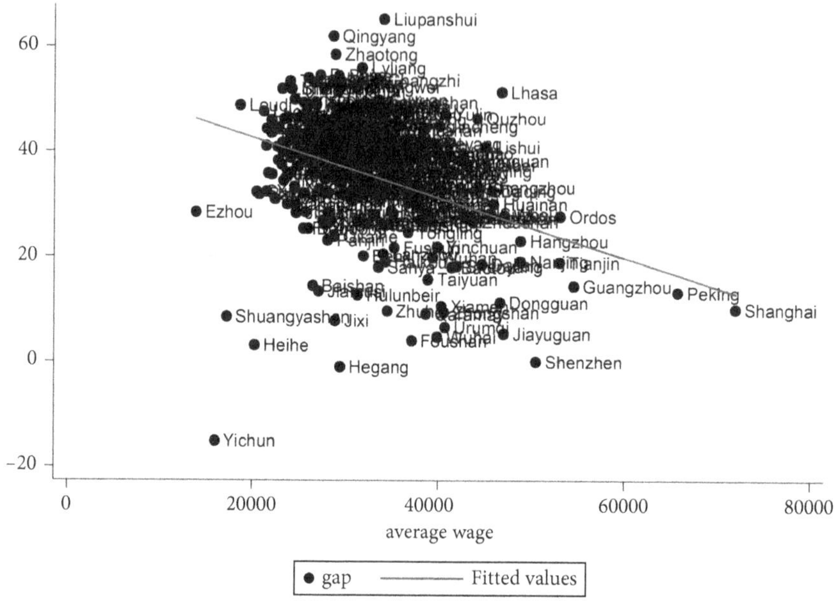

Figure 2.13. The urbanization–industrialization gap and average wage level

Source: (1) Y-axis denotes the gap between industrialization and urbanization. The urbanization rate is computed from the 2010 national population census; industrialization is represented by the ratio of secondary and tertiary industries' output value to GDP, using data from NSBC (2011b).

(2) Average wage data is from the 2011 *China City Statistical Yearbook*.

cities did not adopt labour-intensive production methods. The migrant workers that flooded into the cities, beginning in the 1990s, just happened to work in labour-intensive industries. The key to the issue is that when cities are attracting rural surplus labour, they do not have a plan to let these people take root in the city as 'urban residents'. Outsiders find it difficult to truly settle in the city, which necessarily makes mobility to urban areas incomplete.

Chinese urbanization is propelled not by population growth but administrative changes at the district level. This implies that each region's local government may cause the expansion of an urban area to become disjointed with local population density and industrial development in pursuit of rapid urbanization. Data in the introduction of the National Bureau of Statistics' 'Provisions Regarding Statistically Demarcating Urban and Rural Areas (1999 Trial Implementation)' show that after the State Council approved the Ministry of Civil Affairs' 'Report Regarding Adjustment of the Standard for Designating Townships' and 'Report Regarding Adjustment of the Standards for Creating Municipalities and the Conditions for Municipalities Leading Counties' in November 1984 and April 1986 respectively, there was a widening of the former standards for designating municipalities and townships. Subsequently, actions to retract counties and designate municipalities, and retract *xiang* and designate townships were pervasive, causing a nationwide increase in the number of municipalities and townships. The designation distributes the urban population to relatively smaller municipalities and townships to support their growth, causing the urban population density to decline at the district administration level. According to statistics, since the mid-1990s, the area of 338 municipalities nationwide at the prefectural level and above grew from 16,000 sq. km to 25,000 sq. km, an increase of 60 per cent. In the same time period, the urban district population (including migrant workers) of the 338 cities rose from 270 million to 300 million, an increase of only about 10 per cent. The rate of increase in urban areas is six times that of the rate of increase in the urban district population (Yan and Jiang 2007). Most cities' population density has significantly reduced in recent years (Lu 2013a). This indicates that the PRC's urbanization of people lags far behind its urbanization of land (Lu 2011; World Bank 2014).

This is a very thought-provoking phenomenon. On the one hand, Chinese urbanization is lagging behind. On the other hand, under an economically decentralized system, local governments pursue a larger urban area in an unbalanced manner and obtain revenue from land lease during the process of turning agriculture-use land into construction-use land. In particular, since the aggregate amount of construction-use land quota is regulated in the PRC, the government provides comparatively more construction-use land quotas for inland areas than areas in the eastern region in order to facilitate industrial development in the former and promote balanced regional development. This is a vital measure to support the growth of underdeveloped areas. After 2004, the proportion of development zones in inland areas rose strikingly due to the policy inclination of directing construction-use land quotas towards underdeveloped areas. However, more construction-use land quotas in inland areas have led to inefficiency in land use. Local governments conduct construction-use land quotas as the tools for attracting investment. As inland regions are underdeveloped, governments can finish construction-use land quotas by lowering land use prices and then attract investment for the local economy. Local governments also compete with each other through some preferential policies including subsidizing enterprises and reducing land price. As a result, the land price has been restrained and inefficient companies are more willing to move to inland areas. These preferential policies have caused severe loss of land assets and inefficient land use. As the distribution of construction-use land quotas are relatively inclined towards the inland regions, the phenomenon of the expansion of constructed urban areas exceeding the growth of the non-agricultural population is even more severe in the western regions, followed by the central regions, whereas the gap between the two figures is relatively small in the eastern provinces (Lu 2011). While developed areas have higher labour productivity, relatively reducing construction-use land quotas has increased the land price (Sridhar et al. 2013) and driven enterprises to be more efficient in the east. Therefore, a more even allocation of construction-use land quotas is widening the gap of economic development between developed and laggard regions.

2.5 Rural Development

Urbanization is not only a process of the development of secondary and tertiary industries in cities but also of rural development. Rural areas have also witnessed a great advance in agricultural productivity, capital investment, and agricultural organizations. First, in the urbanization process, more rural labour was attracted to work in non-agricultural industries and live in cities even if they did not have local urban Hukou. Per capita resources such as agricultural output and grain production are increasing, which can further drive the large scale of agricultural operations. Second, with the rise of rural labour working and living in cities, cities' capital accumulation gradually spills over to the countryside, where urban-to-rural remittance is a significant channel. During the process of capital deepening and upgrading the production scale, agricultural technology like mechanization could markedly improve and attract more capital to rural areas. So agricultural productivity, capital investment, and agricultural organizations are linked, influencing the process of urbanization and promoting rural development.

2.5.1 Growth, Productivity, and Income

2.5.1.1 Urbanization and the Agricultural Output from 1980

Many people, especially those in favour of national food security, worry that urbanization and rural-to-urban migration would hurt agriculture, but up to now this has not happened in the PRC (see the Appendix). Agricultural output has risen, thus propelling urbanization (see Figure 2.14). More importantly, agricultural output per capita has presented similar trends with the urbanization rate and is growing faster than urbanization since 1980 (see Figure 2.15).

2.5.1.2 Income and Consumption Level in Rural Households from 1980

In line with productivity growth, the income level of rural households has improved in the urbanization process, which can spur rural consumption and make rural people better off. Moreover, income level rises more quickly than consumption, in accordance with saving behaviour to guarantee a better future (see Figure 2.16). Figure 2.17 further illustrates the relationship between rural income and urbanization. At the city level, the positive connection between rural income and urbanization is manifested in the 2005 national population census. This evidence reveals that urbanization not only promotes agricultural output but also improves income and quality of life in the countryside.

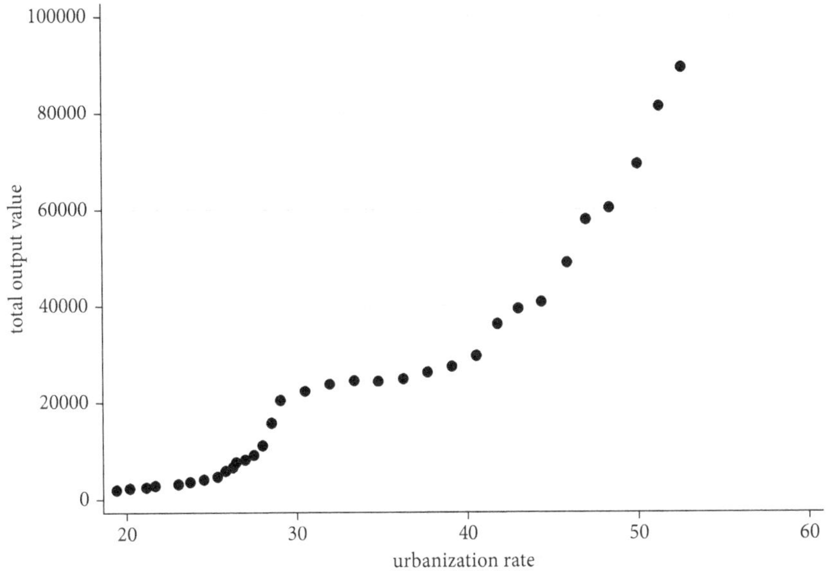

Figure 2.14. Total agricultural output and the urbanization rate

Source: Urbanization is denoted by the ratio of urban permanent residents to total permanent residents. Total agricultural output value, urban permanent residents and total permanent residents come from database of the National Bureau of Statistics, <http://www.gov.cn/shuju/>. This database is consistent with the *China Statistical Yearbook*.

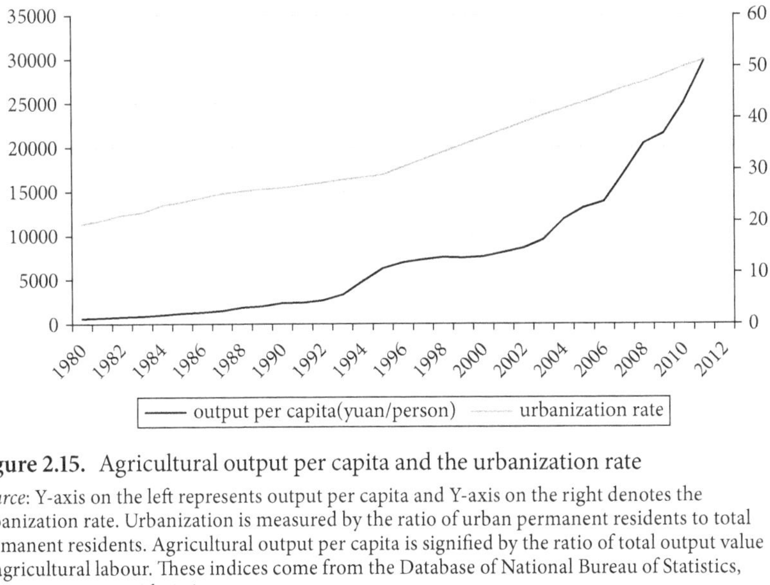

Figure 2.15. Agricultural output per capita and the urbanization rate

Source: Y-axis on the left represents output per capita and Y-axis on the right denotes the urbanization rate. Urbanization is measured by the ratio of urban permanent residents to total permanent residents. Agricultural output per capita is signified by the ratio of total output value to agricultural labour. These indices come from the Database of National Bureau of Statistics, <http://www.gov.cn/shuju/>.

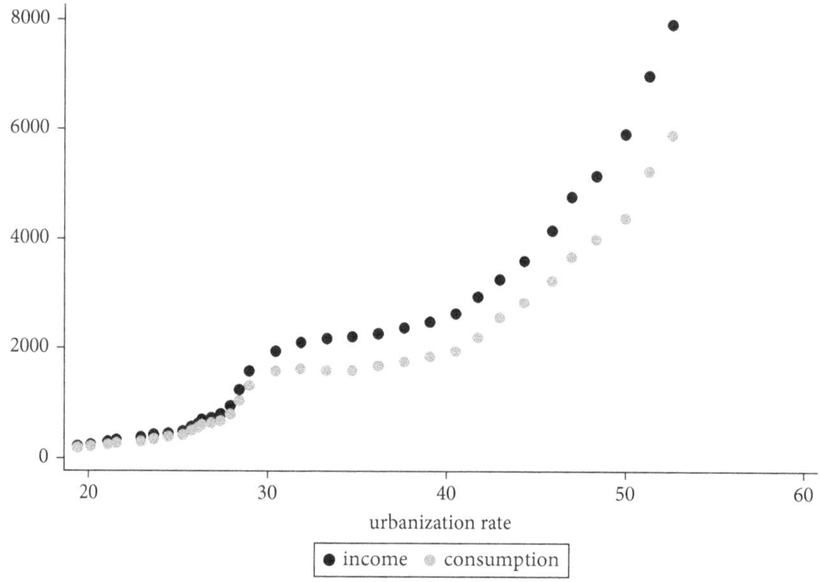

Figure 2.16. Income and consumption of rural households

Source: Database of the National Bureau of Statistics, <http://www.gov.cn/shuju/>.

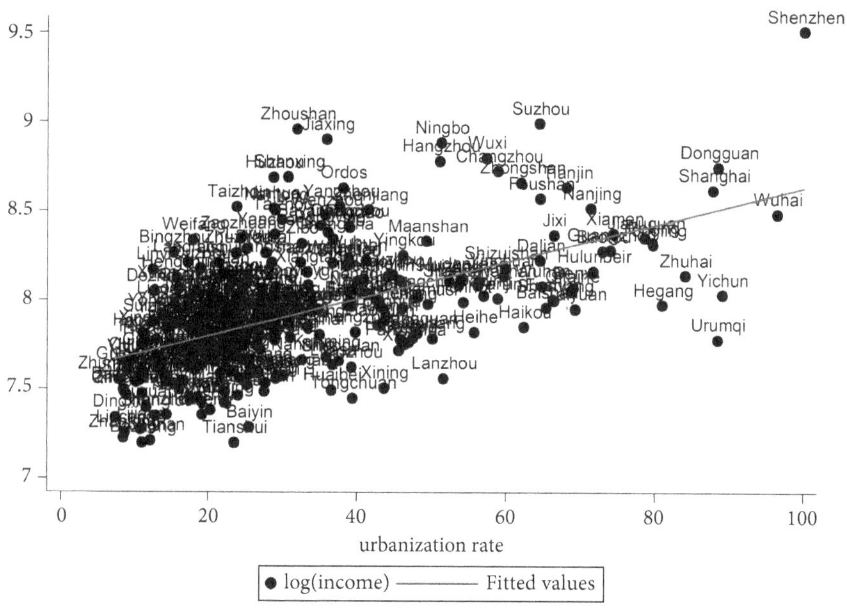

Figure 2.17. Income level in rural households and urbanization in 2005

Source: Authors' estimation based on the 2005 national population census. Urbanization rate = (local urban residents + migrant permanent residents)/(local residents + Migrant permanent residents). Income of rural residents = total income of rural residents/number of rural residents.

2.5.2 Capital Deepening

With the spread of urbanization, capital deepening and migrants' remittance are outstanding phenomena for rural development. Capital investment plays an important role in agricultural labour productivity.

2.5.2.1 Capital–Labour Ratio and Agricultural Productivity During Urbanization from 1980

First, we examine capital deepening in agricultural sectors in the PRC. The measurement of capital deepening is the capital–labour ratio (Kumar and Russell 2002). For the agricultural sector, capital deepening indicates an increase in the ratio of agricultural capital stock to labour engaging in agriculture.

From 1990, the capital–labour ratio ascended at a fast pace, denoting the existence of capital deepening in the agricultural sector. The extent of capital deepening is also growing, which results from the increase in agricultural investment and the transfer of rural labour to other non-agricultural industries. Agricultural capital deepening takes on two forms. The first is the enhancement of agricultural infrastructure and tools of production at the material level. The second is the increase in value of productive fixed assets to rural households (Luo 2013).

As the level of capital accumulation in the urban sector continuously escalates, rural labour is increasingly attracted to work and live in cities, forming the group of 'rural migrant workers'. The trend of capital–labour ratio is, therefore, concordant with the rising number of rural migrant workers. The same mounting tendency of capital–labour ratio and the number of rural migrant workers corresponds with the findings that capital deepening induces a reallocation of capital and labour in general (Acemoglu and Guerrieri 2008).

What is the effect of capital deepening in the agricultural sector? The most significant influence is the great advancement of agricultural output per capita whose growth is strikingly fast (see Figure 2.18). So capital deepening in the agricultural sector, an increasing number of rural migrant workers, and agricultural output per capita are closely linked with each other. Furthermore, increasing capital can partly explain the growth of agricultural labour productivity. (See the Appendix for an econometric model of the evidence.)

2.5.2.2 Remittance of Rural Migrant Workers

The term 'remittance' refers to the money that rural migrant workers send and take back to their communities of origin (Murphy 2006). Since the group of rural migrant workers emerged, remittance has become the most vital source of capital to improve rural household life and stimulate the rural economy. More importantly, remittance has been the main channel of capital accumulation for rural households. Since the mid-1990s, cities have attracted a lion's share in physical

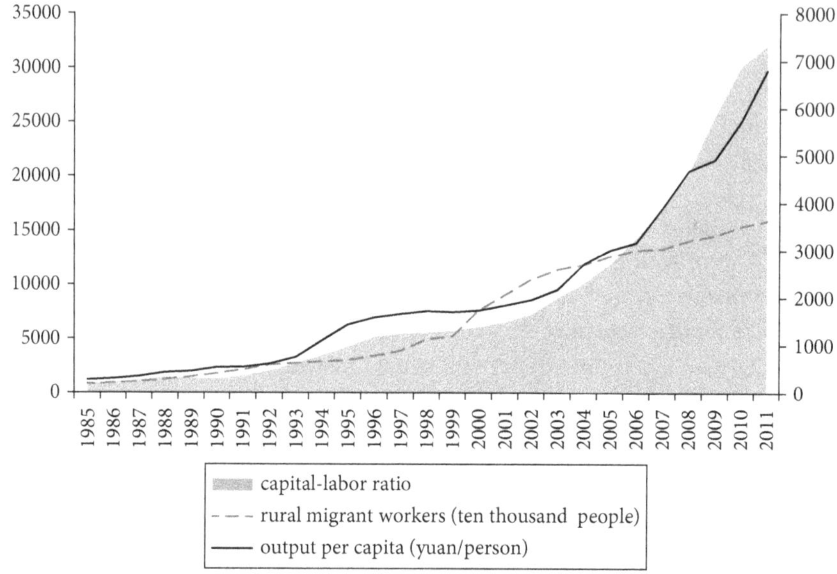

Figure 2.18. Capital–labour ratio and urbanization

Source: Y-axis on the left represents rural migrant workers and output per capita; Y-axis on the right represents capital–labour ratio.

(1) Capital–labour ratio is shown by the ratio of agricultural capital to rural labour. Collective and individual fixed assets data from the *China Rural Statistics Yearbook* (NBSC 2019b) make up agricultural capital. Rural labour data is from the Database of the National Bureau of Statistics, <http://www.gov.cn/shuju/>.

(2) Output per capita is denoted by the ratio of total agricultural output to rural labour and the data is from the Database of the National Bureau of Statistics, http://www.gov.cn/shuju/

(3) Rural migrant workers refers to labour with rural Hukou working out of rural communities. The data from 1985 to 2005 are from Lu (2013b); the data from 2006 to 2012 are from the *Peasant Worker Report* of the National Bureau of Statistics, <http://finance.people.com.cn/n/2013/0527/c1004-21624982.html;http://www.stats.gov.cn/tjsj/tjgb/nypcgb/qgnypcgb/200802/t20080227_30465.html>.

capital formation. Consequently, there was a shortage of investment in the countryside. Remittance can play a role in redistributing capital between different areas and in leading capital back to rural areas (Li 2001).

Following the large-scale migration of rural labour, rural migrant workers' income has been the major source of income in their communities of origin, especially in the middle and western areas, where the total earnings of rural migrant workers exceed the local fiscal revenues (Yu 2006). Compared with other countries, Chinese rural migrant workers send or take a larger proportion of earnings back to their home towns, accounting for 20 to 50 per cent in the rural household income (Fang 2005). According to the survey of the agricultural team in the National Bureau of Statistics and the Agricultural Ministry, the annual average remittance of rural migrant workers is in the range of RMB 3,200 to RMB 4,600, and total remittance could reach RMB 270 billion to RMB 520 billion from

1997 to 2004 (Hu et al. 2008).[2] In terms of individual rural migrant workers' remittances, most of them remit in the range of RMB 2,000 to RMB 8,000 annually and the average remittance in the sample is RMB 4,538 (Hu et al. 2008).

As immigrants in inland provinces make up about 50 per cent of total immigrants and the majority of them head to big cities in eastern areas for working opportunities and higher earnings, rural migrant workers in inland provinces remit more money. In 2000, total remittance in Sichuan Province reached RMB 202 billion, which is equivalent to the local fiscal revenue, while in Anhui the remittance of RMB 174 million surpassed the local fiscal revenue (Murphy 2006). Remittance is more likely to flow into low-income and mostly agricultural rural households, inland areas, and villages rather than cities or towns, accounting for regional differences in remittance (Li 2001).

The majority of remittances are used for living expenses, mainly for building houses, purchasing consumer goods, and education expenditure (Murphy 2006). Some remittances are put into production and investment, spurring local economic development. Married and older rural migrant workers tend to utilize remittance in health and education expenditure, while migrants with higher education and longer working experience are likely to utilize remittance for future venture investment (Hu and Shi 2013). Li et al. (2008) gathered data on the use of remittance from September 2006 to September 2007 and found that the top three preferable uses of remittance are providing for the elderly, family support, and educational fees.

Given the capital deepening in agricultural sectors, the use of agricultural investment needs further exploration. According to Li et al. (2008), only about 3 per cent of remitters they surveyed put agricultural investment in first place, and agricultural investment ranks as the fifth most important use of remittance. However, they pointed out that the proportion of remittance use in agricultural investment is gradually increasing. It demonstrates that agriculture is still given importance due to the guarantee that land provides, the interests of big families in the countryside, and its connection with the migrants' origins.

Considerable remittances have relieved the pressure of capital demands and become important sources of educational, medical, and living expenditure for rural households, encouraging the rural economy (Cheng 2006). Remittance exerts an indirect influence on rural social progress, mainly in the field of consumption, family education, supporting the family, and income. In rural consumption, building houses accounts for a large proportion of capital investment,

[2] According to Cheng (2006), apart from remittances through regular financial institutions, including commercial banks, rural post offices, and rural credit cooperatives, rural migrant workers take a part of their income back home by themselves, accounting for 25 per cent. Since it is hard to estimate the capital taken home, the actual capital amount from rural migrant workers to rural communities could be much larger.

which can propel markets of building materials, decorative objects, household furniture, electrical equipment, and items for daily use. In this way, remittances significantly push the advancement of the local and rural economy. On the other hand, remittances are used for supporting the elderly, weakening the public pressure of social security for the elderly in the countryside (Li et al. 2008). Remittances also offer children more educational opportunities, reduce the dropout rate, and lessen children's working time in agriculture (Hu and Li 2009). Remittance directly increases rural income (Taylor et al. 2003). The income transfer of comparatively poor rural families is higher than that of wealthy families (Du and Park 2003). This denotes that the poverty rate can decline with the use of remittance. But effects of remittances are limited for rural households with low income because this group lacks the resources and capabilities to work in cities far away (Hu 2010).

Agricultural production and productive investments highlight the importance of remittance. Remittances substitute rural labour. As a result, increasing remittances counteract the negative effects that reducing rural labour has on agricultural production (Rozelle et al. 1999; Li 2001). An investigation by the Rural Economic Research Center of the Agricultural Ministry shows that additional cash inputs bring more marginal benefits for agricultural production than additional labour does (Li 2001).

Overall, remittances play a distinctive role in the rural economy including social advancement, capital accumulation, agricultural production, and productive investments.

2.5.3 Agricultural Organization and Production Scale

2.5.3.1 Scale of Operation in Agriculture

With an increasing proportion of the rural population migrating to the cities, their land is transferred to local rural residents. As a result, more cultivated land is concentrated on a decreasing proportion of rural labour, which makes large-scale production and organization possible, giving an impetus to agricultural growth. The shifting of rural labour to non-agricultural industries is the fundamental premise of agricultural scale of operation (Han 1998). Furthermore, operation scale of land is limited by circulation speed. If the number and rate of urbanizing rural labour speeds up, more land can be transferred, making large-scale operations possible (Liu 2006). Figure 2.19 shows that grain output per capita dropped partly due to the rising numbers of rural migrant workers during the period 1995 to 2002, but it gradually goes up thereafter. The large-scale fiscal transfer to support agriculture since 2003 and the agriculture tax abolition in 2006 can partly explain the recent growth of per capita agricultural production.

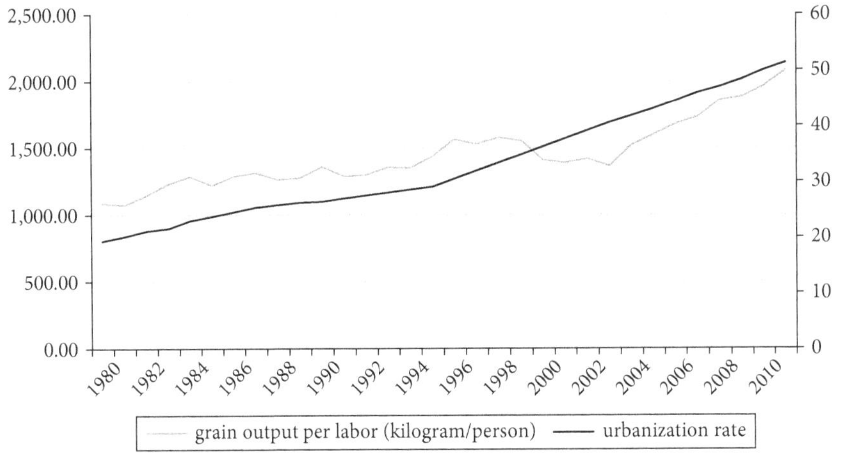

Figure 2.19. Grain output per labour and urbanization

Source: Y-axis on the left represents grain output per labour and Y-axis on the right represents the urbanization rate. The data of grain output per labour are from the Database of the National Bureau of Statistics, <http://www.gov.cn/shuju/>.

However, the increasing operation scale of land and the mechanized substitution for labour can also explain the agricultural productivity growth when labour is no longer critical in agricultural production (see the Appendix for more evidence).

2.5.3.2 Mechanization in Agricultural Production

Agricultural mechanization is the replacement of rural labour, along with large-scale cultivation (Liu 2006). Total output power applied in agriculture is gradually ascending with the growth of rural migrant workers (see Figure 2.20). Apart from the total output power, it is more appropriate to use output power per capita to represent mechanization (see Figure 2.21). The trend has been that mechanization grows faster than the urbanization rate, stressing the striking improvement of agricultural mechanization. So agricultural mechanization in the substitution of labour has advanced following the urbanization process.

2.5.3.3 Farmland in Rural Households

The agricultural production scale is closely related to the number of farmlands in rural households. Since 1982, the Household Contract Responsibility System has been officially issued for the reform of collective land management, spurring the increase of farmland for rural households. Also, after 2003, the quantity of farmland experienced the second impetus with the rising numbers of rural migrant workers (see Figure 2.22). In some sense, this concentration of farmland provides the space for large-scale agricultural operations.

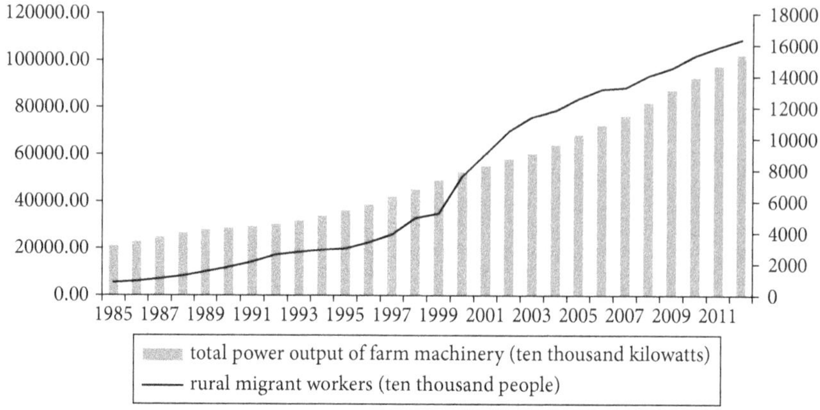

Figure 2.20. Total power output and rural migrant workers

Source: Y-axis on the left represents total power output of farm machinery and Y-axis on the right represents rural migrant workers. The data of total power output of farm machinery are from the Database of the National Bureau of Statistics, <http://www.gov.cn/shuju/>. Rural migrant workers refer to labour with rural Hukou, working out of rural communities. The data from 1985 to 2005 are from Lu (2013b); the data from 2006 to 2012 are from *Peasant Worker Report* of the National Bureau of Statistics. <http://finance.people.com.cn/n/2013/0527/c1004-21624982.html; http://www.stats.gov.cn/tjsj/tjgb/nypcgb/qgnypcgb/200802/t20080227_30465.html>.

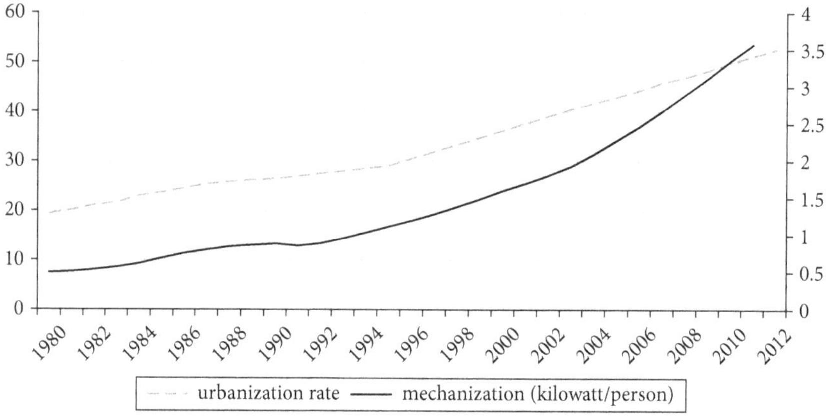

Figure 2.21. Mechanization and urbanization

Source: Y-axis on the left represents the urbanization rate and Y-axis on the right represents mechanization. Mechanization is represented by the ratio of total power output of farm machinery to rural labourers. Urbanization is denoted by the ratio of urban permanent residents to total permanent residents. The data are from the Database of the National Bureau of Statistics, <http://www.gov.cn/shuju/>.

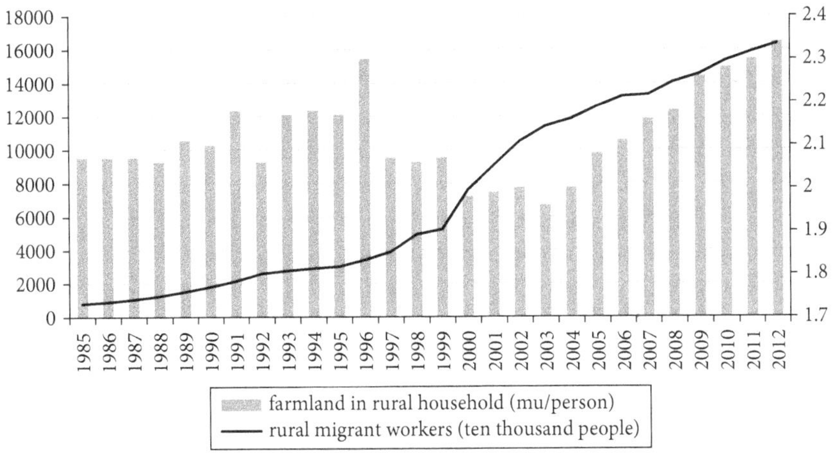

Figure 2.22. Rural farmland and rural-to-urban migration

Source: Y-axis on the left represents rural migrant workers and Y-axis on the right represents farmland in rural households. Farmland in rural households is denoted by cultivated land per capita in rural households. The data are from the Database of the National Bureau of Statistics, <http://www.gov.cn/shuju/>. Rural migrant workers refer to labour with rural Hukou, working out of rural communities. The data from 1985 to 2005 are from Lu (2013b); the data from 2006 to 2012 are from *Peasant Worker Report* of the National Bureau of Statistics, <http://finance.people.com.cn/n/2013/0527/c1004-21624982.html>; <http://www.stats.gov.cn/tjsj/tjgb/nypcgb/qgnypcgb/200802/t20080227_30465.html>.

2.6 Conclusion

This chapter studies how urbanization enhances economic growth. Through agglomeration effects, employment opportunities and income levels can largely increase. In addition, the mechanism of sharing, matching, and learning are greatly strengthened in cities, especially large cities, which can further bring exchange of information, knowledge spillover, and human capital externalities.

However, when taking a close look at the urbanization level, speed, and regional variations, we see that the PRC's urbanization level lags behind that of many developing countries at a similar stage of development, let alone developed countries, although the urbanization process in the PRC has been fast. An examination of regional variations reveals that the urbanization level and speed was higher in the eastern area on average at the city level during the period of 2000 and 2010. Another characteristic of the PRC's growth is that urbanization lags behind industrialization, in a way that is similar to countries like India. Institutional barriers to rural-to-urban and interregional migration, such as the Hukou system, have reduced the ability of urban growth to absorb rural labour. If these institutions can be reformed, urbanization in the PRC still has the potential to develop according to a more efficient, equitable, and sustainable pattern.

As for rural development, urbanization has propelled agricultural productivity and will continue pushing agricultural productivity in the future. Also, rural income and consumption levels have been boosted during urbanization. Moreover, agricultural productivity is significantly driven by capital accumulation. The degree of capital deepening is growing in the agricultural sector mainly because urbanization promotes the rise of rural migrant workers to other non-agricultural industries. Another vital source of capital investment is remittance. Agricultural organizations, urbanization, and outflow of migrant workers make it possible for large-scale production and organization. Agricultural mechanization functions as the force in the substitution of labour and concentration of farmland provides the space for large-scale agricultural operations.

In general, urbanization in the PRC has taken advantage of agglomeration effects and has brought the benefits of economic growth to both urban and rural areas. However, problems of urbanization, including below average urbanization level and urbanization lagging behind industrialization, need to be solved by institutional reforms for sustainable development.

Appendix

Here we use provincial-level data to investigate the effects of agricultural capital, rural labour engaging in agricultural production, and rural land on agricultural output in the PRC during 1998 to 2010.

In rural development, agricultural output and farmers' income are the two main concerns. So two models for total and per capita agricultural production are estimated, respectively. We take the log of every variable.

In the model of total output, we explore how total agricultural capital, rural labour engaging in agricultural production, and rural land influence total agricultural production. In the per capita output model, the effects of agricultural capital per capita and the area of cultivated land per capita on agricultural output per capita are estimated. We also control other variables which are likely to affect total agricultural output or agricultural output per capita. The variables used in the two models are shown in Table A.2.1.

In consideration of price fluctuations, the provincial-level GDP deflator is used in total agricultural output, total agricultural capital, total government expenditure in agriculture, agricultural output per capita, agricultural capital per capita, and government agricultural expenditure per capita to get comparable variables.

As for the data sources, except for educational year[3] and GDP deflator,[4] the other variables come directly from the *China Statistical Yearbook* for the period from 1999 through 2011 (NBSC 2019a). Most variables correspond exactly to the variables in the *China Statistical Yearbook*, while total agricultural capital is measured by the original value of productive fixed assets in agriculture, and the total area of cultivated land represents rural land. For the variables per capita, we use total variables divided by rural labour engaged in agricultural activities.

[3] Average educational year comes from Pinggu bbs, which is computed from the *China Statistical Yearbook* and *China Education Statistical Yearbook*. The website is <http://bbs.pinggu.org/forum.php?mod=viewthread&tid=2138991>.

[4] GDP deflator is computed using 1995 as the base year. The data source comes from the website <http://wenku.baidu.com/link?url=cu8Nr6qAP894YJHuGM_Ae2dsJE8LCZ2MNlD5a_cBU7sLBwkK8VBCpSsamslaMZ0g4kWBjQ5vOZL4JafMDqp3sFbZnh86em8cxPMMyazO7RS>.

Table A.2.1. Variables used in the two models

Variables in total output model	Definition	Variables in per capita output model	Definition
Dependent variable		Dependent variable	
Y	Total agricultural output	PY	Agricultural output per capita
Independent variables		Independent variables	
Capital	The original value of total productive fixed assets in agriculture	Pcapital	Agricultural capital per capita
Land	Total area of cultivated land	Pland	Area of cultivated land per capita
Labour	Rural labour engaging in agricultural production		
Education	Average educational years	Peducation	Average educational years
Finance	Total government expenditure in agriculture	Pfinance	Government agricultural expenditure per capita
Fertilizer	Total consumption of chemical fertilizers	Pfertilizer	Consumption of chemical fertilizers per capita
Road	Total highway mileage in countryside	Road	Total highway mileage in countryside
Railway	Total railway mileage in countryside	Railway	Total railway mileage in countryside

In these panel data models, we also control the fixed effects of year. The results of fixed effects and random effects are both presented in Table A.2.2. According to the Hausman test, the models of fixed effects are preferred.

From this empirical study, we find that agricultural capital and area of cultivated land can improve agricultural output. Columns (1) and (2) in Table A.2.2 represent the regressions for total output with fixed effects and random effects respectively. The results of fixed effects and random effects indicate the positive influence of total agricultural capital and area of cultivated land on total agricultural output. However, the coefficient of rural labour engaged in agricultural production is negative to the development of agricultural output. This implies that labour is no longer the most important factor in agricultural production.

Columns (3) and (4) contain the models for output per capita with fixed effects and random effects respectively. In the results of fixed effects and random effects, the coefficients of agricultural capital per capita and area of cultivated land per capita are significantly positive, illustrating their positive effects on the agricultural output per capita.

Table A.2.2. Regression results

VARIABLES	(1) FE Ln Y	(2) RE Ln Y	VARIABLES	(3) FE Ln PY	(4) RE Ln PY
Ln capital	0.601***	0.521***	Ln Pcapital	0.417***	0.390***
	(0.0329)	(0.0332)		(0.0308)	(0.0307)
Ln land	0.157*	0.0943	Ln Pland	0.253***	0.0178
	(0.0869)	(0.0793)		(0.0734)	(0.0656)
Ln labour	−0.747***	−0.290***	Ln Peducation	−0.109	−0.135
	(0.147)	(0.0983)		(0.147)	(0.146)
Ln education	0.178	−0.0112	Ln Pfinance	0.358***	0.406***
	(0.161)	(0.163)		(0.0363)	(0.0349)
Ln finance	0.136***	0.225***	Ln Pfertilizer	0.143	0.385***
	(0.0466)	(0.0489)		(0.0890)	(0.0757)
Ln fertilizer	0.115	0.304***	Ln road	0.124***	0.141***
	(0.0957)	(0.0859)		(0.0406)	(0.0364)
Ln road	0.106**	0.187***	Ln railway	0.0137	−0.0203
	(0.0449)	(0.0432)		(0.0432)	(0.0395)
Ln railway	0.00120	−0.000203	Constant	6.047***	6.210***
	(0.0466)	(0.0463)		(1.457)	(0.713)
Constant	−3.218**	−6.987***			
	(1.242)	(0.770)			
Hausman test for FE vs RE models	69.25***		Hausman test for FE vs RE models	42.58***	
Observations	382	382	Observations	382	382
R-squared	0.976	0.974	R-squared	0.976	0.975
Number of region	30	30	Number of region	30	30

Notes: Standard errors clustered at the region level are in the parentheses. ***, **, and * represent statistical significance at 1%, 5%, and 10% levels, respectively.

Therefore, agricultural capital and area of cultivated land account for promoting agricultural output more than agricultural labour. The capital deepening in agriculture and the operation scale of cultivated land have become the major forces for agricultural labour productivity. This implies that urbanization of the population will not adversely impact total agricultural production, but will enhance agricultural productivity by increasing capital and land per capita.

References

Acemoglu, D. and V. Guerrieri. 2008. 'Capital Deepening and Nonbalanced Economic Growth'. *Journal of Political Economy 116* (3): 467–98.

Au, Chun-Chung and J. V. Herderson. 2006. 'How Migration Restrictions Limit Agglomeration and Productivity in China'. *Journal of Development Economics 80* (2): 350–88.

Chen, Zhao, Xiaofeng Liu, and Ming Lu. 2013. 'Beyond Lewis: Rural-to-Urban Migration with Endogenous Policy Change'. *China Agricultural Economic Review* 5 (2): 213–30.

Cheng, Enjiang. 2006. 'Domestic Money Transfer Services for Migrant Workers in China- A Report to CGAP (in Chinese)'. Consultative Group to Assist the Poor, World Bank. <http://wenku.baidu.com/view/6e41fbfcf61fb7360b4c6595.html>.

Du, Yang and Albert Park. 2003. 'Migration and Poverty Reduction (in Chinese)'. *China Rural Survey* 5: 2–17.

Fang, Hua. 2005. 'Report of Remittances by Rural Migrant Workers Shows: income inflow of this group mainly depends on remittance (in Chinese)'. *Financial Times*, 27 November. <http://finance.sina.com.cn/g/20051027/01142067896.shtml>.

Glaeser, E. L. and Giacomo A. M. Ponzetto. 2010. 'Did the Death of Distance Hurt Detroit and Help New York?' In *Agglomeration Economics*, edited by E. L. Glaeser, University of Chicago Press.

Glaeser, E. L. and Ming Lu. 2013. 'Human Capital Externalities in China'. Harvard University and Fudan University Working Paper.

Han, Jun. 1998. 'Land Policy: From Land Equalization System to Moderate Large-scale Operation (in Chinese)'. *The World of Survey and Research* 5: 8–9.

Henderson, J. V. 2009. 'Urbanization in China: Policy Issues and Options'. Report for China Economic Research and Advisory Programme.

Hu, Feng. 2010. 'Migrant Remittances and Household Income Inequality: A Counterfactual Analysis (in Chinese)'. *Population Research* 3: 89–100.

Hu, Feng and Shantong Li. 2009. 'The Influence of Parents' Working Out on Left-behind Children: Based on Empirical Analysis of Rural Migrant Workers in Five Cities (in Chinese)'. *Management World* 2: 67–74.

Hu, Feng and Yupeng Shi. 2013. 'Remittances of Rural Migrant Workers and Economic Development of Origin Communities: Based on the Analysis on Factors Influencing the Use of Remittances (in Chinese)'. *World Economic Papers* 2: 80–95.

Hu, Feng, Yupeng Shi, and Qiwen Wang. 2008. 'Are Remittance of Rural Migrant Workers Altruistic? Based on the Analysis of Interval Regression Model (in Chinese)'. *Journal of Financial Research* 1: 175–90.

Jian, Xinhua and Kun Huang. 2010. 'Empirical Analysis and Forecast of the Level and Speed of Urbanization in China (in Chinese)'. *Economic Research Journal* 3: 28–39.

Kumar, S. and R. R. Russell. 2002. 'Technological Change, Technological Catch-up, and Capital Deepening: Relative Contributions to Growth and Convergence'. *The American Economic Review* 92 (3): 527–48.

Lewis, W. A. 1954. 'Economic Development with Unlimited Supplies of Labour'. *The Manchester School* 22 (2): 139–91.

Li, Qiang, Xuefeng Mao, and Tao Zhang. 2008. 'Decisions, Quantities and Use of Rural Migrant Workers' Remittances (in Chinese)'. *China Rural Survey* 3: 2–12.

Li, Qiang. 2001. 'The Research of Chinese Rural Migrant Workers and Their Remittances (in Chinese)'. *Sociological Studies* 4: 64–76.

Liu, Fengqin. 2006. 'A Study of the Conditions of the Scale Operation of Farmland and of the Effect Thereof: Taking the Northeastern Countryside as a Case (in Chinese)'. *Management World* 9: 71–9.

Lu, Ming, Hong Gao, and Hiroshi Sato. 2012. 'On Urban Size and Inclusive Employment (in Chinese)'. *Social Sciences in China 10*: 47–66.

Lu, Ming. 2011. 'Reallocation of Rights of Construction Land Usage Across Areas: New Engines of China's Economic Growth (in Chinese)'. *World Economy 1*: 107–25.

Lu, Ming. 2013a. *The Power of Space*, Shanghai People Press.

Lu, Ming. 2013b. 'Labor Mobility and Laggard Urbanization under Institutional Restrictions'. In *China's Regional Development: Review and Prospect*, edited by Lu Ming et al., Routledge.

Luo, Haoxuan. 2013. 'Empirical Research on the Influence of Agricultural Capital Deepening on Chinese Agriculture Economic (in Chinese)'. *Issues in Agricultural Economy* 9: 4–14.

Moretti, E. 2004a. 'Workers' Education, Spillovers, and Productivity: Evidence from Plant-Level Production Functions'. *The American Economic Review 94* (3): 656–90.

Moretti, E. 2004b. 'Estimating the Social Return to Higher Education: Evidence from Longitudinal and Repeated Cross-Sectional Data'. *Journal of Econometrics 121* (1–2): 175–212.

Moretti, E. 2004c. 'Human Capital Externalities in Cities'. In *Handbook of Urban and Regional Economics, Volume 4: Cities and Geography*, edited by Henderson J. V. and Jacques-Francois Thisse, Elsevier.

Murphy, R. 2006. 'Domestic Migrant Remittances in China: Distribution, Channels and Livelihoods'. *International Organization for Migration (IOM), Migration Research Series 24.*

NBSC (National Bureau of Statistics, China). 2011a. 'Communiqué of the National Bureau of Statistics of People's Republic of China on Major Figures of the 2010 Population Census (No. 1)'. <https://web.archive.org/web/20131108022004/http://www.stats.gov.cn/english/newsandcomingevents/t20110428_402722244.htm>.

NBSC (National Bureau of Statistics, China). 2011b. *China City Statistical Yearbook.* <http://tongji.cnki.net/kns55/Navi/YearBook.aspx?id=N2012020070&floor=1>.

NBSC (National Bureau of Statistics, China). 2013. *China Statistical Yearbook.* <http://www.stats.gov.cn/tjsj/ndsj/>.

NBSC (National Bureau of Statistics, China). 2019a. *China Statistical Yearbook.* <http://www.stats.gov.cn/tjsj/ndsj/>.

NBSC (National Bureau of Statistics, China). 2019b. *China Rural Statistics Yearbook.* <http://tongji.cnki.net/kns55/navi/HomePage.aspx?id=N2017030076&name=YMCTJ&floor=1>.

Rauch, J. E. 1993. 'Productivity Gains from Geographic Concentration of Human Capital: Evidence from the Cities'. *Journal of Urban Economics 34* (3): 380–400.

Rozelle, S., J. E. Taylor, and A. de Brauw. 1999. 'Migration, Remittances and Agricultural Productivity in China'. *The American Economic Review 89* (2): 287–91.

Sridhar, K. S., Shuzhong Gu, and Shujie Yao. 2013. 'Land Sales as a Public Financing Tool in China and India'. In *China's Development and Harmonization*, edited by Bin Wu, Shujie Yao, and Jian Chen, Routledge.

Sveikauskas, L. 1975. 'The Productivity of Cities'. *The Quarterly Journal of Economics 89* (3): 393–413.

Taylor, J. E., S. Rozelle, and A. de Brauw. 2003. 'Migration and Incomes in Source Communities: A New Economics of Migration Perspective from China'. *Economic Development and Cultural Change 52* (1): 75–101.

World Bank. 2014. 'Urbanization and Economic Growth'. Development Research Center of the State Council.

World Bank. 2019. 'World Development Indicators Online'. <http://www.worldbank.org/data>.

Yan, Wei and Nan Jiang. 2007. 'Land Usage Must be Strictly Saved in Accelerating the Process of Urbanization'. *Social Science Weekly*, 9 August.

Yu, Ronghua. 2006. 'Where does Rural Migrant Workers' Money Flow (in Chinese)'. *People's Daily*, 9 February. <http://finance.people.com.cn/BIG5/1045/4076128.html>.

3
Costs and Benefits of Urbanization
The Indian Case

Kala S. Sridhar

3.1 Introduction and Scope

Urbanization has both benefits and costs. In a market economy, the trade-off between benefits and costs determines the level, speed, and pace of urbanization. This chapter summarizes research findings on how urbanization enhances productivity and economic growth in both rural and urban sectors. I examine the relationship between urbanization and growth, using data from India. Given that urbanization cannot be viewed in isolation, this chapter also studies how urban areas are affected by migration from rural areas and how rural areas, in turn, are benefited by urbanization in terms of remittances made by urban migrants to their homes.

This chapter is organized as follows. First, evidence on urban agglomeration economies and economic growth, growth and productivity, and sharing/matching/learning is briefly discussed, within each section first internationally and then in terms of evidence from the Indian context. Following that, the level, speed, and regional variation in urbanization for India are described. Then the urbanization–industrialization gap in the Indian context is summarized, followed by a presentation of the empirical findings with respect to urbanization, which is dependent on benefits and costs. Chapter 21 in this volume examines the impact of urbanization on growth, inequality, and poverty in the Indian context. However, that chapter examines the relationship between growth, poverty, inequality, and urbanization, while this chapter focuses more tightly on a benefit–cost framework for urbanization.

Urbanization cannot be viewed in isolation; hence the last section focuses on rural development in India's context, taking the case of the erstwhile Mahatma Gandhi National Rural Employment Guarantee Scheme (MGNREGS), whose objective is to arrest rural–urban migration by alleviating rural poverty. Here, some evidence on remittances by urban migrants to rural areas is summarized. Following this, the policy implications of the research are summarized.

Kala S. Sridhar., *Costs and Benefits of Urbanization* In: *Cities of Dragons and Elephants: Urbanization and Urban Development in China and India. Edited by:* Guanghua Wan and Ming Lu, Oxford University Press (2019).
 DOI: 10.1093/oso/9780198829225.003.0003

3.2 Evidence on Urban Agglomeration Economies and Economic Growth

While much of the literature on urbanization in different parts of the world focuses on the relationship between urbanization and growth (Henderson 2004; Krugman 1995; Zhang 2002; Lanaspa et al. 2005; Bertinelli and Strobl 2007; Sridhar and Sridhar 2007; Gilbert and Gugler 1982; McGee 1971), the causes of urbanization are understudied, especially in the framework of benefits and costs. Henderson (2004) gives credence to this. Brueckner (1990) studies urbanization in the cross-national context in a benefits–costs framework. Theories that are adequate to describe urbanization in the West are not necessarily applicable to the developing cities of Asia. This lends additional support to investigating the question as to whether the causes of urbanization for Indian states are different from those for the developed world. Besides, there is also evidence from Zhang (2002) and Henderson (2004) that the causal link runs from economic growth to urbanization and not vice versa.

3.2.1 Growth and Productivity

What do we know about the relationship between urbanization and economic growth in India?

Urbanization enhances economic growth. At the global level, the urbanization rate and GDP per capita are positively related, but the position of India is below the average level when compared with that of other countries, which means India's urbanization at 31 per cent lags behind its development stage (with a per capita GDP of $1,503) by about ten percentage points (see Figure 3.1). One reason why this has occurred is because of the government of India's inadequate attention to urbanization and its long-term problems since independence. India was believed to live primarily in its villages. There is surplus labour in India's rural areas, which, however, has usually been absorbed by the services sector in urban areas, as Sridhar and Reddy (2014) find with respect to the poor in Bangalore. Paul et al. (2012) and Sridhar and Kashyap (2014) also confirm that services account for the employment of most of India's urban labour force, clarifying that most Indian cities bypassed the classic transfer of surplus labour from agriculture to manufacturing as demonstrated by the Lewis model and the transition to urbanization.

Among other reasons why India is less urban than what is suggested by the level of income is that successive governments (save the current one) have been pessimistic about urbanization, being guided by Todaro's model, which suggested

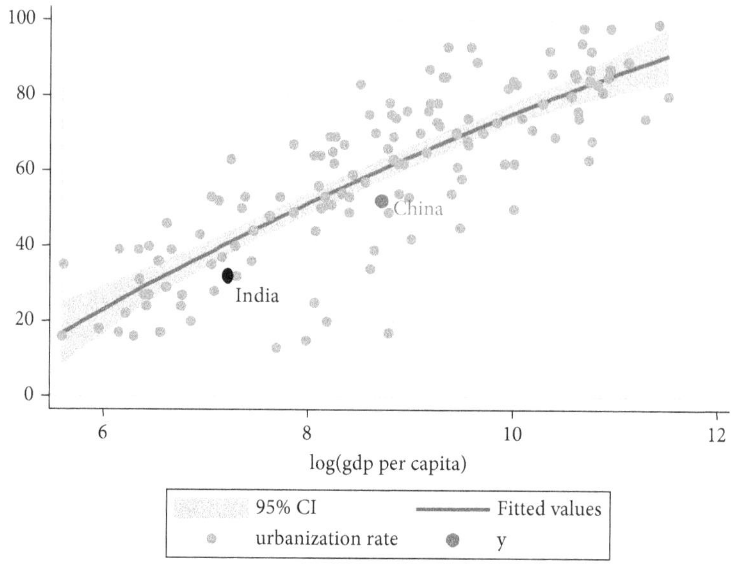

Figure 3.1. Global urbanization and GDP per capita in 2012

Source: Data from the 2012 urbanization rate and GDP per capita in the World Development Indicators (World Bank 2013) analysed by the author. Liechtenstein and Monaco as outliers and typical city states including Hong Kong, China; Macao; Singapore; Taiwan, China; Vatican City; Malta; Di San Marino; and the Maldives have been eliminated.

that urban areas which increase job opportunities will attract greater migration from rural to urban areas, which would, in turn, paradoxically increase their unemployment rate. This model provided a negative view of urbanization since it implied that no matter what urban areas did, it would be futile to improve their liveability.

While empirical evidence supporting Todaro's model has been limited, even using Indian data, Indian urban development policies have implicitly been guided by such a model for a long time. For this reason, it was believed that rural–urban migration has to be 'checked' as may be seen in the case of programmes such as the MGNREGS, which is discussed at the end of this chapter.

Mills and Becker (1986) point out how, even historically, several policies/programmes were in place to 'control' urbanization and city size in India. While there is no single document that describes the Indian government's policies on city size, as they point out, the earliest national government programmes to influence the location of industry made use of industrial licences. In 1977, it was decided that industrial licences would be denied in large metropolitan areas and urban agglomerations.

Second, direct investment in government-owned enterprises was another means through which the government of India restricted the growth of large cities. Preference for the location of government-owned industry was given to low-income areas, rural areas, or small cities and towns.

Further, a locational programme, according to Mills and Becker (1986), which referred to government encouragement of small-scale industry to locate in small towns and rural areas, was yet another tool used to control city sizes. Under these locational programmes, a large number of specific instruments such as concessionary finance, input allocations, technical and marketing assistance, training programmes, and the development of industrial estates were provided to small industries.

A final locational programme of the government of India, also provided by state governments, was to develop 'backward' districts, with tools such as subsidies for capital investment, transport subsidy, income tax concessions, and concessional loans.

Thus, programmes and policies of the Government of India have tried to limit the size and growth of large cities and urbanization, by dispersing the location of industry from large cities to smaller towns and rural areas or to poorer states and districts.

Despite such policies to 'control' urbanization and city size in India, within the country urbanization is positively related to economic development, measured by average wage and urbanization at the state level (see Figure 3.2).

Given the policies and programmes to control the city size, what is the evidence from India regarding Zipf's law? As Gabaix (1999) points out, Zipf's law is the most consistent empirical regularity that characterizes the cities of most countries—the US in 1790 and India in 1911. Gabaix (1999) argues that Zipf's law is a prerequisite for local growth to occur.

Zipf's law has been studied by Basu and Bandyapadhyay (2009) in the context of the size distribution of Indian cities, using data from the Indian censuses of

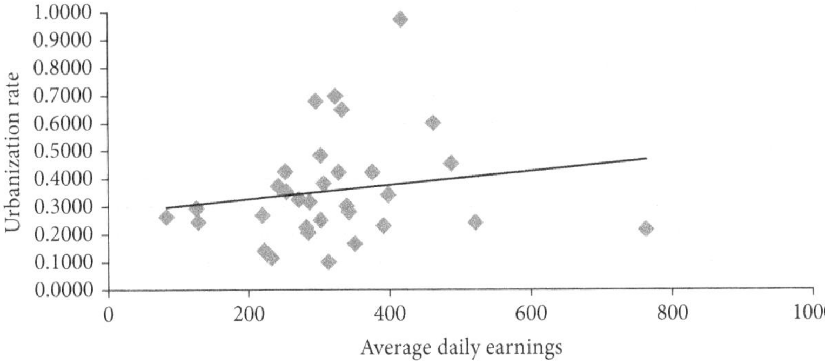

Figure 3.2. Relationship between urbanization and income, Indian states

Notes: All employees include directly employed workers, contract workers, supervisory, managerial, and other staff for 2009–10. Urbanization data are projected for 2009, based on the Census of India data on urbanization for the Indian states for 2001 and 2011. The daily earnings data are in Indian rupees.

Sources: <http://www.indiastat.com> for average daily earnings (2009–10), Census of India 2011 for urbanization, and author's analyses.

1981, 1991, and 2001. Their analysis showed that the population distribution in Indian cities does follow a power law similar to the ones found in other countries.[1] Chapter 5 in this volume estimates Zipf's law for Indian cities and finds that large Indian cities are not big enough and the smaller ones are too small, indicated by the rank-size rule, while finding that there is considerable variation in the degree of primacy across Indian states. For instance, Mathur finds that states such as Karnataka and Tamil Nadu have primate cities, with their capital cities Bangalore and Chennai being several times larger than the second-ranked cities (Mysore and Coimbatore respectively) in these states, in a manner that does not conform to Zipf's law.

Duranton and Puga (2003) study mechanisms that provide the microeconomic foundations of urban agglomeration economies. They distinguish three types of micro-foundations, based on sharing, matching, and learning mechanisms. They do this first by understanding the reasons for the existence of cities. Brueckner (2011) highlights the importance of scale economies and agglomeration economies respectively as causes for the existence of factory towns and large cities.

To justify the existence of cities, a simple argument is to invoke the existence of indivisibilities in the provision of certain goods or facilities. It is clear that there is a trade-off between the gains from sharing the fixed cost of the facility among a larger number of consumers and the costs of increasingly crowding the land around the facility (e.g. because of road congestion). We may think of a city as the equilibrium outcome of such a trade-off. Cities facilitate the sharing of many indivisible public goods, production facilities, and marketplaces.

Duranton and Puga (2003) conclude that different microeconomic foundations may be used to justify the existence of cities. Second, they find that heterogeneity (of workers and firms) is at the root of most, if not all, mechanisms that underlie the existence of cities. They find that interactions within an 'army of clones' could hardly generate sufficient benefits to justify the existence of modern cities. Third, incomplete information often plays a crucial role. Cities make it easier to find inputs (be it workers or intermediate goods) and customers to experiment and discover new possibilities. Fourth, due to the above reasons, sharing and matching mechanisms are well developed. However, the micro-foundations of learning mechanisms, especially of knowledge spillovers, are far less satisfactory. Given the importance that such spillovers appear to play in our perception not only of cities but also of growth and innovation, better and more micro-founded models of learning and spillovers ought to be an important priority for research in this area. We also know much more about the sources of agglomeration economies at the level of cities (or for that matter, at the level of regions) than at smaller spatial scales.

[1] The scaling exponents are found to be 2.15 ± 0.01 for 1981, 2.11 ± 0.01 for 1991, and 2.05 ± 0.02 for 2001 from their linear fit.

As in other countries, India's urbanization also serves as the impetus for agglomeration economies, improving employment opportunities and income level (Figure 3.2). The trend line fitted to the data from Indian states in Figure 3.2 shows that there is a positive relationship between urbanization and the average daily earnings of employees (directly employed, contract, supervisory, managerial, and other). We expect such a relationship because urbanization enhances productivity, attracts more talented workers, and encourages innovation. However, as the *India Labor and Employment Report 2014* (Institute for Human Development 2014) points out, India's labour market inequalities are large. The most striking is the disparity between the regular/casual and organized/unorganized sector workers: the average daily earnings of a casual worker stood at Rs 138 in rural areas and Rs 173 in urban areas in 2011–12, and that of a regular worker at Rs 298 in rural areas and Rs 445 in urban areas, while that of a central public sector enterprise employee was Rs 2,005 per day. Moreover, the public sector employee has many other benefits as well as a secure job. Thus, a rural casual worker earned less than 7 per cent of the salary of a public sector employee.

Castells and Royuela (2011) estimate various econometric specifications by using different measures of agglomeration (urbanization and urban concentration rates) at the cross-country level to examine how inequality and agglomeration influence economic growth. They find that while inequality is a limiting factor for long-run economic growth, increasing inequality and agglomeration[2] enhance growth in low-income countries where income distribution remains equal, but can result in congestion diseconomies in high-income countries.

To assess the relationship between agglomeration and productivity, correlations between state urban population densities (agglomeration) and the net state domestic product per capita (indicator of productivity) were computed for Indian states using data from 2011 (based on thirty-one observations). However, disappointingly, this turned out to be negative (–0.20). Hence, correlations were computed between urban density and urban productivity (GDP per capita for manufacturing and services) at a much smaller administrative level closer to the city—the district level (499 observations). This also turned out to be negative, but smaller in absolute value (–0.15; –0.17 when the largely rural north-eastern districts were excluded). This could be due to the fact that while the district is much closer to the city than the state as an administrative unit, the district is still quite large in geographical area when compared with the city—hence we find this unexpected result. If city-level income were to be available, then we may have concluded definitely regarding its relationship with population density in India's context. While there is evidence of a positive relationship between urban density and

[2] They include the Gini coefficient and measures of agglomeration—the urbanization rate and urban concentration (population in agglomerations of more than a million, as a proportion of the urban population)—as two independent variables.

productivity in the People's Republic of China (PRC) (see Chapter 2 in this volume), the negative relationship in India's context, if it really holds, could be because: (1) people trade income to enjoy a better quality of life and public services; (2) density also brings competition in a given area reducing its productivity.

Quigley (2009) considers the mechanisms that increase economic efficiency in cities. This paper examines the record of cities in improving economic output and making available consumption opportunities to urban residents. Considering both developed and developing countries, the analysis supports the evidence that cities are facilitators of increasing economic output, productivity, and rising incomes in poor and rich regions alike. Hence, Quigley (2009) concluded that policies that encourage rather than inhibit urbanization in countries would improve the economic conditions.

Empirical evidence on agglomeration, sharing, and learning is rich with a large number of studies that throw light on this in the Indian context. Tripathi (2012) finds that agglomeration economies are policy induced as well as market driven, and offers evidence for the strong positive impact of agglomeration on urban economic growth in the Indian context. Sridhar (2011) found that the higher the distance to a large city, the smaller is a city's (non-agricultural) output per capita, finding specifically that for every kilometre that an Indian city was away from a large city, there was a Rs 1,088 reduction in its non-agricultural output per capita. This emphasizes the importance of agglomeration economies in reinforcing city output.

Figure 3.3 demonstrates the relationship between smaller cities with distance to a city of greater than 100,000 population and non-agricultural output per capita. It shows a negative relationship, indicating the strength of agglomeration.

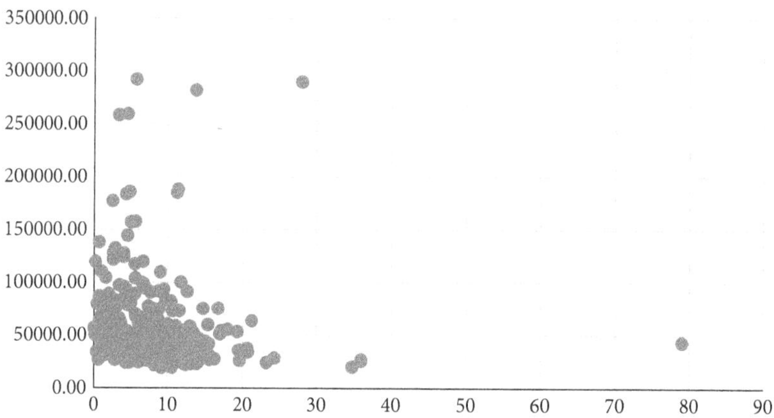

Figure 3.3. Proximity to a large city and city output

Sources: Data on District Domestic Products from the CSO, data on distances from large cities from the Census of India and author's analyses.

Mills and Becker (1986) analysed and estimated city growth in India, first using a national sample of large Indian cities and then using a sample of cities in a large Indian state, Madhya Pradesh. They found that the rapid growth of a city's manufacturing employment and of the national population induced fast growth in a city's population. They further found that a large initial population stimulated growth at low initial population levels. Their results implied that cities grow faster in higher-income states than they do in lower-income states. Both their equations (4.4 and 4.5) indicated that the effect of a large initial population on population growth turned negative at modest initial population levels: 780,000 and 890,000.

Mills and Becker's (1986) findings were different for different categories of cities when they took the case of the Indian state of Madhya Pradesh, where they found statistically significant and negative impacts of distance to the nearest class I city on city growth (taking into account all city sizes), implying that as distance to large cities increased, the growth of cities also diminished (Tables 3.5–3.7 in their book). This emphasizes agglomeration effects and the importance of density.

Au and Henderson (2005) model and estimate net urban agglomeration economies for the PRC's cities. They find that urban agglomeration benefits are high—real incomes per worker rise sharply with increases in city size from a low level. They find that real incomes (per worker) level out nearer the peak and then decline very slowly past the peak. They find that a large fraction of cities in the PRC are undersized, due to nationally imposed, strong migration restrictions, resulting in large income losses. Hence, the PRC needs to free up the Hukou system to reform it, as is currently being done.

Using Chinese city-level data from 1990 to 2006, Chen et al. (2011) estimate the impact of spatial interactions in the PRC's urban system on urban economic growth, and find that proximity to major ports and international markets is essential for urban growth.

Hence, the evidence on agglomeration economies is unquestionable, the only caveat being that micro-level evidence in India's context is quite limited.

3.2.2 Sharing, Matching, and Learning

Urban areas improve labour productivity through the mechanisms of sharing, matching, and learning (see Puga 2009). Enterprises can reduce production costs through these mechanisms. For consumers, big cities supply more diversified products to meet demand. Besides, workers will find it easier to get jobs, accumulate experiences, and acquire knowledge. These three mechanisms bring about scale economies in cities, especially for transportation infrastructure facilities and diversified consumer goods. As sharing is obvious, recent empirical research focuses on the mechanisms of learning (Puga 2009).

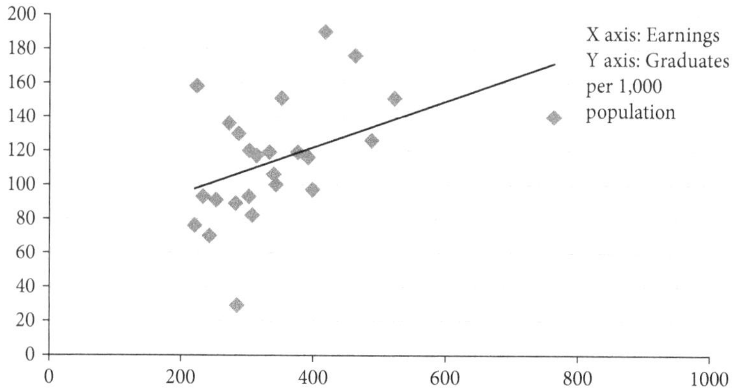

Figure 3.4. Relationship between education and earnings, Indian states

Sources: <http://www.indiastat.com> for the data on both earnings and education which are for 2009–10 and author's analyses.

Empirical studies have proven the existence of human capital externalities (Rauch 1993). In the US, a 1 per cent increase in the university graduate ratio is shown to boost labour productivity by 0.6 to 0.7 per cent (Moretti 2004a) and wage levels by 0.6 to 1.2 per cent (Moretti 2004b). In India, as in other countries, there is a positive relationship between education and earnings. Figure 3.4 shows a scatterplot of the relationship between the number of graduates per 1,000 population (greater than seven years of age) and the average daily earnings of all employees at the state level. This is positive, as we expect and find from other countries. Unfortunately, data on education and earnings are not available for Indian cities.

Section 3.3 summarizes the level, speed, and regional variation with respect to urbanization in the Indian context.

3.3 Urbanization: Level, Speed, and Regional Variation

India's urbanization level is low, at 31 per cent as of the 2011 census, but is high in absolute terms.[3] Over 370 million people live in the cities and towns of India. This is more than the population of the United States. For the first time, the absolute growth in India's urban population, 91 million, is more than its rural counterpart. The urban growth rate, which had decreased in the last couple of decades, rose in

[3] In the Census of India 2011, the definition of urban area is as follows:

1. All places with a municipality, corporation, cantonment board, or notified town area committee.
2. All other places which satisfied the following criteria:
   (a) A minimum population of 5,000
   (b) At least 75 per cent of the male main working population engaged in non-agricultural pursuits
   (c) A density of population of at least 400 persons per sq. km.

the 2011 census. India's urbanization is expected to present not only greater challenges but also higher opportunities due to India's higher population density (411 persons per sq. km) compared with that of the PRC (144 persons per sq. km as of 2011, where the low density of cities is now being criticized).[4] The density of urban population in India was 3,659 persons per sq. km of land area in 2001. In 2011, this increased to 4,767, if the land area is assumed to be the same.

Table 3.1 describes the size distribution of India's cities. It shows that there is nearly a twentyfold increase in the number of class I cities in the country during the century.

Before examining regional variations in urbanization, we study the relationship between national income and urbanization in India over the period

Table 3.1. Size distribution of India's cities, 1901–2011

	Class I	Class II	Class III	Class IV	Class V	All cities*
1901	25	44	144	427	771	1,917
1911	26	38	158	388	750	1,909
1921	29	49	172	395	773	2,047
1931	31	59	218	479	849	2,219
1941	49	88	273	554	979	2,424
1951	76	111	374	675	1,195	3,060
1961	107	139	518	820	848	2,700
1971	151	219	652	988	820	3,126
1981[Ψ]	226	325	883	1,247	920	3,949
1991[Δ]	322	421	1,161	1,451	973	4,615
2001	448	498	1,389	1,564	1,043	5,177
2011	505	605	1,905	2,233	2,187	7,933

* It should be noted that while all cities include cities in class sizes I–VI, columns 2–5 report only class sizes I–V.

The Census of India's definition for various class sizes of cities is as follows:
Class I: Population > 100,000
Class II: Population of 50,000–99,999
Class III: Population of 20,000–49,999
Class IV: Population of 10,000–19,999
Class V: Population of 5,000–9,999
Class VI: Population < 5,000.

Ψ In 1981, no census was held in Assam due to the existence of disturbed conditions there. Thus while during 1901–71, and 1991–2001, the number of cities reported include those in Assam, in 1981 they exclude Assam.

Δ In 1991, in Jammu and Kashmir (J&K), there was no census held owing to disturbed conditions there. So it should be clear that while during 1901–81 and in 2001, the number of cities includes those in J&K, the 1991 list of cities excludes those in J&K.

Source: Compiled from the Census of India for various years.

[4] The low density could be due to the fact that the PRC's city population includes the agricultural population within its jurisdiction. Another reason for the significant drop in density in recent years is because the PRC's cities have expanded fast without creating enough jobs.

1951–2011. Figures 3.5 to 3.7 demonstrate the empirical relationship between total national income (in current prices) and per capita income (in constant, 1993–4 prices) and urbanization. The trend lines fitted show a steeply positive relationship between the two, being an exponential curve in the case of total national income (Figure 3.5) and perfectly positive in the case of per capita income (Figures 3.6 and 3.7).

What can we forecast about the future of urbanization in India? This chapter has argued that Asia's urbanization will be led by megacities to achieve efficiency, equity, and sustainability. The Census of India projected the number of cities in India by 2015, according to which it is expected that there will be roughly forty-one cities with a population of 1–2 million, approximately thirteen cities with a population of 2–5 million, and more or less nine cities with a population of 5 million and over, broadly consistent with the rank-size rule.

Lusome and Bhagat (2006) report that while there has been a substantial increase in the proportion of rural–urban migrants during 1971–2001, there has

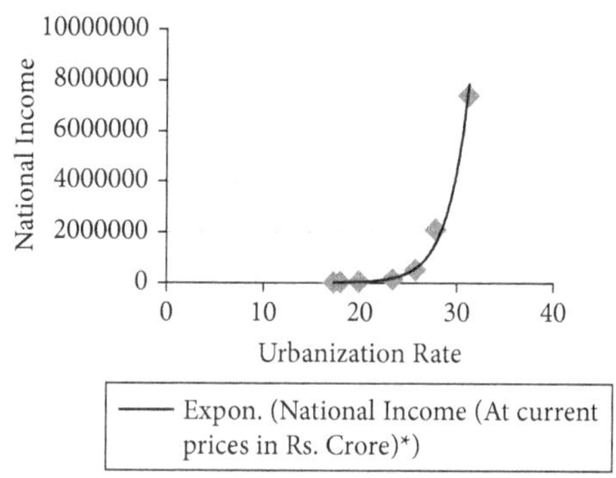

Figure 3.5. National income and urbanization, India, 1951–2011
Sources: The Erstwhile Planning Commission of India, the Census of India, and author's analyses.

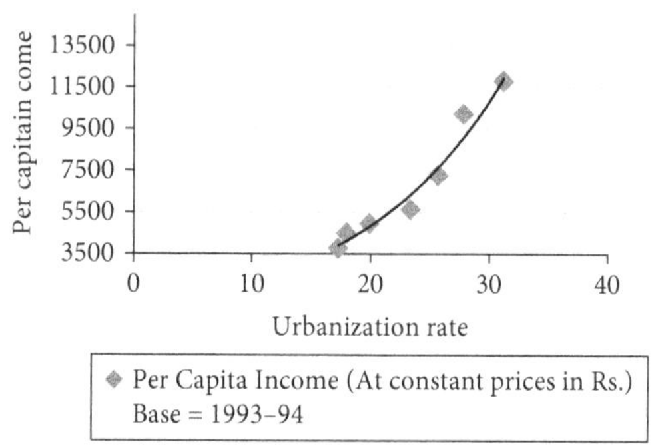

Figure 3.6. Per capita income and urbanization, India, 1951–2004
Sources: The Erstwhile Planning Commission of India, the Census of India, and author's analyses.

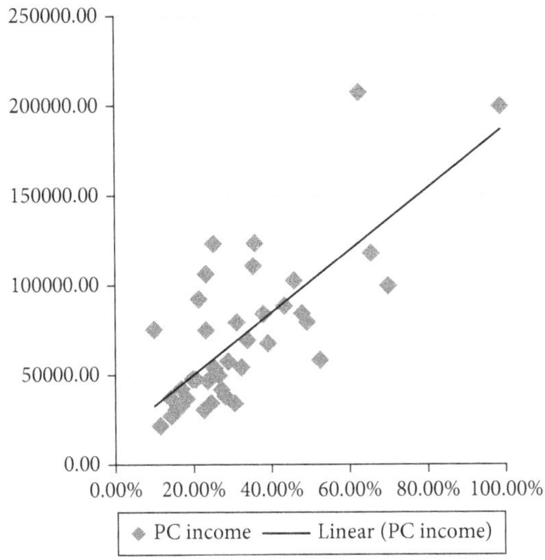

Figure 3.7. Per capita income and urbanization, Indian states, 2011
Sources: The Erstwhile Planning Commission of India, the Census of India, and author's analyses.

also been an increase in the proportion of urban–urban migrants during this period. Lusome and Bhagat's paper finds that the share of urban–urban migration of both males and females was comparatively low in the intra-district stream, but it increased substantially in the inter-district and interstate streams. As institutions of higher learning, particularly professional and technical institutions, are not available in each district, an urge for higher education motivates urban dwellers as well as some of the rural folk to migrate over long distances. This is also partly due to the creation of jobs in the modern sector in major metropolises and big cities (Premi 1990).

Based on the above and several other advantages of megacities that have been discussed in this chapter, I predict that megacities will continue to be important for India's urban growth.

3.3.1 Regional Variation

Table 3.2 describes the regional variation in urbanization across Indian states. The state of Delhi is the most urbanized with 98 per cent urbanization, followed by Chandigarh at 97.25 per cent.

The least urbanized is the hilly state of Himachal Pradesh at 10 per cent urbanization. It does appear that agglomerations such as Delhi, where there are conurbations of economic activity, sharing of knowledge, and learning on a large scale, are highly urban. Physical barriers such as mountainous and hilly terrain

Table 3.2. Regional variations in urbanization, 2011

State/ UT code	India/state/union territory[#]	% urban
	India	**31.16**
01	Jammu and Kashmir	27.21
02	Himachal Pradesh	10.04
03	Punjab	37.49
04	Chandigarh	97.25
05	Uttarakhand	30.55
06	Haryana	34.79
07	Nct Of Delhi	97.50
08	Rajasthan	24.89
09	Uttar Pradesh	22.28
10	Bihar	11.30
11	Sikkim	24.97
12	Arunachal Pradesh	22.67
13	Nagaland	28.97
14	Manipur	30.21
15	Mizoram	51.51
16	Tripura	26.18
17	Meghalaya	20.08
18	Assam	14.08
19	West Bengal	31.89
20	Jharkhand	24.05
21	Orissa	16.68
22	Chhattisgarh	23.24
23	Madhya Pradesh	27.63
24	Gujarat	42.58
25	Daman & Diu	75.16
26	Dadra & Nagar Haveli	46.62
27	Maharashtra	45.23
28	Andhra Pradesh	33.49
29	Karnataka	38.57
30	Goa	62.17
31	Lakshadweep	78.08
32	Kerala	47.72
33	Tamil Nadu	48.45
34	Puducherry	68.31
35	A & N Islands	35.67

Source: Census of India and author's analyses

increase the costs of urbanization, hence states such as Himachal Pradesh are largely rural.

Figures 3.6 and 3.7 show that the relationship between urbanization and per capita income for Indian states is positive, as may be seen in the linear trend line fitted to the data.

It is interesting to examine that across the world, there are a large number of countries, including those in Africa, which have attained a high level of urbanization at fairly low per capita incomes and low degrees of industrialization. This has been termed as the urbanization–industrialization gap, which is observed in the Indian context as well.

3.3.2 The Urbanization–Industrialization Gap

It is assumed that urbanization and industrialization are highly correlated, as observed in the case of the developed countries. In the context of the Indian states, the correlation was computed between the share of industry and services in its NSDP (net state domestic product) and its urbanization for the period 2004–11. The correlation between urbanization and the share of industry/services was positive, being a high 0.74. Urbanization is only at 31 per cent, on average, for India as a whole, but the share of industry and services in Indian states' domestic product is 80 per cent. Hence India's urbanization is significantly lower than what is suggested by its industrialization, which is largely led by the services sector. This suggests that there is a large urban–rural income gap. Taking into account intermittent periods—2004–5, 2009–10, and 2011–12—for major Indian states, while the urban monthly per capita consumption expenditure[5] was Rs 1,712, per capita rural expenditure was only Rs 1,020, accounting only for 60 per cent of per capita urban expenditure.[6]

Next we move to a discussion of the determinants of urbanization in the Indian context, taking into account its benefits and costs.

3.4 Benefits and Costs of Urbanization: Analytical Framework

This part of the chapter is motivated by the theoretical framework provided by Brueckner (1990), which imbeds the monocentric city model in an economy experiencing rural–urban migration. When urban and rural real incomes are set equal in the model to guarantee migration equilibrium, an equilibrium city population is determined. This equilibrium city size depends on three key variables: the ratio of urban–rural income, the ratio of agricultural rent to urban income, and commuting costs. The analysis in Brueckner (1990) shows that city size varies inversely with the rural–urban income ratio and the commuting cost, and

[5] We have extensively surveyed the literature and expenditure has been used to represent income in all cases, since reliable income data are not available.

[6] This is using the assumption of a uniform recall period (URP) under which consumption expenditure data for all items is collected for a thirty-day recall period. Data were available on consumption expenditure using a mixed recall period (MRP), under which consumer expenditure data for five non-food items—namely, clothing, footwear, durable goods, education, and institutional medical expenses—are collected for a 365-day recall period and the consumption data for the remaining items are collected for a thirty-day recall period). But there was missing data for Chhattisgarh, Uttarakhand, and Jharkhand for 2004 if MRP were to be used; hence URP is used.

directly with the ratio of agricultural rent to urban income. The intuition for this expectation is clear. First, an increase in the urban income level raises the urban standard of living relative to that in rural areas, which creates an impetus for migration, as highlighted by the Todaro (1969) model, and increases the urban population. Hence the expected impact of the urban–rural income ratio on urbanization is positive.

Similarly, an increase in the commuting cost reduces the real income of the city residents and leads to an equilibrating migration flow to the countryside—hence the expected impact of commuting cost on urbanization is negative.

When agricultural rent rises relative to urban income, real incomes decline for both urban and rural residents. However, since nominal income stays constant in the countryside, while the disposable income of the resident at the urban boundary rises, it follows that real income falls less in the city than in the countryside. The result is migration towards the city, which proceeds until living standards are equalized. Therefore, the expected impact of the agricultural rent to urban income on urbanization is positive.

The model is stated as follows:

$$U = f(Y,T,R) \tag{1}$$

where U refers to urbanization, Y is the urban–rural income ratio, T refers to commute cost, and R is the ratio of agricultural rent to urban income.

While equation (1) is written as if the rural–urban income ratio (Y) determines urbanization unilaterally, there could be a two-way, possibly non-linear relationship between urbanization and the urban–rural (u-r) income ratio. We need to clarify this further. In theory, we can have the following two expectations.

(1) When we are examining the impact of u–r ratio (Y) on urbanization, the expected impact is positive—since migrants will perceive the income differential and move to cities. The higher the income differential, the higher would be the urbanization rate.

(2) The u–r ratio (Y) could be endogenous. The expected impact of urbanization on the u–r ratio is negative because we expect urbanization to reduce the inequality; a positive impact is possible if urbanization aggravates the rural–urban inequality. Thus the u–r ratio could be endogenous since rural–urban migration, the consequent urbanization, and the demand for and supply of labour could equalize urban–rural incomes and their ratio. If such a thing were to occur, the u–r ratio (Y) is endogenous and would be determined within the model.

Both these expectations may or may not be met in reality, but the expectation depends on what our policy variable is. Hence equation (1) is empirically implemented with data from Indian states by OLS (ordinary least squares) first. In the next step, in order to account for the endogeneity of the u–r ratio (Y), an instrumental variables (IV) estimation is performed, whereby instruments such as the predicted urbanization from the first-stage OLS regression and its squared (to test for non-linearity), commuting cost, the ratio of agricultural rent to urban income and the state's population are used as exogenous variables and regressed on the u–r ratio as the dependent variable. Thus the predicted value of urbanization from the OLS regression is used to instrument for its endogeneity in the second step to get unbiased estimates of the impacts of urbanization.

3.5 Data and Sources

The dataset consists of cross-sectional data for major Indian states on the urbanization rate, urban and rural monthly per capita expenditure (MPCE),[7] the ratio of agricultural rent to urban income, and commuting cost (cost per passenger km), for 2004–5, 2009–10, and 2011–12, given these were the only years for which the MPCE data were available from the National Sample Survey Organization (NSSO). The data on urbanization rates for the Indian states are from the Census of India (2001 and 2011). Total state population and urbanized population for the states, and for the largest cities in the states, for the intervening years (2004–5 and 2009–10) were projected, using an exponential rate assumption. Data on agricultural rent (income) were from the Central Statistical Office (CSO).

The commuting cost, the cost per passenger km variable, was purchased from the Central Institute of Road Transport (CIRT), Pune, which publishes these data for the State Road Transport Undertakings (SRTUs). Several states disaggregate this cost per km separately for rural and urban areas. Several states publish data separately for the SRTUs in their biggest cities—such as the BEST (Brihanmumbai Electricity Supply and Transport) Undertaking in Mumbai, DTC (Delhi Transport Corporation) in Delhi, BMTC (Bangalore Metropolitan Transport Corporation) in Bangalore, and AMTS (Ahmedabad Municipal Transport Service) in Ahmedabad. The cost per passenger km was derived from the fare structure published by the SRTU. The fare structure on the ordinary city bus services for the first 2 km of the journey were used as the basis for commuting cost per passenger km.[8] For instance, if the fare for the first 2 km on the city ordinary buses was Rs 4, then the cost per passenger km was deemed to be Rs 2. Again, commuting cost in metropolitan areas (such as Bangalore, Delhi, Mumbai, and Ahmedabad) would be higher compared with other urban areas. In states for which I had data for several SRTUs

[7] While we attempted using the ratio of urban–rural incomes in many earlier versions of this chapter, there was considerable urban–rural variation across the states, when Indian national accounts data were used by sector, which was not consistent with the evidence from the PRC. Based on an extensive review of the Indian literature on the subject, we decided to use the monthly per capita consumption expenditure for rural and urban areas at the state level, which is much more stable across the Indian states and, possibly for this reason, more extensively used.

[8] The metro express and metro deluxe fares were not taken into account.

(for instance, Maharashtra, where there was a state urban fare for ordinary city services and several city SRTUs such as the Thane Municipal Undertaking, Kolhapur Municipal Undertaking, Pune Municipal Undertaking, and the BEST Undertaking), the cost per passenger km was computed as the average for these several undertakings. Further, several states did not have data on fare structure for the years 2004, 2009, and 2011, which were used for the estimation.[9] Given this, I assumed that the average urban fare per passenger km for all India[10] holds good for these states for the respective years.

3.6 Empirical Results

The ensuing discussion reports empirical results based on the full sample of sixty observations. First, we report descriptive statistics, followed by scatter plots (Figures 3.8 through 3.15) and the results from the estimations. Table 3.3 summarizes the basic characteristics of the distribution—mean, median, minimum, and maximum—for the key variables used in the analysis for Indian states for the years 2004, 2009, and 2011; this is the sample which is used for the estimation.

In terms of the urban–rural per capita MPCE ratio, the state with the highest ratio of per capita urban–rural expenditure is Chhattisgarh, a state characterized by a significant tribal population. This state, with only 21 per cent urban population in 2004, has one major city—Raipur. This state is characterized by very low rural (Rs 425 in 2004) as well as urban MPCE (Rs 990 in 2004) in most NSS surveys. The poor rural MPCE has been attributed to the decline in per capita food production, the poor state of rural infrastructure such as power and roads, and underperformance of social safety net programmes like rural job schemes and public distribution systems, which have apparently restricted rural income growth.

When we examine the ratio of agricultural rent to urban income, the highest is 0.5 in Punjab, an agriculturally rich state. When we examine commuting cost, the most expensive is Maharashtra, due to the fact that the fare per passenger km

[9] Data on fare structure for the following states were missing for 2004, 2009, and 2011, except where indicated: Jammu and Kashmir; Himachal Pradesh, Punjab, Uttarakhand, Haryana, UP, Bihar, Assam, Jharkhand, Chhattisgarh, and Madhya Pradesh; for Kerala, the fare structure was missing only for 2004. Based on my discussions with the CIRT from where I purchased the data, most of the states for which the fare structure was not published were those which did not offer commuter services in their urban areas—they ran only rural or long-distance services (this was the case with Haryana, Punjab, Bihar, Uttarakhand, and Himachal Pradesh). States such as Jharkhand and Chhattisgarh had no independent public bus services or state transport undertakings at the time the research for this chapter was completed. While in Assam, Guwahati city's urban bus service was outsourced to a private operator, that agency had not sent the data on fare structure to the CIRT. In Uttar Pradesh, the city of Lucknow started offering urban bus services only around 2008–9.

[10] This was determined on the basis of the average fare per passenger km for all the states for which the data was available for the respective years.

Table 3.3. Summary statistics

	Urbanization rate	U–R per capita MPCE ratio	Agr. rent–urban income ratio	Cost (paise) per passenger km (in Rs)	State population (in 10,000)	Largest city population (in 10,000)
Mean	0.28	1.74	0.25	1.33	5,595.61	280.36
Median	0.28	1.74	0.26	1.38	4,765.04	159.11
Standard Deviation	0.11	0.29	0.10	0.31	4,277.30	298.17
Minimum	0.10	1.16	0.09	0.50	630.12	15.02
Maximum	0.49	2.33	0.50	2.01	19,958.15	1,247.84

Sources: Census of India, CSO, National Sample Survey Office, Central Institute of Road Transport, and author's analyses

in Mumbai and Pune was Rs 2.50 even for ordinary services—this includes the passenger tax and surcharge, which is not there in most other states. The most urbanized state in the sample is Tamil Nadu at 49 per cent urbanization in 2011. As discussed earlier, Himachal Pradesh is the least urbanized state.

While Figures 3.8 through 3.11 show the relationship between urbanization and the urban–rural MPCE ratio, urbanization and the urban commuting cost, urbanization and the ratio of agricultural rent to urban income, and urbanization and the population of the state's largest city, Figures 3.12 through 3.15 show these relationships between the population of the state's largest city and the other variables indicated above.

Figure 3.8 shows that there is a weak negative relationship between urbanization and the urban–rural MPCE ratio, with a negative correlation of –0.04, which is unexpected since a higher urban consumption expenditure (used to indicate income), relative to that of rural areas, would imply that the incentive to migrate and urbanize is minimal and vice versa. However, this relationship is weak and not significant.

Figure 3.9 shows a weak positive relationship between urbanization and the urban commute cost, which is natural to expect, with a positive correlation of 0.02, with the caveats of the data on commute costs—they are for cities in some cases, whereas in some other cases they represent an overall urban commuting cost for the state as a whole. As urbanization and city size increases, we expect that the commuting cost also commensurately increases.

Further, Figure 3.10 shows a negative relationship between urbanization and the agricultural rent–urban income ratio, which is, as expected, with a correlation of –0.35.

Figure 3.11 shows the relationship between urbanization and state population, demonstrating that there is usually a positive relationship between the two, other things remaining constant. This is reasonable to expect as large states are usually

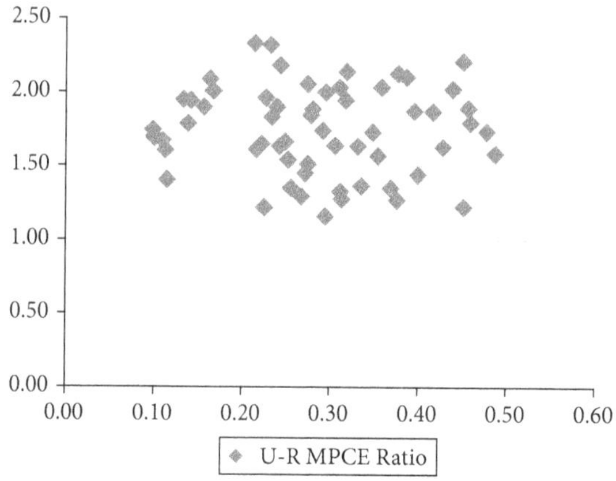

Figure 3.8. Urbanization and U–R MPCE ratio
Source: Census of India, NSSO various rounds, and author's analyses.

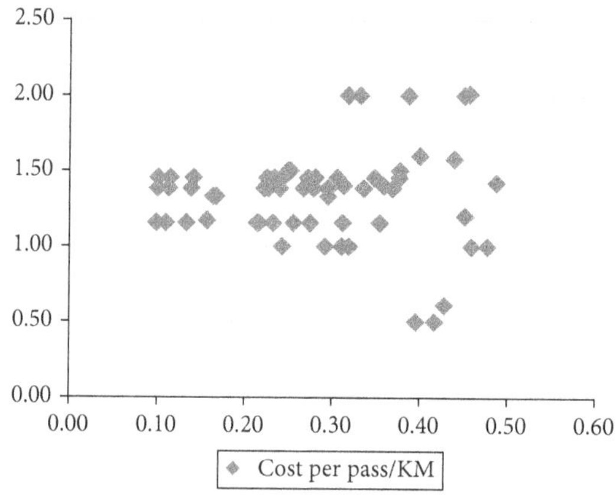

Figure 3.9. Urbanization and commuting cost (Rs) per km
Sources: Census of India, CIRT, and author's analyses.

more urban, with the exception of states such as Uttar Pradesh, which is the largest, but has a low urbanization rate. Hence we may expect large states to be more urban if their income level is also higher. There is a weak positive correlation of 0.11 between the two.

Figure 3.12 demonstrates the relationship between the urban–rural MPCE ratio and the population of the state's largest city. In this and Figures 3.12 through 3.15, the population of the state's largest city is taken to be the indicator of urbanization. As we expect, there is a positive relation between the two (with a positive correlation of 0.35).

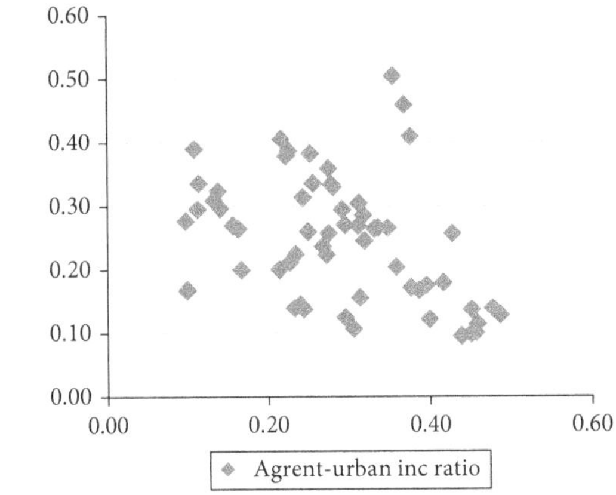

Figure 3.10. Urbanization and ratio of agricultural rent–urban income
Sources: Census of India, CSO, and author's analyses.

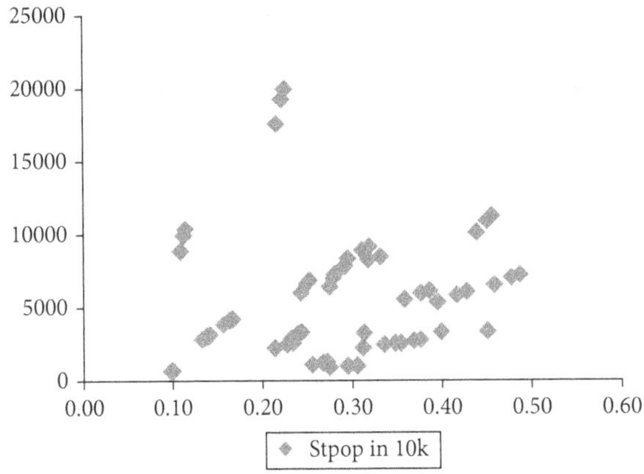

Figure 3.11. Relationship between urbanization and state population
Source: Census of India and author's analyses.

Figure 3.13 shows the relationship between the state's largest city and the ratio of agricultural rent to urban income. As in the case of urbanization, this relationship is negative, as expected for reasons discussed earlier. There is a negative correlation of −0.31 between the two. Figure 3.14 shows the relationship between the population of the state's largest city and the urban commuting cost. This is broadly positive, as we expect, with a correlation of 0.31, since when cities grow beyond a certain size, the costs outweigh the benefits. Figure 3.15 shows the relationship between population of the state's largest city and state population. There is a positive relationship, as we would expect, with the highest positive correlation (0.50) of any variable.

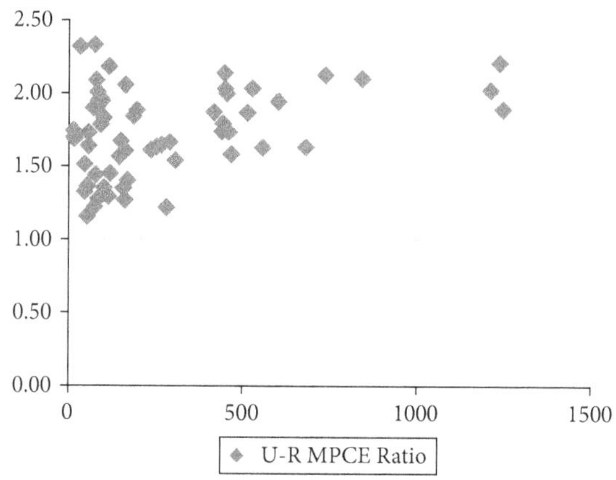

Figure 3.12. U–R MPCE ratio and population of the state's largest city (in 10,000)
Sources: NSSO, Census of India, and author's analyses.

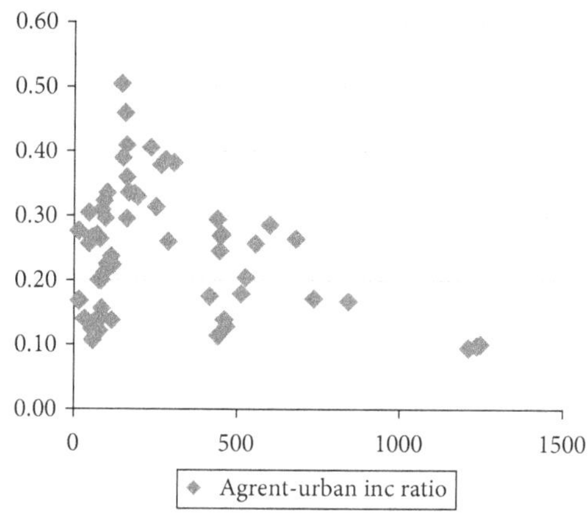

Figure 3.13. Population of the state's largest city (in 10,000) and ratio of agricultural rent and urban income
Source: CSO, Census of India, and author's analyses.

3.6.1 Results from Regressions

As discussed earlier, equation (1) was estimated first by ordinary least squares (Table 3.4). We report four specifications with two dependent variables and two specifications each—the dependent variables are the urbanization rate of the state and the population of the largest city in the state. The exogenous variables are the urban–rural MPCE ratio, the state population, the commuting cost, and the ratio of agricultural rent to income. In one specification, the commuting cost has been excluded since for nearly half of the sample, the cost per passenger km

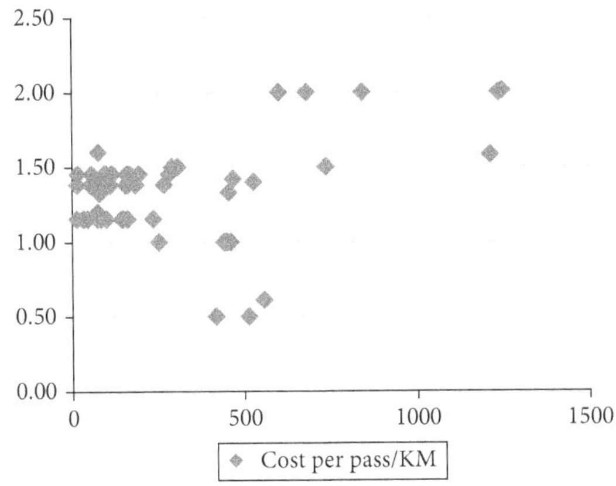

Figure 3.14. Population of the state's largest city (in 10,000) and urban commuting cost

Source: CIRT, Census of India, and author's analyses.

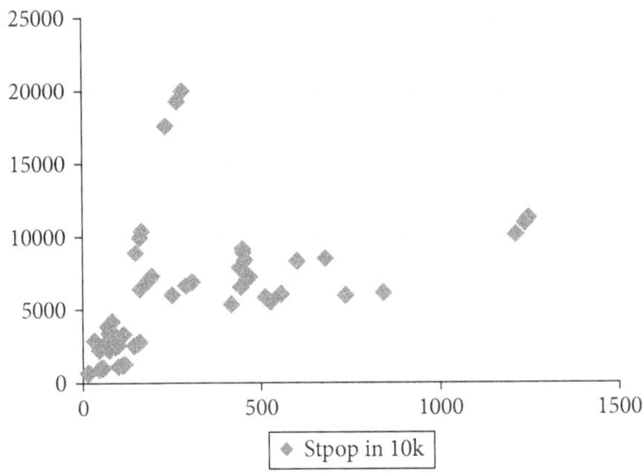

Figure 3.15. Relationship between population of the state's largest city (in 10,000) and state population

Source: Census of India and author's analyses.

had to be extrapolated using the all-India average, given that data were missing for several states.

In both the specifications (with and without the commuting cost), the u–r ratio has no impact on urbanization. This shows that the u–r ratio alone is not adequate to impact the urbanization rate, which is plausible. Urbanization depends on various other enabling conditions, and it would be naïve to assume that the u–r ratio impacts urbanization. It is possible that rural residents also do not have perfect information regarding urban incomes to enable them to make a

Table 3.4. Urbanization regressions (t ratio in parentheses)

Dependent variable	U–R monthly per capita expenditure (MPCE) ratio	Agr. rent–urban income ratio	Cost per passenger km	State pop. (10,000)	R-squared	F statistic
Urbanization rate	−0.07 (−1.61)	−0.52 (−3.71)***	–	0.00 (1.85)*	0.21	4.91
Urbanization rate	−0.07 (−1.62)	−0.53 (−3.73)***	−0.02 (−0.57)	0.00 (1.91)*	0.21	3.72
Pop. largest city	199.12 (1.93)*	−1,176.28 (−3.69)***	–	0.04 (5.66)***	0.47	16.81
Pop. largest city	206.56 (2.06)**	−1,060.58 (−3.38)***	198.15 (2.13)**	0.04 (5.40)***	0.51	14.54

Sources: Census of India, National Sample Survey Office, Central Institute of Road Transport, and author's analyses

Notes: Intercepts are not reported. Sixty observations are used in all the regressions.

decision to migrate to urban areas. Finally, in the context of India, a large part of the observed urbanization is due to a natural population increase and not due to migration. Hence the insignificant impact of the u–r ratio on urbanization makes perfect sense.

Rather, in both the specifications, the ratio of agricultural rent to urban income has a negative and significant impact on urbanization. We would have expected the ratio to impact urbanization positively because when agricultural rent rises relative to urban income, real incomes decline for both urban and rural residents. However, since nominal income stays constant in the countryside, while the disposable income of the resident at the urban boundary rises, it follows that real income falls less in the city than in the countryside. The result is migration towards the city, which presumably proceeds until living standards are equalized. However, it is probable that if migration does not occur, the sign we have found is plausible. State population has the expected positive impact on urbanization, showing that large states are more likely to be urbanized than their smaller counterparts.

When we estimate the population of the largest city in the state, either with or without controlling for commuting costs, the impacts on urbanization are as expected. The u–r ratio has the expected positive impact on urbanization, which has a sharper focus, implying that if rural incomes are higher relative to urban incomes (measured by expenditures), migrants would certainly prefer to move to the biggest city in the state. However, the ratio of agricultural rent to urban income has an unexpected negative impact, showing that migration towards the biggest city does not continue until living standards equalize across rural and urban areas in the event of a rise in agricultural rents at the boundary. Hence, this does not translate into higher population of the largest city in the state.

The unexpected finding is the impact of the commuting cost on the size of the largest city, which is positive. This means that a higher commuting cost actually leads to a bigger size of the city, whereas we would have expected a smaller city with higher commuting costs. This is, in fact, consistent with the literature; Brueckner (1990) finds this strikingly similar, but unexpected finding. One reason why we encounter this finding here is the way in which commuting costs are measured. As explained earlier, in some cases (such as Maharashtra where cost per passenger km is the average of all the SRTUs in that state), the commuting cost is a representative urban commuting cost for the entire state, whereas in some other states, such as Punjab and Rajasthan, the all-India urban commuting cost per passenger km is used, since a commuting cost specific to various urban areas in these states was not reported. In other cases (including Karnataka and Maharashtra), we had city-specific commuting costs (for Bangalore and Mumbai respectively). Another caveat of the commuting data is that the cost per km is for all passengers incurred by the SRTU. The fare structure was available for all the SRTUs, but there was not much variation in the cost per passenger km across the states (it was close to Rs 1 for most states, consistent with the assumption made by

Brueckner and Sridhar (2012). Another reason could be that the commuting cost is the result of a large city. If we had measured the commuting cost more precisely and uniformly for all states, our results may have been as we expect.

The total state population has a positive and significant impact on the size of the largest city in the state, implying that it is highly likely for large states such as Uttar Pradesh to have large cities, which is consistent with the corresponding research using cross-national data.

The unexpected performance of the ratio of agricultural rent to urban income variable in the urbanization regression suggests that migration does not play an important role in determining the rate of urbanization in India. This is consistent with the insignificant role played by the u–r ratio in the urbanization regressions. However, the u–r ratio has a positive impact on the largest city's population, endorsing the idea that while migration does not occur towards urban areas in general, they will likely occur towards the largest city in the state. Further, commuting cost has a positive impact on the largest city population, part of which may be due to the data caveats—in the case of many states, we had to make do with overall state commuting costs, rather than a cost variable applied to urban areas, as explained earlier.

As already discussed, there could be a two-way relationship between urbanization and the per capita u–r ratio. For this, the first-stage OLS regressions were used to predict the urbanization rate (or largest city population) for each of the states. The predicted urbanization rate (or largest city population) was used as an exogenous variable along with commuting cost and the state population in the second-stage regression in which the per capita u–r ratio was the dependent variable. Table 3.5 summarizes the results from the second-stage regressions.

The results from the second stage show that the now exogenous (predicted from the first-stage OLS regression) urbanization (or the largest city population) has a positive impact on the (per capita) u–r ratio. This implies that urbanization or the largest city population (corrected for its endogeneity) increases the u–r ratio. While we had expected urbanization to reduce urban–rural inequality (Lu and Chen (2006) point out that urbanization narrowed urban–rural inequality in the PRC), the finding we get in the Indian context could be due to the fact that rural residents do not move to cities adequately, and the ones who move to the city are either richer or have the potential to become rich (either educated or highly motivated to study or work hard). This is consistent with the assertion made by Kuznets (1966) that inequality may increase, particularly in the initial stages. However, the predicted urbanization squared has a negative impact on the u–r ratio, implying that beyond a certain level of urbanization (which we've confirmed is 25 per cent, see note 11), the urban–rural inequalities will be reduced.[11]

[11] We report the optimal impact of urbanization on the u-r (expenditure) ratio, using the equation:

per capita urban – rural MPCE ratio = 17.42 (predicted) urbanization – 35.55 (predicted) urbanization squared (from Table 3.5).

Table 3.5. Second-stage regressions

Model using	(Predicted) urbanization	(Predicted) urbanization squared	Cost per passenger km	State population (10,000)	R-squared	F statistic
1	17.42 (2.79)**	−35.55 (−2.94)***	–	0.00 (0.29)	0.11	3.33
2	11.12 (1.70)*	−20.99 (−1.83)*	0.03 (0.21)	0.00 (0.61)	0.01	1.15
Model using	**(Predicted) largest city population**	**(Predicted) largest city population squared**	**Cost per passenger km**	**State population (10,000)**	**R-squared**	**F statistic**
3	0.00 (4.48)***	0.00 (−1.33)	–	0.00 (−3.39)***	0.39	12.17
4	0.00 (5.00)***	0.00 (−0.14)	−0.38 (−3.23)***	0.00 (−4.56)***	0.49	13.28

Sources: Census of India, CSO, National Sample Survey Office, Central Institute of Road Transport, and author's analyses

Notes: Dependent variable is the per capita urban–rural MPCE ratio in all the regressions. Intercepts are not reported. All regressions are based on sixty observations

This is what we expect since urbanization not only increases the incomes of the urban residents, but also the rural population shares the growth eventually. As Todaro (1969) pointed out, in a dual economy with expected urban–rural gaps in earnings, labour flow equalizes the returns to factors and narrows urban–rural inequality. On the one hand, wages in the urban labour market will fall with more migration and increased labour supply. On the other hand, the outflow of rural workers reduces the surplus labour in the countryside, effectively upgrading productivity and the incomes of remaining rural labourers. Hence falling urban and rising rural incomes close the gap. The results we find are consistent with this evidence and show that integrated markets are needed to allocate capital, land, and labour between rural and urban areas and across cities. These results are consistent with the effects found by Mitra in Chapter 7 of this volume, who uses data at the district level, in addition to those at the state level.

The state population has a negative impact on the u–r ratio, but it is economically insignificant. If it had been economically significant, it would have implied that large states have plenty of opportunities for reducing urban–rural inequalities. In the specification where the predicted value of the largest city population and its squared are used, the commuting cost has a negative impact on the u–r ratio, implying that lower commuting costs lead to a higher urban–rural inequality and vice versa.

Given the significant linkages we find in the regressions between rural and urban areas, and since urbanization cannot be viewed in isolation, Section 3.7 focuses on rural employment, taking the case of India's Mahatma Gandhi National Rural Employment Guarantee Scheme (MGNREGS) and looking at the positive impacts of migrant remittances on rural areas.

3.7 Rural Employment and Remittances

Affirming the trend of migration of people from villages to big cities and towns, the Census of India 2011 shows that for the first time, India has added more people in urban centres than in rural areas over a decade. Between 2001 and 2011, the number of people living in urban areas increased from 286 million to 377 million,

This equation enables us to compute the optimal impact of urbanization on u-r inequality in the following way). Based on the equation estimated above, the derivative with respect to *urbanization* is

$$\delta u\text{–}r\ ratio/\delta urbanization = 17.42 - 2 \times 35.55\ urbanization.$$

Solving for *urbanization* by setting the above equation equal to 0 gives:

$$\delta u\text{–}r\ ratio/\delta urbanization = 17.42 - 2 \times 35.55\ \text{urbn} = 0$$
$$\text{urbanization} \approx 0.25.$$

The above shows that at about 25 per cent urbanization, u–r inequality is maximum, beyond which we may expect urban–rural inequality to decline.

a rise of 91 million. In comparison, the rural population increased by 90 million, up from 743 million in 2001 to 833 million now (*Indian Express* 2011).

Based on the assumption that migration to cities makes them more congested, making it necessarily bad, the government of India has been trying to counter the trend of rural residents migrating to urban areas in search of jobs, and it has initiated programmes to promote rural employment, as discussed in Section 3.1. The most important rural employment scheme is the Mahatma Gandhi National Rural Employment Guarantee Scheme (MGNREGS), a flagship programme of the Government of India. Under MGNREGS, rural households willing to do unskilled manual labour are constitutionally entitled to demand employment up to hundred days in a year from their respective Gram Panchayats (GPs). The main objectives of NREGS are rural poverty alleviation, prevention of rural–urban migration (similar to the rural subsidy programmes in the PRC, sometimes in the name of 'New Countryside Construction'), creation of durable and productive assets, and environmental conservation. Another key aspect of NREGS is the guarantee of 33 per cent reservation of work opportunities for women and equal wages.

The works undertaken through MGNREGS give priority to activities related to water harvesting, groundwater recharge, drought proofing, and tackling flooding. Its focus on eco-restoration and sustainable livelihoods implies that its success should spur private investment by farmers on their lands. The assumption is that such activities would lead over time to an increase in land productivity, generating a natural demand for labour, which would automatically reduce dependence on MGNREGS as a source of work.

Sridhar and Reddy (2014) answer questions such as whether the MGNREGS wages have been above their reservation wages. They estimate the reservation wages as dependent on individual and labour market characteristics, being one of the few studies to do this using Indian data, and compute net benefits from NREGS jobs. Next, they investigate what demand-side (individual) and supply-side (programme) characteristics determine enrolment in the programme and determine NREGS wages.

Using data from large primary surveys of MGNREGS beneficiaries and non-beneficiaries in Chitradurga district of Karnataka in India, Sridhar and Reddy (2014) find that the wages MGNREGS beneficiaries got were well below their asking wage (which was Rs 207 a day), being only Rs 98 on average. Their estimation of reservation wages showed that higher current wages increase reservation wages. The elasticity of reservation wage with respect to work experience was found to be negative, implying that those with higher work experience have lower asking wages, which could be a reflection of the fact that for unskilled rural workers, higher work experience just means older age, which presumably decreases their asking wage.

Further, Sridhar and Reddy (2014) estimated a two-step regression model to understand the determinants of participation in the programme and of

NREGS wages. They found demand-side characteristics such as age, gender, and the individual's reservation wages had a significant impact on enrolment in the programme. Supply-side factors such as per capita programme expenditure and percentage of delay in payment of wages had significant impacts on participation. They concluded that the programme has had a favourable impact on reducing poverty.

This evidence from India's (erstwhile) MGNREGS, along with the findings from the regressions for urbanization, indicates that rural incomes, when they are high relative to urban incomes, prevent urbanization. The evidence from MGNREGS seems to indicate that it has impacted poverty by raising rural wages, given that in the case of most of the states, the MGNREGS wages were higher than the minimum wages specified. This prevents migration into cities, which is what the regressions also indicate. Thus, if rural employment programmes such as the MGNREGS reduce poverty, these would be adequate to make rural residents refrain from migrating to urban areas. Since its inception in 2006, a total of Rs 2,690 billion (approximately $44.8 billion) had been spent on the programme. Reports of the impact of the programme on poverty have been varied. Niehaus and Sukhtankar (2013) found that 89 per cent of workers reported receiving a wage at least as high as their reservation wage in their restricted sample. A study by India's Institute for Applied Manpower Research (2008) commissioned by the Planning Commission carried out in twenty districts spread throughout India by targeting 300 beneficiaries from each district found that one-fourth of the families surveyed opined that there is migration from their respective village to towns/cities in search of jobs. Almost 50 per cent of the households in the western region expressed that there is migration from their villages. In the north-eastern region, in the district of North Lakhimpur, everyone agreed that there is migration from their villages. There is migration from districts such as South Garo Hills (Meghalaya), Medak (Telangana), and Dahod (Maharashtra), in addition to almost all the districts from the eastern region. In some of these districts, the out-migration is as much as 40 per cent. Hence there is reason to believe that migration to urban areas continues despite the programme, and this is consistent with the evidence from Sridhar and Reddy (2014) that their asking wage was well above that offered by the NREGS.

However, what is it that healthy urbanization entails, which rural development or rural poverty alleviation cannot do? (See Sridhar 2014.) First, urbanization implies the existence of scale economies, which are possible because of division of labour and specialization. Scale economies explain the existence of factory towns. The existence of large metropolitan areas such as Mumbai, Shanghai, or Chicago is explained by the prevalence of agglomeration economies, the economic efficiencies that arise when firms and people locate in close proximity to one another. Agglomeration economies can be either pecuniary or technological in nature. Pecuniary economies reduce the cost of inputs for firms due to their location in close proximity to each other, while technological economies make inputs more productive.

Further, there are a large number of studies that show the impact of density on productivity (Trubka 2007; Carlino et al. 2007). It may be noted here that all countries, including India, have a density (of 400 persons per sq. km in India) or minimum population (of 5,000 in the Indian context) criterion to define their urban areas. While the data from Indian cities do not permit us to examine the productivity impacts of density conclusively, studies from around the world show that high-productivity areas are characterized by high density, whether they are measured by population or employment size and/or employment density.

While wages and land rents are higher in metropolitan areas, there should be inherent advantages to firms and residents in locating there; if the costs of locating in metropolitan areas were higher than the benefits, they would not locate in places that would make them worse off.

Even when rural–urban migration takes place, there is evidence to show that the rural migrants in urban areas send back remittances to the rural economy. An NSSO report (2008) estimates that around 58 per cent of domestic migrants send money home with an average remittance size of Rs 13,000 in a year (NSSO 2010) This survey found that, on average, during the last 365 days male out-migrants from urban areas and residing within India had remitted on average nearly Rs 28,000.[12] Tumbe (2011) confirms this and estimates the domestic remittance market in India to be $10 billion in 2007–8, with 60 per cent being interstate transfers and 80 per cent being directed towards rural households. Migrant earnings and remittances are used to repay debt, purchase basic necessities, and invest in health, education, and enterprise. The study by Tumbe found that domestic remittances financed over 30 per cent of household consumption expenditure in remittance-receiving households, which formed nearly 10 per cent of rural India.

Figure 3.16 shows the historical movement of per capita availability of cultivable arable land area and per capita production of food grains for rural India. While capturing the historical trend, the graph demonstrates that even while per capita availability of arable and cultivable land declined over the period 1961–2010, per capita production of food grains has remained stable.

Hence these results are a clear indication that urbanization should not be planned in isolation, but should take into account rural employment and incomes. Urbanization benefits not only urban area residents and firms through scale economies, agglomeration economies, sharing, matching, and learning, but also rural areas by increasing their incomes, through remittances and financing their expenditures.

[12] NSSO (2010).

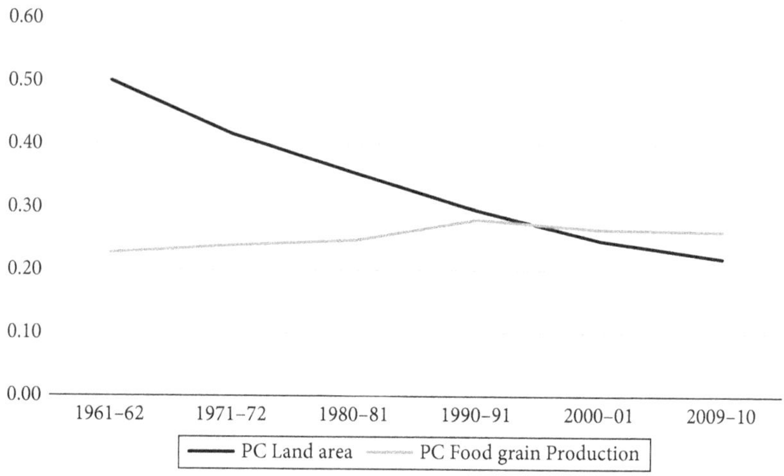

Figure 3.16. Per capita land area and food grain production over time

Sources: Reserve Bank of India's *Handbook of Statistics on the Indian Economy*, www.indiastats.com, Census of India, and author's analyses.

3.8 Policy Implications

A majority of the population in Asia is set to be urban, and the sustainability of growth in the countries of the region depends on their urban areas as their engines of growth. While cities in the PRC account for 70 per cent of the nation's GDP, urban areas in India currently contribute about 65 per cent of GDP (see Sridhar and Wan 2010a and 2010b).

Based on several regressions of urbanization, which reflect its benefits and costs in this chapter, we find a positive impact of the crucial u–r ratio on the population of the largest city in the state, but not on urbanization. This indicates that while the u–r ratio is not strong enough to impact urbanization of the state, it impacts the largest city's population positively, which is plausible.

When accounted for in the two-way relationship between urbanization and the u–r ratio, we find that urbanization (or the largest city's population) increases the urban–rural inequalities. However, at higher levels urbanization can be expected to reduce urban–rural inequalities. This is what we expect since urbanization not only increases incomes of the urban residents but also the rural population shares the growth, due to the equilibrating labour flows and subsequent equalization of incomes.

(1) The results suggest that commuting costs are not important in determining the standard of living in urban India, given the data caveats. Nonetheless, there is a strong case for believing that India can and should support the benefits of urbanization and the development of large cities, due to the

following reasons: while the supporting data are not available at the city level, there are strong reasons to believe that cities are the engines of economic growth in India, which may be seen by the fact that they contribute to nearly two-thirds of the country's GDP. Hence if India is to sustain its macroeconomic growth targets, it is essential to support urbanization.

(2) In the case of Indian cities, there is a positive relationship between urbanization and per capita income, and also between national income and urbanization. This is due to the fact that urbanization enables the better matching of labour markets and skills, sharing, and learning, which enable the workforce in urban areas to be more productive compared with their rural counterparts.

(3) There is a large rural–urban income gap in India, with rural incomes being significantly lower than urban incomes, which leads to migration towards urban areas in the expectation of equalizing the income differential. Although migration is not the primary source of urbanization in the country, this is confirmed by the regression results.

Nonetheless, it should be remembered that subsidizing rural areas or even urban areas for that matter is problematic. This is because rural employment guarantee or assured income for a limited time period is acceptable, but not sustainable. Rural youth and workers have to find their own employment as market conditions improve in the long run. Similarly, urban areas should grow and contribute to output, income, and productivity based on the strengths of scale economies and agglomeration. In the long run, both market and political economy considerations prevent subsidization of one at the cost of the other, failing which it may lead to polarization of interest groups and social conflicts.

It is tempting to believe that commuting and its costs would slow the growth of cities. Savage and Dasgupta (2006) report that Bangalore's travel time (one-way work trip) increased from twenty-four minutes in 1991 to forty minutes in 2001–2. In the UK, some estimates show that 2.5 hours are added to work-related journeys each week because of congestion. But there is hope with technology.

Given the penetration of the computer, Internet, and use of smartphones with 3G and 4G connectivity in urban areas, it is possible for commuters to telecommute to work, which can possibly obviate the negative impacts of commuting on urban growth.[13] Sridhar and Sridhar (2003) find, using data from the Survey of

[13] By definition, telecommuting is the process of commuting to work through communication links rather than through one's physical presence. Telecommuting refers to working at home, non-traditional satellite offices, telecottages, or neighbourhood offices. Teleworking refers to the partial or complete substitution of telecommunications technology for the trip to and from the workplace. Ubiquitous broadband connectivity; powerful computers, smartphones, and tablets with productivity- and communication-enhancing applications; sophisticated remote access and monitoring tools; and enterprise-enabled cloud computing have reduced the physical barriers that formerly required employees to always be in their offices.

Income Program and Participation of the United States, that telecommuting can at best be a complement, not a substitute, for face-to-face interaction. However, the US Department of Transportation data for 2000–10 shows that the increase in the number of people telecommuting is larger than the increase in number of people using transit over the same period.

Telecommuting increases employee productivity by reducing the need to travel, by allowing them to work at times they are likely to be their best, and by reducing office distractions. National Panasonic found through its research that 50 per cent of employee time in branch offices was spent on administrative work that was non-productive. So it is looking at the small office home office concept as one of the measures to increase productivity in the times to come. British Telecom (BT) increased the use of phone conferencing among its staff in the UK by 30 per cent, where 75 per cent of all phone conferences are replacements for face-to-face meetings. A study that looked at the impact of this decision found that BT reduced carbon dioxide emissions by 54,000 tonnes that year alone, besides a saving of 12 million litres of car fuel, costing an estimated £9.7 million, due to a reduction of a staggering 220 million miles of travel and 1,800 years of staff time over that year.

Telecommuting not only benefits employees but also organizations, which can cut costs on office space. IBM recently reported savings of $75 million in real estate expenses related to office space because of telecommuting. Contrary to perceptions, telecommuting could also increase employee participation in organizational activity. BT found that the average conference call involved eight participants, whereas if face-to-face meetings were held, only five travelled on average.

According to the Gartner Group, as early as 2002, more than 108 million users worldwide were working outside the boundaries of their enterprise. Evidence of such teleworking has been found in India and Malaysia. Estimates for European countries vary for teleworkers of all types at 4 per cent of the workforce. Estimates of the number of telecommuters in the US vary and range between 3 and 9 million people, roughly 3 to 8 per cent of the workforce. Other studies for the US predict that the penetration rate of telecommuting may vary between 5.2 and 10.4 per cent of the workforce compared to the very low levels of about 1.6 per cent projected. A Forrester Research study points out that about 10 per cent of US households maintain a second office at home, bringing about nine hours of work per week.

Summarizing, the important opportunities that would be made possible by telecommuting include cutting down on real estate costs, increasing employee productivity, reducing carbon emissions, and making our environment cleaner. Telecommuting can also be a productive way of engaging women and other minorities in the labour force since they may not be able to participate in the labour market otherwise.

Everything said and done, it should be noted that employee telecommuting implies remote supervision that presents monitoring challenges for the employer, while physical isolation may impede the employee's involvement in determining valued organizational outcomes. It might also make it difficult for the company to ensure the quality of its services and their delivery time. Thus it should be noted that telecommuting entails a significant change in management culture, trust on the part of employers, motivation on the part of employees, teamwork, and networking (see Sridhar and Sridhar 2013).

Taking the above into account, it is clear that investments in infrastructure will improve travel time and mobility, which is important to address as cities grow, to keep enlarging the size of the functional labour market (see Bertaud 2014). However, the knee-jerk reaction of policymakers in developing countries is such that they always respond to reducing 'congestion' when a city grows, but not necessarily for improving mobility. This should change since improvement in mobility makes a city more productive and enhances its liveability (see Bertaud 2014; Sridhar 2014).

The lesson that India should learn from the PRC's urbanization is to facilitate greater understanding of Indian cities by enabling data gathering and dissemination about various aspects of urbanization such as education and income at the city level or, even better, at the individual household level. Currently some of these data are gathered by India's NSSO and census town directories, but even as of late 2014, the Census of India's 2011 town directories had still not been released. The NSSO data unfortunately cannot be aggregated with confidence at the city level, due to the inadequate number of observations represented from cities. If these data are gathered and published in a timely and regular fashion periodically, it will be possible to ascertain the relationship between human capital, density, productivity, and the growth of cities.

Research on the PRC's city sizes and the optimum value of output for a certain size by Au and Henderson (2005) indicated that the PRC's cities are undersized, leading to huge welfare losses. Hence the lesson that the PRC should learn from India's urbanization experience is to gradually remove restrictions on rural–urban migration by reforming the Hukou, which is currently being done.

Acknowledgements

I thank Guanghua Wan of Fudan University, for motivating me, and for the opportunity to be involved in this People's Republic of China–India urbanization project and work on this chapter. Lu Ming of Shanghai Jiaotong University and Fudan University gave a lot of interesting ideas and feedback during the initial discussions during the Wuhan workshop, and post-Wuhan, I thank him for his comments regarding the draft chapter. Thanks are due to

Raju Mote in the data bank in the Central Institute of Road Transport (CIRT), Pune, India, for patiently answering many of my questions pertaining to the commute cost data for the State Road Transport Undertakings. I thank Sudhir Krishna for his comments. I am grateful to all other participants at the Wuhan and Sri Lanka workshops, where this chapter was presented, for their comments. I thank Khalil Musa Shaha at the Institute for Social and Economic Change for helping with data on monthly per capita expenditure for all the states. Any errors remain mine.

References

Au, Chun-Chung and J. Vernon Henderson. 2005. 'Are Chinese Cities Too Small?' Brown University Working Paper, 5 October.

Basu, B. and S. Bandyapadhyay. 2009. 'Zipf's Law and Distribution of Population in Indian Cities'. *Indian Journal of Physics 83* (11): 1575–82.

Bertaud. 2014. 'Cities As Labor Markets, Marron Institute on Cities and the Urban Environment'. *Working Paper 2.* Marron Institute on Cities and the Urban Environment, New York.

Bertinelli, Luisito and Eric Strobl. 2007. 'Urbanisation, Urban Concentration and Economic Development'. *Urban Studies 44* (13): 2499–510.

Brueckner, Jan and Kala Seetharam Sridhar. 2012. 'Measuring Welfare Gains from Relaxation of Land-use Restrictions: the Case of India's Building-height Limits'. *Regional Science and Urban Economics (Special issue in honor of Jacques Thisse) 42* (6): 1061–67.

Brueckner, Jan. 1990. 'Analyzing Third World Urbanization: a Model with Empirical Evidence'. *Economic Development and Cultural Change 38*: 587—610.

Brueckner, Jan. 2011. *Why Cities Exist? Lectures in Urban Economics*, MIT Press.

Carlino, Gerald A., Satyajit Chatterjee, and Robert M. Hunt. 2007. 'Urban Density and the Rate of Invention'. *Journal of Urban Economics 61* (3): 389–419.

Castells, David and Vicent Royuela. 2011. 'Agglomeration, Inequality and Economic Growth'. *Research Institute of Applied Economics Working Paper, 2001/14*, Barcelona.

Chen, Zhao, Ming Lu, and Zheng Xu. 2011. 'Agglomeration Shadow: A Non-Linear Core–Periphery Model of Urban Growth in China (1990–2006)'. Paper presented at the ADB Workshop on Green Urbanization in Asia, Honolulu, Hawaii, December.

Duranton, Giles and Diego Puga. 2003. 'Micro Foundations of Urban Agglomeration Economies'. *National Bureau of Economic Research (NBER) Working Paper 9931.*

Gabaix, Xavier. 1999. 'Zipf's Law and the Growth of Cities'. *American Economic Review 89* (2): 129–32.

Gilbert A. and J. Gugler. 1982. *Cities, Poverty, and Development: Urbanization in the Third World*, Oxford University Press.

Henderson, Vernon J. 2004. 'Urbanization and Growth'. In *Handbook of Economic Growth*, volume 1, edited by P. Aghion and S. Durlauf, North-Holland.

Indian Express. (2011). 'Census Data Shows Numbers Rising More in Urban Areas'. Express News Service, 16 July. <http://archive.indianexpress.com/news/census-data-shows-numbers-rising-more-in-urban-areas/818130/>.

Institute of Applied Manpower Research. 2008. *All-India Report on Evaluation of NREGA: A Survey of Twenty Districts*, Institute of Applied Manpower Research.

Institute for Human Development (2014) *India Labor and Employment Report 2014*. Academic Foundation, New Delhi.

Krugman, Paul. 1995. 'Urban Concentration: The Role of Increasing Returns and Transport Costs'. *Proceedings of the World Bank Annual Conference on Development Economics 1994, @1995*, The International Bank for Reconstruction and Development/ The World Bank.

Kuznets, S. (1966). *Modern Economic Growth: Findings and Reflections*. Stockholm: Nobel Foundation.

Lanaspa, L., F. Pueyo, and F. Sanz. 2005. 'Patrones de urbanización y nivel de desarrollo. Unaaplicaciónempírica'. *CuadernosAragoneses de Economía 15* (1): pp. 83–92.

Lu, Ming and Zhao Chen. 2006. 'Urbanization, Urban-Biased Policies and Urban-Rural Inequality in China: 1987–2001'. *Chinese Economy 39* (3): 42–63.

Lusome, R. and R. B. Bhagat. 2006. Paper presented at the Annual Conference of Indian Association for the Study of Population (IASP) during 7–9 June, Thiruvananthapuram. <http://community.eldis.org/.59b6a372/Trends%20and%20Patterns%20of%20Internal%20Migration%20in%20India%201971-2001.pdf>.

McGee, T. G. 1971. *The Urbanization Process in the Third World: Explorations in Search of a Theory*, G. Bell and Sons.

Mills, E. S. and C. M. Becker. 1986. *Studies in Indian Urban Development*, World Bank and Oxford University Press.

Moretti, E. 2004a. 'Workers' Education, Spillovers, and Productivity: Evidence from Plant-Level Production Functions'. *The American Economic Review 94* (3): 656–90.

Moretti, E. 2004b. 'Estimating the Social Return to Higher Education: Evidence from Longitudinal and Repeated Cross-Sectional Data'. *Journal of Econometrics* 121 (1–2): 175–212.

Niehaus, P. and S. Sukhtankar. (2013). 'The Marginal Rate of Corruption in Public Programs: Evidence from India'. *Journal Of Public Economics*, 104, 52–64.

NSSO (National Sample Survey Office). 2010. 'Migration in India 2007–2008'. *NSS Report No. 533* (64/10.2/2), June 2010, National Sample Survey Office, Ministry of Statistics & Programme Implementation, Government of India, New Delhi.

Paul, Samuel, Kala Seetharam Sridhar, A. Venugopala Reddy, and Pavan Srinath. 2012. *The State of Our Cities: Evidence from Karnataka*, Oxford University Press.

Premi, M. K. 1990. 'India'. In *International Handbook on Internal Migration*, edited by Charles B. Nam, William J. Serow, and David F. Sly, Greenwood Press.

Puga, Diego. 2009. 'The Magnitude and Causes of Agglomeration Economies'. Paper written for the *Journal of Regional Science*'s 50th Anniversary Symposium, April. <https://ideas.repec.org/a/bla/jregsc/v50y2010i1p203-219.html>.

Quigley, John. 2009. 'Urbanization, Agglomeration and Economic Development'. In *Urbanization and Growth: Commission on Growth and Development* edited by Michael Spence, Patricia Clarke Annez, and Robert M. Buckley, World Bank, Washington, DC. https://openknowledge.worldbank.org/handle/10986/2582>.

Rauch, J. E. 1993. 'Productivity Gains from Geographic Concentration of Human Capital: Evidence from the Cities'. *Journal of Urban Economics 34* (3): 380–400.

Savage, David and S. Dasgupta. 2006. 'Governance Framework for Delivery of Urban Services'. In *India Infrastructure Report. 2006: Urban Infrastructure* edited by 3i Network, Oxford University Press.

Sridhar, Kala S. 2011. 'Addendum to Determinants of City Growth and Output in India'. *Review of Urban and Regional Development Studies 23* (2–3): 162–5.

Sridhar, Kala S. 2014. 'How To make our cities more productive?' *The Financial Express*, 10 September. <http://www.financialexpress.com>.

Sridhar, Kala S. and V. Sridhar. 2003. 'The Effect of Telecommuting on Suburbanization: Empirical Evidence'. *Journal of Regional Analysis and Policy 33* (1): 1–25.

Sridhar, Kala S. and Nivedita Kashyap. 2014. 'Benchmarking Cities: Evidence from India'. In *Urbanization in Asia: Governance, Infrastructure and the Environment*, edited by Kala S. Sridhar and Guanghua Wan, Springer.

Sridhar, Kala S. and A. V. Reddy. 2014. 'Contribution of the Urban Poor: A Pilot Study from Bengaluru, India'. In *Inclusive Urban Planning: State of the Urban Poor Report 2013*, Ministry of Housing and Urban Poverty Alleviation, Government of India, Oxford University Press.

Sridhar, Kala S. and V. Sridhar. 2007. 'Telecommunications Infrastructure and Economic Growth: Evidence from Developing Countries'. *Applied Econometrics and International Development 7* (2): 37–56.

Sridhar, Kala S. and V. Sridhar. 2013. 'Telecommuting is the Way to Go'. *The Financial Express*, 27 November.Sridhar, Kala S. and Guanghua Wan. 2010a. 'Firm Location Choice in Cities: Evidence from China, India, and Brazil'. *China Economic Review 21*: 113–22.

Sridhar, Kala S. and Guanghua Wan. 2010b. 'Firm Location Choice in Cities: Evidence from China and India'. In *The Rise of China and India: Impacts, Prospects and Implications*, edited by Amelia U. Santos-Paulino and Guanghua Wan, Palgrave Macmillan.

Todaro, Michael P. 1969. 'A Model of Labor Migration and Urban Unemployment in Less Developed Countries'. *American Economic Review 59* (March): 138–48.

Tripathi, Sabyasachi. 2012. 'Do Large Agglomerations Lead to Economic Growth? Evidence from Urban India'. *MPRA Paper* No. 38227, posted 20 April.

Trubka, Roman. 2007. 'Productivity and the Density of Economic Activity: Preliminary Estimates of Agglomeration Benefits in Australian Cities'. Curtin University's Sustainability Policy Institute.

Tumbe, Chinmay. 2011. 'Remittances in India: Facts and issues'. *Indian Institute of Management Bangalore Working Paper 331*, Bangalore.

World Bank. 2013. 'World Development Indicators Online'. Washington DC, The World Bank.

Zhang, Kevin Honglin. 2002. 'What Explains China's Rising Urbanisation in the Reform Era?' *Urban Studies 39* (12): 2301–15.

PART II

URBAN SYSTEM

4
Urban System and Urban Development in the People's Republic of China

Zhao Chen and Ming Lu

4.1 Urban System

4.1.1 The Distribution of Cities of Different Size

In the People's Republic of China (PRC), a city refers to an administrative area with more than 100,000 residents. Cities in the PRC can be categorized into three different administrative levels: county-level city, prefecture-level city, and municipalities. Due to the high speed of interregional migration from rural to urban areas, urban population has been growing at a fast pace since the mid-1990s when rural migrant workers could find jobs in non-agricultural sectors in urban regions. As Table 4.1 shows, the number of cites has also been changing, with prefecture-level cities increasing faster due to the administrative upgrading of county-level cities.

In 2012, the PRC established the prefecture-level city of Sansha in Hainan province, and merged Wujiang city (county level) into SuZhou city (prefecture level) in Jiangsu province as Wujiang district, which increased the number of cities in the PRC to 656. Table 4.2, where cities are grouped according to their population size, shows that from 1978 to 2012, the number of cities more than doubled and the share of larger cities increased faster.

The urban system in China has a clear geographical pattern. As Figure 4.1 shows, most of the larger cities (indicated by darker shades) are located in the eastern part of the country. This is probably the result of two geographical factors. First, the eastern part of the PRC is more productive in agriculture. Second, the eastern part is closer to the major seaports, which has played a very important role during the era of globalization when the PRC opened its doors to the rest of the world.

Another feature of the urban system in China is that most of the large cities are provincial capital cities or municipalities, because resource allocation was biased towards cities at a higher administrative level during the planned era. These cities have also played a significant role since the reforms and opening up.

Zhao Chen and Ming Lu., *Urban System and Urban Development in the People's Republic of China* In: *Cities of Dragons and Elephants: Urbanization and Urban Development in China and India. Edited by:* Guanghua Wan and Ming Lu, Oxford University Press (2019). © Oxford University Press. DOI: 10.1093/oso/9780198829225.003.0004

Table 4.1. Number of Chinese cities at different administrative levels

Year	Total	Municipality	Prefecture-level city	County-level city
1990	467	3	182	279
1995	640	3	207	427
2000	663	4	255	400
2005	657	4	282	370
2010	654	4	286	367

Note: Dates of Hong Kong, China; Macau; and Taipei, China are not included.
Source: National Bureau of Statistics of the PRC, *China City Statistical Yearbook* (1991–2011) (NBSC Various Years).

Table 4.2. Number of Chinese cities with different population size

	Year 1978	%	Year 2012	%
City (Organized by population)	**193**	–	**656**	–
More than 10 million people	0	0.00	11	1.68
5–10 million people	2	1.04	92	14.02
3–5 million people	2	1.04	76	11.59
1–3 million people	25	12.95	164	25.00
0.5–1 million people	35	18.13	177	26.98
Less than 0.5 million people	129	66.84	136	20.73

Data sources: The data in 2012 are based on *China City Statistical Yearbook* (2013) (NBSC Various Years). The data in 1978 are from the State Council (2014).

Figure 4.1. The spatial pattern of urban permanent residents in 2010
Source: The data on urban permanent residents in 2010 are based on the sixth national population census.

4.1.2 The Core–Periphery Pattern of the Urban System

In this section, I further investigate the geographical pattern of the PRC's urbanization. There is no doubt that the PRC will continue its fast pace of urbanization in the future. However, whether a higher population should further agglomerate in megacities in the coastal regions in the eastern part of the PRC still remains a matter of policy debate.

According to Fujita et al. (1999), international trade plays a very important role in reshaping the spatial pattern of urban systems. The PRC's experience after reforms and opening up also shows a trend of agglomeration towards coastal regions (Chen and Lu 2008). During the early stage of reforms and opening up, privileged policies were first applied to coastal cities by means of different types of economic zones. When economic reforms started, the Chinese government implemented an export-oriented strategy, which also benefited coastal regions more than the hinterland. This was reinforced with the PRC joining the World Trade Organization in 2001. Coastal regions developed faster also because they absorbed more foreign direct investment due to their advantage in location. As a result, a lot of new cities emerged in regions close to major seaports, for example, the Pearl River Delta near Hong Kong, China (Wei 1995; Anderson and Ge 2005). As a result, the spatial pattern of the urban system in the PRC shows a core–periphery structure. Table 4.3 separates cities into two groups according to their distance from the nearest major ports—Hong Kong, China; Shanghai; or Tianjin. We can see from Table 4.3 that for both cities with more than one or two million non-agricultural population, those regions closer to the major ports witnessed faster increases in the number of large cities. In particular, from 2005 to 2009, the number of large cities in regions farther to the major ports even decreased, which reflects the fact of interregional labour migration from the hinterland to coastal areas.

There can be said to be two hierarchical monocentric urban systems in the PRC. The first is the national urban system, the cores of which are the major ports, like Shanghai and Hong Kong, China. The distance to these ports is a measure of the remoteness of cities to the global market. The second is the regional urban system(s), the cores of which are large cities like Guangzhou, Chongqing, and Wuhan. The spatial interaction within each urban system exhibits the core–periphery structure. We use the distance to the nearest 'big' city to measure the interaction within regional urban systems, and the distance to the nearest major port to measure the interaction within national urban systems.

We simulate the correlation between the distances to the major ports and the urban economic growth rate (Xu et al. 2010). In Figure 4.2, the horizontal axis represents the distance (kilometres) away from the nearest major ports (Hong

Table 4.3. Number of large cities and distance to major ports

Year	Non-agricultural population > 2 million		Non-agricultural population > 1 million	
Distance to the three major ports	< 500 km	500 km	< 500 km	> 500 km
1990	5	4	13	18
1995	5	5	13	19
2000	6	7	16	22
2005	14	7	30	23
2009	16	6	34	22

Source: National Bureau of Statistics of the PRC, *China City Statistical Yearbook* (1991–2010) (NBSC Various Years), and the author's statistics.

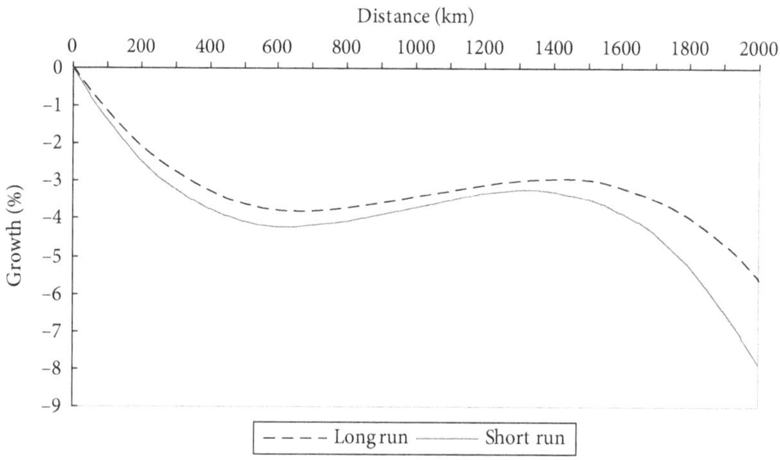

Figure 4.2. Distance to the major ports and urban economic growth
Source: Author's estimation based on original data from the *China City Statistical Yearbook* (1991–2007) (NBSC Various Years).

Kong, China or Shanghai),[1] and the vertical axis is the urban economic growth rate (percentage). A core–periphery pattern of urban system can be seen in the figure.

The dashed line in Figure 4.2 suggests that the impact of distance to the major ports on urban economic growth has basically the same shape as the market potential curve of the core–periphery model in the urban system (Fujita and Mori 1997; Fujita et al. 1999). The solid line simulates the relationship between

[1] According to the *China Statistical Abstract 2009*, in 2008, Hong Kong, China, and Shanghai account for 10.8 per cent and 10.6 per cent of overall Chinese cargo throughput respectively. We also add Tianjin as a major port in the robustness check, which accounts for 7.4 per cent.

distance-to-ports and growth in the short run. The two curves lie close to each other, showing that the long-run relationship between distance and growth is the accumulative effect of that in the short run.

When a city is located within about 600 km from a major port, the closer it is to the major port and international markets, the larger market potential and the higher economic growth rate it has. When the distance is more, international market access is no longer that important. Therefore, a location far away from a port may promote the accumulation of regional and domestic market potential, as well as the development of local economies. When distance is sufficiently long (more than 1,500 km from a port), cities remote from both the domestic and international markets suffer from low market potential and a lower economic growth rate.

Based on the above discussion, we can safely conclude that the national urban system in the PRC is characterized entirely by a core–periphery structure because of the adjustment of urban economies to international markets. We also find evidence for the agglomeration shadow modelled by Krugman (1993) in the Chinese urban system. This suggests that being closer to an agglomeration centre is not always good news for the local economy.[2]

4.1.3 Trends Towards Concentration of the Urban Population in Large Cities

The PRC is also characterized by the trend of urban population being concentrated in coastal cities. The correlation between the urbanization rate and the distance to the nearest port (Tianjin, Shanghai or Hong Kong, China) in 2010 is shown in Figure 4.3. We can see that cities closer to the major ports have a higher level of urbanization. Figure 4.4 further verifies that cities closer to the major ports are more likely to be larger ones.

The following two figures show that this pattern is still being reinforced. Figure 4.5 indicates that cities closer to the major ports have a faster speed of increase in urban permanent residents. This is because cities closer to the major ports have a higher per capita GDP as well as better local public services, where most of the graduate students find their first job. Besides, coastal cities are also the industrial agglomeration centres in the PRC, where most of the rural migrant workers find jobs.

Since cities closer to the major ports are on average larger that those farther away, the correlation in Figure 4.5 suggests that larger cities in the PRC will have a faster speed of population growth. Figure 4.6 shows that cities with more residents have a faster speed of increase in urban permanent residents.

[2] This finding adds new evidence in helping solve the paradox that Partridge et al. (2009) found between the positive closeness–growth relationship when using real data and the theoretical hypothesis of an 'agglomeration shadow'.

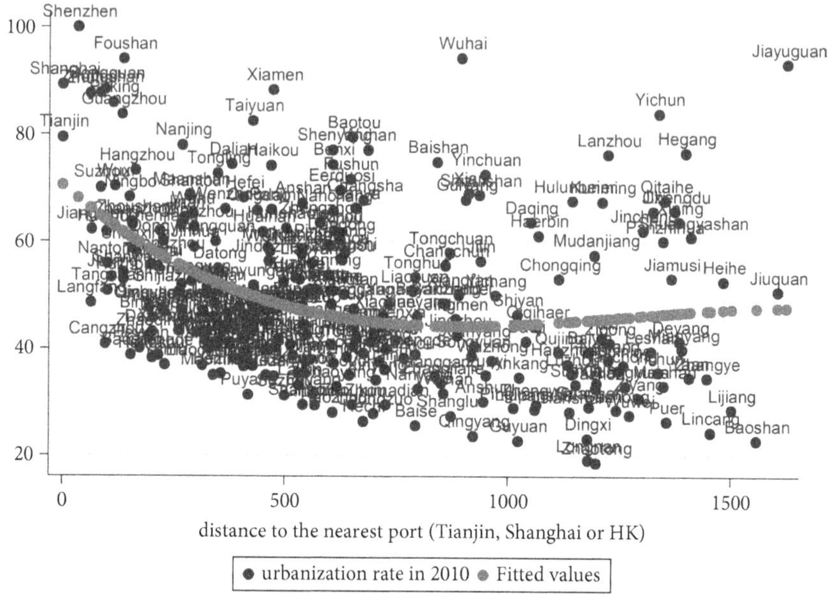

Figure 4.3. The correlation between the urbanization rate and the distance to the nearest port (Tianjin, Shanghai or Hong Kong, China) in 2010

Source: Computed from the 2010 national population census.

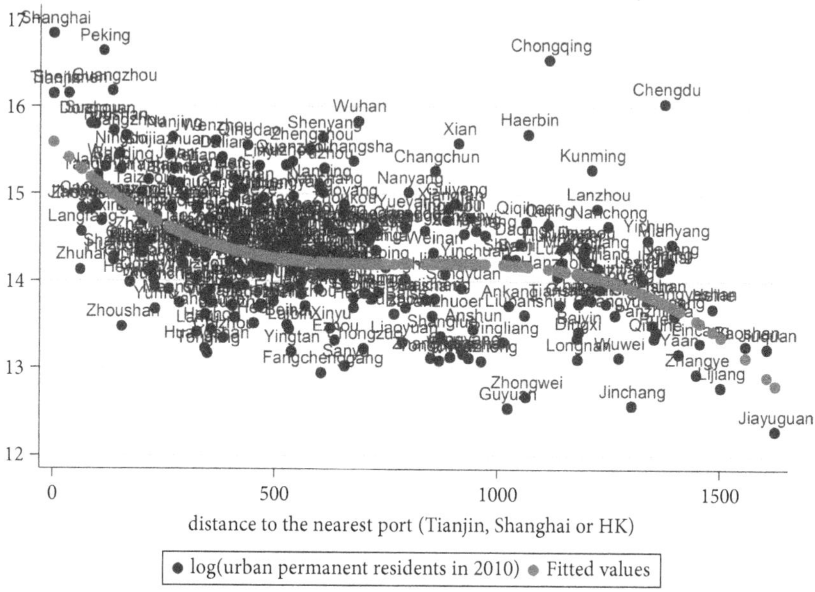

Figure 4.4. The correlation between urban permanent residents and distance to the nearest port (Tianjin, Shanghai or Hong Kong, China) in 2010

Source: Computed from the 2010 national population census.

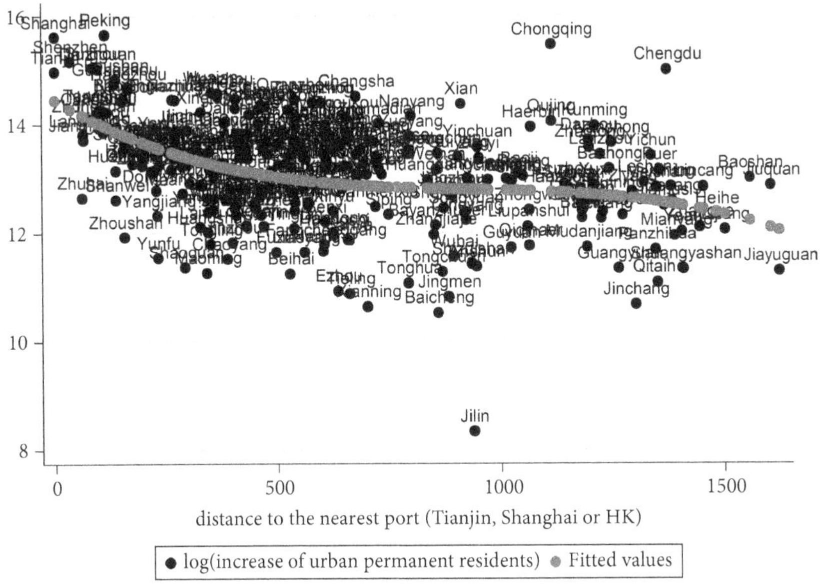

Figure 4.5. The correlation between increase in urban permanent residents from 2000 to 2010 and distance to the nearest port (Tianjin, Shanghai or Hong Kong, China)

Source: Computed from the 2000 and 2010 national population census.

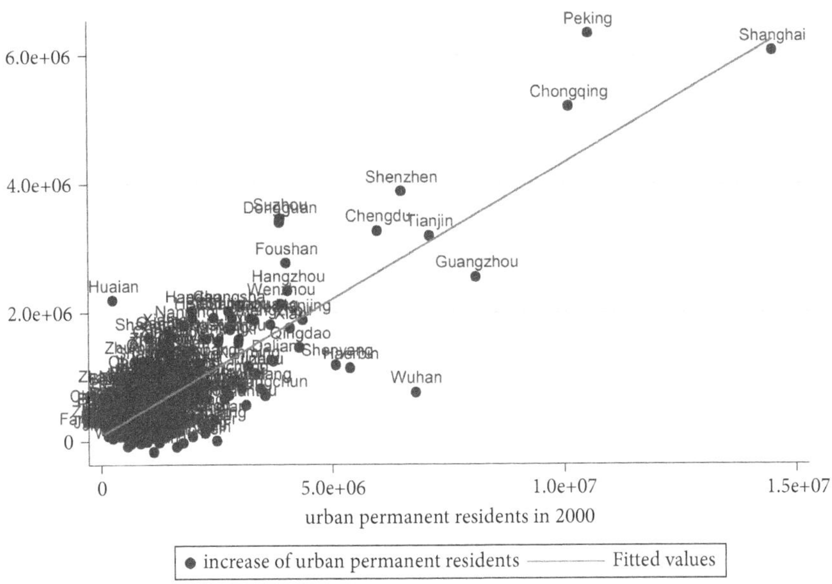

Figure 4.6. The correlation between increase in urban permanent residents from 2000 to 2010 and urban permanent residents in 2000

Source: Computed from the 2000 and 2010 national population census.

4.2 Rank–Size Relationship in the Urban System

An important question that policymakers grapple with in the context of urbanization is what the urban system in the PRC should be like. In this section, we first test whether Zipf's law, which is a statistical rule describing an urban system in a county, exists in the PRC. We then answer the same question by undertaking a cross-country comparison.

4.2.1 A Test of Zipf's Law

Zipf's law can be expressed as the rank–size rule: the *r*th largest city has a size equal to $s = r$ times the size of the *s*th largest city. That is to say, the following equation holds if Zipf's law exists:

$$\ln \text{POP}i = \ln \text{POP}_1 - \ln i,$$

where POP*i* is the population of the *i*th largest city and POP_1 is the population of the largest city in the country.

So, we can simply test Zipf's law by drawing the log value of city rank and the log value of city population in one figure. The closer the coefficient is to –1, the more likely it is that Zipf's law holds. We depict this in Figure 4.7a by using census data from 2000 and 2010. We can see from Figure 4.7a that in order to meet Zipf's law better, the population size in larger cities should be larger (as is the case), while those in smaller cities should be smaller (as it is).

Since China is such a large country, we further separate all the cities into three subgroups according to which major port (Hong Kong, China; Shanghai; or Tianjin) they are closest to. Based on these subsamples, we draw Figure 4.7b and Figure 4.7c. We can see that the dotted lines now become closer to the red line, which implies that in order to understand the urban system in China, it is important to group all the cities into different groups according to their location.

Figure 4.7b and Figure 4.7c also indicate that if Zipf's law is a general law for all countries, there must be some policy constraints that limited population size in the larger cities. We will provide more evidence about the distortion of city size in the PRC next.

4.2.2 Description of the Distortion of City Size

Modern urban economies are mainly composed of secondary and tertiary industries. As the economy transitions to the post-industrial phase, the big cities become even more important in the development of services. There is a misconception in

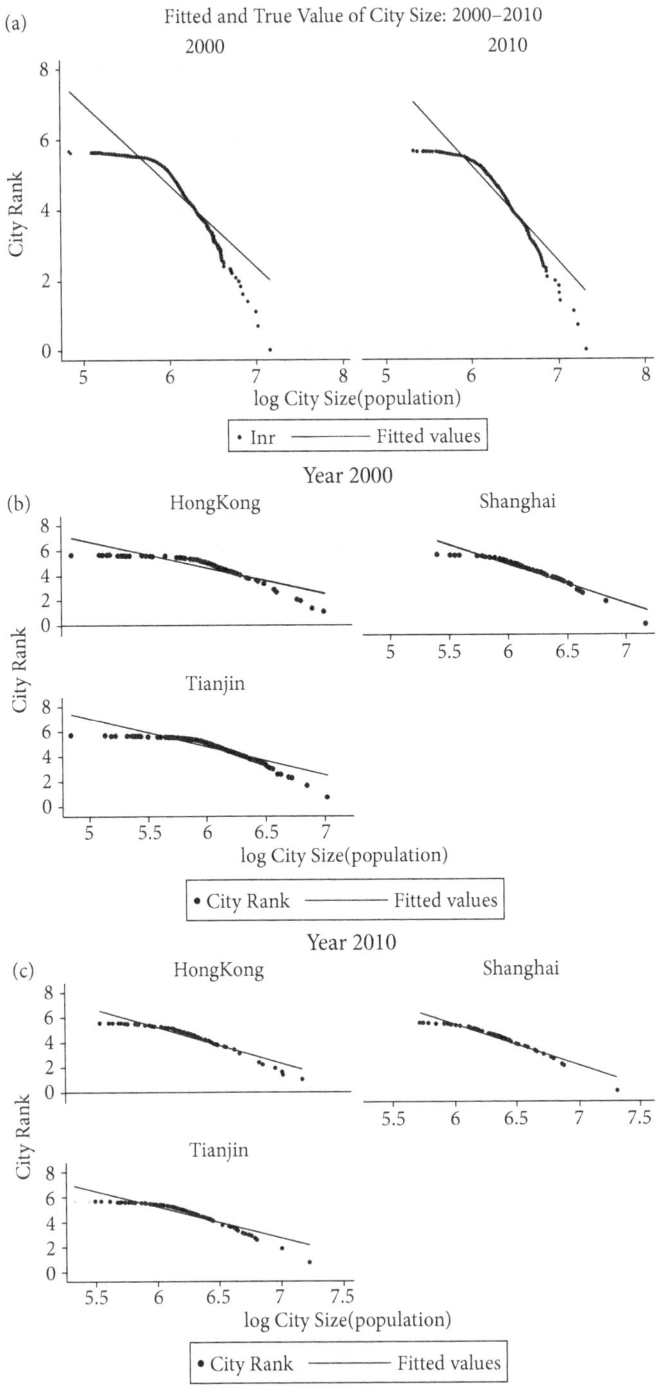

Figure 4.7. Testing Zipf's law

(a) All cities (2000 and 2010)
(b) Cities grouped into three subgroups (2000)
(c) Cities grouped into three subgroups (2010)

Source: The fifth and sixth national population census.

Chinese society that the population density in the big cities is too high. The truth, however, is that, in terms of international standards, other than the Chinese megacities with above ten million population, the average Chinese 'big' city still has a lot of room for growth.

Though the PRC has megacities such as Shanghai, Beijing, and Guangzhou, Au and Henderson (2006) suggest that, in 1997, many prefecture-level cities were about half their efficient sizes. A doubling of the population in such cities would lead to a 20–35 per cent increase in real output per worker. Although some cities have experienced heavy in-migration in the last few years, it seems that much of the PRC still has too many cities with too few people.

Henderson and Wang's (2007) study on 142 countries found that there were ninety-four cities with an urban population of over three million in 2000, and 324 cities with a 1–3 million urban population, and the ratio between the two was 0.29. When we performed the same calculation with Chinese data, we arrived at a ratio of 0.12 in 2000 and 0.17 in 2009. From Figure 4.8, we can also see that the relative number of cities in the megacity group is much smaller than that of the world average, while that of cities in the small city group is larger than that of the world average.

Henderson and Wang (2007) have pointed out that the distribution of the Chinese urban population is not concentrated enough. The spatial Gini coefficient for the global urban population was 0.5619. Among the seven countries with the largest population, namely, the PRC, India, the US, Indonesia, Brazil, Russia, and Japan, Japan has the highest spatial Gini coefficient at 0.6579, while China has the lowest spatial Gini coefficient at 0.4234. According to Fujita et al.'s (2004) calculations, the difference in population size between Chinese cities is far lower

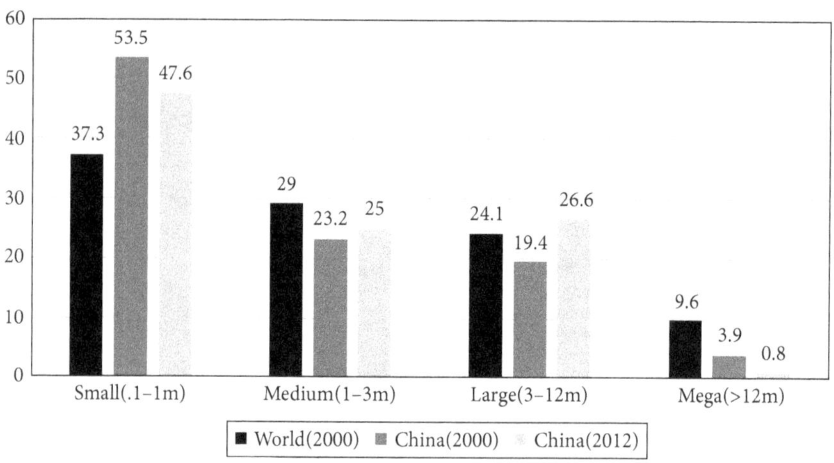

Figure 4.8. Share of cities in different population size: world vs China

Source: The 2000 data are from Henderson (2009); the 2012 data are calculated by the author from *China City Statistical Yearbook* (2013) (NBSC Various Years).

than other market economies and is only close to that of Central Asian and other former planned economy countries. In short, Chinese big cities are not large enough and the number of Chinese big cities is inadequate.

With respect to megacities, the conclusion that their size has become too big cannot simply be drawn from the total population statistics. Chinese cities are defined according to administrative jurisdiction. Megacities (especially the municipalities with province-level status) have a very large area and, strictly speaking, are city clusters instead of individual cities. Thus, when making comparisons, distinctions should be made between the core urban district, suburbs, and satellite cities. To this end, we regard Beijing, Shanghai, and Guangzhou as the core region of the Bohai Rim, Yangtze Delta, and Pearl Delta city clusters respectively, and compare them with Tokyo and New York.

It can be observed from Table 4.4 that if the population density of Shanghai, Beijing, and Guangzhou are calculated by simply using statistical figures, then the population density of these cities will be significantly lower than that of Tokyo and New York. However, the jurisdiction area of these Chinese cities far exceeds that of Tokyo and New York. Therefore, we specifically calculated the population density of the core urban district of these cities using an area comparable to Tokyo and New York. It was discovered that Beijing and Shanghai's central urban district population density is basically equivalent to that of Tokyo and New York, though Guangzhou's population density is still low. If the Tokyo circle is used as the comparison, then it would be more or less equivalent to the area of Beijing's jurisdiction, Shanghai plus Suzhou, or Guangzhou plus Foshan. It can be observed that the population density within Shanghai and Suzhou's boundaries is already equivalent to that of the Tokyo circle, while there is still an obvious gap between the population density of Beijing's jurisdiction and Guangzhou plus Foshan and that of the Tokyo circle. This gap mostly comes from the area outside the central urban area.[3]

4.3 The Primary City

We now look at the question of how large a country's urban primacy should be. This is particularly important for policymakers in the PRC since the officials in megacities such as Shanghai, Beijing, or Guangzhou all want to control the city's population size.

[3] It needs to be mentioned that the source of Chinese urban development lies in the population distribution of the planned economy era. During the process of urban expansion, new population enters the city, while the original population does not sufficiently disperse towards the urban periphery or other areas. If China's future provision of public services between cities and within cities can be further equalized, then a portion of the original downtown population in big cities can disperse towards the urban periphery or other areas and there will still be room in the downtown area to accommodate the newly arrived population.

Table 4.4. China's three city clusters compared with Tokyo (circle) and New York

	Tokyo	New York	Tokyo core districts	Tokyo Circle	Tokyo circle excluding Tokyo
Population	1,298.88	817.51	880.21	3,500.00	2,201.12
Area	2,187.65	783.84	621.9	13,400.00	11,212.35
Population density	5,937.33	10,429.63	14,151.69	2,611.94	1,963.12
	Shanghai	**Shanghai's densest districts including Pudong**	**Shanghai's core 12 districts excluding Pudong**	**Shanghai + Suzhou**	**Beyond Shanghai's core 12 districts + Suzhou**
Population	2,302.66	1,784.15	1,279.42	3,239.61	1,960.19
Area	6,340.50	2,065.97	855.56	11,219.92	10,364.36
Population density	3,631.67	8,635.90	14,954.18	2,887.37	1,891.28
	Beijing	**Beijing core 6 districts**		**Beijing**	**Beyond Beijing core 6 districts**
Population	1,961.20	1,171.60		1,961.20	789.60
Area	16,410.54	1,368.32		16,410.54	15,042.22
Population density	1,195.09	8,562.32		1,195.09	524.92
	Guangzhou	**Guangzhou ten districts**	**Shenzhen**	**Guangzhou + Foshan**	**Beyond Guangzhou ten districts + Foshan**
Population	1,270.08	1,107.07	1,035.79	1,989.08	882.01
Area	7,434.40	3,843.43	1,952.80	11,282.89	7,439.46
Population density	1,708.38	2,880.41	5,304.13	1,762.92	1,185.59

Source: Tokyo's data from <http://quickfacts.census.gov/qfd/states/36/3651000.html>; Shanghai's data from *Shanghai Statistical Yearbook* (NBSC 2011); the rest are from the respective city official websites and the sixth national population census.

4.3.1 A Country's Total Population and Urban Primacy

Different countries have diverse political systems, economic systems, and cultures. However, the determinant of the population size of a country's primary city is basically the same—it is linked to how the total population is distributed within the country. The size of the primary city is a balance of both positive and negative marginal effects on population size. So it is natural that we first look at the relationship between the population of a primary city and that of the whole country, which is shown in Figure 4.9.

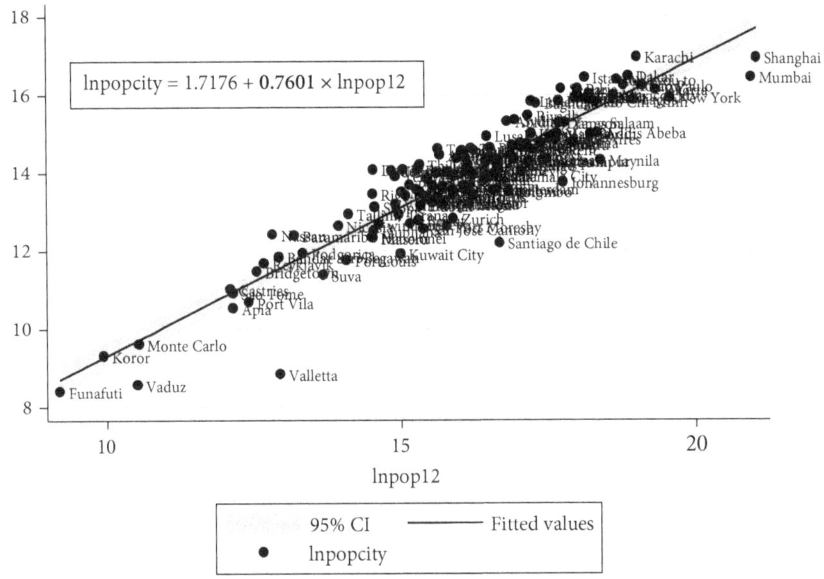

Figure 4.9. A country's population and population of the primary city
Source: The World Bank and Wikipedia's information for each city.

According to Figure 4.9, it is surprising that the population of a primary city and that of the whole country are highly correlated. If we use the log value of the country's total population as a single independent variable, based on observations from 142 countries or economies, the R^2 is as high as 0.85. Therefore, to a large extent, we can predict the population size of a country's primary city on the basis of the country's total population.

Since Asian countries or economies might be different, Figure 4.10 presents observations from subsamples from Asia. Here too we find that the population of a primary city and that of the whole country are highly correlated.

One might argue that the primary city has a large population size because the country's total area is limited. Alternatively, a country's population might be more equally distributed among small and medium-sized cities if it has a larger total area. As a result, the population size of the primary city might be smaller in this case. However, as shown in Figure 4.11, there also exists a positive correlation between the population size of the primary city and the country's total area. There are two possible explanations for this finding. First, a country with a larger area has a larger total population size, which will make the primary city larger (as shown in Figure 4.9 and Figure 4.10). Second, the area of the primary city will also be larger for countries with larger total area. As a result, the primary city with a larger area could have a larger population size. In the case of the PRC, since quite a lot of its area is not feasible for dwelling, a larger total area does not necessarily mean the population is more equally distributed nationwide.

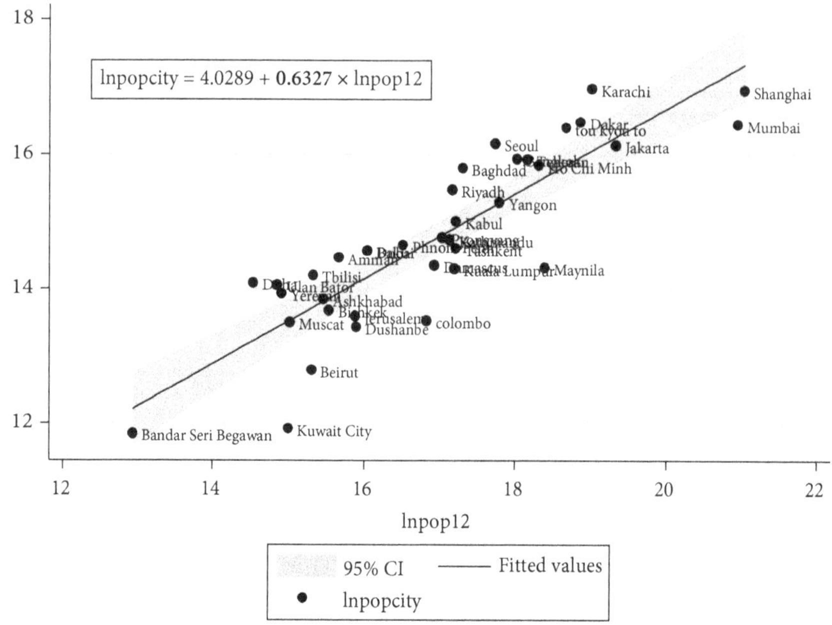

Figure 4.10. Country's population and population of the primary city in Asia
Source: The World Bank and Wikipedia's information for each city.

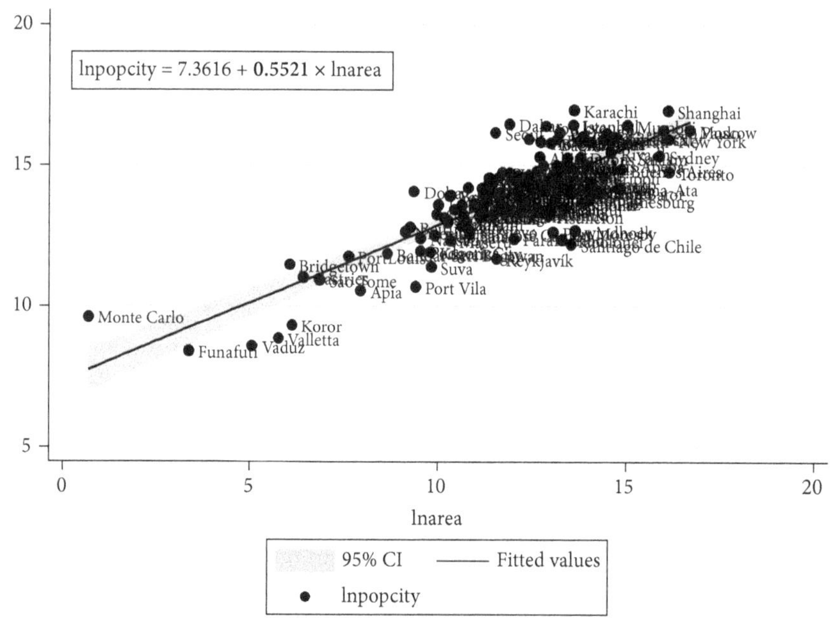

Figure 4.11. Country's area and population of the primary city in Asia
Source: World Bank and Wikipedia's information for each city.

4.3.2 Urbanization, Openness, and Primacy

Two other factors, urbanization and openness, might affect the size of the primary city. A higher level of urbanization means larger agglomeration effects and a higher labour productivity (World Bank 2009; Lu 2013), which results in larger megacities. During the process of urbanization, more migrants settle down in cities, which also enlarges the size of the primary city, where migrants are more likely to find promising jobs because of human capital externalities in large cities. More openness means a higher ratio of trade to GDP, which implies that the services sector will be more important for the whole country. In reality, most primary cities are also trade centres, especially in the case of cities with seaports or riverports. Among the primary cities in the 147 sample countries (or economies), about a third are cities with seaports and 7.5 per cent with riverports.

Figure 4.12 shows the relationship between the population share of the primary city and the urbanization level. The higher the population share of the primary city, the more population is concentrated within it. Figure 4.12 shows a positive correlation with limited fitness. This is mainly because a country's total population is the most important factor that affects the size of the primary city. In Figure 4.12, countries (or economies) with a larger total population are depicted with larger circles. From the figure, we can see that most of the large circles are below the linear fitted line, which indicates that the population shares of primary cities in

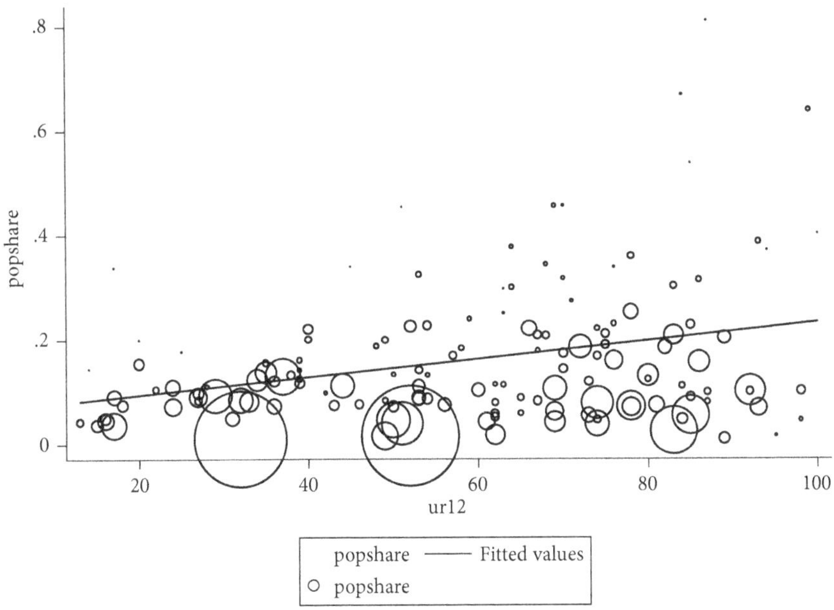

Figure 4.12. Urbanization and population share of the primary city

Source: World Bank and Wikipedia's information for each city.

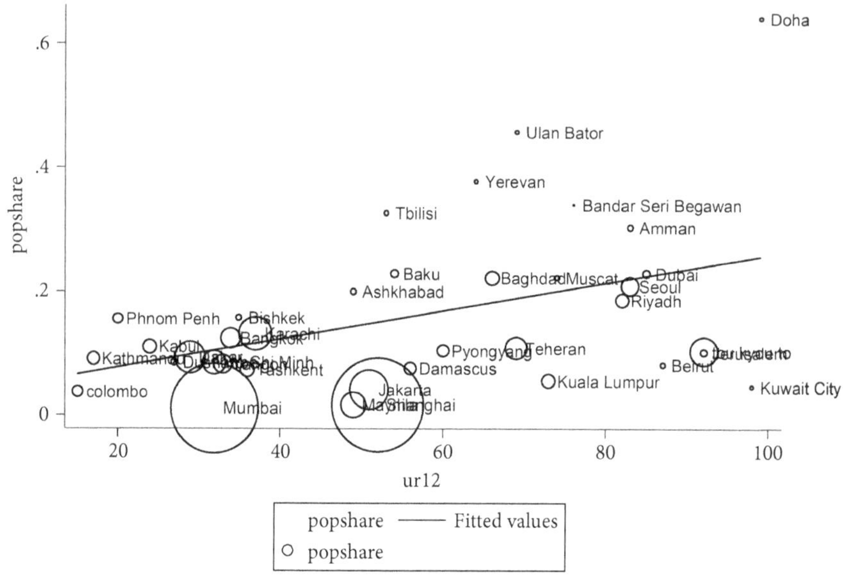

Figure 4.13. Urbanization and population share of the primary city in Asia

Source: World Bank and Wikipedia's information for each city. Larger countries (with larger circles) are below the fitted line.

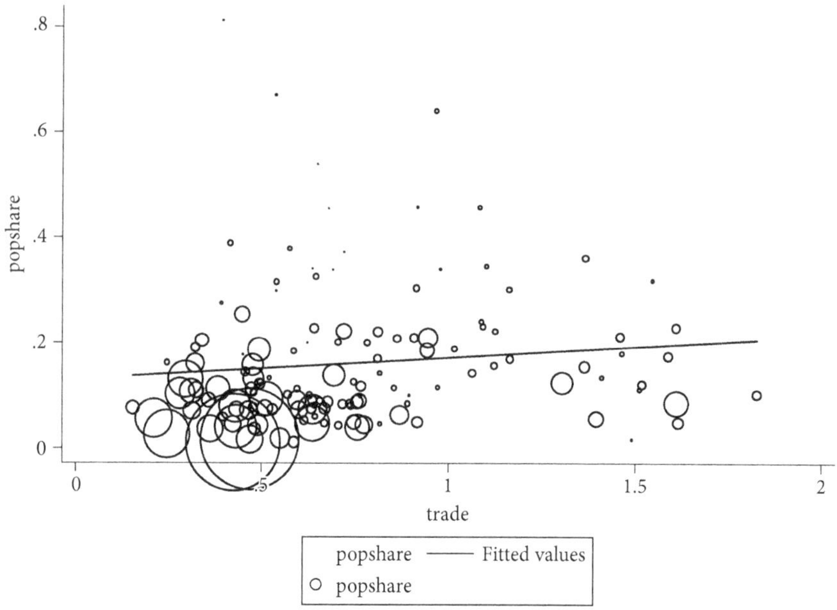

Figure 4.14. Openness and population share of the primary city

Source: World Bank and Wikipedia's information for each city. There was further concentration in some of the regional primary cities, while others had a smaller population share in 2010 than in 2000.

larger countries are below average. Figure 4.13 shows the same result when we use only Asian subsamples.

A similar pattern holds for the correlation between openness and population share of the primary city. We can see from Figure 4.14 that countries with a higher level of openness, measured by the trade–GDP ratio, have a higher share of population in primary cities. Again, the R^2 for the OLS regression is quite limited because total population is the most powerful explanatory factor. Similarly, larger countries (with larger circles) are below the fitted line.

4.3.3 Regional Primacies: Trends Over Time

The PRC is a large country with different regions at different development stages, and cities in the PRC's hinterland are less developed than cities in the coastal region. So we investigate the regional primacies for different provinces and its trend over time. Table 4.5 shows the primary city for each province and its population share in the province for 2000 and 2010. The basic finding is that there was further concentration in some of the regional primary cities, while others had a smaller population share in 2010 than in 2000.

In Table 4.6, we use the population share of the top two populous prefecture-level cities instead of the regional primary city. The result is almost the same as that in Table 4.1. The trend of the change in population proportion varies over different provinces.

In order to find how the population proportion changes for the regional primary cities in different provinces, we draw Figure 4.15, where the horizontal axis is the proportion change and the vertical axis is the province name. Provinces are listed according to their location. From top to bottom, provinces are grouped into western, central, and eastern.

We can see from Figure 4.15 that most western provinces have experienced a decrease in the population proportion of the regional primary city. In central and eastern provinces, on the other hand, the average trend is further population concentration towards the regional primary city. This is in line with the core–periphery pattern of the urban system we discussed before.

4.4 Policy Recommendations

Since the reforms and opening up, the urban system in China has reflected a core–periphery pattern, with cities in coastal regions showing a greater concentration of population than those in the PRC's hinterland. Compared with Tokyo (circle) and New York, there is no evidence that the PRC's three city clusters are too large in population size.

Table 4.5. Population proportion of the most populous prefecture-level cities in a province

Province	Primacy city in 2000	Proportion in 2000 (%)	Primacy city in 2010	Proportion in 2010 (%)
Hebei	Shijiazhuang	18.44	Shijiazhuang	16.29
Shanxi	Taiyuan	24.11	Taiyuan	20.21
The Nei Monggol Autonomous Region	Hulun Buir	17.58	Baotou	15.36
Liaoning	Shenyang	22.06	Shenyang	22.98
Jilin	Changchun	26.69	Changchun	29.07
Heilongjiang	Tsitsihar	28.76	Tsitsihar	30.49
Jiangsu	Nanjing	14.11	Suzhou	15.47
Zhejiang	Hangzhou	18.04	Hangzhou	18.99
Anhui	Hefei	12.46	Hefei	15.20
Fujian	Fuzhou	23.48	Fuzhou	22.55
Jiangxi	Nanchang	18.91	Nanchang	16.99
Shandong	Qingdao	12.48	Qingdao	12.04
Henan	Zhengzhou	17.14	Zhengzhou	15.12
Hubei	Wuhan	28.18	Wuhan	26.51
Hunan	Changsha	15.77	Changsha	16.75
Guangdong	Guangzhou	17.06	Guangzhou	15.42
The Guangxi Zhuang Autonomous Region	Nanning	14.46	Nanning	19.43
Hainan	Haikou	24.64	Haikou	35.22
Sichuan	Chengdu	26.75	Chengdu	28.56
Guizhou	Guiyang	26.93	Guiyang	24.98
Yunnan	Kunming	32.08	Kunming	27.18
Tibet Autonomous Region	Lhasa	37.48	Lhasa	35.40
Shaanxi	Xi'an	35.93	Xi'an	34.25
Gansu	Lanzhou	34.41	Lanzhou	30.01
Qinghai	Sining	65.71	Sining	55.91
The Ningxia Hui Autonomous Region	Yinchuan	36.76	Yinchuan	47.83
The Xinjiang Uygur Autonomous Region	Urumchi	27.83	Urumchi	30.69

Source: The fifth and sixth national population census.

Cross-country analysis also indicates that the population size of the primary city in the PRC is smaller than its predicted value. Moreover, there is a distortion of city size towards small cities in the PRC. That is to say, urban population in China should further concentrate in large cities rather than be more equally spread out.

However, in reality, there exist restrictions on the population size of big cities in China. For example, the 12th Five Year Plan promotes the development of small and mid-sized cities and towns, and restricts the development of megacities. The discussion in this chapter suggests that the Chinese government should adjust the

Table 4.6. Population proportion of the top two populous prefecture-level cities in a province

Province	Top two cities in 2000	Proportion in 2000 (%)	Top two cities in 2010	Proportion in 2010 (%)
Hebei	Shijiazhuang Baoding	32.22	Shijiazhuang Baoding	30.04
Shanxi	Taiyuan Datong	35.53	Taiyuan Yucheng	31.45
The Nei Monggol Autonomous Region	Hulun Buir Hohhot	29.85	Baotou Hohhot	28.41
Liaoning	Shenyang Dalian	38.32	Shenyang Dalian	41.29
Jilin	Changchun Jilin	45.34	Changchun Jilin	46.04
Heilongjiang	Haerbin Tsitsihar	40.75	Haerbin Tsitsihar	41.59
Jiangsu	Nanjing Suzhou	26.68	Suzhou Nanjing	28.64
Zhejiang	Hangzhou Wenzhou	35.45	Hangzhou Wenzhou	36.94
Anhui	Hefei Fuyang	23.61	Hefei Fuyang	24.55
Fujian	Fuzhou Quanzhou	43.30	Fuzhou Quanzhou	43.48
Jiangxi	Nanchang Ganzhou	32.49	Nanchang Ganzhou	33.10
Shandong	Qingdao Weifang	22.52	Qingdao Linyi	21.54
Henan	Zhengzhou Nanyang	26.16	Zhengzhou Nanyang	24.33
Hubei	Wuhan Xiangfan	38.26	Wuhan Xiangfan	36.19
Hunan	Changsha Hengyang	26.18	Changsha Hengyang	27.93
Guangdong	Guangzhou Shenzhen	30.72	Guangzhou Shenzhen	30.42
The Guangxi Zhuang Autonomous Region	Nanning Yulin	25.29	Nanning Yulin	31.23
Hainan	Haikou Sanya	34.72	Haikou Sanya	45.75
Sichuan	Chengdu Mianyang	34.30	Chengdu Nanchong	35.53
Guizhou	Guiyang Zunyi	44.72	Guiyang Zunyi	43.26

(Continued)

Table 4.6. Continued

Province	Top two cities in 2000	Proportion in 2000 (%)	Top two cities in 2010	Proportion in 2010 (%)
Yunnan	Kunming Qujing	42.47	Kunming Qujing	41.58
Tibet Autonomous Region	Lhasa	37.48	Lhasa	35.40
Shaanxi	Xi'an Xianyang	50.17	Xi'an Xianyang	46.35
Gansu	Lanzhou Tianshui	43.92	Lanzhou Tianshui	40.00
Qinghai	Sining	65.71	Sining	55.91
The Ningxia Hui Autonomous Region	Yinchuan Wuzhong	68.40	Yinchuan Shizuishan	64.31
The Xinjiang Uygur Autonomous Region	Urumchi Karamay	32.16	Urumchi Karamay	34.48

Data sources: The fifth and sixth national population census.

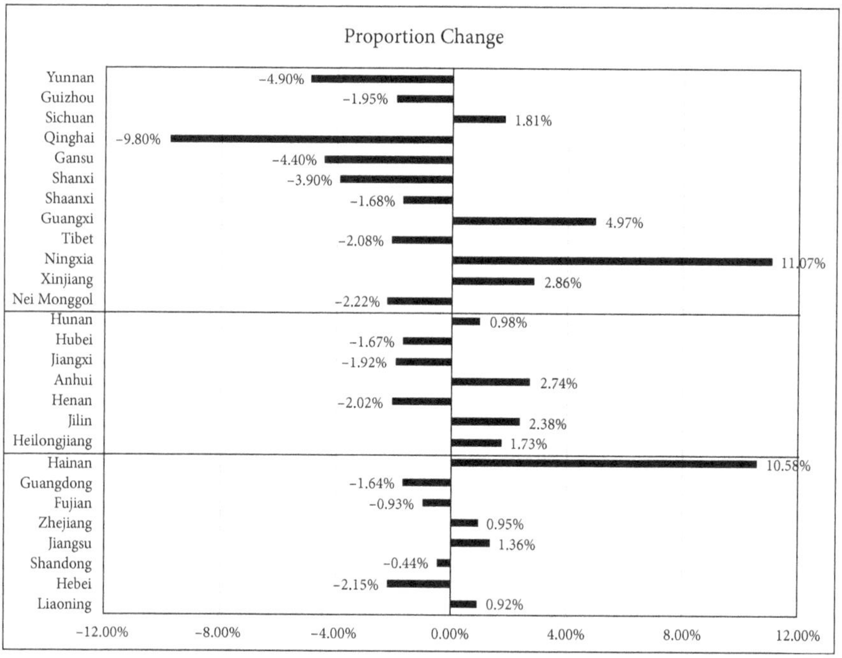

Figure 4.15. Population proportion change, 2000–10

Source: The fifth and sixth national population census.

policies on future urbanization with fewer restrictions on the further growth of megacities. The policy guidelines show allow free factor mobility among regions, especially towards megacities. This means less restrictions regarding Hukou barriers against migrant workers and providing megacities with more discretion in converting agricultural land into non-agricultural land on the basis of market prices rather than quotas by the central government. Given the sharp disparity in the quality and quantity of local public services among different regions in the PRC, the central government should promote a more equal distribution of local public services to ease the burden faced by megacities in providing local public services to the fast-increasing numbers of migrants.

Acknowledgements

I thank Yiran Xia and Dishiya Ren for their very helpful research assistance.

References

Anderson, Gordon and Ying Ge. 2005. 'The Size distribution of Chinese cities'. *Regional Science and Urban Economics 35* (6): 756–76.

Au, Chun-Chung and J. Vernon Henderson. 2006. 'How Migration Restrictions Limit Agglomeration and Productivity in China'. *Journal of Development Economics 80* (2): 350–88.

Chen, Zhao and Ming Lu. 2008. 'Is China Sacrificing Growth when Balancing Interregional and Urban-Rural Development?' In *Reshaping Economic Geography in East Asia*, edited by Yukon Huang and Alessandro Magnoli Bocchi, The World Bank, Washington, DC.

Fujita, M., J. V. Henderson, Y. Kanemoto, and T. Mori. 2004. 'Spatial Distribution of Economic Activities in Japan and China'. In *Handbook of Urban and Regional Economics*, edited by V. Henderson and J. F. Thisse, North-Holland.

Fujita, Masahisa and Tomoya Mori. 1997. 'Structural Stability and Evolution of Urban Systems'. *Regional Science and Urban Economics 27* (4–5): 399–442.

Fujita, Masahisa, Paul Krugman, and Tomoya Mori. 1999. 'On the Evolution of Hierarchical Urban Systems'. *European Economic Review 43* (2): 209–51.

Henderson, J. Vernon and Hyoung Gun Wang. 2007. 'Urbanization and City Growth: The Role of Institutions'. *Regional Science and Urban Economics 37* (3): 283–313.

Henderson, J. V. 2009. 'Urbanization in China: Policy Issues and Options'. Report for the China Economic Research and Advisory Program. <http://www.s4.brown.edu/china2012/Papers/Final%20Report%20format1109summary.pdf>.

Krugman, P. 1993. 'First Nature, Second Nature, and Metropolitan Location'. *Journal of Regional Science 33*: 129–44.

Lu, Ming. 2013. *The Power of Space: Geography, Politics and Urban Development* (in Chinese), Shanghai People's Press.

NBSC (National Bureau of Statistics, China). (2011). *Shanghai Statistical Yearbook*, China Statistical Press.

NBSC (National Bureau of Statistics, China). (Various Years). *China City Statistical Yearbook*, China Statistical Press.

Partridge, M. D., D. S. Rickman, K. Ali, and M. R. Olfert. 2009. 'Do New Economic Geography Agglomeration Shadows Underlie Current Population Dynamics across the Urban Hierarchy?' *Papers in Regional Science* 88: 445–66.

State Council. 2014. *The State's Plan on New Urbanization (2014–2020)*, State Council, People's Republic of China.

Wei, S. J. 1995. 'The Open Door Policy and China's Rapid Growth: Evidence from City-Level Data'. In *Growth Theories in Light of the East Asian Experience*, edited by Takatoshi Ito and Anne Osborn Krueger, NBER-East Asian Seminar on Economics, 4, University of Chicago Press.

World Bank. 2009. *World Development Report. 2009: Reshaping Economic Geography*, World Bank, Washington, DC.

Xu, Z., Z. Chen, and M. Lu. 2010. 'The Core–Periphery Model of China's Urban System: An Empirical Study on Geography and Economic Growth (in Chinese)'. *The Journal of World Economy* 7: 144–60.

5

City-Size Distributions in a Quasi-Open Economy: The India Evidence

Om Prakash Mathur

5.1 Introduction

City-size distributions have been long studied worldwide, India being no exception. In Zipf's seminal work on the theory of human behaviour (1949), where he studied the frequency distribution of expressions of human behaviour and later applied it to city-size distribution, Zipf observed that India's city sizes in 1911 and 1931 followed a primary law distribution, i.e. the sizes of larger cities were inversely proportional to their ranks. Brian Berry's subsequent work on the city-size distributions of thirty-eight countries (1971) came to the conclusion that rank-size regularity was a common feature in countries which were developed and which had high levels of urbanization as well as in countries such as 'India and China' which, in addition to being large, had long urban traditions; conversely, the evidence showed that primacy or some stated degree of primacy was a characteristic of countries which were small and had dual economic structures. Drawing on other studies, Berry put out a general proposition that there was no relationship between the type of city-size distribution and either economic development or the degree of urbanization of countries. 'It appears that there is a scale from primate to lognormal distributions which is somehow tied to the number and complexity of forces affecting the urban structure of countries'; as countries moved up the development ladder, city-size distributions acquired 'rank-size regularity'. Recent India-specific studies, however, show that Indian cities do not conform to rank-size rule as 'most cities in the population size group of >100,000 have populations much higher than would be justified under the rank-size rule'.[1] Nor does India have a primate city at the national level. At subnational, state levels, Ramachandran's study (1989) on urbanization and urban systems shows that 'primacy is observed in a large number of states and rank-size distribution in a small number of states'. Ramachandran further observes that 'rank-size and the

[1] Ramachandran (1989: 202).

Om Prakash Mathur., *City-Size Distributions in a Quasi-Open Economy* In: *Cities of Dragons and Elephants: Urbanization and Urban Development in China and India. Edited by:* Guanghua Wan and Ming Lu, Oxford University Press (2019). © Oxford University Press. DOI: 10.1093/oso/9780198829225.003.0005

primate city concepts are empirical constructs and their objective is to explain the real world structure of settlement systems—In the Indian context, rank-size relationships are an exception, while primate city characteristics appear to be important in a majority of states.'[2]

Two recent papers provide time series evidence on city-size distributions for India (and China); the paper by Schaffar and Dimou (2012)[3] points out that India's city-size distribution is characterized by a dual structure with a substantial presence of small cities and a small group of very large metropolises. They conclude: 'The Indian city-size distribution systematically reject the Zipf law, with a Pareto coefficient higher than 1' (2012: 30). The other paper, by Luckstead and Devadoss (2014), which analysed upper-tail cities (> 750,000 population) for every decade between 1950 and 2010, finds that Zipf's law does not apply to India for the period 1950 to 1990 because of rural predominance but Zipf's law holds for the two recent decades of 2000 and 2010, because of 'increased mobility of workers from rural to urban areas due to economic reforms' (2014: 291).[4]

This chapter undertakes a fresh examination of the city-size distributions from the standpoints of both the Zipf's rank-size rule and Jefferson's thesis on primate city-size distribution. This examination is undertaken at two levels, i.e. (1) at the national level comprising all cities with a population of 100,000 and over; and (2) at subnational, state levels where all cities and towns irrespective of their population size, form part of the examination. City-size distributions are studied for two time periods, i.e. 1991 and 2011, the period during which India substantially liberalized its economy by doing away with what then was a mandatory licensing of industries, by relaxing the foreign exchange regime, and shifting away from import substitution to export-led strategies. During this period, India achieved an annual average growth of 8.4 per cent in its per capita national income (GDP). There several questions that this chapter attempts to answer: Are city-size distributions sensitive to the nature of the economic system? Do city-size distributions change when an economy characterized by controls and regulations of various sorts transits to one which is open or quasi-open? Do faster GDP growth rates lead to a more balanced city-size distribution of cities or create primacies?

The chapter is organized as follows. Section 5.2 outlines the sources of datasets and the methodology employed in the chapter for examining the country's city-size distributions. Section 5.3 gives an overview of the key characteristics of India's urbanization and of its urban system. Section 5.4 analyses the city-size distributions and subjects them to the two tests mentioned earlier—the rank-size test and

[2] Ramachandran (1989: 203).

[3] In their paper, they look at the distributional pattern of cities in China and India in multiple ways: (a) by applying a KS test, (b) by estimating the Pareto coefficient, and (c) by studying intra-distributional dynamics of cities.

[4] The reasoning provided by Luckstead and Devados for the validity of Zipf's law for 2000 and 2010 is questionable. Rural–urban migration in India has not experienced any noticeable appreciation in recent years, notwithstanding economic liberalization.

primacy test—addressing questions such as: Does the city-size distribution of Indian cities conform to Zipf's law or display dominance of primacy? Does the Indian evidence confirm or reject the widely held notions that rank-size distributions are associated with an integrated system of cities as observed in several large, developed countries, and primate cities are symptomatic of small, dual and developing economies? It also brings in, albeit briefly, the link between the shifts in macroeconomic parameters and city-size distributions. Section 5.5 concludes with a brief reference to the implications of the existing city-size distributions for urban policy.

5.2 Datasets and Methodology

As already noted, city-size distributions are studied at two levels, namely the national level and subnational state levels. Studying the dynamics of city-size distributions gives better results if the sample size is sufficiently large. Therefore, all cities with populations in excess of 100,000 are taken into account for the national-level analysis and all cities and towns irrespective of their size form the sample for the state-level analysis. State-level analysis is undertaken for fourteen major states.[5] These states account for 87 per cent of the country's total urban population and 81 per cent of the total number of cities and towns. The administrative unit for sampled cities is a municipality or its variant. Population data are drawn from the Census of India. GDP data are used for economy-wide shifts and analysed for determining if these have any impact on city-size distributions.

City-size distributions are tested for primacy and rank-size regularity. The law of primacy, propounded by Mark Jefferson (1939: 231), stated that 'a country's leading city is always disproportionately large and exceptionally expressive of national capacity and feeling'. The primacy test measures the importance of the largest city relative to the second largest city. Its primacy is established when the second largest city has less than half the population of the largest city. In such a case, the degree of primacy is said to be high. Here, the ratio of the population of the largest to the second largest city, $\frac{P1}{P2}$ (where P_1 is the population of the largest town and P_2 is the population of the second largest town), is calculated for the years 1991 and 2011. Primacy ratios that increase over time demonstrate that the primate city is becoming more important; where primacy ratios decline, the population differences narrow between the two largest places. The two-time period analysis indicates the likely effects of economic growth and economic

[5] India has twenty-nine states and seven union territories. Union territories are governed directly by the federal government. The states that are not studied in this chapter are small border states where the topography limits the physical expansion of cities and towns. The level of urbanization is also very low. Other states that are not covered in this chapter include Chattisgarh, Jharkhand, and Uttarakhand, which were created in 2000 by dividing the larger states of Madhya Pradesh, Bihar, and Uttar Pradesh respectively.

liberalization on the largest city. Also, a simple regression between primacy and GDP per capita is run to see the latter's effect on the primacy level.

Unlike primacy, which measures the importance of the largest city in relation to the second largest city, rank-size looks at the relations between a city's rank (r) with its population (P_1) for a range of cities. Zipf's postulate here is that all cities and towns interact with each other and form part of an integrated social and economic system. If the second-ranking city has half the population of the largest city, the third-ranking city, a third of the largest, and so on down the scale, it is said to have rank-size regularity and meet Zipf's law. Here, for testing the city-size distributions for rank-size rule, populations of cities countrywide and across states are arranged in descending order, the largest city being given rank of 1. On a double logarithmic graph, populations of cities are plotted against their ranks in a graph that has the logarithm of the ranks of cities on the X-axis and the logarithm of the population on the Y-axis. To study the precise nature of the relations between population and their ranks, the ranks and population are converted into logarithms. Then the logarithms of ranks are regressed against the logarithms of population using the equation $Y = a + bx$ ($x = \log r$; $Y = \log Pr$), and the change in the parameters of the equations, i.e. intercept (a) and slope (b) is analysed. The intercept represents the expected values of logarithms of the population of the largest city. A change in the intercept shows the expected growth in the largest city. The slope of the rank-size distribution, Zipf postulated, is the magnitude of the force of diversification divided by the force of unification, and indicates the degree of city-size distribution. If the slope is greater than 1, the city-size distribution is more uneven, and the biggest city is larger than what Zipf's law predicts. Conversely, if the slope is less than 1, the city-size distribution is more even, and the biggest city is smaller than what Zipf's law predicts. Put another way, the slope measuring between 0 and 1 suggests the dominance of the force of diversification, and a slope of greater than 1 implies the force of unification. In addition, an attempt is made to estimate the degree of deviation of the actual population from the expected or predicted population values by using a simple test: $\sum \frac{\textit{actual population} - \textit{expected population}}{\textit{actual population}}$. Section 5.4 gives the results of these tests.

5.3 Urbanization and Urban Systems

5.3.1 Urbanization in India

Urbanization in the sense of more and more people living in urban areas is by far the most important social change that has taken place in India in recent times.[6]

[6] India uses two alternative sets of criteria for designating a settlement as urban. The first set requires three conditions to be met for a settlement to be designated as urban: (a) a minimum population

From a relatively modest base of 78.9 million persons in 1961, the number of Indian urban dwellers has risen to 377.2 million in 2011, signalling a fivefold increase in urban population over a period of five decades. Approximately nine million people are currently added annually to the country's total urban population. The United Nations put India's current urban population (2015) at 419 million, and projects that India will add 395 million persons between 2015 and 2050.[7]

The scale aside, India continues to be a low-urbanized country. In 2011, only 31.2 per cent of India's population lived in urban areas.[8] Also, the pace of its urbanization has, at best, been moderate; between 2001 and 2011, India's urban population increased at an annual exponential rate of 2.76 per cent, compared with the average exponential growth rate of 2.8 per cent for the less developed countries and 3.8 per cent for China.[9] (See Table 5.1.)

There are several distinguishing features of India's urbanization that bear on its urban system. First: India's urbanization is not driven as much by rural–urban migration as by (a) natural increase which, during the decade of 2001–11, added approximately 44 per cent to the increase in urban population; and

Table 5.1. Key characteristics of India's urbanization

Numbers	Years	
	1991	2011
Urban population (million)	217.6	377.2
Level of urbanization (%)	25.7	31.2
Annual exponential growth rate 1991–2001	2.74	–
Annual exponential growth rate 2001–11	–	2.76

Source: Census of India, Registrar General of India, New Delhi.

of 5,000 persons, (b) a density of 400 persons per sq. km, and (c) 75 per cent of male workforce in non-agricultural occupations. In addition, any settlement which is granted a statutory status of a municipality by the state government is 'urban'. This is the second criterion. All urban settlements with a population of 100,000 and over are referred to as cities, and settlements below this population threshold as towns.

[7] United Nations (2014). Figures on India may be seen on p. 219.

[8] Several authors have termed India's low level of urbanization as a statistical artefact. A geo-database called Indiapolis counted 18,365 agglomerations with more than 5,000 inhabitants in 2001 regardless of their census or administrative status, whether rural or urban. Using a threshold of 10,000 inhabitants, the Indiapolis urbanization rate is 10 per cent higher than the official rate. See Swerts et al. (2014). A background paper prepared for the *World Development Report 2009* shows that India's agglomeration index based on (a) population density, (b) population of a large urban centre, and (c) travel time to the large urban centre ranges between 42.9 per cent and 51.9 per cent depending on the threshold size of the large city—42.9 percent at the threshold value of 100,000 and 51.9 percent at the threshold value of 50,000. This does not define urban per se, but is a measure of urban concentration. See Uchide and Nelson (2008).

[9] These averages for China and less-developed countries are drawn from the UN's *World Urbanization Prospects 2014* and refer to the period 1990 and 2010.

Table 5.2. Components of urban population growth (%)

Components	1991–2001£	2001–2011*	2001–2011@
Natural increase	59.2	44.0	56.1
Rural–urban migration	21.1	22.2	24.1
Reclassification of rural into urban settlements	9.9	29.5	10.2
Expansion of boundaries of existing urban settlements	9.7	4.3	9.6

Note: For 2001–11, figures are provisional and taken from a recent paper prepared by the Indian Institute of Human Settlements under a Rockefeller Foundation supported project 'India's Urban Economy'. December 2013. Migration data for 2011 have just been published and are in the process of being studied. @ See Elara Securities (India) Private Ltd. 2013.

Source: Census of India.

(b) reclassification of rural settlements into urban, which contributed an estimated 29 per cent to India's urban population growth.[10] The contribution of rural-to-urban migration to urban population growth has, over the decades, ranged between 20 and 22 per cent. This urban growth pattern has led some analysts to suggest that what India has experienced is not urbanization, which is closely identified with rural-to-urban migration, but urban population growth.[11] Rural-to-urban migration, analysts argue, is central to urban transformation (Table 5.2).

Second: urbanization and its key facets like the level, pace, and composition vary across states of India. Tamil Nadu (48.4 per cent), Kerala (47.7 per cent), and Maharashtra (45.2 per cent) are close to achieving the tipping point of a 50 per cent level of urbanization, while the other extreme is represented by Bihar (11.3 per cent), Orissa (16.7 per cent), and Rajasthan (24.9 per cent) which have not only low levels of urbanization but also low-to-moderate rates of urban population growth (see Appendix, Table A.5.1). Recent trends, however, indicate some convergence in the levels of urbanization across states. As will be discussed later in the chapter, state-level variations in the level and pace of urban population growth are important factors in the determination of their urban systems.

Third: urbanization and economic growth have historically been mutually reinforcing. Urban growth has been rapid where economic growth has been high, which is explained for by the effects of agglomerative features of cities which are the strategic nodes through which much of the economy operates. In India, recent urbanization has lagged behind economic growth—the annual average growth

[10] These are provisional estimates and drawn from a research paper noted with Table 5.2. Another estimate places the contribution of natural increase at 56.1 per cent and that of migration at 24 per cent. See. Elara Securities (India) Private Ltd (2013). The Census of India has just released the 2011 census data on migration, according to which the share of net rural to urban migration in the total increase in urban population in the 2001–11 decade is about 22 per cent.

[11] Urban growth is the rate of change in the urban population; the pace of urbanization is best measured by the rate of change in the proportion of the population that is urban. See Cohen (1996).

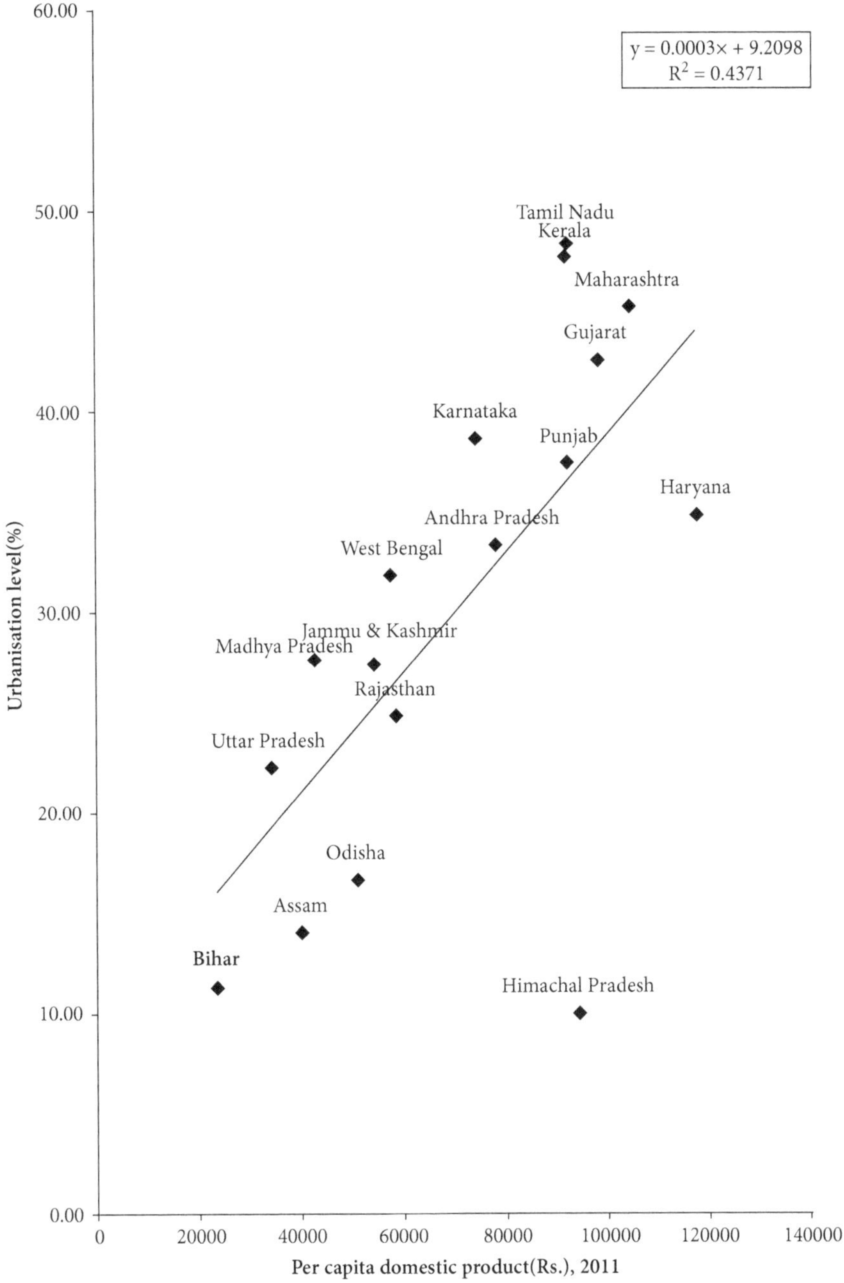

Figure 5.1. Interlinkage effects of per capita income and urbanization levels across seventeen major states, 2011

rate of per capita GDP for the period 1991–2011 has been close to 8.4 per cent; in comparison, urban population growth was about 2.75 per cent annually over this period,[12] much as Sridhar finds in Chapter 3 of this volume regarding the urbanization–industrialization gap. At the state level, urbanization and state domestic products have positive interlinkages, as Chapter 3; it is shown in the Figure 5.1 through the logarithmic regression, providing evidence that cities are important nodes for economic growth. Although the linkages between urbanization and economic growth have grown between 1991 and 2011, these are low by international standards. For developing countries, the explanatory power R^2 is 0.85 compared to 0.64 for India.[13] The lag between growth represented by GDP and urbanization is also substantiated by a low, insignificant R^2 between urban densities and per capita GDP (Figure 5.1).

Another feature that sets India's urbanization apart from other large countries such as China is that in recent years, it has been led by growth in services such as (a) trade, hotels, transport, and communications; (b) financing, insurance, real estate, and business services; and (c) community, social, and personal services. These services added 62 per cent of the net increment to GDP over the 1991–2011 period compared with 27 per cent by manufacturing and the balance of 11 per cent by primary sector activities. The share of these services in GDP (current prices) has risen from 44 per cent in 1991 to 57.4 per cent in 2011–12. The role of manufacturing in the country's growth process was modest in 2011–12, its share was estimated at 26.1 per cent and may, in part, explain a slower pace of urbanization (see Table 5.3).

Table 5.3. Composition of the gross domestic product (%) (current prices)

Structure	1991	2011
Agriculture, forestry and fishing, mining and quarrying	32.1	16.5
Manufacturing, construction, electricity, gas, and water supply	23.8	26.1
Trade, hotels, transport, and communications	17.8	26.7
Financing, insurance, real estate, and business services	12.6	18.0
Community, social, and personal services	13.5	12.7
Total	100.0	100.0

Source: Economic Survey 2013–14, Government of India.

[12] At the current level of per capita GDP, India's level of urbanization is approximately 8 per cent lower than what it should be. This is worked out on the basis of the per capita GDP (PPP) and the level of urbanization for all countries having a population in excess of fifty million.

[13] See Henderson (2000) for figures on the R^2 for developing countries. Figure 5.2 gives the R^2 for Indian states.

Table 5.4. India's urban system

Profile	1991	2011
Megacities (10 million+)		
Number	–	3
Population (million)	–	48.8
% of urban population	–	12.9
Cities (5–10 million)		
Number	2	5
Population (million)	17.5	36.2
% of urban population	8.1	9.6
Cities (1–5 million)		
Number	16	44
Population (million)	32.5	74.6
% of urban population	15.1	19.8
Cities (100,000–1 million)		
Number	304	416
Population (million)	72.6	105.1
% of urban population	33.6	27.9
Towns (less than 100,000)		
Number	4,293	5,705
Population (million)	93.5	112.5
% of urban population	43.2	29.8
Total		
Number	4,615	6,173
Population (million)	215.8	377.2

Note: The 1991 figures exclude the number and population of cities in Jammu and Kashmir.

Source: Census of India.

5.3.2 India's Urban System

India's urban system consists of a small number of large cities and a large number of small towns.[14] In 2011, the numbers of all urban settlements was 7,933; between 2001 and 2011, the numbers increased phenomenally, adding 2,772 urban settlements (see Table 5.4). A significant part of the increase is in the number of small towns (census towns) which account for 94 per cent of all cities and towns; the upper-tail cities have witnessed a transition of cities from one size to the next highest

[14] India's urban system has a strong historical lineage that comprises cities which were set up and developed by (a) the Portuguese who established port towns at Panaji, Goa (1510), and Bombay, now Mumbai (1532); the Dutch who set up factories at Machilipatnam (1605) and Nagapattinam (1658); the British who set up Madras, now Chennai (1639) and Calcutta, now Kolkata (1690); and the French who set up factories at Surat (1668), Pondicherry (1673), and Chandernagore (1690). These cities are all sea ports which served as trading centres. The British were able to later consolidate its supremacy and focused on the development of Kolkata, Chennai, and Mumbai, and later New Delhi. The British also set up a string of Cantonments and hill stations. The introduction of the network of railroads in 1853 altered the relative importance of cities. A large number of cities came up in the nineteenth century.

size category. Small towns (population < 100,000) account for 30 per cent of total urban population. Despite variable growth rates in cities in different size categories, their relative proportions have not changed noticeably over the 2001–11 period. Nor has India witnessed any trends towards convergence of cities to a common size–class category. This stability in the city-size distribution, which is in line with global trends, tends to affirm that cities of different sizes have their ongoing roles and functions.[15]

Population weight has shifted in favour of large cities in recent decades. Large cities with a population in excess of one million account for 42.3 per cent of population; the share of intermediate-sized cities (the range 100,000 to one million) in total urban population is 27.9 per cent, and that of small cities 29.8 per cent. In this transition, cities with a population of over ten million (Mumbai and Delhi) have come to account for 6 per cent of the country's total urban population. However, India displays no significant urban concentration; on the other hand, it is possible be argue that there is an insufficient concentration of population in the category of small towns for them to be able to take advantage of scale economies. The average size of a small town is 20,621 persons.[16]

Metropolitan areas in India, defined as 'areas having a population of one million or more, comprised in one or more districts and consisting of two or more municipalities or Panchayats or other contiguous areas', are an important part of the country's urban system and have gained considerable importance in recent years.[17] The Census of India counted fifty-two urban agglomerations with a population of one million and more in 2011, having risen from thirty-five in 2001 and twenty-three in 1991. The population of such urban agglomerations, assumed here to be metropolitan areas, has risen with every successive decade, and their share in urban population is currently estimated at 42.3 per cent (see Table 5.5).

As generally observed, several metropolitan areas have seen their peripheries posting higher population growth rates in comparison with the 'cores'.[18] Between 2001 and 2011, the population of the core areas of metropolises, which are co-terminus with the municipal boundaries, increased at an annual exponential rate of 3.76 per cent; in comparison, the peripheries posted an annual average increase

[15] See Henderson and Wang (2007). They write: 'Urbanization is not concentrated in mega-cities and urban hierarchies have not become increasingly unbalanced with urbanization—the worldwide relative size distribution of cities has been rock stable over the last forty years' (2007: 284).

[16] Henderson and Wang examine the spatial concentration of population by calculating spatial Gini coefficients. For India, the spatial inequality for all cities and towns is estimated at 0.7250 and 0.5963 for cities with a population in excess of 100,000. For methodology, see Henderson and Wang (2007).

[17] See for definition, Article 243 P(a), Constitution of India. The Census of India provides the population of 'urban agglomerations' which are defined as continuous urban spreads constituting a town and its adjoining outgrowths or two or more contiguous towns together and any adjoining outgrowths of such towns. All urban agglomerations with populations in excess of one million are treated as metropolitan areas in this chapter.

[18] A recent book which studied the five largest metropolitan cities in India points out that some metropolitan cities have seen their core and peripheries growing; in others, population of the core has declined while that of peripheries has risen; and yet there are metropolitan cities whose populations of both core and peripheries have declined in relative terms. See Sivaramakrishnan (2014).

Table 5.5. Metropolitan areas

Key numbers	Years		
	1991	2001	2011
Numbers	23	35	52
Population (million)	70.7	108.3	159.7
Population of the core (%)	–	71.7	73.8
Population of the peripheries (%)	–	28.3	26.2
Annual exponential growth rate, 2001–11 (%)			
Core	–	–	3.76
Periphery	–	–	4.58
Metropolitan area	–	–	3.95
Population share of metropolitan areas in total urban population	32.5	37.8	42.3
Average size (million)	3.09	3.09	3.03

Source: Census of India, 1991, 2001, and 2011.

of 4.58 per cent. Several metropolitan cities in India, notably Bangalore and Hyderabad, have incorporated the peripheries into their municipal limits, with the objective of developing the core and periphery in an integrated manner. The fifty-two metropolitan areas carry a disproportionately large economic weight and are key to the country's economic growth. A recent study by the World Bank (2013) noted that 8 per cent of national employment is in the first ring of 50 km of the seven largest metropolitan areas. Recent years have seen shifts in the population ranks of these cities in response to the increasing competition between them.

Port cities have historically played an important role in India's urbanization. Studies on urbanization, many of which trace India's urban roots to the prehistoric period (2350 to 1800 BC),[19] draw attention to the development of Chennai, Kolkata, Mumbai, and several other port cities for their roles in establishing trade linkages and in the economic and political development of the country. Recent decades have seen the growth and development of several new port towns, notably Kandla port (Gujarat) which also has a special economic zone, Haldia (West Bengal), Paradeep (Orissa), and Nhava Sheva (Maharashtra). What is important to note is that with the exception of the metropolitan cities such as Mumbai, Kolkata, Chennai, Surat, and Vishakapatnam (> 1 million population), other cities have acquired significance as ports rather than as urban centres. Nor are these cities (other than the metropolitan cities) known to have made any significant contribution to the process of urbanization (see Appendix, Table A.5.3). Other inland cities have, in comparison, displayed far greater urbanization vibrancy.[20]

[19] See K. Siddhartha and S. Mukherjee. 1999. Cities, Urbanization and Urban Systems. Kitab Mahal Publishers. Delhi.

[20] The two basic characteristics of India's urbanization, namely the leading role of services in urbanization and a relatively low import–export content in economic growth, partly explain why newly developed port cities have not been at the forefront of India's urban economic development.

Urban systems vary across states. India's federal structure permits each state to formulate its own urban policy, fix urban development priorities, and develop strategies for taking the urban agenda forward in comparison to rural development, which continues to be an important component of development and vis-à-vis small, intermediate, and large cities. Some states, for instance, continue to pursue policies that aim at slowing down rural-to-urban migration and limiting the growth of large cities.[21] For several of them, the primary focus of state interventions is on the physical aspects of urbanization. The role of the central (federal) government with respect to urban development is limited to laying down general policy directions, although in recent years the central government has taken several important initiatives to stimulate urban development, including the development of smart cities. State governments are central to shaping urban development. They are at different levels of urbanization (see Figure 5.2). Tables 5.6 and 5.7

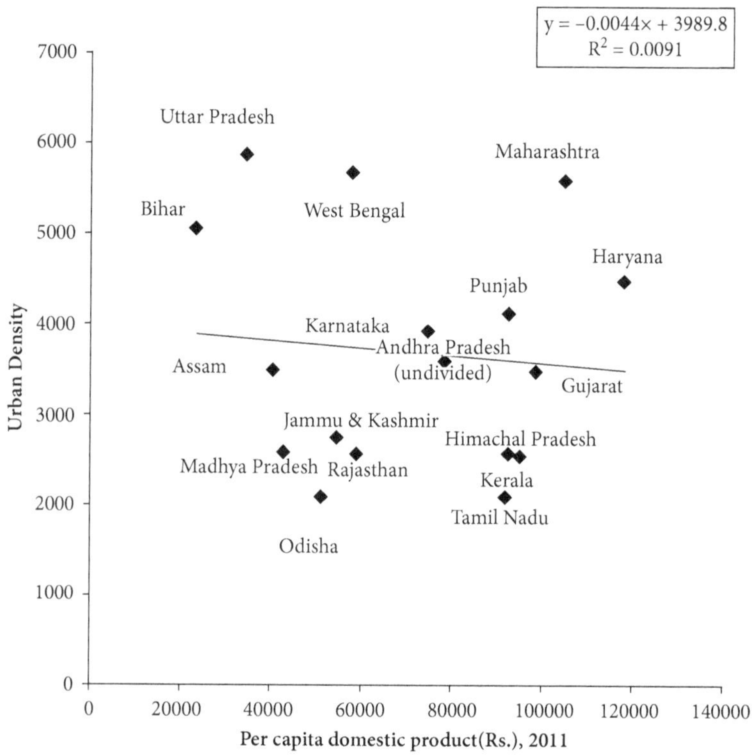

Figure 5.2. Interlinkage effects of per capita income and urban densities across seventeen major states, 2011

[21] See Government of Bihar (2012), as one example where the state government does not consider urbanization important enough to be pursued. Although there are no restrictions on labour mobility in India, programmes such as rural employment guarantee impacts from rural to urban migration. Also see Om Prakash Mathur (2016).

Table 5.6. India's urban system: numbers of cities and towns in different size categories in selected states

State	> 10 million	5–10 million	1–5 million	500,000–1 million	100,000–500,000	< 100,000
	Large			Medium		Small
Andhra Pradesh						
1991	–	–	1	2	32	229
2011	–	1	2	2	37	310
Change	–	+1	+1	–	+5	+81
Bihar						
1991	–	–	–	2	16	253
2011	–	–	1	–	25	173
Change	–	–	+1	−2	+9	−80
Gujarat						
1991	–	–	3	1	12	248
2011	–	1	3	1	25	318
Change	–	+1	–	–	+13	+70
Haryana						
1991	–	–	–	–	10	84
2011	–	–	1	1	18	135
Change	–	–	+1	+1	+8	+51
Karnataka						
1991	–	–	1	1	13	291
2011	–	1	–	3	22	321
Change	–	+1	−1	+2	+9	+30
Kerala						
1991	–	–	–	2	5	190
2011	–	–	–	2	5	513
Change	–	–	–	–	–	+323
Madhya Pradesh						
1991	–	–	2	2	19	442
2011	–	–	4	1	27	444
Change	–	–	+2	−1	+8	+2
Maharashtra						
1991	–	1	3	5	24	304
2011	1	–	9	8	33	484
Change	+1	−1	+6	+3	+9	180
Orissa						
1991	–	–	–	–	7	117
2011	–	–	–	2	8	213
Change	–	–	–	2	+1	+96
Punjab						
1991	–	–	1	2	6	111
2011	–	–	2	1	13	201
Change	–	–	+1	−1	+7	+90
Rajasthan						
1991	–	–	1	2	11	208
2011	–	–	3	2	23	269
Change	–	–	+2	–	+12	+61

(Continued)

Table 5.6. Continued

State	> 10 million	5–10 million	1–5 million	500,000–1 million	100,000–500,000	< 100,000
	Large			Medium		Small
Tamil Nadu						
1991	–	–	1	2	23	443
2011	–	–	3	2	27	1,066
Change	–	–	+2	–	+4	+623
Uttar Pradesh						
1991	–	–	2	6	34	711
2011	–	–	7	8	46	854
Change	–	–	+5	+2	+12	+143
West Bengal						
1991	–	–	1	1	42	338
2011	–	–	2	3	54	850
Change	–	–	+1	+2	+12	+512

Source: Census of India, 1991 and 2011. This table includes all urban settlements including non-statutory towns. The totals in this table, which considers every urban settlement as a discrete unit, may not tally with the numbers in the earlier tables. Earlier tables use the concept of 'urban agglomeration' as one unit.

Table 5.7. India's urban system: population in different size class of cities (million) in selected states

	> 1 million	100,000–1 million	< 100,000
State	Large	Medium	Small
Andhra Pradesh			
1991	2.96	7.33	7.52
2011	9.49	8.57	10.29
Change (%)	220.6	16.9	36.8
Bihar			
1991	–	5.10	6.27
2011	1.68	5.05	5.00
Change (%)	–	–0.98	–20.2
Gujarat			
1991	5.41	2.52	6.23
2011	13.00	4.96	7.75
Change (%)	140.3	96.8	24.4
Haryana			
1991	–	1.52	2.53
2011	1.41	4.55	2.86
Change (%)	–	199.3	13.0
Karnataka			
1991	2.66	3.57	7.62
2011	8.44	7.38	7.76
Change (%)	217.3	106.7	1.8

Kerala			
1991	–	2.05	5.63
2011	–	2.75	13.18
Change (%)		34.1	134.1
Madhya Pradesh			
1991	2.15	4.98	8.22
2011	5.87	5.16	9.03
Change (%)	173	3.6	9.8
Maharashtra			
1991	14.13	8.76	7.61
2011	26.8	11.16	11.88
Change (%)	96.7	−2.40	201
Orissa			
1991	–	1.64	2.59
2011	–	3.01	3.99
Change (%)		83.5	54.1
Punjab			
1991	1.04	2.08	2.88
2011	2.75	3.08	4.56
Change (%)	164.4	48.1	58.3
Rajasthan			
1991	1.46	3.52	5.06
2011	5.08	5.23	6.77
Change (%)	247.9	46.6	26.4
Tamil Nadu			
1991	3.84	5.78	9.41
2011	6.72	7.11	21.12
Change (%)	98.2	23	124.4
Uttar Pradesh			
1991	3.49	10.98	13.18
2011	12.43	14.53	17.51
Change (%)	256.2	32.3	32.8
West Bengal			
1991	4.40	7.54	6.68
2011	5.57	12.42	11.14
Change (%)	26.6	64.7	66.8

Source: Census of India, 1991 and 2011.

provide (a) the numbers of cities and towns in different size categories,[22] and (b) the population of cities and towns in different size categories for 1991 and 2011, which show the extent and nature of changes that have taken place in the urban systems of the fourteen sampled states.

A number of observations are offered here. First, with the exception of Bihar and Madhya Pradesh, which were bifurcated in 2001, other states have registered an expansion in their urban systems. Between 1991 and 2011, Tamil Nadu, West Bengal, Kerala, and Maharashtra added a phenomenally large number of cities

[22] Numbers and population include all cities and towns irrespective of their statutory status.

and towns to their urban portfolio. Second, metropolitan cities are few in numbers but twenty-nine cities were added to this category during 1991–2011. Third, there are striking gaps in the size–class distribution of cities in several states: for example, there is a dearth of cities in the intermediate range in a few states. Actual population distribution for three states is given in Figures 5.3a–5.3c to illustrate the change in the city-size distribution that has taken place between 1991 and 2011.

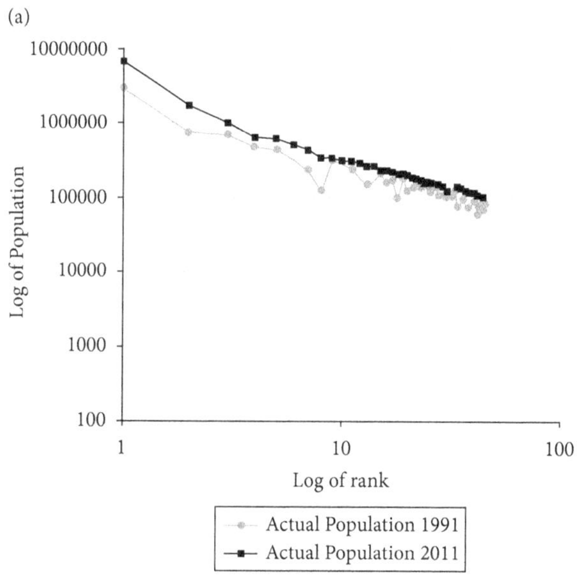

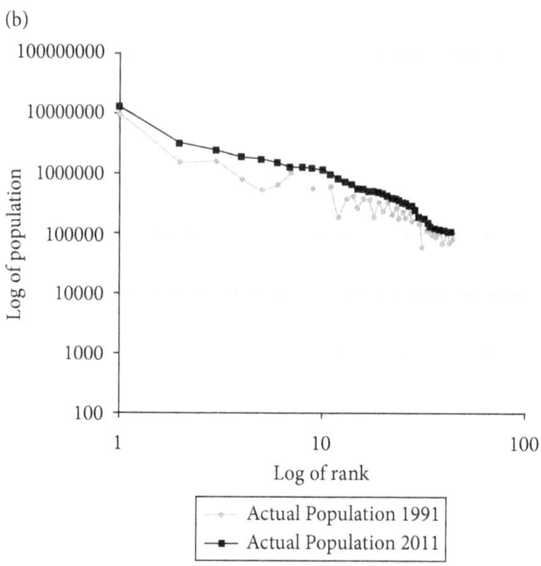

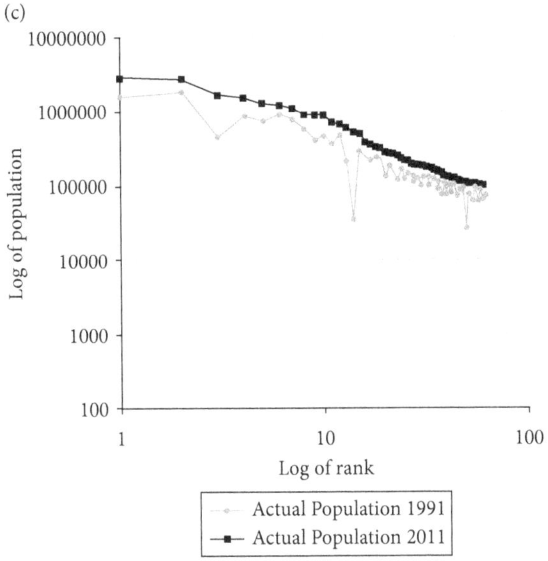

Figure 5.3. Distribution of actual population, 1991 and 2011

Source: Census of India. Actual Population: 1991 and 2011. Andhra Pradesh, Maharashtra, Uttar Pradesh.

5.4 Interpreting the Results: Primacy and Rank-Size Rule Tests

5.4.1 Primacy Test

There is no primate city at the national level in India. The largest city, i.e. Mumbai with a population of 12.44 million (2011), is only 11.3 per cent larger than the second largest city, Delhi, which had a population of 11.03 million (2011). Furthermore, India is a large, federal country where states share developmental responsibilities with the central government, and the absence of primacy in this setup is not unexpected. Two observations are, however, important: (1) recent decades have seen a dip in the primacy of Mumbai, coinciding with the rise of Delhi—the capital city, vis-à-vis Mumbai; and more importantly (2) the population ranks of the seven largest cities (all state capitals) have changed dramatically during 1991–2011, attributable, at least in part, to the development thrust provided to them by respective state governments. Several cities such as Bangalore, Hyderabad, and Ahmedabad have surpassed the populations of the traditionally large cities of Kolkata and Chennai in recent decades (see Appendix, Table A.5.2) and the dominance of Mumbai, Kolkata, and Chennai in India's urban system has declined.

A noted earlier in this chapter, several analysts have pointed to primate city development being an important feature of India's urban system at state levels. The primacy index for the fourteen major states is shown in Table 5.8. As it shows, primacies are strong in seven out of fourteen states, with Karnataka displaying the highest primacy (8.9), suggesting that the population of Bangalore is 8.9 times larger than that of Mysore, which is the second largest city in Karnataka, followed by Tamil Nadu where Chennai's population is 4.42 times higher compared with that of Coimbatore. Other states where primate city development are observed are Andhra Pradesh, Bihar, Maharashtra, and West Bengal. Maharashtra's primacy index has registered a sharp dip, explained in part by the transition of a number of cities from the intermediate size to the large city-size category (Table 5.8), and in part by the slowing down of the growth rate of Mumbai's population, i.e. the core part caused by a process of deindustrialization which idled a large part of the core city land area. The freezing of such an important component of the city's lands combined with restrictions on its real estate development have had profound effects on the city's growth. As a result, the population of 'core' Mumbai increased by only 1.12 per cent on an annual basis during 1991–2011.[23] In Gujarat too, the primacy index has declined in recent decades, explained by the growth of a number of intermediate-sized cities such as Surat, Vadodara, and Rajkot. Several states show stability in the primacy index values—interestingly, these states do not have strong primacy. The conclusion is that while primate city development is an important form of city-size distribution in India, there are trends towards a

Table 5.8. Primacy index

State	Primary index (y)	
	1991	2011
Andhra Pradesh	3.94	3.89
Bihar	1.53	3.56
Gujarat	1.92	1.24
Haryana	1.13	1.61
Karnataka	4.10	8.90
Kerala	1.08	1.2
Madhya Pradesh	1.03	1.09
Maharashtra	6.11	3.98
Orissa	1.02	1.38
Punjab	1.47	1.4
Rajasthan	2.19	2.94
Tamil Nadu	4.08	4.42
Uttar Pradesh	1.16	1.01
West Bengal	4.63	4.17

[23] According to the McKinsey Global Institute (MGI), Mumbai is losing its prominent place in the economy. MGI's study argues that restrictions on the real estate market—for example, placing restrictions on the floor area ratios—are among the key constraints to the city's growth and development. See McKinsey Global Institute (2001).

weakening of primacies in much of the country, exacerbated to some extent by the dismantling of the industrial licensing system. The industrial licensing system required all industrial units to secure a licence for locating their units in large cities. Its abolition has widened the locational choices for the establishment of new enterprises. There is no consistency in the relationship between primacy values and the level of urbanization and between primacy values and per capita GDP. Primacy is a function of multiple factors, affected by a few strong forces; several of them are either 'orthogenetic political and administrative capitals, heterogenetic capitals of the emerging nations, or empire capitals'.[24] R^2 run between primacy and the level of urbanization and per capita GDP are insignificant.[25]

5.4.2 Rank-Size Test

Rank-size tests at the national level are conducted for all cities with a population of more than 100,000, their numbers being 468. City-size distributions are complex; as Ramachandran noted: 'they are empirical constructs and their objective is to explain the real world structure of settlement systems'. Results of the application of the rank-size rule at the national level shows extraordinary heterogeneity in the city-size distribution in that (a) the upper-tail cities are not large enough to fit into the rank-size rule distribution; (b) population sizes of cities at the intermediate range are larger than what would be justified by the rank-size rule, and (c) the population of cities at the lower end are smaller than the predicted population values under the rank-size rule. This is a broad pattern that emerges from the examination. At the aggregate level, India's urban system posts a deficit of 8.049 per cent in its population, i.e. the actual population of cities is lower by 8.049 per cent than the estimated values.

For the fourteen states, the analysis of the rank-size rule is done by plotting the logs of rank and population on Figure 5.4 as well as through an analysis of the regression equations. A visual interpretation of the rank-size graphs, given in the following pages, shows which parts of the city-size distributions are close to the Zipf curve and which parts deviate from the curve. The divergence between the two is observed for most states. A better insight into the urban system is obtained from an examination of the two parameters, namely the intercept and the slope (see Table 5.9). The intercept represents the logarithm of the population of the largest city. That it has risen across states with the exception of Tamil Nadu and West Bengal, where the population of their largest cities have been stagnant, confirms the growth of the largest cities.

[24] Berry (1971: 147).

[25] R^2 between primacy values and the level of urbanization is 0.0197 and with per capita GDP is 0.0028 and is consistent with what Brian Berry had concluded: 'there is no relationship between type of city size distribution and the degree to what a country is urbanized'; 'different city size distributions are in no way related to the relative economic development of countries' (1971: 150).

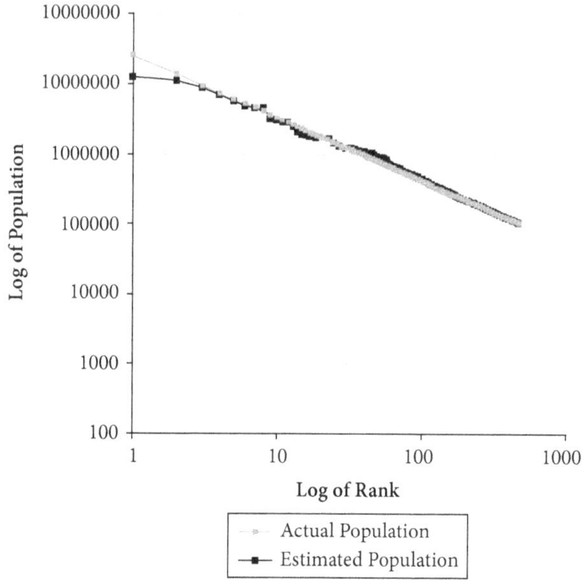

Figure 5.4. Rank-size test, all India, 2011

For both the time points, i.e. 1991 as well as 2011, the coefficient b for seven of the fourteen major states has a value between 0 and 1, namely Andhra Pradesh, Bihar, Kerala, Madhya Pradesh, Orissa, Rajasthan, and Tamil Nadu where, as Zipf's law states, city-size distributions are more even and the largest city is smaller than what it should be under the rank-size rule. For these seven states, the force of diversification has been dominant over the force of unification in determining the size and number of cities at both the time periods. Of this group, the coefficient is seen to decline in the three states of Andhra Pradesh, Bihar, and Tamil Nadu, indicating that the force of diversification has been more dominant over the force of unification recently (2011) as compared to the position prevalent in 1991. Kerala, Madhya Pradesh, Orissa, and Rajasthan registered an increase in the value of the coefficient over the twenty-year period, indicating that the strength of the force of unification has increased in recent years compared with the force of diversification.

The coefficient b has a value greater than 1 for the six states of Gujarat, Haryana, Maharashtra, Punjab, Uttar Pradesh, and West Bengal. According to the rank-size rule, city-size distributions are more uneven in states with b values being greater than 1. The four states of Gujarat, Haryana, Maharashtra, and Uttar Pradesh show an increase in the value of the coefficient, indicating that the force of unification is becoming more dominant than the force of diversification. For the other two states, Punjab and West Bengal, the reverse is seen, with the force of unification diminishing in strength in 2011 as compared to 1991. For the state of Karnataka, the force of unification has become stronger.

Table 5.9. Rank-size tests (actual population and estimated population), fourteen major states, 1991 and 2011

State	Year	Number of observations	b (slope)	a (intercept)
Andhra Pradesh	1991	116	0.918	6.350
	2011	125	0.886	6.445
Bihar	1991	172	0.881	6.111
	2011	139	0.862	6.179
Gujarat	1991	79	1.263	6.566
	2011	195	1.405	7.072
Haryana	1991	84	1.105	6.056
	2011	80	1.152	6.381
Karnataka	1991	179	0.906	6.143
	2011	220	1.013	6.494
Kerala	1991	66	0.808	5.774
	2011	59	0.896	5.959
Madhya Pradesh	1991	389	0.924	6.229
	2011	363	0.961	6.420
Maharashtra	1991	246	1.143	6.786
	2011	256	1.232	7.131
Orissa	1991	102	0.931	5.841
	2011	107	0.981	6.062
Punjab	1991	112	1.110	6.180
	2011	143	1.101	6.365
Rajasthan	1991	193	0.893	6.086
	2011	185	0.965	6.384
Tamil Nadu	1991	112	0.907	6.287
	2011	623	0.822	6.212
Uttar Pradesh	1991	710	1.019	6.675
	2011	648	1.022	6.836
West Bengal	1991	116	1.273	6.889
	2011	129	1.037	6.674

Thus, there is no single dominating force at the level of the states, with a mix of some states with a dominance of the force of unification, and others with a dominance of the force of diversification. A critical factor is that most of the states dominated by the force of unification are the relatively economically developed states and most of the states dominated by the force of diversification are the relatively backward states. For states such as Karnataka, Kerala, Madhya Pradesh, Orissa, Punjab, and Rajasthan, the empirical city-size distribution has moved closer to the theoretical rank-size rule as postulated by Zipf; for other states, the distribution has moved away from the rank-size rule.

The degree to which actual population deviates from the expected population is shown in Table 5.10. Clearly, city-size distributions in several states, notable among them being Gujarat, Karnataka, Haryana, and Andhra Pradesh show significant deviations from the predicted or estimated populations values. In Gujarat and Haryana, actual populations are much lower than the expected values; in

Table 5.10. Degree of deviation from the predicted or estimated population values (%), 2011

Degree of deviation	%
+ States where the actual populations are higher than the predicted values	
Andhra Pradesh	15.05
Karnataka	18.47
Kerala	1.95
Rajasthan	2.77
– States where the actual populations are lower than the predicted values	
Bihar	2.54
Gujarat	41.87
Haryana	16.03
Madhya Pradesh	1.08
Maharashtra	7.18
Orissa	5.72
Punjab	8.90
Tamil Nadu	6.18
Uttar Pradesh	11.35
West Bengal	12.59

Note: The above is worked out by applying a simple test

$$\Sigma \frac{\text{actual population values} - \text{predicted or estimated population values}}{\text{actual population values}}$$

Karnataka and Andhra Pradesh, actual populations are significantly higher than the expected population values. City-size distributions of Kerala, Rajasthan, and Madhya Pradesh show marginal deviations from the expected values.

5.5 Conclusions: Theory to Empirical Evidence

A key consequence of urbanization which is a commonly observed phenomenon accompanying economic growth, the literature underlines, is a change in the distribution of cities in different size categories. Tables 5.4, 5.6, and 5.7 show how city-size distributions have changed between 1991 and 2011; the analysis focuses on whether the city-size distributions have any 'regularity' of the kind Zipf stipulated or whether the distributions have led to a concentration of population in the largest city. The India evidence built on a sample of all cities with a population of over 100,000 for national-level analysis and a sample of all cities and towns irrespective of their population size at state levels, is that while it is possible to identify primate development in several states, city-size distributions need to be understood in terms of their extraordinary heterogeneity—the population of some size categories being greater than what Zipf's law stipulates and the population

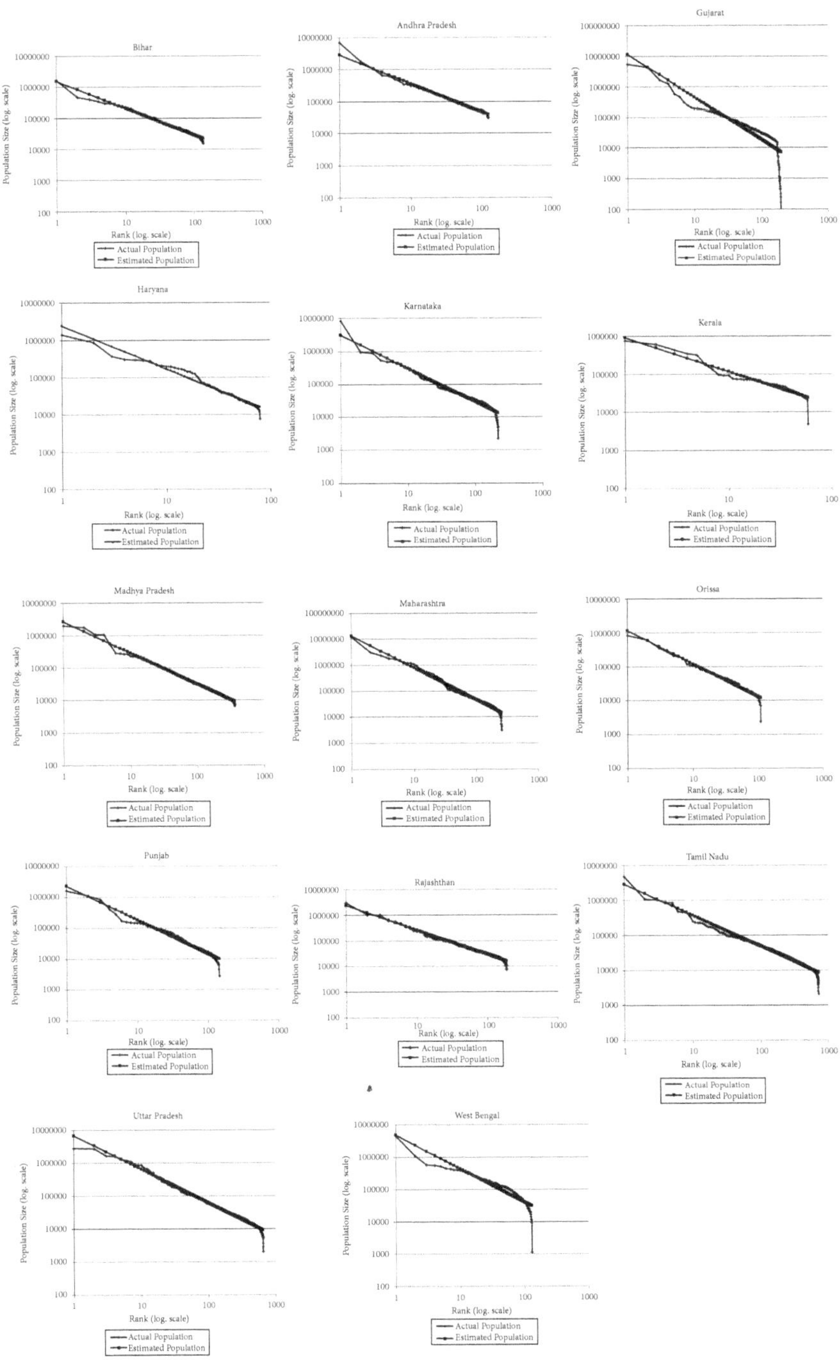

Figure 5.5. Rank-size rule, 2011

of some size categories being lower than the predicted Zipf values. In the aggregate, India's urban system has a population deficit of 8.049 per cent if it is estimated using the predicted values (y = a + bx).

A few features of India's urban system need to be underlined. First, over the period 1991–2011, while the system expanded with the addition of 3,318 towns, the relative proportions of cities and towns in the different size categories remain largely unchanged, and the duality that marks the urban system in India persists. Small cities (< 100,000) account for 94 per cent of the total number of cities and towns. Population shares have shifted in favour of large cities, but population sizes of larger cities are lower if the rank-size rule is taken as a benchmark. The urban structure—which is dominated by small cities on the one hand, and by large cities whose populations are not large enough on the other hand—raises vital issues of scale and agglomeration economies, i.e. whether India's urban system is able to generate enough economies to be able to use urbanization as an instrument for its growth objectives. GDP does not show any sensitivity to urban densities. The one redeeming feature of the urbanization process which is noted is the rise of the intermediate-sized cities (100,000 to one million population) generically called the 'second tier cities', whose numbers increased from 276 in 1991 to 416 in 2011.

Second, India's urban system is not an integrated or unified system of cities.[26] As this chapter shows, it has taken several forms shaped by the urban policies of the constituent states of the country's federation. Several states have primate city development; in a few states, greater evenness is observed in city-size distribution, while in others distribution is uneven. Similarly, the largest city in some states has grown beyond the size indicated by the rank-size rule (Andhra Pradesh, Karnataka, Rajasthan, and Tamil Nadu); in others, the population of the largest city is lower than the predicted values. There are marked differences from the Zipf rank size even when the Zipf coefficient ranges between 0.822 and 1.405. While part of the explanation underlying these forms of city-size distributions may lie in the country's federal structure, its historical and colonial legacy, and its large size, it does not provide adequate understanding of the different forms of distribution, nor does it show their positive or negative characteristics. It is one of the major questions that would call for further research and investigation.

A final point that needs explicit recognition relates to the process of India's recent urbanization which, as this chapter shows, is the outcome of the forces that are at variance with the historical processes. Recent urbanization in India is substantially driven by the natural increase and reclassification of rural into urban settlements. Rural-to-urban migration has played a relatively modest role in the urbanization process. As Elara Securities (India) Private Ltd. (2013) notes: 'Indeed,

[26] The historical lineage of cities developed by the Portuguese, Dutch, British, and French, and the role of the principalities in creating cities such as Jaipur, Udaipur, Jodhpur, Vadodra, Hyderabad, Bhopal, and several others, is an important factor in the development of India's urban system.

it may be concluded that urbanization process in India is less of a migration story than being essentially a product of demographic and organic increase'. It is service-led: the role of manufacturing in the process of urbanization is either stagnant or has been on the decline. A substantial part of the recent urbanization is 'informal'. The overall effects of this process on the urban economic system are not fully evident and are inadequately understood, calling for additional discourse and research.

Appendix

Table A.5.1. State-level urbanization and per capita, GSDP, 2011

States	Primacy index (1)	Level of urbanization (%), 2011	Per capita GSDP (Rs)
Andhra Pradesh	3.89	33.49	67,235
Bihar	3.56	11.30	21,923
Gujarat	1.24	42.58	85,361
Haryana	1.61	34.79	102,016
Karnataka	8.90	38.57	67,415
Kerala	1.20	47.72	76,588
Madhya Pradesh	1.09	27.63	35,771
Maharashtra	3.98	45.23	91,896
Orissa	1.38	16.68	45,608
Punjab	1.43	37.49	76,232
Rajasthan	2.94	24.89	45,008
Tamil Nadu	4.42	48.45	81,350
Uttar Pradesh	1.01	30.55	77,384
West Bengal	4.17	31.89	52,163

Table A.5.2. Population ranks of seven largest cities

Years					
1991			2011		
City	Population (million)	Ratio to the largest city	City	Population (million)	Ratio to the largest city
Mumbai	9.92	1.00	Mumbai (Bombay)	12.44	1.00
Delhi	7.21	0.72	Delhi	11.03	0.89
Kolkata	4.40	0.44	Bangalore	8.44	0.68
Madras	3.84	0.39	Hyderabad	6.73	0.54
Hyderabad	2.96	0.30	Ahmedabad	5.58	0.44
Ahmedabad	2.88	0.29	Chennai (Madras)	4.65	0.37
Bangalore	2.66	0.27	Kolkata (Calcutta)	4.50	0.36

Source: Census of India.

Table A.5.3. Port cities, India

State	Port city	Population (million) 2011	1991
Andhra Pradesh	Vishakapatnam	1.72	0.72
	Machlipatnam	0.17	–
Gujarat	Surat	4.47	1.49
	Bhavnagar	0.48	0.40
	Bharuch	0.17	0.13
	Porbandar	0.15	0.12
Karnataka	Mangalore	0.49	0.27
Kerala	Kochi	0.60	0.56
Maharashtra	Mumbai	12.44	9.92
Tamil Nadu	Chennai	4.65	3.84
	Tuticorin	0.25	0.20
	Nagapattinam	0.10	–
West Bengal	Kolkata	4.49	4.39
	Chandannagar	0.17	0.12
	Haldia	0.20	0.10
Andaman-Nicobar	Port Blair	0.11	–

Source: Census of India, 2011 and 1991.

References

Berry, Brian J. 1971. 'City Size and Economic Development: Conceptual Synthesis and Policy Problems, with Special Reference to South and South East Asia'. In *Urbanization and National Development*, edited by L. Jakobson and Ved Prakash, Sage Publications.

Cohen, Michael et.al. eds. 1996. *Preparing for the Urban Future: Global Pressures and Local Forces*, The Woodrow Wilson Centre, Washington, DC.

Elara Securities (India) Private Ltd. 2013. 'India's Urban Dividend: A US$974 Billion Opportunity'.

Government of Bihar. 2012. *Approach to the 12th Five Year Plan*, Patna.

Henderson, Vernon. 2000. *The Effects of Urban Concentration on Economic Growth*, National Bureau of Economic Research. Cambridge, MA.

Henderson, Vernon, and Hyoung Gun Wang. 2007. 'Urbanization and City Growth: The Role of Institutions'. *Regional Science and Urban Economics 37* (3): 283–313.

Jefferson, Mark. 19891939. 'Why Geography? The Law of the Primate City'. *Geographical Rreview 79* (2): 226–32.

Luckstead, Jeff and Stephen Devadoss. 2014. 'A Comparison of City Size Distributions for China and India from 1950 to 2010'. *Economics Letters 124* (2): 290–5.

Mathur, Om Prakash. 2016. *Cities and the New Economic Vibrancy*, Institute of Social Sciences, New Delhi.

McKinsey Global Institute. 2001. *India: The Growth Imperative*, Mumbai.

Ramachandran, Ranganathan. 1989. *Urbanization and Urban Systems in India*, Oxford University Press.

Schaffar, Alexandra and Michel Dimou. 2012. 'Rank-size City Dynamics in China and India: 1981–2004'. *Regional Studies 46* (6): 707–21.

Sivaramakrishnan, Kallidaikurichi Chidambarakrishnan. 2014. *Governance of Megacities: Fractured Thinking, Fragmented Setup*, Oxford University Press.

Swerts, Elfie, Denise Pumain, and Eric Denis. 2014. 'The Future of India's Urbanization'. *Futures 56*: 43–52.

Uchide, Hiratsugu and Andrew Nelson. 2008. *Agglomeration Index: Towards a New Measure of Urban Concentration*, The World Bank, Washington, DC.

United Nations. 2014. *World Urbanization Prospects 2014*, United Nations, New York.

World Bank. 2013. *Urbanization beyond Municipal Boundaries: Nurturing Metropolitan Economies and Connecting Peri-Urban Areas in India*, The World Bank, Washington, DC.

Zipf, George Kingsley. 1949. *Human Behavior and the Principle of Least Effort: An Introduction to Human Ecology*, Addison Wesley.

PART III
MIGRATION

6

Migration in the People's Republic of China

Ming Lu and Yiran Xia

6.1 Introduction

The People's Republic of China (PRC) is experiencing rapid urbanization. While urban population accounted for only 20.91 per cent of the PRC's population in 1982, it rose to 52.6 per cent of the population in 2012.[1] Rural–urban migration is synonymous with urbanization. According to the National Bureau of Statistics of China (NBSC 2013), 236 million Chinese people live in a place where they do not have a local Hukou (a household registration system), a majority of whom are rural–urban migrants.[2]

Whether urban economic growth creates jobs for migrants and allows them to become permanent residents in cities depends on institutional constraints. Given the institutional background, labour migration in the PRC, much like anywhere else in the world, is the result of rational decision making by individuals or households after weighing up the costs and benefits. Comprehending this rational decision making is the key to understanding the phenomenon of migration.

This chapter starts with an introduction to the institutions related to rural–urban migration. We then summarize the personal, household, and destination characteristics of migration. The Section 6.4 analyses the relationship between urbanization and employment of migrants. The Section 6.5 summarizes the findings of studies on segmentation and integration in urban societies. The last section concludes.

[1] The urbanization ratio of 1982 is estimated on the basis of the third population census (NBSC 2012) and that of 2012 is from NBSC (2013).

[2] Hukou is a registration identity determined according to an individual's parents' Hukou, usually based on where she was originally from. Hukou is linked with locally financed social security and public services, and results in discrimination against migrants, among whom only a few can change their Hukou. It is especially difficult to change a Hukou in big cities such as Shanghai, Beijing, and Guangzhou.

Ming Lu and Yiran Xia., *Migration in the People's Republic of China* In: *Cities of Dragons and Elephants: Urbanization and Urban Development in China and India. Edited by:* Guanghua Wan and Ming Lu, Oxford University Press (2019).
 DOI: 10.1093/oso/9780198829225.003.0006

6.2 Institutions

Before 'reforms and opening up', the PRC had adopted a 'scissors gap' system that depressed the relative price of agricultural goods and boosted the relative price of industrial goods to achieve capital accumulation in the industrial sector and rapid industrialization. At the same time, the wages of the urban industrial sector were also artificially suppressed in order to increase the profit potential and capital accumulation of the industrial sector. Cities had various welfare programmes such as state-sponsored pension, healthcare, education, and housing. The real income of urban residents was much higher than that of rural residents, which created a huge incentive for rural residents to migrate to the cities. The urban industrial sector's lean towards heavy industry meant that its job creation ability was low. Since achieving full employment for urban residents was already proving difficult, the government rigorously restricted peasants from migrating to the cities through the Hukou system and even attempted to alleviate urban employment pressure through the 'Go to the mountains and countryside' (*Shangshan Xiaxiang*) movement.

After 'the reforms and opening up', the Chinese economy began to gradually participate in the globalization process. The comparative advantage of relatively high-quality and low-cost labour enabled the PRC to enter the labour-intensive link of the global supply chain, especially export-processing manufacturing. Since situating export-processing manufacturing near the eastern and southern coastal regions can save transportation costs, much foreign capital is concentrated in the coastal provinces. Accordingly, most newly created jobs in manufacturing are in these coastal provinces. This causes Chinese labour to migrate from the countryside to the cities, while also migrating from inland to coastal regions (Duan et al. 2008).

In the 1980s, labour migration was strictly constrained by the Hukou system. At that time, since the economy was still in a state of shortage, urban residents purchased grain with grain coupons (*liangpiao*) and even if peasants managed to enter the city to find work, they had to bring their own food or obtain grain coupons in the city, which made the costs of labour migration very high. On 1 April 1993, the state increased the purchase and sale price of grain, while on 10 May, the control over prices of grain and cooking oil were relaxed in Beijing and grain coupons were finally withdrawn. Guangdong had already made a stable transition after relaxing grain price controls a year earlier. 'Grain and oil rationing registration' (*liang you guanxi*) was no longer a restraint on labour mobility and the scale of labour migration grew rapidly.[3] Based on population censuses (or minor censuses) over the years, using persons separated from their Hukou

[3] Refer to Chan and Zhang (1999) for an early introduction to and critique of the Hukou system.

location as a criteria,[4] Duan et al. (2008) estimated the migrant population to be 6.57 million, 18.10 million, 21.35 million, 70.73 million, 102.29 million, and 147.35 million in 1982, 1987, 1990, 1995, 2000, and 2005 respectively, among which the most evident acceleration in the migrant population growth rate appeared during 1990 and 1995.

Rural–urban and interregional labour migration in the PRC provides much labour for the manufacturing industry, propels economic growth, and is conducive to narrowing urban–rural income gaps. After computing relevant figures, Sun (2004) reached the conclusion that migrant workers have made great contributions to the economic development of coastal regions. The GDP created by migrant workers is equivalent to 32 per cent of Beijing's economic aggregate, 31 per cent of Shanghai's, 30 per cent of Guangdong's, 11 per cent of Jiangsu's, 17 per cent of Zhejiang's, and 16.8 per cent of Fujian's. Migrant workers created one-sixth to a third of the social wealth in these provinces. Urbanization and rural resident migration to cities is the key to narrowing urban–rural income gaps. Li (1999) was among the earliest to use data from sample surveys to study the income growth effect and income distribution effect of labour migration. He pointed out that rural labour migration to cities has a positive impact on income growth and income distribution within the countryside and can play a positive role in restraining increases in urban–rural, interregional, and even intra-countryside income gaps—something that is not possible for general income redistribution policies to achieve. Correcting unequal income distribution that emerges during economic development through rural labour migration is undoubtedly an effective rational choice that meets the requirements of marketization. Besides, such a choice is not only harmonious with the whole point of market-oriented economic reforms but also consistent with the strategic goal of urban–rural economic integration.

Migrant workers are believed to have caused a shock to the urban labour market. During the mid to late 1990s, on the one hand, large numbers of migrant workers flooded the cities and, on the other hand, labour market reforms in cities rapidly progressed, with many enterprises laying off redundant employees—this led many people to believe that migrant workers took away jobs from urban residents. It must be pointed out that the oft-held belief of a squeezing effect that

[4] The definition of migrant population slightly differed in each census, but they are largely comparable. In the fifth census, migrant population refers to people with two types of Hukou registration situations (survey item R6): 'Has resided over half a year in this township's neighborhood, Hukou is in another area's neighborhood' and 'Has resided less than half a year in this township's neighborhood, been away from Hukou registration area for over half a year', while eliminating people who live in a place different from their registered residence within a city. According to a 1 per cent sample survey project conducted in 2005, migrant population refers to a population whose 'residence at time of survey' (survey item R7) is at this area, but 'Hukou registration residence' is beyond this township (neighborhood), while also eliminating people that live in a place different from their registered residence within a city. See Duan et al. (2008).

migrant workers have on the employment of urban residents is not supported by empirical studies; if migrant workers have any impact, it is mainly on urban wages. Li's study (1997a) showed that rural labour migration's negative impact on the urban economy is infinitesimal and its employment substitution effect is only around 0.1. In the long run, such migration will depress the trend of urban employee wages rising too fast. Li (1997b) provided a theoretical model and policy simulation analysis showing that the entry of rural labour will increase the income gap between skilled and non-skilled labour within cities, which is a correction of the traditional wage administration apparatus. Liu and Zhao (2009) employed a 1 per cent population census data from 2005 and discovered that the impact of migrant workers on urban wages is larger than its impact on the employment rate, which means that there is a limited reaction of urban labour to migrant labour, and this limited reaction is mainly reflected in reduction of reservation wages, but not in the loss of job opportunities.

Although the impact of migrant labour on urban employment is exaggerated, labour market segmentation policies according to Hukou are still formulated and implemented in cities. Hukou-based identity discrimination still exists and the difficulty of obtaining an urban Hukou varies across different regions. Wu et al. (2010) constructed a 'Hukou Settlement Threshold Index' with four directly administered municipalities, twenty-seven provincial capitals, and fifteen cities of other levels, and found that cities with high Hukou Settlement Threshold Index readings are mainly situated in the eastern coastal regions, while the cities with low index readings are mainly concentrated in the central regions. One view is that the PRC's present-day labour mobility is very free, with interregional labour mobility being especially uninhibited. In fact, without local urban Hukous, migrant workers face at least the following 'three discriminations and one barrier' in Chinese cities, which increases the costs of labour migration, thereby restricting labour mobility and urbanization. Specifically, the 'three discriminations' include:

1. *Employment.* At the early stage of the post-reforms era, city governments attempted to directly restrain firms from recruiting migrant labour through policy restraints, the main method of which was levying extra fees against firms that recruit migrant labour, while at the same time limiting migrant labour entrance to a few specific industries. Today, although most discriminative policies have been rescinded, it is almost impossible for people without local urban Hukous to enter the civil service and high-income monopolistic industries. By employing the China Health and Nutrition Survey data for 2006, it can still be observed that good jobs are almost all occupied by labour with urban Hukous, and even in an inferior labour market, labour with local urban Hukous are at an advantageous position (Qiao et al. 2009). Yao and Lai (2004) analysed data from surveys on

Zhejiang's firms and rural labour and discovered that Hukou discrimination can explain 20–30 per cent of the difference in labour and capital relations between urban and rural workers. Other than labour contracts, migrant workers face Hukou discrimination in aspects such as wages, pension, healthcare, unemployment insurance and trade union participation. Zhou and He (2009) found that the attraction of urban regions to rural migrant labour is closely related to the ownership structure of the urban economy. After the 1990s, rural labour that migrated to the cities tended to work outside the traditional system and few could squeeze into the state-owned enterprises. Démurger et al. (2009) employed nationwide sample data from 2002 to find that in cities, the annual wage of local residents is 1.3 times that of the long-term rural migrant workers. Further decomposition of this differential shows that the migrant population has a comparative advantage in the private sector, while entering the public sector does not increase their average wages and vice versa for local residents. The population factor itself is very important, which is reflected in the fact that the wage differentials between the two groups mainly come from differences before entrance into the labour market (e.g. education opportunities), but not from the market itself. The Hukou system's discrimination is not only reflected in wage differentials but also in discrimination in job opportunities. Based on survey data on Beijing, Wuxi, and Zhuhai, Zhang (2010) discovered that Hukou-based discrimination reduced job opportunities for the migrant population and increased the costs they bore while job hunting and unemployed. Therefore, although short-term migrants might mainly work in jobs that locals are unwilling to perform, they change jobs less often and only when they have stayed in the city for a while and have accumulated enough assets.[5]

2. *Social security*. The PRC's current social security system operates independently on local fiscal support; thus each city's social security mainly serves its local residents. Even if some cities have social security provided especially for non-locals, the level of security provided is low and participation by migrant labour is not high.[6] It is worth mentioning that although the Chinese government is endeavouring to make personal endowment insurance accounts transferrable across regions, this has still not been achieved. For a long period, the general provision was that a non-local worker must pay for fifteen years in the location where he works to enjoy pension

[5] Li's (1999) early studies discovered that the first occupational change by migrant workers achieves a rather large augmentation in occupational status, whereas the second occupational change is horizontal and status augmentation is not attained, mainly due to the lack of status accumulation, status inheritance, and social resources.

[6] Zhang et al. (2007) found that urban–rural segmentation factors and regional segmentation systems all have a negative impact on the non-local urban population's participation in social security.

insurance. Since 1 July 2014, a new rule has come into place, whereby workers are allowed to contribute to the pension system and accumulate their personal accounts in different cities.

3. *Public services, especially education for offspring.* Some public services provided by the local government are not discriminatory and cannot be discriminatory, for example, greenery and public transportation. However, there are some public services that are linked to Hukou, among which offspring education is especially important. Without a local urban Hukou, migrants cannot send their offspring to a public kindergarten at the rate charged to local residents. In the compulsory education phase, especially in large cities, local public schools did not admit children of migrant workers, and even if they did, the fee was higher, which led to the coming up of many schools especially for migrant workers' offspring. Since these schools have limited funds, the educational quality provided is evidently worse. Presently, compulsory education phase schools have already opened up to migrant workers' offspring, but the good schools do not offer them equal treatment. Moreover, cities where higher education resources are concentrated often tend to allocate a much larger university admittance quota to local students. The children of migrant workers must return to their original Hukou location and participate in the higher education entrance examination there, making them face even more severe competition, which creates evident unequal opportunities in higher education and blocks intergenerational income and social mobility.[7] A related result is that high-school education in cities (especially large cities) is de facto not equally accessible to the non-local population.[8]

Rural–urban and interregional labour mobility also faces barriers from the land system. In order to guarantee 'food security', a certain amount of farmland must be maintained; thus a 'construction-use land quota rationing system' was implemented with a total quota for construction-use land development every year that could not be exceeded. Though the allocation of this quota has to take into consideration the different economic development needs of every region, an approach that is inclined towards egalitarianism leads to the following situation: coastal regions that need construction-use land more do not have enough quotas,

[7] There is no unanimous opinion on whether or not higher education is a public service. Recent research shows that higher education has strong externalities, so government input into higher education has certain public service properties.

[8] For an early critique on the social segmentation between populations with different Hukous within cities, see Wang and Zuo (1999). Cai et al. (2001) studied the issue of Hukou system and labour market protection. Regarding the living standards of migrant workers as worrisome, Sheng (2008) summarized the condition of migrant workers according to seven aspects: low compensation and benefits, poor residential conditions, lack of social security, difficulty in offspring education, heavy urban discrimination, and lack of spiritual life.

whereas the inland regions have land quotas, but cannot make sufficient use of them, which results in low efficiency of land use. Suppose a market exchange mechanism exists and regions with higher demand for land quotas can buy them from regions with relatively abundant land quotas, then more farmland can be converted into construction-use land, whereas the regions that have sold construction-use land quotas have to relatively increase the reserves of agriculture-use land. In practice, this is called 'balance between occupation and compensation' of agriculture-use land. But as of now, cross-provincial 'balance between occupation and compensation' of agriculture-use land is still prohibited. Moreover, peasants who enter the city have their own rural residential land, which corresponds to the construction-use land quotas by demolishing their housing. In practice, peasants who enter the city are still prohibited from transferring the construction-use land quotas corresponding to their rural residential land at home. In other words, the rural residential land use rights peasants have at home cannot be traded as an asset.

The aforementioned institutional constraints increase the costs of labour migration and create barriers for the integration of migrant workers into the cities. As time passes, the new generation of migrant workers has evidently stronger aspirations than the previous generation of becoming urbanized; therefore, the barriers placed by institutional constraints on their integration into the cities is even more significant (Liu and Cheng 2008).

6.3 The Profile of Migration

6.3.1 Scale and Trend of Migrants

After 'the reforms and opening up', the scale and share of migrants in the total population have increased rapidly, especially after the 1990s. The scale of migrants has increased from 6.57 million in 1982 to 221.4 million in 2010—by almost thirty-three times. However, the PRC's total population has only increased 0.3 times during the same time. The migrant share of total population has risen dramatically from 0.65 per cent in 1982 to 16.53 per cent in 2010 (see Figure 6.1).

6.3.2 Population Structure of Migrants

6.3.2.1 Sex Ratio of Migrants

The sex ratio of migrants has somewhat fluctuated from 1982 to 2010 (see Figure 6.2). Before 1990, female migrants formed the main proportion of migrants due to social reasons such as marriage, moving with others, and joining relatives and friends (Duan et al., 2008). This kind of gender distribution changed

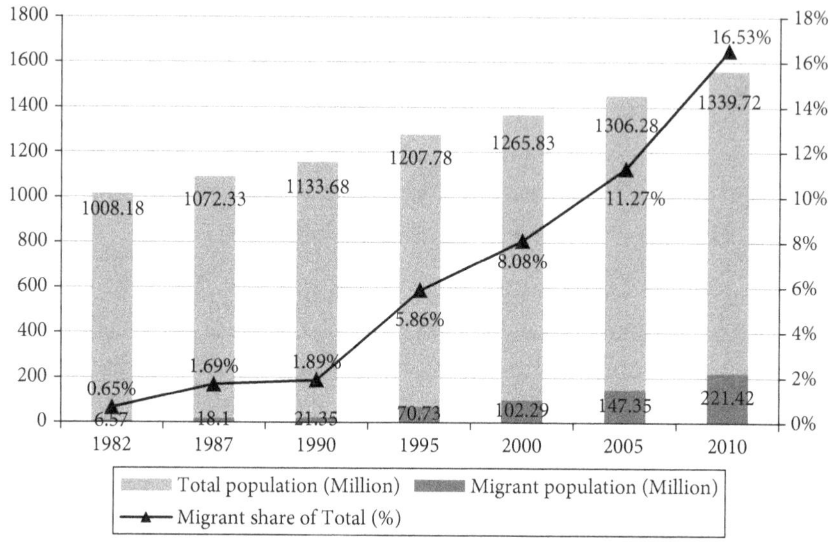

Figure 6.1. The number and share of migrants in the PRC (1982 to 2010)

Source: The data on migrants since 1982 to 2005 are from Duan et al. (2008). The data on migrants in 2010 are from the sixth census in the PRC. The data on total population are from the third census in 1982, 1 per cent population survey in 1987, the fourth census in 1990, 1 per cent population survey in 1995, the fifth census in 1990, 1 per cent population survey in 2005, and the sixth census in 2010.

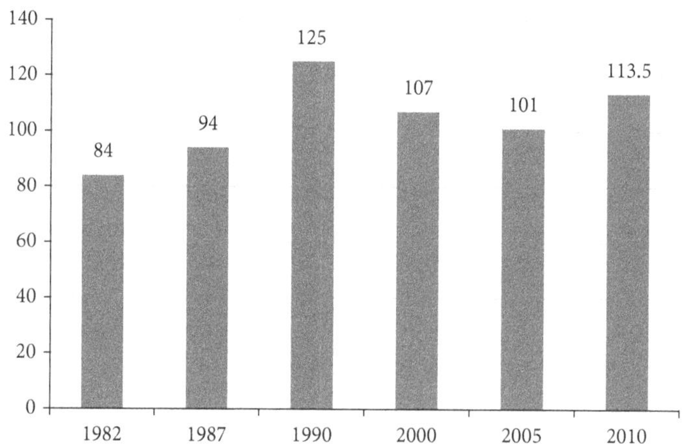

Figure 6.2. The sex ratio of the PRC's migrants (1982 to 2010)

Source: The data on migrants' sex ratio from 1982 to 2005 are from Duan et al. (2008). The data on migrants' sex ratio in 2010 are from Duan et al. (2013a).

fundamentally during the 1990s and the sex ratio became 125, which meant that male migrants formed the main part of migrants. This change was because non-agricultural industries demanded a large number of male workers. After entering the twenty-first century, the sex ratio began falling down to 107 in 2000 and then to 101 in 2005. During this period, female migrants had increased rapidly for two main reasons. First, the labour demand of non-agricultural industries had increased continuously, especially in services. Second, many female migrants left home for reunion with their husbands. In 2010, the sex ratio rose again. The reason for this could be that some female migrant workers went back home because of the financial crisis in 2008 or that the construction industry needed a lot more male workers after the government launched the '4 trillion RMB stimulus package'.

6.3.2.2 Age

We can see in Figure 6.3 that the average age of migrants increased from 28.22 in 1982 to 30.08 in 2010, though with a little decrease during 1987 to 1990. This is relative to the declining fertility rate which is the result of the 'one-child family planning policy' implemented all over the country since the 1980s. With the increasing age of migrants, it is a cause of worry that young migrants will decrease and the supply of labour will be insufficient. At present, this worry is not necessary because the population share of labour aged between 15 and 64 years among migrants rose continuously from 57.89 per cent in 1982 to 85.53 per cent in 2010 (Duan et al. 2013a). This means the working age population is still the main component of migrants and the number of working age migrants is increasing. However, if the low fertility rate trend is maintained in the future, the working age population will eventually reduce.

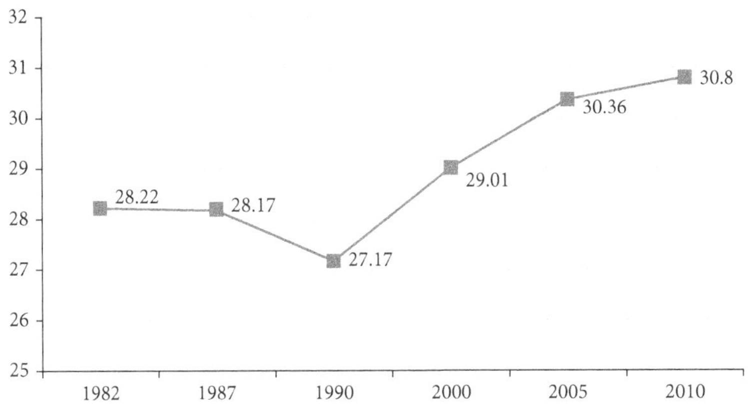

Figure 6.3. The average age of migrants (1982 to 2010)

Source: The data on migrants' average age are from Duan et al. (2013a).

6.3.2.3 Education

The average education level of migrants has improved gradually and has moved from the compulsory education stage into the senior middle-school stage. In Figure 6.4, we can see that the average education year had increased by 4.34 years between 1982 and 2010. The average education year of migrants in 2010 was 9.92 years, which is higher than 8.85 years of the total population and 7.75 years of the rural population.[9] This indicates that migrants can be regarded as 'educated elites' in rural areas and that human capital as a driving force of the PRC's migration has improved greatly. The ratio of migrants with high education has increased, while the ratio of migrants with low education has fallen continuously. The ratio of senior school graduates in migrants had increased from 8.41 per cent in 1982 to 20.63 per cent in 2010. The ratio of college graduates in migrants had increased from 1.04 per cent in 1982 to 15.37 per cent in 2010. According to the PRC's Hukou policy in earlier years, when someone went to college, they could get the non-agricultural Hukou, and when they graduated from college, they would usually be assigned a job in a city; they then got Hukou in that city and would not be counted as a migrant in the census. For this reason, before 1990, there were almost no college graduates among migrants. However, after 1990, college graduates could not get an assigned job. At the same time, more and more college graduates agglomerated to cities, especially the big ones, and many could not get the Hukou

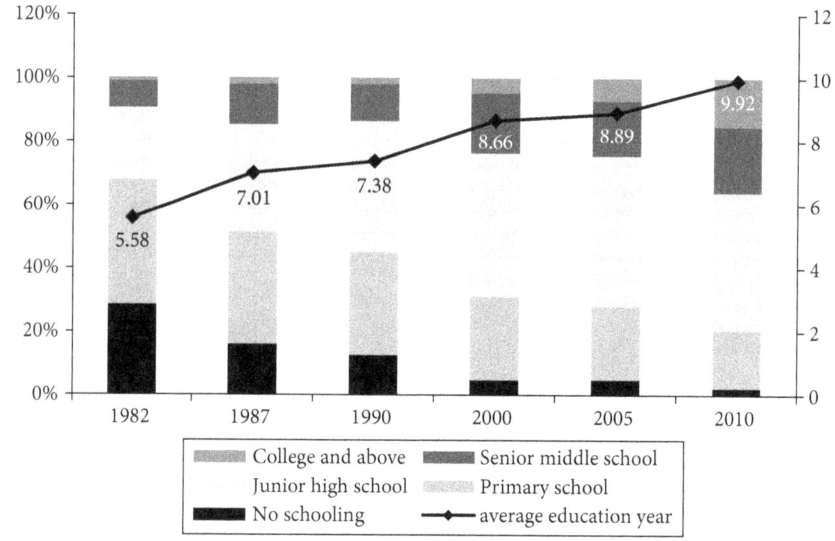

Figure 6.4. The average education years of migrants above six years (1982 to 2010)
Source: The data on migrants' education are from Duan et al. (2013a).

[9] The average educational year of the total population is calculated by data from the Sixth Census Information, <www.stats.gov.cn>.

Table 6.1. Proportion of inter- and intra-provincial migrants in 2010

Intra-provincial (%)	Interprovincial (%)	
Total population	66.94	33.06
No schooling	74.08	25.92
Primary school	65.02	34.98
Junior high school	57.37	42.63
Senior middle school	75.55	24.45
College	79.79	20.21
Bachelor	77.86	22.14
Postgraduate	75.19	24.81

Source: Ma and Chen (2012).

in those cities, as a result of which they were counted into the category of migrants. Table 6.1 shows that migrants with a college education prefer intra-province migration to inter-province migration.

6.3.3 Long-term or Short-term Migration

Figure 6.5 shows that the ratio of migrants who have worked outside their home town for five years and above fell between 1982 and 2010. Does this mean that long-term migrants have decreased during the last thirty years? The answer is negative. The migrant population that has worked outside for five years and above has increased from seven million in 1982 to 68.2 million in 2010 and the scale has increased by almost nine times. The reason for the ratio of long-term migrants falling is that there are more and more new migrants every year who are regarded as 'short term'. Gradually these new migrants will become long-term migrants as time goes by.

6.3.4 Migration With Families

According to the monitoring survey on national rural–urban migrant workers held by NBSC, the ratio of migrants with families has remained steady at around 20 per cent, and the migration like 'migrant birds' leaving families behind is still the most important way. This very low and stable level of migration with family has led to many social problems. According to the sixth population census, there are 61 million left-behind children, who do not live with their parents, but stay in their rural hometowns to study (National Women's Federation Research Group 2013). Duan et al. (2009) estimated there were 10.85 million left-behind

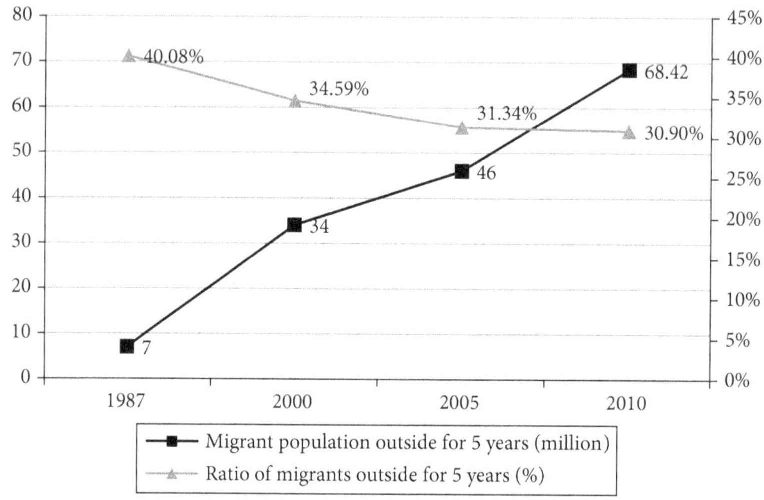

Figure 6.5. The scale and share of migrants working outside for more than five years (1982–2010)

Source: The data are from Duan et al. (2013a).

Source: The data are from Wang et al. (2012).

married women according to the fifth census in 2000, of which women aged between 20 and 49 years accounted for 82.11 per cent. Apart from left-behind children and women, there is another large group that is left behind—the elderly. They are left behind in rural areas because they need to take care of their grand-children who have been left behind by their parents or because they have lost the ability to work in urban areas. In 2012, there were 50 million left-behind elderly, leading to serious concerns about disease and disability problems (Wu 2013).

6.3.5 Flow of Migration

6.3.5.1 Origins of Migration

Table 6.2 shows where migrant workers come from. Migrant workers who migrate outside their original town mainly come from the middle and western regions. Migrant workers who are engaged in non-agricultural activities in their original town mostly come from the eastern region.

According to data on inter-province migration after 1995 (see Table 6.3), the biggest out-migrant provinces in the middle and western regions are Anhui, Jiangxi, Henan, Hubei, Hunan, Guangxi, and Sichuan. The proportion of out-migrants in all these provinces exceeds 5 per cent. Among them, the proportion of out-migrants in the provinces of Anhui, Hunan, and Sichuan was around 10 per cent, and the number of out-migrants in these three provinces was 2.89 million, 3.26 million, and 4.49 million respectively, during 1995 to 2000. In the period of 2000 to 2005,

Table 6.2. The origins of rural–urban migrant workers (%)

	2008		2009		2010		2011		2012	
	Outside	Local	Outside	Local	Outside	Local	Outside	Local	Outside	Local
Eastern	39	63.2	31.9	63.7	31.8	62.9	31.6	61.4	31.5	60.8
Middle	38.5	19.6	36.5	21.9	36.6	22.5	36.6	22.7	36.7	22.9
Western	32.8	15.6	31.6	14.4	31.6	14.6	31.8	15.9	31.8	16.3

Note: Outside migrant workers refer to who migrate outside their original town for more than six months. Local migrant workers refer to those who are engaged in non-agricultural activities for more than six months in their original town.

Source: The reports of monitoring survey on national rural–urban migrant workers between 2008 and 2013, <www.stats.gov.cn>.

Table 6.3. The scale of out-migrants in inter-province migration

Province	1995–2000		2005–10	
	Scale of out-migration (10,000)	Share of total nation (%)	Scale of out-migration (10,000)	Share of total nation (%)
Beijing	17.44	0.54	40.6	0.74
Tianjin	10.43	0.32	21.34	0.39
Hebei	87.22	2.70	201.74	3.67
Shanxi	33.36	1.03	79.37	1.44
Inner Mongolia	44.11	1.37	64.76	1.18
Liaoning	37.99	1.18	68.54	1.25
Jilin	52.93	1.64	85.39	1.55
Heilongjiang	93.98	2.91	146.32	2.66
Shanghai	16.29	0.50	40.1	0.73
Jiangsu	124.1	3.84	189.35	3.44
Zhejiang	96.98	3.00	133.94	2.44
Anhui	289.3	8.96	552.56	10.05
Fujian	62.45	1.93	111.37	2.03
Jiangxi	268.06	8.30	348.33	6.33
Shandong	87.82	2.72	201.5	3.66
Henan	230.9	7.15	543.04	9.87
Hubei	221.02	6.85	380.42	6.92
Hunan	326.12	10.10	459.19	8.35
Guangdong	43.8	1.36	161.29	2.93
Guangxi	183.81	5.69	282.05	5.13
Hainan	12.96	0.40	23.59	0.43
Chongqing	110.31	3.42	184.41	3.35
Sichuan	439.55	13.62	498.81	9.07
Guizhou	123.19	3.82	268.08	4.87
Yunnan	39.81	1.23	108.91	1.98
Xizang	3.54	0.11	6.25	0.11
Shaanxi	71.93	2.23	134.75	2.45
Gansu	56.08	1.74	104.69	1.90
Qinghai	12.32	0.38	15.0	0.27
Ningxia	8.74	0.27	15.07	0.27
Xinjiang	21.68	0.67	28.67	0.52
Total nation	3,228.21	100	5,499.39	100

Source: Wang et al. (2012).

the population of out-migrants in the provinces Anhui, Hunan, and Sichuan increased to 5.52 million, 4.59 million, and 4.98 million respectively. Sichuan had the largest number of out-migrants in 1995–2000, while in the period 2000 to 2005, Anhui became the province with the most out-migrants.

6.3.5.2 Destinations of Migration

In the last thirty years, the most prominent feature of migration is that the migrants are more concentrated, flowing into the south-east coastal areas, especially in the Yangtze River Delta and the Pearl River Delta regions (see Figure 6.6).

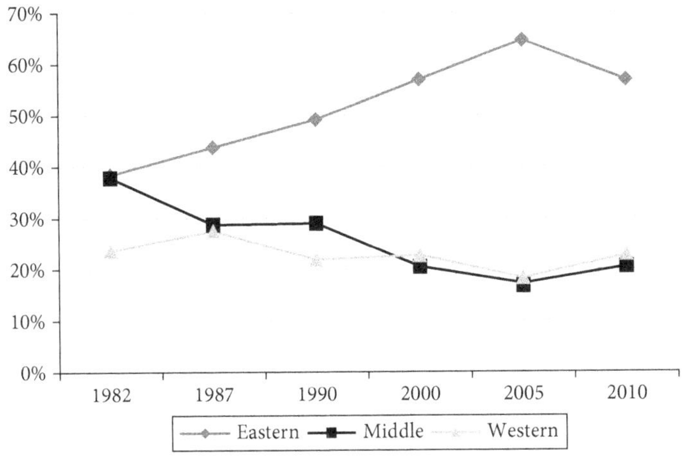

Figure 6.6. The destination regions of migrants (1982 to 2010)
Source: The data on migrants' destination region from 1982 to 2005 are from Duan and Yang (2009). The data on migrants' destination region in 2010 are from Duan et al. (2013b).

In the 1980s, migrants were drawn to the traditional industrial regions, with the old industrial base in the north-east region absorbing 38.14 per cent of total migrants in 1982 (Duan and Yang 2009). After the 1990s, the south-east coastal areas absorbed more and more migrants. The number of migrants flowing to the old industrial base in the north-east declined. Guangdong province absorbed most migrants in 2005. Migrants to Guangdong accounted for 5.23 per cent of total migrants in 1982 and the figure rose to 22.37 per cent in 2005. The proportion of migrants to the Yangtze River Delta region of Shanghai, Jiangsu, and Zhejiang rose from 11.27 per cent to 20.58 per cent during the same period (Duan and Yang 2009).

To get a micro-level understanding, we calculated the migrant population of the PRC's 287 prefecture-level cities using the data from the 2000 and 2010 population census data (Xia et al. 2015). Figure 6.7 shows the spatial distribution of the PRC's migrants in 2000 and 2010. Moving from the left map to the right one, we see that most of the cities' colour becomes darker, indicating that the number of migrants in most cities increased in this decade. The number of cities having more than one million migrants increased from 12 in 2000 to 41 in 2010. In terms of the spatial distribution of migrants, after 2000 the trend of most migrants agglomerating in the eastern coastal areas, a few provinces, and a few cities has not changed. As shown in Table 6.4, the provinces whose migrants accounted for the highest proportion are still Guangdong, Zhejiang, Jiangsu, and Shanghai. However, some changes in the spatial distribution of migrants in cities did take place between 2000 and 2010. The capacity of the four municipalities for absorbing a floating population increased rapidly. Shanghai and Beijing instead of Shenzhen and Dongguan became the cities with the largest number of migrants. The scale

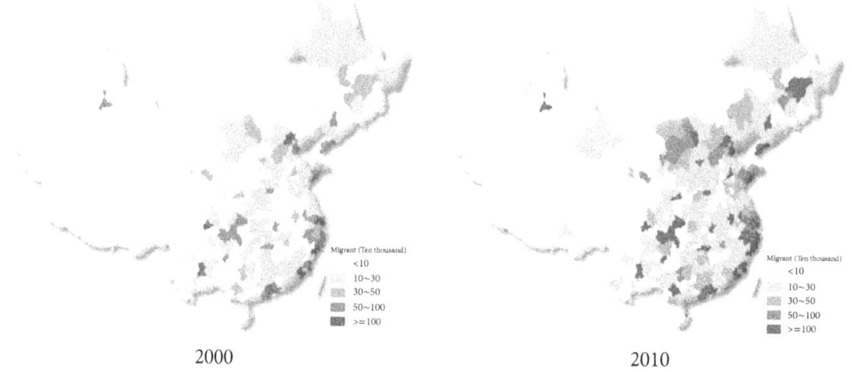

Figure 6.7. Spatial distribution of the PRC's migrants (2000 and 2010)

of migrants in Tianjin and Chongqing also increased at a fast pace. The proportion of the country's total migrants in the south-east coastal cities somewhat declined. The scale of migrants in some big western cities and their proportion has risen significantly. If we rank the leading fifty cities by the scale of migrants, we find that migrants tended to agglomerate in the cities with a higher ranking in 2000, while they were more scattered across these leading fifty cities in 2010 as compared to 2000. This is further reflected in the HHI index of these fifty cities' migrant populations, which decreased from 2.27 in 2000 to 1.96 in 2010.

6.3.6 Determinants of Migration

6.3.6.1 Personal and Family Characteristics

Let us begin with personal characteristics. If the returns on education are higher in industry and services, then one theoretical inference is that education can increase the tendency for labour to migrate from the countryside to the city. In household decision making, better educated family members with comparative advantages in industry and services are preferred for migrant jobs. Empirical studies mostly support this theoretical inference, though there are some findings that differ. Early studies found that formal education's impact on increasing the probability of labour migration was insignificant, though it had a positive impact on increasing the probability of employment in local non-agricultural industries (Zhao 1997; Zhao 1999b); Zhao (2003) found that educational level does not have a significant impact on labour migration. Nevertheless, many empirical studies provide evidence that education significantly impacts labour migration. Du and Park (2003) also found that the high educational level of a household does have a positive impact on migration; Zhu and Zeng's (2004) research found that education only has a positive impact on the reallocation decisions of males, while there

Table 6.4. Scale of migrant population in the top fifty cities and its proportion in the national migrant population

Rank	2000			2010		
	City	Migrant population (10,000)	Ratio (%)	City	Migrant population (10,000)	Ratio (%)
1	Shenzhen	585	7.85	Shanghai	1,102	6.68
2	Dongguan	492	6.61	Beijing	892	5.41
3	Shanghai	436	5.85	Shenzhen	828	5.02
4	Guangzhou	331	4.45	Dongguan	639	3.87
5	Beijing	260	3.49	Guangzhou	542	3.29
6	Foshan	221	2.96	Suzhou	452	2.74
7	Wenzhou	135	1.82	Chendu	387	2.35
8	Quanzhou	129	1.74	Tianjin	386	2.34
9	Chendu	126	1.69	Foshan	358	2.17
10	Suzhou	115	1.55	Wenzhou	324	1.96
11	Kunming	113	1.52	Hangzhou	285	1.73
12	Zhongshan	104	1.40	Chongqing	280	1.70
13	Wuhan	98	1.32	Wuhan	277	1.68
14	Hangzhou	96	1.29	Ningbo	259	1.57
15	Ningbo	94	1.26	Quanzhou	241	1.46
16	Huizhou	91	1.23	Nanjing	225	1.36
17	Chongqing	88	1.19	Wuxi	214	1.30
18	Wuxi	86	1.15	Zhenzhou	200	1.21
19	Fuzhou	83	1.12	Xiamen	199	1.21
20	Nanjing	80	1.07	Xi'an	180	1.09
21	Tianjing	79	1.06	Qingdao	179	1.09
22	Xiamen	75	1.00	Fuzhou	176	1.07
23	Dalian	63	0.85	Shenyang	169	1.02
24	Zhenzhou	62	0.83	Huizhou	167	1.01
25	Urumqi	60	0.81	Kunming	167	1.01
26	Changzhou	60	0.80	Zhongshan	165	1.00
27	Guiyang	58	0.78	Daliang	165	1.00
28	Zhuhai	58	0.78	Jinhua	148	0.90
29	Jinhua	57	0.77	Hefei	148	0.90
30	Taizhou	55	0.73	Changzhou	143	0.87
31	Qingdao	54	0.73	Taizhou	143	0.86
32	Shenyang	52	0.70	Changsha	142	0.86
33	Changsha	52	0.70	Urumqi	131	0.79
34	Xi'an	49	0.66	Jiaxing	130	0.79
35	Harbin	49	0.66	Nanning	128	0.78
36	Shijiazhuang	47	0.63	Jinan	123	0.74
37	Jiangmen	46	0.62	Guiyang	118	0.71
38	Nanning	46	0.62	Harbin	113	0.69
39	Liuzhou	40	0.54	Taiyuan	110	0.67
40	Taiyuan	38	0.51	Hohhot	110	0.67
41	Changchun	36	0.48	Shaoxing	110	0.67
42	Hohhot	36	0.48	Changchun	97	0.59
43	Yantai	34	0.46	Nanchang	92	0.56

(Continued)

Table 6.4. Continued

Rank	2000			2010		
	City	Migrant population (10,000)	Ratio (%)	City	Migrant population (10,000)	Ratio (%)
44	Hefei	34	0.46	Shijiazhuang	91	0.55
45	Baotou	33	0.44	Baotou	80	0.48
46	Shaoxing	33	0.44	Lanzhou	78	0.47
47	Baoding	33	0.44	Yantai	78	0.47
48	Nanchang	33	0.44	Jiangmen	76	0.46
49	Jiaxing	32	0.43	Ordos	76	0.46
50	Lanzhou	32	0.43	Haikou	74	0.45
	Total		69.84	Total		72.74

Note: The scale and share of migrants are calculated on the basis of data from the 2000 and 2010 censuses. Migrants here refer to the migrants moving in from other provinces, cities, or towns in the data.

exists no such impact for females. We employed the Chinese Household Income Project Survey (CHIPS) 2002[10] data in our study and found that, after controlling for other individual, household, and village characteristics, different levels of education have different positive effects on migrant workers. If we use illiteracy as a reference, then middle-school education increases the probability that rural labour will work out of town the most (7.13 per cent more), followed by primary education (5.25 per cent). Compared with illiterates, the tendency for individuals with relatively higher education to work out of town actually shows small increases (the figures for technical schools or higher education schools is 4.75 per cent, while that for high-school education is 4.9 per cent). Of course, this could be due to the fact that rural residents with middle-school education and above find it easier to obtain urban Hukous and, therefore, are no longer classified as rural residents that 'work out of town' (Chen et al. 2014).

Age is an important factor that influences labour migration. Wang and Liu's (2007) study discovered that due to the strong constraints imposed by dual institutions such as the Hukou system on population migration, interprovincial migration is, to a large extent, mainly reflected in young labourers working as migrant labour and the age distribution being highly concentrated in the 20–30 years bracket. The impact of age on labour migration is both positive and negative. On the one hand, an increase in age brings experience, which enables higher returns to be gained; on the other hand, older migrants have higher psychological

[10] CHIPS refers to the Chinese Household and Income Project Survey conducted by the Chinese Academy of Social Sciences.

costs and the period in which they benefit from migration is short (Zhao 1999b). At the same time, the lack of social security and public services that migrant workers face in the city causes bigger problems as age increases. If we take these effects into account comprehensively, the impact of age on the probability of migration may be an inverted U, namely, first ascending and then descending. Studies by Zhu (2002) and Sheng (2008) discovered that age does display an inverted U relationship with the probability of labour migration. We used the CHIPS 2002 data ourselves and found again this inverted U relationship. After controlling for other factors, 33-year-old labour has the highest probability of migration (Chen et al. 2014).

Empirical studies consistently find that the impact of gender and marriage on reallocation decisions is significant. Females and married people have higher migration costs, including monetary and psychological costs. In household decision making, males and singles obviously have a comparative advantage when it comes to working out of town. Zhao (1997) discovered that the migration probability for females is lower than that for males by 7 per cent. Zhao (1999b) points out that compared with the average level, 37.6 per cent of married rural labour is unwilling to reallocate. Similarly, Zhu (2002) also discovered that married status has a significant negative impact on labour migration. In our own study employing CHIPS 2002 data, we found that the migration probability for females is 4.45 per cent lower than that for males, and compared with people of other marital status, the migration probability for the married group drops enormously by 11.76 per cent (Chen et al. 2014). Since the data we employed are newer than Zhao (1997; 1999b) and Zhu (2002), we can perhaps conclude that the effect of gender and marital status on labour migration is declining. This is consistent with the aforementioned trend that the relocation of females and entire families in labour migration are generally increasing.

From the perspective of land and population, all else being equal, more labourers and less land per household implies that the relationship between population and land is tenser, and the probability of labour migration will increase. Studies by Zhao (1997; 1999a) and Zhu (2002) found that households with more land per capita have a lower probability of labour migration. Du and Park's (2003) study on labour migration of the poor also found that household land per capita has a negative impact on migration. In our own study employing CHIPS 2002 data, we found that for every extra labourer in a household, the individual labour migration probability decreases by 4.01 per cent, while, for every *mu*[11] increase in household land per capita, the individual tendency to migrate decreases by 1.25 per cent (Chen et al. 2014).

[11] *Mu* is a Chinese unit of area. 1 *mu* = 666.7m^2.

Of course, government policy variables affect the relative gain between working in agricultural production at home and working outside and are important parameters that affect labour migration decisions. Zhao's (1997; 1999a) studies show that during one period in the 1990s, the burden of agricultural taxes lowered the real income of agricultural production, causing a portion of capable and strong labour to flow into non-agricultural industries, affecting agricultural production. In recent years, the Chinese government placed heavy emphasis on the 'Three Agricultural' issue (issues of agriculture, peasants, and rural areas) and abolished agriculture taxes for the first time in thousands of years, with some grain farmers even receiving subsidies from the government. These policy measures conducive to increasing income from agricultural production brought back some migrant workers to growing crops again. Meng's (2010) study discovered that policy adjustments after 2004 indeed reduced the tendency for migrant workers to work out of town, though the strength of the policy is limited.

The impact on labour migration of factors such as personal characteristics, household land–person ratios, and policy variables still cannot fully reflect the fact that labour migration is the result of household decisions. Even if labour migration is only the result of individual decisions, the aforementioned factors on labour migration still make their impact felt. Differing from orthodox theory, which assumes that individuals are the decision-making entities, new economic migration theory emphasizes the importance of households as decision-making entities, as households determine the relocation or migration of their members in accordance with the principles of maximizing expected income and minimizing risk (Stark and Bloom 1985). This theory has three core concepts. First is 'risk transfer'. Household income is unstable in the hometown, and in order to hedge risks and diversify income sources households will decide to make some of its members work out of town or migrate, so as to reduce the dependence of the household on traditional or single-income sources. Second is 'economic constraints'. Many households face monetary constraints in their home towns, for example, not having crop insurance, unemployment insurance, or enough credit support. In order to break through these constraints to development, households will decide for some of their members to work out of town, in order to obtain the necessary money and technology. Third is 'relative deprivation'. When making migration decisions, households not only take into account the absolute expected income level but also the income level relative to the reference group in the hometowns. Even if a household's income level in its home town sees a large increase, as long as the degree of the increase is below that of the reference group, the household will still feel relatively deprived and its tendency to migrate will increase.

In studies on Chinese labour migration, the fact that labour migration is the result of household decisions is critically reflected in two aspects: diversifying risks and remittances. Du (2001) employed agricultural household survey data and discovered that after inputting the '1996 household asset value' variable into the determinant model of labour's time supply for non-agricultural work, the coefficient of this variable is significantly positive. He believes that the greater the value of household assets, the higher the ability to withstand risk, and the time supply for non-agricultural work is higher. Since the rural labour market is underdeveloped in poor regions, further labour migration is often restricted, making it necessary to reduce welfare losses by effectively enhancing marginal labour productivity through cutting down barriers to labour mobility.

Remittances exhibit the fact that labour migration is the result of household decisions even more clearly.[12] Li (2001) observed that the proportion of migrant workers remitting earnings is higher in the PRC than that in other countries, and the ratio of urban migrant worker remittances to rural resident household income is rather high as well. Du and Park (2003) employed agricultural household survey data on poor countryside areas in the PRC's western regions and discovered that income transfer of migrant labour is an important factor in alleviating poverty. The proportion of relatively poor households that have income transfer among households with migrant workers is higher than that of rich households, which shows that the altruistic nature of migrants has a positive impact on alleviating poverty. Ma et al. (2004) examined the trend of population migration and its impact on local labour and rural income growth and their results show that labour migration has already become a new source of rural income growth for undeveloped regions, and is gradually playing the role of eliminating poverty and checking regional disparities. The remittances of migrant workers play a decisive role in rural life. The younger generation in rural areas is increasingly yearning for a modernized way of life and most of its remittances are used in day-to-day consumption expenditures such as holding weddings and birthday parties similar to urban residents, and renovating their homes. To this end, they often undertake arduous and dangerous jobs in the cities for a long time. These jobs generally do not have signed labour contracts and wages are usually settled together at the Spring Festival. Since most countryside areas do not have medical insurance, many families become poor as a result of illnesses, and remittances from migrant workers play an immense role in paying for their households' medical expenses. Remittances become one of the most important economic activities that connect migrant workers with their households. In terms of lifestyle, remittances and the acceptance of such has already become an important element of migrant worker and rural household life. In a poor Sichuan township in the mid-1990s, the money posted back home by migrant workers every year was five times greater than that of the town government's fiscal revenue. Remittances are only a portion of the money migrants send back home, since when they go home at the Spring Festival

[12] Dustmann and Mestres (2010) found that mostly short-term migrants make remittances, which matches the PRC's situation of migrants mostly being short term.

or autumn harvest, they bring home a portion of the money they have earned. Relatively speaking, among those who work out of town, those working in sectors such as transportation, communications, and industry send more money home, while those working in agriculture send the least home; the closer the location of work and residence from home, the greater the amount of money sent home; the higher the education level, the larger the remittances (Huang 1997). Hu and Wang (2007) discovered that the larger the following variables, the larger the amount of remittances: migrant worker income, rural hometown non-remittance income, size of rural hometown's farmland, and migrant worker age. Migrant workers with higher reallocation costs (transportation expenses), the entire family working out of town together, unemployment experience, and university education are associated with smaller remittances.

The two aforementioned studies have different findings regarding the role of remittances. As time passes, remittance behaviour changes as well. A recent small-scale survey shows that compared with first-generation migrant workers, second-generation migrant workers send less money home, and a smaller proportion of them do so. The survey shows that 30.3 per cent of second-generation migrant workers send back RMB 100–300 every month and 25.8 per cent send RMB 301–500, while 25.8 per cent send no money at all or their family members back home do not need them to send money back, in which case their income is treated as entirely disposable (Liu and Cheng 2008).

6.3.6.2 Destination Characteristics

Studies on the PRC's migration before 2005 found the following characteristics of migrant destinations. Scale of economies is an important factor for a place to attract migrant labour (Wang 1996). Xiao and Liu (2007) found that regions that have a bigger non-agriculture industry, higher expected earnings, and are at a shorter distance to the migrants' original areas are more likely to be chosen by migrants as the flow destination. Fixed assets investment andexport-oriented economies are considered to have strong employment-creation effects. Duan (2001) found that provinces which have higher fixed asset investment absorbed more migrants. Zhu and Zeng (2004) found that provinces with a mainly export-oriented economy absorbed more migrants. However, we find some new changes in the PRC's migrant destinations in 2010. We find that the level of economic development has a positive impact on the number of a city's migrants, but the degree of influence declined between 2000 and 2010. Fixed asset investment and foreign direct investment had significant positive effects in attracting migrants in 2000; however, this effect disappeared in 2010. Between 2000 and 2010, the tertiary industry has replaced the secondary industry to be the main force that attracts migrants to cities. The size of the floating population has increased with the expansion of city population size, but the speed at which the city population size increased descended in 2000 and then rose in 2010 (Xia et al. 2015).

Along with the factors already discussed, people also migrate for public services and human capital externalities (Xia and Lu 2015). Using the micro-data of a 1 per cent population census in 2005 and characteristics of 220 prefecture-level cities, we studied the influence of city characteristics, including public services and wages, on labour flow. We find that people tend to migrate to a city where they can not only get higher wages and job opportunities but also better basic education and medical services, even though in inflow cities migrants cannot enjoy the same public services as local residents because of the constraints of Hukou policies. We also find that migrants are more likely to flow to the cities with higher average educational years and larger population scales. This means cross-regional equalization of public services can mitigate, but not stop, agglomeration in large cities. The regression results are presented in the Appendix.

6.3.7 Rural–Urban Migration and Natural Growth of Population

Large numbers of rural residents have migrated to urban areas since 1949. Figure 6.8 presents the growth trend of the urbanization rate and natural growth rate of the population. In a region, the increased population comes from two sources: natural growing population and migrants from outside. In the PRC, the natural growth rate of populations in urban areas is usually lower than that in rural areas. So when thenatural growth rate of the national population declined after the 1970s, the natural growth rate of the population in urban areas had a

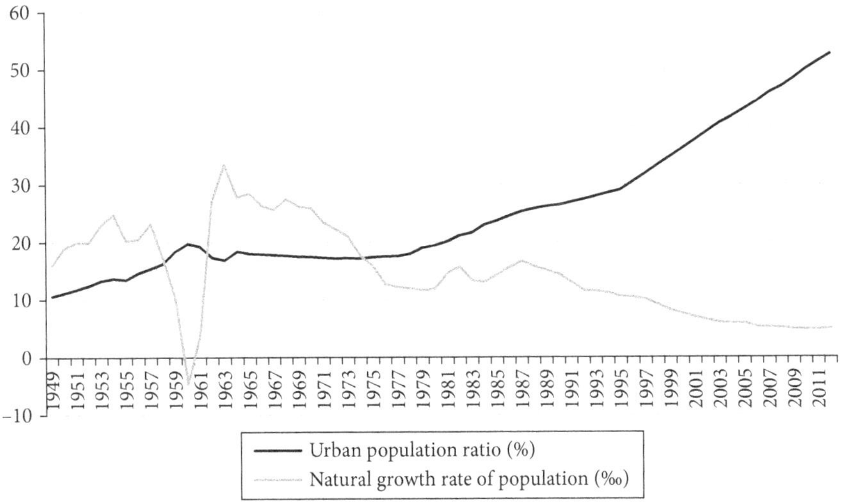

Figure 6.8. Urbanization ratio and natural growth rate of population since 1949

Note: Urban population ratio = urban population at the end of year/total population at the end of year.

Source: The website of NBSC, <www.stats.gov.cn>.

bigger decline. However, after 1970, especially after 1995, the urbanization rate has risen rapidly. We have strong reason to believe that a large part of the increasing numbers of urban residents can be attributed to rural–urban migrants.

6.4 Urbanization and Employment

6.4.1 Employment Growth in Urban Areas

After 'the reforms and opening up', the quantity of employment has increased rapidly from 401.52 million in 1978 to 767 million in 2012. Significant changes have taken place in the employment structure of the three main industries. As shown in Figure 6.9, the proportion of employment in the primary industry has been declining from 71 per cent in 1978 to 34 per cent in 2012. Labour working in the secondary industry and tertiary industry has expanded rapidly since 1978. The increasing speed of employment in the tertiary industry is much faster compared with the secondary industry. Employment in thetertiary industry first surpassed that in the secondary industry in 1995 and then surpassed that in the primary industry in 2011. In 2012, thetertiary industry became the largest industry in absorbing employment. According to Figures 6.9 and 6.10, the proportion of employment and the proportion of GDP in the primary industry have the same declining trends. The rapid development of the secondary and tertiary industries helps absorb large quantities of the rural surplus labour force.

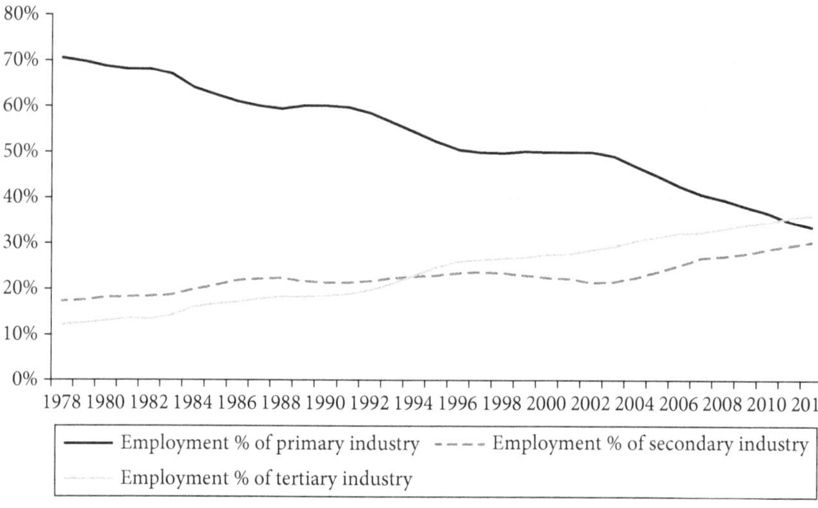

Figure 6.9. The proportion of employment in the three main industries since 1978

Source: The website of NBSC, <www.stats.gov.cn>.

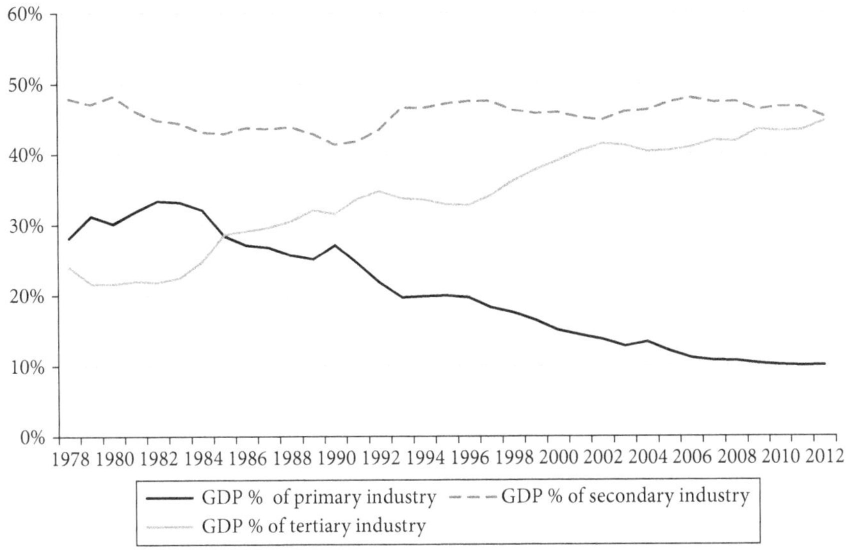

Figure 6.10. The proportion of GDP in the three main industries since 1978
Source: The website of NBSC, <www.stats.gov.cn>.

6.4.2 Urbanization and the Employment Structure of Migrants

Though employment in the tertiary industry surpassed that in the secondary industry in 1995, rural–urban migrants are mainly working in the secondary industry, as shown in Table 6.5. The two largest industries within the secondary industry in which rural–urban migrants work are manufacturing and construction. The proportion of migrants working in the manufacturing industry remained above 30 per cent before 2008. But this proportion started declining after 2008. Construction is the second-biggest industry in which migrant workers are engaged, and the proportion of migrants in construction took a big leap from 13.8 per cent in 2008 to 22.2 per cent in 2010. Migrants increasingly working in the construction industry after 2008 may be the result of the massive investment in infrastructure after the '4 trillion RMB stimulus package'. The proportion of migrants working in services has seen little change in the last six years and has remained around 34 per cent. A remarkable change is that in 2013 the services industry surpassed the manufacturing industry and became the largest industry in absorbing rural–urban migrants. This change is consistent with our findings. Our study finds that cities with a higher ratio of secondary industrial output compared with tertiary industrial output had a stronger ability to absorb migrants in 2000; however, cities with a higher ratio of tertiary industrial output compared with secondary industrial output had a stronger ability to absorb migrants in 2010 (Xia et al. 2015).

Table 6.5. The industry distribution of rural–urban migrant workers (%)

Industry	2008	2009	2010	2011	2012	2013
Manufacturing	37.2	36.1	36.7	36.0	35.7	31.4
Construction	13.8	15.2	16.1	17.7	18.4	22.2
Services	33.1	35.5	35.6	34.2	33.8	34.1
Transportation, storage, and postal	6.4	6.8	6.9	6.6	6.6	6.3
Wholesale and retail trade	9.0	10.0	10.0	10.1	9.8	11.3
Accommodation and catering trade	5.5	6.0	6.0	5.3	5.2	5.9
Resident services and other services	12.2	12.7	12.7	12.2	12.2	10.6
Other industries	15.9	13.2	11.6	12.1	12.1	12.3

Source: The reports of the monitoring survey on national rural–urban migrant workers between 2008 and 2013, <www.stats.gov.cn>.

The employment structure of migrants varies across different regions (see Table 6.6). In the eastern region, migrants mainly work in the manufacturing industry, followed by services and then construction. On the other hand, in the middle and western regions migrants work mainly in services and least in the manufacturing industry. The proportion of migrants working in construction is most in the western region, then the middle, and last the eastern. There is a similar pattern in the proportion of migrants working in services. The different employment structure of migrants is probably caused by most infrastructure investment being concentrated in the middle and western regions as a result of the '4 trillion RMB stimulus package'.

6.4.3 Urbanization and Informalization

6.4.3.1 Earnings of Migrants

After 2008, the earnings of migrants increased rapidly. The monthly earnings of migrants almost doubled during 2008 to 2013—from RMB 1,340 to RMB 2,609 (see Table 6.7). The earnings of migrants exhibit no big difference within different regions. Why do people still migrate to the eastern region even if the earnings do not differ much between different regions? There might be two reasons: first, the similar earnings are just the result of labour mobility across regions; and second, the probability of getting a job is higher in the eastern region and labour migrates for other amenities such as public services or human capital externalities, as already discussed.

6.4.3.2 Social Security of Migrants

In the PRC, we do not have a clear definition of informal employment. However, whether a worker is covered by social security is a very important characteristic of the informalization and instability of jobs. Table 6.8 reports the participation

Table 6.6. The industry distribution of rural–urban migrant workers across different regions (%)

Industry	2011			2012			2013		
	Eastern	Middle	Western	Eastern	Middle	Western	Eastern	Middle	Western
Manufacturing	44.8	23	15.4	44.6	23.2	15.4	43.1	20.1	13.2
Construction	13.4	24.7	27.4	13.9	25.5	28.4	17.5	28.5	30
Services	31	38.5	41.3	30.9	37.9	40.4	30.4	37.5	41.7
Transportation, storage, and postal	5.5	8.1	9.3	5.6	8.2	8.8	5.3	7.3	8.2
Wholesale and retail trade	8.7	13.1	12.5	8.5	12.6	11.9	10.2	12.9	13.2
Accommodation and catering trade	4.5	5.9	7.3	4.4	5.8	7.6	5	6.2	8.1
Resident services and other services	12.3	11.4	12.2	12.4	11.3	12.1	9.9	11.1	12.2
Other industries	10.8	13.8	15.9	10.6	13.4	15.8	9	13.9	15.1

Source: The reports of the monitoring survey on national rural–urban migrant workers since 2011 to 2013, <www.stats.gov.cn>.

Table 6.7. Monthly earnings of rural–urban migrants workers (RMB)

Region	2008	2009	2010	2011	2012	2013
Nation	1,340	1,417	1,690	2049	2,290	2,609
Eastern	1,352	1,422	1,696	2,053	2,286	–
Middle	1,275	1,350	1,632	2006	2,257	–
Western	1,273	1,378	1,643	1990	2,226	–

Source: The reports of the monitoring survey on national rural–urban migrant workers between 2008 and 2013, <www.stats.gov.cn>.

Table 6.8. The participation rate in social security of rural–urban migrants (%)

Insurance	2008	2009	2010	2011	2012	2013
Pension insurance	9.8	7.6	9.5	13.9	14.3	15.7
Occupational injury insurance	24.1	21.8	24.1	23.6	24	28.5
Health care insurance	13.1	12.2	14.3	16.7	16.9	17.6
Unemployment insurance	3.7	3.9	4.9	8	8.4	9.1
Birth insurance	2.0	2.4	2.9	5.6	6.1	6.6

Source: The reports of the monitoring survey on national rural–urban migrant workers between 2008 and 2013, <www.stats.gov.cn>.

rate in social security of rural–urban migrant workers. In the last six years, participation in every type of social security has increased significantly, though the level of participation is still very low. Among the five types of social insurance, the participation rate in occupational injury insurance is the highest. The participation rate in health care insurance and pension insurance in turn rank second and third. The least participation is in birth insurance.

6.4.3.3 Self-employed Migrants

Self-employment constitutes a major part of informal jobs (see Table 6.9). According the national monitoring survey on rural–urban migrant workers in 2013, 83.5 per cent of migrant workers are employed and 16.5 per cent of are self-employed. Among the employed migrant workers, 61.4 per cent are working in the manufacturing and construction industry. Among the self-employed migrant workers, 76.3 per cent are working in the services industry.

6.4.3.4 Occupational Mobility of Migrants

In cities, most migrant workers are in the secondary labour market and are engaged in jobs with low wages, long working hours, poor working environment, and low occupational status (Li 2006). Most migrants work as unskilled workers in the manufacturing industry, service providers in sales and trade, and construction workers (Li 1999; Fu et al. 2012). Migrant workers change jobs frequently.

Table 6.9. The distributions of employed and self-employed migrants in 2013

Industry	Employed	Self-employed
Manufacturing	35.8	10.7
Construction	25.6	5.9
Services	25.3	76.3
Transportation, storage, and postal industry	5.5	39.6
Wholesale and retail trade	4.5	15.1
Accommodation and catering trade	5.3	8.5
Resident services and other services	10	13.1
Other industries	13.3	7.1
Total	100.0	100.0

Source: The report of the monitoring survey on national rural–urban migrant workers in 2013, <www.stats.gov.cn>.

Investigated 728 rural–urban migrants in Beijing, Bai and Li (2008) found that 63.25 per cent of the sample migrants experienced job change, and the average number of changes was 2.06 after working outside their original place of residence. Zhang (2010) found that the mobility rate of migrants (42.3 per cent) greatly exceeds that of urban residents (19.9 per cent). Using an urban household survey for 1999 in the PRC, Knight and Yueh (2004) found that Chinese urban residents have the longest average tenure at 19.9 years, while Chinese rural–urban migrants have the shortest at 4.5 years. Though migrants change jobs frequently, their earnings have not improved significantly and some migrants even suffer income decline after job changes (Bai and Li 2008). Their occupational status change is insignificant (Li 1999). They face a big obstacle in moving to occupations with a higher social status (Fu et al. 2012). Due to limited possibilities of upward mobility, most migrants want to be self-employed and own private enterprises in the future (Xia 2014).

6.4.3.5 Living Conditions of Migrants

In Table 6.10, we can see that renting houses to live in is common for migrants. Half of such migrants share rented accommodation with others, while the other half rents houses independently. The second form of accommodation for migrants is the dorms of employment units—the proportion of these migrants was 28.6 per cent in 2013. In Table 6.10, the data show that fewer migrants purchased houses in their working areas. In fact, according to the Hukou policies in many cities, when people purchase houses they can gain the Hukou of that place, and then they will not be counted as migrants. The living conditions of migrants are different in cities of different sizes. In large cities, the proportion of migrant workers living in dorms, sheds, and rented houses is higher than that in small cities or towns. The proportion of migrant workers living at home and working outside is very high in small towns.

Table 6.10. The accommodation distributions of migrant workers in 2013 (%)

	National total	Municipalities or provincial capital city	Prefecture-level city	Small town
Dorms of employed units	28.6	30.4	33	23
Sheds in construction site	11.9	14.9	10.9	10.4
Working places	5.8	5.9	5.8	5.6
Rent house with others	18.5	21.6	20.5	13.9
Rent house independently	18.2	20.4	19.9	14.9
Purchase house in working areas	0.9	0.7	0.9	1.2
Live at home work and outside	13	3.2	6.4	27.3
Others	3.1	3	2.7	3.8

Source: The report of the monitoring survey on national rural–urban migrant workers in 2013, <www.stats.gov.cn>.

6.4.4 City Scale and Job Creation: Are City Sizes Related to Job Creation?

The relationship between city scale and employment probability is an important topic in urban economics. If increases in city population raise one's employment probability, unemployment is not a major concern in urban population expansion. Using individual-level data from CHIPS 2002 and 2007, Gao et al. (2015) estimated probit models of employment determination. Instrumental variable regression results show that it is more likely for individuals to get employed in big cities. Every 1 per cent growth in the city scale increases one's employment probability by 0.039–0.041 percentage points. Further, we find the scale advantage of big cities being heterogeneous among individuals with different human capital. Both the most and least educated workers benefit from city scale, with the least skilled workers benefiting the most. However, the employment prospects of medium-skilled workers are not affected. Therefore, restricting urban population growth, especially the migration of low-skilled workers, will harm both efficiency and equity, and thus undermine inclusive urban growth (Gao et al. 2015).

Gao (2014) estimated the effect of city scale on income using individual-level data from the 2002 and 2007 Chinese Household Income Project Surveys. Every 1 per cent increase in city population leads to approximately 0.189–0.190 per cent increase in one's nominal income. Even when cities' price differences are considered, city expansion still raises individual incomes. Gao used two different price indices to deflate nominal income and found that when city population grows by 1 per cent, individuals' real incomes rise by 0.082–0.143 per cent. These results show that the effects of city growth on income are heterogeneous across individuals with different income levels. Though everyone benefits from city growth, those with the lowest income levels benefit the least (Gao 2014).

6.5 Urban Segmentation and Market Integration

6.5.1 Labour Market Segmentations

Another manifestation of dual society segmentation in cities is the various segmentations or discriminations seen in the labour market. As Knight and Yueh (2004) pointed out, job stability is worse for non-local people than urban locals, and their job turnover is approximately six times higher than that of urban locals. Even if only the urban locals who entered the labour market after the 'iron rice bowl' system was smashed are taken into consideration, job turnover for non-locals is still twice that of urban locals. Knight and Yueh also discovered that compared with urban locals, job changes for non-locals are more voluntary. Moreover, education and job experience both increase job turnover, as an increase in human capital indeed provides more employment opportunities for non-locals (Knight and Yueh 2004). However, the authors believe that it is hard to view the higher proportion of voluntary job changes for non-locals as evidence of any advantage they hold in the labour market. One explanation for this finding is that urban locals do not want to give up a job they are satisfied with, unless enterprise reforms cause them to face unemployment. A study by Zhang (2010) on the job turnover of Beijing, Wuxi, and Zhuhai discovered that institutional discrimination reduces the job options of non-locals, increasing their costs of job hunting and unemployment. Further, compared with urban locals and the mobile population that has been long-term urban residents, temporary migrants tend to work longer in a firm and experience shorter unemployment. We should not view this as evidence of any advantage enjoyed by temporary urban residents—it is the non-locals who have just arrived in an unfamiliar environment having to accept work even if the working conditions are bad that is probably the cause. Indeed, Zhang's (2010) study discovered that non-locals will switch jobs more often once they have accumulated enough assets after being in the city for a while.

Of course, migrant workers from rural areas are at a disadvantage even before entering the urban labour market. Démurger et al.'s (2009) decomposition of the annual income disparity between urban residents and non-locals who have been employed in the city for a long time shows that the population effect before entering the labour market was the most important and robust factor in explaining the income disparity between the two groups. Although this study argues that the source of urban–rural worker income gaps is mainly due to disparities in aspects such as education opportunities before entering the labour market, we cannot deny that such human resource endowment disparity before entering the labour market is also a result of urban–rural segmentation, which we will discuss in more detail in Section 6.5.2.

More studies stress the discrimination non-local workers face in the cities. For example, Cai et al.'s (2003) study discovered that there exists discrimination in the labour market caused by differences in urban and rural identities. Specifically, in the income disparity between rural migrant labour and urban local labour, only 24 per cent is explained by the variation in personal characteristics and the remaining 76 per cent is explained by discrimination. This implies that under the current system, increasing migrant workers' level of education cannot fully eliminate the income disparity between rural migrants and urban residents. On the contrary, due to the existence of segmentation in the labour market, the gap between labour with local Hukous and labour without local Hukous may continue to expand. Beginning in the mid-1990s, over the next ten years when rural labour began to work in cities on a massive scale, wages for migrant workers in a few relatively developed regions did not change much, but within cities, from 1994 to 2004, the average urban employee's real average salary rose from RMB 4,538 to RMB 11,902 (1994 prices).[13] Meng and Bai (2007) employed payroll data from seven Guangdong enterprises between 2000 and 2004 and discovered that the gap between the wage for migrant workers and Guangdong province's average employee wage kept increasing, and during this period migrant workers' wages did not see a significant gain. Yan (2007) employed data from four major surveys in Shanghai to discover that during 1995 and 2003, the pace at which the rate of return on human capital increased differed for non-local labour and local residents, and the gap between the two is likely to continue increasing. Zhang and Meng (2007) compared data from 1999 and 2002 and showed that the income gap between rural migrant workers and urban residents is increasing, and that this is mainly caused by the relative decline in the educational return of migrant workers. These studies all illustrate the fact that increase in the income gap between workers with different Hukou identities within a city is not just due to the gap in human capital; it is also, to a certain extent, related to the increase in the gap between returns on human capital. Cai and Du (2011) argue that there is some evidence indicating wage convergence between local and migrant workers based on a comparison between wage growth rage of local and migrant workers. However, as figure 2 in their paper shows, only migrant workers at the bottom of the wage distribution have experienced faster wage growth, while migrant

[13] Data are from *China Statistical Yearbook* (NSBC 2005).

workers at the top of the wage distribution have much lower wage growth than local workers. We would rather read this as the result of pro-agriculture policies, which increased the reservation wage of low-income migrant workers, rather than evidence of wage convergence.

Other than income gaps and gaps between the returns on human capital, there also exists dual segmentation in professions, jobs, and industries in the PRC's urban labour market. Labour market segmentation abroad is often related to factors such as sex, race, and union membership (Ashenfelter 1997; Altonji and Blank 1999), while dual segmentation in the PRC's labour market is connected to Hukou. Meng and Zhang's (2001) study found that significant disparities in professional status and income levels exist between non-locals and urban residents, and these disparities mostly cannot be explained by the differences in productivity of the two types of labour. Employing data from the fifth population census as well as survey data from five cities, Wang's (2005) study classified jobs for urban residents and non-locals into five categories: 'self-employed', 'public sector worker', 'public sector administrative and technical personnel', 'non-public sector worker', and 'non-public sector administrative and technical personnel'. The results of relevant empirical studies show that of the income gap between non-local labour and urban local labour, 59 per cent is caused by the income disparity between different jobs and 41 per cent is caused by the income disparity within the type of job. However, 43 per cent of income disparity is caused by unexplainable factors such as discrimination. This reflects that non-locals enter into jobs that are relatively low paid.

6.5.2 Social Segmentation

Due to the dual society segmentation within cities, establishing new urban–rural integrated social networks for migrant workers may be difficult, and this may even result in mutual distrust between urban and rural residents. Generally, migrant workers use kinship or geographical connections to choose their destination and obtain information regarding employment. Such a social network formed in the countryside is brought to the city and the individual ability of migrant workers to withstand risk is increased through mutual help. In comparison, the existence of the Hukou system often prevents social organizations, social activities, and social services of urban communities from sufficiently serving migrant workers. Trade unions do not cover migrant workers either. This causes the urban social capital of migrant workers to be limited to the migrant worker community, and no integration between urban residents and migrant workers is generated in terms of social capital.

The dual society segmentation in cities also fosters distrust among migrant workers towards urban residents and the municipal government, increasing the difficulty of city administration and implementation of public policy, creating immense social losses. Wang et al. (2009) analysed the determinants of resident trust based on survey data from the Shanghai community with an emphasis on the impact of Hukou identity. The study found that, all other conditions being equal, residents without a local Hukou are more distrustful of their neighbours in the community and most people in society, and their trust in the government is even lower. Moreover, Hukou segmentation's negative impact on trust levels will not decline or disappear with the non-local Hukou residents' increase in income or educational level. That is to say, enabling non-locals with relatively higher educational levels and technical skills to work in the cities is unlikely to resolve the problem of social discord that may emerge in cities. Even if non-locals can obtain higher incomes than local residents, if they are not given the same treatment as urban residents, they will still have a significantly lower trust level than urban locals with the same characteristics.

But the impact of Hukou on urban harmonious development does not end there. Employing Chinese provincial-level panel data, Chen's (2010) study discovered that after controlling for the level of urbanization including migrants that insignificantly impacts crime, non-locals without Hukou significantly increase crime rates. In other words, without the distinction between locals and non-locals caused by Hukou, the level of urbanization itself does not significantly impact crime rates. This implies that abolishing Hukou's dual segmentation is also critical to urban harmony and stability from the perspective of crime prevention. Moreover, studies on individual satisfaction also found that non-local Hukou has a significant negative impact on individual satisfaction (Chen et al. 2011; He and Pan 2010). The dissatisfaction of the non-urban Hukou population mainly comes from income and education gaps between people with different Hukou identities. It is worth stressing that the income gap between people with different Hukou identities also has a negative impact on the satisfaction of urban residents with an advantaged status. The explanation is that if identity-induced income gaps lead to problems such as conflict or crime, it will generate negative impacts on urban Hukou residents as well (Jiang et al. 2012).

6.5.3 Residential Segregation

In terms of residential space, the dual society segmentation in cities is strongly reflected in the existence of the so-called 'urban villages'. The 'urban village' itself is a product of the urban–rural segmentation system. Due to the difference between land institutions in the countryside and the city, when rapid urbanization produces large amounts of urban land through changing land usage from agricultural to non-agricultural, such land begins to surround what used to be villages. While urban villages have become 'urban', they are still under the management of their former rural collective land institutions. Dirty and messy urban villages with densely packed, though cheap, housing naturally becomes the residential area of low-income migrant workers. Thus, residential segregation between people with or without local urban Hukou is strikingly evident. Even without urban villages, residential segregation of people with different Hukou in cities still exists. Since most migrant workers belong to the low-income group in cities, their residential location is often clustered on the margins of the urban area and low-cost communities in the urban area where the environment is poor and the density of buildings high. In time, residential segregation within a city will naturally intensify. Under such residential segregation, in low-income communities, the interaction between residents can cause various social problems such as unemployment, poverty, and crime, generating great difficulties for the city's administration. Such residential segregation has economic and socio-psychological reasons. The economic reason is that the high price of housing and services in high-class communities has a squeezing effect on low-income individuals, which means the average person cannot enter this market. Among the various amenities surrounding high-class communities, the most important are quality and expensive schools, hospitals, and public security, and only high-income individuals can bear the corresponding high costs. As for the socio-psychological aspect, residence in high-class communities gives people a superior feeling and usually results in more favourable social networks. In Chinese urban development, the higher the positioning of a community, the more a developer tends to choose locations where the environment is good and high-income individuals are clustered. Meanwhile, the high price of housing forces low-income individuals to migrate towards the margins of the urban area or the suburbs, and the rapid development of the property market accelerates the formation of residential segregation. In Shanghai, empirical analysis has shown that there exists significant residential segregation between people with and without local Hukou (Chen et al. 2012; Chen and Hao 2014).

6.6 Conclusion and Policy Recommendations

Urbanization results from rural–urban migration. Based on various empirical studies on the determinants of migration, we can conclude that migration is not only a personal decision but also a joint decision within households to send members with comparative advantages in manufacturing and services, usually male and young, to work in cities. In the PRC, the coastal regions where manufacturing and services are better developed, especially big cities, are the major destinations of migration. The aspiration for higher incomes and better job opportunities is the major force that drives migration, while public services and urban amenities also partly account for population flows.

However, in the PRC there are still major institutional barriers—especially the Hukou system and related segmentation in the urban labour market, social security, and public services access—that hinder rural–urban and interregional migration. Facing the challenges of fast urbanization, and growing urban diseases, local governments still rely on the current system to control the population flow into the big cities, especially the megacities. Contrary to the view of the government that migration has generated these social problems in cities, we argue that the problems are largely a result of the current discriminative policies rather than urban population growth in itself. As other chapters argue, even if urban population growth is partly the cause of urban diseases, technological progress and management need to be improved to deal with these diseases. Controlling population growth by discriminative policies will only lead to more social problems rather than decrease them, as existing studies have shown. Chinese policymakers should be fully aware of the negative effects of the current policies that are against market forces, and will lead to both inefficiency and unfairness. We suggest that it is time to reconsider the way to achieve an efficient and harmonious urbanization path by shifting to more pro-market policies and reducing the migration costs embedded in the institutional constraints.

Appendix

Table A.6.1. The effects of city characteristics on labour migration

City characteristics	Model 1	Model 2	Model 3	Model 4 (standardized)
Basic education	0.414***	0.237***	0.110***	0.116***
	(0.00748)	(0.00843)	(0.00955)	(0.0101)
Medical services	0.362***	0.0131***	0.0820***	0.118***
	(0.00135)	(0.00389)	(0.00901)	(0.0130)
Wage		0.000105***	0.0000335***	0.151***
		(0.00000157)	(0.00000193)	(0.00866)
Unemployment rate		−7.181***	−2.687***	−0.137***
		(0.200)	(0.207)	(0.0105)
Fixed asset investment ratio		−0.540***	1.137***	0.156***
		(0.0524)	(0.0617)	(0.00850)
Industrial structure		−0.742***	−1.746***	−0.514***
		(0.0239)	(0.0330)	(0.00972)
Distance to nearest seaport		−0.00180***	−0.00411***	−1.630***
		(0.0000643)	(0.0000709)	(0.0281)
Distance to regional large city		−0.00234***	−0.000866***	−0.207***
		(0.0000759)	(0.0000764)	(0.0182)
Scale of population			0.00295***	0.885***
			(0.0000422)	(0.0127)

Average educational years			0.629***	0.474***
			(0.0158)	(0.0119)
House price			0.0000815***	0.0703***
			(0.0000135)	(0.0117)
Distance to Hukou city			–0.407***	–1.343***
			(0.0240)	(0.00731)
Outside province			–0.00225***	–1.435***
			(0.0000123)	(0.0156)
Capital of province (yes = 1)			–1.435***	–0.407***
			(0.0156)	(0.0240)
Province fixed effect	Yes	Yes	Yes	Yes
Chi2	358,831.4	370,373.1	465,278.7	465,278.7
Pseudo R2	0.3288	0.3393	0.4263	0.4263
Observations	22,260,260	22,260,260	22,260,260	22,260,260
Number of cities	220	220	220	220
Number of individuals	101,183	101,183	101,183	101,183

Note: ***, **, and * represent coefficients significant at the level of 1 per cent, 5 per cent, and 10 per cent. Basic education refers to primary school teachers per student and middle-school teachers per student. Medical services refer to hospitals per capita, hospital beds per capita, and doctors per capita. These two variables are constructed using a principal component analysis. Fixed asset investment ratio refers to the ratio of the value of fixed asset investment to GDP. Industry structure refers to the ratio of the production value of the tertiary industry to that of the secondary industry. Distance to nearest seaport means a city's nearest distance to Hong Kong, PRC; Shanghai; or Tianjin—the major seaports in the PRC. Distance to regional large city measures a city's distance to the nearest regional large city among the fourteen cities that had a population of more than four million permanent residents. Distance to Hukou city refers to the distance of the destination city from the city in which the migrant holds Hukou. Outside province means the destination city does not belong to the migrant's original province. The estimation method is the conditional logit model. Model 4 is based on standardized data using the standard deviation of each variable.

References

In English

Altonji, Joseph G. and Rebecca Blank. 1999. 'Race and Gender in the Labor Market'. In *Handbook of Labor Economics*, edited by Orley Ashenfelter and David Card , vol. 3C, Elsevier Science (North-Holland).

Ashenfelter, Orley. 1997. 'Union Relative Wage Effects: New Evidence and a Survey of their Implications for Wage Inflation'. In *The Collected Essays of Orley Ashenfelter* (vol. 1) *Employment, Labor Unions and Wages*, edited by Kevin F. Hallock, Edward Elgar.

Cai, Fang and Yang Du. 2011. 'Wage Increases, Wage Convergence, and the Lewis Turning Point in China'. *China Economic Review 22*: 601–10.

Chan, Kam Wing and Li Zhang. 1999. 'The Hukou System and Rural–Urban Migration in China: Processes and Changes'. *The China Quarterly 160*: 818–55.

Chen, Zhao, Shiqing Jiang, Ming Lu, and Hiroshi Sato. 2014. 'Escaping Low-Level Equilibrium of Urbanization: Institutional Promotion, Social Interaction and Labor Migration'. *China Economist 9* (1): 68–85.

Démurger, Sylvie, Marc Gurgand, Shi Li, and Ximing Yue. 2009. 'Migrants as Second-Class Workers in Urban China? A Decomposition Analysis'. *Journal of Comparative Economics 37* (4): 610–28.

Dustmann, Christian and Josep Mestres. 2010. 'Remittances and Temporary Migration'. *Journal of Development Economics* 92 (1): 62–70.

Gao, Hong, Ming Lu, and Hiroshi Sato. 2015. 'Inclusive Urban Employment: How Does City Scale Affect Job Opportunities for Different People?' *Asian Economic Papers 14* (2): 98–128.

Jiang, Shiqing, Ming Lu, and Hiroshi Sato. 2012. 'Identity, Inequality, and Happiness: Evidence from Urban China'. *World Development 40* (6): 1190–200.

Knight, John and Linda Yueh. 2004. 'Job Mobility of Residents and Migrants in Urban China'. *Journal of Comparative Economics* 32: 637–60.

Meng, Lei. 2010. 'Can Grain Subsidy Impede Rural–Urban Migration in Hinterland China? Evidence from Field Surveys'. Paper presented at 2010 International Workshop on Employment Dynamics and Social Security, Fudan University in Shanghai, 12–14 June.

Meng, Xin and Junsen Zhang. 2001. 'The Two-Tier Labor Market in Urban China Occupational Segregation and Wage Differentials between Urban Residents and Rural Migrants in Shanghai'. *Journal of Comparative Economics 29*: 485–504.

Meng, Xin and Nansheng Bai. 2007. 'How Much Have the Wages of Unskilled Workers in China Increased: Data from Seven Factories in Guangdong'. In *China: Linking Markets for Growth*, edited by Ross Garnaut and Ligang Song, Asia Pacific Press.

Stark, Oded and David Bloom. 1985. 'The New Economics of Labor Migration'. *American Economic Review 75* (2): 173–8.

Wang, Feng and Xuejin Zuo. 1999. 'Inside China's Cities: Institutional Barriers and Opportunities for Urban Migrants'. *American Economic Review 89* (2): 276–80.

Zhang, Dandan and Xin Meng. 2007. 'Assimilation or Disassimilation? The Labour Market Performance of Rural Migrants in Chinese Cities'. Paper presented at the 6th conference on Chinese economy, CERDI-IDREC, Clermont-Ferrand, France, 18–19 October.

Zhang, Huafeng. 2010. 'The Hukou System's Constraints on Migrant Workers' Job Mobility in Chinese Cities'. *China Economic Review* 21: 51–64.

Zhao, Yaohui. 1999a. 'Leaving the Countryside: Rural-to-Urban Migration Decisions in China'. *American Economic Review 89* (2): 281–6.

Zhao, Yaohui. 1999b. 'Labor Migration and Earnings Differences: The Case of China'. *Economic Development and Cultural Change 47*: 767–82.

Zhao, Yaohui. 2003. 'The Role of Migrant Networks in Labor Migration: The Case of China'. *Contemporary Economic Policy 21* (4): 500–11.

Zhu, Nong. 2002. 'The Impact of Income Gaps on Migration Decisions in China: A Verification of the Todaro Model'. *China Economic Review 13* (2–3): 213–30.

In Chinese

Bai, Nansheng and Jing Li. 2008. 'The Study on Migrant Workers' Job Mobility'. *Management World 7*: 70–6.

Cai, Fang, Yang Du, and Meiyan Wang. 2001. 'Household Registration System and Labor Market Protection'. *Economic Research Journal* 12: 41–9.

Cai, Fang, Yang Du, Meiyan Wang. 2003. 'Research Review of Rural Labor Migration in China'. The appendix to *The Political Economy of Labor Migration*, Shanghai Sanlian Press, Shanghai People's Publishing House.

Chen, Binkai, Ming Lu, and Ninghua Zhong. 2010. 'Household Consumption Constrained by Hukou System'. *Economic Research Journal S1*: 62–71.

Chen, Jie and Qianjing Hao. 2014. 'Residential Segregation under Rapid Urbanization in China: Evidence from Shanghai'. *Academic Monthly 5*: 17–28.

Chen, Zhao, Ming Lu, and Jingmin Chen. 2012. 'Hukou and Residential Segmentation: A New Challenge to Public Management in Urban China'. *Fudan Journal (Philosophy and Social Sciences) 5*: 77–86.

Chen, Zhao, Tong Xu, and Xiaofeng Liu. 2011. 'Hukou Identity, Urban Labor Market Segmentation and Citizens' Subjective Well-being: Micro-Evidence from Communities of Shanghai'. *World Economy 4*: 79–101.

Du, Yang. 2001. 'Risk Diversification and Supply of Non-agricultural Labor: Empirical Evidence from Countries of Poor Region'. *Quantitative & Technical Economics 1*: 46–50.

Du, Yang and Albert Park. 2003. 'Migration and Poverty Reduction: Empirical Evidence from Farmer Survey'. *Chinese Journal of Population Science 4*: 56–62.

Duan, Chengrong. 2001. 'Analysis on the Factors of Inter-provincial Migration Destinations Choice'. *Population Research 1*: 56–61.

Duan, Chengrong, Lidan Lv, and Xiangjiang Zou. 2013b. 'Major Challenges for China's Floating Population and Policy Suggestions: An Analysis of the 2010 Population Census Data'. *Population Research 37* (2): 17–24.

Duan, Chengrong and Ge Yang. 2009. 'Trends in Destination Distribution of Floating Population in China'. *Population Research 33* (6): 1–12.

Duan, Chengrong, Ge Yang, Fei Zhang, and Xuehe Lu. 2008. 'Nine Trends of China's Population Flow Since the Reform and Opening-up'. *Population Research 32* (6): 30–43.

Duan, Chengrong, Yan Yuan, and Jing Guo. 2013a. 'The Latest Features of China's Floating Population'. *Northwest Population 34* (6): 1–12.

Duan, Chengrong, Fulin Zhou, and Ge Yang. 2009. 'The Study on the Status of China's Left-behind Women'. <http://www.china.com.cn/news/zhuanti/fnbg/2009-05/07/content_17738716.htm>.

Fu, Ping, Youcai Tang, and Lihua Jiang. 2012. 'Migrants Workers' Occupational Segregation and Upward Mobility'. *Chinese Journal of Population Science* 6: 75–82.

Gao, Hong. 2014. 'City Population and Individual Income'. *World Economy*, forthcoming.

He, Lixin and Chunyang Pan. 2010. 'Explaining China's "Easterlin Paradox": Income Difference, Opportunity Inequality and Citizens' Subjective Well-being'. *Management World* 8: 11–22.

Hu, Feng and Wang Qiwen. 2007. 'An Analysis of Determinants of Remittances of China's Rural Migrants: An Application of Interval Regression Model'. *Statistical Research* 10: 20–5.

Huang, Ping, ed. 1997. *In Search for Survival: A Sociological Study of Rural-urban Migration*, The People's Press of Yunnan.

Li, Chunling. 2006. 'Noninstitutional Paths of Migrants' Status Attainment: Migrant Labors and Non-migrant Labors Comparison'. *Sociological Research* 5: 85–106.

Li, Qiang. 1999. 'Migrant Workers' Occupation Flow in Urban Areas of Mainland China'. *Sociological Research* 3: 93–101.

Li, Qiang. 2001. 'Analysis of the Remittance of the Out-Migrant Workers in China'. *Sociological Research* 4: 64–76.

Li, Shi. 1997a. 'China's Rural Labor Flow and Income Distribution Research Report'. Manuscript, Center for China Studies, Washington, DC.

Li, Shi. 1997b. 'The Model of Labor Mobility in China Economic Transition'. *Economic Research Journal* 1: 23–30.

Li, Shi. 1999. 'Rural Labor Mobility and the Growth and Distribution of Income in China'. *Social Sciences in China* 2: 16–33.

Liu, Chuanjiang and Jianlin Cheng. 2008. 'The Second-generation Rural Migrants Acquiring Citizenship: Analysis of Current Situation and Measure of Progress'. *Population Research* 32 (5): 48–57.

Liu, Xuejun and Yaohui Zhao. 2009. 'The Impact of Labor Migration on Urban Labor Markets in China'. *China Economic Quarterly* 2: 693–710.

Ma, Hongqi and Zhongchang Chen. 2012. 'Patterns of Inter-provincial Migration in China: Evidence from the Sixth Population Census'. *Population Research* 6: 87–99.

Ma, Zhongdong, Weimin Zhang, Zai Liang, and Hongyan Cui. 2004. 'Labour Migration as a New Determinant of Income Growth in Rural China'. *Population Research* 3: 2–10.

National Women's Federation Research Group. 2013. 'Report on the Status of Migrant Children in Urban and Rural Left-behind Children in China'. *Chinese Women's Movement* 6: 30–4.

NBSC (National Bureau of Statistics of China). 2005. *China Statistical Yearbook*, China Statistical Press.

NBSC (National Bureau of Statistics of China). 2012. *China Statistical Yearbook*, China Statistical Press.

NBSC (National Bureau of Statistics of China). 2013. *The Statistical Report of National Economic and Social Development of People's Republic of China in. 2012*. <http://www.stats.gov.cn/tjsj/tjgb/ndtjgb/qgndtjgb/201302/t20130221_30027.html>.

Qiao, Mingrui, Xueya Qian, and Xianguo Yao. 2009. 'Labor Market Segmentation, Hukou and Urban–Rural Difference in Employment'. *Chinese Journal of Population Science 1*: 32–41.

Sheng, Laiyun. 2008. *Flow or Migration: Economic Analysis of the Progress of Rural Labor Mobility*, Shanghai Yuandong Publishing House.

Sun, Ziduo. 2004. 'The Effect of Farmers' Cross-provincial Work on Regional Economic Development'. *Chinese Rural Economy 3*: 28–33.

Wang, Guixin and Jianbo Liu. 2007. 'Inter-provincial Migrations to Yangtze River Delta and Pearl River Delta'. *Chinese Journal of Population Science 2*: 87–94.

Wang, Guixin, Zehao Pan, and Yanqiu Lu. 2012. 'The Changes and Determinants of China's Inter-provincial Migration'. *Chinese Journal of Population Science 5*: 2–13.

Wang, Guixin. 1996. 'Population Migration and Region Economic Development in China'. *Population Research 6*: 9–16.

Wang, Hui, Zhao Chen, and Ming Lu. 2009. 'Hukou, Social Segmentation and Trust: Empirical Evidence from Shanghai'. *World Economy 10*: 81–96.

Wang, Meiyan. 2005. 'Employment Opportunities and Wage Gaps in the Urban Labor Market: A Study of the Employment and Wages of Migrant Laborer'. *Social Science in China 5*: 36–46.

Wu, Kaiya, Li Zhang, and Xiao Chen. 2010. 'The Barrier of Hukou Reform: An Analysis of the Qualifications for the Urban Hukou'. *Chinese Journal of Population Science 1*: 66–74.

Wu, Yushao. 2013. *China Report of the Development on Aging Cause. 2013*, Social Science Academic Press.

Xia, Yiran and Ming Lu. 2015. 'Migrations across Cities——Empirical Study on the Effects of Public Service on Labor Flow'. *Management World 5*: 78–90.

Xia, Yiran, Jinhong Su and Wei, Huang. 2015. 'Where Floating Population Go? The Characteristics and the Changes of Destination Cities'. *Population & Economics 3*: 13–22.

Xia, Yiran. 2014. 'The Difference of Return to Human Capital within Occupations and Migrant Workers' Inclination of Occupational Mobility'. Working paper.

Xiao, Qunying and Huijun Liu. 2007. 'Retesting Dynamical Factor Theories on Inter-provincial Labor Migration with QAP Algorithm'. *Chinese Journal of Population Science 4*: 26–33.

Yan, Shanping. 2007. 'Human Capital, Systems and Differences in Wages: A Case Study on the Dual Labor-Markets in Large Cities'. *Management World 6*: 4–13.

Yao, Xianguo and Puqing Lai. 2004. 'Urban–Rural Hukou Differentials in Chinese Labor Relation'. *Economic Research Journal 7*: 82–90.

Zhang, Zhanxin, Wenshu Gao, and Huili Hou. 2007. 'Urban–Rural Divide, Regional Segmentation and Insufficient Access of Urban Floating Population to Social Security: Evidence from Shanghai and Other Four Chinese Cities'. *Chinese Journal of Population Science* 6: 33–41.

Zhao, Yaohui. 1997. 'China's Rural Labor Flow and the Role of Education: Research Based on the Sichuan Province'. *Economic Research Journal* 2: 37–42.

Zhou, Jingxiang and Yan He. 2009. 'An Empirical Test of Rural Labor Force Employment in Cites and China's Regional Economic Growth: Ownership Transformation among China's Provinces (1990–2006)'. *World Economic Papers* 1: 33–49.

Zhu, Nong and Zhaojun Zeng. 2004. 'The Impacts of Openness on Regional Disparity and Inter-provincial Migratory Flow in China'. *Market and Demographic Analysis* 5: 5–12.

7

Rural-to-Urban Migration and the Urban Labour Market: the Case of India

Arup Mitra

7.1 Migration and Urban Growth

Rural-to-urban movement of a population is an indispensable part of the development process. In the initial stages, as urban–rural development disparities grow, rural residents migrate to urban areas for a variety of reasons, which have been identified in the literature as push–pull factors. Seeking sources of livelihood, better employment opportunities, schooling for children, and remittance to rural relatives, and overcoming rural indebtedness and poverty, are some of the factors which have drawn a great deal of attention in the literature, explaining migration. Also, rural migrants provide an important source of labour to urban areas. In the background to these views and in comparison to the historical experience of the present-day developed countries, India, however, has witnessed sluggish rates of population flow from rural to urban areas, though large/metropolitan cities are an exception. The democratic setup in India allows free flow of population across regions, yet there are a variety of factors that tend to hinder migration, particularly that of the low-income households. Social, cultural, and linguistic barriers are enormous for rural migrants, especially those who originate from states other than the state of destination (i.e. interstate migrants). There is no labour market discrimination as such against migrants in terms of regulations, but the city-spaces in general are shrinking for the low-income households, especially the migrants of rural origin. Even an entry to slums is constrained by a variety of economic and political factors. In some of the large cities, access to space inside a slum cluster is determined by the contacts that the potential migrants have with those who have already migrated. Besides, migrants are required to pay rent to the local muscle-men/slum lords/members of mafia groups (Edelman and Mitra 2006). On the whole, these factors tend to reduce the propensity to migrate. Availability of public services and educational facilities in urban areas can be a driving factor of migration, but in the case of low-income households, this does not have any major impact primarily because they are aware that the slums, characterized by a severe shortage of basic amenities, are their final destination (Mitra 2013). More importantly, job accessibility is their prime concern. But India's urbanization not being prompted by rapid industrialization, and urban

Arup Mitra., *Rural-to-Urban Migration and the Urban Labour Market* In: *Cities of Dragons and Elephants: Urbanization and Urban Development in China and India. Edited by:* Guanghua Wan and Ming Lu, Oxford University Press (2019). © Oxford University Press. DOI: 10.1093/oso/9780198829225.003.0007

areas are less likely to offer productive employment opportunities to the unskilled and semi-skilled variety of workforce. Though an individual merely on the basis of their migration status is not segregated in the cities, their absorption in petty and marginal activities unravels seclusion and vulnerability. In certain instances migration takes place in search of even a low-productivity job in the urban informal sector in order to escape the severity of poverty at the place of rural origin. On the other hand, as Banerjee (1986) pointed out, many among the rural poor cannot afford to migrate as the social and economic costs of migration are enormous:

> The constraints faced by migrants are many—lack of formal residency rights; lack of identity proof; lack of political representation; inadequate housing; low-paid, insecure or hazardous work; extreme vulnerability of women and children to trafficking and sexual exploitation; exclusion from state-provided services such as health and education and discrimination based on ethnicity, religion, class or gender. In the absence of proofs of identity and residence, internal migrants are unable to claim social protection entitlements and remain excluded from government sponsored schemes and programmes. Children face disruption of regular schooling, adversely affecting their human capital formation and contributing to the intergenerational transmission of poverty. Further, migrants are negatively portrayed as a 'burden' to society, discouraged from settling down and excluded from urban planning initiatives. Most internal migrants are denied basic rights, yet internal migration is given very low priority by the government in policy and practice, partly due to a serious knowledge gap on its extent, nature and magnitude. (UNESCO 2013)

The level of urbanization in the Indian context, unlike the experience of several countries at comparable levels of per capita income and growth, has been quite low. It increased sluggishly from 17.29 per cent in 1951 to 27.76 per cent in 2001 and 31.16 per cent in 2011 (Table 7.1). However, the rate of growth of the urban

Table 7.1. Urbanization level and urban growth

Year	% urban	No. of cities or towns	Rate of growth of pop. in urban areas	Rate of growth of pop. in all areas
1951	17.29	3,035		
1961	17.97	2,657	2.37	1.97
1971	19.91	3,081	3.29	2.24
1981	23.34	3,981	3.87	2.23
1991	25.70	4,615	3.16	2.16
2001	27.79	5,161	2.75	1.97
2011	31.16	7,935	2.7	1.62

Note: 1981 and 1991 figures include interpolated population estimates for Assam and Jammu and Kashmir respectively.

Source: Census of India, 2001, 2011.

population has been quite high, notwithstanding a nominal increase in the percentage of the population living in urban areas (see Table 5.8 in Chapter 5). Demographers are quite concerned about this high rate of growth of the urban population, as it tends to create significant pressure on the infrastructure base. The number of cities and towns has also gone up considerably over the years, particularly over the last decade: from 5,161 in 2001 to 7,935 in 2011.

7.2 Different Components of Urban Growth

The change in urban population can be broken down in terms of the following factors: natural growth of population, rural-to-urban migration, and reclassification of rural areas as urban over time. As the decline in the mortality rate has been faster than that in the fertility rate the natural growth of the population in urban areas is seen to be high, which raises the long-run supply of labour substantially. In the Indian case, although the urban birth and death rates were found to be much lower than their rural counterparts for the periods 1971–80 and 1981–9, the urban rates of natural increase were only marginally lower than the rural rates (Mitra 1994). As can be seen from Table 5.8 in Chapter 5, much of the urban growth is attributed to a natural growth of the population. Even during 1991–2001, natural growth contributed to urban growth significantly, though over time this component has shown signs of decline. Around one-fifth of urban population growth is due to rural-to-urban net migration. There was a continuous rise in the contribution of net migration to total urban growth since the 1960s, though between 1991 and 2001 there was a slight decline in the rate compared to the earlier period (refer to Table 5.8 by Mathur on city-size distributions in this volume).

According to the 2011 census, as Bhagat (2011) points out, the increase in urbanization has been faster than expected. In fact since independence this is the first time that the absolute increase in the urban population is seen to be higher than the absolute increase in the rural population. The contribution made by net rural–urban classification and rural–urban migration increased from a little above 40 per cent during the 1990s to 56 per cent during 2001–11. Though the available data from the 2011 census at the moment do not allow for the separation of these two factors, according to Mathur (Chapter 5 in this volume), the contribution of rural–urban net migration to urban growth is around 22.2 per cent (provisional). Also, we saw the emergence of a large number of new towns in 2011 (Bhagat 2011). The number of towns increased from 5,161 to 7,935 over 2001–11, and among the new towns (2,774 in number), 2,532 were census towns and 242 statutory towns.[1] Given the larger contribution made by the reclassification of

[1] The number of non-statutory census towns was 1,362 comprising 21 million people in 2001. In 2011 the corresponding figures were 3,892 and 58.6 million, respectively. This growth of 37.6 million people amounts to 41 per cent of the total growth of urban population in the decade, 2001–11.

areas in the decade 2001–11 compared to the previous one, 1991–2001, it may be safe to infer that net migration has at least not declined, if not increased. It is usually believed that due to a large component of urban growth resulting from natural increase, the contribution made by the rural-to-urban migration flow tends to get suppressed. Even if we account for this fact, the rural-to-urban migration rates in India are still low. Nearly 50 per cent of the workforce is still engaged in the agriculture sector, though the value-added share of this sector has subsided to almost one-fifth. The only exceptions are some of the large cities that have witnessed rapid migration flows (Sundaram 1986).

7.3 Factors Influencing Migration

In this section, we review some of the studies in order to bring out the factors that explain migration from rural areas.

Rural-to-urban migration, which is a response to diverse economic opportunities across geographical areas, has played a significant role in the urbanization process of several countries (Lall et al. 2006). Two important hypotheses have been put forth to explain rapid city growth in developing countries (Williamson 1988): (1) rapid population growth deteriorating the land–man ratio and pushing landless labour into the urban space, and (2) migrants being pulled by economic factors such as a fall in agriculture prices, the import of technology from developed countries favouring urban industries in developing countries, foreign capital flows into urban infrastructure, housing, power, transportation, and large-scale manufacturing.

In India, many of the urban problems are at times attributed to rural spills, i.e. there are considerable overlaps among urban slums, informal sector employment, and rural–urban population mobility. In the face of a high natural growth of population, rural–urban migration is believed to aggravate the situation of excess supply of labour in urban areas. Within the urban informal sector, this tends to reduce the level of earnings and gets manifested in a high incidence of urban poverty. Thus, rural poverty gets transformed into urban poverty—a phenomenon described as 'urbanization of poverty'.[2] But these views seem to be exaggerated. As Mitra (1994) observed, the elasticity of urban poverty with respect to rural poverty, defined as the proportionate rise in the incidence of urban poverty due to a proportionate rise in rural poverty, was highly negligible. Though the

[2] For details see Harris and Todaro (1970) and Ravallion and Datt (2002). Todaro (1969) treats the informal sector as a transitory phenomenon, but in reality it has emerged as a persistent one. Mitra (1994) argued that natural growth of the population maintained the urban supplies of labour at a high level, resulting in informal sector employment and poverty as a persistent phenomenon.

elasticity was positive, indicating a positive association between rural and urban poverty, many among the urban poor have actually been residing in urban areas for a long time and cannot be interpreted as fresh migrants from rural areas. Hence, urban poverty cannot be interpreted as a spillover of rural poverty.

In explaining migration from rural to urban areas income differentials are taken as an important determinant mobilizing people from low-income areas to relatively high-income areas (Harris and Todaro 1970). In rural areas, sluggish agricultural growth and limited development of the rural non-farm sector raises the incidence of rural poverty, unemployment, and underemployment. Given the fact that most of the high-productivity activities are located in urban areas, the rural–urban income differentials, particularly for the poor and unemployed, are enormous. Thus, many of them are believed to migrate to urban areas in search of jobs. However, this is not empirically true as the cost of migration seems to be very high for the poor (Banerjee 1986). Besides, jobs in high-productivity activities are limited in number relative to the supply, and often they are not accessible. This information is not unknown to the individuals who are in the process of taking a decision to migrate. However, this does not rule out the possibility that some of the poor may still flow to urban areas in search of opportunities even in the 'informal sector'.

The paper by Lall et al. (2006) reviewed the literature on migration and synthesized the factors which explain this process of population movement. Some of the questions around which they summarize the findings relate to how internal migrants behave at different stages of the migration process, how migrants prepare for migration, how they migrate, what are the difficulties they face on arriving in urban areas and what links they maintain with rural areas. In an excellent study by de Hann (1994), migration issues in the Indian context are discussed extensively. While economic opportunities play a key role in labour migration, there are varied motivations pertaining to migration, including not only conditions at the place of origin and destination but also patterns of recruitment and migration networks (de Hann 2011). The forced nature of migration has been brought out in the context of western India (Breman 1985). Forced migration refers to displacement of individuals and households due to conflicts, destitution and impoverishment, natural or environmental disasters, chemical or nuclear disasters, famine, or development projects. It is a complex, wide-ranging, and pervasive phenomenon. Though internal migration from poorer areas signifies a form of safety valve, there are many costs of migration which the data on remittances tend to neglect (de Hann 2011). Costs of migration include not only the transportation and resettlement costs at the place of destination but also several social costs such as social exclusion, deprivation from familial bonding and the benefits associated with such bonding, and a variety of harassments that low-income migrants face from labour contractors, slum lords, and city residents

(Mitra 2013). Though there is no city legislation to stop migration legally, these factors tend to discourage the inflow of low-income households to cities.[3]

The literature on migration is based on both field surveys and secondary data. For the sake of comparison non-migrants have also been considered (Mitra and Murayama 2009).

Kundu and Mohanan (2009) argue that migration for employment from rural to urban areas facilitates poverty alleviation, though such opportunities are gradually shrinking. The job prospects are definitely better for the migrants in large cities than those in small towns. But these possibilities are closing down for the unskilled, illiterate population, particularly in large cities where there is resistance to immigration by the unskilled and illiterate male population, prompted by changes in the labour market, especially in relation to skill requirements. The newly emerging activities in urban areas, even including those in the informal sector, are skill-intensive, which the unskilled labour from rural areas cannot match. For example, a number of jobs conducted in the garment sector require experience in tailoring, embroidering, printing, dying, and so on, which the agricultural labour or those who pursued petty jobs as vegetable vendors in the services sector cannot perform.

The study by Kaur (1996) analysed the spatial pattern of rural-to-urban male migration based on the district-wise data from the 1971 population census. She classified the districts into three categories: (a) areas with a relatively high proportion of rural–urban male migrants in the total urban male population (24 per cent and above), (b) areas with a moderate proportion (16 to 24 per cent), and (c) areas with a relatively low proportion (below 16 per cent), each comprising 24.4 per cent, 36 per cent, and 35.7 per cent respectively of the total 356 districts. Districts with rapid migration witnessed rapid development of mining, industrial activities, and the services sector.

The feminist and gender perspective since the 1980s urged that migration studies undervalue women's role as workers (e.g. Fawcett et al. 1984; Chant 1992; Singh 1984; Karlekar 1995). Singh (1984) argued that economic factors do play a significant role in the context of female migration, which is usually taken to be a result of social and cultural practices.

Some of the studies noted that the propensity to migrate increases with education (Connell et al. 1976; Banerjee 1986). Banerjee's study (1986) on the interstate migrants in Delhi found the percentage of matriculates and graduates among

[3] 'The willingness to accept a lower wage in the village reflects the costs of migration as well as the exploitative conditions that labourers face as migrants. The costs of migration include transport costs, uncertain earnings, health hazards, and higher costs of living in urban areas combined with poor living conditions. Migration also results in a breakdown of social life: this is true both in the case of men migrating alone and when entire families migrate. When entire families migrate the situation is even worse: children have to be removed from schools and live in precarious environments. Women and young girls are especially vulnerable to sexual exploitation. Further, urban congestion is a cost of migration that is borne by society at large' (Khera 2006).

migrants in the sample to be many times higher than that in the population from which they originated (in this case, Punjab, Rajasthan, and Uttar Pradesh). Oberai et al. (1989), focusing on the socio-economic characteristics of in-migrants and non-migrants in three states, noted that in the case of Bihar and Kerala the educational level of in-migrants was higher than that of non-migrants, whereas in Uttar Pradesh it was just the opposite.

The importance of social networks in migration has been widely observed. Through caste–kinship bonds and other kinds of rural networks the rural job seekers access urban-based jobs (Banerjee 1986). There is a large concentration of migrants belonging to social backward classes (scheduled castes (SCs) and the scheduled tribes (STs) in the informal sector (Basu et al. 1987; Kasturi 1990; Neetha 2004). This points to the positive effects of networks operating between the backward classes at the places of destination and origin. The study by Bhattacharya (2002) also examined the impact of the SC and ST presence, which showed a positive effect on the migration of SCs from rural areas. Though SC/ST is actually a social identity, the percentage of the population belonging to this social category is taken to explain the prevalence of networks. The underlying idea is that the socially backward classes with inadequate human capital develop networks as survival strategies.

The UNICEF study (2012) argues that in recent years several changes have occurred in India which may have impacted on the pattern and pace of migration. The growth has been accompanied by a widening gap between agriculture and non-agriculture and rural and urban areas besides being concentrated in a few pockets, in an inter-spatial sense. Since migration is a mechanism that equalizes gaps across regions such changes must have influenced population flows. On the other hand, the transport network has expanded significantly with a decline in the real cost of transport and communication. With reduced information asymmetries labour market outcomes are likely to have improved, motivating more migration from rural areas. In addition, the growth pattern is influenced by globalization, resulting in changes in labour demand. For example, skill-intensive growth is likely to generate demand for specific types of employees. On the other hand, in relation to production workers, flexibility is valued by the employers in comparison to the gains accruing from appointing workers on a long-term basis. Consequently, informalization in the formal sector has risen fast, and second, ancillarization or business contracting between the formal and tiny informal sector units has gone up significantly. On the supply side, access to quality education and technical awareness of the workforce has been changing rather sluggishly. Besides, the government policy to make cities attractive for global finance is quite exclusionary, compounded by the politician's move to introduce the 'son of the soil' mindset (UNICEF 2012).

For the first time in India since independence, the urban population increase in the last decade (2001–11) has exceeded its rural counterpart in absolute terms and migration has naturally played an important role (UNESCO 2013). About 30 per cent of the internal migrants are youth (Rajan 2013) and child migrants add up to fifteen million (Daniel 2011). Seasonal and circular migration is quite widespread, especially among the SCs, STs, and other backward castes who are deprived of assets and do not have enough livelihood sources (Deshingkar and Akter 2009). Chandrasekhar and Sharma (2015) documented an increase in two-way commuting across rural and urban areas. Castaldo et al. (2012) urged that the main purpose of rural-to-urban migration is to reduce poverty; remittances do contribute to improving living standards at the place of origin.

7.4 Migration Rates Based on the 2001 Census

7.4.1 State-Level Data

Based on the 2001 population census data, the following are some of the important patterns relating to migration, taken from some of the earlier studies by the author (Mitra and Murayama 2009).

Using the last residence concept of migration (where residence is other than the place of destination), those who migrated in the ten years (1991–2001) preceding the year of the survey, 2001, were identified. The gross decadal inflow of rural-to-urban migrants as a percentage of the total urban population in 2001 turned out to be a little above 7 per cent at the all-India level, with considerable variation across states (Table 7.2). Both industrialized states like Gujarat and Maharashtra and backward states like Orissa and Madhya Pradesh experienced high rates of migration. Similarly, the industrialized states of Tamil Nadu and West Bengal and backward states of Uttar Pradesh, Bihar, and Rajasthan witnessed sluggish rates of migration. Even in terms of the percentage share of each state in the total rural-to-urban migrant population (with the exception of Maharashtra,[4] which alone accounts for around 20 per cent of the total), both the rich and the backward states equally comprise a high relative size (Figure 7.1).

From the census data (2001), we observed that at the class 1 city level, with an increase in city size there is improvement in a number of development indicators such as male and female literacy rates, child–woman ratio, male work participation rate, and percentage of workforce engaged in non-household manufacturing and services. It was only the female–male ratio that deteriorated with an increase in city size, possibly indicating the impact of a greater inflow of single male migration to large cities. In fact, Mitra and Murayama (2009) observed that the

[4] The metropolitan cities in Maharashtra (Mumbai, for example) draw a huge population from within the state as well as outside it.

Table 7.2. Gross decadal rural to urban migrants as a percentage of total urban population, 2001

States	R–U migrants (1991–2001) as a % of urban population
Andhra Pradesh	6.72
Assam	7.12
Bihar	6.28
Gujarat	10.63
Haryana	11.45
Karnataka	7.03
Kerala	6.99
Madhya Pradesh	9.50
Maharashtra	10.41
Orissa	10.97
Punjab	7.63
Rajasthan	6.18
Tamil Nadu	3.34
Utter Pradesh	4.44
West Bengal	4.83
All India	7.32

Note: Migration is defined as the gross decadal (1991–2001) inflow of intrastate and interstate rural-to-urban migration (based on the last residence concept) as a percentage of total urban population (2001). Bihar includes Jharkhand, Madhya Pradesh includes Chhattisgarh, and Uttar Pradesh includes Uttaranchal.

Source: Census of India 2001, Migration Tables, and taken from Mitra and Murayama (2009)

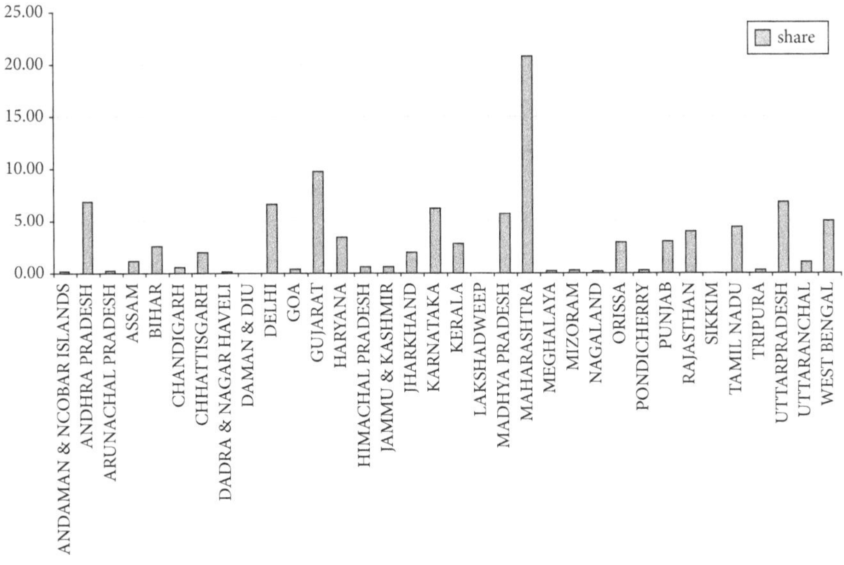

Figure 7.1. Share of each state in the total rural to urban migrant population

Source: Based on Population Census, 2001.

rural-to-urban migration rate was relatively faster in districts which had a class 1 city, particularly so in the case of inter-district migrants coming from rural areas.

The other issue relates to population mobility within urban areas. There is a significant flow from relatively small cities/towns to large/metropolitan cities, suggesting a strong positive relationship between city size and migration. So, large cities tend to get larger supplies of labour, with greater challenges in terms of employment, housing, infrastructure, and amenities. Large cities comprise a number of economic activities, which also give rise to several secondary effects, i.e. an expansion in multinational activities and a rise in the salaries of skilled employees result in a demand for labour providing petty services. All this leads to the migration of even the semi-skilled and unskilled variety of labour, in addition to the skilled ones, into large cities. The fact that such activities can be accessed in large cities seems to have a multiplier effect, i.e. more people tend to move compared to those who can be accommodated (Mitra 2013).

Some of the other distinct patterns that emerged from the 2001 census data on migration are as follows. Among the four streams of migration—i.e. rural-to-rural, rural-to-urban, urban-to-rural, and urban-to urban migration—the first one dominates the rest. The rural-to-rural stream is significant because rural males move in search of jobs from one village to another, while for rural women the main cause of movement is marriage. In 2001, rural-to-rural migration (based on the last residence concept with the duration of residence being 0–9 years at the place of enumeration) accounted for 54.7 per cent of total migration within the country, though the share was on the decline compared to 62 per cent in 1971. Instead, rural-to-urban migration has shown a gradual increase, its share in total migration rising from 16.5 per cent to 21.1 per cent between 1971 and 2001. Urban-to-urban migration also experienced a slight increase to 14.7 per cent from 13.6 per cent over the same period.

In terms of distance the intrastate migration is more prevalent, accounting for 82.1 per cent of migration (duration of 0–9 years). More than half of the migrants at the place of destination came from within the district and the incidence of migration tends to decrease with distance. In India, interstate rural-to-urban migration has always remained modest because of language and cultural barriers. Social and political discriminations exist in subtle forms to discourage the migration of people with certain specific origins (Edelman and Mitra 2006). In recent years, however, there have been instances of migration through labour contractors mitigating the influence of social, cultural, and linguistic differences, which earlier discouraged long-distance interstate rural–urban population movement (Mitra 2013).

Among the intrastate migrants, 60.5 per cent moved from rural to rural areas (duration 0–9 years), followed by 17.6 per cent from rural to urban areas. However, in the case of interstate migrants, the largest proportion (37.9 per cent) migrated from rural to urban destinations (2001 census data, Table 7.3). Among

Table 7.3. Gross decadal intrastate and interstate rural-to-urban male and female migrants as a percentage of total urban male and female population, 2001

State	Intrastate male	Intrastate female	Interstate male	Interstate female	Intrastate + interstate male	Intrastate + interstate female
Andhra Pradesh	6.11	6.59	0.39	0.34	6.5	6.93
Arunachal Pradesh	13.39	14.82	7.67	7.17	21.06	21.99
Assam	5.75	6.22	1.25	0.93	7.01	7.15
Bihar	4.14	6.83	0.42	0.7	4.56	7.53
Chhattisgarh	6.58	8.64	2.22	2.38	8.8	11.02
Gujarat	6.78	8.33	3.89	2.21	10.67	10.54
Haryana	4.56	6.72	6.09	5.38	10.65	12.09
Himachal Pradesh	13.37	14.48	8.09	4.65	21.46	19.13
Jammu & Kashmir	3.03	3.29	1.46	1.48	4.49	4.77
Jharkhand	2.71	3.93	3.02	3.8	5.73	7.73
Karnataka	5.38	6.16	1.36	1.16	6.74	7.32
Kerala	4.81	8.06	0.6	0.4	5.41	8.46
Madhya Pradesh	5.09	6.95	1.26	1.56	6.35	8.51
Maharashtra	5.83	7.18	4.77	2.92	10.6	10.09
Meghalaya	2.26	2.51	2.08	1.47	4.34	3.98
Mizoram	7.08	7.7	2.28	1.15	9.36	8.85
Nagaland	4.11	3.91	3.34	2.53	7.45	6.44
Orissa	9.44	10.31	1.1	1.1	10.54	11.41
Punjab	2.58	4.76	4.8	2.88	7.38	7.64
Rajasthan	4.17	5.92	1.15	1.18	5.32	7.1
Sikkim	7.04	8.2	6.26	5.23	13.31	13.42
Tamil Nadu	2.78	3.44	0.22	0.22	2.99	3.66
Tripura	6.18	8.37	0.4	0.38	6.58	8.75
Uttar Pradesh	2.66	4.33	0.59	0.64	3.25	4.97

(Continued)

Table 7.3. Continued

State	Intrastate male	Intrastate female	Interstate male	Interstate female	Intrastate + interstate male	Intrastate + interstate female
Uttarakhand	5.43	6.04	4.24	4.18	9.67	10.22
West Bengal	2.45	4.23	1.43	1.11	3.88	5.34
Andaman and Nicobar	4.43	4.89	8.81	6.75	13.24	11.65
Chandigarh	0.12	0.1	13.99	12.79	14.11	12.89
Dadra and Nagar Haveli	0.35	0.31	29.15	19.98	29.5	20.29
Daman and Diu	0.24	0.2	8.89	5.96	9.12	6.16
Delhi	0.09	0.14	11.25	9.43	11.34	9.57
Goa	4.4	6.67	6.7	5.46	11.1	12.13
Lakshadweep	11.16	9.56	3.38	0.61	14.54	10.17
Pondicherry	1.68	1.86	4.88	6.2	6.55	8.06

Source: Based on Population Census, 2001 Migration Data, and taken from Mitra and Murayama (2009).

them, the incidence of rural-to-rural and urban-to-urban movement is almost the same, i.e. 26.6 per cent and 26.7 per cent respectively.

Migration streams in India have been dominated by females, who are seen to migrate mainly for social reasons such as marriage (i.e. in a patriarchal society, the woman leaves her paternal house and family to live with her husband and in-laws). Women constituted 66.5 per cent of total migration flows (duration 0–9 years). They outnumbered men in intra-district as well as intrastate migration flows, accounting for 73.9 per cent and 70.3 per cent respectively. However, among the migrants for economic reasons, males outnumbered women. This is somewhat reflected in the interstate migration for economic reasons: with distance the share of male migration tends to increase. Of the total female migration, more than 60 per cent moved from within the district, implying the dominance of short-distance migration among women. In the case of males, while migration within the district is also predominant (43 per cent), the share of longer-distance migration is larger than that among female migrants.

Among the rural-to-urban migrants, the number of males and females was almost equal. While women outnumbered men in intrastate rural–urban flows, the number of males was significantly larger in the case of the interstate rural–urban stream.

7.4.2 District-Level Data

Mitra and Murayama (2009) noted that migration rates, defined in terms of the gross decadal inflow of population as a percentage of the total population at the place of destination, were not high in a large number of districts. The intrastate rates dominated the interstate rates. Second, the male and female migration rates were correlated irrespective of whether they migrated from rural areas within the state or from outside the state. This may be taken to suggest that women usually migrate as dependents and companions of men, though some of the micro surveys have noted the migration of single females in search of jobs (Mitra 2013). Though the districts in many of the relatively poor and backward states show large population mobility primarily in search of livelihoods, the districts in advanced states also witnessed mobility of the male population. Several of the south Indian states in comparison to the north Indian states recorded a high migration rate of females.

As regards the intrastate rural-to-urban migrants, nearly 28 per cent of the districts registered a male migration rate of more than 7 per cent during 1991–2001, whereas less than 8 per cent corresponded to a rate up to 1.5 per cent (Table 7.4). Many of the districts which showed a male intrastate rural–urban migration rate of more than 10 per cent of the urban population are located in the north-east, east, west, and central regions of the country. In the southern region only two

Table 7.4. Intrastate rural-to-urban male migration rate at the district level: migrants over ten years (1991–2001) as a percentage of the total urban population in the district, 2001

Migration rate	No. of districts	Percentage of districts
Up to 1 per cent	20	3.46
More than 1 and up to 1.5 per cent	22	3.81
More than 1.5 per cent and up to 2.5 per cent	70	12.11
More than 2.5 per cent and up to 4 per cent	128	22.15
More than 4 per cent and up to 6 per cent	116	20.07
More than 6 and up to 7 per cent	60	10.38
More than 7 per cent	162	28.03

Note: Percentage figures are calculated relative to a total of 578 districts in all states and union territories (except Manipur).

Source: Based on Population Census Data, 2001 and taken from Mitra and Murayama (2009).

districts of Kerala showed a male intrastate migration rate of more than 10 per cent. Some of the studies showing the impact of the rural employment security programme (called the Mahatma Gandhi National Rural Employment Guarantee Act) on migration are suggestive of a declining trend (Khera 2006).

In reference to intrastate female migrants from the rural to urban areas, nearly 32 per cent of the districts showed a rate of more than 9 per cent and only 5 per cent of the fell below or up to 2 per cent (Table 7.5).

As far as the interstate male migrants are concerned, more than half of the districts recorded a less than 1 per cent migration rate, whereas only around 11 per cent of the districts registered a rate of more than 4.5 per cent (Table 7.6 and Table 7.7). The social, cultural, and linguistic diversity in India tends to reduce the pace of population mobility. Social networks play an important role in the context of migration but they are more prevalent among the short-distance migrants, though there are some exceptions to this phenomenon (migrants from Bihar to Delhi or Maharashtra or West Bengal, for example). As noted in the case of intrastate rural male migrants, the districts in south Indian states do not show a high interstate male migration rate, i.e. more than 7 per cent. In terms of social, cultural, and linguistic variations the north–south divide in India is quite significant with a few exceptions of metropolitan cities. In the context of female interstate migration nearly 55 per cent of the districts are seen to have a rate of less than 1 per cent. On the other hand only 14 per cent recoded a rate of more than 3.5 per cent.

Mitra and Murayama (2009) regressed the rural-to-urban intrastate and interstate male and female migration rate on work participation rate at the place of destination, literacy rate, employment composition, child–woman ratio, and caste composition in terms of the incidence of lower castes. The association between female and male migration rates was also examined. Their findings suggest that prospects for better job opportunities are a major determinant of migration. Low

Table 7.5. Intrastate rural-to-urban female migration rate at the district level: migrants over ten years (1991–2001) as a percentage of the total urban population in the district, 2001

Migration rate	No. of districts	Percentage
Up to 1 per cent	17	2.94
More than 1 and up to 2 per cent	17	2.94
More than 2 to per cent and up to 4 per cent	77	13.32
More than 4 per cent and up to 6 per cent	117	20.24
More than 6 per cent and up to 7 per cent	44	7.61
More than 7 per cent and up to 9 per cent	123	21.28
More than 9 per cent	183	31.66

Note: Percentage figures are calculated relative to a total of 578 districts in all states and union territories (except Manipur).

Source: Based on Population Census Data, 2001 and taken from Mitra and Murayama (2009).

Table 7.6. Interstate rural-to-urban male migration rate at the district level: migrants over ten years (1991–2001) as a percentage of the total urban population in the district, 2001

Migration rate	No. of districts	Percentage
Up to 1 per cent	324	56.06
More than 1 and up to 1.5 per cent	52	9.0
More than 1.5 per cent and up to 2 per cent	43	7.44
More than 2 per cent and up to 3 per cent	46	7.96
More than 3 per cent and up to 3.5 per cent	18	3.11
More than 3.5 per cent and up to 4.5 per cent	32	5.54
More than 4.5 per cent	63	10.90

Note: Percentage figures are calculated relative to a total of 578 districts in all states and union territories (except Manipur).

Source: Based on Population Census Data, 2001 and taken from Mitra and Murayama (2009).

Table 7.7. Interstate rural-to-urban female migration rate at the district level: migrants over ten years (1991–2001) as a percentage of the total urban population in the district, 2001

Migration rate	No. of districts	Percentage
Up to 1 per cent	317	54.84
More than 1 per cent and up to 1.5 per cent	55	9.52
More than 1.5 per cent and up to 2 per cent	43	7.44
More than 2 per cent and up to 2.5 per cent	35	6.06
More than 2.5 per cent and up to 3 per cent	22	3.81
More than 3 per cent and up to 3.5 per cent	24	4.15
More than 3.5 per cent	82	14.19

Note: Percentage figures are calculated relative to a total of 578 districts in all states and union territories (except Manipur).

Source: Based on Population Census Data, 2001 and taken from Mitra and Murayama (2009).

castes and minority groups show a higher propensity to migration through networks. These effects are evident among females as well, though with the inclusion of the male migration rate all other factors tend to become insignificant. This may be taken to suggest that for females who initially migrate as the companions of males the economic factors do not play an important role, though subsequently they may be joining the labour market. After excluding the male migration rate from the female migration function, the effect of economic factors is more or less similar to that in the male migration function.

The policy focus of the study by Mitra and Murayama (2009) shows three different orientations. One relates to the male migrants coming to cities in search of jobs. Through the availability of decent jobs in rural areas in-migration to urban areas can be reduced. Besides, productivity-augmenting strategies can be initiated to help those engaged in residual jobs in the urban informal sector. The other aspect of the policy focuses on the job market prospects of women. Though many of these women from low-income households are engaged in residual activities, several micro studies bring out their importance in meeting the consumption requirements of households (Mitra 2005). These women earners need to access better livelihood opportunities, which they can pursue along with household or domestic work. The third aspect of the policy relates to single-women migrants. Their vulnerability in terms of social crime and housing uncertainty is most serious.

The labour market for casual workers is dominated by migrants of rural origin (Deshingkar and Farrington 2006). Their incomes are highly volatile and they do not receive any social security. They create their own employment opportunities to the extent that their capital and skills permit (Mukherjee et al. 2009) but they often end up earning lower than the minimum wage (Kundu and Sarangi 2007). Evidence on labour exploitation is plentiful. Mukherjee et al. (2009), in their study of migrants in Bombay city, noted that the brokers make migrant labourers work for 18–20 hours but pay nominally.

7.4.3 NSS Data on Migration (2007–8)

The National Sample Survey Organisation (NSSO) conducted a survey on migration in 2007–8 (results published in 2010). If the entire household, as was being enumerated, had moved to the place of enumeration during the last 365 days preceding the date of survey, it was considered as a migrant household. Households in which one member of the household had moved ahead of other members and others had joined subsequently (but all of them during the reference year) were also considered as migrant households. If some members of the household were born or married into households which had moved to the place of enumeration during the last 365 days, the entire household was treated as migrated.

As per this definition, the migrant households of one-year duration constituted nearly 3 per cent of all urban households. Most of the migrant households came from within the state (as 72 per cent of the migrant households in urban areas had moved from within the state). The migration pattern is dominated by those of rural origin: nearly 57 per cent of migrant households in urban areas migrated from rural areas. Further, a majority of the households (nearly 67 per cent in urban areas) migrated for employment-related reasons such as seeking jobs or recruitment in jobs.

As per another definition of migration—one that aims at capturing the long-duration migrants—a household member is defined to be a migrant if his last usual place of residence (UPR), anytime in the past, was different from the present place of enumeration. As per this UPR concept, nearly 29 per cent of the population appeared to be migrants with significant rural–urban and male–female differentials. The migration rate (proportion of migrants in the population) in urban areas turned out to be around 35 per cent, with significant gender differentials: the male *migration rate* was nearly 26 per cent compared to the female *migration rate* of 46 per cent. Further, among migrants in urban areas, nearly 59 per cent migrated from rural areas and 40 per cent from urban areas. Among rural-to-urban migrants, 41.2 per cent came from the same districts; 33.6 per cent from different districts, but within the state; and only 25.2 per cent travelled between states.

The Harris–Todaro framework (1970) suggests that the economically weaker sections of the population migrate from rural to urban areas in search of better livelihood opportunities and to escape poverty. In rural India, since caste and class have a strong association (i.e. lower castes are also economically weak), the migration rate among the disadvantaged social categories is likely to be high. However, contrary to this perception, the migration rate in urban areas was lowest (nearly 33 per cent) among those belonging to the social category comprising 'other backward classes', while it was highest (nearly 38 per cent) among those classified as the general category population, comprising upper castes.

Further, the migration rate was found to be lowest among the bottom monthly per capita consumption expenditure (MPCE) decile class and it had a tendency to increase with an increase in the standard of living. Among urban males, the migration rate in the bottom decile class was 10 per cent and reached 46 per cent in the top decile class, and among urban females the corresponding figures were 36 per cent and 56 per cent respectively. These estimates go against the standard views on migration, which is believed to be high among the poor and disadvantaged classes. Since the 'very poor' cannot afford to meet the cost of migration and take the risk of seeking jobs in an anonymous urban environment, the propensity to migrate among them is low (Banerjee 1986). The other interpretation could be that return migration is possibly high among this class as they are often unsuccessful, which, in turn, results in a relatively lower migration rate *ex post*.

Urbanization and the migration rate do not show a particularly clear-cut relationship as seen from the cross-sectional data, though a mild positive association is discernible (Figures 7.2a and 7.2b).

Again, education and the migration rate show a curvilinear relationship: among urban males, it was relatively high among both the illiterates (17 per cent)

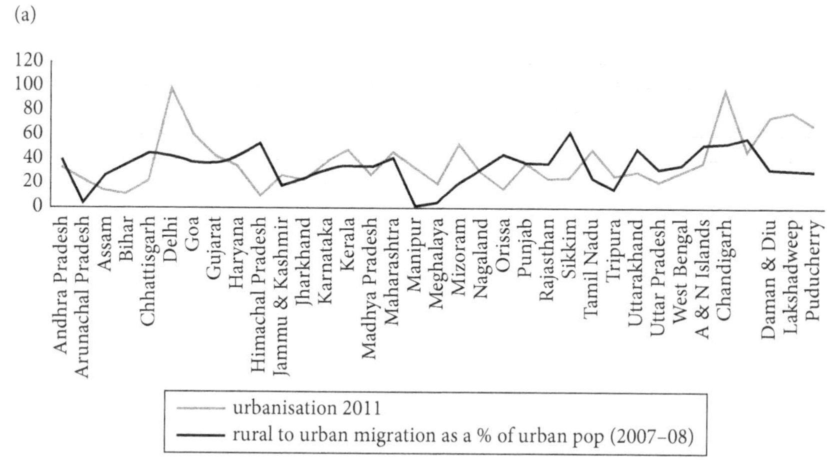

Figure 7.2a. Urbanization and migration across states and union territories
Source: Based on population census and NSS data.

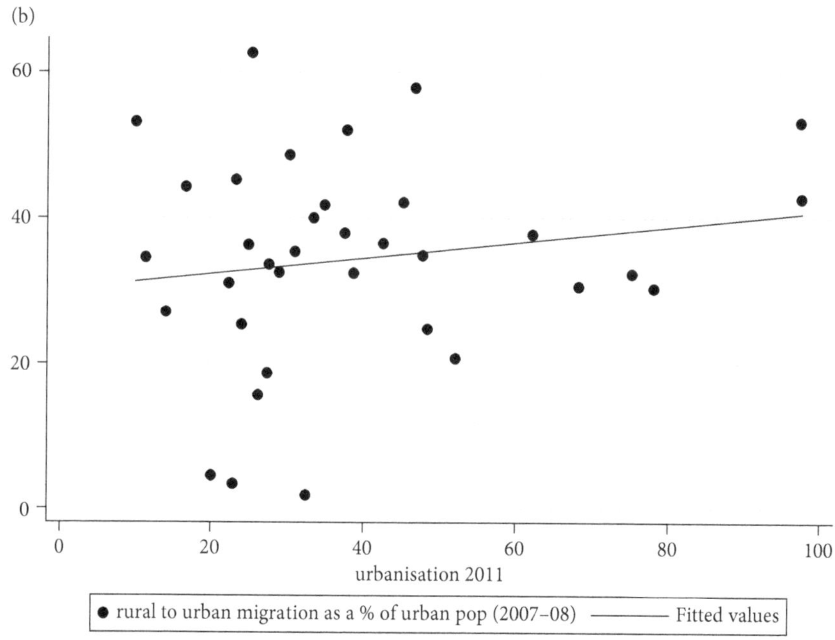

Figure 7.2b. Plot of migration against urbanization
Source: Based on population census and NSS data.

and those with an educational level of graduation or above (38 per cent). Migration involves a cost and therefore not all can afford to migrate to urban areas. As Banerjee (1986) argued, the rich do not have the need to migrate and the poor cannot afford to migrate, while the middle-income group has a higher propensity to migrate.

The quality of migrants in terms of education seems to be inferior in relation to non-migrants. As Table 16.15 in Chapter 16 in this volume indicates, the percentage of illiterates is higher among migrants. Similarly, the share of those with a primary and secondary level of education is smaller among migrants compared to non-migrants.

The most prominent reason for female migration in both rural and urban areas was *marriage*, while the reason for migration among males was dominated by *employment-related factors* (nearly 56 per cent in urban areas). A higher percentage of persons reported to have been engaged in *economic activities* after migration compared to the pre-migration status: for males, the percentage of workers increased from 46 per cent before migration to 70 per cent after migration in urban areas. Srivastava (2011) noted that in 2007–8, excluding seasonal migrants, around 31 per cent of the workforce could be classified as migrants.

In the case of urban males, the percentage of regular wage/salaried employees has shown a major increase—from 18 per cent before migration to 39 per cent after migration. However, there has been an increase in the share of self-employment as well after migration (from 17 per cent to 22 per cent), though the relative size of casual labour declined after migration (from 11 per cent before migration to 8 per cent) at the all-India level.

Is this shift in the occupation of migrants related to the urbanization level?

From the regression based on state-level data, we noted that the higher the level of urbanization, the greater the decline in the unemployment rate after migration in comparison with the unemployment rate prevailing prior to migration. Also, based on the cross-sectional data, the rise in overall labour force participation and the relative size of regular wage employment after migration show a positive relationship with urbanization, though neither of them is found to be statistically significant (Table 7.8). Only the change in self-employment and urbanization level are positively connected. This is evident from the results of factor analysis as well (see factor 2, Table 7.9).

Based on factor analysis, we observe that in factor 1, the change in regular wage employment and the change in unemployment rate after migration are the two most dominant variables, and both are inversely related. Though urbanization is nominally associated with these variables, it takes a positive factor loading, implying that states with higher urbanization levels reveal a greater decline in the unemployment rate and a larger increase in regular wage employment after migration. Besides, the migration rate in urban areas and the urbanization level are positively associated, although moderately (see Table 7.9).

Table 7.8. Urbanization and change in labour market characteristics: regression analysis

Exp. var.	Dep. var. change in LF	Dep. var. change in self-emp.	Dep. var. change in casual emp.	Dep. var. change in reg. wage emp.	Dep. var. change in unemp.
URBN	0.45	0.82	−0.29	0.23	−1.37
	(1.06)	(1.95)*	(−0.89)	(0.29)	(−1.96)*
CONSTANT	−106.47	10.03	0.0325	168.32	−60.14
	(−5.74)**	(0.54)	(0.001)	(4.95)**	(−1.94)*
Adj R2	0.004	0.07	−0.001	−02	0.07
No. of Obs.	36	36	36	36	36

Note: LF is labour force (2007–8), URBN is urbanization (2011), emp. is employment and unemp. is unemployment.

Source: Author's calculation.

Table 7.9. Results from factor analysis: migration and labour market characteristics

Variables	Factor 1	Factor 2
URBN	0.1763	0.3059
CHSELF	0.0577	0.9641
CHREG	0.8960	−0.1944
CHCAS	−0.1087	−0.1178
CHUNEM	−0.9271	−0.2939
CHLF	−0.0417	−0.0580
MIG	0.3679	−0.0928
Eigen value	2.15	1.24
% explained	0.91	0.25

Note: Middle-Income Group (MIG): migration rate (2007–8); CH: change after migration compared with pre-migration; SELF: self-employment; CAS: casual employment; REG: regular wage employment; UNEMP: unemployment; LF: labour force.

Source: Author's calculation.

From the regression analysis, it is evident that the higher the level of urbanization, the higher the rate of male migration in urban areas, though it is not true in the case of females (Table 7.10). Also, the higher male migration rate in urban areas and the higher male migration due to reasons such as employment are positively associated.

Further, from the factor analysis, we observe a strong association between the overall male migration rate and the male migration rate in the bottom two MPCE quintile classes (Table 7.11). Employment as a reason for migration among males and the urbanization level are moderately related to these variables.

Table 7.10. Urbanization and migration: regression analysis

Variable	Dep. Var. MIG MALE	Dep. var MIG FEMALE	Dep. Var. MIG MALE
URBN	2.25	−0.21	2.02
	(2.18)**	(−0.16)	(2.07)**
MIG EMP Male			0.42
			(2.30)**
CONSTANT	186.99	426.68	−30.04
	(4.05)**	(7.07)**	(−0.29)
Adj R2	0.09	−0.03	0.20
No. of Obs.	35	35	35

Note: MIG MALE: migration rate among males (2007–8); MIG FEMALE: migration rate among females (2007–8); MIG EMP Male: males who migrated for employment as a percentage of total male migrants (2007–8); URBN: urbanization (2011).

Source: Author's calculation.

Table 7.11. Factor analysis: poor and migration

Variables	Factor loadings
Q1	0.90
Q2	0.95
MIG MALE	0.85
MIG EMP Male	0.29
URBN	0.15
Eigen Value	2.66
% Explained	0.92

Source: Author's calculation.

7.5 Urban Labour Market

7.5.1 Overall Employment Structure

The employment structure did not shift significantly away from agriculture during the 1980s and 1990s. The share of agriculture was 68 per cent in 1983, which declined to 60 per cent in 1999–2000 and 56 per cent in 2004–5 (Table 7.13). However, the share of manufacturing rose marginally from 11.24 per cent in 1983 to 12.09 per cent in 1999–2000 and 12.2 in 2004–5. On the other hand, the share of services in employment and value-added increased significantly in India even at low levels of per capita income. The share of services (inclusive of electricity, gas, and construction) increased from 21 per cent to around 30 per cent over the same period.

As job opportunities grow sluggishly in urban areas, rural–urban migration flow tends to shrink, though the urban informal sector can residually absorb a large chunk of the workforce. In the rural context the only sector that remains as a last resort for rural job seekers is the rural non-farm sector since the agriculture sector has already reached the point of saturation. Analysing the employment structure for rural and urban areas separately we note that in rural areas the percentage of the usual status male workforce (principal plus subsidiary) engaged in manufacturing increased marginally by 0.3 percentage point between 1993–4 and 1999–2000 (Table 7.13). In urban areas the share of manufacturing in total male workforce dropped from 23.5 per cent to 22.4 per cent during the same period, though a slight improvement is noticed thereafter in 2004–5. Among rural females, the share of manufacturing increased by 0.6 percentage point only. However, among urban females it remained unchanged between 1993–4 and 1999–2000 with a perceptible rise in 2004–5 (Table 7.12).

The share of trade, hotels, etc., in total male employment increased sizably both in urban and rural areas The share of the entire tertiary sector in total male employment also increased both in rural and urban areas over time. Several new activities within the tertiary sector, including information technology and business process outsourcing, are growing rapidly. But trade-related activities account for a sizeable percentage of low-productivity employment (Mitra 1994) as entry to this sector is relatively easy due to nominal requirements in terms of skill and space.

After 2004–5, the value-added structure indicates a sizeable decline in the share of agriculture to around 15 per cent in 2009–10 (Table 7.13). This is in sharp contrast to the share of agriculture in the total workforce. More than 50 per cent of the workforce was still engaged in this sector in 2009–10, indicating low levels of labour productivity. On the other hand, the share of manufacturing in total employment and value-added was 11.5 and 15.7 per cent respectively in 2009–10, and the shares did not change much between 2004–5 and 2009–10, except the fact that the employment share of manufacturing did undergo a marginal fall from 12.2 per cent in 2004–5. Whatever shift has been taking place away from agriculture is mostly towards the services sector. Construction is one activity that recorded a perceptible rise in its employment share during this period. The following two categories—trade, hotel, etc., and other services including finance, real estate, and business services—also show a marginal rise in their employment shares. The value-added share of trade, hotel, etc., however, remained by and large constant, while transport and other services gained by almost two percentage points.

On the whole, economic growth in India is increasingly becoming capital and skill intensive. The high-productivity industrial sector, which could earlier absorb unskilled and semi-skilled labour to a significant scale, is not able to do so anymore due to the adoption of capital-intensive technologies. Further, import of technology from developed countries tends to reduce the labour per unit of output, as such technology is tailored to suit the labour market conditions of developed countries. Given the poor skill base of rural migrants in urban areas, it is unlikely

Table 7.12. Employment structure of male and female workers (UPSS) in rural and urban areas (%)

Activities (Rural)	Male	Male	Male	Male	Male	Female	Female	Female	Female	Female
	1983	1987–8	1993–4	1999–2000	2004–5	1983	1987–8	1993–4	1999–2000	2004–5
Agri. & allied activities	77.5	74.5	74.1	71.4	66.5	87.5	84.7	86.2	85.3	83.3
Mining & quarrying	0.6	0.7	0.7	0.6	0.6	0.0	0.4	0.4	0.3	0.3
Manufacturing	7.0	7.4	7.0	7.3	7.9	6.4	6.9	7.0	7.6	8.4
Utilities	0.2	0.3	0.3	0.2	0.2	0.0	0.0	0.1	0.0	0.0
Construction	2.2	3.7	3.2	4.5	6.8	0.7	2.7	0.9	1.1	1.5
Trade, hotels, etc.	4.4	5.1	5.5	6.8	8.3	1.9	2.1	2.1	2.0	2.5
Transport, etc.	1.7	2.0	2.2	3.2	3.8	0.1	0.1	0.1	0.1	0.2
Services	6.1	6.2	7.0	6.2	5.9	2.8	3.0	3.4	3.6	4.6
Activities (urban)	1983	1987–8	1993–4	1999–2000	2004–5	1983	1987–8	1993–4	1999–2000	2004–5
Agri. & allied activities	10.6	9.1	9.0	6.5	6.1	31.5	29.4	24.7	17.6	18.1
Mining & quarrying	1.2	1.3	1.3	0.9	0.9	0.7	0.8	0.6	0.4	0.2
Manufacturing	26.8	25.7	23.5	22.4	23.5	26.7	27.1	24.1	24.0	28.2
Utilities	1.1	1.2	1.2	0.8	0.8	0.2	0.2	0.3	0.2	0.2
Construction	5.1	5.8	6.9	8.7	9.2	3.2	3.7	4.1	4.8	3.8
Trade, hotels, etc.	20.4	21.5	21.9	29.4	28.0	9.5	9.8	10.0	16.9	12.2
Transport, etc.	10.0	9.7	9.7	10.4	10.7	0.6	1.2	1.3	1.8	1.4
Services	24.7	25.2	26.4	19.0	20.8	26.7	27.8	35.0	34.2	35.9

Source: Employment and Unemployment Situation in India, 2004–5 (Part –I), NSS 61st Round, Government of India, September 2006.

Table 7.13. Value-added share and employment share: 2004–5 and 2009–10

Activities	Employment structure		Value-added structure	
	2004–5	2009–10	2004–5	2009–10
Agriculture	56.5	51.4	20.2	15.5
Mining	0.6	0.6	2.2	1.8
Manufacturing	12.2	11.5	15.1	15.7
Utilities	0.3	0.3	2.3	2.1
Construction	5.7	9.6	6.6	6.8
Trade, hotel, etc.	10.8	11.4	15.5	15.9
Transport, etc.	4.01	4.5	10.2	12.4
Other services including finance, etc.	9.9	10.8	27.8	29.8
Total	100.0	100.0	100.0	100.00

Source: National Accounts Statistics, CSO and NSS.

that they will get absorbed in a significant manner in the high-productivity segment of the services sector. They are rather more likely to get absorbed in the urban informal sector spreading across both manufacturing and services. Within the informal sector, services comprise a large majority of total employment, indicating a greater absorption of migrant labour in activities which do not have significant entry barriers due to nominal skill requirements (Mitra 2013).

The historical experience of the present-day developed nations suggests that industrialization is one of the important determinants of economic growth, creation of high-productivity employment, and enhancement in living standards. The structural change is accompanied by a rise in per capita income and many other development indicators, involving upward mobility of individual occupations and incomes and a shift in the rural–urban composition of the population (Kuznets 1966). However, in the Indian context, the share of manufacturing in the total workforce persists at a low level even after experiencing rapid economic growth in the last several years. The sluggish employment growth in the high-productivity industrial sector, aggravating the mismatch between the overall supply and demand for labour, could be due to the limited spread of the industry and/or the adoption of capital-intensive technology. This leads to a residual absorption of labour in the low-productivity informal sector, with meagre earnings accruing to workers and forcing many to reside in slums.

With globalization, several growth-oriented strategies which include trade openness, foreign direct investment (FDI) inflows, and capital mobility and technology transfer have been initiated. In order to justify technology transfer it is argued that if the wheel has already been adopted somewhere it does not have to be rediscovered for making countries cost-efficient. But the import of new technology, which is primarily capital intensive and skill intensive, does not raise demand for less-skilled workers (Wood 1997). Another argument relates to labour market regulations. Labour laws in the Indian context are believed to be outdated and pro-employee, reducing the pace of labour absorption. Due to the lack of labour market flexibility economic growth is believed to be non-inclusive. However, there are many other factors that affect investment adversely, e.g. the lack of access to land, infrastructure, and a skilled workforce. Another argument refers to skills shortage, pointing to poor employability of workers, forcing many to get residually absorbed in low-productivity activities. Migrants from rural areas are more likely to enter the informal sector and as informal workers in the formal sector such as cleaners, office boys, or contractual or casual labourers in industries or construction companies (Mitra 2013).

7.5.2 Urban Informal Sector Employment

As per the existing literature, the overlaps between the low-productivity informal sector employment and poverty are significant (Mitra 1994; 2001). Based on the NSSO data (1999–2000), the incidence of poverty as well as the intensity of poverty among households dependent on employment in the informal sector were found to be higher in urban areas than in rural areas (Sastry 2004).[5]

Both in rural and urban areas the incidence of informal sector employment, i.e. the proportion of employment in informal sector enterprises (proprietary and partnership enterprises) to total employment, is high (Table 7.15). Not only in agriculture but also in non-agricultural activities, an overwhelmingly large proportion of workers are engaged in the informal sector.

The size of informal employment, which includes casual or short-term contractual or irregular workers in the formal sector and workers in informal sector enterprises and households, can be phenomenally large. In other words, informal sector employment is only a subset of informal employment (see Papola 1981; Mitra 1994; and Sastry 2004). But the estimate of informal sector employment given in Table 7.14 is on the high side, let alone the share of informal employment.

Table 7.14. Relative size of the informal sector in percentages: all-India (2009–10)

Sector	Agriculture			Non-agriculture		
	Male	Female	Person	Male	Female	Person
Rural	90.6	95.0	93.4	73.0	64.1	71.3
Urban	88.3	97.7	92.5	68.3	60.1	66.9

Note: The NSSO's estimates exclude workers employed by households and own-account workers engaged in the production of goods exclusively for own final use by their household.

Source: Based on NSSO (2009–10) unit-level data on employment/unemployment.

[5] Though rural areas are largely characterised by the informal sector (both farm and non-farm activities) hardships involved in the urban-specific informal sector activities could result in such a situation.

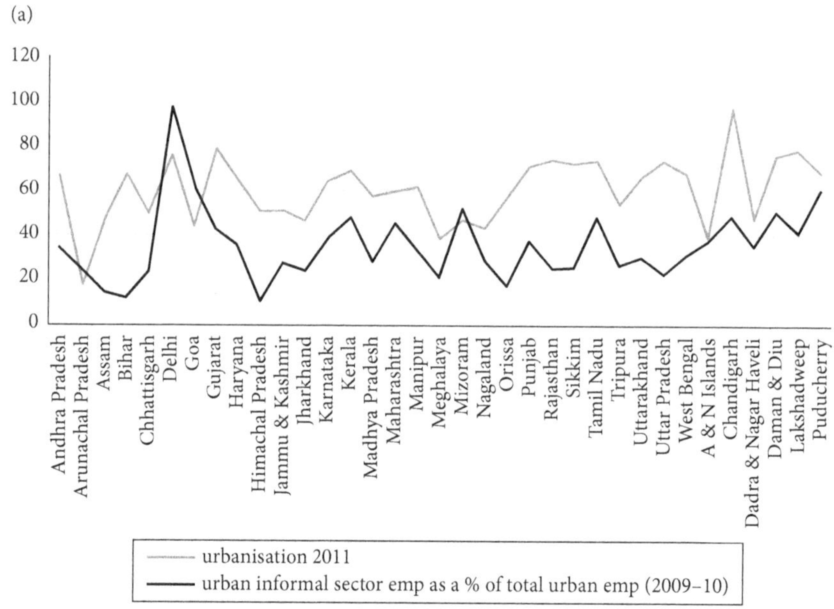

Figure 7.3a. Urbanization and urban informal sector employment across stares and union territories

Source: Based on Population Census (2001) and NSS data (2009–10)

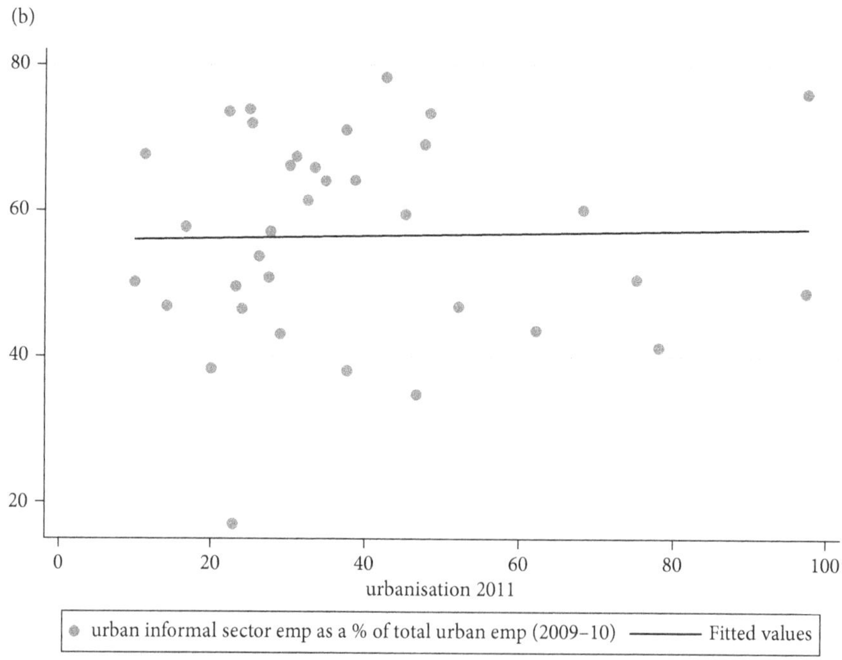

Figure 7.3b. Plot of urban informal sector employment against urbanization

Source: Based on Population Census (2011) and NSS data (2009–10)

The size of the informal sector seems to be large in both high- and low-income states. In the low-income states, it is the residual type of employment which dominates the informal sector, whereas in the high-income states, subcontracting and ancillarization raise the relative size of the informal sector. In relation to urbanization, the share of the informal sector does not show any clear-cut pattern as observed from the cross-sectional information (Figures 7.3a and 7.3b). In other words, both high and low levels of urbanization are associated with a large share of informal sector employment. While rapid flow of population into urban areas can result in excess supplies of labour, the lack of dynamism can also lead to a similar situation of excess supplies of labour, both resulting in a relatively large incidence of informal sector employment.

7.5.3 Migration, Urban Informal Sector Employment, Poverty, and Other Important Correlates

The factor analysis carried out on a large number of variables reveals that higher rural literacy tends to raise the migration rate, although moderately (Table 7.15). The percentage of scheduled castes in rural areas also has a positive impact on the migration rate, supporting the view that the disadvantaged sections migrate to escape their vulnerability (factor 1). The most interesting part is that migration reduces both rural and urban poverty as seen from both factor 1 and factor 4. This is, however, not a very strong pattern emerging from the cross-sectional data.

Higher urbanization and work participation rates in both rural and urban areas are positively associated with migration (factor 2), suggesting that those in the labour market are more likely to migrate and after migration they are likely to continue in the labour market. Such patterns are more prevalent in states that are more urbanized than others.

Migration, urban informal sector employment, and the incidence of SC population (representing lower social categories in terms of caste) in urban and rural areas are all positively connected with each other, suggesting that socially backward groups are more likely to migrate and end up in the urban informal sector. However, this pattern is accompanied by a decline in the incidence of poverty in both rural and urban areas, though in nominal terms only (factor 3).

In factor 4, urbanization takes the highest factor loading and is associated positively with the percentage of the rural and urban workforce engaged in non-household manufacturing and services. Also, urbanization is negatively related to rural and urban poverty.

The relationship between urbanization and informal sector employment is not distinct: the factor loadings of both urbanization and urban informal sector employment do not turn out to be high or moderate simultaneously in any of the four significant factors. In factor 3 or factor 4, only one of the two is closer to

Table 7.15. Factor analysis: migration, urban informal sector, and other rural and urban labour market characteristics

Variables	Factor 1	Factor 2	Factor 3	Factor 4
MIG	−0.1138	0.1812	0.2294	0.1403
UINF	−0.1574	−0.0995	0.6029	−0.0252
MIG EMP MALE	0.1105	0.1661	−0.1277	0.0488
RHHSZ	0.6576	−0.4285	−0.1047	−0.1598
RCHILDWOM	0.8675	−0.2058	−0.1431	−0.1511
RWFPR	−0.1262	0.6799	−.0787	−0.1019
RLIT	−0.5362	0.0718	−0.0909	0.5245
RSC	−0.1469	−0.0411	0.9067	−0.0705
ROTHERACT	−0.1406	0.0425	−0.1517	0.8636
UHHSZ	0.4938	−0.7729	−0.0294	−0.0745
UCHILD–WOM	0.8359	0.0413	−0.1793	0.0322
UWFPR	−0.0001	0.9216	−0.0934	0.1698
ULIT	−0.4368	0.2878	−0.2512	0.2123
USC	−0.0547	−0.0303	0.9247	−0.0724
UOTHERACT	−0.1567	0.1456	−01291	0.4363
RPOV	0.1190	0.1737	−0.1193	−0.2127
UPOV	0.2697	−0.1800	−0.0965	−0.2519
URBN	−0.0244	0.1433	0.0027	0.8671
Eigen value	5.43	2.97	2.18	1.60
% explained	0.3563	0.1951	0.1432	0.1045

Note: R and U prefixes stand for rural and urban areas respectively, MIG: migration rate (2007–8); MIG EMP MALE: migration rate for employment among males (2007–8); UINF: the share of informal sector employment in urban non-agricultural activities (2009–10); CHILD–WOM: child–woman ratio (2011); LIT: literacy rate (2011); SC: % of scheduled caste population (2011); HHSZ: household size (2011); WFPR is work participation rate (2011); OTHERACT: % of workforce in other activities (2011); POV is poverty (2011–12); URBN: % urbanization (2011).

Source: Author's calculation.

unity, while the other is negligible. From this, we may conclude that informal sector employment and urbanization do not show any significant relationship.

Keeping in view the literature suggesting interlinks between rural-to-urban migration, informal sector employment, and poverty (Mitra 1994), we have estimated the following three equations: rural-to-urban migration function, urban informal sector employment function, and urban poverty function. We conceptualized a simultaneous equation system, i.e. rural-to-urban migration impacts urban informal sector employment which, in turn, influences the rural-to-urban migration rate. Further, informal sector employment and rural-to-urban migration both exert effects on urban poverty. Though the Harris–Todaro model (1970) upholds that it is the formal sector which motivates rural-to-urban migration, studies have shown the importance of the urban informal sector in providing sources of livelihood to rural migrants. Even when they do not have the expectation of getting absorbed in the formal sector, migration still takes place precisely because urban informal sector earnings are higher than what the rural economy is able to offer. Further, some of the informal sector jobs enable an above-poverty-line standard of living. Therefore, it is worth examining the nature of the relationship between urban informal sector employment and poverty. Given that both the phenomena—overlaps between informal sector employment and poverty and informal sector enabling some to escape poverty—are prevalent, the relationship may not turn out to be statistically significant.

The findings confirm simultaneity between informal sector employment and the migration rate, both being dependent on each other (Table 7.16).

Table 7.16. Results of the three-equation model (OLS estimates)

Exp. var.	Dep. var. MIG	Dep. var. INF	Dep. var. UPOV
INF	0.38		0.0065
	(2.45)**		(0.93)
RPOV	−1.29		0.59
	(−0.84)		(6.86)**
UOTHERACT	4.27	−9.24	
	(0.95)	(−2.66)**	
RLIT	−0.73		
	(−0.25)		
MIG EMP MALE	0.30		
	(1.41)		
RHHSZ	−95.55		
	(−2.19)**		
RPOPF/M	−578.66		
	(−1.72)*		
MIG		0.32	
		(2.17)**	
USC		8.30	0.004
		(2.74)**	(0.03)
URBN		1.26	
		(1.41)	
UHHSZ		61.46	
		(1.60)	
UCHILD-WOM		−1095.24	
		(−1.85)*	
ULIT			−0.45
			(−2.69)**
PCNETSDP			−0.0004
			(−0.78)
ROTHERACT			0.08
			(1.36)
INTERCEPT	655.31	1,143.57	30.04
	(1.02)	(2.90)**	(2.10)**
Adj R2	0.33	0.42	0.76
N	35	35	31

Note: PCNETSDP is per capita net state domestic product (2010–11) and for other variables see Table 7.15. The OLS estimates provide consistent estimates; hence there is no need to provide system estimates.

Source: Author's calculation.

Migration for employment among males tends to raise the overall migration rate in urban areas, though it is not significant at the 10 per cent level. Large rural households and a higher female–male ratio are associated with reduced rates of migration since a higher level of dependency, captured in terms of a large household size, and higher poverty levels in female-headed households reduce the ability and propensity to migrate.

Other than the migration rate, a higher incidence of SC population is associated with higher informal sector employment. Both urbanization and household size raise the incidence of informal sector employment, though the variables are not statistically significant at the 10 per cent level. Expansion in non-household manufacturing and services activities leads to a decline in the share of informal sector employment, implying that household manufacturing, livestock, and other primary activities constitute a higher incidence of the informal sector. Interestingly, a higher child–woman ratio and informal sector employment are negatively connected, though usually women from large households and children from low-income households are believed to be engaged in the informal sector due to the flexibility the sector offers. However, this result needs to be interpreted carefully. Given the household size, if the child–woman ratio rises, it is indicative of greater domestic responsibility for women, which deprives them even from working in the informal sector.

Finally, there is a strong association between rural and urban poverty: the role of migration cannot be ruled out, though migration may be contributing to a reduction in poverty in both rural and urban areas as seen from the factor analysis. In addition, urban literacy contributes to reduction in poverty significantly. Though the incidence of informal sector employment has a tendency to raise poverty, the coefficient is not statistically significant. Similarly, an enhanced share of non-household manufacturing and services in rural areas is expected to reduce urban poverty, though it is not significant even at the 10 per cent level.

On the whole, based only on the significant results, we conclude that migration and urban informal sector employment are closely connected. Migrants do not necessarily move in search of jobs within the formal sector only; even the possibility to work in the informal sector induces population mobility across space. Further, rural and urban poverty are connected through migration and other state-specific characteristics, though migration and an increased urbanization level tend to reduce both rural and urban poverty, as also observed from the results pertaining to the factor analysis.

The factor analysis carried out for class 1 cities (based on 2011 census data) brings out distinctly that some of the demographic variables such as household size and child–woman ratio decline with city size (Table 7.17). The relative size of some of the residual activities like household manufacturing also tapers off while non-household manufacturing and services rises with an increase in city size.

Table 7.17. Factor analysis: Class I Cities—2011 census

Variables	Factor 1	Factor 2
WFPR	0.0031	0.2070
SC	0.0232	0.0172
LIT	0.3798	0.6327
CHILD-WOM	−0.1683	−0.7684
MFGHH	−0.8589	−0.0776
OTHERACT	0.8612	0.1334
POPF/M	−0.1084	0.6127
HHSZ	−0.2178	−0.4659
POPSZ	0.1002	−0.0385
Eigen Value	3.18	1.35
% Exp.	0.66	0.28

Note: N = 467; class I is each with a population of 100,000 and above.

Source: Author's calculation.

Table 7.18. Self-, casual wage, and regular wage employment across different classes of cities (2009–10)

	Self-EMP	REGULAR	CASUAL
Constant	280.07	366.46	80.46
	(11.65)**	(11.78)**	(4.54)**
DumCity 2	−7.61	−21.36	24.30
	(−0.26)	(−0.57)	(1.15)
DumCity 3	38.09	−70.37	47.18
	(1.35)	(−1.92)*	(2.27)**
Adj R2	0.04	0.04	0.05

Note: No = 77; DumCity 2 and DumCity3 represent dummies for size class 2 (50,000 and above, but less than 1 million) and three towns (less than 50,000) with million-plus cities being the comparison group.

Source: Author's calculation.

The only surprising fact relates to the decline in the gender ratio in large cities, which is mainly because of the predominance of male migration in these cities: with an increase in city size, the male migration rate rises, mainly because employment prospects are better in large cities. At the all-India level, the share of regular wage employment is highest in the million-plus cities and least in class 3 towns (with a population less than 50,000), whereas casual employment and self-employment follow the opposite pattern. Based on the state-level data, it is again distinct that regular wage employment is the highest in the million-plus cities and least in the class 3 towns, though the difference in the magnitude between class 1 and 2 is not statistically significant (Table 7.18). On the other hand, casual employment is the largest in the class 3 towns. Within the million-plus cities, regular employment

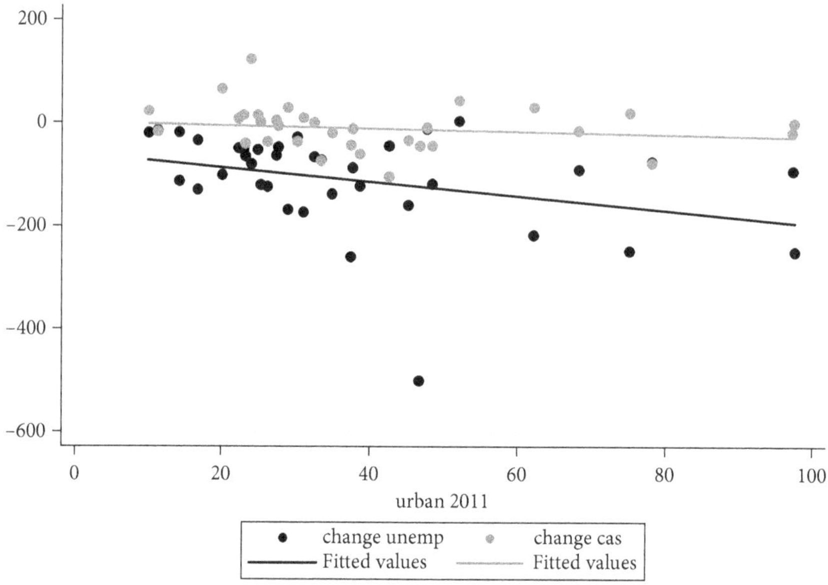

Figure 7.4. Change in the unemployment rate and casual employment after migration (compared to figures before migration) against the urbanization level

Note: The figures on unemployment and causal employment are taken on a per 1,000 basis (not percentage), while the urbanization level is in percent.

Source: NSS (2007–8).

again tends to increase with city size, though it is not statistically significant at the 10 per cent level.[6]

The decline in the unemployment rate and the decline in the percentage of the workforce engaged as casual workers after migration compared with the respective magnitudes prior to migration vary positively with the level of urbanization (see Figure 7.4). Further, we observe that casual employment and self-employment are higher in smaller urban settlements, while regular wage employment is higher in larger urban settlements (see Figures 7.5 to 7.7). From this, we may conclude that individuals in large cities are better off after migration.

On the whole, though the evidence is not highly supportive, the broad patterns are suggestive of population movement to large urban centres which provide better job opportunities compared to the rural job market. Such mobility does not necessarily result in absorption in the formal sector; rather there is an indication of a rise in the incidence of informal sector employment. However, the livelihood opportunities in the urban informal sector could be better than what the migrants accessed at the place of origin, and thus a subtle mechanism which facilitates

[6] REG = 433.49 + 7.12E-06 POPSZ
(11.02)** (1.31) Adj. R2 = 0.03, N = 22; where REG represents regular wage employment and POPOSZ is the population size in the million plus cities.

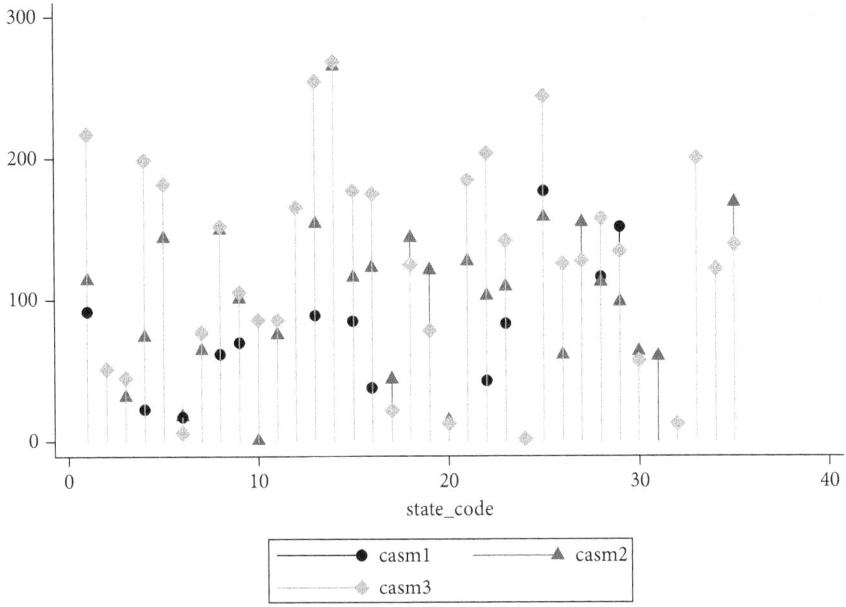

Figure 7.5. Share of casual employment across different classes of cities across states.

Note: Figures are per 1,000. The three types of cities do not exist across all the states and union territories.

Source: NSS (2009–10) Employment-Unemployment Survey.

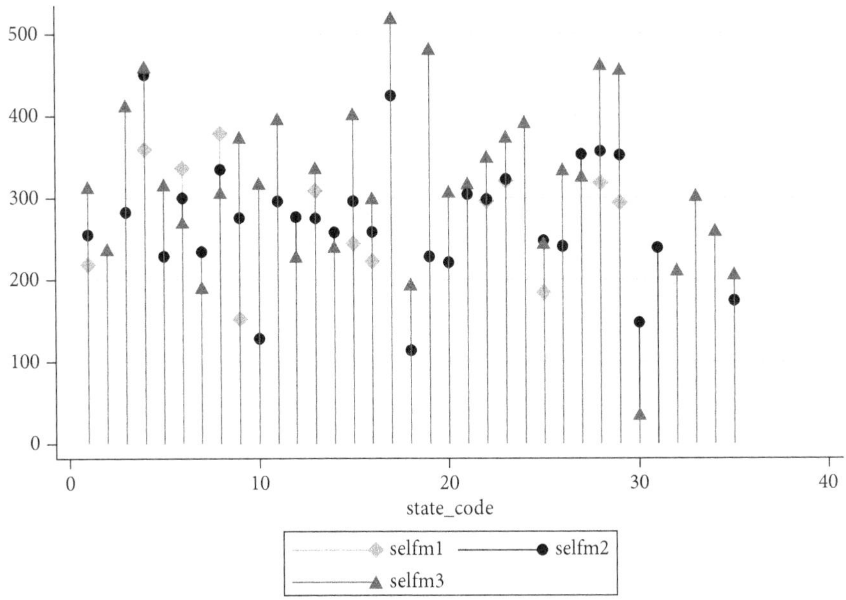

Figure 7.6. Share of self-employment across different classes of cities across states.

Note: Figures are per 1,000. The three types of cities do not exist across all the states and union territories.

Source: NSS (2009–10) Employment-Unemployment Survey.

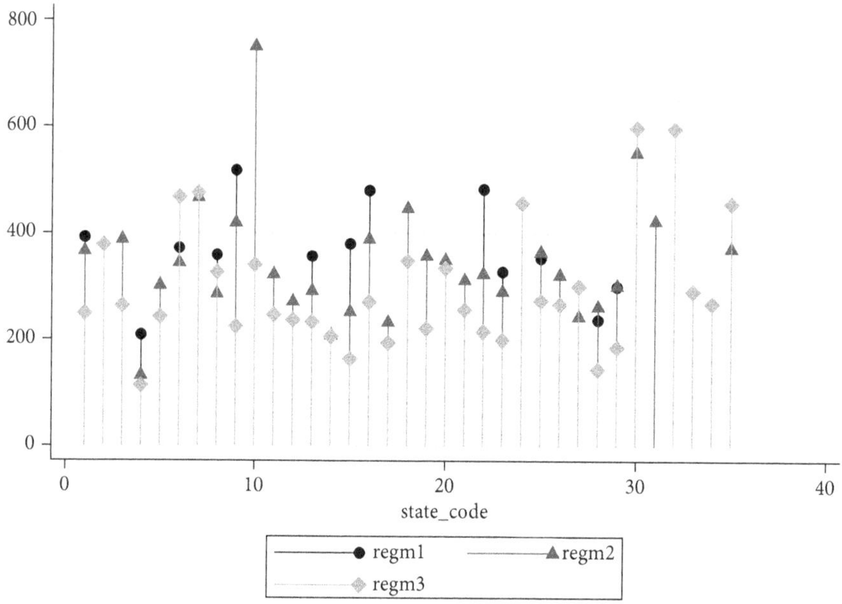

Figure 7.7. Share of regular wage employment across different classes of cities across states

Note: Figures are per 1,000. The three types of cities do not exist across all the states and union territories.

Source: NSS (2009–10) Employment-Unemployment Survey.

poverty reduction after migration seems to exist. But the reduction is nominal and thus the regions even after experiencing a reduction in poverty due to migration may continue to reveal a positive association between rural and urban deprivation. Such observations are substantiated with evidence from the factor analysis as well, confirming the decline in poverty in relation to both migration and urbanization. In order to strengthen these beneficial effects, more policy interventions are required so that migration and urbanization exert their positive spillover effects in both rural and urban areas.

As such, in the Indian context, there is no social security for migrants in particular. The labour market regulations are mostly inapplicable to workers engaged in the informal sector. Though the minimum wage legislation exists for a number of activities, its enforcement is a difficult proposition. As mentioned earlier, even entry to a slum cluster depends on social connections. 'In the absence of a coherent policy framework and strategy, migration imposes heavy costs on human development through poor labour arrangements and working conditions of migrants, and obstacles in their access to shelter, education, healthcare and food' (UNICEF 2012). Internal migration has not received any priority by the government, and policies of the Indian state have not been successful in providing any form of legal or social protection to this vulnerable group (UNICEF 2012).

7.5.4 Job Search Strategies: How Do Informal Sector Workers Access Jobs?

An important question is how the informal sector workers access jobs. Since most of the workers do not possess high levels of education, the possibility of utilizing the formal methods of accessing job market information is rather weak. The percentage of workers accessing informal networks across occupations is given in Table 7.19 based on our survey of slum workers in four cities, which was conducted under a UNDP project. Tailoring and manufacturing were some of the activities in which workers used networks to a larger extent than other activities. On the other hand, those working as construction workers and labourers (excluding Jaipur) seemed to be using networks relatively less. Since the construction sector is predominated by contractors and it operates on the basis of the daily wage labour market, the requirement for networks would be rather less. However, the nature of the city could also be a determinant of network use. A large city with greater economic opportunities attracts larger supplies of labour, and accessibility to the labour market from an individual point of view becomes more difficult. Even the possibility of accessing public space to squat is more difficult in a large city compared with a small one (Edelman and Mitra 2006). Hence, operating through networks among workers is an effective solution. Though we do not have detailed data for different size classes of cities, it is seen widely that low-income households use informal networks even in large cities for accessing labour market information (Banerjee 1986). We are, however, not able to provide any strong evidence in favour of a positive association between network intensity and city size.

Some of the studies have already highlighted the importance of informal networks in accessing jobs in the urban labour market. Networks are an indispensable part of the job search process through which entry is made to the labour market. But, as Mitra (2004) points out, the prevalence of networks—given the specialization of activities in different parts of the city which results in heterogeneity in the city's economic structure—leads to market information asymmetry, leading to physical segmentation of the labour market. Excess supplies of labour in certain activities reduce the scope of upward mobility in terms of income. As the contact persons and the new entrants (migrants) both pursue their jobs in similar activities and in the same neighbourhoods wages remain highly competitive. Social ties often do not release them from the close nexus they share and thus they cannot diversify their job search across space. Elliott (1999) noted that for less-educated workers, the use of informal contacts results in significantly lower wages. Hence, the trade-offs between social ties and economic gains can be significant.

Kono (2006) demonstrates that hiring workers through employee referrals reduces the new applicants' pay-offs, while a diversification of networks can raise their pay-offs. Network extension or pursuance of similar networks reduces the market equilibrium wage, while network diversification raises referral wages

Table 7.19. Distribution of workers by occupation and networks

Occupation	Jaipur		Ludhiana		Mathura		Ujjain		All four cities	
	Self	Networks	Self	Networks	Self	Networks	Self	Networks	Self	Networks
Semi-professional	45.57	54.43	70.37	29.63	74.12	25.88	70.59	29.41	64.26	35.74
Sales & trade	44.17	55.83	62.78	37.22	56.65	43.35	71.74	28.26	57.14	42.86
Personal services	47.22	52.78	72.50	27.50	59.18	40.82	72.58	27.42	58.80	41.20
Manufac. & repair	40.24	59.76	66.45	33.55	44.04	55.96	67.03	32.97	57.25	42.75
Comm. & security	41.38	58.62	70.59	29.41	60.00	40.00	75.00	25.00	62.50	37.50
Transport	58.62	41.38	81.63	18.37	76.71	23.29	78.57	21.43	69.12	30.88
Tailoring	41.89	58.11	64.41	35.59	50.00	50.00	47.37	52.63	54.39	45.61
Construction	63.57	36.43	65.71	34.29	76.09	23.91	90.24	9.76	69.23	30.77
Labour	34.48	65.52	79.49	20.51	75.00	25.00	88.89	11.11	81.71	18.29
Others	51.61	48.39	71.43	28.57	61.70	38.30	76.19	23.81	64.97	35.03
Total	48.33	51.67	67.77	32.23	62.64	37.36	77.57	22.43	63.49	36.51

Source: Slum Survey (2006–7) under the GOI-UNDP Project.

through the bargaining effect. Munshi and Rosenzweig (2006) noted that male 'working-class-lower-caste-networks' in Bombay send boys to local language schools as a result of which they end up in traditional occupations, though the non-traditional white-collar occupations were on the rise in the 1990s.

In order to identify the determinants of upward mobility Mitra (2010) used a binomial logit framework and showed that networks operating through close relatives neither enhance nor reduce the probability of experiencing upward mobility. This is evident despite the fact that informal networks are essential to enter the urban job market. However, younger workers are able to form new networks, particularly through new communication technologies. As a result of this, the duration of job searching seems to have come down, though with increased competition between young workers and the elderly workers who have been forced to participate in the labour market in search of a livelihood, real income levels have not increased widely. Hence, government intervention is important from the long-term developmental point of view. These interventions can be manifested in terms of housing support, provision of health, skill formation and education, dissemination of job market information (pertaining to the informal sector) through effective channels, and a range of livelihood support schemes including marketing and credit assistance and assurance of minimum wages.

7.6 Conclusion and Policy

The overall conclusions are indicative of certain patterns which are important both from analytical and policy points of view. First of all, rural-to-urban migration in the Indian context is not exceptionally high if we consider the aggregate rates for all urban areas. However, when it comes to large cities, the rates are higher. Such city size bias enters into the decision-making process of the migrants because large cities are endowed with higher levels of infrastructure, investment, and job opportunities. Though migrants are not able to graduate to the organized or high-productivity sector, they seem to be better off even in the informal sector, after migration, and particularly in large cities compared to small towns.

From the state-level data, we noted that the higher the level of urbanization, the greater is the decline in the unemployment rate after migration in comparison to the unemployment rate prevailing prior to migration. Also, based on the cross-sectional data, the rise in overall labour force participation and the relative size of regular wage employment after migration show a positive relationship with urbanization, though neither of them is found to be statistically significant. However, based on factor analysis, the change in regular wage employment and the change in unemployment rate after migration are found to be highest and both are inversely related. Though urbanization is nominally associated with these variables, it takes a positive factor loading, implying that states with higher urbanization levels experience a greater decline in the unemployment rate and a larger increase in regular wage employment after migration. Besides, the migration rate to urban areas and the urbanization level are positively associated, though moderately.

The data for class 1 cities brings out distinctly that some of the demographic variables such as household size and child–woman ratio decline with city size. The relative size of some of the residual activities like household manufacturing also tapers off, while that of non-household manufacturing and services rises with an increase in city size. The only surprising fact relates to the decline in the gender ratio in large cities, which is mainly because of the predominance of male migration in these cities. On the whole, with an increase in city size, the migration rate rises mainly because employment prospects seem to be better in large cities. The share of regular wage employment is highest in the million-plus cities and the least in smaller cities, whereas casual employment and self-employment follow just the opposite pattern.

Migration, urban informal sector employment, and the incidence of SCs in urban and rural areas are all positively connected, suggesting that the socially backward groups are more likely to migrate and end up in the urban informal sector. This pattern is accompanied by a decline in the incidence of poverty in both rural and urban areas: the informal sector activities in large cities are able to provide relatively better job opportunities and higher living standards. Urbanization and migration show beneficial effects in terms of reduction in both rural and urban poverty, though this process is not strongly evident. Also, states with a higher poverty incidence in rural areas experience a similar situation in urban areas.

Many rural migrants are not highly educated or skilled, and as a result they get absorbed into the urban informal sector. However, the informal sector also constitutes certain productive activities, which help workers escape poverty. On the whole, though, the evidence is not highly supportive, and the broad patterns are suggestive of a movement of the population to large urban centres as they provide better job opportunities. Such mobility does not necessarily result in absorption in the formal sector, rather there is an indication of a rise in the incidence of informal sector employment. However, livelihood opportunities in the informal sector could be better than what the migrants accessed at the place of origin, and thus a subtle mechanism working towards poverty reduction after migration seems to exist, notwithstanding a positive correlation between rural and urban poverty. The reduction is nominal and thus the regions even after experiencing a reduction in poverty due to migration may continue to reveal a positive association between rural and urban deprivation. Such observations are also substantiated with evidence from the factor analysis, confirming the decline in poverty in relation to both migration and urbanization. This is, however, not to deny the fact that the informal sector comprises vast stretches of low-productivity activities as well, which, in turn, explain considerable overlaps between migration, informal sector employment, and poverty. In order to strengthen the beneficial effects, more policy interventions are required so that migration and urbanization exert their positive spillover effects in both rural and urban areas.

Overall employment growth, particularly in the large-scale manufacturing sector, has not been high enough to provide job opportunities to those who migrate from the agriculture sector. Besides, the manufacturing base in several Indian states is perceptibly low. Rising capital and skill intensity in the growth process has further reduced the labour-absorbing capacity of the manufacturing sector. The informal sector, on the other hand, faces several constraints in terms credit, infrastructure, diversification and marketing of products, lack of information on consumer demand, and management skills. Also, many of the informal sector activities are of the residual type, particularly within the realms of the services sector, though several new services have emerged in the growth process, which are being increasingly consumed by urban middle-class households. Similarly, though the ancillarization and business contractualization processes have enabled some small manufacturing firms to receive greater work consignments from large businesses, such beneficial effects are limited.

On the whole, urbanization due to limited demand for labour is not able to absorb rural surplus labour productively. States with both higher and lower levels of urbanization seem to be experiencing poor quality employment, which explains why there is no relationship between the level of urbanization and the incidence of the informal sector. Further, from the supply point of view, the labour migrating to urban areas demonstrates poor employable skills. Third, there are costs associated with migration which discourage the flow of populations from rural to urban areas. So the major policy challenge is how to raise the level of urbanization and make it of better quality so that the enhanced level of urbanization can be taken as a positive indicator of development. The agglomeration benefits can be utilized in the direction of poverty reduction, which would indeed be cost effective. Expansion in labour-intensive and productive activities is a prerequisite. Besides, the productivity growth that takes place in large cities can partly be utilized for providing social and infrastructure support and training facilities to low-income households. The land market, which is under severe speculation, has reduced the accessibility of low-income migrants to city space. In terms of housing and neighbourhood characteristics, employment and earnings, and accessibility to public services, there is glaring evidence on a segregation process alongside the growth process. Therefore, the policy focus needs to be developed to make the overall urbanization process generative so that it results in better labour market outcomes and becomes inclusive by creating a more conducive environment for rural migrants rather than treating rural to urban population movement as a negative epithet.

Overall, urbanization, as perceived in the light of the historical experience of the present-day developed nations, is a strong indicator of development, which has facilitated population flow from the less developed to developed regions, integrated them into mainstream activities, and provided productive sources of livelihood. In this respect, the Indian experience does not seem to have been promising. The contribution of urbanization as far as rural–urban migration, better labour market outcomes, and livelihood sources are concerned is rather nominal. There is government failure in a number of areas including housing, skill development, health accessibility, and employment creation. On the other hand, the distortions involved in various product and factor markets are enormous. The intermediaries in various markets and their rent-seeking behaviour have added to the vulnerabilities of low-income households and retarded the positive role that urbanization is likely to play in the context of the overall development of an economy. The lack of appropriate technology did not allow urbanization to follow as a concomitant of industrialization, and for this both the government and the market are responsible. The Indian urbanization experience, in fact, stands in sharp contrast to the positive outcomes observed elsewhere. More government action is required for eliminating the distortions in a number of areas. For example, strict regulations are required for curtailing the speculative activities in the land and housing market and more interventions are essential for improving the accessibility of low-income households to employment, earnings, housing, basic amenities, health, and skills. For all this, huge investment is required which, in turn, can contribute to growth and urban development, on the one hand, and make the city space liveable for low-income households, on the other. In other words, there is a huge need for making urbanization inclusive. This can be pursued by focusing on a strategy that aims at targeting the very large cities because that would be cost effective. Some of the large cities are possibly saturated and, in this situation, the nearby areas in the periphery deserve a great deal of investment for reaping the potential benefits which may still exist. In addition, there are several big cities that need to receive quantum investment for reaping the agglomeration economies. The benefits of scale economies in the large cities can reduce the per capita cost and at the same time contribute to growth and development by enhancing the total factor productivity growth. On the whole, integrated markets are needed to allocate capital, land, and labour between rural and urban areas and across cities. The government must play a better role to improve the connectivity of different regions and cities and the liveability and sustainability of cities.

Some of the recent policies in India such as Skill India, Digital India, and Smart Cities are noteworthy. The Smart Cities are supposed to offer world class business environments. Both FDI and domestic investment are expected to flow into these cities. With concentration of economic activities job opportunities are expected to grow. But these investments of world class order will require a skilled workforce. Besides, local governments will be vigilant regarding the growth of slums and squatter settlements. This would mean that rural unskilled labour is less likely to benefit in the process of new growth because of the lack of a suitable entry point. However, with access to skill their employability is expected to improve, and rural–urban migration among the younger population may rise significantly. City authorities will have to plan for greater investment in affordable housing and basic amenities so that future urbanization in India does not present a gloomy scenario.

References

Banerjee, B. 1986. *Rural to Urban Migration and the Urban Labour Market: A Case Study of Delhi, Bombay and New Delhi*, Himalaya Publishing House.

Basu, Alaka Malwade, Kaushik Basu, and Ranjan Ray. 1987. 'Migrants and the Native Bond: An Analysis of Microlevel Data from Delhi'. *Economic and Political Weekly*: 145–54.

Bhagat, Ram B. 2011. 'Emerging Pattern of Urbanisation in India'. *Economic and Political Weekly*: 10–12.

Bhattacharya, Prabir C. 2002. 'Rural-to-Urban Migration in LDCS: A Test of Two Rival Models'. *Journal of International Development 14* (7): 951–72.

Breman, J. 1985. *Of Peasants, Migrants and Paupers: Rural Labour Circulation and Capitalist Production in West India*, Oxford University Press.

Castaldo, Adriana, Priya Deshingkar, and Andy McKay. 2012. 'Internal Migration, Remittances and Poverty: Evidence from Ghana and India'. *Migrating out of Poverty Working Paper 7*, University of Sussex.

Chandrasekhar, S. and Ajay Sharma. 2015. 'Urbanization and Spatial Patterns of Internal Migration in India'. *Spatial Demography 3* (2): 63–89.

Chant, S. (ed.). 1992. *Gender and Migration in Developing Countries*, Belhaven Press.

Connell, J., Dasgupta, B., and Laishley, R. 1976. *Migration from Rural Areas: The Evidence from Village Studies*, Oxford University Press.

Daniel, U. 2011. 'Update on National Workshop on Child Migration, Education and Protection. 29–30 November. 2011, New Delhi'. Presentation at the UNESCO-UNICEF National Workshop on Internal Migration and Human Development in India, 6–7 December, New Delhi.

De Hann, A. 1994. *Unsettled Settlers, Migrant Workers and Industrial Capitalism in Calcutta*, Verloren.

De Hann, A. 2011. 'Inclusive Growth? Labour Migration and Poverty in India'. *The Indian Journal of Labour Economics 54*: 387–409.

Deshingkar, P. and S. Akter. 2009. 'Migration and Human Development in India'. *Human Development. UNDP (Human Development Research Paper, 2009/13.* <http://hdr.undp.org/en/reports/global/hdr2009/papers/HDRP_2009_13.pdf>.

Deshingkar, Priya and John Farrington. 2006. 'Rural Labour Markets and Migration in South Asia-Evidence from Indian and Bangladesh'. *Background paper for the World Development Report*, India.

Edelman, Brent and Arup Mitra. 2006. 'Access to Basic Amenities: The Role of Political Contact, its Determinants and Adverse Effects'. *Review of Urban and Regional Development Studies 18* (1): 25–40.

Elliott, James R. 1999. 'Social Isolation and Labour Market Isolation: Network and Neighbourhood Effects on Less-educated Urban Workers'. *Sociological Quarterly 40* (2): 199–216.

Fawcett, James T., Siew Khoo, and Peter Colin Smith, eds. 1984. *Women in Cities of Asia: Migration and Urban Adaptation*, Westview Press.

Harris, John R. and Michael P. Todaro. 1970. 'Migration, Unemployment and Development: A Two-sector Analysis'. *The American Economic Review 60* (1): 126–42.

Karlekar, M. 1995. 'Gender Dimensions in Labour Migration: An Overview'. In *Women and Seasonal Labour Migration*, edited by L. Schenk-Sandbergen, Sage Publications.

Kasturi, L. 1990. 'Poverty, Migration and Women's Status'. In *Women Workers in India: Studies in Employment and Status*, edited by V. Majumdar, Chanakya Publication.

Kaur, G. 1996. *Migration Geography*, Anmol Publications.

Khera, Reetika. 2006. 'Employment Guarantee and Migration'. *The Hindu*, 13 July.

Kono, Hisaki. 2006. 'Employment with Connections: Negative Network Effects'. *Journal of Development Economics 81*: 244.

Kundu, A. and P. C. Mohanan. 2009. 'Employment and Inequality Outcome in India'. OECD Conference, Paris.

Kundu, Amitabh and Niranjan Sarangi. 2007. 'Migration, Employment Status and Poverty: An Analysis Across Urban Centres'. *Economic and Political Weekly*: 299–306.

Kuznets, S. 1966. *Modern Economic Growth: Rate, Structure and Spread*, Yale University Press.

Lall, S. V., Harris Selod, and Z. Shalizi. 2006. *Rural–Urban Migration in Developing Countries: A Survey of Theoretical Predictions and Empirical Finding*. Development Research Group, The World Bank, Washington, DC.

Luke, Nancy and Kaivan Munshi. 2006. 'New Roles for Marriage in Urban Africa: Kinship Networks and the Labour Market in Kenya'. *The Review of Economics and Statistics 88* (2): 264–82.

Mitra, Arup. 1994. *Urbanisation, Slums, Informal Sector Employment and Poverty: An Exploratory Study*, D. K. Publishers.

Mitra, Arup. 2001. 'Employment in the Informal Sector'. In *Informal Sector in India: Perspectives and Policies*, edited by A. Kundu and A. N. Sharma, Institute for Human Development and Institute of Applied Manpower Research, New Delhi.

Mitra, Arup. 2004. 'Informal Sector, Networks and Intra-City Variations in Activities: Findings from Delhi Slums'. *Review of Urban and Regional Development Studies 16* (2): 154–69.

Mitra, Arup. 2005. 'Women in the Urban Informal Sector: Perpetuation of Meagre Earnings'. *Development and Change 36* (2): 291–316.

Mitra, Arup. 2010. 'Migration, Livelihood and Well-being: Evidencc from Indian City-Slums'. *Urban Studies 47* (7): 1371–90.

Mitra, Arup. 2013. *Insights into Inclusive Growth, Employment and Wellbeing in India*, Springer Science & Business Media.

Mitra, Arup and Mayumi Murayama. 2009. 'Rural to Urban Migration: A District-level Analysis for India'. *International Journal of Migration, Health and Social Care 5* (2): 35–52.

Mukherjee, Piu, G. B. D. Paul, and J. I. Pathan. 2009. 'Migrant Workers in Informal Sector: a Probe into Working Conditions'. *The Adecco-TISS Labour Market Research Initiative (ALTMRI) Discussion Paper Series. Discussion Paper 9.* Tata Institute of Social Sciences, Mumbai.

Munshi, Kaivan and Mark Rosenzweig. 2006. 'Traditional Institutions Meet the Modern World: Caste, Gender, and Schooling Choice in a Globalizing Economy'. *American Economic Review 96* (4): 1225–52.

Neetha, N. 2004. 'Making of Female Breadwinners: Migration and Social Networking of Women Domestics in Delhi'. *Economic and Political Weekly*: 1681–8.

Oberai A. S., H. P. Prasad, and M. G. Sardana.1989. *Determinants and Consequences of Internal Migration in India: Studies in Bihar, Kerala and Uttar Pradesh*, Oxford University Press.

Papola, T. S. 1981. *Urban Informal Sector in a Developing Economy*, Vikas Publishing House.

Rajan, S. I. 2013. *Internal Migration and Youth in India: Main Features, Trends and Emerging Challenges*, United Nations Educational, Scientific and Cultural Organization (UNESCO), New Delhi.

Ravallion, Martin and Gaurav Datt. 2002. 'Why Has Economic Growth Been More Pro-poor in Some States of India Than Others?' *Journal of Development Economics 68* (2): 381–400.

Sastry, N. S. 2004. 'Estimating Informal Employment and Poverty in India'. *United Nations Development Programme India, Discussion Paper Series-7*, December.

Singh, Andrea Menefee. 1984. 'Rural-to-Urban Migration of Women in India: Patterns and Implications'. In *Women in the Cities of Asia: Migration and Urban Adaptation*, edited by J. T. Fawcett, S. E. Khoo and P. C. Smith, Westview Press.

Srivastava, Ravi. 2011. 'Labour Migration in India: Recent Trends, Patterns and Policy Issues'. *The Indian Journal of Labour Economics 54*: 411–40.

Sundaram, K. 1986. 'Agriculture–Industry Inter-relations: Issues of Migration'. In *World Congress of the International Economic Association, 1986, Proceedings: Balance between Industry and Agriculture in Economic Development, Manpower and Transfers*, vol. 3, edited by S. Chakravarty, Macmillan.

Todaro, Michael P. 1969. 'A Model of Labor Migration and Urban Unemployment in Less Developed Countries'. *American Economic Review* 59 (1): 138–48.

UNESCO. 2013. *Social Inclusion of Internal Migrants in India*, United Nations Educational, Scientific and Cultural Organization.

UNICEF. 2012. *Internal Migration in India Initiative Internal Migration in India Initiative Policy Briefs For a Better Inclusion of Internal Migrants in India*, United Nations Educational, Scientific and Cultural Organization.

Williamson, J. G. 1988. 'Migration and Urbanisation'. In *Handbook of Development Economics*, edited by H. Chenery and T. N. Srinivasan , vol 1, Elsevier Science Publishers.

Wood, A. 1997. 'Openness and Wage Inequality in Developing Countries: The Latin American Challenge to East Asian Conventional Wisdom'. *World Bank Economic Review* 33: 33–57.

PART IV

LAND AND HOUSING

8

Housing System and Urbanization in the People's Republic of China

Jie Chen

8.1 Introduction

The transformations in the Chinese urban housing system over the last three decades are clearly the result of the People's Republic of China's (PRC) economic restructuring and the urbanization process. With the housing system changing, it has contributed strongly to reshaping the mode of urbanization.

First, a shift in the provisional responsibility of urban housing from work units to the market was a precondition of the market-oriented reforms of state-owned enterprises in the early 1980s (Wu 1996; Shaw 1997; Wang et al. 2005), which made the revitalization of the Chinese urban economy possible. Second, the transformation of urban housing from a welfare good to a commodity good greatly helped drive a consumption boom and economic prosperity in urban PRC (Song et al. 2004; Chen et al. 2011). Further, an increasingly flexible housing market with responsive supply elasticity is a key force in propelling rural–urban population mobility as well as intercity labour mobility in the PRC. In addition, local state revenue from the sale of residential housing land has played a crucial role in financing Chinese cities' infrastructure investment since the 1998 reforms (Wang et al. 2011; Ye and Wu 2014). As this chapter will show, the great housing market boom in the PRC is not only a consequence but also a source of the PRC's great leap forward in urbanization in the new century. In short, the changing functions of state intervention in the Chinese housing sector have yielded far-reaching impacts on the mode of urbanization. Nonetheless, the Chinese post-reform urban housing system has put too much priority on economic functions, while largely overlooking the needs of migrants, especially rural-to-urban migrants. This imbalance has produced severe obstacles for the sustainability of urbanization in the PRC.

Against this background, this chapter focuses on investigating why the Chinese government recently adopted a radical shift of post-reform housing policy and launched a massive construction plan of 36 million units of public housing between 2011 and 2015. This programme is widely regarded in the PRC as an economic vehicle to counteract the shocks of the global economic downturn and a

Jie Chen., *Housing System and Urbanization in the People's Republic of China Market* In: *Cities of Dragons and Elephants: Urbanization and Urban Development in China and India. Edited by:* Guanghua Wan and Ming Lu, Oxford University Press (2019). © Oxford University Press. DOI: 10.1093/oso/9780198829225.003.0008

regulation tool to cool down the overheating residential property markets (Naughton 2010; J.P. Morgan 2011). This chapter notes that the latest developments in the Chinese housing system should be closely connected to the adoption of the 'harmonious society' development ideology of 2006 as well as the new urbanization strategy formally launched in 2013, which is essentially a reorientation of the development strategy of the Chinese economy (World Bank and DRC 2013). In its focus, the recent public housing programme serves as a propelling engine to promote accommodating millions of low-income migrants in cities permanently under the new urbanization strategy. Interestingly, the literature suggests that housing practices in the PRC at the moment are actually not very different from those in Western countries if we take the stage of development of urbanization in the PRC into consideration (Chen, Stephens, et al. 2014). In many Western countries, public housing was developed at a similar stage of rapid industrialization to accommodate industrial workers (Malpass and Murie 1999; Chen, Stephens, et al. 2014). From this perspective, one may conclude that governments across the world are adopting 'similar strategies' to address similar housing issues when facing the pressures of rapid urbanization (Chen, Stephens, et al. 2014). However, the Chinese experience of achieving a balance between economic prosperity and housing affordability during the rapid urbanization process is still unique and thus may carry wide policy implications.

The remaining sections of this chapter are organized as follows: Section 8.2 provides a rough introduction of the institutional framework of the Chinese housing system as well as its evolution from 1949 until now. Section 8.3 investigates the performance of the Chinese housing sector. Section 8.4 explores the interaction between the housing system and urbanization in China, with a focus on how the marketization of housing provision drives urbanization. The associated problems of this approach are currently being partly corrected by the re-emergence of state provision. Section 8.5 discusses lessons from the Chinese experience of housing system development, and, finally, Section 8.6 provides policy recommendations for establishing a housing system that is supportive of urbanization in developing economies.

8.2 The Institutions of the Chinese Housing System

The Chinese urban housing system can be divided into four principal periods (Chen and Han 2014): (1) the development of the socialist state welfare system from the late 1940s until 1978; (2) the dual-track system until 1998, which included the mass privatization of state-owned and other forms of public housing during the reforms of the 1980s and 1990s; (3) the market-dominated system between 1999 and 2006, which included the fully fledged development of the housing market and the marginalization of state provision; and finally (4) the ongoing new dual regime, seeking to rebalance the state and market in the provision of urban housing, which includes the promotion of 'everyone should be housed' (*zhu you suo ju*) since the 17th national congress of the Chinese Communist Party (CCP) in 2007 and the adoption of a mass public housing programme in 2010. The latest developments in the Chinese housing system should be understood against the background of the new urbanization strategy launched in 2013 (World Bank and DRC 2013).

8.2.1 Housing Provision System: Pre-reform and Reform Era

The Maoist urban housing regime was mainly shaped by ideological and political considerations (Chen and Gao 1993). However, the state provision of housing was also aimed at addressing the urgent need to accommodate the growing population of urban workers at a low cost (Lim and Lee 1990). The integration of work and living under the work-unit-based quasi-clan system effectively depressed population mobility across regions (Zhang 2000). Thus, the work-unit-based public housing provision comprised an essential component of social organization and labour production in pre-reforms urban China (Wu 1996). We can interpret the Maoist housing provision system as a part of the development strategy of 'industrialization without urbanization'.

The heavy dependence of housing construction on the state budget and centralized planning led to deteriorating housing conditions in Maoist urban China (Shaw 1997; Chen and Gao 1993). The average floor space per capita in urban China decreased from 4.5 sq. m in 1952 to 3.6 sq. m in 1978 (World Bank 1992). The severe shortage of housing space heavily constrained the expansion of the urban population in Maoist urban China. Over the period of 1949–78, the urbanization rate achieved only marginal growth, from 10.64 per cent to 17.92 per cent.

Against the backdrop of the reforms of the urban economy, the Chinese government launched the reforms of the urban housing system in 1978. There are three basic policy components to the Chinese housing reforms: rent reform, the privatization of public housing, and the establishment of a housing market. Changing the concept of urban housing from a 'welfare good' (or a socialist welfare right) to a 'market good' (or a commodity) constituted the essential spirit of the Chinese urban housing reforms (Lim and Lee 1990). As a key component of the Chinese government's stimulus package to counteract the negative shocks of the 1997 Asian financial crisis (Man 2011; Wang et al. 2012), the distribution of welfare housing in kind was formally terminated by the State Council in July 1998. With employers no longer bound to provide housing to urban workers, the drastic restructuring of the urban housing provision system greatly facilitated rural–urban migration as well as intercity labour mobility.

8.2.2 The Housing Provision System: Post-reform Era

Since 1998, the housing provision system has evolved gradually with economic development and the urbanization process. In addition to the market housing system, a two-tier public housing system consisting of Cheap Rental Housing (CRH) and Economic Comfortable Housing (ECH) was introduced in 1998 (cf. Table 8.1 and Figure 8.1). ECH was designed as the predominant form of post-reform housing provision in the official document (SC[1998]No.23). However, with the pressure of boosting GDP growth through a real estate boom (Rosen and Ross 2000), the importance of public housing rapidly waned after 1998. In 2003, the State Council formally gave up the idea of ECH as the main form of post-reform housing (SC[2003]No.18). Public housing has since been substantially downgraded to playing a supportive role in the housing provision system.

The shift in the provision responsibility of urban housing from work units to the market has made rural-to-urban migration and labour mobility much easier than before. However, the housing market boom has also been accompanied by a rapid increase in house prices, making home purchase increasingly unaffordable

Table 8.1. Types of public housing in post-reform urban China

Type	Description	
Old public housing	Housing built by the state between 1949 and 1998	
Privatized	Sold to sitting tenants at heavily discounted prices	
Non-privatized	Remained under the control of local housing authorities	
New public housing	Housing built or subsidized by the state after 1998	
	Target group	**Eligibility requirement**
For sale		
Economic Comfortable Housing (ECH)	Low-income "house-poor" urban households	Residence permit (Hukou), income and asset threshold, living space per person threshold
Capped-Price Housing (CPH)	Low-to-middle-income and middle-income urban households	Residence permit (Hukou), income threshold, without owned-home
Shantytown Renovation Housing (SRH)	Households relocated due to urban revitalization and major construction projects	Owners of expropriated homes
For renting		
Cheap Rental Housing (CRH)	Lowest-income "house-poor" urban households	Residence permit (Hukou), income and asset threshold, living space per person threshold
Public Rental Housing (PRH)	Wide range of urban population, including migrants	No residence permit required, flexible or no income threshold

Source: Author's own summary based on various official documents.

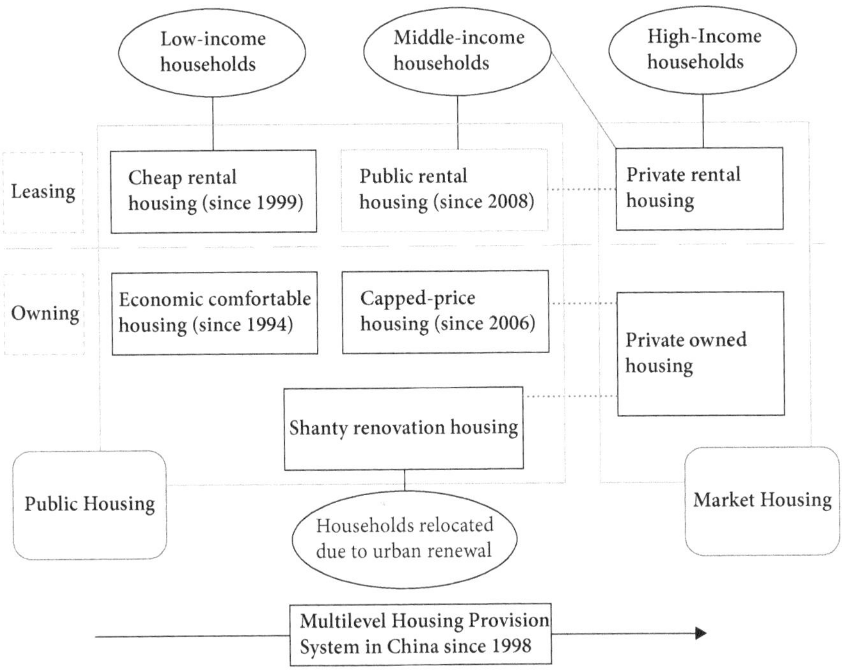

Figure 8.1. The post-reform housing provision system in China

for low- and middle-income households and, in particular, for young workers and migrants (Chen et al. 2010; Yang and Shen 2008). The housing market is thus polarizing property wealth between different tenures and different socio-economic and demographic cohorts (Logan et al. 2010; Man 2011). Meanwhile, the lack of affordable housing provision has produced severe obstacles for the sustainability of urbanization in the PRC. The Chinese central government has over time reached a consensus that the imbalance between the housing sector and socio-economic development can be largely attributed to the insufficiency and inefficiency of the state provision of housing (Qi 2009; MOHURD 2011; Li 2011).

In August 2007, the central government again committed itself to meeting the basic housing needs of low-income 'house-poor' urban households by developing public housing (SC[2007]No.24). This milestone document signalled the turning point of the Chinese post-reform housing system and essentially reversed the downward trend of public housing since 1998 (cf. Table 8.2). Over the last few years, the construction of public housing has experienced a 'Great Leap Forward'. In January 2011, Premier Wen Jiabao announced a five-year plan to construct 36 million units of public housing from 2011 to 2015, aimed at accommodating a fifth of the Chinese urban population by 2015. How this programme affects the urbanization process in the PRC is the focus of this chapter.

Table 8.2. Milestone housing policy documents in post-reform PRC

Date	Issuing authority and policy document	Objectives and implications
July 1998	State Council: Notification on deepening the urban housing reforms and accelerating housing construction (SC[1998]No. 23)	The welfare-based public housing system was to be completely abolished; ECH was designed to dominate the whole housing system
August 2003	State Council: Notification on continuing accelerating healthy and sustainable development of real estate markets (SC[2003]No.18)	Market solutions dominate the housing sector; ECH and other public housing programmes were downgraded to marginal sectors
August 2007	State Council: Opinions on tackling housing difficulties of low-income families in urban areas (SC[2007]No.24)	The government would again intervene in the housing sector through public housing; CRH was chosen as the premier public housing scheme; the ECH scheme was significantly modified
December 2008	State Council General Office: Opinions on promoting steady and healthy development of real estate markets (SCGO[2008]No.131)	Strove to solve the housing difficulties of 7.47 million low-income "house-poor" urban families by 2011
January 2010	State Council General Office: Notification on steady and healthy development of real estate markets (SCGO[2010]No.4)	Strove to meet the housing needs of 15.4 million low-to-middle-income "house-poor" urban families by 2012
September 2011	State Council General Office: Guidelines on the construction and management of public housing (SCGO[2011]No.45)	Public housing planned to host 20 per cent of urban households by 2015; growing attention shifted to PRH

Source: Author's own summary based on various official documents.

8.2.3 Housing Policy Framework

Currently, at the central government level, MOHURD (Ministry of Housing and Urban-Rural Development) plays a leading role in designing and implementing housing policy, with responsibilities ranging from housing market regulation to public housing development. Nonetheless, the land policy is under the control of MLR (Ministry of Land Resource) and the Central Bank—POB (People's Bank of China)—regulates all policies regarding housing finance issues. Figure 8.2 shows the general policy regulatory framework of the housing sector in contemporary PRC. This framework shows a hierarchical and top-down system, with relevant government departments at different levels divided by policy design and regulatory responsibilities. There are also important interactions between the central government, local government, developers, property management companies, recipients, and other involved parties such as banks and other funding providers.

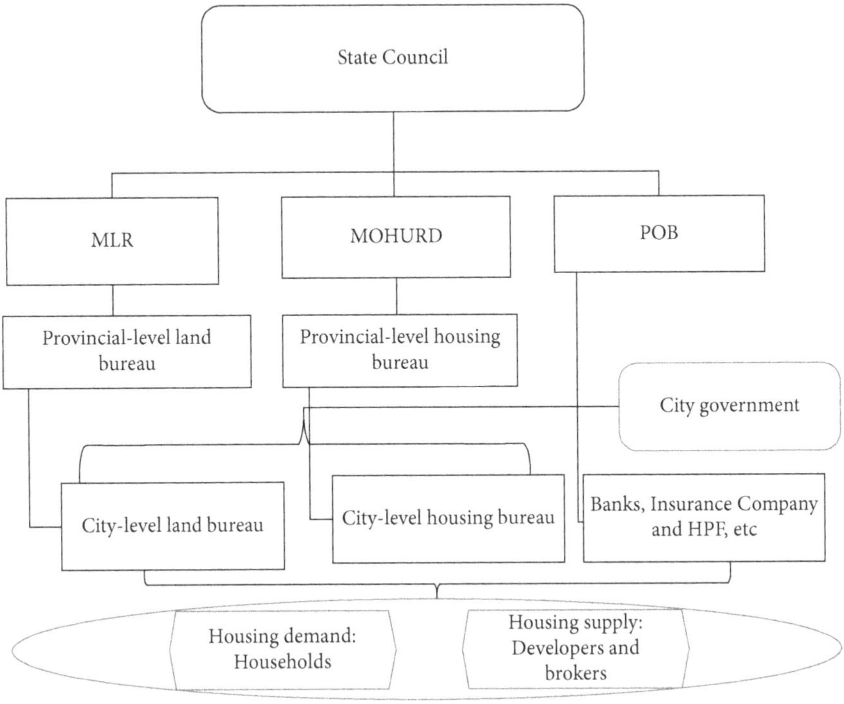

Figure 8.2. Post-reform housing policy regulatory framework in the PRC

Notes: MOHURD, Designing principal guidelines and taking up the general supervision responsibility; MLR, setting the annual quota of land supply, which is detailed at the provincial level, designing principal guidelines, and supervising the allocation of land resource; POB, setting benchmark interest rates, designing mortgage policy, and supervising the allocation of capital funding towards market housing and public housing.

Thus, in tandem with the dissolution of 'unit-based society' under the market economy (Zhao and Bourassa 2003), the division of housing provision responsibility is shared between the market, work units, households, and the state. The regulatory responsibility rests almost entirely in the local government's housing bureaus under the guidelines of central government command.

In the new housing policy framework, in addition to the traditional role of general policy formulation and strategic guidance, the central government is also heavily involved in decision making, both long term and in the annual provision plan of public housing for each province. Since 2009, MOHURD, for example, has signed agreements with each provincial government to guarantee the construction target for public housing (MOHURD 2011). If local leaders fail to complete the tasks assigned by the central government, they will face administrative punishment, including demotion or dismissal (SCGO[2010]No.4; SCGO[2011]No.45). This top-down approach is possible only under a centralized state system, such as that of the PRC. For the central government, the timely supply of sufficient numbers of housing units has been a key concern under the increasing pressure to maintain economic sustainability and society stability (SCGO[2010]No.4; SCGO[2011]No.45).

8.3 The Performance of the Chinese Housing Sector

The dominant role of the market in housing provision spurred one of the most unprecedented construction booms in human history. Housing development has also become more closely bound to economic growth and the urbanization process (Yang and Chen 2014).

8.3.1 Housing Market

Clearly, rapid urbanization is one of the fundamental driving forces behind the recent developments in the urban housing market in the PRC (World Bank and DRC 2013). Since 1999, the housing prices in urban PRC have maintained a strong upward trend, with the exception of a slight downward price adjustment in 2008 due to the shock of the global financial crisis. At the national level, the mean housing price in 2013 was approximately 3.15 times that in 1999 and 1.6 times that in 2008 (cf. Figure 8.3). In large cities such as Beijing and Shanghai, housing prices have risen much higher than the national average (cf. Figure 8.3). A persistent increase in housing prices, particularly in the PRC's major cities after 2008, affects both the sustainability of the property market and social stability (Yang and Chen 2014). The central government took several measures to curb the soaring housing prices, including monetary policies, household purchasing restrictions, and regulations related to the behaviour of real estate developers (Chen and Han 2014). Moreover, experiments with property tax were introduced in Shanghai and Chongqing in 2010 (Chen and Han 2014).

Households' purchasing power varies significantly across regions, and widening differences in regional housing markets have created a volatile context for local housing affordability (Figure 8.4). Examining the regional variations in the price to income ratio, we find it is highly positively correlated with the urbanization rate (Figure 8.4), which suggests that cities experiencing faster urbanization are more likely subject to housing affordability pressures and thus need more flexible modifications in local housing systems. A recent study also shows that migration has significantly contributed to the upsurge of housing prices in Chinese cities since 2000: every 10 per cent increase in the share of migrants in the local population growth in a city between 2000 and 2005 led to a 16.17 per cent increase in housing prices in the city in 2005 (Lu et al. 2014). However, the study also finds that the contribution of migrants to housing price growth is primarily driven by high-income urban-to-urban migrants rather than low-income rural-to-urban migrants (Lu et al. 2014).

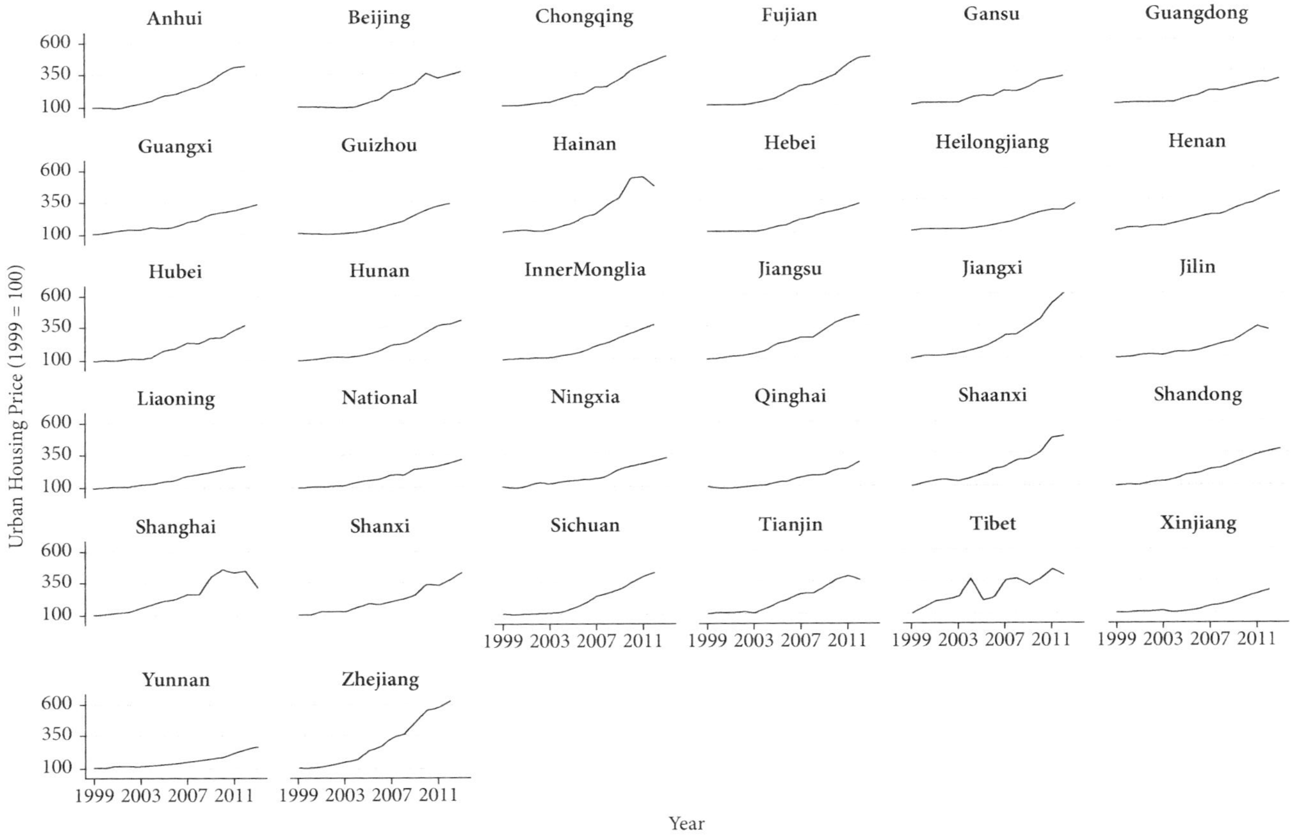

Figure 8.3. The national and regional trend of housing price in urban China (1999–2013)

Source: Statistics Yearbooks published by the National Bureau of Statistics China (NBSC 2013).

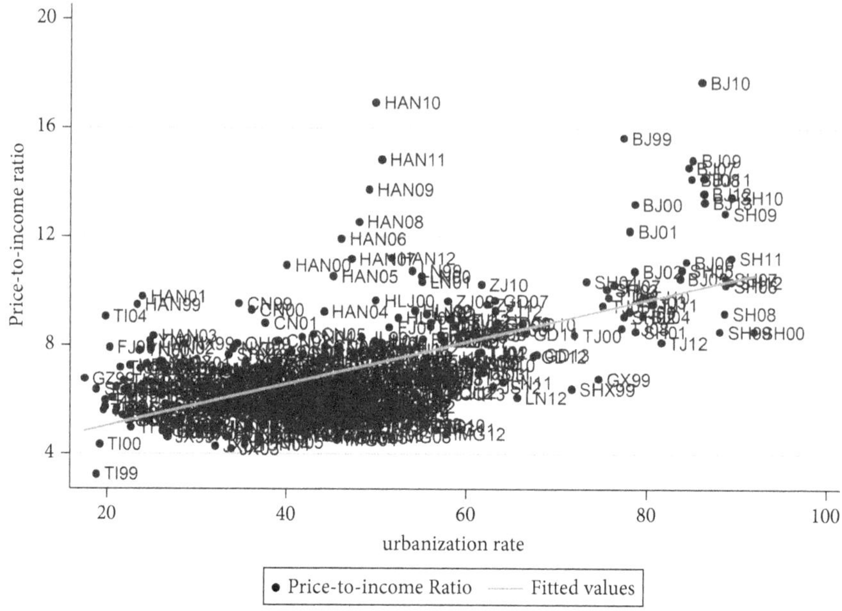

Figure 8.4. Housing affordability and urbanization in China (province-year observations, 1999–2013)

Source: Author's own calculation based on the raw data from the Statistics Yearbooks published by the National Bureau of Statistics China (NBSC 2013).

8.3.2 Housing Stock

An overwhelming majority of the public housing stock was quickly privatized within a few years after 1998. It is estimated that the size of the privatized public urban housing stock at the end of the twentieth century was 2.5 million sq. m (roughly 70 per cent of total public housing stock) and associated with an implicit market value of approximately RMB 2.5 trillion, or approximately 32 per cent of China's GDP in 1998 (Adams 2009). Privatization has helped raise home ownership levels among the permanent urban population to approximately 90 per cent (cf. Table 8.3). It is estimated that 40 per cent of (permanent) urban residents live in privatized housing. Enjoying a form of 'state legacy welfare', they are protected from the rising costs of housing in the market sector (Chen et al. 2010).

In tandem with the massive construction boom since the 1998 reforms, the improvement in housing conditions in urban PRC is substantial. According to the sixth national census (2010) (NBSC 2012), the total construction space of the occupied housing stock in urban PRC doubled from 10.3 billion sq. m in 2000 to 20.3 billion sq. m in 2010, and the average housing space per person in urban PRC resulted in a 35.6 per cent growth over the same period (22.36 sq. m vs 30.33 sq. m) (cf. Table 8.3).

However, the improvement in housing conditions in urban PRC is substantially uneven across regions. The housing conditions are generally quite good in the developed eastern region, but much poorer in the underdeveloped western area (cf. Figure 8.5). Further, there are vast variations in housing conditions across cities with different sizes. Generally speaking, the prevalence of housing overcrowding is still high in large cities where the migrant population grows fast, for instance, Shanghai and Beijing (cf. Table 8.4).

Table 8.3. Tenure distribution of housing in urban PRC, 2011

Tenure type	Description	Share (%)
Owner-occupied		89.3
Owned private housing	Self-built after 1949 or old private housing built before 1949	11.2
Owned market housing	Bought through the market and built by developers	38.0
Privatized public housing	Bought during the 1980–2000 housing reforms	40.1
Rental lease	Including both private and public rental housing	10.7

Source: NBSC (2011).

Table 8.4. Housing conditions in urban PRC and four major cities, 2000–10

Y2000	**Urban area**					
Region	**Families (in thousand)**	**Persons (in thousand)**	**Room numbers per family**	**Housing space per person (sq. m)**	**Housing-poor ratio (%)**	**Housing-difficult ratio (%)**
The PRC	131,298	408,814	2.39	22.36	**11.6**	**39.0**
Beijing	3,231	9,079	2.30	20.01	17.7	41.5
Tianjin	2,211	6,504	1.94	18.32	14.2	46.8
Chongqing	3,156	9,241	2.23	23.37	11.3	36.8
Shanghai	4,671	12,985	1.94	**21.52**	**16.8**	**44.4**
Y2010	Urban area					
China	207,189	590,124	2.65	30.33	**8.4**	**23.5**
Beijing	5,803	13,966	2.09	28.23	14.6	32.0
Tianjin	2,876	77,426	2.00	26.11	7.0	23.9
Chongqing	5,086	13,646	2.53	32.05	7.8	18.8
Shanghai	7,302	18,343	1.93	**25.84**	**15.6**	**35.7**

Note: (1) In the Chinese statistical system, there are two types of households—family households and collective households (*Jiti hu*), where many people share one Hukou (household registration status) collectively. The data here refer only to family households; thus, the number of "persons" in the table is slightly less (*c*.10 per cent) than the number of total persons reported in the census publications. (2) Housing-poor: families with housing space per person of less than 8 sq. m; housing-difficult: families with housing space per person of less than 16 sq. m.

Source: The fifth national census (2000) and sixth national census (2010) (NBSC 2012).

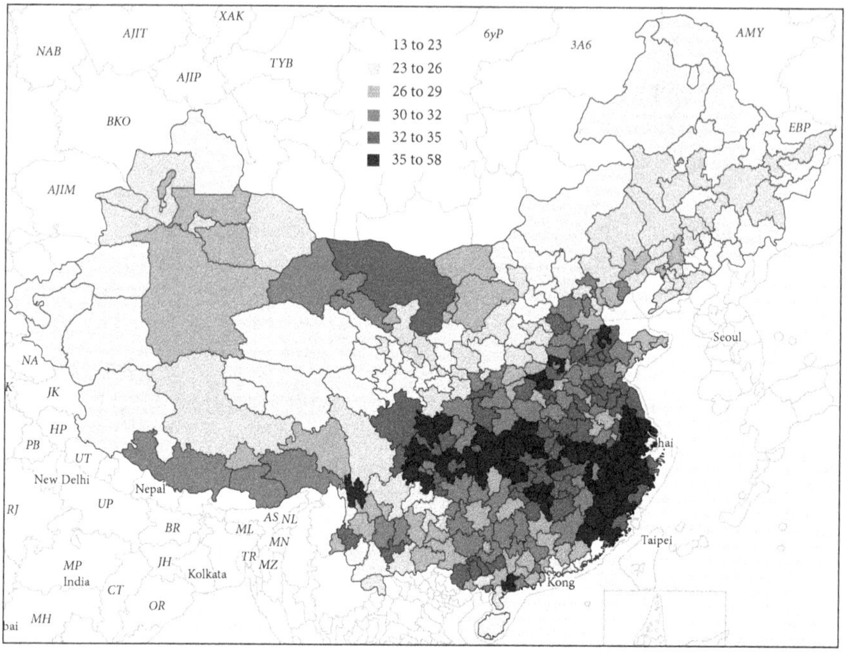

Figure 8.5. Housing space per person at the prefectural-city level in the PRC (2010) (unit: sq. m).

Source: Chinadataonline, University of Michigan, <http://chinadataonline.org/cge/cityclient95/#>.

8.4 The Interactions Between the Housing System and Urbanization

Urbanization has been high up on the policy agenda of developing countries since the 1950s (United Nations 2012; Cohen 2004). Glaeser regards cities as the greatest human invention and believes it is the 'proximity' in cities, bringing people into contact, that enables people to interact in productive ways (Glaeser 2010). However, few studies have examined the pivotal role of the housing system in the urbanization process.

8.4.1 Housing and Urbanization: An Analytical Framework

The housing system can affect urban development and urbanization through several channels. We now discuss four major channels that link the housing system to urbanization (cf. Figure 8.6).

First, the housing system affects the scale and structure of housing construction, which provides the most fundamental physical foundation to urban expansion (Mayer and Somerville 2000). Second, the housing system affects how the housing

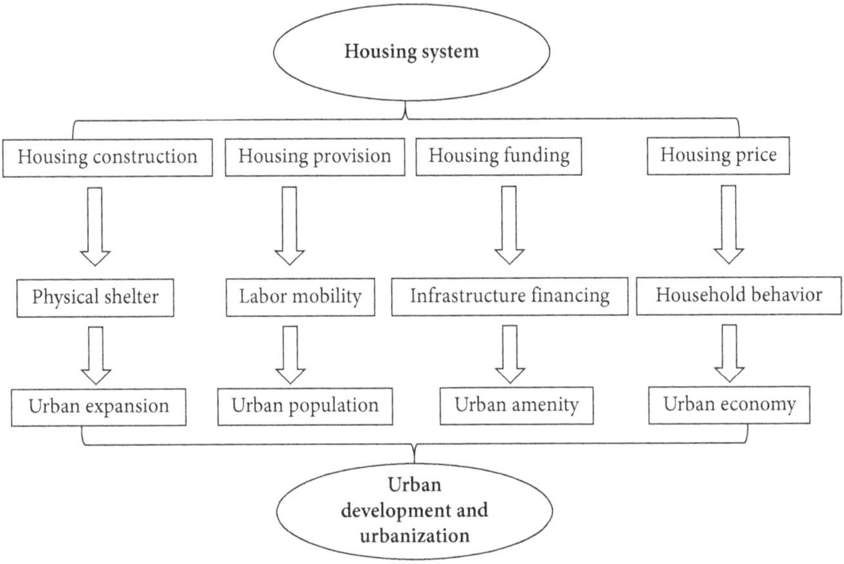

Figure 8.6. The linkage between housing system and urban development

is produced and delivered to the labour force and their families, which directly determines the size and spatial allocation of the urban population. For example, the responsiveness of housing supply plays a crucial role in determining housing prices and then affects urban employment growth (Glaeser et al. 2006). There is evidence that, in areas with an inelastic housing supply, labour demand shocks can more easily translate into lower employment growth (Saks 2008). The elasticity of the housing supply can also be severely land constrained by geography and then contribute to reshaping the spatial distribution of the urban population and urban economy (Saiz 2010). Third, the funding of housing investment is highly integrated with the financing of general urban infrastructure and urban public services, which underpins the formation of urban amenities and eventually affects the relative attractiveness of cities. Fourth, the housing system has a direct impact on the price movements of housing assets. Through household consumption or saving behaviour (wealth effects), borrowing or lending behaviour, and asset-building or asset-consuming behaviour (reverse mortgage), the fluctuations in housing prices deeply affect the trend and business cycles of the urban economy.

8.4.2 Housing Market Developments as Driving Forces of Urbanization

Research points out that the launch of the reforms of the Chinese urban housing system in the 1980s and 1990s was mainly driven by economic reasons (Wang et al. 2005; Man 2011). The direct goal was to reduce the soaring fiscal burden on urban housing subsidies (World Bank 1992). However, the Chinese government has for decades used the development of a commercialized housing sector as a motor to drive the urban economy (Wang and Murie 1999).

8.4.2.1 Housing Investment as a Driving Force of the Urban Economy

By any standard, the housing sector has become a leading pillar industry in the Chinese urban economy since the market-oriented reforms. Since the late 1990s, real estate investment has consistently accounted for approximately 10 per cent of Chinese GDP (NBSC 2013). Several empirical works confirm that housing investment has played a pivotal role in the Chinese economy (EIU 2011; Chen et al. 2011). In addition, some research also demonstrates that housing investment plays an active role in driving the PRC's economic fluctuations (Chen et al. 2011). However, the dependence of the local economy on real estate varies greatly across regions (cf. Figure 8.7). For example, as predicted by previous research (Chen et al. 2011), there does exist an inverted U-shape in the relationship between the ratio of real estate investment in local GDP with respect to the level of local GDP per capita (cf. Figure 8.7). This figure suggests that the importance of real estate investment in driving the Chinese urban economy would gradually lose its momentum in the future.

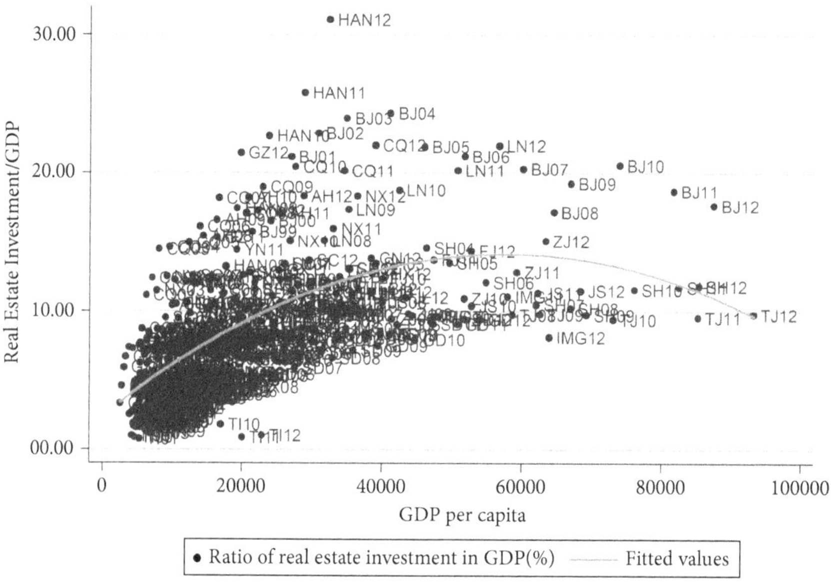

Figure 8.7. The ratio of real estate investment in GDP vs GDP per capita (province level, 1999–2013)

Source: Author's own calculation based on the raw data from the Statistics Yearbooks published by the National Bureau of Statistics China (NBSC 2013).

Data show that the real estate industry alone created 2.73 million jobs in 2012, which was 1.53 million higher than that in 2003 (NBSC 2013). The construction industry is perhaps the industry that benefited most from the housing market boom. Most jobs in the Chinese construction industry are taken up by rural-to-urban migrants. According to a survey published by the National Bureau of Statistics China (NBSC 2014), 22 per cent of rural migrant workers were employed in the construction industry, and this number amounted to 59.7 million.

8.4.2.2 Property-led Urban Redevelopment

The marketization of housing provision has led to great transformations in urban regeneration and urban redevelopment in Chinese cities. Since the early 1990s, urban redevelopment has been largely privately funded and property-led rather than driven by the government (Dowall 1994; Shin 2009). Subordinate to the local development strategy, urban renewal has been extensively used by municipal governments as a 'growth machine' (Wu et al. 2006). Property-led urban regeneration reflects the emergence of the entrepreneurial and profit-seeking behaviour of local governments in Chinese cities (Yang and Chang 2007).

Driven by diverse motivations of different levels of the entrepreneurial state as well as the profit-seeking motivations of investors, pro-growth coalitions between local governments, developers, and government enterprises are formed and exert powerful influence on urban redevelopment (He and Wu 2005). During the so-called 'property-led regeneration', old dilapidated houses in downtown areas were expropriated, original households were relocated to suburban areas, and residential communities in downtown areas were converted to shopping centres or other more profitable projects. By doing so, local governments obtained substantial revenues and funding sources to invest in the development of urban infrastructure and thereby increase the city's competitiveness.

China's market-oriented reforms of housing provision has also actively contributed to transforming the spatial landscape of Chinese cities (Wang and Murie 2000; Li and Wu 2006; Li and Wu 2008). In particular, jobs–housing linkages, transport modes, and commuting behaviour have greatly changed with increasing access to housing from the market rather than work units (Wang and Chai 2009).

8.4.2.3 Housing Supply as a Supporting Apparatus of Urban Expansion

Liberalizing housing markets is a critical step in promoting labour mobility across regions and between rural and urban areas. Empirical research provides evidence that interprovincial migration in the PRC was affected by the quantity of available housing in cities, but not the costs of housing (Fleisher et al. 1997). Figure 8.8 suggests that the expansion of the urban labour force is highly positively correlated with the growth of the local housing supply.

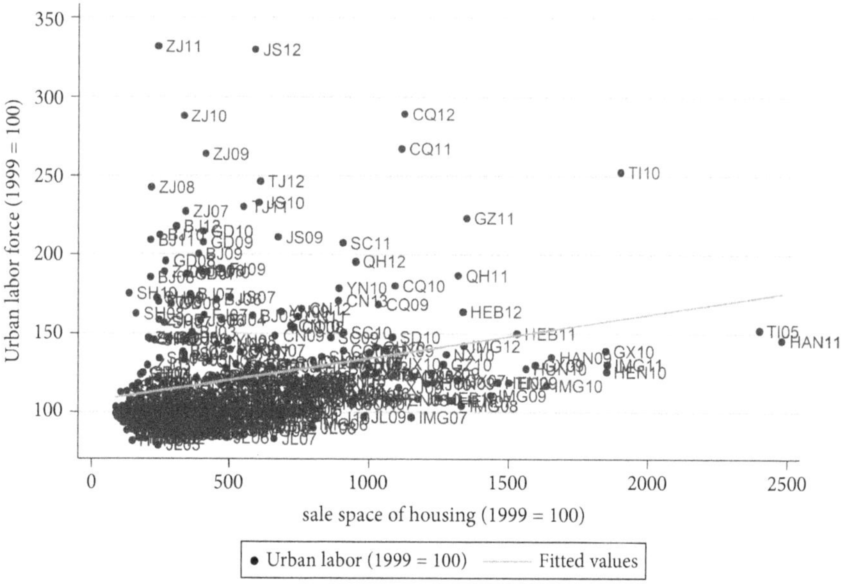

Figure 8.8. Housing supply and urban labour growth (province-level observations, 1999–2013)

Source: Author's own calculation based on the raw data from the Statistics Yearbooks published by the National Bureau of Statistics China (NBSC 2013).

8.4.2.4 Housing Capitalization as a Financial Engine of Urban Development

Encouraging private ownership of housing is another salient component of the Chinese transition from a socialist regime to a market economy (World Bank 1992). The emergence of a liberalized housing market and the related liberalization of land use rights were instrumental in promoting a market-driven urban economy and enabling a 'growth-first' model of urban governance. In a fast-growing economy, the commoditization and capitalization of urban housing makes it easy for the housing sector to attract speculative funding. Then, housing inevitably becomes an attractive source of investment (Chen 2011). At the end of 2013, approximately 21 per cent of banking loans in China were issued to the real estate sector, with 13.6 per cent going to home mortgages and 6.4 per cent going to loans for property and land development (People's Bank of China 2014). The ratio of the outstanding balance of home mortgages as a percentage of GDP rose from 1.41 per cent in 1999 to 17.23 per cent at the end of 2013 (People's Bank of China 2014).

Under the unique urban land system in the PRC where the local states hold a full monopoly over urban land, the capitalization of urban housing leads to the capitalization of urban land. To be exact, with a booming housing market, local

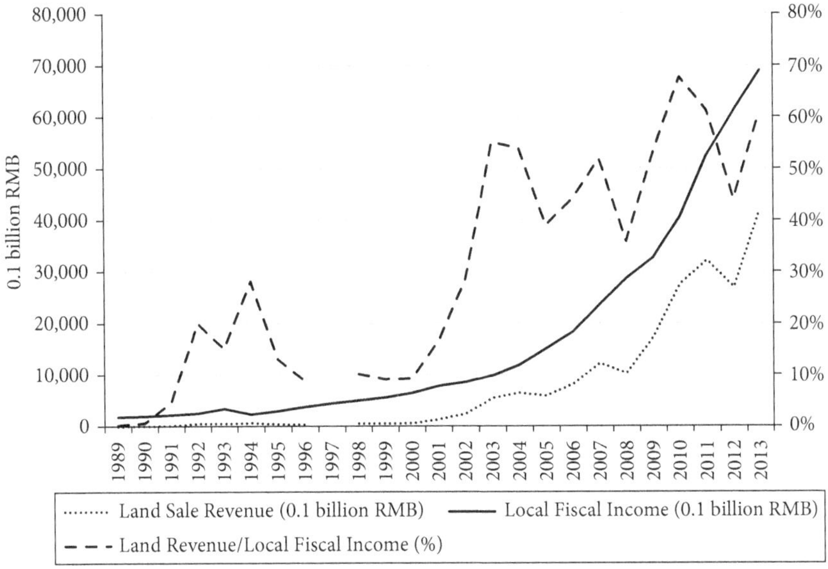

Figure 8.9. Land revenue and its importance to local public finance in the PRC, 1989–2013

Source: Statistics Yearbooks published by the National Bureau of Statistics China (NBSC 2013).

states can both receive enormous amounts of direct funding through land sale revenue and use high-valued land as collateral to borrow money from banks (Tao et al. 2010). Figure 8.9 suggests that the land sale revenue in the PRC has grown at a spectacular speed since the early twenty-first century and currently stands at approximately 3–4 trillion RMB, accounting for roughly a third of local states' total income. In contrast, through local government-backed investment units, the debt that the Chinese local states have a responsibility to repay reached the substantial amount of 1 trillion RMB in June 2013, and approximately 37 per cent of such debts are pledged on future expected land sale revenue (National Audit Office 2013).

Supported by funding from these sources, the entrepreneurial local states fiercely compete for profitable industrial investment on a global scope by either providing subsidies and tax temptation (Lichtenberg and Ding 2009) or enhancing urban amenities through large investments in local urban infrastructure (Wang et al. 2011). For example, according to the audit result report published by the National Audit Office, 86.8 per cent of the funds that the local states borrowed through their investment units were invested in urban infrastructure or the improvement of urban amenities (National Audit Office 2013). Thus, land-based financing of urban development has been identified as the most significant feature of the PRC's urbanization (Ye and Wu 2014).

8.4.3 Housing Market Development as a Constraint to Urbanization

While the marketization of housing provision has greatly helped facilitate rural-to-urban migration and also created millions of job opportunities for migrants, the upsurge in housing prices also makes decent housing accommodation increasingly unaffordable for migrants (Chen et al. 2010; Yang and Shen 2008). Over time, the lack of affordable housing provision has posed severe challenges for the sustainability of urbanization in the PRC.

8.4.3.1 Housing-based Social Stratification

It has been noted that the PRC is 'the only large country... to urbanize without the creation of large slum areas or informal settlements' (UN-HABITAT 2003). This achievement should be qualified because it refers to a period before half the population lived in urban areas and is in any case not attributable to the housing system alone.

Since the socialist economic period, there has clearly been an emphatic shift from the state to the market in the provision of housing welfare (Wang et al. 2012). However, the state remains the ultimate source of housing welfare for a large minority of the urban population benefiting from the state legacy welfare implied by discounted privatization. Beneath the tiers of marketized, subsidized, and social housing remains a fourth tier associated with the migrant population.

The post-reform housing system thus exhibits at least three insider–outsider divides. First, there is a clear insider–outsider divide between households protected from the market and those who have to enter it paying market prices or rents (Huang and Jiang 2009). A second divide reflects the combined impact of the growth in income inequality and rising house prices under the marketization process—a growing wealth gap is emerging between those who can afford to purchase multiple properties and those who cannot afford to purchase at all, so housing perpetuates inequality (Li 2012b). The third divide is between the permanent and migrant population, whose housing options are quite different.

Meanwhile, regional inequality in housing is a salient feature of urbanization in the PRC (cf. Figure 3–4). At the household level, the inequality of housing in urban PRC has continued to rise since the marketization of housing provision (Li 2012b). A recent empirical investigation shows that the Gini coefficient of housing space per person in Shanghai was more than 0.5 in 2010, significantly higher than that in 2000 (Zhang and Chen 2014b).

8.4.3.2 The Problems of Migrants in Local Housing Markets

Despite rapid urbanization, migration in the PRC is still subject to many institutional restraints. The Hukou system, the urban registration system that was introduced in 1958 (although it had precedents), has been promulgated as an official tool to control the free movement of people between urban and rural areas

(Chan and Buckingham 2008). Administration regulations issued in 1982 known as 'custody and repatriation' (C&R) authorized the police to detain migrants if they did not have a local residence permit (Hukou) or temporary living permit in the city and repatriate these 'illegal migrants' to the settlements where their permanent Hukous were issued (Chan and Buckingham 2008). Although the C&R law was formally abolished in 2003, the Hukou system remains in force today and continues to constrain population mobility. Under the Hukou system, migrants are largely excluded from the welfare package reserved for local residents, including unemployment insurance, health care, pension, housing benefits, and even their children's right to enter local schools (PFPC 2012).

The Hukou system has been constantly noted as a major constraint in the housing consumption of migrants (Wu 2004; Hiroshi 2006). A recent investigation based on census data (2010) reveals substantial disparities in housing conditions across residents with different Hukou statuses in Shanghai: whereas the mean housing space per person among Shanghai natives was 29.44 sq. m in 2010, it was only 14.68 sq. m for migrants (Zhang and Chen 2014a). The gap is still substantial even after adjusting for differences in human capital (Zhang and Chen 2014a). At the national level, an official survey indicates that the homeownership ratio among migrants was around just 10 per cent in 2010 (PFPC 2012), which is in sharp contrast with the figure of 89 per cent among permanent urban residents (NBSC 2011). The exclusion of migrants from the local housing welfare system further exacerbates migrants' difficulties in the Chinese urban housing market (Hiroshi 2006).

Several micro studies show that migrants in major cities are not spatially well integrated with local residents (Li and Wu 2008; Liu et al. 2014; Chen and Hao 2014). They generally live outside the expensive downtown areas and cluster heavily in the cheaper suburban areas, which offer low-skilled job opportunities and informal housing accommodation solutions. For example, in 2010, the dissimilarity index between migrants and local residents in Shanghai was measured to be between 0.3373 and 0.4562, depending on the scale of the community (Chen and Hao 2014). These measurements are much higher than what was found for the same city in 2000 (Li and Wu 2008), indicating a large growth in residential segregation in Shanghai since the market-oriented development of housing provision. The rise of Hukou-based residential segregation is not only a self-sorting market equilibrium but also a result of discriminating institutional forces because the migrants are constrained in their housing choices under the Hukou system (Chen and Hao 2014). This is a strong indicator of the Chinese mode of urbanization being neither pro-poor nor inclusive.

8.4.3.3 Urban Villages and Rural Migrants' Informal Housing Solutions

By 2013, there were approximately 240 million migrants in PRC. More than 80 per cent of them were rural-to-urban migrants, and the rest were urban-to-urban migrants (NBSC 2014). Rural migrants are mainly housed in two broad types of housing. Many are housed in dormitories and other forms of temporary accommodation (e.g. semi-completed buildings on construction sites) provided by employers (PFPC 2012). Others are housed in so-called 'urban village' areas that represent two of the underlying dynamics of urbanization: the rapid expansion of cities into former farmland and the urgent need for migrants to find affordable shelter (Wang et al. 2009).

Urban villages (literally: 'villages in a city') are a unique phenomenon in the Chinese urbanization process. They usually refer to villages that were originally located on the outskirts of the city, but have changed to encircled segments situated in the midst of the urban area under rapid urban sprawl. With all surrounding farmland converted into urban land, the villages themselves are reserved as 'rural' and villagers still have a traditional agricultural lifestyle and hold agriculture Hukou. This unique phenomenon in urbanization has challenged the simple dichotomy between the rural and the urban (Wang et al. 2009). It usually occurs when the local government fails to find sufficient funding to compensate the villagers for their lost dwellings with jobs and apartments in the city. At first glance, insufficient planning is to blame for the emergence of semi-urbanized spaces and population. However, the development of urban villages is found to be driven by an intertwined complex of institutional settings, including the dual land system, the Hukou system, weak village governance, and a scarcity of migrant worker housing (He et al. 2010).

Former farmers owning the land of urban villages construct low-quality, but often multistorey properties and rent them to impoverished migrants at low prices. Urban villages in the PRC share many features with the shantytowns found in other developing countries (Wang et al. 2009). Most of the housing in Chinese urban villages is substandard, intensely developed, and densely populated; has poor infrastructure; and is often illegal in the sense that they are not recognized by any form of urban planning (Zheng et al. 2009). Urban villages also often become the breeding grounds for social problems such as crime, drug addiction, alcoholism, and prostitution. Some researchers consider urban villages to be a form of slums with Chinese characteristics. However, urban villages provide cheap accommodation for the transient population and allow migrants to access local labour and other markets (Song et al. 2008). Thus, urban villages are notable hubs for providing economic opportunities to newcomers to the city. Meanwhile, by providing a way of life, urban villages are also enclaves for landless villagers (He et al. 2010).

8.4.4 Public Housing Development and Urbanization in the PRC

A clear shift in political priorities occurred in 2006 when President Hu Jintao's doctrine of the 'harmonious society' was adopted by the ruling Communist Party

(World Bank and DRC 2013). Initially, housing did not feature significantly in the doctrine of 'harmonious society' in urban areas. However, a rapid upsurge in housing prices in most major Chinese cities since 2003 has made housing affordability issues become one of the PRC's top social concerns (Chen et al. 2010).

In 2008, a programme of 7.5 million units of public housing was formed as part of China's stimulation package in response to the Global Financial Crisis (Chen, Yang, et al. 2014). At that time, this was widely thought to have been a temporary intervention in much the same manner as the intervention in response to the Asian financial crisis a decade earlier. However, in 2009, the target was doubled and in 2011, a huge public housing programme of 36 million units was later announced for the plan period 2011–15. If fulfilled, the programme would be the largest ever, outstripping even the Soviet Union's Khrushchev public housing programme in the 1950s (Smith 2010). With this, the proportion of the country's formal housing stock through public provision would almost double from 11 per cent to 20 per cent by the end of 2015 (MOHURD 2011). The Chinese public housing programme includes a mix of 'products' for different segments of the market (cf. Table 8.2). Chen et al. (2014) estimate that in 2011, approximately 60 per cent of public housing provisions were forms of subsidized ownership and 40 per cent were for rent.

8.4.4.1 The Rationale of the New Public Housing Programme

Official statistics suggest that the PRC is currently experiencing the largest scale of urbanization ever known in human history: the urbanization ratio in the PRC will reach 69 per cent in 2030, and the urban population will increase by more than 300 million over the period of 2011–30 (United Nations 2012), which implies that there will be a strong and sustained momentum for the expansion of housing demand and consumption in urban PRC in the next few decades. However, the land available for urban residential use in the PRC is small compared to its fast-growing urban population. Moreover, to ensure its own food security, the PRC has a strict quota on agricultural land development (Ding and Lichtenberg 2011). Thus, there is a decreasing supply of suitable sites for residential development. The expansion of low-cost public housing programmes, however, is expected to increase the supply of affordable housing to meet the accommodation needs of a growing number of new entrants who have little hope of purchasing homes at market prices.

'The recent emphasis on public housing for the poor is a good example of how government resources can be used to address a pressing social need' (World Bank and DRC 2013). Nevertheless, there continues to exist a wide suspicion that in the PRC, state housing provision is just an important economic driver rather than socially necessary (Wang and Murie 2011). The new public housing programme was once more commonly considered a regulation tool to control spiralling housing prices after several rounds of regulations failed to cool down the overheating residential property markets as well as an economic vehicle to counteract the shocks of the global economic downturn. It appears that the Chinese central government juggles the provision of low-income housing towards conflicting economic and socio-political goals and, therefore, creates constant changes in low-income housing policy (Huang 2012).

8.4.4.2 Urban Development Concerns

For local governments, the major interest in supplying public housing is driven by the urgent need to smooth relocation costs, which have soared due to the rapid increase in market housing prices. The emphasis on shantytown resettlement is thus a striking feature of the Chinese public housing programme. There are reasons to believe that the dominance of Shantytown Renovation Housing (SRH) in recent public housing development (cf. Table 8.5) is directly tied to the local governments' goal to promote urban redevelopment by providing low-cost housing to relocated residents.

This finding, however, should not be surprising because the state provision of resettlement housing has been a critical factor underlying the so-called property-led massive urban redevelopment in the PRC ever since the mid-1990s (He and Wu 2005; Shin 2009). Assistance for shantytown dwellers is linked to resettlement, which can take the form of low-cost home ownership, low-cost rental housing, or cash compensation (Chang and Chen 2013). The local governments simply cannot afford for compensation to grow at the same

Table 8.5. Configuration of the Chinese public housing programme, 2011–15

Type of housing	Function	Proportion of programme (%)[a]
Shantytown resettlement	Households displaced by shantytown clearance offered either ECH or price-capped housing or financial compensation.	40
Low rent	Government-owned housing leased on low rents to the poorest urban residents. Limited to 50 sq. m. Financed mainly by the local government, but with an increasing central government component.	39
Economic and comfortable	Limited to 60 sq. m sold at prices 20–30 per cent below market levels. Developers' profit margins usually capped at 3–4 per cent.	12
Price capped	Housing targeted at middle-income households. Limited to 90 sq. m. Prices capped by local government when land sold to developer. Price usually between ECH and market.	9

Note: [a] These numbers are a percentage of the units of new housing construction.

Source: MOHURD (2011); Chen et al. (2015).

rates as the soaring prices of market housing. Thus, the main function of SRH is to rehouse expropriated urban and rural households at low costs and thus help to facilitate 'growth-promoting' urban regeneration.

8.4.4.3 Urbanization Concerns

It should be noted that the primary objective of the Chinese public housing programme of 36 million units is to ensure the success of the new urbanization strategy (MOHURD 2011; Li 2011). The shift in housing policy after 2007 recognized the importance of cheap rental housing for the segment of the migrant population that cannot afford to purchase subsided-ownership housing, which is reflected in the relatively high priority attached to it within the programme (Chen, Yang, et al. 2014). In the ECH scheme, the main qualifications for eligibility include residence status (Hukou), household income, the number of people, average living area per capita, and the total value of assets of a family (Yang and Chen 2014). For PRH, however, the general rule regarding qualification is not very clearly defined by the central government, which leaves local governments with substantial freedom to make their own allocation policies.

The eligibility conditions are much broader and vary substantially from city to city. In Beijing, Guangzhou, and Shenzhen, income per capita, total assets, and current living floor space are assessed. In Beijing, applicants who are qualified for the CRH, ECH and Capped-Price Housing (CPH) can apply for PRH. However, in Shanghai and Chongqing, the current living area is the only eligibility condition for PRH. In addition, urban migrant workers without local Hukou, but with a stable job and income sources, are allowed to apply for PRH in Beijing, Shanghai, Chongqing, and Chengdu, but not in Guangzhou, Shenzhen, or Hangzhou (Chen, Yang, et al. 2014). The variations in allocation criteria for PRH reflect different local political preferences.

For many cities, PRH is regarded not simply as a residual safety net for low-income households, but more as a tool to support local economic development (Chen 2014). According to guidelines on accelerating the development of PHR released by MOHURD and six other departments in July 2010 (MOHURD[2010] No.87), PRH was introduced with the main purpose of solving the temporary and interim accommodation needs of migrants, new workers, and house-poor households (Li 2011). However, local governments are more likely to allocate public housing as subsidized benefits to specific target groups that they prefer, such local civil servants, highly educated people, and skilled labour that they want to attract and retain (Wang and Murie 2011). The provision of public rental housing is thus an effective selective tool used by policymakers to retain skilled or semi-skilled workers in large cities. For example, a study shows that the recent development of PRH projects in Shanghai is mainly the result of a deliberate urban development policy in line with other strategies such as city marketing and gentrification (Chen 2014). Because there is a very limited security of tenure in the private rental housing market in the PRC (Man 2011), PRH in the form of 'gated communities' is very attractive for the middle class (Wu 2005), who highly value residential stability. In this respect, PRH provides an alternative to homeownership with an affordable and guaranteed leasing contract, offering decent housing to the newly emerged middle class.

It is worth noting that the current housing provision system in the PRC is actually not very different from those in Western countries if one considers the stage of development of the country (Chen, Yang, et al. 2014). The PRC is at a stage of rapid industrialization and urbanization. The social composition of the urban population not only includes the emerging middle class but also a re-emerging and ever-expanding working class (which differs from the socialist workers of the pre-reforms period). Though commercial housing targeting the new middle class in cities flourished during the first decade of the twenty-first century, the working-class housing problem was not properly addressed. The poor quality private rental housing offered by the urban villages provided a temporary solution in the past, but has resulted in great social costs over time. For example, many urban villages are unregulated and have become havens for illegal activities and even crimes. Typically, few public amenities are available in urban villages, and the community environment is particularly hazardous for tenants' children (Zheng et al. 2009; PFPC 2012). The alliance of local landless farmers, rural-to-urban migrants, and young educated professionals now represents a large proportion of the expanding urban population (PFPC 2012). The new public housing programme is aimed at this group of people (MOHURD 2011; Li 2011).

8.4.5 The Role of the Chinese Public Housing Programme

The multiple objectives of the public housing programme were best interpreted by the Chinese Primer Keqiang Li himself in 2011:

> The new public housing programme is more than a major enhancement of social welfare, a vehicle to adjust income inequality and a crucial channel to improve social stability; it is also an important pillar of economic growth for the next several years as it has many economic functions such as a tool to dampen price increases in the private housing market. [I]mplementing the massive public housing programme is an effective approach to switch the economic growth model and improve economic structure. Public housing projects bridge economic growth and welfare, enable investment and promote consumption, and thus are decisive in expanding domestic demand. (Li 2011)

The 2011–15 mass public housing programme should thus be interpreted as a key component of the new urbanization strategy adopted by the new Chinese leadership in 2013. It should also be noted that the Chinese mode of providing urban housing is heavily influenced by the political, fiscal, financial, and land-ownership structure (Wu et al. 2006; Naughton 2010). The transfer of state-owned land in free or cheap ways consists of the largest form of government support in promoting public housing development, a feature that is also shared with East Asian 'productivist' regimes, such as Hong Kong, China, and Singapore (Wang and Murie 2011).

8.5 Lessons from the Chinese Housing System

This chapter shows that the balance of several overriding policy objectives has determined the direction of the housing system in urban PRC. The priorities of the Chinese housing policy agenda include promoting economic growth and urbanization through the efficient allocation of housing-related resources and ensuring political consolidation and social stability by maintaining housing affordability for mainstream society (Wang et al. 2012). In this section, we discuss what lessons we can draw from the Chinese housing system in the urbanization process in general.

8.5.1 Achieving a Balance Between Different Policy Priorities in the Housing System

The priority of Chinese urban housing policy in the first decade of 2000 was exclusively to develop for-profit property development that could help generate enormous taxes and increase land revenue. The housing affordability issue of low-income disadvantaged groups, particularly rural-to-urban migrants, has been largely neglected in Chinese urban housing policy so far. This mode of housing regime is clearly unsustainable because it has produced too many social conflicts and even threats to political stability (Chen, Yang, et al. 2014). Heavy reliance on the real estate sector also makes the Chinese urban economy too susceptible to the risks of property cycles. In addition, the Chinese banking system has accumulated undue risks from investing too much credit in mortgages and other forms of real estate loans (People's Bank of China 2014). This model also hinders urbanization in the PRC by not only making the costs of decent accommodation increasingly unaffordable for migrants but also pushing up local wages, deterring labour mobility, hampering large cities from achieving the full potential of the agglomeration effect, and reducing the competiveness of these cities. For example, a recent study notes that the severe constraint of land supply in the east is a key reason housing prices, and consequently wages, have increased in these cities, which has damaged the competitiveness of the Chinese urban economy (Lu et al. 2014).

So far urbanization in the PRC features a clear 'dual-track' pattern, in the sense that migrants do not have access to urban welfare in the same manner as the permanent residents of the cities (Shen 2006). With the slogan of 'human being-oriented urbanization', the new urbanization strategy appears to represent a 'critical juncture' in Chinese public policy. The primary objective of this strategy is to promote inclusive urban growth so that an increasing number of migrants can finally settle in the cities (Koen et al. 2013; OECD 2014). The strategy eventually aims to reorient the economy away from being based on exporting goods cheaply to the rest of the world to greater orientation towards boosting domestic consumption (Li 2012a; World Bank and DRC 2013). It is expected that domestic consumption will be raised through the development of more public services, the lack of which are perceived as a major cause of the PRC's very high savings rate (i.e. people save for old age, medical care, and children's education) (OECD 2014). There is also ample evidence that the Hukou system severely constrains and depresses migrants' consumption propensity. A recent study shows that the consumption of migrants is 16–20 per cent lower than that of local urban residents, even after adjusting for incomes and family characteristics (Lu et al. 2014). Allowing migrants to settle in the cities and increasing their demand for public services is a key to the success of the national economic rebalance.

There is also growing discussion that the Chinese government's overriding development priority of economic growth has been partly shifted to social development in recent years (World Bank 2006; World Bank and DRC 2013). The ideology of a 'harmonious society' and the 'scientific concept of development' put forward by President Hu Jintao in 2006 stresses that promoting people's welfare and social harmony should be placed ahead of pursuing pure economic growth. This change appears to indicate that the Chinese ruling party's welfare ideology is shifting from a type of 'productivist welfare' to a type of 'developmentalist welfare', the latter based on the assumption that 'social expenditures in the form of social investment do not detract from but contribute positively to economic development' (Midgley and Tang 2001). The 18th national congress of the CCP in 2012 confirmed this change by proclaiming the new slogan that 'the ultimate goal of economic development is to promote human development'.

From these perspectives, Chinese housing policy is no longer subordinated to economic policy, but is rather an integrated part of economic policy. Nonetheless, the Chinese housing system is still undergoing drastic transformations, and it is obviously too early to draw any definite conclusion. Further research is needed to identify whether and how the Chinese housing system has shifted from 'productivism' to 'developmentalism'. However, because the switch in the housing regime is already an important part of this macro political and economic transition, the recent transformations of the Chinese urban housing system must be understood within the overall transformation of China's development ideology from 'productivism welfare' to 'developmental welfare' (Chen, Yang, et al. 2014).

8.5.2 Achieving a Balance Between the Market and the State in the Housing System

How should we understand the relationship between the market and state in the PRC's post-reform housing system? The growth of market forces dilutes and erodes the power of the state. The functioning of the housing market becomes increasingly dependent on the governance of market institutions, which are adjusted by the shifting balance between demand and supply. For example, the performance of the market since 2010 has been largely influenced by the central government's policy package to cool the property sector, including the quota restriction for home purchasing and harsh terms for mortgage borrowing (Chen and Han 2014). Nonetheless, it is easy to discern that the state has continued to be the 'builder of the market' in the Chinese housing sector after the 1998 reforms (Zhang 2006). Some literature has alleged that the presence of 'authoritarian centralized control' in the PRC's post-reform economy is a reaction to marketization rather than a socialist legacy (Halper 2010; Xu 2011; Witt and Redding 2013). However, some others interpret the swift responses of the PRC's housing policy to internal and external economic shocks as evidence of a contingent rather than ideal type of neoliberalism (He and Wu 2009; Wang et al. 2012).

In short, the urban Chinese housing system underwent a rapid shift from a state-dominated system to one in which market-like mechanisms determined the production and consumption of housing. Since 2008, and especially after 2010, the state has reasserted its role in the housing market and clearly intends to do so in ways that will shape the whole housing system for decades to come. However, it is clear that the housing programme does not represent a reversion to the type of state-socialist system that operated before 1998 (Chen, Yang, et al. 2014).

At a stage of fast industrialization and rapid urbanization, the social composition of Chinese cities includes not only the emerging middle class (ADB 2010) but also a new working class (different from the socialist workers of the pre-reforms period). Special attention should be given to rural-to-urban migrants and young educated professionals flowing into large cities from small cities. The pressing need to solve the housing needs of the new working class has become a very urgent political challenge (Chen, Yang, et al. 2014).

The Chinese government's greater commitment to supply-side subsidies is said to be partly due to the specific demographic and rapid urbanization pressures in the PRC. For example, given the soaring prices and declining availability of urban land, nearly all for-profit developers tend to build large luxury high-end apartments, and no one has an incentive to construct small-sized affordable housing units, even though the average family size of the new generation urban population is quickly becoming smaller under the one-child policy. Thus, in Chinese political leaders' minds, increasing public provision of small-sized affordable housing units is an effective way to correct 'market failures' in the housing stock and help to alleviate the shortage of urban housing stock in the face of rapid urbanization in the next two decades (Li 2011; World Bank and DRC 2013). Meanwhile, the shift in housing policy exemplifies many of the trends in Chinese social and economic policies that have emerged since the global financial crisis. Over the last few years, the Chinese government has apparently become more cautious of market failure and has increasingly regained more direct control of resource allocation in many economic and social sectors (Naughton 2010). These socio-economic and political backgrounds have pushed the state to not only take major steps to intervene in the housing market but also again take up a significant role in the provision of urban housing.

8.6 Policy Recommendations

The Chinese experience regarding the interaction between the housing system and urbanization is unique, but it clearly indicates that an effective housing system that can responsively provide sufficient affordable housing is an essential component to the success of inclusive and equitable urbanization. We offer some policy recommendations for establishing a housing system that is more supportive to urbanization.

8.6.1 Put Housing Affordability as the Primary Priority of Housing Policy

It is true that housing policy may need to meet several policy objectives, but ensuring affordability should always be the primary priority. The massive public housing programme is designed to help balance economic growth and provide stability in light of the increasingly short supply of low-cost housing, high levels of inflation, and a growing wealth gap. Fortunately, the new urbanization strategy has openly put accommodating low-income migrants in the cities as a central target, and various solutions, including developing massive-scale public housing, have been attempted. The current national prioritization of public housing in the PRC signals a sharp change in the housing policy of previous decades, addressing negative externalities and inefficiencies in the PRC's short-lived post-housing reforms period. To make the affordable housing movement sustainable, there is a need to promote the UN-honoured concept of 'housing rights', where adequate housing is considered a basic human right and is to be protected not only by governmental measures but also by laws (UN-HCHR 2009). However, housing sector complexities can never be totally coordinated by a central authority, and a legal system that ensures the delivery of sufficient affordable housing should be established.

8.6.2 Reduce the Local State's Fiscal Dependence on Land Revenue

The conflict between affordability concerns and the objective of economic growth within the Chinese housing system is largely due to the local state's heavy reliance on land-based urban financing, which is contingent on housing market booms. Land and housing policies are among the Chinese government's most important tools for fine-tuning the economy. A housing policy that addresses the needs of the majority is critical for any government during the transition. Today the government is looking at a long-term land allocation plan oriented towards economic restructuring as a tool to control economic cycles. Nonetheless, to promote human-based urbanization rather than 'land urbanization', the state needs to restructure the central–local fiscal relationship, reform the tax system of local states, and encourage experimental innovations in urban infrastructure financing, i.e. new forms of PPP (public–private partnership). For example, several hybrid arrangements of PPP between local governments and private investors have emerged in the last decade (ADB 2008). However, an enabling setting of the regulatory and policy arrangements is a precondition to the success of any type of PPP project. Meanwhile, there is a need for concerted attempts to develop the Chinese municipal bond market.

8.6.3 Establishing an Effective and Efficient Housing Finance System

The current plan to rapidly increase investment and construction in public housing may result in an increased supply of affordable housing for needy families. However, we believe that the establishment of a finance system for such affordable housing is at least equally important. The Chinese government should promote the use of a variety of financing tools and instruments to attract social capital to public housing investment and lower the cost of borrowing for low- and middle-income families. A well-functioning housing finance system will contribute to the expansion of home ownership, the development of housing markets and employment, economic growth and wealth accumulation, and social and political stability. Several options are worthy of the Chinese government's consideration and experimentation. For example, based on the experience of public housing management in Hong Kong, China, Chinese local governments may try financing public rental housing projects from the private capital market, i.e. through some form of Real Estate Investment Trusts. Another possibility is to restructure HPF (housing provident fund—the worker's compulsory saving scheme) so that it can work as a long-term stable and cheap funding pool for financing public housing development and operation (Chen and Deng 2014), similar to the integrated Central Provident Fund, the public housing model in Singapore.

References

Adams, Bill. 2009. 'Macroeconomic Implications of China Urban Housing Privatization, 1998–1999'. *Journal of Contemporary China 18* (62): 881–8.

ADB. 2008. *Public–Private Partnership (PPP) Handbook*, Asian Development Bank.

ADB. 2010. 'The Rise of Asia's Middle Class'. In *Key Indicators for Aisa and the Pacific. 2010*, Asian Development Bank.

Chan, Kam Wing and Will Buckingham. 2008. 'Is China Abolishing the Hukou System?' *The China Quarterly 195* (6): 582–606.

Chang, Ying and Jie Chen. 2013. 'Public Housing in Shanghai: A Tool with Multiple Purposes'. *Housing Finance International 27* (Winter): 68–85.

Chen, Binkai, Ming Lu, and Ninghua Zhong. 2015. 'How Urban Segregation Distorts Chinese Migrants' Consumption?' *World Development 70*: 133–46.

Chen, Jie. 2011. 'Home Mortgage and Real Estate Market in Shanghai'. In *Global Housing Markets: Crises, Policies, and Institutions*, edited by A. Bardhan, R. Edelstein, and C. Kroll, Wiley.

Chen, Jie. 2014. 'The Development of New Public Rental Housing in Shanghai'. *Critical Housing Analysis 1* (1): 26–34.

Chen, Jie and Lan Deng. 2014. 'Financing Affordable Housing through Compulsory Saving: The Two-decade Experience of Housing Provident Fund in China'. *Housing Studies 29* (7): 937–58.

Chen, Jie, Feng Guo, and Aiyong Zhu. 2011. 'The Housing-led Growth Hypothesis Revisited: Evidence from the Chinese Provincial Panel Data'. *Urban Studies 48* (10): 2049–67.

Chen, Jie and Xufei Han. 2014. 'The Evolution of Housing Market and Its Socio-Economic Impacts in Post-Reform China: A Survey of the Literature', *Journal of Economic Survey 28* (4): 652–70.

Chen, Jie and Qianjin Hao. 2014. 'Residential Segregation under Rapid Urbanization in China: Evidence from Shanghai (in Chinese)'. *Academic Monthly 46* (5): 17–28.

Chen, Jie, Qianjin Hao, and Mark Stephens. 2010. 'Assessing Housing Affordability in Post-reform China: A Case Study of Shanghai'. *Housing Studies 25* (6): 877–901.

Chen, Jie, Zan Yang, and Ya Ping Wang. 2014. 'The New Chinese Model of Public Housing: A Step Forward or Backward?' *Housing Studies 29* (4): 534–50.

Chen, Xiangming and Xiaoyuan Gao. 1993. 'Urban Economic Reform and Public-Housing Investment in China'. *Urban Affairs Review 29* (1): 117–45.

Cohen, Barney. 2004. 'Urban Growth in Developing Countries: A Review of Current Trends and a Caution Regarding Existing Forecasts'. *World Development 32* (1): 23–51.

Ding, Chengri and Erik Lichtenberg. 2011. 'Land and Urban Economic Growth in China'. *Journal of Regional Science 51* (2): 299–317.

Dowall, David E. 1994. 'Urban Residential Redevelopment in the People's Republic of China'. *Urban Studies 31* (9): 1497–516.

EIU. 2011. *Building Rome in a Day: The Sustainability of China's Housing Boom*, Economist Intelligence Unit, London.

Fleisher, Belton M., Yong Yin, and Stephen M. Hills. 1997. 'The Role of Housing Privatization and Labor-market Reform in China's Dual Economy'. *China Economic Review 8* (1): 1–17.

Glaeser, Edward. 2010. *Triumph of the City*, Penguin.

Glaeser, Edward L., Joseph Gyourko, and Raven E. Saks. 2006. 'Urban Growth and Housing Supply'. *Journal of Economic Geography* 6 (1): 71–89.

Halper, S. A. 2010. *The Beijing Consensus: How China's Authoritarian Model Will Dominate the Twenty-first Century*, Basic Books.

He, Shenjing and Fulong Wu. 2005. 'Property-led Redevelopment in Post Reform China: A Case Study of Xintiandi Redevelopment Project In Shanghai'. *Journal of Urban Affairs 27* (1): 1–23.

He, Shenjing and Fulong Wu. 2009. 'China's Emerging Neoliberal Urbanism: Perspectives from Urban Redevelopment'. *Antipode 41* (2): 282–304.

He, Shenjing, et al. 2010. 'Social Groups and Housing Differentiation in China's Urban Villages: An Institutional Interpretation'. *Housing Studies 25* (5): 671–91.

Hiroshi, S. A. T. O. 2006. 'Housing Inequality and Housing Poverty in Urban China in the Late 1990s'. *China Economic Review 17* (1): 37–50.

Huang, Youqin. 2012. 'Low-income Housing in Chinese Cities: Policies and Practices'. *China Quarterly 212* (4): 941–64.

Huang, Youqin and Leiwen Jiang. 2009. 'Housing Inequality in Transitional Beijing'. *International Journal of Urban and Regional Research 33* (4): 936–56.

J.P. Morgan. 2011. *China's Affordable Housing Program: Picking up Momentum.*

Koen, Vincent et al. 2013. *Policies for Inclusive Urbanisation in China*, OECD, Paris.

Li, K. 2011. 'Implementing the Massive-Scale Public Housing Program and Improving Housing Policy and Housing Provision System Step-by-Step (in Chinese)'. *Qiu Shi 53* (8): 3–8.

Li, K. 2012a. 'Deepening the Strategy of Expanding Domestic Consumption Through Furthering the Reform and Openness (in Chinese)'. *Qiu Shi 54* (4): 3–10.

Li, Si-Ming. 2012b. 'Housing Inequalities Under Market Deepening: The Case of Guangzhou, China'. *Environment and Planning A 44* (12): 2852–66.

Li, Zhigang and Fulong Wu. 2006. 'Socio-spatial Differentiation and Residential Inequalities in Shanghai: A Case Study of Three Neighbourhoods'. *Housing Studies 21* (5): 695–717.

Li, Zhigang and Fulong Wu. 2008. 'Tenure-based Residential Segregation in Post-reform Chinese Cities: A Case Study of Shanghai'. *Transactions of the Institute of British Geographers 33* (3): 404–19.

Lichtenberg, Erik and Chengri Ding. 2009. 'Local Officials As Land Developers: Urban Spatial Expansion in China'. *Journal of Urban Economics 66* (1): 57–64.

Lim, Gill-Chin and Man-Hyung Lee. 1990. 'Political Ideology and Housing Policy in Modern China'. *Environment and Planning C: Government and Policy 8* (4): 477–87.

Liu, Yafei, Martin Dijst, and Stan Geertman. 2014. 'Residential Segregation and Well-being Inequality Between Local and Migrant Elderly in Shanghai'. *Habitat International 42* (2): 175–85.

Logan, John R., Yiping Fang, and Zhanxin Zhang. 2010. 'The Winners in China's Urban Housing Reform'. *Housing Studies 25* (1): 101–17.

Lu, Ming, Haijun Ou, and Binkai Chen. 2014. 'Rationality or Bubble? An Empirical Study on Urbanization, Migration and Housing Price (in Chinese)'. *World Economy 36* (1): 30–54.

Malpass, P. and A. Murie. 1999. *Housing Policy and Practice*, 5th edition, Palgrave Macmillan.

Man, J. Y. ed. 2011. *China's Housing Reform and Outcomes*, Lincoln Institute of Land Policy, Cambridge, MA.

Mayer, Christopher J. and C. Tsuriel Somerville. 2000. 'Residential Construction: Using the Urban Growth Model to Estimate Housing Supply'. *Journal of Urban Economics 48* (1): 85–109.

Midgley, James and Kwong-leung Tang. 2001. 'Social Policy, Economic Growth and Developmental Welfare'. *International Journal of Social Welfare 10* (2): 244–52.

MOHURD. 2011. 'The Minster of MOHURD's Report of Latest Progress of Public Housing Program on the Meeting of the 11th NPC (National People's Congress) Standing Committee held in 27 October 2011'. *Sina*. <http://finance.sina.com.cn/focus/rdxwbzf/index.shtml>.

National Audit Office. 2013. 'The Audit Results of National Governmental Debt (Audit Report No.2013–32)'. The Official Website of National Audit Office of China. <http://www.audit.gov.cn/n1992130/n1992150/n1992500/3432077.html>.

Naughton, Barry. 2010. 'The Turning Point in Housing'. *China Leadership Monitor 33* (1): 1–10.

NBSC. 2011. 'Series Reports on China's Economic and Social Development Achievements During the 11th Five-year Planning Period (2006–2010): No.9'. The Official Website of National Bureau of Statistics of China (NBSC). <http://www.stats.gov.cn/ztjc/ztfx/sywcj/201103/t20110307_71321.html>.

NBSC. 2012. 'Tabulation on the 2010 People Census of the People's Republic of China'. The Official Website of National Bureau of Statistics of China (NBSC). <http://www.stats.gov.cn/tjsj/pcsj/rkpc/6rp/indexch.htm>.

NBSC. 2013. *China Statistical Yearbook 2013*. The Official Website of National Bureau of Statistics of China (NBSC). <http://www.stats.gov.cn/tjsj/ndsj/2013/indexch.htm>.

NBSC. 2014. 'The Monitoring Report on Rural Migrant Workers 2013'. The Official Website of National Bureau of Statistics of China (NBSC). <http://www.stats.gov.cn/tjsj/zxfb/201405/t20140512_551585.html>.

OECD. 2014. China: Structural Reforms for Inclusive Growth, OECD.

People's Bank of China. 2014. 'The 2013 Report on the Use of Credit by Financial Agencies'. <http://www.pbc.gov.cn/publish/diaochatongjisi/3172/2014/20140124171309833823834/20140124171309833823834_.html>.

PFPC (National Population and Family Planning Commission of P.R. China) ed. 2012. *Report on China's Migrant Population Development 2012*, China Population Press.

Qi, J. 2009. 'Housing Problems of Low-income Families in China'. In *The 22nd Session of the Governing Council of UN-Habitat*, The Governing Council of UN-Habitat, Nairobi.

Rosen, Kenneth T. and Madelyn C. Ross. 2000. 'Increasing Home Ownership in Urban China: Notes on the Problem of Affordability'. *Housing Studies 15* (1): 77–88.

Saiz, Albert. 2010. 'The Geographic Determinants of Housing Supply'. *Quarterly Journal of Economics 125* (3): 1253–96.

Saks, Raven E. 2008. 'Job Creation and Housing Construction: Constraints on Metropolitan Area Employment Growth'. *Journal of Urban Economics 64* (1): 178–95.

Shaw, V. N. 1997. 'Urban Housing Reform in China'. *Habitat International 21* (2): 199–212.

Shen, Jianfa. 2006. 'Understanding Dual-Track Urbanisation in Post-Reform China: Conceptual Framework and Empirical Analysis'. *Population, Space and Place 12* (5): 497–516.

Shin, Hyun Bang. 2009. 'Residential Redevelopment and the Entrepreneurial Local State: The Implications of Beijing's Shifting Emphasis on Urban Redevelopment Policies'. *Urban Studies 46* (13): 2815–39.

Smith, M. B. 2010. *Property of Communists: The Urban Housing Program from Stalin to Khrushchev*, Northern Illinois University Press.

Song, Shunfeng, S.-F. Chu George, and Xiangming Chen. 2004. 'Housing Investment and Consumption in Urban China'. In *Urbanization and Social Welfare in China*, edited by A. Chen, G. G. Liu, and K. H. Zhang, Ashgate.

Song, Yan, Yves Zenou, and Chengri Ding. 2008. 'Let's Not Throw the Baby Out with the Bath Water: The Role of Urban Villages in Housing Rural Migrants in China'. *Urban Studies 45* (2): 313–30.

Tao, Ran et al. 2010. 'Land Leasing and Local Public Finance in China's Regional Development: Evidence from Prefecture-level Cities'. *Urban Studies 47* (9): 2217–36.

UN-HABITAT. 2003. *The Challenge of Slums: Global Report on Human Settlements 2003*, Earthscan.

UN-HCHR. 2009. *The Right to Adequate Housing*, The Office of the United Nations High Commissioner for Human Rights, United Nations Office at Geneva.

United Nations. 2012. *World Urbanization Prospects: The 2011 Revision*, United Nations, New York.

Wang, D. et al. 2011. 'Urban Infrastructure Financing in Reform-era China'. *Urban Studies 48* (14): 2975–98.

Wang, Donggen and Yanwei Chai. 2009. 'The Jobs–Housing Relationship and Commuting in Beijing, China: The Legacy of Danwei'. *Journal of Transport Geography 17* (1): 30–8.

Wang, Ya Ping and Alan Murie. 1999. *Housing Policy and Practice*, 5th ed., Hampshire: Palgrave Macmillan.

Wang, Ya Ping and Alan Murie. 2000. 'Social and Spatial Implications of Housing Reform in China'. *International Journal of Urban and Regional Research 24* (2): 397–417.

Wang, Ya Ping, and Alan Murie. 2011. 'The New Affordable and Social Housing Provision System in China: Implications for Comparative Housing Studies'. *International Journal of Housing Policy 11* (3): 237–54.

Wang, Ya Ping, Yanglin Wang, and Glen Bramley. 2005. 'Chinese Housing Reform in State-owned Enterprises and its Impacts on Different Social Groups'. *Urban Studies 42* (10): 1859–78.

Wang, Ya Ping, Yanglin Wang, and Jiansheng Wu. 2009. 'Urbanization and Informal Development in China: Urban Villages in Shenzhen'. *International Journal of Urban and Regional Research 33* (4): 957–73.

Wang, Ya Ping et al. 2012. 'The Maturation of the Neo-liberal Housing Market in Urban China'. *Housing Studies 27* (3): 343–59.

Witt, M. A. and G. Redding, 2013. 'China: Authoritarian Capitalism'. In *Oxford Handbook of Asian Business Systems*, edited by M. A. Witt and G. Redding, Oxford University Press.

World Bank. 1992. *China: Implementation Options for Urban Housing Reform*, The World Bank, Washington, DC.

World Bank. 2006. *China Governance, Investment Climate, and Harmonious Society: Competitiveness Enhancements for 120 Cities in China*, The World Bank, Washington, DC.

World Bank and DRC. 2013. *China 2030: Building a Modern, Harmonious, and Creative High-Income Society*, The World Bank, Washington, DC.

Wu, Fulong. 1996. 'Changes in the Structure of Public Housing Provision in Urban China'. *Urban Studies 33* (9): 1601–27.

Wu, Fulong. 2005. 'Rediscovering the "Gate" Under Market Transition: From Work-Unit Compounds to Commodity Housing Enclaves'. *Housing Studies 20* (2): 235–54.

Wu, Fulong, Jiang Xu, and Anthony Gar-On Yeh. 2006. *Urban Development in Post-Reform China: State, Market, and Space*, Routledge.

Wu, Weiping. 2004. 'Sources of Migrant Housing Disadvantage in Urban China'. *Environment and Planning A 36* (7): 1285–304.

Xu, Chenggang. 2011. 'The Fundamental Institutions of China's Reforms and Development'. *Journal of Economic Literature 49* (4): 1076–151.

Yang, You-Ren and Chih-hui Chang. 2007. 'An Urban Regeneration Regime in China: A Case Study of Urban Redevelopment in Shanghai's Taipingqiao Area'. *Urban Studies 44* (9): 1809–26.

Yang, Zan and Jie Chen. 2014. *Housing Affordability and Housing Policy in Urban China*, Springer.

Yang, Zan and Yue Shen. 2008. 'The Affordability of Owner Occupied Housing in Beijing'. *Journal of Housing and the Built Environment 23* (4): 317–35.

Ye, Lin and Alfred M. Wu. 2014. 'Urbanization, Land Development, and Land Financing: Evidence From Chinese Cities'. *Journal of Urban Affairs 36* (S1): 1–15.

Zhang, Xing Quan. 2006. 'Institutional Transformation and Marketisation: The Changing Patterns of Housing Investment in Urban China'. *Habitat International 30* (2): 327–41.

Zhang, Xing Quan. 2000. 'The Restructuring of the Housing Finance System in Urban China'. *Cities 17* (5): 339–48.

Zhang, Yina and Jie Chen. 2014a. 'Housing Poverty in Post-Reform Shanghai: Profiles in 2010 and Decompositions'. *Open House International 40* (4).

Zhang, Yina and Jie Chen. 2014b. 'The Changing Prevalence of Housing Overcrowding in Post-Reform China: The Case of Shanghai, 2000–2010'. *Habitat International 42* (2): 214–23.

Zhao, Yingshun and Steven C. Bourassa. 2003. 'China's Urban Housing Reform: Recent Achievements and New Inequities'. *Housing Studies 18* (5): 721–44.

Zheng, Siqi et al. 2009. 'Urban Villages in China: A 2008 Survey of Migrant Settlements in Beijing'. *Eurasian Geography and Economics 50* (4): 425–46.

9

Land Policy and Urbanization in the People's Republic of China

Li Zhang and Xianxiang Xu

9.1 Introduction

The pace and scale of urban growth, infrastructure development, and spatial restructuring have together become a metaphor for the People's Republic of China's (PRC's) economic miracle. Some emphasize the 'dominance of the government' in urban landscapes and economic growth (Rithmire 2013), which is often related to the PRC's 'urban-biased' land policy (Davis and Henderson 2003). This chapter analyses the land policies associated with urbanization, including dual urban and rural landownership, the local government's dual monopoly over land exchanges, expropriation, open lease, and the central government's administrative allocation of construction land quotas. This chapter also summarizes findings related to central and local government involvement in the process of urbanization. In addition, we describe trends in urban expansion, including the establishment of economic development zones and the creation of new towns within the expanding sprawl of industrial, commercial, and residential land.

In particular, we explore the relationship between urbanization and land leasing. The urbanization rate and land-leasing revenue are positively related, and land leasing provides financial support for Chinese urbanization. The positive feedback mechanism between land financing and investment in urban infrastructure (Zheng et al., 2014) encourages local governments to expropriate rural land to capture the land value-added, which in turn accelerates urbanization. We also investigate the gap between urbanization and industrialization. Under the dual price system for land, prices of industrial land are much lower than those of commercial or residential land, which is associated with the lag between urbanization and industrialization. Finally, we investigate the administrative allocation of construction land quotas as a means of balancing regional disparities—a policy that diminishes the agglomeration effects of urbanization.

Li Zhang and Xianxiang Xu., *Land Policy and Urbanization in the People's Republic of China* In: *Cities of Dragons and Elephants: Urbanization and Urban Development in China and India. Edited by:* Guanghua Wan and Ming Lu, Oxford University Press (2019). © Oxford University Press. DOI: 10.1093/oso/9780198829225.003.0009

9.2 Institutions and Stylized Facts

9.2.1 Landownership

Property rights are the foundation of the institution of land. Over the last half century, the structure of the PRC's landownership has been dualistic, comprising state-owned urban land and collective-owned rural land. The emergence of an economy including diverse forms of enterprise ownership following reforms and opening up has promoted the separation of landownership and land use rights because the new private firms demanded urban construction land for development. 'During the 1980s, China implemented two key reforms to provide land for expanding private sector activity. First, it set aside land in economic development zones and industrial development zones to provide space for foreign direct investment and other private sector economic activity. Enterprises in these zones were granted tax exemptions and readier access to credit in addition to land' (Ding and Lichtenberg 2008). Compared to state-owned urban land, the property rights system for collective-owned rural land is more complicated.[1] A three-class system of collective ownership exists in the PRC's rural regions and includes (a) peasant collective ownership of farms in villages-natural villages; (b) peasant collective ownership of more than two rural collective economic organizations in villages-administrative villages; and (c) peasant collective ownership in townships-towns. This three-class system makes property rights over rural collective-owned land difficult to discern. The term 'collective' is not clearly defined, nor is the relationship between the collective and the farmers. This leads to ambiguous property rights and makes it difficult for rural land to enter the market.

Unequal, dualistic rights to urban land and ill-defined rights over rural land severely weaken farmers' bargaining power in transactions involving the expropriation and requisition of rural land for urbanization. The requirement that rural land be nationalized before entering the urban land market is indicative of the inequitable treatment of rural property owners. The village collectives that own and administer rural land are subject to oversight by higher-level government. Although the village collectives have the authority to allocate rural land for certain limited purposes other than agriculture, such as housing, public works, and village enterprises, the allocation of rural land for uses other than these designated purposes requires that the land be converted from collective ownership to state ownership. Thus, the development of land for most residential, commercial, and

[1] In many cases, the administrative village issues land leases, even though the land belonged to the natural village in the past. It is like the ownership rights to land have been silently stolen from the natural village and vested in a level higher (Ho 2001).

industrial uses is permitted only after a change in ownership status, which is accomplished through the requisition of rural land by urban government officials (Ding and Lichtenberg 2008), and the land value-added accrues to the local government (Qu and Tian 2011). Through land expropriation and requisition, rural agricultural land is converted to urban construction land or other non-agricultural land. In the process of land expropriation, village cadres represent the peasants of the collective in negotiations with the local government. In the current administrative hierarchy that exists in rural PRC, village cadres tend to acquiesce to the demands of higher government authorities or seek personal gain from the expropriation and requisition process. In either case, farmers' interests are ignored (Zhou 2004; Jiang et al. 2007; Cai et al., 2013). In addition, the ambiguity in rural property rights complicates the compensation scheme for land expropriation.[2]

9.2.2 Land Expropriation Policies

The land requisition system has existed since the creation of the PRC in 1949. The Measures of Land Requisition for State Construction (MLRSC) issued in 1953 comprised the first land requisition regulations and legitimized land expropriation for economic development. The MLRSC set forth the basic principles, compensation standards, and approval procedures for land requisitions. After the Three Major Socialist Transformations, farmland ownership was transferred from private individuals to collectives, and in 1958, the MLRSC was revised to reflect this change. In 1978, certain land management regulations were even added to the constitution, including the mandate that, 'based on legal requirements and other conditions, the state may purchase, requisition or nationalize the land'. In 1982, the constitution was further modified so that 'The government may, in the public interest, requisition land'. The Regulations on Land Requisition for State Construction (RLRSC) promulgated the same year emphasized the enforceability of land requisition by the government, stating that 'all that conform to these regulations, including cadres of communes and the masses, shall be subject to the needs of the country, and obstruction or interference is forbidden'. The RLRSC also elaborated on land expropriation compensation, which included compensation for the land as well as resettlement fees. In 1987, the Land Administration Law (LAL) was implemented. This law stated that 'the government can expropriate collective-owned land for the purpose of economic construction, cultural

[2] Before 30 October 1998, the party interested in leasing rural land negotiated a price directly with villagers, while the land administration played a limited role as mediator. This negotiation process resulted in increased compensation to farmers. However, after the revised Land Management Law was adopted in 1999, 'Land Agreement Leasing' (*xie yi chu rang*) became 'Land Notice Leasing' (*gong gao chu rang*). Under Land Notice Leasing, the land administration section negotiates on behalf of the government with the interested party, and land buyers and farmers are no longer permitted to meet.

construction, national defence and social public undertakings' and 'any unit or individual who needs land for construction must apply for the right to use state-owned land according to the relevant laws'. The Property Law (PL) enacted in 2007 contains more detailed provisions and states, for example, that

> to meet the needs of public interests, collective-owned lands, premises owned by entities and individuals, or other real properties may be expropriated in accordance with the power, scope and procedures provided by law. As for the expropriation of collective-owned land, it is necessary, according to law and in the full amount, to pay fees such as land compensation fees, placement subsidies, and compensation for above-ground fixtures and seedlings on the land; to arrange for social security benefits for the farmers whose lands are expropriated; to secure the farmers' livelihood; and to safeguard the farmers' legitimate rights and interests.

The combined effect of these institutional arrangements is that urban construction land has to be acquired from the state. However, the supply of state-owned land depends on the non-agriculturalization of farmland, and the state, represented by local governments, is the sole decision maker with respect to the use of farmland for non-agricultural purposes.

In sum, the conversion of farmland to construction land is subject to mandatory state directives and can be implemented without the consent of peasant collective economic organizations or the farmers.

As the PRC's economic system transformed from a planned economy into a socialist market economy, the land expropriation compensation system transitioned through three stages: employment resettlement with little economic compensation; employment resettlement with increased economic compensation; and economic compensation only. In the 1980s, the RLRSC (1982) and the LAL (1986) both emphasized job placement as well as economic compensation for land expropriation. Thus, these laws gained the support of unemployed farmers and avoided massive social opposition. In 1998, the LAL was revised to adjust land expropriation compensation standards, but the revisions failed to address problems such as the unemployment of landless peasants and the lack of a social security system. Although farmers who had lost land received one-off compensation, they had no long-term sources of income or guarantees of social security, which led to significant problems caused by a massive increase in the number of landless peasants. Before the modern social security system was implemented in rural PRC, land was the primary asset owned by farmers and it guaranteed their livelihoods. Therefore, land expropriation without rational compensation drove farmers who had lost land into both homelessness and joblessness.

The compensation provided by the PRC's requisition laws includes compensation for the land (*tu di bu chang fei*), resettlement allowances for farmers who have lost land (*an zhi bu zhu fei*), and compensation for above-ground assets (e.g. young crops, structures, and water wells) (*di shang fu zhuo wu bu chang fei*). Land compensation and resettlement allowances are calculated on the basis of a benchmark price and a multiplier. The most significant change in the PRC's requisition laws was the transformation from a non-compulsory standard to a compulsory standard with ceilings. While the 1953 and 1958 versions of the MLRSC merely set a reference compensation standard, the 1982 RLRSC introduced two compensation ceilings. The first ceiling limited the maximum resettlement allowance to ten times the annual value of the land's agricultural production; the second limited the sum of the resettlement allowance and land compensation to twenty times the annual value of the land's agricultural production. The 1999 LAL raised the ceiling for total compensation to thirty times the annual value of agricultural production and stipulated that the State Council could increase the multiplier under certain conditions; subsequent reforms similarly entitled local governments to exceed the compensation ceiling. Specifically, in 2004, the State Council permitted local governments to increase the multiplier above thirty and required local governments to formulate either a unified annual output standard or integrated land expropriation price to ensure that similar land received similar compensation. Until last year, the compensation standard with ceilings was removed from the LAL, which is progress.

The acceleration of urbanization caused land values to increase after expropriation. As indicated earlier, the standard compensation paid to farmers who had lost land generally could not exceed thirty times the average annual value of agricultural production over the previous three years. However, current land expropriation compensation standards do not adequately account for the land value-added after expropriation (Qian 2004). Specifically, this compensation system does not consider the location, development potential, or market value of the expropriated land. In short, the government makes decisions regarding land expropriation compensation that denies farmers who have lost land an appropriate share of the land value-added revenue. The World Bank estimates that from 1990 to 2010, local governments paid approximately 2 trillion RMB below market value for expropriated rural land (World Bank and DRC 2014). Ren and Hao (2003) found that land requisition compensation, calculated by using multiple compensation methods, was equivalent to one-fifth of the land value. Moreover, land requisition compensation only pays farmers for property income losses, while ignoring their non-production income. Rural land, being dominated by the government, is expropriated at prices far below market value, which produces an unreasonable distribution of the wealth derived from the land value increment. Figures disclosed in the 2005 *Green Book of China's Rural Economy* (Chinese Academy of Social Sciences and National Bureau of Statistics of the PRC 2005) clearly illustrated this unreasonable distribution: local governments took 20–30 per cent of the land value increment, enterprises received 40–50 per cent, village-level organizations received 25–30 per cent, and farmers received only 5–10 per cent.

This unfair distribution of the land value increment further widens the income gap between urban and rural areas, which causes numerous social conflicts (Rithmire 2013). In 2003, disputes over farmers' land rights and interests became the subject of Zhejiang province's first mass petitions. In Zhejiang, complaint letters about land acquisition and resettlement compensation problems numbered 586 in 2001 and 1,058 in 2002, which represented an increase of 14.5 per cent and 80.55 per cent over the previous year, respectively (Jiang et al., 2007). The *China Social Situation Analysis and Forecast 2004–2005*, issued by the Chinese Academy of Social Sciences (2005), identified social contradictions and conflicts caused by the expropriation of farmland as one of the six major issues facing contemporary PRC. Poor compensation for land expropriation and unreasonable distribution of the land value increment inflame these social conflicts.

9.2.3 Land Leasing

The land-leasing system parallels the land expropriation system. Based on the experience of Hong Kong, the PRC developed a system of long-term leases for land use rights that gave private investors secure tenure and control over land, albeit for a limited period (Ding and Lichtenberg 2008). The LAL clearly states that 'any unit or individual who needs land for construction must apply for the right to use state-owned land according to relevant laws' and thereby legally secures the local government's position as a monopoly supplier of urban land. With the rapid development of the PRC after reforms and opening up, the land-grant system changed from free to paid transfer. In 1980, the state council noted that 'joint venture enterprises should pay site-use fees for either newly expropriated land or originally owned enterprise land' and began the process of charging fees for the use of urban state-owned land (Table 9.1). Hence, free state-owned land was transformed into property with a price tag.

In 1988, the LAL stated that 'The state shall practice a system of paid use of state-owned land in accordance with the law', which legally prescribed the paid transfer of rights to use state-owned land. In 1999, the revised LAL (RLAL) established new regulations. With the exception of the four types of construction land-military use; municipal infrastructure; energy and power industries; schools, hospitals, and other public facilities that can be transferred through allotment, 'Construction units are permitted to use state-owned land only by means of a paid transfer'. Provisions introduced by the State Council in 2001 indicated that the PRC not only strictly limited the administrative allotment of state-owned land but also set the minimum grant price based on a combination of the standard land price and the demarcated land price, limited the scope of land use, and

Table 9.1. City-level initiatives

Year	City	Reform
1984	Fushun, Niaoning Province	Implemented a pilot land use tax system and thus realized the paid use of state-owned land
1987	Shenzhen, Guangdong Province	First leased land through agreement, tender or auction and set time limits on transfers
1988	Guangzhou, Xiamen, Zhuhai, Fuzhou, and other coastal cities	Conducted pilot projects to realize the paid use of urban state-owned land with favourable results

vigorously promoted the tender and auctioning of state-owned land. Decree No. 11 of the Ministry of Land and Resources, which was implemented on 1 July 2002, stipulated that 'profit-oriented land, such as land for business, tourism, entertainment and commercial housing, can only be transferred by means of tender, auction, or listing'. Urban state-owned land is now transferred through open-market tender; local governments already monopolized the primary urban land market.

Section 9.2.3 maintains that the local government is a monopoly supplier in the construction land market under current land policy. Provisions introduced by the State Council in 2001 state clearly that if two or more persons want the same piece of land after the publication of plans for commercial real estate development or other land supply, the administrative department of land for the municipality or county must lease the land by tender or auction. Subsequent laws and regulations, particularly the 2007 PL, have made adjustments to market allocation. The PL states that if 'two or more persons want the same piece of land that is designated as industrial, commercial, tourism, entertainment, residential or other commercial land, the local government shall lease the land through tender, auction or other public process'. The local government leases land under a dual price system, pursuant to which lands leased for military use; municipal infrastructure; energy and power industries; schools, hospitals, and other public facilities are transferred at cost, whereas commercial land is sold at market prices through tender, auction and listing.[3]

Land leasing by the local government is selective. In practice, local governments use agreement and tender for most industrial land leasing transactions, whereas auctions are used for commercial and residential land leasing to ensure that the highest tenderer acquires the land and that there is no price cap (Table 9.2). Due to the public financing of land development projects, some real estate

[3] In mid-September 2011, the Ministry of Land and Resources revealed that 'the next step, according to the basic principles of market allocation of resources, [is to] narrow the scope of allocated land and expand the coverage of paid land, and ultimately abolish the dual system of land supply. The military, affordable housing, and other special land will continue to be allocated for use free of charge, but other uses of land should incur charges.'

Table 9.2. Land-leasing mode, area, and revenue (%)

	Leasing area				Leasing revenue			
	Agreement	Tender	Auction	Listing	Agreement	Tender	Auction	Listing
2003	0.72	0.03	0.05	0.19	0.43	0.12	0.16	0.29
2004	0.71	0.02	0.05	0.21	0.45	0.08	0.15	0.33
2005	0.65	0.03	0.06	0.26	0.29	0.08	0.16	0.48
2006	0.69	0.01	0.05	0.24	0.28	0.04	0.16	0.52
2007	0.50	0.01	0.06	0.43	0.18	0.04	0.21	0.58
2008	0.16	0.02	0.06	0.76	0.07	0.05	0.13	0.74

Source: Data used are from the *China Land and Resources Yearbook* and the authors' own calculations.

developers will tender for land regardless of the market price; some developers even deliberately boost prices at the behest of local governments. In addition, the current lax economic environment enables developers to tender fiercely regardless of market risk because higher prices are expected in the future. This practice results in high premium transactions. By strictly controlling the supply of commercial and residential land, local governments can increase land-leasing revenues.

Since 2003, local governments have used tender, auction, listing, and other methods to lease state-owned land. As shown in Figure 9.1, from 2003 to 2008, small, expensive land parcels were generally leased by auction, whereas large, inexpensive lots were leased by listing. As shown in Figure 9.1a the land areas leased by listing are on average approximately twice as large as those leased by auction, and Figure 9.1b indicates that the average transaction price for listed land is only approximately 60 per cent of the price obtained through auction.[4]

In short, local governments have monopsony power in the rural land market and monopoly power in the urban land market. The local government obtains significant amounts of land and funds and functions as a single-plank bridge between the urban and rural land markets (see Figure 9.2).

With its monopoly on land expropriation and transaction, local governments have held down land expropriation prices to acquire large amounts of rural land and turned them into urban lands, which directly leads to the excessive expansion of urban land area, as in the massive construction of development zones and new towns. As the Hukou system hinders rural–urban migration, it can be predicted that land urbanization will outpace population urbanization with decreasing density of urban population and low efficiency of land use. As governments of higher levels allocate construction land quotas, it is impossible to improve land use efficiency through exchange land quotas among regions.

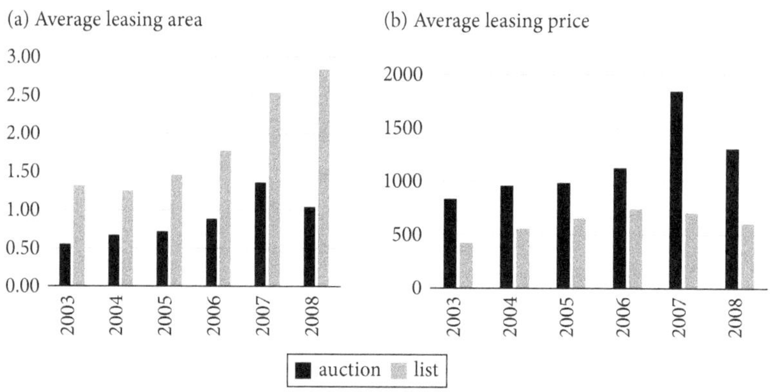

Figure 9.1. Leasing areas and prices

Source: Data used are from the *China Land and Resources Yearbook* and the authors' own calculations.

[4] This percentage decreased to 38 per cent in 2007.

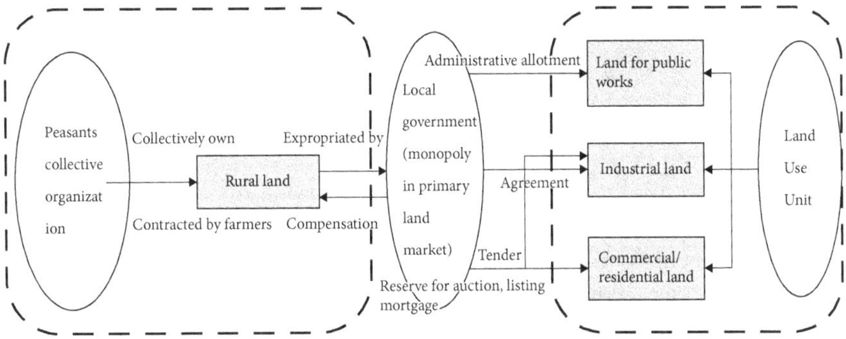

Figure 9.2. The status of local governments the Chinese land market

9.2.4 Administration of Land Planning

Chinese construction land use planning is administered mainly pursuant to the National General Land Use Plan (NGLUP) and annual land use plans. The NGLUP 1997–2010 regulates the quantity of new construction land within a region over the long term, whereas annual land use plans regulate the quantity of new construction land on an annual basis. The NGLUP 1997–2010 determines the total amount and spatial layout of construction land based on an index system that considers the amount of arable land currently occupied by construction, the necessity of protecting basic farmland, and the total amount of arable land (Wang and Tao 2009).

Land quota allocation is biased towards inland PRC. Although local governments determine the land supply, annual construction land quotas are controlled by the central government. Therefore, local land supply largely reflects the local government's implementation and oversight of land quotas allocated by the central government. The proportion of land supply allocated to the central and western provinces (inland PRC) increased significantly after 2003 (Lu and Xiang 2014). The central government intensified its balance policy after 2000. However, both before and after 2003, the central government implemented several considerable changes to the regional allocation of economic resources (including construction land quotas and capital). In particular, the allocation of construction land was reconfigured as a policy tool to support the economic development of mainland PRC. The NGLUP 1997–2010 highlighted the coordination of land use in different regions and strengthened restrictions on construction land in the south-east coastal and Bohai Sea regions (Lu and Xiang 2014). For example, the Zhejiang province has experienced rapid modernization and industrialization. However, the central government has allocated smaller quotas to Zhejiang since 1999, and the construction land supply in Zhejiang has consequently struggled to meet demand. In Zhejiang, the planning and administration of construction land was inconsistent with its rapid industrialization and urbanization (Wang and Tao 2009).

9.3 Trends in Urban Expansion

9.3.1 The Speed of Urbanization

The urbanization of the Chinese population has been rapid since the reforms and opening up of the PRC. The urban population (permanent residents) has increased from less than 20 per cent of the total population in 1978 to 52 per cent of the total population in 2012, representing an increase of 15 million people annually. It is expected that the PRC's urbanization rate will reach 70 per cent by 2030 (World Bank and DRC, 2014). From 2000 to 2008, the urbanization rate increased by an average of 3.78 per cent per year.

Land urbanization has proceeded much more quickly than population urbanization, a phenomenon known as 'the urbanization of land rather than peasants'. Between 2000 and 2010, the built-up area of PRC's cities increased at a compound annual growth rate of 6 per cent and nearly doubled in size, expanding from 22,000 sq. km to 40,000 sq. km. The average 6 per cent annual growth rate of the built-up area of the PRC's cities significantly exceeds the 3.78 per cent growth rate of the urban permanent resident population,[5] indicating that local governments promote land urbanization to a greater extent than population urbanization. In addition, rather than developing existing construction land, which is expensive, local governments tend to expropriate relatively inexpensive rural land. Consequently, urban land continually spreads outwards, and although the pace of land urbanization is rapid, the quality is low (World Bank and DRC 2014). This process decreases urban population density, produces urban sprawl and leads to inefficient land use. Urban population density has exhibited a downward trend in recent years; from 2000 to 2008, urban population density decreased by approximately 27.6 per cent (Xu 2011).

A geographic comparison of population urbanization in the PRC indicates that the eastern region has experienced a higher level of population urbanization and that its urban population is quite evenly distributed along a ribbon-shaped band. In contrast, the urban population in central PRC has a fragmented distribution and is characterized by significant interregional differences (Xu 2011). Urban agglomerations of different levels, sizes, and degrees of development currently exist in the PRC. For example, the urban agglomerations of the Yangtze River and Pearl River deltas are relatively mature and contain a dense network of cities and towns.

Urban agglomerations attract a greater labour force, enhance the efficiency of resource allocation, and promote urbanization and economic development.

Land urbanization occurred at a similar pace in the eastern and western regions, whereas the pace of land urbanization in central PRC is relatively slow.

[5] Data are sourced from CEInet Statistics Database. Ratio is calculated by the authors.

Table 9.3. Average expansion rates of built-up land and non-agricultural populations, 1990–2008 (%)

Average rate	National	East	Central	West
Built-up land expansion	5.63	6.49	4.43	6.17
Non-agricultural population growth	3.79	4.78	2.98	3.39
Difference	1.84	1.71	1.45	2.78

Source: CEInet Statistics Database. The ratio is calculated by the authors.

Population urbanization is most rapid in eastern PRC, and the gap between the population urbanization rates of central and western PRC is small. The difference between the population growth rate and land expansion rate in eastern PRC is 1.71 per cent, which is quite consistent with the national average of 1.84 per cent, whereas this gap in central PRC is slightly lower than the average level and that of western PRC is 2.78 per cent (Table 9.3). Western PRC has a non-agricultural population growth rate that is nearly twice the land urbanization expansion rate, which makes it the region in which a bias towards population urbanization over land urbanization is most evident. This characteristic is related to current government allocation methods for land quotas. Since 2003, construction land quotas have favoured the central and western provinces; construction land quotas in the eastern region have experienced a corresponding decrease (Lu and Xiang 2014).

Long et al. (2014) assessed urban land area in the PRC at the prefectural level and above for the period 1980–2010 using remotely sensed images. The ratio of urban land area in 2010 to that in 1980 approximates the degree of urban expansion in each city. Inland PRC has experienced greater urban expansion than the coastal region during this period. Huang et al. (2007) observed that although the expansion of construction land across the PRC accelerated from 1989 to 2000, expansion trends varied significantly by region. For example, the rate of expansion slightly decreased in the eastern region, but increased in the western region. Huang et al. (2007) analysed the relationship between density, available construction land per capita, and land expansion, and their model indicated that the intensity of land use and maintenance of construction land per capita in eastern PRC were the main reasons for its declining land expansion rate, whereas economic growth and increment of construction land per capita in western PRC (likely due to laxer policies and relatively low prices of land) were the primary reasons for the increased rate of land expansion rate in this region. Therefore, the expansion of construction land and the corresponding reduction of arable land driven by economic growth may exert profound influences on the future development in the central and western regions.

Population aggregation has not kept pace with the urbanization process because the population growth rate is slower than the urbanization rate. Figure 9.3

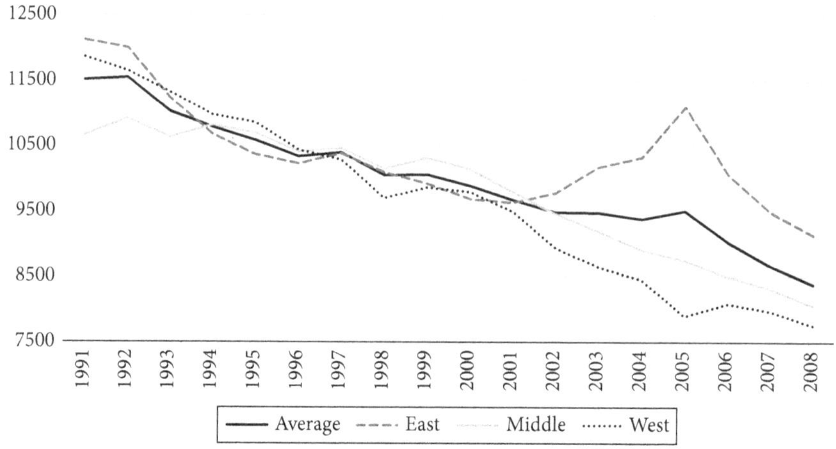

Figure 9.3. National and regional population density
Source: CEInet Statistics Database. The density is calculated by the authors.

indicates that the national average population density in the PRC decreased from 11,600 people per sq. km in 1990 to 8,400 people per sq. km in 2008, which represents a reduction of 27.6 per cent. From 1990 to 2000, regional differences between eastern and western PRC were less obvious. Between 2000 and 2005, the average population density remained relatively stable, although the population density of the eastern region increased because construction land use was limited. However, average population density in the PRC continued to decline after 2005. Population density in the central region decreased at a stable rate, whereas the western region experienced a significant drop, falling to nearly 8,000 people per sq. km—its lowest historical level—in 2005. The decline of national and regional population density between 1990 and 2008 also reflects the inability of population urbanization to keep pace with land urbanization, and the west experienced the greatest annual rate of decline at 2.42 per cent. The decline of population density in eastern PRC was consistent with the national average, whereas the rate of decline in central PRC was relatively low. Decreases in population density are detrimental to the quality of urbanization because agglomeration effects are more evident in cities with high population densities. Agglomeration can reduce the cost of providing services and infrastructure in cities.

9.3.2 Land Use Efficiency

Differences in land use efficiency among the PRC's regions are significant. Eastern PRC has the greatest utilization efficiency, and the gap between the central and western regions is widening. Figure 9.4 displays the trends in the PRC's urban

Figure 9.4. Average land use efficiency, 1990–2011 (billion RMB/sq. km)
Source: CEInet Statistics Database. Density is calculated by the authors.

land use efficiency since 1990. Land use efficiency is defined as the ratio of the output value of the city's secondary and tertiary industries to the area of built-up land (Lu 2011; Shao et al. 2011; Zhang and Xu 2011). Both national and regional land use efficiency have increased. Before 2003, the increasing trend was slight; however, in 2003, the government began to reorganize open economic zones and reduced urban construction planning land by 74 per cent (Lu and Xiang 2014). This policy enhanced the utilization of urban land, increasing land use efficiency dramatically. In 2003, the difference between the values added by the respective secondary and tertiary sectors of eastern and western PRC was RMB 135 million per sq. km. In 2011, this difference was RMB 323 million, which represents an increase of 139.3 per cent. However, the increased land use efficiency in eastern PRC is inconsistent with the current administrative allocation of construction land quotas. Specifically, most construction land quotas have been allocated to the central and western regions in recent years, implying that although the eastern region generates the highest land value-added, it is allocated the lowest land quotas. This allocation policy violates market rules and creates land resource waste and land use inefficiency. Since all of the PRC's largest cities are located in the eastern region, this policy will not help the country's largest cities to improve urbanization quality or generate greater agglomeration effects.

9.3.3 Urban Sprawl

The PRC's urbanization process has been accompanied by urban sprawl. Urban sprawl is caused by the large-scale formation of new towns and development zones. These processes will now be discussed in detail.

9.3.3.1 New Towns

The tremendous transformation of agricultural areas into commercial and residential areas has stimulated the construction of new towns. In 2013, the City and Town Reform and Development Center of the National Development and Reform Commission conducted a survey on the planning and construction of new towns. The survey included 156 prefecture-level cities and 161 county-level cities in twelve provinces. This survey revealed that 90 per cent of the prefecture-level cities had planned for new town construction and that most of these plans had been implemented. Ninety-six of the 255 plans for new town construction revealed their expected construction scale. The total area covered by these ninety-six planned new towns was 6,105 sq. km, on an average of 63.6 sq. km per town. According to the *City Statistical Yearbook of China* (NBSC 2012), the average urban built-up area of all prefecture-level cities in the twelve sampled provinces is 115 sq. km, which means that the average planned area for new urban districts is more than half of the existing urban area. Moreover, some cities had planned for the construction of more than one satellite town. Among the 145 prefecture-level cities that planned to construct new urban areas, 121 cities totally or partially promulgated the expected populations of the new towns. The total expected population of these new towns is 96.72 million people, on an average of 800,000 people per town. However, the yearbook statistics also reveal that the average population of all prefecture-level cities in the twelve sampled provinces is 884,000 people, which means that the expected population per new town is nearly equal to the population of existing towns.

Has China achieved its goals? Due to unrealistic development as well as the extreme scarcity of supporting industries and public facilities, a great number of newly constructed towns have become so-called 'ghost towns' or 'sleeping cities'. For instance, KangBashi, a new town in Ordos, was planned and constructed beginning in 2003 on a planned urban area of 32.23 sq. km. KangBashi's population was expected to grow to 300,000 by 2020 and reach 1 million in the long term. However, the town had only 28,000 residents by 2010, resulting in a small population lost in a big city.[6]

9.3.3.2 Development Zones

Urban sprawl can also result from constructing new development zones on large areas of land converted from agricultural to industrial use. The policies for development zones are extensions of the successful special economic zone (SEZ) policies implemented by the Chinese government. With the advancement of reforms and opening up policies, development zones have been transformed from test fields shouldering the task of economic reforms and institutional innovation into a major policy instrument for boosting regional economic development

[6] <http://www.yicai.com/news/2010/04/336567.html>, 2014-8-30.

(Lu and Xiang 2014). As state-level development zones are established on the construction standards of SEZs, they enjoy similar preferential policies, including tax privileges and favourable land pricing. These preferential policies reduce the cost of land transfers by RMB 10,000–50,000 per unit area, depending on the scale and availability of the investment, and reductions of RMB 30,000–60,000 per unit area are possible if the project is considered high-tech by the local Science and Technology Committee (Ge and Tian 2008). Moreover, because the economic basis and development demands vary from town to town, local governments can make moderate adjustments to their preferential policies. In addition to state-level development zones, three types of provincial development zones are recognized by the central government: provincial economic development zones, high-tech industrial zones, and characteristic industrial zones. Due the unequal tax powers of local governments and the central government, the degree of tax allowances in provincial development zones differs significantly from that of state-level development zones. To attract more enterprises to province-level development zones, some local governments provide unqualified industries with allowances such as land premium refunds, corporate income tax exemptions, and the construction of supporting facilities. The scale of development zones has expanded rapidly and blindly since the first coastal development zones were established in 1984, resulting in an uncontrolled wave of development zone construction. Local governments use these zones to attract private investment and to transform large areas of agricultural land into industrial land. Even if no immediate investment is made in these zones, the land can be reserved for future financing.

Development zones are obviously advancing inland. Wang (2013) cited data from the 2006 *China Developing Zones Audit Announcement Directory* related to 1,568 development zones and outlined the geographical advancement of the reforms and opening-up policy. These data show that the number of cities taking advantage of the opening-up policy has increased dramatically and that only a minority of urban areas has not yet established any development zones. The data also show that the inland advancement of the PRC's development zones increased significantly after the opening-up policy went into effect in 1992.

The clean-up and rectification of development zones strengthen regional balance. At present, the PRC's national ministries and commissions recognize only national development zones and three types of provincial development zones. The clean-up and rectification of development zones conducted by the Ministry of Land and Resources and State Council during 2003–6, following the blind expansion of development zones, has been the most significant undertaking since the development zone policy was implemented. By 2006, the number of national development zones decreased by 77.2 per cent, going down from 6,866 to 1,568, and the planning area decreased by 74 per cent, going from 38,600 sq. km to 9,949 sq. km (Lu and Xiang 2014). The clean-up and rectification of development zones from 2003 to 2006 not only successfully contained the excessive expansion of development zones but also strengthened the regional balance of provincial development zones.

Lu and Xiang (2014) calculated the number of the enterprises in eastern development zones both before and after the rectification and calculated the proportion of counties in the PRC that have development zones. Their study found that although the rectification significantly reduced the number of development zones in eastern China, the number increased in the mid-west. The PRC's regional balance strategy prioritizes development inland to promote equality among regions. This policy allocates more resources to the mid-west and promotes relatively rapid development of this region over the short term. However, this policy conflicts with market dynamics because resource use efficiency is higher in the PRC's east coast, resulting in the loss of macroeconomic efficiency. The spatial distribution of the provincial development zones reflects the PRC's regional balance strategy.

9.4 Land and Urbanization

9.4.1 Land Leasing and Urbanization

Urbanization rates and land-leasing revenue are positively related. The booming real estate markets in most Chinese cities increase the value of urban construction land, which is the primacy resource of local governments, and increases local government revenue, especially since 2003. Figure 9.5 shows that the land-leasing income in 2013 (RMB 2.71 trillion) was nearly forty-five times the land-leasing income in 1999 (RMB 59.6 billion).

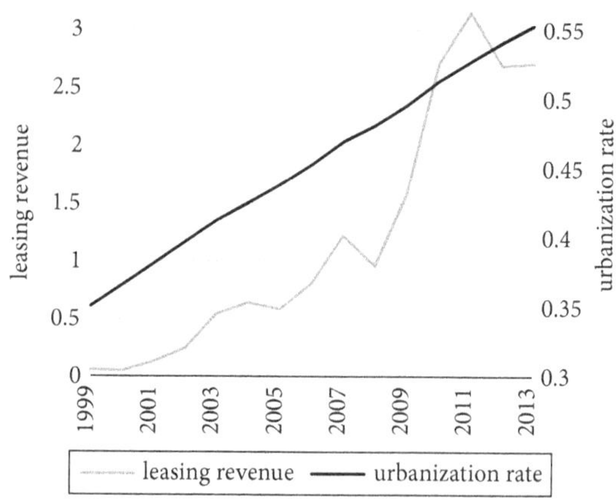

Figure 9.5. Land-leasing revenue and urbanization rates

Source: Leasing data are from the *China Land and Resources Yearbook*; urbanization data are from CEInet Statistics Database and the authors' own calculations.

The amount of land leased by local governments and the average price of land leases transitioned through three stages, as shown in Figure 9.6a. During the period 1999–2002, local governments transferred between 45,000 ha and 124,000 ha of land each year, reaching an average total leased area of approximately 200,000 ha, and the price of leased land soared. In 2010–13, the area of leased land increased to more than 300,000 ha; by 2013, the area of leased land had grown to 367,000 ha, approximately eight times the area of leased land in 1999.[7] Leasing prices gradually increased from an average of RMB 1,133 thousand per hectare in 1999 to RMB 7,384 thousand per hectare in 2013, an increase of nearly 600 per cent.

Land-leasing revenue has become an important source of local government income. On average, the ratio of land-leasing revenue to local fiscal revenue is approximately two-fifths, and the ratio of land-leasing revenue to national fiscal revenue is approximately one-fifth, as shown in Figure 9.6b. As the direct embodiment of land premiums, local governments' land-leasing revenue corresponds to a sustained increase in land prices and has become the most important source of extra-budgetary revenue for local governments. Statistical data indicate that gross land-leasing revenues represented 50.9 per cent of local general budget revenue during the period 2004–11 and represented more than 60 per cent in 2010 and 2011 (Zheng et al. 2014).

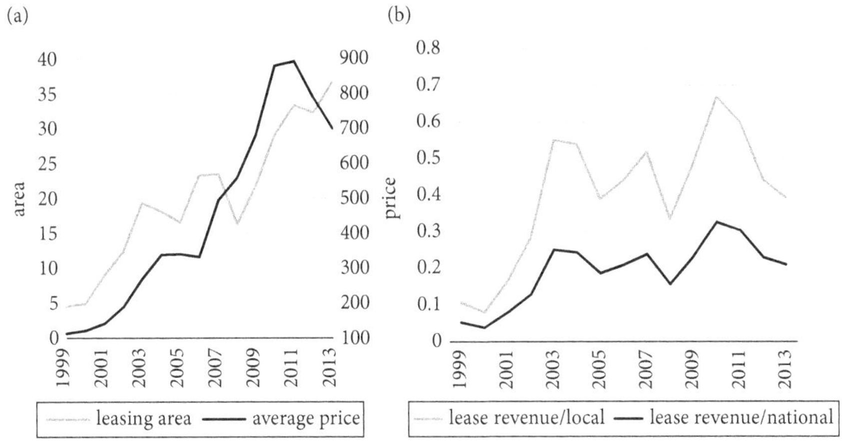

Figure 9.6. Leasing revenue/fiscal income

Source: Leasing data for 1999–2002 are sourced from the *China Land and Resources Yearbook*; leasing data for 2003–7 are sourced from <http://www.bjinfobank.com/>; leasing data from 2009–13 are sourced from the Chinese land resources bulletin; and fiscal data are sourced from <http://www.stats.gov.cn>. Average price = leasing revenue/leasing.

[7] <http://gks.mof.gov.cn/zhengfuxinxi/tongjishuju/201401/t20140123_1038541.html>, <http://finance.sina.com.cn/g/20110107/12029219005.shtml>, <http://www.mlr.gov.cn/xwdt/jrxw/201301/t20130125_1178667.htm>, 2012 <http://www.mlr.gov.cn/xwdt/jrxw/201004/t20100409_144481.htm> 2009 <http://www.stats.gov.cn/tjsj/zbjs/201310/t20131029_449552.html>.

Land leasing provides financial support for the PRC's urbanization. Local governments continue to directly or indirectly control infrastructure investment projects in the vast majority of Chinese cities; however, given the current tax system and the property tax vacancy situation, traditional budget revenue does not provide adequate and sustained funding for local development. This means that other modes of financing city construction—modes with 'Chinese characteristics'—must exist. Land-leasing income is considered extra-budgetary revenue, and local governments can use this money with few constraints. The apportionment of land-leasing revenue between the central and local governments has been adjusted several times. Currently, 30 per cent of new construction land-leasing revenue is paid to the central government and the remainder belongs to the local government.

There is an important indirect, or collateral, effect of the land bonus. Land that has been expropriated and reserved, but not yet leased to private actors, represents the most important asset of most local governments, and increases in land prices enhance the ability of local governments to engage in debt financing (Barro 1976; Stiglitz and Weiss 1981). This combination of land-leasing revenue and land mortgaging provides an important source of funds for much urban infrastructure investment—this method of financing infrastructure is called 'land financing' (Fan and Mo 2014; Zheng et al. 2014). By stimulating local economic growth and improving the quality of life in cities, urban infrastructure investment causes land prices to increase further, which enables local governments to conduct additional, large-scale land financing. This positive feedback relationship between land finance and urban infrastructure investment (Zheng et al. 2014) incentivizes local governments to expropriate additional rural land to capture land value-added income and accelerate urbanization.

9.4.2 Land Supply Structure and Price

Land policies and the local governments' land supply jointly determine the supply of urban construction land in a particular area. Industrialization and urbanization increase the demand for industrial, commercial, and residential land, which in turn affects the price of a city's land.

As Figure 9.7 indicates, the proportion of industrial land declined during 2006–12, going down from 45 per cent to less than 30 per cent. In contrast, the proportion of land used for roads and squares rose rapidly, which reflects local governments' pursuit of enhanced city image and infrastructure construction. Although the proportion of industrial and warehouse land decreased to less than 30 per cent by 2012, this proportion remains much higher than the foreign average of 10–15 per cent.

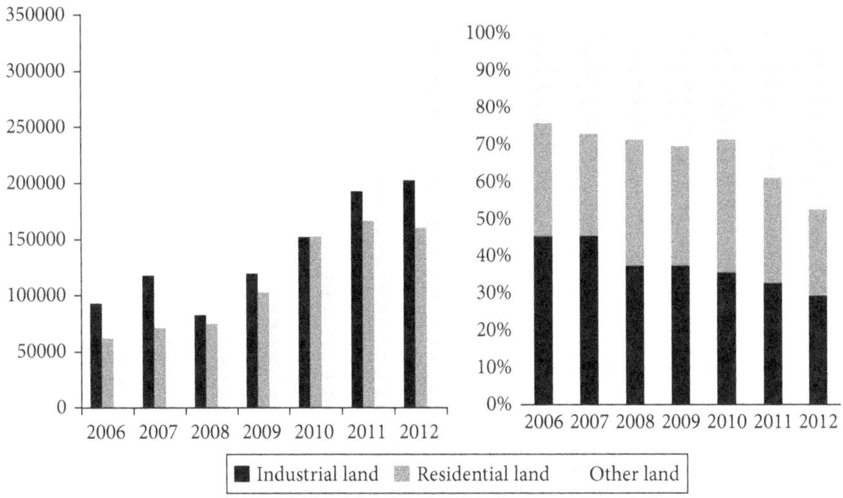

Figure 9.7. Land supply structure

Note: Other land uses include public facilities, public buildings and transportation.

Source: <http://www.landchina.com/default.aspx?tatender=325&WebShieldDRSessionVerify=9Pem7QKq1FfSzYAPMVd7>.

A high proportion of industrial land has resulted from the rational choices of local governments (Tao et al. 2009). The proportion of industrial land is much higher than that of commercial land, which lowers the price of industrial land and increases the price of commercial land. Since the amount of industrial land is large and its price is low, it attracts investment. Conversely, the amount of commercial and residential land is small and its price is expensive. Accordingly, governments either lease commercial and residential land to obtain revenue or reserve the land to obtain financing. Figure 9.8 shows that the price of industrial land is much lower than that of commercial and residential land.

Attracting investment with industrial land has strong external benefits. Such investment can rapidly increase investment in local capital assets, contribute to GDP growth, and facilitate the attainment of political performance goals. Moreover, it can help increase employment and tax revenues. However, using this approach to attract investment creates excess industrial land. Local governments monopolize the transfer of local urban land, and local government intervention affects land use during the process of urbanization.

According to National Land Use Planning 2006–20, the volume rate of industrial land was only 0.3 to 0.6 in 2005. However, over the past six years the volume rate increased to 1.26, which means that the volume rate of early industrial land represented a significant amount of waste. In addition, industrial land supply has continued to grow rapidly in subsequent years; in 2012, industrial, warehouse, and mining land accounted for 40.9 per cent of nationally approved new construction

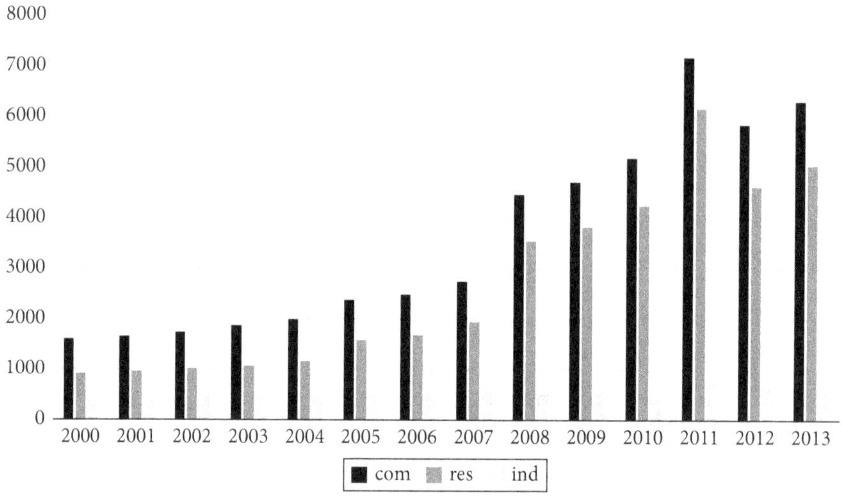

Figure 9.8. The price of land for different uses (2000–13) in urban PRC
Source: <http://www.landvalue.com.cn>, 2014-9-2.

land. At this time, an overall industrialization strategy was being pursued regardless of endowments, and all regions committed to the development of similar industries. This strategy contributed to a race to the bottom, characterized by low-level, redundant construction and low overall land use efficiency; it also severely hampered sustainable industrialization and urbanization.

Land transfer income is derived primarily from commercial and residential land and from subsidies for industrial land (Tao et al. 2009). Local governments supply a significant amount of industrial lands at low prices to attract investment and spur industrialization. Industrialization substantially increases the demand for labour, which prompts landless peasants and farmers to enter cities to seek employment. The expropriation of farmland for land urbanization thus encourages landless farmers to leave rural areas and establish residency in cities as non-agricultural labour, thereby promoting human urbanization. It is evident that local governments use land supply to spur industrialization, which acts like a 'switch' in the PRC's industrialization and urbanization process.

The acceleration of urban development increases the demand for real estate, which causes land prices to rise. Increased urbanization leads to higher numbers of immigrants entering cities, which sustains residential demand growth. Since housing is a mortgage commodity, when investors rationally anticipate sustained residential demand growth, they will invest in housing. Thus, residential prices may increase faster than per capita GDP (and income) increases, especially in the coastal area, where land supply has been restricted in recent years (Lu et al. 2014a). The Research Group on China's Economic Growth (2011) found that because the supply of land is limited, the intertemporal allocation of residential land increases market risk. If real estate prices increase too quickly, urban population and industrial growth are hindered. The Research Group on China's Economic Growth (2011) demonstrates that the expansion of land finance and increased public expenditure directly spur urbanization, but if urbanization does not produce increasing returns to scale and government revenue and expenditure remain unchanged, the sustainable development of cities is threatened.

9.4.3 Land Price Variation and Location Choices of Enterprises and Workers

Industrial, commercial, and residential land prices in the PRC vary widely by region. Land prices in the east are much higher than those in the mid-west, especially the price of residential land. Figure 9.9 shows that the gap between industrial, commercial, and residential land prices in eastern and the mid-west PRC.

The price gap between the east and inland has widened in recent years. Figure 9.10 indicates the industrial, commercial, residential, and combination land price ratio of the east to the average of the middle and west—the wider price gap is related to land allocation being biased towards the mid-west. The central government intensified its regional balance policy after 2000, and in 2003 significantly altered the regional allocation of economic resources (including construction land quotas and capital). In particular, the allocation of construction land was reconfigured as a policy tool to support economic development in the mainland. The Outline of National Land Use Planning 1997–2010, which was approved by the State Council in April 1999, emphasized the coordination of land use among regions and strengthened restrictions on the amount of construction land in south-east coastal areas and the Bohai region. Although local governments determine land supply, annual construction land quotas are controlled by the central government. Therefore, local land supply largely reflects the oversight and

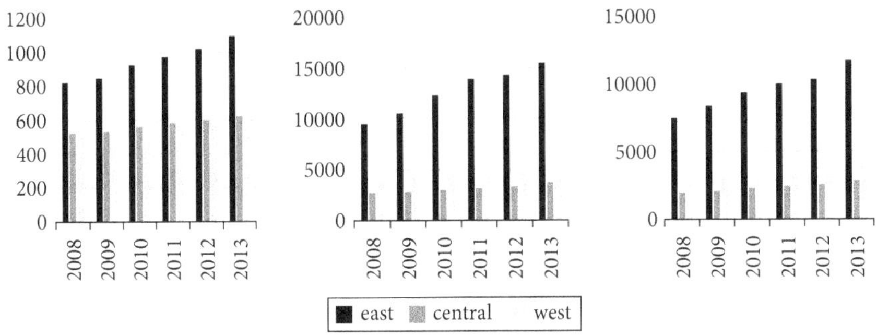

Figure 9.9. The price of industrial, commercial, and residential land by region
Source: <http://www.landvalue.com.cn>, 2014-9-2.

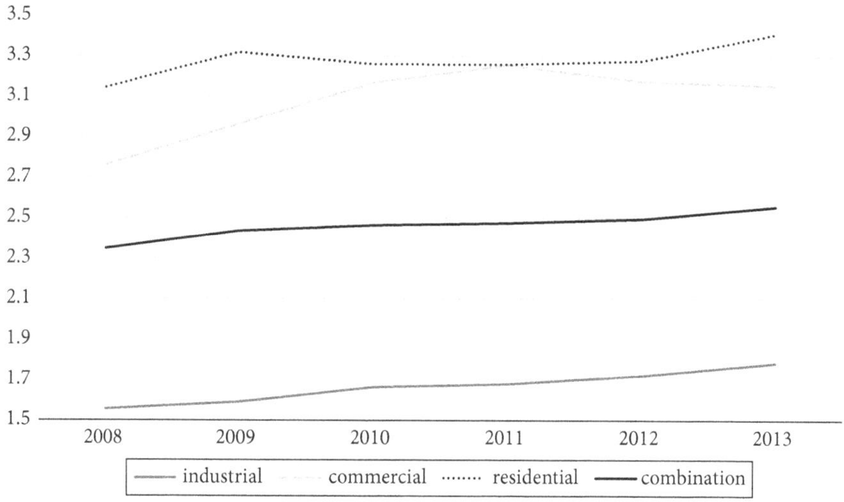

Figure 9.10. The price ratio of the east to the mid-west
Source: <http://www.landvalue.com.cn>, 2014-9-2.

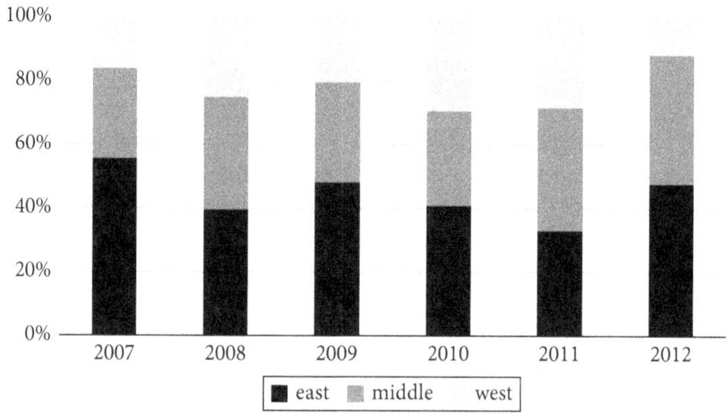

Figure 9.11. Allocation ratio of industrial land area by region
Source: <http://www.landchina.com>, 2014-9-2. The average ratio is calculated by the authors.

implementation of land quotas established by the central government. Figure 9.11 depicts the distribution of industrial land quotas. At first, there is no indication of growth in the mid-west area. However, a gradual upward trend in the industrial land allocated to mid-west areas occurs in two stages, one from 2007 to 2008 and the other from 2009 to 2011. In 2012, the allocation of industrial land quotas to the eastern region increased, but remained below its 2007 level. Thus, the mid-west regions not only enjoyed an advantage in land quota distribution but also benefited from substantial increases in annual new industrial land after 2008. The current

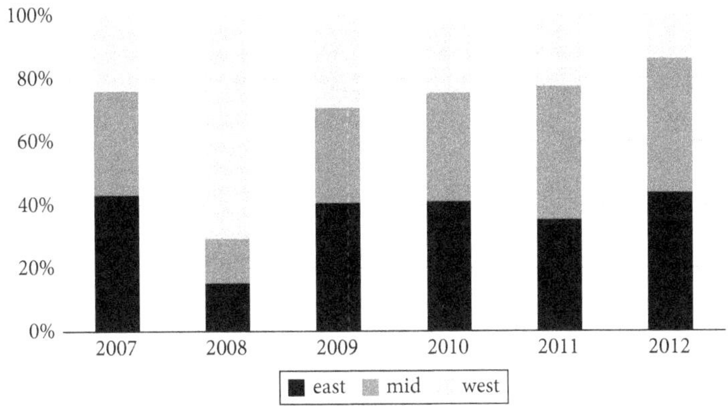

Figure 9.12. Allocation ratio of commercial and residential land by region
Source: <http://www.landchina.com>, 2014-9-2. The average ratio is calculated by the authors.

administrative allocation of construction land is inconsistent with land use efficiency, that is, increasing amounts of construction land have been allocated to the mid-west regions, which has resulted in the waste of land resources and demonstrates a lack of allocation efficiency. Since urban agglomeration is greatest in eastern PRC, this system of land allocation will not promote greater agglomeration effects or improve the quality of urbanization in eastern cities.

The high price of commercial and residential land is associated with high housing prices and rents (Figure 9.12). There is some debate over the precise mechanism by which land prices influence housing prices, but the positive correlation between them is obvious (Kuang 2005). According to the Fischer–DiPasquale–Wheaton model, an increase in housing prices produces an increase in rents. As most migrant workers live in villages, factory dormitories, and workplaces (e.g. shacks on the construction site), as well as other informal dwellings, they are insensitive to housing prices. Nonetheless, rents will increase as housing prices rise (as indicated in our survey of rents for village houses in Guangzhou), rising rents will increase the cost of living for the labour force, and the increased cost of living will trigger worker demands for higher wages. When the price of industrial land is low, enterprises with constant productivity can afford to increase wages. However, if the price of industrial land increases, enterprises will be unable to afford increased labour costs. In this scenario, the substitution effect concept suggests that enterprises will either use capital to substitute for labour inputs or leave the city. The labour force will then also leave the city because of fewer jobs and higher living costs, which will have a negative influence on urbanization.

Under the central government's regional balance policy, land controls in the eastern region differ from those in the mid-west. The PRC's central government manages urban land and controls the scale of each province's construction land based on an index system. Recently, the central government has introduced a series of policies that support the transfer of industry to the mid-west. For example, the allocation of new construction land, and particularly construction land zoned for industrial development, clearly favours the mid-west. Due of the relatively high level of industrialization and urbanization in eastern PRC, these allocation policies initially led to a significant gap between the supply and demand of construction land in eastern areas. Specifically, during the rectification of development zones that occurred after 2003, land planning in the mid-west was strictly implemented and the allocation of land supply was significantly biased towards the mid-west. This biased land policy caused the price of land in eastern PRC to increase and limited the tools available to local governments in eastern PRC to attract investment. A combination of these factors influences enterprises' location selection and shifts industry away from eastern PRC to inland regions. This industry shift affects cities' urbanization and industrialization.

The significant gap between the prices for land used for different purposes in the mid-west attracts business investment. Specifically, the price of land drives housing prices and rents, which affects wages and enterprise production, and thus influences location selection. Lu et al. (2014b) found that wages and housing prices are positively correlated. In eastern PRC, housing prices have increased faster than wages after 2003, especially in 2007 and 2010, due at least in part to the relatively tight land supply. Therefore, although the labour force continues to flow to eastern PRC because of agglomeration effects, the land in eastern cities is under stricter control and the portion of available land is decreasing. When housing prices and rents increase, migrant workers face higher costs of living in eastern cities; simultaneously, increased local government investment in inland areas provides more job opportunities in these areas. Thus, migrant workers can opt to work in their respective local cities, creating a shortage of migrant workers in the coastal areas. In this situation, enterprises in the coastal areas must use higher wages to recruit a labour force. In short, housing prices and wages have a positive feedback relationship.

Is the increased investment in mainland PRC efficient? Lu and Xiang (2014) calculated the average capital productivity of each prefecture-level city using enterprise data. It is clear that investment efficiency in the coastal area is much higher than that in the hinterland of the mid-west. If factors flow freely, then theoretically the returns on capital in different regions should converge. In practice, the Chinese restrictions on land and investment lead to the survival of enterprises with higher productivity. This strategy decreases investment efficiency in the mid-west and highlights the distortive effect of government intervention on efficient resource allocation.

Although businesses that shift to mainland PRC tend to be attracted by the low price of land, the efficiencies achieved by such transfers are insubstantial. The relatively high cost of logistics in the mainland and the lack of competition in its institutional environment dissuade many enterprises from transferring to the mainland to escape increasing cost pressures in eastern PRC, as policymakers expect; instead, these enterprises relocate to the South East Asian countries around the PRC because the cost of labour in these countries is much lower. Moreover, the pressure on local government officials to achieve success based on the PRC's performance assessment index has prompted some mid-west cities to increase their tolerance of industries with high levels of energy consumption and pollution. Therefore, the quality of investment attracted to the mid-west is often low.

To sum up, current land and household registration policies hinder the mobility of factors, including construction land and the labour force, and distort the process of urbanization and industrialization. Current land policy essentially grants local governments the dual monopoly over the urban construction land market, in which local governments lease land to generate funding for urban infrastructure, preventing efficient land transactions. On the other hand, improved urban infrastructure increases house and land prices and attracts investment. This cycle promotes land-financing strategies and provides a source of funding for the expansion of cities. Combined with the Hukou system, these developments have decreased urban population density. In addition, local governments transfer land strategically; specifically, they lease below average amounts of commercial and residential land, which enhances the already substantial price gap between industrial and commercial/residential land. This gap produces a lag between urbanization and industrialization. Meanwhile, the central government allocates land quotas in a manner intended to balance regional development gaps and reduce regional income disparities, which has amplified the misallocation of construction land among regions. Therefore, a series of policy reforms, including land and fiscal reforms, should be implemented on an expedited basis to stimulate urbanization and city system adjustment rather than simply relying on the administration to guide the flow of resources appropriately.

9.5 Conclusion

Current land policy essentially grants local governments a dual monopoly over the urban construction land market, in which local governments lease land to generate funding for urban infrastructure, preventing efficient land transactions. On the other hand, improved urban infrastructure increases house and land prices and attracts investment. This cycle promotes land-financing strategies and provides a source of funding for the expansion of cities. Poor compensation for land expropriation and unreasonable distribution of the land value damage landless peasants' interests and inflame social conflicts.

There has been an inflow of population to eastern PRC, while land has been vacated in the west. Since eastern PRC, its big cities in particular, has stronger agglomeration effects, we find that the market power has driven the population to migrate to the east, but more construction land quotas are allocated to inland PRC. Such policies have intensified the shortage of construction land in eastern PRC, resulting in much higher land and house prices than that in inland PRC. Due to high costs in the east, firms move to inland cities, but as the agglomeration effect there is not strong enough, few firms stay except those with low efficiency and high pollution.

Population urbanization lags behind land urbanization. The current land and Hukou system distorts the flow of factors of production. On the one hand, the local government has dual monopoly power over the land market—motivated by the strategy of 'Land Finance', preferring to expand its urban area, which leads to excessive land urbanization. On the other hand, the Hukou system has restricted immigrant urbanization. These two opposite forces have made population urbanization lag far behind land urbanization. Prices in the land market are distorted and hinder the effective allocation of land. The local government knowingly distorts the supply structure of land, chooses the land-leasing mode to push up the prices of commercial and residential land, holds down the price of industrial land, and distorts the land cost of urbanization and industrialization, damaging the interests of landless peasants.

First and foremost, the land policy should be revised such that the market determines the allocation of land resources, which will create a unified, competitive urban–rural land market. This is a long-term, arduous task, but it may begin with the following two measures.

First, linking land reform with Hukou reform offers the most effective way to solve these problems. Under the current landownership system, a national construction land quota trading system can be established for the market to decide the allocation of construction land quotas and encourage simultaneous population migration. At present, when peasants migrate to cities, they cannot make the best use of their homesteads and farmlands. Land is not mobile, but construction land quotas can be traded. The experiments in Chengdu and Chongqing are restricted within their respective regions, inconsistent with the interregional labour flow, and thus fail to fully demonstrate the advantages of matching flowing populations with land quotas. Circumventing the provincial boundaries and allowing peasants to exchange their land quotas of homesteads for entry into cities can help fix this problem. The homesteads can be recycled for land reclamation and the farmlands can be priced and sold to the local community or other villagers. In this way, the population-receiving governments can have more construction land quotas.

Second, farmers whose land has been expropriated should participate equally in the expropriation process to curb the exploitation of farmers by local governments. In this regard, the government should abandon the notion that land use rights and interests can be acquired in exchange for the mere establishment of a social security or compensation system.

Furthermore, our proposal is to change the local government's pattern of 'Land Finance' to reduce factor misallocation of construction land. By opening up a variety of other financing channels in support of urban development and reducing the local government's overdependence on land for financing, we can change the local government's role in the land market as a monopolist to simply that of an agent.

References

Barro, Robert. 1976. 'The Loan Market, Collateral, and Rates of Interest'. *Journal of Money, Credit and Banking 8* (4): 439–56.

Cai Hongbin, J. Vernon Henderson, and Qinghua Zhang. 2013. 'China's Land Market Auctions: Evidence of Corruption?' *The Rand Journal of Economics 44* (3): 488–521.

Chinese Academy of Social Sciences. 2005. *The China Social Situation Analysis and Forecast 2004-2005*, Social Science Academic Press.

Chinese Academy of Social Sciences and National Bureau of Statistics of the PRC. 2005. *Green Book of China's Rural Economy 2005*, Social Science Academic Press.

Davis, James C. and J. Vernon Henderson. 2003. 'Evidence on the Political Economy of the Urbanization Process'. *Journal of Urban Economics 53* (1): 98–125.

Ding, Chengri and Erik Lichtenberg. 2008. 'Using Land to Promote Urban Economic Growth in China'. Department of Urban Studies and National Center for Smart Growth. Mimeo.

Fan, Jianyong and Jiawei Mo. 2014. 'Local Government Debt, Land Market Institution and Regional Industrial Growth'. *Economic Research Journal 1* (014).

Ge, Shunqi and Guiming Tian. 2008. 'The State Economic and Technological Development Zone's Economic Development and Problems'. *The World Economy Research 12*: 10–16.

Ho, Peter. 2001. 'Who Owns China's Land? Property Rights and Deliberate Institutional Ambiguity'. *The China Quarterly 166*: 394–421.

Huang, J., L. Zhu, and X. Deng. 2007. 'Regional Differences of Chinese Construction Land Expansion and its Influence Factor'. *Science in China Series D: Earth Sciences 50*: 1835

Jiang, Shengsan, Shouying Liu, and Qing Li. 2007. 'The Land Reform and the Growth of National Economy'. *Management of the World 9*: 1–9.

Kuang, Weida. 2005. 'A Study on the Relationship between Housing Pricing and Land Pricing: Basic Model and Evidence from China'. *Finance & Trade Economics 11*: 56–63.

Long, Y., J. Wang, and K. Wu. 2014. *PM2.5 Pollution of Chinese Cities*. Ranking at Beijing City Lab. <http://www.beijingcitylab.com>.

Lu, Ming. 2011. 'Interregional Reallocation of Construction Land Use Rights: A New Dynamic of Chinese Economic Growth'. *The World Economy Research 1.*

Lu, Ming, Haijun Ou, and Binkai Chen. 2014a. 'Rationality or Bubble? An Empirical Study on Urbanization, Migration and Housing Prices'. *World Economy 1*: 30–54.

Lu, Ming and Kuanhu Xiang. 2014. 'Solving the Dilemma between Efficiency and Balance: On China's Regional Development Strategy Comparative'. *Economic & Social Systems 4:* 1–16.

Lu Ming, Hang Zhang, and Wenquan Liang. 2014b. 'Housing Price Threatens Competitiveness: How Did China's Land Policy After 2003 Raise its Wage?' Working paper.

NBSC (National Bureau of Statistics of China). 2012. *City Statistical Yearbook of China*, China Statistical Press.

Qian Zhonghao. 2004. 'Land Expropriation: Equilibrium and Nonequilibrium—Analysis of Current Chinese Land Requisition System'. *Management of the World 12*: 50–9.

Qu, Futian and Guangming Tian. 2011. 'The Coordination Urban Growth between Rural Development, and the Reform of the System of the Property Right of the Rural Collective Land'. *Management World 6*: 34–6.

Ren, Hao and Jing-min Hao. 2003. 'The Impact of Scissors Difference on Rural Land Value'. *China Land Science 17* (3): 38–43.

Research Group on China's Economic Growth (CASS). 2011. 'Urbanization, Fiscal Expansion and Economic Growth'. *Economic Research Journal 11*: 4–20.

Rithmire, Meg. 2013. 'Land Politics and Local State Capacities: The Political Economy of Urban Change in China'. *The China Quarterly 216*: 872–95.

Shao, Ting, Cui Fan, Ying Fan, and Qi Xu. 2011. 'Land Use Efficiency, Regional Disparities and the Requisition-Compensation Balance among Regions'. *China Economic Quarterly 10*: 1087–104.

Stiglitz, Joseph E. and Andrew Weiss. 1981. 'Credit Rationing in Markets with Imperfect Information'. *American Economic Review 71* (3): 393–410.

Tao, Ran, Xi Lu, Fubing Su, and Wang Hui. 2009. 'China's Transition and Development Model Under Evolving Regional Competition Patterns'. *Economic Research Journal 7*: 21–33.

Wang, Hui and Tao Ran. 2009. 'Zhejiang Model of Land Development Right and Exchange: The Origin of System, Operation Mode and its Meaning'. *Management World 8*: 39–52.

Wang, Jin. 2013. 'The Economic Impact of Special Economic Zones: Evidence from Chinese Municipalities'. *Journal of Development Economics 101* (3), 133–47.

World Bank and DRC. 2014. *Urban China: Toward Efficient, Inclusive, and Sustainable Urbanization*, World Bank, Washington, DC.

Xu, Xianxiang. 2011. 'Land Finance and Supporting Reform of Taxation System of China Local Government'. Working paper.

Zhang, Li and Xianxiang Xu. 2011. 'Spatial Re-disposition as a New Force Promoting the Local Regional Economy'. *Academic Research* 2: 014.

Zheng, Siqi, Weizeng Sun, Jing Wu, and Yun Wu. 2014. 'Infrastructure Investment, Land Leasing and Real Estate Price: A Unique Financing and Investment Channel for Urban Development in Chinese Cities'. *Economic Research Journal* 8: 14–27.

Zhou, Qiren. 2004. 'Property Rights and Land Requisition System: A Critical Choice for China's Urbanization'. *China Economic Quarterly* 4 (1): 193–210.

10

Urbanization, Land, and Housing in India: Options Amid the State and the Market Failures

Darshini Mahadevia

10.1 Introduction

Housing or shelter security is the key to rapid as well as inclusive urbanization, which different countries have addressed in their own way in the course of modern history. Public housing supply was important in the post–Second World War economic reconstruction efforts in Western European countries, creating housing and social security and supporting industrialization. The socialist countries in Eastern Europe and Asia (People's Republic of China (PRC) and Vietnam) and the former United Soviet Socialist Republic and later its breakaway republics provided housing as a wage good as well as an entitlement to the industrial workers, thereby ensuring that every urban household as well as individual had housing access. After the opening up of the economy in the PRC, housing provision has become an important incentive to attract rural migrants as workers in industries in the process of rapid industrialization. South Africa, after the apartheid regime ended in 1994, has taken up public housing provision as an important welfare measure, particularly for those discriminated during apartheid. In post-military regime Brazil, with an 85 per cent urbanization level, urban housing rights movements were important component of the 'Right to the City' statute followed by tenure security programmes for the *favelas* under the Workers' Party governments. The South East Asian countries, in particular Thailand and Indonesia, have seen government support for participatory slum-upgrading programmes to improve living conditions of the poor in the cities. Singapore housing is mainly public sector driven. Using Keynesian economics, housing was one of the important sectors of investment in bringing the United States of America (USA) out of recession. Thus, in process of industrialization, economic growth and urbanization, housing has played a central role in addressing welfare, asset formation and economic growth.

India, too, after a hiatus of half a century, introduced for the first time a large public housing programme aimed at the urban poor under the Basic Services

Darshini Mahadevia., *Urbanization, Land, and Housing in India* In: *Cities of Dragons and Elephants: Urbanization and Urban Development in China and India. Edited by:* Guanghua Wan and Ming Lu, Oxford University Press (2019).
 DOI: 10.1093/oso/9780198829225.003.0010

for the Urban Poor (BSUP) of the Jawaharlal Nehru Urban Renewal Mission (JNNURM) followed by the Rajiv Awas Yojana (RAY) and ongoing Housing for All by 2022 named as Prime Minister Awas Yojana (PMAY). In the first two decades of Indian independence, the economy driven through public sector enterprises had introduced employee housing, wherein housing was part of the wage good. In the new towns and the national capital, housing development was envisaged as provided by the public agencies such as the Development Authorities (for example the Delhi Development Authority). In the existing cities, respective state Housing Boards and Slum Clearance Boards provided housing to the urban poor and low-income households. But, the efforts were fragmented and insignificant. Hence, BSUP, then RAY, and now PMAY have brought a national-level framework and financial mechanism for large-scale intervention in the urban housing market for the benefit of the urban poor.

Although India is at a low level of urbanization—31.7 per cent of its population lived in urban areas in 2011—there is significant housing distress, particularly in the metropolitan and large cities. The housing shortage calculated for the Twelfth Five Year Plan is 18.8 million households[1] in 2012 (NBO 2012), which is about 23.8 per cent of the total housing stock in the 2011 census.[2] The population census of 2011 gives a figure of 13.36 million households as living in slums, which is 16.9 per cent of the total households.[3] Thus, there are also non-slum households living in cramped and/or unserviced housing, qualifying to be considered as part of the housing shortage. A revealing fact of the housing census of 2010 is the availability of 11 million vacant houses,[4] which, if put to use, could take care of about 85 per cent of households living in slums in urban India. This arithmetic does not work in reality and therein is located the urban housing question. Explaining this paradox is the first objective of this chapter. The second section presents dimensions of this paradox, while the third section provides the explanation of the paradox in the context of limited effects of state policies and programmes. Mahadevia (2009) calculated that 2–3 per cent land is required in major cities in India to house the existing slum population. The fact that even this small amount of land is not available for housing the slum dwellers is itself a paradox, which requires answers, which we seek in Section 10.5 where land policies and related issues are discussed.

[1] The housing shortage includes temporary housing, housing with age above 80 years, and housing that is congested, that is, where married couples do not have an independent room.

[2] Proportion calculated with total housing stock data of Housing Census of 2010, undertaken as a part of the Population Census 2011 enumeration. Housing census data available from <http://www.censusindia.gov.in/2011census/hlo/hlo_highlights.html> (accessed 15 February 2014).

[3] The number of households living in slums is from <http://www.censusindia.gov.in/2011census/hlo/Slum_table/hl-slum/SHH0101-crc.pdf> (accessed 15 February 2014).

[4] Data from <http://www.censusindia.gov.in/2011census/hlo/hlo_highlights.html> (accessed 15 February 2014).

The relationship between urbanization, land, and housing in India is tenuous and mediated by state-level[5] land policies and politics. While the national government from time to time does announce policies and programmes, these are mediated through state-level dynamics. Each state government also has its own policies and programmes. Hence, there is a mosaic of policies and programmes, on one hand, and differential levels of implementation of these across the states, on the other. Section 10.3 discusses housing policies and their achievements. In general, there is a state failure in making available decent housing to the low-income households. Housing for the urban poor is largely contingent upon land-related policies and legislation, which are presented in Section 10.4 to set the stage for discussion on informal housing in Section 10.5.

Unlike the European and socialist countries' experiences, in developing countries such as India, people themselves are engaged in the production of their own housing, what J.F.C. Turner termed 'housing by the people for the people' (Turner 1967; 1968). The majority of the housing in this segment is built without obtaining necessary development permissions as mandated under the planning and municipal governance statutes and is generically called informal housing. In all, informal housing is much larger than just slum housing. Section 10.5 is on housing submarkets and presents the estimates, the process of formation and mobility within informal housing, and its spread across different states in India.

Because housing policy and its implementation are largely dependent on the state governments' interests, the achievements across the states in housing indicators are varied. India is typically a market economy, and hence housing supply is also largely through market mechanisms, formal or informal, mediated through state policies. This is in contrast to the housing supply processes in the PRC. Housing, in a market economy, is a heterogeneous good. Its components comprise the structure (walls, roof, and floor); area; services such as water supply, sanitation, and electricity; location, which determines neighbourhood characteristics and accessibility to employment and social amenities at the city level; and tenure status (ownership or rental) and tenure security (legal or illegal/formal or informal). Informal housing is largely incremental, and hence, in India, as in other developing countries, housing is a process and not a product (Turner 1967; 1968). Therefore, any study of housing in countries such as India has to evolve the indicators portraying all the above dimensions of housing. Section 10.6 provides the present status of housing indicators disaggregated by geographic regions.

Attempt to analyse the linkages of housing status indicators with the urbanization level and economic growth of the state is presented in Section 10.7 using

[5] A 'state' in India is equivalent to a province in the PRC. However, they have different powers, primarily emanating from different taxation systems (Mahadevia 2006). In the recent years in India there has been very high decentralization of political power, largely on account of the race for economic growth. In the PRC, there has been political and administrative decentralization for a long time now (Qian 2000).

state-level data. Some aspects of housing-related services are a function of the household income and some are a function of state policy priorities, i.e. whether the state is instrumental in extending subsidized water and sanitation to slums, or whether the state is able to set aside land for housing the poor. Section 10.7, through statistical test, attempts to establish these linkages. Section 10.8 summarizes the overall trends in urban housing policies in India and suggests way forward for making 'Housing for All' happen.

The objectives of the chapter are to answer the questions (1) why there has been the state and market failure in meeting the housing needs of the urban poor, (2) what explains different levels of housing achievements by different states in India, (3) how do the urban poor access housing, and (4) what are the policy implications of going forward in the context of the current shortages with regards to housing and basic services, pricing out of vast segments of urban population from the housing market in India?

10.2 The Market Failure

Formal housing supply is largely through markets, with the exception of public housing programmes in the last decade, discussed in Section 10.3. The state has little role except in regulating land supply, use, and transfer, which is discussed in Section 10.4. The data on housing markets are available from real estate databases: one of the universally used is Numbeo, which gives data on housing rent and property prices by geographic location and average income for individual cities.

The rental data (Table 10.1) are for apartment buildings where the house size is presented in terms of the number of rooms; for example, 1BHK refers to a one bedroom, kitchen, and hall unit and 3BHK is a large unit with three bedrooms, kitchen, and hall. A 1BHK dwelling unit in the Indian market would be about 30 to 35 sq. m and a 3BHK unit would be about 100–120 sq. m built-up area. Rent, on its own, does not make sense unless compared with monthly household income. We have done just the same using the average monthly disposable income in hand (after tax) available in the dataset for each city. The ratio of rent to income indicates housing affordability. We have assumed that the affordable ratio will be 20 per cent for low-income households and 35 per cent for high-income households.

Mumbai is the most expensive city in the rental market wherein, in the 1BHK segment, the monthly rents in the central city areas are 71 per cent of the city's average monthly income and in the 3BHK segment are 199 per cent of the same. The other four cities in the top five in the 1BHK segment are Patna, Thane, Kolkata, and Goa in both central city as well as peripheral rental markets. If we consider that 20 per cent of the income can be spent towards rent in the 1BHK segment, central city renting by a household with average income is affordable only in Udaipur, but renting is affordable in the periphery for an average income

Table 10.1. Rent to income ratio for select cities

	Rent as % of income			
	1BHK		3BHK	
	Centre	Periphery	Centre	Periphery
India	33.7	20.6	81.8	49.7
Mumbai	71.4	37.3	199.3	90.4
Patna	54.5	26.3	103.5	54.5
Thane	51.1	33.8	125.8	78.1
Kolkata	44.1	25.2	106.3	57.6
Goa	39.2	30.2	113.2	84.0
Delhi	39.1	22.9	97.7	56.2
Navi Mumbai	38.2	23.4	90.8	55.4
Vishakhapatnam	37.5	21.5	93.5	45.2
Indore	36.6	22.9	87.6	49.1
Ahmedabad	35.6	22.8	90.9	56.7
Kochi	34.4	25.3	76.6	46.2
Bhopal	32.7	19.2	70.3	44.4
Bhubaneshwar	32.4	18.5	82.2	47.0
Guwahati	32.2	19.7	84.2	50.8
Chandigarh	31.8	17.0	86.0	47.4
Chennai	31.7	17.7	80.1	44.7
Nagpur	31.1	17.6	66.5	35.8
Hyderabad	30.6	18.9	79.6	44.4
Faridabad	30.3	17.9	64.3	49.2
Bangalore	30.1	18.0	76.8	47.0
Thiruvanathapuram	29.3	20.5	65.1	43.1
Surat	27.0	18.1	73.6	47.8
Pune	27.0	17.7	56.0	36.0
Gurgaon	26.2	15.8	63.1	38.5
Gaziabad	25.2	16.5	59.0	40.9
Rajkot	23.2	15.9	64.4	45.5
Jaipur	22.1	13.5	62.4	36.6
Vadodara	21.5	14.7	50.7	32.4
Udaipur	19.7	11.4	48.8	36.9

Note:

(1) These are dynamic data and change as per the market situation. The dataset also has data on monthly disposable income after tax.

(2) In March 2017, US$1 = Rs 65 approx.

(3) BHK = Bedroom + Hall + Kitchen; 1BHK means one Bedroom + Hall + Kitchen

(4) Monthly rents are given in the Appendix, Table A.5.1

Source: <http://www.numbeo.com/cost-of-living/country_result.jsp?country=India> (accessed 7 February 2017).

household in eighteen of the twenty-nine cities in the list (Table 10.1). Thus, the households with incomes less than a city's average cannot afford even 1BHK in these cities, certainly not in the centre, and renting 3BHK even on the periphery is out of question. Such households would then prefer to find housing in the informal markets, rental, or self-built ownership housing.

Another measure of housing affordability is the house-value to income ratio. Using the per sq. m price of property from the same database we have calculated prices of Economically Weaker Section (EWS) Dwelling Units (DUs), (30 sq. m); Low-Income Group (LIG) DUs (45 sq. m) and Middle-Income Group (MIG) DUs (70 sq. m). The prices are available for central and peripheral locations for the twenty-nine cities. Mumbai is the most expensive city, with property prices reaching close to Rs 500,000 per sq. m in central city and Rs 180,000 per sq. m in the peripheral area (Figure 10.1); these rates are far higher than comparable location rates in all other cities in the database. Delhi is the second most expensive city in terms of property prices, albeit in the central parts and then followed by two suburbs of Mumbai, Thane, and Navi Mumbai.

In the Indian context, the accepted affordable house-value to income (annual) ratios are 3 for the low-income groups[6] and 4 for the MIG segments. The average-income household in the Indian cities would fall into the LIG category and hence for analysing whether the markets would serve the low-income segment or not, we have assumed that properties valued at three times the annual income of an

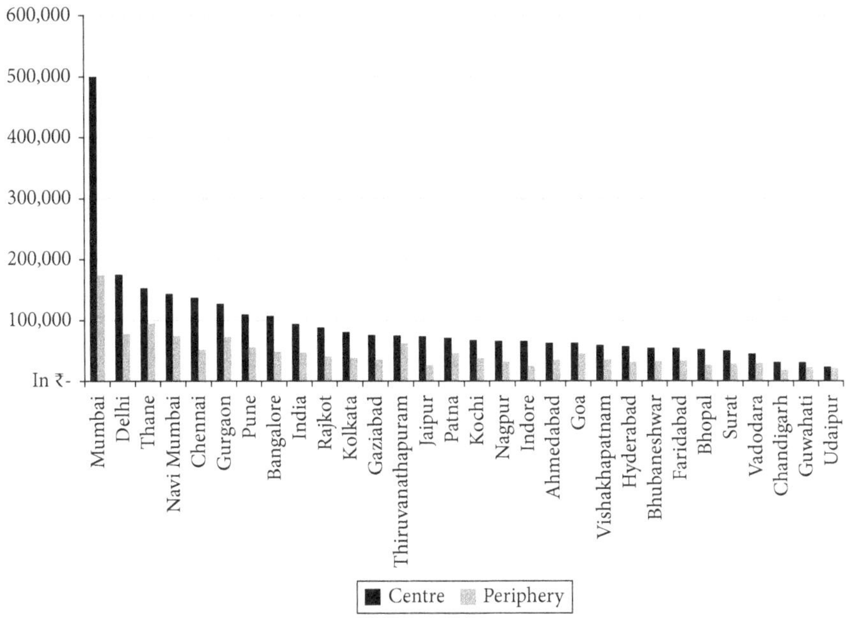

Figure 10.1. Property prices (in Rs) per sq. m by location in select cities in February 2017

Note: Exchange rate in March 2017, US$1 = Rs 65 approx.

Source: <http://www.numbeo.com/cost-of-living/country_result.jsp?country=India> (accessed 7 February 2017).

[6] These sites give the thumb rule in the US context: (1) <http://realestate.aol.com/blog/2012/04/10/home-affordability-house-apartment-mortgage-cost/>, (2) <http://www.financialrx.com/buying-first-house/article/how-much-house-can-i-afford-based-on-my-income> (both accessed 24 October 2014).

Table 10.2. House value to average income ratio for select cities, 2017

	Rent as % of income			
	1BHK		3BHK	
	Centre	Periphery	Centre	Periphery
India	33.7	20.6	81.8	49.7
Mumbai	71.4	37.3	199.3	90.4
Patna	54.5	26.3	103.5	54.5
Thane	51.1	33.8	125.8	78.1
Kolkata	44.1	25.2	106.3	57.6
Goa	39.2	30.2	113.2	84.0
Delhi	39.1	22.9	97.7	56.2
Navi Mumbai	38.2	23.4	90.8	55.4
Vishakhapatnam	37.5	21.5	93.5	45.2
Indore	36.6	22.9	87.6	49.1
Ahmedabad	35.6	22.8	90.9	56.7
Kochi	34.4	25.3	76.6	46.2
Bhopal	32.7	19.2	70.3	44.4
Bhubaneshwar	32.4	18.5	82.2	47.0
Guwahati	32.2	19.7	84.2	50.8
Chandigarh	31.8	17.0	86.0	47.4
Chennai	31.7	17.7	80.1	44.7
Nagpur	31.1	17.6	66.5	35.8
Hyderabad	30.6	18.9	79.6	44.4
Faridabad	30.3	17.9	64.3	49.2
Bangalore	30.1	18.0	76.8	47.0
Thiruvanathapuram	29.3	20.5	65.1	43.1
Surat	27.0	18.1	73.6	47.8
Pune	27.0	17.7	56.0	36.0
Gurgaon	26.2	15.8	63.1	38.5
Gaziabad	25.2	16.5	59.0	40.9
Rajkot	23.2	15.9	64.4	45.5
Jaipur	22.1	13.5	62.4	36.6
Vadodara	21.5	14.7	50.7	32.4
Udaipur	19.7	11.4	48.8	36.9

Note:

(1) These are dynamic data and change as per the market situation. The dataset also has data on monthly disposable income after tax.

(2) Economically Weaker Section (EWS) house size recommended in the PMAY guidelines is 30 sq. m, Low-Income Group (LIG) is recommended to be up to 60 sq. m but in large cities as in this table, LIG houses are about 45 sq. m and Middle-Income Group (MIG) housing units are about 70 sq. m See PMAY guidelines of March 2016, source <http://mhupa.gov.in/writereaddata/HFA_guidelines_March2016-English.pdf> (accessed 21 March 2017).

average income household are affordable in the EWS and LIG categories of DUs. The house value to annual income ratios are given in Table 10.2. In only two of the twenty-nine cities, the house value to income ratio is less than three for the EWS category (30 sq. m.) of unit and in just one city the same is affordable in the LIG category, if the housing is located in the central city. Thus, central locations of

EWS and LIG categories of housing are ruled out in all the cities in this list and similar size cities not in the list. In thirteen cities of the total twenty-nine, peripheral location is affordable for EWS DUs, but only if the household with average income is expected to live there and not the households in the EWS category income (Table 10.2).

The housing constructed under the PMAY (discussed in Section 10.4), which subsidizes the private developers for providing housing to the EWS and LIG sections, has set normative income limits. The annual income norm to be categorized as an EWS household is Rs 300,000 and as a LIG household is Rs 600,000.[7] Assuming the affordability to be three times the annual income for these two segments, an EWS household would be able to afford a house/DU valued Rs 900,000 and a LIG household would be able to afford a house/DU valued Rs 1,800,000. In that case, in eight cities only (Table 10.3), an EWS household would be able to afford a formal sector DU constructed for them on the respective city's periphery. In the case of LIG segment, a DU constructed for them on the respective city's periphery would be affordable in seventeen of the twenty-nine cities listed in Table 10.3. Thus, EWS households are totally priced out of the formal housing market in most cities, even after subsidized interest housing loans are made available to them. The probability of an LIG household finding a house, but on the city's periphery, is higher; in two-thirds of the cities in the Table 10.3, this is possible. Thus, housing markets are distorted and the EWS households, which form at least 25 per cent of the urban population,[8] are priced out of the formal housing market, and another 25 per cent, which forms the LIG segment, is priced out of the formal housing market in a third of the cities. Thus, the informal sector remains a major supplier of housing in all cities in India. This calls for a housing policy that addresses this market distortion.

The larger the city size, the higher is the pricing-out of the EWS and LIG segments. In Table 10.3, we see that the EWS and LIG segments are unable to afford formal housing even on the city's periphery in Mumbai, Delhi, Thane, Navi Mumbai, Chennai, Gurgaon, Pune, Bangalore, Rajkot, and Goa. Thane and Navi Mumbai, as mentioned earlier, are Mumbai's suburbs and Gurgaon is Delhi's suburb. Interestingly, rental housing, as seen above, is not affordable to EWS and LIG segments in Mumbai and her suburbs while this is possible in Delhi's suburb of Gurgaon.

For those not familiar with these cities, it is important to understand how different these cities are. Mumbai is the largest metropolis of India and is a commercial hub, with an urban agglomeration population of 18.41 million in 2011.

[7] Source: <http://mhupa.gov.in/writereaddata/HFA_guidelines_March2016-English.pdf> (accessed 21 March 2017).

[8] Official estimate of urban poverty, defined as inability to consume minimum 2,100 kcal per capita per day, is 26.4 per cent; i.e. urban population living below the poverty line of Rs 1,407 (US$ 29.38) per capita per month in 2011–12 (Press Information Bureau 2014).

Table 10.3. House price in select cities, 2017

Cities	Value to income ratio (for average income households)					
	Centre			Periphery		
	EWS (30 sq. m)	LIG (45 sq. m)	MIG (70 sq. m)	EWS (30 sq. m)	LIG (45 sq. m)	MIG (70 sq. m)
India	**6.86**	**10.30**	**16.02**	**3.40**	**5.09**	**7.93**
Mumbai	24.77	37.16	57.80	8.66	12.98	20.20
Thane	13.97	20.96	32.60	8.66	12.99	20.21
Delhi	10.40	15.60	24.27	4.64	6.95	10.82
Patna	10.37	15.56	24.20	6.68	10.02	15.58
Chennai	9.02	13.52	21.04	3.40	5.10	7.93
Indore	8.72	13.08	20.35	3.21	4.82	7.49
Navi Mumbai	8.65	12.97	20.18	4.49	6.74	10.48
Rajkot	8.20	12.30	19.14	3.76	5.64	8.77
Kolkata	7.63	11.45	17.81	3.53	5.29	8.23
Thiruvanathapuram	6.39	9.58	14.90	5.29	7.93	12.34
Kochi	6.05	9.08	14.13	3.38	5.06	7.88
Jaipur	5.92	8.88	13.82	2.09	3.14	4.88
Goa	5.90	8.85	13.77	4.17	6.26	9.74
Ahmedabad	5.88	8.82	13.72	3.22	4.84	7.52
Bhubaneshwar	5.83	8.74	13.60	3.47	5.21	8.11
Vishakhapatnam	5.80	8.70	13.53	3.51	5.26	8.19
Bangalore	5.61	8.41	13.09	2.53	3.80	5.91
Bhopal	5.59	8.38	13.04	2.81	4.22	6.57
Pune	5.48	8.22	12.79	2.80	4.20	6.53
Nagpur	5.44	8.16	12.70	2.60	3.90	6.07
Gaziabad	5.25	7.87	12.25	2.40	3.60	5.60
Faridabad	5.09	7.64	11.88	3.12	4.68	7.29
Gurgaon	4.95	7.42	11.54	2.84	4.26	6.62
Surat	4.89	7.33	11.41	2.79	4.19	6.51
Hyderabad	4.52	6.78	10.54	2.47	3.70	5.75
Guwahati	3.87	5.81	9.04	2.85	4.28	6.65
Vadodara	3.51	5.27	8.20	2.30	3.46	5.38
Chandigarh	2.35	3.53	5.49	1.36	2.05	3.18
Udaipur	1.96	2.94	4.58	1.82	2.74	4.26

Note:

(1) These are dynamic data and change as per the market situation. The dataset also has data on monthly disposable income after tax.

(2) Economically Weaker Section (EWS) house size recommended in the PMAY guidelines is 30 sq. m, Low-Income Group (LIG) is recommended to be up to 60 sq. m but in large cities as in this table, LIG houses are about 45 sq. m and Middle-Income Group (MIG) housing units are about 70 sq. m
See PMAY guidelines of March 2016, source <http://mhupa.gov.in/writereaddata/HFA_guidelines_March2016-English.pdf> (accessed 21 March 2017).

Source: <http://www.numbeo.com/cost-of-living/country_result.jsp?country=India> (accessed on 7 February 2017).

Urban agglomeration includes all the contiguous areas of the main municipal limits of the city. Mumbai is a peninsular city with a limited land supply, pushing the land and property prices beyond the reach of the average income household and even others.

Since there is a demand for housing among the new middle class, new constructions are being purchased, some by investors and some by users. One measure of housing purchased by users is that they tend to take housing loans. On the whole, of the total gross bank credit, just 9.25 per cent was for housing in 2013, while the figure was 9.21 per cent in 2012.[9]

10.3 Housing Policies and Programmes: The Case of State Failure

In this section we briefly present the last National Urban Housing and Habitat Policy (NUHHP) of 2007; the National Rental Housing Policy, 2015; and the last three national-level housing programmes with focus on the EWS and LIG households and their achievements at the national level.

10.3.1 National Urban Housing and Habitat Policy

The NUHHP, 2007, is prepared by the Ministry of Housing and Urban Poverty Alleviation (2007), based on which the state governments have been asked to make their own policies. Its preamble states: 'Shelter is one of the basic human needs just next to food and clothing.' It recognizes that the new and poorer urban settlers are unable to access formal land markets in urban areas due to high costs and their own lower incomes, leading to a non-sustainable situation. One of the aims of this policy is: 'Facilitating accelerated supply of serviced land and housing with particular focus to EWS and LIG categories and taking into account the need for development of supporting infrastructure and basic services to all categories' (p. 8) at affordable prices (p. 3).

Land being a major constraint in the urban poor accessing secure housing, this leads to many suggestions: (1) the state government should amend the existing laws and procedures or promulgate legislation for the effective implementation of State Urban Housing and Habitat Policy with a particular reference to easy and affordable access to land by government/private sector (p. 11); (2) the local government should devise programmes to meet housing shortages and augment supply of land for housing, particularly for the vulnerable groups, and support private

[9] These data are from the National Housing Bank, India. Source: <http://www.nhb.org.in/Whats_new/Report-on-Trend-and-Progress-of-Housing-in-India-2013.pdf> (accessed 27 November 2014).

sector participation in direct procurement of land and subsequent development of housing (p. 12); (3) the public agencies and parastatals should redefine their role as that of facilitating land assembly, development, and provision of infrastructure and not direct acquisition of land (p. 12) and should use land as a resource for the LIG and EWS sections (p. 13); and (4) the private and cooperative agencies should undertake an active role in terms of land assembly, construction of houses, and development of amenities within the projects, and work out schemes in collaboration with public sector institutions for slum reconstruction on a cross-subsidization basis (p. 13).

The policy also recommends certain specific action areas: (1) land acquisition by public agencies through more feasible alternatives like land sharing and land pooling arrangements, particularly in the urban fringes, through public and private initiative with appropriate statutory support (p. 13); (2) encouragement of land assembly and development by the private sector; (3) earmarking of a portion of land (e.g. 20 per cent to 25 per cent in a new housing colony), to be made available at affordable rates, for the EWS and LIG; (4) action plan for granting tenurial rights to the slum dwellers in-situ and relocation of slum dwellers wherever required at affordable prices with tenurial security; (5) increase in Floor Space Index (FSI)/Floor Area Ratio (FAR) along with ensuring adequacy of social and physical infrastructure to increase supply (p. 18); (5) amending the existing rules, guidelines, and government orders with regard to the Land Acquisition Act to acquire land for the private real estate companies so that they can play a role in increasing housing supply.

The policy also has suggestions for slum improvement and up-gradation (pp. 23–4): (1) land-sharing and -pooling arrangements to facilitate development of land and improvement of basic amenities in slums; (2) Transfer of Development Rights (TDR) and additional FAR as incentives to the private sector, community-based organizations, non-governmental organizations (NGOs) and self-help groups for providing shelter to the poor; and (3) use of land as a resource while taking up slum rehabilitation, which has been adopted by the PMAY as one of the programme verticals.

10.3.2 National Urban Rental Housing Policy (NURHP) (Draft), 2015

The NUHHP, 2007 had identified the need of promoting rental housing, which this policy attempts to address. The NURHP is premised on an understanding of the infeasibility to provide ownership housing for all on one hand, and also demand of rental housing from a large segment of urban population on the other. Given the magnitude of the housing shortage and the inability of the central and state budgets to meet the financial requirements to address it, the NURHP, 2015 has adopted a multipronged approach such as enabling legal and regulatory measures, encouraging the involvement of the private sector, cooperative, non-governmental sector, industrial sector (for labour housing), and the services/ institutional sector (for employee housing), to promote rental housing. The policy therefore seeks to promote public-private partnerships (PPPs) in the rental housing segment to achieve the Housing for All by 2022 policy (discussed next).

The NURHP's aim is to create a vibrant, sustainable, and inclusive rental housing market in India through (1) promoting Social Rental Housing (SRH) with direct or indirect support from the government (at state level) keeping in mind the affordability of the vulnerable urban groups and the poor; (2) promoting need-based rental housing for specific target groups such as migrant labour, single women, single men, students, and others; (3) enabling institutional rental housing (hostels/ paying guests/dormitories) for the working class with special focus on low-earning employees working with government/Public Sector Units (PSUs)/corporate houses/ industries/NGOs etc. (any other category as defined by the state government from time to time); (4) removing legal, financial, and administrative barriers for facilitating access to tenure, land, finance, and technology; (5) improving existing rental housing through adoption of Model Tenancy Act, 2015; and (6) promoting PPPs in constructing, managing, maintaining, and operating rental housing stock wherein the cooperative societies, neighbourhood associations, and resident welfare associations can partner with the local government.

The role of different levels of governments in enabling the rental housing stock creation is also mentioned. Among the important roles ascribed to the central government is to facilitate income tax concessions for institutional owners who would create mass rental housing catering to the affordable SRH sector and extend fiscal and non-fiscal concessions for PPPs in rental housing. The state governments and the Urban Local Bodies (ULBs) have been ascribed a very important role. They have to prepare a state rental housing policy, to undertake appropriate reforms for creating conducive environment for SRH viability; to create legal instrument to earmark or reserve a certain percentage of newly built housing or developed land for SRH in the statutory plans; provide incentives such as exemption from stamp duty, registration charges, property taxes, etc. to boost SRH; amend or repeal the outdated rent control legislation; and many others. The ULBs in particular have implementation roles through identifying target groups and proposing schemes for the same. The policy also states that the Housing Finance Institutions should promote innovative financial instruments to finance SRH schemes.

10.3.3 Affordable Housing Programmes

This subsection discusses briefly three large nationally funded urban housing programmes: (1) the BSUP and Integrated Housing and Slum Development

Programme (IHSDP) under the largest national-level urban development programme, the JNNURM launched in 2005 December; (2) RAY, a slum redevelopment programme and affordable housing in partnership, both launched in 2009 but subsumed under (3) the Housing for All by 2022, named as PMAY. The first two have, in a limited way, increased publicly provided housing supply for low-income households (the EWS and LIG) and the last one is expected to do so through private sector participation in this segment. Also, BSUP was meant for the mission cities which were largely the metropolitan and capital cities and IHSDP for all others (largely small and medium towns). In the BSUP and IHSDP, the national government contributed about 80 per cent of the DU cost, which has been brought down under the PMAY to about 25 per cent.[10] Over time, the real cost far exceeded the approved cost in many BSUP projects, and the states were expected to fill up this gap. Thus, Mahadevia (2010b) has shown that in Patna, as a result, the BSUP projects did not take off. In Ahmedabad, the city government is meeting this gap. The main deficiency of the BSUP was its location way outside the city. The RAY was designed to address the lessons learnt from the BSUP projects in particular, and undertake in-situ redevelopment of existing slums at the same time as creating a new stock of housing for the EWS and LIG segments.

The PMAY takes these ideas forward and has made the scheme demand-based by reducing the central government share. The PMAY is a mission to be implemented during 2015–22 period, which includes central government assistance to the ULBs through state governments and to the Union territories for the following purposes:

(1) In-situ rehabilitation of existing slum dwellers using land as a resource and through private sector participation.
(2) Credit-linked subsidy.
(3) Affordable housing in partnership.
(4) Subsidy for beneficiary led individual house construction/enhancement (extension).

The credit-linked component is implemented as central sector scheme while the other three are Centrally Sponsored Schemes (CSS). The CSS is one that has defined state government share while Central Sector Schemes are fully funded by the central government. Multiple options have been given for obtaining central subsidies for affordable housing, so that the slum dwellers and other low-income groups are able purchase a house from the market. The implementation of the programme has been left to the state governments who will decide the beneficiaries of the programme through declaring cut-off dates.

[10] Calculated by the author from the PMAY data; source: <http://mhupa.gov.in/writereaddata/PMAY_%20Progress.pdf> (accessed 16 March 2017).

The BSUP projects had different approaches in different cities. In Ahmedabad and Surat, these were new units.[11] In all cases in Surat and some in Ahmedabad, some were constructed on the city periphery. In Hyderabad the BSUP units were located on the periphery (Mahadevia and Gogoi 2010). In Bangalore and Pune, the units were constructed on the same site where the slum was located. In Madhya Pradesh, slums were redeveloped on-site. In-situ redevelopment of slums means that the city is willing to give prime lands to poor communities. Putting BSUP housing on the periphery means that the cities are pushing the poor out from the prime lands. At the national level, therefore, there is a mixed picture once again. In many cities, the BSUP units are being used for rehabilitating those affected by the infrastructure and city beautification projects.

A total of 1,065,536 units have been constructed and another 150,320 were under construction in 2017 through funds available under BSUP and IHSDP programmes (Table 10.4). To understand the coverage of existing housing shortfalls we can compare them with total urban slum households in the country or the housing shortage. The new housing constructed under the JNNURM (BSUP + IHSDP) amounts to 8.73 per cent of the slum household in the 2011 census or 6.47 per cent of the housing shortage in 2011. If DUs constructed or upgraded under the RAY are included then the total achievement amounts to 9.32 per cent of slum households and 6.9 per cent of 2011 housing shortage. The progress in reaching to the low-income groups through the BSUP, IHSDP, and RAY has been slow. This called for a reduction in central government assistance per DU and spreading the

Table 10.4. Affordable housing programmes in urban India in last decade

Programme	Central assistance in billion Rs	Houses sanctioned	Construction of houses ongoing	Houses constructed
BSUP*	112.40	788,953	87,034	687,232
IHSDP**	61.61	451,951	63,286	378,304
RAY***	34.66	117,707	57,502	24,603
PMAY@	246.95	1,563,150	437,766	74,505
Total		**2,921,761**	**645,588**	**1,164,644**

Sources:

*** As of 1 March 2017; source: <http://mhupa.gov.in/writereaddata/Ray_State_Wise.pdf> (accessed 16 March 2017).

* As of 1 March 2017; source: <http://mhupa.gov.in/writereaddata/City_wise_BSUP.pdf> (accessed 16 March 2017).

** As of 1 March 2017; source: <http://mhupa.gov.in/writereaddata/City_wise_IHSDP.pdf> (accessed 16 March 2017).

@ As of 6 February 2017; source: <http://mhupa.gov.in/writereaddata/PMAY_%20Progress.pdf> (accessed 16 March 2017).

[11] From the personal visit of this author.

available finances wide through ensuring investments by households in their housing. This is the thrust of the PMAY. We need to wait for some years to see how the PMAY unfolds.

The BSUP housing has been constructed, but there were some follies of the programme. First, there were erroneous inclusions and exclusions in the way the allocations were done, that is, wrong households were allotted the subsidized houses and those eligible to obtain the subsidy were excluded. As on 1 March 2017, 122,743 BSUP units remained unoccupied, that is 15.5 per cent units were not yet occupied.[12] Delhi led with 53.3 per cent DUs under the BSUP remaining vacant.[13] The main reason for the BSUP units remaining unoccupied for a long time is that these schemes were located on the urban periphery and hence were inconvenient to the urban poor, whose employment continued in the city centre. The dwelling units provided were very small, about 22.5 sq. metres, and unsuitable for joint families. In some places, the construction was very poor and certainly post-occupancy maintenance was extremely poor (Kumar and Singh 2014). It was realized that an urban housing programme should have buy-in from the people.

In IHSDP, only 12.7 per cent of DUs have remained unoccupied.[14] The IHSDP had a variety of housing options; in some states only construction materials were provided to those who had plots and in some states DUs were constructed. Location is not a major issue in small and medium-sized towns and hence the new housing constructed was willingly occupied by the beneficiaries.

RAY was the first urban housing programme that had a bottom-up and participatory approach to shelter security, through extension of tenure security to the existing slum dwellers irrespective of their migration to the city. The purpose was to make cities slum free through slum upgrading or redevelopment. The central government component in this programme has been reduced to 50 per cent and the remaining funds are expected to come from the slum dwellers themselves or the private sector that could be brought in as a partner or the local government or all of them. The key to the programme was extending the tenure security for which the MoHUPA has framed the Model Property Rights Act, which the state governments could adopt or adapt to suit their needs.

This analysis shows a general limited reach of the state in reaching the urban poor and improving their living conditions. If economic growth and urbanization have to occur, the state needs to take the responsibility of ensuring minimum living conditions, through extending basic services in deprived areas. Besides the efforts already underway, there is a need to bring other actors on board as in case of the PRC wherein the private sector, particularly in manufacturing, has been

[12] As of 1 March 2017; source: <http://mhupa.gov.in/writereaddata/City_wise_BSUP.pdf> (accessed 16 March 2017).

[13] As of 1 March 2017; source: <http://mhupa.gov.in/writereaddata/City_wise_BSUP.pdf> (accessed 16 March 2017).

[14] As of 1 March 2017; source: <http://mhupa.gov.in/writereaddata/City_wise_BSUP.pdf> (accessed 16 March 2017).

mandated to provide employee housing, which has taken care of significant proportion of housing needs of low-income migrant labour.

10.4 Land Policies and Legislation: Impact on Housing

Although the land is privately owned in most states of India except the present and former Union Territories such as the National Capital Territory (NCT) of Delhi, it is in the 'eminent domain' of the state. Thus, state legislation regulates the use, land use conversion and transfer/sale of land through zoning, Development Control Regulations (DCRs), and land revenue codes. The last one regulates conversion of land use from agriculture to non-agriculture (NA), used for regulating the uncontrolled urbanizing of rural lands. The land use zoning and DCRs are part of the city or city-region level Master/Development Plans and sub-city plans called zonal plans in some and Town Planning Schemes (TPSs) in some others. In situations where the land is privately held, called 'freehold' lands, they are managed through land records regimes wherein the owner's or joint owners' names are entered in these records. The non-freehold lands are given out on periodic leases by the public agency (the central, state, and local governments) and are called 'leasehold' lands. Public lands owned by the central government and its departments are rarely available for general housing purposes except for their own employees.

The discussion in this section is to explain the reasons as to why lands end up in the informal sector, which are then accessed by the urban low-income households for their use. In this section we also discuss why land markets in India have become speculative and have priced out a large segment of the urban population from the formal housing market, a discussion partly held in Section 10.2. Pricing out low-income households from the housing market feeds into informal sector development. It also leads to high vacancy rates in the formal housing market. The housing census of 2010 puts the figure of vacant housing at 11 million.[15]

10.4.1 Processes of Urban Informal Housing Formation

The land legislations pertain to:[16] (a) ownership (land records, tenancy act, and inheritance laws)[17]; (b) use (Town Planning Act, DCRs including TDRs,[18]

[15] Data from <http://www.censusindia.gov.in/2011census/hlo/hlo_highlights.html> (accessed 15 February 2014).

[16] There are many studies on land legislation. The most comprehensive one, where all the legislations are discussed at length, is by Ansari (1998).

[17] In addition, the Urban Land Ceiling and Regulation Act, 1976 was also applicable to urban lands. This legislation has been repealed now in all states.

[18] TDR is a land management tool that permits development in other parts of the city in lieu of the part where the owner holds land. TDR is often used for decongesting some areas, vacate plots for public purposes, protecting heritage sites, and other public purposes.

zoning, building bye-laws,[19] and NA permission in case of change in use from agriculture to urban); (c) acquisition and assembly (Land Acquisition Act, Town Planning Act, and DCRs such as TDR); (d) transfer and registration (Income Tax Act, capital gains tax, stamp duty, No Objection Certification from revenue department, NA permission, and inheritance laws); and (e) disposal (wherever public agencies are directly involved in land supply). Some of the important legislations are discussed below.

The land records are important in the case of 'freehold' land. These are with the revenue department of the state government. Land records have information related to current and past owners and tenant-cultivators in the case of agriculture lands. Under the tenancy laws as a part of the land reforms process in the agriculture sector, lands held by tenant-cultivators were transferred to their ownership. But, these land rights were granted under the conditions that the tenant-cultivators would not sell them in the land markets. Such lands on the periphery of fast-growing cities came under urbanization pressure and such tenant-cultivators owning the lands are given lucrative offers by land developers to purchase such lands, albeit through informal mechanisms such as transfers that are prohibited under the tenancy laws. When such transactions occur then such lands developed for residential purposes become informal. Realizing such informal transactions, some state governments have reformed their tenancy laws and have lifted the restrictions on use and transfer of land held by tenant-cultivators. But, if such transactions have occurred prior to the tenancy law reform, the developments on such lands continue to be informal.

If agriculture land has to be developed for urban use, the developer has to obtain an NA permission from the revenue department. The process is cumbersome and costly (payment of bribes to the local officials) and hence attracts illegal means. Instead, the land owners prefer to informally give rights of development to a land developer through a legal instrument called Power of Attorney; the latter then sub-plotting the agriculture lands, selling them to those interested in self-constructing housing on the plot. Such developers may choose to even construct houses (DUs) on them and sell constructed houses to the home-buyers. These become informal commercial subdivisions on an urban periphery. The developers of such developments do not apply for permissions as required under the concerned Town Planning legislation related to zoning, DCRss and building use, thereby making such developments informal. The urban peripheries thus develop as 'auto-constructed' or 'self-constructed' peripheries offering ownership housing to new migrants and settled urban dwellers intending to shift from rental to house ownership or to a larger house than their current one.

[19] These pertain to building construction and specify margins and open spaces to be maintained when a plot of land is developed, minimum room sizes, projections into margin, floor heights, etc. The Development Controls specify Floor Space Index (ratio of built-up to plot area), land use, etc.

Even if the Master Plan/Development Plans are available, the costs of obtaining permissions are high as there is also a component of 'rent' in it. As it is known, multiple permissions to be taken from multiple windows add to the cost of a real estate development. Interestingly, the urban reforms ongoing in India are moving towards simplified online single window clearance systems,[20] which might then offer possibilities of moving away from the cumbersome regulatory mechanism of development permissions.

House prices in the informal housing markets are low compared to formal markets. Such developments have various levels of basic services, largely self-provided or provided by informal sector service providers. The prices of plots or constructed houses in such developments depend on the location and extent of services available in them.

Informal housing also develops when public lands are encroached upon. The encroachments can be by the poor for their use or by the non-poor for informal developments then made available to low-income households for purchase or renting. But not all public lands can be encroached upon or are allowed to be encroached upon. The lands owned by the national government ministries are generally unavailable for regularizing slums on them if any, although the lands of the railway ministry are the most encroached upon among all national government ministries. In Guwahati, an estimated 40 per cent of slum households live on railway lands (Desai and Mahadevia 2013). Within the state government departments, lands of the housing board, slums clearance board, and development authority could be available for housing purposes if these authorities are able to withstand the pressure for profiteering.[21] The local governments and the development authorities have pressure to raise finance for capital investments such as for infrastructure, and tend to then auction the lands rather than allocate them for low-income housing. Hence, it is becoming increasingly difficult to regularize slums that have been built on public lands.

10.4.2 Land Speculation

Two pieces of legislation, one still in effect and another one repealed, had a great impact on housing markets by pushing lands into the informal sector. In a way,

[20] See the news for Mumbai, the most expensive real estate city in India: 'applications for permissions related to building projects will no longer be accepted by the building proposals department of the civic body as the clearance system is now completely online, from submission of application till the approvals are granted. By integrating 14 departments including the fire, traffic, garden, property tax among others into the online system, the BMC hopes to cut down the time required to process the application by half and add transparency to the system' (Express News Service 2016). Many other cities have moved to this system to increase transparency and reduce the time and cost (including 'rents') of obtaining development permissions.

[21] They are unable to do. See Ramakrishnan (2007).

these pieces of legislation made lands available for encroachment or informal developments, making housing affordable to low-income groups. But they also distorted the formal land markets wherein land availability declined, thereby pushing up property prices. These are discussed below.

Land Acquisition Act, 1894, amended in 1984. Private lands can be acquired by the revenue department for public purpose, such as industries and housing. This legislation has been under dispute for a long time, with those affected and rights activists questioning the definition of 'public purpose' and protesting against acquisitions at rates lower than market prices. These agitations have resulted in state governments offering 'fair market price' for land acquisition. There are many suggestions on how farmers could benefit from the process while the city gets the land. These are: (a) to let the industry/land developer directly purchase the land from the market through direct land price negotiations with the farmers; (b) to let farmers collectivize their lands and then develop the same for the new use, industry, IT enclave, or any other real estate project;[22] (c) to share the benefits of the new land development with the farmers—e.g. in Jaipur, where 25 per cent of the land acquired is given back to the farmer after development for the farmer to reap benefits (which could be more than the price that the farmer would have got from a market rate sale). Before these reforms, the farmers preferred to informally bring their lands onto the private market if they received notifications for acquisition from the state government.

This Act was further amended in 2013 December to introduce new rules towards liberalizing the acquisition and giving a fair compensation to the farmers[23] to reduce litigations in acquiring lands for the urbanization and industrialization process. This will further increase land prices and cities' ability to expand through land amalgamation, as is ongoing in the PRC, may not be feasible.

Urban Land Ceiling and Regulation Act, 1976. This is the most controversial of all land legislation. First enacted at the union government level, in the spirit of the philosophy of socialism enshrined in the constitution in 1976 through a Constitutional Amendment Act, and subsequently approved by the state legislatures, this act put a limit on the amount of vacant land that a family could hold (the amount depending on the size of the city). Any land in excess could be acquired by the Urban Land Ceiling authority. The legislation had certain loopholes in the form of exemptions[24] that were widely used by developers to bring these lands into use. Large amounts of lands notified for acquisition under this

[22] As in case of Hadapsar township in Pune; see Mahadevia and Parashar (2008).

[23] The rules are called 'The Right to Fair Compensation and Transparency in Land Acquisition, Rehabilitation and Resettlement (Social Impact Assessment and Consent) Rules, 2014'. Source: <http://rural.nic.in/sites/downloads/NewReleases/Noti_Commencement_LR19dec13.pdf> (accessed 18 July 2014).

[24] The land developers used the exemptions provided in the legislation, namely, section 19 (public lands use), section 20 (if land acquisition causes undue hardship), and section 21 (if land is developed for EWS housing).

legislation were sold off informally to low-income households, or slums were encouraged to be built on them, in many cities. In effect, due to insincere framing of the legislation itself, followed by insincere implementation, the public agencies could not access land for housing the poor. The poor, however, benefited indirectly from this legislation. For example, in Ahmedabad, Mehta and Mehta (1987) found that large chunks of land were available for low-income housing in the informal sector after 1976 till the early 1980s.

While it existed, it artificially decreased the land supply, creating scarcity and increased prices. It also created a situation wherein only a few actors could negotiate deals with the authorities to obtain the exemptions mentioned above, creating cartelization in land supply in the process and thereby benefiting the large land developers. It also artificially increased land prices and thereby housing prices in the cities.

Black Money Adjustment. This is an important reason as to why the land markets in India are speculative, besides the regulations and vested interests operations—this market is where the shadow economy functions. A white paper on black money by the Finance Ministry of the Government of India[25] in May 2012 states that its extent was about 20 per cent of GDP. It also stated that real estate accounted for 50 per cent of the black money. Also, black money accounted for 30 per cent of the real estate prices on average.[26] Hence, in spite of economic slowdown the real estate markets have remained speculative, and that has priced out large segments from the housing markets, in particular the low-income households who have remained outside its ambit, as explained in Section 10.3.

10.5 Housing Sub-Markets

10.5.1 Different Housing Sub-Markets

The restrictive land regimes, speculative land markets, and restrictive planning, as discussed in Section 10.4, have made land outside the reach of the urban poor, in particular the new migrants. Hence, they tend to live in informal housing. There is a large informal housing sector in the cities of India, which also includes the slums. For analysing housing in the Indian context, as also in the context of other developing countries with private landownership, we use the concept of submarkets. This is because, as stated at the beginning of this chapter, housing is a heterogeneous good and hence a household opts for a mix of components from

[25] Source: <http://www.finmin.nic.in/reports/WhitePaper_BackMoney2012.pdf> (accessed 23 March 2017).

[26] Source: <http://indianexpress.com/article/india/india-news-india/the-un-real-estate-demonetisation-process-100-500-rupee-note-narendra-modi-black-money-4372286/> (accessed 23 March 2017).

the bundle suiting its affordability. Also, households improve their living conditions incrementally. Hence, in the housing market there is a demand for different components of housing and not for any uniform good. There is, therefore, no single housing market, and housing researchers often use the term submarkets (Mehta and Mehta 1987; Desai and Mahadevia 2013). A submarket is one where there are certain common characteristics with regard to components of housing. Housing submarkets can be categorized in various ways.

One categorization is: (1) formal, where land is legally procured, and all approvals for its transfer and development are obtained and (2) informal, wherein none or a few of the approvals are obtained. Housing submarkets are also classified as ownership markets and rental markets. The formal housing markets are further categorized depending on the supply dynamics; there are housing units provided by commercial markets or by developers, and there is self-built housing wherein the owners procure land and build a house, generally an independent house. Housing submarkets are also categorized by housing typology, such as independent house, semi-independent (or semi-detached) house, row house, low-rise apartments, high-rise apartments, slum, *chawls*, and old city housing (traditional housing). Lastly, housing submarkets are categorized by income class and user class such as EWS housing, LIG housing, MIG housing, and High-Income Group housing, or industrial housing and dormitory housing for migrant workers.

As per the latest available statistics, 58.1 per cent of the dwelling units in urban India in 2008–9 were independent houses, 24.4 per cent were apartment buildings, and 17.4 per cent were other types, including semi-detached houses, row houses, and traditional housing in the old parts of the city (NSSO 2010: 67). Interestingly, a shift to apartment housing, which is always provided by developers, is preferred by and affordable to higher-income groups. Hence, 43 per cent of the top twentieth percentile households lived in apartment housing, while for the bottom twentieth percentile the proportion was 11.8 per cent (NSSO 2010: 67). The poorest urban population tends to live in independent houses—66.4 among the bottom twentieth percentile, 67.8 per cent among the bottom twentieth to fortieth percentile and 44.9 per cent among the top twentieth percentile (NSSO 2010: 67). Further, only high-income groups can afford to live in multistorey buildings, which are, on the one hand, commercially provided and, on the other, have high maintenance costs. These data suggest that independent houses dominate the housing typology in the bottom fortieth percentile of the urban population. Hence, contrary to the PRC's situation, wherein independent houses are villas, in the Indian context the middle classes are moving to group housing, largely apartment type housing, whereas the poor tend to live in informal housing, which are independent units. The independent houses in the informal sector are encroachments.

The housing tenure situation also varies by income group: 61.1 per cent households are living in their own dwellings, and among them 97.5 per cent are living on lands on freehold basis (Table 10.5). On the whole, 35.4 per cent households live in rented premises. Of that, just 10.7 per cent households lived in

Table 10.5. Tenure status of households, 2012

Tenure status	MPCE percentile					All Households
	0–20	20–40	40–60	60–80	80–100	
Own dwelling—freehold	65.6	64.1	60.4	57.4	54.4	59.6
Own dwelling—leasehold	1.9	1.5	1.7	1.8	1.0	1.5
Total own dwelling	**67.5**	**65.6**	**62.1**	**59.2**	**55.4**	**61.1**
Employer's quarters	1.9	1.8	3.1	5.1	5.7	3.8
Hired dwelling with contract	1.3	2.8	4.7	6.4	13.1	6.4
Hired dwelling without contract	20.8	25.8	26.0	27.2	25.2	25.2
All hired (rented) dwellings	24.0	30.4	33.8	38.7	44.0	35.4
Others	8.4	4.0	4.1	2.2	0.6	3.4
Total	100.0	100.0	100.0	100.0	100.0	100.0

Note: MPCE = monthly per capita expenditure.
Source: NSSO (2014b: A-6).

employer-provided housing. Of the total households, just 3.8 per cent are living in employer-provided housing. The bulk (71.2 per cent) of rented housing is of the informal type, that is, without any contract. The bulk of own housing on a freehold basis is also of the informal type.

A few interesting observations can be made from Table 10.5:

(1) The proportion of households living in their own dwelling declines with the increase in the expenditure class or the income class, and living in hired dwelling increases with income. In the top twentieth percentile group, 44 per cent households live in rented premises, whereas only 24 per cent live in rented housing in the bottom twentieth percentile.
(2) Beneficiaries of employer housing are those in the top fortieth percentile households. Even among the top twentieth percentile group, about 57 per cent of households live in rented housing without holding any contract and hence are in informal arrangements. This is the effect of the restrictive rent control act.
(3) The lower the income, the higher is the extent of informality. The category of others would include squatting, wherein the household cannot be considered to be occupying freehold land for own dwelling—8.4 per cent households in the bottom twentieth percentile group are occupying such housing.

10.5.2 Informal Housing Market

All forms of land transfer, subdivision, or house construction that take place without official approval are part of urban informality. Informal housing is explained by UN-Habitat (2003) as that which does not conform to the laws and regulatory frameworks of the city. The majority of housing in Indian cities, be it of the poor, middle class, or elite, has an element of informality according to this definition, although not all of it is viewed as such. Informal housing has developed because the people themselves have made efforts to build on their own in the face of a weak state with regard to housing supply and unaffordable housing prices in the formal sector. UN-Habitat (2003) states that the 'poor are the largest producers of shelter and builders of cities in the world'. A segment of informal housing is slums, which many consider as assets built by the poor. All informal housing is not slums, but all slums are informal housing.

Informal housing largely develops incrementally. A new household in a city tends to squat on open land, largely public, if available, and then moves on to consolidate the housing by obtaining tenure security. Tenure security is seen as:

> a complex entity which provides protection to a household or individual against their involuntary removal from their house or land without due process of law. In absence of such security policy, the urban poor and low-income migrants seek to consolidate their urban citizenship through political citizenship in an electoral democracy, welfare interventions by the state, organized grassroots movements and, in the absence of all the above, through their own subversions of urban legalities. (Mahadevia 2011a: 6)

With an increase in the level of tenure security, the household invests more and more in housing, eventually converting the house into a permanent dwelling with all the basic services and paying local government taxes. Households move from insecure tenure to a higher order of tenure security. If there is a tenure regularization programme, that is, a programme of extending the right to own or use land on which the dwelling unit exists, the households are able to quickly improve their housing conditions, followed by improvement in living standards and income. This is called the 'housing mobility' process and the housing is called incremental housing, which is tied to the household's employment mobility and local government policy. While we do not have estimates of informal housing in Indian cities, one can safely assume that about three-fourths of the urban housing in India is informal (25 per cent of rental housing without contract and 50 per cent in the 61 per cent of self-owned housing as per Table 10.5).

10.5.3 Housing for Migrants

There are three types of rural to urban migrants in India: (1) long-term or permanent migrants with the intention of settling down in urban areas, many getting into regular employment, but keeping strong links with native villages/towns, which is possible due to free migration rights in India; (2) seasonal migrants, defined as those who go to cities to tide over lean agricultural seasons and stay in urban areas for more than sixty days in a year, but return back for some period, mainly during monsoons; and (3) migrants tied to their employers, who move from one place of employment to another (no estimates are available for this category). But, in general, if migrants are able to assimilate in the urban economy, they do not return to rural areas.

These three types of migrants in urban India face different types of challenges in accessing housing in urban areas. The permanent migrants tend to enter the urban labour market at the lower end as temporary workers, eventually working their way up into the system, first improving their employment and then housing. Many permanent migrants come to urban areas without their families as single male migrants, largely at a young age, and call their families once they are secure financially, socially, and shelter-wise.

When migrants first come to the city, they squat on public land or stay on a rental basis in some existing settlement or stay with a friend/family member, paying some rent to them. They then move to purchasing a plot of land in an informal settlement. There is no regular legal document of such a purchase. They will then erect a temporary roof over temporary walls. From then on, as and when they have savings, these would be invested in incremental improvements of the house; for example, walls constructed of temporary materials are made permanent, temporary roofs are made permanent, and so on. If the policy supports their shelter security, they are able to improve their living conditions faster than otherwise (Mahadevia 2010a; 2011a). Those intending to return back to their native villages on retirement do not invest in housing in the city and tend to rent.

Temporary migrants prefer rental housing. They stay in shared rental units, largely four to six people sharing one room on the lower end of the employment ladder. Those at the higher end of the employment ladder also rent a house and also often share. But they may share an apartment unit. At the low end of the labour market, in a study of the Indian city Surat, Mahadevia et al. (2012) find that migrants tend to spend about 13–17 per cent of their monthly income on rent for housing. In study of Guwahati city, Desai and Mahadevia (2013) find that family households are paying an average of 12 per cent of their household income as rent and house sharers are paying an average of 5 per cent of their monthly income as rent.

10.5.4 Slum Housing

On the whole, 13.9 million households were living in slums[27] in urban India in 2011. This is 17.7 per cent of the total urban households (Figure 10.2). The housing

[27] Slums are defined as a cluster of a minimum of twenty dwelling units, with temporary or permanent structures, with poor living conditions on account of lack of services and informal land tenure. The definition is fluid. Urban local governments declare such settlements as slums and then attempt to

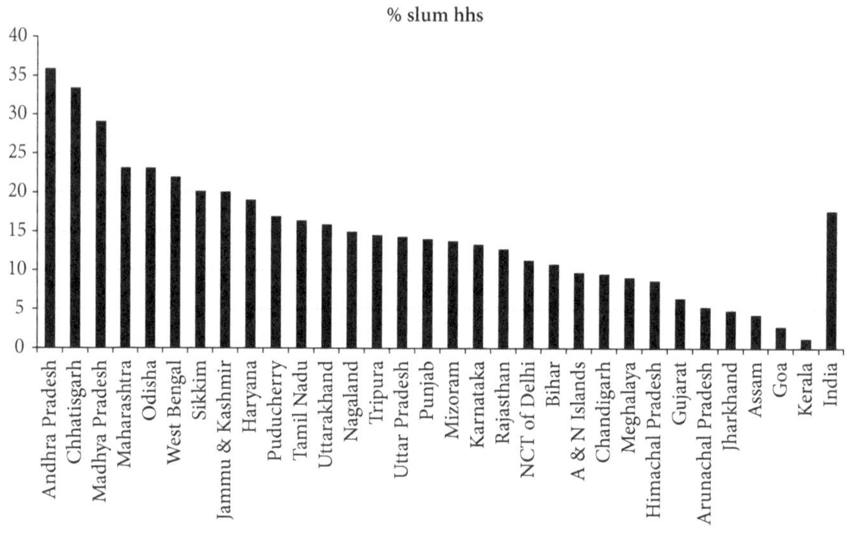

Figure 10.2. Proportion of households living in slums, 2010
Source: Population Census.

shortage estimate of 18.8 million dwelling units in 2012 mentioned before (NBO 2012), includes *katcha*[28] houses (5.3 per cent), obsolescent houses (12.1 per cent),[29] and congested houses[30] (79.8 per cent), as well as homeless households (2.8 per cent). The urban housing shortage calculation is a supply-side approach, but with an understanding that the households in India in general and the low-income households in particular adopt an incremental housing approach and gradually improve their living conditions as per their affordability.

provide basic services to them. The process is called notification of slums. Once any settlement is notified as a slum, even after improving the living conditions, the local governments do not denotify. Hence, it is nearly impossible to have an exact estimate of households living in slums in any city in India. Mahadevia (2009) has shown that the estimates for a city vary significantly if estimated by different agencies.

[28] Katcha housing is defined in India as dwelling units constructed from temporary materials, such as plastic sheets, mud, thatch, and straw for walls, and thatch and plastic sheets as roof materials, along with a lack of water supply and sanitation.

[29] Obsolescent housing consists of all houses aged eighty years and above and houses forty years in age but in bad condition, as defined in the housing census by the population census exercise.

[30] Congested housing is defined from a physical and socio-cultural point of view. The socio-cultural definition is wherein the household has married couples sharing a room. Physically, if married couples are sharing a room in a dwelling unit of less than or equal to 30 sq. metres, then it is not possible to divide the house into smaller rooms, forcing the couples to share a room. Housing supply at the lower end of the market in India is self-built and incremental housing, and hence, when an additional couple gets added to a household, the household puts up a partition to create an additional room for the couple. In very small dwelling units this is not feasible. Such dwelling units are considered crowded, and it was assumed by this report that an additional dwelling unit would be required for such households.

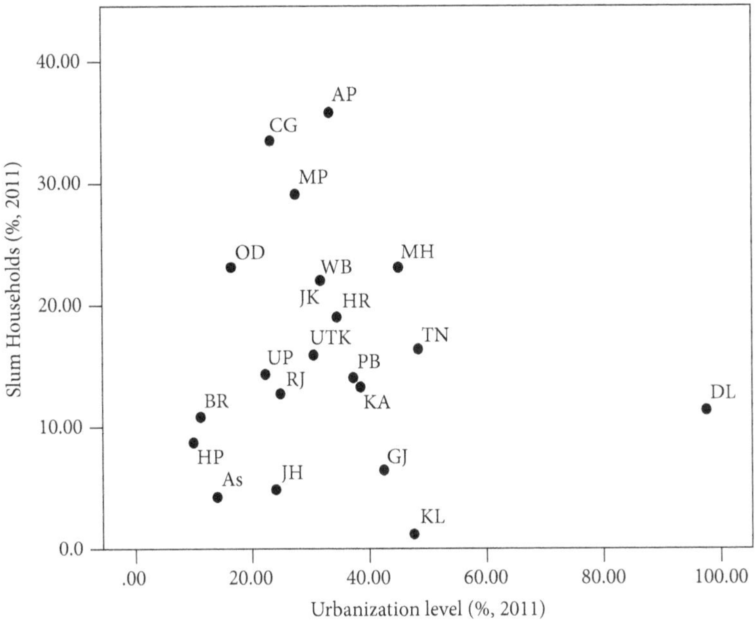

Figure 10.3. Relationship of urbanization level and percentage of households living in slums

The housing shortage is larger than the number of slum dwelling population. There are slum households that are not crowded and there is crowding outside the slums. Slums tend to be in both types of states, ones with a higher level of urbanization and ones with a lower level of urbanization. For example, in Figure 10.3, states with more than 20 per cent of their urban populations living in slums are: Andhra Pradesh, Chhatisgarh, Madhya Pradesh, Maharashtra, Odisha, West Bengal, and Jammu and Kashmir, which are high- as well as low-income states and high- as well as low-urbanization-level states. The relationship between the level of urbanization and the proportion of households living in slums is weak (Figure 10.3). The relationship between the proportion of households living in slums and the state per capita income (PCI) is also weak (Figure 10.4) due to intermediating factors such as land prices in the cities of the state and proactiveness of state policies in addressing slum housing.

10.6 Housing Status Indicators

Considering housing as a heterogeneous good, we have used the following indicators for analysis: (1) quality of dwelling units (DUs), (2) crowding, (3) safe drinking water, (4) access to toilets and type of toilets, (5) access to electricity,

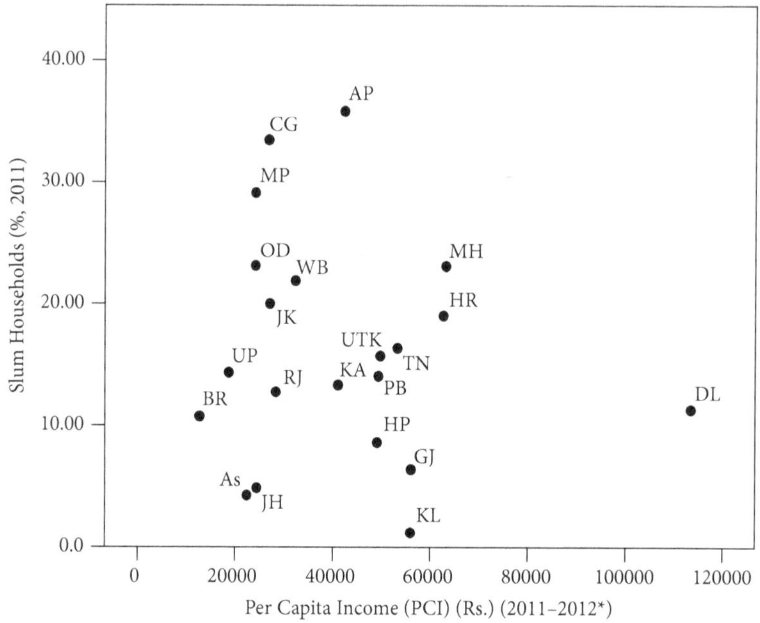

Figure 10.4. Relationship of PCI and percentage of households living in slums

(6) access to bathing facility and its type, and (7) drainage connection and its type. Largely, we have used positive indicators for the purpose. The data are available for two time points, 2001 and 2011, which will also give us an idea of the extent of change in the last decade, which has experienced the fastest rate of economic growth till now. The data used are from the population census.

10.6.1 Quality of Dwelling Unit

Two indicators define the quality of housing: the quality of built structure and crowding. The proportion of households living in good housing was 68.44 per cent in 2011, which is a small increase from 64.16 per cent in 2001 (Table 10.7). The Compound Annual Growth Rate (CAGR) of households living in good housing is 4.59 per cent (Table 10.9), which is higher than the urbanization rate of 2.82 per cent (Table 10.6). Hence, the improvement in housing structures has been higher than the urban population growth rate, which is positive, but the rate of growth is low and lower than the GDP growth rate.

The proportion of households living in good housing is the highest in the Southern states (75.69 per cent), followed by Northern Hill states (73.71 per cent) and Western states (73.43 per cent). The best improvement during 2001–11 was in the Western states by about ten percentage points and the CAGR was the highest

Table 10.6. Urbanization level, rate, PCI and PCI growth rate by regions, India

Region	Urbanization level		Urban population CAGR	Per capita income (PCI) (Rs)		CAGR* (2004–5 to 2011–12)	
	2001	2011	2001–11	2004–05	2011–12*	PCI	NSDP
North-hilly	21.4	24.4	3.1	25,505	39,938	7.76	10.02
North-plains	27.7	30.0	2.6	21,079	32,028	7.22	9.47
East	18.8	20.7	2.7	15,879	22,544	6.01	8.19
North-east	15.7	18.4	3.2	19,138	27,149	6.00	8.00
Central	24.8	26.5	2.6	16,367	25,006	7.32	9.72
West	36.0	39.0	2.5	30,704	52,046	9.19	11.35
South	33.5	41.0	3.3	28,063	47,181	9.04	10.57
India	**27.8**	**31.2**	**2.8**	**24,451**	**38,010**	**7.63**	**10.08**

Note: The smaller Union Territories (UTs) are included. If the UTs were excluded, the averages do not change. For definition of regions, see Appendix, Table A.5.2.

Source: Calculated by the author from the population census data of 1991, 2001, 2011.

in the North-eastern states, indicating that the incomes matter more than the urbanization levels.

A household is considered to be living in a crowded condition if the DU does not have any exclusive room for living or is living in a one-room unit. This reflects high land and property prices, as DU size is a function of price. Thus, states and regions with high income (PCI) and a high level of urbanization are likely to have more crowding in housing than the low-income and low-urbanized ones. This is what we find. The Western region has the highest crowded housing in both 2001 and 2011 (Table 10.7), and had two-fourths of urban households are living in crowded conditions in 2011 (Table 10.7). The lowest crowding is in northern hilly states where only one in every four household is living in crowded conditions. The central region states have the second lowest crowding in 2011 and the least crowded living condition in 2001. Interestingly, at the all-India level as well as in each of the regions, crowded living conditions have reduced by about two percentage points. The absolute number of households living in crowded housing has reduced by 3.18 per cent per annum from 2001 to 2011 (Table 10.9). The highest decline is in the southern states (3.97 per cent per annum) followed by the central states (3.57 per cent per annum).

To sum up, quality of a dwelling unit is linked to the income level and the crowding of the dwelling unit is linked to the level of urbanization in most states. With increase in urbanization levels, crowding would increase, but if this phenomenon is not linked to an increase in incomes, the number of households living in a better quality of housing will not improve. The target of housing policy should be improvement in both the quality of dwelling units as well as reduction in crowding.

Table 10.7. Housing status by regions—1

Region	% households living in good DUs		% households living in crowded housing*		Tap water		Well water		Hand pump/ tube well		Other sources		Access to toilet	
	2011	2001	2011	2001	2011	2001	2011	2001	2011	2001	2011	2001	2011	2001
North-hilly	73.71	65.49	25.16	28.93	84.48	86.30	0.71	0.72	13.00	10.51	1.76	2.48	90.54	85.40
North-plains	59.92	57.79	32.07	32.96	65.51	63.95	0.51	1.07	31.79	33.62	2.13	1.29	86.91	80.78
East	56.25	53.59	38.36	39.38	46.44	49.08	8.09	12.15	43.68	37.15	1.75	1.63	77.13	76.52
North-east	62.12	55.51	29.09	32.11	44.87	42.01	13.63	19.01	32.50	27.26	9.02	11.71	94.79	94.55
Central	66.78	62.76	27.10	26.72	62.27	66.16	5.40	9.86	30.27	22.41	2.06	1.50	70.79	64.37
West	73.43	63.89	41.01	44.69	87.00	86.03	1.98	2.99	8.79	8.95	2.23	2.03	77.71	66.94
South	75.69	75.09	33.68	36.20	74.72	67.67	11.76	13.16	10.72	16.27	2.78	2.88	83.51	73.53
India	**68.44**	**64.16**	**35.20**	**37.44**	70.62	68.65	6.15	7.70	20.75	21.35	2.46	2.27	81.35	73.71

Source: Calculated using housing census data of respective years.

10.6.2 Access to Basic Services

In this section, we discuss access to basic services such as water supply and sanitation. Sanitation includes access to toilets and bathing facilities. While a discussion of these services is covered by Sarkar in Chapter 14 in this volume, this chapter provides a regional orientation to the coverage of basic services. These services are dependent on household income. However, among these, access to tap water is also dependent on supply and hence linked to the state's capacity to supply piped water. Constructing a bathroom and a toilet is dependent on household income, but sometimes the city-level policy of subsidizing construction of baths and toilets could enhance the household's capacity to improve these services. The type of toilet at the household level is also dependent on whether drainage is available or not. If there is no drainage infrastructure, the households opt for pit toilets or other toilets, whereas if there is a drainage connection, households opt for a water closet, that is, pour-flush toilets. This needs to be kept in mind while interpreting the next set of data.

On the whole, just 71 per cent of urban households are connected to a piped water supply and 21 per cent of them depended on hand pumps or tube wells for water in 2011 (Table 10.7). Another 6 per cent are dependent on well water. This means that about 27 per cent of urban households are dependent on local water sources and have made their own individual arrangements for water. Other sources of water are either water supplied through tankers or open sources of water such as rivers or ponds, on which 2.5 per cent of urban households depend. There was a marginal change in the dependency on different water sources in 2011 compared with 2001, but the number of households getting tap water has increased by 4.2 per cent per annum.

The western region has the largest proportion (87 per cent) of households using tap water, whereas the north-east has the lowest (45 per cent), followed by the east (46 per cent). The north-east states are in mountainous terrain, where it is difficult to get a piped water supply to each house. The lack of tap water in the eastern states is due to the poor financial condition of the city governments in these low-income states as well as the high groundwater table in some. In the eastern states, 52 per cent depended on well, tube well, or hand pump water and only 46 per cent had a tap water connection. In the north-eastern states, 9 per cent of urban households depended on other sources of water. These would be either tanker water or water from natural sources such as streams in the mountains. Our study in Guwahati city, the largest city of the north-east, shows that the households living in the hills were dependent on natural sources of water as it was difficult to bring piped water up in the hills (Desai and Mahadevia 2013; Mahadevia et al. 2014).

On the whole, the number of households with a tap water connection increased at a rate of 4.2 per cent per annum during the 2001–11 period, with the southern states registering the highest CAGR of 5.93 per cent per annum and the central states the lowest at 2.93 per cent per annum (Table 10.9).

Urban India still has some way to go in improving access to toilets—81 per cent of households have access to toilets, which means that still 19 per cent of households defecate in the open (Table 10.7). The best coverage is in the north-east states, followed by north-hilly states (more than 90 per cent in both the regions), and the lowest coverage is in the central states where 29 per cent households still defecate in the open. Surprisingly, the western states, which are highly developed, have only 77 per cent of households with access to toilets. The proportion of households with access to toilets increased by 4.95 per cent per annum during the 2001–11 decade (Table 10.9), with the best improvement observed in the southern states (6.23 per cent per annum), followed by the western states (4.85 per cent per annum), and the worst in the northern hilly states (3.89 per cent per annum), which has already reached about 91 per cent coverage.

There has been remarkable improvement in the type of toilet facility available to the urban population. Of those with access to toilets, 89 per cent in 2011 had access to water closet toilets (Table 10.8). In 2001, only 63 per cent toilets were of the water closet type. There is a remarkable decline in the proportion of toilets that were pit latrines, where manual scavenging of faeces is required; the decline is from 20 per cent to 9 per cent in the period. Although the north-east states have high access to toilets, a quarter of the toilets are pit latrines. The second region that has a low proportion of water closet toilets (80 per cent) and had 18 per cent of pit latrines is the east.

There has been a significant improvement in the availability of bathroom facilities within dwelling units, from 70.5 per cent in 2001 to 87.0 per cent in 2011, registering a CAGR of 6.13 per cent per annum (Table 10.9). The best region is the west (93 per cent), followed by the north-east (92 per cent) and south (91 per cent).

10.6.3 Access to Infrastructure

This section will discuss the availability of drainage connections and electricity. Both are dependent on supply-side dynamics. Access to drainage and electricity is possible if the state has invested in these infrastructures. About 82 per cent of households had access to a drainage connection in 2011 (Table 10.8), which is a four percentage point improvement from 78 per cent in 2001. On the whole, the CAGR of households with drainage connections was 4.43 per cent per annum during 2001–11 (Table 10.9). Households with access to closed drains among those having a drainage connection is just 54 per cent (Table 10.8), which means that 46 per cent of households with drainage connections are connected to open drains. The improvement in this indicator was about ten percentage points between 2001 and 2011, registering a CAGR of 6.6 per cent per annum (Table 10.9). The largest improvement in drainage connections, including closed drain connections, has been in the south, followed by the north-east.

Table 10.8. Housing status by regions—2

Region	Water closet (WC)		Pit latrine		Other toilet		Bathroom within premises		Drainage connection		Closed drains among households connected to drainage		Access to electricity	
	2011	2001	2011	2011	2011	2011	2011	2001	2011	2001	2001	2001	2011	2001
North-hilly	87.28	42.33	5.38	25.39	7.34	32.27	92.4	77.4	89.0	85.2	46.5	34.6	97.32	94.87
North-plains	93.05	47.29	4.28	22.70	2.67	30.01	88.6	69.8	93.5	91.2	48.0	40.3	89.71	87.08
East	80.33	64.99	18.37	22.38	1.29	12.63	69.3	54.2	67.1	66.8	37.0	32.7	81.96	74.98
North-east	73.91	51.27	24.01	36.60	2.08	12.13	80.8	53.7	62.5	57.4	22.5	17.5	87.99	80.15
Central	96.60	63.06	2.19	16.19	1.21	20.75	81.0	60.7	79.1	73.1	35.9	31.3	92.94	90.23
West	94.52	72.40	3.60	14.39	1.88	13.21	93.0	79.7	87.8	83.7	68.3	54.4	96.14	93.35
South	86.82	66.64	11.14	19.49	2.03	13.87	90.8	74.0	78.4	71.6	59.7	48.0	96.64	88.76
India	89.22	62.55	8.71	19.82	2.07	17.63	87.0	70.5	**81.8**	**77.9**	**54.4**	**44.3**	92.67	87.59

Source: Calculated using housing census data of respective years.

Table 10.9. Change in housing status indicator during 2001–11

Region	CAGR of								
	Good DUs	Crowded Housing	Access to tap water	Access to toilet	Access to water closet	Bathroom within premises	Drainage connections	Closed drains among households connected to drainage	Access to electricity
North-hilly	4.51	−1.82	3.06	3.89	11.68	5.13	3.73	6.82	3.54
North-plains	4.06	−3.28	3.93	4.44	11.74	6.17	3.94	5.77	3.99
East	4.06	−3.18	2.98	3.64	5.85	6.14	3.61	4.89	4.48
North-east	5.26	−2.96	4.77	4.11	7.99	8.42	4.98	7.63	5.06
Central	4.20	−3.57	2.93	4.55	9.10	6.58	4.38	5.82	3.86
West	4.74	−2.35	3.41	4.85	7.68	4.90	3.78	6.18	3.60
South	4.97	−3.97	5.93	6.23	9.07	7.05	5.83	8.17	5.78
India	4.59	−3.18	4.20	4.95	8.74	6.13	4.43	6.60	4.51

The last indicator of infrastructure for housing discussed in this chapter is households with access to electricity. The situation in urban India is quite good, with 93 per cent of households having access to electricity in 2011 (Table 10.8), an improvement from 88 per cent in 2001. By regions, the best is the north-hilly region, followed by the west and the south, and the worst region is the east. On the whole, the CAGR of households with access to electricity has been 4.5 per cent per annum, while for the southern region it has been 5.8 per cent per annum (Table 10.9). There is not much of differentiation across the states with regard to access to electricity and hence we have not discussed statewise achievements here.

10.7 Linking Housing, Urbanization, and Income

Housing security is the key to rapid urbanization, as large numbers of migrants move to the cities to fuel industrialization only if housing is available, that is, housing is provided or access to informal housing is facilitated by various actors including the state. In the context of India, scholars have argued that rural-to-urban migration is low, that is, the rate of urbanization is low because the manufacturing sector has not grown and whatever has developed is capital intensive with a low labour absorptive capacity (Mohan 1996). In addition, the urbanization process is hostile to the migrants due to exclusive visions and exclusions (Mahadevia 2011b), largely emanating from real estate interests in urban land (Mahadevia 2009) and lack of political commitment to reach out to the new migrants and the poor. The urban poor and new migrants, if they find a foothold, are left to their own devices to eke out a living and find housing in the informal sector. The NSSO estimates on the informal sector show that 69.1 per cent of urban workers were informally employed in 2011–12, an increase from 67.3 per cent in 2009–10, but a decline from 72.2 per cent in 2004–5 (NSSO 2014a: 51). It is anticipated that the informality will continue in the economy. Hence, there is a need for a housing policy that provides shelter security to the new migrants who are going to fuel urbanization and hence economic growth. This is unlike the case of the PRC, where the first major thrust of urbanization came through the manufacturing sector and industrial workers' housing was taken care of by the employers.

The question is, what macroeconomic factors influence the quality of housing? Is it the PCI of the state or the urbanization level of the state? To which macro factors are the improvements in housing status indicators linked to: urbanization level, PCI, or past achievements? We discuss these below. First of all, urbanization level is strongly related to PCI (r = 0.837), that is, the higher the PCI of a state, the higher the level of urbanization (Table 10.10). The housing status indicators that are significantly related to urbanization level are: per cent households living in good houses, per cent households with access to tap water, per cent households with access to water closet type of toilet, per cent households with bathroom

Table 10.10. Correlation of urbanization level and rate, PCI, and CAGR of PCI with housing status indicators and change in housing status

	Urbanization level (2011)	Urban population growth Rate (2001–11)	PCI (2011–12)	CAGR PCI (2004–5 to 2011–12)
Urbanization level (2011)			0.837**	
% in good houses	0.344*	0.164	0.474**	0.580**
% hhs in crowded housing	0.149	−0.040	0.151	0.238
% hhs with tap water	0.440**	−0.151	0.562**	0.331*
% hhs with toilet access	0.148	0.364	0.212	0.195
% hhs with access to water closet type toilet	0.377*	0.076	0.532**	0.476**
% hhs with bathroom within premises	0.400*	0.012	0.502**	0.450**
% hhs with drainage connections	0.350*	−0.203	0.397*	0.343*
% hhs with access to closed drains among those connected to drainage	0.533**	−0.211	0.620**	0.337*
CAGR good housing	−0.131	0.851**	−0.039	0.445**
CAGR crowded housing	0.152	−0.698**	0.046	−0.459**
CAGR tap water	0.140	0.670**	0.166	0.554**
CAGR access to toilets	0.099	0.836**	0.251	0.718**
CAGR water closet	−0.154	0.274	−0.112	−0.006
CAGR bathroom in premises	−0.172	0.464**	−0.210	0.024
CAGR drainage connection	0.056	0.802**	0.073	0.469**
CAGR closed drains	0.014	0.260	−0.069	0.122

Note: Data are state-level indicators.

* Level of significance 0.05 (single-tailed)

** Level of significant 0.01 (single-tailed)

within premises, and per cent households connected to drains and closed drains. The same indicators of housing are significantly related to the PCI and PCI growth rate. The indicators of crowding and access to toilets are not related to urbanization level, PCI, and PCI growth rate.

Housing in a developing country with a market economy is a heterogeneous good and is incrementally improved by the households with economic mobility. The state generally has had a minimal role in providing housing, at best facilitating housing provision, particularly for the low-income households, and extending basic services in the settlements of the poor. Thus, the quality of house structures and access to water and sanitation at the household level is determined by a household's income. The level of urbanization of a state indirectly impacts household income through the state per capita income. This is happening to some extent, except with regards to access to toilets and level of crowding in the DUs.

The next question is, to which factors are the improvements in housing status indicators linked to? The change represented by the CAGR of the housing status indicators are not related to either the 2011 urbanization level or to the 2011–12 PCI, but are related significantly to the urbanization rate (for all but two indicators) and CAGR of PCI (again all but three indicators) (Table 10.10). The indicators with significant positive relations with the urbanization rate are: CAGR of good housing, CAGR of access to tap water, CAGR of access to toilets, CAGR of bathroom within premises, and CAGR of households having drainage connection. The CAGR of households living in crowded housing is negatively, but significantly, related to urbanization rate; that is, the states with higher urbanization levels have higher crowding. While the urbanization level is not showing any significant relationship with crowding in housing, the urbanization rate is in a negative way. This means that in the early periods of high urban growth rates, households tend to crowd into single dwelling units and then there is gradual improvement with regards to this housing indicator. But, the improvement in crowding conditions does not necessarily happen across states, and hence this indicator does not have any significant relationship with either urbanization level or PCI.

The indicators of CAGR of the households with water closets and of CAGR of households whose toilets are connected to closed drains are also not related to the urbanization rate. They are also not related to increases in PCI (CAGR of PCI) (Table 10.10). The indicators with significant positive relations with the PCI increase are: CAGR of good housing, CAGR of access to tap water, CAGR of access to toilets, and CAGR of households having drainage connection.

Lastly, we also investigated whether the base level status of different housing indicators had any influence in the improvements these have observed in a decade (Table 10.11). We find that most of them are negatively related to the base level status. That is, the states where the housing status indicators performed well in 2001 experienced lower rates of improvements. But the relationships are significant (negatively) with regards to access to water closet type toilet, bathroom within premises, toilets connected to drainage, and toilets connected to closed drains. The states have to go a long way in improving housing status indicators, and this slowing down of improvements in them in the states that have made some progress in the past is worrying and there need to be corrective measures for the same.

India's urbanization process presents a case of both state as well as market failure, particularly with regard to housing. The market prices of housing are unaffordable to the households with an average income and below. The state has been able to reach out only to a small proportion—one out of sixteen households living in inadequate housing and one out of twelve households living in slums as of now. Hence, households make their own housing arrangements—it is housing by the people and housing for the people (as J.F.C. Turner stated), through negotiating the informal market and actors in the informal market. The improvements

Table 10.11. Linking housing status indicators' improvement to base level

Variable 1	Variable 2	r value
% hhs in good houses (2001)	CAGR good housing (2001–11)	−0.075
% hhs in crowded housing (2001)	CAGR crowded housing (2001–11)	−0.153
% hhs with tap water (2001)	CAGR tap water (2001–11)	−0.059
% hhs with toilet access (2001)	CAGR access to toilets (2001–11)	0.051
% hhs with access to water closet type toilet (2001)	CAGR water closet (2001–11)	−0.665**
% hhs with bathroom within premises (2001)	CAGR Bathroom in premises (2001–11)	−0.646**
% hhs with drainage connections (2001)	CAGR drainage connection (2001–11)	−0.483**
% hhs with access to closed drains among those connected to drainage (2001)	CAGR closed drains (2001–11)	−0.184

Note: Data are state-level indicators.

* Level of significance 0.05 (single-tailed)

** Level of significant 0.01 (single-tailed)

in housing conditions are happening through the efforts of households, as and when their incomes improve. All the states with higher PCIs are not necessarily achieving more with regards to housing status. Also, there has been a slowing down of improvements in housing indicators once some achievements have already been made in the situations where there is still some way to go in terms of universalizing basic services.

10.8 Way Forward

The primary and the most important policy efforts have to be with regard to availability of affordable land. The ways in which land legislations and markets interact pose a peculiar paradox. The state interventions through regulations, which in essence are for the purpose of equity, have not helped the poor as the state acts as a rent-seeker rather than a welfare distributor. Land supply has got restricted and prices have increased. Given the nature of the regulatory mechanism, large developers are able to negotiate with the state and increase the land prices through cartelization. If regulations are lifted, there remains no mechanism to reach to the poor.

The simplistic policy recommendation, which has been doing rounds since last two decades, has been to increase land supply through dismantling the regulatory regime. The most battered or vilified legislation was the Urban Land Ceiling and Regulation Act, which has now been repealed, but the outcome has been continued informality and an increase in the vacancy rate due to the accumulation of real estate properties in a few hands. Clearly the answer does not lie in a blanket reduction in regulations, but appropriate regulations to reduce land accumulation in a few hands and speculation on the one hand and facilitating availability of small land plots and small house constructions on the other.

In that case, regulations along with incentives through market mechanisms could help increase land and housing for the urban poor. New reforms have been introduced in this direction along with the housing policies discussed in Section 10.3.

The reforms started with RAY reforms and continued in Housing for All 2022, it has been mandated that 25 per cent of land or FSI/FAR.[31] This is also practised by some cities in the PRC. This will make lands or housing available for the low-income groups. In some states such as Gujarat, there is a planning tool called TPS, which is essentially a land-pooling and readjustment tool in which a certain specified proportion of land is acquired by the planning authority for social and economic amenities and low-income housing and raising finance for infrastructure. In the case of the state of Gujarat, 40 per cent of land is taken away by the planning authority from the private owner at the time of giving permission to build on the land plot. A certain proportion of that land (10 per cent) is then auctioned to raise funds for infrastructure, another 10 per cent is allotted for housing the urban poor, and the rest allotted to public uses including for gardens, education and health institutions, and transport infrastructure (Ballaney 2008). In the state of Maharashtra, 5 per cent land is allotted for the urban poor, while in Madhya Pradesh it is 10 per cent. This mechanism of providing lands for the urban poor was suggested as a mandatory reform under the RAY and continued under the PMAY so that the cost of the DU can be partially recovered from the low-income households and by that enable the markets to work.

As discussed earlier, instruments to do so are available in India through the reforms introduced under the JNNURM, RAY, and PMAY of 25 per cent reservation of land or built-up space in new real estate developments for small housing units or small lots. Many cities in the PRC, too, have resorted to such regulation. In India, in addition, reservation alone is not adequate, but has to be supported through controls on prices and access to credit. The Affordable Housing Programme of subsidizing small house construction by the private sector needs to be monitored for leakages and corruption, and there has to be participation of people in such programmes to ensure that affordable housing units get delivered to those in need. This could be a new form of partnership, which we call PPPP, public–private–people partnership.

[31] The FSI/FAR legally specify maximum built-up permissible on a plot of land in relation to the plot size. If FSI is 1 or if FAR is 100 then maximum built-up on that land allowed is equal to the area of the plot of land.

For existing dilapidated housing and slums, RAY was appropriately designed to offer bottom-up, situation-specific solutions through significant investments coming from the people themselves. Indian per capita incomes are still lower than in the PRC, and hence housing solutions need to match with available incomes rather than aim for modern housing. Indian cities will have to accept and live with incremental housing in the medium term till people's affordability for a formal apartment type of housing is reached. People-constructed housing requires low subsidies. RAY was a good example of PPPP and should not have been abandoned for a 'one size fits all' approach to housing.

Lastly, there has to be a proactive policy to support housing in the manufacturing centres, wherein the private manufacturing companies can be facilitated to provide workers' housing. There is a good lesson to be learnt from the PRC in this regard. India can afford to ignore the question of housing security only at her peril—the price to be paid will be very high in terms of low industrialization, low urbanization, and low economic growth.

Appendix

Table A.10.1. Rent per month by cities (in Rs)

City	1BHK		3BHK	
	Centre	Periphery	Centre	Periphery
India	**11,537.89**	**7,062.77**	**27,979.10**	**17,006.28**
Mumbai	35,982.89	18,805.11	100,488.33	45,560.86
Patna	9,333.33	4,500.00	17,725.00	9,333.33
Thane	14,000.00	9,250.00	34,444.44	21,375.00
Kolkata	11,698.14	6,689.81	28,189.19	15,277.78
Goa	10,388.89	8,000.00	30,000.00	22,250.00
Delhi	16,437.50	9,631.10	41,103.45	23,666.67
Navi Mumbai	15,785.71	9,666.67	37,571.43	22,933.33
Vishakhapatnam	9,500.00	5,444.44	23,666.67	11,444.44
Indore	6,922.22	4,333.33	16,555.56	9,277.78
Ahmedabad	9,534.78	6,100.00	24,333.33	15,173.91
Kochi	9,611.11	7,062.50	21,381.82	12,900.00
Bhopal	7,600.00	4,450.00	16,333.33	10,300.00
Bhubaneshwar	7,500.00	4,272.73	19,000.00	10,863.64
Guwahati	6,333.33	3,875.00	16,571.43	10,000.00
Chandigarh	10,409.09	5,583.33	28,181.82	15,545.45
Chennai	12,050.56	6,714.49	30,454.55	16,976.14
Nagpur	9,428.57	5,333.33	20,125.00	10,857.14
Hyderabad	9,560.81	5,913.33	24,877.65	13,868.75
Faridabad	8,000.00	4,725.00	17,000.00	13,000.00
Bangalore	14,346.15	8,571.43	36,575.61	22,372.51
Thiruvanathapuram	8,625.00	6,045.45	19,166.67	12,681.82
Surat	6,863.64	4,590.91	18,700.00	12,136.36
Pune	13,455.13	8,820.25	27,931.02	17,974.49
Gurgaon	16,774.19	10,116.67	40,410.26	24,685.71
Gaziabad	9,166.67	6,000.00	21,428.57	14,857.14
Rajkot	6,222.22	4,250.00	17,250.00	12,187.50
Jaipur	6,875.00	4,200.00	19,400.00	11,400.00
Vadodara	6,807.69	4,666.67	16,045.45	10,250.00
Udaipur	5,800.00	3,366.67	14,400.00	10,875.00

Source: <http://www.numbeo.com/cost-of-living/country_result.jsp?country=India> (accessed 7 February 2017).

Table A.10.2. Urbanization, income, housing status indicators by states

State	Urbanization level		Urban population Growth Rate	PCI	CAGR PCI	% households							
						In good houses	In crowded housing	With tap water	With toilet access	With access to water closet type toilet	With bathroom within premises	With drainage connection	With access to closed drains among those connected to drainage
	2001	2011	2001–211	2011–12	2004–05 to 2011–12	2011	2011	2011	2011	2011	2011	2011	2011
Andhra Pradesh	27.3	33.5	3.1	42,267	8.8	78.9	34.9	83.5	86.1	79.4	92.6	88.3	56.2
Arunachal Pradesh	20.8	22.7	3.2	37,047	5.5	58.5	22.6	84.2	89.5	74.9	80.6	66.2	23.6
Assam	12.9	14.1	2.5	22,544	5.0	58.9	26.3	30.2	93.7	71.0	84.5	56.3	27.4
Bihar	10.5	11.3	3.1	12,480	8.0	53.1	34.7	20.0	69.0	63.4	68.6	71.4	42.0
Chandigarh	89.8	97.2	2.4	124,886	7.6	69.9	39.9	96.8	87.6	87.0	89.7	96.0	91.0
Chhattisgarh	20.1	23.2	3.6	26,799	6.3	64.2	28.7	62.5	60.2	58.7	67.4	68.9	25.4
Goa	49.8	62.2	3.1	138,690	9.7	76.9	23.9	90.2	85.3	80.6	94.9	78.0	70.2
Gujarat	37.4	42.6	3.1	56,403	9.8	76.5	37.9	85.6	87.7	85.2	90.5	82.6	84.0
Haryana	28.9	34.8	3.7	62,606	8.5	62.9	28.0	77.5	89.9	80.5	92.6	92.2	53.6
Himachal Pradesh	9.8	10.0	1.5	49,092	6.6	80.1	29.2	95.5	89.1	87.0	92.8	93.6	69.5
Jammu & Kashmir	24.8	27.2	3.1	27,137	4.0	70.9	18.0	87.9	87.5	68.5	91.4	83.1	39.4
Jharkhand	22.2	24.1	2.8	24,545	4.9	59.9	25.0	41.6	67.2	64.7	69.8	70.8	35.1
Karnataka	34.0	38.6	2.8	40,882	7.26	72.4	36.7	80.4	84.9	71.6	96.4	87.6	64.5
Kerala	26.0	47.7	6.8	55,942	9.5	72.4	7.2	34.9	97.4	75.3	92.9	54.5	61.5
Madhya Pradesh	26.5	27.6	2.3	24,376	7.7	67.6	26.6	62.2	74.2	71.5	85.3	82.3	38.8

Maharashtra	42.4	45.2	2.1	62,887	9.5	73.1	46.5	89.1	71.3	67.3	95.4	91.2	68.8
Manipur	26.6	30.2	3.6	24,705	3.8	63.4	14.9	56.3	95.8	63.7	65.7	70.4	8.6
Meghalaya	19.6	20.1	2.7	32,685	5.8	69.5	22.4	77.6	95.7	82.9	79.9	80.3	22.3
Mizoram	49.6	51.5	2.5	41,927	8.8	73.6	14.5	74.4	98.5	80.9	89.7	79.5	25.7
Nagaland	17.2	29.0	5.3	44,022	8.3	62.0	23.2	35.7	94.6	79.1	94.4	76.5	11.3
NCT Delhi	93.2	97.5	2.4	113,344	9.9	66.0	33.6	81.9	89.8	86.0	91.3	96.0	62.8
Orissa	15.0	16.7	2.4	24,214	5.4	51.5	30.0	48.0	64.8	58.8	64.3	59.0	33.6
Puducherry	66.6	68.3	2.7	81,291	9.3	80.0	45.1	95.4	82.0	81.1	92.0	82.6	39.2
Punjab	33.9	37.5	2.3	49,328	6.5	57.3	26.6	76.4	93.4	85.6	94.8	90.9	63.4
Rajasthan	23.4	24.9	2.6	28,646	7.4	68.9	27.5	82.6	82.0	73.7	89.2	86.0	40.0
Sikkim	11.1	25.0	9.7	71,341	17.7	80.3	33.2	92.1	95.2	91.8	92.0	92.1	42.9
Tamil Nadu	44.0	48.4	2.4	53,419	10.3	76.4	41.4	80.3	75.1	66.5	85.2	74.9	59.7
Tripura	17.1	26.2	5.8	39,083	8.2	63.6	65.8	54.0	97.9	50.0	64.0	53.4	13.6
Uttar Pradesh	20.8	22.3	2.6	18,428	5.9	57.0	33.7	51.5	83.1	77.2	84.6	93.4	34.5
Uttarakhand	25.7	30.6	3.6	49,636	12.3	74.4	30.3	78.4	93.6	85.9	93.1	92.9	45.5
West Bengal	28.0	31.9	2.7	32,517	6.3	57.5	44.7	55.6	85.0	61.6	70.7	66.8	36.5
India	**27.8**	**31.2**	**2.8**	**38,010**	**7.6**	**68.4**	**35.2**	**70.6**	**81.4**	**72.6**	**87.0**	**81.8**	**54.4**

Source: Housing data from population census; PCI 2011–12 data from Reserve Bank of India (2013); PCI 2004–5 data from Reserve Bank of India (2011)

References

Ansari, J. H. 1998. 'Improving Urban Land Management in India'. In *Urban Land Management: Improving Policies and Practices in Developing Countries of Asia*, edited by J. H. Ansari and N. von Einsiedel, Oxford and IBH Publishing.

Ballaney, S. 2008. *The Town Planning Mechanism in Gujarat, India*, The World Bank Institute, Washington, DC.

Desai, R. and D. Mahadevia. 2013. 'Land and Housing Development Processes as Determinants of Rental Housing for the Urban Poor: The Case of Guwahati City'. *Working Paper 19*, Center for Urban Equity and Faculty of Planning, CEPT University, Ahmedabad. <http://cept.ac.in/UserFiles/File/CUE/Working%20Papers/Revised%20New/19CUEWP%2019_Rental%20Housing%20Guwahati%20City.pdf>.

Express News Service. 2016. 'BMC's Building Proposal Dept: Now, Take Online Permissions for Building Projects'. The Indian Express, 19 May. < https://indianexpress.com/article/cities/mumbai/bmcs-building-proposal-dept-now-take-online-permissions-for-building-projects-2807778/>.

Kumar, Y. and S. Singh. 2014. 'Rehabilitation of Slum Dwellers: A Case Study in Bhopal'. *Social Change 44* (4): 567–78.

Mahadevia, D. 2006. 'Urban Infrastructure Financing and Delivery in India and China'. *China and the World Economy 14* (2): 105–20.

Mahadevia, D. 2009. 'Urban Land Market and Access of the Poor'. In *India: Urban Poverty Report. 2009*, edited by the Ministry of Housing and Urban Poverty Alleviation, India, Oxford University Press.

Mahadevia, D. and A. Parashar. 2008. 'Dynamics of High-Tech Urban Spaces: Case of Pune'. In *High-Tech Urban Spaces: Asian and European Perspectives,* edited by C. Ramachandraiah, Guus van Westen, and Sheela Prasad, Manohar.

Mahadevia, D., R. Desai, and S. Vyas. 2014. 'City Profile: Ahmedabad'. *Working Paper 26*, Centre for Urban Equity, CEPT University. <http://cept.ac.in/UserFiles/File/CUE/Working%20Papers/Revised%20New/26CUEWP%2026_City%20Profile%20Ahmedabad.pdf>.

Mahadevia, D., Z. Liu, and X. Yuan. 2012. 'Housing of Urban Migrants in India and China'. *Environment and Urbanization ASIA 3* (1): 143–63.

Mahadevia, D. 2010a. 'Tenure Security and Urban Social Protection Links: India'. *IDS Bulletin 41* (4): 52–62.

Mahadevia, D. 2010b. 'Urban Reforms in Three Cities: Bangalore, Ahmedabad, and Patna'. In *Public Service Delivery in India: Understanding the Reform Process*, edited by V. Chand, Oxford University Press.

Mahadevia, D. 2011a. 'Tenure Security and Urban Social Protection in India'. CSP Research Report 05, Centre for Social Protection, Institute of Development Studies, Sussex.

Mahadevia, D. 2011b. 'Branded and Renewed? Policies, Politics and Processes of Urban Development in the Reform Era'. *Economic and Political Weekly 46* (31): 56–64.

Mahadevia, D. and T. Gogoi. 2010. 'Assessment of Shelter Programmes in Andhra Prades'. *Working Paper 12*, Centre for Urban Equity, December 2010.

Mehta, M. and D. Mehta. 1987. 'Metropolitan Housing Markets: A Case Study of Ahmedabad'. *Economic and Political Weekly 22* (40): 1707–09.

Ministry of Housing and Urban Poverty Alleviation. 2007. *National Urban Housing and Habitat Policy, 2007*, Government of India, New Delhi.

Mohan, R. 1996. 'Urbanization in India: Patterns and Emerging Policy Issues'. In *The Urban Transformation of the Developing World*, edited by J. Gugler, Oxford University Press.

NSSO (National Sample Survey Organization). 2010. *Housing Condition and Amenities in India, 2008–09, NSS 65th Round, Report No. 535 (65/1.2/1)*, Ministry of Statistics and Programme Implementation, Government of India.

NSSO (National Sample Survey Organization). 2014a. *Informal Sector and Conditions of Employment in India, NSS 68th Round, 2011–12, Report No. 557 (68/10/2)*, Ministry of Statistics and Programme Implementation, Government of India, July.

NSSO (National Sample Survey Organization). 2014b. *Drinking Water, Sanitation, Hygiene and Housing Condition in India, NSS 69th Round, Report No. 556 (69/1.2/1)*, Ministry of Statistics and Programme Implementation, Government of India, July.

NBO (National Building Organization). 2012. *Report of the Technical Group (TG-12) on Urban Housing Shortage (2012–17)*, Ministry of Housing and Urban Poverty Alleviation, Government of India.

Press Information Bureau. 2014. *Report of the Expert Group to Review the Methodology for Measurement of Poverty*, Planning Commission, Government of India, New Delhi.

Qian, Y. 2000. 'The Institutional Foundations of Market Transition in the People's Republic of China'. *ADB Institute Working Paper 9*, ADB Institute, Tokyo.

Ramakrishnan, T. 2007. 'Housing Board Real estate boom puts Housing Board back on road to recovery'. *The Hindu*, 25 May.

Reserve Bank of India. 2011. *Handbook of Statistics on the Indian Economy*, Reserve Bank of India.

Reserve Bank of India. 2013. *Handbook of Statistics on the Indian Economy*, Reserve Bank of India. <http://dbie.rbi.org.in>.

Turner, J. F. C. 1967. 'Barriers and Channels for Housing Development in Modernizing Countries'. *Journal of American Institute of Planners 33* (3): 167–81.

Turner, J. F. C. 1968. 'Housing Priorities, Settlement Patterns, and Urban Development in Modernizing Countries'. *Journal of American Institute of Planners 34* (6): 354–63.

UN-Habitat. 2003. *Rental Housing: An Essential Option for the Urban Poor in Developing Countries*, UN-Habitat, Nairobi.

PART V

CAPITAL FLOW AND FDI

11
Foreign Direct Investment, Capital Flows, and Urbanization: the Case of China

Dan Liu

11.1 Introduction

It has been over three decades since the People's Republic of China (PRC) implemented the reforms and opening-up policy. Over this period, the PRC's urbanization has experienced recovery, stable development, and rapid expansion step by step (Niu et al. 2012). In 1978, less than 20 per cent of the PRC's population lived in cities. In 2012, the PRC's urban population reached over 50 per cent of its total population (Lu and Wan 2014). This implies that more than 500 million people have moved out of rural areas. Undoubtedly, this is one of the biggest achievements for the PRC in the last thirty-five years. Many factors, such as international trade, infrastructure construction, and education, have contributed to this rapid rate of urbanization. In this chapter, we will focus on discussing the role of foreign direct investment (FDI) on the PRC's urban growth and development.

It has been widely documented that FDI brings considerable benefits, such as technology transfer, management expertise, and foreign market access. Many developing and transition economies have placed attracting FDI high on their reform agendas. Policymakers have implemented many policies to encourage FDI. Attracting FDI has become a shortcut for developing countries to close the technology gap with high-income countries. The PRC, from being an economy with virtually no foreign presence in the late 1970s, has now become the largest recipient of FDI among developing countries and the second largest FDI recipient in the world after the United States.

In this chapter, we first examine the spatial and industrial distribution of FDI in the PRC and how this pattern changes over time. We then investigate the role of FDI in urban development in the PRC. Specifically, we examine the effects of FDI on city growth, urbanization, job creation, and migration. We also make a comparison between FDI and domestic capital. Finally, there is some discussion on the distribution of government transfer and local government debts.

This chapter makes three key points. First, FDI is very unevenly distributed across regions and industries. Most FDI firms are located in the coastal areas. This

Dan Liu., *Foreign Direct Investment, Capital Flows, and Urbanization* In: *Cities of Dragons and Elephants: Urbanization and Urban Development in China and India. Edited by:* Guanghua Wan and Ming Lu, Oxford University Press (2019). © Oxford University Press. DOI: 10.1093/oso/9780198829225.003.0011

is consistent with the flow of domestic capital. This implies that the use of capital in the coastal provinces is more efficient. In contrast, government transfers are allocated more to the middle, western, and northern provinces. This shows the efforts of central and local governments in closing the regional gaps.

Second, FDI is positively associated with urban growth. From a simple empirical analysis using city-level data, it was found that FDI has a positive impact on urban growth even after controlling for labour, domestic capital, and productivity. Based on the literature, FDI can promote urban growth through two channels: on the one hand, FDI, a kind of capital, in combination with local labour, can increase domestic outputs directly; on the other hand, the horizontal and vertical spillover effects of FDI can increase overall productivity. The latter could be the reason why the magnitude of the impact of FDI on urban growth is actually small.

FDI plays a significant role in the process of urbanization in at least two ways: first, FDI can provide jobs directly, which is supported by our empirical findings; second, by creating new jobs, FDI can affect the amount and direction of migration. Both inflows and outflows of migration can affect local urbanization.

The remaining chapter is organized as follows: Section 11.2 discusses institutional issues related to FDI; Section 11.3 investigates the trends in FDI and its distribution across regions and industries; Section 11.4 analyses the effects of FDI on urban development; Section 11.5 focuses on the domestic capital flows; and Section 11.6 provides policy recommendations.

11.2 Institutions

Institutions are important in determining the direction of capital flows, especially FDI. Du et al. (2008) find that economic institutions such as interventions from the government, intellectual rights protection, and corruption can affect the location of FDI firms. Li and Shen (2008) show that strategic fiscal policies can decrease the spillover effects from FDI and have a negative impact on FDI's achievements in growth. Wang (2013) shows that fiscal decentralization is an important reason for the difference in FDI attraction between the PRC and India.

Overall, the PRC has formulated favourable policies to attract FDI. In this section, we discuss central and local government policies on attracting FDI, especially policies on taxation, headquarter establishment, and land provision.

11.2.1 Tax Policy

Before 2008, taxation laws in the PRC were different for domestic firms and FDI firms. Among all the tax reductions, FDI firms benefited most from income tax reduction. Specifically, FDI firms enjoyed exemption from income tax in the first two profitable years, followed by a half reduction in next three years. For those FDI firms encouraged by the government in the middle or western regions of the PRC, another three years of income tax exemption could be applicable. If exports accounted for more than 70 per cent of the total revenue, FDI firms could enjoy a half reduction in income tax. In addition, if FDI firms bought equipment domestically, or imported tariff-free equipment, income tax could be deducted accordingly and value-added tax could be returned. It should be noticed that these policies favour the more capital-intensive FDI firms intentionally. Although these tax policies were designed by the central government, some scope was left for the local government when carrying out these policies.

One important incentive for local governments to attract more FDI is to promote competition. Since the 1980s, economic development has become one of the most important considerations for promotion. FDI firms are counted as an achievement of the local government in speeding economic development. Li and Shen (2008) found that taxation was the most important policy instrument for regions to attract FDI. Under the basic framework of national laws, local governments could further reduce the actual tax payments of FDI firms by returning their tax if reinvestment happened or by manipulating the process of tax collection.

Table 11.1 shows the average income tax rate for domestic and FDI firms in different regions from 2000 to 2007. First, FDI firms enjoyed, on average, an income

Table 11.1. Average income tax rate by regions for foreign direct investment firms and domestic firms

Year		2000		2003		2007	
Region	Firm	Mean (%)	SD	Mean (%)	SD	Mean (%)	SD
National	FDI	16.01	0.09	15.98	0.08	15.59	0.09
	Domestic	21.76	0.10	21.26	0.09	20.32	0.10
North	FDI	16.74	0.09	16.06	0.08	16.19	0.08
	Domestic	21.33	0.11	20.47	0.10	20.07	0.10
Northeast	FDI	15.36	0.09	14.04	0.07	15.54	0.09
	Domestic	23.38	0.12	21.67	0.09	19.52	0.09
East	FDI	16.52	0.09	16.42	0.08	16.06	0.09
	Domestic	22.09	0.10	21.99	0.09	21.20	0.09
Middle	FDI	17.18	0.11	15.09	0.08	15.49	0.09
	Domestic	21.45	0.12	19.52	0.10	18.23	0.10
South	FDI	14.72	0.09	15.68	0.08	14.76	0.09
	Domestic	20.33	0.11	21.07	0.10	19.58	0.10
Southwest	FDI	14.25	0.07	12.76	0.06	13.36	0.08
	Domestic	21.44	0.08	19.78	0.09	17.44	0.10
Northwest	FDI	16.12	0.07	14.55	0.08	13.35	0.08
	Domestic	21.82	0.10	19.17	0.09	19.10	0.09

FDI = foreign direct investment, SD = standard deviation.

Note: The figures in this table are calculated from Annual Survey of Manufacturing Firms from 2000 to 2007; only FDI firms over 5 years are included to avoid composition effects.

tax rate that was 5 per cent lower than domestic firms. Second, the average tax rate for both FDI and domestic firms decreased by around 2 per cent in the middle and western areas, while it did not change much in the eastern and southern areas. Third, in the north-east provinces, the income tax rate decreased by 3 per cent on domestic firms, but little on FDI firms. This shows that some regions provide favourable policies for both domestic and FDI firms, while others paid more attention to foreign capital. These differences in tax policies could lead to variation in capital flows.

Figure 11.1 shows the relationship between FDI inflows and average tax reduction on FDI firms. Tax reduction is the difference between the income tax rate for domestic firms and FDI firms. The bigger the difference, the more favourable the tax policy adopted by the local government. It can be seen that there is a weak positive correlation between FDI inflows and tax reduction on FDI firms. We ran a regression to investigate the conditional correlation between these two. The results are shown in Table A.11.1. It can be seen that a more favourable tax policy does lead to more FDI flows, after controlling for government expense, road length, GDP per capita, cumulative FDI, local degree of agglomeration, and also some of the lagged.

Since 2008, a new taxation law has been implemented. It eliminated the old separate laws for FDI firms. Common taxation laws were designed for both

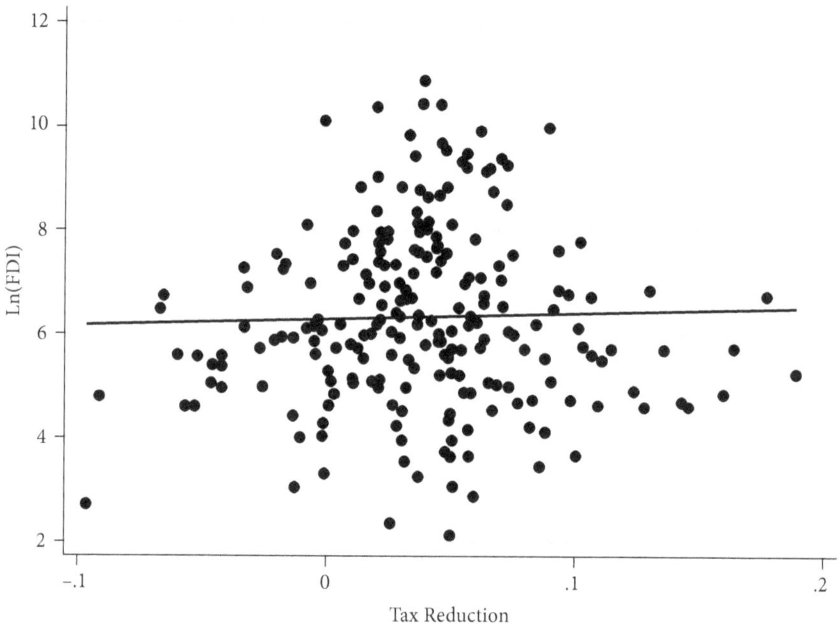

Figure 11.1. FDI inflows and tax reduction on FDI firms, 2007

FDI = foreign direct investment.

Note: Tax reduction is measured by the difference in income tax rate paid by domestic firms and FDI firms. It has been calculated from firm-level data, Annual Survey of Manufacturing Firms, 2007.

domestic firms and FDI firms. However, FDI firms still enjoy a tax reduction in the first five years.

11.2.2 Headquarters Policy

Recently, many cities have started to implement various kinds of beneficial policies to encourage FDI firms to establish or move their headquarters there. Most of these cities have already been the largest recipients of FDI, including Shanghai, Guangzhou, Tianjin, Shenzhen, and Xiamen. Taxation reduction, fiscal subsidy, and even land policies were adopted.

In 2002, the Shanghai government started to carry out 'Temp Regulations on Encouraging Multinational Firms to Establish Regional Headquarters in Shanghai'. The regulations lay down that an FDI firm with headquarters in Shanghai engaged in R&D activities can enjoy all the benefits of high-tech firms. Firms registered in Pudong District can enjoy extra benefits. In addition, if the headquarters provides training on their key technologies, the government could in turn provide financial subsidies.

In 2006, the Tianjin government passed a policy regulation with a similar flavour. The regulation states that the government can provide up to RMB 20 million as a subsidy for a new headquarters set up in Tianjin with registered capital of RMB 1 billion or higher. There are also some other tax exemption policies and housing subsidies for headquarter firms and their workers. In 2003, Guangzhou started implementing fiscally beneficial policies for FDI headquarters. Financial FDI firms were especially encouraged in Guangzhou.

It can be seen from these examples that policies vary from city to city. In addition, competition in attracting high-quality FDI firms is intense among the most developed cities in the PRC. Moreover, local government policies are more favourable to the more capital-intensive firms. As shown in Section 11.4.2, this could affect FDI's role in creating jobs.

11.2.3 Land and Other Policies

Undoubtedly, land policy is another important instrument that the local government can implement in order to attract FDI firms. It includes how much the government charges for land use, the area of the land provided, the location of the land, and the regulations on how to use the land. These policies not only vary across provinces and cities but also change case by case.

In 2003, the Suzhou government started encouraging FDI firms to establish headquarters in the Suzhou Industrial Park. The regulation states that FDI headquarters enjoy a 50 per cent discount on the rent of buildings. If an FDI firm wants to build its own buildings for production or office use, land could be provided at favourable prices. There is no specific regulation on how much the discount on land price could be, which implies that local governments have huge space to manipulate land prices.

In 2003, a regulation was passed that set a price floor for state-owned land. However, this did not stop local governments from implementing other land policies to attract FDI firms. For example, Shenzhen implemented a land-expense-return policy, according to which the government could return up to 30 per cent of land expenses for high-quality FDI firms.

Environmental policies also play a significant role in the competition among cities to attract more FDI. Zhu et al. (2011) show that a strategic choice on environmental policies does exist among cities. The effect of environmental policies on FDI is not significant on average across the country, but it does exist among cities with a median level of FDI or above. This implies that in these cities, local governments tend to lower the threshold on environmental regulations on FDI firms in order to make themselves attractive. This could be effective in the short run in attracting more FDI and promoting GDP growth. However, in the long run, these more favourable environmental policies may not be sustainable.

To sum up, the PRC has implemented aggressive policies to promote FDI. While these policies can encourage FDI inflows and thus increase economic growth and the speed of urbanization, as discussed in detail in Section 11.4, policy distortion in resource allocation can also take place. For example, FDI is more efficient in creating jobs in the eastern provinces, but tax and land policies are more favourable to FDI firms in the middle and western regions. As pointed out by Lu and Ou (2011), government intervention can decrease the job creation ability of FDI. Therefore, local growth and development should not be the only criteria to evaluate FDI policies. Attention needs to be paid to the overall efficiency of capital flows in the PRC as a whole.

11.3 Trends in Foreign Direct Investment

In this section, we investigate the trends in regional and industrial distribution of FDI in the PRC. As shown in Figure 11.2, FDI inflows in the PRC exploded from \$920 million in 1983 to \$111.7 billion in 2012 (Figure 11.2). Before 1992, the increase in FDI was very slow. Since 1992, the total FDI in the PRC has increased dramatically. The average annual rate of increase in FDI from 1992 to 2012 was more than 21 per cent. There have been two booms in FDI over the last thirty years: one in 1992, when the reforms in state-owned enterprises were deepened, and the other in 2001, when the PRC entered the World Trade Organization.

Until the early 2000s, most FDI firms were concentrated along the eastern coastal area of the PRC. In 2001, more than 86 per cent of FDI was invested in the

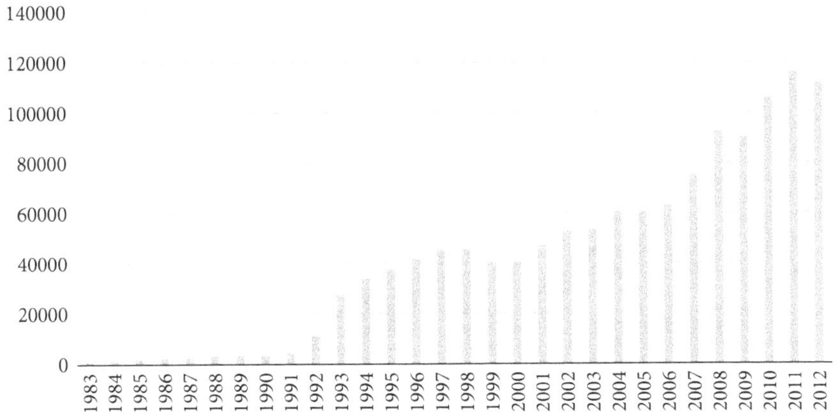

Figure 11.2. FDI in the PRC ($, million)
Source: *China Statistical Yearbook* (1984–2013), National Bureau of Statistics of China.

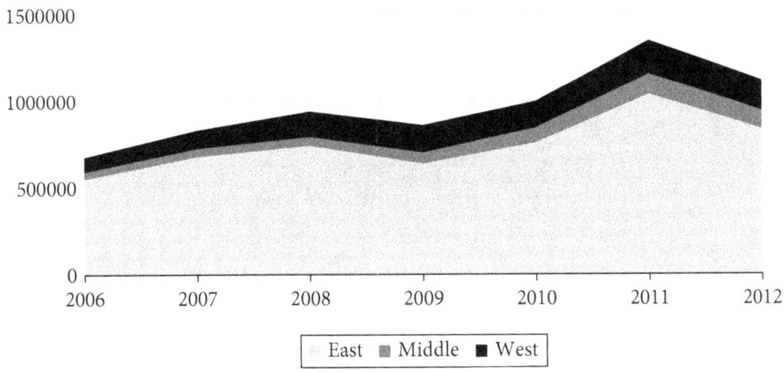

Figure 11.3. FDI by region over time (RMB, million)
Source: *China Statistical Yearbook* (2005–13), National Bureau of Statistics of China.

coastal areas and only around 14 per cent went to middle and western PRC. As shown in Figure 11.3, between 2006 and 2012, FDI in the middle and western provinces increased dramatically. By 2012, the middle and western areas accounted for around one quarter of the total FDI in the PRC. This could be due to the more favourable policies implemented in these provinces, such as tax reduction and land policy.

In addition, there is a trend of moving to the north within the eastern areas. As shown by Figures 11.4–11.6, where darker values represent the range of higher values, since 2001, the rate of increase in FDI around the Yangtze River Delta has been much higher than that around the Pearl River Delta in the farthest south. At the end of 2012, the top three provinces with the largest amount of FDI were

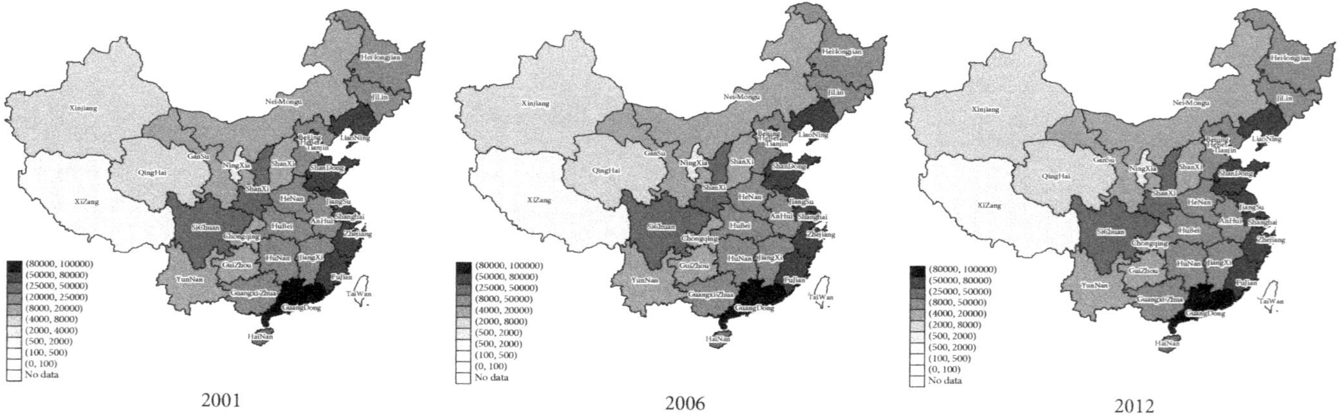

Figure 11.4. Number of FDI firms

Source: *China Statistical Yearbook* (2005–13), National Bureau of Statistics of China.

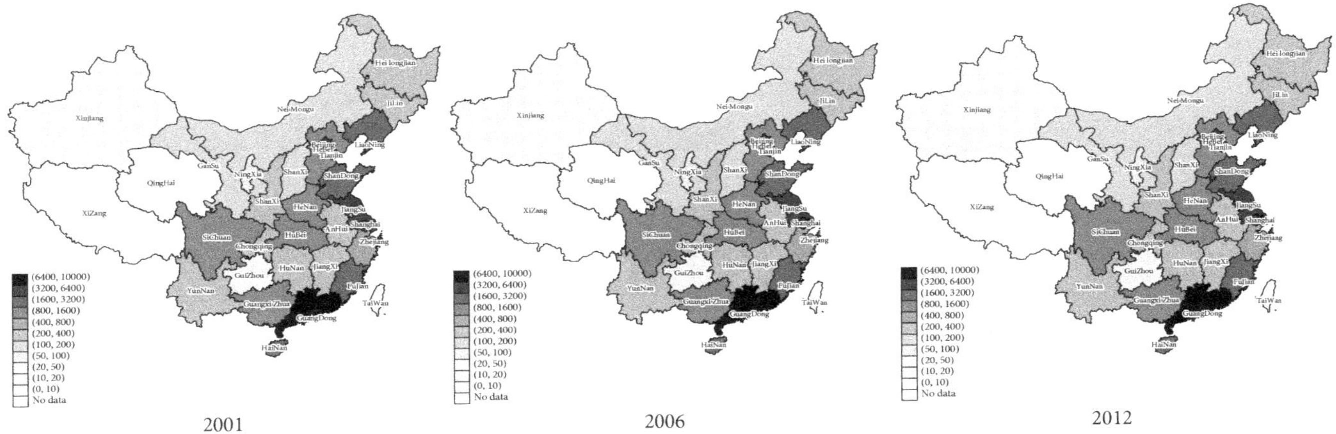

Figure 11.5. Total amount of FDI by year end

Source: *China Statistical Yearbook* (2005–13), National Bureau of Statistics of China.

Figure 11.6. Annual Growth of Foreign Direct Investment

Source: *China Statistical Yearbook* (2005–13), National Bureau of Statistics of China.

Jiangsu (19.9 per cent of total FDI), Guangdong (15.24 per cent), and Shanghai (13.17 per cent). Two of these top three FDI receivers are located in the middle-east area. The proportion of FDI located in Guangdong has been decreasing—it fell from 26.92 per cent in 2000 to 15.24 per cent in 2012. On the other hand, Jiangsu has been attracting more and more FDI, which increased from 9.32 per cent in 2000 to 19.9 per cent in 2012. It has been the largest FDI recipient in the PRC since 2006. At the same time, the provinces around the Bohai Gulf area have also been attracting increasing FDI. The total investment by FDI firms in 2012 around the Bohai Gulf area, including Liaoning, Shandong, Hebei, Tianjing, and Beijin, was comparable to Jiangsu Province.

Overall, the eastern coastal areas have been the main FDI destinations since the 2000s. However, more favourable FDI policies in the middle and western PRC seem to have worked in attracting more FDI. The increase in FDI in the middle and western provinces is higher than in the coastal areas. However, it should be noted that the biggest movement in FDI is along the eastern coast, from the south-east to the middle-east and north-east regions.

Table 11.2 shows the distribution of FDI for Chinese cities and reveals large regional disparities. The major recipients of absolute FDI levels and FDI scaled by GDP are almost always located in the eastern coastal provinces. The top nine cities alone account for more than half of the total inward FDI to the PRC. In contrast, the value of FDI received by the bottom twenty cities accounts for no more than 0.1 per cent of the total FDI. One observation is that cities with the largest absolute levels are not necessarily those with the highest FDI scaled by GDP, suggesting that FDI has a strategic dimension and is not just targeted at the most populous cities. In 2005, the eastern region's average share of FDI in total FDI was 85.11 per cent compared to just less than 15 per cent in the central and western cities. This inequality distribution was even starker in 2013. In 2013, the east's average share of FDI in total FDI was more than 88 per cent. This phenomenon indicates that export-oriented FDI is the key motivation for foreign companies to enter the PRC. Related export statistics also support this point that foreign companies occupy over half of the PRC's total exports. Between 2005 and 2008, the east's average share of exports in total income was more than 70 per cent compared with less than 30 per cent in the central and western regions.

The industrial distribution of FDI is also uneven and changes over time. As can be seen from Figure 11.7, in 2005, over 70 per cent of total FDI in the PRC flowed to the manufacturing industry. The second largest sector is real estate, attracting 8.98 per cent of total FDI. These two sectors account for nearly 80 per cent of total FDI. FDI in the primary sector accounts for only 1.19 per cent. In 2012, manufacturing's share increased by 15.1 per cent, from $42,453 million to $48,866 million, and it remained the largest sector for FDI. Real estate FDI increased dramatically from $5,418 million to $24,125 million, probably due to the surge in the PRC's

Table 11.2. FDI distribution of the top twenty and bottom twenty cities, 2013

FDI inflows ($, million)				FDI/GDP (%)			
Top 20		Bottom 20		Top 20		Bottom 20	
City	FDI ($, million)	City	FDI ($, million)	City	FDI/GDP (%)	City	FDI/GDP (%)
Shanghai	3,027	Bazhong[b]	0.03	Sanya	33.96	Bazhong[b]	0.01
Guangzhou	2,748	Yaan[b]	0.04	Putian	21.20	Yaan[b]	0.01
Tianjin	2,560	Heihe[a]	0.04	Qingyuan	20.51	Hegang[a]	0.01
Beijing	2,378	Hegang[a]	0.06	Suzhou	18.96	Anyang[a]	0.01
Shenzhen	1,961	Baiyin[b]	0.18	Heyuan	16.99	Heihe[a]	0.02
Dalian	1,136	Anyang[a]	0.21	Zhuhai	16.13	Baiyin[b]	0.02
Dongguan	1,087	Qitaihe[a]	0.24	Haikou	16.08	Chifeng[a]	0.02
Xiamen	1,032	Yuncheng[a]	0.26	Meizhou	14.79	Yibin[b]	0.03
Suzhou	1,027	Liaoyuan[a]	0.27	Dongguan	13.75	Qitahe[a]	0.04
Wuhan[a]	754	Chifeng[a]	0.27	Huizhou	13.61	Songyuan[a]	0.05
Qingdao	745	Yibin[b]	0.31	Zhongshan	12.86	Daqing	0.05
Zhuhai	739	Songyuan[a]	0.39	Xiamen	12.73	Panzhihua[b]	0.05
Shenyang	706	Jincheng[a]	0.48	Leshan[b]	11.83	Shiyan[a]	0.05
Zhongshan	650	Xuancheng[a]	0.48	Changzhou	11.58	Yuncheng[a]	0.05
Nanjing	573	Neijiang[b]	0.51	Foshan	11.46	Xuancheng[a]	0.06
Wuxi	516	Jinzhong[a]	0.54	Tianjin	11.38	Liaoyuan[a]	0.06
Ningbo	458	Fuyang[a]	0.76	Yingkou	10.59	Neijiang[b]	0.06
Changzhou	368	Jinchang[b]	0.77	Shiuhing	10.57	Jincheng[a]	0.07
Fuzhou	352	Shiyan[a]	0.80	Shanwei	9.80	Fuyang[a]	0.07
Haikou	347	Panzhihua[b]	0.80	Zhenjiang	9.33	Yangquan[a]	0.08

FDI = foreign direct investment, GDP = gross domestic product.

[a] City in central region; [b] City in western region.

Note: US$ as of 2013. All zero values are regarded as missing.

Sources: China City Statistical Yearbook, 2014 and author's calculation.

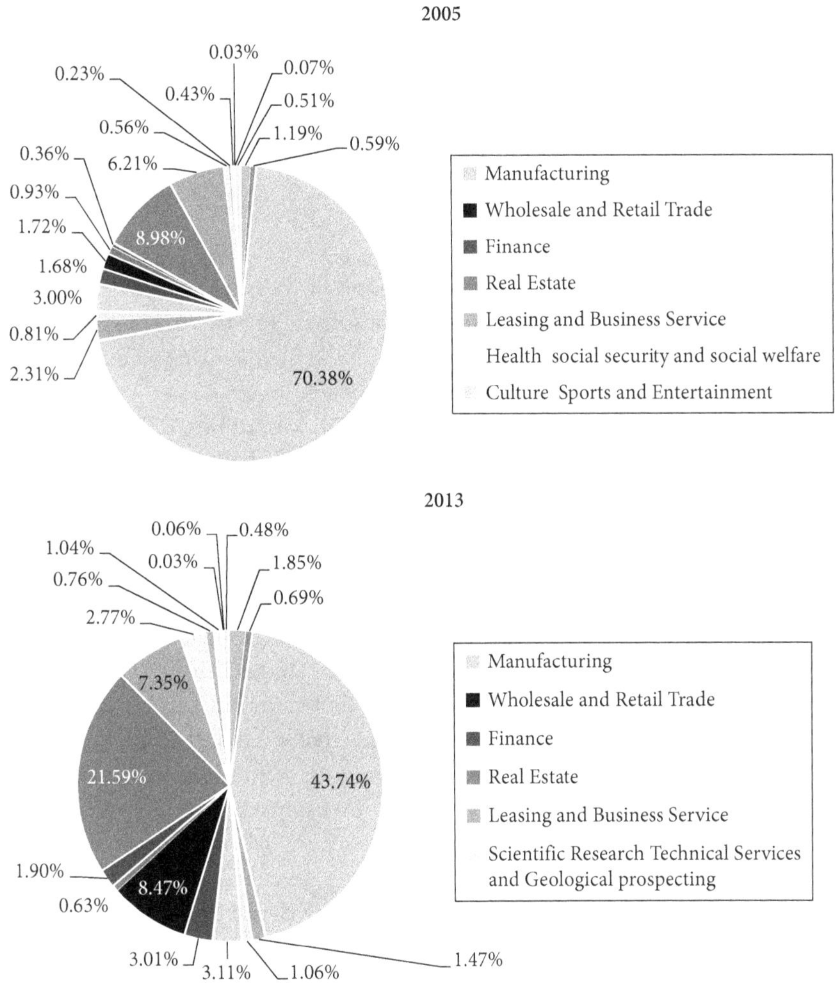

Figure 11.7. Distribution of FDI by industry, 2005 and 2013
Source: *China Statistical Yearbook* (2006, 2013), National Bureau of Statistics of China.

housing prices. It accounted for 21.59 per cent of total FDI in 2012 compared with 8.98 per cent in 2005. The combined share of manufacturing and real estate fell to 65.4 per cent of total FDI in 2012.

In recent years, more and more FDI has started flowing into services, such as wholesale and retailing, finance, and rental and commercial services. From 2004 to 2011, there was a more than tenfold FDI in financial industries, and FDI in the wholesale and retailing industry also increased roughly tenfold during this period. This could be due to the deepening of openness in the PRC from manufacturing to services. It should be mentioned that although FDI in services has increased at a fast pace, it is still concentrated among a few industries within this sector and accounts for a relatively small proportion in the total FDI in the PRC.

11.4 FDI and Development

11.4.1 FDI and Urban Growth

FDI has been viewed as complementary to domestic investment and a shortcut to fill the technology gap with high-income countries. Bhagwati (1994) proposes that FDI inflows vary according to whether a country is following an export push or an import substitution strategy. The PRC's economic growth has been powered by a number of factors including exports and FDI. According to the Ministry of Commerce, foreign-invested enterprises account for over half of the PRC's exports and imports; they provide for 30 per cent of the country's industrial output, and generate 22 per cent of industrial profits while employing only 10 per cent of labour (World Bank 2010).

The PRC has been experiencing fast economic growth in the last thirty years. However, it has been widely documented that the development is quite uneven across regions. Wan et al. (2007) investigated the impact of FDI on regional income inequality in the PRC and found that FDI contributes to rising income inequality across regions. Wei et al. (2009) argue that it is not FDI but the uneven distribution of FDI that contributes to the increase in regional inequality. Lin et al. (2013) examined the distributional effects of FDI using cross-country panel data and found that there is a non-monotonic impact of FDI on income inequality, depending on the level of human capital. Using country-level data, Basu and Guariglia (2007) found that FDI promotes both growth and inequality.

Figure 11.8 shows the relationship between GDP per capita and FDI inflows in 2011. The data are from the *City Statistical Yearbook* (NBSC 2010–12). Each dot represents a prefecture city. There is an obviously strong positive correlation between GDP per capita and FDI across Chinese cities. However, it is hard to see from this unconditional correlation whether FDI promotes development or FDI flows to more developed regions. Thus, we conduct a simple exercise examining the effect of FDI on city development. The details and results are in the Appendix. It can be shown that FDI has a positive impact on GDP growth after controlling for fixed investment, non-agricultural population, education, technology, and infrastructure. In addition, we control for year trend in some specifications, and use random effect and fixed effect models in addition to OLS. The results are consistent and shown in Table A.11.2. Moreover, we also examine the correlation between FDI and urbanization rate. Figure 11.9 shows the connection between the province urbanization rate and the share of foreign investment in total fixed

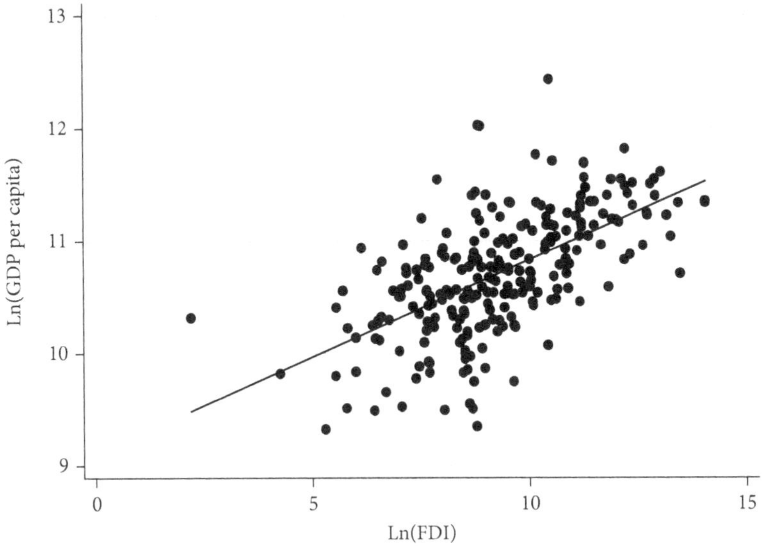

Figure 11.8. The relationship between GDP per capita and FDI inflows in 2011.

The data are from the City Statistical Yearbook. Each dot represents a prefecture city. There is an obviously strong positive correlation between GDP per capita and FDI across Chinese cities. However, it is hard to see from this unconditional correlation whether FDI promotes development or FDI flows to more developed regions. Thus, we conduct a simple exercise examining the effect of FDI on city development. The details and results are in the appendix. It can be shown that FDI has a positive impact on GDP growth after controlling for fixed investment, non-agriculture population, education, technology, and infrastructure. In addition, we control for year trend in some specifications, and use random effect and fixed effect models in addition to OLS. The results are consistent and shown in Table A.11.2. Moreover, we also examine the correlation between FDI and urbanization rate. Figure 11.9 shows the connection between the province urbanization rate and the share of foreign investment in total fixed investment. It can be seen that there is a significant positive correlation between them. This implies that a higher degree of FDI penetration is associated with a higher urbanization rate.

investment. It can be seen that there is a significant positive correlation between them. This implies that a higher degree of FDI penetration is associated with a higher urbanization rate.

There is no doubt that urbanization and economic development are closely connected. Urban growth mainly originates from firms operating in the cities. Usually, firms are more productive in larger cities. This phenomenon can be explained by agglomeration economies and firm selection. Urban agglomeration economies are commonly classified into those arising from labour–market interactions, from linkages between intermediate- and final-goods suppliers, and from knowledge spillovers (Kim 1995; Ellison and Glaeser 1999; Diamond and Simon 1990; Jaffe et al. 1993; Jovanovic and Rob 1989; Duranton and Puga 2004). Besides, FDI in cities greatly exaggerates the scale effect by knowledge transfer, management expertise, and marketing (Javorcik 2004; Blalock and Gertler 2008; Keller 2004; Javorcik and Spatareanu 2008; Havranek and Irsova 2011). Firm selection, as shown in the work

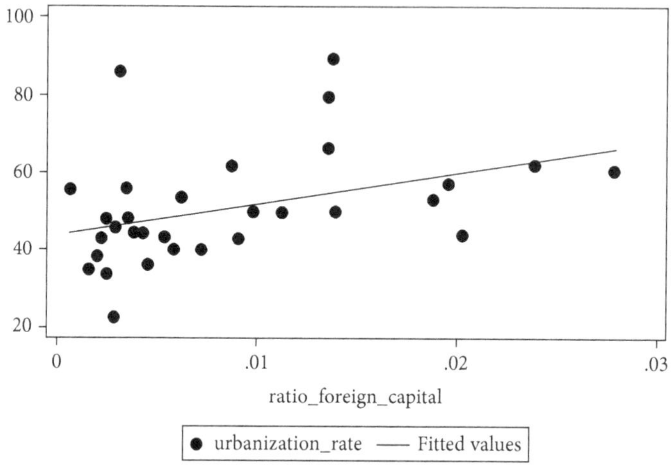

Figure 11.9. Urbanization rate and FDI in fixed investment, 2010

Note: The vertical axis is the urbanization rate, which is calculated from the 2010 census; the horizontal axis is the ratio of foreign capital in fixed investment.

by Melitz (2003), provides an alternative explanation that the least productive firms are forced to exit the market. Melitz and Ottaviano (2008) revised the model with price-cost markups and argue that larger markets attract more firms and that fierce competition between firms can squeeze out the least productive firms. This suggests that the larger the city, the larger the average productivity.

There is some research focusing on the PRC that also finds evidence of the effect of agglomeration on firms. (Li and Lu 2009; Lu and Tao 2007; Lu et al. 2012; Ge 2009; Du et al. 2008). Agglomeration promotes firm size, and firms are more likely to benefit from locating with large firms rather than with a large number of small firms (Lu et al. 2012). Since the beginning of this century, a large number of newly founded firms have had, on an average, higher productivity. As Melitz (2003) mentions, we can predict that a large number of firms would drive competition and force the least productive companies to quit. This kind of dynamic force of creative destruction is confirmed in the PRC and it has helped increase the total factor productivity (TFP) growth in the PRC, where the net entry accounts for over two-thirds of its growth (Zhang et al. 2012). Some research finds that FDI in the PRC has had a positive effect on the productivity of domestic firms (Liu 2008; Wang and Wang 2014). The early industry agglomeration is highly correlated with FDI and trade. Industries dependent on foreign trade and foreign investment tend to locate in regions with easy access to foreign markets. Export-oriented and foreign-invested industries have a higher degree of agglomeration than other industries (Ge 2009). Huang (2009) used provincial-level data and found that FDI has a positive and statistically significant impact on economic growth, which is consistent with our findings here.

11.4.2 FDI and Job Creation

It is obvious that FDI brings job opportunities directly as foreign companies hire local employees. There are also various indirect ways in which FDI increases employment, such as through the purchase of locally produced goods and services, and spillover to its counter-partners, and upstream and downstream firms.

To further investigate the role of FDI in job creation, we first look at the average capital–labour ratio for all FDI firms using information from the Annual Survey of Manufacturing Industries from 2000 to 2007. It should be mentioned that only firms with total revenue higher than RMB 5 million were included in the dataset for all years. Also, since this survey was designed only for manufacturing firms, we have excluded firms in agriculture and services. As shown in Figure 11.7, in 2005, manufacturing firms accounted for more 70 per cent of total FDI in the PRC. Since FDI firms tend to be bigger than domestic firms, this dataset should have included a majority of FDI firms. Table A.11.3 shows the number of FDI firms and domestic firms in the data.

Figure 11.10 shows the average capital to labour ratio of FDI firms and domestic firms from 2000 to 2007 (see Table A.11.4). It can be seen that FDI firms are around twice as capital intensive as domestic firms on average in all the years. This implies that one unit of foreign capital is associated with half the number of jobs created by the same amount of domestic capital. Over time, the average capital intensity increases gradually for domestic firms, while the capital intensity is almost the same for FDI firms. This narrows the gaps in the job-creating ability between domestic firms and foreign firms over time.

We also examine the cross-region pattern in the average capital intensity of manufacturing firms. Figure 11.11 illustrates the average capital intensity for each province in 2000 and 2007. It can be seen that in 2000 the FDI firms in the middle and western provinces were more capital intensive on average than those along the eastern coastal areas. Along the east coast, the FDI firms in the middle-east are more capital intensive than those in the south-east. This implies that in terms

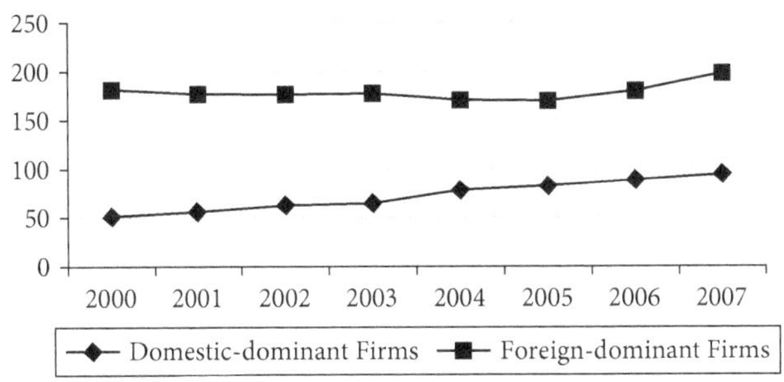

Figure 11.10. Average capital–labour ratio, 2000–7

Note: Foreign-dominant firms are those with foreign capital higher than 50 per cent of the total capital.

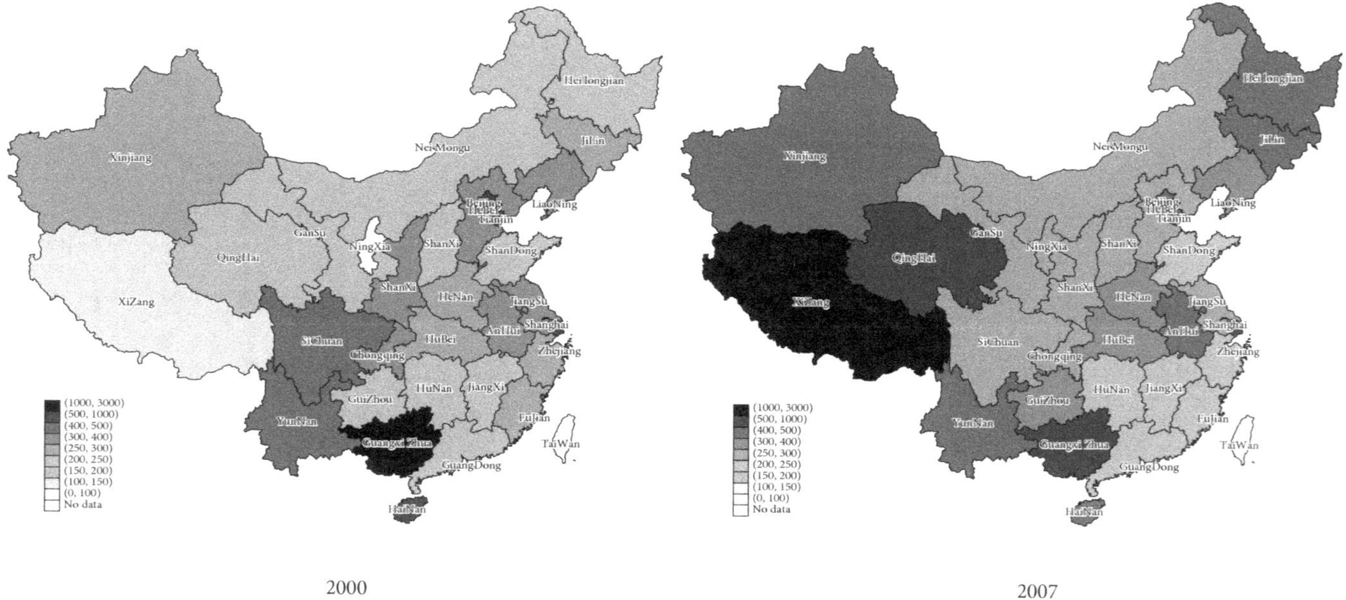

Figure 11.11. Capital–labour ratio of FDI manufacturing firms

Source: Annual Survey of Manufacturing Firms (2000 and 2007).

of job creation, FDI in the middle, west, and middle-east regions was more efficient. From 2000 to 2007, in almost all the provinces, the capital intensity of FDI firms increased, which means that the FDI firms' ability to create jobs actually decreased over time.

The same measure is calculated and shown for domestic firms in Figure 11.12. It can be seen that, on average, firms in the west are more capital intensive than those in the middle regions, which, in turn, are more capital intensive than firms in the east. This is similar to the pattern in FDI firms. However, if within-region patterns are examined, the picture is almost the opposite. For example, along the east coast, it is the firms in the south regions that are more capital intensive than the middle-east provinces, except Shanghai. This implies that within each region, FDI firms and domestic firms could complement each other in creating jobs. However, the big picture is still drawn by the government policies that encourage capital investment in the middle and west regions. This is consistent with the findings of Lu and Ou (2011), who investigated how government policies affect GDP elasticity of employment through its intervention on FDI types. If local governments try to attract more capital-intensive firms to promote GDP growth and increase tax income, FDI could decrease elasticity of employment. Specifically, whether FDI will increase or decrease elasticity of employment depends on the degree of government intervention. Based on Lu and Ou's (2011) empirical analysis, FDI actually decreases elasticity of employment on average.

Figure 11.13 shows the correlation between change in employment and FDI inflows using city-level aggregate data from 2010 and 2011. Change in employment is the change in employment in the second the third industries between the two years. It can be seen that FDI inflows have a significant positive correlation with change in employment in manufacturing and services.

Using the firm-level elements in the data, we investigate the role of FDI in promoting employment. It is clear that some differences in the character of firms have contributed to the ability to create jobs. We first use differences in employment to eliminate the possible firm-specific effects. Controlling for the firm characteristics, industry characteristics, and regional characteristics, we then estimate the effect of firm-specific features. The year, regional, and industry dummies are implemented to capture the time-invariant characteristics. But we do not use the firm-specific dummies since the nature of some firms in the panel may change, such as a shift in ownership. We use two different variables linked to foreign presence to proxy the different channels where FDI may affect employment. The ratio of FDI to capital stock represents the direct channel of foreign companies hiring local employees. Another variable, FDI intensity, measured by the share of sales by FDI firms in total sales at the two-digit industry levels, represents the indirect channel, where a foreign presence can affect the employment of all the firms in an industry due to the spillover effect.

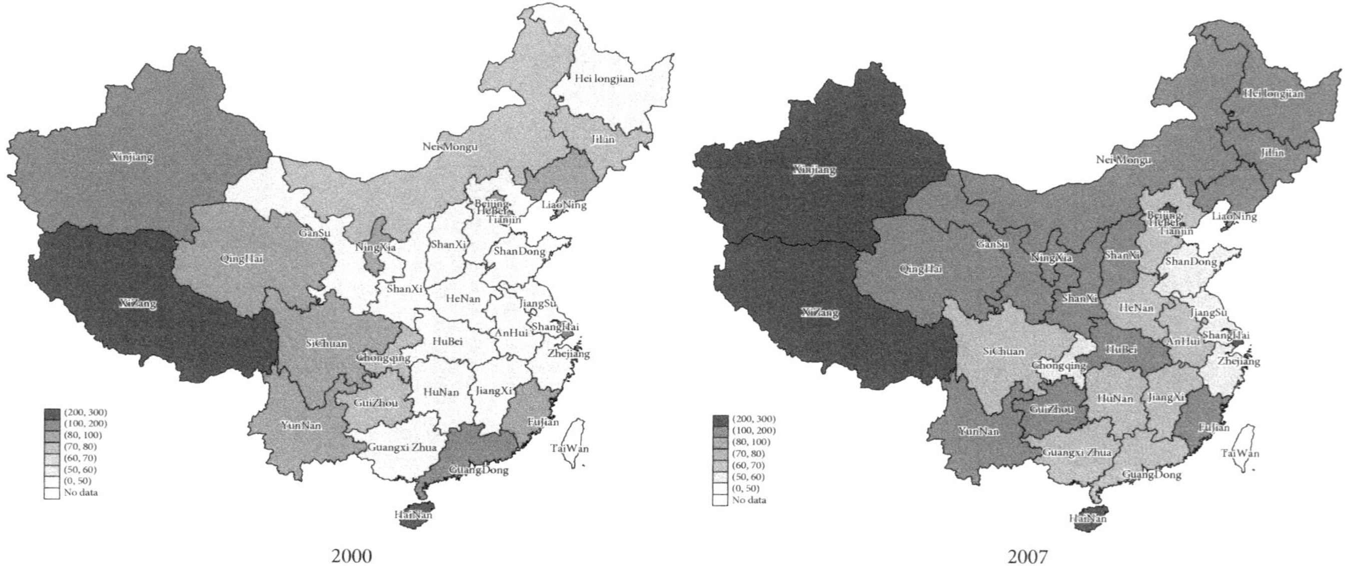

Figure 11.12. Capital–labour ratio of domestic manufacturing firms

Source: Annual Survey of Manufacturing Firms (2000 and 2007).

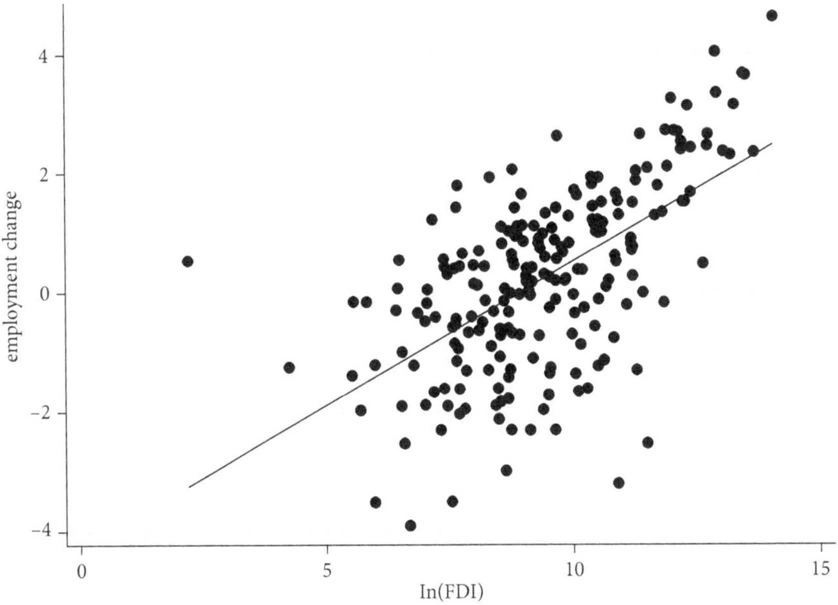

Figure 11.13. Employment change and FDI inflows
Source: *City Statistical Yearbook* (2010 and 2011).

From Table A.11.5 in the Appendix, we find positive effects of FDI in job creation through both direct and indirect channels. The presence of FDI in firms helps increase employment directly and the presence of FDI helps increase an industry's average employment. As to firm characteristics, all the coefficients are positive except the firm size, measured by the total number of employees. However, it should be noticed that the magnitude of the effects from FDI is moderate. This could be due to the complementary roles of FDI and domestic capital in job creation.

11.4.3 FDI and Migration

In this section, we further investigate how FDI affects urbanization by examining the relationship between FDI and migration, both in terms of the extent and direction.

As pointed out in the chapter on migration by Lu and Xia (Chapter 6), the migrant share of total population has risen dramatically from 0.65 per cent in 1982 to 16.53 per cent in 2010. Migration makes a great contribution to the process of urbanization. Figure 11.14 shows the number and geographic distribution of migrants in 2000 and 2010. It can be seen that the coastal provinces are the main

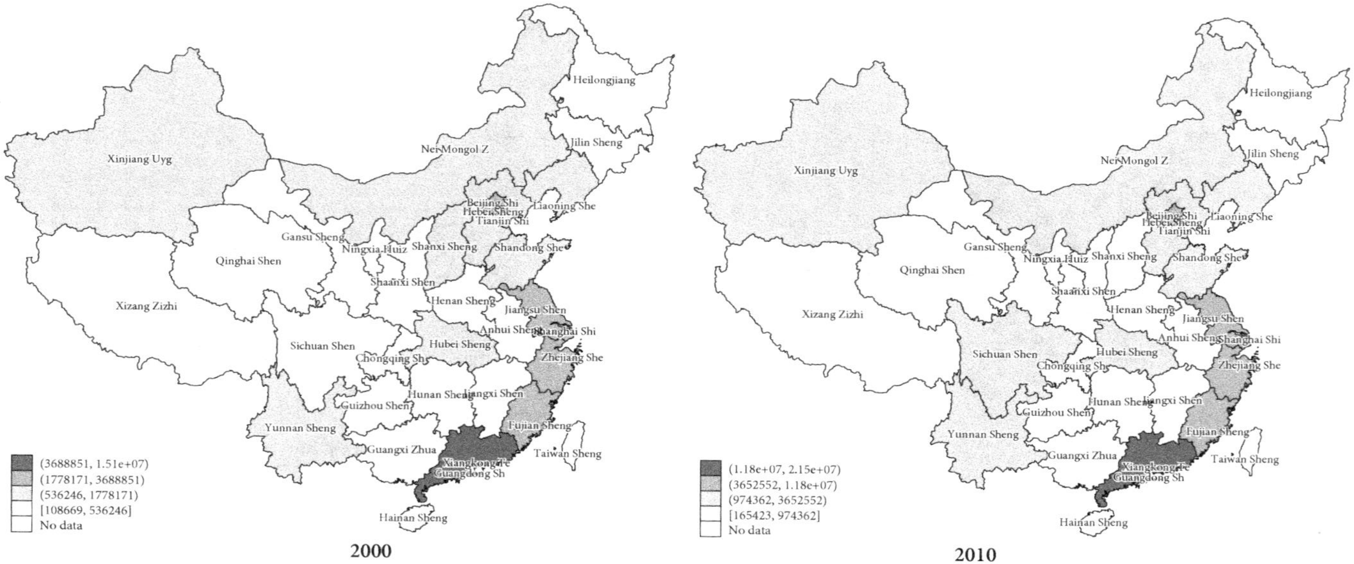

Figure 11.14. Number of Migrants, 2000 and 2010

Notes: The data are from the population censuses of 2000 and 2010, National Bureau of Statistics of China. Migrants include both within-province and between-province migrants.

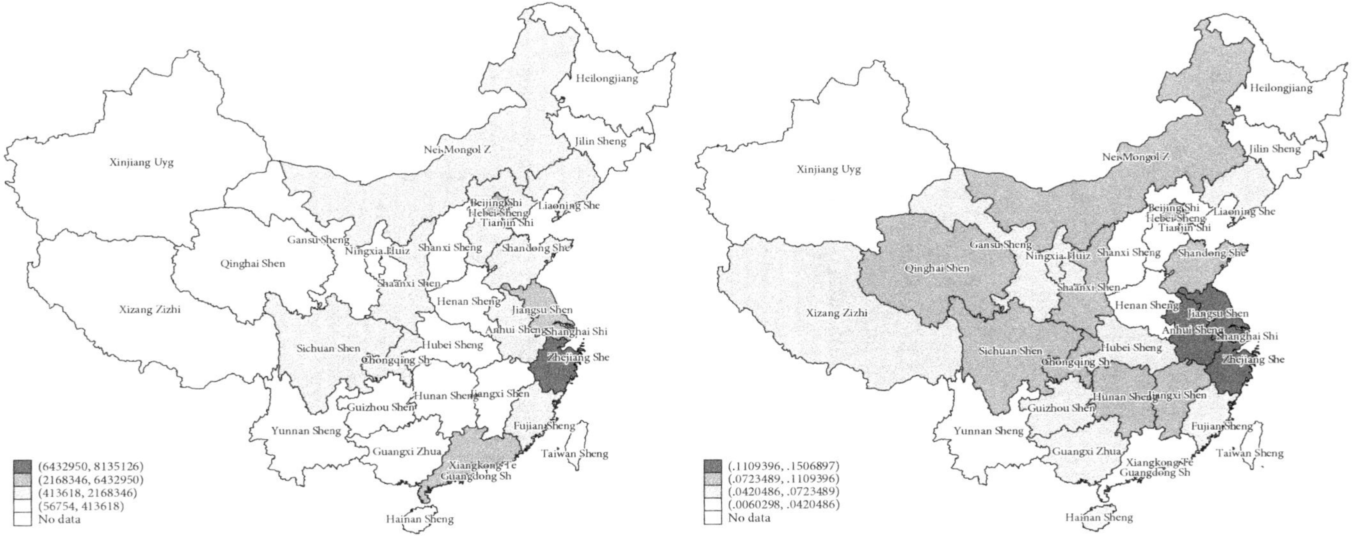

Net migrants, 2000–2010 **Growth rate in migrants, 2000–2010**

Figure 11.15. Change in Migrants from 2000 to 2010

Notes: The data are from the population censuses of 2000 and 2010, National Bureau of Statistics of China. Migrants include both within-province and between-province migrants.

destinations of migrants, and this is highly correlated with the direction of FDI flows. This implies that FDI is indeed attractive to migrants as an important source of capital.

Figure 11.15 shows the change in the number of migrants for each province. In terms of absolute numbers, the south coastal provinces, such as Guangdong, which opened up first, attracted many migrants during this period. However, it should be noticed that middle-east provinces like Jiangsu, Shanghai, and Zhejiang have provided more and more jobs to migrants over this period. In addition, there was a big increase in migrants in Beijing and Tianjin. This is also consistent with the trend of FDI movement from the Pearl River Delta to the Yangtze River Delta and Bohai Gulf provinces during this period. This implies that FDI does play an important role in shaping the pattern of migration, which is consistent with our result that FDI has a positive effect on job creation.

Furthermore, there could be an indirect effect of FDI on urbanization due to the outflow of local rural residents to the FDI firms in other provinces. Figures 11.16 and 11.17 show the pattern in urbanization rate for each province. When these are compared with Figures 11.14 and 11.15, it can be seen that it is mainly the inflow of migrants that contributes to urbanization in the coastal provinces. On the other hand, for some provinces, such as Hunan, Ningxia, and Hebei, which experienced a big increase in the degree of urbanization during this time period, the outflow of rural residents could play a major role.

11.4.4 Impact of FDI on Quality of Urban Growth

From the preceding analysis, it is clear that FDI promotes urbanization by its impact on job creation and migration. The rate of urban growth and the quality of urbanization are both significant. As documented by the literature, FDI could promote both growth and inequality (Wei et al. 2009; Lin et al. 2013; Basu and Guariglia 2007). While the results from the literature do not reach a consensus on how FDI can affect regional inequality, they are in agreement on one aspect—FDI matters to inequality.

FDI has contributed to poverty reduction in the PRC. It has been found that FDI and trade have helped to narrow the poverty difference (Zhang and Wan 2006). But the impact of FDI and trade on poverty is not always consistent. It tends to vary across locations and over time. As dramatically increased trade and FDI inflows are the two most significant aspects of the PRC's integration into the world economy, these findings provide some insights into the much-debated question of whether globalization brings poverty or prosperity. The first point to note is that globalization is a multifaceted process. Evidence on any single aspect of globalization, be it trade, FDI, or integrated financial markets, does not usually suffice for drawing conclusions about the causality between poverty and globalization.

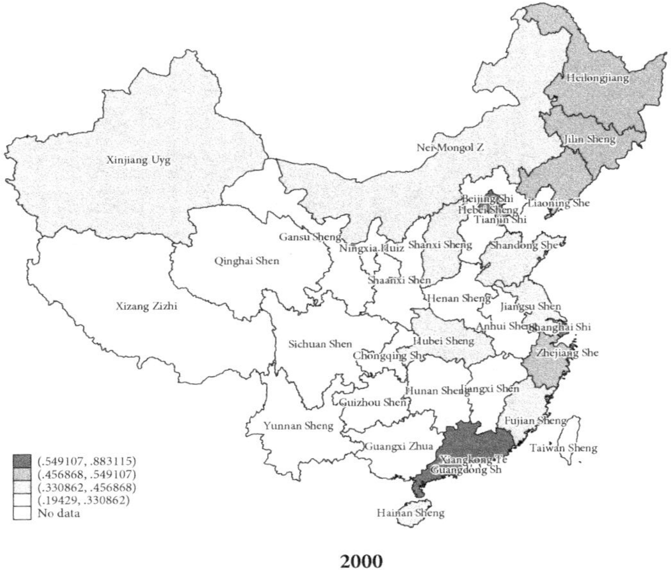

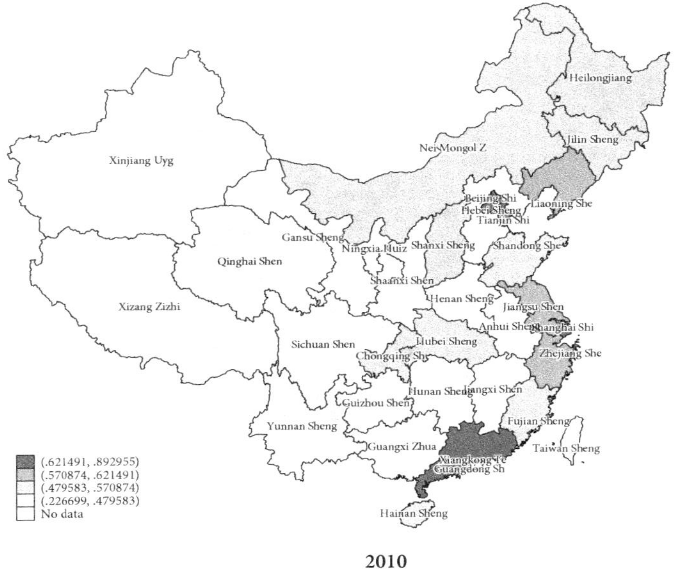

Figure 11.16. Urbanization rates in 2000 and 2010

Notes: The data are from the population censuses of 2000 and 2010, National Bureau of Statistics of China. Migrants include both within-province and between-province migrants.

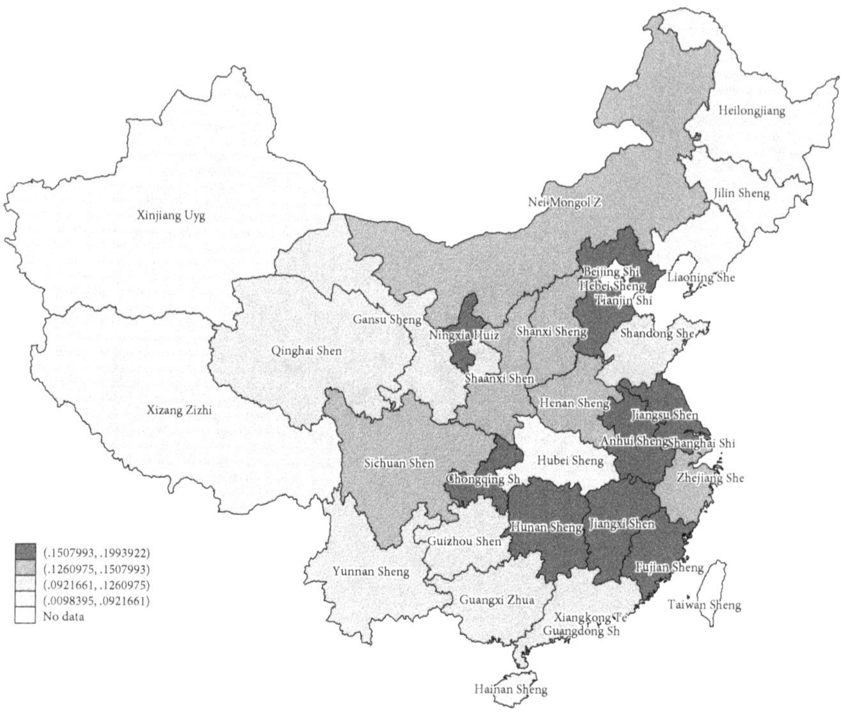

Figure 11.17. Change in urbanization rate from 2000 to 2010

Notes: The data are from the population censuses of 2000 and 2010, National Bureau of Statistics of China. Migrants include both within-province and between-province migrants.

From 2000 to 2008, the PRC experienced a 70 per cent increase in total energy consumption of standard coal at 2.91 billion tons (NBSC 2010), accounting for 17.7 per cent of global energy consumption even though it produces just 8 per cent of the global output (Buyanov 2011). A commonly held view is that the PRC's dependence on imported oil leaves future growth vulnerable to fluctuations in global energy prices and could also be considered an energy security threat.

In the last two five-year plans (2006–10 and 2011–15), the government has been trying to lower the PRC's energy consumption in unit output by encouraging technology innovation, mergers and acquisitions of heavy industries, setting high standards to energy-intensive industries, and developing third industries. Between 1978 and 2001, when economic growth in the PRC averaged around 9 per cent a year, the demand for energy rose by just 4 per cent a year and energy intensity fell from nearly 400 tons of coal equivalent per RMB 1 million to a little over 100 tons. However, after 2001 growth in energy demand began to outstrip GDP growth, with an average growth rate of 14 per cent a year (Rosen and Houser 2007).

Inward FDI has many effects on energy intensity in the PRC. Foreign firms use more advanced and more energy efficient technologies and squeeze

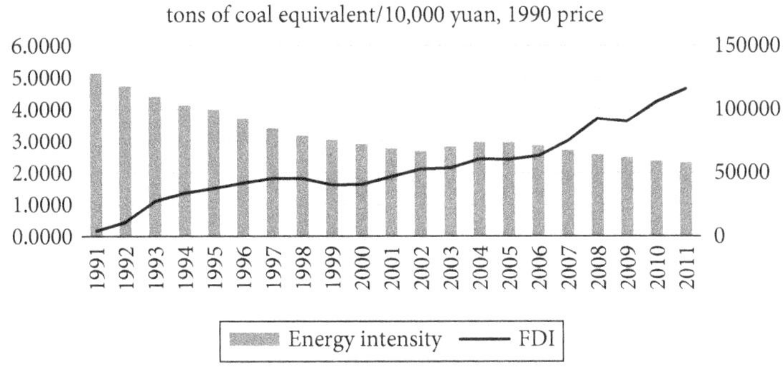

Figure 11.18. Energy intensity and FDI, 1991–2011
Sources: China Energy Statistical Yearbook and *China Statistical Yearbook* (various years).

inefficient domestic firms out of the market. Besides, FDI is a channel through which technology can be transferred from foreign firms to domestic firms. This can be achieved by the transfer of goods, employees, patents, and management experience. Technological progress in domestic firms and the expansion of foreign capital presence can both improve energy efficiency.

Figure 11.18 provides an overview of the changes in energy intensity in the PRC as a whole (measured in tons of coal equivalent). There was a significant downward trend from 1991 to 2001, after which it increased for a few years until 2005, and then decreased again till 2010. The second decreasing subperiod made less progress than the first one. Elliott et al. (2013) have shown that there is a significant and negative relationship between FDI and energy intensity in the PRC.

11.5 Domestic Capital and Urbanization

Although FDI is an important source of capital in the urban development of the PRC, domestic capital still plays a dominant role. There are three main sources of domestic capital: private capital, government budget, and domestic bank loans. Here, due to the limitation in data availability, we will focus on the flow of capital in fixed investments.

As can be seen from Figure 11.19, in both 2004 and 2012, domestic capital, including government budgets, private capital, loans, and others, accounted for more than 95 per cent of the total fixed investment in the PRC. The proportion of FDI in fixed investment fell from around 5 per cent in 2004 to 1 per cent in 2012. At the same time, private domestic capital expanded from 56 per cent to 68 per cent in total fixed investment. This implies that while there are more and more FDI inflows into the PRC, the accumulation of domestic capital in fixed investment is even faster.

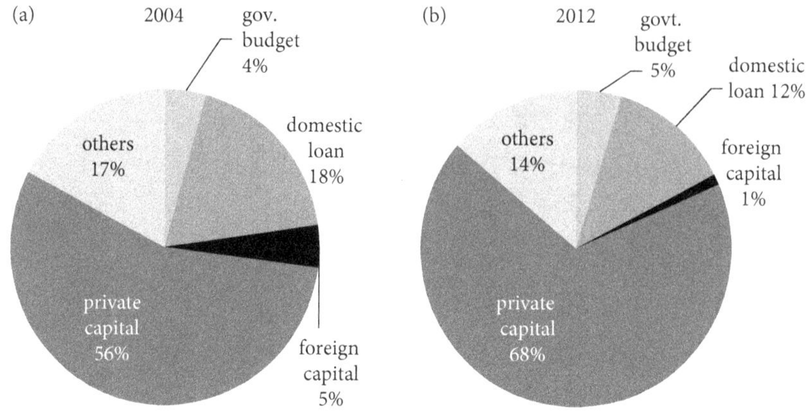

Figure 11.19. Composition of total fixed investment, 2004 and 2012
Source: *China Statistical Yearbook* (2005, 2013), National Bureau of Statistics of China.

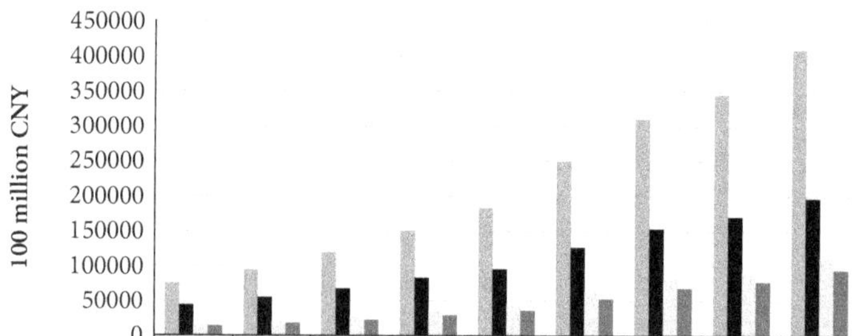

	2004	2005	2006	2007	2008	2009	2010	2011	2012
Total	75195	94591	1E+05	2E+05	2E+05	3E+05	3E+05	3E+05	4E+05
East	43876	54870	67470	82984	95633	1E+05	2E+05	2E+05	2E+05
Middle	15278	20202	26930	35731	46680	64508	82002	91417	1E+05
West	13916	17868	22623	29533	36567	53444	69003	77967	95033

Figure 11.20. Fixed investment across regions, 2004–12
Source: *China Statistical Yearbook* (2005–13), National Bureau of Statistics of China.

Figure 11.20 shows the geographic distribution of fixed investments across regions. The eastern provinces accounted for around half of the total fixed investments in 2012. It can be seen that from 2004 to 2012, total fixed investments increased by 450 per cent overall. The annual growth rate in fixed investment was around 50 per cent on average. While all regions saw a great increase in fixed investment, the growth rate was higher in the middle and western areas than in the eastern areas. The average growth rate was 39 per cent in the east, 70 per cent in the middle, and 65 per cent in the west respectively. The growth rate in the middle region was almost twice that in the east. If we consider the per capita increase, the difference would be even higher. This pattern is exactly the same as the trend in FDI.

Why is an increasing amount of private capital flowing to the middle and western provinces? Is it because the efficiency of capital use in the middle and western regions is much higher? Or is it a consequence of government policy? If it is due to the more favourable policies in the middle and western provinces, would this trend be sustainable in the long run? In this section, we will investigate this issue by comparing the flows of domestic private capital and government budgets and transfers. Also, we will compare the efficiency of investments in creating jobs across regions and their impact on urbanization.

11.5.1 Domestic Private Capital Flows

Here, private capital mainly refers to the capital from private investors. The most important incentive for the flow of private capital is profit. Although it is possible for government policies to guide the direction of private capital flows, the market should play a dominant role in allocating private capital.

Figure 11.21 shows the geographic distribution of private capital in 2004 and 2012. In 2004, Shandong, Jiangsu, and Guangdong were the top three provinces absorbing the largest amount of domestic private capital, and the bottom three were Tibet, Qinghai, and Hainan. In 2012, Liaoning Province went up to third position and Guangdong fell to sixth. Compared with the situation in 2004, domestic private capital moved more to the middle provinces in 2012. This could be due to the crowding out effect of FDI along the coastal areas. It is also possible that the moving-to-the-west policies encouraged domestic capital to flow into these areas.

11.5.2 Fiscal Transfer

Fiscal transfer from central government includes the allocation of government budgets to fixed investment and fiscal subsidies to local governments. The former is usually invested in public transportation and facilities to encourage investments from private parties. In contrast, government subsidies are often allocated to the less developed areas to help them reduce poverty or alleviate suffering from natural disasters. In this section, the distribution of government budgets and transfers will be examined.

As shown in Figure 11.22, the allocation of government budgets has been uneven and varied over time. The middle provinces were allocated more of the government budget over time. Liaoning, Shandong, and Fujian were the top three coastal provinces with the largest amount of the government budget as fixed investment.

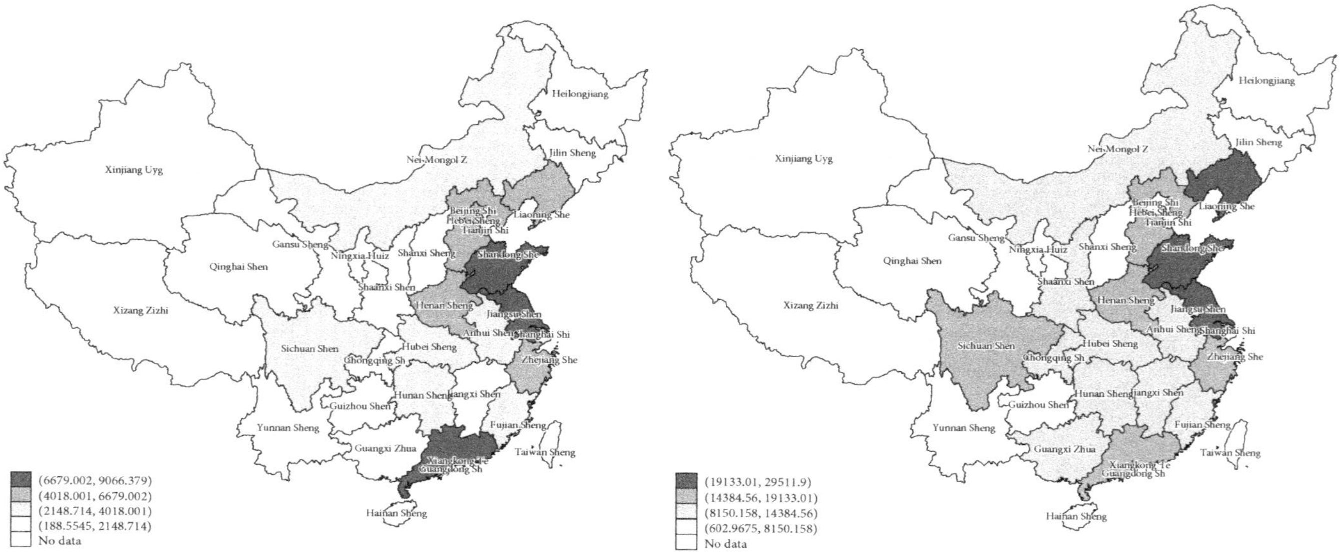

2004 **2012**

Figure 11.21. Geographic distribution of domestic private capital

Source: *China Statistical Yearbook* (2005, 2013), National Bureau of Statistics of China.

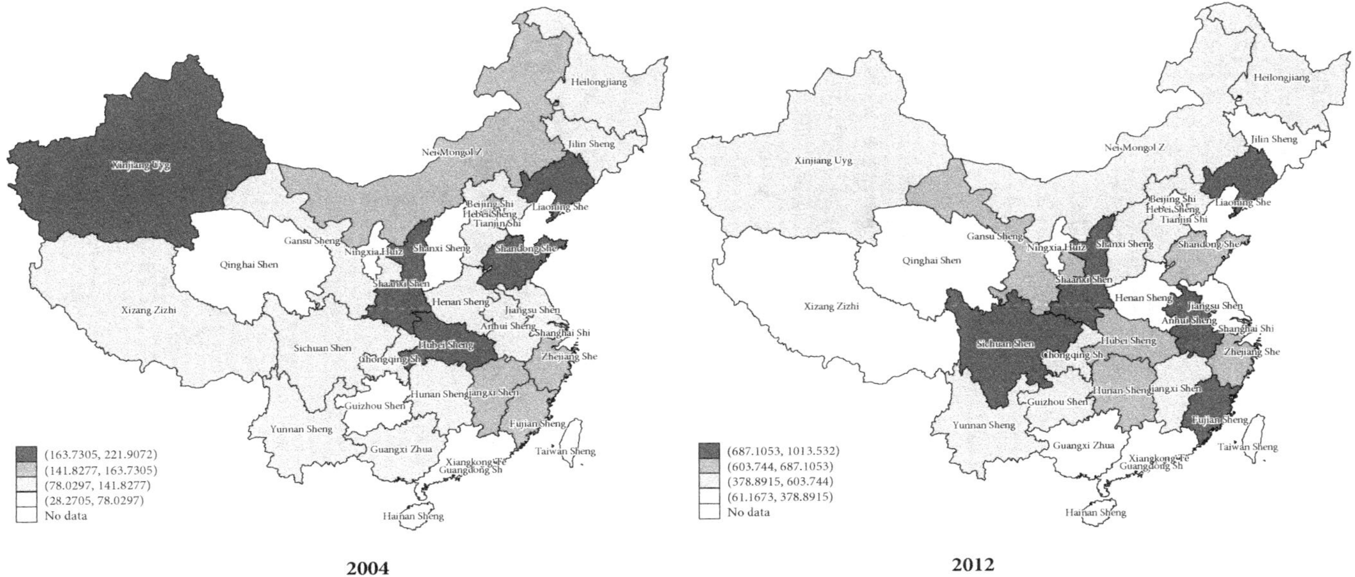

Figure 11.22. Geographic distribution of government budget, 2004 and 2012

This could be the reason why these provinces were also attracting more private capital. On the other hand, Qinghai, Shanxi, and Ningxia received much less of the government budget in all these years. Guangdong was also among the provinces receiving the lowest allocation from the government budget, the reasons for which were obviously different from the other three provinces. The incentives of allocating government budgets are complicated. Economic and political considerations are both important for the central government.

On the other hand, government transfers are usually due to political reasons. As can be seen from Figure 11.23, the western areas received the most transfers from the central government, followed by the middle areas and the east. Generally speaking, the government transfers the most to the less developed regions to balance regional differences, to decrease poverty, or to alleviate suffering from natural disasters. Of course, the amount of government transfer could also depend on the lobbying ability of the local government.

Figure 11.24 shows the geographic distribution of central government transfers per capita in each province. It shows that central government transfers flow mainly into the inland provinces, and this pattern is reinforced from 2000 to 2011. In addition, it can be seen that in 2011 the government transferred more into the north-east areas, especially Heilongjiang and Jilin provinces. All these trends are consistent with government policies of moving to the west and resuscitating the old industrial areas in the north-east. Both Figures 11.23 and 11.24 show that the incentive of government transfer is different from private capital, both domestic and foreign.

Furthermore, we compare the direction of the flows of FDI and government transfers by looking at their relationship with the degree of local urbanization. Figure 11.25 shows that the proportion of central government transfers in total local government revenue was higher in the provinces with lower urbanization rates. This supports our conjecture that government transfers tend to be used for

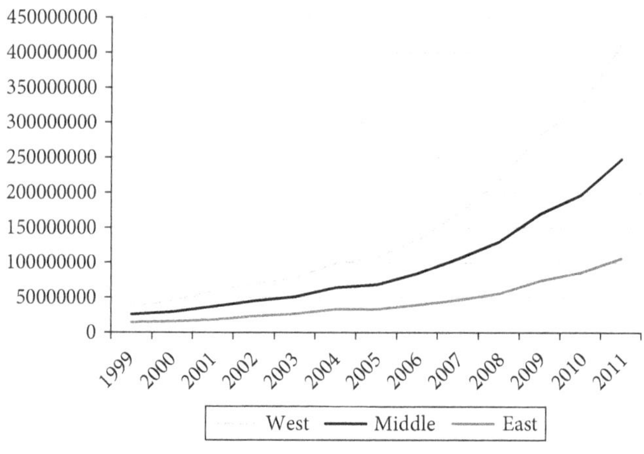

Figure 11.23. Central government transfers, 1999–2011

Source: China Statistical Yearbook (2000–12), National Bureau of Statistics of China.

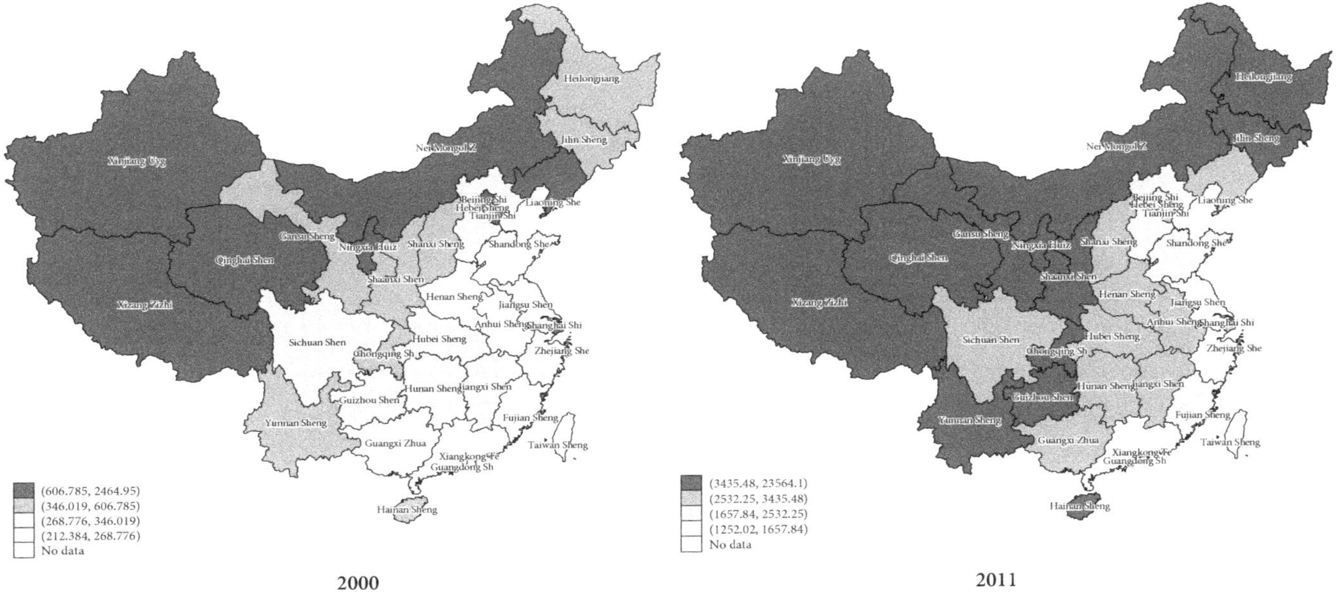

Figure 11.24. Distribution of central government transfers, 2000 and 2011

Source: *China Statistical Yearbook* (2000–12), National Bureau of Statistics of China.

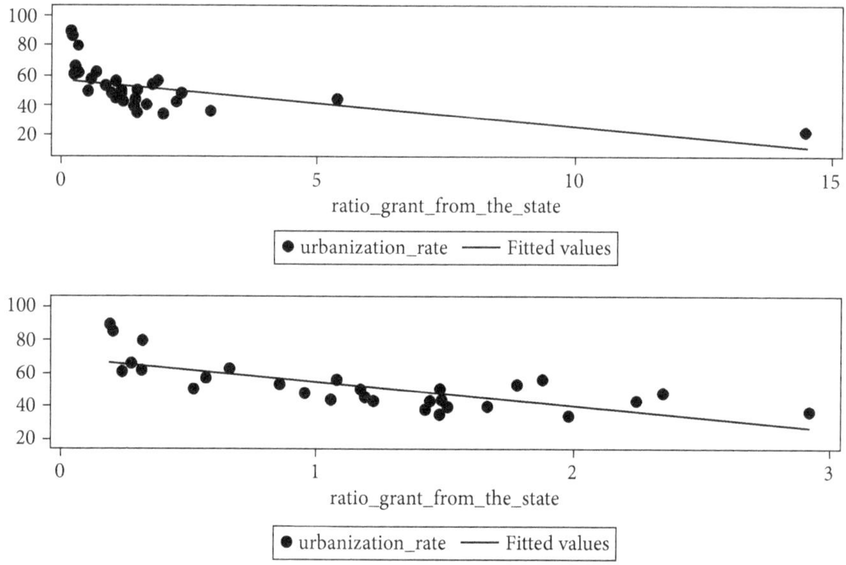

Figure 11.25. Urbanization rate and government transfers, 2010

Note: The vertical axis is the urbanization rate, which is calculated from the 2010 census; the horizontal axis is the ratio of central government transfer to local fiscal income.

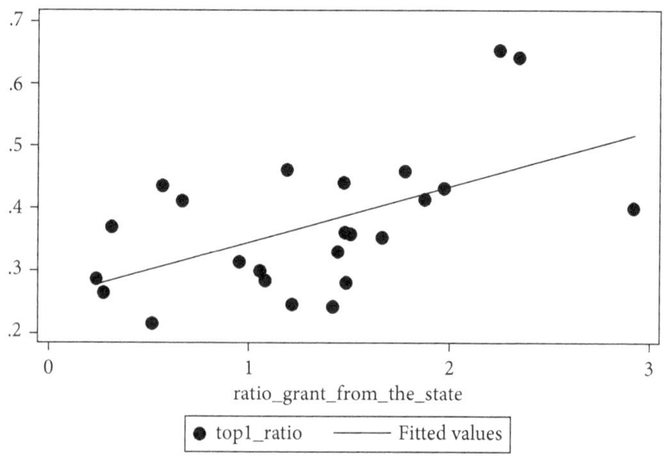

Figure 11.26. Population in the primary city and government transfers, 2010

Note: The vertical axis is the primary ratio, that is, urban population in the largest city divided by the total urban population in the province; the horizontal axis is the ratio of central government transfer to local fiscal income.

balancing regional gaps and helping alleviate poverty. On the other hand, as seen earlier in Figure 11.9, FDI mainly flows to the provinces with a higher degree of urbanization.

We also examine the impact of government transfers on the pattern of urbanization at the province level. One important feature of urbanization is the size of the primary city in each province. Primary ratio, defined as the population ratio of the primary city in the total city, is a measure of the distribution of the size of cities. Figure 11.26 shows the relationship between primary ratio and government transfers. It can be seen that a higher dependence on government funding is connected with a higher primary ratio. Primary ratio tends to be higher in the western provinces, where the per capita income is much lower than in other areas. This is consistent with the argument that government transfers are used to decrease cross-regional inequality. It is also possible that a potential proportion of government transfers was used to promote the development of the primary city, which could lead to a higher primary ratio.

11.5.3 Local Government Debts

In recent years, local government debt has kept surging over time. Local governments raise money through borrowing. There are several instruments that local governments can use: bank loans, local government bonds, build-and-transfer financing, and trust financing. In 2013, the National Audit Office of the PRC conducted a nationwide audit on local government debts. By 30 June 2013, the total local government debt reached almost RMB 11,000 billion, which is more than 20 per cent of the total GDP of the PRC in 2013. The total central government debt was RMB 9,813 billion. In addition, there was around RMB 2,666 billion in debt guaranteed by local governments.

Figure 11.27 shows the composition of the local government debt by level. City governments account for 45 per cent of the total local government debt, followed by counties (36 per cent) and provinces (16 per cent). More than 50 per cent of local government debt came from bank loans, and build-and-transfer financing and government bonds account for another 20 per cent of local government debt. About 37 per cent of local government debt was used in municipal construction, 16 per cent was spent on land acquisition and reservation, and 13.5 per cent was used in transportation construction.

Figure 11.28 shows the geographic distribution of government debts in 2013. It can be seen that government debts are very unevenly distributed across regions. Guangdong, Liaoning, Jiangsu, and Sichuan were the four provinces with the highest amount of total government debts. In addition, it should be noticed that the middle and western provinces such as Hubei, Guizhou, and Chongqing also borrowed a substantial amount. Figure 11.29 shows the government debt–GDP ratio for each province. The ratios for the middle and western provinces are much higher than those for the coastal provinces. This is consistent with the findings in Lu and Xiang (2014), which pointed out that there is an increasing trend in the percentage of debts issued by the inland provinces. In 2012, the number reached over 50 per cent, while these provinces accounted only 41.5 per cent of the total GDP. These inland provinces could try to catch up by borrowing and investing more.

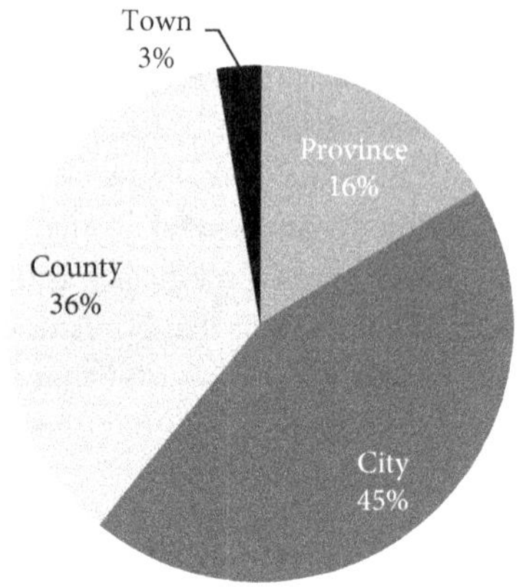

Figure 11.27. Composition of local government debt
Source: All data on debt come from the National Audit Office of the PRC.

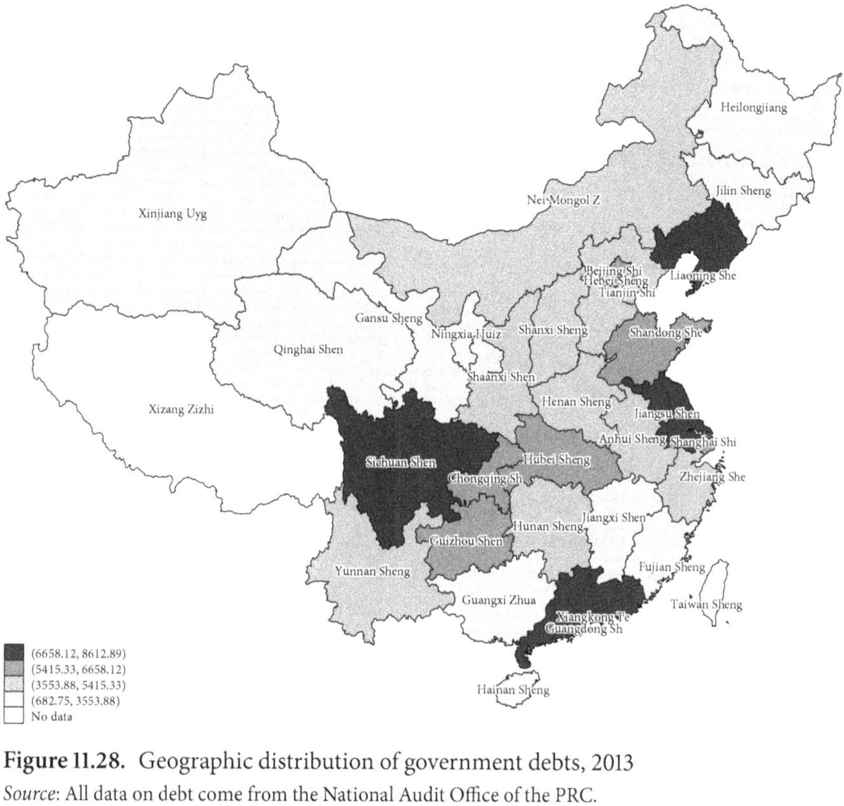

Figure 11.28. Geographic distribution of government debts, 2013
Source: All data on debt come from the National Audit Office of the PRC.

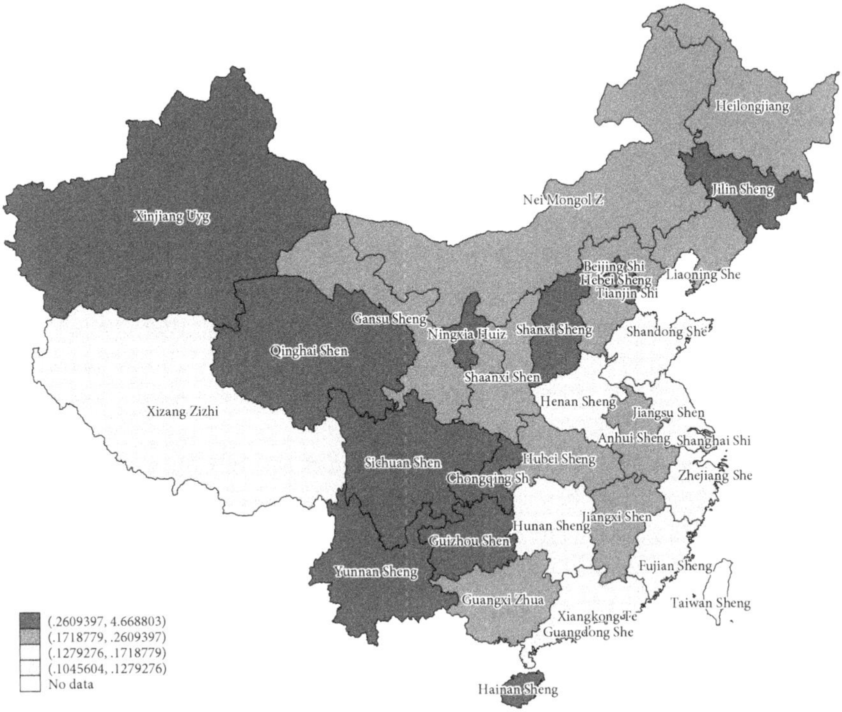

Figure 11.29. Government debt–GDP ratio, 2013
Source: All data on debt come from the National Audit Office of the PRC.

Why were local governments so keen on borrowing? Fan and Mo (2014) argue that government debt has a 'double investment-inducing effect'. Not only can it be used as a kind of investment and to increase local output, it also attracts investment by lowering industrial land costs and promoting infrastructure investment. However, there is a higher potential risk of this massive borrowing behaviour, since the main channel for local governments to repay their debt is the revenue from selling land. Fan and Mo (2014) point out that different types of cities might face different risks. For example, cities with less land endowments might find it more difficult to raise money from selling land to cover their debts, while cities with abundant land might sell too much land for industrial use and leave limited land for residential uses, pushing up housing prices.

11.6 Policy Recommendations

First, policies that conflict with market incentives should be removed. From the preceding analysis, it can be seen that both FDI and private domestic capital flow to the most profitable regions. This is consistent with market forces. At the same time, central government has focused on closing the cross-regional gaps in development. While this is definitely helpful for the development of the middle and western areas, efficiency of capital, in terms of value-added and job creation, should still be considered. Otherwise, the misallocation of capital can cause long-term distortions in the whole economy. If the coastal provinces can use more capital efficiently by creating more jobs and higher value-added, there is no reason for the government to ignore the advantages of this region.

As discussed in Lu and Xiang (2014), there are two ways to close the regional gaps in development: one is to move capital and the other is to let the labour move. Since 2003, the government's policies have focused on moving both public and private capital to the middle and western regions. While these policies are efficient in balancing regional differences in development, both productivity and resource allocation efficiency could worsen due to the distortions in capital and land allocation. As recommended by Lu and Xiang (2014), policies on promoting the movement of labour to the more efficient regions should be considered to avoid the slowing of growth and development.

Second, the government's role should focus on the provision of public goods, such as roads, education, public services, and protection of property rights. Currently, most of the FDI attraction policies focus on reducing the short-run costs of firms, such as tax reduction and free or cheap land policies. These could make some regions in the middle and western areas seem attractive for FDI firms in the short term. However, in order to avoid the flight of capital in the long run, infrastructure, human capital, and public services—which make workers live more comfortably—need to be promoted. The moving costs of workers could be much lower than firms. Therefore, it is easier for good workers to move across regions. The government needs to pay more attention to attracting not only good firms but also good workers. It has been documented that the living costs in coastal areas are much higher than inland provinces. Why, then, do most workers still want to stay in the former? They must enjoy some other benefits, such as good education for children or a more convenient life. When workers are not ready to move, the moving costs for firms would be much higher.

Third, policies that facilitate sustainable FDI inflows should be promoted. In the past, in order to attract more FDI local governments could adopt aggressive policies such as lower environmental restrictions on FDI firms, low land prices, and high tax reductions. While these policies are effective in attracting more capital investment in the short run, what will happen if these favourable policies are removed due to serious pollution and high government debts? How long can these favourable policies last? The government needs to conduct greener capital attraction policies. Only in this way can FDI or private capital lead to sustainable urban growth and urbanization.

Acknowledgements

I am grateful to the comments from all the Chinese and Indian colleagues working on this project, especially Ming Lu and Guanghua Wan for their detailed suggestions. Thanks also to Lu Li, Ziyuan Liu, Fang Zhao, and Chaowen Yuan for their assistance in completing this chapter. All remaining errors are the author's.

Appendix

Table A.11.1. Effect of Tax Rate on FDI

	(1)	(2)
	Model 1	**Model 2**
diff of direct tax	2.786***	1.760**
	(34.19)	(2.13)
lag diff of direct tax	2.234***	1.394*
	(28.76)	(1.81)
real gov expense per capita	0.003***	0.000
	(14.09)	(0.20)
lag real gov expense per capita	0.002***	−0.003
	(11.42)	(−0.37)
road per capita	0.003***	0.022***
	(6.16)	(2.22)
real gdp per capita	6.499***	22.99***
	(33.43)	(5.91)
FDI capital	3.16^{−10}***	−9.91^{−9}***
	(3.97)	(−3.20)
firm_agg_ratio	50.68***	68.19**
	(57.10)	(1.91)
lag firm_agg_ratio	24.34***	103.3**
	(26.16)	(2.78)
Region Fix effect	Yes	Yes
Year Fix effect	Yes	Yes
Constant	2.786***	1.333***
	(104.72)	(5.61)
R^2	0.732	0.503
Log likelihood	−74816.87	–
Observations	1,402	1,402

Notes: The data come from the Annual Survey of Manufacturing Firms (2000–7); t-statistics are reported in brackets; *** $p < 0.01$, ** $p < 0.05$, * $p < 0.1$. The following empirical model is established to investigate the impact of income tax on FDI flows

$$FDI_{it} = \alpha_1 TAX_{it} + \alpha_2 TAX_{it-1} + \beta_1 X_{it} + \beta_2 X_{it-1} + \lambda_t + \theta R + \varepsilon_{it}$$

where i and t represent city and year respectively. FDI is can be measured by the actual amount of FDI invested in the city in the corresponding year (column 1) or the number of FDI contracts signed (column 2). TAX represents the income tax difference in FDI firms and domestic firms.

Table A.11.2. FDI and development

	1	2	3	4
	OLS	OLS	RE	FE
lnFDI	0.063***	0.039***	0.041***	0.030**
	[0.009]	[0.010]	[0.011]	[0.013]
Ln(non-ag-pop)	0.315***	0.255***	0.235***	0.093**
	[0.021]	[0.022]	[0.028]	[0.044]
Ln(fixed investment)	0.402***	0.406***	0.397***	0.171***
	[0.032]	[0.034]	[0.037]	[0.038]
Ln(expend. on tech)	0.092***	0.096***	0.117***	0.091***
	[0.008]	[0.011]	[0.014]	[0.024]
Ln(expend. On edu)	0.083***	0.190***	0.170***	0.071***
	[0.009]	[0.023]	[0.020]	[0.024]
Ln(road per capita)	0.036*	0.053***	0.023	−0.026
	[0.020]	[0.020]	[0.034]	[0.049]
Constant	5.540***	5.225***	5.391***	10.044***
	[0.261]	[0.288]	[0.299]	[0.654]
Obs	2,228	2,228	2,227	524
R-squared	0.869	0.878	0.877	0.968
No. of cities	302	302	302	295

Notes: The data come from the China City Yearbook (2002–12); robust standard errors in brackets; columns 1 and 2 are pooled OLS results; random effect and fixed effect results are reported in columns 3 and 4 respectively; *** $p < 0.01$, ** $p < 0.05$, * $p < 0.1$. The empirical framework is as follows:

$$y_{it} = \alpha_1 fdi_{it} + \alpha_2 fixed\_invt_{it} + \alpha_3 nap_{it} + \alpha_4 edu_{it} + \alpha_5 tec_{it} + \alpha_6 road_{it} + e_{it},$$

where all of the variables are taken in natural logarithm, *i* represents city, *t* is year, and *y* is GDP; fixed_invt represents total fixed investment; nap is non-agriculture population; edu stands for government expenditure on education; and tec is government expenditure on technology.

Table A.11.3. Number of manufacturing firms

	2000	2001	2002	2003	2004	2005	2006	2007
Number of foreign firms	17,985	20,557	22,812	26,448	40,358	40,333	43,929	48,942
Number of domestic firms	137,110	142,070	152,417	165,026	230,898	226,329	252,347	284,940

Notes: The data come from the Annual Survey of Manufacturing Firms (2000–7). Only firms with total revenue higher than 5 million RMB are included; foreign firms are those with foreign capital higher than 50 per cent.

Table A.11.4. Summary statistics of capital/labour

	Domestic firms		Foreign firms	
	Mean	Std. Err.	Mean	Std. Err.
2000	51.31	0.51	181.54	6.00
2001	56.20	0.60	177.04	4.45
2002	62.37	1.16	176.69	4.93
2003	64.66	0.72	177.50	4.75
2004	78.15	1.87	170.56	3.33
2005	82.28	2.49	169.63	3.12
2006	88.55	2.12	179.73	2.86
2007	94.36	1.82	197.71	3.96

Notes: The data come from the Annual Survey of Manufacturing Firms (2000–7). Only firms with total revenue higher than 5 million RMB are included; foreign firms are those with foreign capital higher than 50 per cent.

Table A.11.5. FDI and job creation

	(1)	(2)	(3)
Lagged capital intensity	0.041***	0.041***	0.041***
	(0.000)	(0.000)	(0.000)
Lagged labour productivity	0.044***	0.044***	0.044***
	(0.000)	(0.000)	(0.000)
Lagged employment	−0.056***	−0.056***	−0.056***
	(0.000)	(0.000)	(0.000)
Lagged Herfindahl index	−0.062	−0.138**	−0.137**
	(0.055)	(0.056)	(0.056)
Lagged foreign share of capital	0.008***		0.008***
	(0.002)		(0.002)
Lagged FDI intensity		0.044***	0.043***
		(0.006)	(0.006)
Constant	−0.086***	−0.097***	−0.094***
	(0.003)	(0.004)	(0.004)
Year fixed effect	Yes	Yes	Yes
Regional fixed effect	Yes	Yes	Yes
Industry fixed effect	Yes	Yes	Yes
Observations	1,023,448	1,023,448	1,023,448
R-squared	0.067	0.067	0.067

Notes: Standard errors in parentheses; *** $p < 0.01$, ** $p < 0.05$, * $p < 0.1$. The empirical framework follows the Karlsson et al. (2009).

$$\begin{aligned}\Delta y_{it} &= \ln y_{it} - \ln y_{it-1} \\ &= \alpha + \beta FDI_{it-1} + \gamma X_{it-1} + Year + Region + Industry + \epsilon_{it},\end{aligned}$$

where i is the index for firms, t represents for time, r stands for region, y is firm employment, and j is the industry index. Capital intensity is measured by the ratio of real capital stock to number of employees. Labour productivity is the ratio of real value-added to the number of employees. All the variables except ratios are in logarithm forms. The data used are from the Annual Manufacturing Survey (1999–2007).

References

Basu, P., and A. Guariglia. 2007. 'Foreign Direct Investment, Inequality and Growth'. *Journal of Macroeconomics 29*: 824–39.

Bhagwati, Jagdish N. 1994. 'Free Trade: Old and New Challenges'. *The Economic Journal 104* (423): 231–46.

Blalock, Garrick and Paul J. Gertler. 2008. 'Welfare Gains from Foreign Direct Investment through Technology Transfer to Local Suppliers'. *Journal of International Economics 74* (2): 402–21.

Buyanov, Vladimir. 2011. 'BP: Statistical Review of World Energy 2011'. *Economic Policy 4*: 38–55.

Diamond, Charles A. and Curtis J. Simon. 1990. 'Industrial Specialization and the Returns to Labor'. *Journal of Labor Economics 8* (2): 175–201.

Du, Julan, Yi Lu, and Zhigang Tao. 2008. 'Economic Institutions and FDI Location Choice: Evidence from US Multinationals in China'. *Journal of Comparative Economics 36* (3): 412–29.

Duranton, G. and D. Puga. 2004. 'Micro-foundations of Urban Agglomeration Economies'. In *Handbook of Regional and Urban Economics*, vol. 4, edited by J. V. Henderson and J. F. Thisse, Elsevier.

Elliott, Robert J. R. Puyang Sun, and Siyang Chen. 2013. 'Energy Intensity and Foreign Direct Investment: A Chinese City-level Study'. *Energy Economics 40* (C): 484–94.

Ellison, G. and E. Glaeser. 1999. 'The Geographic Concentration of an Industry: Does Natural Advantage Explain Agglomeration?' *American Economic Association Papers and Proceedings 89*: 311–16.

Fan, Jianyong and Jiawei Mo. 2014. 'Local Government Debt, Land Market Institution and Regional Industrial Growth'. *Economic Research Journal 49* (1): 14.

Ge, Ying. 2009. 'Globalization and Industry Agglomeration in China'. *World Development 37* (3): 550–9.

Havranek, Tomas and Zuzana Irsova. 2011. 'Estimating Vertical Spillovers from FDI: Why Results Vary and What the True Effect Is'. *Journal of International Economics 85* (2): 234–44.

Huang, Shuo. 2009. 'Foreign Direct Investment and Regional Growth in China'. *Proceedings of the German Development Economics Conference, Frankfurt.009*, No. 14.

Jaffe, Adam B., Manuel Trajtenberg, and Rebecca Henderson. 1993. 'Geographic Localization of Knowledge Spillovers as Evidenced by Patent Citations'. *Quarterly Journal of Economics 108* (3): 577–98.

Javorcik, Beata Smarzynska. 2004. 'Does Foreign Direct Investment Increase the Productivity of Domestic Firms? In Search of Spillovers through Backward Linkages'. *American Economic Review 94* (3): 605–27.

Javorcik, Beata Smarzynska and Mariana Spatareanu. 2008. 'To Share or Not to Share: Does Local Participation Matter for Spillovers from Foreign Direct Investment?' *Journal of Development Economics 85* (1–2): 94–217.

Jovanovic, Boyan and Rafael Rob. 1989. 'The Growth and Diffusion of Knowledge'. *Review of Economic Studies 56* (4): 569–82.

Karlsson, Sune, Nannan Lundin, Fredrik Sjöholm, and Ping He. 2009. 'Foreign Firms and Chinese Employment'. *The World Economy 32* (1): 178–201.

Keller, Wolfgang. 2004. 'International Technology Diffusion'. *Journal of Economic Literature 42* (3): 752–82.

Kim, Sukkoo. 1995. 'Expansion of Markets and the Geographic Distribution of Economic Activities: The Trends in U.S. Regional Manufacturing Structure, 1860–1987'. *Quarterly Journal of Economics 110* (4): 881–908.

Li, Ben and Yi Lu. 2009. 'Geographic Concentration and Vertical Disintegration: Evidence from China'. *Journal of Urban Economics 65* (3): 294–304.

Li, Yongyou and Kunrong Shen. 2008. 'Competition among Jurisdictions, Strategical Fiscal Policies, and Regional Characteristics of FDI's Growth Achievements'. *Economic Research Journal* 5: 58–69.

Lin, Shu-Chin, Dong-Hyeon Kim, and Yi-Chen Wu. 2013. 'Foreign Direct Investment and Income Inequality: Human Capital Matters'. *Journal of Regional Science 53* (5): 874–96.

Liu, Zhiqiang. 2008. 'Foreign Direct Investment and Technology Spillovers: Theory and Evidence'. *Journal of Development Economics 85* (1–2): 176–93.

Lu, Ming and Haijun Ou. 2011. 'High Growth and Low Employment: An Empirical Research on Government Intervention and Elasticity of Employment'. *World Economy 12*: 3–31.

Lu, Jiangyong and Zhigang Tao. 2007. 'Trends and Determinants of China's Industrial Agglomeration'. *Journal of Urban Economics* 65 (2): 167–80.

Lu, Ming and Guanghua Wan. 2014. 'Urbanization and Urban Systems in the People's Republic of China: Research Findings and Policy Recommendations'. *Journal of Economic Surveys 28* (4): 671–85.

Lu, Ming and Kuanhu Xiang. 2014. Solving the Dilemma between Efficiency and Balance: on China's Regional Development Strategy'. *Comparative Economic & Social Systems 4*: 1–16.

Lu, Yi, Dongya Li, and Mingqin Wu. 2012. 'Industrial Agglomeration and Firm Size: Evidence from China'. *Regional Science and Urban Economics 42* (1–2): 135–43.

Melitz, Marc J. 2003. 'The Impact of Trade on Intra-Industry Reallocations and Aggregate Industry Productivity'. *Econometrica 71* (6): 1695–725.

Melitz, Marc J. and Gianmarco I. P. Ottaviano. 2008. 'Market Size, Trade, and Productivity'. *Review of Economic Studies 75* (1): 295–316.

NBSC (National Bureau of Statistics of China). Various years. *China Statistical Yearbook*, China Statistical Press.

Niu, Wenyuan, et al. 2012. *China's New Urbanization Development Report*, Science Press.

Rosen, Daniel H. and Trevor Houser. 2007. *China Energy: A Guide for the Perplexed*, Peterson Institute for International Economics.

Wan, Guanghua, Ming Lu, and Zhao Chen. 2007. 'Globalization and Regional Income Inequality: Empirical Evidence from within China'. *Review of Income and Wealth 53* (1): 35–59, 03.

Wang, Jian and Xiao Wang. 2014. 'Benefits of Foreign Ownership: Evidence from Foreign Direct Investment in China'. *Federal Reserve Bank of Dallas Globalization and Monetary Policy Institute Working Paper No. 191.*

Wang, Yong. 2013. 'Fiscal Decentralization, Endogenous Policies, and Foreign Direct Investment: Theory and Evidence from China and India'. *Journal of Development Economics 103* (C): 107–23.

Wei, Kailei, Shujie Yao, and Aying Liu. 2009. 'Foreign Direct Investment and Regional Inequality in China'. *Review of Development Economics 13* (4): 778–91.

World Bank. 2010. *Foreign Direct Investment: The China Story*, World Bank, Washington, DC.

Zhang, Jin, Lanfang Wang, and Susheng Wang. 2012. 'Financial Development and Economic Growth: Recent Evidence from China'. *Journal of Comparative Economics 40* (3): 393–412.

Zhang, Yin and Guanghua Wan. 2006. 'Globalization and the Urban Poor in China'. *World Institute for Development Economic Research (UNU-WIDER) Working Paper RP2006/42*, UNU-WIDER, Helsinki.

Zhu, Pingfang, Zhang Zhengyu, and Guolin Jiang. 2011. 'Empirical Study of the Relationship between FDI and Environmental Regulation: An Intergovernmental Competition Perspective'. *Economic Research Journal* 6: 133–45.

12

Regional and Urban Impacts of Foreign Direct Investment in India

Om Prakash Mathur

12.1 Introduction

International movement of capital has historically been an integral constituent of the global economic system. According to the United Nations Conference on Trade and Development, global foreign direct investment (FDI) flows amounted to \$1.45 trillion (1.9 per cent of the global GDP) in 2013. It projected it to rise to \$1.60 trillion in 2014 and \$1.75 trillion in 2015 (UNCTAD 2014).

Capital movements in the form of FDI flows and their rationale have been extensively studied.[1] Classical theories showed that cross-border capital flows occur due to variations in resource endowments and the differences in the rates of return on capital between capital-exporting and -importing countries. More recent work, especially that of Hymer (1976), Sen (1998), and Denisia (2010) suggested that the motivations underlying capital movements across borders are far more diverse than just the differentials in the rates of return. He identified the 'level of control' that a firm in a capital-exporting country acquires in a host country as one of the principal motivating factors.

Wheeler and Mody (1992) explained FDI flows in terms of variables, such as geographical features, labour and transport costs, and market size, and also in terms of externalities that emerge from investment in firms experiencing agglomeration economies (i.e. the clustering effects of FDI).[2] Dunning (1993) provided a comprehensive analysis of FDI, based on ownership, location, and the internationalization paradigm, and highlighted the ownership- and location-specific advantages that emerge from FDI. He classified the principal motivations of FDI into three parts: (a) resource seeking, which is promoted by the availability of

[1] International investments prior to the Second World War consisted largely of portfolio investments, i.e. funds moved from low interest rate areas to high interest rate areas. Since then, a major component of capital flows has been FDI. See Aliber (1970), Hansen and Rand (2006), Kurtishi-Kastrati (2013), and Forte and Moura (2013).

[2] According to Wheeler and Mody (1992), variables (e.g. geographical features, labour, and transport costs) are a part of the ergodic system, while factors (e.g. externalities) belong to the nonergodic system.

Om Prakash Mathur., *Regional and Urban Impacts of Foreign Direct Investment in India* In: *Cities of Dragons and Elephants: Urbanization and Urban Development in China and India. Edited by:* Guanghua Wan and Ming Lu, Oxford University Press (2019). © Oxford University Press. DOI: 10.1093/oso/9780198829225.003.0012

natural resources, cheap labour, and physical infrastructure; (b) market seeking, which looks for the host country's market size, per capita income, and market growth; and (c) efficiency seeking, in which the motivation is to rationalize investments in such a way that the firm in the capital-exporting country can gain from geographically dispersed activities.

Most scholars consider FDI to be an instrument to enhance a host country's economic growth, and it involves a transfer of capital, advanced technology, and know-how. Questions have, however, been raised about the effects of FDI on growth and the channels through which FDI leads to economic growth. Scholars, such as Denisia (2010), have concluded, after several empirical studies on the relationship between FDI and economic development, that the effects of FDI are complex.

Chowdhury and Mavrotas (2005) showed that it is not FDI that causes economic growth, but the opposite—the host country's economic growth attracts FDI.[3] In addition, according to De Mello (1997), FDI increases economic growth through capital accumulation in the host country; it increases the stock of knowledge and, consequently, results in an increase in the total factor productivity through the transfer and dissemination of knowledge.

FDI does contribute to the integration of the host country into the global economy, however. Mencinger (2003) showed a link between the increase of FDI and rapid integration into global trade. Yet FDI is also said to crowd out local enterprises and have a negative impact on economic development. In fact, Hanson considered the positive effects of FDI to be few (2001), while Lipsey (2004) concluded that there is no consistent relationship between FDI and economic growth.

Studies on the urban and spatial impacts of FDI have been few and sporadic. Brülhart's (2010) recent survey of literature on the implications of trade liberalization for international economic geography showed that (a) import restrictions tend to increase the number of cities that specialize in protected industries, implying that protectionism has spatial effects; and (b) when the Heckscher–Ohlin and Rybczynski theorems are used trade liberalization increases the number of cities that specialize in the production of capital-intensive goods if the country is relatively capital abundant and that specialize in labour-intensive goods if the country is labour abundant (Brülhart 2010). Brülhart also found that the effects of trade on urban concentration depends on a country's relative factor endowments and that trade liberalization can accentuate intranational inequalities across industries, occupational groups, and regions (Brülhart 2010).

The openness to trade and capital flows that makes markets more global also makes subnational disparities in income larger in today's developing countries.

[3] While many studies show positive effects of FDI, others point out the absence of consensus on the degree of these effects. Wang (2009) concluded that the results on the effects of FDI on growth are ambiguous.

Not all parts of a country are suited for accessing world markets, and coastal and economically dense places do better (World Bank 2008:12).

According to Brülhart, the above is representative of mainstream economic thought, because it makes two central assertions: (a) that trade liberalization increases within-country spatial inequality, and (b) that it favours regions with better access to international trade routes (2010).

Noting that trade openness and urbanization have grown together since the 1970s, Ramírez Grajeda and Sheldon's work (2015) in eighty-four countries concluded that main cities reduce in size and secondary cities grow when urban trade openness is increased. Thus, trade openness undermines advantages of urban concentration, and restrictive trade policies lead to the development of metropolitan cities.

This chapter examines the regional and urban impacts of FDI in India. Parallel to the trends observed globally and following the process of liberalization of India's economy—which began in 1991, comprising a shift from import substitution to export-led strategies, relaxation of foreign exchange regulations, and dismantling of the industrial licensing regime—FDI has risen phenomenally in India. In 1991, FDI amounted to $162 million in India, increasing to $27.99 billion in 2012, peaking in 2008 at $42.70 billion. The economic liberalization measures have had large impacts on FDI, as well as on indicators, such as the export and import of services and goods, stock market capitalization, and average import tariff rates (Table A.12.1).

Nunnenkamp and Stracke (2008) analysed the locational choices of foreign investors in India and found that (a) FDI flows are heavily concentrated in a few states; (b) more advanced states attract more FDI; and (c) in all estimations with overall FDI as the dependent variable, the coefficient of per capita income is significant at the 1 per cent level. Similarly, Goldar (2007), using an econometric analysis of the interregional pattern of FDI based on the location pattern of 1,000 firms of which 40 per cent were foreign,[4] found that the state pattern, as well as the city pattern, of plant location of foreign companies is similar to that of domestic companies. The econometric analysis of plant location across the one hundred largest cities in seventeen states showed that city size is an important factor influencing location decisions of industrial plants, and the presence of a metropolitan city in a state has a favourable influence (Goldar 2007). In addition, according to Morris (2007), regions with metropolitan cities have attracted the bulk of FDI in India.

Mathur (2005) explored the implications of India's post-1991 liberalization measures on India's urban areas. Using FDI data for 1991–2002 as a key indicator of globalization, he concluded that (a) the scale of globalization in India, as

[4] Defined as companies with over 25 per cent equity.

measured by FDI, has been small and has not led to acceleration in urban growth or growth of large cities; (b) globalization has not percolated to sectors such as land and water, which are crucial for freeing city economies from the rigidities of existing laws and regulations; and (c) globalization has led to a selective expansion of opportunities in trade, communications, banking, and real estate, including the development of high-quality residential and office space on city outskirts, but has not resulted in any expansion of overall employment opportunities. With the exception of new physical development and some spatial restructuring, no landmark shifts have occurred in the urban form. The changes appear to be isolated and added on, rather than signalling a structural shift in the economy of cities (Mathur 2005).

In this study, the regional and urban impacts of FDI are examined. It observes the pattern of regional distribution of FDI, urbanization, and GDP; simple regressions are run between FDI and urbanization, and FDI and economic growth. Then, it expands the examination by looking at (a) interlinkages between the regional distribution of FDI and selected demographic and economic variables, using a bivariable correlation; and (b) the determinants of FDI and the relative importance of the explanatory variables. A multiple linear regression analysis is undertaken to define the determinants of FDI across states.[5]

The study has five sections, beginning with a brief account of FDI policy in India (Section 12.2). Section 12.3 provides basic information on the scale of FDI and its sector and regional distribution, which is then analysed to ascertain the degree of linkages between them in Section 12.4. Section 12.5 analyses the determinants of FDI, and conclusions and implications for urbanization and urban policy are presented in the last section.

12.2 Foreign Direct Investment Regulatory Frameworks

Regulation of FDI is a ubiquitous practice in most, if not all, countries. Regulatory frameworks relate mostly to sector-specific limitations on FDI, the degree of control and ownership allowed to foreign investors, repatriation of dividends and earnings, conditions of entry, performance requirements, and miscellaneous entry and procedural rules. While the purpose underlying regulatory frameworks is to create an investor-friendly environment for FDI, procedural rules impose considerable costs on the potential FDI. The World Bank (2010) found that restrictive, obsolete laws and regulations often impede FDI, and red tape and poor implementation of laws create barriers. It further noted that the purpose of

[5] Data on FDI are drawn from the Department of Industrial Promotion and Policy, government of India. Data on GDP, urbanization, and other variables are drawn from the concerned departments of the government of India.

rules and procedures should be to set efficient processes and effective institutions for fostering FDI.

FDI policies and regulatory frameworks in India are concerned mainly with sectors or activities open to FDI, limits on FDI across sectors or activities, degree of control and ownership, and entry routes and procedures.[6] Currently, all sectors are open to FDI, except those on the 'negative list'.[7] This list of eight sectors includes the lottery; gambling and betting, including casinos; chit funds; *nidhi* companies; trading in transferable development rights; construction of farm-houses; manufacturing of cigars, cheroots, and tobacco substitutes; and activities that are not open to private sector investment, such as atomic energy.[8]

FDI equity caps or limits reflect the level of control a foreign investor is permitted to exercise in a company operating within this sector. The FDI policy incorporates equity caps at four levels: 26 per cent, 49 per cent, 51 per cent, and 74 per cent. Any equity holding in excess of 25 per cent gives the right to block a 'special resolution', 49 per cent equity represents a level just short of ownership, and 51 per cent signifies ownership and a right to pass all ordinary resolutions.[9]

An entry route relates to whether FDI can be brought in via the 'automatic route' or 'government route', that is, whether prior approval of the government is necessary. The list of activities and sectors permitted under the automatic route has, in recent years, been expanded. There are conditionalities, such as a lock-in period, minimum investment, and nationality criteria on FDI in selected activities. For example, the government, faced with political resistance, has adopted a gradual approach to opening the retail sector and has simultaneously introduced specific regulations that cover issues such as the minimum amount of investment, location of operation, mode of entry, and share of local sourcing.[10]

Policies also relate to fiscal, financial, and regulatory incentives that are offered to attract FDI. Fiscal incentives are key; India offers tax incentives to encourage FDI (and also to domestic investors) in special economic zones (SEZs) and priority industries, and to promote industrialization. The SEZ Act of 2005 provides

[6] The evolution of FDI policy in India has passed through four distinct phases: (1) 1948–69, in which the Industrial Policy of 1948 outlined that the conditions under which foreign capital and enterprise may participate will be regulated in the national interest; (2) 1969–91, which witnessed the setting up of the Monopolistic and Restrictive Trade Practices Act that imposed severe restrictions on the size of operations, pricing of products, and services of foreign companies; (3) 1991–2000, in which FDI was allowed on the automatic route, up to 51 per cent, in thirty-five high-priority industries, later expanded to 111 industries with distinct caps; and (4) post-2000, in which, except for the negative list, all other activities were placed under the automatic route (DIPP 2000).

[7] Early on, the FDI policy enumerated the sectors and activities that were open to FDI. Currently, the policy lists only those sectors and activities that are closed to FDI (i.e. 'the negative list'). Other than the liberalization of FDI policy, the simplification and rationalization of FDI policy have also been important parts of the reform of the FDI policy regime.

[8] A chit fund is a kind of savings scheme in India. *Nidhi* companies refer to mutual benefit societies, which are created to cultivate the habit of thrift.

[9] The relevance of such caps has often been questioned.

[10] For further details, see Sharma and Singh (2013).

concessions for the establishment, development, and management of SEZs for the promotion of exports, and the units are eligible for a fifteen-year tax benefit in relation to export profits.[11] Several states have also introduced their own versions of SEZ policies, which relate to state-specific tax incentives. There is a high degree of interstate variation in tax and other regulatory incentives to attract FDI and domestic investments. However, such incentives are economically inefficient and often lead to misallocation of resources. Although these are supposed to be compensation for information asymmetries between the investor and host government, as well as weak infrastructure and risks, they have not been major determinants of FDI, and their cost-effectiveness has been questioned (Palit and Bhattacharjee 2008).[12]

According to the FDI Regulatory Restrictiveness Index developed by the Organisation for Economic Co-operation and Development (OECD), India is extremely closed compared to the other fifty-seven countries in its database. The index gauges the restrictiveness of a country's FDI rules by looking at foreign equity limitations, screening and approval mechanisms, restrictions on the employment of foreigners as key personnel, and operational restrictions. As a result, while the volume of FDI has seen a phenomenal rise in recent years, India's share in global FDI is less than 2 per cent of total flows (OECD 2014).

12.3 Foreign Direct Investment in India: Size, Sector, and Regional Distribution

In 1991, total FDI in India was estimated at $162 million. Since then, a significant surge in FDI flows has occurred, measuring $27.99 billion in 2012. Average FDI flows between 2007 and 2012 formed 2.16 per cent of the country's GDP, 6.96 per cent of gross fixed capital formation, and 15.5 per cent of total merchandise trade.

However, India's share in global flows was only 1.97 per cent in 2011, which is disproportionately low in relation to India's share in global GDP (2.63 per cent) and urban population (10.6 per cent) (Table 12.1). Also, in comparison with some countries—such as the United States, which accounted for 17.2 per cent of the cumulative FDI flows between 1990 and 2012, and the People's Republic of China (PRC), which attracted 9.2 per cent—India's share was a lacklustre 1.21 per cent.

[11] It includes exemption from payment of capital gains, dividend distribution tax, and interest incomes.

[12] A recent report noted: 'The main objective of special economic zone policy was to generate additional economic activity in self-sustaining industrial townships so that no extra pressure is created on existing infrastructure. These zones are supposed to promote exports and investment and create employment. An analysis of currently approved SEZs, however, shows a worrying picture of the 388 notified SEZs, less than half were exporting as of June 2014. Also, exports from SEZs seem to have plateaued.'

Table 12.1. India's share in global FDI, urban population, and GDP (%)

Share of	Years		
	1991	2001	2011
FDI flows	0.05	0.75	1.97
Cumulative FDI inflows over ten years	0.11	2.14	1.48
Urban population	9.88	10.22	10.58
GDP	1.18	1.51	2.63

Note: Cumulative FDI flows are for 1982–91, 1992–2001, and 2002–11.

Source: Author's calculations based on World Bank (nd) and UNCTAD Statistics, <http://unctad.org/en/Pages/Statistics.aspx>.

Table 12.2. Sector distribution of FDI in India, major sectors

Sectors	Cumulative FDI, 1991–1999 (Rs billion)	% Share in Total	Cumulative FDI, 2000–2013 (Rs billion)	% Share in Total
Services	389.80	18.60	4,626.00	46.30
Manufacturing and mining	1,619.60	77.30	3,863.70	38.70
Construction and real estate	–	–	1,173.40	11.70
Agriculture	87.20	4.10	327.10	3.30
Miscellaneous	–	–	6.20	0.06
Cumulative total	2,096.60	100.00	9,996.50	100.00

Source: Secretariat for Industrial Assistance, Department of Industrial Policy and Promotion, Government of India.

Table 12.2 shows that the composition of FDI in India has changed dramatically. The period 1991–9 was dominated by FDI flows into manufacturing and mining, which accounted for 77 per cent of the total FDI flows, while services measured only about 18 per cent. In the subsequent period, FDI flows to services increased phenomenally, accounting for 46 per cent of the total, while the share of manufacturing dipped to 38.7 per cent. This period also saw FDI flows into construction and real estate, which accounted for 11.7 per cent.

Further details on the sector distribution of FDI indicate that the three subsectors that accounted for the largest FDI in 1991–9 were fuel (i.e. refineries and power), telecommunications, and power; in the subsequent period these were replaced by services (i.e. financial, banking, insurance, outsourcing, research and development, couriers, and technology and testing), construction and real estate, and telecommunications. The sectors that attracted the most FDI during 1991–9 had stronger backward and forward linkages, while such linkages were weak in sectors that attracted FDI in the subsequent period (NCAER 2010). These sectors had greater capital intensity and low labour intensity. At the same time, these had higher urban and large city bias.

During 1991–9, the four states of Delhi, Karnataka, Maharashtra, and Tamil Nadu[13] accounted for 63.4 per cent of total FDI flows; 2000–12 saw a concentration of FDI in just two states, Delhi and Maharashtra, which accounted for 67.4 per cent of total FDI flows.

As evidenced by Table 12.3, the regional distribution of FDI in India is highly uneven. The nineteen states and regions of India with close to 50 per cent of the country's population accounted for only 24 per cent of FDI during the 1990s; in the subsequent decade, these states, accounting for 63 per cent of the total

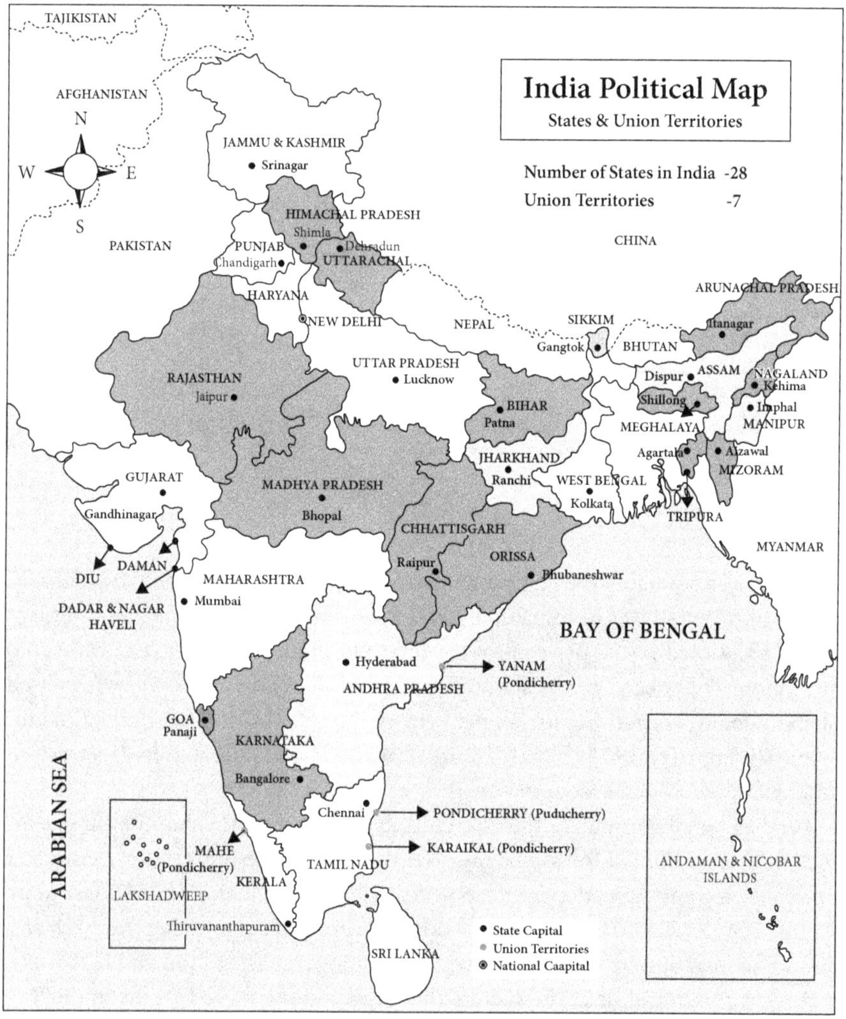

Figure 12.1. Regional distribution of FDI in India states (%)

[13] Maharashtra, Karnataka, and Tamil Nadu have long coastlines.

Table 12.3. Regional distribution of FDI inflows into India

States	1999–2000	2000–13
Maharashtra (Mumbai)	23.5	42.4
Delhi (Delhi)	18.1	25.0
Karnataka (Bangalore)	11.2	7.8
Tamil Nadu (Chennai)	10.6	8.1
Andhra Pradesh (Hyderabad)	6.8	5.4
Gujarat (Ahmedabad)	6.3	6.0
Madhya Pradesh (Bhopal)	5.1	0.7
West Bengal (Kolkata)	4.7	1.7
Odisha[a] (Bhubaneswar)	4.5	0.2
Uttar Pradesh (Kanpur)	2.3	0.2
Haryana (Chandigarh) and Punjab	2.8	0.8
Rajasthan (Jaipur)	1.5	0.5
Kerala (Kochi)	0.7	0.6
Bihar (Patna)	0.4	
Other states	1.5	0.6
Total	100.0	100.0

Note: FDI data for 2000–13 are compiled at the level of the principal city in the concerned region. Mumbai, for instance, combines the FDI flows of Maharashtra, the small Union Territory of Delhi covers parts of Uttar Pradesh adjoining Delhi, and Chennai refers to the state of Tamil Nadu and Puducherry. FDI flows are located mainly in the principal city.

[a] In 2011, the Government of India approved the name change of the State of Orissa to Odisha. This chapter reflects this change.

Source: Secretariat for Industrial Assistance, Department of Industrial Policy and Promotion, Government of India.

population, attracted just about 5 per cent of total FDI. It is important to note that with the exception of the Chandigarh belt (comprising Haryana and Punjab) and Kerala, other states in this category rank low in terms of per capita income and the level of urbanization.

All of the top six states in terms of FDI flows have at least one metropolitan city with a population greater than five million. Maharashtra, in fact, has two such cities, and the eight largest cities in India (with populations of more than four million) are all located in these seven states (see Table 12.3).[14] The presence of such cities can be construed to be vital to the location of FDI.

The National Council of Applied Economic Research (NCAER 2010) studied 1,240 FDI manufacturing plants and found that FDI in manufacturing and the services sectors are concentrated in large cities. Similarly, Ernst & Young (2012) showed that the large cities of Bangalore, Chennai, Delhi, Mumbai, and Pune alone attracted 42 per cent of investment projects, 28 per cent of the value of FDI, and 36 per cent of the jobs created by FDI in India in 2012.

[14] City size distribution of FDI is not available in India.

12.4 Urbanization and Structural Change in Periods of Increasing Foreign Direct Investment Flows

12.4.1 Urbanization

India's post-1991 urbanization is marked, most notably, by the scale of urban population change. Between 1991 and 2011, the urban population increased from 217.6 million to 377.2 million at annual rates of 2.74 per cent during 1991–2001 and 2.76 per cent during 2001–11 (Table 12.4). The net increase in the urban population during 2001–11 outstripped that in the rural population, suggesting that the future demographic change in India would be urban.[15]

Another important feature of India's urbanization is the increasing concentration of the urban population in cities with over one million people. In 2001, the population of these cities was 110.2 million or 37.8 per cent of the total urban population; in 2011, the number of such cities had risen to fifty-two from thirty-five in 2001, and the population to 160.7 million, accounting for 42.6 per cent of the total urban population (Table 12.5). The major states, with the exception of Odisha, have metropolitan cities, which account for significant proportions of their urban population. However, the average size of a metropolitan area did not increase between 2001 and 2011.

A third feature of India's urbanization is urban population growth beyond municipal boundaries, which is setting a new trend in the spatial spread of urbanization. Urban peripheries are expanding, with a consequential decline in overall urban densities.

The seven largest cities with populations of over four million persons (i.e. Ahmedabad, Bangalore, Chennai, Delhi, Hyderabad, Kolkata, and Mumbai) have expanded outwards to become extended urban regions or urban corridors of interconnected cities and towns, exercising a degree of influence that transcends borders. Many of these corridors have emerged at the intersection between cities and their hinterlands that are neither urban nor rural in any conventional sense. These cities now occupy important positions in the larger contexts of regional networks of trade, finance, and information.

Fourth, the composition of urban population growth has not undergone any noticeable shift, indicating that economic liberalization and FDI have not impacted the various growth constituents of the urban population. Rural–urban

[15] At the same time, however, these rates of urban population change were lower than the rates registered in the two decades preceding economic liberalization. This decline at such an early stage of India's urban transition—and when factors such as relatively high GDP growth and greater openness to external trade and flow of capital and technology—has been a matter of debate, with scholars attributing it to a number of factors, such as constricted urban demand for labour, the capital-intensive nature of economic growth, a general decline observed in the manufacturing sector, and increased commuting between larger cities and hinterlands.

Table 12.4. Scale and rate of urban population change

Year	Population increase (million)	Annual exponential growth rate (%)
1981–91	58.1	3.09
1991–2001	68.5	2.74
2001–11	91.1	2.76

Table 12.5. Level of concentration of population in cities with populations over one million (% of population in metropolitan cities to total urban population)

State	2001	2011
Andhra Pradesh	39.1	38.7
Bihar	19.6	17.4
Gujarat	51.9	55.0
Haryana	17.3	15.9
Karnataka	31.7	36.1
Kerala	16.4	76.2
Madhya Pradesh	25.5	32.0
Maharashtra	56.9	58.9
Punjab	29.1	26.9
Rajasthan	17.6	30.5
Tamil Nadu	33.6	38.2
Uttar Pradesh	28.1	31.5
West Bengal	63.6	52.7
All-India	37.8	42.6

migration has been stagnant at 20 per cent—22 per cent in the total population increase. Also, the overall urban system, which is dominated by a large number of small towns and a small number of large cities, has not undergone any noticeable change during this period (Mathur 2014).

Finally, India is characterized by extreme diversity with respect to levels of urbanization and urban growth patterns. Some states, such as Goa, Gujarat, Kerala, Maharashtra, and Tamil Nadu, have attained an over 40 per cent level of urbanization and are continuing to register high urban population growth rates. The other extreme is represented by Bihar (11.3 per cent), Odisha (16.7 per cent), and Uttar Pradesh (20.8 per cent), states that have low levels of urbanization and do not display much buoyancy in urban population growth except that attained by their low urban population base.

Research on urban economic structures has suggested that urban areas are generators of income and employment, and that the urban and non-primary sector shares of GDP in most countries are higher than their population share. Recent research has also shown that the urban labour markets globally, as in India, are becoming increasingly segmented into formal and informal groups, and barriers of different kinds continue to exist that impede movement between the two (Institute for Human Development 2014).

12.4.2 Gross Domestic Product

India has also witnessed rapid growth in its GDP during the past two decades, a trend that first arose in the 1980s and picked up pace in the latter half of the 1990s until 2008 (Table 12.6. The average rate of GDP growth was close to 8.0 per cent; since 2008, it has fallen to 5.3 per cent. Despite the slowdown, during 2001–2011, the growth rate was 7.8 per cent per year. Along with the high GDP growth rate, the economy has become globally integrated, that is, imports as a proportion of GDP have vastly increased from less than 7 per cent in 1991 to 25 per cent in 2013, and exports have risen from 10 per cent of GDP to 28 per cent in 2013 (See Table A.12.1).

12.4.3 Labour Market

The two decades of growth have, however, not brought about any significant change in the composition of labour market and employment conditions. India's urban labour market is still characterized by a low worker–population ratio. The overall urban participation rate was 35.5 per cent in 2011–12, which is lower compared to the 36.5 per cent recorded in 2004–5. Moreover, while 48.9 per cent of the workforce remains in agriculture, manufacturing employs only 12.8 per cent of the labour force—the genesis of the phenomenon of jobless growth. Finally, the

Table 12.6. Economic restructuring: change in the structure of GDP, all India (%)

Sector	1993–4	2011–12
Agriculture and allied services	28.4	14.1
Mining and quarrying	3.3	2.1
Manufacturing	14.6	15.7
Electricity, gas, and water supply	2.2	1.9
Construction	6.6	7.9
Trade, hotels, and restaurants	12.6	16.9
Transport, storage, and communications	5.5	10.6
Financing, real estate, and business services	13.3	18.1
Community, social, and personal services	13.5	12.8
Total	100.0	100.0

Sources: Central Statistical Organization. Various Issues. National Accounts Statistics.

Table 12.7. Economic restructuring: change in the proportion of the workforce, all India (%)

Sector	1993–4	2011–12
Agriculture, forestry, and fishing	64.8	48.9
Mining and quarrying	0.7	0.5
Manufacturing	10.5	12.8
Electricity, gas, and water supply	0.4	0.4
Construction	3.1	10.6
Trade, hotels, and restaurants	7.4	11.4
Transport, storage, and communications	2.8	4.4
Other services	10.3	10.9
Total	100.0	100.0

Source: National Sample Survey Organisation.

industrial structure of the workforce has not witnessed any notable shifts between 2004–5 and 2011–12, except a decline in the proportion of the workforce in agriculture and other primary sector activities (Table 12.7).

12.4.4 Regressions

In sum, the changes in urbanization, GDP, and labour force in India are not significant. GDP has unquestionably risen at rates which, in relative terms, are high, but neither these rates, composition of urbanization, nor labour market have shown any buoyancy.

Table 12.8 summarizes the state shares of FDI, urban population, and GDP, and regressions are run between FDI and urbanization, and FDI and GDP. As expected, these are positive; states with higher shares of FDI are also those that have higher shares of urban population and GDP.[16] Yet while the Mumbai and New Delhi regions have garnered large proportions of FDI relative to their population and GDP shares, the other four regions (i.e. Ahmedabad, Bangalore, Chennai, and Hyderabad) have been able to attract FDI roughly close to their shares in the urban population and GDP. Other regions have little space for FDI.

12.5 Foreign Direct Investment Linkages and Determinants

This section focuses on two exercises: (a) a bivariate correlation analysis between FDI flows and key demographic, economic, and social variables; and (b) a multiple linear regressions analysis to examine the determinants of FDI flows across states in India. Central to these exercises is the selection of variables.

[16] These results should be read with the usual caution. The R2 do not indicate any causality.

Table 12.8. Shares of FDI, urbanization, and gross state domestic product (% share)

State	FDI, 2000–2013	Urban population, 2011	Gross state domestic product, 2011
Ahmedabad	6.0	6.8	7.6
Bangalore	7.8	6.3	5.8
Bhopal	0.7	6.9	5.7
Bhubaneswar	0.2	1.9	2.7
Chandigarh	0.8	3.2	4.4
Chennai	8.2	9.5	8.6
Guwahati	0.05	2.2	2.6
Hyderabad	5.4	7.5	8.4
Jaipur	0.5	4.5	5.1
Kanpur	0.2	12.6	9.9
Kochi	0.6	4.2	3.9
Kolkata	1.7	7.8	7.0
Mumbai	42.4	13.6	15.2
New Delhi	25.0	6.7	7.6
Panaji	0.5	0.2	0.5
Patna	0.02	5.2	5.0

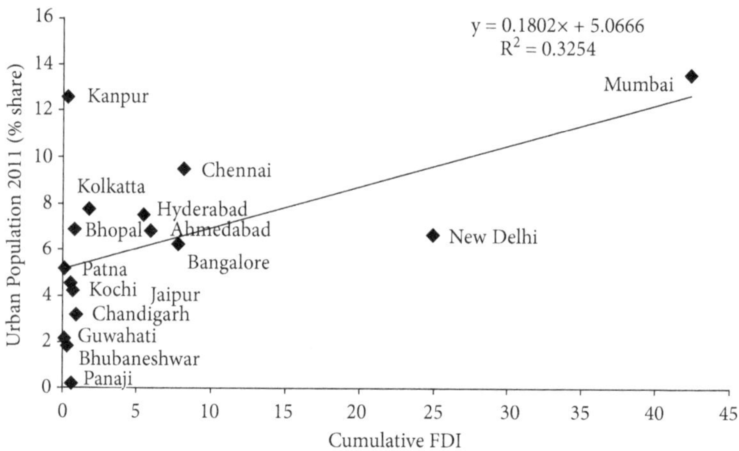

Figure 12.2. Regression: FDI and urbanization

12.5.1 Selection of Variables

Many analytical studies focus on the identification of factors affecting FDI flows within countries. A 1989 study in the United States showed that state per capita incomes, manufacturing density, and transport infrastructure are positively linked to FDI flows (Coughlin et al. 1989). Xu et al. (2008) indicated that agglomeration economies influence the location choice of FDI in the PRC, and

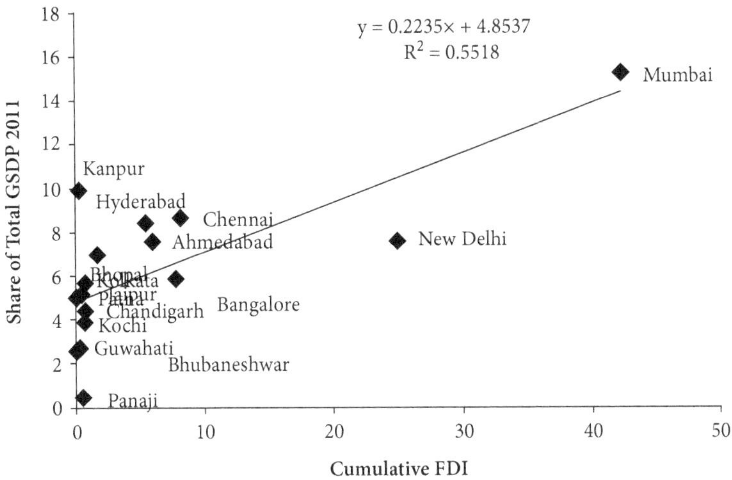

Figure 12.3. Regression: FDI and gross state domestic product
SDP = state domestic product.

cumulative FDI has a crucial demonstrative effect on the decision making of new FDI entrants. Also in the PRC, Boermans et al. (2009) found, in line with predictions, that foreign investors prefer to invest in provinces with better institutions, lower labour costs, and larger market size. In fact, much of the FDI in the PRC and India have accrued to the relatively developed regions; factors such as high per capita income, better socio-economic indicators, better infrastructural facilities, and higher international orientation in terms of per capita international trade are important in attracting FDI (Goldar 2007).

All of this evidence suggests that the most important determinants of the regional distribution of FDI flows within a country include the size and growth of the local market, level of industrial activity, growth of the services sector, availability of quality infrastructure, labour market conditions, policy environment and tax incentives, and presence of agglomeration economies and metropolitan cities. This study draws on the conclusions reached in these studies and examines the interlinkages between FDI inflows and selected variables. The categories of variables are given in Table 12.9.

Multiple sources were used to obtain the data on the explanatory variables: the census for population (MOHA 2011), National Accounts Statistics for per capita incomes and variables relating to economic structure,[17] Reserve Bank of India (2011), road density from the Ministry of Road Transport and Highways, and teledensity from the Telecom Regulatory Authority of India. Raw data on these variables are in Tables A.12.2 and A.12.3 in the Appendix.

[17] Reserve Bank of India, *Handbook of Statistics on Indian Economy.*

Table 12.9. Explanatory variables used in the econometric analysis

Block	Variable	Code
Urbanization and agglomerative economies	% urbanization level, 2011	URBLEVEL 2011
	% urbanization level, 2001	URBLEVEL 2001
	% annual exponential growth rate of urban population, 2001–11	AEGR 2001–2011
	% metropolitan population to total population, 2011	METRO 2011
	% city population to total population, 2011	CITY 2011
	Per capita real estate output (Rs) 2011–12	PCREALESTATE 2011
Market size and economic growth	Population density	POPDENSITY 2011
	Per capita net state domestic product	PCNSDP 2011
	% annual average growth in per capita net state domestic product, 2004–13	GROWTH-PCNSDP 2004–2013
Natural resources endowment	Per capita mining output, 2011–12	PCMINING 2011
Economic activity orientation	Per capita manufacturing sector output, 2011–12	PCMANUFACTURING 2011
	Per capita services sector output, 2011–12	PC SERVICES 2011
Social and physical infrastructure	% literacy rate, 2011	LITERACY 2011
	Road density, 2011	ROAD DENSITY 2011
	Per capita power consumption (kilowatt hours), 2011	PCPOWER CONS PV 2011
	Teledensity, 2011	TELE DENSITY 2011

12.5.2 Bivariate Correlation Exercise

Table 12.10 shows the results of the bivariate correlation exercise. The results are:

(1) there is high positive correlation between per capita FDI and urbanization levels across states for 2001 and 2011 (0.821 and 0.813 respectively, significant at 99 per cent confidence level);
(2) there is negative correlation between per capita FDI and rate of growth of the urban population across states (–0.188), but faster-urbanizing regions have not received higher levels of FDI;
(3) there is high and significant correlation between per capita FDI and the percentage of metropolitan (0.925) and city population (0.910) to the total urban population;
(4) per capita FDI and per capita real estate output are highly and significantly correlated (0.953 at 99 per cent confidence level);
(5) population density across states, taken as a measure of the market size, is highly correlated with FDI (0.960) and is a vital factor in FDI decisions;
(6) there is moderate correlation between per capita FDI and per capita net state domestic product (0.615);

(7) insignificant correlation exists between per capita FDI and rates of gross state domestic product growth; thus, while states like Bihar and Gujarat registered high-income growth rates, Maharashtra, which has a large size and market base, attracted a high proportion of FDI;
(8) there is weak and insignificant correlation among per capita, FDI, and natural resources endowment (–0.096), indicating that mining as a sector for FDI has lost out to other sectors;
(9) significantly, per capita FDI and manufacturing output are weakly correlated (0.146), and one of the significant structural changes in the economy relates to the decline of manufacturing in recent years;
(10) high and significant correlation between per capita FDI and per capita services output (0.829) suggests the rise of the services sector in the economy, consistent with economic growth and urbanization in the country being led recently by services;
(11) the literacy rate is weakly correlated with per capita FDI, suggesting that it is not an important factor in determining the location choice of FDI, nor has FDI caused any significant improvement in the stock of human capital;
(12) there is high and significant correlation between per capita FDI and indicators of physical infrastructures of road density (0.934) and teledensity (0.921); and
(13) power consumption is not a crucial variable in FDI location choices; the correlation of 0.354 is moderately and insignificantly correlated.

12.5.3 Multiple Regression Analysis

The complementary exercise to understand what determines FDI inflows across states is the multiple regression analysis. The aim is to examine the relative importance of a set of explanatory variables in determining the FDI inflows.[18] The explanatory variables consist of the urbanization index (URBANIZATION), market size index (MARKET SIZE), natural resources endowment (MINING), services sector orientation (ECOORIENTATION), literacy rate (LITERACY), and physical infrastructures index (INFRASTRUCTURE).

The results of the multiple regression analysis point out that the fitted model is a good fit, with R^2 of 0.949 and an adjusted R^2 of 0.915 (Table 12.11). On a relative

[18] Minor changes were made in the list of explanatory variables. An urbanization index was arrived at by applying the dimension reduction technique of the principal component method on the six variables listed in Table 12.9. A market size index was built on population density and per capita income. National resource increase was proxied by the per capita mining output. The services–manufacturing output ratio was taken as one of the explanatory variables and is referred to as 'economic activity orientation'. The literacy rate was taken as an outcome indicator for education. A physical infrastructure index was arrived at by using the principal component approach on the three explanatory variables as listed in the table.

Table 12.10. Bivariate correlation matrix: per capita FDI and explanatory variables

	(1)	(2)	(3)	(4)	(5)	(6)	(7)	(8)	(9)
PC FDI 2011	1	0.821**	0.893**	−0.188	0.925**	0.910**	0.953**	0.960**	0.615*
URB LEVEL 2011	0.821**	1	0.956**	0.105	0.814**	0.903**	0.898**	0.713**	0.884**
URB LEVEL 2001	0.893**	0.956**	1	−0.141	0.840**	0.902**	0.940**	0.803**	0.848**
AEGR 2001–2011	−0.188	0.105	−0.141	1	0.097	0.150	−0.043	−0.105	0.085
METRO 2011	0.925**	0.814**	0.840**	0.097	1	0.977**	0.905**	0.900**	0.547*
CITY 2011	0.910**	0.903**	0.902**	0.150	0.977**	1	0.947**	0.866**	0.692**
PC REAL ESTATE 2011	0.953**	0.898**	0.940**	−0.043	0.905**	0.947**	1	0.880**	0.759**
POP DENSITY 2011	0.960**	0.713**	0.803**	−0.105	0.900**	0.866**	0.880**	1	0.521*
PC NSDP 2011	0.615*	0.884**	0.848**	0.085	0.547*	0.692**	0.759**	0.521*	1
GROWTH PC NSDP 2004–2013	0.318	0.610*	0.529*	0.176	0.367	0.449	0.416	0.226	0.589*
PC MINING 2011	−0.096	0.241	0.177	−0.005	−0.247	−0.118	−0.011	−0.122	0.544*
PC MANUFACTURING 2011	0.146	0.550*	0.483	0.034	0.032	0.200	0.292	0.058	0.822**
PC SERVICES 2011	0.828**	0.932**	0.934**	0.044	0.756**	0.851**	0.912**	0.765**	0.944**
LITERACY 2011	0.399	0.715**	0.592*	0.485	0.534*	0.628**	0.542*	0.320	0.715**
ROAD DENSITY 2011	0.934**	0.729**	0.793**	0.016	0.905**	0.877**	0.869**	0.977**	0.556*
PC POWER CONS PN 2011	0.354	0.679**	0.645**	−0.078	0.270	0.432	0.516*	0.221	0.837**
TELE DENSITY 2011	0.921**	0.934**	0.950**	0.045	0.923**	0.963**	0.965**	0.871**	0.773**

	(10)	(11)	(12)	(13)	(14)	(15)	(16)	(17)
PC FDI 2011	0.318	−0.096	0.146	0.828**	0.399	0.934**	0.354	0.921**
URB LEVEL 2011	0.610*	0.241	0.550*	0.932**	0.715**	0.729**	0.679**	0.934**
URB LEVEL 2001	0.529*	0.177	0.483	0.934**	0.592*	0.793**	0.645**	0.950**
AEGR 2001–2011	0.176	−0.005	0.034	0.044	0.485	0.016	−0.078	0.045
METRO 2011	0.367	−0.247	0.032	0.756**	0.534*	0.905**	0.270	0.923**
CITY 2011	0.449	−0.118	0.200	0.851**	0.628**	0.877**	0.432	0.963**
PC REAL ESTATE 2011	0.416	−0.011	0.292	0.912**	0.542*	0.869**	0.516*	0.965**
POP DENSITY 2011	0.226	−0.122	0.058	0.765**	0.320	0.977**	0.221	0.871**
PC NSDP 2011	0.589*	0.544*	0.822**	0.944**	0.715**	0.556*	0.837**	0.773**
GROWTH PC NSDP 2004–2013	1	0.237	0.500*	0.511*	0.421	0.190	0.478	0.455
PC MINING 2011	0.237	1	0.889**	0.358	0.307	−0.049	0.493	0.029
PC MANUFACTURING 2011	0.500*	0.889**	1	0.628**	0.535*	0.107	0.795**	0.326
PC SERVICES 2011	0.511*	0.358	0.628**	1	0.688**	0.791**	0.687**	0.909**
LITERACY 2011	0.421	0.307	0.535*	0.688**	1	0.458	0.473	0.621*
ROAD DENSITY 2011	0.190	−0.049	0.107	0.791**	0.458	1	0.204	0.882**
PC POWER CONS PN 2011	0.478	0.493	0.795**	0.687**	0.473	0.204	1	0.530*
TELE DENSITY 2011	0.455	0.029	0.326	0.909**	0.621*	0.882**	0.530*	1

** Correlation is significant at the 0.01 level (two-tailed).
* Correlation is significant at the 0.05 level (two-tailed).

Table 12.11. Multiple linear regression model: model summary and coefficients

Model	R	R2	Adjusted R2	Std Error of Estimate	Change statistics					Durbin–Watson
					R2 change	F change	df1	df2	Sig. F change	
1	0.974[a]	0.949	0.915	1,038.21061	0.949	27.989	6	9	0.000	1.601

Predictors (Constant) = INFRASTRUCTURE, MINING, LITERACY, ECOORIENTATION, URBANIZATION, MARKETSIZE.
Dependent variable = PCFDI.

Model		Unstandardized Coefficients		Standardized Coefficients	t	Sig.	99.0% Confidence Interval for B	
		B	Std error	Beta			Lower bound	Upper Bound
1	(Constant)	7,920.739	3,653.664		2.168	0.058	−3,953.067	19,794.546
	URBANIZATION	1,706.122	1,381.887	0.478	1.235	0.248	−2,784.783	6,197.027
	MARKETSIZE	1,089.715	1,924.204	0.306	0.566	0.585	−5,163.630	7,343.061
	MINING	0.000	0.001	−0.073	−0.459	0.657	−0.002	0.001
	ECOORIENTATION	589.204	538.015	0.151	1.095	0.302	−1,159.256	2,337.663
	LITERACY	−99.457	48.761	−0.229	−2.040	0.072	−257.921	59.008
	INFRASTRUCTURE	798.124	1,916.133	0.224	0.417	0.687	−5,428.992	7,025.240

Dependent Variable: PCFDI.

scale, urbanization emerges as the most important factor in determining FDI location choices, with a standardized β coefficient of 0.478; it indicates that holding other things constant, an increase in the urbanization scenario index by one unit would result in an increase of Rs47.8 in per capita FDI. Market size index also emerges as a key factor in explaining FDI location choices; an increase in the index by one unit is estimated to result in an increase in per capita FDI by Rs30.6, holding other things constant. Natural resources endowment is found to be insignificant in explaining FDI location distribution among states.

Economic orientation in favour of the services sector is found to be a significant factor in explaining FDI across states, with an increase in the ratio by one unit estimated to result in an increase of Rs15.1 in per capita FDI. The literacy rate has no role in attracting FDI across states. Physical infrastructure is an important factor while making FDI location choices, and an increase in the physical infrastructure index by one unit is estimated to result in an increase in per capita FDI by Rs22.4, holding other factors constant.

12.5.4 Conclusion

The conclusions of the bivariate correlation and multiple regression analysis endorse urbanization as the most important variable in determining regional distribution of FDI in India. The correlation exercise indicates that out of the six variables, the degree of interlinkages is the highest for metropolitan cities and per capita real estate output across states. Market size also emerges as a crucial indicator in explaining FDI location choices. State per capita incomes have a weak role in FDI locations, and FDI inflows do not seem to propel economic growth in states.

12.6 Conclusions: Implications for Urbanization and Urban Policy

FDI flows into India have registered an impressive surge over the past two decades. Although India's share in global FDI flows, relative to its shares in the global total population (or urban population) and GDP, is small, FDI is seen as an integral part of the country's development process. Using the maxim that not all parts and regions of a country are suited for FDI, this study looks at, first, the regional and urban distribution of FDI, and second, the role of urbanization in determining the locational choices of FDI. Three sets of results stand out.

First, the regional or spatial distribution of FDI in India is highly uneven. Only four regions—centred around Bangalore (Karnataka), Chennai (Tamil Nadu), Delhi, and Mumbai (Maharashtra), three of which happen to have long coastlines—have been the principal destinations of FDI in the country. These regions account for 83.4 per cent of total FDI that accrued to India between 2000 and 2012. If regions centred around Ahmedabad (Gujarat) and Hyderabad (Andhra Pradesh) are added, the FDI proportion rises to 98.8 per cent. Notably, these states are more urbanized, have larger proportions of populations living in metropolitan areas, and have higher per capita incomes. Supplementary evidence confirms that most FDI has accrued to large, metropolitan areas in these states, clearly affirming the role of such cities as FDI locations.

Second, urbanization and allied characteristics (e.g. population density, market size proxied by per capita GDP, and infrastructure like road and teledensity) are the key determinants of FDI flows. Correlation and regression exercises carried out to determine the interdependencies between per capita state average FDI flows and a range of variables show that urbanization is the most important explanatory variable in determining FDI's regional distribution in India. The exercise shows that out of the urbanization and agglomeration economies cohort, the proportion of the population living in metropolitan areas and market size emerge as strong explanatory variables of FDI location, indicating FDI flows to India aim at market seeking.

Third, FDI has not led to accelerated urban population growth; in fact, the post-economic liberalization period has seen a deceleration in the rate of urban population growth compared with the preceding period. Nor is FDI accompanied by any noticeable shift in the urban system, which continues to be dominated by a few large cities (where the numbers of such cities have risen, but the average size has remained largely unchanged) and a large number of small cities.

Most cities in India have huge infrastructure and services deficits. One report estimated that India needs $650 billion (2009–10 prices) to offset the urban infrastructure deficits and infrastructure needs of the incremental urban population between 2011 and 2031, and the investments needed to offset the accumulated deficit and infrastructure backlogs are $206 billion (HPEC 2011). The McKinsey Global Institute (2010) estimated that India needs a capital investment of $1.2 trillion (an eightfold increase in spending from $17 per capita today to $134 per capita) and must complement this investment with strategies on improving urban governance, planning, and a major programme for affordable housing.

Other studies have identified the distorted land market as a severe constraint to urbanization and urban investments. Studies of Mumbai's land market, which is characterized by very low consumption of floor space coupled with very high real estate prices, point to supply bottlenecks. Comparing Mumbai with other Asian metropolitan cities, Bertaud (2011) identified four factors that contribute to this kind of land market distortion: (a) an exceptional topography that limits the amount of developable land, (b) a draconian and ill-conceived land policy restricting the area of floor space, (c) muddled property rights preventing free trade in land and floor space, and (d) a failure to develop primary infrastructure networks. Reaping the potential benefits of FDI, in this context, requires the elimination of various kinds of land and other market-related distortions and inefficiencies.

Appendix

Table A.12.1. Economic components of globalization in India

Indicators	1990	2000	2013
Merchandise exports			
Volume ($ million)	17,975	42,295	313,235
% manufacturing	71	79	65
Merchandise imports			
Volume ($ million)	23,642	50,455	466,042
% food	3	7	4
% fuel	27	31	43
% manufacturing	51	51	43
Exports commercial services (2012)			
Volume ($ million)	4,610	17,670	145,029
% others*	45.4	71.4	76.0
Imports of commercial services (2012)			
Volume ($ million)	5,943	19,601	128,955
% others*	35.9	45.8	43.0
Exports of goods and services			
Volume ($ million)	23,028	63,764	465,729
As % GDP	7	14	25
Imports of goods and services			
Volume ($ million)	31,485	75,656	533,217
As % GDP	10	17	28
External debt			
Volume ($ million)	83,628	100,367	427,562
Debt service as % of GNI	2.6	2.2	23.0
Debt service as % of exports of goods and services	32.4	12.8	8.6
FDI			
Volume ($ million)	162	23,152	28,153
% of world's total FDI	0.08	0.20	1.61
Gross private capital flows (2010)			
% of GDP	0.8	3.0	3.0
Stock market			
Volume ($ million)	38,567	110,396	622,479
% of GDP	6.9	48.4	33.5
Gross international reserves			
$ million	5,637	41,059	298,092
Tariff barriers (2009)			
Simple mean tariff	80.2	32.8	11.5
Weighted mean tariff	69.9	32.7	8.2

GNI = gross national income.

Table A.12.2. Statistics on key development indicators

State	Per Capita Annual Average FDI Flow, 2011–13 (Rs)	Urbanization level, 2011 (%)	Urbanization level, 2001 (%)	Annual exponential growth rate of urban population, 2001–2011 (%)	Metropolitan population, 2011 (% of total population)
Andhra Pradesh	563.53	33.49	27.30	3.09	12.85
Assam	7.70	14.01	12.90	2.44	0.00
Bihar	6.19	11.30	10.46	3.01	1.97
Delhi	14,458.36	97.50	93.18	2.36	97.59
Goa	767.86	62.17	49.76	3.01	0.00
Gujarat	710.04	42.58	37.36	3.06	23.45
Haryana	230.65	34.79	28.92	3.66	5.58
Karnataka	1,189.89	38.57	33.99	2.72	13.94
Kerala	304.97	47.72	25.96	6.56	36.36
Madhya Pradesh	121.93	27.63	26.46	2.28	8.85
Maharashtra	3,291.59	45.23	42.43	2.12	26.63
Odisha[a]	41.07	16.68	14.99	2.37	0.00
Rajasthan	52.19	24.89	23.39	2.57	7.56
Tamil Nadu	1,490.83	48.45	44.04	2.40	18.41
Uttar Pradesh	16.15	22.28	20.78	2.53	7.03
West Bengal	217.43	31.89	27.97	2.62	16.75

State	City population 2011 (% of total population)	Per capita real estate output, 2011–12 (Rs)	Population density, 2011 ('000 square kilometres)	Per capita net state domestic product, 2011–12 (Rs)
Andhra Pradesh	25.00	1,055,067	308	69,742
Assam	6.02	116,441	397	36,415
Bihar	7.04	188,412	1,102	22,913
Delhi	97.59	5,238,998	11,297	166,883

(*Continued*)

Table A.12.2. Continued

State	City population 2011 (% of total population)	Per capita real estate output, 2011–12 (Rs)	Population density, 2011 ('000 square kilometres)	Per capita net state domestic product, 2011–12 (Rs)
Goa	22.13	1,363,919	394	174,645
Gujarat	32.91	735,608	308	87,175
Haryana	24.95	1,379,842	573	107,051
Karnataka	26.80	1,545,845	319	68,227
Kerala	44.73	1,210,847	859	78,387
Madhya Pradesh	16.43	452,034	236	37,979
Maharashtra	35.40	1,936,179	365	95,339
Odisha[a]	7.98	363,457	269	41,876
Rajasthan	15.68	570,943	201	52,735
Tamil Nadu	29.37	1,380,341	555	88,697
Uttar Pradesh	14.55	371,959	828	29,785
West Bengal	23.61	579,804	1,029	54,714

Table A.12.3. Additional statistics on key development indicators

State	Annual average growth in per capita net state domestic product (at constant 2004–5 prices), 2004–13 (%)	Per capita Mining Output, 2011–12 (Rs)	Per capita Manufacturing Sector Output, 2011–12 (Rs)	Per capita Services Sector Output, 2011–12 (Rs)	Literacy Rate, 2011 (%)
Andhra Pradesh	7.06	277,892	2,284,795	4,388,227	67.7
Assam	4.32	303,744	1,118,396	2,461,915	73.2
Bihar	8.33	1,392	580,872	1,610,648	63.8
Delhi	8.01	0	3,921,951	18,312,738	86.3
Goa	8.54	4,603,589	12,459,523	12,324,066	87.4
Gujarat	8.48	229,283	4,582,521	5,083,971	79.3
Haryana	6.71	40,606	3,995,558	7,363,738	76.6
Karnataka	5.92	68,421	2,433,951	4,868,988	75.6
Kerala	7.33	61,243	2,144,892	6,258,691	93.9
Madhya Pradesh	6.84	170,784	1,462,208	2,342,293	70.6
Maharashtra	7.92	45,965	3,470,341	7,371,786	82.9
Odisha	4.40	619,162	2,108,072	2,737,644	73.5
Rajasthan	5.58	310,940	2,043,693	3,186,245	67.1
Tamil Nadu	8.56	61,428	3,300,288	5,961,867	80.3
Uttar Pradesh	4.66	27,326	895,878	1,989,598	69.7
West Bengal	5.77	33,712	1,221,979	3,896,718	77.1

(*Continued*)

Table A.12.3. Continued

State	Literacy rate, 2011 (%)	Road density, 2011 (kilometre per 1,000 sq. km)	Per capita power consumption, 2011–12 (kilowatt hours)	Overall teledensity, 2011 (telephone connections per 100 population)	Per capita transport, storage, and communication output, 2011–12 (Rs)
Andhra Pradesh	67.7	865	1,156.5	76.88	690,695
Assam	73.2	3,084	249.8	46.50	334,803
Bihar	63.8	1,388	133.6	46.53	139,298
Delhi	86.3	21,177	1,586.7	220.00	1,619,647
Goa	87.4	2,872	2,025.5	96.71	3,716,917
Gujarat	79.3	797	1,663.2	85.19	759,112
Haryana	76.6	944	1,628.3	76.72	1,172,323
Karnataka	75.6	1,470	1,081.4	91.26	549,907
Kerala	93.9	5,186	593.8	100.76	956,499
Madhya Pradesh	70.6	640	671.5	52.23	275,469
Maharashtra	82.9	1,335	1,204.4	88.75	853,927
Odisha	73.5	1,662	1,145.8	59.70	518,664
Rajasthan	67.1	705	927.4	68.31	358,668
Tamil Nadu	80.3	1,480	1,276.6	109.64	786,958
Uttar Pradesh	69.7	1,620	449.9	56.20	328,778
West Bengal	77.1	3,373	563.8	73.19	503,900

References

Aliber, Robert Z. 1970. 'A Theory of Direct Foreign Investment'. In *The International Corporation: A Symposium*, edited by C. P. Kindleberger, MIT Press.

Bertaud, A. 2011. *Mumbai FSI/FAR Conundrum*. Unpublished.

Boermans, Martijn, H. J. Roelfsema, and Zhang Yi. 2009. 'Regional Determinants of FDI in China: A New Approach with Recent Data'. *Tjalling C. Koopmans Research Institute Discussion Paper 09-23*, Tjalling C. Koopmans Research Institute, Utrecht, Netherlands.

Brülhart, M. 2010. *The Spatial Effects of Trade Openness: A Survey*. Unpublished.

Chowdhury, Abdur and George Mavrotas. 2005. 'FDI and Growth: A Causal Relationship'. *WIDER Research Paper. 2005/25*, World Institute for Development Economic Research, Helsinki.

Coughlin, Cletus Charles, Joseph V. Terza, and Vachira Arromdee. 1989. 'State Characteristics and the Location of Foreign Investment within the United States: Minimum Chi-Square Conditional Logit Estimation'. *Federal Reserve Bank of St. Louis Working Paper 1987-006B*, Federal Reserve Bank, St Louis, MO.

De Mello Jr, Luiz R. 1997. 'FDI in Developing Countries and Growth: A Selective Survey'. *Journal of Development Studies 34* (1): 1–34.

Denisia, Vintila. 2010. 'Foreign Direct Investment Theories: An Overview of the Main FDI Theories'. *European Journal of Interdisciplinary Studies 2* (2): 104–10.

DIPP (Department of Industrial Policy and Promotion). 2000. 'Ministry of Commerce and Industry, Government of India'. *Press Note No. 2 (2000 Series).*

Dunning, John H. 1993. *Multinational Enterprises and the Global Economy*, Addison Wesley.

Ernst & Young. 2012. 2012 *India Attractiveness Survey: Ready for the Transition*, Emerging Markets Center, Delhi.

Forte, Rosa and Rui Moura. 2013. 'The Effects of Foreign Direct Investment on the Host Country's Economic Growth: Theory and Empirical Evidence'. *The Singapore Economic Review 58* (03): 1350017.

Goldar, Bishwanath. 2007. 'Location of Plants of Foreign Companies in India'. Seminar on India and Globalisation: A Seminar in Honour of Professor N. S. Siddharthan, New Delhi.

Hansen, Henrik and John Rand. 2006. 'On the Casual Links between FDI and Growth in Developing Countries'. *World Economy 29* (1): p. 21.

Hanson, Gordon H. 2001. 'Should Countries Promote Foreign Direct Investment?' *G-20 Discussion Paper 9*, United Nations Commission on Trade and Development (UNCTAD), Geneva.

HPEC (High Powered Expert Committee). 2011. *Report on Indian Urban Infrastructure and Services.*

Hymer, S. 1976. *The International Operations of National Firms: A Study of Foreign Direct Investment*, MIT Press.

Institute for Human Development. 2014. *India, Labour and Employment Report 2014*, Academic Foundation, Delhi.

Kurtishi-Kastrati, Selma. 2013. 'Impact of FDI on Economic Growth: An Overview of the Main Theories of FDI and Empirical Research'. *European Scientific Journal 9* (7).

Lipsey, Robert E. 2004. 'Home-and Host-country Effects of Foreign Direct Investment'. In *Challenges to Globalization: Analyzing the Economics*, edited by Robert E. Baldwin, University of Chicago Press.

Mathur, Om Prakash. 2005. 'Impact of Globalization on Cities and City-Related Policies in India'. In *Globalization and Urban Development*, edited by H. Richardson and C. Bae, Springer.

Mathur, Om Prakash. 2014. *City Size Distribution in a Quasi-Open Economy: The India Evidence*. Unpublished.

McKinsey Global Institute. 2010. *India's Urban Awakening: Building Inclusive Cities, Sustaining Economic Growth.*

Mencinger, Jože. 2003. 'Does Foreign Direct Investment Always Enhance Economic Growth?' *Kilkos 56* (4): 491–508.

MOHA (Ministry of Home Affairs). 2011. *Census of India 2011*, Government of India, Delhi.

Morris, S. 2007. 'A Study of the Regional Determinants of Foreign Direct Investments in India and the Case of Gujarat'. *IIM Working Paper 2004/03/07*, Indian Institute of Management, Ahmedabad.

NCAER (National Council of Applied Economic Research). 2010. *FDI in India and its Growth Linkages. Sponsored study by Department of Industrial Policy and Promotion*, Ministry of Commerce and Industry, Government Of India, Delhi.

Nunnenkamp, Peter and Rudi Stracke. 2008. 'Foreign Direct Investment in Post-Reform India: Likely to Work Wonder for Regional Development?' *Kiel Working Paper 1375*, Kiel Institute for the World Economy.

OECD. 2014. *FDI Regulatory Restrictiveness Index*, OECD, Paris.

Palit, Amitendu and Subhomoy Bhattacharjee. 2008. *Special Economic Zones in India: Myths and Realities*, Anthem Press.

Ramírez Grajeda, Mauricio and Ian M. Sheldon. 2015. 'Trade Openness and City Interaction'. *The Region and Trade: New Analytical Directions*: 267–318.

Reserve Bank of India. 2011. *Handbook of Statistics on Indian Economy 2010–11.*

Sen, Hüseyin. 1998. 'Different Arguments For and Against the Role and Impact of Foreign Direct Investment on the Development Potentials of Developing Countries: An Overview'. *Journal of Economics and Administrative Sciences 13* (1): 181–90.

Sharma, Mamta and Satbir Singh. 2013. 'Foreign Direct Investment in India: Regulatory Framework, Issues and Current Status'. *International Journal of Management and Social Science Research 2* (8): 108–20.

Wang, Miao. 2009. 'Manufacturing FDI and Economic Growth: Evidence from Asian Economies'. *Applied Economics* 41 (9): 991–1002.

Wheeler, David and Ashoka Mody. 1992. 'International Investment Location Decisions: The Case of US Firms'. *Journal of International Economics 33* (1–2): 57–76.

World Bank. Nd. 'World Development Indicators'. <http://data.worldbank.org/data-catalog/.world-development-indicators>.

World Bank. 2008. *World Development Report 2009*, World Bank, Washington, DC.

World Bank. 2010. *Investing Across Borders. 2010: Indicators of Foreign Direct Investment Regulation in 87 Economies*, World Bank, Washington, DC.

Xu, Kangning, Xiuyan Liu, and Bin Qiu. 2008. 'Spatial Determinants of Inwards FDI in China: Evidence from Provinces'. In *ETSG 2009 Rome Eleventh Annual Conference*. <http://www.etsg.org/ETSG2009/papers/xu.pdf>.

PART VI
INFRASTRUCTURE

13
Infrastructure in China

Zhigang Li

13.1 Introduction

Generally, infrastructure is defined as the provision of basic services to industries and households (Lee and Martini 1996). It typically includes energy (power generation and supply), transport (toll roads, light rail systems, bridges, and tunnels), water (sewerage, waste water treatment, and water supply), and telecommunications (telephones) (Grimsey and Lewis 2002). To provide a broad picture on the development of infrastructure in the People's Republic of China (PRC), in this section, we first summarize its major trends and features in the past two decades. We then conduct a cross-country comparison to gauge the infrastructure status of the PRC. In this comparison, we shall pay particular attention to the PRC and India in their infrastructure development progress (further detail on infrastructure development and institutions of India can be found in Chapter 14). This provides supplementary information on the general comparison of the urbanization processes of these two countries, as is the major theme of this project (see Chapter 2 for a detailed introduction to urbanization in the PRC).

13.1.1 An Overview of Infrastructure Development in the PRC

Except for waterways, all types of transport infrastructure have registered growth in the PRC since 1978, especially roads, airports, and petroleum and gas pipelines. From 1978 to 2013, the length of roads, railways in operation, civil aviation routes, and petroleum and gas pipelines have increased from 0.9 to 4.4 million km,[1] from 51,700 to 103,100 km, from 148,900 to 4,106,000 km, and from 8,300 to 98,500 km respectively. Figure 13.1 shows the log lengths of alternative transportation routes, and Figure 13.2 shows their growth rates.

Among highways of different grades, expressways have grown the most rapidly. Their length increased from 100 km in 1988 to 104,438 km in 2013, showing a

[1] Until 2005, the China Statistics Yearbook did not include statistics on roads built to connect villages in the measure of road length. Consequently, reported road length increased by 1.47 million km in 2005 alone.

Zhigang Li., *Infrastructure in China* In: *Cities of Dragons and Elephants: Urbanization and Urban Development in China and India. Edited by:* Guanghua Wan and Ming Lu, Oxford University Press (2019). © Oxford University Press.
DOI: 10.1093/oso/9780198829225.003.0013

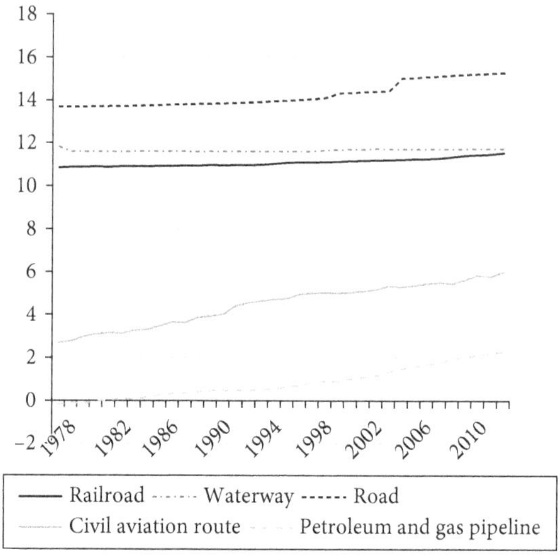

Figure 13.1. Logarithm of the length of different transport infrastructure
Source: Statistics Yearbook of China, various years.

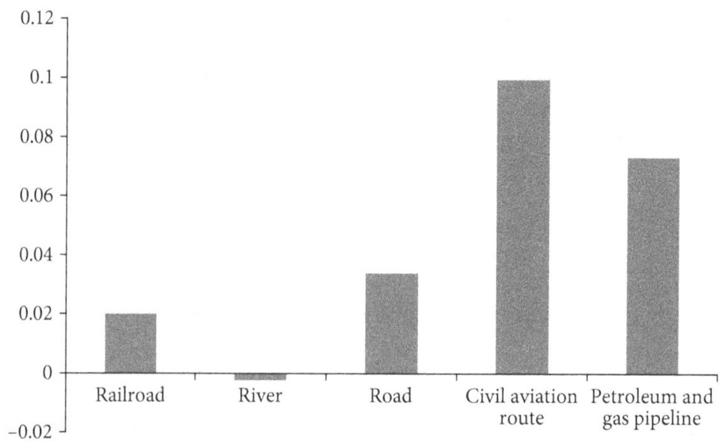

Figure 13.2. Average growth rate of infrastructure, 1978–2013
Source: Statistics Yearbook of China, various years

staggering annual compound growth rate of 32.1 per cent. In contrast, the length of all highways (excluding village roads) grew at an annual compound rate of less than 4 per cent.

As a result of the differential growth rates of different transport infrastructure, their relative share in passenger transport volume has changed significantly, as highways have overtaken railways as the most important mode of passenger transportation, accounting for nearly 55 per cent of total passenger traffic, while

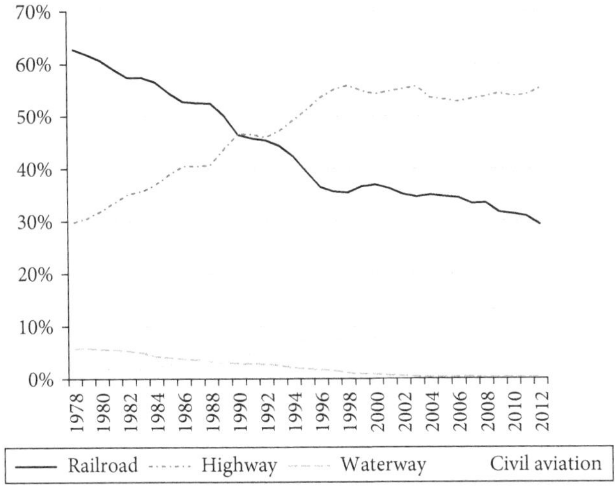

Figure 13.3. Relative importance of different infrastructure in passenger transport
Source: Statistics Yearbook of China, various years.

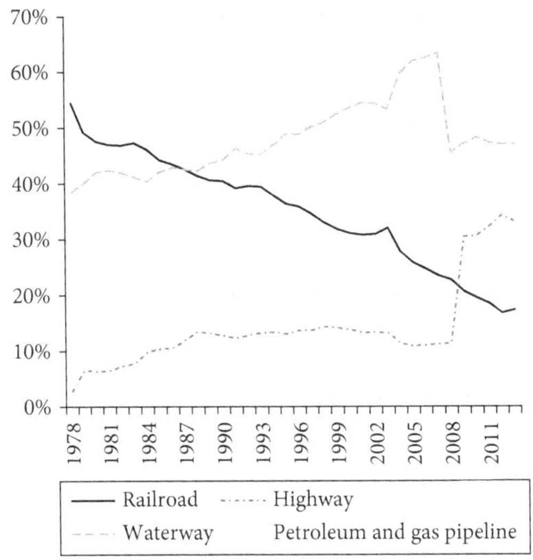

Figure 13.4. Relative importance of different infrastructure in freight transport
Source: Statistics Yearbook of China, various years.

the share of railways has declined (Figure 13.3). The importance of civil aviation has also increased dramatically (Figure 13.3).

In terms of freight transportation, the importance of railroads has also declined steadily over the past three decades, while that of highways has increased (Figure 13.4). Interestingly, there was a sudden and seemingly permanent shock to both waterway and highway shipping in 2008. It could be an impact of the global financial crisis, but we need to treat this explanation cautiously, as it could also be due to changes in statistics methodology (such as a change in the criteria for classifying transport as waterway or highway shipping in the case of the mixed transport mode).

Other than transport infrastructure, investment in electricity generation capacity has also increased steadily and rapidly, registering an average compound growth rate of approximately 9.2 per cent from 1971 to 2011 (Figure 13.5).

To provide an overview of the relation between urbanization and urban infrastructure development in the PRC, in Figure 13.6 we compare the urbanization

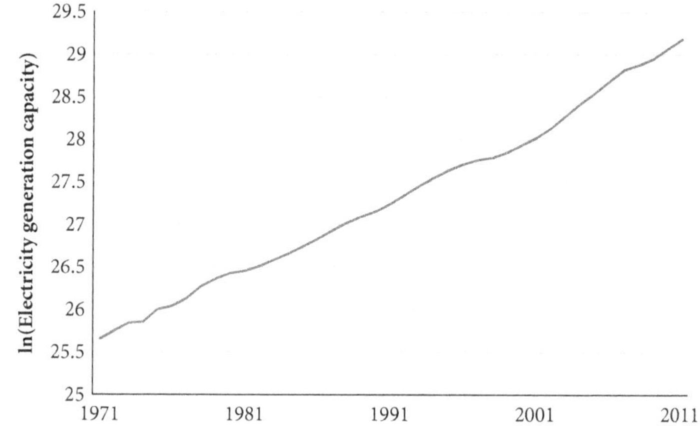

Figure 13.5. Electricity generation capacity of the PRC, 1971–2011
Source: World Development Indicators (WDI), the World Bank, various years.

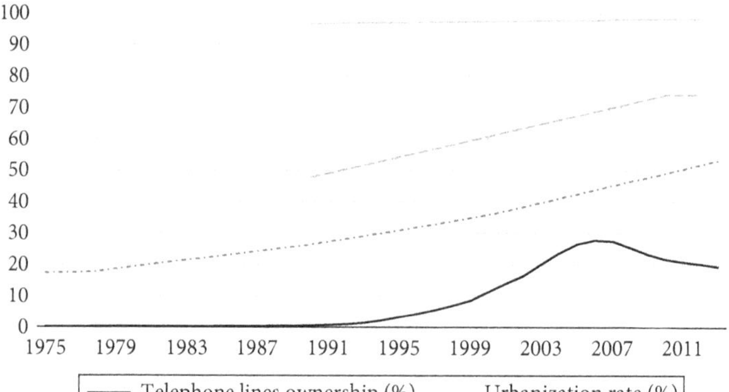

Figure 13.6. Urbanization and urban infrastructure development in the PRC, 1975–2013
Source: WDI, the World Bank, various years.

process of the PRC with telephone ownership, access to water facilities, and access to sanitation facilities in urban PRC. In general, we find that urban infrastructure in the PRC has improved with more urbanization. The improvement in urban infrastructure has been evident in telecommunication and sanitation, while water facilities of Chinese cities have improved after 1990. Note that the telephone ownership rate started to decline in the mid-2000s, which should reflect the impact of adoption in mobile telecommunication technologies.

13.1.2 Cross-Regional Distribution of Infrastructure

Given the vast scope of the PRC and its highly uneven natural and social endowments across different regions, infrastructure investment has also been highly unbalanced. Cities in the much more developed eastern region of the PRC enjoy higher levels of services across different infrastructure types, while in inland provinces infrastructure conditions are much worse.

If we take interregional transport infrastructure as an example, the majority of it connects central PRC with eastern PRC (He and Duchin 2009). In 1997, the transport infrastructure capacity between central PRC and western PRC was more than three times of that of the central-west transport capacity (Figure 13.7). This implies that the density of transport infrastructure is much higher in eastern PRC, which is endowed with less than 10 per cent of the total land area and 34 per cent of the population of the PRC. In contrast, the western region of the PRC occupies 59 per cent of the land area and 27 per cent of the population of the PRC. Nevertheless, in terms of the economic development level, the higher density of transport infrastructure in eastern PRC could be seen as reasonable, as the

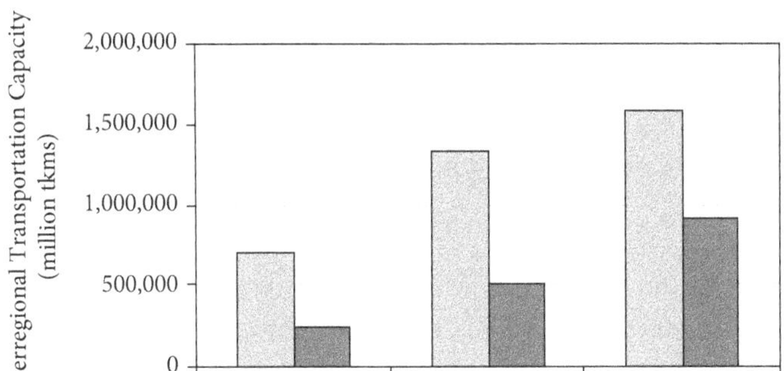

	1997	2010	2020
□ East-Center	713,971	1,322,485	1,586,981
■ Center-West	234,757	506,629	911,932

Figure 13.7. Relative transport density is unbalanced across the PRC
Source: He and Duchin (2009).

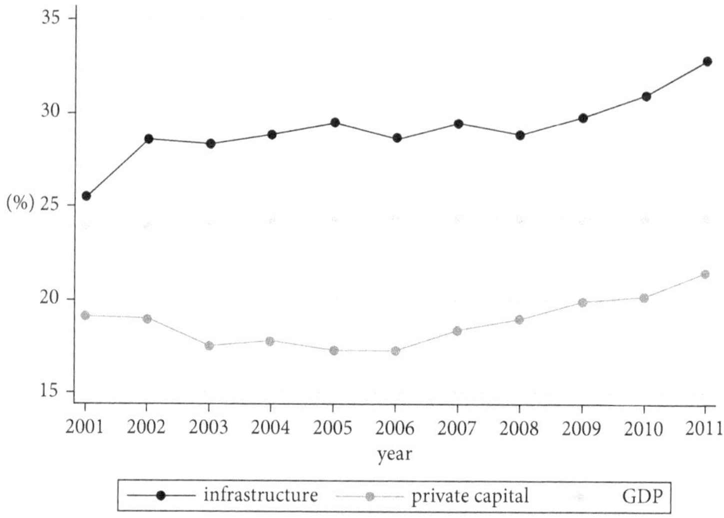

Figure 13.8. Infrastructure versus private capital investment in the western provinces, 2001–11

Note: Calculations are based on the real value of provincial infrastructure investment, private capital investment, and GDP (Shi and Huang 2014). All three lines correspond to the share of western provinces.

western region's GDP per capita was about a third that of the Eastern region (National Statistical Bureau 1998).

Over time, investment in transport infrastructure in western PRC is expected to catch up. According to the official plan, the east–west gap in transport infrastructure is expected to significantly narrow by 2020 (Figure 13.7).[2] This is consistent with the actual infrastructure investment trend, as indicated by Figure 13.8. The percentage of infrastructure investment in the western provinces has increased over the period 2001–11, exceeding the western share of private capital investment and of GDP by wide margins (Shi and Huang 2014).

13.1.3 Cross-Country Comparison of Infrastructure Development

In this section, we gauge the infrastructure development of the PRC from a global perspective. This shows us that the development of infrastructure in the PRC has been unbalanced for different types of infrastructure. Moreover, it also provides us with some insight to explain why the growth rates of different types of infrastructure since the mid-1990s have varied significantly.

[2] The future transportation capacity for 2020 is projected by He and Duchin (2009) based on the National Trunk Expressway Network Plan (Ministry of Communications 2004; Ministry of Railways 2005).

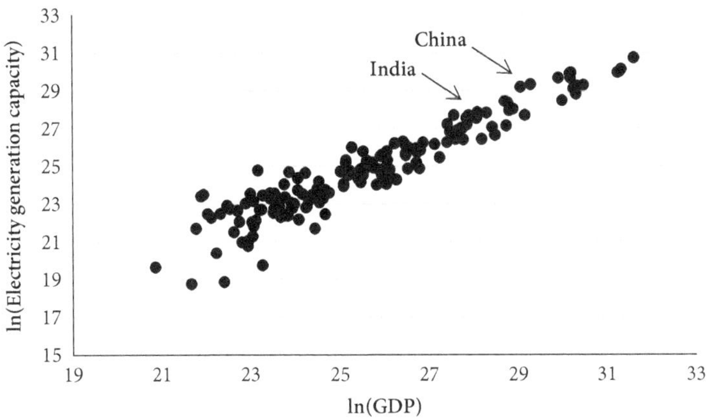

Figure 13.9. Cross-country comparison in electricity generation capacity, 2011
Source: WDI, the World Bank; GDP in 2005 constant US$.

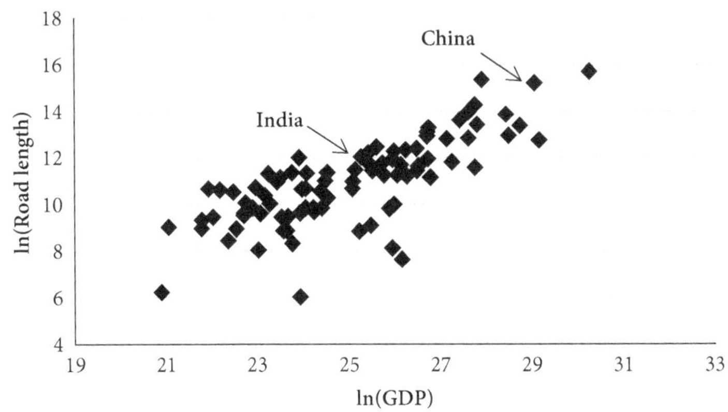

Figure 13.10. Cross-country comparison in roads, 2011
Source: WDI, the World Bank; GDP in 2005 constant US$.

In Figure 13.9, we plot the country-level log electricity capacity against log GDP using data from 2011. There is clearly a positive relationship between electricity infrastructure and GDP. The electricity capacity level of the PRC is higher than other countries with comparable economic size, including India. The advantage of the PRC in electricity infrastructure is consistent with its aggressive investment in electricity generation capacity as shown in Figure 13.5.

Figure 13.10 plots the country-level log length of roads against log GDP using data from 2000. There is clearly a positive relationship between roads and GDP. Although the road stock of the PRC is significantly higher than that of India, it is well in line with the cross-country relationship between roads and GDP, which does not suggest that the PRC has overinvested in roads.

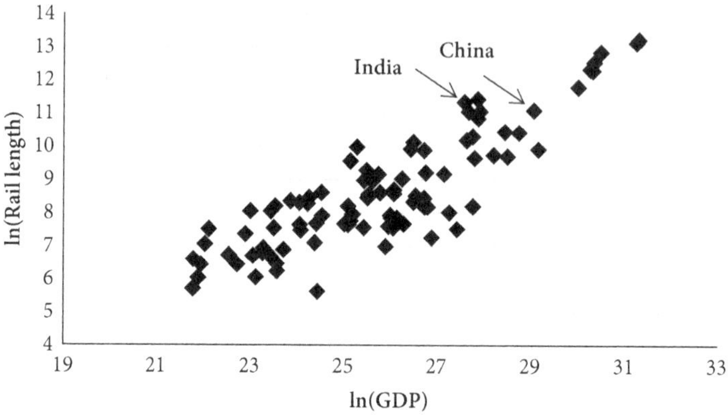

Figure 13.11. Cross-country comparison in railways, 2011
Source: WDI, the World Bank; GDP in 2005 constant US$.

In contrast, the railway network of India appears to be more extensive than that of the PRC (Figure 13.11). Again, the railroad stock of the PRC is well in line with the worldwide average railroad–GDP relationship.

In Figure 13.12, we plot the electricity capacity growth rate at the country level against the GDP growth rate during the 1990–2011 period. We find that electricity growth is positively associated with the GDP growth of a country (with a correlation of 0.73). The PRC stands out with a high GDP growth rate of 10 per cent. Its electricity infrastructure growth, at 10 per cent, is also significant, but it appears in line with the worldwide electricity supply growth–GDP growth relationship. India has a slower growth in electricity generation capacity, but it is consistent with its GDP growth rate. The services of the electricity sector are perceived to be less satisfactory in India than in the PRC according to the World Bank Investment Climate Surveys conducted in 2003. The share of loss of sales due to power outage, as reported by surveyed managers, is 9 per cent in India and 2 per cent in the PRC. This indicates that the service quality of electricity infrastructure is better in the PRC.

We next turn to road investment (Figure 13.13). We find that road growth in the PRC is positively associated with GDP growth (a correlation of 0.39). Despite the commonly reported boom in road investment in the PRC, we find that road growth was actually slightly below the worldwide average. The road length growth of India is also higher than that of the PRC (Figure 13.10).

Next, we examine railroad growth and find that it is also positively associated with GDP growth (a correlation of 0.21). Railroad infrastructure growth in the PRC is broadly in line with the worldwide average and is faster than that of India (Figure 13.14). Given that the stock of railroad in the PRC is below that of India, it is conceivable that the incentive for the PRC to catch up in railroad development is stronger than that of India.

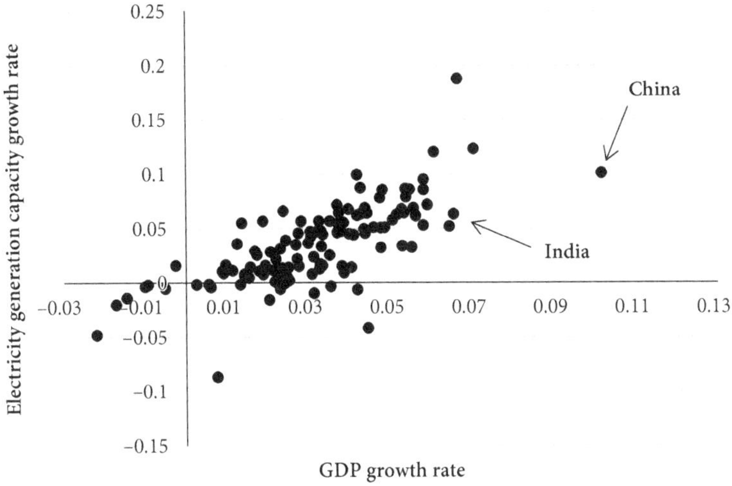

Figure 13.12. Electricity generation capacity growth against GDP growth, cross-country

Source: WDI the World Bank.

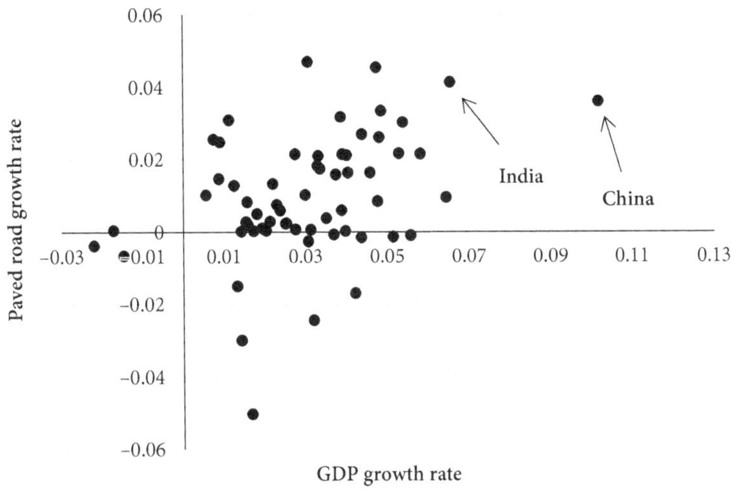

Figure 13.13. Cross-country scatter plot of road growth against GDP growth, 2011

Source: WDI, the World Bank.

To summarize, the cross-country comparison of three types of infrastructure (electricity generation, roads, railways) suggests no sign that the PRC has overinvested in its infrastructure, despite its active investment in infrastructure in the past two decades.

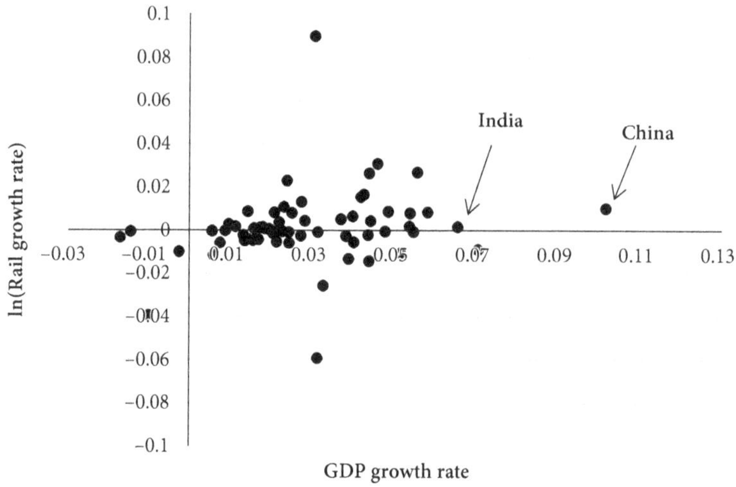

Figure 13.14. Cross-country scatter plot of railroad growth against GDP growth, 2011
Source: WDI, the World Bank.

13.2 Institutional Changes and Infrastructure Development

The economy of the PRC has achieved high-speed growth for over three decades. Besides productivity growth, investment has been the major driving engine of this growth. The investment/GDP ratio in the PRC increased substantially in the 1990s, from approximately 35 per cent in the 1980s to above 40 per cent in the 2000s, with the government having a very high share of investments. An important reason for the high share of public investment, as pointed out by Huang (2008), is the top-down system of the PRC, in which the government, not the private sector or the market, has the main responsibility for economic growth. The main purpose of infrastructure investment by the government has often been to stimulate short-run GDP growth. In addition, GDP growth and investment have been important indicators used for official promotion. Encouragingly, the past two decades have seen institutional changes that have gradually weakened the influence of state power and strengthened the role of the market in infrastructure investment. In this section, we summarize major policy trends for three key infrastructure sectors in the PRC: electricity generation, transport, and telecommunication.

13.2.1 Electricity Generation Infrastructure

The development of electricity infrastructure in the PRC over the past six decades can be divided into three phases, with market forces playing a progressively more important role. The first is the pre-reforms period before 1978, when all activities were under rigid state plans. Business activities and government functions, such as formulating and enforcing regulations, were both undertaken by one government agency, the Ministry of Electricity Industry. The annual growth rate for total installed capacity was 12.6 per cent during this period.

The second period is between 1978 and 2002, in which the state plan was loosened, and government functions and business activities began to separate. Nevertheless, competition was limited and the government agency still played an overwhelmingly dominant role. The growth rates of the sector fluctuated during this period. During 1979–84, the annual growth rate of total installed capacity declined to 4.9 per cent. In the period of 1984–97, the growth rate returned to 9.2 per cent. In 1997, the sector experienced surplus supply, and the government decided not to approve new investment in electricity generation for the next three years. By 2003, twenty-two provinces experienced a severe shortage of electricity supply and electricity had to be rationed again (Bai and Qian 2010).

The third period started from 2002. More players, including private investors, were allowed to invest in electricity infrastructure, significantly increasing the number of parties involved. At the end of 2007, there were more than 4,000 generators with an installed capacity above 6 MW in this sector. Nevertheless, the state still maintained a dominant position in this market. Central government-controlled generators accounted for 54 per cent of the installed capacity, while those controlled by local governments comprised 41 per cent (Bai and Qian 2010). The transmission and distribution sector was mainly controlled by two state grid corporations. Each of them is a monopoly transmitter, distributor, and retailer of electricity in its region. Generators sell power to the power grid companies.

13.2.2 Highways and Railroads

The dominant role of the state has also been the key feature of highway and railroad investment in the PRC. While investments in railways are mainly supported by the central government, most highways in the PRC are supported by local governments, while the central government targets strategically important national highways.

Since the economic reforms started in 1978, the railways sector has been gradually marketized, but progress has been slow relative to other infrastructure regulation reforms in the PRC. During 1949–82, the railways sector featured rigid planning and unprofitably low prices, which were uniformly set by the central authority. During 1982–5, some autonomy on planning, finance, employment, and personnel decisions was given to the local railway bureaus. At the same time, the railways system could retain some profit according to a formula after tax payment. Railway service prices were raised, but still lagged behind the general price level. Compared with 1955, the 1986 freight price dropped by 20.8 per cent relative to the consumer price index and passenger price by 15.7 per cent (Bai and Qian 2010).

In 1993, the railways system started experimenting with corporatization. The Guangdong railway bureau was restructured into a corporate group in February 1993. Then the Dalian railway bureau became Dalian Railway Limited in 1995. The Guangzhou–Shenzhou railway was publicly listed in Hong Kong, PRC, and New York in 1996. The whole system went through corporatization in 1999 with the objective of separating government functions from business activities in the system. In the same period, the price policy became more flexible. Prices were allowed to depend on the quality, route, and season of the services.

The marketization trend also occurred in road investment. Before 1980, road investment funds came from state budgets in the form of grants that did not carry any financial cost. Users did not pay any toll, but they paid a monthly highway maintenance fee based their vehicle tonnage. During the next stage, state investment funds in local projects were changed from grants to loans in 1980, and the cost of investment was shifted to local governments. New fees were introduced in the following years to increase the amount of funds available to local governments in constructing highways. Among the newly introduced fees was vehicle purchase surcharge, which was started in 1985. The surcharge was 10 per cent of the price for domestically produced vehicles and 15 per cent for imported vehicles. This surcharge goes into the State Highway Construction Fund.

Highway tolls were first used experimentally in Guangdong province in 1981. Gradually, toll collection became a widespread practice over the whole country. Currently, highway tolls are regulated by the Highway Law, which was promulgated in 1997 and revised in 1999 and 2004. Among other aspects, the law regulates the types of highway that are eligible for a toll, the number of years in which tolls can be collected on a highway, the toll rates, the transfer of the right for toll collection, the setting up of toll gates, and the coordination between provinces when the highway crosses a provincial border (see Bai and Qian 2010 for more details on the toll regulation policy).

13.2.3 Telecommunication Infrastructure

For a long time, the PRC's telecommunication sector was viewed as an instrument of government control and national defence. The telecommunication sector remained under tight control and was not opened to foreign investors until the 1990s, when the reforms process started. A round of reforms was started by the State Council in 1998 involving the separation of government and enterprise functions, the improvement of market competition, and the removal of monopoly power. The country's entry into the World Trade Organization in 2001 has hastened the reforms process and stimulated the development and growth of the telecommunications sector. Since 2001, the PRC's telecommunications system has expanded significantly and the number of subscribers has increased rapidly. In 2003, the number of subscribers for mobile phone services surpassed that for fixed-line services (Shiu and Lam 2008).

13.3 Infrastructure Financing

The rapid growth in infrastructure investment in the PRC has been supported by a unique financing system, which is not limited to standard fiscal resources but utilizes a number of non-budgetary sources of revenues. In this section, we summarize the structure and major features of this system.

13.3.1 Development of the Infrastructure Financing System in the PRC

The urban infrastructure finance system of the PRC has undergone a series of major changes. Between 1949 and 1978, municipal authorities collected fiscal revenue and remitted it to the central government for reallocation; infrastructure investment funds were then allocated to local governments in the form of grants based on the expenditure needs of local jurisdictions (Wu 1999). This period was characterized by a lack of both political and financial support of urban infrastructure development. From the 1950s to the 1970s, investment in urban infrastructure was RMB 12 billion in total, which was 1.43 per cent of total fixed investment and 0.23 per cent of GDP at the national level. These proportions are much lower than those in other countries (Chan 1998; Hua 1993).

Between 1978 and 1994, the central government intensified its efforts to promote urban infrastructure development through laws and regulations. The central–local government relationship began to change when fiscal decentralization was introduced and local governments began to retain a higher rate of revenue and enjoy more freedom in discretionary spending. State investment funds in local projects were changed from grants to loans in 1980 and the cost of investment was shifted to local governments.

The Urban Maintenance and Construction Tax (UMCT) was imposed in 1985 after a trial period of approximately five years (Chan 1998). The UMCT was the only earmarked tax in the fiscal system and became an important tool for infrastructure funding.

The Land transfer fee is also a major source of funds for infrastructure investment in the PRC. It was introduced in 1981 in Shenzhen foreign enterprises-funded projects and then expanded to other cities (Chan 1998). Two laws were enforced in 1988 and 1990 that provided the legal foundation for land leasing as an infrastructure-funding tool by Chinese municipalities. In addition, the central government set its share of land-leasing revenues at 60 per cent at the beginning and then gradually reduced it to 40 per cent, 32 per cent, and 5 per cent (Peterson 2006). By 1994, all land-leasing revenues were assigned to municipal governments.

In the 1980s, fees and user charges were also introduced, including wastewater treatment charges and user charges for toll bridges (Chan 1998). The State Council introduced infrastructure connection fees in 1984. It was started in several cities and became popular in the early 1990s (Chan 1998). An infrastructure connection fee was charged on new construction and immigrants. It was also always linked with the sale of urban residency rights (Hukou) (Chan 1998).

After the fiscal decentralization reforms of 1994, rather than sharing total tax revenues between local and central government informally, the new fiscal system formalized the sharing scheme of tax revenues between local and central government (Bird and Wong 2005). As a result, local governments gained more autonomy in urban infrastructure finance, strengthening their incentive to collect revenue for infrastructure development (Wu 1999, 2008; Chan 1998).

To summarize, sources of urban infrastructure financing in the PRC include both pay-as-you-go fiscal revenues and market financing approaches (Table 13.1). Pay-as-you-go fiscal revenues include central and local budgetary allocations, the Urban Maintenance and Construction Tax, public utility surcharges, water resource fees, infrastructure connection fees, user charges, land transfer fees, and assets exchange revenues. Market financing approaches include domestic loans, foreign capital, bonds, stock financing, and self-raised funds.

The total amount of urban maintenance and construction revenues has increased thirteenfold from 1990 to 2005 (constant price). Per capita funding increased from RMB 33 in 1990 to RMB 372 in 2005 (the exchange rate between RMB and US dollars was about 8 to 1 during 1990–2005 and, thus, the per capita funding increase was equivalent to about \$4 in 1990 and about \$45 in 2005). Urban maintenance and construction revenues as a percentage of GDP increased from 1.8 per cent in 1999 to 2.9 per cent in 2005. Importantly, the average annual growth rate of fiscal revenue from 1990 to 2005 was 12.8 per cent, which was less than the growth rate of market financing at 17.1 per cent (Figure 13.15).

Figure 13.16 breaks down the fiscal revenues by different sources in 2007. The most important source of urban infrastructure finance was the land transfer fees introduced in the 1980s, accounting for over a third of the fiscal revenues for urban infrastructure financing. Its annual average growth rate was 54.3 per cent, much higher than that of fiscal revenue funds for infrastructure investment (Zhao and Cao 2011; also see Chapters 8 and 9 in this book for more details on land market development and institutions of the PRC). Local budgetary allocation as well as the maintenance and construction tax are also significant, accounting for 33 per cent and 14 per cent of fiscal revenue for infrastructure investment respectively. These three items together contribute to 84 per cent of the fiscal revenue source

Table 13.1. Urban infrastructure financing instruments

Sources of funds	Nature of fund
Pay-as-you-go fiscal revenues	
Budgetary allocation	Earmarked grants from central government for urban maintenance and construction take the form of fiscal transfer and special funds, including irrigation works funds, road funds, and rural construction funds. Local budgetary allocation takes the form of special grants (Wang and Zhang 2009).
Urban Maintenance and Construction Tax	Collected by local governments as a surcharge on top of Value-Added Tax, product tax, and business tax—7 per cent in cities, 5 per cent in towns, and 1 per cent elsewhere.
Land transfer fee	Revenues from leasing land use rights and charging land use fees. Since the introduction of land leasing in the 1980s, it has gradually become one of the most important revenue items for urban infrastructure for local governments.
Public utility surcharges	A surcharge fee collected by local governments for goods and services to cover industrial and domestic uses of electricity, water, natural gas supplies, public transportation, and local telephone services.
Water resource fees	Charged to enterprises and public institutions for exploiting underground water resources in a programming zone of the city (Ministry of Housing and Urban-Rural Development of PRC 2001).
Infrastructure connection fees	Charged to enterprises, institutions, or individuals who engage in construction projects (including construction and expansion of land use) in the programming zone of the city. The charges are levied according to the building area or amount of the investment used for urban infrastructure including roads, water, sewerage, gases, heating, public transportation, sanitation, and parks (Ministry of Housing and Urban-Rural Development of PRC 2001).
Market financing	
Self-raised funds	Self-raised funds are from the accumulated capital of enterprises and public institutions for the purposes of expanded reproduction (Ministry of Housing and Urban-Rural Development of PRC 2001).

Source: Zhao and Cao (2011).

of funds for infrastructure investment. The amount of central budgetary allocation towards local infrastructure is very limited compared to other resources.

We now turn to market financing channels for infrastructure in the PRC (Figure 13.17). Debt financing includes domestic loans as well as other bonds. Domestic loans include bank loans and nationally issued bonds. Given the underdeveloped financial market of the PRC, bank lending still plays a dominant role, accounting for over a half of the total market financing. In terms of the growth rate, domestic loans are also the major source of growth in market financing.

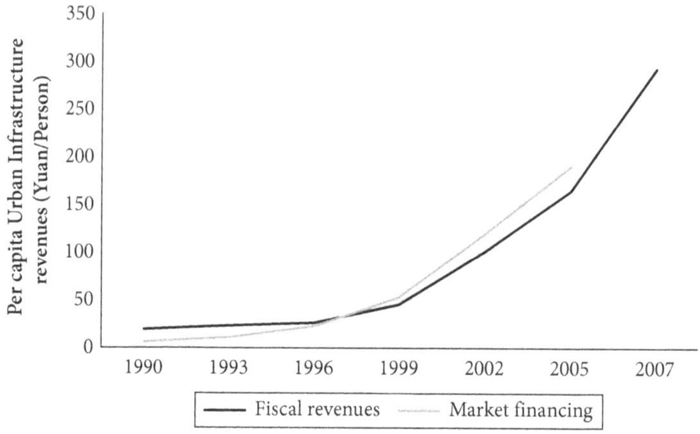

Figure 13.15. Per capita urban infrastructure revenue growth by sources
Source: Wu (2008).

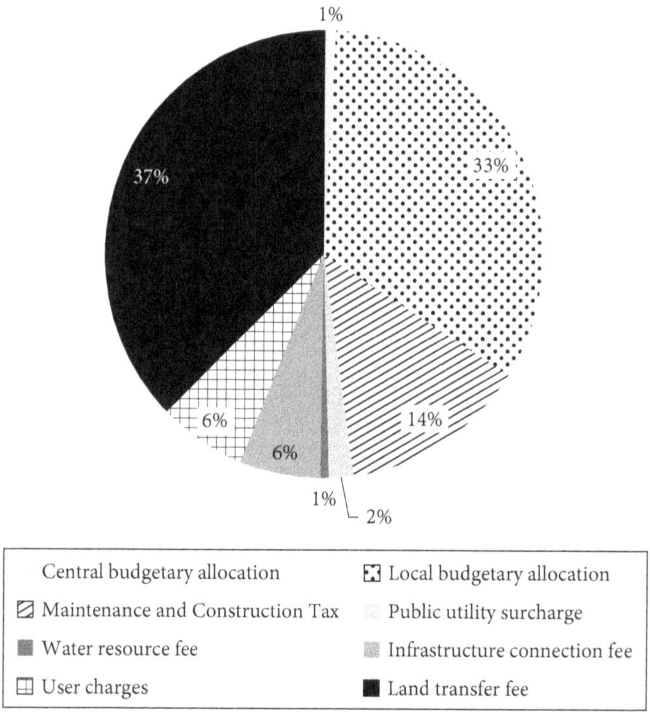

Figure 13.16. Pay-as-you-go fiscal revenues for urban infrastructure financing in the PRC, 2007
Source: Zhao and Cao (2011).

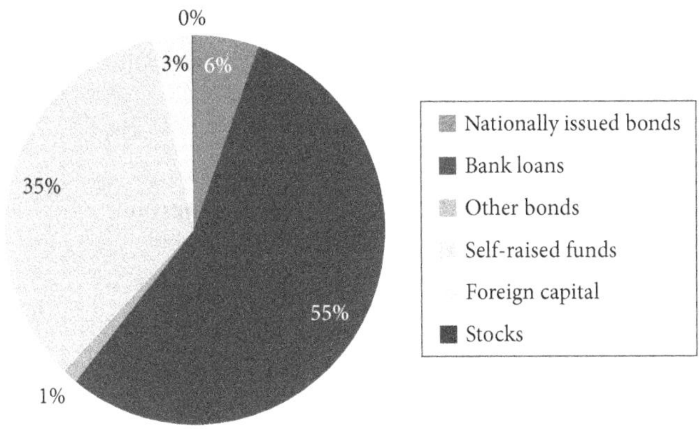

Figure 13.17. Market financing for urban infrastructure financing in the PRC, 2006

Their average annual growth rate from 1990 to 2005 was 24 per cent, while the growth rate of the overall market financing was 17.1 per cent (Zhao and Cao 2011).

Because local governments are not allowed to borrow money directly from commercial banks, Urban Development and Investment Companies are established to justify this way of financing urban infrastructure. Moreover, as infrastructure investment projects usually cannot recover costs within the maturity period of commercial bank loans, local governments always roll over the loans rather than repay them (Su and Zhao 2006). Since the implementation of higher credit standards for commercial banks, local governments' political control over commercial banks has weakened and it has become harder to obtain loans from these banks (Su and Zhao 2006).

In 1998, the Ministry of Finance began to increase nationally issued bonds and grant loans to provincial governments for the purpose of local economic and social development. Local governments are responsible for repaying capital with interest, but the repayment of these loans has typically been waived in the process of political negotiations with central government (Su and Zhao 2006).

Equity financing includes self-raised funds, foreign capital, and stock financing. Self-raised funds refer to those from the accumulated capital of enterprises and public institutions for the purpose of expanded reproduction. The average annual growth rate of self-raised funds is 14.3 per cent, which is lower than the 17.1 per cent of market financing. According to Wang and Zhang (2009), about two-thirds of self-raised funds come from the direct investment of private enterprises.

Foreign investment usually takes the form of public–private partnerships, in which the Chinese government provides the land and foreign companies provide the funds needed (Bird and Wong 2005; Bellier and Zhou 2003). Foreign capital accounts for a relatively low proportion of total infrastructure funding, at about 1–2 per cent.

Compared to other market financing approaches, the use of stock financing is minimal. In most years, it accounted for less than 5 per cent of the overall urban maintenance and construction revenues.

13.3.2 Decentralized Infrastructure Financing in the PRC

Before 'reforms and opening up', the PRC's transport investment was mainly centrally planned (Gao 2005).[3] After the reforms, the financing structure of infrastructure in the PRC has gradually shifted from central financing to local financing, but this centralization process varied widely across different types of infrastructure. Investment in railways is still mainly controlled by the central government, accounting for around 90 per cent of government investment in railways in recent years. In contrast, road investment is mainly local, with local fiscal funds accounting for around 95 per cent of total government investment. This difference in the central–local financing structure may have a large impact on investment efficiency, as local governments are less likely to be concerned about the interregional spillover effect of road infrastructure. Similar to road investment, local investment in waterway transportation has been maintained at about 80–90 per cent of total public investment. Electricity and heat generation are slightly more centrally controlled, with central government financing accounting for 35 per cent and local government financing accounting for 65 per cent of government investment (see Table 13.2).

Table 13.2. Transportation, warehousing, and postal actual fixed asset investment (unit: hundred million RMB)

	2004		2012	
	Central	Local	Central	Local
Railway transportation	752.73 (88.9%)	93.57 (11.1%)	5,045.2 (85.3%)	869.7 (14.7%)
Road transportation	200.69 (4.3%)	4,464.84 (95.7%)	479.6 (3.5%)	13,376.7 (96.5%)
Water transportation	106.58 (19.9%)	428.05 (80.1%)	268.4 (14%)	1,653.3 (86%)
Electricity and heat generation	1,699 (35%)	3,155 (65%)	4,311.7 (37%)	7,291.7 (62%)

Source: Yearbook of China Transportation and Communications, corresponding years.

[3] During the Great Leap Forward, local governments became the main source of financing. See Gao (2005), for a comprehensive review of the financing of Chinese transportation infrastructure investment.

In the latest reforms of the PRC since 2013, the Chinese government proposed the encouragement private investment in the infrastructure sector. The State Council published eighty projects in 2014 to invite private investment. On 12 June 2014 the investment director of the National Development and Reform Commission confirmed that in the long run, the government would continue to encourage private investment.[4]

In sum, the infrastructure financing system of the PRC has made progress in allowing the participation of private funds, but local governments still play the most important role in allocating infrastructure capital. This is helpful for rapid urbanization as local governments have a strong incentive to build transport infrastructure to facilitate urbanization so as to increase fiscal revenue from land sales. However, due to the lack of a system to assess the effectiveness of local governments' investment, overinvestment is likely, resulting in the overexpansion of urban areas. This may be a key reason for the lack of urban agglomeration in the PRC (see Chapter 4 for details), because small cities overexpand due to the financial motive of infrastructure investment.

13.4 Infrastructure–Growth–Urbanization Relationship

The rapid infrastructure investment in the PRC is closely tied to two other important trends: economic growth and urbanization. It is crucial to understand their interrelation in order for policymakers, not only in the PRC but also other developing economies, to make efficient infrastructure investment policies. Although the available empirical evidence is still very limited due to the lack of data and empirical research, a number of recent studies have advanced our understanding of this field. Below we summarize them and discuss their policy implications.

13.4.1 Infrastructure Investment and Growth in the PRC

Inspired by the unprecedented scale of infrastructure investment in the PRC, a rising number of econometric studies have been conducted on the effect of infrastructure investment on the growth of the PRC. In this section, we summarize the major findings in this small but rapidly growing literature.

An important question, in this context, is whether infrastructure investment in the PRC has helped to promote growth. This appears to be the case according to studies available. Démurger (2001) shows that transport infrastructure

[4] <http://www.chinairn.com/news/20140612/113418879.shtml>.

and telecommunication facilities are important factors related to the growth performance of provinces in the PRC (transport infrastructure is particularly important). More recently, Shi and Huang (2014) improved the estimates to assess the causal effect of infrastructure on economic growth, and their results suggest that when the general infrastructure level increases by 1 per cent, the GDP of a province in the PRC can increase by around 0.25 per cent. In contrast, Banerjee et al. (2012), who examined the effect of rail transport connections in the PRC after the mid-nineteenth-century advent of treaty ports, did not find any significant effect on counties that got railways compared with those farther off the grid.

These findings lead to a question: How has the infrastructure investment in the PRC affected economic growth? A number of recent studies have shed light on this question by econometrically examining the mechanisms for infrastructure to affect growth. Below we summarize the major findings.

Mechanism 1: *Transaction cost reduction.*

For infrastructure investment to affect the economy, a direct channel is needed to reduce transaction costs. According to Li et al. (2012), who used survey data on agricultural traders in the PRC in 2004, transport costs in the PRC are non-trivial, accounting for around 8 per cent of agricultural goods' trading value. In theory, transportation investment can improve the productivity of the economy by promoting trade patterns and reduce the prices of traded goods (Limao and Venables 2001).

Evidence from the PRC indeed supports this cost-reduction effect. In terms of road infrastructure, Li et al. (2012) show that road quality has been crucial for reducing transport costs within the PRC: by increasing transport speed by 1 km per hour, the total transport costs for Chinese agricultural traders would decrease by 0.6 per cent, mainly due to improved fuel-burning efficiency and reduced labour requirements.

Some evidence is also available for cost savings via railroad investment. Li and Chen (2013) examine the cost saving due to reduced congestion by expanding the transport capacity of a thousand-mile-long railroad that connects Xinjiang and Gansu provinces, both in north-west PRC. They find that, after this investment in 1994, the shipping volume increased by around 40 per cent and the between-destination price differences of goods dropped by about 30 per cent. This implies a sizeable social return of approximately 30 per cent per year for this particular investment.

Besides saving transport costs for tradable goods, transport infrastructure can also save costs through facilitating the specialization of production to regions with comparative advantages. He and Duchin (2009) find that each dollar of investment in the interregional transport infrastructure of the PRC can generate as much as \$3.9 of total benefits through the cost saving of the specialization effect. Note that, unlike previous studies, the findings of He and Duchin (2009) are derived from the optimization of a multi-region trade model based on linear programming for the period of 1997–2020, and not econometric analysis of the actual impact of transport infrastructure.

Transport infrastructure can also reduce the commuting costs of passengers, thus improving the efficiency of spatial distribution in economic activities. Zheng and Kahn (2013) show that the high-speed rail infrastructure has integrated housing markets between the city core and the surrounding second- and third-tier cities by reducing time costs for passengers. A key consequence and evidence of this cost saving is the rise of housing prices in the peripheral areas. Hence, investment in high-speed trains has played an important role in integrating the PRC's cities into a system of open cities.

In sum, the available econometric evidence suggests that transport infrastructure investment in the PRC has contributed to the productivity of the economy by reducing transport costs for goods and passengers, as well as the further spatial specialization of industries. The evidence available is far from comprehensive and representative as it largely focuses on transport infrastructure. Further research to assess the total costs saved for the PRC by different types of infrastructure, as well as its economic impact, is urgently needed.

Mechanism 2: Spatial redistribution of economic activities.

Given the trade costs reduction, as suggested by the studies reviewed earlier, there should be a redistribution effect according to the theory of Krugman (1980). Existing evidence generally suggests that urban agglomeration of the PRC is insufficient due to institutional constraints, such as local protectionism (see Chapter 4 for a detailed discussion and empirical evidence on the PRC).

Although the available evidence is very limited, it is generally in favour of the hypothesis that market integration can reinforce the concentration of economic activity, thus increasing the productivity of the economy. Specifically, the National Trunk Highway System (NTHS) of the PRC has encouraged industrial production activities to move from peripheral counties to metropolitan areas. As a result, the industrial output of metropolitan areas connected by the NTHS has increased by around 30 per cent (Faber 2009). The reduction of transport costs, as well as the agglomeration effect, has helped to lower product prices by around 1 per cent nationwide, thus increasing aggregate welfare. This price effect is much more significant in peripheral areas.

What if the road does not directly pass by a jurisdiction? The available empirical evidence does not provide a clear answer. Banerjee et al. (2012) estimate that the effect of distance to transportation networks on local economic outcomes in the PRC has been positive, but the magnitude of the effect was modest. The elasticity of per capita GDP with respect to distance from historical transportation networks is approximately –0.07. Moreover, the authors find no effect of proximity to a road on per capita GDP growth.

An important aspect of this spillover effect is that between countries, as shown by Conley and Ligon (2002). Within the context of the PRC, although Shi and Huang (2014) find little spillover effect of infrastructure investment, Li and Li (2013) show a significant spillover effect of road investment on firms in neighbouring provinces, which contributed to around two-thirds of the total inventory decline. These spillover benefits are likely to be even larger if the PRC can further remove its domestic trade barriers caused by local protectionism.

Mechanism 3: Productivity growth.

The aforementioned evidence on the distributional effect of transport infrastructure investment implies productivity gains through the agglomeration effect. In addition to this redistribution effect, transport infrastructure improvements may also be able to raise the productivity of firms. Li and Li (2013) provide an example of this by examining the effect of road investment on the inventory holding of manufacturing firms. In particular, one dollar of road investment in the PRC was able to decrease input inventory by around two cents each year during the 1998–2007 period. The implied that inventory saving is around a third of the estimate for the United States in the 1970s and is well below the capital costs. These estimates suggest that road investments in the PRC have improved the productivity of firms through inventory saving, although the investment efficiency was relatively low. The results also indicate that state-owned enterprises responded little to road improvement, while private entrepreneurs benefited much more. This implies that in order to improve benefits from road investments, the Chinese government may want to push the market reforms further and allocate more resources to the private sector instead of building more roads. This would allow thriving private enterprises to realize more benefits from infrastructure investments and contribute to economic growth.

Li et al. (2017) provide an alternative estimate of the effect of road investment on the productivity of firms in the PRC. They find that road investment in the PRC has modestly raised the productivity of firms. The implied aggregate rate of returns averaged 12 per cent. This is consistent with the findings in Li and Li (2013), suggesting that road investment in the PRC may have been less efficient than that in the US.[5]

[5] Vijverberg et al. (2011) also examine industrial enterprises, using province-level data from 1993 to 2003, but find the rate of returns to be 23–5 per cent. One possibility of this relative small rate of returns is the endogeneity in the infrastructure variable, such as measurement errors, which bias the estimates negatively.

By region, the productivity gain of road investment appeared to be much weaker in inland PRC than in coastal regions around the end of the 1990s, but the productivity gain of road investment in inland PRC picked up in the 2000s faster than in coastal regions (Li et al. 2017), suggesting improved road investment efficiency in inland PRC. This is contrary to the common criticism that roads have been oversupplied in inland PRC. In contrast, Shi and Huang (2014) find that most provinces in the PRC exhibited a clear shortage of infrastructure before 2008. After 2008, most of the western provinces already exhibited an oversupply of infrastructure relative to private capital, whereas some eastern and central provinces still showed a clear shortage of infrastructure. The seemingly contradicting findings of these two studies are due to the former study's focus on roads, while the latter study examines general infrastructure. For some infrastructure, such as telecommunication, the available evidence does suggest that it helps to improve GDP growth in eastern PRC, but not in the inland region (Shiu and Lam 2008).

Importantly, both Li et al. (2017) and Li and Li (2013) also find that the social returns to road infrastructure investment have been relatively modest. Hence, future road investment in the PRC needs more scientific planning in order to achieve an optimal investment scale.

13.4.2. Infrastructure Investment and Urbanization

The evidence for transport infrastructure investment having an effect on the centralization of economic activities, as discussed earlier, suggests that transport infrastructure has facilitated urbanization in the PRC. In this section, we shall provide further evidence on the relationship between general infrastructure investment and urbanization. The available evidence on this topic is scarce. An exception is Démurger (2001), who shows that infrastructure investments that are urban biased have led urbanized provinces to grow at a higher rate than rural provinces. A causal relationship, however, is unclear from this study. To shed further light on the interrelationship between urbanization and infrastructure, we provide additional evidence by analysing city-level data for the PRC.

In theory, infrastructure investment can facilitate urbanization by increasing the attractiveness and capacity of urban areas. On the other hand, urbanization can also affect infrastructure investment by increasing the demand for infrastructure investment. Below we provide a simple analysis of the relationship between infrastructure investment and urbanization in the PRC. In particular, we propose two alternative hypotheses.

Hypothesis 1: Infrastructure investment drives urbanization in the PRC, with decreasing marginal effect.

According to Hulten (1994), building one network may have a very high rate of return, but building a second network may have a lower marginal return. This implies that the marginal effect of infrastructure investment is likely to decrease, i.e. there is an inverse U-shape effect of infrastructure investment on urbanization.

> Hypothesis 2: Urbanization drives infrastructure investment through a demand-side effect, with decreasing marginal return.

We also expect the effect of urbanization on infrastructure investment to have decreasing marginal return (an inverse U-shape pattern) because an infrastructure network requires a large amount of initial capital, but incremental investment should be less costly.

It is important to note that if we examine the reduced form relationship between infrastructure investment and urbanization, only one of the above two hypotheses can hold, depending on which hypothesis is stronger in reality. This is because the inverse U-shape relationship suggested by the two hypotheses cannot hold at the same time.

We plot the ratio of infrastructure investment over GDP against the urbanization rate at the province level in 2007 to provide an overview of the data (Figure 13.18).[6] The pattern appears to favour the second hypothesis, showing that the ratio of infrastructure investment over GDP first increases in urbanization, but then declines. In contrast, when the infrastructure ratio rises, we do not observe a systematic pattern of urbanization. This data pattern generally holds for other years before 2007.

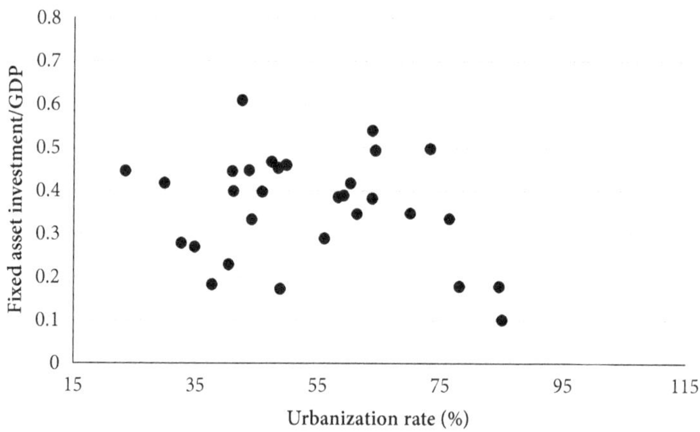

Figure 13.18. Infrastructure investment–GDP ratio vs. urbanization rate, 2007

[6] Infrastructure investment is approximated by city-level fixed asset investment value.

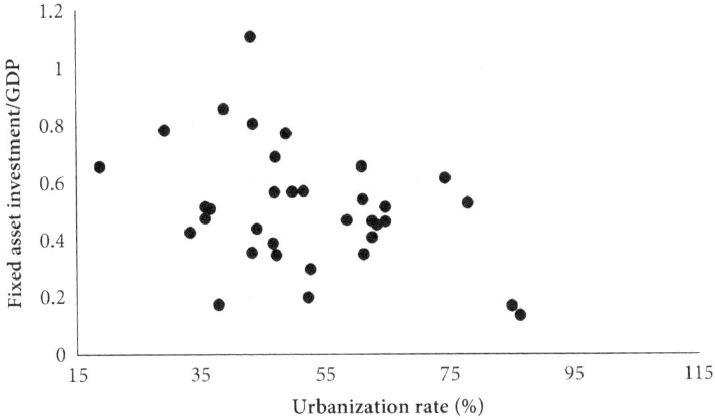

Figure 13.19. Infrastructure investment–GDP ratio vs. urbanization rate, 2009

Interestingly, after 2008, the year of the global financial crisis, the inverse U-shaped relationship between urbanization and infrastructure disappeared (Figure 13.19). This may suggest that after the financial crisis, the Chinese government used a large-scale fiscal stimulus to support the economy, providing easy credit nationwide for infrastructure investment. Hence, after 2008, infrastructure investment across the PRC became supply driven, rather than demand driven. This effect outweighed the strength of the mechanism suggested by hypothesis 2.

More rigorous regression estimates using fixed-effect panel data regressions (robust standard errors clustered at the city level) support the graphical patterns presented above (see Appendix). The estimates suggest that before 2007, when the urbanization rate of a Chinese province was lower than 0.47, rising urbanization was accompanied by rising infrastructure investment intensity in GDP. After the urbanization rate surpassed 0.47, infrastructure investment intensity started declining due to decreasing demand.

13.5 Policy Recommendations

Recommendation 1: Infrastructure investment and urbanization are mutually beneficial and jointly promote economic growth.

Existing evidence suggests the following interrelationship between infrastructure investment, urbanization, and growth in the PRC, which can be used for designing regional development policies. First, urbanization generates demand for infrastructure investment. Although this mechanism has weakened in cities with high urbanization rates, such as Shanghai, the demand for infrastructure in most Chinese cities is still strong as they are still in the middle of urbanization. Second, empirical evidence also suggests that infrastructure investment can facilitate urbanization by increasing economic agglomeration. Third, there is strong evidence in the literature that infrastructure investment in the PRC has promoted economic growth through various mechanisms: market integration, agglomeration, and productivity growth. These linkages together suggest that urbanization and infrastructure investment can jointly promote economic growth.

> Recommendation 2: Policymakers should encourage research on the marginal social returns to infrastructure investment to achieve efficient infrastructure investment.

Due to the limited research available, evidence is still largely lacking on the returns to infrastructure investment in the PRC and a consensus has not yet been reached. Nevertheless, existing evidence (Li and Chen 2013; Li and Li 2013; Li et al. 2017; Shi and Huang 2014) generally suggests that the social returns to transport infrastructure investment have been relatively modest. Hence, in the case of road infrastructure, future investment needs to be carefully studied so as to avoid overinvestment. Empirical evidence on the social returns to other infrastructure, including railroads, urban infrastructure, electronic grids, and telecommunication networks, is largely lacking. As these infrastructure investments may have large externalities and the prices are regulated, their private returns do not provide sufficient information on the returns to their marginal investment. Further studies are needed to answer this question.

> Recommendation 3: The market or the government alone is not sufficient to provide optimal infrastructure investment, and a public–private partnership mechanism is needed.

Existing studies have a number of important implications for infrastructure financing in the PRC. First, infrastructure investment is currently monopolized by governments, especially local governments. Compared with other economies, participation of private investment on infrastructure investment is very limited. This lack of private financing may be a key reason for the low productivity of road infrastructure investment, especially in the coastal regions of the PRC. Hence, reducing the barriers for private investment into infrastructure sector can help to increase the efficiency of investment.

Second, infrastructure may have strong spillover benefits across provinces. For example, both Li and Li (2013) and Li et al. (2017) find that road investment in a province of the PRC can affect the productivity of manufacturing firms in other provinces. Road investment, however, is mainly financed by local governments (Table 13.2). Hence, local governments may have little incentive to take other provinces' benefits into account when they decide on road investment. This issue cannot be addressed by allowing private investments. One possible solution is to increase the share that central government contributes to infrastructure financing. Alternatively, taxes may be levied on firms in other provinces that benefit from road investment in local provinces (such as establishing toll stations between the borders of provinces). Although the evidence available is only on roads, it is likely that a similar situation may occur for other types of infrastructure. More studies are also needed in this direction.

Recommendation 4: When investment incentives are distorted, infrastructure investment will be biased by local institutional quality and financing ability, and correction is needed.

There has been much discussion on whether infrastructure is oversupplied or undersupplied in inland PRC, but the available evidence is very limited. Shi and Huang (2014) find that before 2008, infrastructure was generally undersupplied across the PRC. However, after 2008, most of the western provinces already exhibited an oversupply of infrastructure relative to private capital, whereas some eastern and central provinces still showed a clear shortage of infrastructure. It is important to note that this unbalanced investment across the PRC may vary across different types of infrastructure. For some infrastructure, such as telecommunication, the available evidence suggests that it does help to improve GDP growth in the provinces in the affluent eastern region, but not in the low-income central and western provinces (Shiu and Lam 2008). However, in terms of road investment, Li et al. (2017) found that road infrastructure in inland PRC may still be undersupplied. These findings suggest that there may not be a uniform policy to improve the infrastructure investment efficiency in the PRC. Instead, different policies need to be designed for different types of infrastructure.

Appendix

Hypothesis 1: Infrastructure investment drives urbanization in the PRC, with decreasing marginal effect.

Hypothesis 1 suggests an inverse U-shaped effect of infrastructure investment on urbanization, which can be tested using the following simple regression model:

$$U_{it} = \alpha_0 + \alpha_1 I_{it} + \alpha_2 I_{it}^2 + \alpha_3 X_{it} + \alpha_i + \alpha_t + \epsilon_{it} \tag{A.1}$$

Here, U_{it} is the urbanization rate of city i in year t. I_{it} is the infrastructure investment–GDP ratio of city i in year t. Note that we include the quadratic term of infrastructure investment–GDP ratio to capture the declining marginal effect of infrastructure investment. If the hypothesis holds, we expect α_1 to be positive and α_2 to be negative. In this model, we can also include other factors that may affect the urbanization level of a city, as reflected in X_{it}. With panel data at the city level, we control for city and year fixed effects.

> Hypothesis 2: Urbanization drives infrastructure investment through a demand-side effect, with decreasing marginal return.

In contrast, Hypothesis 2 suggests the following regression model:

$$I_{it} = \beta_0 + \beta_1 U_{it} + \beta_2 U_{it}^2 + \beta_3 Z_{it} + \beta_i + \beta_t + \epsilon_{it} \tag{A.2}$$

Here, U_{it} and I_{it} are defined as above. If hypothesis 2 holds, we expect β_1 to be positive and β_2 to be negative. Other factors that may affect the infrastructure investment level are captured in Z_{it}. With panel data at the city level, we control for city and year fixed effects. Robust standard errors clustered at the city level are reported to test the significance of our estimates.

It is important to note that hypotheses 1 and 2 are contradictory, as the inverse U-shape relationship in the two hypotheses cannot hold at the same time. Hence, by estimating models (A.1) and (A.2), we can shed light on which of the two hypotheses may hold in the PRC in reality.

Data on urbanization, infrastructure investment, and GDP at the city level are obtained from the City Statistics Yearbook for corresponding years.[7]

To provide more a rigorous analysis, we conducted fixed effect panel data regressions of models (A.1) and (A.2), with results summarized in Table A.13.1 and Table A.13.2. Robust standard errors clustered at the city level are reported to test the significance of our estimates.

We find that hypothesis 1 is not supported by the data. In contrast, hypothesis 2 is supported by data before the financial crisis, but not afterwards. Specifically, the effect of infrastructure investment on urbanization is highly insignificant throughout the sample period (Table A.13.1).

In contrast, before 2007, the effects of both the urbanization rate and its quadratic term on infrastructure investment are significant (Table A.13.2). The implied turning point of the inverse U-shape relationship is 0.47. In other words, when the urbanization rate of a Chinese city is lower than 0.47, rising urbanization is accompanied by rising infrastructure investment intensity in GDP. After the urbanization rate surpasses 0.47, the infrastructure investment intensity starts to decline due to decreasing demand.

[7] As data on infrastructure investment are not available at the city level, we provide a proxy by subtracting real estate investment from total fixed asset investment at the city level. Hence, our measure of infrastructure investment also contains fixed asset investment by firms. Nevertheless, we believe the effect of this may be limited, as manufacturing fixed investment should not have an inverse U-shaped relationship with urbanization.

Table A.13.1. Effect of infrastructure investment–GDP ratio on urbanization rate

Dependent variable: urbanization rate	**(1)**	**(3)**
	2000–7	**2008–12**
Infrastructure investment–GDP	0.11	−0.42
	(0.27)	(0.37)
Infrastructure investment–GDP^2	−0.31	−0.31
	(0.32)	(0.29)
Observations	133	105
R-squared	0.97	0.97

Note: City- and year-specific fixed effects are controlled. Robust standard errors in parentheses; *** p < 0.01, ** p < 0.05, * p < 0.1.

Table A.13.2. Effect of urbanization rate on infrastructure investment–GDP ratio

Dependent variable: infrastructure investment–GDP	**(1)**	**(3)**
	2000–7	**2008–12**
Urbanization rate	1.40**	−3.43
	(0.69)	(7.84)
Urbanization rate^2	−1.48***	2.74
	(0.42)	(6.33)
Observations	133	105
R-squared	0.89	0.92

Note: City- and year-specific fixed effects are controlled. Robust standard errors in parentheses; *** p < 0.01, ** p < 0.05, * p < 0.1.

References

Bai Chong'en and Qian Yingyi. 2010. 'Infrastructure Development in China: The Cases of Electricity, Highways, and Railways'. *Journal of Comparative Economics* 38 (1): 34–51.

Banerjee Abhijit, Esther Duflo, and Nancy Qian. 2012. 'On the Road: Access to Transportation Infrastructure and Economic Growth in China'. *NBER working paper no. w17897*, National Bureau of Economic Research.

Bellier, Michel and Yue Maggie Zhou. 2003. *Private Participation in Infrastructure in China: Issues and Recommendations for the Road, Water and Power Sectors*, The World Bank and International Finance Corporation, Washington, DC.

Bird, Richard M. and Christine C. P. Wong. 2005. 'China's Fiscal System: A Work in Progress'. *Working paper 0520, International Studies Program*, Andrew Young School of Policy Studies, Georgia State University, Atlanta.

Chan, Kam Wing. 1998. 'Infrastructure Services and Financing in Chinese Cities'. *Pacific Rim Law and Policy Journal 7* (3): 503–28.

Conley, Timothy G. and Ligon, Ethan. 2002. 'Economic Distance and Cross-Country Spillovers'. *Journal of Economic Growth 7* (2): 157–87.

Démurger, Sylvie. 2001. 'Infrastructure Development and Economic Growth: An Explanation for Regional Disparities in China?' *Journal of Comparative Economics 29* (1): 95–117.

Faber, Benjamin. 2009. 'Integration and the Periphery: The Unintended Effects of New Highways in a Developing Country'. *LSE Working Papers*, London School of Economics.

Gao, Feng. 2005. *Transportation Infrastructure Investment and Economic Growth*, China's Financial and Economic Publishing House.

Grimsey, Darrin and Mervyn K. Lewis. 2002. 'Evaluating the Risks of Public Private Partnerships for Infrastructure Projects'. *International Journal of Project Management 20* (2): 107–18.

He, Lining and Faye Duchin. 2009. 'Regional Development in China: Interregional Transportation Infrastructure and Regional Comparative Advantage'. *Economic Systems Research 21* (1): 3–22.

Hua, Kuiyuan. 1993. 'Urban Infrastructural Construction, Development Problems and Prospects in China'. In *Urban and Regional Development in China: Looking into the 21st Century* edited by Yue-man Yueng, Zhanwenershiyishiji.

Huang, Yasheng. 2008. *Capitalism with Chinese Characteristics: Entrepreneurship and the State*, Cambridge University Press.

Hulten, Charles R. 1994. 'Optimal Growth with Infrastructure Capital: Theory and Implications for Empirical Modeling'. Working paper, University of Maryland.

Krugman, Paul. 1980. 'Scale Economies, Product Differentiation, and the Pattern of Trade'. *The American Economic Review 70* (5): 950–59.

Li, Han and Zhigang Li. 2013. 'Road Investments and Inventory Reduction: Firm Level Evidence from China'. *Journal of Urban Economics 76*: 43–52.

Li, Zhigang and Yu Chen. 2013. 'Estimating the Social Return to Transport Infrastructure: A Price-Difference Approach Applied to a Quasi-Experiment'. *Journal of Comparative Economics 41* (3): 669–83.

Li, Zhigang, Mingqin Wu, and Chen Bin. 2017. 'Is Road Infrastructure Investment in China Excessive? Evidence from Productivity of Firms'. *Regional Science and Urban Economics 65*: 116–26.

Li, Zhigang, Xiaohua Yu, Yinchu Zeng, and Rainer Holst. 2012. 'Estimating Transport Costs and Trade Barriers in China: Direct Evidence from Chinese Agricultural Traders'. *China Economic Review 23* (4): 1003–10.

Limao, Nuno and Anthony J. Venables. 2001. 'Infrastructure, Geographical Disadvantage, Transport Costs, and Trade'. *The World Bank Economic Review 15* (3): 451–79.

Martini, C. A. and Lee, D. Q. 1996. 'Difficulties in Infrastructure Financing'. *Journal of Applied Finance and Investment 1* (1): 24–7.

Peterson, George E. 2006. *Land Leasing and Land Sale as an Infrastructure-Financing Option*, The World Bank, Washington, DC.

Shi, Hao and Shaoqing Huang. 2014. 'How Much Infrastructure is Too Much? A New Approach and Evidence from China'. *World Development 56*: 272–86.

Shiu, Alice and Pun-lee Lam. 2008. 'Causal Relationship between Telecommunications and Economic Growth in China and its Regions'. *Regional Studies 42* (5): 705–18.

Su, Ming and Quanhou Zhao. 2006. 'China: Fiscal Framework and Urban Infrastructure Finance'. In *Financing Cities: Fiscal Responsibility and Urban Infrastructure in Brazil, China, India, Poland and South Africa*, edited by George E. Peterson and Patricia Clarke Annez, Sage Publications and the World Bank.

Vijverberg, Wim P. M., Feng-Cheng Fu, and Chu-Ping C. Vijverberg. 2011. 'Public Infrastructure As a Determinant of Productive Performance in China'. *Journal of Productivity Analysis 36* (1): 91–111.

Wang, De and Zhao Zhang. 2009. 'A Research on the Mechanism of Urban Infrastructure Funding and Financing in China (Woguo chengshi jichusheshi jianshe zijin yunzuo moshi yanjiu)'. *Planning Research (Guihua Yanjiu) 3*: 9–16.

Wu, Weiping. 2008. 'Urban Infrastructure Financing and Regional Economic Performance under China's Fiscal Decentralization'. In *Symposium on Local Public Finance and Property Taxation in China, Lincoln Institute of Land Policy, May* (vol. 12).

Zhao, Zhirong Jerry and Chengxin Cao. 2011. 'Funding China's Urban Infrastructure: Revenue Structure and Financing Approaches. *Public Finance and Management 11* (3): 284–305.

Zheng, Siqi and Matthew E. Kahn. 2013. 'China's Bullet Trains Facilitate Market Integration and Mitigate the Cost of Megacity Growth'. *Proceedings of the National Academy of Sciences 110* (14): E1248–E1253.

Zhu, Xiaodong., 2012. 'Understanding China's Growth: Past, Present, and Future'. *Journal of Economic Perspectives 26* (4), 103–24.

14
Infrastructure and Urbanization in India
Issues and Challenges

Sandip Sarkar and Balwant Singh Mehta

14.1 Introduction

Urbanization is one of the most enabling parallel processes for rapid growth. Historically, no country has achieved higher incomes or sustained rapid economic growth without urbanization. Clear linkages exist between per capita income and level of urbanization; all middle-income countries and areas are at least 50 per cent urbanized, and high-income countries are at least 70–80 per cent urbanized.

High, sustained growth, which makes countries move up the per capita income ladder, requires a growth process that is led by manufacturing and services. Improvement in agricultural productivity frees up the labour force in rural areas, which is then absorbed into the manufacturing and services sectors in urban areas. No amount of growth in the rural sector matches the increase in productivity that is facilitated by people moving into this higher productive employment in urban areas (Spence et al. 2009). As a country becomes more urbanized and cities become larger, faster gains in urban productivity become more predominant.

Yet these processes do not happen automatically. The first challenge is enabling the growth of high-productivity activities that benefit from agglomeration and scale economies arising out of a larger city size. The second challenge is managing the likely side effects of the economic success of cities, such as congestion and high prices of land and housing. Higher productivity in cities also occurs due to the reduction in transport costs that comes from clustering economic activities, cheaper infrastructure, and other public services for a densely packed population, and benefits from knowledge spillovers (Spence et al. 2009).

Rapid urbanization, either through migration or through the conversion of rural areas into urban, often requires large investments in infrastructure and in public goods and services, which tests government capacity to mobilize resources and to shift the balance of spending to urban areas. Overcrowding, slum development, and rising crime often accompany urbanization, and providing infrastructure and public services are possibly the only antidotes to these problems. Therefore,

Sandip Sarkar and Balwant Singh Mehta., *Infrastructure and Urbanization in India* In: *Cities of Dragons and Elephants: Urbanization and Urban Development in China and India. Edited by:* Guanghua Wan and Ming Lu, Oxford University Press (2019). © Oxford University Press. DOI: 10.1093/oso/9780198829225.003.0014

discovering ways of financing the vast expenditures on urban infrastructure and public services is the biggest challenge for urbanization policy in developing countries such as India.

14.2 Urbanization

During the last three decades, India has experienced high economic growth without a significant rise in urbanization. The urban share of population only rose by 8 per cent, from 23 per cent in 1981 to 31 per cent in 2011 (MOHA 2011). To some extent, this is due to the downward bias of India's urban statistics, caused by a delay in drawing urban boundaries as those areas expanded. This created a measurement challenge, as the peripheries of large urban areas that attracted many people and businesses remained officially classified as rural.

Interestingly, the World Bank (2011) presented the spatial profiles of urban areas of the People's Republic of China (PRC), India, and the United States. Unlike the PRC and United States, in which major population concentrations exist along the coasts, urban areas are much more dispersed in wider geographical regions throughout India.

There is substantial variation in the urbanization process in different parts of India. The western, southern, and northern zones are relatively more urbanized than other zones (Figure 14.1). The pace of urbanization was highest in the southern region and lowest in the central and eastern regions between 1991 and 2011.

Despite a slow urbanization process, 87 million people were added to the urban population between 2001 and 2011 (an increase from 290 million to 377 million), and urban areas are likely to house another 250 million people by 2030 (HPEC 2011). For the first time since independence, the absolute decadal increase in the urban population was higher than that in the rural population during 2001 and 2011, which has significant implications for providing infrastructure and other amenities in urban

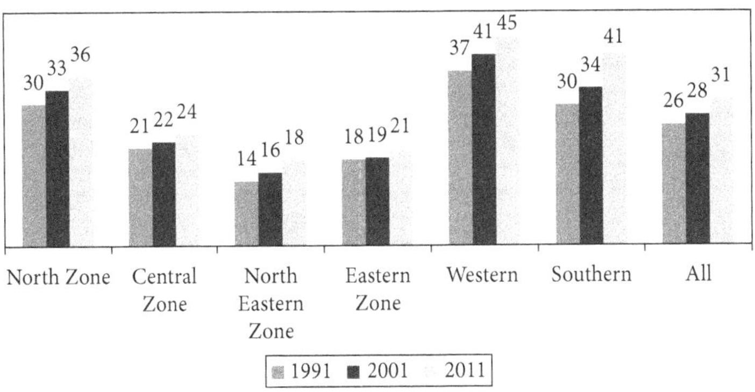

Figure 14.1. Pace of urbanization across regions in India
Source: Compiled from various censuses of India: 1991, 2001 and 2011.

Table 14.1. Infrastructure facilities in India versus the PRC, 2010–11

Infrastructure	India	PRC
Roads, total network ('000 km)	4,582	4,008
Roads, passengers carried (million passenger km)	1,266,588	1,502,081
Roads, goods transported (million ton per km)	1,106,500	4,338,967
Rail lines (total route, '000 km)	64	66
Railways, passengers carried (million passenger km)	903,465	791,158
Railways, goods transported (million ton per km)	600,548	2,451,185
Air transport, passengers carried (million)	74	269
Air transport, freight (million ton per km)	1,631	17,194
Electric power consumption (kWh per capita)	684	3,298
Mobile cellular subscriptions (per hundred people)	73	72

Source: World Bank. World Development Indicators, <http://data.worldbank.org/data-catalog/world-development-indicators> (July 2014), and the Central Statistics Organisation.

areas (Bhagat 2011). Against this background, this chapter explores India's urban infrastructure financing and public services delivery problem.

14.3 Infrastructure Development in India

It is essential to strengthen transport infrastructure facilities, such as rail, roads, and air, to improve India's overall competitiveness in the global market, thereby lowering trade and transaction costs. Table 14.1 compares the infrastructure facilities of India with the PRC according to indicators of various modes of transport, telecommunications, and electricity.

India substantially lagged behind the PRC in terms of goods transported by rail, roads, and air, and electric power consumption in 2011. The major factor responsible seems to be the low manufacturing base of India.

14.3.1 Roads

Road networks have played an important role in developing the country's transport infrastructure. National and state highways connect every state and town or city of India from north to south to east to west. A small proportion of highways is four or six lanes, and a negligible proportion is express ways. In fact, India has the world's second largest road network, with its national highways covering 92,000 kilometres (km), and the length of highway roads has increased almost three times during the last forty years (Figure 14.2). It grew by 4.6 per cent per year from 1970 to 1980, slowed down with 2.5 per cent growth from 1980 to 1990, and had just 1.4 per cent growth from 1990 to 2000. However, the pace has again grown by 2.24 per cent per year from 2000 to 2012.

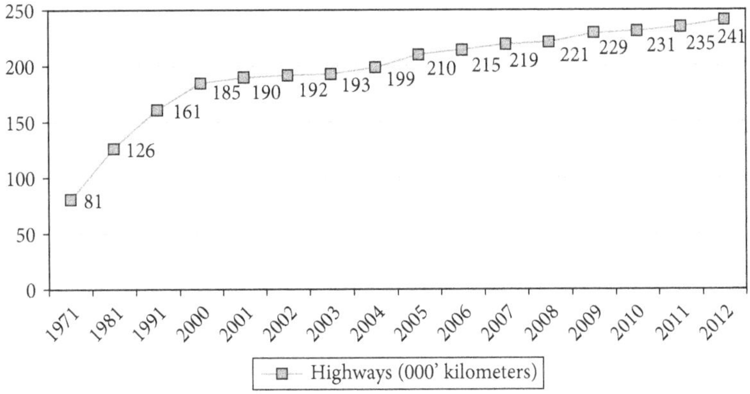

Figure 14.2. Change in highways (national and state) length ('000 kilometres)
Source: Infrastructure Statistics 2014, Central Statistical Office, Government of India.

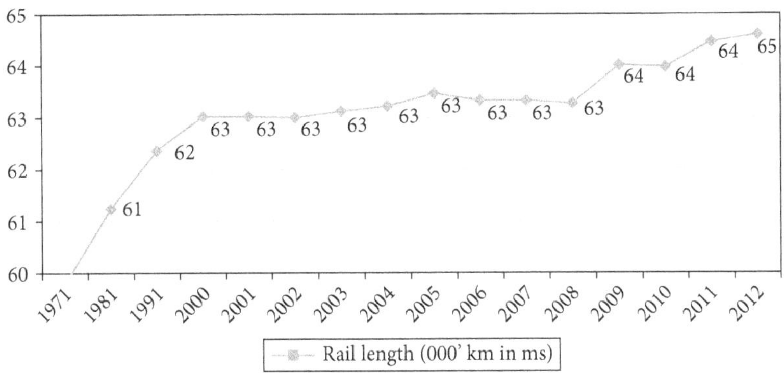

Figure 14.3. Change in rail route length ('000 kilometres)
Source: Infrastructure Statistics 2014, Central Statistical Office, Government of India.

14.3.2 Rail

The railroads have a vast network (the fourth largest in the world), encompassing 64,000 km. This rose from 54,000 km just after independence in 1950 to 60,000 km in 1971, but further increased only by 5,000 km in the next forty years (Figure 14.3). However, during this period, electrification of the routes was substantial.

14.3.3 Waterways

An inland waterway forms a common frontier between two countries or places within a country. It is fuel-efficient, environment friendly, and more economical than rail and road transport. India is richly endowed with navigable waterways, comprising rivers, canals, backwaters, and creeks, with 7,500 km of coastline and about 32,000 km of inland waterways. However, it is a minor mode of goods transport in India, and it carried only 54 million tons of cargo in 2011–12. Waterway length showed an increase only between 2006 and 2007, and remained stagnant thereafter (Figure 14.4).

14.3.4 Pipelines

The pipeline industry has grown in parallel with the development of the global oil industry over the last century. In India, the pipeline length has continuously increased during the last seven years to 41,000 km in 2014 from 25,000 km in 2007 (Figure 14.5).

14.3.5 Electricity Consumption

The per capita consumption of electricity is continuously increasing in India. It more than doubled between 2003 and 2012, from 373 kilowatt hours to 884 kilowatt hours, with the maximum increase occurring only in the last few years (Figure 14.6).

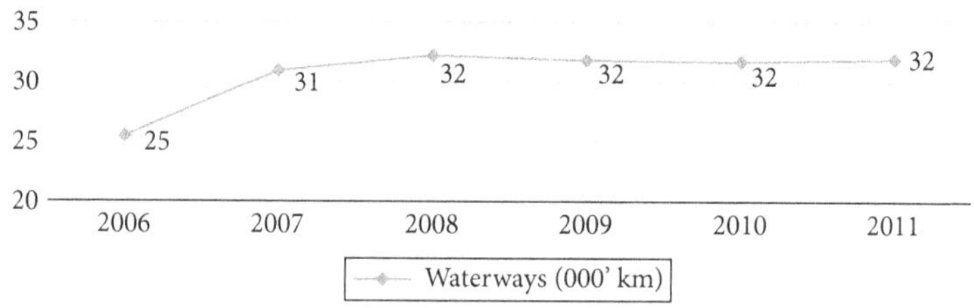

Figure 14.4. Change in waterway length ('000 kilometres)
Source: Infrastructure Statistics 2014, Central Statistical Office, Government of India.

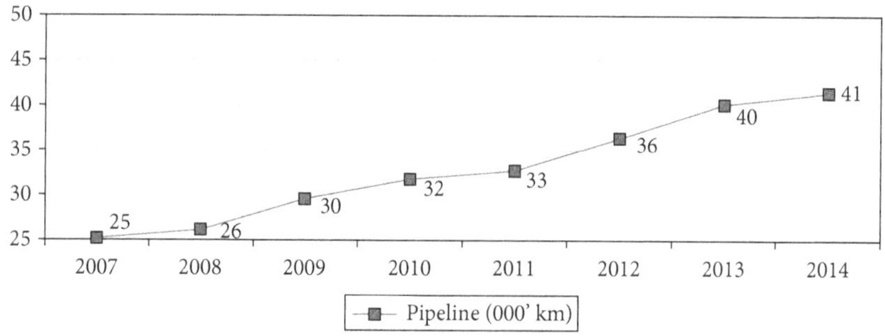

Figure 14.5. Change in pipeline length ('000 kilometres)
Source: Infrastructure Statistics 2014, Central Statistical Office, Government of India.

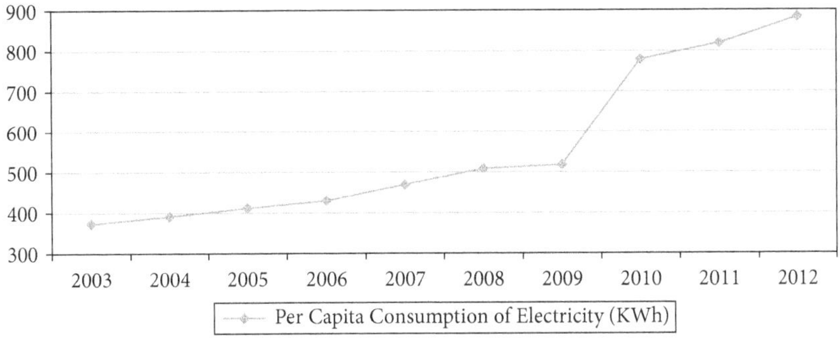

Figure 14.6. Per capita consumption of electricity (kilowatt hours)
Source: Infrastructure Statistics 2013, Central Statistical Office, Government of India.

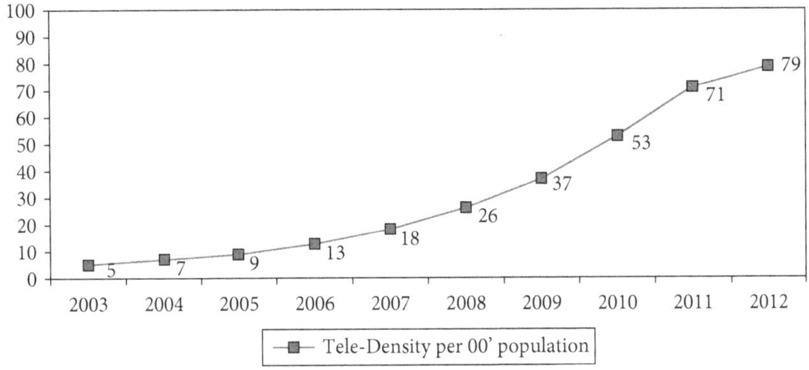

Figure 14.7. Teledensity (per hundred people)
Source: Infrastructure Statistics 2014, Central Statistical Office, Government of India.

14.3.6 Communications

Communication services have increased almost fifteenfold during the last decade—from just 5 per cent teledensity (subscribers per hundred people) in 2003 to 79 per cent in 2012. This increase is mainly attributed to high diffusion and adoption of mobile phones (Figure 14.7).

14.4 Urbanization–Growth–Infrastructure

As discussed earlier, the process of urbanization is directly associated with economic growth in that people migrate from rural to urban areas in search of better or more productive work; the incremental contribution of workers' productivity results in higher economic output[1] (Figure 14.8). This is important to not only

[1] Rural–urban breakdown of GDP is not available for more than a decade.

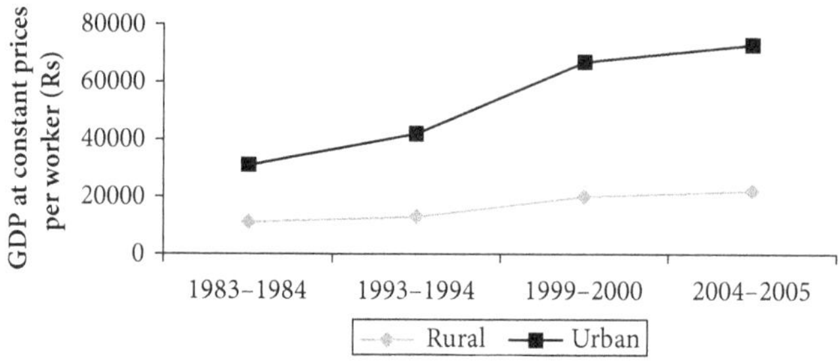

Figure 14.8. Rural–Urban Productivity
Sources: Central Statistical Organisation and National Sample Survey Organisation.

sustain India's economic growth but also inclusive growth, given the strong positive effects that a prosperous urban sector has on rural areas. Mazumdar and Sarkar (2008) showed that the elasticity of rural per capita expenditure with respect to urban per capita expenditure in India was as high as 0.435 in 1999–2000. While Chapters 3 and 21 in this volume examine the relationship between growth and urbanization, and effects of urbanization on inequality, this chapter dwells on the urbanization growth relationship via the infrastructure route.

The launch of the Jawaharlal Nehru National Urban Renewal Mission (JNNURM) in 2005 signalled the growing importance of urban areas and cities in the country's economic growth, which accounted for 62–3 per cent of GDP in 2009–10 (Planning Commission 2012). Accordingly, the High-Powered Expert Committee (HPEC 2011) report on urban infrastructure and services also indicated that the contribution of urban areas is expected to rise to 70–5 per cent of GDP by 2030. Both studies also clearly pointed to the statistically significant relationship between a higher urbanization level and higher per capita income.

14.4.1 Relationship Between Urbanization and the Level of Income

The National Institute of Urban Affairs (2011) found, from across-section regression analysis undertaken at three points of time (1991, 2001, and 2011), that while the per capita GDP level and urbanization were closely linked and became stronger over the years (from increasing R^2 values), the interlinkages were low by international standards. The impact of economic growth on cities in India is thus not strong enough, and the impact of agglomeration economies on urbanization is far from being saturated.

The estimated correlation between the level of per capita income and urbanization in India is presented in Figure 14.9, which indicates that economic growth has a significant and positive association with the urbanization rate. The correlation

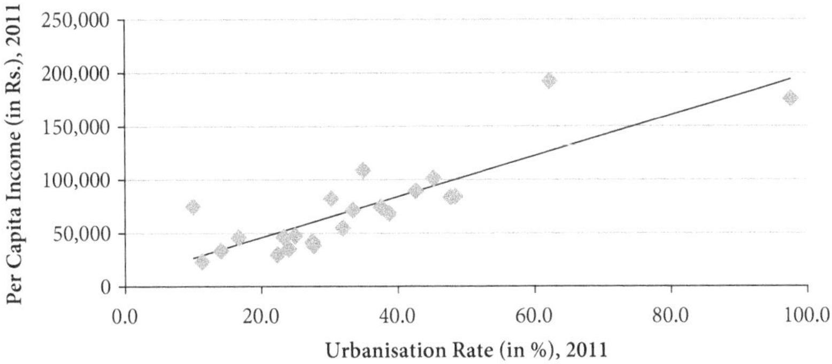

Figure 14.9. Correlation between the urbanization rate and level of per capita income across states, 2011

Source: Census of India, 2011 and Economic Survey of India, 2012–13.

coefficient has increased from 2001 to 2011, which also reflects the growing importance of urbanization in the economy. Chapter 3 in this volume also offers evidence of the positive relationship between urbanization and per capita income nationally and at the state level.

14.4.2 Relationship Between Availability of Infrastructure and Economic Development

There have been few attempts to study the link between infrastructure availability and economic development in India, mostly due to unavailable data. One of the most recent attempts was undertaken by Agarwalla (2011), who examined this relationship within a growth-accounting framework, using panel data for a long-term span of twenty-seven years (1980–1 to 2006–7) in twenty-five major states of India. She divided the whole period into two parts—pre-reform (1980–92) and post-reform (1992–2006). Her production function of regional economy was:

$$Q = A(X,t), F(K,L),$$

where Q = gross output, X = vector of infrastructure services, K = capita, and L = labour input.

The contribution of infrastructure to productivity was assumed to be manifested as an outward shift in the production function. Assuming a multiplicative production function and measuring the Hicksian shift term A(X,t) with the help of the Solow model of residual total factor productivity (TFP) growth, she estimated the following contribution of labour, capital and TFP (Table 14.2).

Table 14.2. Average annual growth rates (% contribution)

Year	Output	Labour	Capital	Total factor productivity growth
1980–92	100	10.60	46.06	43.34
1993–2007	100	15.19	48.66	36.15

Source: Agarwalla (2011).

Table 14.3. Results from panel data analysis of twenty-five states

Serial number	Dependent variable: total factor productivity	1980–92	1992–2006
1	Intercept	0.1990 (0.026)*	0.4440 (0.022)*
2	Public expenditure on infrastructure	0.0180 (0.007)**	0.0001 (0.015)
3	Health infrastructure availability	0.0490 (0.010)*	−0.0030 (0.019)
4	Education infrastructure availability	−0.0050 (0.026)	0.0450 (0.007)*
5	Transport infrastructure availability	0.2370 (0.037)*	0.1320 (0.007)*
6	Power infrastructure availability	0.0540 (0.011)*	0.0300 (0.009)*
7	R^2	0.8200	0.9400

Note: Standard errors are reported in parentheses, and * and ** represent significance levels at 1 per cent and 5 per cent, respectively.

Source: Agarwalla (2011).

After obtaining estimates of TFP and infrastructure availability of each state for all twenty-seven years, she regressed the log of TFP on different infrastructure parameters over time with a constant term (Table 14.3).

The results showed that transport and power infrastructure variables were significant for both periods. In the pre-reform period, public (revenue) expenditure on infrastructure and health infrastructure were significant. In the post-reform period, both of these variables became insignificant, but educational infrastructure became significant. The importance of transport infrastructure showed a decline from the pre- to the post-reform period. In the pre-reform period, the impact of one unit increase in transport infrastructure availability led to a 24 per cent increase in the index of TFP, but in the post-reform period its impact came down to 13 per cent. One reason could be that in post-reform period the TFP growth was clearly led by the service sector (Bosworth and Maertens 2010), which relies more on the availability of an educational infrastructure.

Table 14.4. Correlation between urbanization and infrastructure variables, 2010–11

Variables	Urbanization	Teledensity	State highways	Electricity
Urbanization	1.000	0.844**	−0.059	0.459
Teledensity	0.844***	1.000	0.014	0.505*
State highways	−0.059	0.014	1.000	0.267
Electricity Consumption	0.459*	0.505**	0.267	1.000

Notes:

N (number of major states in India) = 17.
*** Correlation is significant at the 0.01 level (two-tailed).
** Correlation is significant at the 0.05 level (two-tailed).
* Correlation is significant at the 0.10 level (two-tailed).
The variables of teledensity, state highways, and electricity consumption are measured in terms of the standard unit of population size to bring uniformity.

14.4.3 Relationship of Different Forms of Infrastructure with Urbanization

The correlation between urbanization rates and several infrastructure variables, such as state highways, electricity consumption, and communications, is presented in Table 14.4. The results show that communications are positively and significantly correlated with urbanization. Electricity consumption and urbanization rates are also positively correlated, but the significance level is much less. The other infrastructural variable of state highway length is not associated with the urbanization rate.

The contribution of migration to the urbanization process is low in India, but it has increased the pressure on urban infrastructure and services delivery. A major challenge faced by cities and metropolises is how to channel increasing migration. The World Bank (2011) found that the scope lies in accommodating a good proportion of migrants in and around large cities, as economic activities are highly concentrated around large cities and their neighbourhoods. The 50 km periphery (from the city centre) of the seven largest cities in 2001 held a population of 92 million (9 per cent of the total population), a quarter of India's urban population, and a little less than 3 per cent of the rural population (World Bank 2011). These regions provide the opportunity to transform land use and to expand infrastructure in these large cities and suburbs to accommodate a much larger migrant population and to take advantage of agglomeration economies.

14.5 Infrastructure Development

14.5.1 Sector Coverage of Urban Infrastructure

The first issue is defining the sectors covered under urban infrastructure, which have expanded over the years in India (see Table 14.5).

Table 14.5. Sector coverage of urban infrastructure in different reports and studies

Serial number	Source	Year	Sectors covered
1	Committee of Ministers Constituted by the Central Council of Local Self-Government	1963	1. Water supply 2. Sewerage 3. Urban roads 4. Street lighting
2	Indian Infrastructure Report	1996	1. Water supply 2. Sewerage 3. Urban roads 4. Solid waste management
3	Mohanty et al.	2007	1. Water supply 2. Sewerage 3. Urban roads 4. Solid waste management 5. Storm water drains 6. Urban transport
4	McKinsey Study	2010	1. Water supply 2. Sewerage 3. Urban roads 4. Solid waste management 5. Storm water drains 6. Urban transport
5	The High-Powered Expert Committee (HPEC) for Estimating the Investment Requirement for Urban Infrastructure Services	2011	1. Water supply 2. Sewerage 3. Urban roads 4. Solid waste management 5. Storm water drains 6. Urban transport 7. Street lighting 8. Traffic support infrastructure 9. Renewal and development 10. Other sector

Source: Compiled from the five reports mentioned in the table.

In this study, the sectors covered in the HPEC report are the focus: water supply, sewerage, urban roads, solid waste management, storm water drains, urban transport, street lighting, traffic support infrastructure, and renewal and development. This leaves out several large infrastructure sectors such as power, ports, post, and telecommunications, where the level of commercialization is comparatively higher and there is a greater presence of financial institutions.

14.5.2 Urban Services Delivery and Establishment of Norms

The state of urban services delivery in India is less than expected at the country's current level of economic development. This is reflected in the incidence of floods, traffic jams, accumulated waste on roadsides, and people queuing up for water from stand posts and tankers across cities and towns. The Ministry of Urban Development (MUD 2009) found that 23 million children under the age of fourteen in urban India are at risk from poor sanitation, and eight million children in urban areas are at risk from a poor water supply. Further, infant mortality is at forty-two deaths per 1,000 live births in urban areas, which is unacceptably high (Ram et al. 2009).

The government first attempted to reveal the gap in services in 1963 through the formation of the Zakaria Committee, which laid down the physical norms and corresponding expenditure norms for five services (i.e. water supply, sewerage, storm water drainage, urban roads, and street lighting). The committee adopted a demand-driven approach for estimating services standards and per capita investment requirements for urban India. The standards were derived from actual data collected on the quantum of basic urban services, demand for services, cost of provision, maintenance of services, and municipal finances from a sample of cities of different sizes. The financial norms of the committee, adjusted for inflation, are still widely used as benchmarks for assessing infrastructure needs in urban areas. Today, however, they are outdated and do not measure up to the standards relevant for an economy at India's current level of development.

Government institutions, such as the Town and Country Planning Organization in 1979, Planning Commission in 1999, and various state governments at different times have also created modified norms for services. The Ministry of Urban Development undertook the most recent initiative, thanks to the population's rising expectations. After several rounds of consultations with the central and state governments and other stakeholders, the ministry prescribed a new services benchmark in December 2008. These benchmarks, also endorsed by the Thirteenth Finance Commission, assert the necessary conditions for urban local bodies to obtain performance-linked grants, and are also used for estimating infrastructure investments (Table 14.6).

14.5.3 Water Supply

The drinking water supply in urban areas continues to be a major problem. According to the 2011 census, about only 64 per cent of the urban population was covered by individual water connections in 2001, increasing to 71 per cent in 2011. The duration of water supply in cities ranged from one hour to six hours, and the per capita supply of water ranged from 37 to 298 litres per capita per day

Table 14.6. Service norms of the Ministry of Urban Development, 2008

Urban infrastructure services	Norms
Water supply	100 per cent piped water, continuity of water supply twenty-four hours and per capita consumption norms of 135 litres per capita per day for cities.
Sewerage and wastewater treatment	Underground sewerage system and 100 per cent collection and treatment of wastewater.
Storm water drains	Drainage network covering 100 per cent road length on both sides of the roads in all cities.
Solid waste	One hundred per cent of solid waste collected, transported, and treated for all cities.
Urban roads	Area under roads of city size classes IA, IB, and IC should be 11 per cent with road density of 12.5, and for town size classes II–IV, area under roads should be 7 per cent with road density of 7 per cent.
Urban transport	Rail-based and road-based mass rapid transit system for class IA and IB cities, and city bus services for other city classes.
Street lighting	Illumiance-35 lux for all road categories in all cities. Spacing between street lights: 40 metres for major roads, 45 metres for collector roads, and 50 metres for access road spaces.

Source: The High-Powered Expert Committee (HPEC) for Estimating the Investment Requirement for Urban Infrastructure Services (2011).

(Planning Commission 2010). Most cities do not have metering for residential water connections, and household access to tap water has only increased marginally in non-metropolitan[2] areas and has remained almost stagnant in urban areas from 1993 to 2008–9. Overall, around three-quarters of households had access to tap water in urban areas in 2012 (Table 14.7). This indicates that the pace of enhancing safe drinking water supply facilities in urban areas cannot offset the population growth rate there.

Further, access to water within premises over time in both metropolitan and non-metropolitan areas was stagnant between 1993 and 2002, increasing between 2002 and 2008–9. Overall, only about three-quarters of the urban households had access to water within the premises in 2008–9 (Table 14.8).

Overall, households reporting adequacy of drinking water increased from 1993 to 2008–9, improving significantly between 2002 and 2008–9 in metropolitan areas. More households in metropolitan areas reported adequacy of drinking water compared with those in nonmetropolitan areas (Table 14.9). But in 2012, this adequacy seems to have marginally declined overall in urban areas.

[2] Non-metropolitan towns or cities are those urban areas whose urban population is up to one million. All small and medium towns and large cities fall into this category. Metropolitan cities are cities whose urban population is more than one million.

Table 14.7. Access to tap water by size class over time (%)

Size	1993	1998	2002	2008–9	2012
Urban	70.1	70.1	73.6	76.9	74.3
Metropolitan	85.1	78.9	83.8	85.8	
Non-metropolitan	66.1	67.2	69.7	73.8	

Sources: Calculated from unit-level data of 49th round (1993), 54th round (1998), 58th round (2002), 65th round (2008–9), and 69th round (2012) of National Sample Surveys.

Table 14.8. Access to water within premises over time (%)

Size	1993	1998	2002	2008–9
Urban	66.2	65.7	70.3	74.5
Metropolitan	76.3	76.0	76.8	83.6
Non-metropolitan	63.1	62.3	67.8	71.3

Sources: Calculated from unit-level data of 49th round (1993), 54th round (1998), 58th round (2002), and 65th round (2008–9) of National Sample Surveys.

Table 14.9. Households reporting adequacy of drinking water over time (%)

Size	1993	1998	2002	2008–9	2012
Urban	83.7	85.1	89.2	91.1	89.6
Metro	85.2	85.4	90.4	94.5	
Non-metro	83.2	85.0	88.8	89.9	

Sources: Calculated from unit-level data of 49th round (1993), 54th round (1998), 58th round (2002), 65th round (2008–9), and 69th round (2012) of National Sample Surveys.

14.5.4 Sewerage and Storm Water Facilities

Sanitation is a major problem in urban areas. In India, 4,861 out of the 5,161 cities and towns did not have even a partial sewerage network; almost 50 per cent of households in cities such as Bangalore and Hyderabad did not have sewerage connections (Planning Commission 2010). About 18 per cent of urban households did not have access to any form of latrine facility, and members defecated in the open (MOHA 2011). The percentage of households with access to latrines in metropolitan areas almost reached 100 per cent, but in non-metropolitan areas it was only around 86 per cent in 2008–9 (Table 14.10). Households' access to sewerage facilities has increased substantially in both metropolitan and non-metropolitan

Table 14.10. Households with access to latrines over time (%)

Size	1993	1998	2002	2008–9	2012
Urban	69.4	74.5	82.1	88.7	91.2
Metro	82.5	87.3	92.5	97.5	
Non-metro	65.5	55.2	78.2	85.6	

Sources: Calculated from unit-level data of 49th round (1993), 54th round (1998), 58th round (2002), 65th round (2008–9), and 69th round (2012) of National Sample Surveys.

Table 14.11. Households without access to drainage over time (%)

Size	1993	1998	2002	2008–9	2012
Urban	26.8	20.6	18.5	14.8	12.5
Metro	9.2	8.5	8.1	2.9	
Non-metro	32.0	24.6	22.4	19.0	

Sources: Calculated from unit-level data of 49th round (1993), 54th round (1998), 58th round (2002), 65th round (2008–9), and 69th round (2012) of National Sample Surveys.

areas, with the increase substantially higher in non-metropolitan areas. In 2012, access to latrine facilities showed a further increase.

Less than 20 per cent of road networks are covered by storm water drains, and only 21 per cent of wastewater generated is treated (Central Pollution Control Board 2009). Households without access to drainage in urban areas have declined in both metropolitan and non-metropolitan areas, although access had reached almost 100 per cent in metropolitan areas in 2008–9 (Table 14.11). However, around one-fifth of the households in nonmetropolitan areas did not have access to drainage in 2008–9. The access to drainage facilities showed further improvement in 2012 in urban areas.

14.5.5 Solid Waste Management

The quantum of waste generated in India's urban areas is significantly lower compared with other countries; less than 30 per cent of solid waste is segregated (MUD 2010b). Neither households nor municipalities practice segregation of biodegradable waste, and scientific disposal of waste is almost never practised. Municipal Solid Waste Rules were put in place in 2000, but their enforcement has been poor.

Waste collection coverage ranged from 70 per cent to 90 per cent in major cities, and was less than 50 per cent in smaller cities (Planning Commission 2010). A report card based on the Municipal Solid Waste Rules showed that only 38 per cent of solid waste is collected; 33 per cent of recyclables are segregated; sweeping takes place in 72 per cent of streets; 52 per cent of solid waste is transported; and only 9 per cent of solid waste is processed, and hardly 1 per cent is disposed of (HPEC 2011). Even with the current level of highly inadequate services, solid waste management accounts for 25–50 per cent of the expenditure of an urban local body (ULB) (World Bank 2006). However, cities recover less than 50 per cent of the operation and maintenance costs (MUD 2010a). Clearly, the distribution of the expenditure is heavily loaded in favour of collection and transport, and little attention is paid to processing and proper disposal.

14.5.6 Urban Transport and Road Infrastructure

The state of urban transport and roads in India has improved over the years, yet public transport accounts for only 27 per cent of urban transport in India (MUD 2009). Only twenty out of India's eighty-five cities with a population of 0.5 million or more had a city bus services in 2009 (Aggarwal 2009). Moreover, road density (per sq. km) in cities is extremely varied, measuring 3.8 in Chennai and 19.2 in New Delhi (HPEC 2011).

14.5.7 Gaps in Infrastructure Provisioning from the Norm

Water supply in urban India is still lagging behind the benchmark set by the Ministry of Urban Development. Almost a quarter of urban households do not have piped water; per capita water supply ranges from 37 litres per capita per day to 298 litres per capita per day, for just one to six hours. The 100 per cent norms set by the ministry for sewerage, storm water drainage, and waste management are not met in urban areas. Metropolitan areas are very close to the norms, while nonmetropolitan areas are substantially lagging behind (see Table 14.12).

There are several reasons for the insufficiency of infrastructure. First, parastatal bodies and specialized agencies of the state and central government have steadily encroached on ULBs, which has weakened the base and capacity of ULBs. Second, most ULBs are not professionally managed, necessitating important reforms to improve services delivery. Third, in India's federal system, the central government has enormous power to raise resources, while the next layer, state governments, has relatively less elastic sources of revenue. The last layer of government, ULBs, cannot have a deficit in their budget as stipulated under law. Fourth, *octroi*[3] and property taxes have been major sources of revenue of ULBs, and *octroi* is the only tax within the jurisdiction of city governments that has the potential to grow over

[3] *Octroi* is a duty levied on various goods entering into a town or city.

Table 14.12. Gap of infrastructure between actual and normal

Indicators	Normal	Actual	Gap
Water supply	100% piped water	74.5%	26.5%
Sewerage	100% underground sewerage system and treatment of wastewater	79%	21%
Water drainage	Drain network covering 100% of road length	14.8%	85.2%
Solid waste	100% solid waste collection	79–90% in metros, 50% in smaller cities	10–21% in metros, 50% in smaller cities
Urban Transport	100% covered by city bus services	23.5% cities	76.5%

Source: Planning Commission (2011) and National Sample Survey 65th Round (2008–9).

time with economic activities. However, this has been abolished in most states (except Gujarat and Maharashtra), and no credible alternative devolution of major tax sources to ULBs has taken place. Lastly, the need for providing good infrastructure and proper basic services in an integrated fashion has not been clearly defined in India's growth process. For example, the central government created a dedicated fund for building a hundred 'smart' cities in India—but only in the budget of 2014, and smart cities are in the initial stages of implementation.

14.6 Financing of Urban Infrastructure

As seen in the previous Section 14.5, a substantial deficiency exists in the provision of urban infrastructure in India in all size classes of cities; urbanization demands infrastructure investment as soon as possible. Over the years, several studies have estimated the total investment requirements, and these estimations differ in not only their period of estimation but also their coverage (Table 14.13).

The Constitution (74th) Amendment Act (1992) accorded ULBs a constitutional status as the third tier of government. It incorporated the 12th schedule into the Constitution, containing a list of eighteen functions as the legitimate functional domain of ULBs. It, however, made no provision for a corresponding municipal finance list. Assignment of finances has been left to the discretion of state governments, except that such assignment shall be 'by law'. Thus, ULBs depend upon state governments for assignments of revenue sources, provision of intergovernmental transfers, and allocation for borrowing with or without state guarantees. Funds from central government are devolved to state governments, and state governments are required to devolve resources to their local bodies. However, due to resource constraints, they have not been in a position to allocate adequate resources to ULBs (Mohanty et al. 2007).

Table 14.13. Different estimations of total costs to meet the urban infrastructural deficiency

Serial number	Source	Year	Period	Estimate (Rs million/$ million)
1	Committee of Ministers Constituted by the Central Council of Local Self-Government	1963	Annual	2,113 at 1960–1 prices
2	Indian Infrastructure Report	1996	1996–2006 (ten years)	560,000 at 1995–6 prices
3	Mohanty et al.	2007	2004–14 (ten years)	6,300,000 at 2004–5 prices
4	HPEC Report	2011	2012–31 (twenty years)	30,981,410 at 2009–10 prices
5	McKinsey Study	2010	2010–30 (twenty years)	$787,000 at 2008 prices excluding affordable housing and operating expenses
6	HPEC	2011	2012–16	3,213,780 capital expenditure; 1,942,780 operation and maintenance
7	12th Five Year Plan Estimates	2012	2012–17 (five years)	3,825,760, assuming backlog to be cleared in fifteen years rather than twenty years as estimated by HPEC, and excludes capacity building of urban transport

Source: Compiled from all seven reports mentioned in the table.

Some recent reports have highlighted that the internal resources of ULBs are falling short of the requirements to meet the past, current, and growth needs of infrastructure and services. Some ULBs have begun resorting to borrowing in recent years, often with state government guarantees, from housing and urban development corporations, financial institutions, banks, the open market, and external leading agencies such as the Asian Development Bank (ADB) and World Bank. Similarly, the central government has recognized the need for urban infrastructure development, launching the JNNURM in 2005 to support ULBs to improve infrastructure facilities.

Thus, as defined below, infrastructure financing in urban areas comes from three streams: (1) internal funding, (2) external funding, and (3) other central funding.

14.6.1 Internal Funding

Internal financing includes own revenue and other revenue. In 2011–12, the estimated investment was 0.6 per cent of GDP in the urban sector. While this was significantly higher than investments made before, it was much less than other emerging economies. For example, the PRC invested as much as 2.7 per cent of its GDP in the urban sector during 2000–7 (Finance Commission 2007).

Internal resources generated from own revenue come from tax and non-tax income, while other revenue includes that from outside projects or direct financing. The contribution of total expenditure to GDP increased from 0.9 per cent in 2002–3 to 1.1 per cent in 2008–9, which was further projected by HPEC to be 1.7 per cent in 2012–13 (Figure 14.10). The own revenue and expenditure of ULBs were in constant proportion until 2006–7, but the gap widened after that, reflecting the paucity of own resources in meeting the gap in urban infrastructure financing.

Table 14.14 presents the percentage distribution of revenue and expenditure for urban infrastructure development. The sourcing of expenditure, which includes transfers from state governments, the Central Finance Commission, and government, reveals a clear picture of constraining resources for urban financing. The share of sources of expenditure from state government transfers declined from 10.8 per cent in 2002–3 to 4.9 per cent in 2013–14. On the other hand, the share of funding from central government rose, with the share of other funds estimated to be almost three times as much (5.4 per cent to 14.3 per cent) from 2003–4 to 2012–13.

As ULBs predominantly depend on central and state governments for transfers of funds and grants to move forward, they need to cultivate new, sustainable own revenue streams to help finance urban infrastructure investments. The local administrations can also access market funds on the back of their own financial strength.

The share of own revenue for ULBs has declined significantly, from 63 per cent in 2002–3 to 53 per cent in 2007–8. However, it is expected to increase to about 68 per cent in 2013–14 (HPEC 2011) (Table 14.14). The decline from 2002–3 to 2007–8 was driven by underperformance of both tax-based and other revenue streams. The HPEC report quoted a survey of thirty-six cities that highlighted the issues in

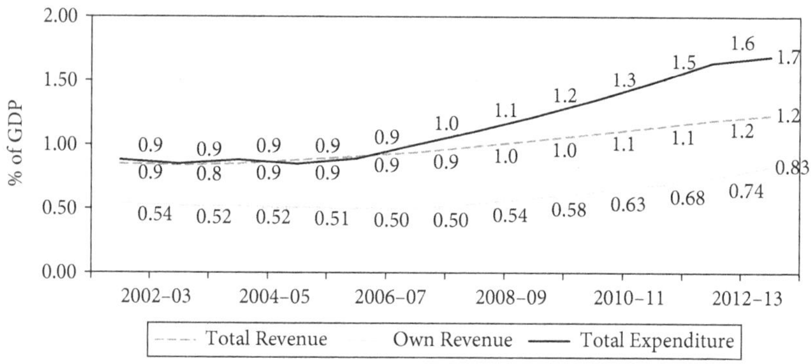

Figure 14.10. Total revenue and expenditure of urban finances from 2002–3 to 2012–13 (% of GDP)

Table 14.14. Distribution of urban infrastructure financing (%)

Financing	2002–3	2007–8	2011–12	2012–13	2013–14
Total revenue	100.0	100.0	100.0	100.0	100.0
1. Own revenue	63.5	52.9	60.2	62.2	67.5
a. Tax	42.2	34.4	43.6	46.2	52.0
b. Non-tax	21.2	18.6	16.5	16.0	15.4
c. Other revenue	36.5	47.1	40.2	38.7	33.3
Subtotal	100.0	100.0	100.0	100.0	100.0
2. Assignment and devolution	17.5	20.6	29.3	31.9	26.8
a. Transfers from state government	10.8	12.8	6.1	5.0	4.9
b. Transfers from Central Finance Commission	1.3	2.0	6.3	8.4	8.1
c. Transfers from government of India	1.5	5.3	4.4	4.2	4.1
d. Others	5.4	6.3	12.1	14.3	9.8
Total expenditure	100.0	100.0	100.0	100.0	100.0
Revenue expenditure	72.5	60.5	71.8	83.3	87.8
Capital expenditure	27.5	39.5	21.6	16.7	12.2

Sources: Finance Commission (2007) and HPEC (2011).

Table 14.15. Cross section regression from states, 2001–2

Serial number	Dependent variable: share of internal revenue of ULB in total revenue	
1	Intercept	25.76 (13.09)***
2	Urbanisation rate, 2001	0.94 (0.435)**
3	R square	0.226

Note: Standard errors are reported in the parenthesis and *, ** and *** represent significance level at 1 per cent, 5 per cent, and 10 per cent respectively.

Source: Census of India 2011 and Thirteenth Finance Commission (2009).

collection of property taxes based on poor assessment rate, weak collection efficiency, flawed methods for property valuation, loss on account of exemptions, and poor enforcement (Mohanty et al. 2007). Also, user charges remained low, which coupled with collection inefficiency has resulted in the low share of the non-tax base of own revenues for ULBs.

But the experience varies from state to state. Are ULBs in more urbanized states in a better position in generating own revenue? It is examined in Table 14.15 through cross-section regression for the year 2001–2 when information on consolidated revenue and expenditure of ULBs across major states are available.

The cross-section regression across eighteen states shows that the urbanization rate positively and significantly affected the share of internal finance of ULBs, implying that more urbanized states can generate a higher share of internal revenue in total revenue (Table 14.15). This is expected, as more urbanized states have higher per capita income and are better administered.

The 74th Amendment introduced two features to strengthen municipal finances: (1) State Finance Commissions (SFCs) that meet every five years to bring certainty, clarity, and consolidation in transfers to ULBs; and (2) measures to augment the State Consolidated Fund to supplement ULB resources as per the Central Finance Commission. However, most SFCs are plagued by inadequate technical and financial support, and, while most have made recommendations, most states have not implemented a formula-based revenue-sharing arrangement with ULBs. Some states have partly devolved funds, while others have cited a strained resource base as the reason for non-compliance. Further, the flow of finances to local bodies is neither predictable nor regular, and does not follow a clear devolution concomitant with their responsibilities.

Private investors have also shied away from investing in urban infrastructure. This is largely due to poor governance at the ULB level, leading to a perception of uncertainty for private investors. Also, there is a lack of clear guidelines for public–private partnerships (PPPs), which makes it difficult for ULBs to design projects that are viable for PPPs. Local agencies seldom use debt financing to fund their requirements, partly driven by the lack of a vibrant debt market in India but mostly because the majority of ULBs are not bankable due to their limited ability to raise revenues.

Further, many small ULBs do not have strong balance sheets or the ability to pay the transaction costs associated with debt financing. As mentioned earlier, the 74th Amendment provided the legitimate functional domain of ULBs, but non-provision of a corresponding Municipal Finance List led to substantial discretion in the hands of state governments to devolve the power of financing urban infrastructure provisions. Thus, the uncertainty in the future stream of income generation of ULBs has affected the investment and maintenance of infrastructure.

14.6.2 External Funding

14.6.2.1 Traditional Financial Institutions

Financial institutions that lend to urban infrastructure projects by providing term loans and investing in their issues include public institutions, such as the Housing and Urban Development Corporation and Life Insurance Corporation of India, and commercial banks and other specialized infrastructure finance bodies such as the India Infrastructure Finance Company, Infrastructure Development Finance Company, and Infrastructure Leasing and Financial Services. Term lending to ULBs is limited, although it is a relatively easier mode than issuing bonds.

Over time, the Housing and Urban Development Corporation's lending to urban infrastructure projects has lessened due to the lack of good projects in urban infrastructure and diminishing abilities of state government guarantees as security in supporting the borrowing agencies, like ULBs and water supply and sewerage boards. The latter phenomenon emerged primarily due to the enactment of the fiscal responsibility legislation that reduced the capacity of state governments to explicitly provide state guarantees for municipal borrowing (Khan 2013).

14.6.2.2 Market-Based Financing System

From the 1990s, a shift can be discerned regarding policy perceptions of the commercial financing of urban infrastructure. The government, recognizing the key role of infrastructure in the process of economic development, set up the Expert Group on the Commercialisation of Infrastructure, popularly known as the Rakesh Mohan Committee, in 1994.

In 1995, a national workshop on municipal bonds explored the possibility of using municipal bonds for accessing capital markets for urban infrastructure. In 1995, the Indo–US Financial Institution Reforms and Expansion (FIRE-D) project supported acredit-rating agency, CRISIL, to develop a methodology for carrying out municipal credit ratings based on a study of ULBs.

In 1996, the Rakesh Mohan Committee advocated commercial finance as a means to meet the large deficit in urban infrastructure finance. PPPs in urban infrastructure were envisaged as a method to mobilize resources and to improve efficiency in the delivery of services. A task force to assist SFCs also recognized the need for municipal bonds. In 1997, the Ninth Five Year Plan approach paper recommended issuance and trading of municipal bonds.

In January 1998, the Ahmedabad Municipal Corporation was first the ULB to access the capital market. It issued Rs 1 billion in bonds to partially finance a Rs 4.390 billion water supply and sewerage project without a state guarantee. Following the Ahmedabad Municipal Corporation, other cities accessed the capital market through municipal bonds without state guarantees. In most cases, the bond proceeds were used to fund water and sewerage schemes or road projects. ULBs have mobilized Rs 4.450 billion through taxable municipal bonds between 1997 and 2004. Out of the eight bonds issued, only two were guaranteed by a state government (Vaidya and Vaidya 2008).

To boost the municipal bond market, the government issued guidelines for the issue of tax-free municipal bonds in February 2001. From 2002 to 2007, eleven ULBs were able to get Rs 6.495 billion in tax-free bonds, and most of the funds were used for water supply, sewerage, drinking water, and road projects.

14.6.2.3 New Market-Based System

Specialized infrastructure financial institutions mostly prefer to lend to special-purpose vehicles and private infrastructure providers—not directly to ULBs—unless it is through some specific intermediation mechanism. The India Infrastructure Finance Company, Infrastructure Development Finance Company, Infrastructure Leasing and Financial Services, and several domestic commercial banks started a

Rs 30 billion pooled municipal debt obligation facility in 2008, which is pan-India in scope. Their list of projects includes development of common infrastructure for small and medium-sized enterprises, solid waste management, power generation, wastewater treatment, and other urban infrastructure facilities like city bus transport.

Infrastructure Leasing and Financial Services also took on some state-specific initiatives. The Tamil Nadu Urban Development Fund was the first PPP between the Tamil Nadu government and three financial institutions—ICICI Bank, HDFC Bank, and Infrastructure Leasing and Financial Services—to provide long-term debt for civic infrastructure in a non-guaranteed mode.

Multilateral institutions, such as ADB and the World Bank, have also financially supported some urban infrastructure development projects. ADB funded the Bangalore Metro Rail Transit System Project and is currently funding the North-Eastern Region Urban Development Program. The World Bank also provided $300 million in capital grants and loans to the Tamil Nadu Urban Development Fund.

14.6.2.4 Pooled Financing

Most of the small and medium ULBs are unable to directly access capital markets on the strength of their balance sheets. In 2003, the Tamil Nadu Urban Development Fund issued a bond of Rs 304 million by pooling fourteen municipalities for commercially viable water and sewerage infrastructure projects. The Water and Sanitation Pooled Fund, a special-purpose vehicle, was set up to issue the municipal bonds. Subsequently, the Karnataka government used the concept of pooled financing to raise debt for the Greater Bangalore Water Supply and Sewerage Project, covering eight municipal towns around Bangalore with a project cost of Rs 6 billion. A debt fund, the Karnataka Water and Sanitation Pooled Fund, was created, and it successfully raised Rs 1 billion of tax-free municipality bonds (Vaidya and Vaidya 2008; Mehta and Mehta 2010).

14.6.2.5 Public–Private Partnerships

Insufficient provision of basic urban services and a lack of access to finance and other resources led ULBs to access PPPs. Several types of PPPs were put into operation, including service contracts, performance-based service contracts, joint sector companies to implement and finance projects, management contracts for operations and maintenance, and construction or build–operate–transfer contracts.

14.6.3 Additional Central Assistance

India had a population of 1.027 billion, with 285 million (28 per cent) living in urban areas, in 2001. It was estimated that by 2011, urban areas would contribute about 65 per cent of GDP. After economic liberalization, it was estimated that the share of the urban population could increase to about 40 per cent of the total population by 2021, but this higher productivity is contingent on availability and quality of infrastructure services.

In 2002–3, the central government set up the Urban Reform Incentive Fund, with an allocation of Rs 5 billion to provide reforms-linked central assistance to states. These reforms were market-linked: (a) enabling the housing and land markets through repealing the Urban Land Ceiling and Regulation Act at the state level, rationalizing the stamp duty, reforming rent control laws, and computerizing land registration; and (b) increasing the financial base of ULBs through property tax reform, increasing the collection efficiency of property taxes, levying user charges on certain services to reach full cost recovery of operation and maintenance costs, and introducing double-entry accounting. The fund was so small, however, that the Urban Reform Incentive Fund did not attract the states.

With a view to make it attractive and make quality infrastructure available, the JNNURM was launched in December 2005 for seven years. The objective of the scheme included empowerment of ULBs, planned and holistic development of cities, and making cities inclusive. The scheme mandated preparation of city development plans and a set of urban reforms at the state and municipal levels. This scheme was introduced in sixty-three cities across India.

It was estimated that over a seven-year period, the ULBs would require a total investment of over Rs 1.2 trillion, which translates into annual funding of over Rs 172 billion in basic infrastructure and services (Table 14.16). It had two focuses: (1) urban infrastructure and governance relating to water supply and sanitation, sewerage, solid waste management, road networks, urban transport, and redevelopment of old city areas; and (2) basic services to the urban poor.

A parallel programme, the Urban Infrastructure Development Scheme for Small and Medium Towns, also started to bridge the gap between the metropolitan

Table 14.16. Urban infrastructure investment requirement (Rs 10 million)

Category	Number of cities	Investment requirement (over seven years starting 2005–6)	Annual fund requirements
Cities with over 4 million population	7	57,143	8,136.3
Cities with 1–4 million population	28	57,143	8,613.3
Selected cities with less than 1 million population	28	6,250	892.9
Total	63	120,536	17,219.5

Source: Ministry of Urban Employment and Poverty Alleviation (2005).

and large cities[4] and small[5] and medium-sized towns.[6] The objectives of the scheme were to (a) improve infrastructure and help create durable public assets and quality-oriented services in cities and towns, (b) enhance PPPs in infrastructural development, and (c) promote the planned, integrated development of towns and cities. The ACA (Additional Central Assistance) under this programme is 80 per cent of project funds, while another 10 per cent are state government funds and 10 per cent are from the ULB. Prior to this scheme, a centrally sponsored scheme, Integrated Development of Small and Medium Towns, occurred.

Both the JNNURM and Urban Infrastructure Development Scheme for Small and Medium Towns have similar mechanisms. After the preparation of a comprehensive development plan, the city- or state-level nodal agency prepares a detailed project proposal, which is then submitted to the Central Sanctioning and Monitoring Committee. The states and cities then enter into a memorandum of agreement with the government, indicating their commitment to implementing identified reforms through specific milestones. The central government gives the funds as ACA, and the memorandum is necessary to access ACA. Essentially, the project proposals and, hence, identification of the projects is done by either the state-level nodal agency or concerned ULB (in states where the ULBs are powerful).

The project proposals articulate the priority of the state and/or the ULB with regard to urban development. Project proposals are by cities and towns, and some have priority. If the state gives priority to small and medium towns, then many applications would go for Urban Infrastructure Development Scheme for Small and Medium Towns funds, and if the state gives priority to the metros and the large cities, then the applications would go to the JNNURM.

Interestingly, the financing pattern recognizes the weak financial base of the small and medium-sized towns. The cities with populations of more than four million only receive 35 per cent of the project funds as ACA, the cities with populations of 1–4 million get 50 per cent of funds as ACA, and others get 80–90 per cent as ACA.[7]

Table 14.17 shows the physical and financial progress under the urban infrastructure schemes. A central allocation of Rs 429 billion for the JNNURM led to an overall commitment of investment of over Rs 807 billion. However, the share of ACA released for infrastructural projects was 73.2 per cent of the sanctioned amount. The performance of the Urban Infrastructure Development Scheme for

[4] Large cities have urban population of more than 200,000 and up to one million.

[5] Small towns are towns with populations up to 50,000. Medium towns are towns that have an urban population of more than 50,000 and up to 200,000.

[6] For details, see <http://urbanindia.nic.in/programme/ud/uidssmt_guidelines.htm> (accessed 26 March 2011).

[7] Ministry of Urban Development, Government of India, Jawaharlal Nehru National Urban Renewal Mission, <http://jnnurm.nic.in/nurmudweb/toolkit/modified_guidelines.pdf> (accessed on 26 March 2011).

Table 14.17. Physical and financial progress under urban infrastructure schemes, up to July 2013 (Rs 10 million)

	JNNURM	UDISSMT	Total	Share
Seven-year allocation	31,500	11,400	42,900	73.4
Number of projects sanctioned	550	806	1,356	40.6
Total cost of projects	66,754	14,011	80,765	82.7
Total ACA committed	31,006	11,313	42,319	73.3
Total ACA released	21,286	9,691	30,977	68.7
ACA released to ACA sanctioned (%)	68.7	85.7	73.2	
Number of projects completed	198	393	591	33.5

Note: ACA = Additional Central Assistance, JNNURM = Jawaharlal Nehru National Urban Renewal Mission, UDISSMT = Urban Infrastructure Development Scheme for Small and Medium Towns.

Source: Ministry of Urban Development, 2013. Presentation on Project Management System, <http://pmis-jnnurm.nic.in/PMIS_Secy_UD_12July13.pdf> (accessed 20 May 2014).

Table 14.18. Sector share under Urban Infrastructure Development Scheme for Small and Medium Towns, 2010

	Water supply	Sewerage	Storm water	Water body management	Solid waste management	Heritage	Roads	Total approval	No. of towns
All India	61.2	22.5	5.8	0.2	2.5	0.3	7.4	100	640

Note: No parking projects were sent for approval under the scheme.

Source: Mahadevia and Sarkar (2012).

Small and Medium Towns was better. A delay in securing land for projects and obtaining approval from various regulatory authorities led to late implementation of some of the projects, but the proportion of ACA committed and released for larger towns was more than two-thirds of the total ACA.

Further, the sector share of the Urban Infrastructure Development Scheme for Small and Medium Towns in 2010 showed that more than half of the fund was spent on water supply, followed by a quarter on sewerage, whereas the share of other sectors like roads, storm water, solid waste management, and heritage consisted of a small part of the total (Table 14.18).

Kundu and Samanta (2011: 62–3) showed that only 58 per cent of the urban population has been covered under JNNURM, the coverage being high in the developed states and metropolitan cities. Of the 5,161 towns/cities, 4,207 are yet to be covered under the programme. An analysis of the JNNURM funding pattern, which is inbuilt in the component-wise indicative allocation, clearly brings out the big city bias. In fact, the developed states have had a larger share of the pie because of their ability to introduce the reforms as per their committed timeline. Moreover, a closer examination of the comprehensive development plans and detailed project proposals, along with the mandatory reforms, makes it obvious that the mission has a clear-cut mandate of producing 'global cities', disciplining them enough to adhere to the rigours of the credit rating agencies, which is a precondition for accessing capital markets and other innovative sources of funding.

By the end of August 2010, proposals were sent for 640 towns under the scheme for 763 projects (Mahadevia and Sarkar 2012). This means that only a few towns have sent funding applications (i.e. detailed project proposal) and that too for only one project. The average number of project proposals sent per small or medium town was 1.2. This is unlike the proposals sent under the JNNURM for the mission cities, in which case many proposals per city have been sent for funding to the Ministry of Urban Development.

The policy context clearly indicates a bias in favour of metropolitan and large cities in terms of urban development issues and financing. From another perspective, it could be more efficient to solve the congestion problem and shortage of urban facilities in large cities and to create conditions for agglomeration effects, given the limited availability of resources.

Most of the ACA released largely went to two schemes: water supply and sewerage (Table 14.19). The impact of this larger allocation can be seen (Table 14.19) in the continuous improvement in tap water supply and the substantial improvement in household access to latrine and drainage facilities in metropolitan and non-metropolitan areas over the last decade. The unavailability of data beyond 2008–9 does not allow examination of the changes that have taken place in the most recent years.

These constituted more than 80 per cent of total ACA funds released under the Urban Infrastructure Development Scheme for Small and Medium Towns. Yet under JNNURM, the share was comparatively less, because twenty-one projects, including the Bus Rapid Transit System (BRTS), with an approved cost of over

Table 14.19. Share of ACA released under urban infrastructure schemes, as of July 2013

Sector	JNNURM	UDISSMT	Total
Water supply	37.2	65.8	46.8
Sewerage	23.2	17.9	21.4
Share in total ACA released	60.3	83.7	68.2

Note: ACA = Additional Central Assistance, JNNURM = Jawaharlal Nehru National Urban Renewal Mission, UDISSMT = Urban Infrastructure Development Scheme for Small and Medium Towns.

Source: Ministry of Urban Development, 2013, Presentation on Project Management System, <http://pmis-jnnurm.nic.in/PMIS_Secy_UD_12July13.pdf> (accessed 20 May 2014).

Rs 52 billion, were sanctioned. Besides, 15,260 low-floor and semi-low-floor buses were sanctioned to sixty-five cities with central assistance of over Rs 20 billion, which enabled thirty-four cities to organize city bus services for the first time. Another 123 projects, involving roads, flyovers, road-over bridges, and parking projects, with an approved cost of over Rs 101 billion, were sanctioned for traffic improvement and parking.

In last few years further steps have been taken to improve urban infrastructure. To encourage public transport, BRTS has been approved for eleven cities under the JNNURM programme. A new programme, the Atal Mission for Rejuvenation and Urban Transformation, was launched in June, 2015 to improve basic infrastructure in 500 cities/towns, the total outlay for five years from 2015–16 to 2019–20 has been fixed at Rs 500 billion.

14.7 Lessons from Success Stories and Future Strategies

Despite several constraints, government organizations, private bodies, and others have made many successful efforts to ease urban congestion and to develop urban infrastructure in India. Some of these are discussed here to understand their operations, so that future strategies can be suggested in a similar direction to make efficient development of urban infrastructure (Box 14.1).

Efforts have also been made to provide underground sewerage networks by direct public participation. One such case is a residential suburb of Chennai in Kanchipuram District (Box 14.2).

Box 14.1. Bangalore Municipal Corporation has reorganized

Bangalore went through administrative reforms in 2007 by merging its surrounding municipalities. The Bangalore Municipal Corporation was changed to the Greater Bangalore Municipal Corporation when it was merged with seven neighbouring city municipal councils as well as eleven villages around Bangalore. In addition, the Bangalore Metropolitan Regional Development Authority was formed as an autonomous body under the Karnataka state government to coordinate regional investment projects. The municipal corporation has thus eased the pressures of population by merging the neighbouring villages, by decreasing population density from 19,012 persons per sq. km in 2001 to only 11,470 persons per sq. km in 2011, with the merged city's geographical area expanding from 226 sq. km in 2001 to 740.6 sq. km in 2011.

Box 14.2. Construction of underground sewerage in a residential suburb of Chennai, Kanchipuram District

A residential suburb of Chennai in Kanchipuram District, with a population of 150,000, had no underground sewerage until 2000. Almost 80 per cent of the households had to depend on septic tanks with soak pits. The urban landscape of Alandur was transformed by an infrastructure project, which provided a comprehensive underground sewerage network and a sewage treatment plant. This was accomplished over five years with direct public participation. The project was expected to cost Rs 3.4 billion, and the financing was arranged so half of the amount would come from the government of India's megacity programme, a precursor to the JNNURM; Rs 1.36 billion from the World Bank; and Rs 340 million from resident deposits. The residents contributed Rs 1.19 billion, so only Rs 30 million was drawn from the World Bank and Tamil Nadu Urban Infrastructure Financial Services.

This project involved the construction of a sewer line covering the entire road length of 137 kilometres, a pump house, 5,650 manholes, and 23,700 home service connections. The network construction contract was awarded to IVRCL, a private infrastructure company. Consulting Engineering Services was appointed as the project management consultant. A major contributing factor to the success of the initiative was the dynamic leadership of the directly elected mayor of Alandur (HPEC 2011).

The other successful case studies are Delhi's rail-based Mass Rapid Transit System and Ahmedabad's BRTS), which have successfully contributed to improving the situation with respect to public transport. In addition, Indore, which did not have a public transport system until 2006, now has a city bus service with 104 buses run by a special-purpose vehicle under Indore City Transport Services. Surat's bus fleet of 125, established in 2008, carries 70,000 passengers every day. In both cases, the option of the bus services has been outsourced to the private sector (Box 14.3).

14.8 Conclusion and Policy Recommendations

In the last three decades, India has experienced high growth without a significant rise in urbanization. However, substantial changes in infrastructure facilities can be observed. The length of highways has doubled, and the rail route length has increased marginally with substantial improvement in the electrification of the routes. The length of navigable waterways has also marginally increased. Other

Box 14.3. The success of city bus services in Indore and Surat

Indore and Surat developed their city bus services through a transparent, competitive bidding process for service providers. Both now have private bus operators running services on routes determined by the urban local body, and bus stops have been built on a build–operate–transfer basis.

The marketing of the city bus services in Indore is done by a vendor who issues at least 15,000 monthly and daily passes at agreed rates every month, ensuring a monthly income of Rs 4 million for Indore City Transport Services. Indore runs 104 buses on twenty-four routes, with 300 bus stops built on a build–operate–transfer basis. The net profits of Indore City Transport Services rose from Rs 3.4 million in 2006–7 to over Rs 10 million in 2009–10. A GPS tracking system is used to monitor the bus services, but the high maintenance cost of the technology (at 55 per cent of Indore City Transport Services' total costs) is justified by its ability to put in place a monitoring mechanism that helps oversee the service standards set by the company.

Surat has 125 buses running on forty-four routes, carrying 70,000 passengers every day. There are eighty-seven bus stops on a build–operate–transfer basis, each of them earning revenue of Rs 40,000 per year. The urban local body gets a premium of Rs 20,000 per bus from the operator for the contract period of five years. All city buses are run on compressed natural gas and are owned, operated, and maintained by private operators (HPEC 2011).

facilities, such as the length of pipelines, electricity consumption, and teledensity, have improved substantially even in the last decade. India does not lag much behind the PRC in terms of passenger traffic, but does substantially lag behind it in terms of goods transported by roads, rail, and air, and electric power consumption. The low manufacturing base of India seems to go along with the lower level of goods transport movement and electricity consumption.

The relationship between urbanization and road density across the seventeen major states of India in 2011 is not found to be significant. Yet the urbanization rate has a significant positive relationship with teledensity and electricity consumption per capita. However, per capita income positively and significantly affected the urbanization rate (examined through regression across states). Similarly, transport and power infrastructure availability are significant explanatory factors for TFP (i.e. the proxy for economic development). Thus, infrastructure positively affects urbanization through promoting faster economic growth.

This chapter shows that urbanization in India does create demand for infrastructure investment, but it is not financed sufficiently, resulting in gaps in provision of infrastructure. This gap of infrastructure provisioning also varies across states.

Apart from the issue of financial devolution to ULBs, several other strategies need to be adopted: (a) strengthening various aspects of urban governance, (b) establishing adequate urban planning with proper city development plans and not implementing urbanization efforts through disjointed activities, and (c) building capacity to manage urbanization.

The primary requirement of financing urban infrastructure is to strengthen the financial base of ULBs so that they can generate a predictable quantum of funds over a certain specified period. This would create a sufficient base on the basis of which external financing requirements can be planned and executed. The following steps are needed to realize this.

(1) *Assign a revenue base to ULBs.* Today, ULBs depend on state governments to assign revenue sources, transfer state and central financing, and permit borrowing with or without state guarantees. The Twelfth Five Year Plan proposed creating a constitutional amendment that would clearly delineate the domain of ULBs by providing a local bodies finance list, which would define the various tax and non-tax revenue streams for ULBs. It further suggested that the list should include property, entertainment, professional, motor vehicle, advertising taxes, and stamp duties, as well as entitling ULBs to collect appropriate user charges and trade licence fees, and to use land-based instruments to augment their revenues. Further, these taxes and user charges are needed to be regularly updated using scientific principles.

(2) *Make revenue sharing more predictable.* The Twelfth Five Year Plan suggested that even revenue sharing from the state to ULBs needs to be made more predictable by sharing 25 per cent of the goods and services tax with rural and urban local bodies, and this should be enforced through an appropriate constitutional mechanism.

(3) *Collect user fees.* ULBs should also take appropriate measures to collect outstanding dues of user charges for water supply, sewerage, and garbage collection for the high operational and maintenance requirement of these facilities. As discussed earlier, there is substantial scope of generating resources through this mechanism. It should be targeted to at least cover the operation and maintenance cost of these facilities, which takes up a substantial proportion of the expenditure budget of ULBs.

(4) *Generate more non-budgetary resources.* ULBs should be encouraged to generate additional non-budgetary resources through measures such as monetization of land and other land value instruments like betterment charges, land use conversion charges, and appropriate development charges, which have already been successfully implemented in various cities. These enhanced and predictable revenue sources would enable ULBs to explore various mechanisms of external financing (both private and public) to raise a considerable amount of funds for financing infrastructure.

References

Agarwalla, Astha. 2011. *Estimating the Contribution of Infrastructure in Regional Productivity Growth in India*, Indian Institute of Management, Ahmedabad.

Aggarwal, O. P. 2009. *Sustainable Urban Transport in India: Current Challenges and Directions for the Future*, Urban Mass Company, Delhi.

Bhagat, Ram B. 2011. 'Emerging Pattern of Urbanisation in India'. *Economic and Political Weekly 46* (34): 10–12.

Bosworth, B. and A. Maertens. 2010. 'Economic Growth and Employment Generation: The Role of Service Sector in Eja Ghani'. In *The Service Revolution in South Asia*, edited by Ejaz Ghani and Homi Kharas, Oxford University Press.

Central Pollution Control Board. 2009. *Annual Report of CPCB for 2008–9*, Ministry of Environment and Forests, Government of India, Delhi.

Finance Commission, India. 2007. *Report of the Thirteenth Finance Commission, 2010–2015*, Delhi.

Finance Commission. 2009. 'Report of the Thirteenth Finance Commission', New Delhi.

HPEC (High-Powered Expert Committee). 2011. *2011 Report on Indian Urban Infrastructure and Services*, Delhi.

Khan, H. R. 2013. 'Financing Strategies for Urban Infrastructure: Trends and Challenges'. Inaugural address at the Centre for Advanced Financial Research and Learning Conference on Financing Strategies for Urban Infrastructure, Mumbai, 18–19 July.

Kundu, Debolina and Dibyendu Samanta. 2011. 'Redefining the Inclusive Urban Agenda in India'. *Economic and Political Weekly in India 46* (5): 55–63.

Mahadevia, Darshini and Sandip Sarkar. 2012. *Handbook of Urban Inequalities*, Oxford University Press.

Mazumdar, Dipak and Sandip Sarkar. 2008. *Globalization, Labour Market and Inequality in India*, Routledge.

Mehta, Meera and Dinesh Mehta. 2010. 'A Glass Half Full? Urban Development (1990s to 2010)'. *Economic and Political Weekly 45* (28): 20–3.

MUD (Ministry of Urban Development). 2009. *National Urban Sanitation Policy: A Perspective*, Government of India, Delhi.

MUD (Ministry of Urban Development). 2010a. *National Rating and Award Scheme for Sanitation for Indian Cities*, Government of India, Delhi.

MUD (Ministry of Urban Development). 2010b. *Improving Service Outcomes 2008–9*, Government of India, Delhi.

Ministry of Urban Employment and Poverty Alleviation. 2005. *Jawaharlal Nehru National Urban Renewal Mission*, Government of India, Delhi.

MOHA (Ministry of Home Affairs). 2001. *India 2001 Census*, Government of India, Delhi.

MOHA (Ministry of Home Affairs). 2011. *India 2011 Census*, Government of India, Delhi.

Mohanty P. K., B. M. Misra, R. Goyal, and P. D. Jeromi. 2007. *Municipal Finance in India: An Assessment*, Department of Economic Analysis and Policy, Reserve Bank of India, Mumbai.

National Institute of Urban Affairs. 2011. *India's Urban Demographic Transition: 2011 Census Results*, Delhi.

Planning Commission. 2010. *Mid Term Appraisal for Eleventh Five Year Plan*, Government of India, Delhi.

Planning Commission. 2011. *Report of the Steering Committee on Urbanisation*, Government of India, Delhi.

Planning Commission. 2012. *Twelfth Five Year Plan, 2012–17*, Government of India, Delhi.

Ram, F., S. K. Mohanty, and Usha Ram. 2009. *Progress and Prospects of Millennium Development Goals in India*, International Institute for Population Sciences, Mumbai.

Vaidya, Chetan and Hitesh Vaidya. 2008. 'Creative Financing of Urban Infrastructure in India through Market Based Financing and Public–Private Partnership Options'. In *9th Metropolis Congress of Metropolis, Sydney, 22–25 October.*

World Bank. Nd. 'World Development Indicators'. <http://data.worldbank.org/data-catalog/world-development-indicators>.

World Bank. 2006. 'Improving Management of Municipal Solid Waste Management in India: Overview and Challenges', World Bank.

PART VII

HUMAN CAPITAL

15
Human Capital and Urbanization in the People's Republic of China

Chunbing Xing

15.1 Introduction

Human capital refers to the knowledge, skills, and strength accumulated by an individual to enhance his/her productivity, which are embedded in human bodies. It plays an essential role in economic development and the urbanization process. The modern economic sector has a greater demand for labour with more human capital. Urban areas with a large population and high population density are ideal places for people to accumulate human capital. In particular, cities provide places for knowledge, skills, and ideas to influence individuals informally, creating large spillover (external) effects. In developing countries like the People's Republic of China (PRC), human capital also facilitates the process of population shifts from rural to urban areas.

The interaction between human capital development and urbanization is influenced by institutional arrangements and government policies. In the PRC, the decentralized fiscal system and the Hukou system have major impacts on this relationship.

In this chapter, we address the following issues. First, how does educational development perform in the PRC's urbanization process? We examine this issue by looking at the changes in education levels for rural and urban PRC and for different provinces/cities. Second, how do the returns to education vary between rural and urban areas and across different provinces/cities? Are the external returns to education large in urban PRC? As cities are different in terms of geographical location, economic structure, and historical legacy, they have different optimal population sizes and education levels. Therefore, we are interested in whether the labour force with different education levels can move freely to meet the demand for it by cities of different sizes. In particular, we examine the responsiveness of the labour force of different education levels to regional labour demand shocks. The distribution of human capital and human capital returns in rural and urban PRC and across cities provide hints for evaluating and reforming policies affecting labour mobility.

Chunbing Xing., *Human Capital and Urbanization in the People's Republic of China* In: *Cities of Dragons and Elephants: Urbanization and Urban Development in China and India. Edited by:* Guanghua Wan and Ming Lu, Oxford University Press (2019). © Oxford University Press. DOI: 10.1093/oso/9780198829225.003.0015

As most of the population growth in urban PRC comes from rural-to-urban migration, it is important to examine the characteristics of rural-to-urban migrants in comparison to rural and urban residents. To be specific, we ask whether there are selection effects in terms of education levels in the urbanization process. Finally, we discuss whether migrant households face problems (or discrimination) in education and training, and how to improve efficiency and equality in education and health.

To address these issues, we first provide an analysis on the institutional background of the relationship between human capital and institutions, such as the role played by governments at various levels in allocating educational resources and the role of the PRC's household registration (Hukou) system in determining migrants' access to education and health care. We then discuss educational development in the context of rapid urbanization. In particular, we describe the educational developments in rural and urban PRC and across different regions. To see the role of human capital in urban development, we emphasize the following: (1) large and educated cities provide higher returns to education and attract more educated workers. However, the Hukou system is still a factor impeding sufficient labour mobility, which is especially true for educated workers, implying that the returns to education in cities are not fully realized; (2) there are large external returns to education in urban areas; and (3) rural-to-urban migration is positively selected in terms of human capital levels. Issues in human capital development in the urbanization process are then discussed.

Health issues might be slightly different from education or other types of skills. We analyse its relationship with urbanization in Section 15.6. Policy implications are discussed in Section 15.7.

15.2 Institutional Background

One important feature in the PRC's urbanization process is that labour mobility is controlled by the Hukou system, which has greatly influenced the pace and pattern of the PRC's urbanization (Au and Henderson 2006). Traditionally, one's Hukou status is categorized by both socio-economic eligibility ('agricultural' and 'non-agricultural' Hukou) and registered residential location (local and non-local Hukou) (Chan and Buckingham 2008).[1] Hukou status is primarily determined by birth and is passed on from one generation to the next (Wu and Treiman 2004).

[1] The first classification determined entitlement to state-subsidized food grain and other prerogatives. The second classification defines one's rights for many activities in a specific locality. One's Hukou status (locality and socio-economic categories either agricultural or non-agricultural) is determined by birth, following his/her parents.

By controlling migration, the Hukou system has been an essential factor in the PRC's rural–urban divide (Knight and Song 1999; Zhao 2000; Lu 2003). Hukou status not only signifies differences in occupation and location but also differences in many other areas, with urban Hukou being associated with better paid and more secure jobs, access to better public services, and more welfare and subsidies. Only a small number of rural residents with special achievements can obtain urban Hukou. Going to college or professional school has been a major channel of Hukou conversion. Other channels that increase the probability of Hukou conversion include joining the army, being promoted as a cadre (Wu and Treiman 2004; Fan 2008), purchasing urban housing (Deng and Gustafsson 2006), and land conversion as a result of city expansion (Wong and Huen 1998).

In the Hukou-reforming process since the early 1980s, one major change was the localization of Hukou management, with many local governments receiving full power to determine their own criteria and the number of new local permanent Hukou they would grant. It has become easier for workers and households to transfer their registrations to other locations (in particular, to small- to medium-sized cities), and temporary residence permits are being granted more often. Also, it became possible for some to migrate and get a job without a valid permit.

Many migrants without urban Hukou are excluded from formal urban sectors and earn significantly less than native workers (Meng and Zhang 2001; Meng 2001; Maurer-Fazio and Dinh 2004; Gagnon et al. 2014; Démurger et al. 2009). In most cases, migrant workers are not covered by urban social security systems and are not entitled to local welfare programmes, subsidies, and public services, including education (Gagnon et al. 2014).

Educational development and its role in the urbanization process are closely related to this institutional background. In the PRC, primary school education and lower middle school have been compulsory since the late 1980s. As a public service, the operation of the schools was mostly financed by local governments. To be specific, the county governments are mainly responsible for financing the functioning of these schools. Before 2000, local governments in rural areas could collect agricultural taxes or fees for education expenditures, but these taxes and fees were cancelled in the following years, putting financial stress on many local governments. This decentralized feature, combined with the Hukou system, caused several problems regarding the allocation of educational resources. First, a large gap in education resources has emerged not only between rural and urban areas but also across different regions, and even across different districts within a city. Second, the education expenses of local governments tend to be based on the number of residents with local Hukou, making it hard for residents without local Hukou to send their children to local schools. In the early reforms period, most migrant workers had to leave their children back home in rural areas. Although the situation has improved in recent years with the building of migrant schools (mostly in suburban areas and privately run) and some local public schools opening access to migrant children, the school quality is lower for migrants without local Hukou than for local residents, and extra fees are often required. More and more children are migrating with their parents, and attending schools at their destination location. However, they are required to take the college entrance examinations at the Hukou registration province.

Colleges and universities were mainly located in cities, especially in municipalities and provincial capitals. Under the earlier central planning regime, higher education had been heavily subsidized. With economic reforms and the enlargement of the scale of higher education, the Chinese government gradually lowered subsidies for higher education. In 'Guidelines for China's Education Reform and Development' published in 1993, the central government made it clear that higher education is non-compulsory, and students should pay tuition in principle (State Council 1993). From 1995 to 2004, tuition fees increased from 800 RMB per person per year to 5,000 RMB per person per year on average (Yang 2006). Expenditures on education ranked first in total household expenditure in the 10th Five Year Plan (CYCRC 2007).

Another major reform of higher education in the 1990s was to cancel the planning system for allocating college graduates. The new system is thus effectively a two-sided market. Graduates find jobs based on mutual agreement with employers, with much less intervention from the government. But equally, college graduates face more severe competition, putting pressure on the labour market, especially in urban areas.

Universities are administered by different levels of government. Elite universities are generally funded by both the central government (through the management of the Ministry of Education) and provincial governments, while many other local universities are mainly funded by the provincial-level government. Universities admit students from all over the PRC, but usually the admission quota is higher for the province of location than for other provinces, which is true even for elite universities managed by the Ministry of Education. In the last two decades, the central government has initiated two major projects (the 211 project and the 985 project), aiming at improving the quality of universities. The aim of these two projects is to promote the quality of teaching and research by building high-quality or first-class universities in the world. Universities in these projects were mainly elite universities. There are currently very few privately run universities in the PRC.

Higher education is closely related to the PRC's urbanization process because it not only produced graduates with higher human capital levels, but has also been one of the major channels through which rural individuals get urban local Hukou.

15.3 Educational Development in the Urbanization Process

15.3.1 Human Capital Development in the PRC

15.3.1.1 Educational Expansion

The PRC has experienced tremendous educational expansion in recent decades. In the period 1990–2012, the PRC's GDP grew at an annual rate of 10 per cent, and the amount of fiscal expenditure on education also grew rapidly. In the mid-1990s, the share of fiscal expenditure on education in GDP was below 2.5 per cent, and by 2011 it had reached 4 per cent (see Figure 15.1). Figure 15.2 shows that local government has been responsible for around 90 per cent of the fiscal expenditure on education. Figure 15.3 shows the shares of the fiscal expenditure on different education levels in total education expenditure. The share of primary education has declined continuously from around 35 per cent to 30 per cent, while that of tertiary education has increased significantly in recent years.

Figure 15.4 shows that the share of primary school graduates admitted to middle school increased from 80 per cent in the early 1990s to around 98 per cent in the early 2010s due to the enforcement of the Law of Compulsory Education and increased subsidies, especially in poor regions. The change in the case of higher education was more dramatic. In 1998, less than 50 per cent of high-school graduates were admitted to college. The percentage increased to 65 per cent in 1999, and it kept rising in subsequent years. The share of the middle-school graduates admitted to high school increased continuously from around 50 per cent in the

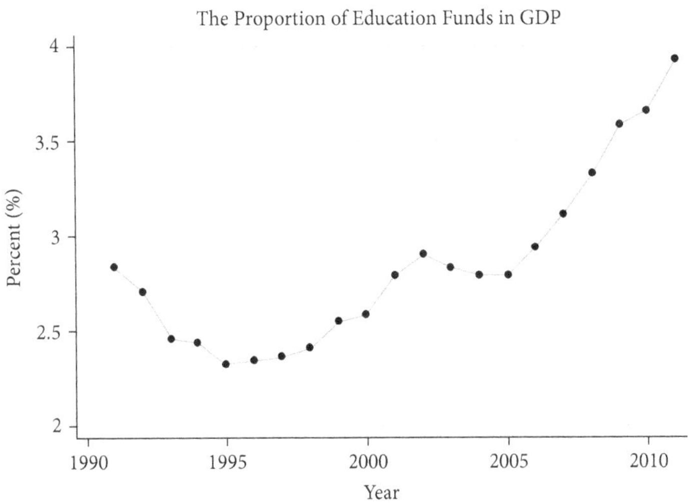

Figure 15.1. The share of fiscal expenditure on education in GDP
Source: Ministry of Education of China (2013).

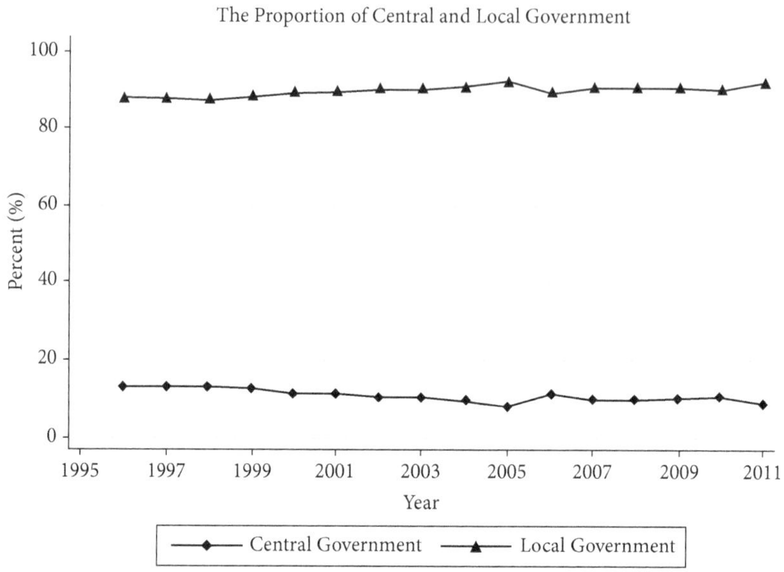

Figure 15.2. Share of fiscal expenditure on education by central and local governments
Source: Ministry of Education of China (2013).

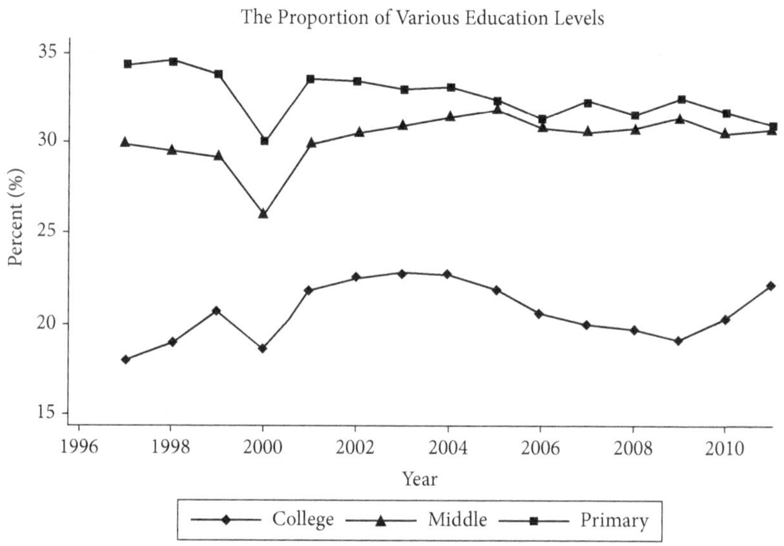

Figure 15.3. The share of education fiscal expenditure in different levels of education
Source: Ministry of Education of China (2013).

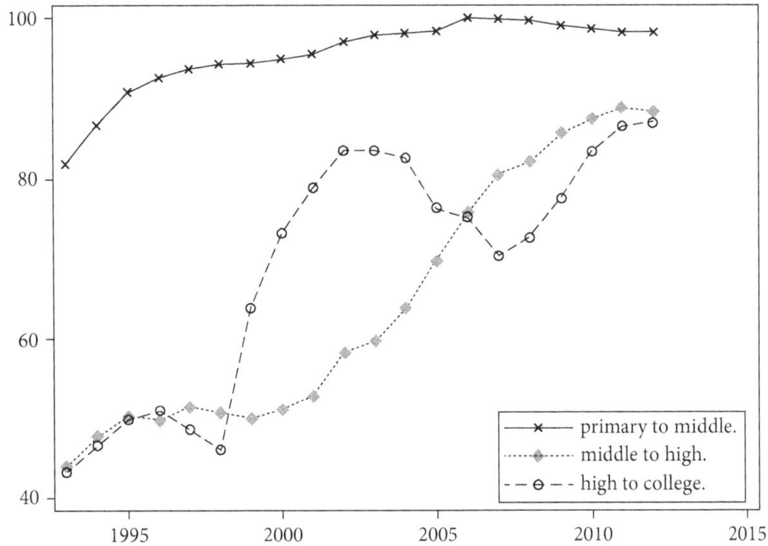

Figure 15.4. Admission rates at various education levels
Source: *China Statistical Yearbook* 2013 (NBSC Various years).

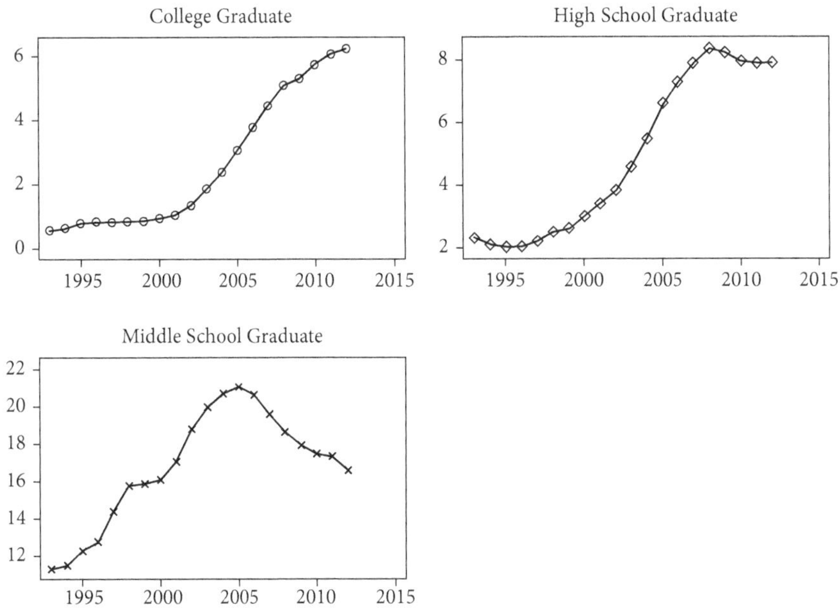

Figure 15.5. The number of graduates at various levels of education (in million)
Source: *China Statistical Yearbook* 2013 (NBSC Various years).

late 1990s to nearly 90 per cent in the early 2010s. As the returns to high school are relatively low and the main function of high schools is preparation for college examinations, the expansion in high school can be largely regarded as a response to the expansion in tertiary education. Between 2003 and 2007, the increase in the number of high-school graduates (and the middle-school to high-school admission rate) was so dramatic that the share of high-school graduates admitted to college decreased. However, the number of students admitted to universities kept increasing. Starting from around 2008, the number of high-school graduates stopped rising and the admission rate into universities increased again.

As a result of educational expansion, the number of college graduates increased dramatically starting from early 2000. For example, the number of college graduates in 2000 was 1.03 million. By 2012, the number reached 6.25 million (see Figure 15.5).

15.3.1.2 Human Capital in Rural and Urban PRC

In this section, we use two nationally representative datasets to show that human capital development is unbalanced between rural and urban areas. The first dataset we use is from three waves of the China Household Income Project (CHIP) in 1995, 2002, and 2007. Table 15.1 shows the distributions of different education levels in rural and urban areas throughout this period for individuals aged 22–54. The increase in the level of human capital is dramatic in urban PRC. The share of the sample with university degrees increased from 7 per cent in 1995 to 16 per cent in 2007. If we consider the education levels above professional school (inclusive), the increase is even more dramatic, with the share increasing from 22 to 40 per cent between 1995 and 2007. In contrast, the share of the sample with tertiary education in rural areas increased only slightly, from 0.6 per cent in 1995 to 2.6 per cent in 2007.

This pattern is also observed in our second dataset, the 2000 census data and the 1 per cent population survey for 2005 (see Table 15.2). Between 2000 and 2005, the share of population aged 22–54 with professional school degrees and above

Table 15.1. Distribution of education levels (%), 1995–2007

	1995		2002		2007	
	Urban	Rural	Urban	Rural	Urban	Rural
Primary and below	6.6	47.9	4.4	36.6	2.3	25.8
Middle school	32.0	40.7	27.9	47.4	19.9	55.2
High school	24.1	9.6	28.0	11.8	27.5	12.6
Technical school	15.3	1.3	11.0	3.0	10.6	3.8
Professional school	15.0	0.4	19.7	1.0	24.2	1.7
University and above	7.0	0.2	9.0	0.3	15.5	0.9

Note: Observations are restricted to those aged 22–54, who are able to work and are out of school.
Source: Calculated using CHIP 1995, 2002, and 2007.

Table 15.2. Distribution of education levels (%), 2000 and 2005

	2000		2005				
	By Hukou type		By Hukou type		By type of residence		
	Non-agricultural	Agricultural	Non-agricultural	Agricultural	Urban (city)	Suburban (town)	Countryside (village)
	Share of various education levels within agricultural/non-agricultural Hukou or rural/urban areas (%, column total=100)						
Below primary	1.3	8.0	1.3	8.6	2.1	4.5	10.1
Primary	9.2	39.0	7.9	34.3	13.2	21.7	37.1
Middle school	36.5	46.4	34.3	49.0	42.0	47.5	45.6
High school	22.5	5.8	32.4	7.5	26.1	17.4	6.3
Technical school	13.2	0.7					
Professional	12.3	0.2	15.8	0.5	10.3	6.8	0.8
University and above	5.1	0.0	8.5	0.1	6.4	2.1	0.1
Total	100	100	100	100	100	100	100
	Agricultural Hukou–non-agricultural Hukou or rural–urban distribution for different education levels (%, row total=100)						
Below primary	5.5	94.5	5.8	94.3	10.8	12.0	77.2
Primary	7.7	92.3	8.7	91.4	16.3	14.0	69.7
Middle school	21.7	78.4	22.4	77.7	31.0	18.2	50.9
High school	57.8	42.2	64.1	35.9	58.4	20.2	21.4
Technical school	86.2	13.8					
Professional	95.9	4.1	92.8	7.2	68.2	23.6	8.3
University and above	99.2	0.9	98.0	2.0	83.7	14.0	2.3
Total	26.0	74.0	29.2	70.8	33.0	17.1	49.9

Note: Observations are restricted to those aged 22–54, who are able to work and are out of school.

Source: Calculated using random samples of the 2000 census and the 2005 1 per cent population survey.

Table 15.3. Education levels for population aged above six, 2000 and 2010

	2000				2010			
	Urban	Rural	Urban	Rural	Urban	Rural	Urban	Rural
	10,000		%		10,000		%	
Illiterate	1,165	6,930	4.2	9.8	803	4,417	2.1	7.2
Primary school	6,132	33,359	22.4	47.1	6128	23,207	16.0	38.1
Middle school	10,145	26,025	37.0	36.7	13,859	27,381	36.1	44.9
High school	4,569	3,307	16.7	4.7	9,363	4,710	24.4	7.7
Technical (*zhongzhuan*)	2,176	849	7.9	1.2				
Professional	1956	325	7.1	0.5	4,375	942	11.4	1.5
University	1,208	52	4.4	0.1	3,509	302	9.1	0.5
Graduate	84	2	0.3	0.0	378	12	1.0	0.0
Total	27,435	70,849	100	100	38,415	60,971	100	100

Source: Calculated from the 2000 and 2005 censuses.

increased from 18 per cent to 26 per cent in urban areas. In contrast, the share only increased from 0.2 per cent to 0.6 per cent in rural areas. The last four columns in Table 15.2 indicate that a majority of the less educated population (middle-school graduates and below) is concentrated in rural areas, while highly educated workers mostly reside in urban areas.

This pattern remains true when we look at the population aged above six, rather than the restricted sample of the working age population (see Table 15.3). Even in the most recent data of the 2010 census, there still is a huge gap in education, especially in tertiary education.

15.3.1.3 Human Capital Across Provinces/Cities

Within urban areas, how are individuals of different education levels distributed across cities? Using the random samples of the 2000 census data and the 2005 1 per cent population survey, we calculate the size of the working age population (defined as those aged 23–55 and not in school) and the share of workers with college degrees or above for each prefecture-level city.[2] Figure 15.6 shows the relationship between this share and the population for 2000 (panel A) and 2005 (panel B). The figure suggests that individuals of different education levels are not randomly located in different cities, there is a positive correlation between the share of college graduates and population size, and the correlation seems to be stronger for 2005 than for 2000.

Figure 15.7 further shows the changes in the share of college graduates in each prefecture-level city against the city's initial share of college graduates in 2000.

[2] As the sample is random, we count the number of observations in each city and use it as the city's population.

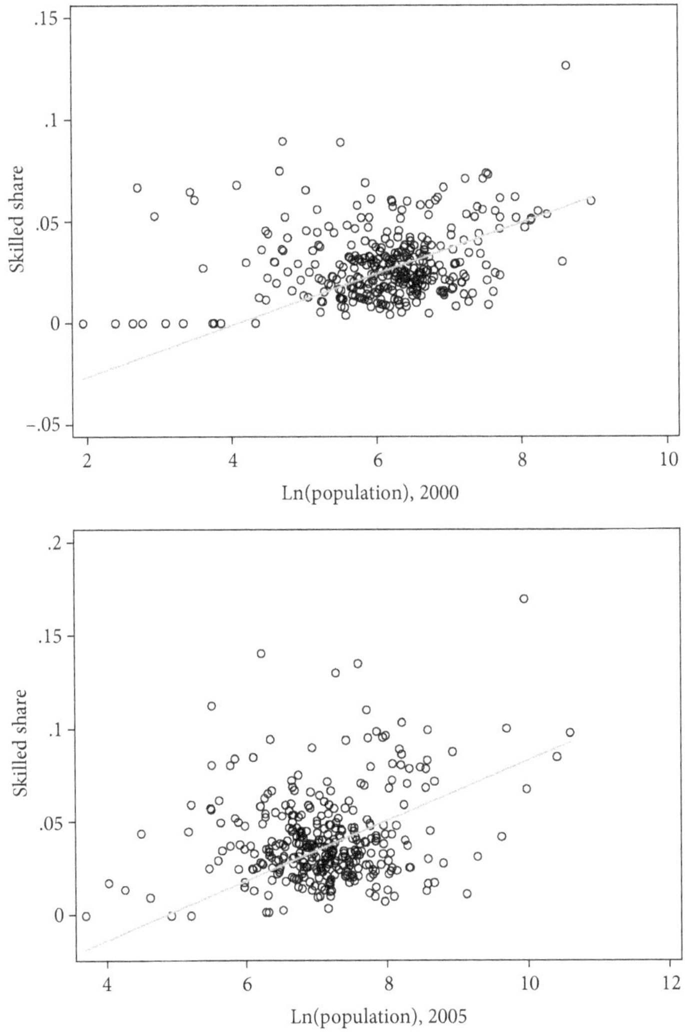

Figure 15.6. Share of skilled workers and population, 2000 and 2005

Note: Population refers to the number of observations in each city in our dataset. Skilled share refers to the share of observations with college or above degrees.

Source: Calculated from the 2000 census and the 2005 1 per cent population survey.

There is a significantly positive relationship between the share of college graduates in 2000 and the subsequent change in the share of skilled workers. Figure 15.8 shows that there is also a positive correlation between the change in the share of college graduates and the share of college graduates in 2000. In summary, the evidence suggests that large cities attract more educated workers. Between 2000 and 2005, large and educated cities became more educated.

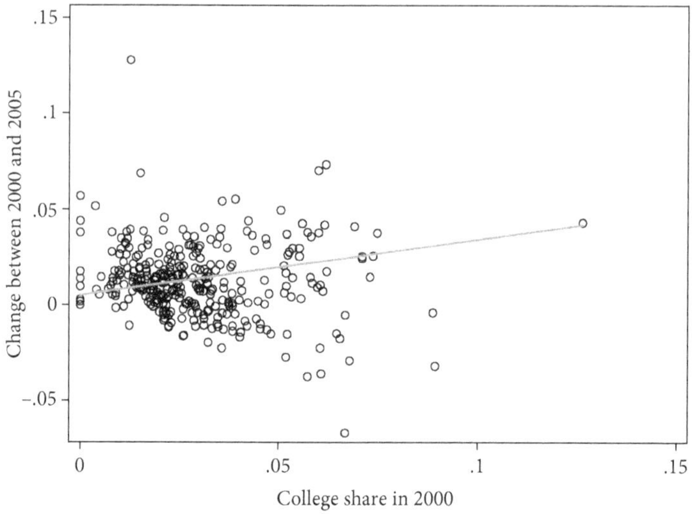

Figure 15.7. Changes in the share of college graduates and the education levels in 2000

Source: Calculated from the 2000 census and the 2005 1 per cent population survey.

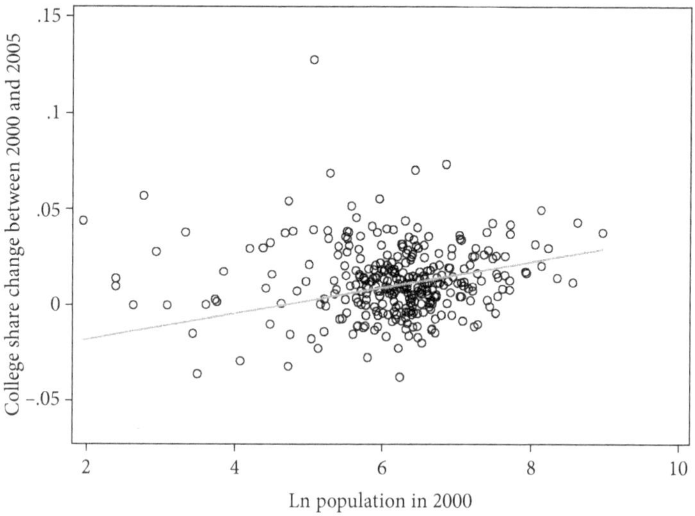

Figure 15.8. Changes in the share of college graduates and population, 2000

Source: Calculated from the 2000 census and the 2005 1 per cent population survey.

Source: CHIP 1995, 2002, and 2007.

15.3.2 The Returns to Education

Since education is a major form of human capital, educated workers, on average, earn more than the less educated. The returns to education (that is, the wage increase associated with a certain number of years of schooling; for example, four years of college education) depend on the circumstances such as infrastructure, economic structure, and population. In Section 15.3.2.1, we show that the returns to education are significantly higher in urban than in rural areas, and within urban areas they are significantly higher in larger and more educated cities.

15.3.2.1 The Returns to Education in Rural and Urban Areas

To estimate the returns to education for rural and urban PRC separately, we use the rural and urban surveys of the CHIP data for 1995, 2002, and 2007. We also use the 2005 1 per cent population survey, which covers both rural and urban PRC. The returns to education are estimated by running OLS regressions of the wages in log form on years of schooling and other standard controls including gender, experience, experience squared, and region dummies. The returns to education are significantly higher in urban than in rural areas and that the gap seems to have increased from the 1990s (Table 15.4). In the mid-1990s, for example, the returns to education were around 5 per cent in urban PRC, while for rural areas they were 2 per cent. By 2007, the returns to education increased to 11 per cent in urban areas, while remaining low at 2.7 per cent in rural areas. The gap is also large in 2005, for which year the data of the 1 per cent population survey was used (13 vs. 4 per cent).[3]

Table 15.4. The returns to education in rural and urban PRC (coefficients on years of schooling in wage equations)

	1995 (1)	2002 (2)	2005 (3)	2007 (4)
Urban	0.049***	0.094***	0.125***	0.111***
	(0.002)	(0.003)	(0.000)	(0.003)
Rural	0.020*	0.034***	0.042***	0.027***
	(0.010)	(0.004)	(0.001)	(0.004)

Note: (1) We control for experience, experience squared, gender, and provincial dummies in our OLS regressions; (2) the sample is restricted to those aged 22–54, who are able to work and are not in school; (3) * and *** are significance levels at 10 per cent and 1 per cent respectively; (4) standard errors are in parentheses.

Source: CHIP data are used to get the 1995, 2002, and 2007 results, and the 1 per cent population survey data are used for the 2005 data. The dependent variable is log of hourly wage, except for 2007, for which we use annual wage.

[3] We also use the Heckit model to correct for selection bias and get similar results. The results from another dataset (CHNS) show similar patterns of rural and urban returns to education.

There are two important (related) aspects that need to be pointed out. First, the returns to education in rural areas do not take into consideration the role of education in increasing the probability of rural people migrating to urban areas. Chen and Xing (2006) show that the probability of having a non-farm job increases significantly with educational level. More importantly, as mentioned earlier, going to college has been a major channel of converting Hukou status from rural to urban. We will come to this point later.

15.3.2.2 College Premium

Within urban areas, educational expansion was accompanied by a continuous increase in the returns to higher education. Figure 15.9 summarizes several studies and shows that the college premium increased dramatically in the 1990s. By the end of the 1990s, the returns to college education reached 30 to 50 per cent (Zhang et al. 2005; Li and Ding 2003; Meng et al. 2010). Possibly due to the expansion policy, the increasing trend stopped after 2003, but college premia were still approaching 40 per cent (Meng et al. 2010). These results are usually obtained using employee observations. Recent research shows that the unemployment rate increased for young college graduates. However, even with an unemployment rate of 20 per cent, the expected returns from college education could still be as high as 30 per cent. In fact, the unemployment rate for older college graduates was much lower than other education levels. Therefore, urban areas provide ample rewards to college graduates.

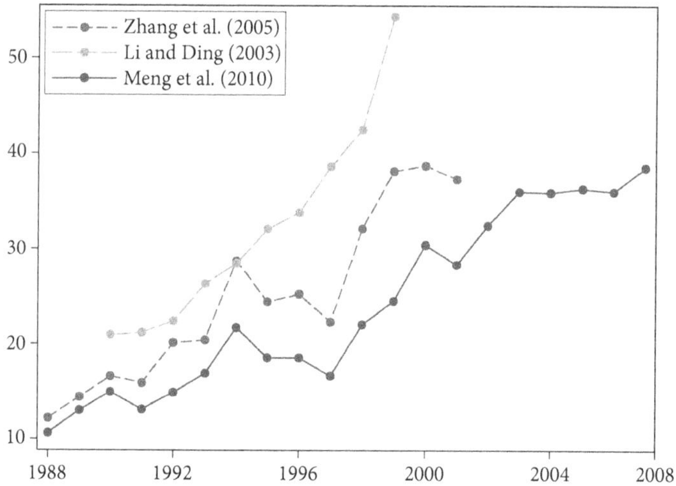

Figure 15.9. The returns to college from 1988 to 2008 (%)

Note: The reference group is high school graduates.

Source: Zhang et al. (2005), Li and Ding (2003), and Meng et al. (2010).

15.3.2.3 The Returns to Education Across Regions/Cities

As a large developing country in economic transition, the PRC's various regions have very different levels of economic development. Given the considerable effort devoted to estimating the returns to education, the extension to include the regional dimension is a natural next step. Possible reasons for the regional dispersion in the returns to education include institutional factors such as different shares of the private sector across regions, different degrees of openness (in terms of trade activity and foreign direct investment), and a set of 'place-based' policies. For a more detailed discussion, see Whalley and Xing (2014).

Evidence from the CHIP Data (1995, 2002, and 2007)

We estimate the returns to years of schooling and the returns to various levels of education for a number of provinces using two different models:

$$\ln(WAGE) = \beta_0 + \beta_1 * SCHOOLING + \gamma X + \varepsilon \quad (1)$$

$$\ln(WAGE) = \beta_0 + \sum_i \gamma_i * EDU_i + \gamma X + \varepsilon \quad (2)$$

In model (1), *SCHOOLING* is years of formal schooling, and in model (2), EDU_i are dummies for various education levels. X controls for the same factors as in model (1).

Results for these models are reported in columns 4–9 of Table 15.5. For the earlier period (1995–2002, columns 4–5), the returns to years of schooling increased sharply across all regions. There also is large variation across regions in the returns to education. In 1995, the returns to years of schooling vary by around 3 to 4 per cent. In 2002, Guangdong had the highest returns to schooling (8.4 per cent), while Hubei and Yunnan had the lowest returns (around 4.6–4.7 per cent). For the period between 2002 and 2007 (columns 5 to 6), there are signs that the returns to education stopped rising or even declined in the central and western provinces (for example, Anhui and Gansu). For coastal regions, the returns to education kept rising, and in some cases the increase was dramatic. For example, the returns to education increased from 6 per cent to 11 per cent in Beijing. Jiangsu province experienced a similar increase. It is obvious that the regional dispersion in the returns to education has become larger.

The college premia show similar patterns, but their dispersion increased only slightly (columns 7 to 9). Due to the limitation of space, the returns to other education levels are not reported, though some features of these returns are worth noting. First, most of the increases in the returns to education are concentrated in higher levels of education, especially college education. Second, coastal regions witnessed rising returns for almost every tertiary education level. Finally, the returns to high school decreased between 1995 and 2007.

Table 15.5. The returns to education and college premium in urban PRC, by province, 1995–2007

Province	Skilled workers' share			Returns to years of schooling			College premium (college vs. high school)		
	1995	2002	2007	1995	2002	2007	1995	2002	2007
	(1)	(2)	(3)	(4)	(5)	(6)	(7)	(8)	(9)
Beijing*	51.6	47.7	61.2	0.026	0.059	0.114	0.207	0.414	0.618
Shanxi	43.4	44.0	49.9	0.037	0.059	0.066	0.193	0.315	0.470
Liaoning*	39.2	41.0	48.6	0.048	0.075	0.078	0.333	0.602	0.510
Shanghai*			46.8			0.135			0.895
Jiangsu*	32.9	36.4	45.4	0.034	0.058	0.117	0.057	0.537	0.657
Zhejiang*			43.7			0.114			0.574
Anhui	34.0	41.8	47.0	0.031	0.072	0.053	0.248	0.401	0.345
Fujian*			51.9			0.091			0.442
Henan	38.8	42.2	62.6	0.039	0.056	0.066	0.325	0.445	0.504
Hubei	41.3	51.3	55.3	0.027	0.046	0.080	0.334	0.365	0.499
Hunan			53.0			0.077			0.513
Guangdong*	36.3	41.2	52.7	0.037	0.084	0.117	0.433	0.684	0.700
Chongqing	42.8	40.3	48.4	0.039	0.056	0.066	0.164	0.559	0.587
Sichuan	41.6	36.9	51.4	0.028	0.058	0.089	0.199	0.495	0.640
Yunnan	45.6	51.7	52.3	0.027	0.047	0.090	0.219	0.332	0.566
Gansu	37.4	43.1	48.7	0.039	0.074	0.072	0.367	0.504	0.457
Standard dev.	40.2	43.4	51.6	0.007	0.012	0.024	0.104	0.113	0.127
			(52.4)			(0.022)			(0.101)

Note: For each province, we run an OLS regression of wage equations to get the returns to education. We also control for experience, experience squared, gender, industry, and ownership dummies. In the first three columns, skilled labour includes those with college degrees (three or four years) or above and technical school graduates. Those with high-school degrees or below are classified as unskilled workers. Numbers in parentheses are calculated by excluding the newly added provinces in 2007. Coastal provinces are marked with an asterisk.

We also estimate wage equations for sixty-two, sixty-one, and ninety-one cities for 1995, 2002, and 2007 respectively, using the same specification as in model (1). After calculating the returns to education, we estimate their yearly kernel densities non-parametrically, each city being treated as an observation without using city population or employment as weight. We use the Epanechnikov kernel function and the bandwidth set at 0.02. The distributions are reported in Figure 15.10.[4] Apparently, they are non-degenerate in all three years. The distribution moved to the right and became more dispersed between 1995 and 2002. In the second period (2002 to 2007), it moved slightly to the right. A fatter right tail is observed

[4] We also estimate kernel densities of the returns to education across cities using cities that are covered in all three surveys. While only thirty-three cities remained and the estimates became less accurate, the regional distribution evolved in a similar pattern. We do not report it here due to space constraints.

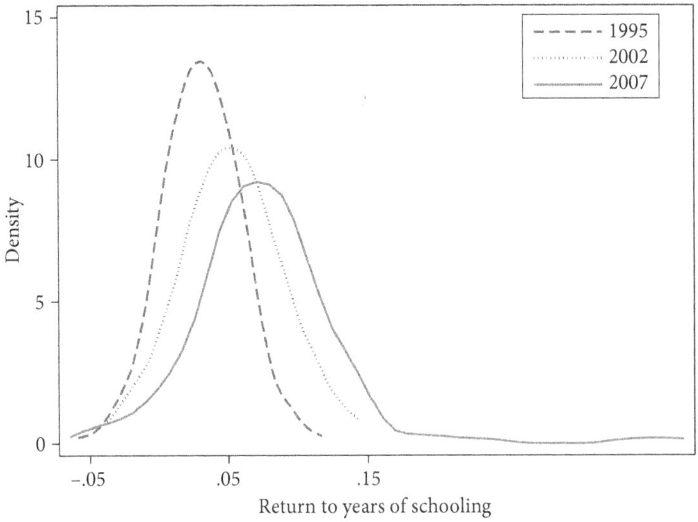

Figure 15.10. Distribution of the returns to years of schooling at the city level
Sources: CHIP 1995, 2002, and 2007.

in the 2007 distribution, which is likely due to the fairly high returns to education of some coastal cities.

Evidence from the 1 Per Cent Population Survey in 2005

The 1 per cent population survey of 2005 allows us to estimate the returns to education for all prefectural-level cities. Using the sample for each city (individuals aged 22–55 and out of school), we run regressions of the individual income in log terms on years of schooling, age, age squared, and gender. The estimated returns (the coefficients on years of schooling) show a large regional variation, with the returns for most cities ranging from 5 to 15 per cent. We are particularly interested in the correlation between the returns to education and city size and the education level of the city population.

Figure 15.11 shows that the returns to years of schooling are positively correlated with city population: larger cities have higher returns. Of course, there is large heterogeneity in cities of similar size. Figure 15.12 also shows a positive correlation between the returns to years of schooling and the share of college graduates in a city.

The returns to education can be regarded as the price for human capital. Our evidence suggests that large and more educated cities have higher prices for human capital. From the perspective of the private returns for individuals, it is a rational choice for educated workers to choose large cities with more educated populations.

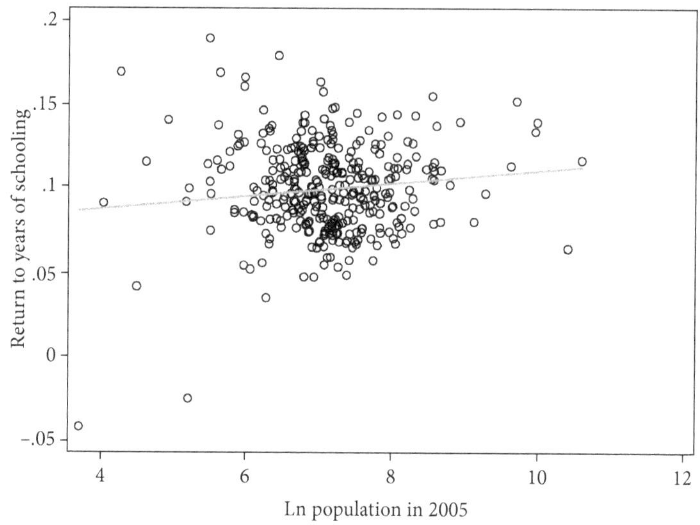

Figure 15.11. The returns to education and population, 2005
Source: Author's calculation using the 2005 1 per cent population survey.

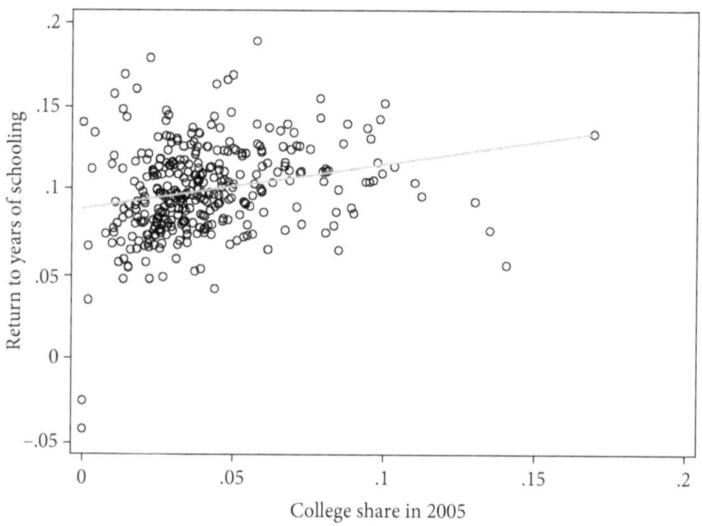

Figure 15.12. The returns to education and share of college graduates, 2005
Source: Author's calculation using the 2005 1 per cent population survey.

The fact that the returns to education have not been equalized across provinces/cities indicates that across-region mobility of skilled labour is insufficient to meet the regional demand shocks. Figure 5 provides further evidence supporting this conclusion. The upper panel of Figure 5 shows that around a third of the skilled workers are migrants in Beijing, Shanghai, and Guangdong, and over 10 per cent

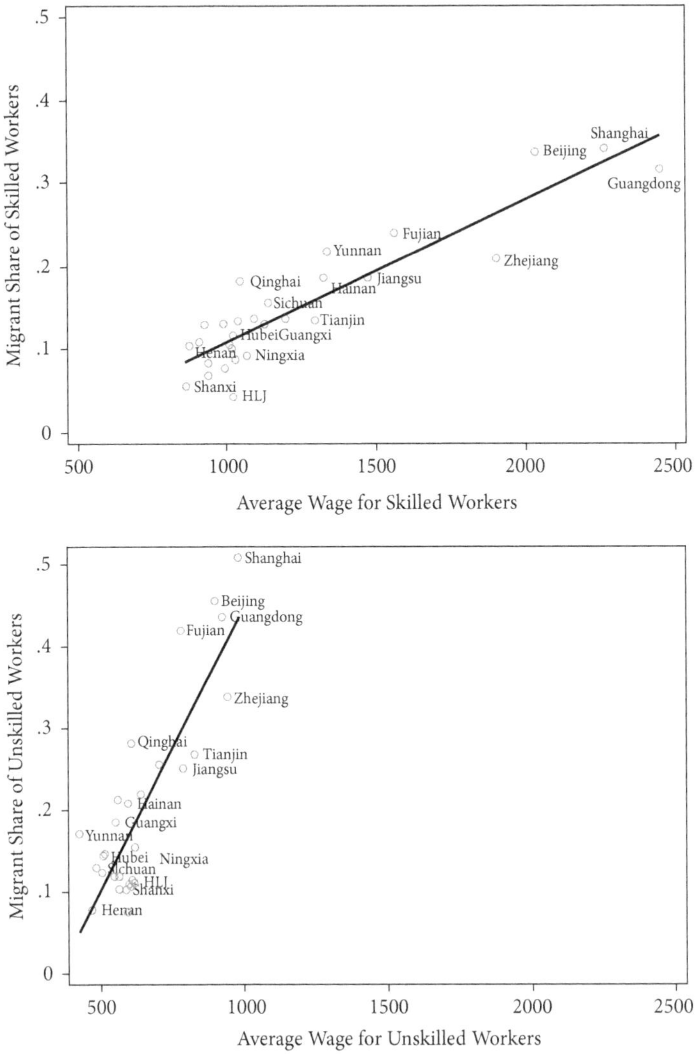

Figure 15.13. The relationship between real wages and migrant shares of skilled and unskilled workers

Note: Wages are deflated using provincial-level urban consumer price indices. The price levels for all provinces are normalized to one in 1995. Skilled workers are those having degrees higher than high-school graduates and with positive wage income. Migrants are those who have left their Hukou registration location and have been working in another city for more than half a year.

Source: 1 per cent population survey for 2005 and *China Statistical Yearbook* 1997–2006 (NBSC Various years).

of skilled workers in twenty-three provinces are migrants; these shares are much lower than those for unskilled workers, especially in coastal regions (see the bottom panel of Figure 15.13). Taking into consideration the large difference in the number of skilled and unskilled workers, skilled migrants are much lower in number than unskilled migrants.[5] Figure 15.13 also reports the relationship between these shares and the real wages of skilled and unskilled workers. The results suggest that skilled workers are less responsive to regional income differentials than unskilled workers. While wage differences are much larger for skilled workers, their migrant share differences are lower than the share for unskilled workers.[6]

These results point to how college graduates should be allocated under the educational expansion policy, favouring coastal regions over non-coastal regions. As it still poses high costs for a large proportion of skilled workers, relaxing the Hukou system could help facilitate the migration of skilled workers.

Skilled workers seem to have a greater potential to move than unskilled workers. By 2007, they had larger regional wage differentials than unskilled workers. The expanded wage differentials mainly reflect local wage increases among skilled workers in coastal regions, suggesting a lower geographic mobility among skilled workers.[7]

The results in Table 15.6 indicate that skilled migrant households have a stronger preference for permanent housing, social security, and public services that are closely related to Hukou status.[8] We define skilled households as those whose household heads have higher than professional school degrees (inclusive) and unskilled households as those with lower education degrees. Panel A in Table 15.6 shows that skilled migrant households are more likely to purchase permanent housing rather than rent an apartment or live at construction site dormitories. Around 54 per cent of the skilled migrant households purchased permanent housing, and the percentage is only 24 per cent for unskilled migrant households. In large cities, the percentages for both skilled and unskilled migrant households are significantly lower than in mid-sized and small cities. This may be due to high housing prices and discrimination against migrant households. Panel B shows that 64 per cent of the skilled migrant households are willing to stay in cities for over five years, and the percentage is 59 per cent for unskilled migrant households. The skilled migrant households have an even stronger willingness to stay in the

[5] According to our calculation based on the 2005 1 per cent population survey, the ratio of unskilled to skilled migrants is 5.8 to 1 in the urban labour market.

[6] Regressing the provincial incomes of skilled workers on migrant shares of skilled urban workers, we get a coefficient of 0.00017(0.000015), which is much smaller than the results for unskilled workers: 0.00068(0.00008). Dropping Yunnan province produces the results 0.00017(0.000014) and 0.00072(0.000080), respectively. Tibet is dropped in all regressions.

[7] This is consistent with Topel (1986), which shows that the largest local wage adjustments occur among workers who exhibit the least geographic mobility.

[8] Panel A uses the 2005 1 per cent population survey; panels B and C use the floating population monitoring data for 2012 compiled by the National Population and Family Planning Commission. Corresponding regression results can be found in the Appendix.

Table 15.6. Migrants' propensity to purchase housing and their willingness to settle down and change Hukou

	Top ten largest	11th–50th	Remaining	Total
	A: share of migrant household purchasing permanent housing (2005 1 per cent population survey)			
Unskilled	17.54	24.05	30.80	23.92
Skilled	48.96	57.75	58.14	53.63
Total	24.53	30.07	35.27	29.61
	B: share of migrant household willing to stay for 5+ years (2012 migrant survey data)			
Unskilled	64.49	57.28	57.23	59.34
Skilled	72.35	60.57	56.99	64.48
Total	66.11	57.74	57.2	60.13
	C: share of migrant household willing to change Hukou (2012 migrant survey data)			
Unskilled	60.37	45.64	41.55	48.48
Skilled	72.66	51.36	43.50	58.07
Total	62.90	46.44	41.78	49.95

Note: The *skilled* are households whose household heads have professional degrees or above.
Source: Author's calculation using 2005 1 per cent population survey and the 2012 migrant dynamic monitoring survey.

top ten largest cities relative to unskilled migrant households (72 per cent vs. 64 per cent). For small cities, the percentages are roughly the same for both household types. Panel C shows that the skilled migrant households are more willing to change Hukou registration than the unskilled. In the top ten largest cities, 73 per cent of skilled households want to change their Hukou registration, and the percentage for the unskilled is 60 per cent. The percentages are much lower in mid-sized and small cities for both skilled and unskilled migrant households, and the difference between skilled and unskilled households becomes smaller as the city size decreases.

The difference in the willingness to settle down or convert their Hukou status may be due to the fact that migrants with higher education levels are better treated in the destination cities. In some big cities, for example, migrants with college degrees are more likely to get an urban local Hukou. This might provide an explanation for their greater willingness to settle down in their workplaces. If this is true, educated workers without a local urban Hukou would be willing to accept a job with lower wages in exchange for the chance to convert Hukou in the future. However, the results in Gagnon et al. (2014) indicate that urban migrants (migrants with urban Hukou) earn significantly more than urban native workers. One explanation is that urban residents who usually have higher education levels often need to sacrifice Hukou-related benefits in their origin Hukou registration locations to move to other places (big cities, for example). They must be compensated in monetary terms to make a move. An alternative explanation is that workers must earn significantly more than local workers to pay for local Hukou-related services. This latter explanation is less likely to hold because we do not observe a wage premium for rural migrants. Either explanation means that the wage premium for urban migrants actually indicates high opportunity costs for educated workers in migration. Finally, the fact that there is a considerable number of skilled migrants without local Hukou suggests that the Hukou system restricts the mobility of the skilled migrants.

These results suggest that relaxing the Hukou system, in particular the Hukou restriction in large cities, will probably encourage more skilled rather than unskilled workers to move to high-premium cities. Such reforms will not only let skilled workers respond to regional demand changes more completely, but also help reduce inequality in high-premium cities. This, of course, does not mean that the mobility of unskilled workers should be restricted, nor does it mean that the current restriction on the mobility of unskilled workers need not be reformed. On the contrary, given the complementarity between skilled and unskilled workers and the shortage of migrant workers, Hukou restrictions should also be relaxed for unskilled workers and they should be treated more equally in large cities.

15.3.3 Externalities of Human Capital

Although there has been a growing literature trying to estimate the external returns to education, little is known about this aspect of human capital in the PRC, except through studies like Liu (2007) and Glaeser and Lu (2013). Both studies find that the external returns to education in cities are significantly high. For example, Liu uses the CHIP data from 1988 and 1995 and finds that the external returns are at least as high as the private returns to education. In particular, OLS estimates of the external returns range from 4.9 per cent to 6.7 per cent. He also uses the compulsory education law as an instrumental variable. The two-stage least square estimates indicate that a one-year increase in city average education could increase individual earnings by between 11 and 13 per cent. Glaeser and Lu (2013) use more recent data and employ another strategy to address the endogeneity issue. Using university relocation in the 1950s as an instrumental variable, they find that the external returns to education in urban PRC are large—the OLS regressions show that one more year in city-level education leads to a 11.9 per cent increase in hourly wage. After using the instrumental variable, the human capital externality is raised to 21.9 per cent, almost twice of the OLS estimates. The change in the estimate of human capital externality is greater for the most skilled workers.

Given large external returns to education, governments should subsidize human capital investment. Whether local (provincial) or central governments should fund this subsidy depends on the mobility of educated workers. If the educated workers are highly mobile (similar to many developed countries like the US), the central government should take more responsibility in subsidizing higher education. If, on the other hand, highly educated workers tend to stay where they get educated, local governments should share more responsibility.

Disregarding the financing of higher education, local governments should bring forth a series of measures to attract educated workers. Such measures include relaxing Hukou restrictions to reduce the cost of moving, industrial policies that can create jobs for educated workers, and also efforts to provide more amenities valued by educated workers (for example, cleaner air, quality education, museums, and libraries).

15.4 Human Capital and Urban Development

15.4.1 Selectivity of Rural-to-Urban Migration

In the 2002 urban survey of CHIP, urban residents were asked: 'When did you get urban Hukou?' Those who answered with a specific year were former rural residents who had successfully obtained urban Hukou. This information helps us to identify permanent migrants. As shown in Table 15.7, around 20 per cent of urban residents were not born with urban Hukou, among whom over half obtained urban Hukou within the last two decades, a figure consistent with the fact that the Hukou system has become less restrictive in the post-reforms period.

Table 15.7 also describes channels through which rural residents obtained urban Hukou. The largest share obtained urban Hukou through formal education and the second largest share through joining the army. Other channels take up a relatively small share of the permanent migrant population.

Different channels of Hukou conversion play different roles in different time periods.[9] Education plays an important role in most of the time periods. Among those who obtained urban Hukou in the 1980s, more than 30 per cent did so through education. Even during the 1960s, when joining the army was the major channel, more than 18 per cent of permanent migrants still obtained their Hukou via education. Membership in a cadre and joining the army both played a smaller role in the post-reforms period. From the 1970s to the 1990s, the number of rural residents who gained their urban Hukou after having their lands occupied or after

[9] Nearly half of the permanent migrants did not report how they obtained their urban Hukou. Here, we only consider those who reported this information.

Table 15.7. Using urban survey to identify permanent migrants

Time of obtaining urban Hukou		Ways former rural residents get urban Hukou (%)							
		Education	Cadre promotion	Join army	Lose land	Buy housing	Others	Missing	Total
born urban	16,278	–	–	–	–	–	–	–	–
–1950	133	18.05	8.27	15.79	2.26	9.02	37.59	9.02	100
1951–60	509	28.29	4.91	13.36	0.59	3.93	40.86	8.06	100
1961–70	484	18.18	3.93	31.82	1.45	2.27	33.88	8.47	100
1971–80	839	23.60	4.53	14.18	2.86	1.91	49.70	3.22	100
1981–90	1,312	33.16	1.45	5.34	8.08	3.96	43.45	4.57	100
1991–	884	16.52	0.68	2.71	12.44	7.81	53.05	6.79	100
Missing	193	–	–	–	–	–	–	–	–
Total	20,632								

Source: CHIPS 2002.

purchasing housing in urban areas grew significantly, from less than 5 per cent to more than 20 per cent.

In the following analysis, we restrict the data to individuals aged 18 to 60 who are not in school.[10] The shares of the rural and urban samples remain almost unchanged. To avoid the endogeneity problem of education, we also drop permanent migrants who obtained their urban Hukou when they were under the age of sixteen. Next, we compare our subsamples with the first two (urban natives and permanent migrants) having urban Hukou and the last two (rural residents and temporary migrants)[11] having rural Hukou.

Panel A of Table 15.8 presents statistics for men. We first compare urban natives and rural residents (without migrants). The urban natives are better educated than rural residents, with the average number of years of schooling for the two groups being 11.1 and 7.7 respectively. In terms of age, ethnicity, and political status, the urban natives are older, less likely to be minorities, and more likely to have party memberships. Finally, around 81 per cent of urban natives had wage incomes in 2002, while this percentage was only 42 per cent for rural residents.

Migrants without local urban Hukou are slightly more educated than rural residents, much younger, and less likely to have party memberships. Among permanent migrants, more than 40 per cent have education above a college degree—a figure much higher than that for urban natives. Permanent migrants' share of party memberships is also much higher than that of urban natives. The dissimilarities are more significant when comparing permanent migrants with rural residents. These characteristics indicate that permanent migrants are positively selected, and that the selection effect is larger for permanent migrants than for temporary migrants.

Panel B of Table 15.8 presents the statistics for women. The contrasts between rural women and urban women are similar to those between rural and urban men. Urban women have higher levels of education, are less likely to be minorities, and are more likely to be party members and wage earners. However, in the case of female urban residents, the differential patterns for natives and migrants are dissimilar to those in the case of men. Both the migrants' education level and labour participation rate are slightly lower than those of their urban native counterparts, and their likelihood of being party members is almost the same as that of the natives.

Table 15.9 gives summary statistics for wage earners (workers). Wage earners have a slightly higher level of education compared to the whole sample, and this is especially true for women. The contrasts between urban and rural residents, and

[10] The results are unaffected by increasing the cut-off age to twenty-two. When using per capita income, we try to include all dependents in the calculations. We will point this out when necessary.

[11] The rural resident sample does not include migrants.

Table 15.8. Summary statistics for rural and urban residents and migrants aged 18 to 60

	A: Male				B: Female			
	Urban residents		Rural residents w/o migrants	Mig. w/o Hukou	Urban residents		Rural residents w/o migrants	Mig. w/o Hukou
	Natives	Mig. w/Hukou						
Years of schooling	11.14	11.67	7.67	8.18	10.65	9.9	6.33	7.52
By education level								
Primary and below	0.03	0.05	0.27	0.19	0.06	0.13	0.50	0.31
Middle school	0.29	0.20	0.53	0.60	0.30	0.33	0.40	0.55
High school	0.39	0.31	0.18	0.19	0.42	0.35	0.10	0.13
College and above	0.29	0.44	0.02	0.02	0.22	0.19	0.01	0.01

Note: The 'high school' category includes professional schools.

Source: CHIP 2002.

Table 15.9. Summary statistics for wage earners aged 18 to 60

	A: Male				B: Female			
	Urban natives	Mig. w/Hukou	Rural Local workers	Mig. w/o Hukou	Urban natives	Mig. w/ Hukou	Rural Local workers	Mig. w/o Hukou
Years of schooling	11.42	12.06	8.00	8.16	11.51	11.12	7.60	7.64
By education level								
Primary and below	0.02	0.04	0.21	0.19	0.02	0.04	0.33	0.30
Middle school	0.26	0.16	0.54	0.60	0.20	0.25	0.44	0.56
High school	0.39	0.30	0.23	0.19	0.47	0.41	0.21	0.13
College and above	0.33	0.49	0.02	0.02	0.31	0.30	0.02	0.02

Note: The 'high school' category includes professional schools.

Source: CHIP 2002.

between urban natives and permanent migrants, are similar to those presented in Table 15.8. Because the labour participation rate is relatively high for urban residents and migrants, statistics for wage earners are very similar to those in Table 15.8.

The above analysis uses the CHIP data for 2002, which is relatively old. However, the following evidence is consistent with the existence of positive selection in recent years. First, categories like buying a house and losing land have become increasingly important. Although migrants of these categories are less educated than those who change Hukou status through the educational channel, they remain positively selected from the rural population. Second, as shown previously, the rural population had an extremely low share of college graduates, and this situation has improved only marginally since the early 1990s.[12] Meanwhile, the number of rural high-school graduates taking college entrance exams has increased dramatically since the late 1990s. There must have been positive selection in recent years. Third, the returns to education (both private and external) have been significantly lower in rural compared to in urban areas, which provides an incentive for more educated workers to migrate to cities.

The selectivity in migration has a major impact on the pattern of urbanization. One major implication for education policy in urbanization is that the education for rural residents is important because they constitute a reservoir for urban population growth. Improving the quality of rural education should be a policy priority given the large rural–urban gap in this aspect. One alternative option is to let rural children get education in cities. But the financial and psychic costs are usually high, especially for primary and secondary education.

15.4.2 Higher Education Expansion Promotes Urbanization

As mentioned earlier, the PRC's higher education expansion not only increased the education levels of the labour force but also accelerated the urbanization process. It had differential impacts not only on the education levels of both rural and urban areas but also on the education levels and regional development across different regions. To see these effects more clearly, we take into consideration the facts that higher education plays an important role in helping rural residents get urban Hukou and that higher education expansion is unevenly distributed across provinces.

Figure 15.14 shows the number of college students per capita in different provinces between 1998 and 2005. The left panel indicates that the number of students in colleges is strongly correlated between 1998 and 2005, and the educational

[12] While the share of college graduates increased from 7 to 18 per cent in urban PRC between 1993 and 2006, the same for rural PRC only increased from 0.1 to 1.3 per cent.

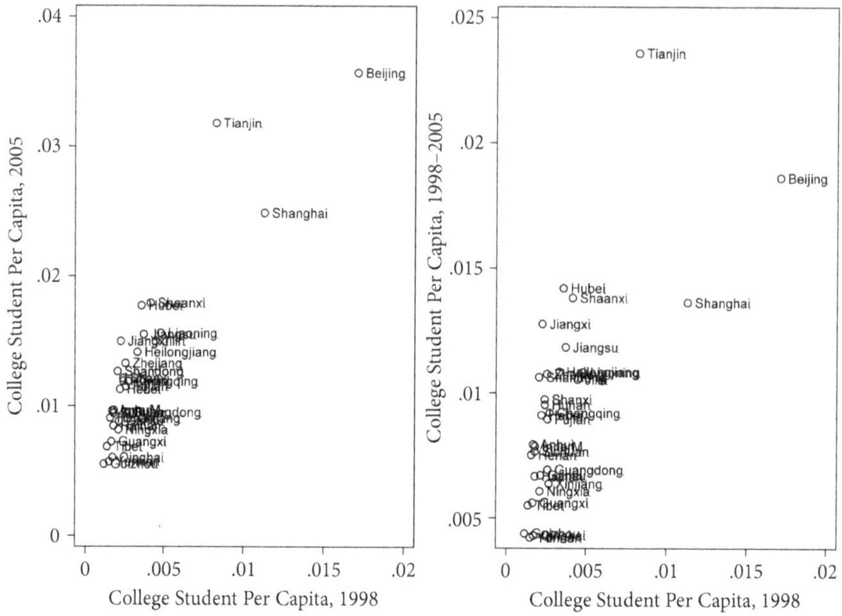

Figure 15.14. Numbers of college students in school and the changes between 1998 and 2005, by province

Source: *China Statistical Yearbook* 1999 and 2006 (NBSC Various years).

expansion since 1999 has increased rather than reduced the regional gap in the number of students. The right panel shows that the more students a province had in 1998, the larger was the increase in that province between 1998 and 2005. This feature is mainly driven by the fact that the PRC's higher education expanded by increasing admission quota of existing universities (rather than establishing new universities).

In a recent empirical study, Xing (2013) explores this regional variation in higher education expansion and finds that this policy significantly increased the probability of an urban resident having a college degree. The research suggests that the probability of rural residents going to college also increased significantly and those who were admitted to colleges stayed on in urban areas. Without higher education expansion, they may not have migrated out of rural areas or they may have worked in urban areas as 'peasant workers' rather than in the formal sector. Therefore, educational expansion is a major policy instrument that facilitates the PRC's urbanization process. In this sense, the education policy should offer equal education opportunities for rural residents who are the major source of urban population growth. This policy could potentially guarantee qualified skilled workers for urban growth. For the youth from rural PRC, three to four years of college education also means a process of assimilation. Other policies that could help college graduates find jobs should also be designed. In particular, college graduates from rural areas should not be discriminated against in finding jobs in the urban labour markets.

15.5 Other Educational Issues in Urbanization

The PRC's urbanization has created various challenges in human capital development, sometimes at the price of sacrificing or threatening the human capital of the next generation. Many of these problems are caused by institutional arrangements, in particular the Hukou system and the fiscal arrangement.

Due to the restrictions of the Hukou system, the majority of rural migrants in cities do not have access to pensions, health care, public education, and other social benefits at the place they live. The number of migrant children aged six to fourteen is estimated at approximately 15 million (All China Women's Federation 2013). However, funding for elementary education is mainly determined by the number of children with local Hukou and is not portable across administrative units. Therefore, local authorities lack the incentives and financial resources to accommodate migrant children into public schools. Three options are available for migrant families. They can send their children to local public schools (school-choice fees are required sometimes) or privately run migrant schools, or leave their children at home under the custody of the elders or relatives.

There has been a growing literature trying to assess the impact of migration behaviour on children's human capital. For example, Chen and Feng (2013) found that migrant students who are unable to enrol in public schools perform significantly worse than their more fortunate counterparts in both Chinese and mathematics. An earlier study by Liang and Chen (2007) shows that temporary migrant children are much less likely to be enrolled in school compared with local children. Temporary migrants with less than one year of residence in cities suffer the most. Perhaps somewhat surprisingly, permanent migrant children are more likely to be enrolled in schools than local children largely due to the highly selective nature of their parents. The situation for migrant children may be worse in Beijing. Goodburn (2009) concludes that administrative and financial barriers, as well as discrimination, prevent migrant children from entering public schools. The quality of education available in unlicensed private schools is generally poor.

In recent years, the urban population increased dramatically in many cities, especially in the large ones. Due to inelastic housing supply in urban centres, most newly arrived migrants live in suburban or newly converted urban areas, where the public schools or newly established migrant schools are of low quality. On the contrary, high-quality educational resources tend to be distributed in urban centres. As a consequence, spatial sorting in terms of both residence and education emerges. Breaking this spatial sorting and promoting equal distribution of educational resources is a major policy challenge for many large cities.

15.6 Health and Urbanization

Urbanization and health also influence each other significantly. Economists have realized for a long time that better health can improve productivity and income levels (Strauss and Duncan 1998). Economic development, urbanization in particular, can impact health, either positively or negatively, through several channels: (1) higher income with urbanization enables individuals and households to invest more in nutrition and health; (2) better health/medical facilities help urban residents to improve health; (3) living conditions for migrants are generally disadvantaged; (4) migrant workers tend to work in economic sectors that are bad for health or have higher risks (for example, construction); (5) newly arrived migrants bear psychological costs because of the new environment and possible discrimination against them; (6) urban areas have higher risks of epidemic diseases. This section will examine the issues regarding the relationship between health and urbanization, paying particular attention to issues related to migrant workers.

15.6.1 Health/Medical Facilities and their Inelastic Supplies

In contrast to the tremendous expansion in education, the PRC's health services sector has not witnessed significant growth in the last two decades. Figure 15.15 shows the number of hospitals (A), hospital beds (B), and doctors (C) in different cities in 1997 and 2007. From panel A, we can see that the relative number of hospitals increased in small cities (former cities with less number of hospitals), but for large cities, the relative number of hospitals actually decreased.

If we look at the relative number of hospital beds (B) and doctors (C), the change was even smaller. For most of the large cities, the relative number of doctors actually decreased. This suggests that the supply of medical or health-related services is inelastic to the increased demand. This will be a major constraint for cities (especially large ones) in accommodating more immigrants. Another explanation for this is that there is scale economy in medical services. Unfortunately, we cannot tell which explanation dominates.

15.6.2 Urbanization, Migration, and Health

15.6.2.1 Living Conditions

Migrants face high living costs, which can affect their health. Li (2013) uses the 1 per cent population survey for 2005 conducted by National Bureau of Statistics of China and the Dynamic Monitoring Data of Migrants conducted by National Health and Family Planning Commission to look at the living conditions of rural-to-urban migrants. He shows that a majority of migrant households live in rented

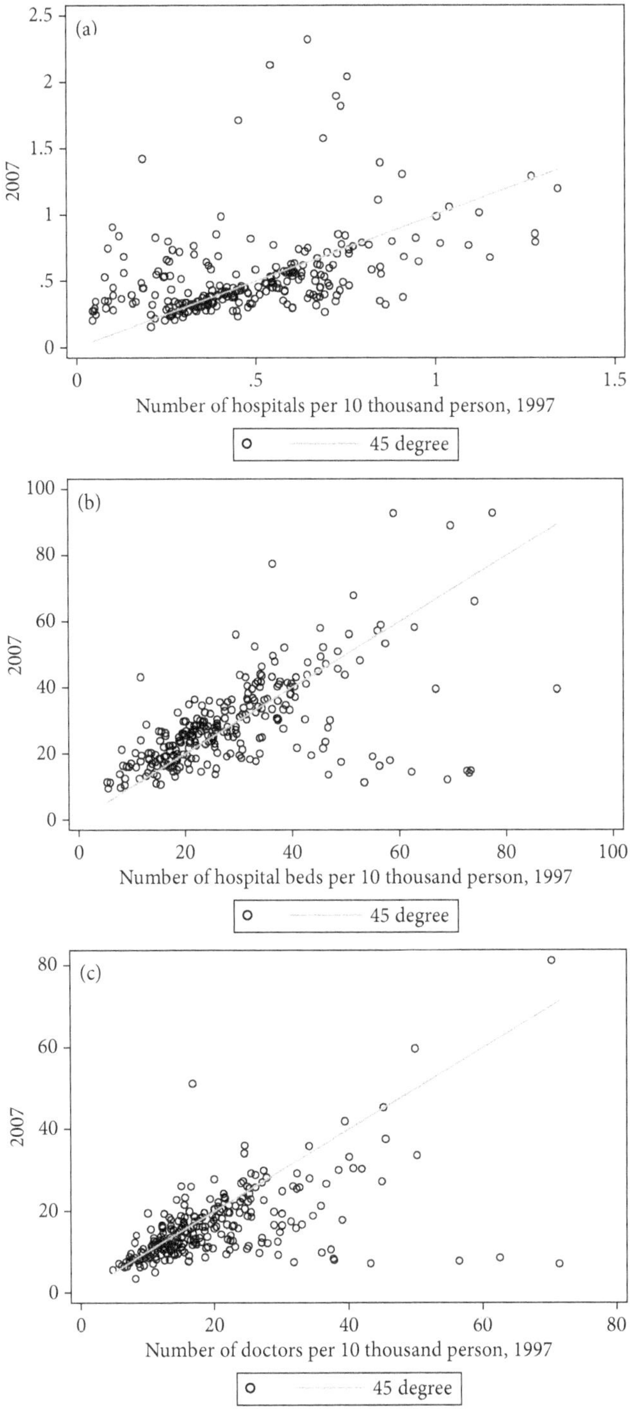

Figure 15.15. Growth in the medical services sector between 1997 and 2007 in different cities

Sources: China Statistical Yearbook 1998 and 2008 (NBSC Various years).

apartments provided by private landlords. Very few (less than 10 per cent) can afford buying an apartment. The government plays a minor role in helping migrants get housing. Importantly, although the income levels increased for migrants between 2005 and 2010, living conditions have not improved.

Existing research also looks at the facilities inside living places to examine the living conditions of migrants. Li (2013) shows that around 30 per cent of the migrant households live in houses without toilets, another 40 to 50 per cent of them live in places with shared toilets. This reflects the poor living conditions of the migrants.

Next, we look at the living areas per capita of the migrant households, which is another aspect reflecting the living conditions of migrant households. Li (2013) shows that in 2005, the average living areas for those living in rented rooms was around 12 to 13 sq. m. According to Li (2013), around 30 per cent of the migrant workers' living area per capita is below 6 sq. m, which is the poverty line in terms of size of living area. From 2005 to 2010, the living areas increased slightly for those renting houses. But for those living in purchased housing, the area actually decreased slightly. This might be due to the increased housing prices in many cities. Generally speaking, the living conditions for rural migrants are poor, which may have negative impacts on their health. This also is supported by existing studies (Niu et al. 2011; Wang et al. 2011).

15.6.2.2 Medical Insurance

Due to the Hukou system, many migrant workers are disproportionately distributed in the informal sector, with many not covered by medical insurance. Table 15.10 shows that according to the 2005 1 per cent population survey, less than 10 per cent of the rural migrant workers working in the informal sector (self-employed or those without formal labour contracts) have medical insurance. The situation is better if they have jobs with formal contracts, with the share increasing to 71 per cent. For urban residents with local Hukou, 54 per cent of this population has medical insurance. If we look at urban residents with formal contracts, the percentage is around sixty. Urban migrants who have urban Hukou but have migrated lie in-between, with less than 20 per cent of people working in the informal sector having medical insurance. Table 15.11 shows that less than 20 per cent of rural migrant workers have medical insurance in urban areas, and the situation improved only slightly in recent years.

A major issue for the medical insurance system is that this insurance is largely immovable and confined within the locality of the working place. By 2010, most rural residents were covered by the New Rural Cooperative Medical Insurance (NRCMI). Rural migrant workers in city areas are covered by the NRCMI in their respective Hukou registration places. If a rural migrant visits a hospital in another county, he/she must pay first and the cost is later reimbursed by the insurance from his/her Hukou registration place, and the process is usually complicated and time-consuming.

Table 15.10. Share of people having medical insurance (%), 2005

	Total	Employees with formal contract	Self-employed	Employees without contract
Urban residents	54	59	19	48
Rural migrants	15	29	6	7
Urban migrants	36	52	16	17

Source: 2005 1 per cent population survey.

Table 15.11. Share of rural migrants having medical insurance (%), 2008–12

	2008	2009	2010	2011	2012
Urban medical insurance	13.1	12.2	14.3	16.7	16.9
Urban insurance for injuries	24.1	21.8	24.1	23.6	24.0

Source: NBSC (2013).

15.6.2.3 Health Consequences of Migration

Health and migration behaviour are closely related. As we have argued, migration (urbanization) can influence health through several channels. Empirically, researchers examine this effect by comparing the health conditions of migrant workers and urban residents or rural non-migrant residents. Zhou and Lu (2014) use the China General Social Survey data to investigate the effect of migration on health. They find that migrant workers' health conditions are significantly better than urban natives (see Table 15.12). This mainly is a selection effect: rural people migrating to cities tend to be younger and more healthy. This is clearer in Table 15.13, where we report the health conditions by age group. In most of the cases, self-reported health is actually better for rural migrants than for urban native workers.

The selection process happened not only at the beginning but also after the migrants arrived at urban areas. Among migrants, it is those with bad health who tend to return home (early) after spending some time in urban areas. Table 15.14 shows that over 80 per cent of the migrant workers with bad health returned home. This share is around 50 per cent for those with good health.

In addition to the selection effect, working conditions in specific industries in urban areas tend to have negative effects on the health of migrant workers. Zhou and Lu (2014) find that the health of those working in the construction industry tends to deteriorate more rapidly than for other urban residents. Niu (2013) also finds that the migration experience could be detrimental to migrants' health. If we think of health as another type of human capital, the depreciation rate is higher for migrant workers.

Table 15.12. Self-reported health of migrant workers and urban natives

	The whole sample N = 3,439	Rural migrant workers N = 668	Urban native workers N = 2,771
Self-reported health	3.99 (0.94)	4.12 (0.89)	3.96 (0.94)

Note: Rural migrant workers are those with rural Hukou, but are working outside or have returned temporarily. Urban native workers are those with urban Hukou who are working. Self-reported health takes values from 1 to 5, representing poor health, fairly poor, so so, fairly good, excellent. Standard deviations are in parentheses.

Source: Zhou and Lu (2014).

Table 15.13. Self-reported health of migrant workers and urban natives, by age group

age	Migrant workers		Urban native workers	
	# of obs.	Health	# of obs.	Health
<=30	230	4.42 (0.77)	589	4.31 (0.81)
31–40	209	4.06 (0.85)	843	4.10 (0.85)
41–50	152	3.91 (0.93)	796	3.86 (0.94)
51–60	62	3.74 (1.04)	418	3.60 (1.03)
>=61	15	4.07 (0.96)	123	3.24 (0.95)

Note: Rural migrant workers are those with rural Hukou, but are working outside or have returned temporarily. Urban native workers are those with urban Hukou who are working. Self-reported health takes values from 1 to 5, representing poor health, fairly poor, so so, fairly good, excellent. Standard deviations are in parentheses.

Source: Zhou and Lu (2014).

Table 15.14. Health and return migration

	# of obs.	Share of return migrants
Healthy	532	0.49
Fairly healthy	565	0.56
So so	315	0.64
Fairly poor	170	0.81
poor	36	0.92

Note: Migrants are defined as those working outside, those who return temporarily, and those who return permanently. The last category is regarded as returnees.

Source: Zhou and Lu (2014).

Another strand of literature looks at the effect of migration on the health (both subjective and objective) of two groups of children, namely migrant children and left-behind children. Xu and Xie (2013) investigate the effect of migration on children's well-being using the China Family Panel Studies data for 2010. For children, migration may be a double-edged sword. On the one hand, migration to cities exposes children to an urban environment that is characterized by new ideas, more permissive social norms, expanded peer networks, better schools, nutrition-rich food, and modern hospitals. In these respects, migration can be an empowering experience for children. On the other hand, migrant children are confronted with the challenge of assimilating into a new social environment, which is somewhat alien to and perhaps even discriminatory towards them (this is especially true considering the PRC's Hukou system). Xu and Xie (2013) pool the origin–destination child samples to form appropriate comparisons and apply propensity score matching methods to estimate the average treatment effects for the treated. They find significant positive effects of child migration on their objective well-being, but no negative effects on their subjective well-being. They also find little difference between the left-behind and non-migrant children across multiple life domains. These findings highlight the important role of migration in narrowing the longstanding rural–urban gap in child development in the PRC.

Ren and Treiman (2013) use the same dataset to look at the effect of migration on left-behind children's emotional well-being. While the expected effect is negative, the empirical results suggest that migration has not affected the health of those left-behind children.

15.7 Policy Implications

Human capital is an important factor in the urbanization process. Policies and institutional arrangements during this process also influence the human capital of both rural and urban residents. According to our analysis, several policy implications emerge:

(1) The Hukou system is still a major barrier to the mobility of the labour force and needs to be reformed. Both rural and urban migrant workers seem to be hindered by this system. Conventional wisdom seems to be that the Hukou system imposes higher costs on unskilled workers. Our results suggest that the costs for skilled workers are also high.

(2) The provision of both educational and medical service are inelastic to emerging demand in city areas, especially large cities. Institutional reforms (including the Hukou reforms) are needed to make the supply more elastic to surging demand. Private investment should be encouraged,

and the government should subsidize such investment and play the role of supervision.

(3) The central government should take more responsibility in financing education at various levels, due to the fact that education has externalities and educated workers are highly mobile across regions.

(4) Education and health resources should be allocated more equally across regions.

(5) Housing is also a major obstacle for migrants. Bad housing is also a major factor influencing migrants' health. Housing supply should be more elastic. The current land regime should be reformed.

(6) Rural areas are and will still be the reservoir of labour force in the urbanization process. Education and medical services in rural areas should be improved.

(7) A portable and nationally coordinated health care system should be established.

Appendix

Table A.15.1. Migrants' propensity to purchase housing and their willingness to settle down and change Hukou

	2005 1% population survey	2012 floating population monitoring data	
	Purchase permanent housing (yes = 1/no = 0)	Willing to stay over five years (yes = 1/no = 0)	Willing to change Hukou location (yes = 1/no = 0)
	(1)	(2)	(3)
Skilled	0.122***	0.056***	0.060***
	(0.006)	(0.004)	(0.005)
Pseudo R2	0.274	0.080	0.100
N	76,934	132,623	132,684

Note: All regressions are run for migrant household head, controlling for cubic age, gender, ethnicity, Hukou status, marital status, quadratic log of monthly income, and city dummies. Column 1 also controls for family size, but columns 2 and 3 do not for the lack of data. The *skilled* are individuals with college degrees (three or four years) or above and technical school graduates. Probit models are estimated and the marginal effects are reported. *** is significance level at 1 per cent.

References

All-China Women's Federation. 2013. 'Report on the Status of Rural Migrant and Left-Behind Children in China'. *Chinese Women's Movement* 6: 30–4.

Au, Chun-Chung and J. Vernon Henderson. 2006. 'Are Chinese Cities Too Small?' *Review of Economic Studies* 73: 549–76.

Chan, Kam Wing and Will Buckingham. 2008. 'Is China Abolishing the Hukou System?' *China Quarterly* (195): 582–606.

Chen, Yuyu and Chunbing Xing. 2006, 'Human Capital, Rural Industrialization and China's Labor Market in. 1990s'. In *China's Rural Economy after WTO: Problems and Strategies*, edited by Song Shunfeng and Chen Aiming, Ashgate.

Chen, Yuanyuan and Shuangzhang Feng. 2013. 'Access to Public Schools and the Education of Migrant Children in China'. *China Economic Review 26*: 75–88.

CYCRC. 2007. 'Report on the Development of the China Youth During the 10th and 11th 5-Year-Plan (in Chinese)'. China Youth and Child Research Center.

Deng, Q. and Gustafsson B. 2006. 'China's Lesser Known Migrants'. *IZA Discussion Papers 2152*, IZA.

Démurger, S., Gurgand M., Li S., and Yue X. 2009. 'Migrants As Second-class Workers in Urban China? a Decomposition Analysis'. *Journal of Comparative Economics 37* (4): 610–28.

Fan, C. 2008. *China on the Move: Migration, the State, and the Household*, Routledge.

Gagnon, J., T. Xenogiani, and C. Xing. 2014. 'Are Migrants Discriminated Against in Chinese Urban Labour Markets?' *IZA Journal of Labor and Development 3*: 17.

Glaeser, Ed and Ming Lu. 2013. 'Human Capital Externalities in China'. Working paper.

Goodburn, Charlotte. 2009. 'Learning from Migrant Education: A Case Study of the Schooling of Rural Migrant Children in Beijing'. *International Journal of Educational Development 29* (5): 495–504.

Knight, J. and L. Song. 1999. *The Rural–Urban Divide: Economic Disparities and Interactions in China*, Oxford University Press.

Li, Shi. 2013. 'Current Situation of Rural Migrant Workers in the Chinese Labor Market'. *Studies in Labor Economics 1* (1): 51–68.

Li, Shi and Sai Ding. 2003. 'Long-term Change in Private Returns to Education in Urban China (in Chinese)'. *Social Science in China 6*.

Liang, Zai and Yiu Por Chen. 2007. 'The Educational Consequences of Migration for Children in China'. *Social Science Research 36* (1): 28–47.

Liu, Zhiqiang. 2007, 'The External Returns to Education: Evidence from Chinese Cities'. *Journal of Urban Economics 61*: 542–64.

Lu, Yilong. 2003. *Huji Zhidu: Kongzhi yu Shehui Chabie (Hukou System: Control and Social Disparity)* (in Chinese), The Commercial Press.

Maurer-Fazio, M. and N. Dinh. 2004. 'Differential Rewards to, and Contributions of Education in Urban China's Segmented Labor Markets'. *Pacific Economic Review 9* (3): 173–89.

Meng, X. 2001. 'The Informal Sector and Rural–Urban Migration: A Chinese Case Study'. *Asian Economic Journal 15* (1): 71–89.

Meng, X. and J. Zhang. 2001. 'The Two-tier Labor Market in Urban China: Occupational Segregation and Wage Differentials Between Urban Residents and Rural Migrants in Shanghai'. *Journal of Comparative Economics 29* (3): 485–504.

Meng, Xin, Kailing Shen, and Xue Sen. 2010. 'Economic Reform, Education Expansion, and Earnings Inequality for Urban Males in China 1988–2007'. *IZA Discussion Paper No. 4919.*

Ministry of Education of China. 2013. *Educational Statistics Yearbook of China*, China Statistics Press.

NBSC (National Bureau of Statistics of China). 2013. 'National Migrant Workers Monitoring Survey Report'. <http://www.gov.cn/xinwen/2014-05/12/content_2677889.htm>.

NBSC (National Bureau of Statistics of China). Various years. *China Statistical Yearbook*, China Statistics Press.

Niu, Jianlin, Zhenzhen Zheng, Linghua Zhang, and Xuchun Zeng. 2011. 'Labor Migrants' Working and Living Environments and the Related Health Impacts'. *Population Studies 3*: 64–75.

Niu, Jianlin. 2013, ' Migration and its Impact on the Differences in Health between Rural and Urban Residents in China'. *China Social Science* (2): 46–63.

Ren, Qiang and Donald Treiman. 2013. 'The Consequences of Parental Labor Migration in China for Children's Emotional Well-being'. *PSC Research Report No. 13-799.*

State Council. 1993. 'Guidelines for China's Education Reform and Development (in Chinese)'. <http://www.moe.edu.cn/edoas/website18/level3.jsp?tablename=208&infoid=3334>.

Strauss, John and Duncan Thomas. 1998. 'Health, Nutrition, and Economic Development'. *Journal of Economic Literature 36* (2): 766–817.

Topel, Robert. 1986. 'Local Labor Markets'. *Journal of Political Economy 94* (3): S111–S143.

Wang, Guixin, Xiaoxin Su, and Ming Wen. 2011, 'Urban Migrants' Living Conditions and Impact on Health Status: The Case of Shanghai'. *Population Studies 35* (2).

Whalley, John and Chunbing Xing. 2014, 'The Regional Distribution of the Skill Premia in Urban China and its Implications for Growth and Inequality'. *International Labour Review 153* (3): 395–420.

Wong, L. and W. Huen. 1998. 'Reforming the Household Registration System: A Preliminary Glimpse of the Blue Chop Household Registration System in Shanghai and Shenzhen'. *International Migration Review 32* (4): 974–94.

Wu, X. and D. Treiman. 2004. 'The Household Registration System and Social Stratification of China 1955–1996'. *Demography 41* (2): 363–84.

Xing, C. 2013. 'Education Expansion, Migration and Rural–Urban Education Gap: A Case Study on the Effect of University Expansion (in Chinese)'. *China Economic Quarterly (Jingjixue Jikan) 13* (1): 207–32.

Xu, Hongwei and Xie Yu. 2013. 'The Causal Effects of Rural-to-Urban Migration on Children's Wellbeing in China'. *PSC Research Report No. 13–798.*

Yang, Dongping. 2006. *Transition and Development of China's Education* (in Chinese), Social Science Academic Press.

Zhang, Junsen, Yaohui Zhao, Albert Park, and Xiaoqing Song. 2005. 'Economic Returns to Schooling in Urban China 1988 to 2001'. *Journal of Comparative Economics 33*: 730–52.

Zhao, Y. 2000. 'Rural-to-Urban Labor Migration in China: The Past and the Present'. In *Rural Labor Flows in China*, edited by L. A. West and Y. Zhao, University of California Press.

Zhou, Xiaogang and Lu Ming. 2014. 'Health of Rural Migrant Workers'. Working paper.

16
Human Capital and Urbanization in India

Sandip Sarkar

16.1 Introduction

Urbanization and growth are usually expected to go move together. Industry and services grow more rapidly than other sectors and these are concentrated in and around cities. A large range of literature explains the role of agglomeration economies and the functioning of labour markets in cities that make cities engine of growth. These are supposed to work through better productivity impacts and linkages with the growth process in cities. Many economies that developed late, such as those of countries in East Asia, witnessed high rates of urbanization during their growth experience.

A city-led growth strategy requires labour from rural areas to work in more productive industries in urban centres. Human capital is the most important engine in urban development. Cities also amplify returns to human capital through the 'human capital externality'. Urban production processes require labour with some level of human capital, i.e. education, skill, and health. Development of human capital thus becomes a prerequisite for such a growth strategy.

A lot needs to be done to improve the levels of education and healthcare in India, and these are the areas which the private sector is not capable of handling. Therefore, the government needs to invest in human capital (education, health) and remove the institutional barriers to help rural–urban migrants accumulate human capital and improve human capital externalities.

While Chapter 7 in this volume studies urbanization and migration and finds beneficial effects in terms of reduction in both rural and urban poverty as labour market outcomes tend to improve, this chapter attempts to analyse the human capital base in general and that of the migrants in particular. It compares the human capital base of the population and workers in rural and urban areas. The role of human capital in the knowledge-based sector of information and communication technology (ICT) is also analysed. The nature and extent of the private sector's role in human capital formation are also looked at to assess the levels and areas of intervention that are required by the government. The government's contribution in this regard is examined to identify the gaps as well.

Sandip Sarkar., *Human Capital and Urbanization in India* In: *Cities of Dragons and Elephants: Urbanization and Urban Development in China and India. Edited by:* Guanghua Wan and Ming Lu, Oxford University Press (2019).
 DOI: 10.1093/oso/9780198829225.003.0016

The rest of this chapter is divided into five sections: Section 16.2 focuses on human capital and growth, Section 16.3 highlights the changes in India's population and economy, Section 16.4 presents the status of human capital in the country, Section 16.5 discusses the financing of human capital formation, and Section 16.6 concludes with some policy interventions.

16.2 Human Capital and Growth

Traditional growth theories focused on capital, labour, and technology as determinants of growth, but capital, labour, and technical progress alone were not sufficient to explain the growth patterns across countries. According to Becker (1964: 10):

> Throughout history, few countries have experienced long periods of persistent growth in per capita income. Economic theory can explain this easily enough, because if per capita income growth is caused by the growth of land and physical capital per worker, diminishing marginal returns will eventually eliminate further growth. What classical economic theory cannot explain is the fact that the United States and other countries have had continuous economic growth in per capita income over the past century and continue to grow.

Becker (1964) also noted that all countries that have had continuous GDP per capita growth have simultaneously devoted great amounts of resources to nationwide education.

Since the 1960s, human capital has been one of the central issues of neoclassical growth theory. Theodore Schultz and Gary Becker did much of the work on the subject of human capital in the early 1960s. Schultz (1961) focused on education as a form of human capital, and Becker built on Schultz's work by developing a broader theory of human capital.

Different grades of labour enter the production function differently and affect the rates of return to capital. According to Psacharopoulos (1987), 'Differences in the level of ability and per capita productivity from country to country are the result of variances in the level of human capital investments, rather than genetic endowment.'

Human capital increases the productivity of workers. Some activities that increase human capital include acquiring health care, additional education, and training. The theory of human capital states that investments can be made in human beings, as well as in physical capital, which yield a future stream of returns or dividends to the initial investment. The theory of human capital bases itself on the assumption that after an initial investment in human capital is made, a stream of higher future income can be generated from both expansion of education and improvements in health. 'Human capital plays a dual role in the process of economic growth. As a stock of knowledge, it is a source of technological change. At the same time, the formation of adaptable skills in the work force is, in part, induced by changes in technology' (Mincer 1989).

Returns to education are private as well as social. Private returns accrue to workers as earnings increase with the rise in human capital. However, there are positive externalities associated with human capital formation, which leads to additional gains for the economy as a whole. Investment in human capital has been one of the major sources of growth in modern economies during the twentieth century, though the process of investing in human capital normally takes much longer than physical capital.

Individuals make investments in human capital based on private returns to education. Households' decision to invest in human capital, especially education, is guided by several other factors as well. The opportunity cost of getting education is the most obvious with regard to foregone earnings. Not being able to invest and spend in other avenues, such as in physical capital or consumption expenditure, is another important opportunity cost of investment in human capital. Paucity of resources is a major deterrent to human capital formation in developing countries. For this reason, the government's role in facilitating human capital formation becomes even more important in developing countries. The limitation of resources even at the national level means that public investment in human capital formation has to compete with physical capital formation.

There are strong reasons for considering health to be a crucial aspect of human capital and, therefore, a critical ingredient of economic growth. Healthier workers are physically and mentally more energetic and robust. They are more productive and earn higher wages. They are also less likely to be absent from work because of illness (or illness in their family) (Bloom et al. 2001). This study considers physical capital, labour, and human capital as inputs in production. It takes life expectancy along with education and experience as human capital, and finds that health has a positive and statistically significant effect on economic growth. It suggests that a one-year improvement in people's life expectancy contributes to a 4 per cent increase in output. Unfortunately, there are few estimates of social returns to education in India. Psacharopoulos (1994) calculated private and social returns to capital for the year 1978. His estimation of social returns to investment in primary, secondary, and higher education were 29.3 per cent, 13.7 per cent, and 10.8 per cent, respectively. Corresponding private returns to investment in education in primary, secondary, and higher education were higher at 33.8 per cent, 19.8 per cent, and 13.2 per cent, respectively. Both social returns and private returns to education were highest for primary education. Schündeln and Playforth (2014) analysed the interrelationship between education growth and economic growth on the basis of panel data across states of India at five points of time (1961, 1971, 1981, 1991, and 2001). They found evidence that the effect of the government sector size on education's effectiveness in promoting growth was negative, economically large, and statistically significant. It suggested that the government absorbed human capital in low-productivity activities. Once the effect of government sector size on educational effectiveness was controlled, the result indicated that the effect of education in India was positive and significant for a wide range of Indian states. They felt that after the faster growth of the 1980s, there was a possibility of educational expansion having a more positive effect on economic growth. However, the micro-evidence on public–private wage differentials showed that the large positive wage differential between the public and private sector persisted through the 1990s with the public sector wage premium going up to 140 per cent. They concluded that, on average, outside opportunities for educated workers were still unattractive relative to the government sector, which otherwise would have led to significant social returns in economic growth.

However, the recent growth pattern suggests that since the last decade, corporate jobs in certain sectors are paying far better than government jobs with a similar level of education. The ICT sector has turned out to be one of the high-growth sectors. The contribution of the ICT sector to GDP was 4.2 per cent in 2001–2, and it increased its share to 8 per cent in 2013. Employment in the ICT sector went up from 1.09 million in 1999–2000 to 3.91 million in 2011–12. In 2011–12, 87.1 per cent of ICT sector workers were located in urban areas. The activities of this sector are metro-centric, with 41 per cent of all workers working in metros. Of all workers working in metros, 81 per cent are located in the six large cities of Bangalore, Delhi (including satellite cities of Gurgaon and Noida), Hyderabad, Pune, Mumbai, and Chennai. The share of information technology (IT) and IT-enabled services (a dominant subset of the ICT sector) is even more urban-oriented, with 95.5 per cent of all workers working in urban areas and 72 per cent of all workers working in metros in 2011–12. The share of graduates in all workers in the ICT sector has risen from 44.4 per cent in 1999–2000 to 58.5 per cent in 2009–10. The share of workers in public enterprises within ICT has declined from 28 per cent in 1999–2000 to 8 per cent in 2009–10. In 2009–10, this sector was driven by the private corporate sector, which employed 56 per cent of all workers. The wage premium of the private corporate sector over the public sector for regular wage workers was 10 per cent in 2009–10. Chapter 3 in this volume studying the relationship between the number of graduates per 1,000 population (greater than seven years of age) and the average daily earnings of all employees at the state level, is quadratic, decreasing first with education, and then increasing.

Another study based on multi-country data showed that benefits of health apply primarily to poor countries. The chapter also argues that other measures of health, such as disease prevalence rates and cognitive functioning, are important for maintaining a steady supply of skilled labour (Bhargava et al. 2001).

One major criticism of human capital models is that they ignore the labour market situation. Demand for labour plays a very important role in economies like India and varies for different levels of education. The threshold level of education for entry into the workforce has been going up over time. This is not entirely due to requiring more educated and skilled labour as this threshold has gone up for unskilled workers as well. Any policy formulation with respect to the role of human capital formation must, therefore, take labour market considerations into account.

16.3 Change in India's Population and Economy

The two main drivers for change in human capital are demographic and economic change. Currently, more than half of India's population is under the age of twenty-five, and by 2020 India is likely to become the world's third largest economy, with a correspondingly rapid growth in the size of its middle classes. India is expected to outpace the People's Republic of China (PRC) as the country with the largest tertiary-age population. The Organisation for Economic Co-operation and Development estimates that in 2020, 200 million of the world's 25–34 year olds will be university graduates, and 40 per cent of these will be from the PRC and India, representing a huge proportion of the global talent pool. With the emergence of India as a knowledge-based economy, human capital has now become its major strength.

The process of urbanization in India so far has been low. According to the census of India, 68.7 per cent of India's population resides in rural areas. It is reasonable to argue that simply having people move to cities does not guarantee growth. The latter depends on the nature of urbanization and the manner in which it is managed. It depends on the absolute quality of urban opportunities. People move to the cities to seek better opportunities relative to rural ones, but it is the absolute quantity of opportunities in urban areas that determines the outcome in growth.

Table 16.1 shows that in India, the process of urbanization so far has been low. The growth of the population has been higher in metropolitan cities with a population of one million and above. Some portion of this higher growth is due to the addition of newer cities (Table 16.2). Still, the rate of population growth has been historically higher. The share of metropolitan cities in the urban population in 2011 was 42.3 per cent.

In this regard, it is useful to see the extent to which migration played a role in the rise in population in urban areas, as presented in Part III in this volume.

A large majority of the countries from different geographic regions of Asia have recorded a deceleration in urban growth and migration in recent years that cannot be fully explained in terms of a decline in natural growth, declassification of towns, and definitional or boundary adjustment factors. One can postulate a thesis of exclusionary urban growth, stipulating that the negative

Table 16.1. Growth of population in urban areas by size and rural areas (%)

Areas	1971–81	1981–91	1991–2001	2001–11
Rural	1.8	1.8	1.7	1.2
Urban	3.9	3.2	2.8	2.4
Total	**2.2**	**2.1**	**2.0**	**1.5**
Towns	2.7	2.4	1.5	1.6
Cities	4.4	3.7	3.5	2.7
Metropolitan	4.2	4.9	4.2	3.5

Notes: City = population 100,000 or more; metropolitan = population one million or more; towns = population less than 100,000.

Source: Calculated from Census of India; 2011 values are projected.

Table 16.2. Growth of metropolitan cities

Items	1981	1991	2001	2011
Share of metropolitan Population in urban (%)	27.7	32.9	37.8	42.3
Number of metropolitan cities	12	23	35	53

Source: Census documents.

policy perspective on migration and increased unaffordability of land and basic amenities by the rural poor have led to a deceleration in urban growth (Kundu 2009).

In this context, it is necessary to examine India's economic growth over the years, which is strongly associated with urbanization and human capital. For the first time, during 1981–91, India grew by more than 5 per cent per annum. The growth rate marginally went up in the next decade to 5.6 per cent, and it further accelerated to 7.7 per cent during 2001–11. A gradual process of dismantling the highly restrictive trade policy regime began in 1991, and it got implemented over a decade. The gradualist nature of the reforms, structural rigidities in the economy, and the time taken to establish the creditability of a new policy regime meant a strong pick-up of private investment after some years.

The acceleration in non-agricultural GDP after 2001 was predominantly driven by the private sector, particularly in some states that led the process of market orientation and built the necessary infrastructural and supportive investment environment in their urban areas. The rapid growth since the early 1980s led to a significant structural transformation—the share of agriculture in GDP declined from 34 per cent in 1983–4 to 15 per cent in 2009–10. The corresponding share of services in GDP rose from 45 per cent to 64 per cent and that of construction from 6 per cent to 8 per cent, while the share of manufacturing remained relatively constant at 15 per cent.

Table 16.3 compares the patterns of sector growth in the last two decades. Two sectors, services and construction, recorded higher than GDP growth in the last decade. A more detailed examination shows that the contribution to services sector growth by real estate, renting, and business services was 12.7 per cent during 1981–2000, but it rose substantially to 18.9 per cent during 2000–12. The only other services subsector that could raise its contribution in services sector growth was trade, hotel, and restaurants, whose contribution went up from 31.3 per cent during 1981–2000 to 33.7 per cent during 2000–12 (Ghose 2013). India's experience of economic growth and structural transformation in 1980–2005 is associated with only a moderate decline in the share of agriculture in total employment. The decline in the agriculture sector's share in employment in the 1980s was small. Even during 1993–4 to 2004–5, it fell from 64 per cent to 52 per cent. The share of industry in total employment marginally decreased and services were the principal sector recording a sharp increase in the share of total employment. Since GDP growth was coming from highly skilled sectors like IT, telecoms, and banking, or highly skilled manufacturing like engineering and pharmaceuticals, it did not draw much labour from rural areas. This is reflected in the continuously higher share of urban areas in GDP as shown in Figure 16.1. This process quickened after the economic reforms that began in the early 1990s.

Table 16.3. Sector growth in the last two decades

Period	Agriculture growth	Manufacturing growth	Construction growth	Services growth	GDP growth
1991–2001	2.8	5.7	5.1	7.3	5.6
2001–11	3.1	6.9	10.0	9.4	7.7

Source: Calculated from various issues of *Economic Survey of India* (Government of India Various years).

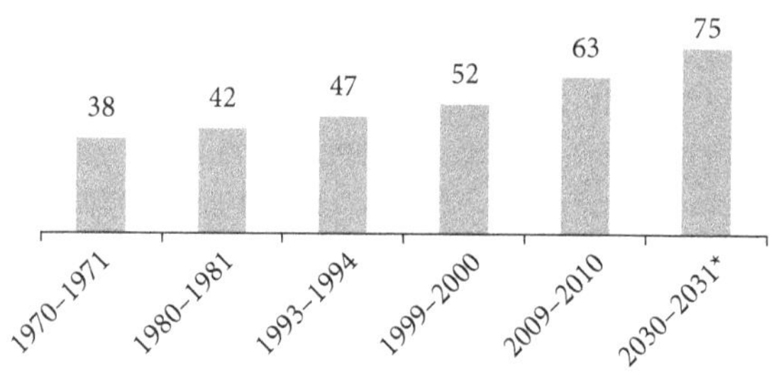

Figure 16.1. Urban GDP share

Note: * = estimated.

Source: Central Statistical Office, Eleventh Five Year Plan, 2007–12, and the Mid-Term Appraisal of the Eleventh Five Year Plan, 2007–12.

Manufacturing has never played a leading role in India's economic development. It can be seen that the share of manufacturing in GDP hovered at around 14–16 per cent and that the share of manufacturing in India's employment moved in a narrow range of 11–13 per cent in the last three decades. Three decades of rapid economic growth would normally have propelled migration from rural areas, but growth in India has not had this effect thus far. This is because industrialization has been capital intensive and has failed to become a leading sector for growth, and the services boom fuelled by the knowledge economy has also been skill intensive. A few cities of India have acted as centres of knowledge and innovation. As more cities provide economies of agglomeration and scale for clusters of industries and other non-agricultural economic activities, the urban sector will become the principal engine for stimulating national economic growth.

In consequence, the rural–urban differentials in productivity in India, as shown in Figure 16.2, have widened over time, indicating considerable scope for migrants to take advantage of the higher-productivity non-agriculture sectors if they can be equipped with the skills and education relevant for employment in urban areas. The economy seems to be far from reaching a saturation point in migration, and it is reasonable to expect a hastening in the pace of urbanization.

India's economic growth momentum cannot be sustained if urbanization is not actively facilitated. Nor can poverty be addressed if the needs of the urban poor are isolated from the broader challenges of managing urbanization. Cities will have to become the engines of national development. India cannot afford to get its urban strategy wrong, but it cannot get it right without bringing about a fundamental shift in the mindset that separates the rural from the urban.

The McKinsey Report (McKinsey Global Institute 2010) on India's urbanization prospects estimates that over 2010–30, urban India will create 70 per cent of all new jobs in India and these urban jobs will be twice as productive as equivalent jobs in the rural sector. In a bid to attract private capital, urban centres have become less accommodating to the poor, restricting their entry and thereby increasing rural–urban economic inequalities.

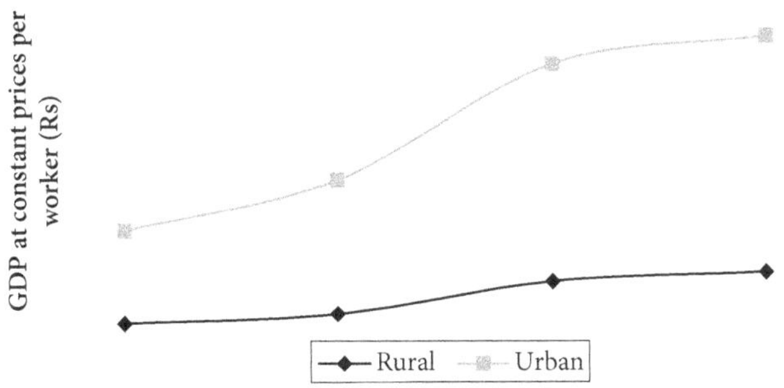

Figure 16.2. Rural–urban productivity

Source: Central Statistical Office and National Sample Survey Office.

The McKinsey Report argues that the challenge of managing urbanization will have to be addressed through a combination of increased investment, strengthening the framework for governance and financing, and a comprehensive capacity-building programme at all levels of government. The fact that higher urbanization levels have been associated with higher levels of per capita income in several other countries suggests that higher levels of income resulting from the faster GDP growth rates of India's economy in the years to come should result in higher levels of urbanization in India.

16.4 Status and Development of Human Capital in India

In the context of the discussion in Section 16.3, this section takes stock of the current human capital base of India. This section covers the level of general education, technical and vocational education, enrolment, rural–urban differences of skill acquisition, and the human capital base of knowledge economy.

16.4.1 General Education

The educational level among people of seven years and above across gender and sector for 2011–12 is shown in Table 16.4. About a quarter of the population was still illiterate and another third had up to primary-level education. Males were considerably more educated than females. Even illiteracy among females was almost double that of male counterparts.

Table 16.4. Distribution of population (7+ years) by educational level, 2011–12 (%)

Educational level	All India		
	Male	Female	Total
Not literate (0)	17.3	33.7	25.2
Below primary (1–4)	18.0	16.4	17.3
Primary (5)	16.7	15.0	15.9
Middle (8)	17.5	13.9	15.7
Secondary (10)	13.1	9.3	11.3
Higher secondary (12)	9.5	6.6	8.1
Graduate + (15 and above)	7.9	5.1	6.5
Total	**100**	**100**	**100**

Note: Figures in parentheses show minimum years of schooling.

Source: Calculated from various years of unit-level data of the National Sample Survey Office.

16.4.1.1 Higher Enrolment of Primary Education

Since the 1990s, universal primary education has been one of the major thrusts of the government. India's National Policy on Education, which was formulated in 1986 and revised in 1992, had resolved to ensure free and compulsory education for all children up to fourteen years of age by the end of the last century. Sarva Shiksha Abhiyan (SSA), launched in 2001–2, revised the goals to ensure provision of useful and relevant elementary education for all children aged 6–14 years by 2010. In 2009, the Right of Children to Free and Compulsory Education (RTE) Act was passed, which put the compulsion on the government to ensure the right for every child aged 6–14 years to receive at least eight years of child-friendly education in a neighbourhood school.

The net enrolment ratio (NER) at the primary and upper primary (middle) levels is shown in Table 16.5. This shows that the NER was almost 100 per cent at the primary level in 2009–10, while it was only 58 per cent at the upper primary level (middle school). The NER at both the primary and upper primary levels (middle) had gone up over the years.

Figure 16.3 shows adjusted net attendance ratios for children in the primary age group (6–10) and the upper primary age group (11–14) separately. The adjusted net attendance ratio for the primary age group is defined as the ratio of number of children attending primary or higher grades and the total number of children in the 6–10 age group and similarly for the upper primary age group. These ratios

Table 16.5. Net enrolment ratio at the primary and upper primary levels (%)

Item	2007–8	2008–9	2009–10
Net enrolment ratio at the primary level	95.9	98.6	98.3
Net enrolment ratio at the upper primary level	52.6	56.2	58.3

Source: Government of India, Planning Commission, 2014.

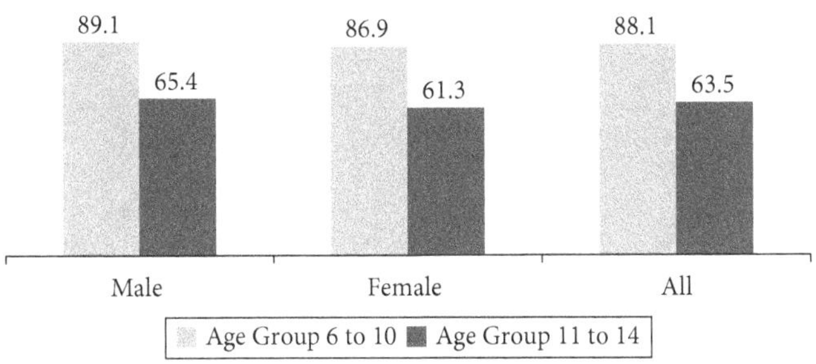

Figure 16.3. Adjusted net attendance ratio in the primary and upper primary age group, 2007–8

Note: Adjusted net attendance ratio adjusts for students who study in higher classes compared to official age groups.

Source: Calculated from National Sample Survey Office unit-level data (2007–8).

are different from the normal net attendance ratios in the sense that they include underage enrolment in the numerator.

As can be seen from Figure 16.3, enrolment for the upper primary age group was far below the primary age group. Gender differences in enrolment at these levels are not very stark. Since 2007–8, there has been improvement at the upper primary level as a result of initiatives taken by the government, most notable among these being the introduction of the RTE Act.

16.4.1.2 Net Attendance

Figure 16.4 compares attendance rates in the two sectors for the primary and upper primary age groups between rural and urban areas. The rates are significantly higher for urban children at the upper primary level. The net attendance rate in urban areas was twelve points higher than rural areas for the upper primary age group, and it was 3.2 per cent for the primary age group.

The net attendance ratio for the higher secondary level was just 23 per cent in rural areas and almost 50 per cent in urban areas in 2007–8. The percentage of the population aged fifteen years and above also showed that only about 18 per cent in rural areas and 44.7 per cent in urban areas had more than secondary-level qualifications (not presented here). In India, there is no special government funding for urban areas, although most of the better schools are located in urban areas, where even students from rural areas attend. Further, job opportunities for the educated mostly exist in urban areas except for some government jobs that are available in rural areas. So, the incentive for education is less in rural areas.

16.4.1.3 Gross Attendance

Education plays an important role in growth and any strategy of urbanization-linked growth must be based on the assessment of human capital endowments of people in the urban sector vis-à-vis the rural sector. Gross attendance ratios for

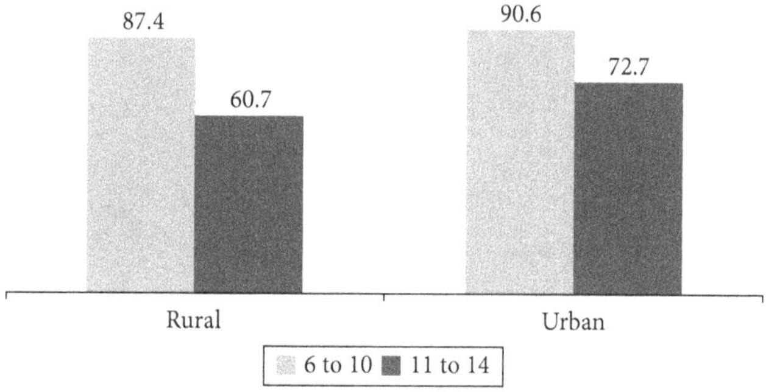

Figure 16.4. Adjusted net attendance rate by sector for the primary and upper primary age group population, 2007–8

Source: Calculated from National Sample Survey unit-level data (2007–8).

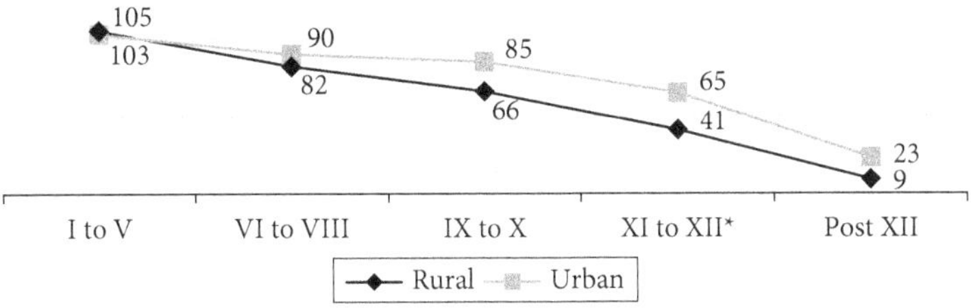

Figure 16.5. Gross attendance ratio, 2007–28

Note: * Implies completion of school education of 10th standard.

Source: Calculated from National Sample Survey unit-level data (2007–8).

Table 16.6. Distribution of currently attending (aged 15–29 years) by type of education (%)

Location	General	Technical/vocational
Rural	98.3	1.7
Urban	94.9	5.1
Total	**97.2**	**2.8**

Source: Calculated from National Sample Survey Office unit-level data (2011–12).

urban areas are consistently higher than rural areas across education levels except for the primary level of education as shown in Figure 16.5. Though urban areas fare better in comparison rural areas, the trend of decline over levels of education is very similar for both sectors. Attendance ratios at the tertiary level were pretty low at 23 per cent for the urban population and even lower (not even double digit) for their rural counterparts.

16.4.1.4 Current Attendance

Table 16.6 presents the rural–urban comparison with respect to attendance of technical or vocational courses among people aged between 15 and 29 years.[1] Here we find that overall attendance of these courses is quite low and the levels

[1] The National Sample Survey Office (NSSO) broadly divides education into three categories: (1) general education, (2) technical and professional education, and (3) vocational education. General education, in this survey, includes general school education from the primary to the higher secondary level and normal university education for a degree, whereas technical/professional courses involve hands-on training in addition to theoretical classes. Engineering, medicine, agriculture, management, chartered accountancy, and cost accountancy are examples of technical/professional courses. The education that aims to impart training in very specific fields through providing significant 'hands-on' experience in acquiring necessary skills, which will make the students employable or create for them opportunities of self-employment, and the degree/diploma/certificate awarded by the institutes which have recognition by the state/central government/public sector or similar employers, is included under vocational education. Education offered by industrial training institutes and polytechnics are examples of vocational courses.

are far below the desired levels. Within the overall very low levels, the rural–urban gap is quite stark.

16.4.1.5 Type of Management

This chapter discusses the issue of deficiencies in technical and vocational education and the financing of these in detail in Section 16.4.2. Figure 16.6 shows the extent of privatization at different levels of education in rural and urban areas. Though degrees of privatization for the rural population have been more or less consistent across levels of schooling, these have been quite low in comparison with the urban sector. If we look at the pattern of privatization in the urban sector, it provides some interesting insights. Enrolment has been higher in the urban sector not only in private-unaided but also private-aided[2] schools. Only at the secondary and higher secondary levels do we notice some significant contribution of private schools for the rural population, both aided and unaided.[3] The share of private-unaided schools in total private school attendance is quite significant even at the upper primary level.

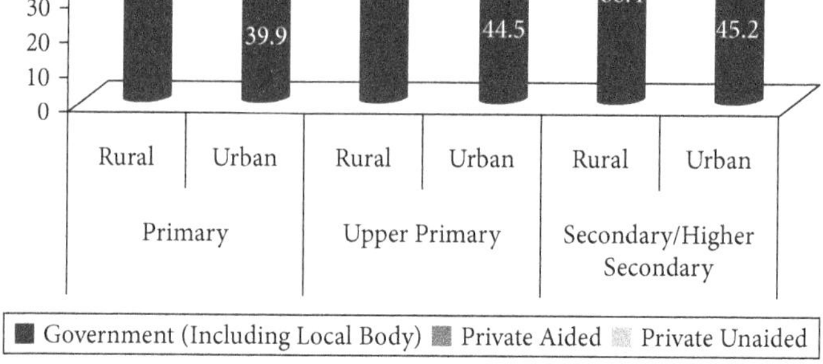

Figure 16.6. Distribution of currently attending students (aged 5–29 years) by management (%)

Source: Calculated from National Sample Survey Office unit-level data (2007–8).

[2] All schools run by an individual or a private organization and which receive a grant from the government/local body.

[3] This could partially be a result of rural children at the secondary/higher secondary levels attending nearby urban schools as the NSSO collects data by place of residence.

16.4.2 Technical or Professional Education

With the changing production structure, technical and vocational skills are becoming increasingly important sources of productivity growth. Any economy aspiring to be competitive needs to not only build a pool of skilled workers but also identify the appropriate types of skills by production requirements. This section examines the current stock of skills in India.

The technical and professional qualifications for 2011–12 in India is given in Table 16.7. Overall, around only 2 per cent were technically qualified people in the country, with little over 4 per cent in urban areas and less than 1 per cent in rural areas.

Figure 16.7 shows further technical education by type of certification. More than half of the technically qualified people were technical diploma/certificate holders below the graduate level. About a quarter of them were technical diploma holders above the graduate level, and 16 per cent held technical degrees. The percentage of technical diploma holders above the graduate level was relatively higher in urban areas, while technical diploma or certificate holders below the graduate level in rural areas were much higher than the overall average.

Table 16.7. Technical education in India, 2011–12 (%)

Technical	Rural	Urban	Total
Technical education	0.7	4.1	1.7
No technical education	99.3	95.9	98.3
Total	**100.0**	**100.0**	**100.0**

Source: Calculated from National Sample Survey Office unit-level data (2011–12).

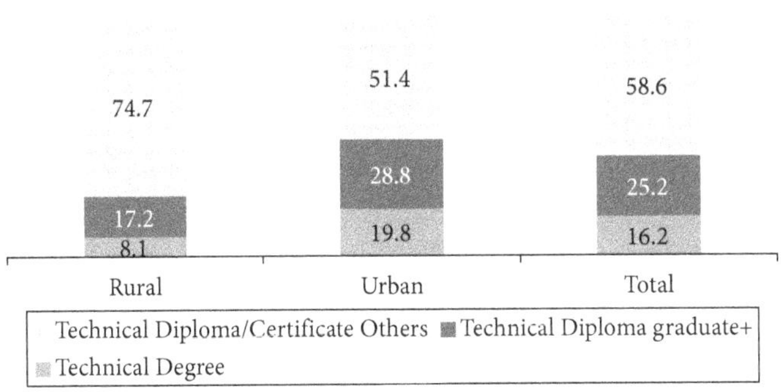

Figure 16.7. Technical education by type, 2011–12 (%)
Source: Calculated from National Sample Survey Office unit-level data (2011–12).

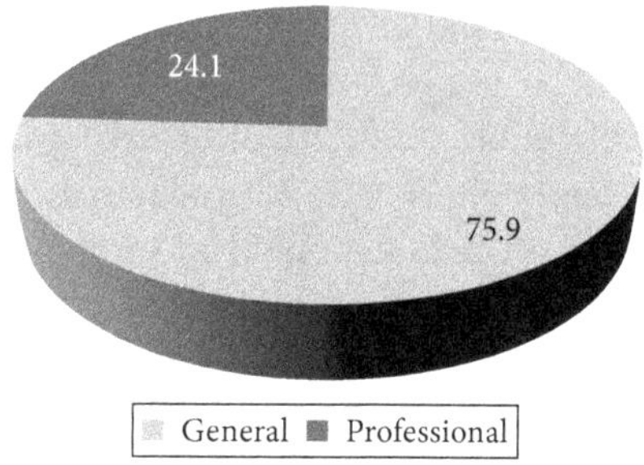

Figure 16.8. Distribution of enrolment in higher education, 2009–10 (%)
Source: Department of Higher Education, Ministry of Human Resource Development.

16.4.2.1 Enrolment

Figure 16.8 gives the breakup of those enrolled beyond the senior secondary level in general and professional education in 2009–10. The share of enrolment in professional courses may appear reasonable at 24 per cent, but as seen in Section 16.4.2, the overall participation in tertiary education is so low that it cannot make a substantial contribution.

India falls far behind countries like the PRC when it comes to skill development in the education system. A study on the PRC concludes that India cannot match the scale and size of the PRC's technical and vocational education and training system without ensuring that India's 10,000 secondary and senior secondary schools have a vocational education stream. Currently, vocational education is offered only at the senior secondary level in India (Government of India, Planning Commission 2013).

16.4.2.2 Type of Professional Education

In 2010–11, among those attending technical education, a huge majority were those with diplomas (84 per cent). Certificate holders and those with postgraduate diplomas came next, in almost equal proportion of 7 per cent each. Those with integrated degrees formed a minuscule proportion of the group. Further exploration of these diplomas needs to be done to be able to gauge their usefulness.

16.4.2.3 Management Type

Figure 16.9 compares the contributions of the government and the private sector in general and professional education. As discussed, the size of technical and vocational education is very small in India. Within this small sector of education, the direct contribution of the government is much lower than its contribution to general education. The share of unaided private institutions in imparting technical and vocational education was not substantially smaller than the government and the private-aided sector put together. The way the National Sample Survey Office (NSSO) defines technical and vocational education gives reason to believe

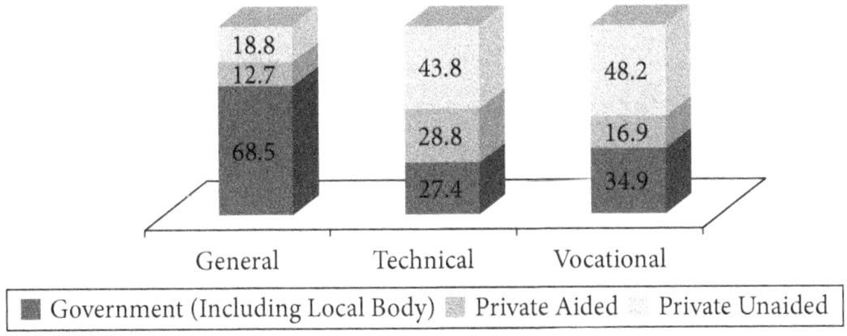

Figure 16.9. Management by type of current education (aged 5–29 years) (%)
Source: Calculated from National Sample Survey Office unit-level data (2007–8).

that professional education could be a very heterogeneous category in terms of duration and quality. In 2010–11, six major urbanized states with an urbanization rate of more than 35 per cent had a 50.6 per cent share in the total higher educational institutions of all types. These states had a share of 30.3 per cent in India's population in 2011.

16.4.3 Recent Performance in the Education Sector

School enrolment has witnessed a steady though modest rise over the years, and this is true across grades. What is also noticeable is that the difference in enrolment from primary to higher secondary over the years has remained almost the same, with primary school enrolment remaining the highest followed by much lower levels of upper primary, secondary, and higher secondary (Figure 16.10).

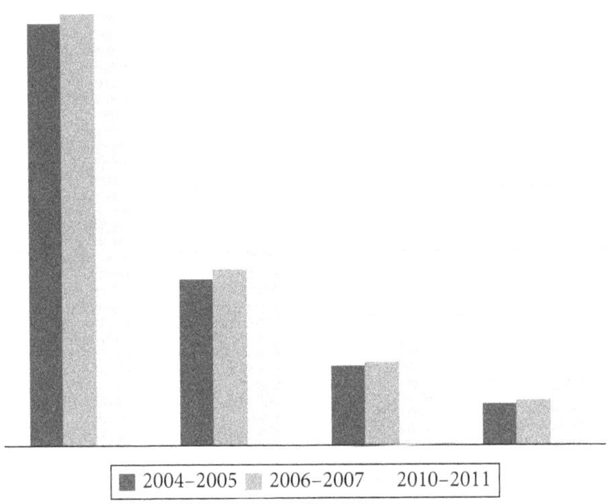

Figure 16.10. School enrolment by grades (million)
Source: Department of Higher Education, Ministry of Human Resource Development.

But the implication of this moderate growth in educational performance is reflected in a substantial increase when presented in absolute numbers. Enrolment in higher education in the general stream shows an increase of five million in the last decade from a modest level of seven million and that of professional education from less than two million to four million (Figure 16.11).

A breakup of the professional education stream shows that most of the increase has been quite lopsided and it has taken place in the engineering/technical stream (Figure 16.12). But the overall increase in the mean years of schooling was quite modest in the last decade (Table 16.8).

To sum up, despite many gains during the Eleventh Five Year Plan (2007–12), education in India faces several challenges. The country's mean years of schooling at 5.12 years is well below that of other emerging market economies such as the PRC (8.17 years) and Brazil (7.54 years) and significantly below the average for all

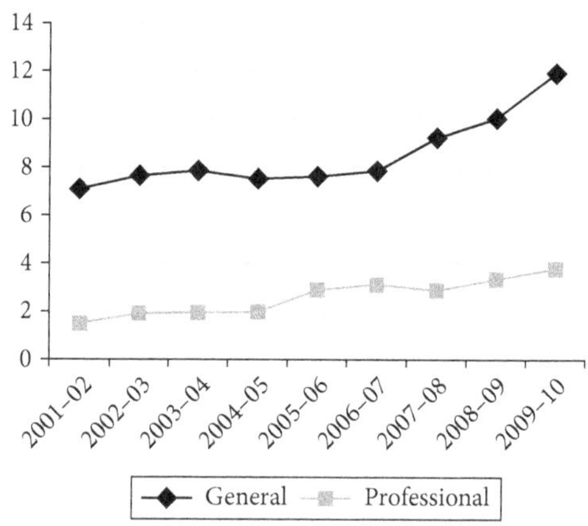

Figure 16.11. Enrolment in higher education (million)
Source: Department of Higher Education, Ministry of Human Resource Development.

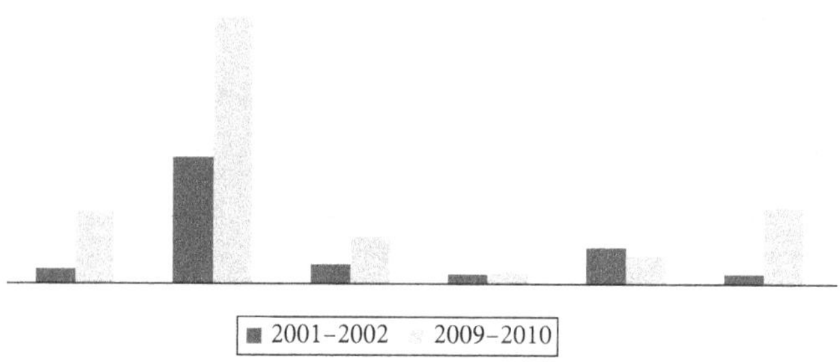

Figure 16.12. Enrolment in professional education by stream (million)
Source: Department of Higher Education, Ministry of Human Resource Development.

Table 16.8. Mean years of schooling (aged 7+ years)

	Rural	Urban
1999–2000	2.7	5.5
2007–8	3.5	6.2

Source: National Sample Survey Office, 52nd and 64th rounds.

developing countries (7.09 years).[4] A matter of particular concern is the steep dropout rate after the elementary level. The sharp drop-off in enrolment at the middle-school level and the increasing enrolment gap from middle to higher secondary suggests that the gains at the elementary level have not yet impacted the school system as a whole.

16.4.4 Human Capital in Rural and Urban India

In Section 16.4.1, we observed a substantial rural–urban difference in gross and net attendance rates of school-going children. Here we examine its implication on the quality of human capital. Table 16.9 presents the composition of educational status of persons aged seven years and above. The spread of college-level education is very low in rural areas, and it was a meagre 3 per cent compared with 15 per cent for urban areas in 2011–12. The share of persons with education below the primary level was almost half in rural areas compared with little over a quarter in urban areas.

Table 16.9. Composition of education level of persons (age 7+ years) in rural and urban areas, 2011–12

Educational level	Rural			Urban		
	Male	Female	Total	Male	Female	Total
Not literate (0)	20.9	39.5	30.0	8.9	19.7	14.0
Below primary (1–4)	19.8	17.7	18.8	14.0	13.3	13.7
Primary (5)	17.7	15.5	16.6	14.2	13.9	14.1
Middle (8)	17.9	13.3	15.7	16.3	15.1	15.8
Secondary (10)	12.1	7.6	9.8	15.5	13.5	14.5
Higher secondary (12)	7.6	4.5	6.1	14.0	11.8	12.9
Graduate+ (15 and above)	4.0	1.9	3.0	17.1	12.7	15.0
Total	100.0	100.0	100.0	100.0	100.0	100.0

Note: Figures in parentheses show the minimum number of years of schooling.
Source: Calculated from unit-level data of National Sample Survey Office, 68th round.

[4] 12th Five Year Plan documents of India.

Table 16.10. Composition of the education level of persons (age 7+ years) in metros and non-metros, 2011–12

Educational level	Metro			Non-metro		
	Male	Female	Total	Male	Female	Total
Not literate (0)	6.7	16.2	11.2	9.8	21.2	15.4
Below primary (1–4)	12.7	12.4	12.5	14.5	13.7	14.1
Primary (5)	13.2	13.3	13.3	14.7	14.1	14.4
Middle (8)	14.8	14.5	14.7	17.1	15.4	16.2
Secondary (10)	16.2	13.6	15.0	15.2	13.4	14.3
Higher secondary (12)	15.0	13.2	14.1	13.5	11.2	12.4
Graduate+ (15 and above)	21.4	16.8	19.2	15.2	11.0	13.2
Total	**100.0**	**100.0**	**100.0**	**100.0**	**100.0**	**100.0**

Notes: Figures in parentheses show the minimum number of years of schooling; metro means a city with a population of one million or more.

Source: Calculated from unit-level data of National Sample Survey Office, 68th round.

Table 16.11. Results from cross section regression from twenty-two states, 2011–12

Serial number	Dependent variable: share of graduates in total population, 2011–12	
1	Intercept	3.127 (1.739)***
2	Urbanization rate, 2001	0.128 (0.045)*
3	R square	0.292

Note: standard errors are reported in the parenthesis, and * and *** represent significance level at 1 per cent and 10 per cent respectively.

Source: Census of India 2011; National Sample Survey, 2011–12.

The difference between metros and non-metros in the composition of the human capital stock is less stark (Table 16.10). The major difference can be observed in the share of graduates and above. The share of graduates in metropolitan areas is one and half times that of non-metro areas.

The substantial difference in the higher level of education in rural and urban areas allows us to postulate that urbanization provides the necessary condition for enhancing quality of human capital. This difference is examined across twenty-two major states of India in 2011–12. The regression analysis showed that urbanization indeed contributed significantly in improving the quality of human capital, captured through the share of graduates in the total population. The relationship is plotted in Table 16.11.

Alternatively, improvement in human capital also attracts the modern services sector and high-quality manufacturing activities to establish units in those areas, which leads to further urbanization. However, this relationship is not particularly direct as urbanization is closely related to the level of economic development. Therefore, we have to control the impact of economic development through variable per capita income to establish this relationship statistically. It is observed from cross-section regression across the twenty-two major states that better endowment of human capital captured through the share of graduates in the total population positively and significantly affects urbanization after controlling for the level of per capita income. This is shown in Table 16.12.

We have earlier observed a substantial and growing divergence of labour productivity between rural and urban areas. The educational gap between workers in rural and urban areas makes this clear. Nearly a quarter of all workers in urban areas were graduates and above compared with only 4 per cent in rural areas (Table 16.13). In rural areas, the major gains can be observed in the share of middle-school educated workers between 1993–4 and 2004–5 and that of secondary educated between 2004–5 and 2011–12. But the gap between rural and urban areas in the share of those that are highly educated (graduate and above) increased over the years.

The level of education has a substantial impact on the level of earnings. In India, earnings of the self-employed are not available, so we restrict our analysis of returns to education to the category of regular workers.

From Figure 16.13, it can be observed that incremental net additions to earnings went up at each successive level of education from middle school. In 1999–2000, addition to earnings went up substantially from secondary to higher secondary compared with that from higher secondary to graduate and above. But over the years, only the net addition to earnings of regular workers with graduate-and-above degrees has been going up continuously.

Table 16.12. Regression results showing human capital influencing urbanization, 2011–12

Serial number	Dependent Variable: urbanization rate, 2011	
1	Intercept	−249.65 (51.68)*
2	Share of graduates in total population	1.103 (0.572)***
3	Log per capita income, 2011–12	57.341 (11.091)*
4	R square	0.706

Note: standard errors are reported in the parenthesis and * and *** represent significance level at 1 per cent and 10 per cent respectively.

Sources: Census of India 2011; National Sample Survey, 2011–12.

Table 16.13. Composition of the education level of UPS workers (15 years and above)

		1993–4	2004–5	2011–12
Rural	Not literate (0)	54.5	44.3	35.0
	Below primary (1–4)	13.1	12.2	12.2
	Primary (5)	11.8	14.0	14.1
	Middle (8)	10.6	15.0	16.9
	Secondary (10)	5.6	7.3	11.0
	Higher secondary (12)	2.4	4.3	6.4
	Graduate+ (15 and above)	1.9	2.9	4.3
	Total	**100.0**	**100.0**	**100.0**
Urban	Not literate (0)	23.7	17.7	14.0
	Below primary (1–4)	11.3	8.6	7.6
	Primary (5)	13.4	13.7	11.3
	Middle (8)	15.6	17.7	16.5
	Secondary (10)	14.0	13.4	15.1
	Higher secondary (12)	8.0	11.9	13.0
	Graduate+ (15 and above)	14.0	16.9	22.5
	Total	**100.0**	**100.0**	**100.0**

Note: Figures in parentheses show the minimum years of schooling; UPS workers = workers who have worked for a major part of the year.

Source: Calculated from various years of unit-level data of National Sample Survey Office.

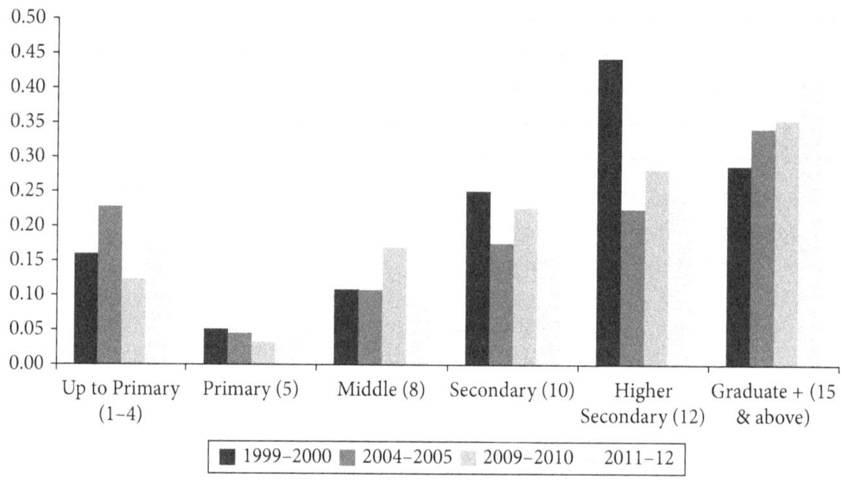

Figure 16.13. Incremental net additions to log earnings for successive levels of education for regular workers

Note: This has been derived after controlling for factors like age, rural–urban location, gender, industry groups, formal–informal sector, and employment status in the regression equation of log earnings of regular workers.

Source: Mazumdar et al. (2017b)

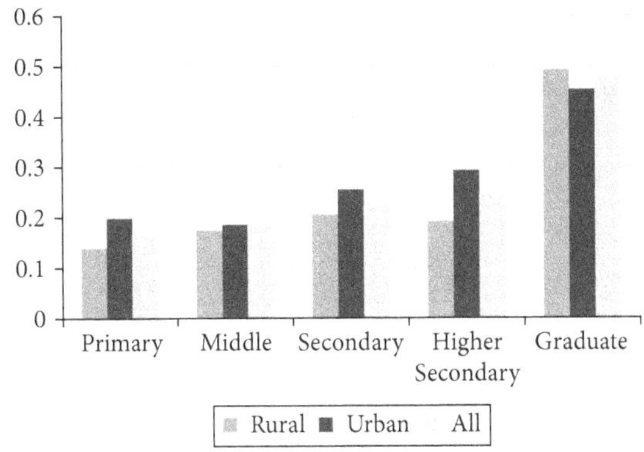

Figure 16.14. Incremental returns to education at different educational levels
Source: Computed from Agrawal (2011).

In the earnings regression, Mazumdar et al. (2017a) used rural dummies and showed that the rural dummy (in relation to the omitted urban dummy) had been negative for all these three years. But the estimated value of the rural dummy went up from −0.182 in 1999–2000 to −0.242 in 2004–5 and further to −0.305 in 2009–10, reflecting rural–urban differences.

Agrawal (2011) estimated the private returns to education using data from the India Human Development Survey, 2005. She used selectivity-corrected (Heckman) augmented Mincer functions for wage earners to arrive at her estimates.

She found similar results in that earnings went up substantially at each successive level of education and returns were far higher at the graduate-and-above level (Figure 16.14). Returns to education at all levels except for the graduate-and-above level were higher in urban areas than in rural areas. Higher returns to education for graduates in rural areas can be explained by the fewer jobs that are available at this level, which are mostly government jobs where there is a premium of earnings compared with most of the private sector jobs. The low private returns to education at the lower level of education makes poorer families less inclined to educate their children beyond primary education except for children who are brighter and more likely to complete the tertiary level of education.

16.4.5 Selectivity of Rural–Urban Migration

In Section 16.4.4, we observed the substantial difference in the educational level of workers between rural and urban areas. It will be interesting to examine whether any selectivity bias exists in migration from rural to urban areas.

It can be seen from Table 16.14 that the share of migrant workers vis-à-vis non-migrants was higher in two extreme levels of education qualification—not literate and graduate and above. Not literate migrants constituted 18 per cent of migrant workers compared with 15 per cent for non-migrant workers. Even the

Table 16.14. Composition of the education level of UPS workers (15 years and above) in urban areas by migration status, 2007–8) (%)

Educational level	Migrants	Non-migrant
Not literate (0)	18.1	14.5
Below primary (1–4)	7.0	7.6
Primary (5)	10.8	13.1
Middle (8)	16.4	19.4
Secondary (10)	14.3	15.8
Higher secondary (12)	12.5	12.1
Graduate + (15 and above)	20.9	17.5
Total	**100.0**	**100.0**

Note: UPS workers = workers who have worked for the major part of the year.

Source: Calculated from unit-level data of National Sample Survey Office, 64th round.

proportion of migrants with an educational qualification of at least a graduate degree constituted 21 per cent of the total migrant workers compared with 18 per cent for non-migrant workers. It can be seen that cities attract both not literate and highly educated migrants in large proportions, but the share of highly educated migrants was higher than not literate migrants from a very low base of the highly educated human capital stock that exists in rural areas. In that sense, the selectivity bias favouring highly educated migrants exists in India.

The migration data for India do not capture the proper magnitude of migration from rural to urban areas. It captures only long-term migrants and leaves out a sizeable proportion of short-term and circular migrants. Another section that constitutes a sizeable proportion of the urban workforce is commuting workers. As the results are based on household surveys, they capture the residential status, but not workplace location. The cross-tabulation of residential status and workplace location can capture the section of workers who commute from rural to urban areas and contribute to the urban GDP.

It can be seen from Table 16.15 that the distribution of commuting workers was quite even across different educational levels. Nearly two-thirds of commuting workers were at most middle-school educated compared with half of urban resident workers. Hardly one-tenth of commuting workers had a graduate degree compared with more than two-fifths of urban resident workers.

Chandrasekhar (2011) found from an analysis of unit-level NSSO data for 2009–10 that 33 per cent of commuting workers were engaged in elementary occupation, 25 per cent in craft and related trades, and 12 per cent were service workers or engaged in shop market sales.

In 2011–12, commuting workers constituted 7.9 per cent of urban-located work. Again, the share of migrant workers in total urban workers was 36.7 per cent in

Table 16.15. Composition of the educational level of workers and commuting workers, 2011–12 (%)

Educational level	Workers	Commuting workers
Not literate (0)	14.0	18.0
Below primary (1–4)	7.6	9.3
Primary (5)	11.3	16.1
Middle (8)	16.5	18.9
Secondary (10)	15.1	15.7
Higher secondary (12)	13.0	11.8
Graduate + (15 and above)	22.5	10.2
Total	**100.0**	**100.0**

Source: Calculated from unit-level data of National Sample Survey Office, 68th round.

2007–8. It can be concluded that there is a systematic pattern of exclusionary urbanization growth in India by selectively allowing the highly educated to be urban residents and allowing lower-skilled workers to commute from rural areas. This is fuelled by increased unaffordability of land and basic amenities in urban areas, particularly in metropolitan cities.

16.5 Financing and Provision of Education in India

It is widely accepted that there is an acute shortage of resources in the education sector in India. There are several important sources of education finance—the public sector, which includes expenditure by central government, state governments, and local bodies; foreign aid, which is transferred primarily through central government budgets; and the private sector, which is financed largely by individual households and, to a smaller extent, by the non-profit and for-profit private sectors.

In spite of the crucial importance of private sources in several countries, public expenditure is still the main source of educational funds in India. In more developed countries for which data are available, public financing represents most of the total education financing in 2009–10 (Figure 16.15).

Comparing three large developing countries in 2000, India's public expenditure on education as a percentage of GDP was the lowest, as shown in Figure 16.16. South Africa's spending was the highest. By 2005, however, India's public expenditure had plummeted. In the same period, however, Brazil increased its public expenditure, while South Africa's expenditure fell, though slightly. In the subsequent years, i.e. between 2005 and 2010, while both South Africa and Brazil significantly pushed up their public expenditure on education as a percentage of GDP, India recorded only a small increase.

The share of public expenditure on education in GDP in India has been continuously increasing from 0.6 per cent in 1951 to 3.8 per cent in 2000, after which

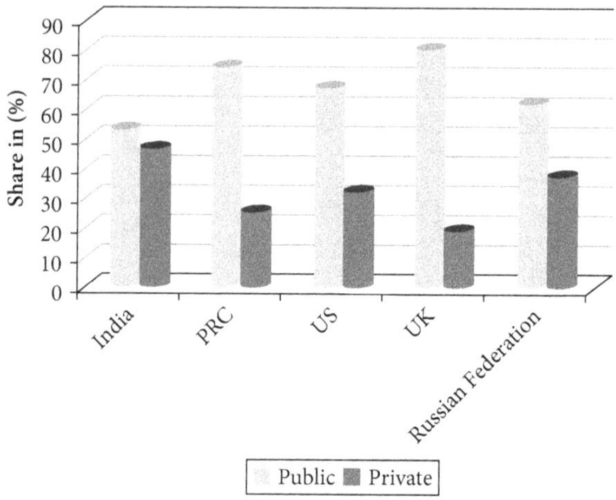

Figure 16.15. Financing education across major countries, public versus private
Source: Indiastat, <http://www.indiastat.com/default.aspx>.

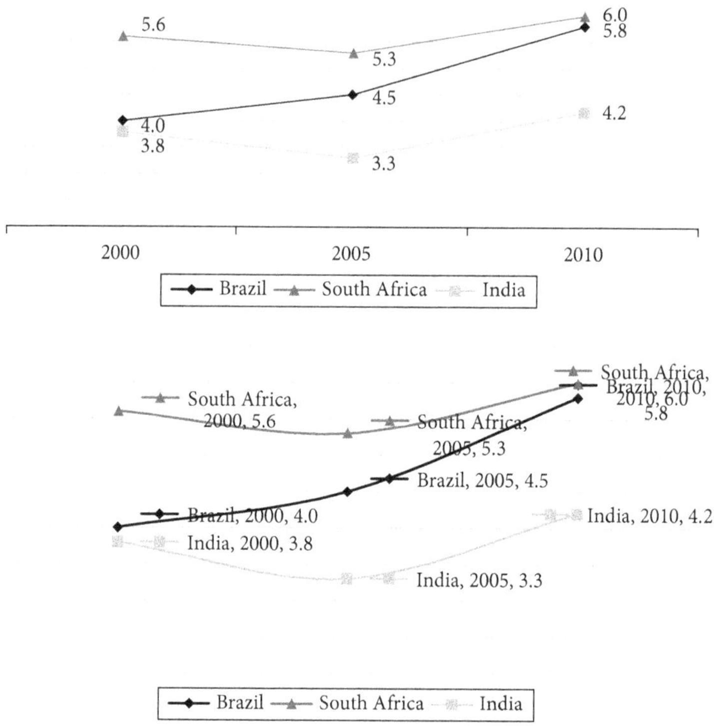

Figure 16.16. Public expenditure on education as a percentage of GDP
Source: Indiastat, <http://www.indiastat.com/default.aspx>.

it suffered a decline until 2008 and increased thereafter, as shown in Figure 16.17. However, it may be noted that although education has always been given high priority by the Government of India since independence, the public expenditure target of 6 per cent of GDP is still nowhere in sight. Consequently, the enrolment rates are still low, particularly in tertiary education and the inhabitants of rural areas. The role of public spending on education, though not complete per se, remains important in accelerating the growth in school enrolment.

The total public expenditure on education and the shares borne by the centre and the states, respectively are shown in Figure 16.18. The states still bear a lion's

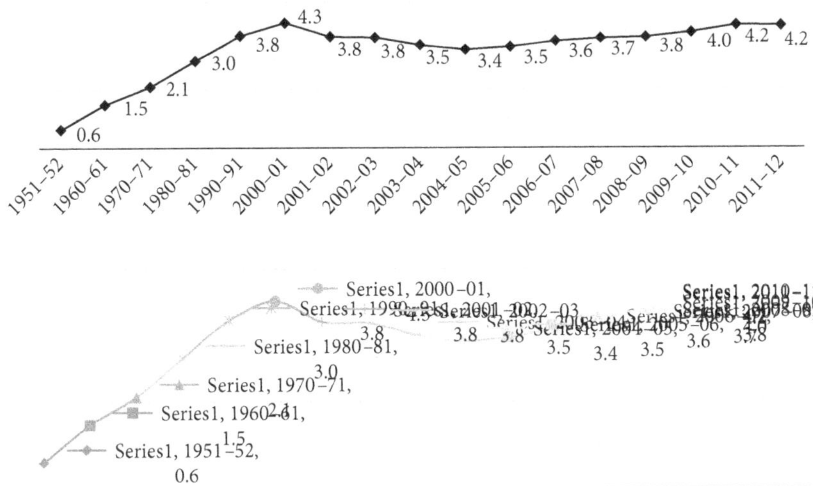

Figure 16.17. Trend of public expenditure on education as a percentage of GDP
Source: Indiastat, <http://www.indiastat.com/default.aspx>.

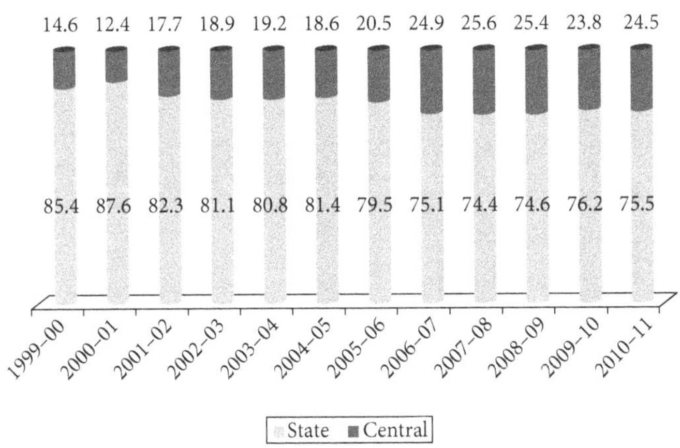

Figure 16.18. Trends in the share of central and state public expenditure
Source: Indiastat, <http://www.indiastat.com/default.aspx>.

share of the expenses on education; their share in the total has been declining continuously (from 85.4 per cent in 1999–2000 to 75.5 per cent in 2010–11), while the centre's share has shown a jump (from 14.6 per cent to 24.5 per cent during the same period).

In 2011–12, half of the money spent on education (centre and states combined) went towards elementary education. Secondary education is observed to have received the next largest share of the combined expenditure, i.e. 30 per cent (Figure 16.19). While the government spent only one-eighth of the allocated amount on university-level education, technical education and others received far less priority.

It is evident from Figure 16.20 that both the centre and state governments have also invested in elementary education programmes. The government has devoted a huge amount of money to promoting elementary education by investing in

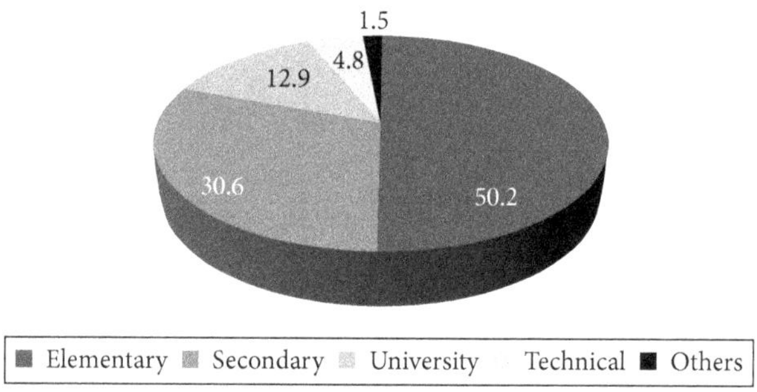

Figure 16.19. Distribution of educational expenditure (centre and states combined), 2011–12 (%)

Source: Indiastat, <http://www.indiastat.com/default.aspx>.

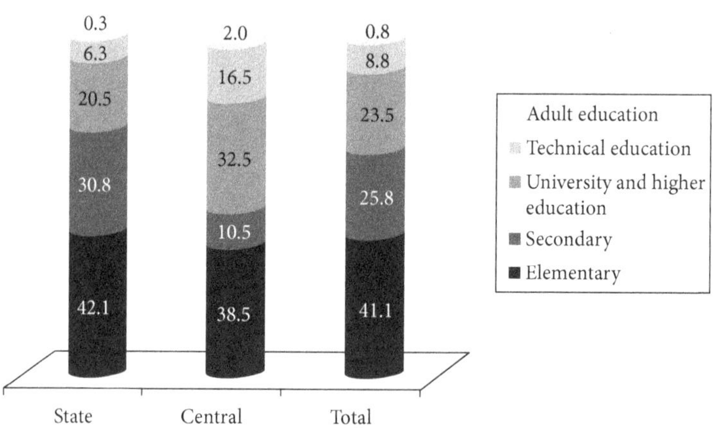

Figure 16.20. Distribution of Educational expenditure by centre and states, 2009–10

Source: Indiastat, <http://www.indiastat.com/default.aspx>.

flagship programmes like the SSA to achieve the target of universalization of education among children. While elementary education benefits from this, the government, on the other hand, is forced to spend less on higher education.

16.5.1 Education Cess

An important aspect of budget expenditure on elementary education is the source of funds. While most sectors receive funds from the overall budgetary support, elementary education receives substantial resources from an earmarked tax, namely the education cess. The education cess, introduced in 2004, is a cess levied at the rate of 2 per cent on all major central taxes—income tax, corporation tax, excise duties, customs duties, and service tax. The revenue from cess is meant for elementary education.

The Prarambhik Shiksha Kosh was set up in 2005 as a dedicated non-lapsable fund, with the revenues of the education cess. The Kosh is to fund the two major schemes in elementary education, namely the SSA and midday meals. These two schemes are actually expected to be largely financed out of the gross budgetary support. Only after exhausting the funds provided by the gross budgetary support is the balance of the expenditure to be financed from the Kosh. It appears that exactly the opposite has happened. A disproportionately large amount of expenditure on SSA and midday meals is being met out of revenues collected from the education cess. As high as 74 per cent of the expenditure on SSA and midday meals in 2008–9 was met by the Kosh, i.e. by the revenues received from the education cess, and the balance out of general budgetary support. The corresponding figure, i.e. the share of the Kosh, was 69 per cent in 2007–8. In other words, the two major components of elementary education receive very little resources from general tax and non-tax revenues.

A secondary and higher education cess, introduced in 2007, at the rate of 1 per cent on all major central taxes, additionally yielded Rs 17.36 billion in 2007–8. It was supposed to be used to finance the Scheme for Universal Access and Quality at the Secondary Stage for which an allocation of Rs 22.30 billion is made in the 2009–10 budget.

16.6 Conclusion and Policy Interventions

Urbanization and growth move together. The role of agglomeration economies and the functioning of labour markets in cities make cities more conducive to growth. The rural–urban differentials in productivity have widened over time. Human capital plays an important role in increasing the productivity of workers. This study finds that earnings of workers increased substantially at each successive level of education and returns were far higher at the graduate-and-above level. But returns to education at all levels except for the graduate-and-above level were higher in urban areas than in rural areas. Higher returns to education for the graduate-and-above level in rural areas can be explained by the few jobs that are available in rural areas, which are mostly government jobs that carry a premium over most of the private jobs available in rural areas. Earlier studies showed that social returns to capital had been lower than private returns to education. One study concluded that, on average, outside opportunities for educated workers were unattractive relative to the government sector, which otherwise would have led to significant social returns in economic growth. The recent growth pattern suggests that this has started happening. ICT largely located in urban areas, and mostly concentrated in metros, is dominated by the private corporate sector, which pays workers higher wages than the government sector.

In India, in the last four decades, the contribution of rural–urban migration towards increasing the urban population has been around one-fifth. In that sense, urban growth has been exclusionary. As most of the GDP growth came from the highly skilled sectors of ICT, banking, and financial services, and highly skilled manufacturing like engineering and pharmaceuticals, it did not draw much labour from rural areas.

There is still a substantial rural–urban difference in the gross and net attendance rates of school-going children. The spread of college-level education is very low in rural areas, and it was a meagre 3 per cent compared with 15 per cent for urban areas in 2011–12 for those aged seven years and above. The difference between metros and non-metros in the composition of the human capital stock is less stark.

The substantial rural–urban difference in higher education allows us to postulate that urbanization provides the necessary condition for enhancing the quality of human capital. This characteristic is examined across the twenty-two major states of India in 2011–12. The regression analysis showed that urbanization indeed contributed significantly in improving the quality of human capital, captured through the share of graduates in the total population. Improvement in human capital also attracts the modern services sector and high-quality manufacturing activities to establish units in those areas, leading to further urbanization. However, this relationship is not that direct as urbanization is closely related to the level of economic development; we have to control the impact of economic development through variable per capita income to statistically establish this relationship. It is observed from the cross-section regression across the twenty-two major states that better endowment of human capital captured through the share of graduates in the total population positively and significantly affects urbanization after controlling for the level of per capita income.

Consequently, there is a substantial and growing divergence of labour productivity between rural and urban areas. The educational gap between workers in rural and urban areas makes this clear. Nearly a quarter of all workers in urban areas consisted of graduates and above compared with only 4 per cent in rural areas. The substantial difference in the educational level of workers between rural and urban areas can be explained to some extent through the selectivity bias in migration from rural to urban areas.

The share of migrant workers vis-à-vis non-migrant workers was higher in the two extreme levels of education qualification—not literate and graduate and above. Not literate migrants constituted 18 per cent of migrant workers compared with 15 per cent for non-migrant workers. The proportion of migrants having an educational qualification of at least a graduate degree constituted 21 per cent of the total migrant workers compared with 18 per cent for non-migrant workers. It can be seen that cities attract both not literate and highly educated migrants in large proportions, but the share of highly educated migrants was higher than not literate migrants from a very low base of the highly educated human capital stock that exists in rural areas. In that sense, the selectivity bias favouring highly educated migrants exists in India. But commuting workers were quite evenly distributed across different educational levels. Nearly two-thirds of commuting workers were at most middle-school educated compared with half of urban resident workers. Hardly one-tenth of commuting workers had a graduate degree compared with more than two-fifths of urban resident workers. The selectivity bias is far less for commuting workers.

India substantially lags behind even other comparable developing countries in educational performance. The mean years of schooling of 5.12 requires a substantial increase in the amount of public funds to be devoted to educational development. Despite setting a target to spend at least 6 per cent of the GDP on education, public expenditure from GDP has hovered at around 4 per cent for the last decade. This expenditure needs to be stepped up substantially if we want to develop a modest level of human capital.

The thrust given by the government in achieving universal elementary education in the last decade has led to an almost universal enrolment rate at the elementary level of education, but the biggest concern is the poor level of learning among students. The evidence suggests that learning outcomes of children in schools in India are far below corresponding class levels in other countries. Building educational infrastructure and providing modern educational accessories (interactive smart boards, computer labs, math labs, etc.) are of the utmost importance in elementary schools.

One of the most important causes of the low mean years of schooling in India is the high dropout rate at the lower primary level (after standard V) as we have observed in Section 16.4.1. Urgent steps are needed to reverse this alarming trend. One important policy step that can be taken is to implement vocational education after standard VIII, instead of the practice of introducing vocational education after standard X. Such a job-oriented educational channel will be helpful in reducing dropout rates as it would open up better job opportunities for students not interested in going into the general stream. To make it successful, better linkages with employers in both industry and the services sector will be required.

We have seen that the share of private education in India, starting from the elementary to the tertiary education level, is far higher than in other developing and developed countries. We have also seen that better performance in tertiary education, particularly in the engineering/technical streams, has been achieved in the last decade. But unfortunately evidence shows that this has mostly taken place in the private sector. It is urgently required that public-funded institutes open up these streams in greater numbers so that bright students from economically weaker sectors can enrol in these courses in larger numbers.

We have observed that urban areas are not only considerably better endowed with the quality of human capital, but also that the average returns to education are higher in urban areas compared with rural areas. It has also been observed that the urban–rural gap of average returns to education has been increasing over the years. This calls for active policies to promote rural–urban migration that will boost urban as well as national income. In this regard, an active policy of promoting the labour-intensive manufacturing sector is required, which is likely to promote more migration and reduce the selectivity bias in rural–urban migration.

References

Agrawal, Tushar. 2011. 'Return to Education in India: Some Recent Results'. *Working Paper WP-2011-017*, Indira Gandhi Institute of Development Research (IGIDR), Mumbai.

Becker, Gary S. 1964. 'Human Capital: A Theoretical and Empirical Analysis with Special Reference to Education'. National Bureau of Economic Research, New York.

Bhargava, Alok, Dean T. Jamison, Lawrence J. Lau, and Christopher J. L. Murray. 2001. 'Modeling the Effects of Health on Economic Growth'. *Journal of Health Economics 20* (3): 423–40.

Bloom, David E., David Canning, and Jaypee Sevilla. 2001. 'The Effect of Health on Economic Growth: Theory and Evidence'. *Working Paper No. 8587*, National Bureau of Economic Research, Cambridge.

Chandrasekhar, S. 2011. 'Workers Commuting Between the Rural and Urban: Estimates from NSSO Data'. *Economic and Political Weekly 66* (46): 22–5.

Ghose, A. 2013. 'India's Service-Led Growth and its Discontents'. IGIDR Conference on Labour and Employment, Mumbai, 5–6 September.

Government of India. Various years. *Economic Survey of India*, Ministry of Finance, Economic Division, Department of Economic Affairs, Delhi.

Government of India, Planning Commission. 2013. *Twelfth Five Year Plan (2012–2017): Faster, More Inclusive and Sustainable Growth*, vols 1–3.

Kundu, Amitabh. 2009. 'Exclusionary Urbanisation in Asia: A Macro Overview'. *Economic and Political Weekly 44* (28): 48–58.

Mazumdar, Dipak, Sandip Sarkar, and Balwant Singh Mehta. 2017a. 'Inequality in India—I'. *Economic and Political Weekly 52* (30): 47–56.

Mazumdar, Dipak, Sandip Sarkar, and Balwant Singh Mehta. 2017b. 'Inequality in India—II—The Wage Sector'. *Economic and Political Weekly 42* (30): 58–66.

McKinsey Global Institute. 2010. 'India's Urban Awakening: Building Inclusive Cities, Sustaining Economic Growth'. McKinsey & Co.

Mincer, Jacob. 1989. 'Human Capital and the Labor Market: A Review of Current Research'. *Educational Researcher 18* (4): 27–34.

Psacharopoulos, George, ed. 1987. *Economics of Education: Research and Studies*, Pergamon Press.

Psacharopoulos, George. 1994. 'Return to Investment in Education: A Global Update'. *World Development 22* (9): 1321–43.

Schultz, T. 1961. 'Education and Economic Growth'. In *Social Forces Influencing American Education*, edited by N. B. Henry, University of Chicago Press.

Schündeln, Matthias and John Playforth. 2014. 'Private versus Social Return to Human Capital: Education and Economic Growth in India'. *European Economic Review 666*: 266–83.

PART VIII

CONGESTION AND POLLUTION

17
Congestion and Pollution in Chinese Cities

Siqi Zheng, Cong Sun, Jianghao Wang, and Xiaoke Hu

17.1 Introduction

In 2010, there were twenty-three cities in the world whose population exceeded ten million, with ten of them located in Asia, of which four are cities in the People's Republic of China (PRC).[1] These megacities are the engines of economic growth in Asia. Urban growth offers potentially large benefits as cities provide greater opportunities to trade, learn, and specialize in diverse occupations. On the other hand, rapid urbanization, especially in developing nations, involves large social costs. The quality of life in megacities suffers from a fundamental tragedy of the commons. Urban air, water, and infrastructure such as roads are local public goods. An unintended consequence of daily urban activity is to exacerbate pollution and congestion challenges. Such degradation of non-market local public goods means that as the megacities grow, their standard of life suffers (Zheng and Kahn 2013a).

During recent decades, congestion and pollution have become major challenges faced by many large cities in the PRC. A rapid increase in car ownership and usage, combined with lagged transportation infrastructure supply, has led to heavy traffic congestion in these cities. The average one-way commuting time in Beijing reached fifty-two minutes in 2012, which was much higher than that in New York City (at thirty-one minutes).[2] During the morning rush hours, the average speed of motor vehicles is less than 20 km/h on the main roads in Beijing's downtown area. It is estimated that fifteen cities at the top of the traffic congestion list suffer a total loss of one billion RMB every day in terms of the travel time wasted on roads in the PRC.[3]

Traffic congestion is a major contributor to air pollution in the cities of the PRC. Industrial production, construction sites, and winter heating with coal are the other major sources of air pollution. Breathing polluted air, measured in terms of the concentration of particulate matter, raises one's risk of heart and lung

[1] Source: UN Database <http://esa.un.org/unpd/wup/index.htm>.
[2] Data source: <http://www.census.gov/prod/2011pubs/acs-15.pdf>.
[3] <http://www.china.org.cn/top10/2012-11/02/content_26980425.htm>.

Siqi Zheng, Cong Sun, Jianghao Wang, and Xiaoke Hu., *Congestion and Pollution in Chinese Cities* In: *Cities of Dragons and Elephants: Urbanization and Urban Development in China and India. Edited by:* Guanghua Wan and Ming Lu, Oxford University Press (2019). © Oxford University Press. DOI: 10.1093/oso/9780198829225.003.0017

disease (Chay and Greenstone 2003; Evans and Smith 2005; Moretti and Neidell 2011). The Asian Development Bank reports that less than 1 per cent of the 500 largest cities in the PRC meet the air quality standards recommended by the World Health Organization, and seven of these cities are ranked among the top ten polluted cities in the world (Asian Development Bank 2012). In 2013, about half of the PRC suffered from a heavy haze in December.[4] Pollution exposure significantly impacts people's quality of life.

This chapter looks at the issues of urban congestion and pollution resulting from the PRC's rapid urbanization. We will use a 'demand–supply–government' framework to analyse the PRC's experience on how cities make trade-offs between the positive and negative externalities associated with fast urban growth. We will also discuss the roles of the market and the government in mitigating such social costs, and how the government can play a better role in improving the liveability and sustainability of cities.

Sections 17.2 and 17.3 provide an overview of the urban congestion and pollution problems, and how they are driven by the demand and supply factors associated with the PRC's fast urbanization. Section 17.4 discusses the effectiveness of various policy measures, and management and technology innovations aimed at reducing such social costs.

17.2 Urban Congestion

17.2.1 Rising Travel Demand Driven by Fast Urbanization

The PRC's urbanization rate has been increasing by about one percentage point per year, from 26 per cent in 1990 to 53.7 per cent in 2013.[5] This means 10–15 million people move into cities every year. Such a huge migration inflow, especially rural–urban migration, has contributed to the PRC's astounding 10 per cent annual economic growth rate in the past two decades.

With rising incomes and the declining cost of owning a private car, a typical urban household's demand for cars has also increased. Based on a cross-sectional micro dataset of 25,000 urban households, Zheng et al. (2011) find that the income elasticity of car ownership is 0.63. The price of an ordinary private car has declined since the PRC became a member of the World Trade Organization. The personal annual income–car price ratio was less than 10 per cent in the last decade, but more than 60 per cent in many large cities of the PRC in 2010. Thus private cars have become quite affordable for the middle class in the cities of the PRC. The growing urban population, combined with the rising car purchase propensity

[4] <http://usa.chinadaily.com.cn/china/2013-12/09/content_17160658.htm>.

[5] The PRC's Statistical Abstract (2014).

of a typical urbanite, has triggered the vast demand for driving. According to the National Bureau of Statistics of the PRC (NBSC), the total number of private cars in the cities of the PRC increased from 6.25 million in 2000 to 73.27 million in 2011, with an average annual growth rate of 22.76 per cent.[6] It is worth noting that due to the very low car ownership rate at the beginning of the 1990s, though the growth rate was very high in the past decade, currently the car ownership rate is still relatively low (11.2 per cent in 2010 for all municipalities)[7] compared with developed countries. This means that we may see a further big increase in the demand for private cars if no car ownership restriction policies are implemented. The city-specific car ownership rates are shown in Figure 17.1. This rate is higher in high-income and highly populated coastal cities. Those cities also have larger urbanized areas. We also observe a positive correlation between city population size and average one-way commuting time, keeping city income constant (Figure 17.2).

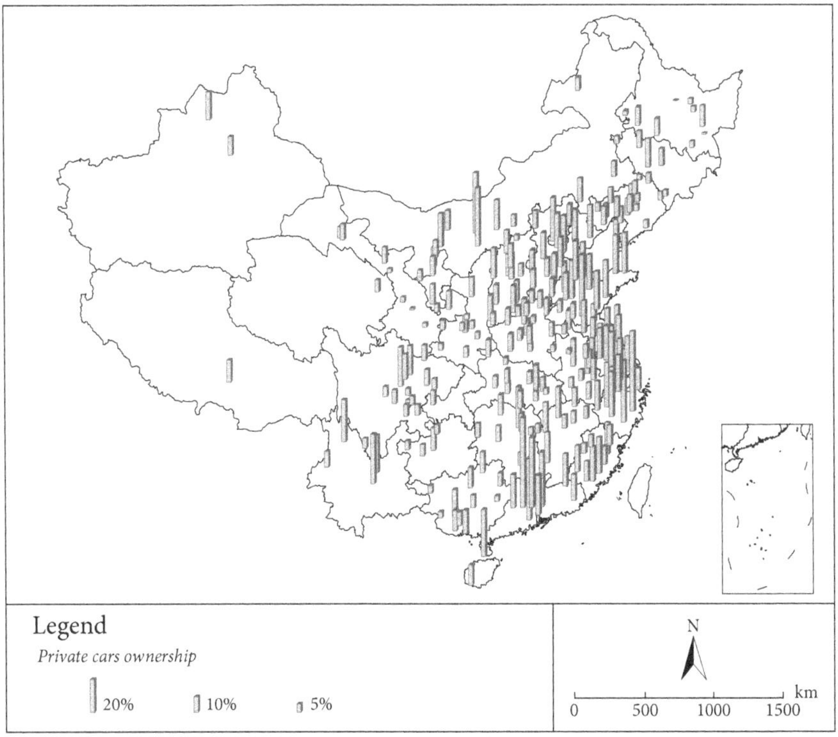

Figure 17.1. Car ownership rates in the cities of the PRC, 2010
Source: 2010 Urban Household Survey of the PRC (NBSC).

[6] The PRC's Statistic Yearbook (2001–12).
[7] Calculated from the 2010 Urban Household Survey data of the PRC.

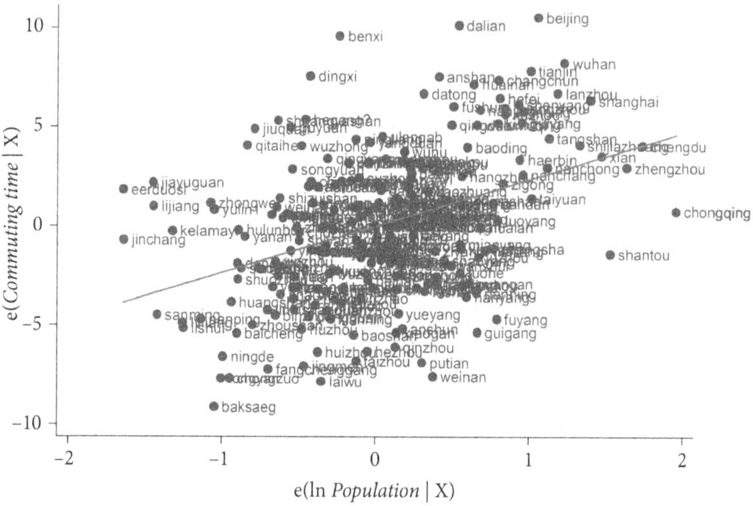

coef = 2.3528107, se = .34582958, t = 6.8

Figure 17.2. Relationship between city population and commuting time in the PRC, 2010

Source: 2010 Urban Household Survey of the PRC (NBSC).

The evolving spatial structure in the cities of the PRC also contributes to the increasing travel demand. Prior to the 1980s, different levels of government assigned firm location. Firms then set aside a portion of their land to build residential dwellings and distributed those dwellings to their employees at highly subsidized rents. Thus, the city spatial structure in the planned economy era was typically very compact, with a predominantly mixed pattern of residential and non-residential land uses and thus minimal commuting demand (Sit 1985). The majority of the urban workforce would commute by foot or bicycles to work near their homes. Such a land use pattern, although largely an outcome of central planning, would be consistent with the endogenous urban spatial model predicted by Fujita and Ogawa (1982) and Lucas and Rossi-Hansberg (2002) under the conditions of high commuting costs and low external economies in production. With rising agglomeration benefits enjoyed by skill-intensive industries and declining travel costs per unit of distance, a more specialized land use pattern has emerged: the central business district (CBD) has greatly expanded and residential land use has extended into the suburbs, whereas industrial land use has been pushed towards outlying urban locations (Zheng et al. 2006). With this ongoing suburbanization trend, jobs and housing are more and more spatially separated, inducing longer commuting distances for workers. For instance, Beijing is a typical monocentric city with half its jobs located within three miles from the city centre.[8]

[8] Calculated by the authors using Economic Census data.

The population density gradient with respect to the distance to CBD was −0.156 in 2000, shrinking to −0.123 in 2010.[9] Zheng et al. (2010) tested Lucas and Rossi-Hansberg's (2002) model in Beijing and found that skill-intensive firms do tend to cluster together to enjoy agglomeration benefits, and thcy are willing to a pay higher wage premium to compensate their employers' longer commuting time. In this sense, a longer commuting time (and the possible congestion induced) is the cost for a city's productivity gain through fostering high-density employment centres.

Another cause for the rising travel demand is the rising diversity of people's daily life. After all, according to Beijing 2010 Transportation Survey the proportion of home-to-work commuting in the total urban traffic flow has been declining in major cities of the PRC, with this share now less than 40 per cent in Beijing. In this regard, urbanites are willing to bear higher transportation costs (in terms of both time and money) to get access to a high-quality and more vibrant urban life.

A large segment of non-commute travel comprises travel to access local public services, such as schools and hospitals. Within the cities in the PRC, the spatial mismatch between high-quality local public services and population induces a vast traffic flow of sending children to schools during rush hours. Here we use the example of schools as a case to explain such a spatial mismatch. Few schools are built by the private sector[10] and these cannot compete with good public schools in terms of the educational quality.[11] Most of these public schools were built before the 1980s, and the high-quality ones were clustered in the inner city when the urban spatial scale was quite small. Further government funding for public education could only maintain the operation of the original good schools, but could not finance building any new good ones during the period of rapid urban expansion. For instance, more than 60 per cent of key primary schools were located in the Beijing central area (within the third ring road) in 2010, but only 32 per cent of the urban population was concentrated in this central area (Figure 17.3). According to the Fourth Beijing Transportation Survey, school buses are not common in the PRC, and less than 3 per cent of school children use school buses. Many middle-class and high-income parents in the PRC believe that studying in good schools is crucial for their children not only for receiving a good education but also for their futures. However, it is quite possible that the school zones in which they reside cannot satisfy their demand for high-quality education and high-quality living conditions simultaneously because most of the housing units in downtown are very old and small in size. As a result, many medium- and high-income households choose to live in places with better quality

[9] Calculated by the authors using Population Census data.

[10] Some educational websites collect the basic information on private schools in the cities of the PRC. See, for example, <http://xuexiao.51sxue.com/schoolByArea/p_2_areaCodeS_11_t_2.html>.

[11] Due to long-term public investment and preferential policies, good schools have more advantages in terms of social reputation, teacher quality, and financing channels than ordinary schools built in the suburban area.

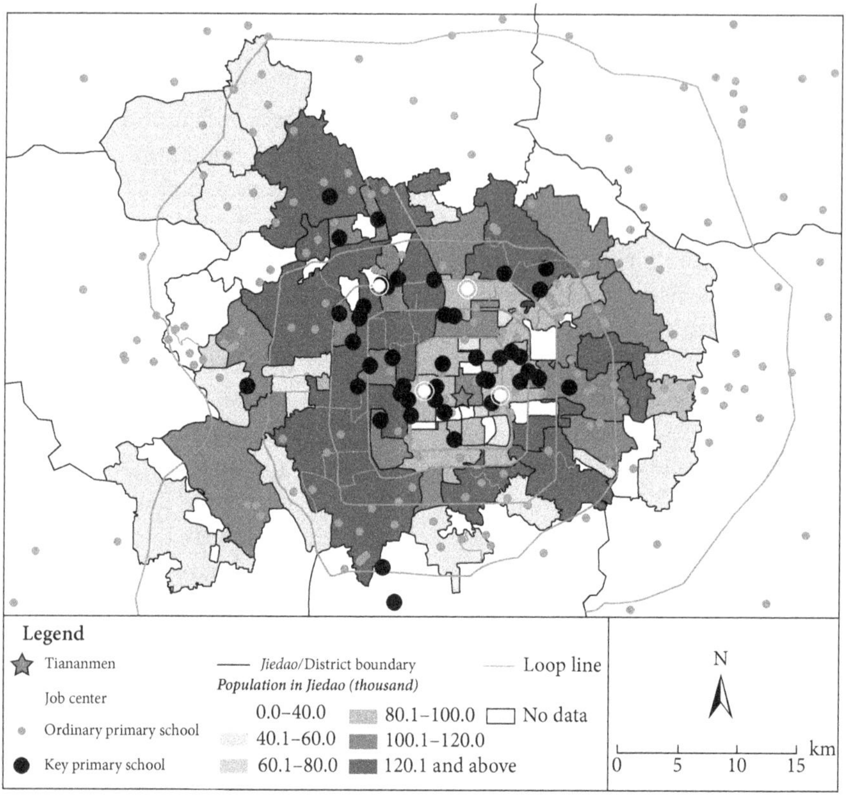

Figure 17.3. Spatial distribution of primary schools and urban population in Beijing, 2010

Source: Authors' data collection and calculation.

and larger size housing, and drive their children to the high-quality schools in other school zones ('cross-zone schooling'), paying a high admission fee and without owning a housing unit in the respective school zone. In addition, high-quality middle schools also expect to enrol excellent students from other zones and districts. According to the Fourth Beijing Transportation Survey, students who take private cars to primary and secondary schools account for 14.8 per cent of overall driving journeys in morning rush hours. Lu et al. (2014) employ a quantitative analysis to suggest that the spatial mismatch of school supply and demand in Beijing has indeed triggered the traffic flow and congestion level increase during rush hours on school days in Beijing. During school holidays, the morning traffic congestion index fell by about 20 per cent of the average value on school days.

Planning and transportation researchers point out that land use and built environment have significant effects on motorization and a broad set of travel behaviour. Most studies have shown that high-density cities (compact cities) always have lower private car ownership and are more 'public transit-oriented',

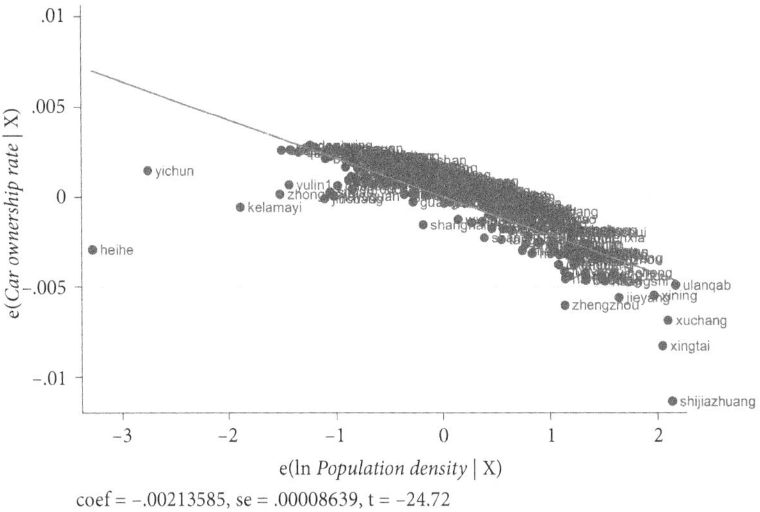

Figure 17.4. Negative correlation between population density and private car ownership rate in the cities of the PRC

Source: 2010 Urban Household Survey of the PRC conducted by NBSC, the PRC's Statistic Yearbook.

and thus are 'greener' (Crane 2000; Ewing and Cervero 2001, 2010). Using micro household survey data in seventy-four cities of the PRC, Zheng et al. (2011a) show that city population density is associated with lower levels of emissions from taxi uses. Figure 17.4 clearly shows the negative correlation between city population density and private car ownership level (both in logs), keeping city average income constant.

17.2.2 Undersupply of Transport Infrastructure in Cities

Given the rising travel demand associated with the PRC's rapid urbanization, the supply of transportation infrastructure and smart transportation planning and management are crucial for easing traffic congestion. In the PRC's current local public finance system, local expenditure on public services is determined by the size of the population with local urban Hukou, rather than the total urban population. However, fast urbanization brought a vast 'floating population' (a large section of them being rural migrants) without local urban Hukou. Local city governments have weak incentives to supply public services to non-local residents without Hukou. This leads to a significant undersupply of local public services, especially in megacities with a large share of floating population. As a typical public good, transportation infrastructure, especially public transit such as buses and subways, has lagged behind the fast urbanization of many cities, which may be a cause of traffic congestion.

It is worth noting that, in many cases, the construction of new roads will induce more traffic on these roads because more people will buy cars and will live further away from their jobs. This is the so-called lock-in effect. Transportation investment in suburban highways encourages suburbanization. Baum-Snow et al. (2012) have studied how the PRC's urban form has been affected by its highway investment. They reported evidence that urban compactness is reduced by radial and ring road construction, but enhanced by public transport.

Given that private vehicles are significant contributors to local traffic congestion and air pollution, the introduction of subways and other high-quality public transit can play a significant role in improving urban environmental performance. The PRC is in the midst of a major subway construction period. In 1980, only Beijing had subway lines. In 2000, three cities had subways. In 2010, twelve cities had subways and another sixteen cities had lines under construction. In the case of Beijing, the construction of new subways has attracted private developers and new restaurants to locate in close proximity, reinforcing the desire to live close to public transit (Zheng and Kahn 2013b). Zheng et al. (2017) use a micro dataset in Beijing to find that better subway accessibility reduces a typical resident's probability of owning a car after controlling for possible endogeneity and, thus, encourages 'green' travel behaviour. Therefore, the development of urban rail in Beijing does discourage driving by reducing car ownership, and results in positive congestion-mitigating and environmental consequences. In fact, in the megacities of the PRC such as Beijing and Shanghai, subway trains are very congested, indicating that there is still a big gap between the demand and supply of subway travel.

17.3 Urban Pollution

17.3.1 The Level of Urban Pollution in the Cities of the PRC

Traffic congestion leads to air pollution. Besides transportation, manufacturing production, electricity generation (especially using coal), and winter heating are the other major causes of urban pollution in the cities of the PRC (Zheng and Kahn 2013a), and these are all associated with the ongoing fast urbanization process.

17.3.1.1 Transportation

Motorization has not only contributed to traffic congestion but also air pollution and greenhouse gas emissions in the course of the PRC's urbanization. In large cities like Beijing, the share of pollution produced due to vehicle exhaust emissions has reached 31 per cent of the total local $PM_{2.5}$ (fine particulate matter) emissions, which is almost equal to or even higher than the share from industrial activities.[12] Rapid growth in car ownership is believed to be behind the haze that

[12] For details, see <http://www.china.org.cn/environment/2014-01/03/content_31078855.htm>.

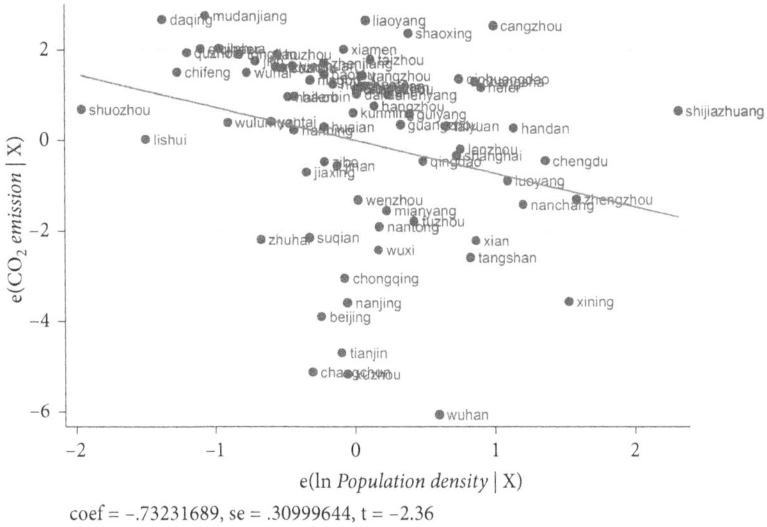

Figure 17.5. Population density and residential carbon emission
Source: Authors' data collection and calculation (based on Zheng et al. 2011a)

has occurred here in recent years. High-density cities with lower car ownership rates are expected to have less transportation-related energy consumption and pollutant emissions. Figure 17.5 shows the clearly negative correlation between population density and per capita residential carbon emission in the cities of the PRC, after controlling for city income (2010 data).

17.3.1.2 The Economic Geography of Industrial Pollution

The PRC's phenomenal industrial growth has been accompanied by fast urbanization over the last three decades. At the beginning of the PRC's economic reforms, eastern coastal regions with good access to the global market became the most attractive locations for manufacturing firms. Cheap land and labour, and favourable industrial policies, also attracted foreign direct investment (FDI) and fostered industrial clusters in coastal cities. The huge across-city population flow towards coastal cities provided sufficient cheap labour to the labour-intensive manufacturing industries located there. In the mid-2000s, more than 65 per cent of manufacturing employment in above-scale (with annual sale above RMB 5 million) industrial firms was located in the coastal region, as compared with 42 per cent in 1980 (NBSC). The PRC was then known as 'the world's factory', with 68 per cent of computers and 40 per cent of clothes being 'made in China'.[13]

Booming industrialization and urbanization bring new economic opportunities, but cause environmental deterioration. The links between industrial production

[13] The PRC's Textile Industry Development Report (2010–11).

and local pollution are well known from the experience of many developed countries. According to the national energy consumption and emissions inventory in 2010, industrial activities were responsible for almost 90 per cent of total energy consumption and 65 per cent of the total emissions in the cities of the PRC.[14] In 1973, the PRC's energy consumption only accounted for 7.9 per cent of the world's total, but this proportion rose to 21.3 per cent in 2011 (Zheng et al. 2014a).

Industrial pollution is highly correlated with energy consumption. The effects of scale, composition, and technique together determine the total energy consumption of a city's industrial sector. Scale refers to the sheer count of jobs and output located in a city, while composition refers to a city's set of industries and the vintage of its capital stock. Technique represents emissions per unit of economic activity. This decomposition logic is very useful when considering the role that FDI plays in determining the PRC's industrial pollution levels. In the PRC in the 1980s, attracting FDI meant more factories and thus more pollution. Conversely, it is possible that FDI provides the financial capital and access to developed nations' technologies, which allows cleaner factories to be built. The existing literature has generated mixed findings on the FDI flows' environmental consequences. Wang and Jin (2007) find that foreign firms exhibit better environmental performance than state-owned and privately owned firms because they use cleaner technology and are more energy efficient. Zheng et al. (2010) use data across thirty-five major cities in the PRC over the years 2003 to 2006 and report a negative correlation between a city's FDI inflows and its ambient air pollution level. Using data from the 1990s and early 2000s, He (2006; 2009) finds evidence that pollution and FDI are positively correlated. One possible explanation for these facts is that, up until the early 2000s, FDI increased the scale of industrial activity in the cities of the PRC and this increased pollution, while in recent years FDI has improved the technologies used in the PRC's industrial sector, resulting in a decline in the pollution per unit of industrial production (Zheng et al. 2010).

If we look at the total pollution emissions, the geographic concentration of manufacturing activities did have significant local environmental consequences in coastal cities. However, when evaluating the marginal cost of urban growth, and the quality of life urbanites enjoy, scholars always prefer to use pollution emissions per capita or per unit of industrial output. This 'per unit' measure contains the composition and technique effects mentioned earlier. The installation and use of pollution treatment infrastructure (such as waste water treatment equipment and sulfur dioxide (SO_2) scrubbers) need the economies of scale, which means that only large cities can afford such infrastructure and technologies (Lu and Feng 2014; Bao et al. 2013). Using the PRC's provincial panel data from 1993 to 2006, Lu and Feng (2014) measure the degree of spatial agglomeration

[14] The PRC's Energy Statistical Yearbook (2011).

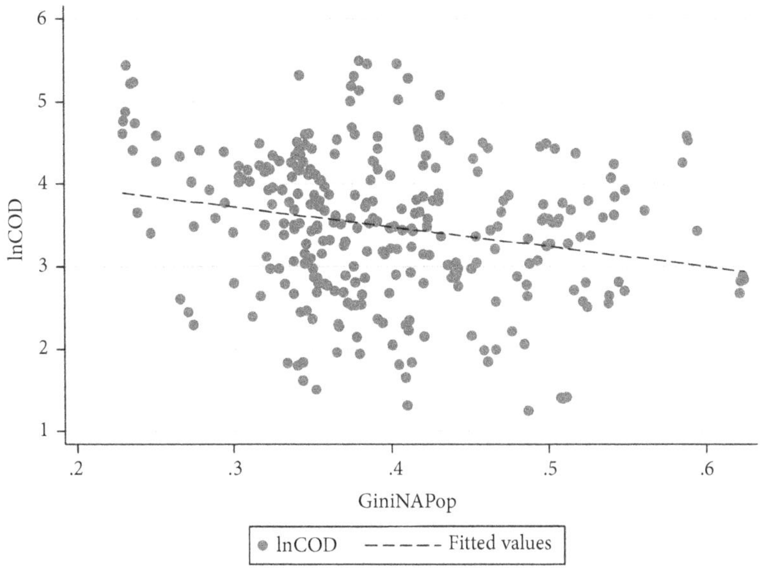

Figure 17.6. Agglomeration and industrial COD treatment efficiency
Source: Authors' data collection and calculation.

within a province by the within-province inequality of city-level population size (x-axis in Figure 17.6) and find that spatial agglomeration of population and economic activities have negative effects on the industrial chemical oxygen demand (COD) emission per unit of industrial GDP (y-axis in Figure 17.6). Similarly, Figure 17.7 shows that the removal rate of industrial SO_2 (Y-axis) is higher in denser cities (x-axis in Figure 17.7 is the city's population density).

Since the mid-2000s, the rising social costs (including pollution) associated with the industrial agglomeration in large coastal cities began to drive a shift in the country's industrial geography. Labour and land costs have been increasing dramatically in these cities. The 2008 global financial crisis shrank international demand and hit export-oriented and labour-intensive industries. Moreover, environmental regulations are more stringent in these cities. As a result, many large cities in the PRC's eastern region have undergone deindustrialization, while the less developed inland cities in the central and western regions are experiencing fast industrialization. Many labour-intensive firms in large coastal cities either upgraded their capital and technology or moved to nearby small cities and inland cities such as Wuhan and Zhengzhou. Manufacturing's share in the GDP of the central and western regions (inland region or inland area) grew from 36 per cent in 2004 to 44 per cent in 2010, but declined in the eastern region (coastal region or coastal area) after 2008.[15]

[15] The PRC's Statistic Yearbook.

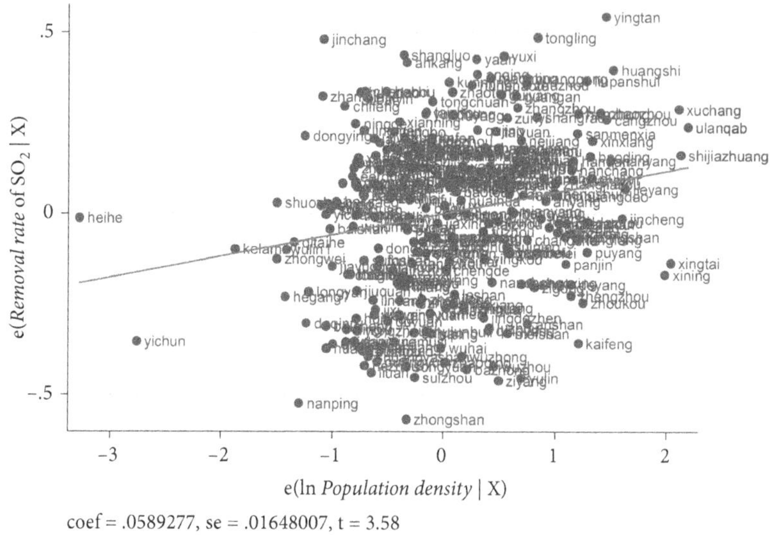

Figure 17.7. Agglomeration and industrial SO_2 treatment efficiency
Source: Authors' data collection and calculation.

Under this 'manufacturing on the move' scenario, if the technique effect remains constant over time, the increases in both scale and share of energy-intensive manufacturing industries in the inland cities of the PRC will lead to rising energy consumption and energy intensity (energy consumption per GDP dollar). Since the mid-2000s, the scale of industrial production in inland cities has been rising faster than that in coastal cities. In Table 17.1, we do a simple decomposition exercise on energy intensity (energy consumption per GDP dollar) from the industrial sector in these two regions. It shows that the composition effect increases inland cities' energy intensity, while it reduces that in coastal cities. Between 2006 and 2011, keeping technique effect constant, the change in manufacturing share in output contributed to a 3.17 tce (tonne coal equivalent) decline and a 6.83 tce increase in coastal and inland cities, respectively. The good news is that technology upgrading has made a major contribution to energy intensity decline in both regions. Our own calculations show that inland cities enjoyed a 19.8 tce energy intensity decrease, which outweighed the positive composition effect so that the net change in energy intensity is negative for the inland area. One possible reason for this is that FDI-based manufacturing firms bring advanced clean technology and environmental management to inland cities and promote technological innovation. Many manufacturing firms also upgrade their technology and equipment during the relocation process.

This calculation highlights that the migration of industrial factories towards the west does induce a 'zero-sum pollution game'. With coastal cities such as Shanghai growing cleaner due to deindustrialization, there are social marginal

Table 17.1. Energy consumption and energy intensity changes in coastal and inland cities

	Year/period	Coastal cities	Inland cities
Manufacturing share in output	2006	46%	41%
	2011	44%	45%
Composition effect (tce per million RMB)	2006–11	−3.17	6.83
Technique effect (tce per million RMB)	2006–11	−22.4	−19.8

Source: Zheng et al. (2014a).

benefits from reducing the pollution exposure of millions of wealthy Shanghai residents to industrial pollution.

A pessimist would posit that an equal amount of damage is created in the inland area where the factory moves. This logic is false because more people live in the large coastal cities such as Shanghai and thus exposing them to less pollution reduces the Pigovian social cost of industrial production in the PRC (Zheng et. al., 2014a).

17.3.1.3 Power Plants and Winter Heating Using Coal

Power plants in the PRC have generated the electricity that has fuelled the PRC's fast industrialization and urbanization. Coal-fired power plants generate 80 per cent of the PRC's electricity. The number of coal-fired power plants increased significantly in the past decades, in order to meet the energy consumption needs mainly from booming industrial activities (NBSC 2011). Conversely, since coal-fired electricity was cheap, it further encouraged the energy- and pollution-intensive manufacturing industries to build factories.[16] In 2010, more than 6,000 power plants consumed 1.55 trillion tons of coal and accounted for 30.5 per cent of the total national emissions of SO_2 (Cao et al. 2011). Based on the calculations using geographical data on the location of the PRC's power plants, 46 per cent of these plants are built around large and medium-sized cities with five million people or above (especially the coastal cities and coal-mining cities). Some public health studies have examined how such geographical distribution of the PRC's coal-fired power plants and their activities affect public health (Zhou et al. 2006; Tang et al. 2008).

Winter heating, relying on coal, also produces substantial air pollution in the cities of north PRC. Winter heating is subsidized for homes and offices in northern PRC—above the Huai River and Qinling Mountains—where the average January temperature is roughly 0°C. This region creates a high level of emissions because the main energy source of heating is coal. As a result, during the winter heating

[16] According to International Energy Agency's statistics, the price of electricity in the PRC was RMB 0.587 per kWh, equivalent to 0.54 times Japan's price or 0.63 times England's price, in 2009.

season, the contributions from coal combustion and biomass aerosol to $PM_{2.5}$ mass increase significantly in northern cities. Northern cities' per capita residential carbon emission was 0.64 tons compared with 0.37 tons for southern cities in 2006 (Zheng et al. 2011a). This gap between northern and southern cities can largely be explained by the central heating in the northern region as discussed. The PRC's fast urbanization triggered a huge amount of new construction of residential and commercial buildings in the last three decades. In northern cities, the floor area of all buildings covered by central heating increased from 11.67 million sq. m in 1981 to 4.36 billion sq. m in 2010, and thus the total demand for winter heating also increased proportionally. A recent study by Chen et al. (2013) focuses on the health implications of coal-fired winter heating. The results of the study estimate that life expectancies are significantly lower in the north owing to an increased incidence of cardiorespiratory mortality, due to the ambient concentration TSPs at about 184 $\mu g/m^3$ or 55 per cent higher in the north.

17.3.1.4 Cross-boundary Pollution

As opposed to traffic congestion, pollution has a unique feature of cross-boundary externality. It means that local pollution (such as air and water) is not only determined by local emissions but also influenced by emissions from nearby jurisdictions. Cai et al.'s (2013) study on water pollution documents that polluting sources are located at political boundaries so that the social costs of industrial activity are borne by downstream areas adjacent to cities in the PRC. Zheng et al. (2014b) also point out that cities suffer from cross-boundary spillovers of industrial smoke from nearby manufacturing regions. A 10 per cent decrease in industrial smoke emissions may reduce local PM_{10} concentration by 1.7 per cent. Moreover, as estimated by the Beijing Environmental Protection Bureau, about a third of Beijing's $PM_{2.5}$ pollution is currently contributed by industrial activities in Tianjin and Hebei provinces.[17] That is to say, even if some polluting factories have moved out from large cities to nearby small cities and towns, the cross-boundary spillovers of pollution emissions still affect those large cities. This means that intercity and interregional cooperation is very important to combat such pollution problems with clear cross-boundary externalities.

17.3.2 Rising Demand for Green Cities

The PRC's urbanites' demand for environmental quality has been rising in recent years. In the old days, the poor urbanites focused on earning money and sometimes compromised on their quality of life, of which environmental quality is a key component. Educational attainment in major cities of the PRC has been

[17] <http://english.people.com.cn/90882/8600714.html>.

rising sharply during the rapid urbanization process. In 2000, 11 per cent of people older than twenty-five had college or higher degrees in the cities of the PRC, while in 2010 this share increased to 21.2 per cent.[18] This means that the new cohorts of urbanites are richer and better educated, which leads to a rising demand to live in 'green cities'.

Information asymmetry may prevent urbanites from knowing the real pollution challenges and health risks they are facing. In the past, the PRC's state monopolized news coverage and this meant that environmental disasters caused by industrial negligence did not generate the same attention as a similar event taking place in the United States or Europe. In the absence of media attention and public outrage, officials would have less incentive to nudge polluting industries to invest in costly precautions. As the new urban cohorts in the PRC become richer and more educated, they have a greater willingness to pay for avoiding risks, and thus their demand for information and political accountability is likely to rise.

The rise of demand for environmental information creates incentives for the media to cover such stories (Gentzkow and Shapiro 2010). In recent years, the PRC's media has devoted greater attention to environmental issues. For instance, there were 240 times as many Google news items about 'environmental pollution' in 2011 as there were ten years ago (Zheng et. al. 2014c). With developments in modern media and information technology, such as WeChat (a mobile text and voice messaging service) and Weibo (a micro blogging service—the equivalent of Twitter in the PRC), and mobile phone messaging, the government no longer has a monopoly over information, making suppression of information difficult. This should incentivize politicians to invest more effort in providing environmental regulation. One salient example is the 2011 Internet criticism that pushed the government to report on $PM_{2.5}$ air pollution in many cities of the PRC.

Environmental quality is a typical type of public good without market price. However, we can observe people's demand for it using the compensation differentials methodology in the housing market. Using standard revealed preference methods, new research is documenting local public goods demand in the cities of the PRC. An intra-urban study by Zheng and Kahn (2008) finds that proximity to fast public transit, clean air, high-quality schools, major universities, and environmental amenities are capitalized into home prices in Beijing. An intercity study of thirty-five large cities by Zheng et al. (2010) finds that home prices are lower in cities with higher ambient pollution levels (Figure 17.8), and the marginal valuation for green amenities is rising over time. They report evidence of an Environmental Kuznets Curve (EKC) such that the richer cities are beyond the turning point at a much lower level of per capita income than has been estimated in a cross-country study (Grossman and Krueger 1995).

[18] Source: Population Census of the PRC (in 2000 and 2010).

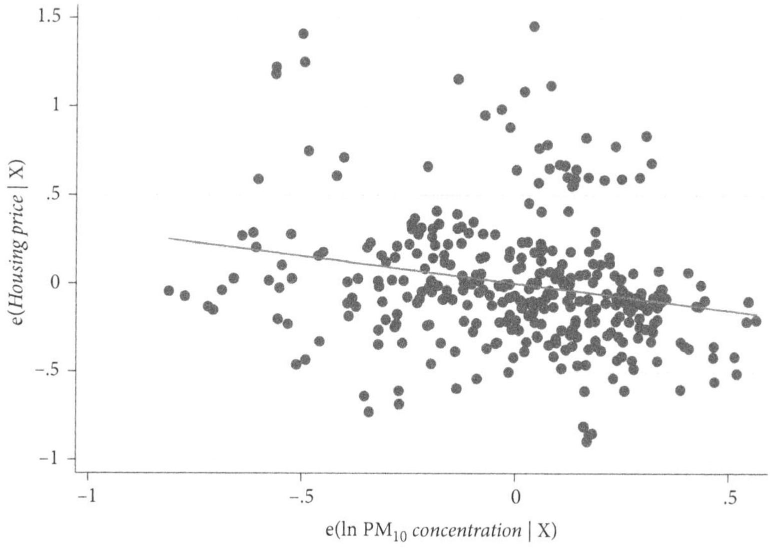

Figure 17.8. Air pollutant concentration and housing prices in the cities of the PRC, 2006–9

Source: NBSC, Ministry of Environmental Protection of the PRC.

Other evidence for the PRC's urbanites' rising demand for clean air is that they are increasingly investing in self-protection goods including masks and air filters to avoid pollution exposure. The PRC's largest online shopping platform (Taobao.com) estimated that the PRC's consumers spent RMB 870 million (US$143 million) on 4.5 million online transactions purchasing anti-smog products in 2013. During the haze week in December 2013, the mask and air filter consumption was ten to fifteen times of that of the previous week.

17.4 Policies and Regulations to Mitigate Urban Congestion and Pollution

Prominent studies on the EKC describe an inverse U-shaped relationship between per capita income and different indicators of pollution (Grossman and Krueger 1995; Hilton and Levinson 1998; Harbaugh et al. 2002). Using the PRC's data, Zheng et al. (2010) and Zheng et al. (2014c) both find empirical evidence supporting the contention that the EKC regularity also holds for the cities of the PRC. Per capita indicators of urban pollution (such as PM_{10}, $PM_{2.5}$, and SO_2 concentration in the air) had first risen with city GDP or average income per capita and then started falling in recent years. The EKC theory points out that consumers' rising demand for quality of life is the most important underlying driving force for the turning point—people will push the government to implement stringent environmental regulations and the market will also respond to consumers' demand for green products.

In Section 17.3 we presented evidence showing that the PRC's urbanites' demand for green cities is rising as the new cohorts in cities become more educated and richer, which is now incentivizing the PRC's central and local governments to address urban congestion and pollution problems. In recent years, the PRC's central and local governments have adopted a wide range of anti-pollution and anti-congestion policies, including public investments such as SO_2 scrubbers and transportation infrastructure, car ownership and usage restrictions, and some demand-side pricing tools. Given the PRC's central–local government structure and the local public finance system, whether local governments have real and strong incentives to address the congestion and pollution problems in their jurisdictions is the key determinant of the effectiveness of such regulations. In addition, without enough information, expertise, and management skills, local governments have sometimes done 'too much' and 'created' inappropriate policies that generate unintended negative consequences.

17.4.1 Local Governments' Incentives for 'Going Green'

The PRC has a very strong one-party central government, and hundreds of local city governments are the real executives of city management and governance. For a long time, during the period of rapid urbanization and industrialization, the PRC's central government focused on economic growth with an emphasis on GDP as the key evaluation criteria of local officials' performance. Therefore, local officials (especially city mayors) whose cities boomed with higher GDP growth rate were more likely to be promoted, rather than on the basis of their performance in improving the local quality of life. Wu et al. (2014) argue that city mayors focus on transportation investment rather than environmental protection because transportation leads to more immediate GDP gains for the city. As we mentioned earlier, investment in roads is not always a good way of reducing congestion.

In recent years, the central government realized that pure GDP-oriented growth will not be sustainable and started emphasizing the importance of energy saving and environmental protection. There are two major incentives to encourage local governments to pursue this national goal: changing the promotion criteria of local officials and the transfer payments from central government to local governments. At the same time, with rising media transparency, urbanites' demand for 'blue skies' can be more easily and directly addressed by central and local governments, which also generates an 'invisible' pressure on local governments. The pressures from central government and citizens form a 'sandwich' structure to nudge local governments to pursue environmental sustainability goals by improving urban governance and implementing effective policies during the new urbanization era (Zheng et al. 2014c).

It should be noted that the rich coastal areas are now moving polluting firms out of their cities, but at the same time the cities in underdeveloped areas still welcome these firms because they need industrial output, tax revenue, and employment opportunities—their 'golden goose'. The PRC is a big country and has more than 600 cities. This means that the cities will be located in different points on the EKC curve, and each one is moving on its unique path. We should expect that the richer cities in the eastern coastal area will pass the turning point earlier than the poorer ones in inland PRC.

17.4.2 Supply-Side Policies: Infrastructure Investment and Facility Installation

As mentioned in Section 17.2, the introduction of subways and other public transit systems can effectively improve urban traffic and environmental performance. The PRC is in the midst of a major subway construction period. Today, many major cities, such as Beijing and Shanghai, have the longest subway line operations in the world.

Subway refers to a high-speed transportation technology to move people within a city. High-speed rail (HSR, 'bullet train') is a similar technology, but it can move people between cities. The PRC's recent investment in bullet trains allows individuals to move at speeds of roughly 175 miles per hour and this increases the number of locations that have access to megacities. The Ministry of Railway announced its ambitious bullet train plan in 2006.[19] The first set of bullet train lines opened in April 2007, boosting the speed of some major trains to 200–50 km/h. In August 2008, to coincide with the 2008 Beijing Olympic Games, new bullet trains opened between Beijing and Tianjin. They reached a higher top speed of about 350 km/h. By the end of 2010, the PRC's bullet train service length reached 8,358 km. By 2020, the PRC's total service HSR length will reach 12,000 km.[20] This transportation technology innovation allows individuals to access a megacity without living within its boundaries and thus offers potentially large social benefits—individuals can enjoy the benefits of urban agglomeration without having to pay megacity real estate rents and suffering from the city's social costs (Zheng and Kahn 2013c).

[19] The typical financing arrangement for constructing bullet train lines is that the Ministry of Railway pays 50 to 60 per cent of the total cost and the destination cities pay the remainder. See <http://finance.people.com.cn/GB/1037/8743758.html>.

[20] The average construction cost is about RMB 100 million per kilometre for newly constructed bullet train lines, and this cost is much lower for upgraded railway lines. The average operating cost is about RMB 0.3 per person per kilometre.

The PRC has invested extensively on SO_2 scrubbers since 2006, and innovative policies were enacted in 2007 to increase the likelihood that these installed scrubbers actually operate (Xu et al. 2009). The share of coal power plants with SO_2 scrubbers increased from 10 per cent to 48 per cent betwecn 2005 and the end of 2007 (Xu et al. 2009). The two enforcement policies are as follows. First, all coal power plants with SO_2 scrubbers must install continuous monitoring systems and transfer real-time data to the government. Second, an incentive scheme that varies with the scrubber's operation rate was set up—for a 100 per cent operation rate, electricity can be sold to the grid at a \$2.0/MWh price premium compared with a plant without scrubbers, but the premium falls to zero at an 80 per cent operation rate. Figure 17.9 shows the spatial distribution of the installed capacity of desulfurization equipment in coal-fired power plants in 2011.

To change the coal-based urbanization and industrialization pattern, the PRC's government has gradually adjusted the energy structure through substantial adjustments on hydropower and wind power generation. In the past few years, the PRC increased its production capacity for producing renewable power equipment such as wind turbines and solar panels. Those types of equipment are

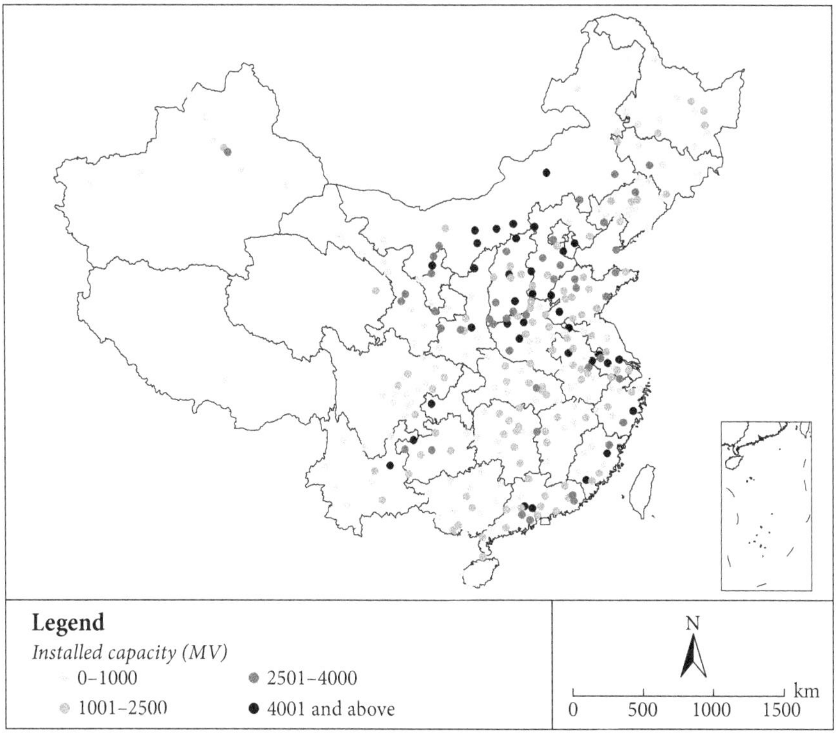

Figure 17.9. The installed capacity of desulfurization equipment in coal-fired power plants

Source: Zheng et al. (2014b)

both exported globally and are sold in the domestic market. The PRC is now the world's largest exporter of solar panels, with over 40 per cent of the global market share. The rapid growth in the PRC's wind turbine production has focused on the domestic market. It shows that the PRC's energy consumption has transformed to a greener and cleaner energy pattern.

17.4.3 Demand-Side Policies: Command-and-Control Regulations and Market-Oriented Policies

There are two major types of demand-side policies to address urban congestion and pollution problems: command-and-control regulations and market-oriented policies. The PRC is an emerging market economy, which transited from the old central planning economy, and the current policy package is a mixed one with policy tools in both categories. However, in the future market-oriented policies will gradually dominate. Such policies are aimed at changing the behaviour of firms and individuals by changing the incentives for them.

Here, we use the transportation sector in Beijing as an example to show how such regulations and policies are designed and implemented, and also to evaluate their effectiveness. We will also discuss a typical market-oriented policy type—pricing the negative externalities and charging the firm or the individual who produces such externalities accordingly.

17.4.3.1 Transportation Demand Management Policies in Beijing

Cities in the PRC have adopted a wide range of transportation policies in the recent past to address the road congestion problem. Beijing is the most congested city in the PRC, so its city government has implemented a long list of transportation regulations (Table 17.2). Some of these regulations were later replicated in other major cities.

Among the regulations listed in Table 17.2, driving restriction is a popular command and control to reduce traffic congestion, which has been used in many cities around the world since it is easy and cheap to implement. Nowadays, driving restrictions are used in about ten large and medium-sized cities in the PRC where automobiles are taken off the road on each workday according to the last digit of their licence plates. Sun et al. (2014) and Lu et al. (2014) find that driving restrictions significantly reduced Beijing's traffic congestion during rush hours in the short run, from 2009 to early 2011. However, its long-term effectiveness is widely questioned by many scholars and the public. For instance, such a regulation encourages high- and middle-income households to buy a second car, which increases the total traffic flow as an unintended consequence.

To avoid this unintended consequence of the 'second car' effect, many city governments later implemented the 'lottery' (such as in Beijing) or 'auction' system

Table 17.2. Transportation and environmental policies/actions in Beijing, 2007–11

Category	Policy/action	Start time (end time)
Fare subsidy	Bus	January 1, 2007
	Subway	January 10, 2007
New subway	No. 5	July 10, 2007
	No. 10 and Airport line	July 19, 2008
	No. 8	10-September 2008
	No. 4	September 28, 2009
	No. 15 and suburban line	December 30, 2010
	No. 9	December 31, 2011
Driving and ownership restrictions	Odd-even	July, 20, 2008 (September 20, 2008)
	One day per week (6 am-9 pm)	October 11, 2008 (April 10, 2009)
	One day per week (7 am-8 pm)	April 11, 2009
	Private car licence plate lottery	January 1, 2011
Parking fee increase	Selected areas in central city	April 1, 2010 (March 31, 2011)
	Non-residential areas in central city	April 1, 2011
Taxi fuel surcharge for trips over 3 km	1 RMB	November 25, 2009 (April 8, 2011)
	2 RMB	April 9, 2011
Environmental policies	Improved light-duty vehicle emission standards	March 1, 2008
	Improved commercial vehicle emission standards	July 1, 2008
Others	Gasoline price adjustments, increases in bus-only lanes	Various times

Source: Sun et al. (2014).

(such as in Shanghai) of private car licence plates to control the absolute growth rate of the total cars in stock. Although this regulation has directly slowed down the growing number of cars and reduced road congestion, it has certain side effects. One side effect is that when a household acquires a licence plate, it is more likely to buy a more expensive and larger car with larger engine displacement, which will produce more emission. Another side effect is that restricting the number of private car licences transfers the pressure to other transportation modes such as subways and buses. In Beijing, the subway capacity cannot meet passengers' rising demand, and passengers have to squeeze into subway cars during rush hours. In this sense, Shanghai's 'auction' system is better than Beijing's 'lottery' system because the former generates considerable revenue, which can then be used to build more subway lines (Li 2014).

17.4.3.2 Price Negative Externalities

It is the government rather than the market that sets up most energy prices in the PRC. Therefore, energy pricing is a typical tool to internalize the congestion and pollution externalities and change the PRC's urbanites' driving and energy consumption behaviours.

Before 2005, fuel prices in the PRC had been much lower than that in the West. Such prices were once highly subsidized. In recent years, fuel prices in the PRC have increased to roughly 30 per cent higher than that in the US, but it is still lower than that in Japan, the Republic of Korea, the United Kingdom, and France (International Energy Agency 2011). This underpricing encouraged people to commute long distances from low-density suburban areas. As estimated, the PRC's gas tax as a share of the total price of a gallon of gasoline is about 45 per cent, which is about twice that in the US, but lower than that in Europe.[21] Anas et al.'s (2008) study compares the effectiveness of congestion tolls and fuel taxes in reducing traffic congestion and finds the latter more effective. This finding is crucial for predicting how changes in the PRC's public policies directed at increasing the cost of driving will affect the pollution produced by the vehicle sector. Similarity, residential electricity and water use have also been underpriced in the cities of the PRC for a long time. The central government recently launched the 'multistep' electricity price scheme in order to help reduce power consumption.

Beijing's transportation regulation of increasing the parking fee in the central city is also a typical pricing regulation. This will encourage those who need to go to the CBD to take public transits rather than driving there. Several cities are discussing the possibility of implementing congestion pricing, similar to what Singapore and London are doing, but up to now no city of the PRC has started it yet.

17.4.4 Technology and Management Innovations

The government should encourage technology and management innovations, which can change technique and composition effects to achieve energy saving and environmental progress, given the scale of the whole economy.

Technological advance and the diffusion of existing technologies could break the link between private motorization growth and increased pollution (Acemoglu et al. 2012). If electric vehicles replace gasoline vehicles and if electricity is generated by renewable energy sources, then the miles driven would not lead to large-scale local air pollution or emission of greenhouse gases. Rapid transit such as subways and high-speed rail are other examples of how technology can reduce congestion

[21] See <http://news.163.com/special/reviews/youjiagaige.html>.

and pollution without constraining urban growth. Such huge infrastructure investment projects need economies of scale, so they are more feasible in large cities. Such technological progress would shift the classic EKC curve down so that less pollution is produced during the early phase of economic growth (Zheng and Kahn 2013b).

Another key determinant of the energy consumption per unit of output or per capita is management quality. A promising trend in the PRC is the rising quality of its universities and the professionalization of the managerial class as more MBAs graduate from elite universities. If energy prices rise in the PRC, there will be a premium for managers who figure out strategies for economizing energy consumption. Zheng et al. (2014c) examine the role of city leadership (city leaders' human capital level, measured by years of schooling) in determining the city's energy/environmental actions and outcomes. They find that if a new mayor has a higher educational attainment than the former mayor, the city enjoys a significant air quality improvement. This means that better educated leaders may devote more effort to protecting the environment, and thus their cities may benefit from their leadership and enjoy progressive approaches to energy and the environment.

17.5 Conclusion

The PRC's remarkable economic performance in the past three decades has been fuelled by urban industrial growth. However, many of the most polluted and congested cities in the world are located in the PRC. Over the next thirty years, hundreds of millions of households in the PRC are expected to urbanize. Employing a demand–supply–government framework, this chapter has reviewed the congestion and pollution consequences of the PRC's fast urbanization, and how governments have coped with such challenges.

We have investigated the regularities in the congestion and pollution problems that the PRC's urban growth has generated. The interaction of rising travel demand and lagged supply of public transits causes traffic congestion. Constructing more high-speed public transits such as subways can effectively alleviate traffic congestion. The fast growth of industrial production, motorization, and energy consumption leads to acute pollution problems, but with new cohorts of urbanites becoming more educated and richer, their demand for green cities is also rising.

We find that larger and denser cities generally have lower energy consumption and pollution emission per capita (or per GDP dollar), due to the scale economies in transportation and anti-pollution infrastructure construction, and that there is a higher probability of technology and management innovations in such megacities. Since Asia's urbanization will be led by megacities to achieve efficiency, these cities can also achieve the goal of sustainability.

We have highlighted the roles of the market and the government in mitigating such negative externalities. The central government and the public are now both pushing local governments to achieve the goal of energy saving and environmental protection and improve urbanities' quality of life. This forms a 'sandwich' structure, which incentivizes local governments to implement more stringent anti-congestion and anti-pollution regulations. However, some of these policies, especially the command-and-control ones, were not carefully designed and have led to unintended consequences, which means that the government may have 'done too much'.

Our analysis of the causes of congestion and pollution can perhaps be generalized across cities in the developing world. While we recognize that a specific city's own geographic and natural attributes play a key role in determining the congestion and pollution problems it faces, all growing cities face the tragedy of the commons with increasing population, industrial production, motorization, and energy consumption. With increasing technology innovations and carefully designed policies that can change firms' and individuals' incentives in a positive direction, the problem of congestion and negative externalities of urban growth can be effectively mitigated and the goal of efficient and sustainable urban growth achieved.

References

Acemoglu, Daron, Leo Bursztyn, Philippe Aghion, and David Hemous. 2012. 'The Environment and Directed Technical Change'. *American Economic Review 102* (1): 131–66.

Anas, Alex, Govinda R. Timilsina, and Siqi Zheng. 2008. 'Effects of a Toll on Congestion versus a Tax on Gasoline on Car Travel, Fuel Consumption and CO2 Emissions in Beijing'. *World Bank Working Paper WPS5068.*

Asian Development Bank. 2012. 'Toward an Environmentally Sustainable Future: Country Environmental Analysis of the People's Republic of China'. <http://www.adb.org/sites/default/files/pub/2012/toward-environmentally-sustainable-future-prc.pdf>.

Bao, Chenggang, Zhao Chen, and Jianfeng Wu. 2013. 'Chinese Manufacturing on the Move: Factor Supply or Market Access?' *China Economic Review 26*: 170–81.

Baum-Snow, Nathaniel, Loren Brandt, J. Vernon Henderson, Matthew A. Turner, and Qinghua Zhang. 2012. 'Roads, Railroads and Decentralization of Chinese Cities'. Working paper.

Cai, Hongbin, Yuyu Chen, and Qing Gong. 2013. 'Polluting Thy Neighbor: The Case of River Pollution in China'. Working paper, Peking University.

Cao, Guoliang, Xiaoye Zhang, Sunling Gong, Xinqin An, and Yaqiang Wang. 2011. 'Emission Inventories of Primary Particles and Pollutant Gases for China'. *Chinese Science Bulletin 56* (8): 781–8.

Chay, Kenneth Y. and Michael Greenstone. 2003. 'The Impact of Air Pollution on Infant Mortality: Evidence from Geographic Variation in Pollution Shocks Induced by a Recession'. *Quarterly Journal of Economics 118* (3): 1121–67.

Chen, Yuyu, Avraham Ebensteinb, Michael Greenstone, and Hongbin Li. 2013. 'Evidence on the Impact of Sustained Exposure to Air Pollution on Life Expectancy from China's Huai River Policy'. *Proceedings of the National Academy of Sciences 110* (32): 12936–41.

Crane, Randall. 2000. 'The Influence of Urban Form on Travel: An Interpretive Review'. *Journal of Planning Literature 15* (1): 3–23.

Evans, Mary F. and V. Kerry Smith. 2005. 'Do New Health Conditions Support Mortality–Air Pollution Effects?' *Journal of Environmental Economics and Management 50* (3): 496–518.

Ewing, Reid and Robert Cervero. 2001. 'Travel and the Built Environment: A Synthesis'. *Transportation Research Board 178* (1): 87–114.

Ewing, Reid and Robert Cervero. 2010. 'Travel and the Built Environment'. *Journal of the American Planning Association 76* (3): 265–94.

Fujita, Masahisa and Hideaki Ogawa. 1982. 'Multiple Equilibria and Structural Transition of Non-monocentric Urban Configurations'. *Regional Science and Urban Economics 12* (2): 161–96.

Gentzkow, Matthew and Jesse, Shapiro. 2010. 'What Drives Media slant? Evidence from U.S. Daily Newspapers'. *Econometrica 78* (1): 35–71.

Grossman, Gene M. and Alan B. Krueger. 1995. 'Economic Growth and the Environment'. *The Quarterly Journal of Economics 110* (2): 353–77.

Harbaugh, William T., Arik Levinson, and David Wilson. 2002. 'Reexamining the Empirical Evidence for an Environmental Kuznets Curve'. *The Review of Economics and Statistics 84* (3): 541–51.

He, Jie. 2006. 'Pollution Haven Hypothesis and Environmental Impacts of Foreign Direct Investment: The Case of Industrial Emission of Sulfur Dioxide in Chinese Provinces'. *Ecological Economics 60* (1): 228–45.

He, Jie. 2009. 'China's Industrial SO2 Emissions and its Economic Determinants: EKC's Reduced vs. Structural Model and the Role of International Trade'. *Environment and Development Economics 14* (2): 227–62.

Hilton, F. G. Hank and Arik Levinson. 1998. 'Factoring the Environmental Kuznets Curve: Evidence from Automotive Lead Emissions'. *Journal of Environmental Economics and Management 35* (2): 126–41.

International Energy Agency. 2012. *Key World Energy Statistics, 2011*. <https://www.iea.org>.

Li, Shanjun. 2014. 'Better Lucky than Rich? Welfare Analysis of Automobile License Allocations in Beijing and Shanghai'. SSRN Working Paper. <http://papers.ssrn.com/sol3/papers.cfm?abstract_id=2349865>.

Lu, Ming and Hao Feng. 2014. 'Spatial Agglomeration and Pollution Reduction: An Empirical Analysis of Industrial Pollution Based on Provincial Panel Data'. *The Journal of World Economy 7*: 86–114.

Lu, Ming, Cong Sun, and Siqi Zheng. 2014. ' "Monocentric Schools" in Beijing: The Congestion and Pollution Consequences of Driving Children to Schools'. Working paper.

Lucas, Robert E. and Esteban Rossi-Hansberg. 2002. 'On the Internal Structure of Cities'. *Econometrica 70* (4): 1445–76.

Moretti, Enrico and Matthew Neidell. 2011. 'Pollution, Health, and Avoidance Behavior Evidence from the Ports of Los Angeles'. *Journal of Human Resources 46* (1): 154–75.

NBSC (National Bureau of Statistics of China). 2011. *China Energy Statistical Yearbook 2010*, China Statistics Press.

Sit, Victor Fung Shuen, ed. 1985. *Chinese Cities: The Growth of the Metropolis Since 1949*, Oxford University Press.

Sun, Cong, Siqi Zheng, and Rui Wang. 2014. 'Restricting Driving for Better Traffic and Clearer Skies: Did it Work in Beijing?' *Transport Policy 32*: 34–41.

Tang, Deliang, Tin-yu Li, Jason J. liu, Zhi-jun Zhou, Tao Yuan, Yu-hui Chen, Virginia A. Rauh, Jiang Xie, and Frederica Perera. 2008. 'Effects of Prenatal Exposure to Coal-Burning Pollutants on Children's Development in China'. *Environmental Health Perspectives 116* (5): 674–9.

Wang, Hua and Yanhong Jin. 2007. 'Industrial Ownership and Environmental Performance: Evidence from China'. *Environmental and Resource Economics 36* (3): 255–73.

Wu, Jing, Yongheng Deng, Jun Huang, Randall Morck, and Bernard Yeung. 2014. 'Incentives and Outcomes: China's Environmental Policy'. *Capitalism and Society 9* (1).

Xu, Yuan, Robert H. Williams, and Robert H. Socolow. 2009. 'China's Rapid Deployment of SO2 Scrubbers'. *Energy & Environmental Science 2*: 459–65.

Zheng, Siqi and Matthew E. Kahn. 2008. 'Land and Residential Property Markets in a Booming Economy: New Evidence from Beijing'. *Journal of Urban Economics 63*: 743–57.

Zheng, Siqi and Matthew E. Kahn. 2013a. 'Understanding China's Urban Pollution Dynamics'. *Journal of Economic Literature 51* (3): 731–72.

Zheng, Siqi and Matthew E. Kahn. 2013b. 'Does Government Investment in Local Public Goods Spur Gentrification? Evidence from Beijing'. *Real Estate Economics 41* (1): 1–28.

Zheng, Siqi and Matthew E. Kahn. 2013c. 'China's Bullet Trains Facilitate Market Integration and Mitigate the Cost of Mega City Growth'. *Proceedings of the National Academy of Sciences of the United States of America 110* (14): 1248–E1253.

Zheng, Siqi, Cong Sun, Ye Qi, and Matthew E. Kahn. 2014a. 'The Evolving Geography of China's Industrial Production: Implications for Pollution Dynamics and Urban Quality of Life'. *Journal of Economic Surveys 28* (4): 709–24.

Zheng, Siqi, Jing Cao, Matthew E. Kahn, and Cong Sun. 2014b. 'Real Estate Valuation and Cross-Boundary Air Pollution Externalities: Evidence from Chinese Cities'. *Journal of Real Estate Finance and Economics 48* (3): 398–414.

Zheng, Siqi, Matthew E. Kahn, and Hongyu Liu. 2010. 'Towards a System of Open Cities in China: Home Prices, FDI flows and Air Quality in 35 Major Cities'. *Regional Science and Urban Economics 40* (1): 1–10.

Zheng, Siqi, Matthew Kahn, Weizeng Sun, and Danglun Luo. 2014c. 'Incentives for China's Urban Mayors to Mitigate Pollution Externalities: The Role of the Central Government and Public Environmentalism'. *Regional Science and Urban Economics 47*: 61–71.

Zheng, Siqi, Rui Wang, Edward L. Glaeser, and Matthew E. Kahn. 2011. 'The Greenness of China: Household Carbon Emissions and Urban Development'. *Journal of Economic Geography 11* (5): 761–92.

Zhang, Yingjie, Siqi Zheng, Cong Sun, and Rui Wang. 2017. 'Does subway proximity discourage automobility? Evidence from Beijing'. Transportation Research Part D: Transport and Environment *52*: 506–17.

Zheng, Siqi, Yuming Fu, and Hongyu Liu. 2006. 'Housing-Choice Hindrances and Urban Spatial Structure: Evidence from Matched Location and Location-Preference Data in Chinese Cities'. *Journal of Urban Economics 60* (3): 535–57.

Zhou, Ying, Jonathan I. Levy, John S. Evans, and James K. Hammitt. 2006. 'The Influence of Geographic Location on Population Exposure to Emissions from Power Plants Throughout China'. *Environment International 32* (3): 365–73.

18
Urbanization, Water Supply, and Sanitation in India

Surender Kumar

18.1 Introduction

Urbanization in a country confers advantages in harnessing economies of scale, scope, and connectedness, and thus raises standard of living. Availability and efficiency in the provision of basic amenities such as water and sanitation are essential for realizing advantages of urbanization.

In India, about 31 per cent of the population lives in urban areas (Census of India 2011), and it is expected that this figure will reach about 40 per cent by 2030. Note that despite the low level and pace of urbanization in the country in comparison with other developing countries such as Indonesia, Brazil, China, Mexico, Nigeria, and South Africa, basic amenities are seriously inadequate. In urban areas, about 97 per cent of the population has access to safe drinking water and 60 per cent enjoy sanitation facilities. Even in urban areas about 12 per cent of people defecate in the open, without any dignity or privacy (WHO-UN 2014).

A large number of Indian cities are experiencing moderate to severe water and sanitation deficiencies due to low levels of urban-centric economic growth. These deficiencies are expected to multiply with dwindling fresh water resources. Due to the inadequacy of water and sanitation facilities, urban India annually loses about 90 million working days (World Bank 2013). Improving efficiencies and minimizing losses in provisioning could help in addressing these challenges. The power-law scaling relationship between water and sanitation services and level of urbanization reveals that autonomy in management helps in improving efficiency. Estimates of technical efficiency disclose that an average Indian urban water utility could provide 37 per cent more services with available resources, of which 22 per cent of the efficiency can be accomplished by improving management, and the remaining 15 per cent could be achieved by operating at an optimal scale. Similarly, sanitation providers have the potential to increase their efficiency level by about 48 per cent. Moreover, financial sustainability could be realized by charging for services following the marginal cost-pricing rule; most urban utilities are operating at decreasing returns to scale in India.

Surender Kumar., *Urbanization, Water Supply, and Sanitation in India Cities* In: *Cities of Dragons and Elephants: Urbanization and Urban Development in China and India. Edited by:* Guanghua Wan and Ming Lu, Oxford University Press (2019). © Oxford University Press. DOI: 10.1093/oso/9780198829225.003.0018

The chapter is organized as follows: an overview of the institutional arrangements and the extent of water and sanitation facilities in urban areas is provided in Section 18.2. A case study on the technical efficiency of water and sanitation providers is presented in Section 18.3. Policy initiatives undertaken in the country are analysed in Section 18.4. Section 18.5 concludes the chapter.

18.2 Overview of Urban Water and Sanitation in India

18.2.1 Institutional Provisions

India has three-tier system of governance. Providing water and sanitation facilities in urban areas is a responsibility of local governments. At the federal level, two ministries, the Ministry of Urban Development and Ministry of Housing and Urban Poverty Alleviation, are the nodal agencies. The central government is responsible for the formulation of policies or guidelines for the overall development of the water and sanitation sector. The central government provides technical assistance and funding support to the sector through state governments. State governments prescribe specified policies and the institutional setup for proper development and management of the sector. Note that responsibility for regulating discharge of wastewater lies with the Ministry of Environment, Forest and Climate Change.

The institutional setup for delivering water and sanitation services varies from state to state. In some states the services are provided by state-level public health engineering departments, in others specialized state-wide water supply and sewerage boards (WSSBs), specialized city-level WSSBs, municipal corporations, and urban local bodies (ULBs) are the main agencies for delivering of these services. Moreover, other ministries and departments, financial institutions, external support agencies, non-governmental organizations, and private sector also help directly or indirectly in providing these services.

Although, according to the 74th Amendment of the Indian Constitution, providing water and sanitation facilities is a responsibility of municipal or local governments, the real task of providing these services lies with state governments. Generally, it has been observed that a state-level agency is involved in planning and investment, but responsibility for maintenance and operation lies with local urban bodies. In some big cities such as Delhi, delivery of these services is not a responsibility of ULBs, and is provided by some autonomous bodies known as parastatal bodies, e.g. the Delhi Jal Board in Delhi. Note that though there is decentralization in provision of these services, local bodies have to depend on state governments for finance since they remain financially weak. It has also been observed that tariffs are generally set by state governments far below operating expenses, and low recovery of tariffs further deteriorate the financial conditions of local bodies and result in lower-quality service delivery.

Note that the institutional setup in the country is afflicted by the existence of multiple agencies, and there is a lack of clear responsibilities between these multiple agencies. Therefore, local governments should be given autonomy in provision and cost recovery of these services. State and central governments should assist local governments following the principles of fiscal federalism and recommendations of successive Finance Commissions.

18.2.2 The State of Urban Water and Sanitation

A brief description of the extent of access to water and sanitation facilities and impacts due to inadequacy is provided in this section. The description has been provided at two levels: state level and city level. Leading indicators of water and sanitation are used to assess the existing situation on a comparative basis.

18.2.2.1 State-level Description

About 97 per cent of the urban population has access to potable drinking water (Census of India 2011), and about 29 per cent of households have to get water from outside their premises. About 21 per cent of households get water from within 100 metres of their premises and about 8 per cent of households have to bring water from more than 100 metres away from their premises (Figure 18.1), as Chapter 10 in this volume also testifies. Note that availability of water within premises is not uniform throughout the country; as Chapter 10 demonstrates there are significant regional variations. The 2011 population census reveals that in Punjab, about 93 per cent of households get water within their premises, but in Nagaland, Manipur, and Orissa, more than 20 per cent of households have to get water from more than 100 metres away from their premises. Figure 18.2 shows that there is a positive association between availability of water within premises

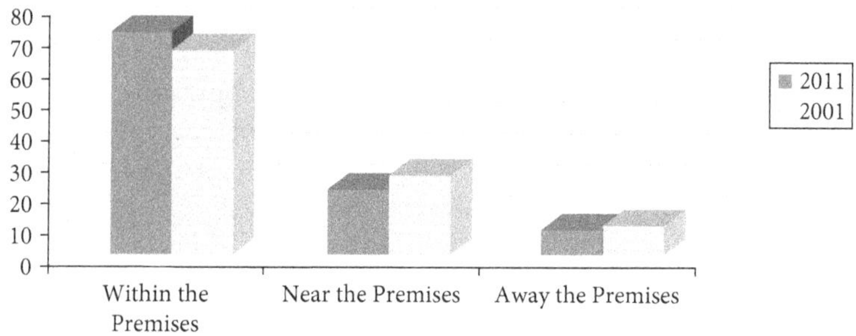

Figure 18.1. Availability of drinking water to urban households
Source: Census of India 2011.

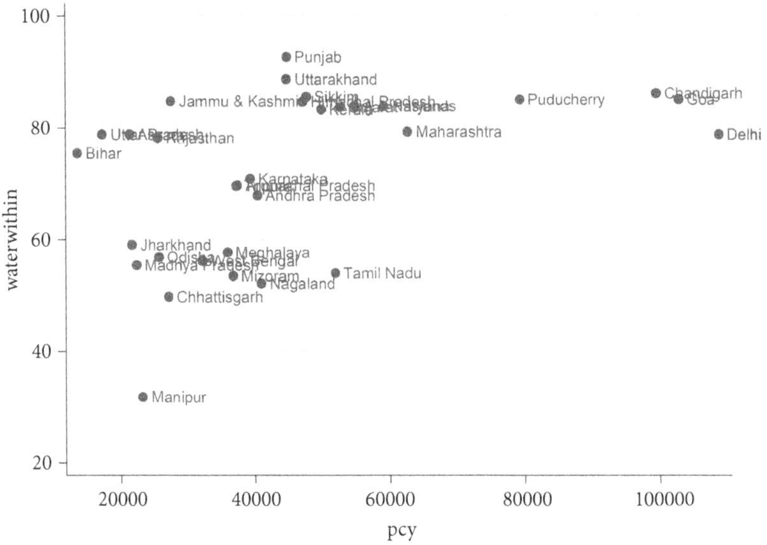

Figure 18.2. Association between water availability within premises and per capita income

Source: Constructed on the data from Census of India 2011 and Reserve Bank of India.

and per capita state income, as also found in Chapter 10 in this volume. We also observe a positive relationship between levels of urbanization and availability of water within a household's premises. States with a higher level of urbanization have a lower number of households that have to get water from outside of their premises.

Figure 18.3 provides a report card of progress in availability of drinking water in urban areas in the country. It reveals that only 54 per cent of households are able to get piped water supply in their premises, and the rest have to use untreated water for their daily needs. In some states, such as Himachal Pradesh and the union territories of Chandigarh and Puduchery, more than 90 per cent of households get treated tap water, whereas in Nagaland and Bihar only 6 and 15 per cent of households respectively get treated tap water. Similarly, in Uttar Pradesh, Arunachal Pradesh, Tripura, Jharkhand, Tripura, Assam, Orissa, and Chhattisgarh, and in some union territories, less than 50 per cent of households get treated tap water. This again reveals the fact that economically backward states have less access to treated tap water supply in urban India.

We keep the analysis confined to the management of human excreta and wastewater, though sanitation covers many other aspects such as hygiene practices, management of domestic, industrial, and medical wastes, animal wastes, and drainage, among other things. The Total Sanitation Campaign was started in 1991 with an objective of universal household sanitation coverage to be achieved by 2012. Though the scheme was implemented in 606 districts spread across thirty states and union territories, twenty states were not able to meet the target

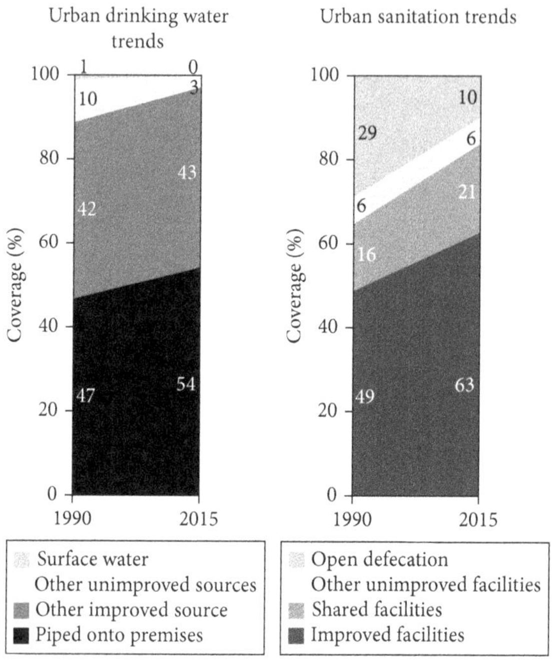

Figure 18.3. Progress in urban water and sanitation in India
Source: WHO-UNICEF (2015) (as taken from TERI 2016).

(Census of India 2011). Only the states of Tripura, Haryana, Himachal Pradesh, Kerala, Goa, Uttarakhand, Sikkim, and Mizoram were able to meet the target.

As stated earlier, in India a substantial proportion, about 10 per cent, of the urban population have yet to defecate in the open (Figure 18.3). About 77 per cent of households had access to improved latrine facilities within household premises in 2011 (Figures 18.4 and 18.5). Note that despite various programmes initiated by governments, only 6 per cent urban households are using public toilets. The Census of India 2011 household amenity data also shows that there is huge interstate variation in availability and type of latrine facilities in India. Figure 18.6 illustrates the extent of households having toilet facilities within premises. In Jharkhand about 31 per cent of households defecate in the open, followed by Odisha (33 per cent), and Chhattisgarh (34 per cent). On the other side, in Kerala the smallest percentage of households are practising open defecation, followed by Mizoram, Manipur, Sikkim, Tripura, Goa, Nagaland, and Punjab. Among the northeastern states of India, unimproved/traditional latrine facilities within premises are very common.

Table 18.1 helps in explaining variation across states in availability of improved latrine facilities in urban India. To have improved sanitation facilities within the premises of a household, the convenience of drinking water within the premises of household is a necessity. We have already observed that economically better-off

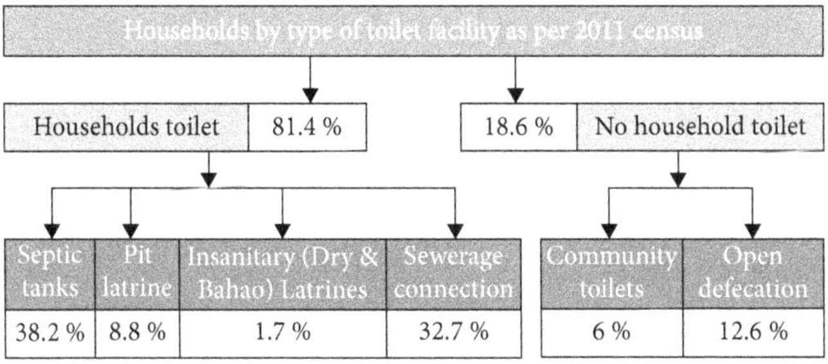

Figure 18.4. Latrine facilities available in urban India in 2011
Source: Census of India 2011 (as taken from TERI 2016).

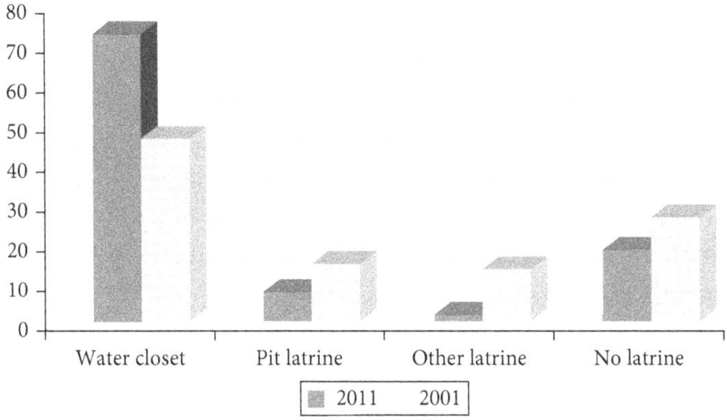

Figure 18.5. Latrine facilities in urban India
Source: Census of India 2011.

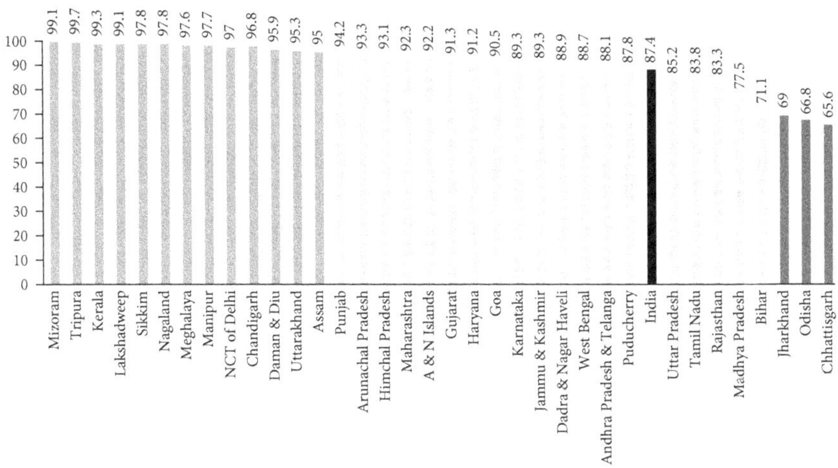

Figure 18.6. Toilet coverage at the state level (%)
Source: TERI (2016).

Table 18.1. Determinants of the closet latrine facility in urban India

	Coefficient	Standard error	z-statistics
Water within premises	0.34***	0.08	4.03
Ln(Sex Ratio)	47.97*	26.19	1.83
Literacy rate	−0.05	0.18	−0.3
Ln(per capita non-agricultural income)	15.11***	2.75	5.5
Constant	−440.16***	189.77	−2.32
No. of observations	64		
R^2: within	0.76		
between	0.44		
overall	0.58		

*** 1 per cent level of significance, * 10 per cent level of significance.

states have higher access to potable drinking water facilities. The availability of improved latrine facilities is also linked to social factors. Indian society is predominantly patriarchal, and women suffer the most in the absence of improved latrine facilities within premises. Therefore, it is expected that states with a higher sex ratio (women per 1,000 men) have better availability of improved sanitation facilities. Similarly, if people in a state are more educated, they are expected to be aware of the consequences of lack of sanitation facilities.

Using state-level panel data from the 2001 and 2011 censuses, we regress the availability of closet latrine facilities on its determinants, i.e. availability of water within premises, sex ratio, literacy rate, and per capita non-agricultural income. The results of the random effect panel data model are presented in Table 18.1. Rather than using per capita gross state domestic product, we use per capita state non-agricultural product as most urban income arises from non-agricultural sources. As expected, we find a positive association between closet latrine facility in a household and availability of water within premises. States with a higher per capita non-agricultural income also have a higher number of households with closet latrine facilities. Moreover, as hypothesized, states with a higher sex ratio have a higher level of closed latrine facilities among households. This explains the higher percentage of households with closed latrine facilities in the north-eastern states and Kerala. This finding corroborates the observations of Mehta and Mehta (2014).

18.2.2.2 City-Level Description

Generally, it is observed that cities are more concerned about water, but pay less attention towards the waste this water generates. In the absence of proper disposal facilities, sewage generated by households goes into streams, ponds, lakes, and rivers, polluting waterworks and compromising health. Therefore, it is imperative to provide hygienic and pollution-free sanitation to all citizens. To understand the situation comparatively at the micro level, we use data from pilot cities.

The water sector in India suffers from multiple problems such as intermittent and irregular water supply, low tariffs, poor management, low concern for consumers, high coping costs, etc. Therefore, to improve water and sanitation services, the government of India agreed to a service-level benchmarking (SLB) scheme and applied it in twenty-eight cities, known as pilot cities, spread over fourteen states and one union territory. The Ministry of Urban Development in partnership with the Water and Sanitation Program (WSP) (2010) collected information on twenty-eight indicators for these pilot cities and published a data book on the water and sanitation situation of these cities.

The per capita water supply in twenty-eight cities in India is illustrated in Figure 18.7. An average city provides 130 lpcd (litres per capita per day) against the norm of 140 lpcd decided in 1980s by the National Drinking Water Mission. But distribution across cities is not uniform; it varies from 37 litres for Chas to 298 litres for Bokaro. Only about a third of the cities meet the national norm.

As stated earlier, the sector suffers from the problem of intermittent water supply, and a 24/7 water supply is only available in a few cities, e.g. Pimpri. Cities such as Chandigarh and Trivandarum have better water supplies whereas Bhopal, Indore, Berhampur, Guntur, and Ujjain experience a very poor situation, ranging between twenty-five minutes to one hour per day (see Figure 18.8). Indian cities have an average water supply of five hours per day, which is much lower than other Asian cities, e.g. Singapore, Hong Kong, Seoul, and Kuala Lumpur have 24/7 water supplies (Kumar and Managi 2010; Gupta et al., 2012).

The Indian water sector is prone to inefficiency that is mirrored in terms of the large quantity of non-revenue water (NRW). NRW is water that is produced but does not reach consumers. In the cities analysed, average water loss, measured as NRW, is more than 43 per cent of the water produced. In some cities such as Bangalore, Delhi, Bhubaneswar, Bokaro, Guntur, Imphal, Indore, Jalandhar, Nashik, Palampur, and Ujjain, NRW is more than 50 per cent of produced water (see Figure 18.9).

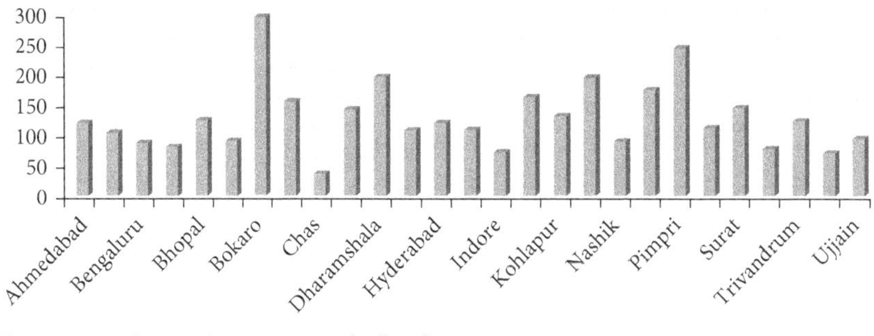

Figure 18.7. Per capita water supply (lpcd)

Source: Based on data from the Ministry of Urban Development in partnership with the Water and Sanitation Program (WSP) (2010).

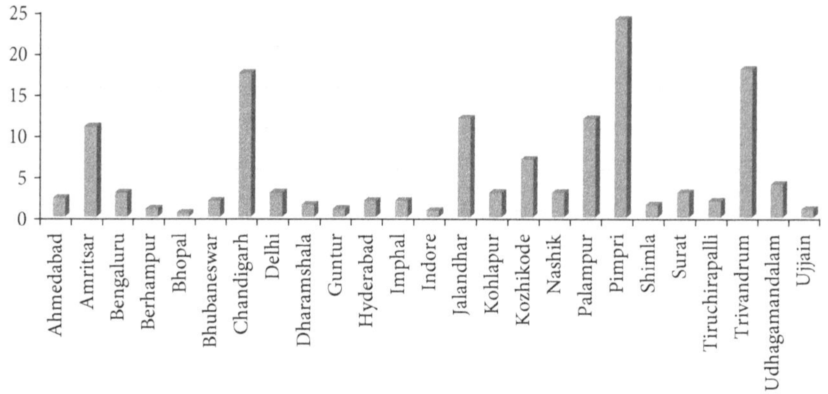

Figure 18.8. Water availability (hours/day)

Source: Based on data from the Ministry of Urban Development in partnership with the Water and Sanitation Program (WSP) (2010).

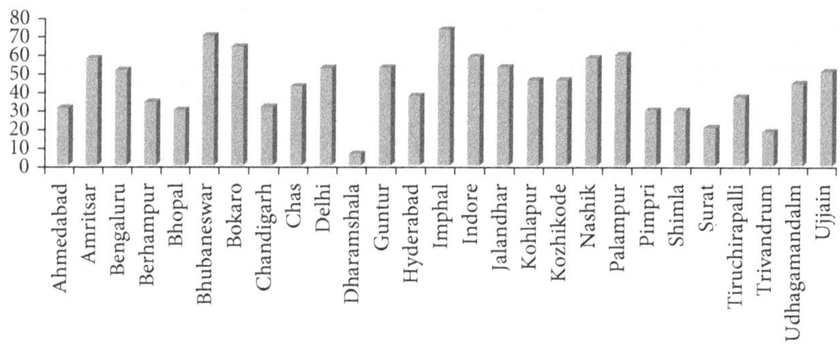

Figure 18.9. Non-revenue water (percentage of produced water)

Source: Based on data from the Ministry of Urban Development in partnership with the Water and Sanitation Program (WSP) (2010).

The average level of water metering is about 33 per cent in the country (Figure 18.10). Only in Kolhapur are all water connections metered. In Kozhikode, Nasik, Bangalore, Trivandrum, and Udhagamandalam, more than 80 per cent of water connections are metered. In some places such as Ahmedabad, Chas, Raipur, Palampur, Imphal, and Berhampur metering is completely absent. This explains the existence of such high levels of NRW in Indian cities, since in the absence of consumption metering, service providers have little incentive for improving service levels in a city.

Having a water connection is not a guarantee of water availability. A comparative assessment of the data for twenty-eight cities for water connections shows that the number of connections per 1,000 people is the highest in Ujjain (530), and the lowest in Chas and Raipur (eleven and forty-four respectively) (Figure 18.11).

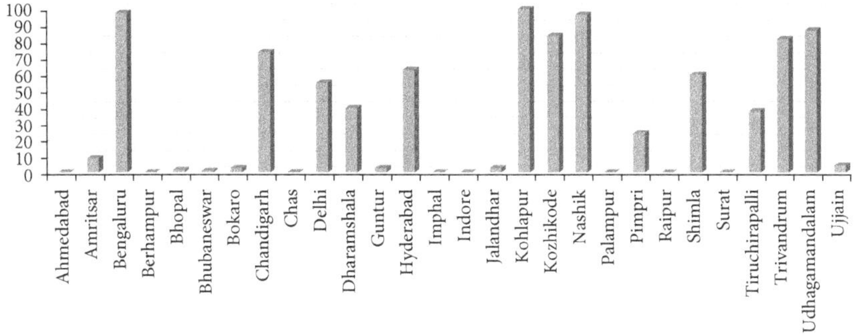

Figure 18.10. Consumption metering (%)

Source: Based on data from the Ministry of Urban Development in partnership with the Water and Sanitation Program (WSP) (2010).

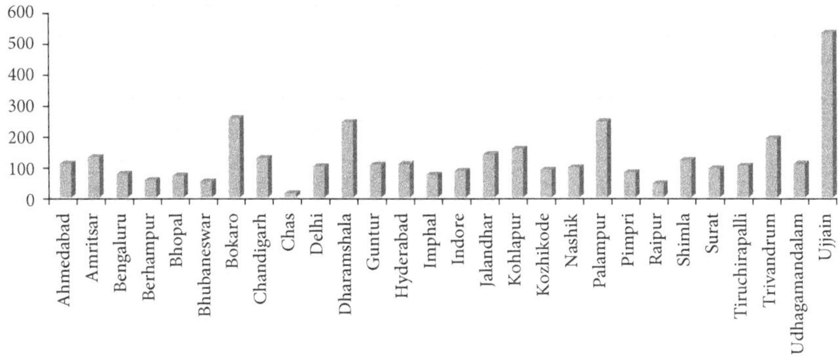

Figure 18.11. Water connections per thousand persons

Source: Based on data from the Ministry of Urban Development in partnership with the Water and Sanitation Program (WSP) (2010).

In Bokaro, Nashik, Shimla, and Dharamshala everyone is served by an organized water supply system, whereas in Chas, Berharmpur, and Raipur, less than 30 per cent of the total population is served by a water supply system (Figure 18.12). Note that rapid population growth in cities distorts this indicator significantly.

Figure 18.13 shows O&M (operations and maintenance) expenditure per connection. O&M expenditure on utilities comprises energy (40 per cent), personnel (27 per cent), establishment costs, debt servicing, and so on. In Shimla, most of the expenses are attributed to personnel, whereas they are due to energy costs in Surat. Annual per connection expenditure is calculated by dividing total O&M expenditure by number of connections. An analysis of twenty-eight cities shows that annual per connection expenditure is highest in Bangalore (Rs 6,873), trailed by Bhubaneswar (Rs 6,627) and Imphal (Rs 6,359), and lowest in Chas (Rs 904). Mean annual per connection O&M expenditure is Rs 3,415.

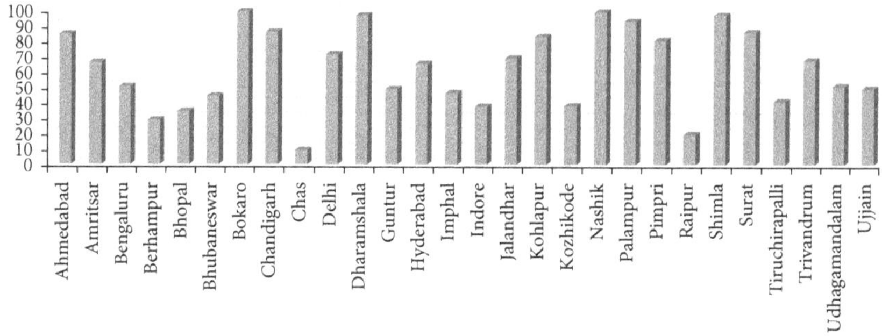

Figure 18.12. Water supply coverage (% population served)

Source: Based on data from the Ministry of Urban Development in partnership with the Water and Sanitation Program (WSP) (2010).

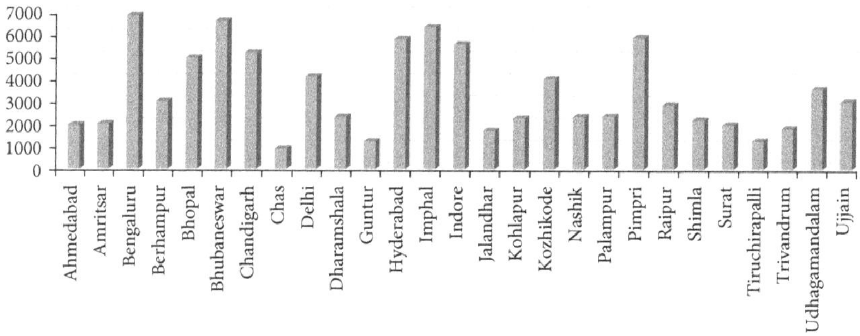

Figure 18.13. O&M expenditure per connection (Rs)

Source: Based on data from the Ministry of Urban Development in partnership with the Water and Sanitation Program (WSP) (2010).

Figure 18.14 presents the sewerage networks of twenty-eight cities. On average, the network covers 61 per cent of properties. Here again, like water services, we observe a great variability among cities. There are cities like Chandigarh and Bokaro where almost all properties are connected to a sewerage network. On the other hand, there are cities like Bhopal, Guntur, and Bhubaneswar where even 20 per cent of properties are not covered by a sewerage network.

Wastewater generation is linked to availability of water for use. Wastewater collection efficiency is defined as the quantity of wastewater collected as a percentage of average sewage generation in a ULB. Wastewater collection efficiency in Indian cities is generally poor. The average efficiency is about 55 per cent, with the highest efficiency being that of Nashik. Cities like Bhubaneswar, Bhopal, Shimla, and Dharamshala report less than 20 per cent efficiency in collection of wastewater (Figure 18.15).

Figure 18.16 shows O&M expenditure per connection. O&M expenditure of utilities comprises energy, personnel, etc. Annual per connection expenditure is

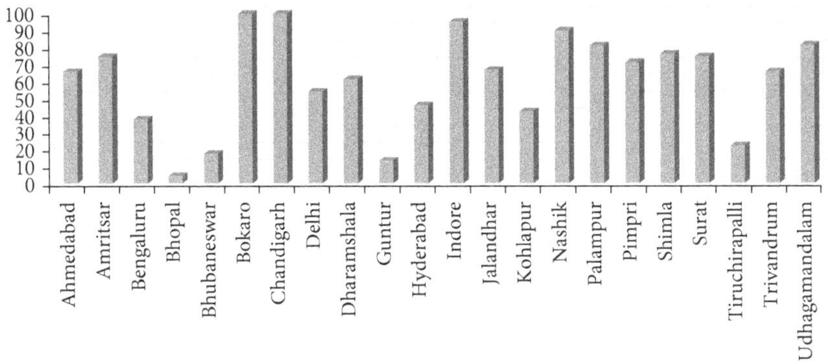

Figure 18.14. Sewerage network coverage (%)

Source: Based on data from the Ministry of Urban Development in partnership with the Water and Sanitation Program (WSP) (2010).

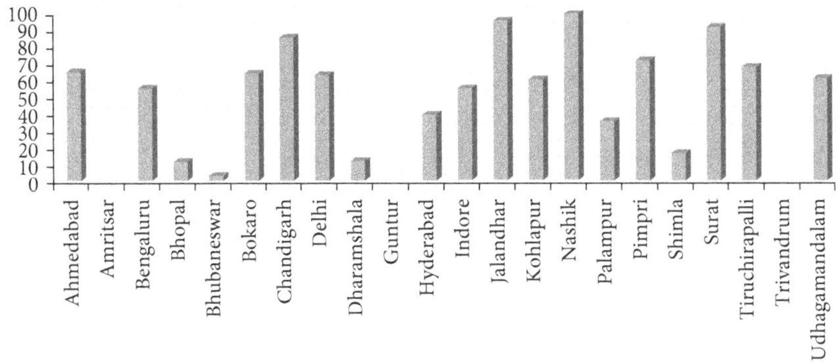

Figure 18.15. Water collection efficiency (%)

Source: Based on data from the Ministry of Urban Development in partnership with the Water and Sanitation Program (WSP) (2010).

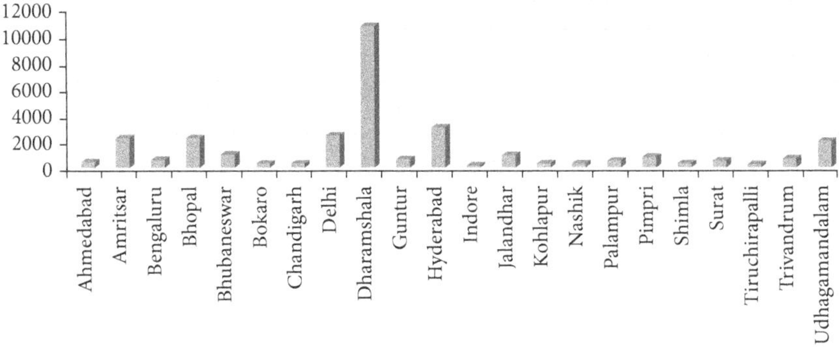

Figure 18.16. Expenditure per connection (Rs)

Source: Based on data from the Ministry of Urban Development in partnership with the Water and Sanitation Program (WSP) (2010).

calculated by dividing total O&M expenditure by number of connections. An analysis of twenty-eight cities shows that annual per connection expenditure is highest in Dharamshala, which is more than Rs 10,000, followed by about Rs 3,000 in Hyderabad, with the lowest in Indore (Rs 125). Mean annual per connection O&M expenditure is Rs 1,360.

18.2.3 Loss Due to Inadequacy of Services

Diarrheal diseases are major causes of death due to lack of proper water and sanitation facilities across countries (World Bank 2011). Many epidemiological studies show a relationship between water and sanitation amenities and human capital; these studies argue that there exists a causal relationship between lack of water and sanitation facilities and prevalence of diarrheal diseases. A study using country-level data from demographic and health surveys shows that open defecation is a main cause of child stunting (Spears et al. 2013). Spears et al. (2013) show a positive association between the rate of open defecation and the number of stunted children at district level (Figure 18.17). Note that vulnerable sections of society, such as the poor, women, and children, are affected more in comparison

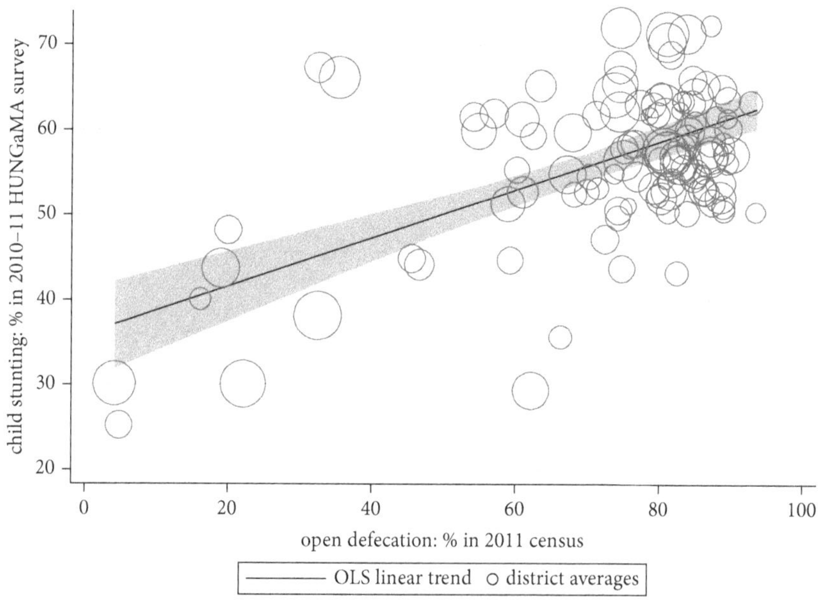

Figure 18.17. Relationship between open defecation and child stunting in India
Source: Spears et al. (2013).

to other groups in society. A National Sample Survey Organization (NSSO 2010) survey shows that between 10 and 20 per cent of notified and non-notified slums, respectively, had no latrine facilities.

Epidemiological studies have established a link between water and sanitation facilities and human health; these studies have not estimated the economic costs of the inadequacy of these services. There is a scarcity of studies on the benefits of water and sanitation provision in India, especially in the urban sector. Zérah (2000) estimated that an average household in Delhi spent about Rs 2,000 annually as coping costs due to the unreliable water supply in the city, which is more than five times the amount they were paying to municipalities as water charges. Similarly, in a household survey, Misra and Goldar (2008) find that an average household in Delhi used to pay Rs 16 per kilolitre as a managing cost against Rs 6 per kilolitre incurred by the Delhi Jal Board as an operating cost, reflecting the fact that consumers in Delhi have been paying almost three times the operating cost in terms of managing strategies to mitigate the effects of poor delivery. McKenzie and Ray (2009) estimate that India loses about Rs 6 billion annually due to unsafe and contaminated water supplies delivered to urban of households.

Anselin et al. (2008) estimate marginal willingness to pay for an increase of one day per week in water availability using a hedonic approach for Bhopal and Bangalore. Note that these cities are not getting water seven days a week. On average, households have access to water around three days per week in both cities. However, distribution of water availability is quite diverse for Bhopal and Bangalore. While for Bhopal, more than 80 per cent of households are concentrated on the tails of water access distribution, having either zero or seven days of water availability, in Bangalore, 50 per cent of households have water available four days in a week. In both the cities, the contingent valuation method using a stochastic payment card was used to value access to improved water supply. For Bangalore, the resulting point estimate of willingness to pay is Rs 119.62 for 'definitely yes', while for Bhopal it is Rs 45.14. For 'probably yes', they are Rs 170.12 and Rs 119.34 respectively.

All these estimates of city-specific case studies shows that in the absence of adequate water facilities, urban households have to bear a substantial monetary loss. These coping costs are well below the water supply costs that urban water utilities have to incur. But none of the studies provide estimates of economic costs at the country or state level. Moreover, there is a need for more studies to understand the real economic costs of inadequacy in water services.

Though there are few studies measuring the economic costs of inadequacy of safe water services, we located a single study that has estimated the economic cost of the inadequacy of sanitation facilities in India. WSP (2010) estimates economic costs for both rural and urban areas using secondary data. This study finds that

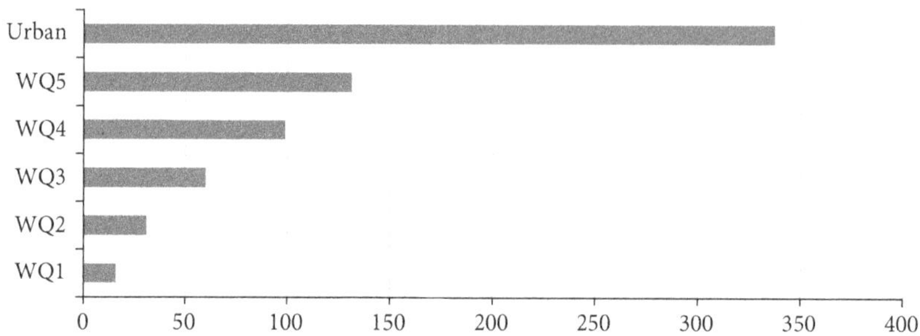

Figure 18.18. Economic effects of inadequate sanitation in urban India, 2006 (Rs billion)
Source: WSP (2010).

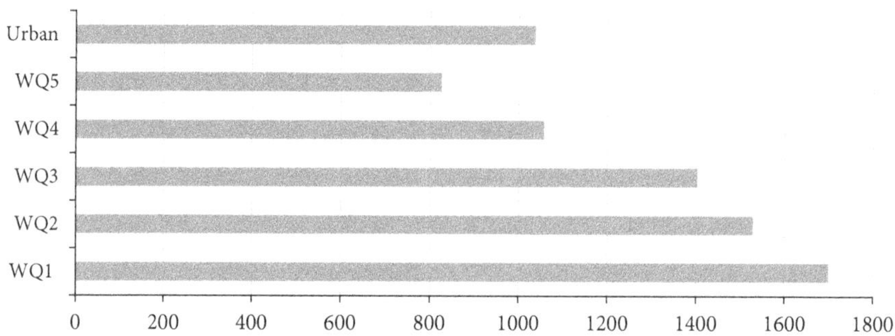

Figure 18.19. Per capita economic effects of inadequate sanitation in urban India 2006 (Rs)
Source: WSP (2010).

the country lost 6.4 per cent of GDP in terms of immature deaths and diseases in 2006. Health-related economic impacts account for about 72 per cent of total economic costs that India has to bear in the absence of adequate sanitation facilities. Figure 18.18 and Figure 18.19 present aggregate and per capita economic impacts for urban areas for 2006. Notice that the poor are disproportionately affected due to the lack of these basic sanitation facilities. Figure 18.19 shows that per capita loss in the lowest wealth quintile (WQ1) is much higher in comparison to the highest wealth quintile (WQ5) and the national average.

Similarly, the World Bank (2013) provides estimates of economic impacts arising due to the inadequacy of water, sanitation, and hygiene. The total economic impact that urban India has to bear amounts to Rs 155 billion in 2009. These impacts include mortality and morbidity losses. In addition to that, urban India has to spend Rs 38 billion on the activities which they have to perform due to the absence of safe drinking water such as purchasing bottled water and purification of drinking water.

18.2.4 Urbanization, Water, and Sanitation in India

The Census of 2011 shows that absolute growth of the urban population was more than that of the rural population in last decade. As cities become bigger, they generate various kinds of economies and diseconomies of scale. There is a need to understand the implications for urban infrastructure such as water and sanitation facilities. Bettencourt et al. (2007) and Bettencourt (2013) show that varied urban features, for example infrastructure, water and sanitation, energy consumption, employment, and innovation, are related to population size, and there is a power-scaling relationship between many of features of a city and its population size (i.e. $Y(t) = Y_0 N(t)^{\beta}$). It is expected that β usually equals one for individual human needs, while its value is less than one for infrastructural features, implying economies of scale. For features such as knowledge, and innovations that are associated with the intrinsically social nature of cities, its value is generally greater than one, implying higher returns to scale.

Table 18.2 shows a log–log relationship between water consumption in a city and its population size. The approximate linear relationship suggests a dependence of urban water consumption upon population, following a power-law scaling relationship. Here it should be noted that though the β value is 0.93, it is not statistically different from one, implying an absence of economies of scale. But it becomes significantly less than one as we control for a city's water supply management (having a dummy equal to one if a city's water supply is managed by the city board in place of a municipality or state government) and a city's participation in the Jawaharlal Nehru National Urban Renewal Mission (JNNURM). In our sample, four cities have city boards for managing the water supply system and sixteen cities have participated in the JNNURM. This implies that management structure or other forms of policy interventions are required to solve city problems (Batty 2013), that is, effective and autonomous management of water supply plays an important role in harnessing economies of scale associated with urbanization.

Table 18.2. Relationship between population and water consumed

Dependent variable: ln (total water consumed)			
Intercept	−7.69***	−7.19***	−6.34***
	(−6.03)	(−5.60)	(−5.64)
ln(population)	0.93***	0.89***	0.80***
	(10.85)	(10.03)	(9.57)
City board dummy		0.58	0.64
		(1.67)*	(1.56)
JNNURM dummy			0.55
			(1.63)*
R^2	0.83	0.84	0.85
Number of observations	28		

Box 18.1. A power-law relationship in sanitation infrastructure

$$\ln(\textit{waste water collection}) = -8.77 + 0.966 \ln(\textit{population}) + 0.479 \textit{ City board Dummy}$$

(t-stat) (−6.25) (10.13) (2.21)

R^2: 0.83, Number of Observations: 27

As far as the application of the power-scaling relationship is concerned with respect to sanitation infrastructure, we find an absence of economies of scale in Indian cities (Box 18.1). As discussed later, we observe that most Indian sanitation providers are working under increasing returns to scale, i.e. they are not optimally utilizing their plant sizes; therefore, to realize economies of scale in the use of sanitation facilities, we need effective public policy interventions.

18.3 Performance of Urban Water and Sanitation Utilities in India

18.3.1 Water

The above discussion reveals that there is a severe shortage of water, that sanitation facilities adversely impact the living standards of people in urban India, and that solutions may be found in improving the efficiency of water and sanitation providers. Therefore, it is imperative to measure the level of inefficiency of these service providers given the scarcity of resources. Measuring the efficiency of service providers will also help in finding appropriate policy measures to help improve the efficiency of providing these services. We use data envelopment analysis (DEA) for calculating technical efficiency estimates of water and sanitation service providers in twenty-eight pilot cities. An attempt is also made to find the determinants of service providers' performance.[1] Surprisingly, we could not find any performance measurement for sanitation facility providers using a total factor productivity approach, and the present study fills this gap in the policy and academic utility performance literature.

We follow the output-oriented DEA approach for measuring technical efficiency and consider a service provider to be a service-producing unit. In this case study we consider three outputs and two inputs. The two inputs considered are: O&M expenditure during a year as a proxy for variable inputs, and water treatment capacity as representing the capital stock of a utility. O&M expenditure includes

[1] See Kumar (2010), Kumar and Managi (2010), and Gupta et al. (2012) for applications of performance measurement of Indian water utilities.

energy, personnel, and other expenses of a utility. We have taken three outputs: water delivered to consumers, hours of supply, and water quality. The first output is considered as a proxy for the quantitative output of service providers, but the last two outputs capture quality dimensions of the service delivered. Note that consumers in urban India generally get intermittent supplies and near to ground-water quality, therefore the hours of supply and pass rates of chlorine tests are satisfactory measures of quality (Picazo-Tadeo et al. 2008; Kumar and Managi 2010).

We compute the technical efficiency of both water and sanitation utilities using three scenarios: only delivered water; delivered water and pass rate of chlorine tests; and delivered water, pass rate of chlorine tests, and hours of daily water supply. Note also that technical efficiency of water utilities has been computed under constant returns to scale (CRS), variable returns to scale (VRS), and non-increasing returns to scale (NRS). Figures 18.20 through 18.22 present estimates of pure technical efficiency (i.e. VRS), scale efficiency, and optimal technical efficiency (i.e. CRS) of water utilities.

Technical efficiency estimates. Figure 18.20 provides estimates of technical efficiency under the first scenario when only the quantity of delivered water has been considered as an output of the utilities. Estimates show that water utilities of Palampur and Dharamshala are the most efficient both in terms of technical as well as scale efficiencies. In Palampur, O&M expenditure per MLD (million litres per day) of water is lowest, which is Rs 1.10 million. Similarly, in the case of Dharamshala, we find that the ratio of delivered to total water produced is the highest, followed by Palampur. Imphal and Bhubaneswar are the utilities that are found to be least efficient, where these utilities have the lowest ratio of delivered to total water produced. Average urban water utilities in India operate at two-thirds of their potential under the CRS scenario and the level of efficiency increases to

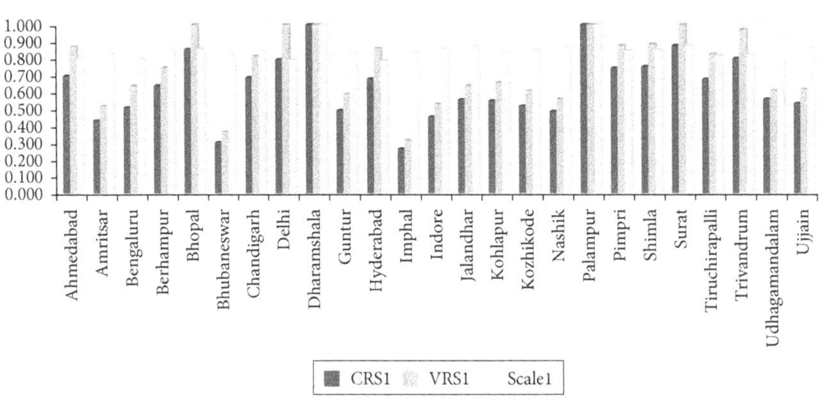

Figure 18.20. Technical efficiency of urban water utilities (only delivered water included as output)

CRS1 = constant returns to scale, VRS1 = variable returns to scale, Scale1 = scale efficiency.

Source: Author's computation.

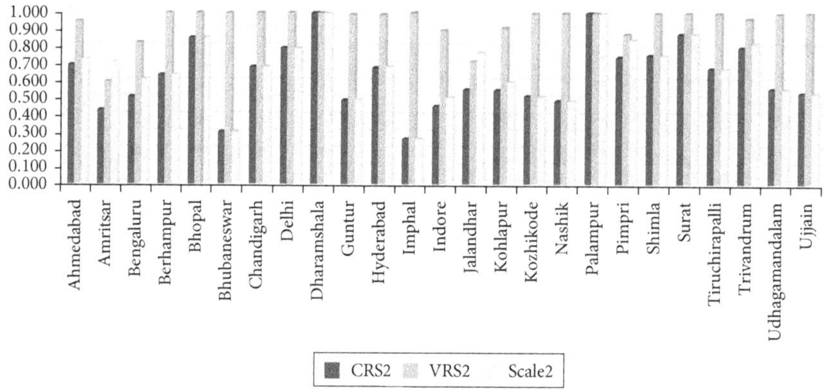

Figure 18.21. Technical efficiency of urban water utilities (delivered water and pass rate of chlorine test included as outputs)

CRS2 = constant returns to scale, VRS2 = variable returns to scale, Scale2 = scale efficiency.

Source: Author's computation.

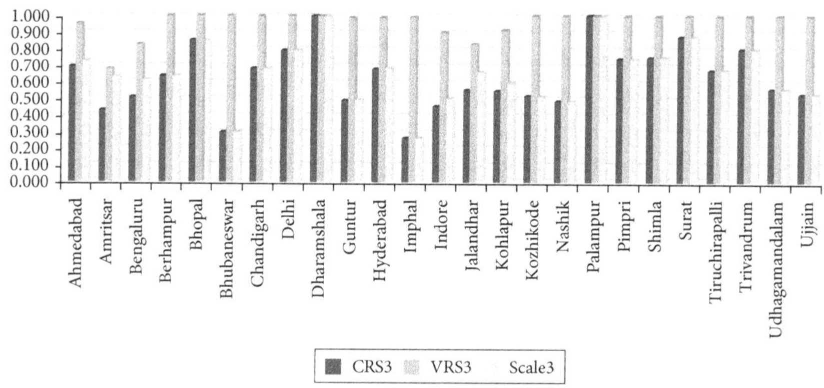

Figure 18.22. Technical efficiency of urban water utilities (delivered water, pass rate of chlorine tests, and hours of supply included as outputs)

CRS3 = constant returns to scale, VRS3 = variable returns to scale, Scale3 = scale efficiency.

Source: Author's computation.

0.74 if the restriction of CRS is relaxed and the utility is allowed to operate under the VRS scenario. This implies that about 15 per cent inefficiency exists, since utilities are not operating at an optimal scale and the rest of the inefficiency may be due to non-professional management of Indian urban water utilities.

Figures 18.21 and 18.22 present quality-adjusted estimates of technical efficiency. Palampur and Dharamshala again come out on the frontier when both water quantity and quality parameters are considered. The mean technical efficiency under CRS, VRS, and scale efficiency is 0.63, 0.95, and 0.67, respectively, when adjusted for the pass rate of chlorine tests only, and are 0.63, 0.96, and 0.66, respectively, when adjusted for both pass rate of chlorine tests and hours of supply. Quality-adjusted statistics of performance show that although adjustment for quality does not change the overall performance of utilities, pure technical and scale efficiencies are affected. About a third of inefficiencies can be attributed to the inappropriate scale of operations. Improving the management of these utilities can reduce the remaining inefficiencies. To understand the significance of adjusting for qualitative factors, let us choose a utility randomly. For Chandigarh, a conventional measure of pure technical and scale efficiency levels are 0.81 and 0.84 respectively, implying that a proper scale operation could increase its performance by 16 per cent, but when we adjust for quality parameters the utility comes out as efficient in terms of pure technical efficiency, and the inefficiency could be attributed to scale parameters. Under VRS, the potential cost of maintaining quality is about 19 per cent of its potential output. To confirm the results that quality does matter in performance measurement, we conduct tests for equality of means and variances of performance results under different scenarios. To understand that quality does matter in the ranking of utilities, we conduct the Spearman's rank correlation between conventional and quality-adjusted measures of performance. Moreover, we also conduct the Spearman's rank correlation test to judge whether the sample water utilities rank differently according to their conventional and quality-adjusted measures of performance. Tests results are provided in Table 18.3. Table 18.4 shows that management also matters in the performance of a water utility. We find that utilities managed by city boards are doing better than their peers managed by either state governments or municipalities. Note that city boards have some amount of managerial autonomy in comparison to utilities managed by state governments or municipalities.

Scale economies: Estimates of scale efficiency provide an idea about whether a utility has been using its resources optimally. Figures 18.17 to 18.19 provide estimates of scale efficiency under different scenarios. These figures show that

Table 18.3. Quantity-based and quality-adjusted (for both hours of supply and positive rate of quality tests) measures of technical efficiency

	t-test[a] (t-statistics)	F-test[b] (z-statistics)	Spearman test[c] (Spearman ρ)
Quantity-based versus quality-adjusted (VRS)	1.878 (−0.067)	6.995 (0.000)	0.332 (0.105)
Quantity-based versus quality-adjusted (scale)	5.190 (0.000)	0.085 (0.000)	0.134 (0.523)

Notes: [a] H_0: means are equal. [b] H_0: both distributions are same. [c] H_0: both variables are independent. Values in parentheses are p-values.

Source: Author's computations.

Table 18.4. Technical efficiency by management group

Management	CRS1	VRS1	Scale1	CRS2	VRS2	Scale2	CRS3	VRS3	Scale3
City board	0.66	0.83	0.79	0.66	0.94	0.70	0.66	0.94	0.70
State board	0.56	0.67	0.84	0.56	0.99	0.57	0.56	1.00	0.56
Municipality	0.64	0.74	0.87	0.64	0.94	0.69	0.64	0.96	0.67
Overall Average	0.63	0.74	0.85	0.63	0.95	0.67	0.63	0.96	0.66

Source: author's computations.

Table 18.5. Returns to scale (water utilities)

Returns to scale	City
Constant returns to scale (optimal scale)	Dharamshala, Palampur
Decreasing returns to scale	Ahmedabad, Amritsar, Bengaluru, Bhopal, Chandigarh, Delhi, Hyderabad, Indore, Jalandhar, Kohlapur, Nashik, Pimri, Surat, Trivandrum, Bhubaneswar, Tiruchirapalli, Ujjain, Bokaro, Chas, Shimla, Udhagamandalam

Source: Author's computations.

except for the utilities of Dharamshala and Palampur (Table 18.5), none of them are operating at an optimal scale. This implies that these utilities can improve their performance by changing the level of their operation. The results indicate that most urban water utilities are operating under decreasing returns to scale (DRS). Economic efficiency can be ensured by following the rule of marginal cost pricing if utilities are operating under DRS.

Another objective of the case study is to understand the underlying factors that cause variation in measures of performance of these water utilities, i.e. utility-specific attributes that contribute to the level of performance. Therefore, we regress various performance measures against utility-specific attributes, and regress various measures of efficiency on utility-specific variables such as management, NRW, and consumption metering.[2] To examine the relationship between different measures of performance and management, we included a dummy for management: 1 for the utilities where parastatals (city boards) either completely or partially manage a utility and 0 for others, per capita per day water supplied (lpcd), non-revenue water, consumption metering, labour per connection, JNNURM dummy, network length, and lpcd.

Table 18.6 provides the regression results. We observe a negative association between NRW and various measures of efficiency. We find that city board management is positively associated with performance of water utilities in all three regressions. Utilities that are providing higher lpcd hire less labour per connection and their participation in the JNNURM enhances their performance. Lengthy network and groundwater sources of water decrease the performance of water utilities, although the coefficients are not statistically significant.

[2] Truncated regression with bootstrapped standard errors is often used with censored data and is suitable for analysis of efficiency scores (Khanna and Kumar 2012). Therefore, in the present study, truncated regression with bootstrapped standard errors has been used to find the determinants of inefficiency of water utilities.

Table 18.6. Determinants of technical efficiency of water providers in India

	Constant returns to scale		Variable returns to scale		Scale efficiency	
	Coefficient	z-statistics	Coefficient	z-statistics	Coefficient	z-statistics
Non-revenue Water (%)	−0.0079***	−2.89	−0.0012	−0.96	−0.0071***	−2.93
Consumption metering (%)	0.0014*	1.95	0.0001	0.37	0.0013*	1.66
Water source: surface (%)	0.0011	0.9	0.0018*	1.8	0.0000	−0.02
Labour per connection	−5.6636	−0.71	4.2138	1.52	−8.1703	−1.11
City board dummy	0.2416*	1.89	−0.0408	−0.64	0.2648**	2.04
JNNURM dummy	0.0413	0.43	−0.0247	−0.44	0.0551	0.59
ln(length of network)	−0.0635	−1.14	0.0049	0.26	−0.0656	−1.41
ln(Lpcd)	0.1480	1.11	0.0176	0.25	0.1392	1.27
Intercept	0.6389	0.86	0.7327**	2.02	0.7909	1.51
Sigma	0.0931***	4.03	0.0473***	5.62	0.0898***	4.58
Log likelihood	23.522		40.680		24.216	
Number of observations	24		24		24	

*** 1 per cent level of significance, ** 5 per cent level of significance, * 10 per cent level of significance.
Source: Author's computations.

18.3.2 Sanitation

For measuring the performance of sanitation providers, we consider wastewater collection as single output produced using two inputs: O&M expenditure and water consumed in the jurisdiction of a utility. As mentioned earlier, wastewater generation is linked to water consumption in a household. We measure performance under CRS, VRS, and NRS, like water utilities. Table 18.7 provides estimates of the technical efficiency, pure technical efficiency, and scale efficiency of sanitation providers in pilot cities. Efficiency estimates reveal that Ujjain, Tiruchirapalli, Bhubaneswar, Bhopal, Delhi, Bangalore, Chas, and Palampur are operating at the frontier in terms of pure technical efficiency. Three cities, namely, Ujjain, Tiruchirapalli, and Bhubaneswar, are also operating at the optimal scale of operation. In Ujjain and Tiruchirapalli, O&M expenses are negligible, at least among the sample cities. On the other side, Amritsar, Dharamshala, Shimla, and Udhagamandalam are operating at less than 40 per cent of their potential in terms of pure technical efficiency. These cities have the potential to increase

Table 18.7. Technical efficiencies of urban sanitation providers in India

Management	ULB	Pure technical efficiency	Scale efficiency	Technical efficiency at CRS*
City board	Bengaluru	1	0.595	0.595
	Bokaro	0.521	0.99	0.515
	Delhi	1	0.412	0.412
	Hyderabad	0.943	0.477	0.45
	Average	0.866	0.619	0.493
Municipality	Ahmedabad	0.752	0.477	0.358
	Amritsar	0.372	0.964	0.358
	Bhopal	1	0.629	0.629
	Chandigarh	0.98	0.618	0.606
	Chas	1	0.358	0.358
	Dharamshala	0.385	0.925	0.356
	Guntur	0.461	0.986	0.455
	Indore	0.787	0.962	0.758
	Jalandhar	0.513	0.907	0.465
	Kohlapur	0.763	0.956	0.73
	Nashik	0.541	0.749	0.405
	Palampur	1	0.275	0.275
	Pimpri	0.585	0.602	0.352
	Shimla	0.364	0.982	0.357
	Surat	0.781	0.574	0.448
	Tiruchirapalli	1	1	1
	Udhagamandalam	0.311	0.939	0.292
	Ujjain	1	1	1
	Average	0.700	0.772	0.511
State board	Bhubaneswar	1	1	1
	Trivandrum	0.526	0.681	0.358
	Average	0.763	0.841	0.679
Overall average		0.731	0.753	0.522

*CRS = constant returns to scale.

Source: Author's computations.

wastewater collectionby about 2.5 times through better managerial practices. Udhagamandalam is the least efficient in collection of wastewater. This city has the second highest collection cost per MLD, followed by Chandigarh. For the sample utilities average performance is 0.52, implying that utilities on average can collect about 48 per cent more wastewater with given resources. About 25 per cent of the potential could be realized by better managerial practices, and to harness the remaining potential utilities have to operate at the desired scales.

To understand the role of managerial autonomy in the performance of a sanitation service provider, utilities are divided into three categories: utilities managed by municipalities, state boards, and parastatal bodies. Note that parastatal bodies are relatively functionally autonomous in comparison to their counterpart utilities managed by municipalities and state boards. The results provided in Table 18.7 show

Table 18.8. Returns to scale of sanitation utilities

Returns to scale	City
Constant returns to scale (optimal scale)	Bhubaneswar, Tiruchirapalli, Ujjain
Increasing returns to scale	Bokaro, Chas, Dharamshala, Palampur, Shimla, Udhagamandalam
Decreasing returns to scale	Ahmedabad, Amritsar, Bengaluru, Bhopal, Chandigarh, Delhi, Hyderabad, Indore, Jalandhar, Kohlapur, Nashik, Pimri, Surat, Trivandrum

Source: Author's computations.

that utilities managed by city boards are doing better than their peers managed by municipalities and state boards in terms of pure technical efficiency. This implies that they follow better managerial practices. However, the overall technical efficiency of these utilities is lower than their peers because they do not operate at the required scale.

Table 18.8 indicates that only three of the utilities are functioning at an optimal scale and six cities are working under IRS (increasing returns to scale). But all remaining cities, that is, fourteen water utilities, are functioning under DRS. Scale of operation, per se, is linked with size of a utility measured in terms of population served by it. Smaller utilities are functioning at IRS. These results have implications for urban sanitation pricing. Note that utilities operating under IRS are generally smaller in comparison to their counterparts, but to get economic efficiency in provision of sanitation facilities utilities operating under DRS can follow the marginal cost-pricing rule.

18.4 Central Government's Policy Initiatives and Gaps

As stated in Section 18.2.1, providing water and sanitation services is a responsibility of local governments, but central and state governments also play a pivotal role in the provision of these services. In this section, we briefly review the steps taken by the central, states and local governments for augmenting the services. Note that the central government has been a main source of finance in the area and stipulates universal norms and guidelines across the country. Figure 18.23 shows the initiatives of the central government.

The central government initiated efforts for providing water and sanitation facilities way back in the late 1970s. To provide drinking water in cities and towns the central government launched programmes such as Integrated Development for Small and Medium Towns in 1979 and the Accelerated Urban Water Supply

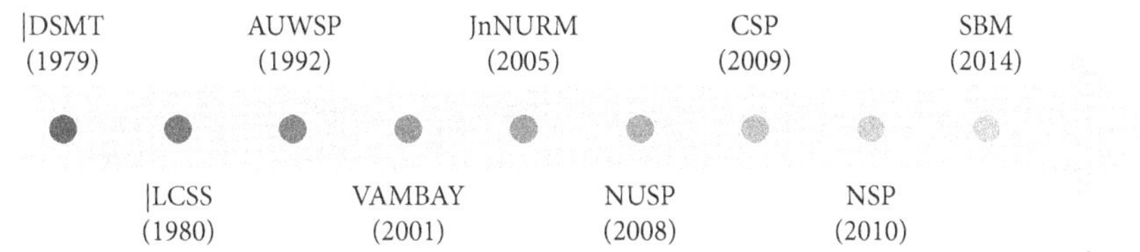

Figure 18.23. Evolution of central government-sponsored schemes in urban water and sanitation
Source: TERI (2016).

Programme in 1992. Similarly, in the sanitation sector, the first central government effort was an initiation of Integrated Low Cost Sanitation Scheme in 1980. The scheme was aimed at providing subsidies to households for buying low-cost toilets. The National Slum Development Project was started to construct community toilets in slum areas and was later replaced with a programme known as Valmiki Ambedkar Awas Yojana in 2001.

A landmark shift in urban reforms came with the unveiling of the JNNURM in 2005. The JNNURM was aimed at providing basic amenities like housing, water supply, sanitation, road networks, urban transport, and the development of inner city areas in sixty-three cities. The government of India created an Inter-Ministerial Task Force to frame national policy on universal urban sanitation with an objective of community-driven, totally sanitized cities and towns known as Nirmal Shahar in 2005. Since, initially, the JNNURM was aimed at large cities, in 2005 the Urban Infrastructure Development Scheme for Small and Medium Towns was started with a focus on urban infrastructure provisions. Within this scheme a subscheme known as 'Basic Services for Urban Poor' was initiated targeting the neglected urban poor.

Similarly, to create cities free from open defecation, the National Urban Sanitation Policy (NUSP) was initiated in 2008. Note that the NUSP was a paradigm shift in the Indian approach towards sanitation since this policy emphasizes both developing infrastructure and behavioural change. The policy provides a framework for developing city sanitation plans. About 150 city governments were funded for preparing city sanitation plans.

Note that the central government's efforts for providing universal urban water and sanitation facilities do not remain confined to investment programmes such as JNNURM, Swachh Bharat Mission (SBM), and policies and advisories such as NUSP, but also take initiatives for creating a sense of competition among the cities, that is ranking of cities and SLB. In 2010, a National Sanitation Rating Survey was conducted in 423 cities for raising awareness about urban sanitation and recognizing the performance of cities. The SLB was initially piloted for twenty-eight cities, which was scaled up to more than 1,756 cities in 2012.

These plans have shifted their focus from just developing infrastructure to including service delivery. However, note that these plans have fallen short of the required investments at municipal level, implying that more finance and guidelines are needed to ensure consistency and quality of city-level water and sanitation reforms (TERI 2016).

The present government is specifically focusing on these areas, and on 2 October 2014 it launched the biggest drive to accelerate efforts towards eliminating open defecation, obtaining universal sanitation coverage, and improving cleanliness by 2 October 2019, known as SBM. Under the mission to develop infrastructure the government is supposed to spend about US$10 billion. The mission is targeted at introducing new toilet technologies and bringing about behavioural changes through campaigns and public awareness programmes.

The Atal Mission for Rejuvenation and Urban Transformation is another important initiative in this area. Moreover, the Ministry of Urban Development has recently started an initiative for ranking seventy-three cities with a population of more than one million on cleanliness and sanitation. This initiative is known as Swachh Survekshan 2016. This initiative would help cities to know their absolute and relative status in providing basic water and sanitation facilities.

Note that all these initiatives from the central government are aimed at providing the infrastructure and guidelines to provide basic clean water and sanitation facilities. All programmes from the central government recognize the importance of providing basic services to the poor. For example, aiming at universal coverage of water supply and toilets recognizes the centrality of delivering services to the poor. These programmes and policies also need to recover operation and maintenance expenses as user charges, but are not clear on whether local city governments have the required resources, personnel, and operating systems to manage their systems properly. Similarly, SLB programmes give an idea of the delivery of services without giving due consideration to resource utilization. There is a need to improve the efficiency of urban water and sanitation facilities. Note that the guidelines provided in these initiatives generally do not recognize local needs and conditions, that is, 'one size fits all' cannot work and they need to provide functional autonomy to local bodies in the provision of these services.

18.5 Conclusions

Over the years, many epidemiological studies have reflected on the significance of interventions in areas of sanitation, hygiene, and water quality and quantity that help realize the benefits of urbanization. The present study shows that the management and governance of basic amenities like water and sanitation services play a significant role in realizing the economies of scale offered by urbanization. The power-law scaling relationship between water supply and urbanization reveals that in the water supply sector, economies of scale are linked to the management of these services. Autonomy in management and incentives in the water and sanitation sector are important for harnessing the benefits of urbanization.

Efficiency results show that, at the mean level, an average Indian water utility provider has substantial potential for increasing the service level. The potential can be realized by functioning at the optimal level, since many water utilities are functioning at decreasing returns to scale. Moreover, efficiency results also have implications for urban domestic water pricing. The sample utilities are functioning either at constant or decreasing returns to scale, implying that water should be priced following the rule of marginal cost pricing.

The regression results disclose that NRW and metering of water connections are major determinants of performance for water utilities. Reduction in NRW should be an area of concern for water utilities. Note that reduction in NRW requires resources. The results also reveal that metering helps in improving the technical efficiency of water utilities. Metering and proper pricing could help in reducing the NRW of utilities. Both these factors are linked with the governance and management of a water utility.

Untreated wastewater from urban settlements is one of the key challenges for better management of water and sanitation facilities in urban India. Note that in India less than 30 per cent of wastewater can be treated and most of this treatment capacity is confined to big metropolitan cities (Murty and Kumar 2011). Therefore, it should be emphasized that substantial investments are needed in the sector. Moreover, effective monitoring networks also help in moving in the desired direction.

There are both public and private dimensions to the challenge and a multi-pronged approach is required to address problems of inadequacy in water and sanitation services. There is a need to make substantial investments in the infrastructure of these facilities, not only to create new facilities but also for O&M of the existing ones. Proper tariff mechanisms based on principles of 'user pays' ensure improved cost recovery and better utilization of facilities. Moreover, sustained public awareness campaigns on links between health, water supply, sanitation, and hygiene are required.

Acknowledgements

I am thankful to Ms. Prerna Prabhakar for providing excellent research assistance, and the Asian Development Bank for financial support under the project technical assistance 8522: The Urbanization–Poverty–Inequality Triangle in Asia and the Pacific.

References

Anselin, L., N. Lozano-Gracia, U. Deichmann, and S. Lall. 2008. 'Valuing Access to Water: A spatial Hedonic Approach Applied to Indian Cities'. *World Bank Policy Research Working Paper 4533*.

Batty, Michael. 2013. 'A Theory of City Size'. *Science 340*: 1418–19.

Bettencourt, Luís M. A. 2013. 'The Origins of Scaling in Cities'. *Science 340*: 1438–41.

Bettencourt, L. M. A., J. Lobo, D. Helbing, C. Kuhnert, and G. B. West. 2007. 'Growth, Innovation, Scaling, and the Pace of Life in Cities'. *Proceedings of the National Academy of Sciences 104* (17): 7301–6.

Census of India. 2011. *2011 Census Data*, Ministry of Home Affairs, Government of India, New Delhi.

Gupta, Sreekant, Surender Kumar, and Gopal K. Sarangi. 2012. 'Measuring the Performance of Water Service Providers in Urban India: Implications for Managing Water Utilities'. *Water Policy 14* (3): 391–408.

Khanna, M. and S. Kumar. 2012. 'Corporate Environmental Management and Environmental Efficiency'. *Environmental and Resource Economics 50* (2): 227–42.

Kumar, Surender. 2010. 'Unaccounted for Water and Performance of Water Utilities: An Empirical Analysis from India'. *Water Policy 12*: 710–21.

Kumar, Surender and Shunsuke Managi. 2010. 'Service Quality and Performance Measurement: Evidence from Indian Water Sector'. *International Journal of Water Resources Development 26* (2): 173–91.

McKenzie, David and Isha Ray. 2009. 'Urban Water Supply in India: Status, Reform Options and Possible Lessons'. *Water Policy 11* (4): 442–60.

Mehta, M. and D. Mehta. 2014. 'Open Defecation in Cities: a Faltering India Story'. <http://ideasforindia.in/article.aspx?article_id=276>.

Ministry of Urban Development and Water and Sanitation Program (WSP). 2010. *Improving Service Outcomes. 2008–09, Service Level Benchmarking Data-book*, Water and Sanitation Program, New Delhi.

Misra, Smita and Bishwanath Goldar. 2008. 'Likely Impact of Reforming Water Supply and Sewerage Services in Delhi'. *Economic and Political Weekly 11*: 57–66.

Murty, M. N. and S. Kumar. 2011. 'Water Pollution in India: An Economic Appraisal, India Infrastructure Report. 2011'. *India Infrastructure Report 19*: 285–98.

NSSO (National Sample Survey Organization). 2010. 'Some Characteristics of Urban Slums 2008–09: NSS 65th Round (July. 2008-June. 2009) Report (No 534)'. National Sample Survey Office, National Statistical Organization, Ministry of Statistics and Programme Implementation, Government of India.

Picazo-Tadeo, Andrés J., Francisco J. Sáez-Fernández, and Francisco González-Gómez. 2008. 'Does Service Quality Matter in Measuring the Performance of Water Utilities?' *Utilities Policy 16*: 30–8.

Spears, Dean, Arabinda Ghosh, and Oliver Cumming. 2013. 'Open Defecation and Childhood Stunting in India: An Ecological Analysis of New Data from 112 Districts'. *PLoS One 8* (9): e73784.

TERI. 2016. 'Swachh Bharat Mission (Urban) Towards Cleaning India: A Policy Perspective, A Policy Brief, February'.

Water and Sanitation Program (WSP). 2010. *Economic Impact of Inadequate Sanitation in India, Water and Sanitation Program*, Delhi.

WHO-UN. 2014. *Progress on Drinking Water and Sanitation: 2014 Update*, World Health Organization, Geneva.

WHO-UNICEF. 2015. *Joint Monitoring Programme Update 2015*, World Health Organization and United National Children Fund.

World Bank. 2011. *Sanitation and Hygiene: Why They Matter*, World Bank, Washington, DC.

World Bank. 2013. *India Diagnostic Assessment of Select Environmental Challenges: An Analysis of Physical and Monetary Losses of Environmental Health and Natural Resources*, Disaster Management and Climate Change Unit, Sustainable Development Department, South Asia Region, New Delhi.

Zérah, Marie-Hélène. 2000. 'Household Strategies for Coping with Unreliable Water Supplies: the Case of Delhi'. *Habitat International 24*: 295–307.

19
Air Pollution and Traffic Congestion in Urban India

Surender Kumar

19.1 Introduction

Cities in India house nearly 31 per cent of country's population and generate about 58 per cent of GDP (MGI 2010). In cities people earn higher incomes and experience better quality of life. Positive benefits are realized since cities offer increasing returns to innovations and wealth creation and economies of scale in infrastructural facilities (Bettencourt et al. 2007; Bettencourt 2013). However, these positive benefits are restricted by the costs and frictions arising from congestion, such as crime, diseases, and pollution (Bettencourt et al. 2007; Bettencourt 2013; Desmet and Rossi-Hansberg 2013). These frictions are known as urban diseases.

Though urban India has been able to attract investment and talent, particularly in the last two decades, these attractions are not accompanied by the required infrastructural and basic amenities. The result is increased levels of urban air pollution and traffic congestion. According to a recent report from the World Health Organization, Delhi is the worst city in terms of air quality among 1,600 cities worldwide (WHO 2014). Delhi observed the levels of 153 and 286 micrograms per cubic metre ($\mu g/m^3$) of $PM_{2.5}$ and PM_{10} respectively, which were far above the prescribed limits. Similarly, monetary losses attributed to urban air pollution amount to Rs 1,103 billion or 1.7 per cent of GDP in 2009 (World Bank 2013).[1]

Industrialization and vehicular pollution are considered to be the main sources of urban air pollution; therefore, environmental regulations have been targeted at these specific areas. Note that the government approach towards control of pollution has mostly been based on legislation-based command-and-control measures. Though the need to use economic and fiscal instruments for pollution control was realized during the 1990s, their use has been limited (Kumar and Managi 2009). Moreover, note that an active judiciary and people's participation have been playing a considerable role in environmental protection in the country. To stem the tide of rising pollution in critically polluted cities, the Supreme Court

[1] In this chapter we concentrate particularly on the air pollution and traffic congestion problem in urban areas. For details on issues relating to water and sanitation, please see Chapter 18.

Surender Kumar., *Air Pollution and Traffic Congestion in Urban India* In: *Cities of Dragons and Elephants: Urbanization and Urban Development in China and India. Edited by:* Guanghua Wan and Ming Lu, Oxford University Press (2019). DOI: 10.1093/oso/9780198829225.003.0019

asked for city-specific action plans. Delhi was the first city to develop an action plan in 1996. According to Greenstone and Hanna (2014), so far the Supreme Court has asked seventeen cities to develop action plans. Further, in 1995, the Supreme Court ordered all new petrol-fuelled cars in the four major metro cities (Delhi, Mumbai, Kolkata, and Chennai) to be fitted with catalytic converters. In 1998, the policy was extended to forty-five other cities.

This chapter critically analyses the state of urban air pollution and traffic congestion in India. It has been divided into six sections, including the present one. Section 19.2 provides a description of temporal and spatial variations in the level of urban air pollution in the country and its sources, and provides an analysis of drivers of urban air pollution in the country. A descriptive analysis of the traffic congestion problem in the country is given in Section 19.3. Section 19.4 describes the extent of the economic consequences of these problems in the country. Steps taken by the government and society to lower the impacts of these problems are discussed in Section 19.5. Section 19.6 offers some concluding remarks.

19.2 Urban Air Pollution

The Central Pollution Control Board (CPCB 2012) provides an analysis of air quality level in 167 cities. It shows that SO_2 levels are within permissible limits for most of the cities (only 1 per cent are exceeding the National Ambient Air Quality Standards (NAAQS)); in about 12 per cent of the cities, air quality is either in the high or critical range with respect to NO_2 emissions; and as far as respirable suspended particulate matter (RSPM) is concerned, about 78 per cent of the cities are crossing the permissible limit of 60 $\mu g/m^3$. The CPCB report also reveals that levels of RSPM in most of the state capitals and industrial cities are in the critical region.

CPCB (2012) also provides an analysis of trends in emissions in thirty-five metropolitan cities—of these, five (15 per cent) and thirty-two (94 per cent) cities exceed the NAAQS with respect to NO_2 and PM_{10}. Figure 19.1 presents a picture of some major metropolitan cities in India. This figure reveals that ambient air quality has been improving in the cities of Delhi, Mumbai, and Chennai in recent years. In Mumbai, the emissions of sulfur and nitrogen are increasing but RSPM reveals a declining trend. Kolkata observes a very volatile trend in RSPM and a decreasing trend in sulfur emissions, but an increasing trend in nitrogen emissions. The recent increasing trend in air pollution level in Delhi could be attributed to increasing new vehicles, especially diesel vehicles, and unchecked emissions from industries and non-compressed natural gas (CNG) heavy vehicles (Kumar and Foster 2009).

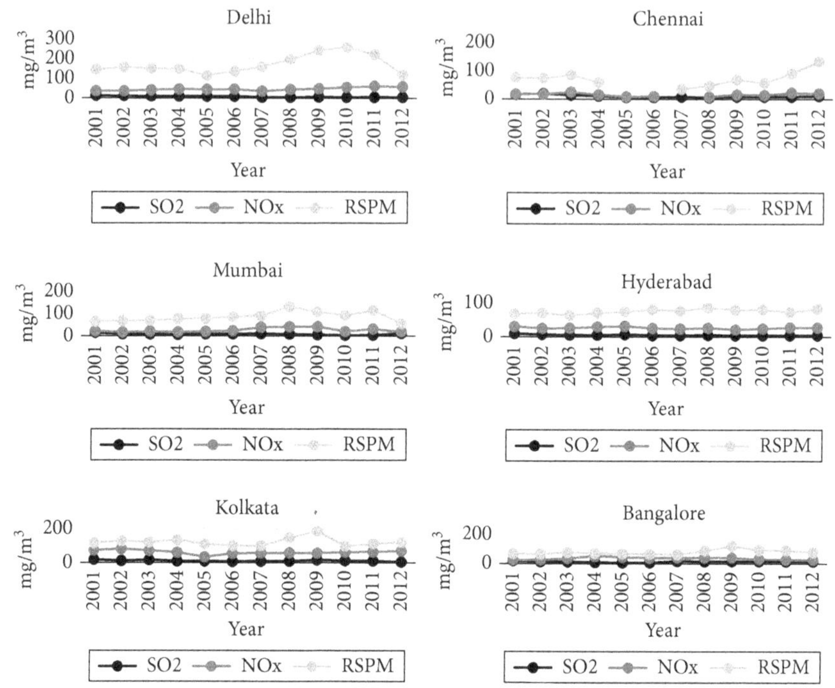

Figure 19.1. Emission trends in major metropolitan cities

NO_2 = nitrogen dioxide, RSPM = respirable suspended particulate matter, SO_2 = sulfur dioxide.

Source: Based on data downloaded from the Central Pollution Control Board, <http://cpcbedb.nic.in> (accessed 24 August 2014).

19.2.1 Sources of Air Pollution

Vehicular pollution. A CPCB (2010) study reveals that in six cities—Bangalore, Chennai, Delhi, Kanpur, Mumbai, and Pune—the transport sector contributes more than 30 per cent of ambient air pollution either directly from vehicle exhaust or indirectly via the resuspension of dust on roads due to vehicle movements. Guttikunda and Mohan (2014) find that in major cities for which the data of registered vehicles are available, vehicular pollution accounts for 30–40 per cent of the national on-road total emissions.[2]

Figures 19.2 and 19.3 show a distribution of vehicular pollution in Delhi according to vehicles and fuel types. These figures show that though the share of two-wheelers is the largest in population of vehicles, four-wheelers contribute the

[2] These major cities are Agra, Ahmedabad, Bangalore, Bhopal, Bhubaneswar, Chandigarh, Chennai, Coimbatore, Delhi (including its satellite cities), Dhanbad, Guwahati, Hyderabad, Indore, Jaipur, Kanpur, Kochi, Kolkata, Lucknow, Ludhiana, Mumbai, Nagpur, Patna, Pune, Ranchi, Surat, Trivandrum, Vadodara, Varanasi, and Vishakhapatnam.

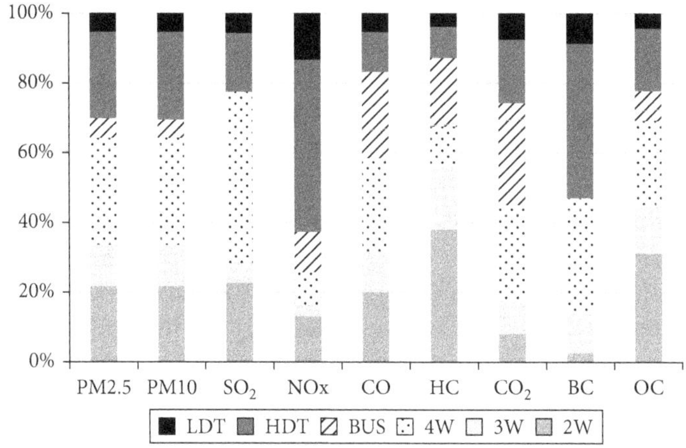

Figure 19.2. Share of emissions from passenger and freight vehicles in Delhi, 2011

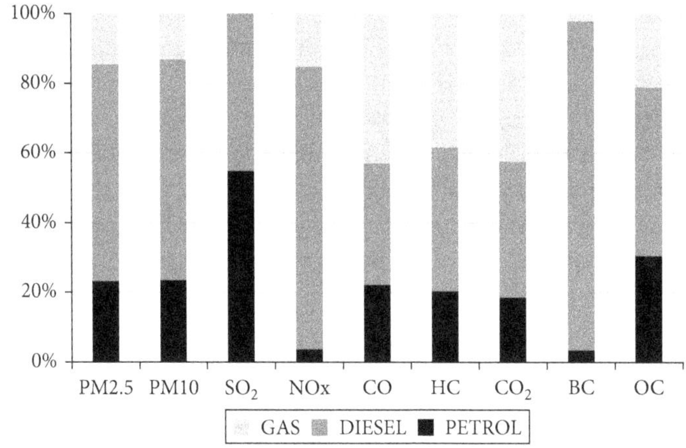

Figure 19.3. Share of emissions according to fuel type from vehicles in Delhi, 2011

BC = black carbon, BUS = buses, CO = carbon monoxide, CO_2 = carbon dioxide, HC = hydro carbon, HDT = heavy duty trucks, LDT = light-duty trucks, NO_x = nitrogen oxide, OC = organic compounds, PM = particulate matter, SO_2 = sulfur dioxide.

Source: Guttikunda and Mohan (2014).

most to particulate and sulfur emissions, while heavy-duty trucks are major contributors to the emissions of nitrogen oxides. Note that diesel-fuelled vehicles are the biggest contributors to total vehicular pollution in the capital city of Delhi. The same is true for all the major cities in the country. Factors contributing to high air pollution from vehicles are: a high proportion of old vehicles on road using outdated technology, two-stroke engined two-wheelers, a high number of personalized vehicles, high passenger kilometre demand, and poor public transport infrastructure (Ghosh and Kansal 2014).

Pollution from industrial and power plants. The industrial sector accounts for about 15 per cent of national GDP and contributes substantially to air pollution. The CPCB has categorized industrial units into seventeen categories that account for about 60 per cent of industrial output, and the remaining 40 per cent comes from small- and medium-scale units, which number more than three million (Kandlikar and Ramachandran 2000). A recent economic boom has resulted in increasing investment in construction, mining, and the iron and steel sectors, which has resulted an an increase in pollution in these industries. The scattered distribution of small and medium-sized units makes pollution control more difficult and financially non-viable. According to Kansal et al. (2011), industrial and power generation contribute about 20–40 per cent to urban air pollution. Gujarat, Maharashtra, Uttar Pradesh, Bihar, West Bengal, and Madhya Pradesh are relatively industrialized, and hence are the most polluted and populated states in India. These states have the highest levels of SO_2 and NO_x emissions (ADB and CAI-Asia 2006).

Emissions from the power sector have increased dramatically in the last two decades. Thermal power plants generate about 67 per cent of total power generation in the country, and these plants are a main source of air pollution. More than 99 per cent of the coal used in thermal power plants is domestic steam coal, which has very high ash content. Lu and Streets' (2012) estimates show that there was an increase of at least 70 per cent in NO_x emissions during 1996–2010, and thermal power plants contribute about 96 per cent to total power sector emissions. Similarly, Lu et al. (2013) developed a unit-based inventory of SO_2 emissions for India's thermal power sector. Their estimates show that SO_2 emissions increased dramatically by 71 per cent during 2005–12.

Pollution from domestic sector. Unlike developed countries, the domestic sector is also a significant contributor to air emissions in India, though its share is small relative to the transport, industry, and power sectors. Smoke emissions arising from burning coal, wood, cattle dung, and other biomass are significant sources of particulate matter. The pattern of various kinds of energy use by households is a key determinant of domestic air pollution. Figure 19.4 shows energy-use patterns of urban households for cooking purposes. This figure reveals that about a third of urban households are using non-clean sources of energy for cooking purposes. Of these non-clean sources, about 27 per cent of total households are using wood, coal, or other biomass sources, which are highly particulate matter-intensive. Note that the fuel-use pattern is linked to the income levels of households, and following the energy ladder, as incomes increase, households move from biomass sources to clean sources such as liquefied petroleum gas (LPG) or piped natural gas (PNG). Therefore, the energy-use pattern reveals that low-income households are more prone to the ill effects of indoor air pollution in urban India too.

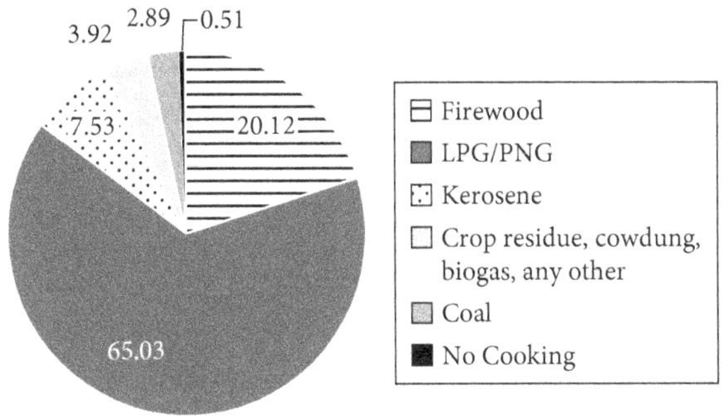

Figure 19.4. Household energy-use pattern in urban India (%)
LPG = liquefied petroleum gas, PNG = piped natural gas.
Source: Based on Census of India 2011 data.

19.2.2 Drivers of Urban Air Pollution

To understand the determinants of urban air pollutants in India, we postulate that urban air pollution is a function of demographic, socio-economic, geographic, and governance factors. To account for demographic factors, we consider two variables: population and population density in a city. Population growth exerts a burden on natural resources, thereby affecting the quality of the environment. However, population density reduces pollution. This may be due to disincentives for using private vehicles that might cause congestion, thereby resulting in greater use of public transport. Less vehicles on the roads implies lower emission levels (Marshall et al. 2005).

Focusing on the impact of a city's income on pollution level, the environment Kuznets curve (EKC) argument given by Grossman and Krueger (1995) can be applied. As income increases, the pollution level is expected to increase. However, with income crossing a certain limit, it can be expected that efforts will be made to improve environmental quality through stringent regulations, thereby lowering the pollution level. Greenstone and Hanna (2014), using city-level data of air pollution, find that environmental regulations are effective even when a country has not reached the level of the EKC's turning point, as has been observed in developed countries. Therefore, we assume only a log-linear relationship between air pollutants and non-agricultural per capita income. Moreover, we take the share of the services sector in state GDP as one of the determinants of a city's pollution level. Services are considered less polluting relative to manufacturing or other industrial activities.

We incorporate sex ratio and literacy as other determinants of urban air pollution, expecting that high sex ratios and literacy levels indicate high awareness and hence sensitivity towards environmental issues. Note that women played a leading role in environmental movements in India, as in case of the famous Chipko Movement or the Narmada Bachao Andolan. Dasgupta and Wheeler (1997) argue that regulators need to be informed about problems for further inspections. However, poorly educated regions remain silent because of ignorance, resulting in a lower allocation of resources in the area. Therefore, to limit this process, outreach programmes are needed to encourage poorly educated people to voice their complaints. In line with our expectation, literacy helps in decreasing pollutants. We include a state-specific dummy to account for geographic and governance factors. Note that environmental regulation is a state subject in India, so the level of implementation of environmental laws differs from state to state.

Data. To conduct a regression analysis using city-level data, the choice of cities is constrained by the availability of data. We obtained data on ambient emission levels from the CPCB (2012), which is available for 117 cities for PM_{10} and for 114 cities for the pollutants of SO_2 and NO_2. Population, sex ratio, and literacy rate data are obtained from the Census of India 2011 for all these cities for which pollution data are available. Economic data at city level are not available; therefore, we have taken state non-agricultural per capita income as a proxy for city-level per capita income, since most of non-agricultural income arises in urban areas. Similarly, we use share of the services sector in state GDP as a determinant of a city's air quality. Note that we have used population density (persons per kilometre) as one of the determinants in regression analysis, but data on the area of a city are available only for seventy-one cities. Thus, we end up with a sample size of seventy-one cities spread over eighteen states and one union territory.

Table 19.1 provides descriptive statistics of the final dataset. With a mean population of more than two million people, the sample accounts for about 39 per cent of the total urban population in India. From descriptive statistics of pollutants, it can be said that in the sample, no city crosses the prescribed limit of SO_2 levels, but in the case of PM_{10} and NO_x, there are cities that cross the NAAQS. Moreover,

Table 19.1. Descriptive statistics of variables used in the regression analysis

Variable	Mean	Std. Dev.	Minimum	Maximum
SO_2 ($\mu g/m^3$)	10.39	7.16	2	35
NO_2 ($\mu g/m^3$)	27.25	13.37	7	66
PM_{10} ($\mu g/m^3$)	122.08	64.07	31	308
Persons (million)	2.08	2.87	0.102	16.3
Sex ratio (females per thousand males)	920	66.02	754	1,117
Literacy rate (%)	87	5.41	64.61	96.38
Services sector/SGDP (%)	59.27	12.44	8.692928	92.57361
Per capita income (Rs)	45,863	28,251.24	12,923.51	175,813.5
Population density (persons/km^2)	8,117	5,398	338.4	24,115

NO_2 = nitrogen dioxide, PM = particulate matter, SGDP = state gross domestic product, SO_2 = sulfur dioxide, Std. Dev. = standard deviation, ug/m^3 = microgram per cubic metre.

based on the standard deviation of the three pollutants, it can be said that there is high variability with respect to the pollutants PM_{10} and NO_x across the sample cities.

Table 19.2 presents the regression results, which display a positive relationship between the level of air pollution and population in a city. This is statistically significant with regard to PM_{10} and NO_x. The positive, but less than one, value of the regression coefficient implies that as the size of a city in terms of population increases, the level of pollution increases, though at a decreasing rate, that is, population has a less than proportional impact on emissions in cities. The relationship between population and ambient PM_{10} emission levels is presented in Figure 19.5. The results indicate a 'sublinear' scaling from population size (i.e. economies of scale), after controlling for other plausible factors like infrastructural variables (Bettencourt et al. 2007). Similar to other public goods (e.g. infrastructural facilities), emission levels are local public bads, and there are diseconomies of scale in release of emissions. A value of less than one indicates decreasing per capita emission level contribution with increasing population size. The policy implication of such a result is that the physical form of a city plays a role in reducing urban air pollution.

The power-law scaling relationship between local pollutants and population observed in the present study corroborates the results of Lamsal et al. (2013). Lamsal et al. observe power-law scaling between emission of nitrogen oxide and population for the US, Europe, China, and India, using city-level satellite data. However, the value of the coefficient in the present study is lower than that observed by them. The reasons for this difference can be found in the data sources and control variables.

The second demographic variable we have used is population density. The application of power-law scaling between pollution level and population implies a negative relationship. Figure 19.6 shows the relationship between population density and level of PM_{10} in urban India. The regression results confirm this argument. A higher population density is significantly associated with lower pollution levels for PM_{10} and NO_2. Relative to sprawling cities, dense cities may require less energy as their residents have to travel less for domestic and business purposes, and the result is lower emissions (Gonzalez 2005; Sarzynski 2012). On the other hand, higher density also reflects a higher slum population, which consumes less energy than other forms of urban development (Jorgenson et al. 2010). Moreover, emission control strategies like fast and convenient transport, vehicle mileage standards, and energy efficient buildings are implemented in dense areas or megacities relative to small and medium-sized cities (Parrish and Zhu 2009; Parrish et al. 2009).

We take the per capita non-agricultural income of a state as a proxy for per capita income of a particular city, assuming that most non-agricultural income arises in urban areas. In all three regressions, we find a positive association between level of emissions in a city and per capita income, but this relationship is not

Table 19.2. Regression results

Variable	Ln (PM_{10})		Ln (SO_2)		Ln (NO_X)	
	Coefficient	t-statistics	Coefficient	t-statistics	Coefficient	t-statistics
Ln (persons)	0.113[a]	1.94	0.085	0.87	0.134[b]	2.29
Ln (sex ratio)	–1.26	–0.98	–1.523	– 1.22	–1.882	–1.49
Ln (per capita income)	0.317	1.38	0.156	0.49	0.147	0.65
Services sector/SGDP (%)	–0.012[c]	–5.24	–0.035[c]	–8.59	–0.011[c]	–4.6
Ln (population density)	–0.01[a]	–1.77	0.001	0.09	–0.01[b]	–2.03
Literacy rate (%)	–0.004[a]	–1.67	0.007	0.3	0.004	0.35
Assam	0.389	1.22	0.537	1.05	0.008	0.03
Bihar	0.913[a]	1.68	0.839	1.21	0.933[a]	1.95
Chhattisgarh	1.411[c]	6.17	1.13[c]	3.04	1.051[c]	4.82
Gujarat	–0.162	–1.16	0.689[c]	4.09	0.077	0.38
Haryana	0.475[c]	6.64	1.308[c]	12.05	0.421[c]	5.81
Himachal Pradesh	–0.309	–1.08	–0.519	–1.23	–0.269	–0.93
Jharkhand	0.819[c]	2.92	1.373[c]	2.84	0.871[c]	2.97
Karnataka	–0.29	–1.5	0.737[a]	1.71	0.205	0.81
Kerala	–0.202	–0.73	0.223	0.5	0.126	0.39
Madhya Pradesh	0.723[b]	2.15	0.654	1.11	0.192	0.65
Maharashtra	0.088	0.61	1.372[c]	5.16	0.589[c]	3.47
National Capital Territory of Delhi	0.848[c]	5.07	0.801[c]	2.82	0.985[c]	5.72
Odisha[d]	0.246	0.89	–0.63	–1.29	0.337	1.02
Punjab	0.633[c]	3.42	0.522[b]	2.11	0.485[c]	3.01
Rajasthan	0.625[c]	2.58	0.323	0.88	0.592[b]	2.26
Tamil Nadu	–0.182	–0.9	0.875[b]	2.42	0.474[b]	2.43

Uttar Pradesh	0.786[b]	2.23	0.332	0.66	0.515	1.45
West Bengal	0.677[c]	3.24	0.954[c]	2.8	1.62[c]	8.3
Constant	9.1	0.83	10.5	0.91	12.5	1.15
R-squared	0.822		0.694		0.749	
Root MSE	0.279		0.520		0.314	
No. of observations	71		71		71	

Ln = natural logarithm, MSE = mean square error, NOx = nitrogen oxide, PM = particulate matter, SGDP = state gross domestic product, SO_2 = sulfur dioxide.

[a] $p \leq 0.1$.

[b] $p \leq 0.05$.

[c] $p \leq 0.01$.

[d] In 2011, the government of India approved the name change of the state of Orissa to Odisha. This document reflects this change. However, when reference is made to policies that predate the name change, the formal name Orissa is retained.

Source: Author's calculations.

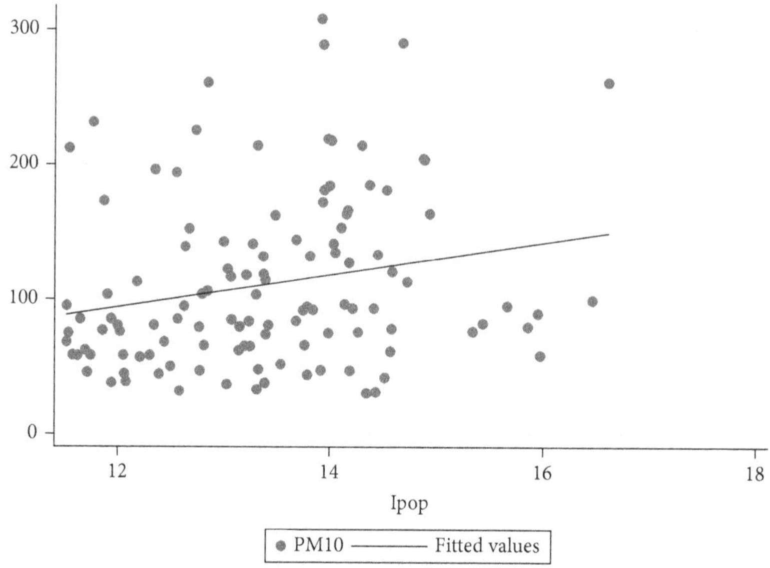

Figure 19.5. Population and level of ambient PM_{10} in cities in India
lpop = natural logarithm of the population, PM = particulate matter.
Source: Author's computations.

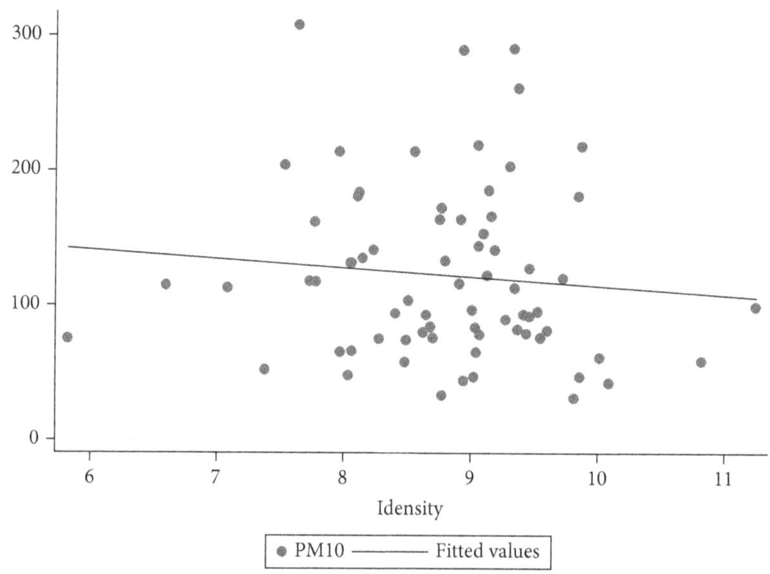

Figure 19.6. Population density and PM_{10} level
Ldensity = natural logarithm of the population density, PM = particulate matter.
Source: Author's computation.

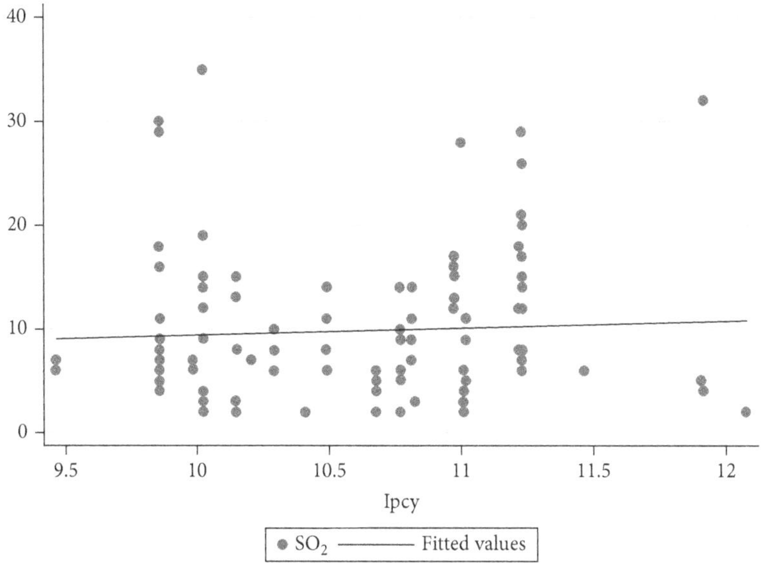

Figure 19.7. Pollution and income relationship in urban India
lpcy = natural logarithm of the per capita income, SO_2 = sulfur dioxide.
Source: Author's computation.

statistically significant, as presented in Figure 19.7, contrary to the EKC relationship observed in various studies. This finding corresponds to Greenstone and Hanna (2014). Using city-level information, Greenstone and Hanna find that environmental regulation with respect to air pollution is effective, and cities in India experience a higher reduction in air pollution before reaching the peak of the EKC, as opposed to situations observed in developed countries.

We find a negative and statistically significant relationship between emission levels in a city and the share of the services sector in state GDP (Figure 19.8), as services are considered to be less polluting relative to manufacturing or agriculture.

We have taken two social factors, sex ratio and literacy rate, to understand the levels of emissions in Indian cities. It is expected that these variables help reduce emission levels, as a higher value for these variables indicates that people are more informed about and sensitive to environmental conditions. Jalan et al. (2009) find that in urban India, the probability of water purification by a household increases by ten percentage points if a female member of a household reads a newspaper at least once a week. We find the signs of these variables are as expected in all the three models, but literacy rate is a statistically significant determinant of PM_{10} level (Figure 19.9) since education appears to be a determinant of environmental preferences and willingness to pay worldwide (Jalan et al. 2009).

In all the three models, we observe that most of the state dummies are statistically significant, implying that state-specific geographic and governance variables are

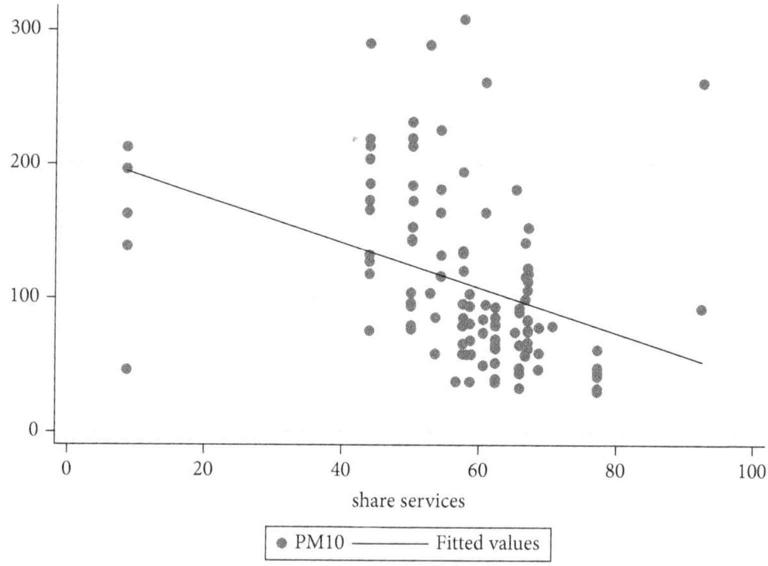

Figure 19.8. Relationship between share of the services sector (%) in GDP and pollution

PM = particulate matter.

Source: Author's computation.

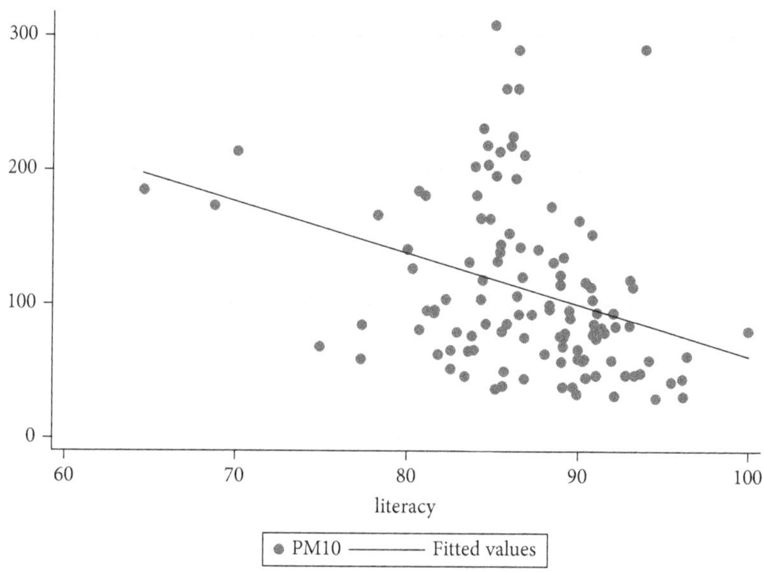

Figure 19.9. Relationship between urban pollution level and literacy rate (%)

PM = particulate matter.

Source: Author's computation.

important determinants of air quality in a city. This finding again corroborates the finding of Greenstone and Hanna (2014), as environmental regulation in India is controlled by the states. It is observed from the regression results that the coefficient value is negative, though insignificant, for the states that are relatively more urbanized except Delhi. We find positive and significant state dummies for the states where power plants and industrial production are concentrated. This implies that the government needs to focus more in these areas as it is expected that the share of industrial production in GDP will increase in the coming years and coal will remain the country's main source of electricity. Monitoring activities in these states need to be extended in order to regulate urban air pollution.

19.3 Traffic Congestion

Higher rates of growth of urbanization and population have put substantial pressure on urban transport systems. However, most cities in India have not been able to meet the growing demand for mobility and suffer from traffic congestion and air pollution. Public transport systems in Indian cities have been unable to keep pace with increasing demand for mobility. Bus services have declined greatly, and passengers have turned to personalized vehicles, adding to traffic congestion.

Another remarkable feature of India's urbanization is that cities have expanded horizontally, partly due to restrictions on vertical expansion and an increase in passenger travel demand.[3] The average trip length in India's megacities is substantially higher than in European cities. For example, an average trip length in Bangalore is 12–13 kilometres, in Mumbai 12.4 kilometres, and in Delhi ten kilometres; vehicular travel demand is about 4,200 million passenger kilometres (Ghosh and Kansal 2014); the average time required to complete one trip in these cities during peak hours varies between thirty-eight and forty-five minutes or more. Therefore, as a result, in the absence of proper enforcement and infrastructure, average mobility has slowed down. Though the per capita trip rate in India's cities is low relative to developed countries, it ranges between 1 and 1.7 kilometres. The per capita trip rate is low since small and medium-sized enterprises employ a significant number of people and are often located in or near residential areas.

Wilbur Smith Associates and MoUD (2008) prepared an index of congestion for thirty Indian cities . They define congestion as the inverse of mobility, that

[3] There are regulations on the vertical expansion of buildings in some cities in India. For example, in Delhi, according to the Master Plan 2021, buildings taller than fifteen meters without stilts and 17.5 meters with stilts are considered high-rise buildings, and there is no provision for high-rise buildings in the Master Plan. See also <http://indianexpress.com/article/cities/delhi/dda-invites-feedback-on-master-plan-2021-modifications/> (accessed 26 August 2014).

is, congestion is the gap between desired and observed levels of mobility. The index is defined as,

$$Congestion\ index = 1 - \frac{A}{M},$$

where A is observed and M is desired (30 kilometres per hour) travel speed on a major corridor of a city during peak hours.

Figure 19.10 shows that smaller cities generally have a lower index value, implying they have a lower level of traffic congestion, as expected. Delhi and Mumbai have the highest index value, implying that these cities are suffering the most with regard to traffic congestion. Though cities like Bangalore, Kolkata, Varanasi, and Guwahati have a lower index value compared with Delhi and Mumbai, they have considerable levels of congestion that require attention. Chandigarh has almost zero index value. This implies that the city has very good road networks. Moreover, note that the congestion index is closely associated with the availability of public transport—cities with better public transport facilities have lower traffic congestion problems (Wilbur Smith Associates and MoUD 2008).

Urbanization, coupled with motorization and dependence on traditional fuels, has resulted in rising congestion and emission levels (CAI-Asia Center 2010). Table 19.3 presents the regression results, showing a relationship between urbanization factors and congestion index. The regression results reveal that bigger and crowded cities face higher levels of congestion (Figures 19.11 and 19.12). Generally, in a dense city people use more public transport and less private vehicles on the assumption that a large proportion of employment is concentrated in the central area of a city and that most of the urban area is accessible by public transport; hence, congestion levels are low. In India's cities, a higher average trip length encourages the ownership and use of private vehicles. Increasing incomes induce people to

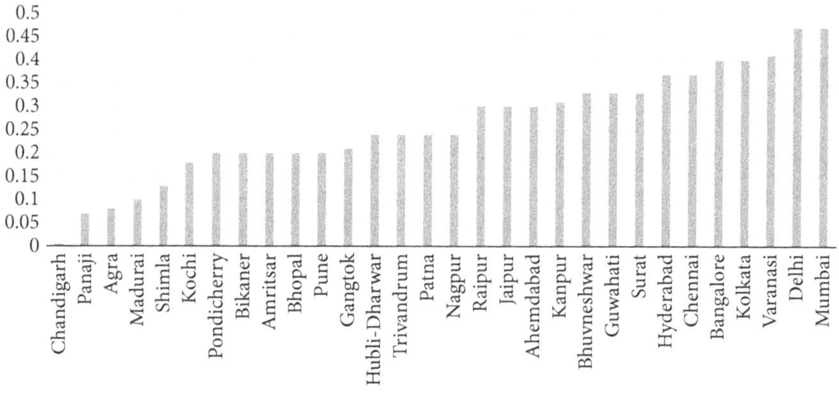

Figure 19.10. Congestion index of cities in India

Source: Wilbur Smith Associates and MoUD (2008).

Table 19.3. Congestion index and urbanization

Variable	Coefficient	Standard error	t-statistics
Ln (population)	0.37[a]	0.200	1.85
Ln (population density)	0.29[a]	0.139	2.09
Ln (public transportation)	−0.01	0.075	−0.18
Ln (private transportation)	0.42[b]	0.168	2.47
Intercept	−2.48[a]	1.103	−2.25
R^2	0.56		
N	14		

[a] $p \leq 0.1$.

[b] $p \leq 0.05$.

Ln = natural logarithm, N = number of observations, R^2 = coefficient of determination.

Source: Author's calculations.

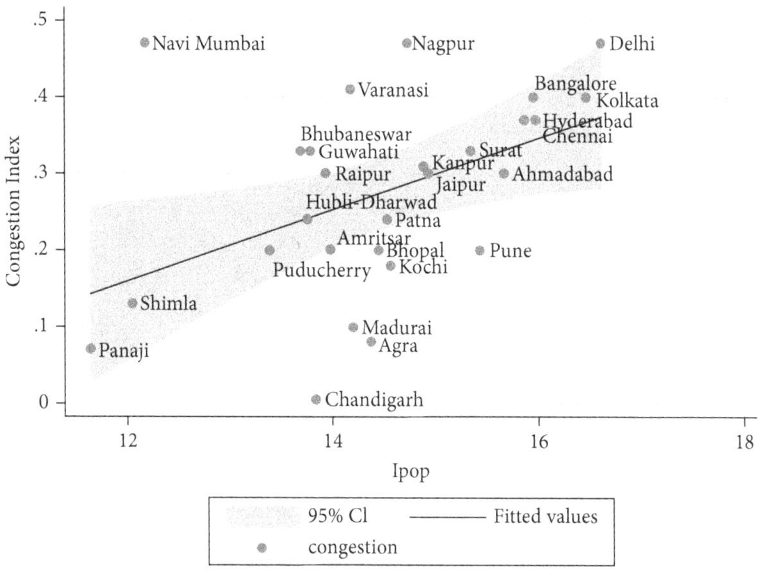

Figure 19.11. Level of congestion and population in urban India

CI = confidence interval, Ipop = natural logarithm of population.

Source: Author's computation based on data from Wilbur Smith Associates and MoUD (2008) and Census of India 2011.

shift towards private vehicles in the absence of safe and convenient commuting facilities. Figure 19.13 reveals that during 2001–11, the percentage of households owning cars has almost doubled. Moreover, growth in sprawls has been causing longer per capita trip length in cities and reducing the number of walking and cycling trips. Two-wheelers and cars are becoming the predominant means of

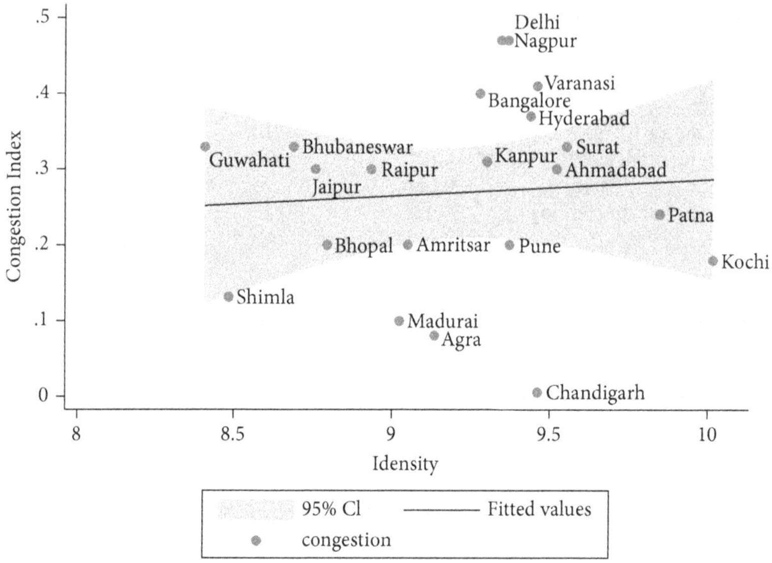

Figure 19.12. Level of congestion and population density

CI = confidence interval, Idensity = natural logarithm of population density.

Sources: Author's computation based on data from Wilbur Smith Associates and MoUD (2008) and Census of India 2011.

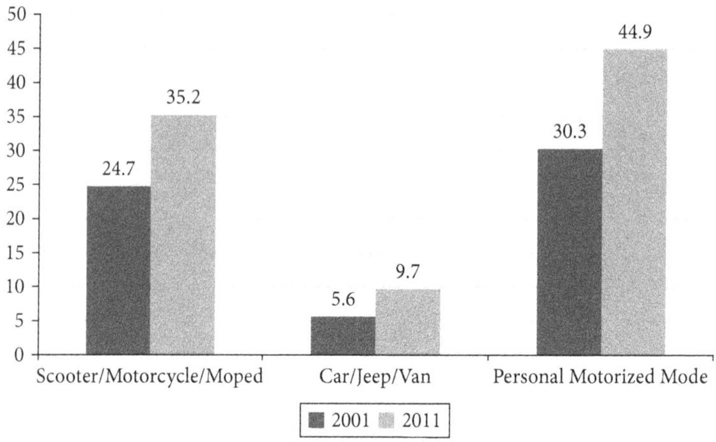

Figure 19.13. Mode of transport in urban India (% households)

Source: Census of India 2011.

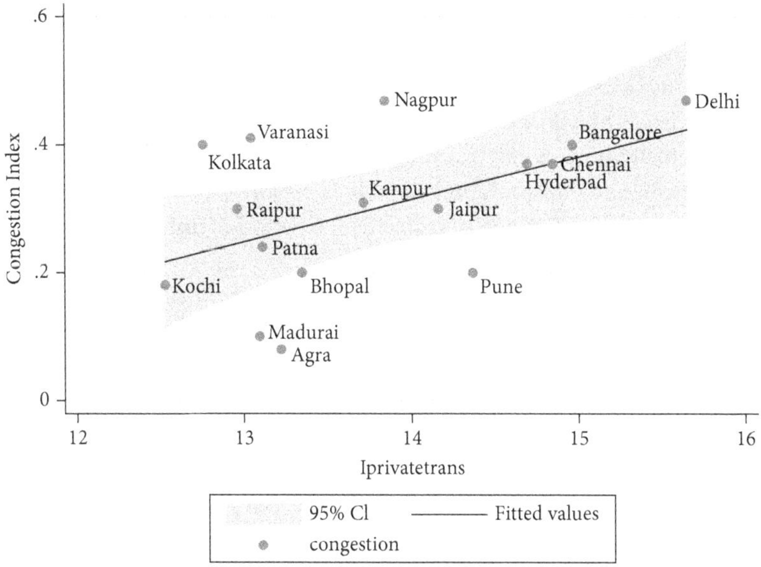

Figure 19.14. Level of congestion and private transportation in urban India

CI = confidence interval, lprivate trans = natural logarithm of private vehicles.

Source: Author's computation based on data from Wilbur Smith Associates and MoUD (2008), and Offices of State Transport Commissioners/Union Territories Administrations and Basic Road Statistics of India, 2009–11.

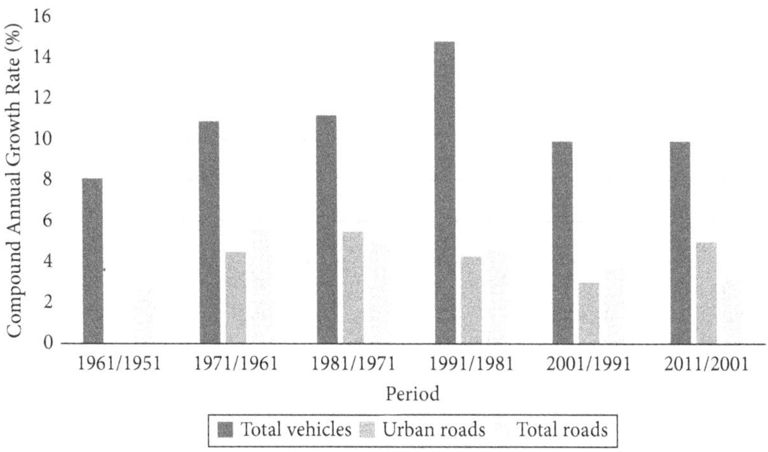

Figure 19.15. Growth rates for total vehicles and roads in India

Source: Based on Offices of State Transport Commissioners/Union Territories Administrations and Basic Road Statistics of India, 2009–11.

transport for individual trips in India's cities. This results in higher traffic volume per sq. km in bigger and denser cities.

The positive and statistically significant coefficient of private transportation testifies to this observation, that is, there is a positive association between number of private vehicles (mainly cars) and congestion level in India's cities (Figure 19.14). Note that the public transportation variable is negative, as expected, but it is not statistically significant. Further, note that over a period of time, the growth rate of length of urban roads could not match the increasing growth of vehicles (Figure 19.15. This implies that reliable, convenient, comfortable, and affordable public transportation needs to be developed to lower the level of traffic congestion in Indian cities. The discussion in Section 19.4 reveals that commuters are willing to shift to public transportation from the use of private cars.

19.4 Consequences of Urban Air Pollution and Traffic Congestion

Epidemiological studies show that air pollution is a significant determinant of respiratory diseases that affects individuals' productivity at work and increases medical expenses. Higher levels of ambient air pollution causes mortality and morbidity (Krupnick et al. 1990; Cropper et al. 1997; Chhabra et al. 2001). A recent review by the Centre for Science and Environment[4] of about eighty studies conducted across cities in India reveals that although studies evaluating the effects of urban air pollution on health started in the early 1990s, more than 70 per cent of the studies have taken place in 2000s. All these studies reveal significant health effects of urban air pollution. Note that these studies do not remain confined to megacities, but also cover small and medium-sized cities. It is also worth noting that although early studies were evaluating the health impacts of suspended particulate matter and emissions of sulfur dioxide, recent studies cover the health effects of smaller particulates, NO_x, ozone, volatile organic compounds, etc. About 59 per cent of the studies focused on the effects of exposure to vehicular pollution.

Though globally there are many studies measuring the value of damage due to air pollution on human health, there have been relatively few comprehensive studies in this area in India. Among earlier studies, Brandon and Hommann (1995) provide tentative estimates of the health costs of urban air pollution as amounting to $1.4 billion. The World Development Indicators indicate that India loses about $7 billion annually due to air pollution (World Bank 2014). Some city-specific studies were conducted to measure the economic consequences

[4] Centre for Science and Environment, <http://www.cseindia.org/userfiles/Air%20pollution%20and%20health%20impact%20evidences-1.pdf> (accessed 9 June 2014).

of air pollution in India (e.g. Cropper et al. 1997; Kumar and Rao 2001; Murty et al. 2003a; Gupta 2008). These studies are based on a health production function, damage function, or cost-of-illness approach, and estimate an individual's willingness to pay for reducing air pollution to a safe level.

Cropper et al. (1997), using a dose-response model, find that a 100 microgram per cubic metre increase in total suspended particulate matter (TSPM) leads to a 2.3 per cent increase in trauma deaths in Delhi. Kumar and Rao (2001), using a microeconomic framework, estimated individual willingness to pay varying between Rs 12 and Rs 53 per month for improving air quality to World Health Organization standards for Panipat. Using a similar model, Murty et al. (2003a) observe that a representative household gains about Rs 2,086 and Rs 950 per annum due to the reduction of air pollution to safe levels in Delhi and Kolkata, respectively.

The World Bank (2013) comprehensively measures the economic impact of urban air pollution in India. This study measures the impact of criteria pollutants PM_{10} and $PM_{2.5}$ and covers all cities that had a population of more than 100,000 in 2001. It follows a cost-of-illness approach to measure morbidity effects and a human capital approach and value of statistical life to evaluate mortality effects. This study finds that urban air pollution causes around 109,000 premature deaths among adults and 7,500 deaths among children aged under five annually. It estimates that every year there are 48,000 new cases of chronic bronchitis; 370,000 new cases of annual hospitalization; and 7,300 cases of emergency room visits/outpatient hospitalizations. In monetary terms, India loses about Rs 1,103 billion, equivalent to 1.7 per cent of GDP, due to urban air pollution. About 93 per cent of costs can be attributed to mortality losses and about 7 per cent to morbidity losses.

Traffic congestion is another urban disease that causes enormous loss. Poor infrastructure adds to the problem of badly managed transport system in cities of India. Road space is grossly insufficient. Therefore, issues of uncompetitive public transport, poor infrastructure facilities, and improper regulations and polices result in traffic congestion.

Direct economic losses from traffic congestion include the wastage of time and fuel (Bertrand 1978)—congestion results in slow traffic speeds, making trip durations unpredictable (Stopher 2004; Wachs 2002). Slow speeds increase fuel costs (Pucher et al. 2005). Indirect costs due to traffic congestion include adverse impacts on health and the environment (Walder 2007; Stopher 2004; Wachs 2002). Congestion costs are also categorized as external and internal. External costs are those that are borne by others and internal costs are the ones incurred by the trip-maker him/herself. Delay costs, pollution, and increased vehicle operation costs for others are considered to be external costs of congestion. In the literature, researchers have developed economic models to estimate external congestion costs (Bertrand 1978; Mayeres 1993). Estimation of external, especially marginal external, costs are relevant due to their direct relationship with efficient pricing

Table 19.4. Relative externalities caused by different vehicles

Externality parameter	Two-wheeler	Car	Bus
Congestion per passenger	7.02	15.93	1
Pollution per passenger	13.35	15.99	1
Road damage per passenger	0.9	16	1

Source: Kharola and Tiwari (2008).

strategies, namely, congestion taxes (Rouwendal and Verhoef 2006; Santos and Newbery 2001). Sen et al. (2010) estimate Rs 0.031 per vehicle kilometre as the marginal congestion cost during peak hours in Delhi.

An analysis of vehicular pollution and congestion problems in India's cities reveals that with higher levels of economic development, the share of personalized vehicles has been increasing disproportionately and at a rapid rate alongside physical infrastructure. The Karnataka Tax Reform Commission carried out an analysis of externalities posed by increasing personalized vehicles relative to public road transport; the findings of the commission are presented in Table 19.4. A challenge for policymakers is to lower the growth in demand for personalized vehicles in a growing economy and to improve commuting efficiency for residents.

19.5 Environmental Quality and Commuting Efficiency: Challenges and Opportunities

Industrial relocation and pollution transfer. The analysis so far shows that industrial and vehicular pollution are the main sources of urban ambient air pollution. The industrial sector accounts for about 45 per cent of total commercial energy consumption in the country. The share of energy-intensive industries in total energy consumed in the industrial sector was about 63 per cent in 2005 (de la Rue du Can et al. 2009).

Since 2000, both income and industrial energy use have been increasing in India. GDP has increased at a rate of about 8.6 per cent per annum and industrial energy consumption has increased at an annual growth rate of 5.8 per cent. Figure 19.16 compares energy intensity in India to the Western world, and shows a decline since the early 1990s; however, there is ample space for improvement. Goldar (2010) shows that a decline in the energy intensity of manufacturing in India in the post-1992 period is attributable mostly to an improvement in the energy-use efficiency of energy-intensive industries. However, note that average intensity lags behind the best-practice levels. To accelerate energy efficiency in a cost-effective way, the Ministry of Power launched a scheme known as Perform, Achieve and Trade (PAT) in 2012.

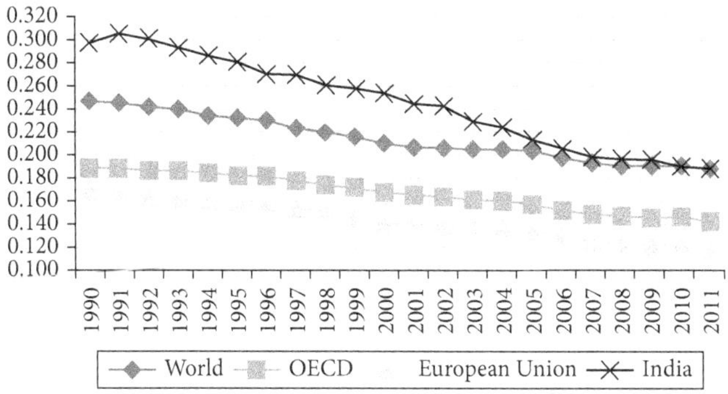

Figure 19.16. Energy intensity of GDP at constant purchasing power parities (kgoe/$2005)

kgoe = kilogram of oil equivalent, OECD = Organisation for Economic Co-operation and Development.

Source: Based on data from Enerdata (2012).

Sridhar and Wan (2010) and Ghani et al. (2012) analyse the locational choices of industries in India. Sridhar and Wan find that Indian firms refrain from locating in capital cities, and labour-intensive firms prefer to locate in medium-sized cities. Moreover, they observe that proximity to inputs is a key determinant in choice of location for a firm in India, and economically efficient firms prefer to settle in medium-sized to large cities. However, Ghani et al. (2012) observe the urbanization of unorganized sector firms and the deurbanization of organized sector firms. They find that from 1989 to 2005, the urban employment share for the organized sector declined from 69 per cent to 57 per cent, while it increased for the unorganized sector from 25 per cent to 37 per cent, i.e. though in value terms India's industrialization has been becoming rural, in terms of employment it has been urbanizing. Very often these industrial units in the unorganized sector operate illegally with primitive technologies and process standards. Due to the higher number of pollution sources, poor technology, and fuel quality, the resulting pollution levels in urban areas are higher (Ghosh and Kansal 2014).

People's rising demand for 'green cities' and efficient commuting. Environmental quality is considered a luxury commodity in the EKC studies, which argue that as average incomes in a society cross a threshold level, demand for environmental quality increases. Similarly, studies measuring the health impacts of air pollution observe that consumers are willing to pay for improved air quality. Improved air quality mitigates morbidity costs and increases the productivity of humans at work. Therefore, it is expected that with increasing incomes and higher information levels, people in urban India will be willing to pay more for a higher level of environmental amenities.

Murty and Gulati (2005) and Murty et al. (2003b) show that residents of Delhi, Kolkata, and Hyderabad are willing to pay more to reside in a better ambient air quality environment and to reduce the exposure of their family members to pollution in the workplace. These studies use hedonic property valuation methods to estimate the benefit to households from reduced pollution. Murty and Gulati (2005) estimate that a representative household in the twin cities of Hyderabad and Secunderabad is willing to pay about Rs 4,500 per year as housing rent for a reduction in RSPM to a safe level. A representative commuter gets a benefit of Rs 7.27 per day for the reduction of RSPM to a safe level. Similarly, Murty et al. (2003b) provide estimates of household marginal annual willingness to pay for a reduction of one microgram of TSPM in the cities of Kolkata and Hyderabad.

It is observed that with increasing incomes in urban areas, more people are shifting to personalized vehicles and, as a result, commuting efficiency has been diminishing. Therefore, shifting urban commuters to public transport can be an effective strategy in dealing with problems of traffic congestion and pollution. To identify commuters' preferences, Jain et al. (2014) conducted a survey in Delhi during January to June 2013 for about 500 commuters in fifty locations using a stratified random sampling technique. Using an analytical hierarchy process, they found that 96 per cent of commuters are willing to shift from personalized vehicles to public transport, provided it is reliable, comfortable, safe, and efficient. Commuters are willing to pay more for improved public transport facilities. This reflects a need to take into account commuters' preferences while planning and designing for commuting facilities in urban areas.

Nearly 17 per cent of urban India lives in slums and about a third of the slum population is concentrated in just 46 million-plus cities (Government of India, Ministry of Home Affairs 2011). It is argued that the poor consume less energy and mostly use public transport for commuting and, therefore, cannot be blamed for urban diseases. Figure 19.4 shows that about 27 per cent of households in urban India use polluting energy sources for domestic cooking, implying that the urban poor are more exposed to indoor pollution. Similarly, only the 'notified' (recognized by the government) slums get security of residential tenure, access to water, sanitation, and electricity, and about 50 per cent of slums in India are 'non-notified' (Subbaraman et al. 2013). Moreover, note that the poor are more exposed to ambient air pollution and they are more adversely affected than better-off households. In a recent study measuring the impact of air quality regulations in Delhi, Foster and Kumar (2011) confirm this hypothesis.

Government reactions to urban environmental and commuting issues. Articles 39(e), 47, and 48A of India's Constitution say that it is a responsibility of the state to secure and improve people's health and environment. Various regulations were enacted during the 1980s and 1990s; pollution levels in India's cities were very high and the ambient air quality in Delhi was alarming.[5] Due to growing public

[5] For details on the institutional setup for environmental regulations in India, see Kumar and Managi (2009: chapter 3).

discontent, which took the form of filing public interest litigation cases against persistent air pollution, the Supreme Court intervened. The Supreme Court directed the government to improve air quality by adopting measures such as the closure of polluting industries in non-conforming areas, switching commercial vehicles from conventional fuel to CNG, and mandating catalytic converters in all vehicles. The Supreme Court directed that city-specific action plans should be prepared, and to date action plans have been prepared for seventeen cities (Greenstone and Hanna 2014). Table 19.5 lists the measures taken by various state governments for curbing air pollution in various cities.

The road transport sector is a major air polluter in urban India. The Auto Fuel Policy (MoPNG 2003) prescribes standards for vehicle emissions in the country. In last decade, it has moved from Euro I to Euro IV emission norms for private, public, and all commercial vehicles. The government has mandated the introduction of Bharat IV (equivalent to Euro IV) emission norms for public, private, and light commercial vehicles in twenty big cities, including Delhi and Mumbai, since 2010. It has been mandatory for two- and three-wheelers to abide by Bharat Stage III emission norms since April 2010.

Moreover, the government introduced low-sulfur fuels and mandated the use of CNG for public transport in the cities of Delhi and Mumbai. In megacities, fifteen-year-old commercial vehicles were phased out. An independent laboratory has been set up for checking fuel adulteration, thus strengthening vehicle inspection programmes. In 2006, the government of India announced the National Urban Transport Policy with the objective of providing safe, comfortable, reliable, convenient, and sustainable transport facilities to the residents of growing cities. The policy was aimed at increasing the share of public transport in commuting, reducing pollution, and encouraging better use of intelligent systems to increase commuting efficiency, among other goals.

As a result of the Supreme Court's intervention, the air quality of cities where the action plans were implemented has improved (Greenstone and Hanna 2014). Most of the evaluation studies are concerned with the impacts of the Supreme Court intervention in Delhi's air pollution. Kumar and Foster (2009) report that although air quality in Delhi was worse in comparison to other cities both before and after the Supreme Court intervention, it improved after the intervention. They also provide a comparison with Kanpur, an industrial city where the Court has not intervened, and find that during post-intervention period, air quality has worsened. Note that before the intervention, air quality was worse inside the city compared to outside city areas of Delhi and its neighbouring towns. But the intervention has reversed the situation since such regulations were absent in neighbouring areas.

These mandated regulations and their effectiveness show that environmental quality has improved, though per capita income has not reached the turning point observed by the EKC in developed countries. It implies that the success of policies depends on institutional setup. The experience of Delhi also calls for

Table 19.5. Measures taken to curb air pollution in different cities in India

City/cities	Measure	Year
Delhi[a,b,c,f]	Phasing out of leaded petrol	1998
	Mandatory conversion of buses and auto-rickshaws to CNG	2000
	Prohibition of the plying and idle parking of heavy goods, medium goods, and light goods vehicles on certain roads and areas during specified times	
	Temporary ban on registration of certain classes of diesel vehicles (lifted for private vehicles in August 2016)	2015
	Ban on firecrackers and diesel-powered generators	2015
	Driving restrictions for vehicles on alternate days, implemented for two fortnights in January and April	2016
	Closure of polluting industries	2016
Mumbai[d]	Restrictions on entry of heavy vehicles between 8.00 am to 12.00 pm and 4.00 pm to 10.00 pm	2016
Bangalore[a,g]	Supply of 5 per cent ethanol-blended petrol in twenty-seven districts	2003
	Mandatory LPG conversion in all auto-rickshaws	2004
	Ban on entry of trucks between 6.00 am and 10.00 pm	2014
Chennai[a,j]	Ban on entry of trucks between 6.00 am and 10.00 pm	2007
	Mandatory LPG conversion in all auto-rickshaws	2008
Hyderabad[a]	Introduced Multi-Model Transport System	2003
	Restrictions on interstate/intercity buses and entry of non-destined vehicles in the city	2003
	Mandatory LPG conversion in all auto-rickshaws	2005
	Phasing out of fifteen-year-old commercial vehicles	2009
Kolkata[k]	Mandatory LPG conversion in all auto-rickshaws	2010
	Conversion of auto-rickshaws using two-stroke engines to four-stroke engines	2010
Ahmedabad[a]	Mandatory CNG conversion in all auto-rickshaws and buses	2005
Lucknow[h]	Mandatory CNG conversion in all auto-rickshaws	2007

Chandigarh[i]	Mandatory LPG conversion in all auto-rickshaws	2009
All major cities[a]	Bharat Stage IV (equivalent to Euro IV standards) implemented for all categories of four-wheelers	2010
Kannur, Kochi, Kollam, Kozhikode, Thiruvananthapuram, and Thrissur[e]	Ban on registration of diesel vehicles and use of diesel vehicles more than ten years old	2016

[a] <http://cpcb.nic.in/upload/NewItems/NewItem_104_airquality17cities-package.pdf>.

[b] <http://www.delhi.gov.in/wps/wcm/connect/doit_transport/Transport/Home>.

[c] <http://timesofindia.indiatimes.com/city/delhi/DPCC-orders-closure-of-146-polluting-units/acticleshow/55057504.cms>.

[d] <http://timesofindia.indiatimes.com/city/thane/No-entry-for-heavy-vehicles-in-city-during-peak-hrs-for-1-month/articleshow/53232573.cms>.

[e] <http://indianexpress.com/article/india/india-news-india/kerala-hc-stays-ngt-order-on-10-year-old-diesel-vehicles-285629>.

[f] <http://delhigovt.nic.in/newdelhi/dept/transport/tr2.asp>.

[g] <http://kspcb.kar.nic.in/annualeng-1.pdf>.

[h] <http://www.cpcb.nic.in/divisionsofheadoffice/pri3/Second-city-report.pdf>.

[i] <http://www.expressindia.com/latest-news/only-lpg-autos-to-ply-on-city-roads/311178>.

[j] <http://www.tn.gov.in/sta/go1158.PDF>.

[k] <https://indiankanoon.org/doc/32078166>.

checking unabated pollution in outside and neighbouring areas of the city. A uniform policy intervention is required for checking the disproportionate distribution of emission sources and resulting air pollution (Nandi 2014). Although air quality in cities has improved because of the Supreme Court's intervention, cost-effectiveness was not a concern since these regulations were command and control in nature.

In last few years, the government of India has expressed a desire to use markets to control point source pollution and to enhance energy efficiency in the country. In 2013, the government launched a pilot emissions trading scheme for particulate matter in Tamil Nadu, Gujarat, and Maharashtra. To increase energy efficiency in energy-intensive industries in a cost-effective manner, the government of India initiated the PAT trading scheme known in 2012. Renewable power obligations are now increasing the share of renewable energy in the country's total electric-energy requirement.

19.6 Concluding Remarks

Increasing levels of urbanization and industrialization have raised concerns about the prevalence of urban diseases such as pollution and traffic congestion in Indian cities. This chapter has provided an overview of urban pollution and congestion problems in the country. Though India has a well-established regulatory institutional setup for addressing environmental concerns dating back to the 1970s, urban air quality was worse during the 1980s and 1990s, and it was alarming in big cities. Though the Supreme Court interventions in the form of city-specific action plans and mandated use of catalytic converters in vehicles has helped improve urban air quality, much more is needed to make India's cities liveable. Delhi is considered one of the most polluted cities in the world.

The application of the power-law scaling relationship between pollution and population suggests that urban expansion to an extent is responsible for urban diseases, but India's cities need something more than intervention in their physical form, though physical plans are useful for a better shape and quality of life in our cities. The urbanization of small-scale industrial units and increasing demand for private vehicles can be considered as reasons for increasing pollution and congestion in urban India that may not necessarily be an outcome of urbanization but of general economic development and governance.

The success of the Supreme Court intervention through action plans for air pollution reduction in India's cities shows the effectiveness of India's institutional setup, i.e. the legitimacy of policy enforcement is a strong predictor of a policy's success. Note that these interventions were in the form of a legislation-based command-and-control framework and were not bothered about cost-effectiveness. Though the government has taken some pilot steps to move towards providing fiscal incentives for the prevention and control of point source emissions, most of the fiscal incentives are in the form of subsidies or tax rebates. There is a need to have economic incentive-based environmental regulation in the country to meet environmental standards cost-effectively.

The city-specific plans mandated by the Supreme Court orders were able to lower pollution levels in the cities concerned, but led to higher levels of pollution in neighbouring areas and non-intervened cities. A uniform policy of implementation will help check disproportional distribution of emission sources and the resulting air pollution. India also needs to optimize its air pollution monitoring network since most of the monitoring stations are located in metropolitan cities and do not reflect a true picture of urban air pollution in the country.

To reduce traffic congestion in cities, India needs to strengthen its road networks and public transportation infrastructure. While developing such infrastructure, the preferences of commuters should be internalized to bring financial sustainability in providing these services. Commuters are willing to pay for convenient, safe, and comfortable mobility.

In the coming years, it is expected that with an increasing share of national income coming from manufacturing, and with increasing levels of income, urban pollution and congestion problems will be issues of concern. However, rising public environmental awareness and demand for quality of life, coupled with information transparency, will bring more accountability in the decision making of governments and businesses. This will help produce environmentally benign technologies and reduce frictions arising from pollution and congestion.

Acknowledgement

I am thankful to Ms. Prerna Prabhakar for providing excellent research assistance, and the Asian Development Bank for financial support under the project technical assistance 8522: The Urbanization–Poverty–Inequality Triangle in Asia and the Pacific.

References

ADB (Asian Development Bank and CAI-Asia (Clean Air Initiative for Asian Cities). 2006. 'Country Synthesis Report on Urban Air Quality Management India'. Discussion draft.

Bertrand, Trent J. 1978. 'Congestion Costs in a Transport System: With an Application to Bangkok'. *Journal of Transport Economics and Policy 12* (3): 244–79.

Bettencourt, Luís M. A. 2013. 'The Origins of Scaling in Cities'. *Science 340*: 1438–41.

Bettencourt, L. M. A., J. Lobo, D. Helbing, C. Kuhnert, and G. B. West. 2007. 'Growth, Innovation, Scaling, and the Pace of Life in Cities'. *Proceedings of the National Academy of Sciences of the United States of America 104* (17): 7301–6.

Brandon, Carter and Kirsten Hommann. 1995. 'The Cost of Inaction: Valuing the Economy-wide Cost of Environmental Degradation in India'. October memo, Asia Environmental Division, World Bank, Washington, DC.

CAI-Asia Center. 2010. *India: Air Quality Profile*, Pasig City, Philippines.

Chhabra, S. K., J. N. Pande, T. K. Joshi, and P. Kumar. 2001. 'Air Quality and Health'. Paper presented at the workshop on Land Use, Transportation and the Environment, Pune, India. <http://www.deas.harvard.edu/TransportAsia/workshop_papers/ChhabraetalFinal2.pdf>.

CPCB (Central Pollution Control Board). 2010. *Air Quality Monitoring, Emission Inventory and Source Apportionment Study for Indian Cities*, Government of India, New Delhi.

CPCB (Central Pollution Control Board). 2012. *National Ambient Air Quality Status and Trends in India—2010*, Government of India, New Delhi.

Cropper, M., N. B. Simon, A. Alberini, A. Seema, and P. K. Sharma. 1997. 'The Health Benefits of Air Pollution Control in Delhi'. *American Journal of Agricultural Economics 79* (5): 1625–9.

Dasgupta, Susmita and David Wheeler. 1997. 'Citizen Complaints and Environmental Indicators Evidence from China'. *Policy Research Working Paper 1704*, World Bank, Washington, DC.

De la Rue du Can, S., M. McNeil, and J. Sathaye. 2009. 'India Energy Outlook: End Use Demand in India to 2020'. Ernest Orlando Lawrence Berkeley National Laboratory.

Desmet, Klaus and Esteban Rossi-Hansberg. 2013. 'Urban Accounting and Welfare'. *American Economic Review 103* (6): 2296–327.

Enerdata. 2012. *Yearbook 2012: Global Energy Market Review in. 2011.* <http://www.enerdata.net/enerdatauk/press-and-publication/publications/world-energy-statistics-supply-and-demand.php>.

Foster, Andrew and Naresh Kumar. 2011. 'Health Effects of Air Quality Regulations in Delhi, India'. *Atmospheric Environment 45* (9): 1675–83.

Ghani, Ejaz, Arti Grover Goswami, and William R. Kerr. 2012. *Is India's Manufacturing Sector Moving Away from Cities?* The World Bank, Washington, DC.

Ghosh, Ruchira and Arun Kansal. 2014. 'Urban Challenges in India and the Mission for a Sustainable Habitat'. *Interdisciplina 2* (2): 281–304.

Goldar, Bishwanath. 2010. 'Input Substitution and Technical Change in Indian Manufacturing'. *The Journal of Industrial Statistics 1* (2): 1973–2007.

Gonzalez, George A. 2005. 'Urban Sprawl, Global Warming and the Limits of Ecological Modernization'. *Environmental Politics 14*: 344–62.

Government of India, Ministry of Home Affairs. 2011. *Census of India 2011*, New Delhi.

Greenstone, Michael and Rema Hanna. 2014. 'Environmental Regulations, Air and Water Pollution, and Infant Mortality in India'. *American Economic Review 104* (10): 3038–72.

Grossman, Gene M. and Alan B. Krueger. 1995. 'Economic Growth and the Environment'. *The Quarterly Journal of Economics 110* (2): 353–77.

Gupta, Usha. 2008. 'Valuation of Urban Air Pollution: A Case Study of Kanpur City in India'. *Environmental and Resource Economics 41* (3): 315–26.

Guttikunda, Sarath K. and Dinesh Mohan. 2014. 'Re-fueling Road Transport for Better Air Quality in India'. *Energy Policy 68*: 556–61.

Jain, S., P. Aggarwal, P. Kumar, S. Singhal, and P. Sharma. 2014. 'Identifying Public Preferences Using Multi-criteria Decision Making for Assessing the Shift of Urban Commuters from Private to Public Transport: a Case Study of Delhi'. *Transportation Research Part F: Traffic Psychology and Behaviour 24*: 60–70.

Jalan, Jyotsna, E. Somanathan, and Saraswata Chaudhuri. 2009. 'Awareness and the Demand for Environmental Quality: Survey Evidence on Drinking Water in Urban India'. *Environment and Development Economics 14* (6): 665–92.

Jorgenson, Andrew K., James Rice, and Brett Clark. 2010. 'Cities, Slums, and Energy Consumption in Less Developed Countries 1990 to 2005'. *Organization & Environment 23* (2): 189–204.

Kandlikar, Milind and Gurumurthy Ramachandran. 2000. 'The Causes and Consequences of Particulate Air Pollution in Urban India: A Synthesis of the Science'. *Annual Review of Energy and the Environment 25* (1): 629–84.

Kansal, Arun, Mukesh Khare, and Chandra Shekhar Sharma. 2011. 'Air Quality Modelling Study to Analyse the Impact of the World Bank Emission Guidelines for Thermal Power Plants in Delhi'. *Atmospheric Pollution Research 2* (1): 99–105.

Kharola, P. S. and G. Tiwari. 2008. 'Urban Public Transport Systems: Are the Taxation Policies Congenial for their Survival and Growth?' *Economic and Political Weekly 11*: 41–7.

Krupnick, Alan J., Winston Harrington, and Bart Ostro. 1990. 'Ambient Ozone and Acute Health Effects: Evidence from Daily Data'. *Journal of Environmental Economics and Management 18* (1): 1–18.

Kumar, Naresh and Andrew D. Foster. 2009. ' Air Quality Interventions and Spatial Dynamics of Air Pollution in Delhi and its Surroundings'. *International Journal of Environment and Waste Management 4* (1–2): p. 85.

Kumar, Surender and D. N. Rao. 2001. 'Valuing the Benefits of Air Pollution Abatement Using Health Production Function'. *Environmental and Resource Economics 20*: 91–102.

Kumar, Surender and Shunsuke Managi. 2009. *Economics of Sustainable Development: The Case of India*, Springer.

Lamsal, L. N. R. V., D. Martin, D. Parrish, and N. A. Krotkov. 2013. 'Scaling Relationship for NO2 Pollution and Urban Population Size: a Satellite Perspective'. *Environmental Science & Technology 47* (14): 7855–61.

Lu, Zifeng and David G. Streets. 2012. 'Increase in NO x Emissions from Indian Thermal Power Plants During 1996–2010: Unit-based Inventories and Multisatellite Observations'. *Environmental Science & Technology 46* (14): 7463–70.

Lu, Z., D. G. Streets, B. de Foy, and N. A. Krotkov. 2013. 'Ozone Monitoring Instrument Observations of Interannual Increases in SO2 Emissions from Indian Coal-fired Power Plants During 2005–2012'. *Environmental Science & Technology 47* (24): 13993–4000.

Marshall, J. D., T. E. McKone, E. Deakin, and W. W. Nazaroff. 2005. 'Inhalation of Motor Vehicle Emissions: Effects of Urban Population and Land Area'. *Atmospheric Environment 39* (2), 283–95.

Mayeres, Inge. 1993. 'The Marginal External Costs of Car Use—with an Application to Belgium'. *Tijdschrift voor economie en management 38* (3): 225–58.

MGI (McKinsey Global Institute). 2010. *India's Urban Awakening: Building Inclusive Cities, Sustaining Economic Growth*, McKinsey & Company.

MoPNG. 2003. *Auto Fuel Policy Report*, Ministry of Petroleum and Natural Gas, Government of India, New Delhi.

Murty, M. N. and S. C. Gulati. 2005. 'A Generalized Method of Hedonic Prices: Measuring Benefits from Reduced Urban Air Pollution'. *Working Paper E/254/06*, Institute of Economic Growth, New Delhi.

Murty, M. N., S. C. Gulati, and Avishek Banerjee. 2003a. 'Health Benefits from Urban Air Pollution Abatement in the Indian Subcontinent'. *Discussion Paper no. 62/2003*, Institute of Economic Growth, Delhi.

Murty, M. N., S. C. Gulati, and A. Banerjee. 2003b. 'Hedonic Property Prices and Valuation of Benefits from Reducing Urban Air Pollution in India'. *Working Paper E 237/2003*, Institute of Economic Growth, Delhi.

Nandi, J. 2014. 'Delhi's Satellite Towns Bearing the Brunt of Increase in Air Pollution?' *Times of India*, 7 July. <http://timesofindia.indiatimes.com/home/environment/pollution/Delhis-satellite-towns-bearing-the-brunt-of-increase-in-air-pollution/articleshow/37928438.cms>.

Parrish, David D. and Tong Zhu. 2009. 'Clean Air for Megacities'. *Science 326*, 30 October.

Parrish, D. D., W. C. Kuster, M. Shao, Y. Yokouchi, Y. Kondo, P. D. Goldan, J. A. de Gouw, M. Koike, and T. Shirai. 2009. 'Comparison of Air Pollutant Emissions Among Mega-cities'. *Atmospheric Environment 43*: 6435–41.

Pucher, J., N. Korattyswaropam, N. Mittal, and N. Ittyerah. 2005. 'Urban Transport Crisis in India'. *Transport Policy 12* (3): 185–98.

Rouwendal, Jan and Erik T. Verhoef. 2006. 'Basic Economic Principles of Road Pricing: From Theory to Applications'. *Transport Policy 13* (2): 106–14.

Santos, Georgina and David M. G. Newbery. 2001. *Urban Congestion Charging: Theory, Practice and Environmental Consequences*, CESifo Group, Munich.

Sarzynski, Andrea. 2012. 'Bigger Is Not Always Better: A Comparative Analysis of Cities and their Air Pollution Impact'. *Urban Studies 49*: 3121.

Sen, Akshaya Kumar, Geetam Tiwari, and Vrajaindra. 2010. 'Estimating Marginal External Costs of Transport in Delhi'. *Transport Policy 17* (1): 27–37.

Sridhar, Kala Seetharam and Guanghua Wan. 2010. 'Firm Location Choice in Cities: Evidence from China, India, and Brazil'. *China Economic Review 21*: 113–22.

Stopher, Peter R. 2004. 'Reducing Road Congestion: A Reality Check'. *Transport Policy 11* (2): 117–31.

Subbaraman, R., S. Shitole, T. Shitole, K. Sawant, J. O'Brien, D. Bloom, and A. Patil-Deshmukh. 2013. 'The Social Ecology of Water in a Mumbai Slum: Failures in Water Quality, Quantity, and Reliability'. *BMC Public Health 13* (1): 173.

Wachs, Martin. 2002. 'Fighting Traffic Congestion with Information Technology'. *Issues in Science and Technology 19* (1): 43–50.

Walder, J. 2007. *Road User Charging*, Transportation Research Board, London.

WHO (World Health Organization). 2014. Ambient (Outdoor) Air Pollution in Cities Database 2014, WHO, Geneva.

Wilbur Smith Associates and MoUD. 2008. *Study on Traffic and Transportation Policies and Strategies in Urban Areas in India*, Wilbur Smith Associates and Ministry of Urban Development, Ministry of Urban Development, Government of India, Delhi.

World Bank. 2013. *India Diagnostic Assessment of Select Environmental Challenges: An Analysis of Physical and Monetary Losses of Environmental Health and Natural Resources*, Disaster Management and Climate Change Unit, Sustainable Development Department, South Asia Region, New Delhi.

World Bank. 2014. 'World Development Indicators'. World Bank, Washington, DC.

PART IX

POVERTY AND INEQUALITY IN URBANIZATION

20
Urbanization, Inequality, and Poverty in the People's Republic of China

Yuan Zhang

20.1 Urbanization, Growth, and Inequality

20.1.1 Urban–Rural/Interregional Inequality

Over the past three decades, although the People's Republic of China (PRC) has made significant achievements in promoting GDP growth and reducing rural poverty, its performance in reducing inequality, especially between urban and rural areas, has been disappointing. Figure 20.1 depicts the urban–rural ratio of per capita consumption and per capita income from 1978 to 2010. It can be seen that the urban–rural gap in the consumption level was more pronounced than in the income level; furthermore, the urban–rural income ratio and consumption ratio experienced two clear decreasing trends in the early 1980s and the mid-1990s, as well as a slight downward trend in the first few years of the twenty-first century. The gap in both income and consumption between urban and rural residents showed an increasing trend, the income ratio rising from 2.57 in 1978 to a maximum value of 3.33 in 2007, and the consumption ratio rising from 2.9 in 1978 to a maximum value of 3.83 in 2003. This indicates that after the reforms and opening up in 1978, the PRC's urban–rural gap in income and consumption expanded overall.

The urban–rural income and consumption ratio cannot provide a comprehensive description of inequality in the PRC. Table 20.1 shows the Gini index published by the World Bank. These Gini coefficients are based on three different data sources. From 1981 to 2002, all Gini coefficients exhibited a clear upward trend, but after 2002, all Gini coefficients began to show a downward trend. Therefore, inequality in the PRC begins to show a decreasing trend at the beginning of the twenty-first century, irrespective of the index used to depict inequality. This trend is believed to be partly associated with a basket of policies favouring peasants and agricultural production, including rural tax reforms and agricultural subsidies (Zhang 2012).

Yuan Zhang., *Urbanization, Inequality, and Poverty in the People's Republic of China* In: *Cities of Dragons and Elephants: Urbanization and Urban Development in China and India. Edited by:* Guanghua Wan and Ming Lu, Oxford University Press (2019). © Oxford University Press. DOI: 10.1093/oso/9780198829225.003.0020

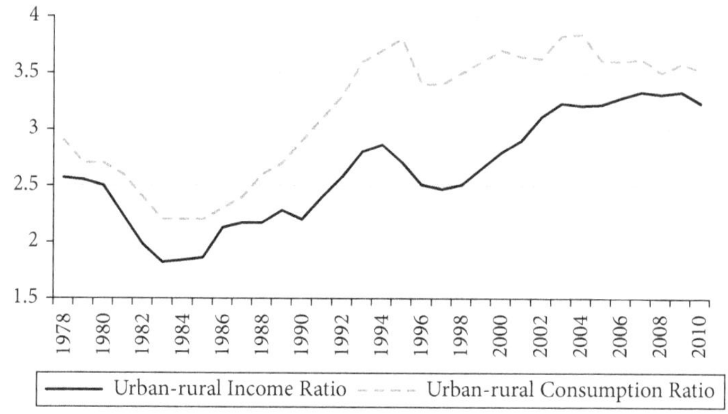

Figure 20.1. Rural–urban income and consumption ratio, 1978–2010

Source: Statistic Yearbook of China, various years.

Table 20.1. Gini index in the PRC, 1981–2005

	1981	1984	1987	1990	1993	1996	1999	2002	2005
Source 1	29.1	27.7	31.7	32.7	38	34.9	38.9	53.6	39.8
Source 2	29.11	27.69	29.85	32.43	35.5	35.7	39.23	42.59	42.48
Source 3	n.a.	n.a.	30.1	34.84	41.96	39.8	41.64	46.3	39.78

Note: Source 1 refers to a new, relatively consistent Gini index created from all eight data sources available to Branko Milanovic, who provides these measures. Source 2 refers to the World Bank-based dataset that covers the period 1978–2011 and includes 124 countries. Source 3 is the World Income Distribution dataset that covers the period 1980–2010 and includes 152 countries.

Source: Website of the World Bank, <http://go.worldbank.org/9VCQW66LA0>.

20.1.2 Poverty in Urban Areas

There is a rich literature explaining the determinants of rural poverty in the PRC (Fan et al. 2000; Jalan and Ravallion 1998, 2000; Montalvo and Ravallion 2009; Chen and Ravallion 2009; Zhang et al. 2003), so this chapter will focus mainly on urban poverty in the PRC. Given the PRC's gradual approach to reforms, its territory and population size, and its very uneven development, serious and significant market fragmentations exist both across provinces and between urban and rural areas. Thus, it is important to consider differences in the price levels between rural and urban areas. Also, in order to compare household income across years, it is necessary to deflate household income with the consumer price index (CPI), using separate urban and rural CPIs with the base year of 2005. To be able to describe poverty in the PRC, we need to convert international poverty lines into local Chinese currency. To begin with, when we measure the poverty rate by the commonly used US$1.25 per day threshold, purchasing power parity (PPP)

Table 20.2. Poor households in urban PRC (%)

Per capita daily income (2005 PPP)	1995	2002	2007
$1.25	3.03	1.87	0.14
$2	16.46	7.26	1.16

Source: Author's calculation based on CHIPS data.

rates reported by the World Development Indicators of the World Bank[1] typically result in a rural poverty rate way beyond what is commonly perceived as the actual poverty rates in rural PRC. Thus, we use PPPs derived from PovcalNet data. These were 4.02 for urban areas and 2.95 for rural areas in 2005, compared to the official PPP rates of 4.09.

We measure poverty by the headcount ratio, using international poverty lines. Table 20.2 presents the profile of urban poverty in the PRC. Several observations are immediately evident from Table 20.2. From 1995 to 2007, urban households experienced phenomenal poverty reduction. In 1995, less than 4 per cent of urban households remained below $1.25 a day, and the proportion of poor urban households under $1.25 a day dropped substantially to only 0.14 per cent in 2007. More impressively, the share of urban households that remained below $2 a day dropped sharply from more than 16 per cent to nearly 1 per cent.

20.1.3 Inequality in Urban Areas

The average money wage of Chinese urban workers increased from 615 to 47,593 RMB from 1978 to 2012 (NBSC 2013a). Accompanying this unprecedented growth was a considerable increase in income inequality. Figure 20.2 depicts the trends of the provincial Gini and Theil indices in urban areas in the past two decades. It shows that inequality in urban PRC has an increasing trend over time. The Gini index has the same pattern as that of the Theil index. So, we can conclude that the increasing inequality in urban areas from the early 1990s is a stylized fact in the PRC. The urbanization process plays an important role in enlarging inequality in the PRC. For example, using the sample of the 2005 population census in the PRC, Chen et al. (2014) examined the relationship between income inequality and city size and found that overall income inequality is higher for larger cities. In addition, they identified the potential channels through which city size can affect inequality and found that education, migration, and the degree of ownership restructuring together can explain most of the correlation between city size and inequality. Rising housing prices during the process of urbanization and marketization can

[1] Based on the findings of the 2005 International Comparison Program.

Figure 20.2. Inequality in urban PRC, 1991–2010

Source: Author's calculation using household grouped data from the Statistic Yearbook of NBSC.[2]

also help explain the increasing inequality in urban China. One important issue is assets inequality. For example, urbanization improves the demand for housing. As a result, it improves the asset inequality of urban citizens. Accompanying this process, the privatization of public houses also plays an important role in enlarging assets inequality. Using CHIPS (China Household Income Project Survey) 1995 and 2002 data, Li et al. (2005) mapped the assets inequality of urban households and found that the privatization of public housing in urban PRC enlarged the rural–urban assets inequality, and that the inequality of financial assets will play a more important role in driving the inequality of gross assets in the PRC. Similarly, using a unique set of repeated cross-sectional data, Meng et al. (2013) examined the causes of this increase in urban workers' earnings inequality and found that the major changes occurred in the 1990s when the labour market moved from a centrally planned system to a market-oriented system.

20.1.4 Spatial Dimensions of Urban Poverty

Given the PRC's territory and population size and very uneven development, poor households are not equally distributed across urban areas. Employing CHIPS 1995 and CHIPS 2002, we have mapped the regional distribution of poverty in urban PRC, where household welfare is measured by consumption expenditure, and both $1.25 and 2$ poverty lines are adopted. Table 20.3 shows that consumption poverty in urban PRC is mainly concentrated in central areas, followed by western areas and then eastern areas.

[2] The data source is described in detail in the Appendix.

Table 20.3. Expenditure cutoffs for defining urban poverty, 1995 and 2002

	Per capita daily consumption	Subtotal (%)	East (%)	Central (%)	West (%)
1995	$1.25	6.18	1.10	3.71	1.36
	$2	25.24	4.54	13.37	7.32
2002	$1.25	3.17	0.51	1.95	0.72
	$2	14.07	2.44	7.85	3.79

Source: Calculated from CHIPS 1995 and CHIPS 2002 urban samples.

Table 20.4. Distribution of income poverty using CGSS 2006 data

Per capita daily income	East (%)	Central (%)	West (%)
$1.25	1.02	2.54	1.81
$2	3.79	9.24	4.40

Source: Calculated from the CGSS 2006 urban sample.

In addition, we employed the China General Social Survey (CGSS) 2006 data to further map urban poverty in the PRC. Table 20.4 presents the results, where we can find that most of the urban households under the $1.25 and $2 poverty lines are distributed in central and western China, and the poverty rate in eastern China is the lowest. So, the regional distribution pattern revealed in Table 20.4 is nearly the same as that in Table 20.3.

20.1.5 Impact of Urbanization on Poverty and Inequality

Before examining the effects of the PRC's urbanization on poverty and inequality, we need to resolve the problem of data issues. The National Bureau of Statistics of China does not report provincial measures of poverty and inequality, such as the Gini or Theil indices. In order to resolve this problem, we first tried to calculate the provincial index of poverty and inequality based on present statistics.[3] These are headcount ratios measured by the $1.25 and $2 poverty lines (2005 PPP), the Gini index, and the Theil index. These values were estimated from grouped household income data published by national and provincial bureaus of statistics in the PRC. With these provincial-level data at hand, we can empirically test the relationship between urbanization, poverty, and inequality in the PRC.

[3] The method of calculating the provincial poverty and inequality index is introduced in the Appendix.

Figure 20.3 describes the relationship between urbanization and headcount ratio in rural PRC measured by the $2 poverty line. From Figure 20.3, we can see that rural poverty is negatively correlated with urbanization on a provincial level, suggesting that urbanization has an effect of reducing rural poverty.

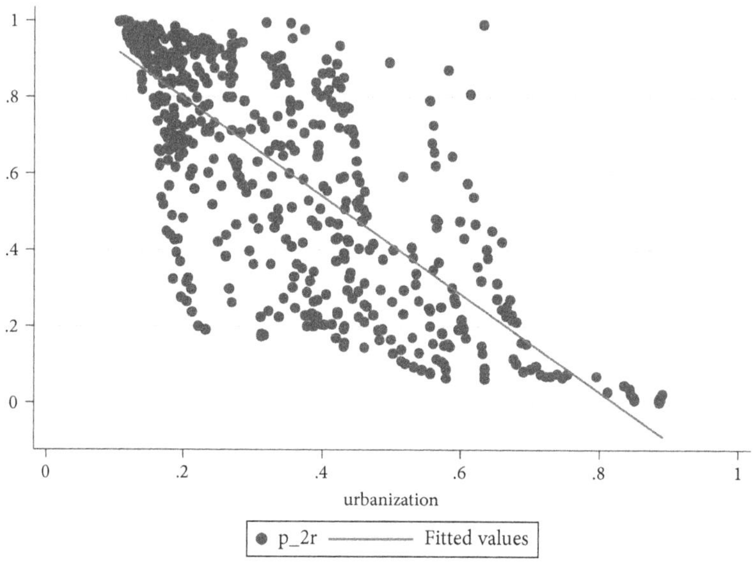

Figure 20.3. Urbanization and rural poverty

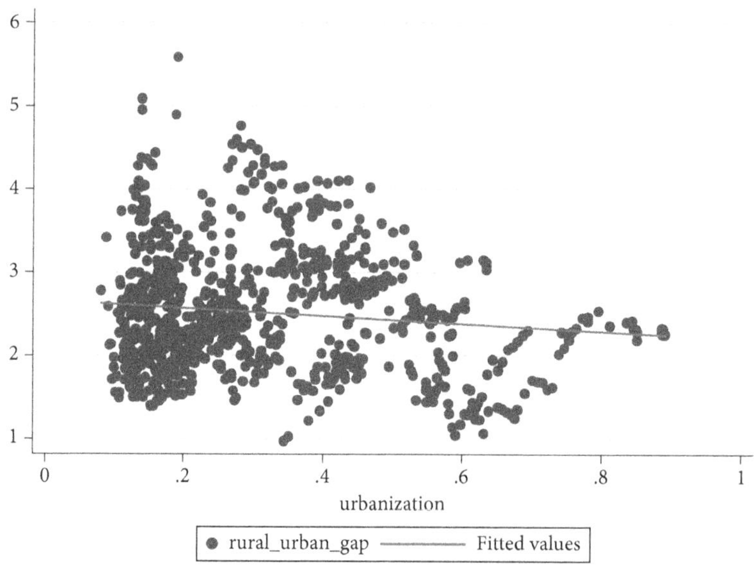

Figure 20.4. Urbanization and the rural–urban income gap

Figure 20.4 depicts the relationship between urbanization and the rural–urban gap, showing a negative relationship between them, which suggests that urbanization also has the effect of reducing rural–urban income gaps. This result is consistent Figure 20.3, which shows that urbanization can reduce rural poverty.

Figures 20.5 and 20.6 describe the relationship between urbanization and the Gini index and the Theil index at the provincial level, indicating a similar conclusion as that from Figure 20.4. These results can be explained by the structural change in urban sectors during the process of urbanization. A large proportion of surplus rural labour migrates to urban PRC and works there with higher-wage incomes. As a result, the migrants suffer less poverty than those staying back in their home towns, and this decreases inequality in the PRC, especially rural–urban inequality.

Figure 20.7 describes the relationship between urbanization and urban poverty, where again we find a negative relationship between them, indicating that higher urbanization is correlated with lower urban poverty.

However, Figures 20.3–20.7 only provide a very preliminary description of the effect of urbanization on poverty and inequality. The negative correlation does not necessarily suggest that urbanization can reduce poverty and inequality in general. In order to get robust conclusions, we ran some regressions to see if these conclusions still hold when some other variables are controlled. All variables in the regressions are defined in Table A.20.2 in the Appendix, and the regression results of the fixed effect and random effect models are presented in Tables A.20.3 and A.20.4 respectively. From these regression results, we can generate the following conclusions: first, urbanization can help reduce rural poverty; second,

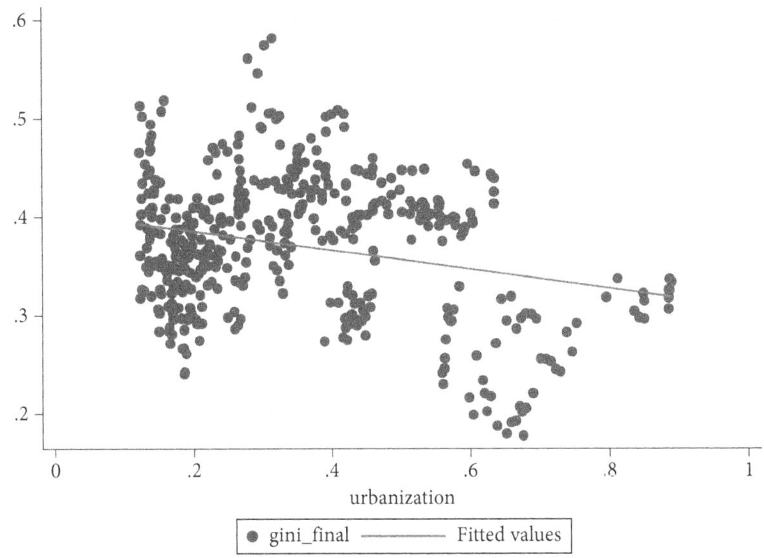

Figure 20.5. Urbanization and the Gini index

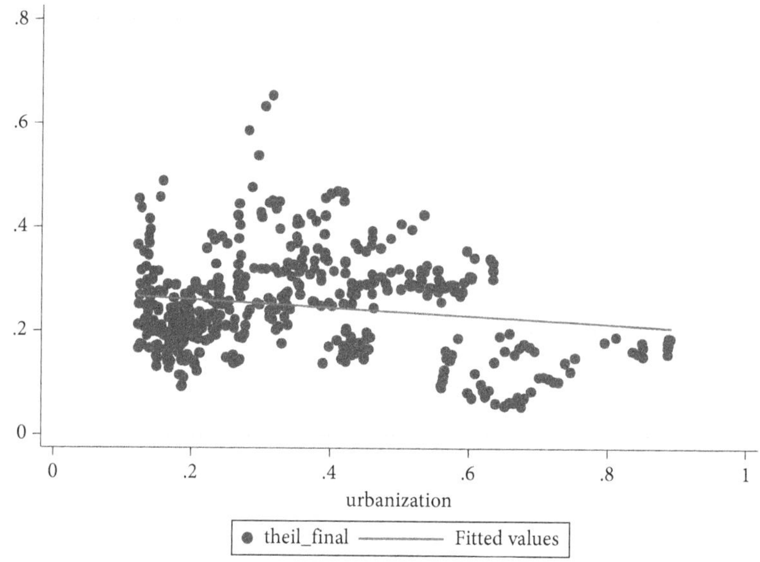

Figure 20.6. Urbanization and the Theil index

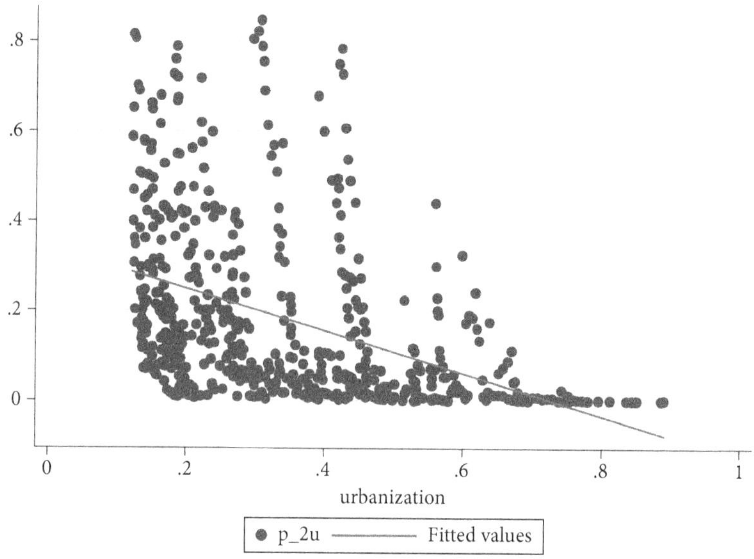

Figure 20.7. Urbanization and urban poverty

urbanization can reduce the rural–urban gap, and the provincial Gini index and Theil index; third, we find that urbanization increases urban poverty rather than reducing it. This can be explained by two facts. First, the structural changes, especially in the late 1990s, created a lot of jobless growth, while the government's social protection system lagged behind the transition of the economy. Consequently, the poverty of urban households increased rather than decreased in some periods. Second, a large number of migrating peasants entered the urban labour market and competed for job opportunities with urban citizens, which decreased the welfare of some urban workers and, as a result, increased urban poverty. Employing the urban sample from the Population Census of 2005, Liu and Zhao (2009) investigated the effect of rural–urban migration on the employment rate and wages of urban workers and found that, other things being equal, a 10 per cent increase in rural–urban labour migration resulted in a 0.3 per cent decrease in the employment rate for urban workers and a 0.65 per cent decrease in the wages of urban workers.

20.1.6 Segregation Issues in Terms of the Location of Poor Households within Cities

Ghetto housing in urban areas is believed to be harmful in reducing poverty and inequality, and is an obstacle to the building of a harmonious society; residential segregation is highly correlated with ghetto housing in developed and developing economies (Collins and Margo 2000; Wilson 1987; Haynie 2002; Haynie and Osgood 2005; Warr 2002). With rapid urbanization in the PRC, residential segregation has become a serious issue. Only micro data with residential locations can be used to measure residential segregation. Unfortunately, we do not have such data. So, we next provide only some evidence of spatial clustering that reflects the residential segregation problem in urban PRC. Using the CHIPS 2002 data, Table 20.5 presents the residential distribution of poor households in urban PRC. Three conclusions can be generalized from this table. First, moving from the centre of the city to the suburbs, the headcount ratio has an increasing trend, with a few exceptions. Second, this pattern does not change whether poverty is measured by the $1.25 poverty line or the $2 poverty line. Third, the distribution pattern also does not change if poverty is measured by daily consumption, rather than daily income, although the absolute level of headcount ratio is much higher when consumption is employed to measure poverty. The pattern indicated in Table 20.5 suggests that there is very clear residential clustering in urban PRC.

During the urbanization process in the PRC, a huge number of peasants migrated to urban labour markets, but they could not join the social protection system meant for urban citizens. So, in urban PRC, residential clustering and segregation not only exists between urban citizens but also between urban citizens and migrating peasants. Using a 2006–7 urban household survey in Shanghai and Shenzhen, Chen et al. (2013) found evidence that residential segregation between migrating peasants and urban households already exists in these two cities, where migrating peasants have worse living conditions, a lower evaluation of their residential quarters, and lower trust in their neighbourhoods. Similarly,

Table 20.5. Residential clustering of poor urban households in the PRC

	Income poverty (%)		Consumption poverty (%)	
	Pov_$1.25	Pov_$2	Pov_$1.25	Pov_$2
Centre of the city	1.34	5.74	3.32	15.03
In city	1.24	6.80	3.75	16.69
In near suburbs	2.07	7.40	4.73	16.72
In outer suburbs	0.78	6.98	16.28	28.68

Source: Calculated by the author using the sample of urban households from CHIPS 2002.

using the samples in Shanghai from the 2010 population census in the PRC, Chen and Hao (2013) found that more migrating peasants live outside the downtown. They further examined the level of residential segregation in 2010 in Shanghai and found that residential segregation between locals and migrating peasants is already serious in Shanghai and has accelerated in recent years.

20.2 Urban Labour Market and Poverty

20.2.1 Urban Informal Sector Employment and Poverty

According to Harris and Todaro (1970), the urban labour market in developing economies is generally segmented into an informal market and a formal market. Specifically, the formal labour market provides high-wage jobs with better working conditions, and workers have more opportunities to be promoted. On the other hand, the informal labour market only provides low-wage jobs with worse working conditions, and workers have very few opportunities to be promoted. So, having opportunities to be employed in the formal labour market is crucial for workers' wages and related welfare and, as a result, it is an important determinant of urban poverty. Most economists agree that the urban labour market in the PRC is a segmented one (Cai 2000; Wang and Zuo 1999; Yang and Chen 2000; Yan 2006; Meng and Zhang 2001).

In order to investigate the role of the informal sector in urban poverty, we first need a classification of the formal and informal sectors. In the present literature, Yan (2006) classifies most of the public sectors and state-owned enterprises (SOEs) as the formal sector, and small and medium enterprises as the informal sector. Following this definition, and taking into account the available information in CHIPS 2002, we classify the following units as comprising the formal sector: first, workers in the party and government bodies; second, workers in governmental or collective institutions; third, workers solely in SOEs; fourth, workers in state-controlled enterprises; fifth, workers in any other unit with more than one hundred employees. Workers who do not belong to any one of these five categories are in the informal sector. Using this definition and the urban household samples from CHIPS 2002,[4] we find that the number of household members being employed in the informal sector is positively correlated with income and consumption poverty, and the ratio of household members in the informal sector is also positively correlated with poverty. So, we can conclude that more household members being employed in the informal sector significantly improves the probability of falling into poverty for an urban household.

In order to get more robust results, we employed Probit models to investigate if being employed by the informal sector increases the probability of falling into poverty for an urban household. In the regression models, the dependent variable is whether an urban household is poor, measured by per capita income or consumption level, using the $1.25 and $2 poverty lines. We measured the effect of employment by the informal sector by two variables. The first one is *No_informal*, indicating the gross number of household members working in the informal sector, and the second one is *Ratio_informal*, indicating the share of household members employed in the informal sector. The variables *Age*, *Age_square*, *Male*, *Edu_year*, *Partymember*, and *Minority*, indicate characteristics of the household head: age, squared term of age, gender, years of schooling, whether a member of the CCP, and whether a minority, respectively. The variable *Depend_ratio* measures the dependent ratio of a household. *East* and *Central* are regional dummies representing eastern and central PRC.

Table A.20.5 in the Appendix presents the regression results of Probit models. The following conclusions can be deduced. First, *No_informal* and *Ratio_informal* are significant in all models, suggesting that more household members being employed in the informal sector significantly improves the probability of falling into poverty for an urban household. Second, most of characteristics of the household head are significant. Age of household head in the equation of $2 poverty has a reversed U-shape relationship with the probability of falling into poverty. Schooling years has a significant effect on reducing poverty. Being a party member of the CCP can also reduce poverty. Higher dependent ratio results in more poverty. These results all coincide with those from the present literature.

20.2.2 Rural-to-Urban Migration and Urban Poverty

In 2012, there were 260 million migrating peasants working in urban labour markets (NBSC 2013b). The present literature on rural poverty generally finds that migrating into urban labour markets can help rural households escape from

[4] The headcount ratio in 2007 was very low, so we only employ CHIPS 2002 rather than CHIPS 2007 to examine the role of the informal sector in poverty and poverty reduction in urban PRC.

poverty. On the one hand, the empirical test in Section 20.2.1 indicates that being employed by the informal sector improves the probability of falling into poverty for urban households. On the other hand, the present literature does not provide evidence that migrating into urban areas can help migrating peasants escape from poverty. So, we next employed household samples in CHIPS 2007 to investigate the determinants of poverty of migrating peasants.

Migrating peasants cannot join the urban social protection system and have no equal access to the public goods in urban PRC. In most cases, the parents and children of migrating peasants do not migrate together with them to urban areas. So, when measuring their poverty, we do not use per capita income, but use individual income to quantify migrating peasants' welfare levels—that is, here we measure individual poverty rather than household poverty.

In the questionnaire of CHIPS 2007 for migrating peasants, there is a very interesting question: if a migrating peasant did not leave his/her home town, how much does he/she earn in a month? This information can be used to measure their poverty at home and compare it with their monthly income after migrating to urban areas. This way, we can gauge the effect of migration on poverty reduction and understand the relationship between rural–urban migration and urban poverty. Table 20.6 presents the headcount ratio of migrating households. Using monthly wage after migrating into urban areas to measure poverty, and adopting the 1.25$ poverty line, we found that only 0.081 per cent of migrants fall into poverty, and adopting the 2$ poverty line, only 0.42 per cent of migrants are poor, which indicates that most migrant workers are not poor at all. However, if we use monthly wage at home to measure poverty, the headcount ratio increases sharply to more than 8 per cent or about 14 per cent, respectively. This comparison suggests that rural–urban migration can help migrating peasants escape poverty.

According to Harris and Todaro (1970), the informal labour market in developing economies is crucial for migrating peasants as it provides them with some jobs at an early stage, although wages are not very high and social protection is not very good. The present literature finds that most migrating workers are employed in the informal sector (Cai 2000; Wang and Zuo 1999; Yang and Chen 2000; Yan 2006; Meng and Zhang 2001). During urbanization, the informal sector plays an important role in providing jobs for migrating peasants.

Table 20.6. Headcount ratio of migrating peasants in 2007

	$1.25	$2
Monthly wage at home (%)	8.04	13.85
Monthly wage after migrating into urban areas (%)	0.081	0.42

Source: Calculated from migrant samples in CHIPS 2007.

Table 20.7. Characteristics of migrating peasants in the informal and formal sectors

	Informal sector	Formal sector
No. of observation	3,639	2,506
Age	31.06	30.53
female	42.07%	35.43%
Health_soso	44.71%	43.38%
Health_bad	15.11%	11.89%
Health_verybad	1.70%	0.92%
Edu_year	8.24	8.84
Experience	3.88	3.37
Work_hour	65.58	55.61
Month_wage	1,655.26	1,485.02
Home_wage	690.72	724.45
Hourwage	6.18	6.65

Source: Calculated from migrant samples in CHIPS 2007.

Table 20.7 presents a statistical description of migrating peasants in the formal and informal sectors.[5]

Table 20.7 indicates that more than half of migrating peasants are in the informal sector. This suggests that although wages are lower in the informal sector, they can provide jobs to migrating peasants with very low education or bad health conditions and provide more job opportunities for male peasants. So, the existence of the informal sector is crucial for migrating peasants, although it has a significant effect on increasing the probability of falling into poverty for urban citizens.

20.3 The Multifaceted Nature of Poverty and Urbanization

20.3.1 Consumption Poverty

Household with a daily income higher than \$2 may consume less than \$2 a day because of illness, lack of social protection, debt crisis, or other negative shocks. In this case, their welfare level is still under the poverty line. So, income poverty may conceal or underestimate the true situation. Employing CHIPS 2002–7, Table 20.8 presents the headcount ratios measured by daily income and daily consumption, where the \$1.25 and \$2 poverty lines are adopted. We can see that headcount ratios measured by consumption level are much higher than those

[5] The questionnaires for migrating peasants and urban citizens are different, so the definition of a formal sector for migrating peasants is slightly different from that for urban citizens in that for migrating peasants, if the gross number of employees of a company or organization is higher than fifty, it is regarded as a formal sector, while for urban citizens, if the gross number of employees of a company or organization is higher than one hundred, it is regarded as a formal sector.

Table 20.8. Consumption vs income poverty in the PRC

			CHIPS 2002	CHIPS 2007
Income	$1.25	Urban (%)	1.87	0.14
		Rural (%)	21.71	2.81
	$2	Urban (%)	5.39	1.02
		Rural (%)	26.33	8.25
Consumption	$1.25	Urban (%)	2.91	3.30
		Rural (%)	58.82	11.30
	$2	Urban (%)	12.99	9.52
		Rural (%)	81.79	34.37

Source: Calculated from the rural and urban samples in CHIPS 2002 and 2007.

measured by income level. This pattern applies to both rural and urban areas in the PRC.

At present in urban PRC consumption poverty is more serious in the case of migrating peasants because while they work in urban areas, they cannot join the social protection system for urban citizens. As a result, they may have a daily income higher than $2, but have daily consumption levels under $2. Using the migrating peasants sample in CHIPS 2007, Table 20.9 presents their income structure and consumption structure.

Table 20.9 shows that in 2007, the household average net income for migrating peasants was 26,270 RMB, where 17,397 came from wage income, accounting for nearly 70 per cent of the total net income. In the total net income, 15,987 RMB was consumed, where consumption on food, clothes, and residence comprised the main component of total consumption expenditure, and the shares of expenditures on durable goods, medicine, and medical services was relatively low.

According to Table 20.9, we can calculate the gross saving rate of migrating peasants at 39.14 per cent. Table 20.10 presents the gross saving rate of urban households and rural households. This comparison shows that the gross saving rate of migrant peasants is the highest. Although the gross saving rate of urban households is higher than that of rural households, it is still much lower than that of migrating peasants.

Contrary to a high saving rate, migrating peasants have very low expenditure on durable goods. Table 20.11 presents the ownership of durable goods for migrating peasants, urban households, and rural households in 2007, respectively. From this table, we can see that ownership of a television, washing machine, motorbike, and refrigerator for migrating peasants is much lower than that for rural households and urban households. There are some exceptions in that migrating peasants are more likely to own a camera, personal computer, air conditioner, and mobile phone than rural households, which can be explained by the fact that the former use these durable goods more often in urban areas than their counterparts in rural areas.

Table 20.9. Net income, consumption, and their composition for migrating peasants (RMB)

Net income	**26,270.28**
Wage income	17,397.12
Net income from household business	8,407.2
Property income	279.84
Transfer income	186.12
Consumption expenditure	15,987.07
Food	6,262.44
Clothes	1,739.88
Living expenditure	3,153.84
Durable goods	820.44
Consumer goods and services	702.19
Medicine and health care	699.55
Traffic expenditure	667.60
Communicational expenditure	890.97
Entertainment and cultural expenditure	245.89
Educational expenditure	557.27
Insurance expenditure	79.90
Other consumption expenditure	167.10
Remittance back to home town	2,458.68
Deposit	1,118.74

Note: We transferred all expenditures calculated monthly into annual expenditure values. There are 5,000 urban household samples in CHIPS 2007.

Table 20.10. Saving rates of migrating peasants, urban citizens, and rural citizens in 2007

	Migrating peasants	**Urban residents**	**Rural residents**
Gross saving rate (%)	39.14	27.48	22.14

Note: Gross saving rates of urban residents and rural residents have been calculated using the *China Statistical Yearbook* (NBSC 2008).

In the present literature, Chen et al. (2014) proposed three channels through which Hukou constraints cause lower levels of consumption among migrating peasants in comparison with urban residents: precautionary saving motivation, lower permanent income, and lower incentive to consume durable goods. Employing CHIPS 2007 data, they provided empirical evidence indicating that these hypotheses cannot be rejected. Table 20.11 suggests that migrating peasants spend much less on durable goods than urban households and much less than rural households. This result can help explain the high and increasing saving rate in the PRC in the past decades.

Table 20.11. Number of durable goods per 100 households in the PRC

	Migrating peasants	Urban residents	Rural residents
Television	58.89	137.8	106.5
Motorbike	6.85	24.8	48.5
Washing machine	18.83	96.8	45.9
Refrigerator	17.80	95.0	26.1
Camera	7.01	45.1	4.3
Personal computer	9.66	53.8	3.7
Air conditioner	15.21	95.1	8.5
Cell phone	118.44	165.2	77.8
Audio	10.85	30.2	–
Car	1.38	6.1	–
Water heater	11.65	79.5	–

Note: Data on ownership of durable goods for urban citizens and rural citizens come from the *China Statistical Yearbook* (NBSC 2008).

20.3.2 Other Dimensions of Poverty

For Sen (1981), poverty is not low well-being, but the inability to pursue well-being because of the lack of economic means. Similarly, Blackwood and Lynch (1994) assert that poverty does not end abruptly once an additional dollar of income raises a family's (or individual's) income beyond a discretely defined poverty line. It is more accurate to conceive of poverty as a continuous function of varying gradation. So, as a multidimensional index, poverty can also be reflected by illness, illiteracy, or having no access to clean water or sanitation.

Li and Knight (2002) examined the nature of poverty in urban PRC. By combining income and consumption criteria, they distinguished between three types of poverty: chronic, transient, and voluntary poverty.[6] Chronic poverty refers to income and consumption levels being lower than the poverty line, transient poverty refers to the income level being lower than the poverty line and the consumption level being higher than the poverty line, and voluntary poverty refers to the income level being higher than the poverty line and the consumption level being lower than the poverty line. Employing 1999 cross-section household survey data covering six provinces of the PRC, Li and Knight (2002) found that a large proportion of the poor are in voluntary poverty.

Another dimension of poverty that needs to be addressed during urbanization of the PRC is housing poverty. For example, until 1978, the average living space per person in urban PRC was only 3.6 sq. m (in terms of housing construction

[6] Using panel data, another study also proposed similar terms with different means to describe the welfare of poor households. For example, a household being poor in most of the observation periods is persistently poor, while a household falling into poverty in a few of the observation periods is transiently poor.

space, 6.7 sq. m), and 47.5 per cent of urban households had living space less than 2 sq. m per person (Hou et al. 1999). Over the last two decades, the PRC has experienced a drastic transformation of the housing system as well as rapid urbanization. A huge number of houses has been built during this time period, accompanied by a rapid increase in housing prices, making home purchases increasingly unaffordable for low-income households and particularly for young workers (Chen et al. 2010). Meanwhile, most migrating peasants are excluded from the formal housing market, and they are concentrated in so-called 'urban villages' (Zheng et al. 2009). According to an official report, in 2011 the private rental market accommodated only 37 per cent of migrating peasants, while the rest mainly lived in overcrowded dorms or shanty sheds at their workplaces (PFPC 2012). Using survey data covering thirteen cities in six provincial-level administrative units in 1999, Hiroshi (2006) provided evidence that a new type of housing poverty was emerging among migrating peasants in the late 1990s. It is not easy to set a relevant measurement of housing poverty applicable to urban PRC. If the proportion of rent actually paid in total household expenditure is used as a simple measurement of housing poverty, and the poverty line is set at the 30 per cent level, Hiroshi (2006) found that 28 per cent of migrating peasants in Beijing are below the poverty line. No urban household in Beijing, by contrast, is under this poverty line. When the same housing poverty line is employed for thirteen cities, 21 per cent of the migrating peasants are in housing poverty, whereas no urban household living in rented housing is below the poverty line. Zhang and Chen (2014) provide further evidence from present-day Shanghai. Using a pool of household-level micro data from three waves of the national population census (2000, 2005, and 2010), they traced the evolution of housing overcrowding conditions in Shanghai and found that the overall incidence of housing overcrowding in Shanghai did not improve over the period from 2000 to 2010. They also found that migrating peasants are more likely to be subject to the risks of overcrowding than urban citizens, other things being equal.

20.4 Anti-Poverty (Inequality) Policies (Short-Run and Long-Run Policies) in the Context of Urbanization

20.4.1 Employment-Related Programs

Reforms in the urban sector, which started from the 1990s, brought not only many benefits to urban citizens but also some challenges. For example, economic reforms in 1995–9 created 24 million laid-off workers, and registered unemployment jumped from 3.8 million in 1990 to 5.8 million in 1999, a more than 50 per cent growth in nine years (NBSC 2000). Being laid off or unemployed is a negative shock, which brings uncertainty to jobs and wages for a household, and, as a

Table 20.12. Headcount ratio of employed, unemployed, and laid-off workers

	Annual income	Age	Years of schooling	Poverty_1.25 (%)	Poverty_2 (%)
Working or employed	12,108.10	40.48	11.41	1.49	3.57
Laid-off (Xia Gang)	3,346.19	41.45	9.71	33.61	47.34
Unemployed (Shi YE)	3,700.40	38.67	9.88	34.16	44.27

Data source: Urban household sample from CHIPS 2002.

result, may increase poverty. Employing a cross-section household survey covering six provinces of the PRC in 1999, Appleton et al. (2005) found that even after being re-employed, wages of the unemployed or laid-off workers still decreased significantly. Table 20.12 shows that the average annual wage of the laid-off workers is only about 27.6 per cent of that of employed workers, and even slightly lower than that of the unemployed. The laid-off workers are older than employed and unemployed workers and have lower schooling years than employed workers. Adopting the $1.25 and $2 poverty lines, the headcount ratio of laid-off workers is surprisingly higher than that of employed workers.

In order to relieve the unrest caused by huge lay-offs, the central and local government established the so-called Service Center of Re-employment (SCR) to provide some help to the laid-off workers. There are some basic differences between laid-off workers and unemployed workers. First, unemployed workers terminate their employment relationship or terminate their contracts with employers, while laid-off workers still have an employment relationship with their employers. Second, laid-off workers can still get some subsidy from their employers or from the SCR, and the SCR pays some insurance to them. Third, the SCR can provide some job opportunities to the laid-off workers. For example, the SCR can allocate some jobs created by local governments to laid-off workers by discriminating against migrating peasants. Some statistics reveal that not all laid-off workers can get subsidy from the SCR. For example, according to the official statistics, in 1999 about 40 per cent of laid-off workers did not get a subsidy or lower subsidy other than the amount specified by the central government (NBSC 2000). This suggests that the effect of subsidies for laid-off workers on reducing urban poverty is not very positive.

20.4.2 Minimum Wage and Poverty Reduction

A minimum wage is a very common policy adopted by developed economies to protect the welfare of low-wage workers and also is used by policymakers to reduce poverty. It is thought to be effective at reducing poverty as it can guarantee the wages of employed workers. However, if the minimum wage is higher than the market-clearing level, disemployment will be boosted in the labour market. So, the net effect of a minimum wage on poverty reduction is not straightforward. Addison and Blackburn (1999) adopted an approach that links increases in both federal and state minimum wages to contemporaneous changes in poverty rates in the US, and found that in the period 1983–96, the minimum wage had a poverty-reducing effect among teenagers and older junior high-school dropouts. However, using data drawn from the March Current Population Survey, Sabia and Burkhauser (2010) found that state and federal minimum wage increases between 2003 and 2007 had no effect on state poverty rates, which suggests that raising the federal minimum wage continues to be an inadequate way to help the working poor. Similarly, using 2004 survey data from Ontario of Canada, Mascella et al. (2009) found that, first, over 80 per cent of low-wage earners are not members of poor households and, second, over 75 per cent of poor households do not have a member who is a low-wage earner. They also presented simulation results which suggested that even without any negative employment effects, planned increases in Ontario's minimum wage will lead to virtually no reduction in the level of poverty.

The Chinese government issued the 'Regulation of Minimum Wages' on 30 December 2003, and put it into force from 1 March 2004. However, there is very little literature investigating the role of a minimum wage in the PRC's urban labour market. Using the 1998–2007 industrial enterprises panel data, Ma et al. (2012) found that a 10 per cent increase in the minimum wage significantly decreased the number of workers by 0.6 per cent. To fill this gap in the literature, this subsection makes use of provincial panel data to investigate the effect of a minimum wage on urban poverty.

We first plot the minimum wage and poverty ratio at the provincial level in Figure 20.8, where we find that there is a clear negative relationship between them, which suggests that the minimum wage has an effect of reducing urban poverty, and this conclusion still holds when poverty is measured by different poverty lines.

In the Appendix, Table A.20.6 presents the regression results, where the dependent variable is the urban poverty rate at the provincial level and the key independent variable is 'logmini_wage', indicating the provincial level of minimum wage, which is collected from the websites of provincial governments. The other ten independent variables are controlled in the regression models, where 'urbanization' measures the share of urban population; 'logavegdp' measures the per capita GDP in logarithm; 'gdp1_ratio' and 'gdp2_ratio' measure the share of primary GDP and industrial GDP in total GDP respectively; 'fdi_gdp', 'export_gdp', and 'import_gdp' measure the ratio of FDI, export, and import to total GDP respectively; and 'east', 'central', and 'timetrend' are regional dummies and time trend, respectively. From the regression results, we can see that the minimum wage is significantly negative in all the models, suggesting that increasing the minimum wage has a

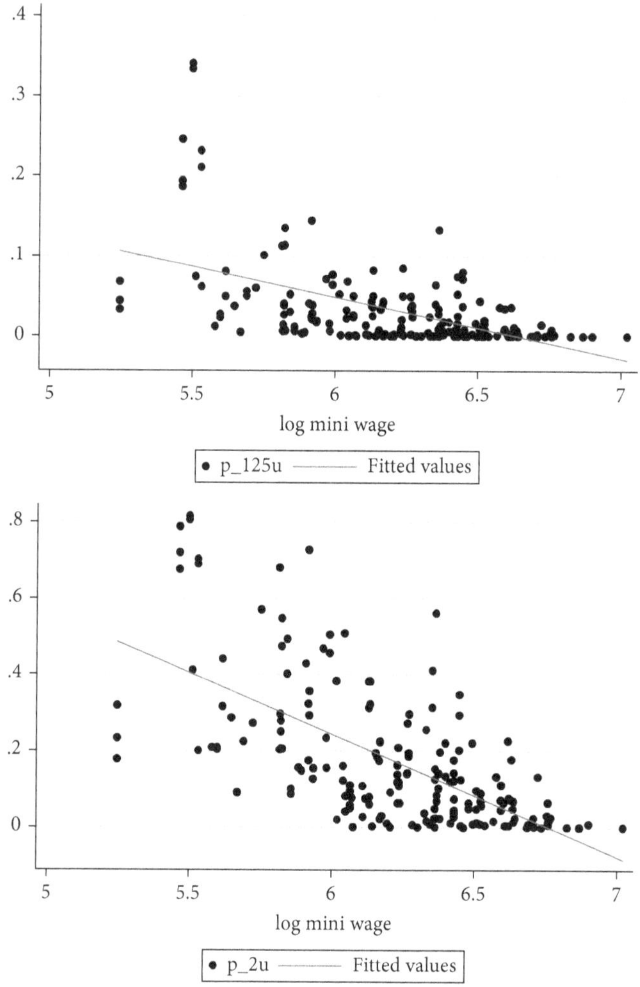

Figure 20.8. Relationship between minimum wage and urban poverty

significant effect on reducing urban poverty. This conclusion still holds even if we further control the disposable income of urban citizens and some other variables.

20.4.3 Social Security

From the 1990s, the economic restructuring and reform of SOEs in urban PRC has led to widespread lay-offs, unemployment, and income insecurity. As a result, urban poverty increased in the 1990s. Using a large, repeated cross-section household survey from 1986 to 2000, Meng et al. (2005) mapped the changes in income, inequality, and poverty over the fifteen-year period and investigated the determinants of poverty in urban PRC, and found that the reduction in social welfare provision, deregulation of grain prices, and increases in income uncertainty in the 1990s increased urban poverty. In order to guarantee the basic needs of urban citizens, central and local governments set up the system of social assistance, Minimum Living Guarantee (Di Bao), in 1999, and brought all urban citizens into this system in 2003. Due to the lack of data, very few studies provide evidence on what effect Di Bao has had on reducing urban poverty. Using a survey covering large parts of urban PRC in 2002, Gustafsson and Deng (2007) investigated the factors affecting receipt and how receipt affects urban poverty. Results from estimating probability models indicate that Di Bao receipt is strongly linked to joblessness among household members. However, Gustafsson and Deng (2007) also found that the Di Bao payments are small and many of the urban poor are not receivers, and, as a result, much urban poverty still remains. This indicates that the effect of Di Bao on reducing urban poverty is very limited.

In urban PRC, another tool in the social security system is the unemployment subsidy or unemployment insurance. Unfortunately, their effect on urban poverty is very weak. Official statistics suggest that in 1999, only 47 per cent of the registered unemployed received an unemployment subsidy, and the level of subsidy was only 1,174 RMB, which is about 12 per cent of an urban citizen's average wage income (NBSC 2000). Similarly, Li and Knight (2002) found that the employers of many of the unemployed did not pay unemployment insurance to them because of the financial squeeze during the 1990s and, as a result, the unemployed had no source of income during unemployment. Taken together, very little literature provides evidence that the effect of the social security system on anti-poverty in urban PRC is effective.

20.4.4 Asset Formation and Empowerment of the Poor

As a productive factor, asset formation plays an important role in determining the daily life of households. On the one hand, it can generate asset income which is usually an important income source for rich households. On the other hand, it can be sold out to hedge against negative shocks, such as illness or unemployment. Moser (1998) illustrates that the urban poor are managers of complex asset portfolios, and asset management affects both household poverty and vulnerability to poverty. In economics and sociology, there are four kinds of productive capitals: human capital, political capital, social capital, and financial capital or financial asset. Economists and sociologists already provide ample evidence indicating the roles of these kinds of capital in the daily lives of poor and non-poor households. In the context of the Chinese economy, financial assets include houses, bonds, deposits, securities, and other valuable assets. The education level of workers or the household head is generally used as a proxy of human capital. Being a member of the CCP or a cadre is generally used as a proxy of political capital. The number of relatives and/or friends is often used to measure social capital.

In order to provide more direct evidence that asset formation is crucial for poor households in urban PRC, we further employed CHIPS 2002 data to investigate the role of financial assets in determining urban poverty. Figure 20.9 presents the relationship between the stock of financial assets and urban poverty, which is measured by the \$2 poverty line in terms of income or consumption. From Figure 20.9, we can see a negative correlation between financial assets and the probability of falling into poverty, indicating that having more financial assets results in lower poverty.

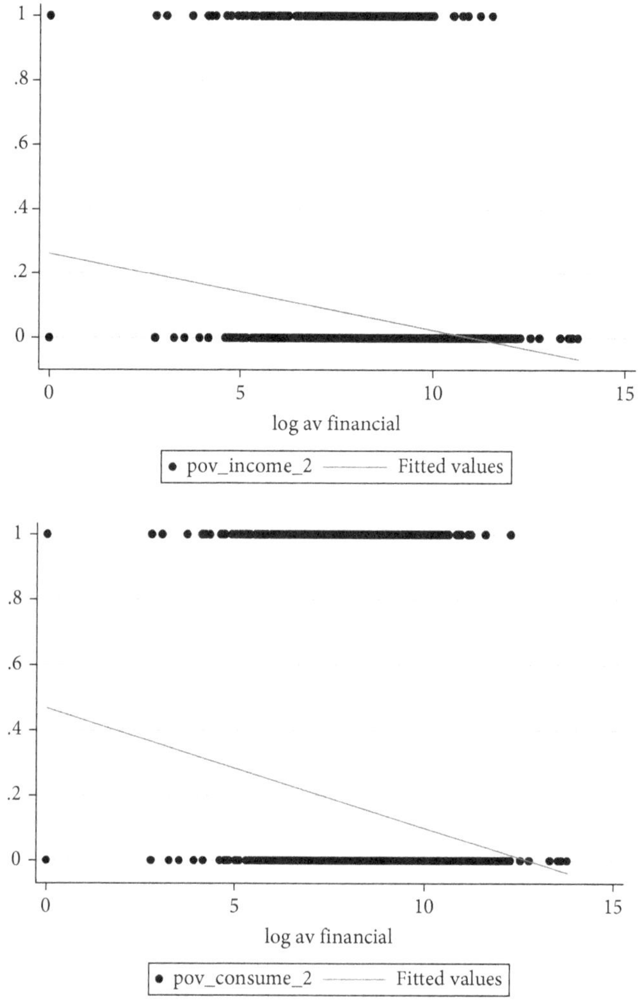

Figure 20.9. Effect of financial assets on urban poverty

Table A.20.7 in the Appendix presents the regression results of Probit models, where the dependent variable is a dummy of whether a household's average income or consumption expenditure is lower than the poverty line. The key independent variable is 'log(financial_K)', which measures the stock of financial assets of an urban household. The other independent variables are same as those in Table A.20.5 in the Appendix. From the regression results, we find that financial assets are significantly negative in all models, suggesting that having more financial assets would decrease the probability of falling into poverty. Similarly, 'Edu_year' and 'Party_member', indexing human capital and political capital, are significantly negative in all regression models, indicating that human capital and political capital can play an important role in reducing urban poverty in the PRC.

20.5 Conclusion and Policy Implications

In the past three decades, the Chinese economy has witnessed radical structural changes, including urbanization, industrialization, and opening up, which created a miracle of economic growth. Until 2012, there were 260 million migrating peasants working in urban labour markets, which is one of the most important determinants of urbanization and economic development in the PRC. However, inequality also increased sharply during this process and urban poverty increased in the late 1990s, although rural poverty has shown an absolute decreasing trend since the early 1980s. So, understanding the role of urbanization in enlarging inequality, in reducing rural poverty, and in increasing urban poverty in the late 1990s is an important mission for development economists. Relying on the present literature, official statistics, and household survey data in the PRC, this chapter has summarized research findings on the relationship between urbanization, interregional/urban–rural inequality, and poverty, and provided further empirical evidence on the role of urbanization and government policies in urban poverty. Several important conclusions can be drawn from our discussion in this chapter.

On the one hand, urbanization has a significant effect on reducing both the poverty of rural residents and the poverty of migrating peasants, and, consequently, has a positive effect on narrowing the rural–urban income/consumption gap. Urban labour markets play a very important role in this effect. The development strategy of giving priority to heavy industries and urban-biased policies adopted by the Chinese government in the early stages created a huge welfare gap between rural and urban citizens. After the opening up and economic reforms in 1978, the development of urban sectors gradually created a demand for rural labour and, as a result, more and more rural surplus labour migrated to urban labour markets. Although rural migrants have very low skills and human capital, they can still find jobs in labour-intensive sectors or the informal sector, where they can earn much higher wages than in rural sectors. We also find that even being employed in the informal sector, migrating peasants can still earn much higher wages than staying in their home towns. Many empirical tests also show that with more and more surplus labour migrating into more productive sectors in urban areas, the left-behind peasants can get more production resources, such as cultivated land and physical capital. As a result, those peasants remaining in rural sectors can also make more money than before. As a result of these channels, the rural–urban income or consumption gaps and provincial inequality measured by the Gini index have begun showing a slight declining trend in the past decade.

On the other hand, this chapter finds that urbanization is positively correlated to urban poverty. This can be explained by the competition between migrating peasants and urban workers in the labour market, and the failure of the government's anti-poverty policies in urban areas. Employing the urban sample from the population census of 2005, Liu and Zhao (2009) found that, other things being equal, a 10 per cent increase in rural–urban labour migration results in a 0.3 per cent decrease in the employment rate of urban workers and a 0.65 per cent decrease in the wages of urban workers. In this chapter, we also find that the existence of an informal sector has a negative effect on the poverty of urban citizens. Being employed by the informal sector significantly increases the probability of falling into poverty for urban citizens. This result seems to be contrary to the effect of being employed by the informal sector on migrants' poverty reduction. Here, should we keep in mind that although most migrating peasants are not in income poverty, but a fairly large share of them are in consumption poverty, suggesting that they restrain their consumption when working in urban PRC. Even though the development of the urban labour market has a negative effect on urban poverty reduction, we find that its effect is actually very small. We believe that if the local or central government proposes suitable or efficient policies, there could end up being no negative effect. Unfortunately, we only find that the minimum wage has a positive effect on reducing urban poverty, while the effect of other policies, such as Di Bao and Minimum Living Standard, is limited.

Although the empirical evidence provided in this chapter does not show a generally positive effect from urbanization on reducing rural and urban poverty and inequality in the PRC, we cannot take for granted that urbanization and urban concentration are harmful to economic development. Rural–urban labour migration and urbanization have important effects not only on reducing rural poverty and rural–urban gaps, but also on providing low-cost labour to urban sectors and providing services to urban citizens. Migrants contribute substantially to taxes to urban governments, but share very few of the public goods in urban areas. So, the urban local government should take the welfare of migrants into account when making policies. If urban governments propose employment policies to protect the employment of urban workers, this will make unemployed migrants more vulnerable than their urban counterparts and may result in a higher crime rate. If urban governments do not pay attention to the residential segregation of migrants, there is danger of fomenting criminal activities, which will pose a great challenge to city management. Therefore, a more inclusive policy package that is not discriminatory towards migrants during the urbanization process could be a win-win strategy.

These conclusions help us understand the role of urbanization, labour markets, and government policies in urban poverty, inequality, and rural poverty in the most populous country in the world, and shed light on policymaking in the PRC and in other developing economies to help find a way for a more balanced and harmonious model of economic growth.

Appendix

Following the methodology described in Box 20.1, the headcount ratio, the Gini index, and the Theil index used in this chapter were deduced from the two grouped household data-sets from the provincial statistic yearbooks. The first set of data is on the share of households within different income intervals, and the second one is on the household size under different income intervals.

Box 20.1. On Shorrocks and Wan's (2008) 'Ungrouping Income Distributions'

Assume a Lorenz curve with $(m+1)$ coordinates (p_k^*, L_k^*), where p_k^* and $L_k^*(k=1,2,\ldots,m)$ refer respectively to the cumulative shares in the total population and in total income of income classes 1 to k. And $p_0^* = L_0^* = 0$. Once all observations are normalized by the overall mean of the distribution, the actual mean μ_k^* of class k becomes:

$$\mu_k^* = \frac{L_k^* - L_{k-1}^*}{p_k^* - p_{k-1}^*} \quad k = 1 \; to \; m \tag{1}$$

The goal is to obtain a synthetic sample of n equally weighted observations whose overall mean is 1. These n observations are partitioned into m non-overlapping and ordered groups, each having $m_k = n(p_k^* - p_{k-1}^*)$ observations. Call x_{ki} the ith observation in class k, the mean of this class based on the synthetic data is μ_k.

The algorithm proposed by Shorrocks and Wan (2008) includes two stages. The first step is to generate an initial sample with a unitary mean based on a parametric model fitted to the grouped data. See Ryu and Slottje (1999) for a survey of various parametrizations of the Lorenz curve.[7] In the second stage, the algorithm adjusts the initial synthetic observations to ensure $\mu_k^* = \mu_k$.

[7] Shorrocks and Wan chose to generate the initial sample on the basis of a lognormal distribution. For more details, see Shorrocks and Wan (2008).

Table A.20.1. Inequality measures in urban PRC

	Gini index	Theil index	Observation
1981	0.3143	0.1709	6
1982	0.2978	0.1571	8
1983	0.2988	0.1543	7
1984	0.3087	0.1643	7
1985	0.2944	0.1560	7
1986	0.2864	0.1525	5
1987	0.3053	0.1703	6
1988	0.2856	0.1490	5
1989	0.2626	0.1288	4
1990	0.2313	0.1089	5
1991	0.1779	0.0542	5
1992	0.1850	0.0567	6
1993	0.1736	0.0553	8
1994	0.1939	0.0638	8
1995	0.1868	0.0569	8
1996	0.2108	0.0739	11
1997	0.2212	0.0814	9
1998	0.2186	0.0799	11
1999	0.2073	0.0714	15
2000	0.2053	0.0698	14
2001	0.2215	0.0820	18
2002	0.2330	0.0933	17
2003	0.2349	0.0927	18
2004	0.2418	0.1008	15
2005	0.2323	0.0921	19
2006	0.2364	0.0988	19
2007	0.2488	0.1072	20
2008	0.2548	0.1120	21
2009	0.2586	0.1150	21
2010	0.2612	0.1159	22

Table A.20.2. Variable definition using provincial panel data

Variable	Variable definition
pov_r_1.25	Headcount ratio in rural areas measured by $1.25 poverty line
pov_r_2	Headcount ratio in rural areas measured by $2 poverty line
pov_u_1.25	Headcount ratio in urban areas measured by $1.25 poverty line
pov_u_2	Headcount ratio in urban areas measured by $2 poverty line
gini_all	Provincial level Gini index
theil_all	Provincial level Theil index
urban_rural_gap	Income ratio between urban and rural citizens
urbanization	Share of urban population
logavgdp	Per capita GDP (RMB, in log)
gdp1_ratio	Share of GDP of the primary industry
gdp2_ratio	Share of GDP of the secondary industry
fdi_gdp	Ratio of FDI to GDP
export_gdp	Ratio of export to GDP
import_agr	Ratio of import to GDP
timetrend	Time trend variable

Table A.20.3. Effect of urbanization on poverty and inequality in the PRC

	Pov_r_2	Pov_u_2	Gini_all	Theil_all	Urban_rural_gap
urbanization	−0.339***	0.713***	−0.143***	−0.131***	−0.970***
	(0.0778)	(0.0669)	(0.0328)	(0.0480)	(0.2030)
logavgdp	−0.179***	−0.183***	0.0344***	0.0479***	0.228***
	(0.0100)	(0.0092)	(0.0044)	(0.0064)	(0.0262)
gdp1_ratio	−0.2400	0.608***	0.0136	0.0653	−2.234***
	(0.1510)	(0.1490)	(0.0684)	(0.1000)	(0.4240)
gdp2_ratio	−0.426***	0.0041	0.0761	0.201***	−0.0014
	(0.1090)	(0.1120)	(0.0487)	(0.0712)	(0.3300)
fdi_gdp	1.16e−05*	0.0000	7.91e−06***	6.90e−06*	8.53e−06*
	(0.0000)	(0.0000)	(0.0000)	(0.0000)	(0.0000)
export_gdp	0.0000	−2.11e−05***	−7.71e−06***	-9.25e−06**	−0.000127***
	(0.0000)	(0.0000)	(0.0000)	(0.0000)	(0.0000)
import_gdp	−1.44e−05**	1.66e−05***	0.0000	0.0000	3.27e−05**
	(0.0000)	(0.0000)	(0.0000)	(0.0000)	(0.0000)
timetrend	0.000511*	−0.0004	−0.000302***	−0.0002	0.00493***
	(0.0003)	(0.0003)	(0.0001)	(0.0002)	(0.0008)
Observation	512	517	418	418	725
R^2	0.886	0.791	0.549	0.528	0.622

Note: Standard errors in parentheses; *** p<0.01, ** p<0.05, * p<0.1.

Table A.20.4. Effect of urbanization on poverty and inequality in the PRC (random effect model)

	Pov_r_2	Pov_u_2	Gini_all	Theil_all	Urban_rural_gap
urbanization	−0.302***	0.671***	−0.187***	−0.179***	−1.613***
	−0.0674	−0.0577	−0.0303	−0.0446	−0.1990
logavgdp	−0.186***	−0.185***	0.0386***	0.0526***	0.273***
	−0.0088	−0.0083	−0.0041	−0.0060	−0.0261
gdp1_ratio	−0.327**	0.498***	0.0186	0.0664	−2.327***
	−0.1410	−0.1370	−0.0668	−0.0977	−0.4330
gdp2_ratio	−0.450***	0.0388	0.0389	0.152**	−0.5440
	−0.1060	−0.1020	−0.0484	−0.0707	−0.3370
fdi_gdp	0.0000	0.0000	8.70e−06***	7.67e−06**	1.06e−05**
	0.0000	0.0000	0.0000	0.0000	0.0000
export_gdp	0.0000	−2.14e−05***	−5.04e−06*	0.0000	−9.79e−05***
	0.0000	0.0000	0.0000	0.0000	0.0000
import_agr	−1.21e−05**	1.43e−05***	0.0000	0.0000	0.0000
	0.0000	0.0000	0.0000	0.0000	0.0000
timetrend	0.000602**	−0.0002	−0.000427***	−0.000335**	0.00269***
	−0.0003	−0.0002	−0.0001	−0.0002	−0.0008

(*Continued*)

Table A.20.4. Continued

	Pov_r_2	Pov_u_2	Gini_all	Theil_all	Urban_rural_gap
east	0.106***	0.0595***	0.0519***	0.0735***	0.507***
	−0.0264	−0.0200	−0.0132	−0.0208	−0.0898
central	−0.302***	0.671***	−0.187***	−0.179***	−1.613***
	−0.0674	−0.0577	−0.0303	−0.0446	−0.1990
constant	1.310**	1.870***	0.900***	0.403	−3.971**
	−0.527	−0.495	−0.228	−0.333	−1.723
Observation	512	517	418	418	725

Note: Standard errors in parentheses; *** p<0.01, ** p<0.05, * p<0.1.

Table A.20.5. Employment in the informal sector and income poverty in urban PRC (probit model)

	Income poverty		Consumption poverty	
	$1.25	**$2**	**$1.25**	**$2**
No_informal			0.387***	0.307***
			(0.0742)	(0.0390)
Ratio_informal	0.474***	0.460***		
	(0.112)	(0.0641)		
Age	0.0871*	0.00791	0.0778**	0.0245
	(0.0495)	(0.0214)	(0.0382)	(0.0181)
Age_square	−0.00116**	−0.000300	−0.00113***	−0.000533***
	(0.000531)	(0.000222)	(0.000393)	(0.000180)
Male	0.101	0.281***	0.210**	0.295***
	(0.114)	(0.0656)	(0.106)	(0.0598)
Edu_year	−0.0840***	−0.0989***	−0.0899***	−0.100***
	(0.0182)	(0.0102)	(0.0159)	(0.00897)
Partymember	−0.488***	−0.440***	−0.596***	−0.477***
	(0.156)	(0.0747)	(0.144)	(0.0664)
Minority	0.0454	−0.227	−0.00323	−0.219
	(0.235)	(0.155)	(0.220)	(0.144)
Depend_ratio	2.058***	1.866***	2.142***	1.738***
	(0.314)	(0.166)	(0.263)	(0.133)
East	−0.324**	−0.415***	−0.346**	−0.348***
	(0.145)	(0.0783)	(0.135)	(0.0717)
Central	0.0518	0.0451	0.0670	0.0841
	(0.121)	(0.0683)	(0.109)	(0.0623)
Constant	−4.074***	−1.320**	−3.889***	−1.590***
	(1.174)	(0.535)	(0.960)	(0.472)
Observation	6,843	5,886	6,843	5,886
Pseudo R^2	0.2032	0.1886	0.2148	0.1788

Data source: CHIPS 2002 urban samples.

Table A.20.6. Effect of minimum wage on urban poverty reduction

	Random effect models		Fixed effect models	
	Pov_u_1.25	Pov_u_2	Pov_u_1.25	Pov_u_2
logmini_wage	−0.0403*	−0.0752	−0.0545**	−0.0963**
	(0.0215)	(0.0459)	(0.0222)	(0.0447)
urbanization	0.149**	0.652***	0.548***	1.446***
	(0.0703)	(0.164)	(0.133)	(0.269)
logavgdp	−0.0051	−0.0853***	0.0306	−0.0062
	(0.0146)	(0.0326)	(0.0219)	(0.0441)
gdp1_ratio	0.319**	1.125***	0.260*	0.885***
	(0.125)	(0.271)	(0.147)	(0.296)
gdp2_ratio	−0.0506	−0.142	−0.231**	−0.604***
	(0.0924)	(0.205)	(0.112)	(0.226)
fdi_gdp	1.92e−07	8.98e−08	4.56e−07	5.56e−07
	(6.84e−07)	(1.46e−06)	(7.01e−07)	(1.41e−06)
export_gdp	−1.29e−06	−9.88e−06	−6.45e−06	−1.58e−05
	(4.59e−06)	(1.04e−05)	(5.87e−06)	(1.18e−05)
import_agr	−2.73e−06	−6.44e−06	−1.93e−06	−3.51e−06
	(3.20e−06)	(6.92e−06)	(3.45e−06)	(6.95e 06)
east	0.0339	0.144*		
	(0.0325)	(0.0855)		
central	0.0320	0.141		
	(0.0347)	(0.0902)		
timetrend	−0.0012	−0.0052	−0.0095**	−0.0238**
	(0.0030)	(0.0065)	(0.0046)	(0.0094)
constant	2.598	11.26	19.00**	48.28***
	(5.779)	(12.65)	(9.113)	(18.37)
Observation	161	160	160	160
R^2			0.475	0.740

Table A.20.7. Asset formation and poverty in urban PRC (probit model)

	Income poverty		Consumption poverty	
	$1.25	$2	$1.25	$2
Ln(Financial_K)	−0.0963***	−0.107***	−0.0854***	−0.0924***
	(0.0130)	(0.00826)	(0.00948)	(0.00698)
Age	0.0810**	0.0249	−0.0187	−0.0151
	(0.0388)	(0.0184)	(0.0195)	(0.0128)
Age_square	−0.00114***	−0.000526***	3.23e−05	−5.94e−05
	(0.000401)	(0.000183)	(0.000191)	(0.000126)
Male	0.166	0.271***	0.532***	0.455***
	(0.108)	(0.0610)	(0.0811)	(0.0459)
Edu_year	−0.0851***	−0.0952***	−0.0811***	−0.0887***
	(0.0165)	(0.00925)	(0.0104)	(0.00673)
Party_member	−0.543***	−0.426***	−0.273***	−0.219***
	(0.150)	(0.0682)	(0.0747)	(0.0452)

(Continued)

Table A.20.4. Continued

	Income poverty		Consumption poverty	
	$1.25	$2	$1.25	$2
Minority	0.136	−0.0988	−0.0559	0.0284
	(0.220)	(0.143)	(0.169)	(0.101)
Depend_ratio	1.300***	1.173***	0.681***	0.680***
	(0.216)	(0.120)	(0.135)	(0.0857)
East	−0.257*	−0.258***	−0.0825	−0.338***
	(0.138)	(0.0735)	(0.0943)	(0.0549)
Central	0.0447	0.0554	0.439***	0.293***
	(0.111)	(0.0634)	(0.0782)	(0.0475)
Constant	−2.632***	−0.400	−0.395	0.873**
	(0.955)	(0.474)	(0.517)	(0.341)
Observation	6,843	6,843	6,843	6,843
Pseudo R^2	0.2377	0.2079	0.1729	0.1615

Source: Urban samples from CHIPS 2002.

References

Addison John T. and McKinley L. Blackburn. 1999. 'Minimum Wages and Poverty'. *Industrial and Labor Relations Review 52* (3): 393–409.

Appleton, Simon, Lina Song, and Qingjie Xia. 2005. 'Has China Crossed the River? The Evolution of Wage Structure in Urban China during Reform and Retrenchment'. *Journal of Comparative Economics 33* (4): 644–63.

Blackwood, D. L. and Robert G. Lynch. 1994. 'The Measurement of Inequality and Poverty: A Policy Maker's Guide to the Literature'. *World Development 22* (4): 567–78.

Cai Fang. 2000. 'Political Economy Analysis on the Constraint of Rural–Urban Labor Migration in China'. *Population Science of China (Zhongguo Renkou Kexue) 4*.

Chen Binkai, Dan Liu, and Ming Lu. 2014. 'Growing Unequal: Why Do Bigger Cities Have Higher Income Disparity in China?' Working paper.

Chen, Binkai, Ming Lu, and Ninghua Zhong. 2015. 'How Urban Segregation Distorts Chinese Migrants' Consumption?' *World Development 70*: 133–46.

Chen Jie and Qianjin Hao. 2013. 'Residential Segregation during Fast Urbanization Process: Empirical Evidence from Shanghai'. *Academic Monthly* 5: 17–28.

Chen, Jie, Qianjin Hao, and Mark Stephens. 2010. 'Assessing Housing Affordability in Post-reform China: A Case Study of Shanghai'. *Housing Studies 25* (6): 877–901.

Chen, Shaohua and Martin Ravallion. 2009. 'China's (Uneven) Progress against Poverty: In Governing Rapid Growth in China'. In *Governing Rapid Growth in China*, edited by Ravi Kanbur and Xiaobo Zhang, Routledge.

Chen Zhao, Ming Lu, and Jingmin Chen. 2013. 'Hukou and Residential Segregation: New Challenge of Management in Urban China'. *Fudan Journal of Social Science 5*: 77–86.

Collins, William J. and Robert A. Margo. 2000. 'Residential Segregation and Socioeconomic Outcomes: When Did Ghettos Go Bad?' *Economics Letters 69* (2): 239–43.

Fan Shenggen, Zhang Linxiu, and Zhang Xiaobo. 2000. 'Growth and Poverty in Rural China: The Role of Public Investments'. EPTD Discussion Paper, No. 66, International Food Policy Research Institute, Environment and Production Technology Division.

Gustafsson Bjorn and Quheng Deng. 2007. 'Social Assistance Receipt and Its Importance for Combating Poverty in Urban China'. *IZA discussion paper, No. 2758.*

Harris, John R. and Michael P. Todaro. 1970. 'Migration, Unemployment and Development: A Two-sector Analysis'. *The American Economic Review 60* (1): 126–42.

Haynie, Dana L. 2002. 'Friendship Networks and Delinquency: The Relative Nature of Peer Delinquency'. *Journal of Quantitative Criminology 18* (2): 99–134.

Haynie, Dana L. and D. Wayne Osgood. 2005. 'Reconsidering Peers and Delinquency: How Do Peers Matter?' *Social Forces 84* (2): 1109–30.

Hiroshi, S. A. T. O. 2006. 'Housing Inequality and Housing Poverty in Urban China in the Late 1990s'. *China Economic Review 17* (1): 37–50.

Hou, X., H. Ying, and Y. Zhang. 1999. *To Meet Housing Needs of All People: Major Breakthroughs of Urban Housing System* (in Chinese), Guangxi Normal University Press.

Jalan, Jyotsna and Martin Ravallion. 1998. 'Transient Poverty in Post-Reform China'. Journal of Comparative Economics 26: 338–57.

Jalan, Jyotsna and Martin Ravallion. 2000. 'Is Transient Poverty Different? Evidence for Rural China'. *The Journal of Development Studies 36* (6): 82–99.

Li, Shi and John Knight. 2002. 'Three Poverties in Urban China'. *Economic Research Journal (Jingji Yanjiu) 10*: 47–58.

Li, Shi, Zong Wei, and Sai Ding. 2005. 'Empirical Analysis on the Causes of Asset Inequality in China'. *Economic Research Journal (Jingji Yanjiu) 6*: 4–15.

Liu, Xuejun and Yaohui Zhao. 2009. 'Effect of Labor Migration on Urban Labor Market'. *Economic Quarterly (Jingjixue Jikan) 8* (2): 693–710.

Ma, Shuang, Ji Zhang, and Xi Zhu. 2012. 'Effect of Minimum Wages on Employment and Wage Level in Urban China'. *Economic Research Journal (Jingji Yanjiu) 5*: 132–46.

Mascella, Allison, Shahzia Teja, and Brennan S. Thompson. 2009. 'Minimum Wage Increases as an Anti-poverty Policy in Ontario'. *Canadian Public Policy 35* (3): 373–9.

Meng, Xin, Kailing Shen, and Sen Xue. 2013. 'Economic Reform, Education Expansion, and Earnings Inequality for Urban Males in China 1988–2009'. *Journal of Comparative Economics 41* (1): 227–44.

Meng, Xin, Robert Gregory, and Youjuan Wang. 2005. 'Poverty, Inequality, and Growth in Urban China 1986–2000'. *Journal of Comparative Economics 33* (4): 710–29.

Meng, Xin and Junsen Zhang. 2001. 'The Two-Tier Labor Market in Urban China: Occupational Segregation and Wage Differentials between Urban Residents and Rural Migrants in Shanghai'. *Journal of Comparative Economics 29* (3): 485–504.

Montalvo, Jose G. and Martin Ravallion. 2009. 'The Pattern of Growth and Poverty Reduction in China'. *World Bank Policy Research Working Paper 5069*, World Bank, Washington, DC.

Moser, Caroline O. N. 1998. 'The Asset Vulnerability Framework: Reassessing Urban Poverty Reduction Strategies'. *World Development 26* (1): 1–19.

NBSC (National Bureau of Statistics of China). 2008. *China Statistical Yearbook*, China Statistical Press.

NBSC (National Bureau of Statistics of China). 2000. *China Labor Statistical Yearbook*, China Statistical Press.

NBSC (National Bureau of Statistics of China). 2013a. *China Statistical Yearbook*, China Statistical Press.

NBSC (National Bureau of Statistics of China). 2013b. *Monitoring Report of Rural Migrants in China-2012*. <http://www.stats.gov.cn/tjfx/fxbg/t20120427_402801903.htm>.

PFPC, ed. 2012. *In PFPC (Ed.), Report on China's Mmigrant Population Development. 2012 National Population and Family Planning Commission of P.R. China*. Beijing: China Population Press.

Ryu, Hang K. and Daniel J. Slottje. 1999. 'Parametric Approximations of the Lorenz Curve'. In *Handbook on Income Inequality Measurement*, edited by Silber Jacques, Kluwer Academic Publishers.

Sabia, Joseph J. and Richard V. Burkhauser. 2010. 'Minimum Wages and Poverty: Will A $9.50 Federal Minimum Wage Really Help the Working Poor?' *Southern Economic Journal 76* (3): 592–623.

Sen, Amartya. 1981. *Poverty and Famines: An Essay on Entitlement and Deprivation*, Oxford University Press.

Shorrocks, Anthony and Guanghua Wan. 2008. 'Ungrouping Income Distributions: Synthesising Samples for Inequality and Poverty Analysis'. *Working Paper Series RP2008/16*, World Institute for Development Economic Research (UNU-WIDER).

Wang, Feng and Xuejin Zuo. 1999. 'Inside China's Cities: Institutional Barriers and Opportunities for Urban Migrants'. *American Economic Review 89* (2): 276–80.

Warr, Mark. 2002. *Companions in Crime: The Social Aspects of Criminal Conduct*, Cambridge University Press.

Wilson, William Julius. 1987. *The Truly Disadvantaged: The Inner City, the Underclass, and Public Policy*, University of Chicago Press.

Yan, Shanping. 2006. 'Labor Mobility and its Determinants in Urban Labor Market, and Neo-Dual Structure in Chinese Cities'. *Management World (Guanli Shijie) 8*: 8–17.

Yang, Yunyan and Jinyong Chen. 2000. 'Segmentation and Competition of Transitional Labor Market: Evidences from Wuhan'. *China Social Science (Zhongguo Shehui Kexue) 5*: 28–38.

Zhang, Linxiu, Jikun Huang, and Scott Rozelle. 2003. 'China's War on Poverty: Assessing Targeting and the Growth Impacts of Poverty Programs'. *Journal of Chinese Economic and Business Studies 1* (3): 301–17.

Zhang, Yina and Jie Chen. 2014. 'The Changing Prevalence of Housing Overcrowding in Post-reform China: The Case of Shanghai, 2000–2010'. *Habitat International* 42: 214–23.

Zhang Yuan, Qing Xu, and Wu Jingjing. 2012. 'A Successful Anti-Poverty War: Experience from China'. Economic Research Journal (Jingji Yanjiu) 11: 76–87.

Zheng, Siqi, Fenjie Long, C. Cindy Fan, and Yizhen Gu. 2009. 'Urban Villages in China: A 2008 Survey of Migrant Settlements in Beijing'. *Eurasian Geography and Economics 50* (4): 425–46.

21

Growth, Inequality, Poverty, and Urbanization: the Case of India

Arup Mitra

21.1 Analytical Framework

In the process of economic growth, inequality may increase, particularly in the initial stages, as seen in the light of the historical experience of developed countries (Kuznets and Murphy 1966). Since urbanization also increases in response to per capita income growth, one may infer that inequality and urbanization go hand in hand. In other words, urbanization is a concomitant of rapid growth and since growth and inequality go hand in hand, at least in the initial phases, rising inequality in the urban context need not come as a major surprise, particularly in the context of developing countries. However, from a different perspective, urbanization and a reduction in interregional inequality may move together. It is usually observed that urban incomes are higher than rural incomes. Therefore, lagging urbanization can lead to rising rural–urban and regional inequality. On the other hand, rapid urbanization encompassing a large population inflow from rural areas benefits many, and thus inequality may decline.

It is, therefore, pertinent to examine the impact of urbanization on growth, inequality, and poverty in India. This is a key question both in urban development research and urban policymaking. Because of the agglomeration effects and rise in total factor productivity growth, economic growth is expected to be positively associated with urbanization. Also, in the process of urbanization, employment opportunities for all sections of the society, including the unskilled and semi-skilled variety of the workforce, are expected to grow through several forward and backward linkages between the dynamic sectors and the informal sector. In other words, even the activities that were residual in nature to begin with may acquire productivity gains in the process of urbanization and, thus, offer better levels of living to the workers located in the lower echelons. Since the cost of providing services in urban areas is usually less than that in rural areas (as a result of agglomeration effects), the decline in the incidence of urban poverty is likely to take place at a higher pace with rapid urbanization. Even the rural poor benefit from the process of urbanization through interlinkage effects. Chapter 3 in this volume deals with the benefit–cost framework for urbanization, whereas this chapter

Arup Mitra., *Growth, Inequality, Poverty, and Urbanization* In: *Cities of Dragons and Elephants: Urbanization and Urban Development in China and India. Edited by:* Guanghua Wan and Ming Lu, Oxford University Press (2019).
 DOI: 10.1093/oso/9780198829225.003.0021

directly assesses the impact of urbanization on economic growth, inequality, and poverty. In the face of agglomeration economies, which vary positively with urbanization, economic growth is expected to shoot up more than proportionately in relation to an increase in inputs.

Inequality and poverty are likely to have a direct relationship. Given the level of per capita income if inequality rises, it results in an increase in poverty. However, when both growth and inequality rise simultaneously, the poverty outcome is a little uncertain. The beneficial effects of growth on poverty tend to get neutralized by the adverse effects of increasing inequality on poverty and thus the net decline in poverty can be quite modest. However, at higher levels of growth, when inequality tends to decline, poverty is certain to fall. One may, therefore, infer that at higher stages of urbanization, overall poverty is also expected to decline substantially.

However, there can be deviations from this postulation. Since urbanization can offer opportunities to rural migrants to escape poverty—more so because of the agglomeration effects in large human settlements—the relationship between urbanization, on the one hand, and rural and urban poverty, on the other, can be an inverse one even at lower levels of urbanization. If rural–urban migration is directed to large cities and much of the economic growth also originates from large cities, the decline in poverty and rise in urbanization can occur simultaneously.

Ferré et al. (2012) provide evidence from eight developing countries in favour of an inverse relationship between poverty and city size. Poverty is both more widespread and deeper in very small and small towns than in large or very large cities and, more importantly, a majority of the urban poor live in medium, small, or very small towns. In other words, the share of small towns in total urban poverty is much more than that of large cities. Also, the authors noted that the greater incidence and severity of consumption poverty in smaller towns is generally compounded by similar or greater deprivation in terms of access to basic infrastructure services, such as electricity, heating gas, sewerage, and solid waste disposal (also see Lanjouw and Murgai 2010).

Since the urbanization level in India is relatively low, the composition of national poverty has a relatively larger rural share and so the policy focus, and thus urban poverty, is often treated as a rural spillover (Dandekar and Rath, 1971), even when rural-to-urban migration has not been rapid. The linkages between rural and urban poverty, therefore, need a thorough investigation, and if the linkages are not found to be strong, more effective strategies need to be initiated for urban poverty reduction specifically.

Mahadevia and Sarkar (2012) pointed out that there has been an increase in inequality between the metros and the non-metros. The beneficiaries of economic reforms comprise only the top 20 and 5 per cent of the population in the metros and the non-metros respectively, while the bottom 40 per cent of the population in these cities witnessed a rise in consumption only at a decreasing rate. The McKinsey Global Institute Report and that of India's High Powered Expert Committee (Report on Indian Urban Infrastructure and Services) vouched for promoting urbanization through metropolization and global linkages of large cities. But in the face of existing inequality, such a recommendation, if implemented, is feared to accentuate the degree of inequality further. Mahadevia and Sarkar (2012) also elucidated in terms of investment the pro-metro bias of the largest urban programme (Jawaharnan Nehru National Urban Renewal Mission, JNNURM).

In a paper by Sharma and Kumari (2012), the authors show a relationship between poverty and weights, which are the combined effect of distance to nearest town and class of towns in India. Higher weights are given to bigger towns and closer rural areas in terms of distance. The authors noted a U-shaped curve, implying that poverty reduces up to a certain point and after that it starts increasing. This has a very interesting policy implication: if the government wants to invest in poverty alleviation in villages, it should be spent directly within the villages that are more than 20 km away from the nearest town. On the other hand, in the case of poor villages located within 20 km of the towns, government investment should be spent on the nearby towns, which will indirectly benefit the surrounding rural areas through spillover effects.

Another important aspect of inequality and poverty in India is the social dimension. Kundu and Mohanan (2009) noted that inequality across social and religious groups has gone up in rural areas and small towns, but not in large cities. Urban poverty is high not only in backward areas/states but also in many developed states, suggesting that lack of development and the nature and pattern of development are both important for poverty reduction. They noted that vertical inequality in urban areas had grown faster than in rural areas. On the other hand, rural poverty is concentrated in a few inaccessible and less developed areas, among which there is a high concentration of socially disadvantaged people.

Using per capita consumption expenditure as a measure of welfare, Deaton and Dreze (2002) noted that interstate inequality increased between 1993–4 and 1999–2000, and that urban–rural inequality increased not only throughout India but also within states. Jha (2002) found higher inequality in both urban and rural sectors during the reforms period compared to the early 1990s. In the context of cities/towns, Kundu (2006) noted gross inequality between the million-plus cities (with one million or more population), medium towns (with 50,000 to one million population), and small towns (with less than 50,000 population) in terms of employment and consumption. In particular, consumption expenditure differences across different size classes of cities/towns are indicative of severe intra-urban inequality. Kundu (2006) further noted that intra-urban inequality has increased over time.

Calì (2008) empirically addressed three important aspects of the urbanization process in India: rural–urban disparities and their relation with economic development; the relation between urbanization and growth; and the convergence hypothesis in cities' growth. The results support the idea of a U-shaped relationship between rural–urban disparities in socio-economic indicators and the level of economic development. Though the level of urbanization and that of economic development go hand in hand across Indian states over time, this relation is not strong. Also the rate of urbanization (change in the proportion of population living in urban areas) and the rate of economic growth appear to be negatively correlated. Finally, the author noted a tendency towards convergence in growth rates among Indian towns: other things being equal, smaller towns grow faster than large ones. Further, Calìand Menon (2012) pointed out that urbanization has a substantial and systematic poverty-reducing effect in the surrounding rural areas. The authors argue that this effect is causal in nature and is largely attributable to the positive spillovers of urbanization on the rural economy rather than to the movement of the rural poor to urban areas. We turn to the quantitative aspects of these views in the following sections.

As regards agglomeration economies, large cities are seen to be more productive though the productivity levels start tapering off beyond a threshold limit (Mitra 2004). There are greater possibilities relating to ancillarization and subcontracting in large cities as the firms are not only large in number but also they tend to encourage interdependency in an attempt to reduce cost and pursue super-specialization (Mitra 2014). Further, the rural–urban distinction has grown sharper in response to globalization as many of the activities are undertaken in other cities across the world. Do substantial productivity gains arise from such concentration and do they actually get translated into higher wages,or are there labour market forces such as informalization and contractualization which tend to slow down the wage growth? If unskilled labour does not gain and wage inequality rises in the process of growth then the role of urbanization in reducing poverty will naturally be curtailed.

How urban poverty is to be conceptualized is also an important question. Housing and access to basic amenities, health, and education are some of the important dimensions in assessing urban poverty rather than simply considering consumption expenditure. The growth of slums is an endemic feature of urbanization. How improvements in living conditions can be attained so that urbanization becomes inclusive and, at the same time, creates world-class cities for future growth to accelerate is a key challenge for the Indian government. Identifying effective ways of providing support (such as asset creation for livelihood promotion and accessibility to inexpensive transport and other infrastructural facilities) to the urban poor is an important issue from the policy point of view.

On the whole, evidence related to growth, inequality, poverty, and urbanization is not scanty. But at the same time, keeping in view some of these pertinent issues, there is a need to pursue fresh research based on recent data from the population census of 2011 and National Sample Survey Office's (NSSO) survey

(2011–12) on consumption expenditure. The focus of this chapter is on growth, inequality, and poverty, particularly in relation to urbanization. The analysis is pursued at three levels of disaggregation—states, districts, and million-plus cities—for which data are available. Three important sources of information are used: (1) NSSO data on consumption expenditure, (2) Central Statistical Office (CSO) data on domestic product per capita (growth), and (3) population census data on urbanization and many other socio-economic and demographic characteristics. The study is organized as follows. In Section 21.2, we present estimates of GDP originating from urban areas. Section 21.3 presents an empirical analysis of growth, inequality, poverty, and urbanization, which is pursued at three levels of disaggregation: states, districts, and million-plus cities. Section 21.4 focuses on the multifaceted nature of poverty, and Section 21.5 summarizes the major findings.

21.2 Contribution of Urban Areas to Overall Growth

The level of urbanization measured in terms of the percentage of the population residing in urban areas is perceptibly low, and it sluggishly increased from around 28 to 31 per cent from 2001 to 2011. However, as Mitra and Mehta (2011) estimated, the amount of GDP originating from urban areas at the national level in nine pre-identified sectors of the economy is considerably high (Table 21.1). Almost 70 per cent of GDP is generated in urban areas as per the first estimate, which uses the ratio of urban wage to all-areas wage in order to adjust for productivity differentials across rural and urban areas. On the other hand, in the second estimate—using the ratio of urban monthly per capita consumption expenditure (MPCE) to all-areas average MPCE—the figure is around 59 per cent. In non-agricultural activities, the share of urban India is 92 per cent and 76 per cent as per estimates 1 and 2 respectively. Urban India's share of the GDP can be attributed to the value created by the manufacturing and services sectors. (Table 21.1 presents the mean values of estimate 1 and estimate 2.)

Table 21.2 presents the proportion of urban areas' GDP as part of state GDP (which is otherwise called state domestic product, SDP) across primary, secondary, and tertiary sectors. The numbers in the table represent the mean value of two different estimates of state domestic product or SDP. It is interesting to see that the urban areas' share of SDP is less than 50 per cent in seventeen states, though in terms of non-agricultural SDP the share is high across most of the states and union territories.

Delhi is the most urban state, with 96 per cent of its GDP coming from urban areas. The contribution of urban areas in rapidly industrializing states such as Gujarat, Maharashtra, Chhattisgarh, and Karnataka is almost 85 per cent of the SDP. The contribution of non-agricultural activities to the SDP averages 93 per cent.

Table 21.1. Percentage of GDP originating from urban areas: all India (2000–1), sector-wise estimation

Agriculture, forestry, and fishing	Mining	Manufacturing	Utilities	Construction	Trade	Transport	Finance	Services	GDP	Non-agricultural GDP
5.1	45.915	74.075	81.09	51.02	83.985	79.22	*	84.585	64.89	83.69

Note: In the percentage of GDP from activities like finance, real estate ownership, and business services, the figures are an overestimation. This is mainly because the same wage rate is assumed to prevail across different areas and activities.

Source: Mitra and Mehta (2011).

Table 21.2. Percentage of state GDP originating from urban areas, 2000–1

State	Primary	Secondary	Tertiary	SDP	Non-agricultural SDP
Delhi	25.52	95.15	97.4	95.90	96.88
Chandigarh	32.27	79.74	97.28	91.85	92.55
Maharashtra	10.59	92.17	*	84.98	*
Karnataka	06.36	89.54	*	82.08	*
Chhattisgarh	27.78	82.18	*	82.03	88.49
Pondicherry	18.82	80.54	92.83	81.38	86.04
Gujarat	12.89	89.12	87.98	79.61	84.37
Mizoram	28.13	85.46	92.36	78.34	91.21
Tamil Nadu	11.15	76.68	96.77	74.80	88.38
Madhya Pradesh	12.34	79.56	99.16	73.18	85.01
Meghalaya	1.7	53.84	94.33	71.92	74.56
Goa	44.82	79.01	66.56	68.71	73.66
West Bengal	5.97	72.37	88.1	62.15	83.34
Jharkhand	41.67	51.5	73.47	60.56	73.27
Andhra Pradesh	8.42	61.35	89.88	57.95	79.20
Rajasthan	5.93	51.69	75.73	49.50	64.52
Uttarakhand	3.67	50.3	72.92	43.01	63.48
Uttar Pradesh	4.12	51.37	70.54	41.81	62.69
Manipur	13.12	33.91	61.56	41.14	53.51
Orissa	8.98	34.08	70.02	40.88	55.45
Punjab	3.47	56.68	70.77	40.46	65.20
Andaman and Nicobar Islands	3.79	37.07	63.95	39.65	55.07
Assam	10.95	47.22	60.23	38.68	57.52
Arunachal Pradesh	3.15	41.05	65.01	38.55	55.83
Nagaland	4.19	44.43	55.86	37.68	53.23
Haryana	5.21	43.72	52.68	34.68	48.94
Kerala	10.47	31.5	41.47	33.35	38.75
Jammu and Kashmir	5.29	37.59	48.17	32.84	45.45
Bihar	4.10	32.65	58.15	32.06	53.40
Sikkim	0.05	19.78	50.03	32.05	41.21
Tripura	2.67	28.69	46.98	31.72	41.16
Himachal Pradesh	1.40	25.27	24.58	19.65	24.60
India	8.73	69.93	83.64	64.89	83.69

Note: The tertiary sector value-added has been grossly overestimated in urban areas in Maharashtra, Karnataka, and Chhattisgarh because of the assumption that the same wage rate prevails across different areas and activities.

Source: Mitra and Mehta (2011).

Big southern states like Andhra Pradesh and Tamil Nadu also have a significant urban contribution to their SDP—58 per cent and 75 per cent respectively. Himachal Pradesh is the least urbanized state, with only 19 per cent of its SDP coming from urban areas. Considering India as a whole, urban areas contributed an estimated 65 per cent of total GDP in 2000–1.

Other studies have also indicated a similarly high level of contribution made by urban areas to national GDP. For example, in a report Barclays said that urban

India's contribution will be around 70 to 75 per cent of its GDP by 2020.[1] As per the Central Statistical Organisation the urban net state domestic product has been greater than its rural counterpart in absolute terms.[2]

In the 2011 census, 475 urban agglomerations (UAs) with 981 outgrowths (OGs) were identified, as against 384 UAs with 962 OGs in the 2001 census (Table 21.3). In total, there are 7,935 towns in the country according to the 2011 census. In fact, the number of towns has increased by 2,774 since the last census. Many of these towns are part of UAs and the rest are independent towns. Around 264.9 million persons, constituting 70 per cent of the total urban population, live in the Class I UAs/towns. This proportion has increased considerably over the last census, while the growth has been nominal in the remaining classes of towns.[3] Out of 468 UAs/towns belonging to the Class I category, fifty-three have a population of one million or above, while eighteen new UAs/towns have been added to this list since the last census. These are the major urban centres in the country, constituting around 160.7 million persons (or 42.6 per cent of the total urban population). There are around 2,500 census towns which have emerged between 2001 and 2011. These towns are not recognized by the government of India (i.e. they continue to be rural) but the population census office identified them as urban areas. Many of them are located on the periphery of large cities and conduct economic activities quite similar to those in the cities. All this suggests that the share of urban GDP in the total will increase further. The Barclays report, as cited by one of the business dailies in India, suggests that the share of urban areas in total GDP will rise to around 70 to 75 per cent by 2020.[4] As per the Mid-Term Appraisal of the Eleventh Five Year Plan the urban share of GDP was around 63 per cent in 2009–10 which is expected to increase to 75 per cent by 2030.

Table 21.3. Type of towns

Type of towns/UAs/OGs	2011 census	2001 census
Statutory towns	4,041	3,799
Census towns	3,894	1,362
Urban agglomeration (UA)	475	384
Class 1 cities/UA	461	394
Outgrowths (OG)	981	962

Source: Census of India 2011: Urban Agglomerations and Cities.

[1] *Business Standard* (2014).

[2] <http://mospi.nic.in/sites/default/files/reports_and_publication/cso_national_accounts/Chapter%2032.pdf>.

[3] Census of India 2011: Urban Agglomerations and Cities, <http://censusindia.gov.in/2011-prov-results/paper2/data_files/India2/1.%20Data%20Highlight.pdf>.

[4] *Business Standard* (2014).

21.3 Empirical Analysis of Growth, Inequality, Poverty, and Urbanization

21.3.1 State-Level Data

Following the economic reforms in India since 1991, growth has been accompanied by a reduction in poverty on a scale which, on an average, is seen to be larger than the corresponding decline in the 1980s (Sundaram and Tendulkar2003). However, Sachs et al. (2002) observed that economic growth across states in the 1990s had a tendency to diverge rather than converge, implying that states with a higher per capita income grew faster than states with lower per capita income. Further, it has been noted that states with higher levels of urbanization have grown faster, meaning that external economies of scale or agglomeration economies result fromthe concentration of population and activities in rich states with strong infrastructure,and have resulted in productivity growth. Hence, the poor in these states, at least in urban areas, might have benefited more than their counterparts in other states. Theoretically, if labour can move freely in large numbers, convergence of income across regions is likely to take place. However, the constraints posed by demand- and supply-side factors and the costs associated with mobility result in income differentials across regions.

Below we present figures on urbanization, per capita net SDP in constant prices, rural poverty, urban poverty, rural inequality, and urban inequality for the years 2004–5 and 2011–12 (or 2010–11). Here, poverty is defined in terms of consumption expenditure (not income because of the lack of data), and it is measured as the percentage of population below the national poverty line set by the government of India.[5] Inequality is measured in terms of the Gini coefficient pertaining to consumption expenditure.

Economic growth in India has been associated with rising inequality as suggested by several indirect indicators (Tables 21.1 and 21.2). Unfortunately, in the Indian context we do not have information on income distribution and, therefore, it is difficult to measure income inequality over time. However, the NSSO gives us data on consumption expenditure and the distribution of households based on expenditure size classes. From this, expenditure inequality has been estimated, though it is believed to be much less than income inequality. Since the upper-income households tend to save more and spend less, expenditure inequality is usually a gross underestimate. But, even then, there is evidence in favour of rising inequality over time across several states.

According to the World Bank, between 1994and 2005, the income share held by the highest 10 per cent of the population increased from 26 per cent to 28.3 per cent

[5] Tendulkar Committee, Planning Commission, Government of India.

> while that of the bottom 20 per cent decreased from 9.09 per cent to 8.64 per cent. According to the OECD, between 1993 and 2008, India's Gini coefficient increased from 0.32 to 0.38. As per the recently released Human Development Report (HDR) 2013, India ranked 136th (134th in 2011) in Human Development Index (HDI). Strikingly, when the HDI is adjusted for inequality, the index loses its value by as much as 29.3 per cent.[6]

India's reforms process resulted in opportunities that could be taken advantage of by a limited few or those who had access to resources. Inequality is being perpetuated by unequal access to health and education between the poor and the rich. As Kundu (2013) points out, inequality in access to education is so glaring that India's education index loses more than 40 per cent of its value once adjusted for inequality. In other words, education and health inequality are much sharper than expenditure inequality.

Many states reported a rise in inequality over 2004–5 and 2011–12. At the all-India level, growth during this period was around 7 per cent per annum, but this growth has been associated with a rise in inequality both in rural and urban areas. India's Gini coefficient has gone from 0.26 to 0.28 and from 0.35 to 0.37 in rural and urban areas, respectively (Table 21.4). There is evidence of growing concentration of wealth among the elite. The consumption of the top 20 per cent of households grew at almost 3 per cent per year in the 2000s as compared with 2 per cent in the 1990s, while the growth in consumption of the bottom 20 per cent of households remained unchanged at 1 per cent per year according to the consumption expenditure surveys of the NSSO.[7]

In fact, at the state level we get to see a very mixed picture. Many states registered rapid growth and witnessed a decline in inequality in either rural or urban areas. On the other hand, there are states that experienced a rise in inequality over time with rapid growth.

Consumption poverty declined over 2004–5 to 2011–12 in a number of states and at the all-India level as well, in both rural and urban areas. The urbanization level, on the other hand, increased at varying levels across states. For example, in Andhra Pradesh, it went up from 32.6 to 37.7 per cent, whereas Odisha, one of the low-income states, witnessed a nominal increase from 15 to 16.7 per cent over 2001–11.

The plot of the growth index, i.e. per capita net SDP against urbanization, shows a positive relationship (Figures 21.1 and 21.2).

Rural and urban poverty tend to vary inversely with urbanization in terms of the fitted line, though the observed points are scattered, and they deviate sizably from the fitted line (Figures 21.3 and 21.4). Further, the fitted line for urban

[6] Kundu (2013). [7] *Times of India*, 7 December2011.

Table 21.4. Growth, inequality, poverty, and urbanization

State	*Level of urban (%) 2001*	Level of urban (%) 2011	Rural poverty, 2004–05	Urban poverty, 2004–05	Rural poverty, 2011–12	Urban poverty, 2011–12	Lorenz ratio rural, 2004–5	Lorenz ratio urban, 2004–5	Lorenz ratio rural, 2011–12	Lorenz ratio urban, 2011–12	Per capita NSDP, 2004–5 (Rs)	Per capita NSDP, 2010–11 (Rs)
Andaman and Nicobar Islands	*32.6*	37.7	4.1	0.8	1.57	0.0	0.2532	0.3048	0.2897	0.3294	40,921	54,765
Andhra Pradesh	*27.3*	33.4	32.3	23.4	10.96	5.81	0.2515	0.3417	0.2434	0.3097	25,321	40,366
Arunachal Pradesh	*20.8*	22.9	33.6	23.5	38.93	20.33	0.2401	0.2132	0.3345	0.3226	26,610	37,417
Assam	*12.9*	14.1	36.4	21.8	33.89	20.49	0.182	0.301	0.2108	0.3447	16,782	21,406
Bihar	*10.5*	11.3	55.7	43.7	34.06	31.23	0.1851	0.3116	0.2038	0.2809	7,914	13,532
Chandigarh	*89.8*	97.3	34.7	10.1	1.64	22.31	0.244	0.3411	0.2694	0.3891	74,173	99,487
Chhattisgarh	*20.1*	23.2	55.1	28.4	44.61	24.75	0.2508	0.354	0.2407	0.3871	18,559	27,156
Dadra & N. Haveli	*22.9*	46.7	63.6	17.8	62.59	15.38	0.324	0.2949	0.3029	0.3094		
Daman & Diu	*36.2*	75.2	2.6	14.4	0.0	12.62	0.209	0.2419	0.1575	0.2645		
Delhi	*93.2*	97.5	15.6	12.9	12.92	9.84	0.2616	0.3243	0.2823	0.3731	63,877	108,876
Goa	*49.8*	62.2	28.1	22.2	6.81	4.09	0.2665	0.3329	0.2795	0.2922	76,968	102,844
Gujarat	*37.4*	42.6	39.1	20.1	21.54	10.14	0.2514	0.2953	0.2465	0.2839	32,021	52,708
Haryana	*28.9*	34.9	24.8	22.4	11.64	10.28	0.2953	0.3257	0.2492	0.3824	37,972	
Himachal Pradesh	*9.8*	10	25	4.6	8.48	4.33	0.2595	0.2609	0.272	0.3288	33,348	47,106
Jammu & Kashmir	*24.8*	27.4	14.1	10.4	11.54	7.2	0.1969	0.2413	0.2454	0.3022	21,734	27,607
Jharkhand	*22.2*	24	51.6	23.8	40.84	24.83	0.1985	0.3259	0.2112	0.3382	18,510	21,734
Karnataka	*34*	38.7	37.5	25.9	24.53	15.25	0.2322	0.3577	0.2605	0.4063	26,882	39,301
Kerala	*26*	47.7	20.2	18.4	9.14	4.97	0.2941	0.3527	0.3507	0.3885	31,871	49,873
Lakshadweep	*44.5*	78.1	0.4	10.5	0	12.62	0.1673	0.2356	0.2431	0.2993		
Madhya Pradesh	*26.5*	27.6	53.6	35.1	35.74	21	0.2365	0.3505	0.2764	0.3608	15,442	22,382
Maharashtra	*42.4*	45.2	47.9	25.6	24.22	9.12	0.27	0.3502	0.2516	0.3581	35,915	62,729
Manipur	*26.6*	32.5	39.3	34.5	38.8	32.59	0.1362	0.1488	0.1928	0.1988	18,640	23,298
Meghalaya	*19.6*	20.1	14	24.7	12.53	9.26	0.1363	0.2403	0.1723	0.2278	24,086	35,932

Mizoram	*49.6*	52.1	23	7.9	35.43	6.36	0.1665	0.2132	0.2434	0.2446	24,662	36,732
Nagaland	*17.2*	28.9	10	4.3	19.93	16.48	0.1729	0.2136	0.1915	0.2277	30,441	40,957
Orissa	*15*	16.7	60.8	37.6	35.69	17.29	0.2535	0.3297	0.2341	0.3452	17,650	25,708
Puducherry	*66.6*	68.3	22.9	9.9	17.06	6.30	0.2813	0.3019	0.2509	0.2684	48,302	79,333
Punjab	*33.9*	37.5	22.1	18.7	7.66	9.24	0.2626	0.3233	0.2691	0.3131	33,103	44,752
Rajasthan	*23.4*	24.9	35.8	29.7	16.05	10.69	0.2041	0.3033	0.2275	0.3065	18,565	26,436
Sikkim	*11.1*	25.2	31.8	25.9	9.85	3.66	0.2358	0.2317	0.1927	0.198	26,693	47,655
Tamil Nadu	*44*	48.4	37.5	19.7	15.83	6.54	0.2584	0.3445	0.2751	0.3297	30,062	51,928
Tripura	*17.1*	26.2	44.5	22.5	16.53	7.42	0.2034	0.2996	0.2074	0.292	24,394	37,216
Uttar Pradesh	*20.8*	22.3	42.7	34.1	11.62	10.48	0.2337	0.3391	0.2478	0.4052	12,950	17,349
Uttarakhand	*25.7*	30.2	35.1	26.2	30.4	26.06	0.2226	0.3017	0.2559	0.3413	24,726	44,723
West Bengal	*28*	31	38.2	24.4	22.52	14.66	0.2411	0.3564	0.2351	0.3816	22,649	32,228
India	*27.8*	31.2	42	25.5	25.7	13.7	0.2655	0.3475	0.2803	0.3673	24,143	35,993

Note: Poverty estimates are based on the national poverty line (Tendulkar methodology).

Source: Data Book, Planning Commission, and official estimates released by the government of India.

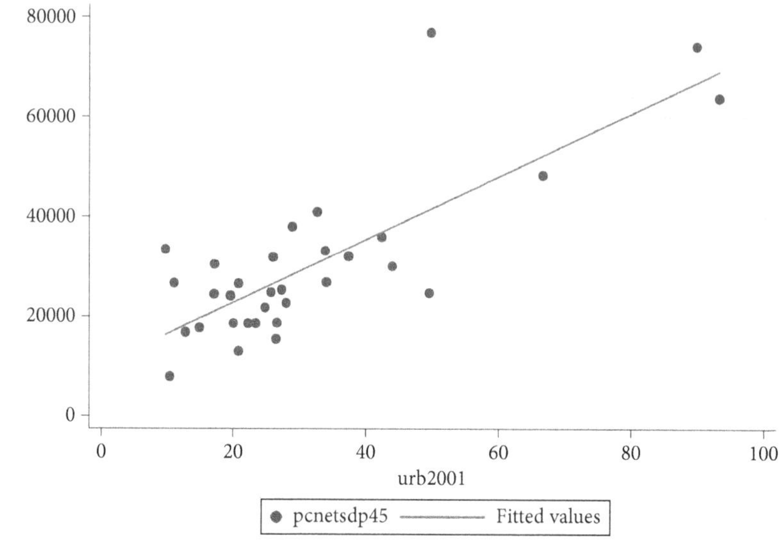

Figure 21.1. Urbanization (2001) and per capita net SDP (pcnetsdp45: 2004–5)
Source: Population census and CSO.

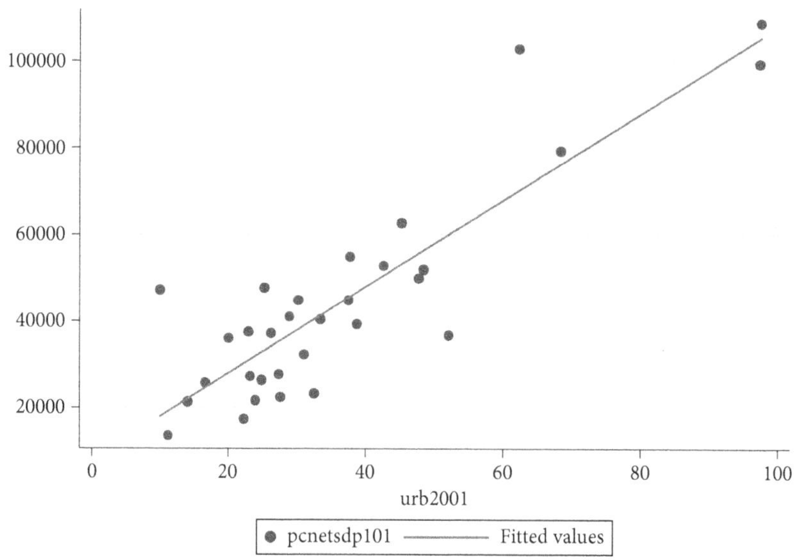

Figure 21.2. Urbanization (2011) and per capita net SDP (pcnetsdp101: 2010–11)
Source: Population census and CSO.

poverty is flatter than its rural counterpart in 2011–12, suggesting a greater decline in rural poverty than urban poverty with respect to urbanization.

The relationship between inequality and urbanization is positive but weak (Figures 21.5 and 21.6). The quadratic fit (an inverted U-shaped curve fitted to the data) does not become distinct either in rural or urban areas for the year 2004–5. However, for 2011–12, while rural poverty shows such an inverted U-shaped relationship remotely, urban poverty tends to follow a U-shaped relationship with respect to urbanization.

Based on the cross-sectional figures, the correlation between growth and inequality seems to be positive and significant in the rural context, while it is insignificant in urban areas. Possibly because rural areas are at lower levels of growth, inequality tends to rise. On the whole, the cross-sectional picture suggests that with economic growth, inequality tends to rise only in rural areas, while in urban areas, which show a higher level of growth than rural areas, inequality does not necessarily rise (Tables 21.5–21.7). However, this is only based on cross-sectional data; over time, at the all-India level, growth and inequality both seemed to have moved together.

Again, from the cross-sectional data, economic growth is seen to reduce poverty, though the role of other factors is also important. Inequality and poverty are mostly unrelated, though for 2011–12 there is a negative relationship in the rural

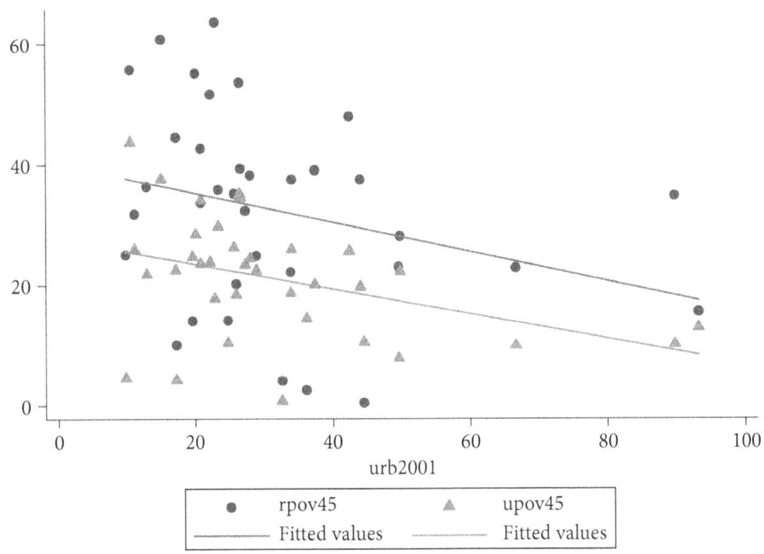

Figure 21.3. Rural (rpov45) and urban (upov45) poverty in 2004–5 and urbanization in 2001 (urb2001)

Source: Population census and NSSO.

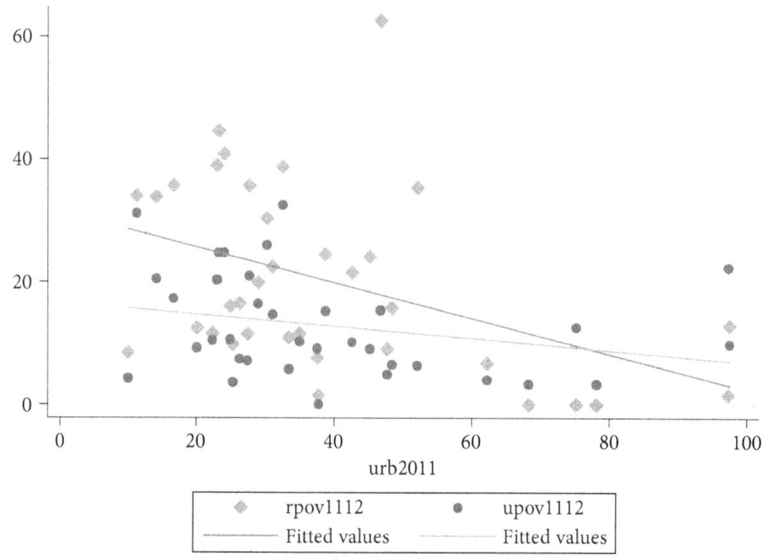

Figure 21.4. Rural (rpov1112) and urban (upov1112) poverty in (2011–12) and urbanization in 2011 (urb2011)
Source: Population census and NSSO.

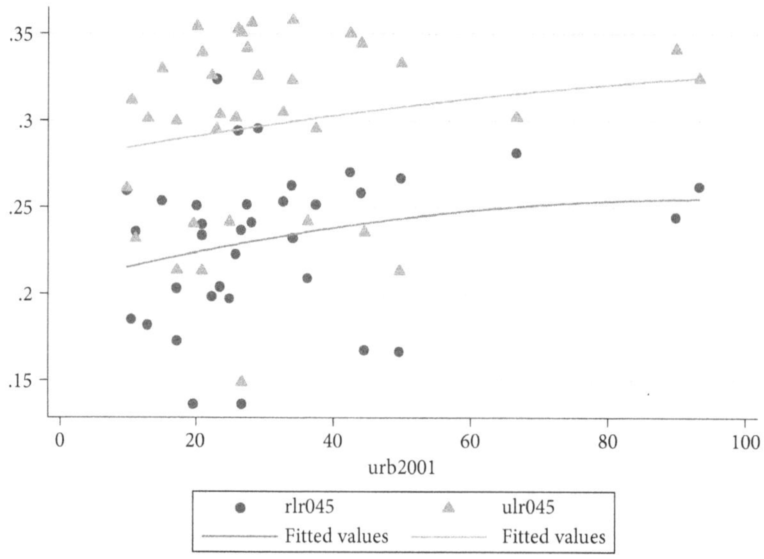

Figure 21.5. Rural (rlr45) and urban (ulr45) inequality in 2004–5 and urbanization in 2001 (urb2001)
Source: Population census and NSSO.

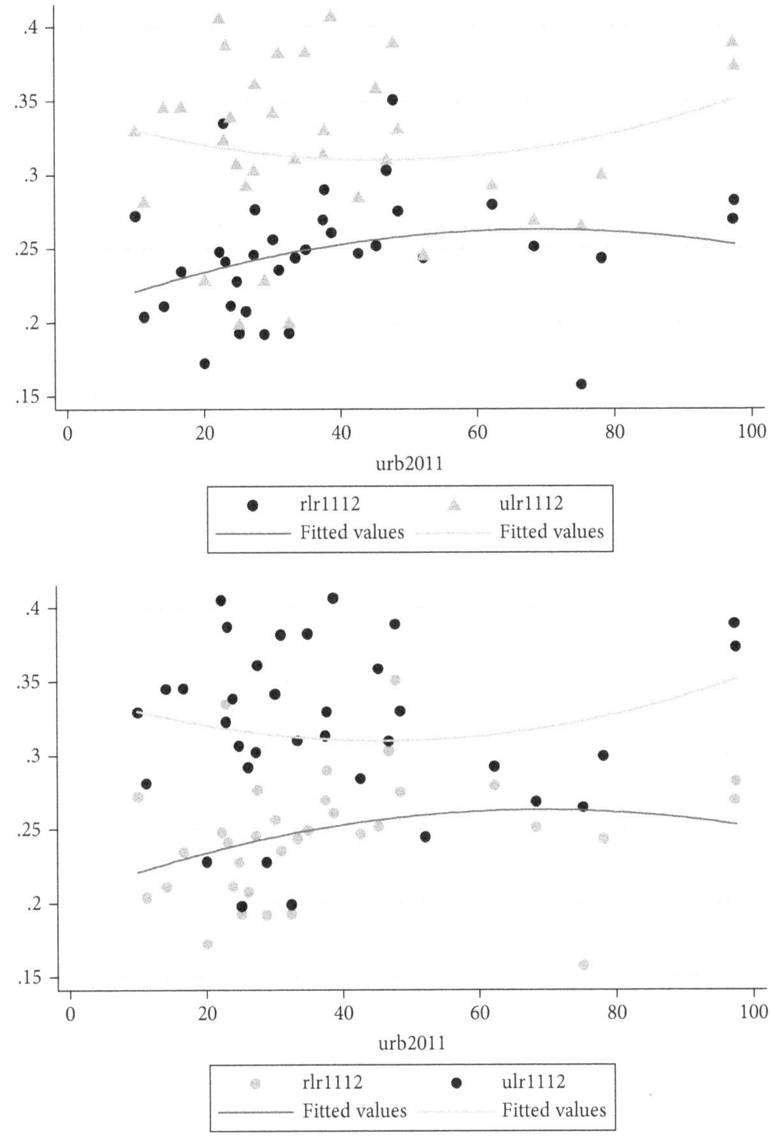

Figure 21.6. Rural (rlr1112) and urban (ulr1112) inequality in 2011–12 and urbanization in 2011 (urb2011)

Source: Population census and NSSO.

context that goes against the stylized factsproposing higher inequality being associated with higher poverty. In the equation for poverty being a function of both growth and inequality, inequality again shows no effect except in the urban context for 2004–5, where it takes a positive coefficient as one would expect, i.e. with an increase in inequality, poverty tends to rise.

Table 21.5. Correlation matrix: poverty, inequality, and agricultural and non-agricultural income per capita and urbanization, 2001

	RPOV, 2004–5	UPOV, 2004–5	Rural inequality, 2004–5	Urban inequality, 2004–5	Non-agr. NSDP per capita, 2004–5	Agr.and allied NSDP per capita, 2004–5
UPOV, 2004–5	0.78					
Rural inequality, 2004–5	−0.003	−0.15				
Urban inequality, 2004–5	0.36	0.20	0.64			
Non-agr. NSDP per capita, 2004–5	−0.36	−0.47	0.44	0.21		
Agr. and allied NSDP per capita, 2004–5	−0.40	−0.26	0.04	−0.35	−0.28	
Urbanization, 2001	−0.26	−0.40	0.32	0.23	0.85	−0.47

Note: The correlation between total net SDP per capita and urbanization is estimated at 0.79, that between total net SDP per capita and rural poverty is –0.43 and that between total net SDP per capita and urban poverty is –0.53.

Source: Author's calculations.

Table 21.6. Correlation matrix: poverty, inequality, and agricultural and non-agricultural income per capita and urbanization, 2011

	RPOV, 2011–12	UPOV, 2011–12	Rural inequality, 2011–12	Urban inequality, 2011–12	Non-agr. NSDP per capita, 2010–11	Agr. and allied NSDP per capita, 2010–11
UPOV, 2011–12	0.75					
Rural inequality, 2011–12	−0.22	−0.27				
Urban inequality, 2011–12	0.03	−0.09	0.56			
Non-agr. NSDP per capita, 2010–11	−0.58	−0.56	0.43	0.13		
Agr. and allied NSDP per capita, 2010–11	0.03	−0.07	0.07	−0.35	−0.38	
Urbanization, 2011	−0.44	−0.23	0.38	0.17	0.90	−0.43

Note: The correlation between total net SDP per capita and urbanization is estimated at 0.88, that between total net SDP per capita and rural poverty is –0.59 and that between total net SDP per capita and urban poverty is –0.40.

Source: Author's calculations.

Table 21.7. Impact of agricultural and non-agricultural growth, inequality, and urbanization on poverty

	RPOV, 2004–5	UPOV, 2004–5	RPOV, 2011–12	UPOV, 2011–12
Urbanization, 2001	0.288	−0.18		
	(−1.40)	(−1.17)		
Agr. NSDP per capita, 2004–5	−0.004	−0.002		
	(−4.29)**	(−2.54)**		
Non-agr. NSDP per capita, 2004–5	−0.0003	−0.002		
	(−1.26)	(−1.20)		
Rural inequality, 2004–5	106.14			
	(2.00)**			
Urban inequality, 2004–5		41.20		
		(1.35)		
Intercept	47.31	30.01		
	(3.82)**	(2.52)**		
Urbanization 2011			0.08	−0.05
			(0.40)	(−0.37)
Agr. NSDP per capita, 2011–12			−0.001	−0.001
			(−1.41)	(−2.09)**
Non-agr. NSDP per capita, 2011–12			−0.0004	−0.0002
			(−2.39)**	(−1.62)
Rural inequality, 2011–12			63.25	
			(0.95)	
Urban inequality, 2011–12				−15.77
				(−0.59)
Intercept			26.50	34.73
			(1.75)*	(3.15)**
Adj R2	0.43	0.38	0.31	0.32
N	31	31	29	29

Source: Author's calculations.

Cross-sectional data pertaining to 2004–5 suggest that rural and urban poverty are both strongly correlated (r=0.78). Both agricultural and non-agricultural income per capita are moderately and negatively associated with rural poverty (r is −0.40 and −0.36 respectively). Urban poverty and urban inequality show a positive correlation (r=0.20). In terms of growth, non-agricultural income per capita shows a relatively stronger effect (r = −0.47) on urban poverty than agricultural income per capita (r = −0.26), though both have a beneficial effect.

The urbanization level in 2001 is seen to be negatively correlated with both rural and urban poverty (2004–5) (r is −0.26 and −0.40 respectively), though rural and urban inequality reveal a positive association with the level of urbanization (r is 0.32 and 0.23 respectively). The most interesting point is that urbanization is strongly and positively related to non-agricultural income per capita (r = 0.85), while it tends to decline with respect to agricultural income per capita (r= −0.47), implying that with agricultural growth, the pace of migration due to rural impoverishment falls, which reduces the urbanization level.

Pertaining to 2011–12, the strong and positive correlation between rural and urban poverty is again very much evident (r = 0.75). Interestingly, neither rural nor urban poverty show any significant association with agricultural growth (0.03 and –0.06 respectively), while non-agricultural income per capita shows a beneficial effect on both rural and urban poverty (r is –0.58 and –0.56 respectively).

Urbanization in 2011 is negatively correlated with both rural and urban poverty (2011–12) (r is –0.44 and –0.23 respectively) and non-agricultural growth enhances urbanization (r=0.90), while agricultural income per capita reduces it.

However, some of these findings related to the impact of sectoral growth on poverty tend to change drastically as we regress rural and urban poverty on urbanization, agricultural income per capita, non-agricultural income per capita, and the inequality index in a multiple regression model. For 2004–5, agricultural income per capita (and not non-agricultural income per capita) is seen to reduce poverty significantly in both rural and urban areas (see Table 21.7). Even in 2011–12, urban poverty fell in response to agricultural income per capita, while non-agricultural income per capita was not significant even at the 10 per cent level. However, in the rural poverty function for 2011–12, non-agricultural income per capita turned out to be highly significant, while agricultural income per capita remained insignificant.

These major deviations from what we observed in terms of the correlation between pairs of variables may be attributed to the problem of multicollinearity, particularly if we keep in view the fact that other variables included in the model are mostly insignificant.

Pertaining to overall growth (net SDP per capita), inequality, poverty, and urbanization, we observe the following patterns based on the results from Tables 21.8 to 21.14.

Urbanization and per capita income are strongly correlated—urbanization turns out to be a significant determinant of growth for both 2004–5 and 2010–11. However, the growth rate in per capita income across states is not significantly related to the changes in the level of urbanization over time. Further, urbanization does not significantly impact inequality. In fact, the correlation between urbanization and urban inequality in 2004–5 and 2011–12 is only 0.22 and 0.17 respectively. However, as mentioned earlier, here inequality is measured merely in terms of consumption expenditure, which is a gross underestimate of income inequality.

The fact that both rural and urban poverty are positively related may imply a similarity in the poverty situation in both rural and urban areas across states. However, it may also reflect the importance of migration of the rural poor to urban areas in search of livelihoods.

Table 21.8. Impact of urbanization on poverty and inequality

Independent variable	Dependent variable							
	RPOV, 2004–5	UPOV, 2004–5	RPOV, 2011–12	UPOV, 2011–12	Rural inequality, 2004–5	Urban inequality 2004–5	Rural inequality 2011–12	Urban inequality, 2011–12
Urbanization, 2001	−0.242 (−1.73)*	−0.21 (−2.54)**			0.001 (1.32)	0.001 (1.08)		
Urbanization, 2011			−0.29 (−2.70)**	−0.10 (−1.73)*			0.0004 (1.27)	0.0002 (0.44)
Constant	40.09 (7.72)**	27.57 (9.16)**	31.57 (6.56)**	16.76 (5.89)**	0.21 (1 5.01)**	0.28 (16.36)**	0.23 (16.25)**	0.31 (15.78)**
Adj. R2	0.05	0.14	0.16	0.04	0.02	0.005	0.02	−0.02
No. of obs.	35	35	35	35	35	35	35	35

Note: ** and * denote significance at 5 and 10 per cent levels respectively.

Source: Author's calculations.

Table 21.9. Effect of urbanization and growth on inequality

Independent variable	Dependent variable			
	Rural inequality, 2004–5	Urban inequality, 2004–5	Rural inequality, 2011–12	Urban inequality, 2011–12
Urbanization, 2001	−0.0002 (−0.04)	0.0006 (0.82)		
Urbanization, 2011			0.0003 (0.43)	0.001 (1.08)
PCNETSDP, 2004–5	1.42e-06 (2.04)**	−7.34e-08 (−0.07)		
PCNETSDP, 2010–11			4.29e-07 (0.73)	−6.63E-07 (−0.73)
Constant	0.195 (13.54)**	0.28 (13.93)**	0.22 (15.22)**	0.31 (13.80)**
Adj. R2	0.16	−0.01	0.10	−0.02
No. of obs.	32	32	31	31

Note: ** and * denote significance at 5 and 10 per cent levels respectively.

PCNETSDP: per capita net state domestic product.

Source: Author's calculations.

Table 21.10. Determinants of urbanization and urban work participation rate

Independent variable	Dependent variable			
	URBN, 2001	URBN, 2011	URBN, 2011	UWFPRM, 2011
GR, 2005–6	2.06 (3.30)**			
GR, 2010–11		−0.43 (−0.51)		
PCNETSDP, 2010–11			0.0009 (11.18)**	−0.0000 (−0.19)
MIG			−0.011 (−0.91)	0.005 (1.22)
UOTHERACTM			−1.03 (−2.98)**	0.29 (2.05)**
URBN, 2011				0.05 (0.67)
ULITM				0.48 (2.84)**
USCM				0.17 (1.74)*
Constant	12.52 (1.92)*	40.62 (4.42)**	93. 19 (3.18)**	−21.43 (−1.25)
Adj. R2	0.24	−0.02	0.82	0.54
No. of obs.	32	32	31	31

Note: UWFPRM: main workforce participation rate in urban areas among males; ULITM: literacy among urban males; USCM: percentage of male scheduled caste population in urban areas; UOTHERACTM: percentage of urban male workers engaged in non-household manufacturing and services; URBN: percentage of population in urban areas; MIG: migration rate in urban areas; PCNETSDP: per capita net state domestic product; GR: annual growth rate in state domestic product. ** and * denote significance at 5 and 10 per cent levels, respectively.

Source: Author's calculations.

Table 21.11. Impact of growth on inequality

Independent variable	Dependent variable			
	Rural inequality, 2004–05	Urban inequality, 2004–05	Rural inequality, 2011–12	Urban inequality, 2011–12
PCNETSDP, 2004–05	0.000001 (2.82)**	0.0000006 (0.95)		
PCNETSDP, 2010–11			0.0000006 (2.33)**	0.0000002 (0.46)
Constant	0.195 (13.72)**	0.218 (14.09)**	0.218 (15.59)**	0.31 (13.97)**
Adj. R2	0.18	0.13	0.13	–.0.03
No. of obs.	32	32	31	31

Note: PCNETSDP: per capita net state domestic product. ** and * denote significance at 5 and 10 per cent levels respectively.

Source: Author's calculations.

The growth index (per capita income) reduces poverty. However, the explanatory power of these equations is extremely low, suggesting that the role of other factors is also important. In fact, factors like infrastructure development, skill formation, asset creation, and health status of the population are some of the most important determinants of poverty (Mitra 2013).The growth index (per capita income) raises inequality only in the rural context, while its impact is insignificant in urban areas.

Inequality and poverty are mostly unrelated in terms of statistical significance, though for 2011–12 only there is a negative and significant relationship in the rural context. In the equation for poverty is taken to be a function of both growth and inequality, inequality again shows no effect except in the urban context for 2004–5, where it takes a positive coefficient.

Urbanization does not show any significant impact on rural poverty, though it tends to reduce poverty in urban areas. However, the R^2 is nominal, indicating the impact of many other factors. After controlling for growth and inequality, the effect of urbanization is insignificant. These estimates are not robust in the sense that the explanatory power of the equations is moderate. Clearly there are several other relevant variables that influence poverty.

We may further note from Table 21.10 that growth positively influences urbanization, while expansion in non-agricultural employment tends to reduce it. Though the latter comes as a major surprise, this needs to be interpreted carefully. Given the economic growth, expansion in non-agricultural employment could be of the residual type, which does not provide productive sources of livelihood, and thus tends to reduce the pace of urbanization. In fact, in the Indian context, employment challenges are severe: a large majority of the workforce, even in

Table 21.12. Impact of growth on poverty

Independent variable	Dependent variable									
	RPOV04–05	UPOV04–05	RPOV11–12	UPOV11–12	RPOV04–05	UPOV04–05	RPOV11–12	UPOV11–12	Change in RPOV	Change in UPOV
GR, 2005–06	−0.35 (−0.69)	−0.47 (−1.32)								
GR, 2010–11			0.81 (1.68)	0.74 (2.36)**						
PCNETSDP, 2004–05					−0.0004 (−2.61)**	−0.0003 (−3.39)**				
PCNETSDP, 2010–11							−0.0003 (−3.90)**	−0.0001 (−2.32)**		
GR in PCNETSDP, 2004–5 to 2010–11									−1.69 (−1.44)	−1.48 (−1.88)*
Constant	36.57 (6.90)**	25.96 (6.99)**	12.56 (2.37)**	5.18 (1.50)	44.69 (9.09)**	31.60 (9.53)**	34.45 (8.45)**	19.52 (6.31)**	−1.75 (−0.22)	0.62 (0.12)
Adj. R2	−0.02	0.02	0.06	0.13	0.16	0.25	0.32	0.0.13	0.03	0.08
No. of obs.	32	32	32	32	32	32	31	31	31	31

Note: PCNETSDP: per capita net state domestic product, GR: annual growth rate in state domestic product. ** and * denote significance at 5 and 10 per cent levels respectively.

Source: Author's calculations.

Table 21.13. Determinants of growth

Independent variable	Dependent variable		
	PCNETSDP, 2004–05	PCNETSDP, 2010–11	PCNETSDP, 2010–11
URBN, 2001	632.70 (7.15)**		
URBN, 2011		1,001.42 (9.80)**	901.09 (10.77)**
ULIT			−13.50 (−0.03)
UHHSZ			−12322.36 (−1.60)
RHHSZ			6,520.48 (1.07)
UOTHERACT			1,033.07 (3.60)**
Constant	10,132.32 (3.07)**	7,898.01 (1.84)*	−54374.18 (−0.91)
Adj. R2	0.62	0.76	0.87
No. of obs.	32	31	31

Note: PCNETSDP: per capita net state domestic product; UHHSZ: household size in urban areas; RHHSZ: household size in rural areas; ULIT: literacy rate; UOTHERACT: percentage of urban workers engaged in non-household manufacturing and services; URBN: percentage of population in urban areas. ** and * denote significance at 5 and 10 per cent levels respectively.

Source: Author's calculations.

non-agricultural activities, is engaged in the informal sector. Further, urbanization has often been accompanied by expansion in the informal sector as the vast supplies of labour relative to demand pick up petty activities in the informal sector for survival.

Migration is also not found to be a significant determinant of urbanization.[8] As natural population growth is more significant thanmigration flows in urban areas, the urbanization level is not significantly influenced by migration. On the other hand, urbanization and expansion in non-agricultural activities both contribute to economic growth (Table 21.11). A rise in demographic pressure, such as urban household size, reduces growth. Economic growth, on the other hand, does not seem to be resulting in a higher work participation rate in urban areas—a phenomenon that has been widely cited in the Indian context. Even urbanization is not seen to have resulted in an enhanced work participation rate.

[8] As per the definition of migration used by NSSO (2007–8), which aims at capturing the long-duration migrants, a household member is defined to be a migrant whose last usual place of residence (UPR), anytime in the past, was different from the present place of enumeration.

Table 21.14. Impact of growth, inequality, and urbanization on poverty

Independent variable	Dependent variable							
	RPOV, 2004–05	UPOV, 2004–05	RPOV, 2011–12	UPOV, 2011–12	RPOV, 2004–05	UPOV, 2004–05	RPOV, 2011–12	UPOV, 2011–12
PCNETSDP, 2004–05	−0.0005 (−2.96)**	−0.0004 (−3.85)**			−0.0006 (−2.60)**	−0.0004 (−2.27)**		
PCNETSDP, 2010–11			−0.0003 (−3.71)**	−0.0002 (−3.81)**			−0.0004 (−2.62)**	−0.0003 (−2.17)**
Rural inequality, 2004–5	83.43 (1.34)				88.19 (1.41)			
Urban inequality, 2004–5			19.50 (0.37)			57.71 (1.96)**		
Rural inequality, 2011–12		57.35 (2.01)*					15.95 (0.30)	
Urban inequality, 2011–12				5.78 (0.25)				3.72 (0.16)
URBN, 2001					0.17 (0.93)	−0.0103 (−0.08)		
URBN, 2011							0.16 (0.82)	0.06 (0.43)
Constant	28.42 (2.17)**	15.31 (1.76)*	30.30 (2.49)***	20.12 (2.63)**	27.21 (2.06)**	15.22 (1.70)*	30.71 (2.50)**	20.62 (2.62)**
Adj. R2	0.18	0.32	0.31	0.29	0.18	0.30	0.30	0.27
No. of obs.	32	32	31	31	32	32	31	31

Note: URBN is the percentage of urban population. ** and * denote significance at 5 and 10 per cent levels respectively.

Source: Author's calculations.

21.3.2 Urban–Rural Inequality

The differences in the rural–urban consumption disparity are enormous and these differences do not seem to be declining over time (Table 21.15). Urban areas reported almost double the MPCE figure as compared with rural areas.

Table 21.15. Proportion of urban (U) to rural (R) average monthly per capita consumption expenditure

States & UTs	U/R MPCE, 2004–5	U/R MPCE, 2011–12
Andhra Pradesh	1.739	1.531
Arunachal Pradesh	1.142	1.489
Assam	1.948	1.796
Bihar	1.669	1.337
Chhattisgarh	2.329	1.819
Delhi	1.436	1.194
Goa	1.453	1.267
Gujarat	1.871	1.680
Haryana	1.324	1.754
Himachal Pradesh	1.742	1.602
Jammu & Kashmir	1.349	1.426
Jharkhand	2.317	2.006
Karnataka	2.032	1.939
Kerala	1.274	1.277
Madhya Pradesh	2.058	1.786
Maharashtra	2.022	1.970
Manipur	1.183	0.987
Meghalaya	1.816	1.652
Mizoram	1.542	1.562
Nagaland	1.482	1.109
Orissa	1.899	1.935
Punjab	1.566	1.191
Rajasthan	1.632	1.528
Sikkim	1.607	1.666
Tamil Nadu	1.793	1.549
Tripura	2.052	1.607
Uttar Pradesh	1.609	1.774
Uttarakhand	1.512	1.355
West Bengal	1.999	2.007
A & N Islands	1.686	1.712
Chandigarh	2.051	1.275
Dadra & N. Haveli	2.470	2.378
Daman & Diu	0.930	0.980
Lakshadweep	1.083	1.124
Pondicherry	1.391	1.480
All India	1.883	1.839

Note: MPCE = monthly per capita consumption expenditure.

Source: Based on National Sample Data.

The urban–rural differences in average per capita consumption expenditure are taken to be a function of non-agricultural income per capita, agricultural income per capita, and also the urbanization level. However, the results pertaining to 2004–5 and 2011–12 do not turn out to be statistically significant. In other words, rural–urban inequality could not be explained by the sector-specific growth index or the urbanization level.

Bhanumurthy and Mitra (2010) made an attempt to assess the impact of economic reforms on poverty in terms of a decomposition analysis by splitting the percentage change in the incidence of poverty between two time points via growth/mean effect, inequality effect, and the population shift effect. This has been pursued for two time periods: one from 1983 to 1993–4 and another from 1993–4 to 1999–2000, described as the pre-reforms period and reforms period, respectively. While the growth/mean effect was seen to be dominant and had resulted in a decline in the incidence of poverty in both periods and in most of the states, inequality, which in general rose during the process of growth, raised the poverty ratio at the all-India level. However, in the rural areas of a large number of states, the inequality effect turned out to be beneficial in the second period. Even in the urban areas of several states and at the all-India level, the adverse inequality effect fell considerably in the second period compared with the first. The population shift effect, which measures the net effect of a rise (and fall) in the percentage of the population residing in urban (and rural) areas on the incidence of poverty, appeared to be beneficial in several major states and at the all-India level, in both the periods. In other words, the overall incidence of poverty in these states fell because of rural–urban migration, though it might have raised urban poverty (Table 21.16).

Economic reforms have been pursued at different levels across states, and this seems to have enhanced the interstate variations in economic growth. Other than the role of agriculture in a few states like West Bengal, the rapid growth of new components in the tertiary sector, such as information technology, business process outsourcing services, financial institutions, and infrastructure services, has impacted upon economic growth at various levels across states. Besides, economic growth is also dependent on industrial productivity, which, in turn, is a function of agglomeration economies. Economic reforms seem to have generated an effect on factors that broadly fall into this class of agglomeration economies, and hence economic growth across states has shown divergence instead of convergence. But, interestingly, the beneficial growth/mean effect on poverty increased in magnitude in most of the states in the reforms period relative to the pre-reforms period and, more importantly, its variation across states dropped considerably. This is possibly because of good governance in the rapidly growing and reforming states, and the demonstration effect of this in the slowly growing states. The deleterious effect of inequality on poverty also shows a declining tendency in several states in the reforms phase compared with the previous period.

Table 21.16. Change in poverty due to population shift or migration

	Change in rural poverty (percentage point) (1983–94	Change in urban poverty (percentage point) 1983–94)	Change in rural poverty (percentage point) (1993–2000)	Change in urban poverty (percentage point) (1993–2000)
Andhra Pradesh	−2.17	3.81	−0.06	0.16
Assam	−1.48	0.5	−1.0	0.18
Bihar	−0.59	0.39	−0.12	0.08
Gujarat	−2.72	3.5	−1.23	1.51
Haryana	−7.21	6.01	−0.16	0.11
Karnataka	−2.06	2.58	−1.29	1.78
Kerala	−4.97	5.38	0.18	−0.22
Madhya Pradesh	−2.50	2.83	−0.96	1.07
Maharashtra	−3.69	3.35	−1.83	1.84
Orissa	−1.49	1.16	−0.95	0.82
Punjab	−1.99	2.78	−2.01	1.88
Rajasthan	−1.40	1.6	−0.22	0.27
Tamil Nadu	−2.74	2.75	−4.37	5.1
Uttar Pradesh	−1.71	1.65	−0.71	0.55
West Bengal	−0.9	0.47	−0.33	0.17
All India	−2.59	2.28	−1.65	1.43

Source: Bhanumurthy and Mitra (2010).

The population shift effect, which showed a tendency of raising urban poverty, also fell in magnitude in the second period compared with the first, across states. And states with greater beneficial growth effects in the second period relative to the first also showed lower adverse population shift effects in urban areas, that is, relatively less of a rise in the incidence of urban poverty caused by the population shift effect (perceived in terms of rural–urban migration). This can be interpreted as the beneficial effects of urbanization, which helped migrants access better employment opportunities in urban areas, and thus contributed to a reduction in poverty. The fact that the extent of the rise in urban poverty due to migration was less in regions that experienced higher beneficial effects of growth on poverty suggests that growth and urbanization moved hand in hand, contributing to poverty reduction.

The *Urban Poverty Report 2009* (Government of India 2010) also noted that across Indian states, poverty is negatively correlated with the level of urbanization, and large and medium cities have a lower incidence of poverty than small cities in India, though large centres have higher levels in inequality. A World Bank study (World Bank 2011) also found more widespread poverty in very small towns than in large cities. Gangopadhyay et al. (2010, 2011) applied the small area estimation methodology in three Indian states in 2004–5 and confirmed that in

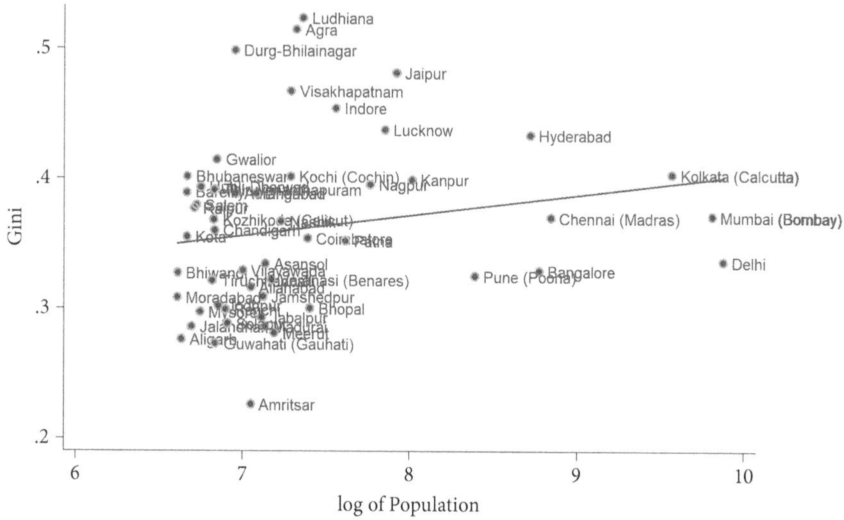

Figure 21.7. Inequality and city size
Source: Tripathi (2013).

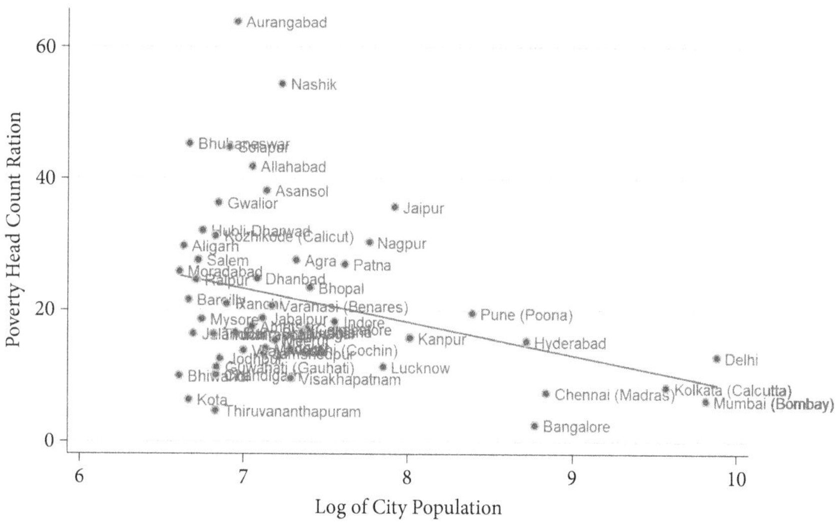

Figure 21.8. Poverty and city size
Source: Tripathi (2013).

the states of West Bengal, Orissa, and Andhra Pradesh, the poverty level in large cities was much lower than in small towns.Tripathi (2013) observed that higher levels of economic growth in cities and large city agglomerations are associated with a reduction in city poverty and an increase in inequality between cities (see Figures 21.7 and 21.8). However, as per the *Urban Poverty Report 2009*

(Government of India 2010), about eighty million people were estimated as poor in the cities and towns of India in 2007–8, and urban poverty in some of the larger states is higher than rural poverty, a phenomenon generally known as the 'urbanization of poverty' and attributed to rural–urban migration (Tripathi 2013). Such rural–urban differences are perceived despite a negative association between urbanization and urban poverty across states, as mentioned earlier. The differences in the findings can be attributed to the fact that the *Urban Poverty Report 2009* refers to all urban areas, while Tripathi (2013) analyses the poverty situation in cities only. Since small towns have a higher incidence of poverty compared to large cities, overall urban poverty can turn out to be on the high side.

21.3.3 Urban Labour Market, Migration, and Poverty

The factor analysis shows that, as per factor 1, the workforce participation rate and literacy in urban areas have a negative association with urban poverty, suggesting the importance of employment generation for poverty reduction (Table 21.17).

Table 21.17. Results from factor analysis (urban)

Variables	Factor 1	Factor 2
MIG	0.2586	0.1808
HHSZ	−0.8945	−0.1621
WFPR	0.7792	0.3300
LIT	0.7326	0.1992
SC	−0.0127	0.0506
OTHERACT	0.3264	0.2910
F/M	0.2294	−0.0504
UPOV	−0.4142	−0.4480
URBN	0.1114	0.9422
UINEQ	−0.0705	0.1066
NSDPPERCAP	0.3120	0.8817
Eigen value	3.83	1.80
Explained variation	0.53	0.25

No. of Observation: 31.

Note: HHSZ: household size; WFPR: main workforce participation rate; LIT: literacy rate; SC: percentage of scheduled caste population; OTHERACT: percentage of workers engaged in non-household manufacturing and services; F/M: female–male ratio in the population, UPOV: percentage of households below the poverty line in urban areas; URBN: percentage of population in urban areas; NSDPPERCAP: net state domestic product per capita; UINEQ: inequality in terms of Gini index in urban areas. The variables are for 2011, 2011–12, or 2010–11.

Source: Author's calculations.

Migration is again positively associated with some of the development indicators, while it has a negative relationship with urban poverty and with some of the variables representing demographic pressure like urban household size. In other words, states with a higher incidence of poverty show lower migration rates, implying that rural migrants are less likely to move to the urban areas of states that do not provide adequate sources of livelihood and are thus characterized by a greater magnitude of urban poverty. However, this negative association can also be interpreted as a positive outcome in terms of a decline in poverty subsequent to migration from rural to urban areas. In factor 2, this pattern is quite pertinent: higher levels of urbanization and growth are associated with higher levels of migration (though the migration rate does not have a high factor loading) and a lower incidence of urban poverty.

The results pertaining to the second factor show that both urbanization and per capita net SDP take a very high factor loading, suggesting a strong association between them. Though inequality is not strongly correlated with urbanization and growth, the relationship is distinct. While poverty tends to decline, inequality rises in the process of growth and urbanization. The work participation rate and the percentage of urban workers engaged in non-household manufacturing and services are also positively associated with growth and urbanization, though in the regression analysis, growth was not found to be a significant determinant of the urban work participation rate. Interestingly, the rural-to-urban migration rate in urban areas also shows a positive relationship with urbanization and the growth index, though it does not have a high factor loading. Even the literacy rate does not take a high factor loading, indicating less significance. Caste does not turn out to be significant in either factor 1 or 2, implying that a lower social category of population is not related to any of the other variables significantly.The results pertaining to the rural specific variables in relation to urbanization are presented in Appendix 1.

In the Indian context, there is no specific policy as such for the migrants except for the notified slum clusters that are entitled to receive support in terms of basic amenities. The migrants specifically are not covered by any social security measure. If they are employed in regular jobs in the formal sector, they are entitled to the benefits that are meant for workers in this sector. Otherwise, there is no special scheme for the migrant workers. There is no legal barrier as such on migrants, though the social, cultural, and linguistic barriers are enormous for the migrants who come from rural areas, especially from other states. The cityspace is shrinking for low-income households and more so for migrants; even entry to slums is becoming difficult due to shortage of space. In some of the large cities, access to space inside a slum cluster is determined by the contacts that the potential migrants have with those who have already migrated and the paying capacity of the newly migrated to the local muscle-men/slum leaders/members of mafia groups/illegal landlords who earn rent on public space (Edelman and Mitra 2006). Though migrants have no legal restrictionson selling their land at their place of origin and moving cities, the practical difficulties tend to reduce migration significantly. Besides, there are instances of harassment caused to migrants by the police authorities, builders, and some of the political parties. The slum demolition squads followed by local governments, which are not often accompanied by resettlement projects, are the biggest factors in discouraging the entry of migrants to cities. Though in a democratic setup it is difficult to pursue any legal mechanism that hinders the mobility of the population across space, certain prevalent practices stop individuals from benefiting in the process of growth, by posing indirect restrictions on their mobility (Mitra 2013). Labour market regulations are not applicable to the informal sector. The low-income migrants who are employed in the informal sector are as vulnerable as the locals engaged in the same sector, though migrant workers are confronted with more challenges, particularly in terms of shelter. At the outset of the 2010 Commonwealth Games, when slums were demolished, the inhabitants tried to enter public parks in the night for rest. However, the police chased them away, which amounts to creating barriers on migration, though in a democratic setup as that of India, no restriction on migration can be posed explicitly.

From the regression analysis, it is observed that higher inequality in urban areas leads to a higher rate of migration. Higher income or wage inequality at the place of destination is also an indicator of dynamism, which, in turn, tends to raise the expected income differential between rural and urban areas, and thuspotential rural migrants are more likely to shift to urban locations. Economic growth too shows a positive impact on migration. A higher level of urbanization tends to reduce migration, whereas the urban work participation rate is not statistically significant. However, it may be argued that inequality is a result of rather than a reason for migration. Respecifying migration as a function of growth, urbanization, and urban informal sector employment, we are able to estimate a better model. Both growth and urban informal sector employment induce migration, while increased urbanization capturing greater demographic pressure suppresses it.

$$\begin{gathered}\text{MIG} = -278.819 + 914.75\ \text{UINEQ} + 0.005\ \text{NSDPPERCAP} \\ -4.16\ \text{URBN} + 5.17\ \text{UWFPR} \\ (-1.02) \quad (2.14)^{**} \quad (2.10)^{**} \quad (-1.74)^{*} \quad (0.64) \\ \text{Adj. R2} = 0.20,\ N=31\end{gathered}$$

$$\begin{gathered}\text{MIG} = -6.337 + 0.005\ \text{NSDPPERCAP} - 5.10\ \text{URBN} + 0.45\text{INF} \\ (-0.06)\ (3.03)^{**} \qquad (-2.24)^{**}\ (2.72)^{**} \\ \text{Adj. R2} = 0.29,\ N=31\end{gathered}$$

In the above equations, MIG = migration rate; UWFPR = main workforce participation rate among urban males; URBN = percentage of population in urban areas; NSDPPERCAP = net state domestic product per capita; UINEQ = inequality in terms of the Gini index in urban areas; and INF = urban informal sector employment. ** and * denote significance at 5 and 10 per cent levels respectively.

One important fact from which gross inequality can be inferred is that an overwhelming proportion of workers are engaged in the informal sector, though in certain situations the informal sector also provides productive sources of livelihood and an abovepovertyline level of living. The 'employment problem' in the Indian context cannot be conceptualized merely in terms of the open unemployment rate because many cannot afford to remain unemployed for long. On the other hand, the set of working poor is prevalent, implying residual absorption of the workforce in low-productivity informal sector activities. Even in non-agricultural activities, the incidence of informal sector employment is over 70 per cent (National Sample Survey 2009–10). The set of informal workers is extremely large, which includes the self-employed in the informal sector (ranging from street vendors to those who operate micro-enterprises with less than ten workers), regular hired workers in the petty enterprises in the informal sector, and casual and contractual workers both in the informal and formal sectors without any employment security or social security.

There are considerable overlaps between urban informal sector employment and urban poverty. Second, rural-to-urban migration has a positive association with urban informal sector employment. Often rural migrants are not able to find jobs in the formal sector and thus pick up menial jobs in the informal sector (Mitra 2013). Though the urban informal sector provides sources of livelihood and helps reduce the incidence and intensity of urban poverty, the overlaps between slum formation, informalization of employment, and poor living standards cannot be overlooked (Mitra 1994). Nearly 80 per cent of low-income migrants are located in slums; 90 per cent of the households from slums are engaged in the urban informal sector; the incidence of consumption poverty in the slums is more than 70 per cent and most slum dwellers are susceptible to poor health outcomes (Mitra 1994). The details on these aspects of the analysis are not presented in this chapter because Chapter 7 deals with some of these issues.

21.3.4 District-Level Data

Given the complex relationship between urbanization, growth, inequality, poverty, work participation rate, caste, literacy, and demographic pressure, as seen from the state-level analysis, we prefer to pursue the multivariate analysis for the district-level data. At the district level, the average MPCE is taken as a proxy for growth and inequality respectively.

The correlation matrix shows that in relation to urbanization, the average consumption expenditure in both rural and urban areas increases, poverty declines, and inequality rises (Table 21.18). The work participation rate and the percentage of workforce engaged in non-household manufacturing and services, both in rural and urban areas, vary positively with urbanization, indicating the importance of diversification away from agriculture that accompanies urbanization. These correlations are, however, observed at a moderate level. Though urban–rural inequality also has a positive association with urbanization, the correlation is very low (0.13).

The rural- and urban-specific growth rates are closely associated with each other. Rural and urban growth is associated with a reduction in poverty in both areas. Poverty is accompanied by a lower work participation rate and less diversification in terms of non-agricultural activities. Poverty and inequality again go hand in hand.

The plot of some of the important variables against urbanization suggests the following patterns (Figures 21.9–21.12). Growth represented by per capita consumption expenditure rises mildly in response to urbanization; poverty both in rural and urban areas tends to decline with an increase in urbanization, though there are too many outliers; urban–rural inequality measured in

Table 21.18. The correlation matrix

	URBN	RAVMPCE	UAVMPCE	RBPL	UBPL
RAVMPCE	0.46				
UAVMPCE	0.44	0.67			
RBPL	−0.31	−0.65	−0.49		
UBPL	−0.34	−0.50	−0.59	0.52	
RINEQ	0.24	0.65	0.41	−0.30	−0.24
UINEQ	0.39	0.41	0.68	−0.23	−0.27
URINEQ	0.13	−0.08	0.68	−0.003	−0.30
RWFPR	0.28	0.31	0.21	−0.22	−0.27
ROTHERACT	0.46	0.56	0.47	−0.35	−0.32
UWFPR	0.35	0.36	0.35	−0.24	−0.37
UOTHERACT	0.29	0.31	0.44	−0.20	−0.39

Note: U and R represent urban and rural areas respectively; HHSZ: household size; CHILDWOM: proportion of children to women; WFPR: main workforce participation rate; LIT: literacy; SC: percentage of scheduled caste population; OTHERACT: percentage of workers engaged in non-household manufacturing and services; MFGHH: percentage of workers in household manufacturing; F/M: female–male ratio in the population, BPL: percentage of households below the poverty line; URBN: percentage of population in urban areas; AVMPCE: average monthly per capita consumption expenditure; INEQ: inequality in terms of the difference between the minimum and maximum value of the consumption expenditure; URINEQ: the urban–rural difference in consumption expenditure, a proxy for urban–rural inequality. The variables are for 2011 or 2011–12.

Source: Census of India 2011 and NSSO Data (2011–12).

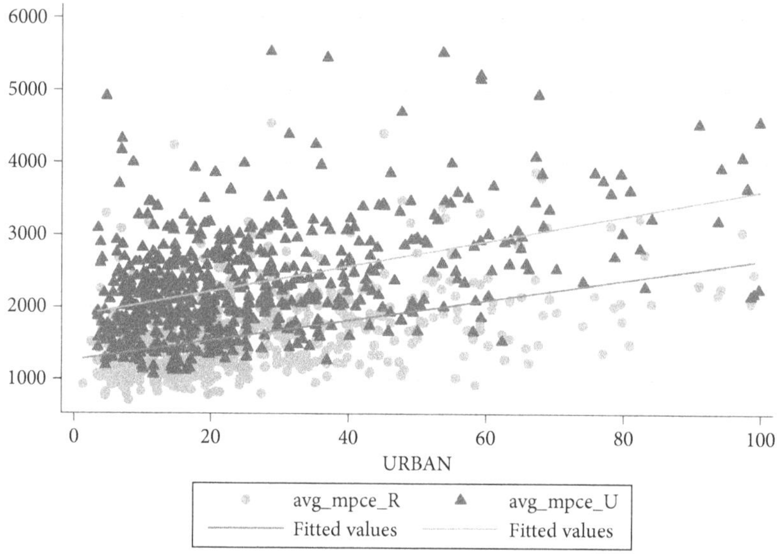

Figure 21.9. Average monthly consumption expenditure per capita in rural and urban areas (2011–12) plotted against urbanization (2011)

Note: R and U stand for rural and urban respectively. Avg_mpce is average monthly per capita consumption expenditure.

Source: Census of India 2011 and NSSO (2011–12).

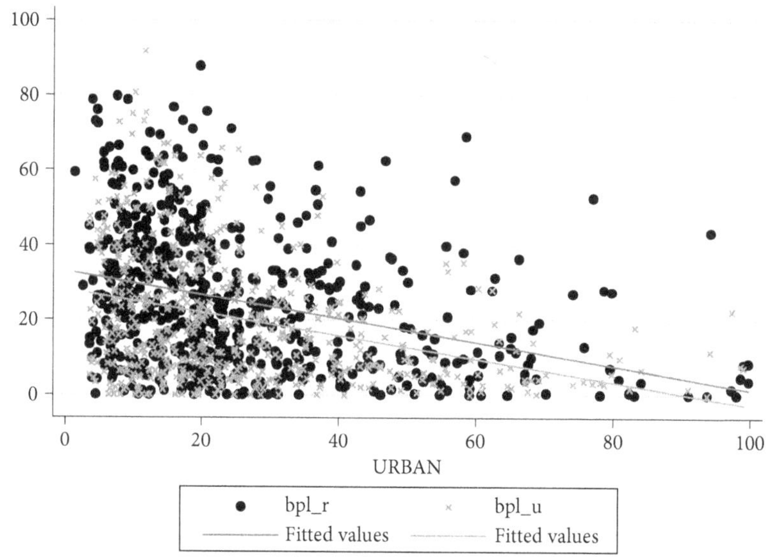

Figure 21.10. Incidence of poverty in rural and urban areas (2011–12) plotted against urbanization (2011)

Note: r and u stand for rural and urban respectively. bpl is below poverty line households.

Source: Census of India 2011 and NSSO (2011–12).

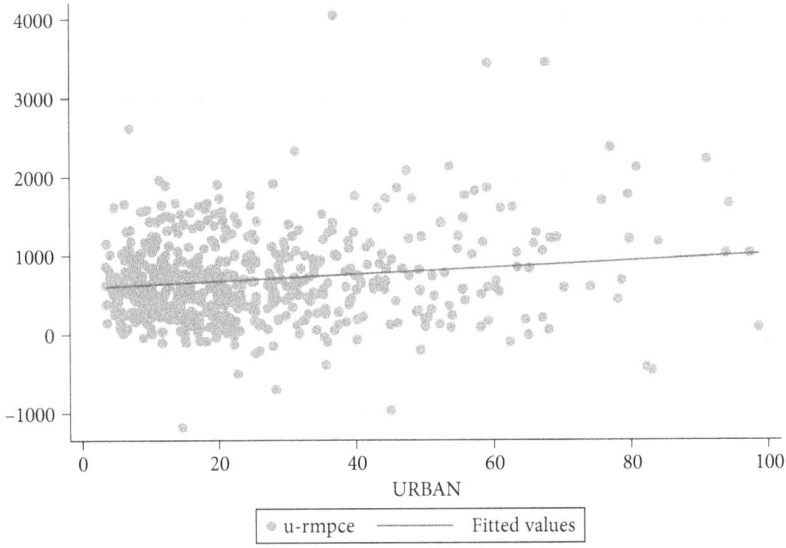

Figure 21.11. Urban–rural inequality (2011–12) in terms of difference between urban and rural average consumption expenditure per capita plotted against urbanization (2011)

Note: u-r mpce represents differences between urban and rural monthly per capita consumption expenditure per capita. A couple of negative figures represent higher rural magnitudes than their urban counterparts.

Source: Census of India 2011 and NSSO (2011–12).

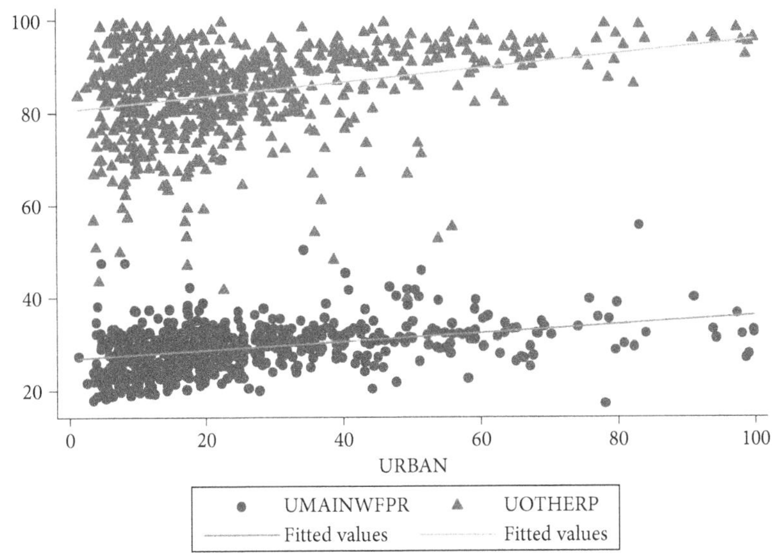

Figure 21.12. Workforce participation rate and percentage of non-household manufacturing and services in total workforce in urban areas plotted against urbanization, 2011

Source: Census of India 2011 .

terms of the differences between the urban and rural average consumption expenditure per capita shows almost no relationship with urbanization; the workforce participation rate and the percentage of the workforce engaged in non-household manufacturing and services both show a rising tendency in relation to urbanization(see Table 21.18).

Based on the district-level data, both factor and regression analyses have been carried out: the results pertaining to the factor analysis are presented Appendix 2.

From the regression analysis, rural poverty is seen to decline in relation to growth, though inequality raises poverty (Table 21.19). Further, male literacy and the work participation rate reduce poverty. The positive relationship between female literacy and rural poverty is indicative of the extensive rural literacy mission aimed at encompassing more women from poor households. Similarly, in urban areas poverty declines in response to rise in growth, male work participation rate, and male literacy rate, though inequality raises it. More importantly, urbanization shows a strong beneficial effect on poverty, as higher levels of urbanization are associated with lower poverty incidence.

The regression analysis of urbanization suggests that both rural and urban growth contribute to urbanization. The rural male work participation rate and rural male literacy also add to urbanization as rural male workers and those that are literate are more likely to migrate to cities in search of better jobs after acquiring work experience and skills. With rural diversification (expansion in non-agricultural activities), the urbanization index also tends to increase, as the rural–urban discontinuum in terms of activities tends to break down. Rural areas start urbanizing and migration also becomes easier, as the differences in the nature of the activities across space get dissipated. However, in relation to the rural male scheduled caste population, urbanization falls, as they represent the socially vulnerable who are less likely to afford the cost of migration. With respect to women, we reserve our comments because female migration is governed more by social factors such as marriage (Mitra 2013).

The regression analysis of economic growth in urban areas again confirms the importance of urbanization. Literacy, increased work opportunities resulting in an enhanced work participation rate, and expansion in activities such as non-household manufacturing and services also contribute to growth. However, economic growth in rural areas is not significantly influenced by urbanization, though the other factors remain pertinent.

Urban inequality rises in response to both urbanization and urban growth. The migration of low-income households from rural to urban areas resulting in higher levels of urbanization manifests itself in a higher level of inequality. However, increased work opportunities reduce urban inequality, while the presence of vulnerable social categories such as the scheduled caste population aggravates urban inequality. In the rural context, inequality is not seen to be influenced by urbanization, meaning out-migration does not result in inequality reduction. A

Table 21.19. Regression results from district-level data: poverty, urbanization, growth, and inequality functions

Independent variables	RPOV, 2011–12	UPOV, 2011–12	URBN	URBN	UAVMPCE	RAVMPCE	UINEQ	RINEQ	URINEQ
RMWFPR	−0.165 (−1.72)*		0.62 (5.90)**	0.71 (6.97)**					
UMWFPR		−0.23 (−2.05)**							
RFWFPR	0.065 (1.01)		−0.26 (−3.51)**	−0.007 (−0.09)					
UFWPR		−0.015 (−0.11)							
RWFPR						23.73 (10.65)**		−148.67 (−3.86)**	
UWFPR					15.43 (2.58)**		−189.55 (−3.08)**		4.25 (0.91)
ROTHERACT				0.37 (7.41)**		16.68 (13.81)**		−55.81 (−2.53)**	
UOTHERACT					20.05 (6.44)**		−44.19 (−1.36)		11.77 (4.86)**
RMLIT	−0.464 2(−3.23)**		0.567 (3.49)**	0.44 (2.81)**					
UMLIT		−0.67 (−2.90)**							
RFLIT	0.398 (3.37)**		−0.22 (−1.68)*	−0.31 (−2.38)**					
UFLIT		0.21 (1.31)							
RLIT						9.81 (4.99)**		50.56 (1.61)	
ULIT					21.61 (4.60)**		10.66 (0.22)		−1.88 (−0.51)

(Continued)

Table 21.19. Continued

Independent variables	RPOV, 2011–12	UPOV, 2011–12	URBN	URBN	UAVMPCE	RAVMPCE	UINEQ	RINEQ	URINEQ
RMSC	−1.64		−8.82	−6.80					
	(−1.04)		(−4.73)**	(−3.77)**					
UMSC		−0.42							
		(−0.31)							
RFSC	1.38		8.66	6.78					
	(0.88)		(4.64)**	(3.76)**					
UFSC		0.39							
		(0.29)							
RSC								−7.60	
								(−0.30)	
USC							103.44		
							(2.53)**		
URBN	0.023	−0.086			11.34	1.54	74.29	−11.85	−4.22
	(0.66)	(−2.51)**			(8.29)**	(1.46)	(4.59)**	(−0.72)	(−3.38)**
RAVMPCE	−0.026		0.006	0.0008				10.63	
	(−17.74)**		(3.48)**	(0.46)				(16.84)**	
UAVMPCE		−0.014	0.004	0.003			7.62		
		(−13.48)**	(3.82)**	(2.98)**			(18.21)**		
RINEQ	0.0005								
	(5.49)**								
UINEQ		0.0005							0.03
		(5.64)**							(13.11)**
INTER	84.44	99.39	−38.998	−37.72	−1,690.19	−235.42	−3199.97	−6709.04	−472.08
	(15.19)*	(11.39)**	(−6.31)**	(−6.38)**	(−5.59)**	(−2.27)**	(−0.99)	(−4.07)**	(−1.99)**
No. of obs.	608	592	592	592	602	608	592	608	592
Adj. R2	0.4927	0.42	0.35	0.40	0.37	0.52	0.49	0.44	0.29

Note: For the definition of variables, see Tables 21.21 and 21.22. While the prefixes RM, RF, UM, and UF represent rural male, rural female, urban male, and urban female respectively, simply R and U refer to rural and urban areas for both the sexes. For other variables, see Table 21.21. ** and * denote significance at 5 and 10 per cent levels respectively.

Source: Author's calculations

greater presence of the scheduled caste population does not add to inequality, suggesting no significant differences in living standards across social categories in rural areas, while in the urban context such differences are more pronounced. Again, greater work opportunities and rural diversification are endemic to controlling inequality in rural areas.

The urban–rural inequality envisaged in terms of the differences in average consumption expenditure per capita rises in response to expansion in employment opportunities in the non-household manufacturing and services sector in urban areas. If the level of inequality in urban areas is high, it tends to raise the rural–urban differences as well. However, urbanization reduces interspatial inequality, implying that urbanization provides livelihood opportunities to the rural population by helping them migrate out from rural areas and also by transforming rural areas into urban.

21.3.5 Million-Plus Cities

Large cities are said to be more productive: more demand-induced employment opportunities are available in large cities, which grow in response to the large quantum of investment undertaken therein. Several socio-economic development indicators tend to improve with an increase in city size (Mitra 2013). Economic globalization has not reduced the intra-urban or rural–urban growth differentials. Agglomeration economies continue to exist because new forces in the present context of economic globalization have emerged to substitute the forces that explained their prevalence around two decades ago and have been on the decline (Mitra 2014). As a backdrop to these views, we therefore take a look at the dataset generated for the million-plus cities in India (Figure 21.12). These cities are scattered across space instead of being concentrated in a few regions. However, it seems they mainly surround seaports, or are state capitals or located in the neighbourhood of state capitals.

The incidence of poverty in million-plus cities is, however, not negligible, as Table 21.20 indicates. In fact, in some of the cities the incidence is more than 25 per cent (Table 21.20), though such cities are very few in number. Within the million-plus cities, there seems to be an inverse relationship between city and poverty (Figure 21.13). Since we do not have such information for other smaller cities or towns it is difficult to make a comparison and conclude whether poverty, unemployment, or informal employment is lower in big cities. The skill levels across various occupations are higher in million-plus cities compared with the other categories of urban settlements and hence it may be inferred that poverty tends to decline with city size (Mitra 2010, Tripathi 2013).

Though city size and poverty or city size and growth (measured in terms of average consumption expenditure per capita) are expected to be strongly associated, the graphs are not indicative of this(see Figures 21.14 and 21.15).

Table 21.20. Poverty in million-plus cities, 2011–12

Less than 3%	3 to less than 5%	5 to less than 10%	10 to less than 25%	25% and above
Hyderabad	Kollam	Surat	Faridabad	Allahabad
Ghaziabad	Rajkot	Jodhpur	Kanpur	Aurangabad
Madurai	Pune	Jaipur	Ranchi	Kota
Greater Mumbai	Thrissur	Vijayawada	Nashik	Agra
Tiruchirappalli	Coimbatore	Visakhapatnam	Nagpur	Jamshedpur
Indore	Kochi	Ahmadabad	Jabalpur	Dhanbad
Bangalore	Meerut	Kannur	Gwalior	
Vasai-Verar	Kozhikode	Srinagar	Varanasi	
Chennai	Kolkata	Malappuram	Lucknow	
Thiruvananthapuram		Amritsar	Durg	
		Bhopal	Chandigarh	
		Patna	Raipur	
		Delhi	Asansol	
		Vadodara		

Source: Based on NSS unit-level data.

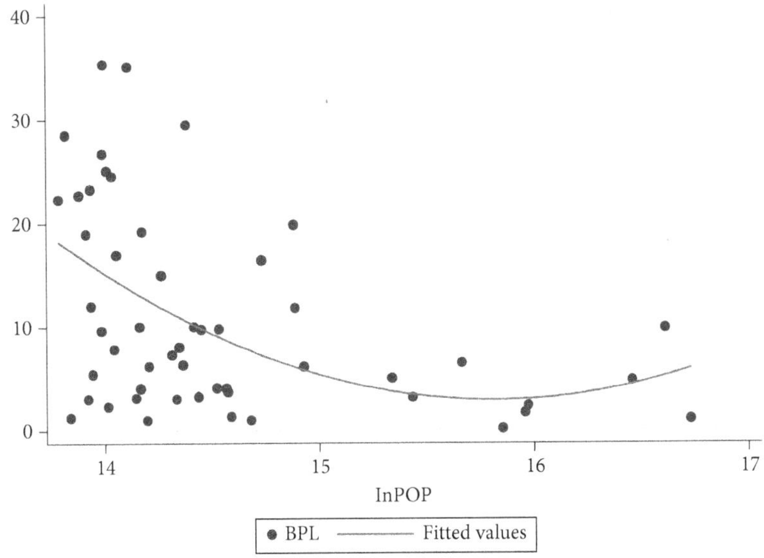

Figure 21.13. City size in 2011 and poverty in 2011–12 (below poverty line, BPL)
Note: In the horizontal axis, we have taken the logarithmic transformation of population.
Source: Census of India 2011 and NSSO (2011–12).

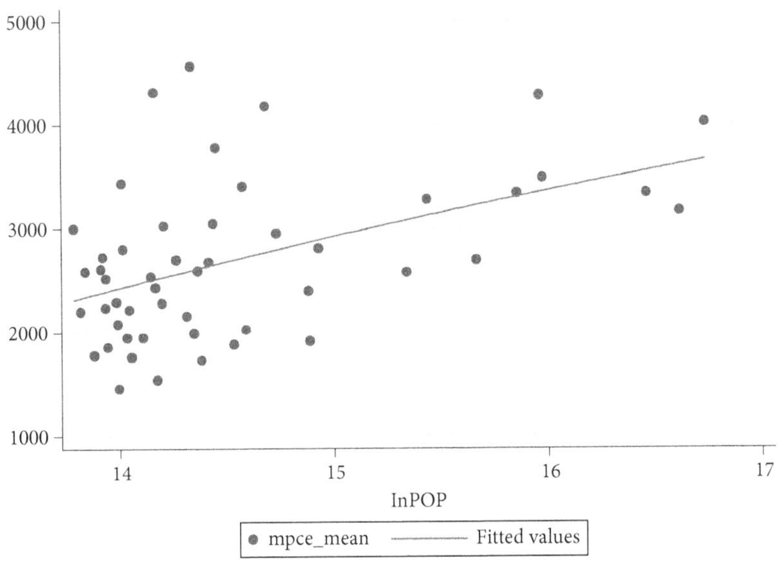

Figure 21.14. City size in 2011 and monthly per capita consumption expenditure in 2011–12 (mpce_mean)
Note: In the horizontal axis, we have taken the logarithmic transformation of population.
Source: Census of India 2011 and NSSO (2011–12).

Figure 21.15. Million-plus cities

Poverty tends to fall with city size and then increase slightly in the case of very large cities. Per capita consumption expenditure figures rise in relation to city size, though the observations are highly scattered instead of being concentrated around the line. In fact, the correlation between log of city size and poverty incidence and log of city size and mean per capita consumption expenditure is seen to be somewhat moderate, i.e. –0.42 and 0.47 respectively.

Based on the factor analysis, though the results do not bring out a strong relationship between city size, growth, and poverty as per the most significant factor (1), the next significant factor (2) elucidates that in the million-plus cities, poverty tends to decline with growth and city size, favouring agglomeration effects. Some of the demographic variables such as household size and child–woman ratio are important determinants of poverty (Table 21.21). Growth and inequality vary positively with each other and literacy varies inversely with poverty. In fact, large

Table 21.21. Factor analysis (million-plus cities)

Variables	Factor 1	Factor 2
HHSZ	−0.5461	−0.7420
CHILD-WOM	−0.7113	−0.2801
WFPR	−0.0477	0.8520
LIT	0.7071	0.3828
SC	−0.1747	0.0131
OTHERACT	0.0872	0.4563
F/M	0.8674	−0.1288
BPL	−0.2519	−0.2939
CITYSZ	−0.0729	0.2287
AVMPCE	0.1162	0.3141
INEQ	0.1539	0.1895
Eigen value	3.90	1.50
Explained variation	0.61	0.23

Note: No. of observations: 50. HHSZ: household size; CHILD-WOM: proportion of children to women; WFPR: main workforce participation rate; LIT: literacy; SC: percentage of scheduled caste population; OTHERACT: percentage of workers engaged in non-household manufacturing and services; F/M: female–male ratio in the population, BPL: percentage of households below the poverty line; CITYSZ: city size; AVMPCE: average monthly per capita consumption expenditure; INEQ: inequality in terms of the difference between the minimum and maximum value of the consumption expenditure.

Source: Author's calculations.

cities are seen to be positively associated with better employment opportunities as reflected in terms of a positive relationship between city size and work participation rate, which again, in turn, varies positively with literacy (in factor 2).

21.3.6 Mobility of Poor Households

Wenoted earlier that the incidence of poverty declined over time, while per capita income rose during the same period. However, what is important to know is whether households that were poor at one time point have become non-poor at another time point and vice versa. If some of the households keep oscillating around the poverty line, the decline in the aggregate incidence of poverty does not speak much in terms of inclusiveness. If some of the poor households have escaped poverty and none of the non-poor have become poor again, then the decline in the incidence could be a matter of success because there is hope that the remaining poor households would gradually escape poverty. But it is difficult to confirm some of these patterns from the secondary data. Our survey data from slum households from different types of cities bring out the fact that both upward and downward mobility have taken place over time, though the extent of upward mobility exceeds the extent of downward mobility (Mitra 2004, 2010). Also, the most dynamic cities have experienced upward mobility to a greater extent than the small cities. This tends to support the agglomeration effects. Rapid urbanization and large cities reduce poverty faster than small towns or rural areas. As regards income mobility, our survey results support the positive effect of saving, asset formation, education, and locational characteristics. Within cities, households living in certain specific pockets have been able to escape poverty possibly because they were able to benefit from intermingling with non-poor households and diversifying their job search networks.

Our survey data, however, do not offer any evidence on mobility from slum to non-slum areas. At most, some of the slum households are seen to have carried out investment activities on their living units, which may be interpreted as a movement from slum to non-slum living conditions. However, cases showing significant improvements in living conditions are limited in number. One important determinant of housing investment is land tenure; since it is difficult for the slum dwellers to get legal ownership over the land, investment in housing is highly limited.

21.4 Multifaceted Nature of Poverty: Well-being of Low-Income Households

The next issue relates to well-being levels, which not only means consumption poverty but also other aspects of the population in different types of cities, with the underlying hypothesis that agglomeration economies in large cities get translated into higher well-being levels. Higher agglomeration economies reflected in terms of higher productivity levels and real earnings imply greater affordability. Nutritional status and accessibility to education and health improve, which in turn contribute to the overall well-being levels of the households. Fertility behaviour, for example, changes and so do the indicators of social development. One important determinant of housing investment is land tenure; since it is difficult for slum dwellers to get legal ownership over the land, investment on housing is highly limited. Educational levels and health outcomes tend to improve.

However, due to the lack of data at the aggregate level or for the total population in a given city, we had to examine this hypothesis indirectly. The question that we pose is: Are the households from low-income clusters better off in large cities compared with their counterparts in relatively small ones? Again, on the aspect of well-being, not much information is available from secondary sources. However, under the UNDP-sponsored project on urban poverty, one survey was undertaken in four cities of different population sizes and economic activities

(Jaipur, Ludhiana, Mathura, and Ujjain).[9] These cities were picked from the list of sixty-four cities prepared specifically for the urban renewal mission (JNNURM). The primary survey enables us to comment on certain aspects of well-being of the slum dwellers in these four cities. While Jaipur and Ludhiana are two million-plus cities, Mathura and Ujjain are relatively small in size. Again, Ludhiana is an industrial city, while Jaipur, as a state capital, a tourist centre, and also a trade centre, has a significant spread of the services sector. Mathura and Ujjain are both religious cities, and between the two the latter is absolutely stagnant. Such a mix of cities enables us to perceive the well-being of slum dwellers in contexts that involve large variations.

From the measurement point of view, various dimensions of poverty, rather than only income or consumption poverty, need to be considered to assess well-being. However, we could consider only those dimensions that are quantifiable. The following variables have been combined to construct the household-specific well-being index: household size; child–woman ratio; per capita consumption expenditure; proportion of persons in the household who reported illness; percentage of household members who acquired at least primary-level education; percentage of members in the age group 15 to 59, which is a proxy for adult potential earners; percentage of working individuals; age of the household head/principal earner taken as a proxy for experience in the job market; health expenditure per capita; and per capita household income.

Household size is likely to reduce well-being because earnings and related gains get distributed among a large number of individuals with an increase in the number of members. Similarly, households with a greater child–woman ratio indicate a higher rate of fertility and thus economic gains get shared among a large number of children. As the percentage of ill members in the household rises, the income loss due to work loss andextra expenditure for curative purposes tend to increase, reducing the well-being level of the household. Health expenditure per capita on a prioritybasis may raise the well-being of the household if it is incurred for protective purposes, enhancing productivity. On the other hand, it may reduce well-being if it is incurred at the expense of consumption of essential items.

The other variables are expected to improve well-being. Per capita household income and per capita consumption expenditure raise well-being because higher income and higher consumption enhance accessibility to a better quality of life and health. Similarly, with a rise in the percentage of household members who acquired at least primary-level education, accessibility to better jobs and incomes and also awareness about health and children's education improves. The percentage of members in the age group 15–59, which is a proxy for adult potential earners, the percentage of working individuals, and the age of the household head/principal

[9] This project and survey sponsored by UNDP-GOI were undertaken by the Institute of Economic Growth, Delhi.

earner, which is a proxy for experience in the job market, contribute positively to household income.

Since these variables are heterogeneous, it is difficult to combine them to indicate an overall living standard of the households. Hence, factor analysis was conducted, and using the factor loadings as weights, variables were combined to generate a composite index of well-being.

The results of the factor analysis are in conformity with our hypothesis. The factor loading of household size is negative, which suggests that it reduces the well-being of the households. Household income per capita and consumption expenditure per capita both take positive factor loadings, though in terms of magnitude they are moderate, like that of household size. On the higher side are the child–woman ratio, the percentage of household members in the age bracket 15–59, and the proportion of the number of working members to total household size. While the child–woman ratio reduces the well-being as reflected in terms of negative factor loadings, the other two variables take a positive coefficient. Education, though moderate in terms of magnitude, shows a positive effect except in Jaipur. Health expenditure per capita also shows a positive effect, though the magnitude of the factor loadings is quite low.

The well-being index has been constructed using the factor loadings as weights. It indicates that in Jaipur and Ludhiana, 26 and 32 per cent of slum households, respectively, are located in the bottom two size classes (Mitra 2014). However, in Mathura and Ujjain, which are much smaller than the other two cities and also lack growth dynamism, the corresponding figures are 57 and 61 per cent respectively. Thus, the well-being index even among low-income households seems to have a positive association with city size, confirming the existence of agglomeration benefits.

It is interesting to note that these figures are substantially lower than the incidence of consumption poverty, which is 66.8 per cent in Jaipur, 43.6 per cent in Ludhiana, 75 per cent in Mathura, and 88.2 per cent in Ujjain. This would tend to suggest that even when consumption poverty is high, many other facilities that are available in the cities contribute to the well-being of the population. Thus, the restrictions on migration, which are many in indirect terms, deprive the population from taking advantage of urban facilities.

21.4.1 Housing Poverty

Housing is an important aspect of well-being. Like food, housing is essential for human existence. Also, as an activity when it expands, it creates employment opportunities for unskilled and semi-skilled workers. It is an indispensable component of urban planning. Any discrepancy between demand and supply can lead to serious problems related to human habitation.

Even in the national capital, there is a severe shortage of housing and basic amenities, let alone the average for all urban areas. At the all-India (urban) level, only 66.1 per cent of the households lived in concrete (pucca) houses, 21.3 per cent in semi-concrete (semi-pucca) houses, and 12.6 per cent in mud-thatched houses (Census of India 2011). The 2011 census also indicates that eleven million housing units are vacant, indicating a paradox of housing shortage of nineteen million vis-à-vis eleven million vacant units. States and cities need to examine their respective status.

Another way of conceptualizing housing poverty is to consider the percentage of the population residing in slums with inadequate living space and basic amenities. At the all-India level, 26.31 per cent of the urban population lived in slums in 2001. In Delhi, the corresponding estimate was a bit lower in magnitude, but still at 18 per cent. In addition to the notified slums, there are also 'slum-like' structures in the city that are unfit for human habitation. If the slum population can be augmented by adding the population living in such structures, the percentage would be even more. Because of an acute shortage of affordable shelter, many migrants tend to encroach on city space and squat on public land. Such unauthorized squatter settlements are not only overcrowded and unhygienic but also prone to various environmental and health hazards.

The slum problem is both a housing problem as well as an 'employment problem'. There are several households that reside in slums because they cannot afford better quality housing because of being engaged in low-productivity jobs. On the other hand, there are households that stay in slums in spite of being engaged in jobs with higher remuneration as there is a severe shortage of housing.

The report of the technical group (for the 12th Five Year Plan on urban housing) estimated that there were 18.78 million households that did not have housing in 2012.[10] In urban Delhi alone, 0.49 million were estimated to have a housing shortage, comprising 2.59 per cent in relative terms of the total scarcity in urban India.

In the equation for slum incidence given below, there seems to be a direct relationship between urbanization and the percentage of the population living in slums across states, though it is not statistically significant. On the other hand, economic growth reduces the incidence of slums, though it is again statistically insignificant. Urbanization without the growth-enhancing channel is seen to reduce the incidence of slums, but it is highly negligible as the correlation is estimated at only −0.05. So we may infer that urbanization does not lead to any rise in the incidence of the slum population. Much of the concern expressed, particularly by demographers and policymakers, seems to be exaggerated. With effective intervention, the slum problem, which is expected to get worse during the urbanization process, can be tackled.

[10] Source: Government of India (Undated).

$$\text{SLUM} = 26.03 + 0.175\text{URB} - 0.0002\ \text{NSDP per cap}$$
$$(6.68)^{**}\ (1.11)\qquad (-1.60)$$
$$\text{Adj. } R2 = 0.02;\ N = 31$$

Delhi and many other million-plus cities continue to face the problem of the mushrooming growth of slum clusters on land belonging to various agencies. Migrants travel to these cities in search of livelihoods, which do not remain confined to the formal economy as the informal economy holds significant possibilities of absorption of unskilled and semi-skilled labour. Besides, there are several residents in the slums who have been staying in such locations for several decades, and some of them were even born in the city. In spite of being in the city for a long time and being aware of the functioning of the labour market and the availability of infrastructural support, these households have not been able to experience any upward mobility. Table A.21.4 in Appendix 3 provides estimates on the projected slum population in different states and union territories, which are indeed phenomenal.

Though a number of slum development schemes and measures to provide housing to the economically weaker section of the population exist, the land and housing market, especially in the large cities, involves a great deal of speculation. In practice, space for the economically weaker sections is shrinking day by day (Mitra 1994). Most of the low-income migrant households end up in slums, which are of two types: registered and unregistered. The registered slums are those that are recognized by the local authorities (municipalities, etc.) and are entitled to receive basic amenities, and in cases of slum demolitionresidents are relocated to an alternative area, which is usually on the outskirts of the cities and, thus, remains least preferred by the inhabitants. On the other hand, unregistered slums do not even have these minimum supports and, thus, run the risk of demolition at any time. Many of the residents of the registered slums are likely to bear initially a 'token' and subsequently a voter's identity card, which recognizes them as the residents of the urban localities and thus provides access to the public distribution system. The functioning of the overall land and housing market aggravates inequality, which reduces accessibility of low-income households to decent living conditions, forcing many to reside in unregistered slums, let alone registered slums.

On the whole there is segregation at least in terms of residence. There are pockets in which low-income households reside with meagre incomes and inadequate amenities. The nexus between the builders, politicians, and elite is on the rise as far as city space is concerned (Edelman and Mitra 2006). The middle-class communities' accessibility to land is also on the rise, as revealed by the increasing expansion of housing societies in the million-plus cities and other large cities. Multiple complexes for commercial purposes are emerging prior to the demolition of slums and squatter settlements. As Kundu (2009) argues, the urbanization process is increasingly becoming exclusionary. Slum rehabilitation programmes, keeping in view the access to basic amenities and inexpensive transport networks, need to be implemented effectively. Some of the city space has to be reserved for the economically weaker sections of the population,otherwise policies to provide housing to these sections can never be implemented successfully on a large scale. The construction of low-cost housing and provision of credit assistance are some of the effective ways of enhancing accessibility to better living conditions. The housing problem, however, cannot be separated from the 'employment problem' because without productive employment and 'decent wages', workers can never upgrade their living conditions.

21.5 Conclusion and Policies

This study has assessed the relationship between urbanization, growth, inequality, and poverty against the backdrop of labour market and demographic characteristics. From the state-level data, urbanization and per capita income are seen to be strongly correlated—urbanization turns out to be a significant determinant of growth for both the years 2004–5 and 2011–12. Urbanization does not impact on inequality significantly. Growth reduces poverty, though the role of other factors is also important. However, growth raises inequality, though only in the rural context.

Inequality and poverty are mostly unrelated. Urbanization does not show any significant impact on rural poverty, though it tends to reduce poverty in urban areas. However, the explanatory power of the equation is nominal, indicating the impact of many other factors. After controlling for growth and inequality, the effect of urbanization is absolutely insignificant. So, we may conclude that urbanization increases both income and inequality. Besides, urbanization reduces poverty, while inequality increases poverty.

We further noted that growth positively influences urbanization. On the other hand, urbanization and expansion in non-agricultural activities both contribute to economic growth. However, economic growth does not seem to be resulting in a higher work participation rate in urban areas. Even urbanization is not seen to have resulted in an enhanced work participation rate.

The results from factor analysis corroborate some of these findings: urbanization and per capita net SDP both take a high factor loading, suggesting a strong association between them. Though urban inequality is not strongly correlated with urbanization and growth, the relationship is distinct. While poverty tends to decline, inequality rises in the process of growth and urbanization. The work participation rate and the percentage of urban workers engaged in non-household manufacturing and services are also positively associated with growth and urbanization. The workforce participation rate and literacy both show a negative association with urban poverty, indicating the importance of employment generation for poverty reduction. Again in relation to urbanization and growth, rural inequality tends to rise and rural poverty declines. Also, there seems to be a positive relationship between the child–woman ratio, household size, poverty, and female–male ratio in factor 1, implying that poverty tends to rise with demographic pressure and is more prevalent in households with a larger number of women.

Migration is not found to be a significant determinant of urbanization. Given the moderate flow of population from rural to urban areas, this is quite an expected phenomenon. However, both rural and urban poverty are positively correlated, implying a similarity in the poverty situation in rural and urban areas across states.

Higher inequality in urban areas is seen to attract more migrants. Higher income or wage inequality at the place of destination is an indicator of dynamism, which, in turn, tends to raise the expected income differential between rural and urban areas and, thus, potential rural migrants are more likely to shift to these urban locations.

Economic growth, too, shows a positive impact on migration. Though a higher level of urbanization tends to reduce migration, from the factor analysis, migration shows a positive relationship with urbanization and the growth index, though it does not have a high factor loading. Migration is seen to be positively associated with some of the development indicators, while it has a negative relationship with urban poverty and some of the variables representing demographic pressure, like urban household size. In other words, states with a higher incidence of urban poverty show lower migration rates, implying that rural migrants are less likely to move to urban areas that do not provide adequate sources of livelihoods to the poor and are thus characterized by a greater magnitude of urban poverty. However, this negative association can also be interpreted as a positive outcome in terms of a decline in poverty subsequent to migration from rural to urban areas.

The district-level data for urban areas confirm a positive association between urbanization, work participation rate, percentage of the workforce engaged in non-household manufacturing and services, literacy, growth, and inequality, though the degree of association is mild as shown by the moderate factor loadings corresponding to many of these variables. Further, urban poverty is also seen to be negatively associated with these variables, though not strongly. However, in the next significant factor, this relationship between growth, inequality, poverty, and urbanization turns out to be much sharper. While growth, inequality, and urbanization tend to move in the same direction, poverty declines.

In the rural context, from the district-level data, though similar findings are discernible between growth, inequality, poverty, and other development indicators including the urbanization level in the district, the factor loadings are much lower in magnitude in the most significant factor. However, in the least significant factor, the growth–inequality–poverty–urbanization nexus gets sharper. On the whole, districts with a higher level of urbanization are associated with reduced rural poverty and higher levels of growth and other development indicators, though inequality is likely to rise in the process.

From the regression analysis of the district-level data, rural poverty is seen to decline in relation to growth, though inequality raises poverty. Further, male literacy and the work participation rate reduce poverty. The positive relationship between female literacy and rural poverty is indicative of the extensive rural literacy mission aimed at encompassing more women from poor households. Similarly, in urban areas poverty declines in response to increases in growth, male work participation rate, and male literacy rate, though inequality raises it. More importantly, urbanization shows a strong beneficial effect on poverty as higher levels of urbanization are associated with a lower poverty incidence.

The regression analysis of urbanization at the district level suggests that both rural and urban growth contribute to urbanization. Rural male work participation rate and rural male literacy also add to urbanization as the rural male workers and those that are literate are more likely to migrate to cities in search of better jobs after acquiring work experience and skills. With rural diversification (expansion in non-agricultural activities), the urbanization index also tends to increase as the rural–urban discontinuum in terms of activities tends to break down. Rural areas start urbanizing and migration also becomes easier as the differences in the nature of activities across space start to dissipate.

The regression analysis of economic growth in urban areas again confirms the importance of urbanization. Literacy, increased work opportunities resulting in an enhanced work participation rate, and expansion in activities such as non-household manufacturing and services also contribute to growth. However, economic growth in rural areas is not significantly influenced by urbanization, though the other factors remain pertinent.

The district-level data also confirm that urban inequality rises in response to both urbanization and urban growth. Migration of low-income households from rural to urban areas resulting in higher levels of urbanization manifests itself in a higher level of inequality. However, increased work opportunities reduce urban inequality, while the presence of vulnerable social categories such as the scheduled caste population aggravates urban inequality. In the rural context, inequality is not seen to be influenced by urbanization, meaning out-migration does not result in inequality reduction. Again, greater work opportunities and rural diversification are endemic to controlling inequality in rural areas.

From the data at the city level (million-plus cities), there is evidence on poverty declining with growth and city size, favouring agglomeration effects. Some of the demographic variables such as household size and the child–woman ratio are also the other determinants of poverty (Table 21.12). Growth and inequality vary positively with each other. Literacy varies inversely with poverty. In fact, large cities are seen to be positively associated with better employment opportunities as reflected in terms of a positive relationship between city size and work participation rate, which, in turn, again varies positively with literacy (in factor 2). Based on the primary survey data, the distribution of slum households across the size classes of the well-being index shows that the percentage of households in the bottom two size classes is much larger in stagnant and small urban settlements compared with large and relatively dynamic ones.

For the urban poor to experience upward mobility, urban employment programmes are pertinent. Most of the urban-specific programmes in India largely emphasize the importance of basic amenities to the urban poor and the infrastructure needs of the cities. However, a safety net for workers in the low-productivity urban informal sector is essential for reducing the intensity and the incidence of urban poverty. Besides, improvements in health and educational support can have a longer-term effect on poverty. The well-known employment guarantee programme (the Mahatma Gandhi National Rural Employment Guarantee Act) is applicable only in the rural context and does not have an urban counterpart. The increasing rural–urban development disparities may result in an increased rate of migration to urban areas in search of jobs. The 'Skill India' programme of the present government may again induce migration, as rural residents after acquiring skills would look for high-productivity jobs in urban areas. The focus on creating world-class cities under the Smart Cities programme may motivate rural aspirants to shift to these locations. But stringent anti-slum policies in the so-called smart cities will possibly lead to exclusionary urbanization unless the other urban centres offer opportunities to low-income households and encourage migration. The 'Make in India' initiative to boost manufacturing growth may, however, offer employment opportunities which in turn may lead to reduction in poverty.

Some of the major programmes of the Ministry of Housing and Urban Poverty Alleviation meant for urban areas are: JNNURM; Basic Services to the Urban Poor and Integrated Housing and Slum Development Programme; Swarna Jayanti Shahari Rozgar Yojana (i.e. employment programmes in urban areas for the low-income households); Affordable Housing in Partnership; Interest Subsidy Scheme for Housing the Urban Poor; Urban Statistics for HR and Assessments; Integrated Low Cost Sanitation Scheme; and projects/schemes for the development of the north-eastern region, including Sikkim. However, the employment programmes in the urban context have hardly been implemented. Only the measures related to urban basic services and slum development are evident across many cities. Even among them, the slum rehabilitation or resettlement schemes have remained mostly unsuccessful as the new areas allotted to slum dwellers are usually outside the city territory, where employment opportunities are scanty. On the other hand, the lack of an inexpensive transport system to reach the city centres and other places where work opportunities exist makes urban survival more stressful for low-income households, particularly those who migrate from other places.

A distinction needs to be made between short-run and the long-run anti-poverty policies. Manufacturing growth is essential for the productive absorption of the unskilled and the semi-skilled variety of labour that shifts out of the agricultural sector. In the long run, for making urbanization more sustainable, growth with employment generation has to be the focus so that agglomeration effects are utilized towards poverty reduction. Provision of mere doles, which do not contribute to asset formationor make the poor self-sufficient in the long run, cannot result in poverty-free cities. Besides, urban transport policies also need to be developed in a more integrated manner so that low-income households are able to access their sources of livelihood in a cost-effective way.

In the historical context, urbanization had mostly been a concomitant of industrialization, and it has absorbed rural migrants to a considerable extent, thus resulting in a sizeable increase in living standards. However, in the Indian context, urbanization and poverty reduction are at the most mildly associated. Though much of the non-agricultural income growth is concentrated in urban areas, inequality is also seen to have increased alongside it. Both the market and the government are required to play a more efficient role so as to enhance the positive spillover effects of urbanization on growth, employment generation, and poverty. The role of the government in making urbanization inclusive has been negligible. Growth and employment-oriented strategies need to be introduced into the urban space, taking advantage of agglomeration economies, so that the relationship between urbanization and poverty can be strengthened substantially.

Infrastructure, education, health, housing, and basic amenities deserve a great deal of attention in the urban space. If the agglomeration benefits are to be reaped, megacities require further investment. New towns, which have been developin-gon the periphery of large cities in response to the exhaustion of space within city territories, require huge investment in terms of liveability and connectivity. Population flow to large urban settlements both from rural and smaller urban settlements has always been rapid in India. In the coming years too, a similar pattern is likely to continue, reassuring the prominence of large cities in the development experience of the Indian subcontinent. Hence, in order to keep pace with supplies of labour and achieve productivity gains through agglomeration economies, newer growth channels and poverty-mitigating strategies need to be explored. Large cities have to emerge as growth poles in a cost-effective manner and, at the same time, they must adopt pro-poor strategies so that the effects of growth can reach out to all sections of society instead of being confined to a limited few. Integrated markets need to develop for such pro-poor growth to take place and to fasten the impact of urbanization on poverty reduction.

Appendix

Appendix 1

State-Level Data: Rural Areas (Factor Analysis Results)

Corresponding to the rural specific variables, literacy and the percentage of workers engaged in non-household manufacturing and services are positively associated (Table A.21.1). Urbanization and growth reveal a strong positive association in relation to which rural

Table A.21.1. Results from factor analysis (rural)

Variables	Factor 1	Factor 2	Factor 3
HHSZ	−0.2555	−0.6846	0.3132
CHILD-WOM	−0.1547	−0.8907	0.0923
WFPR	0.1133	0.1999	−0.8894
LIT	0.5304	0.6314	−0.0599
SC	0.0396	0.1467	0.1218
HHMFG	−0.2061	0.0960	0.5090
OTHERACT	0.8031	0.2337	0.3018
F/M	−0.4439	0.4916	0.1211
RPOV	−0.5206	−0.1914	0.0084
URBN	0.9145	0.0379	−0.2345
RINEQ	0.3515	0.3080	0.0069
NSDPPERCAP	0.8918	0.2039	0.2031
Eigen value	4.33	1.73	1.49
Explained variation	0.48	0.19	0.17

Note: No. of observations: 31. HHSZ: household size; WFPR: main workforce participation rate; LIT: literacy rate; SC: percentage of male scheduled caste population; HHMFG: percentage of workers in household manufacturing; OTHERACT: percentage of workers engaged in non-household manufacturing and services; F/M: female–male ratio in the population, RPOV: percentage of households below the poverty line in rural areas; URBN: percentage of population in urban areas; NSDPPERCAP: net state domestic product per capita; RINEQ: inequality in terms of Gini index in rural areas. The variables are for 2011 or 2011–12 or 2010–11.

Source: Author's calculations.

inequality tends to rise and rural poverty decline. Caste again enters with a negligible factor loading in factor 1, implying no significant association with poverty. Also, there seems to be a positive relationship between child–woman ratio, household size, poverty, and female–male ratio in factor 1, implying that poverty tends to rise with demographic pressure and is more prevalent in households with a larger number of women. This conforms to the view on feminization of poverty and female-headed households being more prone to poverty, though factor 2 does not suggest so.

Appendix 2

District-Level Data (Factor Analysis Results)

Based on the multivariate analysis (factor analysis), the district-level data for urban areas confirm a positive association between urbanization, work participation rate, percentage of workforce engaged in non-household manufacturing and services, literacy, growth, and inequality, though the degree of association is mild as shown by the moderate factor loadings corresponding to many of these variables (Table A.21.2). Further, urban poverty is also seen to be negatively associated with these variables, though not strongly. However, as we move on to the next significant factor 2, this relationship between growth, inequality, poverty, and urbanization turns out to be much sharper. While growth, inequality, and urbanization tend to move in the same direction, poverty declines.

Another interesting finding that emerges is that the dependency ratio (child–woman ratio) and the demographic variable (household size) are the two highly significant variables in factor 1 that have a positive association with each other and with poverty as well. On the other hand, they are negatively connected with many of the development indicators. Besides, poverty tends to increase with a rise in household-based activities represented by household manufacturing share in the workforce. Interestingly, the female–male ratio appears to be higher in districts with improved outcomes in terms of poverty, growth, urbanization, and work participation rate.

In the rural context, though similar findings are discernible between growth, inequality, poverty, and other development indicators, including the urbanization level in the district, the factor loadings are much lower in magnitude in factors 1 and 2, implying the absence of a strong association (Table A.21.3). It is only in factor 3 that the growth–inequality–poverty–urbanization nexus gets sharper. On the whole, districts with a higher level of urbanization are associated with a reduced rural poverty incidence and higher levels of growth and other development indicators, though inequality is likely to rise in the process. Again, such districts with better outcomes also witness a higher female–male ratio in the

Table A.21.2. Results from factor analysis (district: urban)

Variables	Factor 1	Factor 2
UHHSZ	−0.7716	−0.1540
UCHILD-WOM	−0.8534	−0.1684
UWFPR	0.6353	0.1921
ULIT	0.7374	0.2264
USC	0.1201	0.0383
UOTHERACT	0.3282	0.3096
UMFGHH	−0.2011	−0.0983
UF/M	0.3075	0.0014
UBPL	−0.3135	−0.4429
URBN	0.2366	0.4735
UAVMPCE	0.2611	0.8050
UINEQ	0.1276	0.7407
Eigen value	3.97	1.18
Explained variation	0.6374	0.1898

Note: No. of Observation: 592. U represents urban areas; HHSZ: household size; CHILD-WOM: proportion of children to women; WFPR: main workforce participation rate; LIT: literacy; SC: percentage of scheduled caste population; OTHERACT: percentage of workers engaged in non-household manufacturing and services; MFGHH: percentage of workers in household manufacturing; F/M: female–male ratio in the population, BPL: percentage of households below the poverty line; URBN: percentage of population in urban areas; AVMPCE: average monthly per capita consumption expenditure; INEQ: inequality in terms of the difference between the minimum and maximum value of the consumption expenditure. The variables are for 2011, 2011–12, or 2010–11.

Source: Author's calculations.

Table A.21.3. Results from factor analysis (district: rural)

Variables	Factor 1	Factor 2	Factor 3
RHHSZ	−0.6615	−0.1201	−0.0750
RCHILD-WOM	−0.8758	−0.1914	−0.2291
RWFPR	0.4826	−0.2138	0.1992
RLIT	0.6064	0.2863	0.2864
RSC	0.1626	0.0470	0.0835
ROTHERACT	0.1095	0.7814	0.2365
RMFGHH	−0.0320	0.1394	−0.0442
RCUL	−0.1466	−0.9115	−0.1291
RAGLAB	0.0393	0.0829	−0.1217
RF/M	0.4391	−0.0442	0.0058
RBPL	−0.1700	−0.1488	−0.5527
URBN	0.1797	0.3859	0.2479
RAVMPCE	0.2638	0.2676	0.7903
RINEQ	0.1938	0.1964	0.6557
Eigen value	3.92	1.90	1.69
Explained variation	0.4115	0.1987	0.1775

Note: No. of Observation: 608.

R: rural areas, HHSZ: household size; CHILD-WOM: proportion of children to women; WFPR: main workforce participation rate; LIT: literacy; SC: percentage of scheduled caste population; OTHERACT: percentage of workers engaged in non-household manufacturing and services; CUL: percentage of workforce engaged as cultivators; AGLAB: percentage of workforce engaged as agricultural labourers; MFGHH: percentage of workers in household manufacturing; F/M: female–male ratio in the population, BPL: percentage of households below the poverty line; URBN: percentage of population in urban areas; AVMPCE: average monthly per capita consumption expenditure; INEQ: inequality in terms of the difference between the minimum and maximum value of the consumption expenditure. The variables are for 2011, 2011–12, or 2010–11.

Source: Author's calculations.

population. Hence, based on the district-level data, it may be concluded that urbanization not only delivers better outcomes in terms of economic indicators but also social and demographic indicators, though the process of social transformation seems to be taking place at a much slower pace.

Appendix 3

Table A.21.4. Statewise projected slum population, 2011–17

State	2011	2012	2013	2014	2015	2016	2017
Andaman and Nicobar Island	33,722	35,294	36,867	38,265	39,663	41,060	42,633
Andhra Pradesh	8,188,022	8,273,434	8,357,451	8,440,074	8,521,999	8,602,530	8,681,318
Arunachal Pradesh	98,248	103,459	108,669	114,127	119,833	125,788	131,494
Assam	1,070,835	1,100,118	1,129,636	1,159,857	1,190,780	1,222,406	1,253,798
Bihar	1,683,954	1,707,378	1,730,148	1,752,590	1,774,376	1,795,671	1,816,639
Chandigarh	332,473	348,685	365,154	381,881	397,321	411,474	429,744
Chhattisgarh	2,111,546	2,169,237	2,228,058	2,287,634	2,347,964	2,409,802	2,470,886
Dadra and Nagar Haveli	26,083	28,813	31,542	34,424	37,305	40,035	43,219
Daman & Diu	9,187	9,316	9,316	9,445	9,445	9,575	9,575
Delhi	3,163,430	3,260,984	3,360,874	3,463,999	3,570,716	3,681,745	3,793,313
Goa	154,759	161,494	168,229	174,815	180,801	185,741	192,476
Gujarat	4,662,619	4,759,581	4,856,740	4,954,094	5,051,840	5,149,782	5,245,569
Haryana	3,288,292	3,390,907	3,495,059	3,600,364	3,707,207	3,815,202	3,923,582
Himachal Pradesh	87,281	89,143	91,005	92,983	94,845	96,707	98,685
Jammu & Kashmir	494,180	504,243	514,306	524,369	534,275	544,180	553,771
Jharkhand	931,912	948,949	966,239	983,530	1,001,202	1,019,382	1,036,673
Karnataka	3,631,147	3,700,490	3,770,161	3,839,998	3,910,162	3,980,656	4,049,341
Kerala	533,278	536,057	538,776	541,314	543,671	545,906	548,021
Lakshadweep	1,560	1,560	1,498	1,435	1,435	1,435	1,373
Madhya Pradesh	6,393,040	6,523,229	6,654,059	6,785,528	6,917,636	7,050,705	7,181,214
Maharashtra	18,151,071	18,549,628	18,950,624	19,352,665	19,754,009	20,152,914	20,557,046
Manipur	75,197	75,915	76,514	76,993	77,592	78,190	78,789

(*Continued*)

Table A.21.4. Continued

State	2011	2012	2013	2014	2015	2016	2017
Meghalaya	205,176	208,590	212,003	215,416	219,209	222,622	226,415
Mizoram	105,720	107,700	109,679	111,659	113,639	115,619	117,599
Nagaland	83,220	84,292	85,365	86,223	87,295	88,368	89,226
Orissa	1,736,064	1,770,623	1,805,436	1,840,503	1,876,078	1,912,161	1,948,244
Puducherry	136,899	143,316	149,876	156,435	162,282	167,131	174,118
Punjab	2,798,256	2,864,014	2,930,296	2,996,316	3,062,598	3,128,094	3,193,590
Rajasthan	3,826,160	3,894,590	3,962,311	4,029,561	4,095,395	4,160,049	4,224,939
Sikkim	13,321	13,803	14,124	14,605	14,926	15,408	15,729
Tamil Nadu	8,644,892	8,862,969	9,081,045	9,298,651	9,515,080	9,729,624	9,940,165
Tripura	131,080	134,137	137,003	140,061	143,118	146,175	149,232
Uttar Pradesh	10,878,336	11,127,210	11,378,552	11,631,376	11,885,434	12,139,739	12,394,291
Uttarakhand	826,257	846,181	866,105	886,615	906,832	927,342	947,559
West Bengal	8,546,755	8,640,642	8,733,188	8,825,399	8,918,616	9,014,179	9,106,055
India	93,055,983	94,977,993	96,907,923	98,845,216	1.01E+08	1.03E+08	1.05E+08

References

Bhanumurthy, N. R. and A. Mitra. 2010. ‘Globalization, Growth and Poverty in India’. In *The Poor under Globalisation in Asia, Latin America and Africa*, edited by M. Nissanke and Erik Thorbecke, Oxford University Press.

Business Standard. 2014. ‘Urban population to contribute 70-75% of India’s GDP by 2020—Barclays’. 20 march, <http://www.business-standard.com/article/news-cm/urban-population-to-contribute-70-75-of-india-s-gdp-by-2020-barclays-114032000273_1.html>.

Calì, M. 2008. ‘Urbanisation, Inequality and Economic Growth: Evidence from Indian States and Towns’. Background note for the *World Development Report*, Overseas Development Institute, London.

Calì, M. and Carlo Menon. 2012. ‘Does Urbanization Affect Rural Poverty? Evidence from Indian Districts’. *The World Bank Economic Review 27* (2): 171–201.

Dandekar, V. M. and Nilkantha Rath. 1971. ‘Poverty in India, Indian School of Political Economy’. *Economic and Political Weekly 6* (1).

Deaton, Angus and Jean Dreze. 2002. ‘Poverty and Inequality in India: A Re-examination’. *Economic and Political Weekly 37* (36): 3729–48.

Edelman, Brent and Arup Mitra. 2006. ‘Access to Basic Amenities: The Role of Political Contact, its Determinants and Adverse Effects’. *Review of Urban and Regional Development Studies 18* (1): 25–40.

Ferré, Céline, Francisco H. G. Ferreira, and Peter Lanjouw. 2012. ‘Is There a Metropolitan Bias? The Relationship Between Poverty and City Size in a Selection of Developing Countries’. *The World Bank Economic Review 26* (3): 351–82.

Gangopadhyay, Shubhashis, Ghosh Namrata, and Sharma Purti. 2010. ‘Report on “Generating Poverty Maps for India”’. Submitted to Planning Commission.

Gangopadhyay, Shubhashis, Ghosh Namrata, Sharma Purti, and Kumari Niloo. 2011. ‘Report on “Generating Poverty Estimates Using New Poverty Lines”’. Submitted to Planning Commission.

Government of India. 2010. *Report of the Committee on Slum Statistics/Census*, Ministry of Housing and Urban Poverty Alleviation. National Buildings Organisation, New Delhi.

Government of India. Undated. Report of the Technical Group. 2007–12. *On Estimation of Urban Housing Shortage*, Ministry of Housing and Urban Poverty Alleviation, National Buildings Organisation, Government of India, New Delhi.

Jha, R. 2002. *Reducing Poverty and Inequality in India: Has Liberalization Helped?* Oxford University Press.

Kundu, Amitabh. 2006. ‘Urbanisation and Urban Governance: Search for a Perspective Beyond Neo-liberalism’. In *Indian Cities in Transition*, edited by A. Shaw, Orient Longman.

Kundu, Amitabh. 2009. ‘Exclusionary Urbanisation in Asia: A Macro Overview’. *Economic and Political weekly 44* (48): 48–58.

Kundu, Amitabh and P. C. Mohanan. 2009. 'Employment and Inequality Outcomes in India'. In *Joint Seminar on Employment and Inequality*, Employment, Labour and Social Affairs Directorate and Development Centre, Paris, vol. 8:1–43.

Kundu, Kiron K. 2013. 'India Has a Problem with Inequality, and it Won't Be Solved Easily'. *Business* Standard, 25 May. <http://www.business-standard.com/article/opinion/india-has-a-problem-with-inequality-and-it-won-t-be-solved-easily-113052500705_1.html>.

Kuznets, Simon and John Thomas Murphy. 1966. *Modern Economic Growth: Rate, Structure and Spread*, Yale University Press.

Lanjouw, Peter and R. Murgai. 2010. 'Size Matters: Urban Growth and Poverty in India. 1983–2005'. *Development Economics Research Group Working Paper*, World Bank, Washington, DC.

Mahadevia, D. and S. Sarkar. 2012. *Handbook of Urban Inequalities*, Oxford University Press.

Mitra, Arup. 1994. *Urbanisation, Slums, Informal Sector Employment and Poverty: An Exploratory Study*, BR Publishing Corporation.

Mitra, Arup. 2004. 'Informal Sector, Networks and Intra-City Variations in Activities: Findings from Delhi Slums'. *Review of Urban & Regional Development Studies 16* (2): 154–69.

Mitra, Arup. 2010. 'Migration, Livelihood and Well-being: Evidence from Indian City Slums'. *Urban Studies 47* (7): 1371–90.

Mitra, Arup. 2013. *Insights into Inclusive Growth, Employment and Wellbeing in India*, Springer.

Mitra, Arup. 2014. 'Agglomeration Economies and Wellbeing: Evidence from India'. *Athens Journal of Health 1* (1): 23–36.

Mitra, Arup and Barjor Mehta. 2011. 'Cities As the Engine of Growth: Evidence from India'. *Journal of Urban Planning and Development 137* (2): 171–83.

Sachs, Jeffrey D., Nirupam Bajpai, and Ananthi Ramiah. 2002. 'Understanding Regional Economic Growth in India'. *Asian Economic Papers 1* (3): 32–62.

Sharma, P. and N. Kumari. 2012. 'Location as a Poverty Trap'.

Sundaram, K. and Suresh D. Tendulkar. 2003. 'Poverty Among Social and Economic Groups in India in 1990s'. *Economic and Political Weekly 38* (50): 5263–76.

Tripathi, Sabyasachi. 2013. 'Does Higher Economic Growth Reduce Poverty and Increase Inequality? Evidence from Urban India'. *Indian Journal of Human Development 7* (1): 109–37.

World Bank Group. 2011. *Perspectives on Poverty in India: Stylized Facts from Survey Data*, World Bank, Washington, DC.

Index

Note: Tables, figures, and boxes are indicated by an italic *t*, *f*, and *b* following the paragraph number.

For the benefit of digital users, indexed terms that span two pages (e.g., 52–53) may, on occasion, appear on only one of those pages.

The manufacturer's authorised representative in the EU for product safety is Oxford University Press España S.A. of el Parque Empresarial San Fernando de Henares, Avenida de Castilla, 2 – 28830 Madrid (www.oup.es/en or product.safety@oup.com). OUP España S.A. also acts as importer into Spain of products made by the manufacturer.

www.ingramcontent.com/pod-product-compliance
Lightning Source LLC
LaVergne TN
LVHW011852200926
848484LV00002B/445

* 9 7 8 0 1 9 8 8 2 9 2 2 5 *